UNITED NATIONS CONFERENCE ON TRADE AND DEVELOPMENT
CONFÉRENCE DES NATIONS UNIES SUR LE COMMERCE ET LE DÉVELOPPEMENT

UNCTAD
HANDBOOK
OF STATISTICS

MANUEL
DE STATISTIQUES
DE LA CNUCED

2008

UNITED NATIONS
New York and Geneva

NATIONS UNIES
New York et Genève

NOTE

Symbols of United Nations documents are composed of capital letters combined with figures. Mention of such a symbol indicates a reference to a United Nations document.

General disclaimer

The designations employed and the presentation of the material in this publication do not imply the expression of any opinion whatsoever on the part of the secretariat of the United Nations concerning the legal status of any country, territory, city or area, or of its authorities, or concerning the delimitation of its frontiers or boundaries.

Where the designations "economy" or "country or area" appear in tables, they cover countries, territories, cities and areas.

The designations "developed", "in transition" and "developing" are intended for statistical convenience and do not necessarily express a judgement about the stage reached by a particular country or area in the development process.

Material in this publication may be freely quoted or reprinted, but acknowledgement is obligatory, together with a reference to the document number (TD/STAT.33). A copy of the publication containing the quotation or reprint should be sent to the UNCTAD secretariat.

*
*   *

La cote des documents de l'Organisation des Nations Unies se compose de lettres majuscules et de chiffres. La mention d'une telle cote indique qu'il est fait référence à un document de l'Organisation.

Déni de responsabilité

Les appellations employées dans cette publication et la présentation des données qui y figurent n'impliquent, de la part du secrétariat de l'Organisation des Nations Unies, aucune prise de position quant au statut juridique des pays, territoires, villes ou zones, ou de leurs autorités, ni quant au tracé de leurs frontières ou limites.

Les appellations «économie» ou «pays ou zone» figurant dans certaines rubriques des tableaux désignent des pays, des territoires, des villes ou des zones.

Les termes «développés», «en transition» et «en développement» sont utilisés pour plus de commodité dans la présentation des statistiques et n'impliquent pas nécessairement un jugement quant au stade de développement atteint par un pays ou une zone donnée.

Le contenu de la présente publication peut être cité ou reproduit sans autorisation, sous réserve qu'il soit fait mention de ladite publication et de sa cote (TD/STAT.33) et qu'un justificatif soit adressé au secrétariat de la CNUCED.

TD/STAT. 33

UNITED NATIONS PUBLICATION

Sales number / Numéro de vente : E/F.08.II.D.18

ISBN 978-92-1-012069-2
ISSN 0251-9461

The *UNCTAD Handbook of Statistics* provides essential data for analysing world trade, investment, international financial flows and development. Reliable statistical information is often the first step when preparing recommendations or taking decisions that will commit countries for many years as they strive to integrate into the world economy and improve the living standards of their citizens. Whether it be for research, consultation or technical cooperation, UNCTAD requires comparable, often detailed economic, demographic and social data, available if possible over several decades and for as many countries as possible.

In addition to collecting and checking data and calculating related indicators that facilitate the work of the secretariat's economists, the *UNCTAD Handbook of Statistics* provides an opportunity to share a rich statistical database with decision-makers and research specialists – academics, officials from national Governments or international organizations, executive managers or members of NGOs from developing, transition or developed countries. The *Handbook* further offers journalists comprehensive information in a presentation that meets their needs.

In order to provide maximum benefit to all users, the publication is available in three complementary formats: printed copy, DVD and online (www.unctad.org/statistics/handbook).

Particular acknowledgement is due to the Statistics Division of the Department of Economic and Social Affairs of the United Nations, as well as to other international organizations, for their help in preparing this publication.

Le but du *Manuel de statistiques de la CNUCED* est de fournir les données statistiques essentielles à l'analyse du commerce mondial, de l'investissement, des flux financiers internationaux et du développement. Une information statistique fiable est souvent le préalable à la formulation de recommandations et à la prise de décisions qui engageront les pays pour de longues années dans leur processus d'intégration dans l'économie mondiale et l'amélioration des conditions de leurs peuples. Que ce soit pour la recherche, la concertation ou la coopération technique, la CNUCED a besoin de données économiques, démographiques et sociales comparables et souvent détaillées, disponibles si possible sur plusieurs décennies et sur un maximum de pays.

Au-delà de la mobilisation et de la vérification des données, du calcul d'indicateurs dérivés qui alimentent les travaux des économistes du secrétariat, le *Manuel de statistiques de la CNUCED* est l'occasion de partager une base statistique riche les décideurs et les chercheurs, qu'ils soient universitaires, fonctionnaires d'administrations nationales ou d'organisations internationales, cadres d'entreprises ou membres d'organisations non gouvernementales de pays en développement, en transition ou développés. Les journalistes trouvent aussi dans ce manuel une information synthétique dans une présentation bien adaptée à leurs préoccupations.

La publication est disponible dans trois formats complémentaires, l'édition imprimée, le DVD et la version en ligne (www.unctad.org/statistics/handbook), pour que chaque utilisateur, où qu'il soit, puisse en tirer le meilleur avantage.

Le secrétariat de la CNUCED tient à remercier la Division de statistique, Département des affaires économiques et sociales de l'ONU, et diverses organisations internationales du concours qu'elles ont apporté à la préparation de cette publication.

TABLE OF CONTENTS		**TABLE DES MATIÈRES**

PART ONE
International merchandise trade

PREMIÈRE PARTIE
Commerce international des marchandises

TABLE OF CONTENTS

TABLE DES MATIÈRES

PART EIGHT
Development indicators

HUITIÈME PARTIE
Indicateurs du développement

These notes summarize the content of each part of the *Handbook* according to the revised Table of Contents of the present issue of the *Handbook of Statistics*.

The tables included in this book represent analytical summaries of the full time series contained in the *UNCTAD Handbook of Statistics 2008* on DVD and on the statistics portal of the UNCTAD website at www.unctad.org. In certain instances, the two electronic versions might contain different figures from the printed volume, as they are published somewhat later and may reflect more recent data.

PART ONE
International merchandise trade

Tables 1.1 show the value of total exports and imports, expressed in millions of dollars and percentages of the world total, of individual countries and geographical regions (1.1.1), economic groupings (1.1.2), and trade groups (1.1.3). The trade flows shown in table 1.1.1 refer to the General Trade System except for the countries which employ the Special Trade System and which are marked with an asterisk. The General Trade System is used when the statistical territory of a compiling country coincides with its economic territory. Consequently, imports include all goods entering the economic territory of a compiling country and exports include all goods leaving the economic territory of the compiling country. The Special Trade System is used when the statistical territory comprises only a particular part of the economic territory within which "goods may be disposed of without customs restriction". In such a case, imports include all goods entering the free circulation area of the compiling country, which means cleared through customs for home use, and exports include all goods leaving the free circulation area of a compiling country.

Average annual growth rates of international trade derived from table 1.1 are presented in tables 1.2.

Tables 1.3 contain trade balances (exports f.o.b. minus imports c.i.f.) and these balances, as a percentage of imports of individual countries, geographical regions and economic groupings.

Table 1.4 shows the relative importance of trade among group members as compared to the regional or total trade of that group.

PART TWO
International merchandise trade by region

Table 2.1 shows the export and import structure of individual countries by main regions of origin and destination. Data are presented for as many individual countries as possible, while trade partners are grouped in 14 major clusters.

Table 2.2 presents the structure of exports by destination and imports by origin by major commodity groups for 12 selected country groups. The table provides detailed information on the world trade network for 19 regions of origin and destination and six commodity groups.

Totals of international merchandise trade presented in the tables found in parts one and two are not strictly comparable due to complementary but different sources and remaining unallocated trade flows, despite efforts to distribute trade flows by destination, origin and commodity group.

Exports by destination may differ considerably in some cases from data on imports as reported by countries of destination for a variety of factors, among which the following may be of particular importance:

- Most import data are reported on a c.i.f. rather than an f.o.b. basis.

- There is a time lag between the date on which goods are recorded as exports and their arrival at their destination;

- There may be considerable differences between the recorded destination of exports and the actual destination as shown in import statistics.

PART THREE
International merchandise trade by product

Table 3.1 shows the export and import structure of individual economies by commodity groups for selected years for nine commodity groups (total, all food items, agricultural raw materials, fuels, ores and metals, manufactured goods, including chemical products, machinery and transport equipment and other manufactured goods).

Tables 3.2 (A, B and C, respectively) present the structure of exports for the world and for developed and developing economies, by product, at the SITC group (Revision 3, 3-digit) level. Each product share of world exports is calculated for each economic grouping as well as the average annual growth rate and the latter's deviation in relation to the world growth rate.

Table 3.2D establishes for each economy the list of main products exported (SITC group Revision 3, 3-digit level). Each product's share of total exports of individual countries, geographical regions and the world is also indicated.

Table 3.2E lists major exporters of 70 leading products among developing economies at the SITC group (Revision 3, 3-digit) level as well as corresponding shares in world trade.

Table 3.3 provides concentration indices and structural change indices for exports and imports by product group at SITC (Revision 3, 3-digit) level. The first indicator shows how a product market is concentrated in a few countries or homogeneously distributed among several countries. The structural change indicator shows whether the market share for a given product among export countries has changed significantly when compared with a reference year.

Totals of international merchandise trade presented in the tables of this third part may also differ from the data contained in the first and second parts for the above reasons, to which must be added margins of exports and imports not distributed by commodity group or the use of different product nomenclatures by the exporting and importing countries.

PART FOUR
International merchandise trade indicators

Tables 4.1 include calculation results of concentration and diversification indices for individual countries, geographical regions and economic groupings. This concentration index specifically shows how exports and imports of individual countries or country groupings are concentrated on several products or otherwise distributed in a more homogeneous manner among a series of products. The diversification indicator signals whether the structure of exports or imports by product of a given country or country grouping differs from the structure by product shown for the world.

Tables 4.2 contain volume indices of exports and imports, rounding out the unit values available in tables 1.1 and 1.2, and derived terms of trade and purchasing power of exports calculated at the level of individual countries and geographical regions (4.2.1) and economic groupings (4.2.2).

To improve data coverage, especially for the latest periods, the following procedure was used in the calculation of unit value indices::

- A set of average prices indices at SITC (Revision 3, 3-digit) group level was constructed using available sources.

- At the country level, unit value indices were calculated using previous year's trade values at the SITC 3-digit level available in table 3.2 as weights.

In some instances these indices may differ from the estimates published in official sources, since the main aim is to provide tentative estimates for most developing countries on a comparable basis.

Table 4.3 presents average applied import MFN tariff rates for major categories of non-agricultural and non-fuel products by individual markets.

PART FIVE

International trade in services

Tables 5.1.1, 5.1.2, and 5.1.3 present the value of total trade in services by individual country, geographical region, economic grouping and trade group. The tables show values of exports (credits) and imports (debits) of services that were derived from statistics on international service transactions as presented in the IMF's *Balance of Payments Statistics*. Services are defined as the economic output of intangible commodities that may be produced, transferred and consumed at the same time. However, services cover a heterogeneous range of intangible products and activities that are difficult to capture within a single definition and are sometimes hard to separate from goods. Services are outputs produced to order, and they typically include changes in the condition of the consumers realized through the activities of the producers at the demand of customers. By the time production of a service is completed, it must have been provided to a consumer.

Services figures shown here comprise 11 principal services categories according to the concepts and definitions of the IMF *Balance of Payments Manual* (BPM5, 1993). These categories cover transport; travel; communications; construction; insurance; financial services; computer and information services; royalties and license fees; other business services; personal, cultural and recreational services; and government services n.i.e. Given the general difficulties involved in statistically capturing certain aspects of the trade in services, the balance-of-payments figures presented here may be somewhat downward-biased as compared with the actual value of the international trade in services. The aggregate data from tables 5.1 include the UNCTAD secretariat's estimates of missing values that are not shown separately.

Table 5.2 indicates 20 major exporters and importers, among developing economies, for each of the 10 principal services sectors as defined in the IMF *Balance of Payments Manual* (BPM5, 1993), which are transport; travel; communication; construction; computer and information services; insurance; financial services; royalties and licence fees; other business services; and personal, cultural and recreational services. Government services n.i.e. are not included.

Table 5.3 focuses on tourism services in individual countries in recent years. It presents the following statistics: value of total expenditure of visitors, value of visitors' expenditure excluding transportation, number of tourists' overnight stays, and number of arrivals of visitors. All figures refer to non-resident visitors (inbound tourism). The international (non-resident) visitor is an international traveller travelling to a place other than her/his usual environment for a stay of less than 12 months and whose main purpose of a trip is other than exercise an activity remunerated from within the place visited. This includes all persons who arrive in a particular economy to stay for less than a year for business purposes or personal reasons. Tourists are those who stay at least one night in a collective or private accommodation in the country visited. Same-day visitors are persons who do not stay overnight in a country visited.

Table 5.4 concerns international maritime transport. It contains data on the world merchant fleet by flag of registration and by type of ship by region and economy, highlighting the group of major open-registry countries. A ship owner who registers his or her vessel in an open-registry country does not need to have any connection with a country of registry. The number of open-registry countries has varied over the years. In order to better show their relevance, the group of "major open- and international-registry countries" now includes a higher number of countries (10 in total) than the one described in the previous versions of the *Handbook*. Table 5.4 contains consolidated time series from various issues of the UNCTAD *Review of Maritime Transport*. It reports on the worldwide evolution of shipping, ports and multimodal transport related to the major traffics of liquid bulk, dry bulk and containers.

PART SIX

Commodities

Table 6.1 includes aggregated price indices for primary commodity groups such as food, tropical beverages, vegetable oilseeds and oils, agricultural raw materials and minerals, ores and metals, as well as an all groups price index in current US dollars. Also included are the annual and quarterly free-market price indices for selected commodities exported by developing economies. The weight of price indices for the above mentioned commodity groups (2000=100) are based on the value of exports of developing countries from 1999 to 2001. The table is based on data from the *UNCTAD Commodity Price Statistics* database, available on the statistics portal of the UNCTAD website.

Table 6.2 presents instability indices and trends in free-market prices for selected primary commodities that are of particular interest to developing economies.

Table 6.3 presents information on the production of aluminium and copper at different processing stages and consumption by individual country and by geographical region. Figures for the production of bauxite are expressed at gross volume, while those for copper ore production are shown in metal content.

PART SEVEN

International finance

Table 7.1 presents summaries of the current account of the balance of payments for individual countries and territories. Balance-of-payments current account data cover all transactions between residents and non-residents of a reporting economy, involving economic values and mainly concerning goods, services, income and current transfers. Data on these principal categories, with an additional detail on direct investment income, are covered in the table. For information about the concepts regarding the categories mentioned, please see the IMF *Balance of Payments Manual* (BPM5, 1993).

Table 7.2 contains summaries of the capital and financial account of the balance of payments for individual economies. Capital and financial account figures cover transactions in foreign assets and liabilities. Assets represent claims on non-residents, while liabilities are indebtedness to non-residents of the reporting economy. No valuation changes or other non-transaction modifications of net foreign assets are reflected in these accounts. Capital account includes capital transfers and acquisition and disposal of non-produced, non-financial assets. Financial account covers investments (direct, portfolio and other) and reserve assets (comprised of monetary gold, SDRs, foreign exchange and others). Statistics on these principal categories of the capital and financial account are included in the *Handbook*. Detailed notes with explanations of categories and terminology used are provided after the table. For more information, see the IMF *Balance of Payments Manual* (BPM5, 1993).

Tables 7.3.1, 7.3.2 and 7.3.3 contain information on foreign direct investment (FDI) inflows and outflows by individual country, geographical region, economic grouping and trade group. These figures correspond to the Statistical Annexes of the UNCTAD *World Investment Report 2006: FDI from Developing and Transition Economies: Implications for Development*. Foreign direct investment (FDI) is defined as an investment involving a long-term relationship and reflecting a lasting interest in and control by a resident entity in one economy (foreign direct investor or parent enterprise) of an enterprise resident in a different economy (FDI enterprise or affiliate enterprise or foreign affiliate). Such investment involves both the initial transaction between the two entities and all subsequent transactions between them and among foreign affiliates. A direct investment enterprise is defined as an incorporated or unincorporated enterprise in which the direct investor, resident in another economy, owns 10 percent or more of the ordinary shares or voting power (or the equivalent).

Table 7.4 presents values of receipts and payments of workers' remittances for individual economies. It also shows workers' remittances as a percentage of international trade (exports and imports, balance-of-payments data). According to the definition of the IMF *Balance of Payments Manual* (*BPM5, 1993*), workers' remittances are goods and financial instruments transferred by migrants living and working (considered to be residents) in a new economy to residents of the economy in which the migrants formerly resided. A migrant must live and work in the new economy for more than one year to be considered a resident there. The *BPM5* classifies workers' remittances separately from compensation of employees. Table 7.4 includes the sum of the two categories in the values shown, in order to present a clearer picture of the flows that enter or exit economies via transfers by migrant or non-resident workers.

Table 7.5 presents data on international reserves (total reserves minus gold) of developing economies by country, region and economic grouping. Other calculations included show months of imports that these reserves could finance at current import levels, as well as the annual change in total reserves. According to the IMF definition, total reserves minus gold consist of the sum of the country's foreign exchange, its reserve position in the IMF and the US dollar value of SDR holdings by its monetary authorities.

Table 7.6 gives a summary of official financial flows to developing economies by type of flow, country, geographical region and economic grouping. Flows from bilateral and multilateral sources are shown as recorded by the Development Assistance Committee (DAC – OECD).

Table 7.7 presents time series on the external long-term indebtedness of developing economies for major economic groupings. It also provides a detailed breakdown of public and publicly guaranteed debt by source of lending. External debt data in this table are based on the Debtor Reporting System (DRS) maintained by the World Bank.

PART EIGHT
Development indicators

Tables 8.1 provide information on total and per capita nominal GDP by individual country, geographical region and economic grouping. The GDP figures in dollars are derived from GDP data provided in national currencies. The prevailing annual average market exchange rates, as reported by IMF, have been used for the conversion from national currencies to dollars for most countries.

Tables 8.2 contain annual average growth rates of total and per capita real GDP by individual country, geographical region and economic grouping. The growth rates are based on GDP in constant 1990 dollars.

Tables 8.3 provide data on GDP by type of expenditure and kind of economic activity, by individual country, geographical region and economic grouping.

Tables 8.4 provide data on population and labour force: total population, urban population as a percentage of total population, total labour force, female labour force as a percentage of total labour force, total agriculture labour force and female labour force as a percentage of total agriculture labour force.

Basic population and labour data are rounded out by the demographic indicators in table 8.5: population growth rate, natural increase rate per 1,000 inhabitants, net migration rate per 1,000 inhabitants, crude birth and death rate per 1,000 inhabitants, infant mortality rate per 1,000 live births and life expectancy at birth.

OTHER NOTES

Unless otherwise specified, country aggregates are the sums of the relevant country data by group. Calculations of aggregates may in some cases include data estimated by the UNCTAD secretariat that are not necessarily all reported separately.

Because of rounding, details and percentages in tables do not necessarily add up to totals.

Data were collected and checked to ensure that they matched the geographical coverage of the countries, as described at the beginning of the *Handbook*. However, some gaps could not be avoided due to data unavailability and are described in the notes at the end tables.

Unless otherwise stated, dollars ($) refer to US dollars and data in dollars are expressed in current US dollars of the year to which they refer.

Average annual growth rates are defined as the coefficient b in the exponential trend function $y = ae^{bt}$ where t stands for time. This method takes all observations in a period into account. Therefore, the resulting growth rates reflect trends that are not unduly influenced by exceptional values.

EXPLANATION OF SYMBOLS

0   Zero means that the amount is nil or negligible.

_   The symbol underscore indicates that the item is not applicable.

..   Two dots indicate that the data are not available or are not separately reported.

-    Use of a hyphen between years (e.g. 1985-1990) signifies the full period involved, including the initial and final years.

(e)   Estimate

(p)   Provisional data

(r)   Revised data

Some exceptions are indicated in footnotes.

The country distributions presented are for statistical convenience only and follow those used by the Statistics Division, Department of Economic and Social Affairs (DESA), of the United Nations. They are grouped by economic criteria or by adhesion to commercial agreements for the purpose of statistical analysis and research.

The term "economies", as used in this publication, refers to regions, countries and territories.

Country-level data are included where statistics have been reported or where it was possible to make an estimate.

1. Geographical regions, countries and territories

This section includes countries and territories divided into three major categories: developing countries, economies in transition and developed economies. Each category is further divided by geographical regions.

Developing economies:

This category includes countries and territories in America, Africa, Asia and Oceania not specified below. The geographical regions are further subdivided into subregions in order to present more detailed statistics. Exceptions are specified in table footnotes.

Economies in transition:

The economies in transition are subdivided between Asia and Europe.

Developed economies:

This category is subdivided into 4 geographical regions: America, Asia, Europe, and Oceania.

2. Economic groupings of developing countries

The *Handbook* provides numerous and varied groups of countries and territories in order to provide easy access to the statistics necessary for socio-economic analysis and development research.

Developing economies are presented at three levels of aggregation: the total group, the group excluding China (referring to continental China) and the group excluding the least developed countries.

The developing economies are also categorized into three subgroups according to their per capita GDP in 2000: high-income, middle-income and low-income. This breakdown is based on GDP and population data available in 2004 and was not revised in order to maintain the composition of the groups for several editions of the *Handbook of Statistics.*

The category of heavily indebted poor countries (those economies benefiting from the HIPC debt reduction initiative of the World Bank and the International Monetary Fund) includes 40 countries.

Least developed countries and landlocked developing countries are recognized by the United Nations as categories that require special attention from the international community.

Since 1994, the United Nations recognizes the particular problems of the Small Island Developing States (SIDS), even though the criteria for drawing up an official list of SIDS have not yet been determined. The unofficial list is used by UNCTAD for analytical purposes only.

The group of major petroleum exporters consists of countries whose share of petroleum and petroleum products was not less than 50 per cent of their total exports, and whose exports of these products amounted to a minimum average of US$ 2 billion for the period 2003–2005. This group is divided into three geographical zones: Africa, America and Asia.

The group of major exporters of manufactured goods, divided into two geographical zones, America and Asia, consists of economies whose share of manufactured products was not less than 50 per cent of their total exports, and whose exports of these products amounted to a minimum average of US$ 22 billion for the period 2003–2005.

The composition of the groups of emerging economies (in America and Asia) and newly industrialized economies (composed of first and second tier) corresponds to UNCTAD's *Trade and Development Report.*

The different geographical regions are also presented at various levels of aggregation:

- *Africa*: Northern Africa excluding Sudan, sub-Saharan Africa, including Sudan, including and excluding South Africa.

- *America:* Central America and Greater Caribbean Islands excluding Puerto Rico, including and excluding Mexico, South America and Central America, and South America excluding Brazil.

- *Asia:* Eastern and South-Eastern Asia excluding China, and Southern Asia excluding India.

3. Trade groups and interregional groups

Statistics of trade groups with special analytic interest are presented according to their pertinence. These groupings include all relevant economies and are subclassified by geographical regions, with the exception of following interregional groups: African, Caribbean and Pacific Group of States (ACP); Asia–Pacific Economic Cooperation (APEC); Black Sea Economic Cooperation (BSEC); and Commonwealth of Independent States (CIS).

GEOGRAPHICAL REGIONS

Africa

Eastern Africa

British Indian Ocean Territory	Madagascar	Somalia
Burundi	Malawi	Uganda
Comoros	Mauritius	United Republic of Tanzania
Djibouti	Mayotte	Zambia
Eritrea	Mozambique	Zimbabwe
Ethiopia	Rwanda	
Kenya	Seychelles	

Middle Africa

Angola	Chad	Equatorial Guinea
Cameroon	Congo	Gabon
Central African Republic	Democratic Republic of the Congo	Sao Tome and Principe

Northern Africa

Algeria	Morocco	Western Sahara
Egypt	Sudan	
Libyan Arab Jamahiriya	Tunisia	

Southern Africa

Botswana	Namibia	Swaziland
Lesotho	South Africa	

Western Africa

Benin	Guinea	Nigeria
Burkina Faso	Guinea-Bissau	Saint Helena
Cape Verde	Liberia	Senegal
Côte d'Ivoire	Mali	Sierra Leone
Gambia	Mauritania	Togo
Ghana	Niger	

America

Caribbean islands

Greater Caribbean

Cuba	
Dominican Republic	
Haiti	
Jamaica	

Small Caribbean islands

Anguilla	Montserrat
Antigua and Barbuda	Netherlands Antilles
Aruba	Saint Kitts and Nevis
Bahamas	Saint Lucia
Barbados	Saint Vincent and the Grenadines
British Virgin Islands	Trinidad and Tobago
Cayman Islands	Turks and Caicos Islands
Dominica	United States Virgin Islands
Grenada	

Central America

Belize	Guatemala	Nicaragua
Costa Rica	Honduras	Panama
El Salvador	Mexico	

South America

Argentina	Ecuador	Suriname
Bolivia	Falkland Islands (Malvinas)	Uruguay
Brazil	Guyana	Venezuela (Bolivarian Republic of)
Chile	Paraguay	
Colombia	Peru	

GEOGRAPHICAL REGIONS (concluded)

Asia

Eastern Asia

China
Democratic People's Republic
 of Korea
Hong Kong, Special Administrative
 Region of China
Macao, Special Administrative
 Region of China
Mongolia
Republic of Korea
Taiwan Province of China

Southern Asia

Afghanistan
Bangladesh
Bhutan
India
Iran (Islamic Republic of)
Maldives
Nepal
Pakistan
Sri Lanka

South-Eastern Asia

Brunei Darussalam
Cambodia
Indonesia
Lao People's Democratic Republic
Malaysia
Myanmar
Philippines
Singapore
Thailand
Timor-Leste
Viet Nam

Western Asia

Bahrain
Iraq
Jordan
Kuwait
Lebanon
Occupied Palestinian territory
Oman
Qatar
Saudi Arabia
Syrian Arab Republic
Turkey
United Arab Emirates
Yemen

Oceania

American Samoa
Christmas Islands
Cocos (Keeling) Islands
Cook Islands
Fiji
French Polynesia
Guam
Johnston Island
Kiribati
Marshall Islands
Micronesia (Federated States of)
Midway Islands
Nauru
New Caledonia
Niue
Norfolk Island
Northern Mariana Islands
Palau
Papua New Guinea
Pitcairn
Samoa
Solomon Islands
Tokelau
Tonga
Tuvalu
Vanuatu
Wake Island
Wallis and Futuna Islands

ECONOMIES IN TRANSITION

GEOGRAPHICAL REGIONS

Asia

Armenia	Kazakhstan	Turkmenistan
Azerbaijan	Kyrgyzstan	Uzbekistan
Georgia	Tajikistan	

Europe

Albania	Moldova	The former Yugoslav Republic
Belarus	Russian Federation	of Macedonia
Bosnia and Herzegovina	Serbia and Montenegro	Ukraine
Croatia		

DEVELOPED ECONOMIES

GEOGRAPHICAL REGIONS

America

Bermuda	Greenland	United States of America
Canada	Saint Pierre and Miquelon	including Puerto Rico

Asia

Israel
Japan

Europe

Andorra	Gibraltar	Poland
Austria	Greece	Portugal
Belgium	Holy See	Romania
Bulgaria	Hungary	San Marino
Cyprus	Iceland	Slovakia
Czech Republic	Ireland	Slovenia
Denmark	Italy	Spain
Estonia	Latvia	Sweden
Faeroe Islands	Lithuania	Switzerland including Liechtenstein
Finland including Åland Islands	Luxembourg	United Kingdom of Great Britain and
France including French Guyana,	Malta	Northern Ireland including Channel
Guadeloupe, Martinique,	Netherlands	Islands and Isle of Man
Monaco and Réunion	Norway including Svalbard	
Germany	and Jan Mayen	

Oceania

Australia
New Zealand

ECONOMIC GROUPINGS

INCOME GROUPS

2000 per capita current GDP above US$ 4,500: High-income (42)

American Samoa	Hong Kong, Special Administrative	Saint Kitts and Nevis
Anguilla	Region of China	Saint Lucia
Antigua and Barbuda	Kuwait	Saudi Arabia
Argentina	Lebanon	Seychelles
Aruba	Libyan Arab Jamahiriya	Singapore
Bahamas	Macao, Special Administrative	Taiwan Province of China
Bahrain	Region of China	Trinidad and Tobago
Barbados	Mexico	Turks and Caicos Islands
British Virgin Islands	Montserrat	United Arab Emirates
Brunei Darussalam	Netherlands Antilles	United States Virgin Islands
Cayman Islands	New Caledonia	Uruguay
Chile	Northern Mariana Islands	Venezuela (Bolivarian Republic of)
Falkland Islands (Malvinas)	Oman	
French Polynesia	Palau	
Grenada	Qatar	
Guam	Republic of Korea	

2000 per capita current GDP between US$ 1,000 and US$ 4,500: Middle-income (50)

Algeria	Gabon	Peru
Belize	Guatemala	Saint Helena
Bolivia	Iran (Islamic Republic of)	Saint Vincent and the Grenadines
Botswana	Jamaica	Samoa
Brazil	Jordan	South Africa
Cape Verde	Malaysia	Suriname
Colombia	Maldives	Swaziland
Cook Islands	Marshall Islands	Syrian Arab Republic
Costa Rica	Mauritius	Thailand
Cuba	Micronesia (Federated States of)	Tokelau
Dominica	Morocco	Tonga
Dominican Republic	Namibia	Tunisia
Ecuador	Nauru	Turkey
Egypt	Niue	Tuvalu
El Salvador	Occupied Palestinian territory	Vanuatu
Equatorial Guinea	Panama	Wallis and Futuna Islands
Fiji	Paraguay	

2000 per capita current GDP below US$ 1,000: Low-income (65)

Afghanistan	Guinea	Niger
Angola	Guinea-Bissau	Nigeria
Bangladesh	Guyana	Pakistan
Benin	Haiti	Papua New Guinea
Bhutan	Honduras	Philippines
Burkina Faso	India	Rwanda
Burundi	Indonesia	Sao Tome and Principe
Cambodia	Iraq	Senegal
Cameroon	Kenya	Sierra Leone
Central African Republic	Kiribati	Solomon Islands
Chad	Lao People's Democratic Republic	Somalia
China	Lesotho	Sri Lanka
Comoros	Liberia	Sudan
Congo	Madagascar	Timor-Leste
Côte d'Ivoire	Malawi	Togo
Democratic People's Republic of Korea	Mali	Uganda
Democratic Republic of the Congo	Mauritania	United Republic of Tanzania
Djibouti	Mongolia	Viet Nam
Eritrea	Mozambique	Yemen
Ethiopia	Myanmar	Zambia
Gambia	Nepal	Zimbabwe
Ghana	Nicaragua	

ECONOMIC GROUPINGS (continued)

Heavily indebted poor countries - HIPCs (41)

Afghanistan	Gambia	Nepal
Benin	Ghana	Nicaragua
Bolivia	Guinea	Niger
Burkina Faso	Guinea-Bissau	Rwanda
Burundi	Guyana	Sao Tome and Principe
Cameroon	Haiti	Senegal
Central African Republic	Honduras	Sierra Leone
Chad	Kyrgyzstan	Somalia
Comoros	Liberia	Sudan
Congo	Madagascar	Togo
Côte d'Ivoire	Malawi	Uganda
Democratic Republic of the Congo	Mali	United Republic of Tanzania
Eritrea	Mauritania	Zambia
Ethiopia	Mozambique	

Landlocked developing countries - LLDCs (31)

Afghanistan	Kazakhstan*	Rwanda
Armenia*	Kyrgyzstan*	Swaziland
Azerbaijan*	Lao People's Democratic Republic	Tajikistan*
Bhutan	Lesotho	The former Yugoslav Republic
Bolivia	Malawi	of Macedonia*
Botswana	Mali	Turkmenistan*
Burkina Faso	Moldova*	Uganda
Burundi	Mongolia	Uzbekistan*
Central African Republic	Nepal	Zambia
Chad	Niger	Zimbabwe
Ethiopia	Paraguay	

* These countries are classified as economies in transition (neither developed nor developing).
  However, as they are landlocked States, they are also members of this group.

Small island developing States - SIDS (29)

Antigua and Barbuda	Maldives	Samoa
Bahamas	Marshall Islands	Sao Tome and Principe
Barbados	Mauritius	Seychelles
Cape Verde	Micronesia (Federated States of)	Solomon Islands
Comoros	Nauru	Timor-Leste
Dominica	Palau	Tonga
Fiji	Papua New Guinea	Trinidad and Tobago
Grenada	Saint Kitts and Nevis	Tuvalu
Jamaica	Saint Lucia	Vanuatu
Kiribati	Saint Vincent and the Grenadines	

ECONOMIC GROUPINGS (concluded)

Least developed countries - LDCs (49)

Year of inclusion in the group   *Year of inclusion in the group*   *Year of inclusion in the group*

Africa and Haiti

Angola	1994	Gambia	1975	Niger	1971
Benin	1971	Guinea	1971	Rwanda	1971
Burkina Faso	1971	Guinea-Bissau	1981	Senegal	2001
Burundi	1971	Haiti	1971	Sierra Leone	1982
Central African Republic	1975	Lesotho	1971	Somalia	1971
Chad	1971	Liberia	1990	Sudan	1971
Democratic Republic of the Congo	1991	Madagascar	1991	Togo	1982
Djibouti	1982	Malawi	1971	Uganda	1971
Equatorial Guinea	1982	Mali	1971	United Republic of Tanzania	1971
Eritrea	1994	Mauritania	1986	Zambia	1991
Ethiopia	1971	Mozambique	1988		

Asia

		Islands	
Afghanistan	1971	Comoros	1977
Bangladesh	1975	Kiribati	1986
Bhutan	1971	Maldives	1971
Cambodia	1991	Samoa	1971
Lao People's Democratic Republic	1971	Sao Tome and Principe	1982
Myanmar	1987	Solomon Islands	1991
Nepal	1971	Timor-Leste	2003
Yemen	1971	Tuvalu	1986
		Vanuatu	1985

Major petroleum exporters (22)

Africa	**Asia**	**America**
Algeria	Bahrain	Ecuador
Angola	Brunei Darussalam	Trinidad and Tobago
Congo	Iran (Islamic Republic of)	Venezuela (Bolivarian Republic of)
Equatorial Guinea	Iraq	
Gabon	Kuwait	
Libyan Arab Jamahiriya	Oman	
Nigeria	Qatar	
Sudan	Saudi Arabia	
	Syrian Arab Republic	
	United Arab Emirates	
	Yemen	

Major exporters of manufactured goods (12)

America	**Asia**	
Brazil	China	Taiwan Province of China
Mexico	Hong Kong, Special Administrative Region of China	Thailand
	India	Turkey
	Malaysia	
	Philippines	
	Republic of Korea	
	Singapore	

Emerging economies (10)

America	**Asia**
Argentina	Malaysia
Brazil	Republic of Korea
Chile	Singapore
Mexico	Taiwan Province of China
Peru	Thailand

Newly industrialized economies (8)

First tier	**Second tier**
Hong Kong, Special Administrative Region of China	Indonesia
Republic of Korea	Malaysia
Singapore	Philippines
Taiwan Province of China	Thailand

TRADE GROUPS

Africa

Arab Maghreb Union - UMA (5)

	Year of accession
Algeria	1989
Libyan Arab Jamahiriya	1989
Mauritania	1989
Morocco	1989
Tunisia	1989

Common Market for Eastern and Southern Africa - COMESA (19)

Burundi	1994
Comoros	1994
Democratic Republic of the Congo	1994
Djibouti	1994
Egypt	1994
Eritrea	1994
Ethiopia	1994
Kenya	1994
Libyan Arab Jamahiriya	2005
Madagascar	1994
Malawi	1994
Mauritius	1994
Rwanda	1994
Seychelles	1994
Sudan	1994
Swaziland	1994
Uganda	1994
Zambia	1994
Zimbabwe	1994

Economic Community of Central African States - ECCAS (11)

	Year of accession
Angola	1999
Burundi	1983
Cameroon	1983
Central African Republic	1983
Chad	1983
Congo	1983
Democratic Republic of the Congo	1983
Equatorial Guinea	1983
Gabon	1983
Rwanda	1983
Sao Tome and Principe	1983

Economic Community of the Great Lakes Countries - CEPGL (3)

Burundi	1976
Democratic Republic of the Congo	1976
Rwanda	1976

Economic Community of West African States - ECOWAS (15)

Benin	1975
Burkina Faso	1975
Cape Verde	1977
Côte d'Ivoire	1975
Gambia	1975
Ghana	1975
Guinea	1975
Guinea-Bissau	1975
Liberia	1975
Mali	1975
Niger	1975
Nigeria	1975
Senegal	1975
Sierra Leone	1975
Togo	1975

Economic and Monetary Community of Central Africa - CEMAC (6)

	Year of accession
Cameroon	1994
Central African Republic	1994
Chad	1994
Congo	1994
Equatorial Guinea	1994
Gabon	1994

Mano River Union - MRU (3)

Guinea	1980
Liberia	1973
Sierra Leone	1973

Southern African Development Community - SADC (14)

Angola	1992
Botswana	1992
Democratic Republic of the Congo	1992
Lesotho	1992
Madagascar	2005
Malawi	1992
Mauritius	1992
Mozambique	1992
Namibia	1992
South Africa	1994
Swaziland	1992
United Republic of Tanzania	1992
Zambia	1992

West African Economic and Monetary Union - UEMOA (8)

Benin	1994
Burkina Faso	1994
Côte d'Ivoire	1994
Guinea-Bissau	1994
Mali	1994
Niger	1994
Senegal	1994
Togo	1994

America

Andean Community - ANCOM (4)

	Year of accession
Bolivia	1996
Colombia	1996
Ecuador	1996
Peru	1996

Caribbean Community - CARICOM (15)

	Year of accession
Antigua and Barbuda	1974
Bahamas	1983
Barbados	1973
Belize	1974
Dominica	1974
Grenada	1974
Guyana	1973
Haiti	1997
Jamaica	1973
Montserrat	1974
Saint Kitts and Nevis	1974
Saint Lucia	1974
Saint Vincent and the Grenadines	1974
Suriname	1995
Trinidad and Tobago	1973

Central American Common Market - CACM (5)

	Year of accession
Costa Rica	1962
El Salvador	1961
Guatemala	1961
Honduras	1961
Nicaragua	1961

TRADE GROUPS

America (concluded)

Free Trade Area of the Americas - FTAA (34)	Year of accession		Year of accession		Year of accession
Antigua and Barbuda	1994	Paraguay	1994	**Mercado Común del Sur - MERCOSUR (4)**	
Argentina	1994	Peru	1994		
Bahamas	1994	Saint Kitts and Nevis	1994	Argentina	1994
Barbados	1994	Saint Lucia	1994	Brazil	1994
Belize	1994	Saint Vincent and the Grenadines	1994	Paraguay	1994
Bolivia	1994	Suriname	1994	Uruguay	1994
Brazil	1994	Trinidad and Tobago	1994		
Canada	1994	United States of America	1994	**North American Free Trade Agreement - NAFTA (3)**	
Chile	1994	Uruguay	1994		
Colombia	1994	Venezuela (Bolivarian Republic of)	1994	Canada	1994
Costa Rica	1994			Mexico	1994
Dominica	1994	**Latin American Integration Association - LAIA (12)**		United States of America	1994
Dominican Republic	1994				
Ecuador	1994	Argentina	1980	**Organization of Eastern Caribbean States - OECS (9)**	
El Salvador	1994	Bolivia	1980		
Grenada	1994	Brazil	1980	Anguilla	1995
Guatemala	1994	Chile	1980	Antigua and Barbuda	1981
Guyana	1994	Colombia	1980	British Virgin Islands	1984
Haiti	1994	Cuba	1999	Dominica	1981
Honduras	1994	Ecuador	1980	Grenada	1981
Jamaica	1994	Mexico	1980	Montserrat	1981
Mexico	1994	Paraguay	1980	Saint Kitts and Nevis	1981
Nicaragua	1994	Peru	1980	Saint Lucia	1981
Panama	1994	Uruguay	1980	Saint Vincent and the Grenadines	1981
		Venezuela (Bolivarian Republic of)	1980		

Asia

Asia-Pacific Trade Agreement - APTA (6) *	Year of accession		Year of accession		Year of accession
Bangladesh	1975	Myanmar	1997	**Gulf Cooperation Council - GCC (6)**	
China	2001	Philippines	1967	Bahrain	1981
India	1975	Singapore	1967	Kuwait	1981
Lao People's Democratic Republic	1975	Thailand	1967	Oman	1981
Republic of Korea	1975	Viet Nam	1995	Qatar	1981
Sri Lanka	1975			Saudi Arabia	1981
* Former Bangkok Agreement		**Economic Cooperation Organization - ECO (10)**		United Arab Emirates	1981
		Afghanistan	1992		
Association of South-East Asian Nations - ASEAN (10)		Azerbaijan	1992	**South Asian Association for Regional Cooperation - SAARC (7)**	
Brunei Darussalam	1984	Iran (Islamic Republic of)	1985	Bangladesh	1985
Cambodia	1999	Kazakhstan	1992	Bhutan	1985
Indonesia	1967	Kyrgyzstan	1992	India	1985
Lao People's Democratic Republic	1997	Pakistan	1985	Maldives	1985
Malaysia	1967	Tajikistan	1992	Nepal	1985
		Turkey	1985	Pakistan	1985
		Turkmenistan	1992	Sri Lanka	1985
		Uzbekistan	1992		

Europe

European Free Trade Association - EFTA (3)	Year of accession		Year of accession		Year of accession
Iceland	1960	Greece	1981	**Euro zone (12)**	
Norway	1960	Hungary	2004	Austria	2002
Switzerland	1960	Ireland	1973	Belgium	2002
		Italy	1957	Finland	2002
European Union - EU (27)		Latvia	2004	France	2002
		Lithuania	2004	Germany	2002
Austria	1995	Luxembourg	1957	Greece	2002
Belgium	1957	Malta	2004	Ireland	2002
Bulgaria	2008	Netherlands	1957	Italy	2002
Cyprus	2004	Poland	2004	Luxembourg	2002
Czech Republic	2004	Portugal	1986	Netherlands	2002
Denmark	1973	Romania	2008	Portugal	2002
Estonia	2004	Slovakia	2004	Spain	2002
Finland	1995	Slovenia	2004		
France	1957	Spain	1986		
Germany	1957	Sweden	1995		
		United Kingdom	1973		

Oceania

Year of accession

Melanesia Spearhead Group - MSG (4)

Fiji	1998
Papua New Guinea	1993
Solomon Islands	1993
Vanuatu	1993

Interregional groups

African, Caribbean and Pacific Group of States - ACP (79)

Angola	Gambia	Rwanda
Antigua and Barbuda	Ghana	Saint Kitts and Nevis
Bahamas	Grenada	Saint Lucia
Barbados	Guinea	Saint Vincent and the Grenadines
Belize	Guinea-Bissau	Samoa
Benin	Guyana	Sao Tome and Principe
Botswana	Haiti	Senegal
Burkina Faso	Jamaica	Seychelles
Burundi	Kenya	Sierra Leone
Cameroon	Kiribati	Solomon Islands
Cape Verde	Lesotho	Somalia
Central African Republic	Liberia	South Africa
Chad	Madagascar	Sudan
Comoros	Malawi	Suriname
Congo	Mali	Swaziland
Cook Islands	Marshall Islands	Timor-Leste
Côte d'Ivoire	Mauritania	Togo
Cuba	Mauritius	Tonga
Democratic Republic of the Congo	Micronesia (Federated states of)	Trinidad and Tobago
Djibouti	Mozambique	Uganda
Dominica	Namibia	United Republic of Tanzania
Dominican Republic	Nauru	Vanuatu
Equatorial Guinea	Niger	Zambia
Eritrea	Nigeria	Zimbabwe
Ethiopia	Niue	
Fiji	Palau	
Gabon	Papua New Guinea	

Year of accession		*Year of accession*		*Year of accession*	
Asia-Pacific Economic Cooperation - APEC (21)		**Black Sea Economic Cooperation - BSEC (12)**		**Commonwealth of Independent States - CIS (12)**	
Australia	1989	Albania	1992	Armenia	1991
Brunei Darussalam	1989	Armenia	1992	Azerbaijan	1991
Canada	1989	Azerbaijan	1992	Belarus	1991
Chile	1994	Bulgaria	1992	Georgia	1993
China	1991	Georgia	1992	Kazakhstan	1991
Hong Kong, Special Administrative Region of China	1991	Greece	1992	Kyrgyzstan	1991
Indonesia	1989	Moldova	1992	Moldova	1991
Japan	1989	Romania	1992	Russian Federation	1991
Malaysia	1989	Russian Federation	1992	Tajikistan	1991
Mexico	1993	Serbia	2004	Turkmenistan	1991
New Zealand	1989	Turkey	1992	Ukraine	1991
Papua New Guinea	1993	Ukraine	1992	Uzbekistan	1991
Peru	1998				
Philippines	1989				
Republic of Korea	1989				
Russian Federation	1998				
Singapore	1989				
Taiwan Province of China	1991				
Thailand	1989				
United States of America	1989				
Viet Nam	1998				

ACP	African, Caribbean and Pacific Group of States
ANCOM	Andean Community
APEC	Asia–Pacific Economic Cooperation
APTA	Asia-Pacific Trade Agreement (former Bangkok Agreement)
ASEAN	Association of South-East Asian Nations
BPM	*Balance of Payments Manual* (IMF)
BSEC	Black Sea Economic Cooperation
CACM	Central American Common Market
CARICOM	Caribbean Community
CEMAC	Economic and Monetary Community of Central Africa (formerly UDEAC)
CEPGL	Economic Community of the Great Lakes Countries
c.i.f.	cost, insurance and freight
CIS	Commonwealth of Independent States
COMESA	Common Market for Eastern and Southern Africa (formerly PTA)
DAC	Development Assistance Committee (of OECD)
DRS	Debtor Reporting System
ECCAS	Economic Community of Central African States
ECE	Economic Commission for Europe
ECO	Economic Cooperation Organization
ECOWAS	Economic Community of West African States
EFTA	European Free Trade Association
ESCAP	Economic and Social Commission for Asia and the Pacific
ESCWA	Economic and Social Commission for Western Asia
EU	European Union
excl.	Excluding
FAO	Food and Agriculture Organization of the United Nations
FDI	foreign direct investment
f.o.b.	free on board
FTAA	Free Trade Area of the Americas
GATS	General Agreement on Trade in Services
GCC	Gulf Cooperation Council
GDP	Gross domestic product
GFCF	Gross fixed capital formation
GNP	Gross national product
HIPC	heavily indebted poor countries
ILO	International Labour Organization
IMF	International Monetary Fund
LAIA	Latin American Integration Association
LDC	least developed country
MERCOSUR	Mercado Común del Sur
MFN	most favoured nation
MRU	Mano River Union
MSG	Melanesia Spearhead Group
NAFTA	North American Free Trade Agreement
n.e.s.	not elsewhere specified
NIE	newly industrialized economies
n.i.e.	not included elsewhere
NPISHs	non-profit institutions serving households
OA	official aid
ODA	official development assistance
OECD	Organisation for Economic Co-operation and Development
OECS	Organization of Eastern Caribbean States
OOF	other official flows
OPEC	Organization of the Petroleum Exporting Countries
SAARC	South Asian Association for Regional Cooperation
SADC	Southern African Development Community
SAR	Special Administrative Region
SDR	special drawing right
SFR	Socialist Federative Republic of Yugoslavia (former)
SIDS	Small Island Developing States
SITC	Standard International Trade Classification
TFYR	The former Yugoslav Republic of Macedonia
TNC	transnational corporation
UEMOA	West African Economic and Monetary Union
UMA	Arab Maghreb Union
UNAIDS	Joint United Nations Programme on HIV/AIDS
UNCTAD	United Nations Conference on Trade and Development
UN/DESA/SD	United Nations Department of Economic and Social Affairs, Statistics Division
UNDP	United Nations Development Programme
UNESCO	United Nations Educational, Scientific and Cultural Organization
UNICEF	United Nations Children's Fund
UNWTO	World Tourism Organization
USSR	Union of Soviet Socialist Republics
WHO	World Health Organization
WTO	World Trade Organization

Ces notes générales présentent le contenu de chaque tableau du Manuel de statistiques ainsi que les modifications introduites dans cette nouvelle édition, s'il y a lieu.

Les tableaux inclus dans cette publication constituent un résumé analytique des séries chronologiques complètes publiées dans le Manuel de statistiques 2007 de la CNUCED sur DVD et dans la version en ligne sur le portail des statistiques du site internet de la CNUCED à l'adresse suivante : www.unctad.org. Toutefois les données disponibles dans les versions électronique et imprimée pourront, dans certains cas, être différentes en raison de leur mise à jour et de leur publication à des dates différentes.

PREMIÈRE PARTIE
Commerce international des marchandises

Les tableaux 1.1 donnent la valeur des exportations et des importations totales de marchandises, exprimée en millions de dollars et en pourcentage du monde, des pays et régions géographiques (1.1.1), groupements économiques (1.1.2) et groupements commerciaux (1.1.3). Les flux du commerce présentés dans le tableau 1.1.1 se réfèrent au Système du Commerce Général, à l'exception des pays et territoires qui utilisent le Système du Commerce Spécial et qui sont munis d'un astérisque. Le Système du Commerce Général est utilisé lorsque le territoire statistique d'un pays coïncide avec son territoire économique, et en conséquence, les importations comprennent tous les biens admis sur le territoire du pays déclarant et les exportations tous les biens qui le quittent. Le Système du Commerce Spécial est utilisé lorsque le territoire statistique ne comprend qu'une partie du territoire économique à l'intérieur de laquelle « les biens peuvent être écoulés librement sans restriction douanière ». Dans ce cas, les importations comprennent tous les biens qui entrent dans la zone de libre circulation du pays déclarant, c'est-à-dire qui ont été dédouanés pour mise à la consommation et les exportations comprennent tous les biens qui quittent la zone de libre circulation du pays déclarant.

Les taux d'évolution annuels moyens du commerce international des marchandises, calculés à partir des valeurs des tableaux 1.1, figurent dans les tableaux 1. 2.

Les tableaux 1.3 présentent les balances commerciales (exportations f.a.b. moins importations c.a.f.), ainsi que ces mêmes balances en pourcentage des importations des pays, régions géographiques et groupements économiques.

Le tableau 1.4 indique l'importance des échanges entre pays membres de groupements commerciaux par rapport aux exportations régionales et totales de ces groupements.

DEUXIÈME PARTIE
Commerce international des marchandises par régions

Le tableau 2.1 présente la structure des exportations et des importations des pays par régions de destination et d'origine. Le plus grand nombre possible de pays en développement sont inclus tandis que les partenaires commerciaux sont regroupés en 14 groupes considérés comme particulièrement importants pour l'analyse du commerce international.

Le tableau 2.2 indique la structure des exportations par destination ainsi que des importations par origine et par groupes de produits pour le monde et une sélection de 12 groupements de pays. Le tableau fournit une information détaillée sur le réseau du commerce international avec le monde, 19 régions d'origine et de destination, et pour six différents groupes de produits.

Les totaux du commerce international des marchandises présentés dans les tableaux des première et deuxième parties ne sont pas strictement comparables en raison de sources complémentaires mais différentes et d'une marge d'exportations et d'importations non distribuées, en dépit des efforts déployés pour répartir les flux commerciaux par destinations et origines.

Les exportations ventilées par destinations peuvent accuser un écart parfois considérable par rapport aux importations déclarées par les pays destinataires en raison de divers facteurs dont les plus importants sont les suivants :

- Les importations sont déclarées en principe "valeur c.a.f." plutôt que "valeur f.a.b".
- Les importations de marchandises peuvent arriver à destination et être enregistrées longtemps après la date de leur enregistrement à l'exportation.
- D'importantes différences peuvent exister entre la destination des exportations déclarée par les pays exportateurs et la destination réelle telle qu'indiquée dans les statistiques d'importation.

TROISIÈME PARTIE
Commerce international des marchandises par produits

Le tableau 3.1 fournit la structure des exportations et des importations des pays par produits classés en 9 groupes (total, produits alimentaires, matières premières d'origine agricole, combustibles, minerais et métaux, produits manufacturés, dont produits chimiques, machines et matériel de transport, articles manufacturés divers) pour plusieurs années.

Les tableaux 3.2A, B et C présentent respectivement les exportations du monde, des économies développées et en développement, par produits à un niveau très détaillé (CTCI révision 3, position à trois chiffres). Les parts que représente chaque produit dans les exportations du monde et de la région, sont calculées pour chaque groupe d'économies, ainsi que le taux annuel de croissance et l'écart de ce dernier par rapport au taux de croissance mondial.

Le tableau 3.2D établit, pour chaque économie, la liste des principaux produits qu'elle exporte (CTCI révision 3, position à trois chiffres). La part de chaque produit dans le total des exportations du pays, de la région et du monde est également indiquée.

Le tableau 3.2E liste les plus gros exportateurs de 70 produits parmi les produits les plus exportés par les économies en développement (CTCI révision 3, position à trois chiffres), ainsi que les parts correspondantes dans le commerce mondial.

Le tableau 3.3 fournit les indices de concentration et de changements structurels des exportations et des importations des produits au niveau de la CTCI (révision 3, position à trois chiffres). Le premier indicateur a vocation à montrer comment le marché d'un produit est concentré sur quelques pays ou réparti de façon plus homogène entre les pays. L'indicateur de changement structurel indique si la répartition du commerce d'un produit entre les pays exportateurs ou importateurs a connu une évolution importante par rapport à une année de référence.

Les totaux du commerce international des marchandises présentés dans les tableaux de cette troisième partie peuvent aussi être différents des données des première et deuxième parties pour les raisons précédemment citées, auxquelles il convient d'ajouter des marges d'exportations et d'importations non distribuées par groupes de produits ou l'utilisation de nomenclatures différentes de produits par le pays exportateur et le pays importateur.

QUATRIÈME PARTIE
Indicateurs du commerce international des marchandises

Les tableaux 4.1 contiennent les résultats du calcul des indices de concentration et de diversification des pays, régions géographiques et groupements économiques. Cet indice de concentration a vocation à montrer comment les exportations et importations d'un pays ou groupe de pays sont concentrées sur quelques produits ou réparti de façon plus homogène sur une gamme de produits. L'indicateur de diversification indique si la structure par produits des exportations ou importations d'un pays ou groupe de pays diverge de la structure par produits observée au niveau du monde.

Les tableaux 4.2 fournissent les indices de volume des exportations et des importations complétant ainsi l'information en valeur disponible dans les tableaux 1.1 et 1.2, les indices de la valeur unitaire des exportations et importations et les indices de termes de l'échange et le pouvoir d'achat des exportations dérivés des indices de valeur unitaire, calculés au niveau des pays et régions géographiques (4.2.1) et des groupements économiques (4.2.2).

Afin d'améliorer la couverture des données et spécialement pour les années récentes, la méthode suivante a été utilisée pour le calcul des valeurs unitaires :
- Un ensemble d'indices de prix moyens au niveau des groupes de la CTCI (révision 3, position à 3 chiffres) a été construit en utilisant les sources disponibles.
- Au niveau des pays individuels, les indices de la valeur unitaire ont été calculés en utilisant comme pondération les valeurs des exportations et des importations de l'année précédente disponibles dans la table 3.2.

Dans certains cas ces indices peuvent différer des estimations publiées dans les sources officielles, le but principal étant de fournir des estimations approximatives et comparables pour la plupart des pays en développement.

Le tableau 4.3 contient les données sur les droits de douane NPF moyens appliqués à l'importation des principales catégories de produits non agricoles et non pétroliers, par marchés individuels.

CINQUIÈME PARTIE
Commerce international des services

Les tableaux 5.1.1, 5.1.2 et 5.1.3 présentent la valeur des exportations et des importations totales des services par pays, par régions géographiques, groupements économiques et groupements commerciaux. Les tableaux incluent les valeurs des exportations (crédits) et des importations (débits) des services qui proviennent des statistiques sur les transactions internationales de services, telles qu'elles sont présentées dans les Statistiques de la balance des paiements du FMI. Les services sont définis comme rendements économiques de produits intangibles qui peuvent être produits, transférés et consommés au même moment. Cependant, les services recouvrent un groupe large et hétérogène de produits et d'activités que l'on peut difficilement englober dans une définition. Parfois, la démarcation entre les services et les marchandises n'est pas aisée. Les services sont produits sur commande et ils ont généralement pour résultat un changement des conditions des consommateurs qui ont demandé les services. Pour que la production d'un service soit terminée, il doit être fourni au consommateur.

Les chiffres couvrent les 11 catégories principales de services conformément à la définition du Manuel de la balance des paiements du FMI (MBP5, 1993). Ces catégories comprennent : les transports; les voyages; les communications; le bâtiment et les travaux publics; les assurances; les services financiers; l'informatique et l'information; les redevances et droits de licence; les autres services aux entreprises; les services personnels, culturels et relatifs aux loisirs; et les services fournis ou reçus par les administrations publiques. De manière générale, les difficultés à mesurer statistiquement la valeur du commerce des services persistent et les données de la balance des paiements sur les services peuvent être inférieures à la valeur des transactions réelles. Les agrégats inclus dans le tableau 5.1 comprennent les valeurs manquantes, estimées par le secrétariat de la CNUCED, qui ne sont pas présentées séparément.

Le tableau 5.2 liste, parmi les économies en développement, les 20 plus gros exportateurs et importateurs pour chacun des 10 secteurs principaux du commerce des services, c'est-à-dire les transports; les voyages; les communications; le bâtiment et les travaux publics; l'informatique et l'information; les assurances; les services financiers; les redevances et droits de licence; autres services aux entreprises; et les services personnels, culturels et relatifs aux loisirs. Les services fournis ou reçus par les administrations publiques ne sont pas inclus.

Le tableau 5.3 fait apparaître les données sur les services liés au tourisme en présentant, par pays et pour les années récentes, les statistiques suivantes : valeur des dépenses totales des visiteurs, valeur des dépenses des visiteurs sans le coût du transport, nombre de nuitées des touristes et nombre d'arrivées des visiteurs. Tous les indicateurs se réfèrent aux visiteurs non résidents (visiteurs internationaux). Le visiteur international est un voyageur voyageant dans une économie - où il n'est pas résident - pour y rester moins de 12 mois et dont le but principal du voyage est d'exercer une activité qui n'est pas rémunérée par une entité résidente dans l'économie visitée. Cela inclut des personnes qui arrivent sur le territoire d'une économie pour y rester moins d'une année pour affaires ou pour des raisons personnelles. Les touristes sont ceux qui séjournent dans le pays visité au moins une nuit dans un logement collectif ou privé. Les visiteurs d'une journée sont des personnes qui ne passent pas la nuit dans le pays visité.

Le tableau 5.4 concerne le transport maritime international. Il contient des données sur la flotte marchande mondiale par pavillons d'immatriculation et par types de navires et fait spécialement ressortir le groupe des principaux pays de libre immatriculation. Un propriétaire qui enregistre son navire dans un pays "libre d'immatriculation" ne doit avoir aucune relation avec ce pays. Le nombre de pays de libre immatriculation a changé au cours des années. Le groupe de "principaux pays de libre immatriculation" comprend désormais plus de pays (10 au total) que le même groupe paru dans les versions antérieures du Manuel. Le tableau 5.4 incorpore les informations consolidées provenant des différentes éditions de la publication Review of Maritime Transport. Elle rend compte de l'évolution mondiale du transport multimodal, portuaire et maritime concernant les principaux trafics de vracs liquides, de vracs secs et de conteneurs.

SIXIÈME PARTIE
Produits de base

Le tableau 6.1 donne les indices annuels et trimestriels de prix en dollars courants sur le marché libre d'une sélection de produits de base exportés par les économies en développement. Ces indices sont aussi disponibles au niveau des groupes de produits de base suivants : produits alimentaires, boissons tropicales, huiles et graines oléagineuses, matières premières d'origine agricole, minéraux, minerais et métaux ainsi qu'un indice de l'ensemble. Les pondérations ont été calculées à partir de la valeur des exportations des pays en développement de 1999 à 2001 et les indices en utilisant 2000=100 comme année de base. Ce tableau a été établi à partir de données extraites de la base de données en ligne des statistiques de prix des produits de base accessible depuis le portail des statistiques du site web de la CNUCED.

Le tableau 6.2 complète l'information sur les prix des produits de base par les indices d'instabilité et les tendances de prix sur le marché libre d'une sélection de produits de base ayant une importance particulière pour les économies en développement.

Le tableau 6.3 présente la production d'aluminium et de cuivre à différents niveaux de transformation et leur consommation par pays et régions géographiques. Les chiffres de la production de bauxite sont exprimés en volume brut, alors que ceux de la production du minerai de cuivre sont indiqués en métal contenu.

SEPTIÈME PARTIE
Finance internationale

Le tableau 7.1 contient un état récapitulatif du «compte courant» de la balance des paiements des pays et territoires individuels. Les données du compte des transactions courantes de la balance des paiements recouvrent toutes les transactions, entre entités résidentes et non résidentes, portant sur des valeurs économiques, concernant notamment les biens, les services, les revenus et les transferts courants. Ce tableau comprend les statistiques sur ces catégories principales, y compris le détail additionnel sur les revenus d'investissement direct étranger. Pour l'information sur les concepts concernant les catégories mentionnées, veuillez vous référer au Manuel de la balance des paiements du FMI (MBP5, 1993).

Le tableau 7.2 fait apparaître l'état récapitulatif du «compte de capital et d'opérations financières» de la balance des paiements des économies individuels. Les chiffres des comptes de capital et des comptes financiers couvrent les transactions en avoirs et engagements étrangers. Les avoirs représentent des créances sur les non résidents et les engagements des dettes envers les non

résidents. Toutes les réévaluations et autres variations d'avoirs et d'engagements qui ne reflètent pas des transactions sont exclues du compte de capital et d'opérations financières. Le compte de capital est subdivisé en transferts de capital et en acquisitions et cession d'avoirs non financiers non-produits. Le compte financier recouvre les investissements (directs, de portefeuille et autres) et les avoirs de réserve (or monétaire, DTS, devises et autres créances). Ce tableau comprend les statistiques sur ces catégories principales du «compte de capital et d'opérations financières». Pour l'information sur les concepts concernant les catégories mentionnées, veuillez vous référer au Manuel de la balance des paiements du FMI (MBP5, 1993).

Les tableaux 7.3.1, 7.3.2 et 7.3.3 sont consacrés aux investissements directs en provenance de l'étranger (IDE). Ils présentent les flux entrants et sortants de l'IDE par pays et régions géographiques, groupements économiques et groupements commerciaux. Les chiffres correspondent aux données contenues dans l'Annexe statistique du World Investment Report 2006: FDI from Developing and Transition Economies: Implications for Development, de la CNUCED. L'investissement direct étranger (IDE) est un investissement impliquant une relation à long terme et témoignant de l'intérêt durable d'une entité résidant dans un pays (investisseur étranger direct ou société mère) à l'égard d'une entreprise résidant dans un autre pays (entreprise bénéficiaire, entreprise affiliée, ou encore filiale étrangère). Cet investissement englobe à la fois la transaction initiale entre les deux entités et toutes les transactions ultérieures entre elles et entre filiales étrangères, qu'elles soient constituées ou non en sociétés. L'entreprise d'investissement direct est définie comme une entreprise dotée ou non de la personnalité morale, dans laquelle un investisseur direct qui est résident d'une autre économie détient au moins 10% des actions ordinaires ou des droits de vote (ou l'équivalent).

Le tableau 7.4 fournit les informations sur les envois de fonds des travailleurs pour les principales économies en développement concernées. Ces données sont également communiquées en pourcentage du commerce international (total des exportations et importations). Selon la définition du Manuel de la balance des paiements du FMI (MBP5, 1993), les envois de fonds des travailleurs sont les transferts de biens ou d'actifs financiers effectués par les migrants qui vivent et travaillent (considérés résidents) dans une économie en faveur des résidents de leur ancien pays de résidence. Un migrant doit vivre et travailler dans une nouvelle économie durant plus d'une année pour y être considéré résident. Le MBP5 classifie séparément les envois de fonds des travailleurs de la rémunération des salariés. Les valeurs du tableau 7.4 incluent la somme des deux catégories mentionnées, afin de mieux présenter les flux entrants dans ou sortants d'une économie à travers les transferts liés aux travailleurs migrants ou non résidents.

Le tableau 7.5 fait apparaitre les données relatives aux réserves internationales (les réserves totales moins l'or) des économies en développement par pays, par régions et par groupements économiques. Les mois d'importation que ces réserves peuvent financer, dans la situation actuelle du commerce international du pays, sont également indiqués, ainsi que la variation annuelle des réserves totales. Selon la définition du FMI, les réserves totales moins l'or représentent la somme des avoirs du pays en devises, la position de ses réserves au FMI et la valeur en dollars E.U. des avoirs en DTS de ses autorités monétaires.

Les flux financiers publics vers les économies en développement sont retracés dans tableaux 7.6 par catégories de flux, pays, régions géographiques et groupements économiques. La définition des flux bilatéraux et multilatéraux est conforme aux publications du Comité d'aide au développement (CAD – OCDE).

Le tableau 7.7 contient des données sur la dette extérieure à long terme des principaux groupes d'économies en développement, en particulier la ventilation détaillée de la dette publique ou garantie par l'état par sources d'emprunt. Les données de la dette extérieure présentées dans ce tableau se basent sur le Système de notification des pays débiteurs (SNPD), géré par la Banque mondiale.

Les tableaux 8.1 fournissent le produit intérieur brut (PIB) nominal total et par habitant des pays, régions géographiques et groupements économiques. Les données de PIB en dollars ont été obtenues à partir des valeurs de PIB exprimées à l'origine en monnaies nationales. Les taux de change moyens annuels sur le marché libre, obtenus des séries statistiques du FMI, ont été utilisés pour la plupart des pays lors de la conversion en dollars.

Les taux annuels moyens de variation du PIB réel total et du PIB réel par habitant des pays, régions géographiques et groupements économiques sont disponibles dans les tableaux 8.2. Les taux de croissance se basent sur le PIB en dollars constants de l'année 1990.

Le PIB total est décomposé par catégories de dépenses et la valeur ajoutée totale par branches d'activité économique dans les tableaux 8.3, pour les pays, régions géographiques et groupements économiques.

Les tableaux 8.4 fournissent des données sur la population et la main-d'œuvre : population totale, population urbaine en pourcentage de la population totale, main-d'œuvre totale, main-d'œuvre féminine en pourcentage de la main-d'œuvre totale, main-d'œuvre dans l'agriculture, main-d'œuvre féminine en pourcentage de la main-d'œuvre totale dans l'agriculture.

Les données de base sur la population et la main-d'œuvre sont complétées par les indicateurs sur la démographie du tableau 8.5 : taux d'accroissement de la population, taux d'évolution naturelle par 1 000 habitants, taux net de migration par 1 000 habitants, taux de natalité et de mortalité bruts pour
1 000 habitants, taux de mortalité infantile pour 1 000 naissances vivantes, espérance de vie à la naissance.

AUTRES NOTES

Sauf indication contraire, les agrégats de pays sont obtenus en sommant les données des pays composant le groupe. Les calculs d'agrégats peuvent dans certains cas inclure des données estimées par le secrétariat de la CNUCED qui ne sont pas nécessairement toutes rapportées séparément.
Par ailleurs, la somme des chiffres et des pourcentages indiqués dans les tableaux ne correspond pas nécessairement aux totaux en raison des arrondis.

Les données ont été collectées et vérifiées pour qu'elles correspondent à la couverture géographique des pays, telle qu'elle est décrite en début de Manuel. Toutefois certains écarts n'ont pu être évités en fonction de la disponibilité des données. Ils sont alors décrits dans les notes de fin de tableau.

Sauf indication contraire, le terme «dollar» s'entend du dollar des États-Unis d'Amérique et les données en dollars sont exprimées en dollars courants de l'année à laquelle elles se réfèrent.

Les taux moyens d'évolution annuelle sont définis par le coefficient b de la fonction exponentielle de tendance $y = ae^{bt}$, où t représente le temps. Cette méthode permet de prendre en compte toutes les observations concernant une période donnée sans que le taux de croissance obtenu ne soit trop affecté par des valeurs exceptionnelles.

SIGNIFICATION DES SYMBOLES

0   Un zéro signifie que le montant est nul ou négligeable.

_   Un tiret signifie que la rubrique est sans objet.

..   Deux points signifient que les données ne sont pas disponibles ou ne sont pas communiquées séparément.

-    Le trait d'union entre deux millésimes (par exemple 1985-1990) indique qu'il s'agit de la période tout entière, y compris la première et la dernière année mentionnées.

(e) Estimation

(p) Donnée provisoire

(r) Donnée révisée

Les exceptions sont indiquées dans les notes de bas de page.

Les pays et territoires sont présentés suivant des critères géographiques conformes à ceux de la Division de statistique, Département des affaires économiques et sociales (DAES) de l'ONU. Les pays et territoires sont aussi regroupés suivant des critères économiques ou d'adhésion à des accords commerciaux à des fins d'analyse statistique et de recherche.

Dans cette publication, le terme «économie» couvre les régions, les pays et les territoires.

Les pays sont montrés dans les tableaux s'ils ont communiqué des données ou si des estimations ont pu être calculées.

1. Régions géographiques, pays et territoires

Les pays et territoires sont répartis en trois grandes catégories, les économies en développement, les économies en transition et les économies développées, elles-mêmes subdivisées suivant des critères géographiques.

1) Économies en développement :

Ces économies sont réparties entre quatre grandes régions géographiques : Amérique, Afrique, Asie et Océanie elles-mêmes subdivisées en sous-régions pour permettre la présentation de statistiques plus détaillées. Les exceptions à ce classement que l'on retrouve dans certains tableaux sont indiquées dans des notes.

2) Économies en transition :

Ces économies sont réparties entre deux grandes régions géographiques : Asie et Europe.

3) Économies développées :

Ces économies sont réparties entre quatre grandes régions géographiques : Amérique, Asie, Europe et Océanie.

2. Groupements économiques des économies en développement

Dans le *Manuel de statistiques de la CNUCED*, les regroupements des pays et territoires en développement sont nombreux et variés afin de disposer facilement des données statistiques nécessaires à l'analyse socio-économique et aux recherches sur le développement.

Les économies en développement sont présentées à trois niveaux d'agrégation : le groupe dans son intégralité, puis sans la Chine continentale et enfin sans les pays les moins avancés.

Les économies en développement sont également réparties en trois groupes de revenu en fonction du PIB par habitant en 2000 : revenu élevé, revenu intermédiaire et revenu faible. Cette répartition est basée sur les données de PIB et de population qui étaient disponibles en 2004 et elle n'a pas été révisée afin de maintenir la composition des groupes durant plusieurs éditions du *Manuel de statistiques*.

Le groupe des pays pauvres très endettés (PPTE) inclut 40 pays. Ces pays bénéficient de l'initiative de désendettement de la Banque mondiale et du Fonds monétaire international.

Les pays les moins avancés (PMA) et les pays en développement sans littoral sont des groupes de pays qui requièrent une attention particulière de la communauté internationale. Les PMA sont présentés aux niveaux d'agrégation suivants : Afrique et Haïti, Asie et les îles.

Depuis 1994, les Nations Unies ont également pris en compte les problèmes particuliers des petits États insulaires en développement mais n'ont pas établi de liste officielle de ces États. La liste présentée dans le *Manuel de statistiques* est utilisée par la CNUCED à des fins analytiques uniquement.

Le groupement des principaux exportateurs de pétrole comprend les pays dont la part du pétrole et des produits pétroliers ne représentait pas moins de 50 % de leurs exportations totales, et les exportations de ces produits s'élevaient à au moins 2 milliards de dollars en 2003-2005 en moyenne. Les pays composant ce groupement sont répartis en trois zones géographiques : Afrique, Amérique et Asie.

Le groupement des principaux exportateurs d'articles manufacturés, répartis entre Amérique et Asie, comprend les économies dont la part d'articles manufacturés ne représentait pas moins de 50 % de leurs exportations totales, et leurs exportations d'articles manufacturés avaient une valeur moyenne d'au moins 22 milliards de dollars en 2003-2005.

La composition des groupements des économies émergentes (réparties entre Amérique et Asie) et des économies nouvellement industrialisées (première et deuxième génération) correspond à celle utilisée dans le *Rapport sur le commerce et le développement* de la CNUCED.

Les différentes régions géographiques sont également présentées à différents niveaux d'agrégation :

- *Afrique* : Afrique septentrionale sans le Soudan, Afrique subsaharienne, Soudan compris, avec et sans l'Afrique du Sud.

- *Amérique* : Amérique centrale et Grandes Antilles sans Porto Rico, avec et sans le Mexique, Amérique du Sud et centrale, Amérique du Sud sans le Brésil.

- *Asie* : Asie orientale et du Sud-Est sans la Chine et Asie méridionale sans l'Inde.

3. Groupements commerciaux et interrégionaux

Les statistiques des groupements commerciaux sont présentées dès lors qu'elles sont pertinentes et présentent un intérêt analytique. Ces groupements englobent toutes les économies concernées et sont classés selon les grandes régions géographiques utilisées précédemment, à l'exception des groupements interrégionaux suivants : le groupe des États d'Afrique, des Caraïbes et du Pacifique (ACP), le groupe de Coopération économique de l'Asie et du Pacifique (CEAP), le groupe de Coopération économique de la mer Noire (CEMN) et la Communauté des États indépendants (CEI).

ÉCONOMIES EN DÉVELOPPEMENT

RÉGIONS GÉOGRAPHIQUES

Afrique

Afrique orientale

Burundi	Malawi	Seychelles
Comores	Maurice	Somalie
Djibouti	Mayotte	Territoire britannique de l'océan Indien
Érythrée	Mozambique	Zambie
Éthiopie	Ouganda	Zimbabwe
Kenya	République-Unie de Tanzanie	
Madagascar	Rwanda	

Afrique centrale

Angola	Gabon	République démocratique du Congo
Cameroun	Guinée équatoriale	Sao Tomé-et-Principe
Congo	République centrafricaine	Tchad

Afrique septentrionale

Algérie	Maroc	Tunisie
Égypte	Sahara occidental	
Jamahiriya arabe libyenne	Soudan	

Afrique australe

Afrique du Sud	Lesotho	Swaziland
Botswana	Namibie	

Afrique occidentale

Bénin	Guinée	Nigéria
Burkina Faso	Guinée-Bissau	Sainte-Hélène
Cap-Vert	Libéria	Sénégal
Côte d'Ivoire	Mali	Sierra Leone
Gambie	Mauritanie	Togo
Ghana	Niger	

Amérique

Amérique centrale

Belize	Guatemala	Nicaragua
Costa Rica	Honduras	Panama
El Salvador	Mexique	

Amérique du Sud

Argentine	Équateur	Suriname
Bolivie	Guyana	Uruguay
Brésil	Îles Falkland (Malvinas)	Venezuela (République bolivarienne du)
Chili	Paraguay	
Colombie	Pérou	

Caraïbes

Grandes Antilles	**Petites Antilles**	
Cuba	Anguilla	Îles Turques et Caïques
Haïti	Antigua-et-Barbuda	Îles Vierges américaines
Jamaïque	Antilles néerlandaises	Îles Vierges britanniques
République dominicaine	Aruba	Montserrat
	Bahamas	Sainte-Lucie
	Barbade	Saint-Kitts-et-Nevis
	Dominique	Saint-Vincent-et-les Grenadines
	Grenade	Trinité-et-Tobago
	Îles Caïmanes	

RÉGIONS GÉOGRAPHIQUES (fin)

Asie

Asie orientale

Chine	Mongolie
Hong Kong, région administrative spéciale de Chine	Province chinoise de Taiwan
	République de Corée
Macao, région administrative spéciale de Chine	République populaire démocratique de Corée

Asie méridionale

Afghanistan	Inde	Népal
Bangladesh	Iran (République islamique d')	Pakistan
Bhoutan	Maldives	Sri Lanka

Asie du Sud-Est

Brunéi Darussalam	Myanmar	Thaïlande
Cambodge	Philippines	Timor-Leste
Indonésie	République démocratique populaire lao	Viet Nam
Malaisie	Singapour	

Asie occidentale

Arabie saoudite	Koweït	Territoire palestinien occupé
Bahreïn	Liban	Turquie
Émirats arabes unis	Oman	Yémen
Iraq	Qatar	
Jordanie	République arabe syrienne	

Océanie

Fidji	Îles Salomon	Pitcairn
Guam	Île Wake	Polynésie française
Îles Christmas	Îles Wallis-et-Futuna	Samoa
Îles Cocos (Keeling)	Kiribati	Samoa américaines
Îles Cook	Micronésie (États fédérés de)	Tokélaou
Île Johnston	Nauru	Tonga
Îles Mariannes septentrionales	Nioué	Tuvalu
Îles Marshall	Nouvelle-Calédonie	Vanuatu
Îles Midway	Palaos	
Île Norfolk	Papouasie-Nouvelle-Guinée	

ÉCONOMIES EN TRANSITION

RÉGIONS GÉOGRAPHIQUES

Asie

Arménie	Kazakhstan	Tadjikistan
Azerbaïdjan	Kirghizistan	Turkménistan
Géorgie	Ouzbékistan	

Europe

Albanie	ex-République yougoslave de Macédoine	Serbie et Monténégro
Bélarus	Fédération de Russie	Ukraine
Bosnie-Herzégovine	Moldova	
Croatie		

ÉCONOMIES DÉVELOPPÉES

RÉGIONS GÉOGRAPHIQUES

Amérique

Bermudes	États-Unis d'Amérique, y compris	Groenland
Canada	Porto Rico	Saint-Pierre-et-Miquelon

Asie

Israël

Japon

Europe

Allemagne	Grèce	Portugal
Andorre	Hongrie	République tchèque
Autriche	Îles Féroé	Roumanie
Belgique	Irlande	Royaume-Uni de Grande-Bretagne
Bulgarie	Islande	et d'Irlande du Nord, y compris les
Chypre	Italie	îles Anglo-Normandes et l'île de Man
Danemark	Lettonie	Saint-Marin
Espagne	Lituanie	Saint-Siège
Estonie	Luxembourg	Slovaquie
Finlande, y compris les îles d'Åland	Malte	Slovénie
France, y compris la Guadeloupe,	Norvège, y compris les îles Svalbard	Suède
la Guyane française, la Martinique,	et Jan Mayen	Suisse, y compris le Liechtenstein
Monaco et la Réunion	Pays-Bas	
Gibraltar	Pologne	

Océanie

Australie

Nouvelle-Zélande

ÉCONOMIES EN DÉVELOPPEMENT

GROUPEMENTS ÉCONOMIQUES

GROUPES DE REVENU

PIB courant par habitant supérieur à 4 500 dollars en 2000 : Revenu élevé (42)

Anguilla
Antigua-et-Barbuda
Antilles néerlandaises
Arabie saoudite
Argentine
Aruba
Bahamas
Bahreïn
Barbade
Brunéi Darussalam
Chili
Émirats arabes unis
Grenade
Guam
Hong-Kong, région administrative
    spéciale de Chine

Îles Caïmanes
Îles Falkland (Malvinas)
Îles Mariannes du Nord
Îles Turques et Caïques
Îles Vierges américaines
Îles Vierges britanniques
Jamahiriya arabe libyenne
Koweït
Liban
Macao, région administrative
    spéciale de Chine
Mexique
Montserrat
Nouvelle-Calédonie
Oman
Palaos

Polynésie française
Province chinoise de Taiwan
Qatar
République de Corée
Sainte-Lucie
Saint-Kitts-et-Nevis
Samoa américaines
Seychelles
Singapour
Trinité-et-Tobago
Uruguay
Venezuela (République bolivarienne du)

PIB courant par habitant compris entre 1 000 et 4 500 dollars en 2000 : Revenu intermédiaire (50)

Afrique du Sud
Algérie
Belize
Bolivie
Botswana
Brésil
Cap-Vert
Colombie
Costa Rica
Cuba
Dominique
Égypte
El Salvador
Équateur
Fidji
Gabon
Guatemala

Guinée équatoriale
Îles Cook
Îles Marshall
Îles Wallis-et-Futuna
Iran (République islamique d')
Jamaïque
Jordanie
Malaisie
Maldives
Maroc
Maurice
Micronésie (États fédérés de)
Namibie
Nauru
Nioué
Panama
Paraguay

Pérou
République arabe syrienne
République dominicaine
Sainte-Hélène
Saint-Vincent-et-les Grenadines
Samoa
Suriname
Swaziland
Territoire palestinien occupé
Thaïlande
Tokélaou
Tonga
Tunisie
Turquie
Tuvalu
Vanuatu

PIB courant par habitant inférieur à 1 000 dollars en 2000 : Revenu faible (65)

Afghanistan
Angola
Bangladesh
Bénin
Bhoutan
Burkina Faso
Burundi
Cambodge
Cameroun
Chine
Comores
Congo
Côte d'Ivoire
Djibouti
Érythrée
Éthiopie
Gambie
Ghana
Guinée
Guinée-Bissau
Guyana
Haïti
Honduras

Îles Salomon
Inde
Indonésie
Iraq
Kenya
Kiribati
Lesotho
Libéria
Madagascar
Malawi
Mali
Mauritanie
Mongolie
Mozambique
Myanmar
Népal
Nicaragua
Niger
Nigéria
Ouganda
Pakistan
Papouasie-Nouvelle-Guinée
Philippines

République centrafricaine
République démocratique du Congo
République démocratique populaire lao
République populaire démocratique
    de Corée
République-Unie de Tanzanie
Rwanda
Sao Tomé-et-Principe
Sénégal
Sierra Leone
Somalie
Soudan
Sri Lanka
Tchad
Timor-Leste
Togo
Viet Nam
Yémen
Zambie
Zimbabwe

GROUPEMENTS ÉCONOMIQUES (suite)

Pays pauvres très endettés - PPTE (41)

Afghanistan	Guinée-Bissau	Ouganda
Bénin	Guyana	République centrafricaine
Bolivie	Haïti	République démocratique du Congo
Burkina Faso	Honduras	République-Unie de Tanzanie
Burundi	Kirghizistan	Rwanda
Cameroun	Libéria	Sao Tomé-et-Principe
Comores	Madagascar	Sénégal
Congo	Malawi	Sierra Leone
Côte d'Ivoire	Mali	Somalie
Érythrée	Mauritanie	Soudan
Éthiopie	Mozambique	Tchad
Gambie	Népal	Togo
Ghana	Nicaragua	Zambie
Guinée	Niger	

Pays en développement sans littoral (31)

Afghanistan	Kirghizistan*	République centrafricaine
Arménie*	Lesotho	République démocratique populaire lao
Azerbaïdjan*	Malawi	Rwanda
Bhoutan	Mali	Swaziland
Bolivie	Moldova*	Tadjikistan*
Botswana	Mongolie	Tchad
Burkina Faso	Népal	Turkménistan*
Burundi	Niger	Zambie
Éthiopie	Ouganda	Zimbabwe
ex-République yougoslave de Macédoine*	Ouzbékistan*	
Kazakhstan*	Paraguay	

* Ces pays font partie du groupement des économies en transition (ni développées ni en développement).
  Cependant, comme ce sont des pays sans littoral, ils appartiennent aussi à ce groupement.

Petits États insulaires en développement (29)

Antigua-et-Barbuda	Jamaïque	Saint-Vincent-et-les Grenadines
Bahamas	Kiribati	Samoa
Barbade	Maldives	Sao Tomé-et-Principe
Cap-Vert	Maurice	Seychelles
Comores	Micronésie (États fédérés de)	Timor-Leste
Dominique	Nauru	Tonga
Fidji	Palaos	Trinité-et-Tobago
Grenade	Papouasie-Nouvelle-Guinée	Tuvalu
Îles Marshall	Sainte-Lucie	Vanuatu
Îles Salomon	Saint-Kitts-et-Nevis	

GROUPEMENTS ÉCONOMIQUES (fin)

Pays les moins avancés - PMA (49)

Afrique et Haïti

	Année d'inclusion dans le groupe		Année d'inclusion dans le groupe		Année d'inclusion dans le groupe
Angola	1994	Haïti	1971	République démocratique du Congo	1991
Bénin	1971	Lesotho	1971	République-Unie de Tanzanie	1971
Burkina Faso	1971	Libéria	1990	Rwanda	1971
Burundi	1971	Madagascar	1991	Sénégal	2001
Djibouti	1982	Malawi	1971	Sierra Leone	1982
Erythrée	1994	Mali	1971	Somalie	1971
Ethiopie	1971	Mauritanie	1986	Soudan	1971
Gambie	1975	Mozambique	1988	Tchad	1971
Guinée	1971	Niger	1971	Togo	1982
Guinée-Bissau	1981	Ouganda	1971	Zambie	1991
Guinée équatoriale	1982	République centrafricaine	1975		

Asie / Îles

	Année d'inclusion dans le groupe		Année d'inclusion dans le groupe
Asie		**Îles**	
Afghanistan	1971	Comores	1977
Bangladesh	1975	Iles Salomon	1991
Bhoutan	1971	Kiribati	1986
Cambodge	1991	Maldives	1971
Myanmar	1987	Samoa	1971
Népal	1971	Sao Tomé-et-Principe	1982
République démocratique		Timor-Leste	2003
populaire lao	1971	Tuvalu	1986
Yémen	1971	Vanuatu	1985

Principaux pays exportateurs de pétrole (22)

Afrique

Algérie	Gabon	Nigéria
Angola	Guinée équatoriale	Soudan
Congo	Jamahiriya arabe libyenne	

Amérique

Equateur	Venezuela (République bolivarienne du)
Trinité-et-Tobago	

Asie

Arabie saoudite	Iran (République islamique d')	Qatar
Bahreïn	Iraq	République arabe syrienne
Brunéi Darussalam	Koweït	Yémen
Emirats arabes unis	Oman	

Principaux pays exportateurs d'articles manufacturés (12)

Amérique

Brésil
Mexique

Asie

Chine	Malaisie	Singapour
Hong Kong, région administrative	Philippines	Thaïlande
spéciale de Chine	Province chinoise de Taiwan	Turquie
Inde	République de Corée	

Économies émergentes (10)

Amérique	Asie
Argentine	Malaisie
Brésil	Province chinoise de Taiwan
Chili	République de Corée
Mexique	Singapour
Pérou	Thaïlande

Économies nouvellement industrialisées (8)

Première génération	Deuxième génération
Hong Kong, région administrative	Indonésie
spéciale de Chine	Malaisie
Province chinoise de Taiwan	Philippines
République de Corée	Thaïlande
Singapour	

Afrique

Communauté de développement de l'Afrique australe - CDAA (14)

	Année d'adhésion
Afrique du Sud	1994
Angola	1992
Botswana	1992
Lesotho	1992
Madagascar	2005
Malawi	1992
Maurice	1992
Mozambique	1992
Namibie	1992
République démocratique du Congo	1992
République-Unie de Tanzanie	1992
Swaziland	1992
Zambie	1992
Zimbabwe	1992

Communauté économique des États de l'Afrique centrale - CEEAC (11)

Angola	1999
Burundi	1983
Cameroun	1983
Congo	1983
Gabon	1983
Guinée équatoriale	1983
République centrafricaine	1983
République démocratique du Congo	1983
Rwanda	1983
Sao Tomé-et-Principe	1983
Tchad	1983

Communauté économique et monétaire de l'Afrique centrale CEMAC (6)

Cameroun	1994
Congo	1994
Gabon	1994
Guinée équatoriale	1994
République centrafricaine	1994
Tchad	1994

Communauté économique des États de l'Afrique de l'Ouest - CEDEAO (15)

	Année d'adhésion
Bénin	1975
Burkina Faso	1975
Cap-Vert	1977
Côte d'Ivoire	1975
Gambie	1975
Ghana	1975
Guinée	1975
Guinée-Bissau	1975
Libéria	1975
Mali	1975
Niger	1975
Nigéria	1975
Sénégal	1975
Sierra Leone	1975
Togo	1975

Communauté économique des pays des Grands Lacs - CEPGL (3)

Burundi	1976
République démocratique du Congo	1976
Rwanda	1976

Marché commun des États de l'Afrique de l'Est et du Sud - COMESA (19)

Burundi	1994
Comores	1994
Djibouti	1994
Egypte	1994
Erythrée	1994
Ethiopie	1994
Kenya	1994
Jamahiriya arabe libyenne	2005
Madagascar	1994
Malawi	1994
Maurice	1994
Ouganda	1994
République démocratique du Congo	1994
Rwanda	1994
Seychelles	1994
Soudan	1994
Swaziland	1994
Zambie	1994
Zimbabwe	1994

Union du fleuve Mano - UFM (3)

	Année d'adhésion
Guinée	1980
Libéria	1973
Sierra Leone	1973

Union du Maghreb arabe - UMA (5)

Algérie	1989
Jamahiriya arabe libyenne	1989
Maroc	1989
Mauritanie	1989
Tunisie	1989

Union économique et monétaire ouest-africaine - UEMOA (8)

Bénin	1994
Burkina Faso	1994
Côte d'Ivoire	1994
Guinée-Bissau	1994
Mali	1994
Niger	1994
Sénégal	1994
Togo	1994

Amérique

Accord de libre-échange nord-américain - ALENA (3)

	Année d'adhésion
Canada	1994
États-Unis d'Amérique	1994
Mexique	1994

Association latino-américaine d'intégration - ALADI (12)

Argentine	1980
Bolivie	1980
Brésil	1980
Chili	1980
Colombie	1980
Cuba	1999
Equateur	1980
Mexique	1980
Paraguay	1980
Pérou	1980
Uruguay	1980
Venezuela (République	

Communauté andine - ANCOM (4)

	Année d'adhésion
Bolivie	1996
Colombie	1996
Équateur	1996
Pérou	1996

Communauté des Caraïbes - CARICOM (15)

	Année d'adhésion
Antigua-et-Barbuda	1974
Bahamas	1983
Barbade	1973
Belize	1974
Dominique	1974
Grenade	1974
Guyana	1973
Haïti	1997
Jamaïque	1973
Montserrat	1974
Sainte Lucie	1974
Saint-Kitts-et-Nevis	1974
Saint-Vincent-et-les Grenadines	1974
Suriname	1995
Trinité-et-Tobago	1973

GROUPEMENTS COMMERCIAUX

Amérique (fin)

	Année d'adhésion		*Année d'adhésion*		*Année d'adhésion*
Marché commun d'Amérique centrale - MCAC (5)		**Zone de libre-échange des Amériques - ZLEA (34)**			
Costa Rica	1962	Antigua-et-Barbuda	1994	Paraguay	1994
El Salvador	1961	Argentine	1994	Pérou	1994
Guatemala	1961	Bahamas	1994	République dominicaine	1994
Honduras	1961	Barbade	1994	Sainte-Lucie	1994
Nicaragua	1961	Belize	1994	Saint-Kitts-et-Nevis	1994
		Bolivie	1994	Saint-Vincent-et-les Grenadines	1994
Marché commun sud-américain - MERCOSUR (4)		Brésil	1994	Suriname	1994
		Canada	1994	Trinité-et-Tobago	1994
Argentine	1994	Chili	1994	Uruguay	1994
Brésil	1994	Colombie	1994	Venezuela (République bolivarienne du)	1994
Paraguay	1994	Costa Rica	1994		
Uruguay	1994	Dominique	1994		
		El Salvador	1994		
Organisation des États des Caraïbes orientales - OECO (9)		Équateur	1994		
		États-Unis d'Amérique	1994		
Anguilla	1995	Grenade	1994		
Antigua-et-Barbuda	1981	Guatemala	1994		
Dominique	1981	Guyana	1994		
Grenade	1981	Haïti	1994		
Îles Vierges britanniques	1984	Honduras	1994		
Montserrat	1981	Jamaïque	1994		
Sainte-Lucie	1981	Mexique	1994		
Saint-Kitts-et-Nevis	1981	Nicaragua	1994		
Saint-Vincent-et-les Grenadines	1981	Panama	1994		

Asie

	Année d'adhésion		*Année d'adhésion*		*Année d'adhésion*
Accord commercial de l'Asie et du Pacifique - ACAP (6) *		**Association des nations de l'Asie du Sud-Est - ANASE (10)**		**Conseil de coopération du Golfe - CCG (6)**	
Bangladesh	1975	Brunéi Darussalam	1984	Arabie saoudite	1981
Chine	2001	Cambodge	1999	Bahreïn	1981
Inde	1975	Indonésie	1967	Emirats arabes unis	1981
République de Corée	1975	Malaisie	1967	Koweït	1981
République démocratique populaire lao	1975	Myanmar	1997	Oman	1981
Sri Lanka	1975	Philippines	1967	Qatar	1981
* ex-Accord de Bangkok		République démocratique populaire lao	1997	**Organisation de coopération économique - OCE (10)**	
Association de l'Asie du Sud pour la coopération régionale - SAARC (7)		Singapour	1967	Afghanistan	1992
		Thaïlande	1967	Azerbaïdjan	1992
Bangladesh	1985	Viet Nam	1995	Iran (République islamique d')	1985
Bhoutan	1985			Kazakhstan	1992
Inde	1985			Kirghizistan	1992
Maldives	1985			Ouzbékistan	1992
Népal	1985			Pakistan	1985
Pakistan	1985			Tadjikistan	1992
Sri Lanka	1985			Turkménistan	1992
				Turquie	1985

Europe

	Année d'adhésion		*Année d'adhésion*		*Année d'adhésion*
Association européenne de libre-échange - AELE (3)		Grèce	1981	**Zone euro (12)**	
		Hongrie	2004	Allemagne	2002
Islande	1960	Irlande	1973	Autriche	2002
Norvège	1960	Italie	1957	Belgique	2002
Suisse	1960	Lettonie	2004	Espagne	2002
		Lituanie	2004	Finlande	2002
Union européenne - UE (27)		Luxembourg	1957	France	2002
Allemagne	1957	Malte	2004	Grèce	2002
Autriche	1995	Pays-Bas	1957	Irlande	2002
Belgique	1957	Pologne	2004	Italie	2002
Bulgarie	2008	Portugal	1986	Luxembourg	2002
Chypre	2004	République tchèque	2004	Pays-Bas	2002
Danemark	1973	Roumanie	2008	Portugal	2002
Espagne	1986	Royaume-Uni	1973		
Estonie	2004	Slovaquie	2004		
Finlande	1995	Slovénie	2004		

Océanie

Année d'adhésion

Groupe Fer de lance mélanésien - MSG (4)

Fidji	1998
Îles Salomon	1993
Papouasie-Nouvelle-Guinée	1993
Vanuatu	1993

Groupements interrégionaux

Groupe des États d'Afrique, des Caraïbes et du Pacifique - ACP (79)

Afrique du Sud	Guinée équatoriale	République démocratique du Congo
Angola	Guyana	République dominicaine
Antigua-et-Barbuda	Haïti	République-Unie de Tanzanie
Bahamas	Îles Cook	Rwanda
Barbade	Îles Marshall	Sainte-Lucie
Belize	Îles Salomon	Saint-Kitts-et-Nevis
Bénin	Jamaïque	Saint-Vincent-et-les Grenadines
Botswana	Kenya	Samoa
Burkina Faso	Kiribati	Sao Tomé-et-Principe
Burundi	Lesotho	Sénégal
Cameroun	Libéria	Seychelles
Cap-Vert	Madagascar	Sierra Leone
Comores	Malawi	Somalie
Congo	Mali	Soudan
Côte d'Ivoire	Maurice	Suriname
Cuba	Mauritanie	Swaziland
Djibouti	Micronésie (Etats fédérés de)	Tchad
Dominique	Mozambique	Timor-Leste
Erythrée	Namibie	Togo
Ethiopie	Nauru	Tonga
Fidji	Niger	Trinité-et-Tobago
Gabon	Nigéria	Tuvalu
Gambie	Nioué	Vanuatu
Ghana	Ouganda	Zambie
Grenade	Palaos	Zimbabwe
Guinée	Papouasie-Nouvelle-Guinée	
Guinée-Bissau	République centrafricaine	

Année d'adhésion

Coopération économique de l'Asie et du Pacifique - CEAP (21)

Australie	1989
Brunéi Darussalam	1989
Canada	1989
Chili	1994
Chine	1991
Etats-Unis d'Amérique	1989
Fédération de Russie	1998
Hong Kong, région administrative spéciale	1991
Indonésie	1989
Japon	1989
Malaisie	1989
Mexique	1993
Nouvelle-Zélande	1989
Papouasie-Nouvelle-Guinée	1993
Pérou	1998
Philippines	1989
Province chinoise de Taiwan	1991
République de Corée	1989
Singapour	1989
Thaïlande	1989
Viet Nam	1998

Année d'adhésion

Coopération économique de la mer Noire - CEMN (12)

Albanie	1992
Arménie	1992
Azerbaïdjan	1992
Bulgarie	1992
Fédération de Russie	1992
Géorgie	1992
Grèce	1992
Moldova	1992
Roumanie	1992
Serbie	2004
Turquie	1992
Ukraine	1992

Année d'adhésion

Communauté des États indépendants - CEI (12)

Arménie	1991
Azerbaïdjan	1991
Bélarus	1991
Fédération de Russie	1991
Géorgie	1993
Kazakhstan	1991
Kirghizistan	1991
Moldova	1991
Ouzbékistan	1991
Tadjikistan	1991
Turkménistan	1991
Ukraine	1991

AASP	autres apports du secteur public
ACAP	Accord commercial de l'Asie et du Pacifique (ex-Accord de Bangkok)
ACP	Groupe des États d'Afrique, des Caraïbes et du Pacifique
AELE	Association européenne de libre-échange
AGCS	Accord général sur le commerce des services
ALADI	Association latino-américaine d'intégration
ALENA	Accord de libre-échange nord-américain
ANASE	Association des nations de l'Asie du Sud-Est
ANCOM	Communauté andine
anc.	ancien, ancienne, anciennement
AP	aide publique
APD	aide publique au développement
CAD	Comité d'aide au développement (OCDE)
CARICOM	Communauté des Caraïbes
CCG	Conseil de coopération du Golfe
CDAA	Communauté de développement de l'Afrique australe
CEAP	Coopération économique de l'Asie et du Pacifique
CEDEAO	Communauté économique des États de l'Afrique de l'Ouest
CEE	Commission économique pour l'Europe
CEEAC	Communauté économique des États de l'Afrique centrale
CEI	Communauté des États indépendants
CEMAC	Communauté économique et monétaire de l'Afrique centrale (anc. UDEAC)
CEMN	Coopération économique de la mer Noire
CEPGL	Communauté économique des pays des Grands Lacs
CESAP	Commission économique et sociale pour l'Asie et le Pacifique
CESAO	Commission économique et sociale pour l'Asie occidentale
c.a.f.	coût, assurance, fret
CNUCED	Conférence des Nations Unies sur le commerce et le développement
COMESA	Marché commun d'Afrique de l'Est et du Sud
CTCI	Classification type pour le commerce international
DTS	droit de tirage spécial
f.a.b.	franco à bord
FAO	Organisation des Nations Unies pour l'alimentation et l'agriculture
FBCF	formation brute de capital fixe
FMI	Fonds monétaire international
IDE	Investissement direct étranger
ISBLM	institutions sans but lucratif au service des ménages
LERY	L'ex-République yougoslave de Macédoine
MBP	*Manuel de la balance des paiements* (FMI)
MCAC	Marché commun d'Amérique centrale
MERCOSUR	Marché commun sud-américain
MSG	Groupe Fer de lance mélanésien
n.c.a.	non classé ailleurs
n.d.a.	non dénommé ailleurs
NEI	nouvelles économies industrialisées
NPF	nation la plus favorisée
OCDE	Organisation de coopération et de développement économiques
OCE	Organisation de coopération économique
OECO	Organisation des États des Caraïbes orientales
OIT	Organisation internationale du travail
OMC	Organisation mondiale du commerce
OMS	Organisation mondiale de la santé
OMT	Organisation mondiale du tourisme
ONU/DAES/DS	Organisation des Nations Unies, Département des affaires économiques et sociales, Division de statistique
ONUSIDA	Programme commun des Nations Unies sur le VIH/sida
OPEP	Organisation des pays exportateurs de pétrole
PIB	produit intérieur brut
PMA	pays les moins avancés
PNB	produit national brut
PNUD	Programme des Nations Unies pour le développement
PPTE	pays pauvres très endettés
RAS	région administrative spéciale
RSF	République socialiste fédérative de Yougoslavie (anc.)
SAARC	Association de l'Asie du Sud pour la coopération régionale
SNPD	Système de notification des pays débiteurs
STN	société transnationale
UE	Union européenne
UEMOA	Union économique et monétaire des États de l'Afrique de l'Ouest
UFM	Union du fleuve Mano
UMA	Union du Maghreb arabe
UNESCO	Organisation des Nations Unies pour l'éducation, la science et la culture
UNICEF	Fonds des Nations Unies pour l'enfance
URSS	Union des Républiques socialistes soviétiques
ZLEA	Zone de libre échange des Amériques

The *Handbook of Statistics* refers to the Standard International Trade Classification (SITC) Revision 3 detailed below.

Le *Manuel de statistiques* se réfère à la Classification type pour le commerce international (CTCI) révision 3 qui est détaillée ci-dessous.

Depending on the table, nomenclature of statistics is detailed at the 3-digit level or by broad product group as follows:

Les statistiques sont présentées, selon les tableaux, au niveau détaillé de la nomenclature (position à trois chiffres) ou par groupes de produits dont la composition est la suivante :

SITC Codes Codes CTCI	Product groups	Groupes de produits
0 + 1 + 22 + 4	All food items	Produits alimentaires
2 - (22 + 27 + 28)	Agricultural raw materials	Matières premières d'origine agricole
27 + 28 + 68 + 667 + 971	Ores, metals, precious stones and non-monetary gold	Minerais, métaux, pierres précieuses et or à usage non monétaire
3	Fuels	Combustibles
5 to 8 - (667 + 68)	Manufactured goods:	Articles manufacturés :
5	- Chemical products	- Produits chimiques
7	- Machinery and transport equipment	- Machines et matériel de transport
6 + 8 - (667 + 68)	- Other manufactured goods	- Articles manufacturés divers

Codes	Standard International Trade Classification (SITC) Revision 3 (1 to 3 digits)	Classification type pour le commerce international (CTCI) révision 3 (positions de un à trois chiffres)
0	**Food and live animals**	**Produits alimentaires et animaux vivants**
00	**Live animals other than animals of division 03**	**Animaux vivants autres que ceux figurant dans la division 03**
001	Live animals other than animals of division 03	Animaux vivants autres que ceux figurant dans la division 03
01	**Meat and meat preparations**	**Viandes et préparations de viandes**
011	Meat of bovine animals, fresh, chilled or frozen	Viande des animaux de l'espèce bovine, fraîche, réfrigérée/congelée
012	Other meat and edible meat offal	Autres viandes et abats comestibles
016	Meat, edible meat offal, salted, dried; flours, meals	Viandes et abats comestibles salés, fumés; farines et poudres
017	Meat, edible meat offal, prepared, preserved, n.e.s.	Préparations de viandes et d'abats, n.d.a.
02	**Dairy products and birds' eggs**	**Produits laitiers et oeufs d'oiseaux**
022	Milk, cream and milk products (excluding butter, cheese)	Lait et produits laitiers (sauf beurre, fromages)
023	Butter and other fats and oils derived from milk	Beurre et autres matières grasses du lait
024	Cheese and curd	Fromages et caillebotte
025	Birds' eggs, and eggs' yolks; egg albumin	Oeufs d'oiseaux et jaunes d'oeufs frais, blanc d'oeuf
03	**Fish (not marine mammals), crustaceans, molluscs and aquatic invertebrates and preparations thereof**	**Poissons, crustacés et mollusques et préparations de poisons, de crustacés et de mollusques**
034	Fish, fresh (live or dead), chilled or frozen	Poissons frais, vivants ou morts, réfrigérés ou congelés
035	Fish, dried, salted or in brine; smoked fish	Poissons séchés, salés, fumés
036	Crustaceans, molluscs and aquatic invertebrates	Crustacés, mollusques et invertébrés aquatiques
037	Fish, aqua. invertebrates, prepared, preserved, n.e.s.	Poissons, crustacés, mollusques, préparés ou conservés, n.d.a.
04	**Cereals and cereal preparations**	**Céréales et préparations à base de céréales**
041	Wheat (including spelt) and meslin, unmilled	Froment (dont épeautre) et méteil non moulus
042	Rice	Riz
043	Barley, unmilled	Orge non mondée
044	Maize (not including sweet corn), unmilled	Maïs non moulu
045	Cereals, unmilled (excluding wheat, rice, barley, maize)	Céréales non moulues (sauf froment, riz, orge, maïs)
046	Meal and flour of wheat and flour of meslin	Semoules
047	Other cereal meals and flour	Autres semoules et farines de céréales
048	Cereal preparations, flour of fruits or vegetables	Préparations; céréales, fécules de fruit ou légume
05	**Vegetables and fruits**	**Légumes et fruits**
054	Vegetables, fresh, chilled, frozen or simply preserved; roots tubers and other edible vegetable products, n.e.s. fresh, dried	Légumes et plantes potagères, frais, réfrigérés, congelés ou simplement conservés; autres produits végétaux, n.d.a. frais, séchés
056	Vegetables, roots, tubers, prepared, preserved, n.e.s.	Préparations ou conserves de légumes, n.d.a.
057	Fruits and nuts (excluding oil nuts), fresh or dried	Fruits (sauf oléagineux), frais ou secs
058	Fruit, preserved, and fruit preparations (no juice)	Préparations et conserves de fruits (sauf jus)
059	Fruit and vegetable juices, unfermented, no spirit	Jus de fruits, non fermentés, sans alcool
06	**Sugars, sugar preparations and honey**	**Sucres, préparations à base de sucre, et miel**
061	Sugars, molasses and honey	Sucres, mélasses et miel
062	Sugar confectionery	Sucreries
07	**Coffee, tea, cocoa, spices, and manufactures thereof**	**Café, thé, cacao, épices, et produits dérivés**
071	Coffee and coffee substitutes	Café et succédanés du café
072	Cocoa	Cacao

	Product classification for international trade	Classification des produits pour le commerce international
073	Chocolate, food preparations with cocoa, n.e.s.	Chocolat et autres préparations du cacao, n.d.a.
074	Tea and mate	Thé et maté
075	Spices	Épices
08	**Feeding stuff for animals (excluding unmilled cereals)**	**Nourriture destinée aux animaux (sauf céréales non moulues)**
081	Feeding stuff for animals (excluding unmilled cereals)	Nourriture destinée aux animaux (sauf céréales non moulues)
09	**Miscellaneous edible products and preparations**	**Produits et préparations alimentaires divers**
091	Margarine and shortening	Margarine et graisses culinaires
098	Edible products and preparations, n.e.s.	Produits et préparations alimentaires, n.d.a.
1	**Beverages and tobacco**	**Boissons et tabacs**
11	**Beverages**	**Boissons**
111	Non-alcoholic beverages, n.e.s.	Boissons non alcooliques, n.d.a.
112	Alcoholic beverages	Boissons alcooliques
12	**Tobacco and tobacco manufactures**	**Tabacs bruts et fabriqués**
121	Tobacco, unmanufactured; tobacco refuse	Tabacs bruts ou non fabriqués; déchets de tabac
122	Tobacco, manufactured	Tabacs fabriqués (dont succédanés de tabac)
2	**Crude materials, inedible, except fuels**	**Matières brutes non comestibles, sauf carburants**
21	**Hides, skins and furskins, raw**	**Cuirs, peaux et pelleteries, bruts**
211	Hides and skins (except furskins), raw	Cuirs et peaux (sauf pelleteries), bruts
212	Furskins, raw, other than hides and skins of group 211	Pelleteries brutes autres que ceux du groupe 211
22	**Oil seeds and oleaginous fruits**	**Graines et fruits oléagineux**
222	Oil seeds & oleaginous fruits (excl. flour) of a kind used for the extraction of soft' oils	Graines et fruits oléagineux (sauf farines) servant normalement à l'extraction d'autres huiles végétales fixes douces
223	Oil seeds & oleaginous fruits (incl. flour, n.e.s.) of a kind used for the extraction of other fixed vegetable oils	Graines et fruits oléagineux (y compris les farines) servant normalement à l'extraction d'autres huiles végétales fixes
23	**Crude rubber (including synthetic and reclaimed)**	**Caoutchouc brut (y compris synthétique et régénéré)**
231	Natural rubber and similar gums, in primary forms	Caoutchouc naturel, balata, guayule, etc., formes primaires.
232	Synthetic rubber; reclaimed rubber; waste and scrap	Caoutchouc synthétique; caoutchouc régénéré; déchets et débris
24	**Cork and wood**	**Liège et bois**
244	Cork, natural, raw and waste (incl. blocks, sheets)	Liège naturel brut et déchets (dont blocs, feuilles)
245	Fuel wood (excluding wood waste) and wood charcoal	Bois de chauffage (sauf déchets), charbon de bois
246	Wood in chips or particles and wood waste	Bois en plaquettes, particules, déchets de bois
247	Wood in the rough or roughly squared	Bois bruts ou équarris
248	Wood, simply worked, and railway sleepers of wood	Bois simplement travaillés, traverses de bois pour voies ferrées
25	**Pulp and waste paper**	**Pâtes à papier et déchets de papier**
251	Pulp and waste paper	Pâtes à papier et déchets de papier
26	**Textiles fibres and their wastes**	**Fibres textiles et leurs déchets**
261	Silk	Soie
263	Cotton	Coton
264	Jute and other textile bast fibre, n.e.s., not spun; tow, waste	Jute et autres fibres textiles libériennes, n.d.a.; déchets
265	Vegetable textile fibres, not spun; waste of them	Fibres textiles végétales (sauf coton, jute); déchets
266	Synthetic fibres suitable for spinning	Fibres synthétiques discontinues, pour filature
267	Other man-made fibres suitable for spinning and waste	Autres fibres synthétiques ou artificielles pouvant être filées; déchets
268	Wool and other animal hair (including wool tops)	Laines et autres poils (dont rubans de laine)
269	Worn clothing and other worn textile articles, rags	Friperie, drilles et chiffons
27	**Crude fertilizers (excluding div. 56) & crude minerals**	**Engrais bruts saufs ceux de la division 56, et minéraux bruts**
272	Crude fertilizers (excluding those of division 56)	Engrais bruts (sauf ceux de la division 56)
273	Stone, sand and gravel	Pierres, sables et graviers
274	Sulphur and unroasted iron pyrites	Soufre et pyrite de fer non grillées
277	Natural abrasives, n.e.s. (including industrial diamonds)	Abrasifs naturels, n.d.a. (dont diamants industriels)
278	Other crude minerals	Autre minéraux bruts
28	**Metalliferous ores and metal scrap**	**Minerais métallifères et déchets de métaux**
281	Iron ore and concentrates	Minerais de fer et leurs concentrés
282	Ferrous waste and scrap; remelting ingots, iron, steel	Déchets et débris de fer, fonte, acier; lingots
283	Copper ores & concentrates; copper mattes, cement copper	Minerais de cuivre et concentrés; mattes de cuivre; cuivre de cément
284	Nickel ores and concentrates; nickel mattes, etc.	Minerais de nickel et concentrés; mattes, etc.
285	Aluminium ores and concentrates (including alumina)	Minerais d'aluminium et concentrés (dont alumine)
286	Ores and concentrates of uranium or thorium	Minerais d'uranium ou de thorium et concentrés
287	Ores and concentrates of base metals, n.e.s.	Minerais de métaux communs et concentrés, n.d.a.

Product classification for international trade		Classification des produits pour le commerce international
288	Non-ferrous base metal waste and scrap, n.e.s.	Déchets et débris de métaux communs non ferreux, n.d.a.
289	Ores and concentrates of precious metals; waste, scrap	Minerais de métaux précieux et concentrés; débris et déchets
29	**Crude animal and vegetable materials, n.e.s.**	**Matières brutes d'origine animale ou végétale, n.d.a.**
291	Crude animal materials, n.e.s.	Matières brutes d'origine animale, n.d.a.
292	Crude vegetable materials, n.e.s.	Matières brutes d'origine végétale, n.d.a.
3	**Mineral fuels, lubricants and related materials**	**Combustibles minéraux, lubrifiants et produits connexes**
32	**Coal, coke and briquettes**	**Houilles, cokes et briquettes**
321	Coal, whether or not pulverized, not agglomerated	Houilles, même pulvérisées, mais non agglomérées
322	Briquettes, lignites and peat	Briquettes, lignite et tourbe
325	Coke & semi-cokes of coal, lignite or peat; retort carbon	Cokes et semi-cokes de houille, lignite ou tourbe; charbon de cornue
33	**Petroleum, petroleum products and related materials**	**Pétrole et produits dérivés du pétrole et produits connexes**
333	Petroleum oils, oils from bituminous materials, crude	Huiles brutes de pétrole ou minéraux bitumineux
334	Petroleum oils or bituminous minerals > 70 % oil	Huiles de pétrole ou minéraux bitumineux > 70% huile
335	Residual petroleum products, n.e.s., related materials	Produits résiduels du pétrole, n.d.a.; produits connexes
34	**Gas, natural and manufactured**	**Gaz naturel et gaz manufacturé**
342	Liquefied propane and butane	Propane et butane liquéfiés
343	Natural gas, whether or not liquefied	Gaz naturel, même liquéfié
344	Petroleum gases, other gaseous hydrocarbons, n.e.s.	Gaz de pétrole et autres hydrocarbures gazeux, n.d.a.
345	Coal gas, water gas & similar gases (excl. hydrocarbons)	Gaz de houille, pauvre et similaires (sauf hydrocarbures)
35	**Electric current**	**Énergie électrique**
351	Electric current	Énergie électrique
4	**Animal and vegetable oils, fats and waxes**	**Huiles, graisses et cires d'origine animale ou végétale**
41	**Animal oils and fats**	**Huiles et graisses d'origine animale**
411	Animal oils and fats	Huiles et graisses d'origine animale
42	**Fixed vegetable oils & fats, 'soft', crude, refined or fractionated**	**Huiles végétales fixes, douces, brutes, épurées ou raffinées**
421	Fixed vegetable oils & fats, 'soft', crude, refined or fractionated	Huiles végétales fixes, douces, brutes, épurées ou raffinées
422	Fixed vegetable fats & oils, crude, refined, fractionated, other than 'soft'	Huiles végétales fixes, brutes, épurées ou raffineés, autres que douces
43	**Animal and vegetable fats and oils, processed; waxes of animal or vegetable origin**	**Huiles et graisses animales et végétales, préparées et cires d'origine animale et végétale**
431	Animal or veg. oils & fats, processed, n.e.s.; waxes, mixt.	Huiles et graisses animales ou végétales, préparées, n.d.a.; cires
5	**Chemicals and related products, n.e.s.**	**Produits chimiques et produits connexes, n.d.a.**
51	**Organic chemicals**	**Produits chimiques organiques**
511	Hydrocarbons, n.e.s., & halogenated, nitr. derivative	Hydrocarbures, n.d.a. et dérivés halogènes, nitrosés, sulfonés, nitrés
512	Alcohols, phenols, and their derivatives	Alcools, phénols, et leurs dérivés halogénés
513	Carboxylic acids, anhydrides, halides, peroxides; derivatives	Acides carboxyliques, anhydrides, halogénures, péroxydes; dérivés
514	Nitrogen-function compounds	Composés à fonctions azotées
515	Organo-inorganic, heterocyclic compounds, nucl. acids	Composés organo-inorganiques et composés hétérocycliques; sels
516	Other organic chemicals	Autres produits chimiques organiques
52	**Inorganic chemicals**	**Produits chimiques inorganiques**
522	Inorganic chemical elements, oxides & halogen salts	Produits chimiques inorganiques : éléments, oxydes, sels
523	Metallic salts & peroxysalts, of inorganic acids	Sels et persels métalliques des acides inorganiques
524	Other inorganic chemicals; organic & inorganic compounds of precious metals	Autres produits chimiques inorganiques, composés organiques ou inorganiques de métaux précieux
525	Radioactive and associated materials	Matières radioactives et produits associés
53	**Dyeing, tanning and colouring materials**	**Produits pour teinture et tannage et colorants**
531	Synthetic organic colouring matter & colouring lakes	Matières colorantes organiques synthétiques; préparations, laques
532	Dyeing & tanning extracts, synthetic tanning materials	Extraits pour teinture et tannage
533	Pigments, paints, varnishes and related materials	Pigments, peintures, vernis et produits connexes
54	**Medicinal and pharmaceutical products**	**Produits médicinaux et pharmaceutiques**
541	Medicinal and pharmaceutical products, excluding 542	Produits médicinaux et pharmaceutiques (sauf 542)
542	Medicaments (including veterinary medicaments)	Médicaments pour médecine humaine ou vétérinaire
55	**Essential oils and resinoids & perfume materials; toilet, polishing and cleansing preparations**	**Huiles essentielles et produits utilisés en parfumerie; préparations pour la toilette, produits d'entretien et détersifs**
551	Essential oils, perfume & flavour materials	Huiles essentielles, produits pour la parfumerie, la confiserie
553	Perfumery, cosmetics or toilet preparations (soaps exclud.)	Produits de parfumerie ou de toilette; préparations (savons exclus)
554	Soaps, cleansing and polishing preparations	Savons, produits d'entretien et détersifs

Product classification for international trade		Classification des produits pour le commerce international	
56	**Fertilizers (other than those of group 272)**	**Engrais manufacturés (autres que ceux du groupe 272)**	
562	Fertilizers (other than those of group 272)	Engrais (autres que ceux du groupe 272)	
57	**Plastics in primary forms**	**Matières plastiques sous formes primaires**	
571	Polymers of ethylene, in primary forms	Polymères de l'éthylène, sous formes primaires	
572	Polymers of styrene, in primary forms	Polymères du styrène, sous formes primaires	
573	Polymers of vinyl chloride or of halogenated olefins	Polymères du chlorure de vinyle ou d'autres oléfines halogènes	
574	Polyacetals, other polyethers and epoxide resins, polyesters	Polyacetals, autres polyéthers et résines époxydes, polyesters	
575	Other plastics, in primary forms	Autres matières plastiques, sous formes primaires	
579	Waste, parings and scrap, of plastics	Déchets, rognures et débris de matières plastiques	
58	**Plastics in non-primary forms**	**Matières plastiques sous formes autres que primaires**	
581	Tubes, pipes and hoses of plastics	Tubes et tuyaux en matières plastiques	
582	Plates, sheets, films, foil & strip, of plastics	Plaques, feuilles, rubans en matières plastiques	
583	Monofilaments, of plastics, cross-section > 1mm	Monofilaments en plastiques (coupe transversale > 1mm)	
59	**Chemical materials and products, n.e.s.**	**Matières et produits chimiques, n.d.a.**	
591	Insecticides and similar products, for retail sale	Insecticides, produits similaires, conditionnés pour la vente au détail	
592	Starches, wheat gluten; albuminoidal substances; glues	Amidons et fécules, gluten de froment; matières albuminoïdes; colles	
593	Explosives and pyrotechnic products	Explosifs et articles de pyrotechnie	
597	Prepared additives for mineral oils; lubricating preparations;	Additifs pour huiles minérales	
598	Miscellaneous chemical products, n.e.s.	Produits chimiques divers, n.d.a.	
6	**Manufactured goods classified chiefly by material**	**Articles manufacturés classés principalement d'après la matière première**	
61	**Leather, leather manufactures and dressed furskins**	**Cuirs et peaux, préparés et apprêtés**	
611	Leather	Cuirs et peaux préparés	
612	Manufactures of leather, n.e.s.; saddlery & harness	Ouvrages en cuir, n.d.a.; articles de bourrellerie	
613	Furskins, tanned or dressed, excluding those of 8483	Pelleteries tannées ou apprêtées (sauf 8483)	
62	**Rubber manufactures, n.e.s.**	**Caoutchouc manufacturé, n.d.a.**	
621	Materials of rubber (pastes, plates, sheets, etc.)	Produits en caoutchouc (pâtes, plaques, tubes, etc.)	
625	Rubber tyres, tyre treads or flaps and inner tubes	Pneumatiques en caoutchouc	
629	Articles of rubber, n.e.s.	Ouvrages en caoutchouc, n.d.a.	
63	**Cork and wood manufactures (excluding furniture)**	**Ouvrages en liège et en bois (sauf meubles)**	
633	Cork manufactures	Ouvrages en liège	
634	Veneers, plywood, and other wood, worked, n.e.s.	Placage, contre-plaqué et autres bois travaillés, n.d.a.	
635	Wood manufacture, n.e.s.	Ouvrages en bois, n.d.a.	
64	**Paper and paper manufactures**	**Papiers et préparations de papier**	
641	Paper and paperboard	Papiers et cartons	
642	Paper and paperboard, cut to shape or size, articles	Papiers et cartons découpés	
65	**Textile yarn, fabrics, made-up articles, n.e.s., and related products**	**Fils, tissus et articles textiles façonnés, n.d.a., et produits connexes**	
651	Textile yarn	Fils textiles	
652	Cotton fabrics, woven (excluded narrow or special fabrics)	Tissus de coton (sauf petites largeurs ou spéciaux)	
653	Fabrics, woven, of man-made fabrics	Tissus en matières textiles synthétiques ou artificielles	
654	Other textile fabrics, woven	Autres tissus	
655	Knitted or crocheted fabrics, n.e.s.	Étoffes de bonneterie (dont velours), n.d.a.	
656	Tulles, trimmings, lace, ribbons & other small wares	Tulles, dentelles et autres articles de mercerie	
657	Special yarn, special textile fabrics & related	Fils spéciaux, tissus spéciaux et produits connexes	
658	Made-up articles, wholly or chiefly of textile materials, n.e.s	Articles façonnés entièrement ou principalement en matières textiles, n.d.a.	
659	Floor coverings, etc.	Revêtements de sols, etc.	
66	**Non metallic mineral manufactures, n.e.s.**	**Articles minéraux non métalliques manufacturés, n.d.a.**	
661	Lime, cement and fabricated construction materials (excluding glass and clay materials)	Chaux, ciments et matériaux de construction fabriqués (sauf argile et verre)	
662	Clay construction and refractory construction materials	Matériaux de construction réfractaires, en argile	
663	Mineral manufactures, n.e.s.	Articles minéraux manufacturés, n.d.a.	
664	Glass	Verre	
665	Glassware	Ouvrages en verre	
666	Pottery	Poterie	
667	Pearls, precious and semi-precious stones	Perles fines ou de culture, pierres gemmes et similaires	

67	**Iron and steel**	**Fer et acier**
671	Pig iron & spiegeleisen, sponge iron, powder & granules	Fonte, fer spongieux, poudres de fer et d'acier
672	Ingots, primary forms, of iron or steel; semi-finished products	Lingots et autres formes primaires en fer ou acier;
673	Flat-rolled prod., iron, non-alloy steel, not coated	Produits laminés plats, en fer ou aciers non alliés
674	Flat-rolled prod., iron, non-alloy steel, coated, clad	Produits laminés plats, fer, aciers non alliés, zingués
675	Flat-rolled products of alloy steel	Produits laminés plats, en aciers alliés
676	Iron & steel bars, rods, angles, shapes & sections	Barres, profilés en fer ou acier (dont palplanches)
677	Rails & railway track construction mat., iron, steel	Rails et autres éléments de voies ferrées, fer, acier
678	Wire of iron or steel	Fils de fer ou d'acier
679	Tubes, pipes & hollow profiles, fittings, iron, steel	Tubes, profilés creux et accessoires, fer ou acier
68	**Non-ferrous metals**	**Métaux non ferreux**
681	Silver, platinum, other metals of the platinum group	Argent, platine et métaux de la mine du platine
682	Copper	Cuivre
683	Nickel	Nickel
684	Aluminium	Aluminium
685	Lead	Plomb
686	Zinc	Zinc
687	Tin	Étain
689	Miscellaneous non-ferrous base metals for metallurgy	Autres métaux communs non ferreux utilisés en métallurgie
69	**Manufactures of metal, n.e.s.**	**Articles manufacturés en métal, n.d.a.**
691	Structures & parts, n.e.s., of iron, steel, aluminium	Constructions et parties, n.d.a. en fonte, fer, acier
692	Metal containers for storage or transport	Récipients métalliques pour stockage ou transport
693	Wire products (excluding electrical) and fencing grills	Ouvrages en fils métalliques (sauf électriques), grillages
694	Nails, screws, nuts, bolts, rivets & the like, of metal	Pointes, vis, écrous, boulons, clous et similaires
695	Tools for use in the hand or in machine	Outils à main et outils pour machines
696	Cutlery	Coutellerie
697	Household equipment of base metal, n.e.s.	Articles d'économie domestique en métaux communs, n.d.a.
699	Manufactures of base metal, n.e.s.	Articles manufacturés en métaux communs, n.d.a.
7	**Machinery and transport equipment**	**Machines et matériel de transport**
71	**Power-generating machinery and equipment**	**Machines génératrices, moteurs et leur équipement**
711	Vapour-generating boilers, auxiliary plant; parts	Chaudières à vapeur, auxiliaires, parties et pièces
712	Steam turbines and other vapour turbines, parts, n.e.s.	Turbines à vapeur, parties, pièces détachées, n.d.a.
713	Internal combustion piston engines, parts, n.e.s.	Moteurs à explosion ou à combustion interne, n.d.a.
714	Engines and motors, non-electric; parts, n.e.s.	Moteurs et machines motrices, non électrique, n.d.a.
716	Rotating electric plant and parts thereof, n.e.s.	Appareils électriques rotatifs, pièces détachées, n.d.a.
718	Other power generating machinery and parts, n.e.s.	Moteurs et machines motrices, pièces, parties, n.d.a.
72	**Machinery specialized for particular industries**	**Machines et appareils spécialisés pour les industries particulières**
721	Agricultural machinery (excluding tractors) & parts	Machines agricoles (sauf tracteurs), parties, pièces
722	Tractors (excluding those of 71414 & 74415)	Tracteurs (sauf 74414 et 74415)
723	Civil ingineering & contractors' plant & equipment	Appareils, matériel de génie civil et construction
724	Textile & leather machinery, & parts thereof, n.e.s.	Machines pour industrie textile, cuir et peaux, n.d.a.
725	Paper mill, pulp mill machinery; paper articles man.	Machines pour pâte à papier et papier; parties, pièces
726	Printing & bookbinding machinery, & parts thereof	Machines pour imprimerie, brochage, reliure; parties
727	Food-processing machines (excluding domestic)	Machines pour industrie alimentaire
728	Other machinery for particular industries, n.e.s.	Autres machines pour industries particulières, n.d.a.
73	**Metal working machinery**	**Machines et appareils pour le travail des métaux**
731	Machine-tools working by removing material	Machines-outils travaillant par enlèvement de matière
733	Machine.-tools for working metal (exclud.removing material)	Machines pour travail des métaux (sans enlèvement)
735	Parts, n.e.s., & accessories for machines of 731, 733	Pièces, n.d.a., des machines des groupes 731 et 733
737	Metalworking machinery (excluding machine tools) & parts	Machines pour travail des métaux, n.d.a.; pièces détachées
74	**Other industrial machinery and parts**	**Autres machines industrielles et pièces détachées**
741	Heating & cooling equipment & parts thereof, n.e.s.	Appareils de chauffage et de réfrigération, n.d.a.
742	Pumps for liquids; liquid elevators; parts for such pumps	Pompes pour liquides; élévateurs à liquides; parties et pièces
743	Pumps (excluding liquid), air & gas compressors & fans; centrifuges	Pompes (sauf pour liquides), compresseurs; ventilateurs; centrifugeuses
744	Mechanical handling equipment, & parts, n.e.s.	Équipement mécanique de manutention, pièces, n.d.a.

745	Other non-electrical machinery, tools and mechanical apparatus, and parts thereof	Appareils et outils non électriques, pièces, n.d.a.
746	Ball or roller bearings	Roulements à billes, galets, rouleaux ou aiguilles
747	Appliances for pipes, boiler shells, tanks, vats, etc.	Articles de robinetterie, tuyauterie et similaires
748	Transmission shafts and cranks; bearings housings; gears and gearing; flywheels and pulleys; clutches, shaft couplings	Arbres de transmission et manivelles; engrenages et roues de friction; volants et poulies; embrayages, organes d'accouplement
749	Non-electric parts & accessories. of machinery, n.e.s.	Parties, non électriques d'appareils mécaniques, n.d.a.
75	**Office machines and automatic data processing machines**	**Machines et appareils de bureau ou pour le traitement automatique de l'information**
751	Office machines	Machines et appareils de bureau
752	Automatic data processing machines, n.e.s.	Machines automatiques de traitement de l'information, n.d.a.
759	Parts, accessories for machines of groups 751, 752	Parties et pièces détachées pour groupes 751, 752
76	**Telecommunications and sound recording apparatus and reproducing apparatus and equipment**	**Appareils et équipements de télécommunications et pour l'enregistrement et la reproduction du son**
761	Television receivers, whether or not combined	Téléviseurs, même combinés à d'autres appareils
762	Radio-broadcast receivers, whether or not combined	Appareils de radiodiffusion, même combinés à d'autres appareils
763	Sound recorders or reproducers; television image and sound recorders or reproducers, prepared unrecorded media	Appareils d'enregistrement ou de reproduction du son; appareils d'enregistrement ou de reproduction de l'image et du son en télévision
764	Telecommunication equipment, n.e.s.; & parts, n.e.s.	Équipements de télécommunication, n.d.a. et parties
77	**Electrical machinery, apparatus and appliances, n.e.s.**	**Machines et appareils électriques, n.d.a.**
771	Electric power machinery, and parts thereof	Appareils pour production, transformation de l'énergie
772	Apparatus for electrical circuits; switchboard, control panels	Appareils pour circuits électriques; tableaux de commande et parties
773	Equipment for distributing electricity, n.e.s.	Équipement pour distribution d'électricité, n.d.a.
774	Electro-diagnostic apparatus for medical or veterinary sciences and radiological apparatus	Appareils d'électrodiagnostic à usage médical ou vétérinaire et Appareils de radiologie
775	Household type equipment, electrical or not, n.e.s.	Machines et appareils, à usage domestique, n.d.a.
776	Thermionic, cold cathode or photo-cathode valves & tubes; diodes, transistors and similar;	Lampes, tubes, valves électroniques à cathode chaude, froide ou à photocathode; diodes, transistors et dispositifs similaires
778	Electrical machinery & apparatus, n.e.s.	Machines et appareils électriques, n.d.a.
78	**Road vehicles**	**Véhicules routiers**
781	Motor vehicles for the transport of persons	Véhicules automobiles pour transport de personnes
782	Motor vehicles for the transport of goods and special purposes	Véhicules automobiles pour le transport de marchandises et pour usages spéciaux
783	Road motor vehicles, n.e.s.	Véhicules routiers, n.d.a.
784	Parts & accessories of vehicles of 722, 781, 782, 783	Parties, pièces détachées des groupes 722, 781, 782, 783
785	Motorcycles and cycles, motorized or not; invalid carriages	Motocycles et cycles, avec ou sans moteur; fauteuils roulants
786	Trailers and semi-trailers; other vehicles, not mechanically propelled; specially designed & equiped transport containers	Remorques et semi-remorques; autres véhicules non automobiles; cadres et conteneurs conçus et équipés pour le transport
79	**Other transport equipment**	**Autres matériels de transport**
791	Railway vehicles and associated equipment	Véhicules et matériel pour chemin de fer
792	Aircraft and associated equipment; spacecraft and spacecraft launch vehicles, parts thereof	Aéronefs et matériels connexes; véhicules spatiaux et leurs véhicules lanceurs; leurs parties et pièces détachées
793	Ships, boats and floating structures	Navires, bateaux et engins flottants
8	**Miscellaneous manufactured articles**	**Articles manufacturés divers**
81	**Prefabricated buildings, sanitary, heating and lighting fixtures, n.e.s.**	**Constructions préfabriquées, appareils sanitaires de chauffage et d'éclairage, n.d.a.**
811	Prefabricated buildings	Constructions préfabriquées
812	Sanitary, plumbing, heating fixtures, fittings, n.e.s.	Appareils sanitaires, plomberie, chauffage, n.d.a.
813	Lighting fixtures and fittings, n.e.s.	Appareillages d'éclairage, n.d.a.
82	**Furniture and parts thereof**	**Meubles et leurs parties et pièces détachées**
821	Furniture and parts thereof	Meubles et leurs parties et pièces détachées
83	**Travel goods, handbags and similar containers**	**Articles de voyage, sacs à mains et contenants similaires**
831	Travel goods, handbags and similar containers	Articles de voyage, sacs à mains et contenants similaires
84	**Articles of apparel, and clothing accessories**	**Vêtements et accessoires du vêtement**
841	Men's clothing of textile fabrics, not knitted	Articles d'habillement en matières textiles pour hommes
842	Women's clothing, of textile fabrics	Articles d'habillement en matières textiles pour femmes
843	Men's or boy's clothing, of textile, knitted, crocheted	Articles d'habillement, en bonneterie pour hommes

Product classification for international trade		Classification des produits pour le commerce international
844	Women's clothing, of textile, knitted or crocheted	Articles d'habillement, en bonneterie pour femmes
845	Articles of apparel, of textile fabrics, n.e.s.	Vêtements en matières textiles, n.d.a.
846	Clothing accessories, of textile fabrics	Accessoires du vêtement en matières textiles
848	Articles of apparel, clothing access., excluding textile	Vêtements et accessoires en matières non textiles
85	**Footwear**	**Chaussures**
851	Footwear	Chaussures
87	**Professional and scientific instruments, n.e.s.**	**Instruments professionnels et scientifiques, n.d.a.**
871	Optical instruments and apparatus, n.e.s.	Appareils et instruments d'optique, n.d.a.
872	Instruments & appliances, n.e.s., for medical, surgical, dental or veterinary purposes	Appareils, n.d.a. pour médecine, art dentaire, chirurgie ou pour usage vétérinaire
873	Meters & counters, n.e.s.	Compteurs et instruments de mesure, n.d.a.
874	Measuring, analysing & controlling apparatus, n.e.s.	Appareils et instruments de mesure, contrôle, n.d.a.
88	**Photographic apparatus, equipment and supplies and optical goods, n.e.s.; watches and clocks**	**Appareils et fournitures de photographie et d'optique, n.d.a.; montres et horloges**
881	Photographic apparatus and equipment, n.e.s.	Appareils et équipement photographiques, n.d.a.
882	Cinematographic and photographic supplies	Fournitures cinématographiques et photographiques
883	Cinematograph films, exposed & developed	Films cinématographiques, impressionnés, développés
884	Optical goods, n.e.s.	Éléments d'optique et articles de lunetterie, n.d.a.
885	Watches and clocks	Horlogerie
89	**Miscellaneous manufactured articles, n.e.s.**	**Articles manufacturés divers, n.d.a.**
890	Merchandises not classified according to kind	Marchandises non classées par catégorie
891	Arms & ammunition	Armes et munitions
892	Printed matter	Imprimés
893	Articles, n.e.s., of plastics	Ouvrages, n.d.a., en matières plastiques
894	Baby carriages, toys, games and sporting goods	Voitures pour le transport des enfants, jouets, jeux et articles pour divertissements et sports
895	Office and stationery supplies, n.e.s.	Articles de papeterie, fournitures de bureau, n.d.a.
896	Works of art, collectors' pieces & antiques	Objets d'art, de collection et d'antiquité
897	Jewellery and articles of precious material., n.e.s.	Articles de bijouterie et d'orfèvrerie, n.d.a.
898	Musical instruments, parts; records, tapes & similar	Instruments de musique; disques, bandes et similaires
899	Miscellaneous manufactured articles, n.e.s.	Autres articles manufacturés divers
9	**Commodities and transactions, not classified elsewhere in the SITC**	**Articles et transactions, non classés ailleurs dans la CTCI**
91	**Postal packages not classified according to kind**	**Colis postaux non classés par catégorie**
911	Postal packages not classified according to kind	Colis postaux non classés par catégorie
93	**Special transactions and commodities not classified**	**Transactions spéciales et articles non classés par catégorie**
931	Special transactions and commodities not classified	Transactions spéciales et articles non classés par catégorie
96	**Coin (other than gold coin), not being legal tender**	**Monnaies n'ayant pas cours légal**
961	Coin (other than gold coin), not being legal tender	Monnaies n'ayant pas cours légal
97	**Gold, non-monetary (excluding ores & concentrates)**	**Or, à usage non monétaire (à l'excl.des minerais et concentrés)**
971	Gold, non-monetary (excluding ores & concentrates)	Or, à usage non monétaire (à l'exclusion des minerais et concentrés d'or

1

INTERNATIONAL **MERCHANDISE** TRADE

COMMERCE INTERNATIONAL DES **MARCHANDISES**

1.1.1 Exports and imports of countries and geographical regions
Value

Region, country or territory	Exports (f.o.b.) - Exportations (f.a.b.) Millions of dollars							
	1980	1990	2000	2003	2004	2005	2006	2007
WORLD	**2 032 154**	**3 479 591**	**6 455 988**	**7 547 559**	**9 182 967**	**10 474 871**	**12 087 769**	**13 833 041**
DEVELOPING ECONOMIES	597 574	843 904	2 056 407	2 426 752	3 097 429	3 775 908	4 505 697	5 190 026
ECONOMIES IN TRANSITION	85 426	118 709	154 507	206 692	282 017	359 164	449 482	533 684
DEVELOPED ECONOMIES	1 349 154	2 516 978	4 245 074	4 914 115	5 803 521	6 339 799	7 132 590	8 109 330
Developing economies: Africa	**118 981**	**106 983**	**153 072**	**178 383**	**231 869**	**303 036**	**358 998**	**397 457**
Eastern Africa	*7 012*	*7 323*	*10 204*	*12 422*	*14 879*	*16 640*	*20 416*	*23 606*
Burundi*	65	75	50	38	48	57	58	(e)60
Comoros*	11	18	14	27	19	12	10	..
Djibouti*	13	25	75	37	38	40	56	..
Eritrea	–	–	19	9	11	11	11	..
Ethiopia	–	–	486	496	678	903	1 050	(e)1 290
Ethiopia (former)	425	298	–	–	–	–	–	–
Kenya	1 245	1 032	1 734	2 411	2 684	3 293	3 437	(e)4 119
Madagascar*	401	318	824	849	999	853	974	(e)1 156
Malawi	295	417	379	525	483	496	620	(e)813
Mauritius	435	1 194	1 810	1 898	1 993	2 138	2 333	2 054
Mozambique	281	126	364	1 044	1 504	1 745	2 381	(e)2 492
Rwanda	121	109	53	63	98	125	147	177
Seychelles	21	57	193	274	291	340	380	(e)360
Somalia	141	150	193	322	350	460	541	..
Uganda	345	152	460	562	709	863	1 004	1 615
United Republic of Tanzania*	511	331	734	1 216	1 473	1 676	1 723	2 005
Zambia*	1 305	1 309	892	980	1 576	1 810	3 770	4 853
Zimbabwe	1 396	1 713	1 925	1 670	1 926	1 820	1 920	(e)1 995
Middle Africa	*8 856*	*11 772*	*17 112*	*22 167*	*31 751*	*49 625*	*62 515*	*75 129*
Angola*	1 902	3 884	7 921	9 508	13 475	24 109	31 862	(e)41 109
Cameroon*(1)	1 384	2 002	1 833	2 246	2 478	3 104	3 706	(e)3 289
Central African Republic*(1)	116	120	161	127	126	128	158	(e)195
Chad*	71	188	183	601	2 191	3 149	3 410	(e)3 820
Congo*(1)	911	981	2 489	2 677	3 408	4 800	6 780	(e)6 949
Dem. Rep. of the Congo*	2 269	2 326	824	1 374	1 850	2 190	2 319	(e)2 531
Equatorial Guinea	14	62	1 097	2 801	4 599	6 691	8 216	(e)10 142
Gabon*(1)	2 173	2 204	2 602	2 826	3 620	5 450	6 059	(e)7 090
Sao Tome and Principe*	17	4	3	7	4	3	4	4
Northern Africa	*44 042*	*41 055*	*54 361*	*63 525*	*80 313*	*110 512*	*134 891*	*150 907*
Algeria*	13 871	14 707	21 871	24 105	32 324	45 631	53 221	(e)53 718
Egypt*	3 046	4 957	4 689	6 311	7 530	10 672	13 736	16 101
Libyan Arab Jamahiriya	21 910	13 225	12 716	13 761	17 333	28 885	39 253	(e)44 047
Morocco*	2 441	4 265	7 428	8 778	9 663	10 006	11 511	13 884
Sudan*	543	374	1 807	2 542	3 778	4 824	5 657	(e)8 146
Tunisia	2 231	3 527	5 850	8 027	9 685	10 494	11 513	15 011
Southern Africa	*25 540*	*23 568*	*35 225*	*42 660*	*54 139*	*60 687*	*68 257*	*80 192*
Botswana*	..	..	2 796	2 810	3 513	4 404	4 529	4 005
Lesotho	..	..	212	470	702	651	718	(e)795
Namibia	..	..	1 320	1 260	1 829	1 990	2 720	(e)3 433
South Africa	(a)25 540	(a)23 568	29 983	36 482	46 146	51 626	58 175	69 788
Swaziland	..	..	914	1 638	1 949	2 016	2 115	(e)2 171
Western Africa	*33 530*	*23 265*	*36 169*	*37 610*	*50 788*	*65 573*	*72 920*	*67 622*
Benin*	63	288	392	541	567	578	568	631
Burkina Faso	90	152	206	321	479	468	(e)588	679
Cape Verde*	4	6	11	13	15	18	21	19
Côte d'Ivoire*	3 135	3 072	3 888	5 788	6 919	7 477	8 140	(e)8 581
Gambia	31	31	15	8	10	8	10	(e)11
Ghana	1 257	891	1 671	2 562	2 739	2 802	3 726	(e)4 132
Guinea	401	671	666	609	726	890	900	(e)966
Guinea-Bissau	11	19	62	65	76	89	79	118
Liberia*	600	2 207	329	109	104	132	158	(e)205
Mali*	205	359	545	928	977	1 101	1 544	1 460
Mauritania*	194	447	355	318	440	625	1 367	1 343
Niger*	566	283	283	352	437	497	509	653
Nigeria	25 934	13 673	26 449	24 047	35 050	48 490	52 771	(e)45 958
Senegal*	477	762	920	1 257	1 510	1 578	1 556	1 775
Sierra Leone*	224	138	13	92	139	158	216	(e)271
Togo*	338	268	364	599	601	660	(e)767	823

For sources and notes, see end of table 1.1.1.

Imports (c.i.f.) - Importations (c.a.f.) Millions de dollars								Régions, pays ou territoires
1980	1990	2000	2003	2004	2005	2006	2007	
2 073 633	3 590 363	6 653 669	7 771 121	9 462 990	10 776 488	12 337 928	14 056 584	**MONDE**
492 879	800 281	1 914 743	2 254 347	2 876 773	3 397 199	3 971 659	4 632 355	ÉCONOMIES EN DÉVELOPPEMENT
83 598	139 945	104 694	171 830	223 213	272 642	349 782	465 513	ÉCONOMIES EN TRANSITION
1 497 156	2 650 137	4 634 232	5 344 943	6 363 004	7 106 648	8 016 487	8 958 716	ÉCONOMIES DÉVELOPPÉES
93 735	97 057	130 238	173 391	217 515	262 927	300 314	340 949	**Économies en développement : Afrique**
10 706	*12 701*	*16 847*	*20 835*	*26 248*	*31 529*	*37 079*	*42 973*	*Afrique orientale*
168	231	148	157	176	267	431	(e)338	Burundi*
29	52	43	70	85	99	115	..	Comores*
213	215	207	238	261	277	341	..	Djibouti*
–	–	471	433	480	495	(e)562	..	Érythrée
–	–	1 262	2 119	3 087	4 127	4 710	(e)5 230	Éthiopie
722	1 081	–	–	–	–	–	–	Éthiopie (anc.)
2 125	2 223	3 105	3 725	4 553	6 149	7 311	(e)9 160	Kenya
764	566	997	1 295	1 692	1 699	1 789	(e)2 124	Madagascar*
439	575	532	786	933	1 184	1 210	(e)1 184	Malawi
614	1 618	2 207	2 363	2 771	3 157	3 630	3 901	Maurice
800	878	1 162	1 753	2 035	2 408	2 869	(e)2 965	Mozambique
262	287	213	259	284	402	496	590	Rwanda
99	187	343	412	497	676	755	(e)766	Seychelles
435	81	343	459	464	531	740	..	Somalie
293	288	1 538	1 250	2 023	1 895	2 505	(e)3 423	Ouganda
1 258	1 364	1 524	2 164	2 552	3 275	4 440	5 337	République-Unie de Tanzanie*
1 088	1 220	888	1 574	2 152	2 558	3 074	3 991	Zambie*
1 396	1 835	1 863	1 778	2 204	2 330	2 100	(e)2 205	Zimbabwe
5 884	*6 778*	*7 566*	*13 307*	*15 041*	*19 481*	*22 588*	*24 073*	*Afrique centrale*
1 328	1 578	3 040	5 480	5 832	8 353	8 778	(e)9 200	Angola*
1 602	1 400	1 484	2 163	2 406	2 735	3 150	(e)2 785	Cameroun*(1)
81	154	117	118	148	171	203	(e)228	République centrafricaine*(1)
74	286	317	777	953	950	1 309	(e)1 505	Tchad*
562	621	479	856	879	1 457	1 854	(e)2 000	Congo*(1)
1 519	1 739	697	1 594	1 986	2 270	2 800	(e)2 879	Rép. dém. du Congo*
26	61	451	1 236	1 580	2 121	2 859	(e)3 464	Guinée équatoriale
674	918	952	1 043	1 216	1 370	1 561	(e)1 933	Gabon*(1)
19	21	30	41	41	53	73	80	Sao Tomé-et-Principe*
31 553	*44 952*	*48 882*	*58 254*	*74 993*	*91 759*	*100 270*	*123 347*	*Afrique septentrionale*
10 559	9 780	9 201	12 916	18 960	20 718	21 005	(e)24 275	Algérie*
4 860	16 783	14 010	11 139	12 859	19 851	20 614	26 929	Égypte*
6 777	5 336	4 018	6 141	8 735	11 188	13 213	(e)14 535	Jamahiriya arabe libyenne
4 255	6 922	11 534	14 250	17 587	19 458	22 499	30 244	Maroc*
1 576	619	1 553	2 898	4 035	7 367	8 074	(e)8 416	Soudan*
3 526	5 513	8 567	10 910	12 818	13 177	14 865	18 948	Tunisie
19 700	*18 399*	*35 574*	*48 246*	*62 394*	*71 444*	*86 794*	*91 845*	*Afrique australe*
..	..	2 469	2 448	3 231	3 148	3 067	2 756	Botswana*
..	..	809	1 112	1 399	1 436	1 501	(e)1 799	Lesotho
..	..	1 550	1 980	2 420	2 450	2 730	(e)3 175	Namibie
(a)19 700	(a)18 399	29 695	41 084	53 466	62 304	77 280	81 750	Afrique du Sud
..	..	1 052	1 623	1 877	2 106	2 216	(e)2 365	Swaziland
25 893	*14 228*	*21 370*	*32 748*	*38 839*	*48 715*	*53 584*	*58 710*	*Afrique occidentale*
331	265	613	892	894	894	1 006	(e)1 061	Bénin*
359	536	611	925	1 272	1 383	1 426	1 618	Burkina Faso
68	136	230	350	386	438	542	740	Cap-Vert*
2 991	2 098	2 785	3 231	4 292	5 094	5 766	(e)6 339	Côte d'Ivoire*
165	188	187	156	229	237	245	(e)300	Gambie
1 129	1 199	2 974	3 233	4 297	5 347	6 754	(e)7 937	Ghana
270	723	612	640	690	820	900	(e)1 035	Guinée
55	86	49	65	83	106	98	134	Guinée-Bissau
535	210	668	170	337	324	467	(e)555	Libéria*
439	602	806	1 252	1 291	1 612	1 769	(e)2 021	Mali*
286	220	454	542	923	1 428	1 167	1 198	Mauritanie*
594	389	395	622	752	981	996	(e)1 334	Niger*
16 643	5 627	8 721	17 193	19 387	25 371	27 402	(e)28 089	Nigéria
1 052	1 220	1 553	2 399	2 839	3 197	3 434	4 431	Sénégal*
427	149	149	303	286	345	389	(e)446	Sierra Leone*
551	581	562	(e)775	(e)880	(e)1 138	(e)1 224	(e)1 473	Togo*

Pour les sources et les notes, se reporter à la fin du tableau 1.1.1.

Region, country or territory	Exports (f.o.b.) - Exportations (f.a.b.) Millions of dollars							
	1980	1990	2000	2003	2004	2005	2006	2007
Developing economies: America	111 345	143 793	364 482	384 445	474 969	570 768	683 156	765 319
Caribbean	*22 368*	*11 668*	*19 000*	*18 034*	*21 630*	*26 302*	*32 877*	*31 497*
Anguilla	..	..	4	4	6	15	32	(e)10
Antigua and Barbuda*	26	21	52	45	55	58	60	..
Aruba (2)	..	155	2 525	2 052	2 723	3 484	3 669	2 691
Bahamas (3)	5 009	238	576	425	477	562	674	(e)724
Barbados	228	215	272	250	278	359	385	419
Cuba*	5 577	4 910	1 676	1 677	2 332	2 159	(e)2 905	(e)3 690
Dominica*	10	55	56	41	42	43	41	(e)39
Dominican Republic*	962	735	5 737	5 471	5 936	6 145	6 440	7 237
Grenada*	17	28	76	38	32	28	28	(e)41
Haiti	226	160	318	347	391	470	519	(e)519
Jamaica	963	1 158	1 295	1 180	1 390	1 500	1 874	(e)2 172
Montserrat*	1	2	1	2	4	1	1	(e)2
Netherlands Antilles*(4)	(b)5 162	1 790	1 986	1 161	1 409	1 644	1 879	..
Saint Kitts and Nevis*	24	24	49	55	54	58	(e)59	(e)62
Saint Lucia*	70	134	47	62	80	64	72	(e)80
Saint Vincent and the Grenadines*	15	83	47	38	33	40	33	(e)43
Trinidad and Tobago*	4 077	1 960	4 274	5 178	6 374	9 657	14 187	(e)11 813
Turks and Caicos Islands	..	..	9	10	12	15	18	16
Central America	*23 379*	*45 576*	*180 991*	*180 278*	*205 113*	*231 587*	*270 144*	*294 696*
Belize	111	108	218	205	213	208	266	267
Costa Rica*	1 002	1 448	5 850	6 102	6 301	7 026	8 216	(e)9 338
El Salvador*	1 075	644	2 963	3 153	3 339	3 429	(e)3 560	(e)3 953
Guatemala*	1 520	1 163	2 711	2 632	2 939	3 477	3 665	(e)4 530
Honduras*	829	831	1 380	1 321	1 537	1 679	1 929	(e)2 149
Mexico	18 031	40 711	166 367	165 396	189 084	213 891	250 441	272 055
Nicaragua	451	331	643	605	756	858	1 027	1 202
Panama, excl. Canal Zone (former)	361							
Panama*	–	340	859	864	944	1 018	1 039	1 202
South America	*65 598*	*86 549*	*164 491*	*186 134*	*248 227*	*312 880*	*380 136*	*439 126*
Argentina*	8 021	12 353	26 341	29 566	34 576	40 351	46 569	55 642
Bolivia	942	926	1 230	1 598	2 146	2 791	3 863	4 490
Brazil	20 132	31 414	55 086	73 084	96 678	118 529	137 807	160 649
Chile*	4 705	8 373	19 210	21 664	32 520	41 297	58 116	68 296
Colombia	3 924	6 721	13 043	13 080	16 224	21 146	24 388	(e)29 706
Ecuador*	2 481	2 714	4 927	6 223	7 753	10 100	12 728	13 751
Guyana*	389	251	502	513	593	553	596	(e)681
Paraguay	310	959	869	1 242	1 627	1 697	1 906	3 374
Peru*	3 898	3 231	6 955	9 091	12 617	16 587	23 765	27 680
Suriname	514	472	505	638	895	950	1 234	..
Uruguay	1 059	1 693	2 295	2 206	2 931	3 405	3 953	(e)4 459
Venezuela (Bolivarian Rep. of)	19 221	17 444	33 529	27 230	39 668	55 473	65 210	69 165
Developing economies: Asia	365 007	590 417	1 534 755	1 859 413	2 385 427	2 896 196	3 456 391	4 018 909
Eastern Asia	*76 165*	*280 565*	*774 897*	*1 003 970*	*1 285 300*	*1 538 367*	*1 847 451*	*2 187 136*
China	18 099	62 091	249 203	438 228	593 326	761 953	969 380	1 218 000
China, Hong Kong SAR	19 752	82 160	201 860	223 762	259 260	289 337	322 669	344 629
China, Macao SAR	613	1 701	2 547	2 581	2 812	2 476	2 557	2 543
China, Taiwan Province of	19 786	67 079	147 777	143 900	173 909	197 779	224 007	246 723
Dem. People's Rep. of Korea	..	1 857	708	1 066	1 278	1 338	1 830	..
Mongolia	403	661	536	616	870	1 065	1 543	(e)1 857
Republic of Korea (5)	17 512	65 016	172 267	193 817	253 845	284 419	325 465	371 554
Southern Asia	*26 127*	*47 033*	*92 734*	*118 171*	*149 764*	*192 957*	*221 571*	*263 281*
Afghanistan	670	235	137	144	305	384	(e)452	..
Bangladesh	759	1 671	6 399	7 050	8 151	9 294	11 794	12 361
Bhutan	17	70	103	154	183	258	414	..
India (6)	8 586	17 969	42 379	58 963	76 649	99 620	120 861	145 431
Iran (Islamic Rep. of)*	12 328	19 305	28 345	33 991	44 403	60 012	63 247	78 423
Maldives	8	78	109	152	181	162	225	228
Nepal	80	204	803	662	756	830	760	(e)917
Pakistan	2 618	5 589	9 028	11 930	13 379	16 051	16 933	(e)17 400
Sri Lanka	1 062	1 912	5 430	5 125	5 757	6 347	6 886	(e)7 655
South-Eastern Asia	*73 957*	*145 284*	*431 911*	*453 696*	*568 977*	*652 733*	*765 641*	*865 786*
Brunei Darussalam*	4 581	2 213	3 903	4 421	5 057	6 250	7 800	..
Cambodia	16	86	1 397	2 087	2 589	2 910	3 693	(e)4 066
Indonesia	23 950	26 807	65 407	64 109	71 785	86 179	98 548	118 728
Lao People's dem. Rep.*	28	79	330	335	363	553	882	(e)1 139
Malaysia (7)	12 945	29 452	98 229	99 369	125 744	140 870	160 573	176 024

For sources and notes, see end of table 1.1.1.

Imports (c.i.f.) - Importations (c.a.f.) Millions de dollars								Régions, pays ou territoires
1980	1990	2000	2003	2004	2005	2006	2007	
123 588	127 240	392 045	369 101	449 011	530 415	631 683	749 287	**Économies en développement : Amérique**
27 362	*18 702*	*32 390*	*30 827*	*34 863*	*42 420*	*49 287*	*53 415*	*Caraïbes*
..	..	95	77	102	130	(e)175	(e)250	Anguilla
88	255	407	422	454	497	550	..	Antigua-et-Barbuda*
..	581	2 583	2 400	3 005	3 494	3 838	2 851	Aruba (2)
7 546	1 112	2 074	1 762	1 905	2 396	2 828	(e)2 862	Bahamas (3)
525	704	1 156	1 195	1 413	1 604	1 586	1 709	Barbade
6 505	6 745	4 843	4 662	5 610	7 591	(e)9 503	(e)10 083	Cuba*
48	118	148	128	144	165	167	(e)197	Dominique*
1 964	3 006	9 479	7 627	7 888	9 876	11 160	13 817	République dominicaine*
50	106	246	253	250	288	285	(e)379	Grenade*
375	332	1 036	1 188	1 306	1 454	1 875	(e)1 581	Haïti
1 171	1 928	3 301	3 639	3 772	4 460	5 313	(e)6 273	Jamaïque
12	48	22	28	25	26	30	(e)30	Montserrat*
(b)5 676	2 141	2 854	2 606	3 050	3 452	3 911	..	Antilles néerlandaises*(4)
45	110	172	175	175	185	(e)218	(e)235	Saint-Kitts-et-Nevis*
124	271	355	403	459	550	600	(e)633	Sainte-Lucie*
57	136	163	201	226	240	247	(e)318	Saint-Vincent-et-les Grenadines*
3 178	1 109	3 308	3 892	4 858	5 708	6 503	(e)7 155	Trinité-et-Tobago*
..	..	149	169	221	304	498	581	Îles Turques et Caïques
29 743	*51 772*	*207 773*	*207 435*	*239 274*	*269 286*	*311 388*	*347 589*	*Amérique centrale*
150	211	524	552	520	593	676	684	Belize
1 540	1 990	6 389	7 663	8 268	9 812	11 520	(e)12 686	Costa Rica*
966	1 263	4 948	5 754	6 329	6 834	7 628	(e)8 591	El Salvador*
1 598	1 649	5 171	6 722	7 812	8 810	10 157	(e)11 843	Guatemala*
1 009	935	2 855	3 276	3 916	4 613	5 418	(e)6 753	Honduras*
22 144	43 548	182 702	178 503	206 623	231 821	268 169	296 578	Mexique
887	637	1 805	1 879	2 212	2 623	2 988	3 579	Nicaragua
1 449	–	–	–	–	–	–	–	Panama, sans la zone du canal (anc.)
–	1 539	3 379	3 086	3 594	4 180	4 833	6 875	Panama*
66 482	*56 766*	*151 882*	*130 839*	*174 873*	*218 709*	*271 008*	*348 283*	*Amérique du Sud*
10 545	4 078	25 280	13 834	22 445	28 688	34 158	44 780	Argentine*
665	687	1 830	1 616	1 844	2 341	2 819	3 444	Bolivie
24 961	22 522	59 066	50 881	66 433	77 628	95 852	126 581	Brésil
5 797	7 742	18 507	19 322	24 794	32 735	38 409	46 966	Chili*
4 739	5 589	11 539	13 889	16 746	21 204	26 046	(e)33 047	Colombie
2 253	1 865	3 721	6 703	8 226	10 287	12 114	(e)13 308	Équateur*
396	311	653	576	651	787	870	(e)1 040	Guyana*
615	1 352	2 193	2 228	3 097	3 715	6 090	(e)7 532	Paraguay
2 499	3 470	8 888	8 414	10 101	12 502	15 312	19 580	Pérou*
504	472	526	704	742	916	965	..	Suriname
1 680	1 343	3 466	2 190	3 114	3 879	4 757	(e)5 576	Uruguay
11 827	7 335	16 213	10 483	16 679	24 027	33 616	45 463	Venezuela (Rép. bolivarienne du)
272 005	570 895	1 386 764	1 704 105	2 201 735	2 594 651	3 029 655	3 530 946	**Économies en développement : Asie**
85 536	*265 896*	*742 868*	*956 454*	*1 231 634*	*1 411 111*	*1 647 495*	*1 910 060*	*Asie orientale*
19 941	53 345	225 094	412 760	561 229	659 953	791 605	955 800	Chine
22 447	82 490	212 805	231 896	271 074	299 533	334 681	367 864	Chine (RAS de Hong Kong)
543	1 533	2 261	2 755	3 478	3 913	4 565	5 366	Chine (RAS de Macao)
19 764	54 831	139 927	127 366	168 090	182 571	202 725	219 347	Province chinoise de Taiwan
..	2 930	1 686	2 049	2 279	2 718	3 050	..	Rép. populaire dém. de Corée
548	924	615	801	1 021	1 184	1 486	(e)1 986	Mongolie
22 292	69 844	160 481	178 827	224 463	261 238	309 383	356 648	République de Corée (5)
39 540	*57 416*	*96 072*	*136 377*	*178 041*	*237 606*	*284 440*	*326 815*	*Asie méridionale*
841	936	1 176	2 101	2 177	2 740	2 850	..	Afghanistan
2 599	3 618	8 883	10 434	12 036	13 872	16 171	18 530	Bangladesh
50	81	175	249	411	386	420	..	Bhoutan
14 864	23 580	51 523	72 558	99 775	142 842	175 242	215 500	Inde (6)
13 427	18 330	15 207	29 100	35 207	40 969	46 648	43 186	Iran (Rép. islamique d')*
29	137	389	471	642	745	927	1 096	Maldives
342	672	1 574	1 755	1 871	1 860	2 100	(e)2 987	Népal
5 350	7 376	10 864	13 038	17 949	25 357	29 825	(e)31 242	Pakistan
2 037	2 685	6 281	6 672	7 973	8 834	10 258	(e)11 005	Sri Lanka
65 641	*162 292*	*377 683*	*396 757*	*496 193*	*594 331*	*683 017*	*772 366*	*Asie du Sud-Est*
572	1 001	1 107	1 327	1 422	1 491	1 760	..	Brunéi Darussalam*
180	164	1 936	2 668	3 269	3 928	4 749	(e)5 404	Cambodge
10 834	21 837	40 365	39 546	50 554	69 408	75 714	93 088	Indonésie
92	185	535	462	713	882	1 060	(e)1 010	Rép. dém. populaire lao*
10 779	29 258	81 963	81 948	105 298	114 411	131 080	146 770	Malaisie (7)

Pour les sources et les notes, se reporter à la fin du tableau 1.1.1.

Region, country or territory	Exports (f.o.b.) - Exportations (f.a.b.) Millions of dollars							
	1980	1990	2000	2003	2004	2005	2006	2007
Myanmar	477	328	1 646	2 483	2 380	3 813	4 506	(e)6 487
Philippines	5 741	8 117	39 783	36 229	39 680	39 879	47 416	(e)50 761
Singapore (8)	19 375	52 730	137 804	144 181	198 637	229 649	271 807	299 271
Thailand*	6 505	23 068	68 963	80 324	96 248	110 178	130 803	153 103
Timor-Leste	..	..	..	8	8	9	8	..
Viet Nam	339	2 404	14 449	20 149	26 485	32 442	39 605	48 400
Western Asia	*188 758*	*117 535*	*235 213*	*283 577*	*381 387*	*512 139*	*621 728*	*702 706*
Bahrain	3 606	3 761	6 194	6 624	7 556	10 160	12 200	13 634
Iraq*	26 349	10 314	20 380	9 711	18 490	23 697	30 528	(e)33 785
Jordan	574	1 064	1 899	3 082	3 922	4 302	5 175	5 700
Kuwait*	19 842	7 042	19 436	20 675	28 729	45 011	57 266	62 237
Lebanon	955	494	715	1 813	2 199	2 337	2 814	2 816
Oman	2 387	5 508	11 319	11 669	13 342	18 692	21 585	(e)22 127
Qatar*	5 680	3 529	11 424	13 382	18 426	25 339	34 052	(e)37 940
Saudi Arabia*	101 577	44 416	77 481	93 245	125 998	180 572	215 475	230 607
Syrian Arab Republic*	2 108	4 212	4 633	5 731	5 383	6 450	10 919	(e)11 816
Turkey*	2 910	12 959	27 775	46 576	61 683	71 928	81 912	106 851
United Arab Emirates	21 967	23 544	49 878	67 135	90 985	117 238	142 486	(e)167 093
Yemen (former Arab Republic)	777							
Yemen (former Democratic)	25							
Yemen*	–	692	4 079	3 934	4 676	6 413	7 316	(e)8 100
Developing economies: Oceania	**2 242**	**2 710**	**4 098**	**4 510**	**5 163**	**5 908**	**7 152**	**8 341**
American Samoa*	127	311	346	460	446	374	432	..
Cook Islands	4	5	7	9	8	5	4	(e)11
Fiji	377	398	538	674	693	701	679	(e)780
French Polynesia*	30	111	244	151	185	210	236	180
Guam	61	82	74	43	53	52	53	91
Kiribati	3	3	4	3	2	4	6	..
Marshall Islands	..	3	9	..	..	..	..	..
Micronesia (Federated States of)	..	4	17	18	14	13	(e)12	..
Nauru	65	60	28	(e)15	(e)14	(e)12	(e)15	..
New Caledonia*	409	480	606	788	1 026	1 085	1 344	2 045
Niue	..	..	0	0	0	..	..	..
Palau	..	..	12	8	9	(e)13	(e)17	..
Papua New Guinea	1 031	1 144	2 095	2 207	2 552	3 273	4 166	(e)4 551
Samoa*	17	9	14	15	11	12	11	15
Solomon Islands*	74	70	69	74	97	105	122	(e)132
Tokelau	..	..	..	..	..	..	..	..
Tonga	7	11	9	18	15	10	11	(e)7
Tuvalu	..	1	0	0	0	0	(e)0	..
Vanuatu	36	19	26	27	38	39	46	..
Wallis and Futuna Islands	..	..	..	0	0	(e)0	(e)0	..
Economies in transition: Asia	**–**	**–**	**17 782**	**24 864**	**34 854**	**45 278**	**62 173**	**72 519**
Armenia*	–	–	294	686	715	950	1 004	1 219
Azerbaijan*(9)	–	–	1 745	2 590	3 615	4 347	6 372	(e)5 454
Georgia (10)	–	–	323	461	647	867	993	1 240
Kazakhstan*(10)	–	–	8 812	12 927	20 093	27 849	40 470	(e)46 930
Kyrgyzstan	–	–	505	582	719	672	796	1 134
Tajikistan (10)	–	–	780	797	915	909	1 399	(e)1 463
Turkmenistan (10)	–	–	2 506	3 632	3 870	4 935	5 774	7 567
Uzbekistan (10)	–	–	2 817	3 189	4 280	4 749	5 365	(e)7 511
Economies in transition: Europe	**–**	**–**	**136 726**	**181 828**	**247 163**	**313 886**	**387 308**	**461 166**
Albania	..	224	258	448	605	658	798	1 043
Belarus	–	–	7 326	9 946	13 774	15 979	19 739	24 339
Bosnia and Herzegovina*(11)	–	–	1 067	1 340	1 790	2 304	3 428	4 152
Croatia*	–	–	4 432	6 187	8 024	8 773	10 377	12 360
Moldova	–	–	472	789	980	1 091	1 060	1 342
Russian Federation (12)	–	–	105 565	135 929	183 207	243 798	303 926	355 464
Serbia and Montenegro*	–	–	1 711	2 756	4 440	5 013	7 216	(e)9 915
SFR of Yugoslavia (former)	8 978	14 308						
TFYR of Macedonia*	–	–	1 323	1 367	1 676	2 041	2 398	3 302
Ukraine (10)	–	–	14 573	23 067	32 666	34 228	38 368	49 248
USSR (former)	76 449	104 177	–	–	–	–	–	–
Developed economies: America	**293 549**	**521 758**	**1 058 880**	**998 036**	**1 123 608**	**1 267 055**	**1 428 253**	**1 579 896**
Bermuda	37	60	51	60	73	49	25	..
Canada	67 734	127 629	276 635	272 819	304 528	359 431	389 531	416 464
Greenland	211	452	271	380	480	406	407	..

For sources and notes, see end of table 1.1.1.

Imports (c.i.f.) - Importations (c.a.f.) Millions de dollars								Régions, pays ou territoires
1980	1990	2000	2003	2004	2005	2006	2007	
357	273	2 401	2 091	2 196	1 927	2 108	(e)3 069	Myanmar
8 291	13 004	37 027	39 502	42 345	46 964	54 081	(e)56 379	Philippines
24 007	60 774	134 545	127 939	163 854	200 047	238 710	263 150	Singapour (8)
9 214	33 045	61 923	75 824	94 410	118 158	128 723	140 795	Thaïlande*
..	..	242	194	163	137	141	..	Timor-Leste
1 314	2 752	15 638	25 256	31 969	36 978	44 891	60 800	Viet Nam
81 289	*85 291*	*170 140*	*214 518*	*295 867*	*351 604*	*414 704*	*521 705*	**Asie occidentale**
3 483	3 712	4 633	5 657	6 584	9 339	10 515	11 488	Bahreïn
8 707	6 526	13 384	9 934	19 954	23 532	20 892	(e)23 085	Iraq*
2 402	2 600	4 597	5 743	8 128	10 506	11 447	13 531	Jordanie
6 533	3 972	7 157	10 986	12 631	17 488	15 991	19 387	Koweït*
3 650	2 525	6 230	7 315	9 609	9 633	9 647	11 815	Liban
1 732	2 681	5 040	6 572	8 865	8 827	10 915	(e)14 577	Oman
1 447	1 695	3 252	4 897	6 004	10 061	16 441	22 005	Qatar*
30 165	24 107	30 197	36 916	44 745	59 459	69 800	89 153	Arabie saoudite*
4 124	2 400	3 815	5 111	7 049	7 898	11 488	(e)12 867	République arabe syrienne*
7 910	22 302	54 503	65 637	96 368	98 998	133 584	168 527	Turquie*
8 631	11 199	35 009	52 074	72 072	91 150	97 864	(e)128 478	Émirats arabes unis
1 527		–	–	–	–	–	–	Yémen (anc. République arabe du)
978		–	–	–	–	–	–	Yémen (anc. démocratique)
–	1 571	2 324	3 675	3 859	4 713	6 120	(e)6 793	Yémen*
3 550	*5 090*	*5 697*	*7 750*	*8 513*	*9 206*	*10 008*	*11 172*	**Économies en développement : Océanie**
95	360	506	624	604	507	342	..	Samoa américaines*
23	52	51	70	84	87	112	(e)178	Îles Cook
562	754	856	1 209	1 446	1 607	1 802	(e)1 818	Fidji
547	928	1 072	1 568	1 480	1 702	1 547	1 709	Polynésie française*
400	461	421	526	503	533	501	688	Guam
17	27	40	52	59	76	63	..	Kiribati
..	56	55	75	84	(e)120	(e)138	..	Îles Marshall
..	84	107	118	133	130	138	..	Micronésie (États fédérés de)
12	34	27	(e)22	(e)17	(e)15	(e)18	..	Nauru
456	883	922	1 532	1 641	1 782	2 108	2 793	Nouvelle-Calédonie*
..	..	2	2	8	(e)7	(e)7	..	Nioué
..	..	127	82	138	145	(e)170	..	Palaos
1 176	1 118	1 151	1 367	1 680	1 729	2 209	..	Papouasie-Nouvelle-Guinée
63	81	106	152	210	239	275	265	Samoa*
89	91	92	94	122	185	217	(e)278	Îles Salomon*
..	..	1	0	0	..	..	..	Tokélaou
38	62	69	94	105	120	130	(e)133	Tonga
..	4	5	16	11	13	13	5	Tuvalu
73	96	87	106	128	149	160	..	Vanuatu
..	..	..	41	61	(e)60	(e)59	..	Îles Wallis-et-Futuna
–	*–*	*13 515*	*20 228*	*28 340*	*35 703*	*47 643*	*61 469*	**Économies en transition : Asie**
–	–	882	1 280	1 351	1 768	2 194	3 282	Arménie*
–	–	1 172	2 626	3 516	4 350	5 268	(e)5 958	Azerbaïdjan*(9)
–	–	709	1 141	1 848	2 491	3 681	5 217	Géorgie (10)
–	–	5 040	8 409	12 781	17 353	24 956	(e)32 778	Kazakhstan*(10)
–	–	554	717	941	1 108	1 848	2 417	Kirghizistan
–	–	675	881	1 191	1 330	1 725	(e)2 415	Tadjikistan (10)
–	–	1 786	2 512	3 320	3 638	4 056	4 517	Turkménistan (10)
–	–	2 697	2 662	3 392	3 666	3 915	(e)4 885	Ouzbékistan (10)
–	*–*	*91 179*	*151 603*	*194 873*	*236 939*	*302 139*	*404 044*	**Économies en transition : Europe**
..	423	1 090	1 864	2 309	2 618	3 058	4 066	Albanie
–	–	8 646	11 558	16 491	16 708	22 323	28 674	Bélarus
–	–	3 894	5 613	6 650	7 577	7 560	9 720	Bosnie-Herzégovine*(11)
–	–	7 887	14 209	16 589	18 560	21 502	25 830	Croatie*
–	–	776	1 403	1 773	2 293	2 710	3 690	Moldova
–	–	49 125	83 677	107 120	137 977	181 161	245 365	Fédération de Russie (12)
–	–	3 711	7 952	12 013	11 840	15 034	(e)20 852	Serbie-et-Monténégro*
15 076	18 871	–	–	–	–	–	–	RSF de Yougoslavie (anc.)
–	–	2 094	2 306	2 932	3 228	3 752	5 177	LERY de Macédoine*
–	–	13 956	23 020	28 997	36 136	45 039	60 670	Ukraine (10)
68 522	120 651	–	–	–	–	–	–	URSS (anc.)
320 210	*641 358*	*1 505 240*	*1 549 441*	*1 807 270*	*2 065 547*	*2 278 816*	*2 405 993*	**Économies développées : Amérique**
343	595	719	833	988	985	1 094	..	Bermudes
62 544	123 244	244 786	245 028	279 931	331 553	357 651	386 929	Canada
328	445	365	460	601	595	581	..	Groenland

Pour les sources et les notes, se reporter à la fin du tableau 1.1.1.

Region, country or territory	Exports (f.o.b.) - Exportations (f.a.b.) Millions of dollars							
	1980	1990	2000	2003	2004	2005	2006	2007
Saint Pierre and Miquelon	1	26	5	6	(e)7	11	(e)20	..
United States*	225 566	393 592	781 918	724 771	818 520	907 158	1 038 270	1 162 980
Developed economies: Asia	**135 979**	**299 157**	**510 653**	**503 601**	**604 293**	**637 675**	**696 720**	**763 733**
Israel*	5 538	11 576	31 404	31 784	38 618	42 770	46 789	54 065
Japan	130 441	287 581	479 249	471 817	565 675	594 905	649 931	709 668
Developed economies: Europe	**892 261**	**1 646 917**	**2 598 373**	**3 324 405**	**3 968 855**	**4 307 508**	**4 861 890**	**5 597 668**
Andorra	..	..	54	89	122	142	(e)180	..
Austria*	17 489	41 135	67 738	97 113	118 312	· 125 352	136 693	161 843
Belgium*	–	–	–	255 527	306 722	334 859	366 790	427 915
Belgium-Luxembourg*	64 656	118 294	196 830	–	–	–	–	–
Bulgaria*	10 372	4 822	4 809	7 540	9 931	11 739	15 102	18 338
Cyprus*	532	957	951	834	945	1 470	1 330	1 389
Czechoslovakia (former) (13)	14 891	11 906						
Czech Republic*(14)	–	–	28 996	48 709	68 953	78 211	94 886	121 614
Denmark*(15)	16 749	37 037	51 319	66 491	77 047	85 238	92 526	102 772
Estonia*(10)	–	–	3 830	5 623	5 931	7 699	9 714	10 891
Faeroe Islands	187	400	477	599	620	602	631	731
Finland	14 150	26 571	46 126	53 148	61 494	66 115	77 000	89 104
France*	116 409	217 265	327 752	391 901	451 890	464 061	495 677	549 679
Germany (former Dem. Rep.)	17 312	–	–	–	–	–	–	–
Germany (former Federal Rep.)	192 860	–	–	–	–	–	–	–
Germany*	–	410 104	552 053	751 292	909 449	972 247	1 107 663	1 317 604
Greece*	5 153	8 105	11 753	13 377	15 305	17 229	20 747	23 443
Hungary*(16)	8 671	9 598	28 016	42 532	55 538	63 025	75 231	93 991
Iceland*	918	1 592	1 891	2 385	2 896	2 944	3 453	(e)4 282
Ireland*	8 398	23 747	77 450	92 726	104 736	109 805	108 679	120 511
Italy*	78 104	170 486	240 619	299 232	353 607	373 640	416 706	488 239
Latvia*	–	–	1 865	2 893	4 003	5 170	6 150	8 250
Lithuania (10)	–	–	3 548	6 970	9 300	11 823	14 132	17 045
Luxembourg*	–	–	–	13 287	16 237	18 824	22 893	22 286
Malta	483	1 130	2 443	2 467	2 487	2 280	2 661	2 900
Netherlands*	84 948	131 775	233 227	295 908	357 250	406 928	463 446	547 201
Norway	18 543	34 049	60 058	67 479	81 750	101 938	120 464	137 917
Poland*	14 191	13 627	31 651	53 537	75 008	89 561	110 737	137 883
Portugal*	4 640	16 422	24 375	31 742	35 770	38 196	43 314	50 916
Romania*	11 209	5 775	10 367	17 619	23 485	27 730	32 336	40 025
Slovakia*	–	–	11 889	21 966	27 639	32 092	41 832	57 791
Slovenia*			8 732	12 767	16 349	19 273	23 219	29 856
Spain*	20 720	55 521	115 297	156 096	182 529	192 912	213 631	239 416
Sweden	30 906	57 538	87 170	102 066	123 211	130 473	147 738	168 051
Switzerland*	29 634	63 794	81 534	104 972	123 010	130 930	147 856	170 706
United Kingdom*	110 137	185 268	285 553	305 520	347 328	385 002	448 472	434 899
Developed economies: Oceania	**27 365**	**49 146**	**77 168**	**88 073**	**106 765**	**127 561**	**145 727**	**168 033**
Australia*	21 944	39 752	63 870	71 546	86 420	105 832	123 293	141 083
New Zealand	5 421	9 394	13 297	16 527	20 344	21 729	22 434	26 950

For sources and notes, see end of table 1.1.1.

Imports (c.i.f.) - Importations (c.a.f.) Millions de dollars								Régions, pays ou territoires
1980	1990	2000	2003	2004	2005	2006	2007	
10	86	70	69	(e)70	63	(e)60	..	Saint-Pierre-et-Miquelon
256 985	516 987	1 259 300	1 303 050	1 525 680	1 732 350	1 919 430	2 017 330	États-Unis*
151 080	**252 162**	**410 915**	**419 233**	**497 406**	**562 064**	**629 908**	**676 478**	**Économies développées : Asie**
9 784	16 794	31 404	36 303	42 864	47 142	50 334	56 621	Israël*
141 296	235 368	379 511	382 930	454 542	514 922	579 574	619 857	Japon
997 995	**1 705 132**	**2 632 643**	**3 268 626**	**3 925 749**	**4 327 522**	**4 947 720**	**5 680 024**	**Économies développées : Europe**
..	..	1 195	1 511	1 756	1 796	(e)1 919	..	Andorre
24 444	49 088	72 423	99 499	119 842	127 495	137 157	161 271	Autriche*
			234 867	285 487	319 137	351 842	410 421	Belgique*
71 864	120 314	188 866		–		–	–	Belgique-Luxembourg*
9 650	4 710	6 505	10 902	14 467	18 163	23 270	29 787	Bulgarie*
1 202	2 568	3 846	4 288	5 495	6 329	6 928	8 563	Chypre*
12 774	13 106		–		–			Tchécoslovaquie (anc.) (13)
		33 852	53 801	69 936	76 617	93 154	117 121	République tchèque*(14)
19 340	33 248	45 581	57 411	68 120	75 682	85 472	98 960	Danemark*(15)
		4 236	6 480	8 330	10 228	13 442	15 098	Estonie*(10)
219	333	533	740	629	747	783	964	Îles Féroé
15 635	27 001	34 456	42 495	51 423	59 088	68 842	80 949	Finlande
137 554	240 753	339 090	398 697	470 713	504 811	541 701	610 955	France*
19 082	–	–	–	–	–	–	–	Allemagne (anc. Rép. dém. d')
188 002	–	–	–	–	–	–	–	Allemagne (anc. Rép. fédérale d')
–	346 153	497 417	604 401	715 395	778 139	906 320	1 051 545	Allemagne*
10 548	19 777	33 495	44 836	52 728	54 142	63 571	75 027	Grèce*
9 245	8 671	31 955	47 602	60 511	66 638	78 230	94 413	Hongrie*(16)
999	1 680	2 591	2 789	3 553	4 558	6 155	(e)6 007	Islande*
11 153	20 682	51 060	53 871	61 780	68 656	73 084	81 670	Irlande*
100 741	181 968	238 863	297 412	355 124	385 313	442 373	501 104	Italie*
–	–	3 184	5 242	7 087	8 708	11 534	15 152	Lettonie*
–	–	5 219	9 668	12 383	15 573	19 366	24 042	Lituanie (10)
			16 159	20 042	21 926	26 558	27 255	Luxembourg*
938	1 961	3 400	3 398	3 668	3 600	3 979	4 329	Malte
88 419	126 475	218 360	264 607	319 516	364 322	416 668	488 429	Pays-Bas*
16 926	27 221	34 392	39 486	48 085	54 792	63 366	79 769	Norvège
16 690	8 413	48 940	68 004	89 654	101 782	126 941	161 598	Pologne*
9 309	25 264	39 972	47 188	54 917	61 268	66 646	77 273	Portugal*
13 843	9 843	13 055	24 003	32 664	40 463	51 106	69 404	Roumanie*
–	–	13 412	23 760	29 727	35 455	44 807	59 820	Slovaquie*
–	–	10 116	13 853	17 754	20 369	24 136	31 326	Slovénie*
34 078	87 554	156 211	208 531	258 209	289 175	328 560	370 097	Espagne*
33 438	54 245	72 913	83 510	100 384	111 599	127 493	150 353	Suède
36 356	69 691	83 584	100 352	115 969	126 574	141 400	159 937	Suisse*
115 545	224 412	343 922	399 263	470 403	514 378	600 917	615 462	Royaume-Uni*
27 871	**51 486**	**85 434**	**107 644**	**132 579**	**151 515**	**160 043**	**196 221**	**Économies développées : Océanie**
22 399	41 985	71 529	89 084	109 384	125 281	133 613	165 331	Australie*
5 472	9 501	13 905	18 559	23 195	26 234	26 430	30 890	Nouvelle-Zélande

Pour les sources et les notes, se reporter à la fin du tableau 1.1.1.

1.1.1 Exports and imports of countries and geographical regions
Share

Region, country or territory	Exports (f.o.b.) - Exportations (f.a.b.) Percentage - En pourcentage										
	1980	1985	1990	1995	2000	2002	2003	2004	2005	2006	2007
WORLD	100.000	100.000	100.000	100.000	100.000	100.000	100.000	100.000	100.000	100.000	100.000
DEVELOPING ECONOMIES	29.406	25.362	24.253	27.625	31.853	31.770	32.153	33.730	36.047	37.275	37.519
ECONOMIES IN TRANSITION	4.204	4.973	3.412	2.357	2.393	2.510	2.739	3.071	3.429	3.718	3.858
DEVELOPED ECONOMIES	66.390	69.665	72.335	70.018	65.754	65.721	65.109	63.199	60.524	59.007	58.623
Developing economies: Africa	5.855	4.181	3.075	2.083	2.371	2.245	2.363	2.525	2.893	2.970	2.873
Eastern Africa	0.345	0.267	0.210	0.188	0.158	0.184	0.165	0.162	0.159	0.169	0.171
Burundi*	0.003	0.006	0.002	0.002	0.001	0.000	0.000	0.001	0.001	0.000	(e)0.000
Comoros*	0.001	0.001	0.001	0.000	0.000	0.000	0.000	0.000	0.000	0.000	..
Djibouti*	0.001	0.001	0.001	0.000	0.001	0.001	0.000	0.000	0.000	0.000	..
Eritrea	–	–	–	0.002	0.000	0.001	0.000	0.000	0.000	0.000	..
Ethiopia	–	–	–	0.008	0.008	0.007	0.007	0.007	0.009	0.009	(e)0.009
Ethiopia (former)	0.021	0.017	0.009	–	–	–	–	–	–	–	–
Kenya	0.061	0.049	0.030	0.036	0.027	0.033	0.032	0.029	0.031	0.028	(e)0.030
Madagascar*	0.020	0.014	0.009	0.010	0.013	0.013	0.011	0.011	0.008	0.008	(e)0.008
Malawi	0.015	0.012	0.012	0.008	0.006	0.006	0.007	0.005	0.005	0.005	(e)0.006
Mauritius	0.021	0.022	0.034	0.030	0.028	0.028	0.025	0.022	0.020	0.019	0.015
Mozambique	0.014	0.004	0.004	0.003	0.006	0.012	0.014	0.016	0.017	0.020	(e)0.018
Rwanda	0.006	0.007	0.003	0.001	0.001	0.001	0.001	0.001	0.001	0.001	0.001
Seychelles	0.001	0.001	0.002	0.001	0.003	0.004	0.004	0.003	0.003	0.003	(e)0.003
Somalia	0.007	0.005	0.004	0.003	0.003	0.005	0.004	0.004	0.004	0.004	..
Uganda	0.017	0.020	0.004	0.009	0.007	0.007	0.007	0.008	0.008	0.008	0.012
United Republic of Tanzania*	0.025	0.013	0.010	0.013	0.011	0.015	0.016	0.016	0.016	0.014	0.014
Zambia*	0.064	0.040	0.038	0.020	0.014	0.015	0.013	0.017	0.017	0.031	0.035
Zimbabwe	0.069	0.057	0.049	0.041	0.030	0.036	0.022	0.021	0.017	0.016	(e)0.014
Middle Africa	0.436	0.411	0.338	0.220	0.265	0.284	0.294	0.346	0.474	0.517	0.543
Angola*	0.094	0.117	0.112	0.072	0.123	0.128	0.126	0.147	0.230	0.264	(e)0.297
Cameroon*(1)	0.068	0.037	0.058	0.032	0.028	0.028	0.030	0.027	0.030	0.031	(e)0.024
Central African Republic*(1)	0.006	0.005	0.003	0.003	0.002	0.002	0.002	0.001	0.001	0.001	(e)0.001
Chad*	0.003	0.003	0.005	0.005	0.003	0.003	0.008	0.024	0.030	0.028	(e)0.028
Congo*(1)	0.045	0.055	0.028	0.023	0.039	0.035	0.035	0.037	0.046	0.056	(e)0.050
Dem. Rep. of the Congo*	0.112	0.094	0.067	0.032	0.013	0.017	0.018	0.020	0.021	0.019	(e)0.018
Equatorial Guinea	0.001	0.001	0.002	0.002	0.017	0.033	0.037	0.050	0.064	0.068	(e)0.073
Gabon*(1)	0.107	0.099	0.063	0.052	0.040	0.037	0.037	0.039	0.052	0.050	(e)0.051
Sao Tome and Principe*	0.001	0.000	0.000	0.000	0.000	0.000	0.000	0.000	0.000	0.000	0.000
Northern Africa	2.167	1.683	1.180	0.697	0.842	0.772	0.842	0.875	1.055	1.116	1.091
Algeria*	0.683	0.653	0.423	0.216	0.339	0.290	0.319	0.352	0.436	0.440	(e)0.388
Egypt*	0.150	0.189	0.142	0.067	0.073	0.073	0.084	0.082	0.102	0.114	0.116
Libyan Arab Jamahiriya	1.078	0.625	0.380	0.165	0.197	0.152	0.182	0.189	0.276	0.325	(e)0.318
Morocco*	0.120	0.110	0.123	0.133	0.115	0.121	0.116	0.105	0.096	0.095	0.100
Sudan*	0.027	0.019	0.011	0.011	0.028	0.030	0.034	0.041	0.046	0.047	(e)0.059
Tunisia	0.110	0.088	0.101	0.106	0.091	0.106	0.106	0.105	0.100	0.095	0.109
Southern Africa	1.257	0.829	0.677	0.539	0.546	0.536	0.565	0.590	0.579	0.565	0.580
Botswana*	..	..	..	..	0.043	0.039	0.037	0.038	0.042	0.037	0.029
Lesotho	..	..	..	..	0.003	0.005	0.006	0.008	0.006	0.006	(e)0.006
Namibia	..	..	..	..	0.020	0.017	0.017	0.020	0.019	0.023	(e)0.025
South Africa	(a)1.257	(a)0.829	(a)0.677	(a)0.539	0.464	0.458	0.483	0.503	0.493	0.481	0.505
Swaziland	..	..	..	..	0.014	0.016	0.022	0.021	0.019	0.017	(e)0.016
Western Africa	1.650	0.992	0.669	0.439	0.560	0.469	0.498	0.553	0.626	0.603	0.489
Benin*	0.003	0.008	0.008	0.008	0.006	0.007	0.007	0.006	0.006	0.005	0.005
Burkina Faso	0.004	0.004	0.004	0.005	0.003	0.004	0.004	0.005	0.004	(e)0.005	0.005
Cape Verde*	0.000	0.000	0.000	0.000	0.000	0.000	0.000	0.000	0.000	0.000	0.000
Côte d'Ivoire*	0.154	0.151	0.088	0.074	0.060	0.081	0.077	0.075	0.071	0.067	(e)0.062
Gambia	0.002	0.002	0.001	0.000	0.000	0.000	0.000	0.000	0.000	0.000	0.000
Ghana	0.062	0.032	0.026	0.033	0.026	0.029	0.034	0.030	0.027	0.031	(e)0.030
Guinea	0.020	0.025	0.019	0.014	0.010	0.011	0.008	0.008	0.008	0.007	(e)0.007
Guinea-Bissau	0.001	0.001	0.001	0.001	0.001	0.001	0.001	0.001	0.001	0.001	0.001
Liberia*	0.030	0.022	0.063	0.016	0.005	0.003	0.001	0.001	0.001	0.001	(e)0.001
Mali*	0.010	0.006	0.010	0.009	0.008	0.013	0.012	0.011	0.011	0.013	0.011
Mauritania*	0.010	0.019	0.013	0.009	0.005	0.005	0.004	0.005	0.006	0.011	0.010
Niger*	0.028	0.013	0.008	0.006	0.004	0.004	0.005	0.005	0.005	0.004	0.005
Nigeria	1.276	0.665	0.393	0.237	0.410	0.286	0.319	0.382	0.463	0.437	(e)0.332
Senegal*	0.023	0.029	0.022	0.019	0.014	0.016	0.017	0.016	0.015	0.013	0.013
Sierra Leone*	0.011	0.007	0.004	0.001	0.000	0.001	0.001	0.002	0.002	0.002	(e)0.002
Togo*	0.017	0.010	0.008	0.007	0.006	0.007	0.008	0.007	0.006	(e)0.006	0.006

For sources and notes, see end of table.

Imports (c.i.f.) - Importations (c.a.f.) Percentage - En pourcentage											Régions, pays ou territoires
1980	1985	1990	1995	2000	2002	2003	2004	2005	2006	2007	
100.000	100.000	100.000	100.000	100.000	100.000	100.000	100.000	100.000	100.000	100.000	MONDE
23.769	22.995	22.290	28.572	28.777	28.870	29.009	30.400	31.524	32.191	32.955	ÉCONOMIES EN DÉVELOPPEMENT
4.031	4.692	3.898	2.193	1.573	2.026	2.211	2.359	2.530	2.835	3.312	ÉCONOMIES EN TRANSITION
72.200	72.314	73.812	69.236	69.649	69.104	68.780	67.241	65.946	64.974	63.733	ÉCONOMIES DÉVELOPPÉES
4.520	3.568	2.703	2.306	1.957	2.142	2.231	2.299	2.440	2.434	2.426	Économies en développement : Afrique
0.516	0.386	0.354	0.299	0.253	0.274	0.268	0.277	0.293	0.301	0.306	Afrique orientale
0.008	0.009	0.006	0.004	0.002	0.002	0.002	0.002	0.002	0.003	(e)0.002	Burundi*
0.001	0.002	0.001	0.001	0.001	0.001	0.001	0.001	0.001	0.001	..	Comores*
0.010	0.010	0.006	0.003	0.003	0.003	0.003	0.003	0.003	0.003	..	Djibouti*
–	–	–	0.009	0.007	0.008	0.006	0.005	0.005	(e)0.005	..	Érythrée
–	–	–	0.022	0.019	0.024	0.027	0.033	0.038	0.038	(e)0.037	Éthiopie
0.035	0.049	0.030	–	–	–	–	–	–	–	–	Éthiopie (anc.)
0.102	0.071	0.062	0.057	0.047	0.049	0.048	0.048	0.057	0.059	(e)0.065	Kenya
0.037	0.017	0.016	0.012	0.015	0.009	0.017	0.018	0.016	0.014	(e)0.015	Madagascar*
0.021	0.014	0.016	0.009	0.008	0.010	0.010	0.010	0.011	0.010	(e)0.008	Malawi
0.030	0.026	0.045	0.038	0.033	0.032	0.030	0.029	0.029	0.029	0.028	Maurice
0.039	0.021	0.024	0.013	0.017	0.023	0.023	0.022	0.022	0.023	(e)0.021	Mozambique
0.013	0.015	0.008	0.005	0.003	0.004	0.003	0.003	0.004	0.004	0.004	Rwanda
0.005	0.005	0.005	0.004	0.005	0.006	0.005	0.005	0.006	0.006	(e)0.005	Seychelles
0.021	0.013	0.002	0.005	0.005	0.007	0.006	0.005	0.005	0.006	..	Somalie
0.014	0.016	0.008	0.020	0.023	0.017	0.016	0.021	0.018	0.020	(e)0.024	Ouganda
0.061	0.042	0.038	0.032	0.023	0.025	0.028	0.027	0.030	0.036	0.038	République-Unie de Tanzanie*
0.052	0.036	0.034	0.013	0.013	0.017	0.020	0.023	0.024	0.025	0.028	Zambie*
0.067	0.043	0.051	0.051	0.028	0.037	0.023	0.023	0.022	0.017	(e)0.016	Zimbabwe
0.284	0.274	0.189	0.112	0.114	0.160	0.171	0.159	0.181	0.183	0.171	Afrique centrale
0.064	0.069	0.044	0.028	0.046	0.056	0.071	0.062	0.078	0.071	(e)0.065	Angola*
0.077	0.057	0.039	0.021	0.022	0.028	0.028	0.025	0.025	0.026	(e)0.020	Cameroun*(1)
0.004	0.006	0.004	0.003	0.002	0.002	0.002	0.002	0.002	0.002	(e)0.002	République centrafricaine*(1)
0.004	0.008	0.008	0.007	0.005	0.025	0.010	0.010	0.009	0.011	(e)0.011	Tchad*
0.027	0.029	0.017	0.013	0.007	0.010	0.011	0.009	0.014	0.015	(e)0.014	Congo*(1)
0.073	0.061	0.048	0.020	0.010	0.016	0.021	0.021	0.021	0.023	(e)0.020	Rép. dém. du Congo*
0.001	0.001	0.002	0.002	0.007	0.008	0.016	0.017	0.020	0.023	(e)0.025	Guinée équatoriale
0.032	0.042	0.026	0.017	0.014	0.014	0.013	0.013	0.013	0.013	(e)0.014	Gabon*(1)
0.001	0.000	0.001	0.001	0.000	0.000	0.001	0.000	0.000	0.001	0.001	Sao Tomé-et-Principe*
1.522	1.595	1.252	0.932	0.735	0.801	0.750	0.792	0.851	0.813	0.878	Afrique septentrionale
0.509	0.484	0.272	0.243	0.138	0.171	0.166	0.200	0.192	0.170	(e)0.173	Algérie*
0.234	0.546	0.467	0.225	0.211	0.188	0.143	0.136	0.184	0.167	0.192	Égypte*
0.327	0.202	0.149	0.098	0.060	0.083	0.079	0.092	0.104	0.107	(e)0.103	Jamahiriya arabe libyenne
0.205	0.189	0.193	0.192	0.173	0.178	0.183	0.186	0.181	0.182	0.215	Maroc*
0.076	0.038	0.017	0.023	0.023	0.037	0.037	0.043	0.068	0.065	(e)0.060	Soudan*
0.170	0.136	0.154	0.151	0.129	0.143	0.140	0.135	0.122	0.120	0.135	Tunisie
0.950	0.563	0.512	0.584	0.535	0.513	0.621	0.659	0.663	0.703	0.653	Afrique australe
..	..	..	..	0.037	0.028	0.032	0.034	0.029	0.025	0.020	Botswana*
..	..	..	..	0.012	0.012	0.014	0.015	0.013	0.012	(e)0.013	Lesotho
..	..	..	..	0.023	0.020	0.025	0.026	0.023	0.022	(e)0.023	Namibie
(a)0.950	(a)0.563	(a)0.512	(a)0.584	0.446	0.439	0.529	0.565	0.578	0.626	0.582	Afrique du Sud
..	..	..	..	0.016	0.014	0.021	0.020	0.020	0.018	(e)0.017	Swaziland
1.249	0.749	0.396	0.380	0.321	0.395	0.421	0.410	0.452	0.434	0.418	Afrique occidentale
0.016	0.016	0.007	0.014	0.009	0.011	0.011	0.009	0.008	0.008	(e)0.008	Bénin*
0.017	0.016	0.015	0.009	0.009	0.011	0.012	0.013	0.013	0.012	0.012	Burkina Faso
0.003	0.004	0.004	0.005	0.003	0.004	0.005	0.004	0.004	0.004	0.005	Cap-Vert*
0.144	0.086	0.058	0.056	0.042	0.037	0.042	0.045	0.047	0.047	(e)0.045	Côte d'Ivoire*
0.008	0.005	0.005	0.003	0.003	0.002	0.002	0.002	0.002	0.002	(e)0.002	Gambie
0.054	0.043	0.033	0.036	0.045	0.041	0.042	0.045	0.050	0.055	(e)0.056	Ghana
0.013	0.018	0.020	0.016	0.009	0.010	0.008	0.007	0.008	0.007	(e)0.007	Guinée
0.003	0.003	0.002	0.003	0.001	0.001	0.001	0.001	0.001	0.001	0.001	Guinée-Bissau
0.026	0.014	0.006	0.010	0.010	0.003	0.002	0.004	0.003	0.004	(e)0.004	Libéria*
0.021	0.015	0.017	0.015	0.012	0.014	0.016	0.014	0.015	0.014	(e)0.014	Mali*
0.014	0.011	0.006	0.008	0.007	0.006	0.007	0.010	0.013	0.009	0.009	Mauritanie*
0.029	0.018	0.011	0.007	0.006	0.007	0.008	0.008	0.009	0.008	(e)0.009	Niger*
0.803	0.437	0.157	0.157	0.131	0.205	0.221	0.205	0.235	0.222	(e)0.200	Nigéria
0.051	0.041	0.034	0.027	0.023	0.030	0.031	0.030	0.030	0.028	0.032	Sénégal*
0.021	0.007	0.004	0.003	0.002	0.004	0.004	0.003	0.003	0.003	(e)0.003	Sierra Leone*
0.027	0.014	0.016	0.011	0.008	0.009	(e)0.010	(e)0.009	(e)0.011	(e)0.010	(e)0.010	Togo*

Pour les sources et les notes, se reporter à la fin du tableau.

Region, country or territory	Exports (f.o.b.) - Exportations (f.a.b.) Percentage - En pourcentage										
	1980	1985	1990	1995	2000	2002	2003	2004	2005	2006	2007
Developing economies: America	5.479	5.531	4.132	4.436	5.646	5.413	5.094	5.172	5.449	5.652	5.533
Caribbean	*1.101*	*0.706*	*0.335*	*0.251*	*0.294*	*0.246*	*0.239*	*0.236*	*0.251*	*0.272*	*0.228*
Anguilla	..	..	..	..	0.000	0.000	0.000	0.000	0.000	0.000	(e)0.000
Antigua and Barbuda*	0.001	0.001	0.001	0.001	0.001	0.001	0.001	0.001	0.001	0.000	..
Aruba (2)	..	..	0.004	0.026	0.039	0.023	0.027	0.030	0.033	0.030	0.019
Bahamas (3)	0.247	0.138	0.007	0.003	0.009	0.007	0.006	0.005	0.005	0.006	(e)0.005
Barbados	0.011	0.018	0.006	0.005	0.004	0.004	0.003	0.003	0.003	0.003	0.003
Cuba*	0.274	0.304	0.141	0.031	0.026	0.022	0.022	0.025	0.021	(e)0.024	(e)0.027
Dominica*	0.000	0.001	0.002	0.001	0.001	0.001	0.001	0.000	0.000	0.000	(e)0.000
Dominican Republic*	0.047	0.037	0.021	0.073	0.089	0.080	0.072	0.065	0.059	0.053	0.052
Grenada*	0.001	0.001	0.001	0.000	0.001	0.001	0.001	0.000	0.000	0.000	(e)0.000
Haiti	0.011	0.009	0.005	0.002	0.005	0.004	0.005	0.004	0.004	0.004	(e)0.004
Jamaica	0.047	0.029	0.033	0.028	0.020	0.017	0.016	0.015	0.014	0.016	(e)0.016
Montserrat*	0.000	0.000	0.000	0.000	0.000	0.000	0.000	0.000	0.000	0.000	(e)0.000
Netherlands Antilles*(4)	(b)0.254	(b)0.052	0.051	0.029	0.031	0.025	0.015	0.015	0.016	0.016	..
Saint Kitts and Nevis*	0.001	0.001	0.001	0.000	0.001	0.001	0.001	0.001	0.001	(e)0.000	(e)0.000
Saint Lucia*	0.003	0.003	0.004	0.002	0.001	0.001	0.001	0.001	0.001	0.001	(e)0.001
Saint Vincent and the Grenadines*	0.001	0.003	0.002	0.001	0.001	0.001	0.001	0.000	0.000	0.000	(e)0.000
Trinidad and Tobago*	0.201	0.109	0.056	0.047	0.066	0.060	0.069	0.069	0.092	0.117	(e)0.085
Turks and Caicos Islands	..	..	..	..	0.000	0.000	0.000	0.000	0.000	0.000	0.000
Central America	*1.150*	*1.572*	*1.310*	*1.723*	*2.803*	*2.688*	*2.389*	*2.234*	*2.211*	*2.235*	*2.130*
Belize	0.005	0.005	0.003	0.003	0.003	0.003	0.003	0.002	0.002	0.002	0.002
Costa Rica*	0.049	0.050	0.042	0.067	0.091	0.081	0.081	0.069	0.067	0.068	(e)0.068
El Salvador*	0.053	0.034	0.019	0.032	0.046	0.047	0.042	0.036	0.033	(e)0.029	(e)0.029
Guatemala*	0.075	0.054	0.033	0.038	0.042	0.038	0.035	0.032	0.033	0.030	(e)0.033
Honduras*	0.041	0.040	0.024	0.024	0.021	0.020	0.018	0.017	0.016	0.016	(e)0.016
Mexico	0.887	1.358	1.170	1.538	2.577	2.478	2.191	2.059	2.042	2.072	1.967
Nicaragua	0.022	0.015	0.010	0.009	0.010	0.009	0.008	0.008	0.008	0.008	0.009
Panama, excl. Canal Zone (former)	0.018	–	–	–	–	–	–	–	–	–	–
Panama*	–	0.017	0.010	0.012	0.013	0.013	0.011	0.010	0.010	0.009	0.009
South America	*3.228*	*3.252*	*2.487*	*2.462*	*2.548*	*2.478*	*2.466*	*2.703*	*2.987*	*3.145*	*3.174*
Argentina*	0.395	0.426	0.355	0.405	0.408	0.396	0.392	0.377	0.385	0.385	0.402
Bolivia	0.046	0.032	0.027	0.021	0.019	0.020	0.021	0.023	0.027	0.032	0.032
Brazil	0.991	1.301	0.903	0.899	0.853	0.931	0.968	1.053	1.132	1.140	1.161
Chile*	0.232	0.193	0.241	0.310	0.298	0.280	0.287	0.354	0.394	0.481	0.494
Colombia	0.193	0.180	0.193	0.196	0.202	0.184	0.173	0.177	0.202	0.202	(e)0.215
Ecuador*	0.122	0.147	0.078	0.083	0.076	0.078	0.082	0.084	0.096	0.105	0.099
Guyana*	0.019	0.010	0.007	0.009	0.008	0.008	0.007	0.006	0.005	0.005	(e)0.005
Paraguay	0.015	0.015	0.028	0.018	0.013	0.015	0.016	0.018	0.016	0.016	0.024
Peru*	0.192	0.151	0.093	0.106	0.108	0.119	0.120	0.137	0.158	0.197	0.200
Suriname	0.025	0.017	0.014	0.009	0.008	0.007	0.008	0.010	0.009	0.010	..
Uruguay	0.052	0.046	0.049	0.041	0.036	0.029	0.029	0.032	0.033	0.033	(e)0.032
Venezuela (Bolivarian Rep. of)	0.946	0.733	0.501	0.364	0.519	0.413	0.361	0.432	0.530	0.539	0.500
Developing economies: Asia	17.962	15.555	16.968	21.019	23.773	24.059	24.636	25.977	27.649	28.594	29.053
Eastern Asia	*3.748*	*6.096*	*8.063*	*10.879*	*12.003*	*12.684*	*13.302*	*13.997*	*14.686*	*15.284*	*15.811*
China	0.891	1.388	1.784	2.877	3.860	5.021	5.806	6.461	7.274	8.020	8.805
China, Hong Kong SAR	0.972	1.532	2.361	3.360	3.127	3.086	2.965	2.823	2.762	2.669	2.491
China, Macao SAR	0.030	0.046	0.049	0.039	0.039	0.036	0.034	0.031	0.024	0.021	0.018
China, Taiwan Province of	0.974	1.558	1.928	2.157	2.289	2.012	1.907	1.894	1.888	1.853	1.784
Dem. People's Rep. of Korea	..	..	0.053	0.019	0.011	0.016	0.014	0.014	0.013	0.015	..
Mongolia	0.020	0.035	0.019	0.009	0.008	0.008	0.008	0.009	0.010	0.013	(e)0.013
Republic of Korea (5)	0.862	1.537	1.868	2.418	2.668	2.505	2.568	2.764	2.715	2.693	2.686
Southern Asia	*1.286*	*1.480*	*1.352*	*1.261*	*1.436*	*1.545*	*1.566*	*1.631*	*1.842*	*1.833*	*1.903*
Afghanistan	0.033	0.029	0.007	0.003	0.002	0.002	0.002	0.003	0.004	(e)0.004	..
Bangladesh	0.037	0.051	0.048	0.072	0.099	0.094	0.093	0.089	0.089	0.098	0.089
Bhutan	0.001	0.001	0.002	0.002	0.002	0.002	0.002	0.002	0.002	0.003	..
India (6)	0.422	0.464	0.516	0.592	0.656	0.777	0.781	0.835	0.951	1.000	1.051
Iran (Islamic Rep. of)*	0.607	0.719	0.555	0.355	0.439	0.435	0.450	0.484	0.573	0.523	0.567
Maldives	0.000	0.001	0.002	0.002	0.002	0.002	0.002	0.002	0.002	0.002	0.002
Nepal	0.004	0.008	0.006	0.007	0.012	0.009	0.009	0.008	0.008	0.006	(e)0.007
Pakistan	0.129	0.139	0.161	0.155	0.140	0.153	0.158	0.146	0.153	0.140	(e)0.126
Sri Lanka	0.052	0.068	0.055	0.073	0.084	0.072	0.068	0.063	0.061	0.057	(e)0.055
South-Eastern Asia	*3.639*	*3.678*	*4.175*	*6.254*	*6.690*	*6.285*	*6.011*	*6.196*	*6.231*	*6.334*	*6.259*
Brunei Darussalam*	0.225	0.149	0.064	0.046	0.060	0.057	0.059	0.055	0.060	0.065	..
Cambodia	0.001	0.001	0.002	0.017	0.022	0.027	0.028	0.028	0.028	0.031	(e)0.029
Indonesia	1.179	0.943	0.770	0.918	1.013	0.912	0.849	0.782	0.823	0.815	0.858
Lao People's dem. Rep.*	0.001	0.003	0.002	0.006	0.005	0.005	0.004	0.004	0.005	0.007	(e)0.008
Malaysia (7)	0.637	0.777	0.846	1.429	1.522	1.438	1.317	1.369	1.345	1.328	1.272

For sources and notes, see end of table.

Imports (c.i.f.) - Importations (c.a.f.) Percentage - En pourcentage											Régions, pays ou territoires
1980	1985	1990	1995	2000	2002	2003	2004	2005	2006	2007	
5.960	4.119	3.544	4.791	5.892	5.317	4.750	4.745	4.922	5.120	5.331	**Économies en développement : Amérique**
1.320	*0.910*	*0.521*	*0.382*	*0.487*	*0.451*	*0.397*	*0.368*	*0.394*	*0.399*	*0.380*	*Caraïbes*
..	..	..	..	0.001	0.001	0.001	0.001	0.001	(e)0.001	(e)0.002	Anguilla
0.004	0.008	0.007	0.007	0.006	0.006	0.005	0.005	0.005	0.004	..	Antigua-et-Barbuda*
..	..	0.016	0.034	0.039	0.030	0.031	0.032	0.032	0.031	0.020	Aruba (2)
0.364	0.151	0.031	0.024	0.031	0.026	0.023	0.020	0.022	0.023	(e)0.020	Bahamas (3)
0.025	0.030	0.020	0.015	0.017	0.016	0.015	0.015	0.015	0.013	0.012	Barbade
0.314	0.393	0.188	0.054	0.073	0.063	0.060	0.059	0.070	(e)0.077	(e)0.072	Cuba*
0.002	0.003	0.003	0.002	0.002	0.002	0.002	0.002	0.002	0.001	(e)0.001	Dominique*
0.095	0.088	0.084	0.099	0.142	0.133	0.098	0.083	0.092	0.090	0.098	République dominicaine*
0.002	0.003	0.003	0.002	0.004	0.003	0.003	0.003	0.003	0.002	(e)0.003	Grenade*
0.018	0.022	0.009	0.012	0.016	0.017	0.015	0.014	0.013	0.015	(e)0.011	Haïti
0.056	0.055	0.054	0.054	0.050	0.053	0.047	0.040	0.041	0.043	(e)0.045	Jamaïque
0.001	0.001	0.001	0.001	0.000	0.000	0.000	0.000	0.000	0.000	(e)0.000	Montserrat*
(b)0.274	(b)0.068	0.060	0.035	0.043	0.034	0.034	0.032	0.032	0.032	..	Antilles néerlandaises*(4)
0.002	0.003	0.003	0.003	0.003	0.003	0.002	0.002	0.002	(e)0.002	(e)0.002	Saint-Kitts-et-Nevis*
0.006	0.006	0.008	0.006	0.005	0.005	0.005	0.005	0.005	0.005	(e)0.005	Sainte-Lucie*
0.003	0.004	0.004	0.003	0.002	0.003	0.003	0.002	0.002	0.002	(e)0.002	Saint-Vincent-et-les Grenadines*
0.153	0.075	0.031	0.033	0.050	0.055	0.050	0.051	0.053	0.053	(e)0.051	Trinité-et-Tobago*
..	..	..	..	0.002	0.003	0.002	0.002	0.003	0.004	0.004	Îles Turques et Caïques
1.434	*1.266*	*1.442*	*1.758*	*3.123*	*3.054*	*2.669*	*2.529*	*2.499*	*2.524*	*2.473*	*Amérique centrale*
0.007	0.006	0.006	0.005	0.008	0.008	0.007	0.005	0.006	0.005	0.005	Belize
0.074	0.054	0.055	0.078	0.096	0.108	0.099	0.087	0.091	0.093	(e)0.090	Costa Rica*
0.047	0.047	0.035	0.064	0.074	0.078	0.074	0.067	0.063	0.062	(e)0.061	El Salvador*
0.077	0.058	0.046	0.063	0.078	0.095	0.086	0.083	0.082	0.082	(e)0.084	Guatemala*
0.049	0.044	0.026	0.031	0.043	0.045	0.042	0.041	0.043	0.044	(e)0.048	Honduras*
1.068	0.941	1.213	1.450	2.746	2.650	2.297	2.183	2.151	2.174	2.110	Mexique
0.043	0.047	0.018	0.019	0.027	0.026	0.024	0.023	0.024	0.024	0.025	Nicaragua
0.070	–	–	–	–	–	–	–	–	–	–	Panama, sans la zone du canal (anc.)
–	0.068	0.043	0.048	0.051	0.045	0.040	0.038	0.039	0.039	0.049	Panama*
3.206	*1.943*	*1.581*	*2.651*	*2.283*	*1.812*	*1.684*	*1.848*	*2.030*	*2.197*	*2.478*	*Amérique du Sud*
0.509	0.188	0.114	0.385	0.380	0.135	0.178	0.237	0.266	0.277	0.319	Argentine*
0.032	0.034	0.019	0.027	0.027	0.027	0.021	0.019	0.022	0.023	0.025	Bolivie
1.204	0.705	0.627	1.035	0.888	0.746	0.655	0.702	0.720	0.777	0.901	Brésil
0.280	0.151	0.216	0.304	0.278	0.256	0.249	0.262	0.304	0.311	0.334	Chili*
0.229	0.204	0.156	0.265	0.173	0.191	0.179	0.177	0.197	0.211	(e)0.235	Colombie
0.109	0.087	0.052	0.079	0.056	0.096	0.086	0.087	0.095	0.098	(e)0.095	Équateur*
0.019	0.011	0.009	0.010	0.010	0.009	0.007	0.007	0.007	0.007	(e)0.007	Guyana*
0.030	0.025	0.038	0.060	0.033	0.025	0.029	0.033	0.034	0.049	(e)0.054	Paraguay
0.121	0.090	0.097	0.178	0.134	0.112	0.108	0.107	0.116	0.124	0.139	Pérou*
0.024	0.015	0.013	0.011	0.008	0.007	0.009	0.008	0.008	0.008	..	Suriname
0.081	0.035	0.037	0.055	0.052	0.029	0.028	0.033	0.036	0.039	(e)0.040	Uruguay
0.570	0.399	0.204	0.242	0.244	0.178	0.135	0.176	0.223	0.272	0.323	Venezuela (Rép. bolivarienne du)
13.117	15.149	15.901	21.361	20.842	21.318	21.929	23.267	24.077	24.556	25.120	**Économies en développement : Asie**
4.125	*6.155*	*7.406*	*10.848*	*11.165*	*11.596*	*12.308*	*13.015*	*13.094*	*13.353*	*13.588*	*Asie orientale*
0.962	2.079	1.486	2.525	3.383	4.429	5.311	5.931	6.124	6.416	6.800	Chine
1.083	1.462	2.298	3.685	3.198	3.116	2.984	2.865	2.780	2.713	2.617	Chine (RAS de Hong Kong)
0.026	0.038	0.043	0.039	0.034	0.038	0.035	0.037	0.036	0.037	0.038	Chine (RAS de Macao)
0.953	0.990	1.527	1.982	2.103	1.692	1.639	1.776	1.694	1.643	1.560	Province chinoise de Taiwan
..	..	0.082	0.026	0.025	0.028	0.026	0.024	0.025	0.025	..	Rép. populaire dém. de Corée
0.026	0.054	0.026	0.008	0.009	0.010	0.010	0.011	0.011	0.012	(e)0.014	Mongolie
1.075	1.532	1.945	2.583	2.412	2.283	2.301	2.372	2.424	2.508	2.537	République de Corée (5)
1.907	*1.968*	*1.599*	*1.390*	*1.444*	*1.661*	*1.755*	*1.881*	*2.205*	*2.305*	*2.325*	*Asie méridionale*
0.041	0.059	0.026	0.007	0.018	0.037	0.027	0.023	0.025	0.023	..	Afghanistan
0.125	0.125	0.101	0.124	0.134	0.129	0.134	0.127	0.129	0.131	0.132	Bangladesh
0.002	0.004	0.002	0.002	0.003	0.003	0.003	0.004	0.004	0.003	..	Bhoutan
0.717	0.784	0.657	0.663	0.774	0.848	0.934	1.054	1.325	1.420	1.533	Inde (6)
0.648	0.591	0.511	0.244	0.229	0.357	0.374	0.372	0.380	0.378	0.307	Iran (Rép. islamique d')*
0.001	0.003	0.004	0.005	0.006	0.006	0.006	0.007	0.007	0.008	0.008	Maldives
0.017	0.022	0.019	0.025	0.024	0.021	0.023	0.020	0.017	0.017	(e)0.021	Népal
0.258	0.290	0.205	0.219	0.163	0.169	0.168	0.190	0.235	0.242	(e)0.222	Pakistan
0.098	0.091	0.075	0.099	0.094	0.092	0.086	0.084	0.082	0.083	(e)0.078	Sri Lanka
3.165	*3.275*	*4.520*	*6.793*	*5.676*	*5.397*	*5.106*	*5.244*	*5.515*	*5.536*	*5.495*	*Asie du Sud-Est*
0.028	0.030	0.028	0.040	0.017	0.023	0.017	0.015	0.014	0.014	..	Brunéi Darussalam*
0.009	0.006	0.005	0.023	0.029	0.035	0.034	0.035	0.036	0.038	(e)0.038	Cambodge
0.522	0.505	0.608	0.777	0.607	0.535	0.509	0.534	0.644	0.614	0.662	Indonésie
0.004	0.009	0.005	0.011	0.008	0.007	0.006	0.008	0.008	0.009	(e)0.007	Rép. dém. populaire lao*
0.520	0.603	0.815	1.485	1.232	1.198	1.055	1.113	1.062	1.062	1.044	Malaisie (7)

Pour les sources et les notes, se reporter à la fin du tableau.

Region, country or territory	Exports (f.o.b.) - Exportations (f.a.b.) Percentage - En pourcentage										
	1980	1985	1990	1995	2000	2002	2003	2004	2005	2006	2007
Myanmar	0.023	0.016	0.009	0.017	0.025	0.047	0.033	0.026	0.036	0.037	(e)0.047
Philippines	0.283	0.234	0.233	0.338	0.616	0.563	0.480	0.432	0.381	0.392	(e)0.367
Singapore (8)	0.953	1.158	1.515	2.287	2.135	1.930	1.910	2.163	2.192	2.249	2.163
Thailand*	0.320	0.361	0.663	1.091	1.068	1.050	1.064	1.048	1.052	1.082	1.107
Timor-Leste	..	..	..	..	..	0.000	0.000	0.000	0.000	0.000	..
Viet Nam	0.017	0.035	0.069	0.105	0.224	0.255	0.267	0.288	0.310	0.328	0.350
Western Asia	**9.289**	**4.302**	**3.378**	**2.625**	**3.643**	**3.545**	**3.757**	**4.153**	**4.889**	**5.143**	**5.080**
Bahrain	0.177	0.147	0.108	0.080	0.096	0.089	0.088	0.082	0.097	0.101	0.099
Iraq*	1.297	0.528	0.296	0.010	0.316	0.204	0.129	0.201	0.226	0.253	(e)0.244
Jordan	0.028	0.040	0.031	0.034	0.029	0.043	0.041	0.043	0.041	0.043	0.041
Kuwait*	0.976	0.538	0.202	0.247	0.301	0.237	0.274	0.313	0.430	0.474	0.450
Lebanon	0.047	0.015	0.014	0.013	0.011	0.019	0.024	0.024	0.022	0.023	0.020
Oman	0.117	0.200	0.158	0.117	0.175	0.172	0.155	0.145	0.178	0.179	(e)0.160
Qatar*	0.280	0.174	0.101	0.067	0.177	0.169	0.177	0.201	0.242	0.282	(e)0.274
Saudi Arabia*	4.998	1.394	1.276	0.968	1.200	1.117	1.235	1.372	1.724	1.783	1.667
Syrian Arab Republic*	0.104	0.083	0.121	0.069	0.072	0.101	0.076	0.059	0.062	0.090	(e)0.085
Turkey*	0.143	0.404	0.372	0.418	0.430	0.533	0.617	0.672	0.687	0.678	0.772
United Arab Emirates	1.081	0.749	0.677	0.564	0.773	0.804	0.889	0.991	1.119	1.179	(e)1.208
Yemen (former Arab Republic)	0.038	..	–	–	–	–	–	–	–	–	–
Yemen (former Democratic)	0.001	0.030	–	–	–	–	–	–	–	–	–
Yemen*	–	–	0.020	0.038	0.063	0.056	0.052	0.051	0.061	0.061	(e)0.059
Developing economies: Oceania	**0.110**	**0.095**	**0.078**	**0.088**	**0.063**	**0.053**	**0.060**	**0.056**	**0.056**	**0.059**	**0.060**
American Samoa*	0.006	0.010	0.009	0.005	0.005	0.006	0.006	0.005	0.004	0.004	..
Cook Islands	0.000	0.000	0.000	0.000	0.000	0.000	0.000	0.000	0.000	0.000	(e)0.000
Fiji	0.019	0.012	0.011	0.011	0.008	0.008	0.009	0.008	0.007	0.006	(e)0.006
French Polynesia*	0.001	0.002	0.003	0.004	0.004	0.003	0.002	0.002	0.002	0.002	0.001
Guam	0.003	0.001	0.002	0.002	0.001	0.001	0.001	0.001	0.000	0.000	0.001
Kiribati	0.000	0.000	0.000	0.000	0.000	0.000	0.000	0.000	0.000	0.000	..
Marshall Islands	..	..	0.000	0.000	0.000	..	..	..	..	..	..
Micronesia (Federated States of)	..	..	0.000	0.001	0.000	0.000	0.000	0.000	0.000	(e)0.000	..
Nauru	0.003	0.003	0.002	0.001	0.000	0.000	(e)0.000	(e)0.000	(e)0.000	(e)0.000	..
New Caledonia*	0.020	0.014	0.014	0.009	0.009	0.008	0.010	0.011	0.010	0.011	0.015
Niue	..	..	..	..	0.000	0.000	0.000	0.000	..	..	..
Palau	..	..	..	0.000	0.000	0.000	0.000	0.000	(e)0.000	(e)0.000	..
Papua New Guinea	0.051	0.046	0.033	0.051	0.032	0.025	0.029	0.028	0.031	0.034	(e)0.033
Samoa*	0.001	0.001	0.000	0.000	0.000	0.000	0.000	0.000	0.000	0.000	0.000
Solomon Islands*	0.004	0.004	0.002	0.003	0.001	0.001	0.001	0.001	0.001	0.001	(e)0.001
Tokelau	..	..	..	..	..	..	..	..	..	..	..
Tonga	0.000	0.000	0.000	0.000	0.000	0.000	0.000	0.000	0.000	0.000	(e)0.000
Tuvalu	..	0.000	0.000	0.000	0.000	0.000	0.000	0.000	0.000	(e)0.000	..
Vanuatu	0.002	0.002	0.001	0.001	0.000	0.000	0.000	0.000	0.000	0.000	..
Wallis and Futuna Islands	..	..	..	..	..	0.000	0.000	0.000	(e)0.000	(e)0.000	..
Economies in transition: Asia	**–**	**–**	**–**	**0.248**	**0.275**	**0.296**	**0.329**	**0.380**	**0.432**	**0.514**	**0.524**
Armenia*	–	–	–	0.005	0.005	0.008	0.009	0.008	0.009	0.008	0.009
Azerbaijan*(9)	–	–	–	0.012	0.027	0.033	0.034	0.039	0.041	0.053	(e)0.039
Georgia (10)	–	–	–	0.003	0.005	0.005	0.006	0.007	0.008	0.008	0.009
Kazakhstan*(10)	–	–	–	0.102	0.136	0.149	0.171	0.219	0.266	0.335	(e)0.339
Kyrgyzstan	–	–	–	0.008	0.008	0.007	0.008	0.008	0.006	0.007	0.008
Tajikistan (10)	–	–	–	0.014	0.012	0.010	0.011	0.010	0.009	0.012	(e)0.011
Turkmenistan (10)	–	–	–	0.037	0.039	0.044	0.048	0.042	0.047	0.048	0.055
Uzbekistan (10)	–	–	–	0.066	0.044	0.039	0.042	0.047	0.045	0.044	(e)0.054
Economies in transition: Europe	**–**	**–**	**–**	**2.109**	**2.118**	**2.214**	**2.409**	**2.692**	**2.997**	**3.204**	**3.334**
Albania	..	..	0.006	0.004	0.004	0.005	0.006	0.007	0.006	0.007	0.008
Belarus	–	–	–	0.093	0.113	0.124	0.132	0.150	0.153	0.163	0.176
Bosnia and Herzegovina*(11)	–	–	–	0.000	0.017	0.016	0.018	0.019	0.022	0.028	0.030
Croatia*	–	–	–	0.087	0.069	0.076	0.082	0.087	0.084	0.086	0.089
Moldova	–	–	–	0.014	0.007	0.010	0.010	0.011	0.010	0.009	0.010
Russian Federation (12)	–	–	–	1.603	1.635	1.655	1.801	1.995	2.327	2.514	2.570
Serbia and Montenegro*	–	–	–	0.030	0.027	0.035	0.037	0.048	0.048	0.060	(e)0.072
SFR of Yugoslavia (former)	0.442	0.543	0.411	–	–	–	–	–	–	–	–
TFYR of Macedonia*	–	–	–	0.023	0.020	0.017	0.018	0.018	0.019	0.020	0.024
Ukraine (10)	–	–	–	0.254	0.226	0.277	0.306	0.356	0.327	0.317	0.356
USSR (former)	3.762	4.430	2.994	–	–	–	–	–	–	–	–
Developed economies: America	**14.445**	**15.732**	**14.995**	**15.031**	**16.402**	**14.586**	**13.223**	**12.236**	**12.096**	**11.816**	**11.421**
Bermuda	0.002	0.001	0.002	0.001	0.001	0.001	0.001	0.001	0.000	0.000	..
Canada	3.333	4.616	3.668	3.716	4.285	3.892	3.615	3.316	3.431	3.223	3.011
Greenland	0.010	0.009	0.013	0.007	0.004	0.005	0.005	0.005	0.004	0.003	..

For sources and notes, see end of table.

1980	1985	1990	1995	2000	2002	2003	2004	2005	2006	2007	Régions, pays ou territoires
			Imports (c.i.f.) - Importations (c.a f.) Percentage - En pourcentage								

1980	1985	1990	1995	2000	2002	2003	2004	2005	2006	2007	Régions, pays ou territoires
0.017	0.014	0.008	0.026	0.036	0.035	0.027	0.023	0.018	0.017	(e)0.022	Myanmar
0.400	0.268	0.362	0.542	0.556	0.558	0.508	0.447	0.436	0.438	(e)0.401	Philippines
1.158	1.293	1.693	2.380	2.022	1.747	1.646	1.732	1.856	1.935	1.872	Singapour (8)
0.444	0.455	0.920	1.353	0.931	0.970	0.976	0.998	1.096	1.043	1.002	Thaïlande*
..	..	..	..	0.004	0.003	0.002	0.002	0.001	0.001	..	Timor-Leste
0.063	0.091	0.077	0.156	0.235	0.285	0.325	0.338	0.343	0.364	0.433	Viet Nam
3.920	**3.751**	**2.376**	**2.330**	**2.557**	**2.664**	**2.760**	**3.127**	**3.263**	**3.361**	**3.711**	***Asie occidentale***
0.168	0.153	0.103	0.071	0.070	0.075	0.073	0.070	0.087	0.085	0.082	Bahreïn
0.420	0.519	0.182	0.013	0.201	0.147	0.128	0.211	0.218	0.169	(e)0.164	Iraq*
0.116	0.134	0.072	0.071	0.069	0.076	0.074	0.086	0.097	0.093	0.096	Jordanie
0.315	0.295	0.111	0.149	0.108	0.135	0.141	0.133	0.162	0.130	0.138	Koweït*
0.176	0.108	0.070	0.139	0.094	0.098	0.094	0.102	0.089	0.078	0.084	Liban
0.084	0.155	0.075	0.081	0.076	0.090	0.035	0.094	0.082	0.088	(e)0.104	Oman
0.070	0.056	0.047	0.065	0.049	0.061	0.063	0.063	0.093	0.133	0.157	Qatar*
1.455	1.162	0.671	0.537	0.454	0.484	0.475	0.473	0.552	0.566	0.634	Arabie saoudite*
0.199	0.195	0.067	0.090	0.057	0.067	0.066	0.074	0.073	0.093	(e)0.092	République arabe syrienne*
0.381	0.558	0.621	0.683	0.819	0.745	0.845	1.018	0.919	1.083	1.199	Turquie*
0.416	0.322	0.312	0.401	0.526	0.640	0.670	0.762	0.846	0.793	(e)0.914	Émirats arabes unis
0.074	..	–	–	–	–	–	–	–	–	–	Yémen (anc. République arabe du)
0.047	0.092	–	–	–	–	–	–	–	–	–	Yémen (anc. démocratique)
–	–	0.044	0.030	0.035	0.044	0.047	0.041	0.044	0.050	(e)0.048	Yémen*
0.171	**0.159**	**0.142**	**0.113**	**0.086**	**0.093**	**0.100**	**0.090**	**0.085**	**0.081**	**0.079**	**Économies en développement : Océanie**
0.005	0.015	0.010	0.008	0.008	0.007	0.008	0.006	0.005	0.003	..	Samoa américaines*
0.001	0.001	0.001	0.001	0.001	0.001	0.001	0.001	0.001	0.001	(e)0.001	Îles Cook
0.027	0.022	0.021	0.017	0.013	0.014	0.016	0.015	0.015	0.015	(e)0.013	Fidji
0.026	0.027	0.026	0.019	0.016	0.019	0.020	0.016	0.016	0.013	0.012	Polynésie française*
0.019	0.014	0.013	0.008	0.006	0.007	0.007	0.005	0.005	0.004	0.005	Guam
0.001	0.001	0.001	0.001	0.001	0.001	0.001	0.001	0.001	0.001	..	Kiribati
..	..	0.002	0.001	0.001	0.001	0.001	0.001	(e)0.001	(e)0.001	..	Îles Marshall
..	..	0.002	0.002	0.002	0.002	0.002	0.001	0.001	0.001	..	Micronésie (États fédérés de)
0.001	0.001	0.001	0.001	0.000	0.000	(e)0.000	(e)0.000	(e)0.000	(e)0.000	..	Nauru
0.022	0.017	0.025	0.018	0.014	0.015	0.020	0.017	0.017	0.017	0.020	Nouvelle-Calédonie*
..	..	..	..	0.000	0.000	0.000	0.000	(e)0.000	(e)0.000	..	Nioué
..	..	..	0.001	0.002	0.001	0.001	0.001	0.001	(e)0.001	..	Palaos
0.057	0.050	0.031	0.028	0.017	0.019	0.018	0.018	0.016	0.018	..	Papouasie-Nouvelle-Guinée
0.003	0.003	0.002	0.002	0.002	0.002	0.002	0.002	0.002	0.002	0.002	Samoa*
0.004	0.004	0.003	0.003	0.001	0.001	0.001	0.001	0.002	0.002	(e)0.002	Îles Salomon*
..	..	..	..	0.000	0.000	0.000	0.000	..	..	..	Tokélaou
0.002	0.002	0.002	0.001	0.001	0.001	0.001	0.001	0.001	0.001	(e)0.001	Tonga
..	0.000	0.000	0.000	0.000	0.000	0.000	0.000	0.000	0.000	0.000	Tuvalu
0.004	0.003	0.003	0.002	0.001	0.001	0.001	0.001	0.001	0.001	..	Vanuatu
..	..	..	..	..	0.001	0.001	0.001	(e)0.001	(e)0.000	..	Îles Wallis-et-Futuna
–	–	–	**0.202**	**0.203**	**0.238**	**0.260**	**0.299**	**0.331**	**0.386**	**0.437**	**Économies en transition : Asie**
–	–	–	0.013	0.013	0.015	0.016	0.014	0.016	0.018	0.023	Arménie*
–	–	–	0.013	0.018	0.025	0.034	0.037	0.040	0.043	(e)0.042	Azerbaïdjan*(9)
–	–	–	0.007	0.011	0.012	0.015	0.020	0.023	0.030	0.037	Géorgie (10)
–	–	–	0.073	0.076	0.099	0.108	0.135	0.161	0.202	(e)0.233	Kazakhstan*(10)
–	–	–	0.010	0.008	0.009	0.009	0.010	0.010	0.015	0.017	Kirghizistan
–	–	–	0.015	0.010	0.011	0.011	0.013	0.012	0.014	(e)0.017	Tadjikistan (10)
–	–	–	0.015	0.027	0.032	0.032	0.035	0.034	0.033	0.032	Turkménistan (10)
–	–	–	0.055	0.041	0.036	0.034	0.036	0.034	0.032	(e)0.035	Ouzbékistan (10)
–	–	–	**1.991**	**1.370**	**1.787**	**1.951**	**2.059**	**2.199**	**2.449**	**2.874**	**Économies en transition : Europe**
..	..	0.012	0.014	0.016	0.023	0.024	0.024	0.024	0.025	0.029	Albanie
–	–	–	0.106	0.130	0.136	0.149	0.174	0.155	0.181	0.204	Bélarus
–	–	–	0.018	0.059	0.066	0.072	0.070	0.070	0.061	0.069	Bosnie-Herzégovine*(11)
–	–	–	0.141	0.119	0.161	0.183	0.175	0.172	0.174	0.184	Croatie*
–	–	–	0.016	0.012	0.016	0.018	0.019	0.021	0.022	0.026	Moldova
–	–	–	1.316	0.738	1.006	1.077	1.132	1.280	1.468	1.746	Fédération de Russie (12)
–	–	–	0.051	0.056	0.095	0.102	0.127	0.110	0.122	(e)0.148	Serbie-et-Monténégro*
0.727	0.601	0.526	–	–	–	–	–	–	–	–	RSF de Yougoslavie (anc.)
–	–	–	0.033	0.031	0.030	0.030	0.031	0.030	0.030	0.037	LERY de Macédoine*
–	–	–	0.296	0.210	0.255	0.296	0.306	0.335	0.365	0.432	Ukraine (10)
3.304	4.091	3.360	–	–	–	–	–	–	–	–	URSS (anc.)
15.442	**21.347**	**17.863**	**17.969**	**22.623**	**21.440**	**19.938**	**19.098**	**19.167**	**18.470**	**17.116**	**Économies développées : Amérique**
0.017	0.020	0.017	0.011	0.011	0.011	0.011	0.010	0.009	0.009	..	Bermudes
3.016	3.968	3.433	3.212	3.679	3.414	3.153	2.958	3.077	2.899	2.753	Canada
0.016	0.015	0.012	0.008	0.005	0.006	0.006	0.006	0.006	0.005	..	Groenland

Pour les sources et les notes, se reporter à la fin du tableau.

Region, country or territory	Exports (f.o.b.) - Exportations (f.a.b.) Percentage - En pourcentage										
	1980	1985	1990	1995	2000	2002	2003	2004	2005	2006	2007
Saint Pierre and Miquelon	0.000	0.000	0.001	0.000	0.000	0.000	0.000	(e)0.000	0.000	(e)0.000	..
United States*	11.100	11.105	11.311	11.307	12.112	10.688	9.603	8.913	8.660	8.589	8.407
Developed economies: Asia	**6.691**	**9.309**	**8.597**	**8.936**	**7.910**	**6.879**	**6.672**	**6.581**	**6.088**	**5.764**	**5.521**
Israel*	0.272	0.318	0.333	0.368	0.486	0.453	0.421	0.421	0.408	0.387	0.391
Japan	6.419	8.991	8.265	8.568	7.423	6.426	6.251	6.160	5.679	5.377	5.130
Developed economies: Europe	**43.907**	**43.187**	**47.331**	**44.759**	**40.247**	**43.031**	**44.046**	**43.220**	**41.122**	**40.222**	**40.466**
Andorra	..	..	..	0.001	0.001	0.001	0.001	0.001	0.001	(e)0.001	..
Austria*	0.861	0.875	1.182	1.116	1.049	1.212	1.287	1.288	1.197	1.131	1.170
Belgium*						3.329	3.386	3.340	3.197	3.034	3.093
Belgium-Luxembourg*	3.182	2.728	3.400	3.597	3.049	–	–	–	–	–	–
Bulgaria*	0.510	0.677	0.139	0.104	0.074	0.089	0.100	0.108	0.112	0.125	0.133
Cyprus*	0.026	0.024	0.028	0.024	0.015	0.012	0.011	0.010	0.014	0.011	0.010
Czechoslovakia (former) (13)	0.733	0.604	0.342								
Czech Republic*(14)	–	–	–	0.419	0.449	0.594	0.645	0.751	0.747	0.785	0.879
Denmark*(15)	0.824	0.867	1.064	0.984	0.795	0.885	0.881	0.839	0.814	0.765	0.743
Estonia*(10)	–	–	–	0.036	0.059	0.067	0.074	0.065	0.074	0.080	0.079
Faeroe Islands	0.009	0.009	0.011	0.007	0.007	0.008	0.008	0.007	0.006	0.005	0.005
Finland	0.696	0.691	0.764	0.783	0.714	0.695	0.704	0.670	0.631	0.637	0.644
France*	5.728	5.181	6.244	5.838	5.077	5.109	5.192	4.921	4.430	4.101	3.974
Germany (former Dem. Rep.)	0.852	1.282	–								
Germany (former Federal Rep.)	9.490	9.335	–	–	–	–	–	–	–	–	–
Germany*	–		11.786	10.123	8.551	9.485	9.954	9.904	9.282	9.164	9.525
Greece*	0.254	0.230	0.233	0.214	0.182	0.160	0.177	0.167	0.164	0.172	0.169
Hungary*(16)	0.427	0.433	0.276	0.248	0.434	0.532	0.564	0.605	0.602	0.622	0.679
Iceland*	0.045	0.041	0.046	0.035	0.029	0.034	0.032	0.032	0.028	0.029	(e)0.031
Ireland*	0.413	0.526	0.682	0.865	1.200	1.359	1.229	1.141	1.048	0.899	0.871
Italy*	3.843	3.894	4.900	4.521	3.727	3.919	3.965	3.851	3.567	3.447	3.530
Latvia*	–	–	–	0.025	0.029	0.035	0.038	0.044	0.049	0.051	0.060
Lithuania (10)	–	–	–	0.052	0.055	0.081	0.092	0.101	0.113	0.117	0.123
Luxembourg*	–	–	–	–	–	0.157	0.176	0.177	0.180	0.189	0.161
Malta	0.024	0.020	0.032	0.037	0.038	0.034	0.033	0.027	0.022	0.022	0.021
Netherlands*	4.180	3.952	3.787	3.929	3.613	3.759	3.921	3.890	3.885	3.834	3.956
Norway	0.912	1.014	0.979	0.812	0.930	0.921	0.894	0.890	0.973	0.997	0.997
Poland*	0.698	0.583	0.392	0.443	0.490	0.632	0.709	0.817	0.855	0.916	0.997
Portugal*	0.228	0.289	0.472	0.441	0.378	0.399	0.421	0.390	0.365	0.358	0.368
Romania*	0.552	0.618	0.166	0.153	0.161	0.214	0.233	0.256	0.265	0.268	0.289
Slovakia*	–	–	–	0.166	0.184	0.223	0.291	0.301	0.306	0.346	0.418
Slovenia*				0.161	0.135	0.160	0.169	0.178	0.184	0.192	0.216
Spain*	1.020	1.231	1.596	1.892	1.786	1.936	2.068	1.988	1.842	1.767	1.731
Sweden	1.521	1.546	1.654	1.556	1.350	1.255	1.352	1.342	1.246	1.222	1.215
Switzerland*	1.458	1.393	1.833	1.579	1.263	1.419	1.391	1.340	1.250	1.223	1.234
United Kingdom*	5.420	5.144	5.324	4.601	4.423	4.315	4.048	3.782	3.675	3.710	3.144
Developed economies: Oceania	**1.347**	**1.437**	**1.412**	**1.291**	**1.195**	**1.225**	**1.167**	**1.163**	**1.218**	**1.206**	**1.215**
Australia*	1.080	1.147	1.142	1.027	0.989	1.003	0.948	0.941	1.010	1.020	1.020
New Zealand	0.267	0.290	0.270	0.264	0.206	0.222	0.219	0.222	0.207	0.186	0.195

Sources:
- UN, Yearbook of International Trade Statistics
- UN, Monthly Bulletin of Statistics
- IMF, International Financial Statistics
- IMF, Direction of Trade Statistics
- World Trade Organization
- Other international and national sources
- UNCTAD secretariat estimates

Notes:

* Countries which use the Special Trade System as reporting system.
(a) Data refers to South Africa Customs Union (Botswana, Lesotho, Namibia, South Africa and Swaziland)
(b) Including Aruba

(1) Trade with other member countries of CEMAC is excluded.
(2) Prior to 1986, included in Netherlands Antilles. Including exports and imports of crude oil and oil products.
(3) From 1990 onwards, trade statistics exclude certain oil and chemical products.
(4) Prior to 1986, including Aruba.
(5) Excluding imports of goods financed through foreign aid.
(6) Excluding military goods, fissionable materials, bunkers, ships and aircraft.
(7) Inter-trade between the States of Malaysia included. From 1965 onwards, excluding military imports and offshore installations of petroleum industry.
(8) Including trans-shipments to and from peninsular Malaysia.
(9) Excluding military goods, precious metals and goods procured in foreign ports.
(10) Prior to 1994, covers only trade with countries outside the CIS.
(11) Prior to 1998, data refer to the Federation of Bosnia and Herzegovina only. The other entity of Bosnia and Herzegovina, Republika Srpska, is not included.
(12) Prior to 1994, excluding trade with independent states resulting from the former USSR.
(13) From 1985 onwards, data are not comparable to those shown for prior periods due to revisions of the koruna-to-US dollar exchange rate.
(14) From 1995 onward, including goods for processing.
(15) Prior to 1988, excluding ships.
(16) Prior to 1996, excluding customs free zones.

Imports (c.i.f.) - Importations (c.a.f.) Percentage - En pourcentage											Régions, pays ou territoires
1980	1985	1990	1995	2000	2002	2003	2004	2005	2006	2007	
0.000	0.002	0.002	0.001	0.001	0.001	0.001	(e)0.001	0.001	(e)0.000	..	Saint-Pierre-et-Miquelon
12.393	17.343	14.399	14.736	18.926	18.009	16.768	16.123	16.075	15.557	14.351	États-Unis*
7.286	**6.907**	**7.023**	**6.987**	**6.176**	**5.592**	**5.395**	**5.256**	**5.216**	**5.105**	**4.813**	**Économies développées : Asie**
0.472	0.486	0.468	0.565	0.472	0.533	0.467	0.453	0.437	0.408	0.403	Israël*
6.814	6.421	6.556	6.421	5.704	5.059	4.928	4.803	4.778	4.697	4.410	Japon
48.128	**42.492**	**47.492**	**42.842**	**39.567**	**40.756**	**42.061**	**41.485**	**40.157**	**40.102**	**40.408**	**Économies développées : Europe**
..	..	..	0.020	0.018	0.021	0.019	0.019	0.017	(e)0.016	..	Andorre
1.179	1.033	1.367	1.266	1.088	1.173	1.280	1.266	1.183	1.112	1.147	Autriche*
					2.972	3.022	3.017	2.961	2.852	2.920	Belgique*
3.466	2.765	3.351	3.340	2.839	_	_	_	_	_	_	Belgique-Luxembourg*
0.465	0.672	0.131	0.108	0.098	0.120	0.140	0.153	0.169	0.189	0.212	Bulgarie*
0.058	0.061	0.072	0.071	0.058	0.058	0.055	0.058	0.059	0.056	0.061	Chypre*
0.616	0.549	0.365	_	_							Tchécoslovaquie (anc.) (13)
_	_	_	0.504	0.509	0.642	0.692	0.739	0.711	0.755	0.833	République tchèque*(14)
0.933	0.898	0.926	0.878	0.685	0.754	0.739	0.720	0.702	0.693	0.704	Danemark*(15)
_	_	_	0.046	0.064	0.072	0.083	0.088	0.095	0.109	0.107	Estonie*(10)
0.011	0.012	0.009	0.006	0.008	0.007	0.010	0.007	0.007	0.006	0.007	Îles Féroé
0.754	0.651	0.752	0.563	0.518	0.513	0.547	0.543	0.548	0.558	0.576	Finlande
6.633	5.450	6.706	5.671	5.096	4.934	5.131	4.974	4.684	4.391	4.346	France*
0.920	1.153	_	_	_	_	_	_	_	_	_	Allemagne (anc. Rép. dém. d')
9.066	7.798	_	_	_	_	_	_	_	_	_	Allemagne (anc. Rép. fédérale d')
		9.641	8.868	7.476	7.347	7.778	7.560	7.221	7.346	7.481	Allemagne*
0.509	0.499	0.551	0.495	0.503	0.473	0.577	0.557	0.502	0.515	0.534	Grèce*
0.446	0.405	0.242	0.294	0.480	0.567	0.613	0.639	0.618	0.634	0.672	Hongrie*(16)
0.048	0.045	0.047	0.034	0.039	0.034	0.036	0.038	0.042	0.050	(e)0.043	Islande*
0.538	0.493	0.576	0.618	0.767	0.785	0.693	0.653	0.637	0.592	0.581	Irlande*
4.858	4.315	5.068	3.938	3.590	3.702	3.827	3.753	3.576	3.585	3.565	Italie*
_	_	_	0.035	0.048	0.061	0.067	0.075	0.081	0.093	0.108	Lettonie*
_	_	_	0.070	0.078	0.113	0.124	0.131	0.145	0.157	0.171	Lituanie (10)
_	_	_	_	_	0.190	0.208	0.212	0.203	0.215	0.194	Luxembourg*
0.045	0.037	0.055	0.056	0.051	0.043	0.044	0.039	0.033	0.032	0.031	Malte
4.264	3.598	3.523	3.541	3.282	3.286	3.405	3.376	3.381	3.377	3.475	Pays-Bas*
0.816	0.765	0.758	0.630	0.517	0.524	0.508	0.508	0.508	0.514	0.567	Norvège
0.805	0.583	0.234	0.555	0.736	0.827	0.875	0.947	0.944	1.029	1.150	Pologne*
0.449	0.377	0.704	0.623	0.601	0.602	0.607	0.580	0.569	0.540	0.550	Portugal*
0.668	0.554	0.274	0.196	0.196	0.268	0.309	0.345	0.375	0.414	0.494	Roumanie*
_	_	_	0.176	0.202	0.262	0.306	0.314	0.329	0.363	0.426	Slovaquie*
_	_	_	0.181	0.152	0.164	0.178	0.188	0.189	0.196	0.223	Slovénie*
1.643	1.474	2.439	2.171	2.348	2.474	2.683	2.729	2.683	2.663	2.633	Espagne*
1.613	1.405	1.511	1.243	1.096	1.003	1.075	1.061	1.036	1.033	1.070	Suède
1.753	1.512	1.941	1.532	1.256	1.310	1.291	1.226	1.175	1.146	1.138	Suisse*
5.572	5.388	6.250	5.109	5.169	5.456	5.138	4.971	4.773	4.870	4.378	Royaume-Uni*
1.344	**1.569**	**1.434**	**1.438**	**1.284**	**1.316**	**1.385**	**1.401**	**1.406**	**1.297**	**1.396**	**Économies développées : Océanie**
1.080	1.274	1.169	1.172	1.075	1.091	1.146	1.156	1.163	1.083	1.176	Australie*
0.264	0.295	0.265	0.267	0.209	0.226	0.239	0.245	0.243	0.214	0.220	Nouvelle-Zélande

Sources :
- ONU, Annuaire statistique du commerce international
- ONU, Bulletin mensuel de statistique
- FMI, International Financial Statistics
- FMI, Direction of Trade Statistics
- Organisation mondiale du commerce
- Autres sources internationales et nationales
- Estimations du secrétariat de la CNUCED

Notes :

* Pays qui utilisent le système du commerce spécial en tant que système d'enregistrement.
(a) Donnée relative à l'Union Douanière d'Afrique du Sud (Afrique du Sud, Botswana, Lesotho, Namibie et Swaziland)
(b) Y compris Aruba

(1) Non-compris le commerce avec les autres pays membres de la CEMAC.
(2) Avant 1986 compris dans Antilles néerlandaises. Les données comprennent les exportations et importations de pétrole brut et produits dérivés.
(3) À partir de 1990, certains produits pétroliers et chimiques ne sont plus inclus dans les statistiques du commerce.
(4) Avant 1986, y compris Aruba.
(5) Non-compris les biens d'importation financés par l'aide à l'étranger.
(6) Non-compris les biens à usage militaire, le matériel fissile, le combustible de soute et l'avitaillement des navires et aéronefs.
(7) Y compris le commerce entre les États de la Malaisie. Non comprises les importations militaires et l'installation près des côtes de l'industrie pétrolière.
(8) Y compris les transbordements vers et en provenance de la Malaisie péninsulaire.
(9) Non-compris les biens à usage militaire, les métaux précieux et les biens fournis dans les ports étrangers.
(10) Avant 1994, concerne seulement le commerce avec les pays extérieurs à la CEI.
(11) Avant 1998, les données se réfèrent uniquement à la Fédération de la Bosnie-Herzégovine. L'autre entité de la Bosnie-Herzégovine, Republika Srpska, n'est pas incluse.
(12) Avant 1994, non-compris le commerce avec les républiques indépendantes de l'ancienne URSS.
(13) À partir de 1985, les chiffres ne sont pas comparables à ceux des années antérieures à cause des révisions du taux de change couronne par rapport au dollar des États-Unis.
(14) À partir de 1995, y compris les biens destinés à subir des transformations.
(15) Avant 1988, non-compris les navires.
(16) Avant 1996, non-compris les zones franches douanières.

1.1.2 Exports and imports of economic groupings
Value

Economic grouping	Exports (f.o.b.) - Exportations (f.a.b.) Millions of dollars							
	1980	1990	2000	2003	2004	2005	2006	2007
DEVELOPING ECONOMIES	**597 574**	**843 904**	**2 056 407**	**2 426 752**	**3 097 429**	**3 775 908**	**4 505 697**	**5 190 026**
Developing economies excluding China	579 475	781 813	1 807 204	1 988 524	2 504 103	3 013 955	3 536 317	3 972 026
Developing economies excluding LDCs	582 316	824 289	2 020 073	2 380 477	3 036 523	3 693 072	4 401 991	5 064 382
High-income developing countries	325 845	458 599	1 114 408	1 198 033	1 510 380	1 810 579	2 127 250	2 343 560
Middle-income developing countries	131 436	202 218	414 998	493 266	622 630	742 675	861 512	1 003 803
Low-income developing countries	140 294	183 087	527 000	735 453	964 418	1 222 654	1 516 936	1 842 664
Heavily indebted poor countries	20 393	21 822	26 993	35 027	44 708	52 511	64 395	73 147
Landlocked developing countries	7 451	8 307	32 806	42 890	59 006	73 610	96 599	113 146
Small island developing States	12 546	6 994	11 703	12 748	14 771	19 232	25 478	23 717
Least developed countries	*15 258*	*19 615*	*36 334*	*46 275*	*60 906*	*82 836*	*103 706*	*125 644*
Africa and Haiti	12 243	16 047	21 201	29 112	41 143	58 035	73 457	91 258
Asia	2 848	3 365	14 895	16 850	19 403	24 456	29 817	33 937
Islands	166	202	238	313	360	346	432	450
Major petroleum exporters	*294 263*	*195 765*	*356 753*	*391 415*	*530 425*	*743 945*	*898 818*	*985 449*
Africa	67 256	49 110	76 951	82 267	113 587	168 880	203 819	217 158
America	25 779	22 118	42 730	38 630	53 795	75 230	92 125	94 729
Asia	201 228	124 536	237 072	270 518	363 044	499 834	602 874	673 562
Major exporters of manufactured goods	*169 375*	*492 766*	*1 407 492*	*1 703 829*	*2 164 743*	*2 558 032*	*3 043 140*	*3 545 051*
America	38 163	72 125	221 453	238 480	285 762	332 420	388 248	432 704
Asia	131 212	420 642	1 186 040	1 465 349	1 878 981	2 225 612	2 654 892	3 112 347
Emerging economies	*130 912*	*333 426*	*898 998*	*960 391*	*1 213 858*	*1 393 551*	*1 629 353*	*1 830 996*
America	54 788	96 081	273 959	298 801	365 475	430 656	516 698	584 321
Asia	76 124	237 346	625 039	661 591	848 383	962 895	1 112 655	1 246 675
Newly industrialized economies	*125 567*	*354 429*	*932 089*	*985 691*	*1 219 109*	*1 378 290*	*1 581 288*	*1 760 793*
First tier	76 425	266 985	659 708	705 660	885 651	1 001 184	1 143 948	1 262 177
Second tier	49 141	87 444	272 381	280 031	333 458	377 106	437 340	498 616
Developing economies: Africa	**118 981**	**106 983**	**153 072**	**178 383**	**231 869**	**303 036**	**358 998**	**397 457**
Northern Africa excluding Sudan	43 500	40 681	52 554	60 983	76 535	105 688	129 234	142 761
Sub-Saharan Africa	75 481	66 302	100 518	117 401	155 334	197 349	229 764	254 696
Sub-Saharan Africa excluding South Africa	49 941	42 734	70 535	80 919	109 188	145 723	171 589	184 908
Developing economies: America	**111 345**	**143 793**	**364 482**	**384 445**	**474 969**	**570 768**	**683 156**	**765 319**
Central America and Greater Carribean Islands excluding Puerto Rico	31 107	52 539	190 017	188 951	215 163	241 860	281 882	308 314
Central America and Greater Carribean Islands excluding Mexico and Puerto Rico	13 076	11 828	23 650	23 555	26 079	27 969	31 441	36 259
South America and Central America	88 977	132 125	345 482	366 412	453 340	544 466	650 280	733 822
South America excluding Brazil	45 466	55 135	109 405	113 050	151 549	194 351	242 329	278 477
Developing economies: Asia	**365 007**	**590 417**	**1 534 755**	**1 859 413**	**2 385 427**	**2 896 196**	**3 456 391**	**4 018 909**
Eastern and South-Eastern Asia excluding China	132 023	363 758	957 605	1 019 438	1 260 951	1 429 147	1 643 712	1 834 922
Southern Asia excluding India	17 542	29 064	50 355	59 208	73 115	93 337	100 710	117 850

Sources:
- Data in this table are based on trade figures in table 1.1.1.

18

Imports (c.i.f.) - Importations (c.a.f.) Millions de dollars								Groupements économiques
1980	1990	2000	2003	2004	2005	2006	2007	
492 879	**800 281**	**1 914 743**	**2 254 347**	**2 876 773**	**3 397 199**	**3 971 659**	**4 632 355**	**ÉCONOMIES EN DÉVELOPPEMENT**
472 937	746 936	1 689 649	1 841 587	2 315 544	2 737 246	3 180 054	3 676 555	Économies en développement sans la Chine
469 110	775 548	1 870 742	2 194 090	2 804 925	3 309 490	3 870 413	4 517 586	Économies en développement sans les PMA
222 876	399 001	1 009 641	1 043 128	1 296 061	1 511 066	1 741 764	1 992 549	Pays en développement à revenu élevé
144 621	223 964	431 786	491 549	629 911	725 685	860 016	1 005 997	Pays en développement à revenu intermédiaire
125 382	177 316	473 317	719 670	950 802	1 160 448	1 369 880	1 633 809	Pays en développement à revenu faible
25 390	24 438	37 700	49 076	60 396	74 375	86 813	99 025	Pays pauvres très endettés
9 068	12 322	36 793	48 804	64 113	76 392	94 259	115 935	Pays en développement sans littoral
15 717	10 405	17 536	19 357	22 374	25 927	29 813	32 547	Petits États insulaires en développement
23 769	*24 733*	*44 001*	*60 257*	*71 848*	*87 710*	*101 246*	*114 769*	*Pays les moins avancés*
16 485	16 723	23 964	35 629	43 854	55 705	63 686	71 503	Afrique et Haïti
6 966	7 501	19 004	23 434	26 532	30 308	35 577	41 062	Asie
318	509	1 033	1 193	1 462	1 696	1 984	2 204	Îles
136 728	*112 043*	*172 780*	*235 089*	*308 778*	*392 894*	*445 412*	*530 615*	*Principaux exportateurs de pétrole*
38 144	24 540	28 414	47 762	60 623	77 945	84 746	91 911	Afrique
17 258	10 309	23 242	21 078	29 764	40 022	52 233	65 926	Amérique
81 326	77 194	121 124	166 250	218 391	274 927	308 434	372 777	Asie
206 615	*508 542*	*1 401 559*	*1 643 641*	*2 099 962*	*2 434 164*	*2 863 835*	*3 313 939*	*Principaux exportateurs d'articles manufacturés*
47 105	66 071	241 768	229 384	273 056	309 449	364 021	423 159	Amérique
159 510	442 471	1 159 791	1 414 257	1 826 905	2 124 715	2 499 814	2 890 780	Asie
152 003	*329 111*	*873 282*	*862 858*	*1 086 511*	*1 259 799*	*1 462 521*	*1 661 195*	*Économies émergentes*
65 947	81 360	294 443	270 954	330 396	383 374	451 900	534 485	Amérique
86 056	247 751	578 839	591 904	756 115	876 425	1 010 621	1 126 710	Asie
127 629	*365 082*	*869 037*	*902 848*	*1 120 087*	*1 292 330*	*1 475 097*	*1 644 041*	*Économies nouvellement industrialisées*
88 511	267 938	647 758	666 028	827 481	943 389	1 085 499	1 207 009	Première génération
39 118	97 144	221 279	236 820	292 606	348 941	389 598	437 032	Deuxième génération
93 735	**97 057**	**130 238**	**173 391**	**217 515**	**262 927**	**300 314**	**340 949**	**Économies en développement : Afrique**
29 977	44 333	47 329	55 357	70 958	84 392	92 196	114 931	Afrique septentrionale sans le Soudan
63 759	52 724	82 909	118 034	146 557	178 535	208 118	226 018	Afrique subsaharienne
44 059	34 325	53 214	76 951	93 091	116 231	130 838	144 268	Afrique subsaharienne sans l'Afrique du Sud
123 588	**127 240**	**392 045**	**369 101**	**449 011**	**530 415**	**631 683**	**749 287**	**Économies en développement : Amérique**
39 759	63 783	226 433	224 550	257 850	292 667	339 240	379 343	Amérique centrale et Grandes Antilles sans Porto Rico
17 615	20 234	43 731	46 047	51 227	60 846	71 071	82 765	Amérique centrale et Grandes Antilles sans le Mexique et Porto Rico
96 226	108 537	359 654	338 274	414 147	487 995	582 396	695 873	Amérique du Sud et Amérique centrale
41 521	34 244	92 816	79 958	108 440	141 081	175 156	221 702	Amérique du Sud sans le Brésil
272 005	**570 895**	**1 386 764**	**1 704 105**	**2 201 735**	**2 594 651**	**3 029 655**	**3 530 946**	**Économies en développement : Asie**
131 235	374 843	895 457	940 451	1 166 598	1 345 488	1 538 907	1 726 626	Asie orientale et Asie du Sud-Est sans la Chine
24 675	33 836	44 549	63 819	78 265	94 764	109 198	111 315	Asie méridionale sans l'Inde

Sources :
- Les données dans ce tableau ont été calculées d'après les chiffres du tableau 1.1.1.

1.1.2   Exports and imports of economic groupings
Share

Economic grouping	Exports (f.o.b.) - Exportations (f.a.b.) Percentage										
	1980	1985	1990	1995	2000	2002	2003	2004	2005	2006	2007
DEVELOPING ECONOMIES	**29.41**	**25.36**	**24.25**	**27.62**	**31.85**	**31.77**	**32.15**	**33.73**	**36.05**	**37.27**	**37.52**
Developing economies excluding China	28.52	23.97	22.47	24.75	27.99	26.75	26.35	27.27	28.77	29.26	28.71
Developing economies excluding LDCs	28.66	24.69	23.69	27.16	31.29	31.14	31.54	33.07	35.26	36.42	36.61
High-income developing countries	16.03	12.93	13.18	15.32	17.26	16.13	15.87	16.45	17.28	17.60	16.94
Middle-income developing countries	6.47	6.77	5.81	6.18	6.43	6.48	6.54	6.78	7.09	7.13	7.26
Low-income developing countries	6.90	5.66	5.26	6.13	8.16	9.16	9.74	10.50	11.67	12.55	13.32
Heavily indebted poor countries	1.00	0.82	0.63	0.47	0.42	0.46	0.46	0.49	0.50	0.53	0.53
Landlocked developing countries	0.37	0.31	0.24	0.47	0.51	0.54	0.57	0.64	0.70	0.80	0.82
Small island developing States	0.62	0.40	0.20	0.19	0.18	0.16	0.17	0.16	0.18	0.21	0.17
Least developed countries	*0.75*	*0.67*	*0.56*	*0.47*	*0.56*	*0.62*	*0.61*	*0.66*	*0.79*	*0.86*	*0.91*
Africa and Haiti	0.60	0.53	0.46	0.30	0.33	0.38	0.39	0.45	0.55	0.61	0.66
Asia	0.14	0.14	0.10	0.16	0.23	0.24	0.22	0.21	0.23	0.25	0.25
Islands	0.01	0.01	0.01	0.01	0.00	0.00	0.00	0.00	0.00	0.00	0.00
Major petroleum exporters	*14.48*	*7.93*	*5.63*	*3.83*	*5.53*	*4.99*	*5.19*	*5.78*	*7.10*	*7.44*	*7.12*
Africa	3.31	2.23	1.41	0.78	1.19	0.99	1.09	1.24	1.61	1.69	1.57
America	1.27	0.99	0.64	0.50	0.66	0.55	0.51	0.59	0.72	0.76	0.68
Asia	9.90	4.71	3.58	2.56	3.67	3.44	3.58	3.95	4.77	4.99	4.87
Major exporters of manufactured goods	*8.33*	*12.07*	*14.16*	*19.41*	*21.80*	*22.32*	*22.57*	*23.57*	*24.42*	*25.18*	*25.63*
America	1.88	2.66	2.07	2.44	3.43	3.41	3.16	3.11	3.17	3.21	3.13
Asia	6.46	9.41	12.09	16.97	18.37	18.92	19.41	20.46	21.25	21.96	22.50
Emerging economies	*6.44*	*8.82*	*9.58*	*12.64*	*13.93*	*13.14*	*12.72*	*13.22*	*13.30*	*13.48*	*13.24*
America	2.70	3.43	2.76	3.26	4.24	4.20	3.96	3.98	4.11	4.27	4.22
Asia	3.75	5.39	6.82	9.38	9.68	8.94	8.77	9.24	9.19	9.20	9.01
Newly industrialized economies	*6.18*	*8.10*	*10.19*	*14.00*	*14.44*	*13.50*	*13.06*	*13.28*	*13.16*	*13.08*	*12.73*
First tier	3.76	5.78	7.67	10.22	10.22	9.53	9.35	9.64	9.56	9.46	9.12
Second tier	2.42	2.32	2.51	3.78	4.22	3.96	3.71	3.63	3.60	3.62	3.60
Developing economies: Africa	**5.85**	**4.18**	**3.07**	**2.08**	**2.37**	**2.24**	**2.36**	**2.52**	**2.89**	**2.97**	**2.87**
Northern Africa excluding Sudan	2.14	1.66	1.17	0.69	0.81	0.74	0.81	0.83	1.01	1.07	1.03
Sub-Saharan Africa	3.71	2.52	1.91	1.40	1.56	1.50	1.56	1.69	1.88	1.90	1.84
Sub-Saharan Africa excluding South Africa	2.46	1.69	1.23	0.86	1.09	1.04	1.07	1.19	1.39	1.42	1.34
Developing economies: America	**5.48**	**5.53**	**4.13**	**4.44**	**5.65**	**5.41**	**5.09**	**5.17**	**5.45**	**5.65**	**5.53**
Central America and Greater Carribean Islands excluding Puerto Rico	1.53	1.95	1.51	1.86	2.94	2.81	2.50	2.34	2.31	2.33	2.23
Central America and Greater Carribean Islands excluding Mexico and Puerto Rico	0.64	0.59	0.34	0.32	0.37	0.33	0.31	0.28	0.27	0.26	0.26
South America and Central America	4.38	4.82	3.80	4.19	5.35	5.17	4.85	4.94	5.20	5.38	5.30
South America excluding Brazil	2.24	1.95	1.58	1.56	1.69	1.55	1.50	1.65	1.86	2.00	2.01
Developing economies: Asia	**17.96**	**15.56**	**16.97**	**21.02**	**23.77**	**24.06**	**24.64**	**25.98**	**27.65**	**28.59**	**29.05**
Eastern and South-Eastern Asia excluding China	6.50	8.39	10.45	14.26	14.83	13.95	13.51	13.73	13.64	13.60	13.26
Southern Asia excluding India	0.86	1.02	0.84	0.67	0.78	0.77	0.78	0.80	0.89	0.83	0.85

Sources:
- Data in this table are based on trade figures in table 1.1.1.

Imports (c.i.f.) - Importations (c.a.f.) En pourcentage											Groupements économiques
1980	1985	1990	1995	2000	2002	2003	2004	2005	2006	2007	
23.77	**22.99**	**22.29**	**28.57**	**28.78**	**28.87**	**29.01**	**30.40**	**31.52**	**32.19**	**32.96**	**ÉCONOMIES EN DÉVELOPPEMENT**
22.81	20.92	20.80	26.05	25.39	24.44	23.70	24.47	25.40	25.77	26.16	Économies en développement sans la Chine
22.62	22.02	21.60	27.94	28.12	28.11	28.23	29.64	30.71	31.37	32.14	Économies en développement sans les PMA
10.75	9.94	11.11	14.90	15.17	14.05	13.42	13.70	14.02	14.12	14.18	Pays en développement à revenu élevé
6.97	6.50	6.24	7.54	6.49	6.47	6.33	6.66	6.73	6.97	7.16	Pays en développement à revenu intermédiaire
6.05	6.56	4.94	6.13	7.11	8.35	9.26	10.05	10.77	11.10	11.62	Pays en développement à revenu faible
1.22	0.98	0.68	0.59	0.57	0.64	0.63	0.64	0.69	0.70	0.70	Pays pauvres très endettés
0.44	0.45	0.34	0.55	0.55	0.62	0.63	0.68	0.71	0.76	0.82	Pays en développement sans littoral
0.76	0.46	0.29	0.26	0.26	0.27	0.25	0.24	0.24	0.24	0.23	Petits États insulaires en développement
1.15	*0.97*	*0.69*	*0.63*	*0.66*	*0.76*	*0.78*	*0.76*	*0.81*	*0.82*	*0.82*	*Pays les moins avancés*
0.79	0.62	0.47	0.37	0.36	0.43	0.46	0.46	0.52	0.52	0.51	Afrique et Haïti
0.34	0.33	0.21	0.25	0.29	0.31	0.30	0.28	0.28	0.29	0.29	Asie
0.02	0.02	0.01	0.01	0.02	0.02	0.02	0.02	0.02	0.02	0.02	Îles
6.59	*5.43*	*3.12*	*2.66*	*2.60*	*3.04*	*3.03*	*3.26*	*3.65*	*3.61*	*3.77*	*Principaux exportateurs de pétrole*
1.84	1.30	0.68	0.58	0.43	0.58	0.61	0.64	0.72	0.69	0.65	Afrique
0.83	0.56	0.29	0.35	0.35	0.33	0.27	0.31	0.37	0.42	0.47	Amérique
3.92	3.57	2.15	1.72	1.82	2.12	2.14	2.31	2.55	2.50	2.65	Asie
9.96	*11.67*	*14.16*	*20.37*	*21.06*	*20.98*	*21.15*	*22.19*	*22.59*	*23.21*	*23.58*	*Principaux exportateurs d'articles manufacturés*
2.27	1.65	1.84	2.49	3.63	3.40	2.95	2.89	2.87	2.95	3.01	Amérique
7.69	10.02	12.32	17.88	17.43	17.59	18.20	19.31	19.72	20.26	20.57	Asie
7.33	*6.95*	*9.17*	*13.14*	*13.12*	*11.79*	*11.10*	*11.48*	*11.69*	*11.85*	*11.82*	*Économies émergentes*
3.18	2.07	2.27	3.35	4.43	3.90	3.49	3.49	3.56	3.66	3.80	Amérique
4.15	4.87	6.90	9.78	8.70	7.89	7.62	7.99	8.13	8.19	8.02	Asie
6.15	*7.11*	*10.17*	*14.79*	*13.06*	*12.10*	*11.62*	*11.84*	*11.99*	*11.96*	*11.70*	*Économies nouvellement industrialisées*
4.27	5.28	7.46	10.63	9.74	8.84	8.57	8.74	8.75	8.80	8.59	Première génération
1.89	1.83	2.71	4.16	3.33	3.26	3.05	3.09	3.24	3.16	3.11	Deuxième génération
4.52	**3.57**	**2.70**	**2.31**	**1.96**	**2.14**	**2.23**	**2.30**	**2.44**	**2.43**	**2.43**	**Économies en développement : Afrique**
1.45	1.56	1.23	0.91	0.71	0.76	0.71	0.75	0.78	0.75	0.82	Afrique septentrionale sans le Soudan
3.07	2.01	1.47	1.40	1.25	1.38	1.52	1.55	1.66	1.69	1.61	Afrique subsaharienne
2.12	1.45	0.96	0.81	0.80	0.94	0.99	0.98	1.08	1.06	1.03	Afrique subsaharienne sans l'Afrique du Sud
5.96	**4.12**	**3.54**	**4.79**	**5.89**	**5.32**	**4.75**	**4.74**	**4.92**	**5.12**	**5.33**	**Économies en développement : Amérique**
1.92	1.82	1.78	1.98	3.40	3.32	2.89	2.72	2.72	2.75	2.70	Amérique centrale et Grandes Antilles sans Porto Rico
0.85	0.88	0.56	0.53	0.66	0.67	0.59	0.54	0.56	0.58	0.59	Amérique centrale et Grandes Antilles sans le Mexique et Porto Rico
4.64	3.21	3.02	4.41	5.41	4.87	4.35	4.38	4.53	4.72	4.95	Amérique du Sud et Amérique centrale
2.00	1.24	0.95	1.62	1.39	1.07	1.03	1.15	1.31	1.42	1.58	Amérique du Sud sans le Brésil
13.12	**15.15**	**15.90**	**21.36**	**20.84**	**21.32**	**21.93**	**23.27**	**24.08**	**24.56**	**25.12**	**Économies en développement : Asie**
6.33	7.35	10.44	15.12	13.46	12.56	12.10	12.33	12.49	12.47	12.28	Asie orientale et Asie du Sud-Est sans la Chine
1.19	1.18	0.94	0.73	0.67	0.81	0.82	0.83	0.88	0.89	0.79	Asie méridionale sans l'Inde

Sources :
- Les données dans ce tableau ont été calculées d'après les chiffres du tableau 1.1.1.

Trade group	Exports (f.o.b) - Exportations (f.a.b.) Millions of dollars							
	1980	1990	2000	2003	2004	2005	2006	2007
AFRICA								
CEMAC (formerly UDEAC)	4 668	5 558	8 365	11 278	16 422	23 322	28 330	31 485
CEPGL	2 455	2 510	927	1 475	1 996	2 372	2 525	2 768
COMESA	33 847	27 598	29 863	35 466	43 992	61 347	78 850	91 564
ECCAS	9 042	11 956	17 215	22 267	31 896	49 807	62 720	75 366
ECOWAS	33 336	22 818	35 815	37 292	50 348	64 947	71 553	66 280
MRU	1 225	3 015	1 008	810	968	1 180	1 274	1 442
SADC	34 336	35 186	50 897	61 725	79 417	97 523	116 159	139 200
UEMOA	4 884	5 202	6 661	9 851	11 566	12 449	13 752	14 719
UMA	40 648	36 171	48 220	54 990	69 445	95 640	116 865	128 002
AMERICA								
ANCOM	11 246	13 592	26 154	29 991	38 739	50 624	64 744	75 627
CACM	4 877	4 417	13 547	13 812	14 872	16 469	18 397	21 172
CARICOM	11 681	4 909	8 288	9 016	10 912	14 551	20 030	18 155
FTAA	393 904	658 157	1 416 834	1 377 130	1 591 531	1 830 039	2 102 453	2 336 475
LAIA	88 302	131 447	331 527	352 056	438 155	527 427	631 652	712 956
MERCOSUR	29 522	46 418	84 590	106 097	135 811	163 982	190 236	224 124
NAFTA	311 331	561 932	1 224 920	1 162 986	1 312 132	1 480 480	1 678 242	1 851 499
OECS	164	346	332	286	306	307	327	337
ASIA								
APTA	46 045	148 738	476 009	703 519	938 091	1 162 185	1 435 267	1 756 140
ASEAN	73 957	145 284	431 911	453 688	568 969	652 724	765 633	865 778
ECO	18 527	38 088	82 450	116 358	153 262	191 836	222 720	273 185
GCC	155 060	87 800	175 732	212 730	285 035	397 012	483 064	533 638
SAARC	13 129	27 493	64 252	84 036	105 056	132 561	157 872	184 406
EUROPE								
EFTA	49 095	99 434	143 483	174 837	207 656	235 812	271 773	312 905
EU	842 979	1 547 083	2 454 359	3 148 880	3 760 457	4 070 953	4 589 306	5 283 852
Euro zone	624 839	1 219 424	1 893 221	2 451 348	2 913 301	3 120 168	3 473 238	4 038 157
OCEANIA								
MSG	1 518	1 631	2 728	2 982	3 380	4 118	5 013	5 509
INTERREGIONAL								
ACP	95 315	78 581	119 045	136 638	177 972	224 399	264 234	289 376
APEC	627 358	1 332 544	3 114 807	3 340 256	4 059 444	4 686 837	5 461 946	6 220 182
BSEC	29 644	31 886	177 933	249 082	332 840	414 567	502 617	603 668
CIS	..	..	145 717	194 594	265 481	340 375	425 266	502 912

Sources:
- Data in this table are based on trade figures in table 1.1.1.

Imports (c.i.f.) - Importations (c.a.f.) Millions de dollars								Groupements commerciaux
1980	1990	2000	2003	2004	2005	2006	2007	
								AFRIQUE
3 018	3 440	3 799	6 192	7 181	8 805	10 937	11 915	CEMAC (anc. UDEAC)
1 949	2 256	1 058	2 010	2 447	2 940	3 727	3 807	CEPGL
22 946	34 854	35 148	39 854	50 690	68 097	75 947	89 055	COMESA
6 314	7 296	7 927	13 723	15 501	20 150	23 515	25 001	CEEAC
25 607	14 008	20 916	32 206	37 916	47 287	52 417	57 512	CEDEAO
1 231	1 082	1 429	1 113	1 313	1 489	1 756	2 036	UFM
28 906	29 773	48 483	67 034	84 550	98 677	117 484	125 631	SADC
6 371	5 777	7 374	10 160	12 303	14 404	15 718	18 411	UEMOA
25 402	27 771	33 774	44 759	59 023	65 969	72 749	89 200	UMA
								AMÉRIQUE
10 157	11 611	25 977	30 621	36 917	46 334	56 290	69 379	ANCOM
6 001	6 473	21 168	25 294	28 537	32 692	37 711	43 452	MCAC
14 268	7 223	14 091	15 118	16 902	19 870	22 714	24 612	CARICOM
430 925	757 955	1 885 585	1 907 237	2 242 609	2 579 322	2 890 810	3 135 840	ZLEA
94 231	106 276	338 247	312 724	385 712	456 418	546 845	652 939	ALADI
37 801	29 295	90 005	69 133	95 090	113 910	140 858	184 469	MERCOSUR
341 673	683 779	1 686 788	1 726 581	2 012 234	2 295 724	2 545 250	2 700 837	ALENA
423	1 044	1 607	1 688	1 837	2 082	2 272	2 592	OECO
								ASIE
61 826	153 257	452 797	681 713	906 189	1 087 621	1 303 718	1 558 493	ACAP
65 641	162 292	377 441	396 563	496 030	594 194	682 876	772 225	ANASE
27 528	48 944	93 674	127 683	176 841	199 509	254 674	298 775	ECO
51 991	47 366	85 287	117 103	150 901	196 324	221 526	285 086	CCG
25 272	38 149	79 689	105 176	140 657	193 897	234 942	280 779	SAARC
								EUROPE
54 281	98 592	120 567	142 627	167 607	185 923	210 921	245 713	AELE
943 494	1 606 206	2 510 348	3 123 749	3 755 758	4 139 056	4 734 098	5 431 428	UE
710 829	1 245 029	1 870 213	2 312 565	2 765 174	3 033 473	3 423 323	3 935 998	Zone euro
								OCÉANIE
1 900	2 059	2 186	2 776	3 375	3 670	4 387	4 465	MSG
								INTERRÉGIONAUX
88 536	72 108	114 318	149 065	181 317	220 606	257 057	280 222	ACP
669 769	1 405 143	3 340 280	3 672 126	4 457 756	5 137 855	5 835 311	6 493 435	CEAP
41 951	57 056	175 268	260 388	343 140	399 399	514 642	670 993	CEMN
..	..	86 019	139 885	182 720	228 817	298 876	399 868	CEI

Sources :
- Les données dans ce tableau ont été calculées d'après les chiffres du tableau 1.1.1.

1.1.3 Exports and imports of trade groups
Share

Trade group	Exports (f.o.b) - Exportations (f.a.b.) Percentage										
	1980	1985	1990	1995	2000	2002	2003	2004	2005	2006	2007
AFRICA											
CEMAC (formerly UDEAC)	0.23	0.20	0.16	0.12	0.13	0.14	0.15	0.18	0.22	0.23	0.23
CEPGL	0.12	0.11	0.07	0.03	0.01	0.02	0.02	0.02	0.02	0.02	0.02
COMESA	1.67	1.17	0.79	0.44	0.46	0.44	0.47	0.48	0.59	0.65	0.66
ECCAS	0.44	0.42	0.34	0.22	0.27	0.29	0.30	0.35	0.48	0.52	0.54
ECOWAS	1.64	0.97	0.66	0.43	0.55	0.46	0.49	0.55	0.62	0.59	0.48
MRU	0.06	0.05	0.09	0.03	0.02	0.01	0.01	0.01	0.01	0.01	0.01
SADC	1.69	1.20	1.01	0.77	0.79	0.81	0.82	0.86	0.93	0.96	1.01
UEMOA	0.24	0.22	0.15	0.13	0.10	0.13	0.13	0.13	0.12	0.11	0.11
UMA	2.00	1.49	1.04	0.63	0.75	0.67	0.73	0.76	0.91	0.97	0.93
AMERICA											
ANCOM	0.55	0.51	0.39	0.41	0.41	0.40	0.40	0.42	0.48	0.54	0.55
CACM	0.24	0.19	0.13	0.17	0.21	0.19	0.18	0.16	0.16	0.15	0.15
CARICOM	0.57	0.34	0.14	0.11	0.13	0.11	0.12	0.12	0.14	0.17	0.13
FTAA	19.38	20.90	18.91	19.37	21.95	19.92	18.25	17.33	17.47	17.39	16.89
LAIA	4.35	4.89	3.78	4.01	5.14	4.96	4.66	4.77	5.04	5.23	5.15
MERCOSUR	1.45	1.79	1.33	1.36	1.31	1.37	1.41	1.48	1.57	1.57	1.62
NAFTA	15.32	17.08	16.15	16.56	18.97	17.06	15.41	14.29	14.13	13.88	13.38
OECS	0.01	0.01	0.01	0.01	0.01	0.00	0.00	0.00	0.00	0.00	0.00
ASIA											
APTA	2.27	3.51	4.27	6.04	7.37	8.47	9.32	10.22	11.09	11.87	12.70
ASEAN	3.64	3.68	4.18	6.25	6.69	6.29	6.01	6.20	6.23	6.33	6.26
ECO	0.91	1.29	1.09	1.17	1.28	1.40	1.54	1.67	1.83	1.84	1.97
GCC	7.63	3.20	2.52	2.04	2.72	2.59	2.82	3.10	3.79	4.00	3.86
SAARC	0.65	0.73	0.79	0.90	1.00	1.11	1.11	1.14	1.27	1.31	1.33
EUROPE											
EFTA	2.42	2.45	2.86	2.43	2.22	2.37	2.32	2.26	2.25	2.25	2.26
EU	41.48	40.73	44.46	42.33	38.02	40.65	41.72	40.95	38.86	37.97	38.20
Euro zone	30.75	30.21	35.05	33.32	29.33	31.52	32.48	31.73	29.79	28.73	29.19
OCEANIA											
MSG	0.07	0.06	0.05	0.07	0.04	0.03	0.04	0.04	0.04	0.04	0.04
INTERREGIONAL											
ACP	4.69	3.27	2.26	1.68	1.84	1.75	1.81	1.94	2.14	2.19	2.09
APEC	30.87	37.57	38.30	45.52	48.25	45.62	44.26	44.21	44.74	45.19	44.97
BSEC	1.46	1.93	0.92	2.78	2.76	2.99	3.30	3.62	3.96	4.16	4.36
CIS	..	..	..	2.21	2.26	2.36	2.58	2.89	3.25	3.52	3.64

Sources:
- Data in this table are based on trade figures in table 1.1.1.

1980	1985	1990	1995	2000	2002	2003	2004	2005	2006	2007	Groupements commerciaux
Imports (c.i.f.) - Importations (c a.f.) En pourcentage											
											AFRIQUE
0.15	0.14	0.10	0.06	0.06	0.09	0.08	0.08	0.08	0.09	0.08	CEMAC (anc. UDEAC)
0.09	0.09	0.06	0.03	0.02	0.02	0.03	0.03	0.03	0.03	0.03	CEPGL
1.11	1.16	0.97	0.62	0.53	0.56	0.51	0.54	0.63	0.62	0.63	COMESA
0.30	0.30	0.20	0.12	0.12	0.17	0.18	0.16	0.19	0.19	0.18	CEEAC
1.23	0.74	0.39	0.37	0.31	0.39	0.41	0.40	0.44	0.42	0.41	CEDEAO
0.06	0.04	0.03	0.03	0.02	0.02	0.01	0.01	0.01	0.01	0.01	UFM
1.39	0.89	0.83	0.80	0.73	0.74	0.86	0.89	0.92	0.95	0.89	SADC
0.31	0.21	0.16	0.14	0.11	0.12	0.13	0.13	0.13	0.13	0.13	UEMOA
1.23	1.02	0.77	0.69	0.51	0.58	0.58	0.62	0.61	0.59	0.63	UMA
											AMÉRIQUE
0.49	0.41	0.32	0.55	0.39	0.43	0.39	0.39	0.43	0.46	0.49	ANCOM
0.29	0.25	0.18	0.25	0.32	0.35	0.33	0.30	0.30	0.31	0.31	MCAC
0.69	0.39	0.20	0.19	0.21	0.21	0.19	0.18	0.18	0.18	0.18	CARICOM
20.78	24.97	21.11	22.62	28.34	26.61	24.54	23.70	23.93	23.43	22.31	ZLEA
4.54	3.25	2.96	4.13	5.08	4.51	4.02	4.08	4.24	4.43	4.65	ALADI
1.82	0.95	0.82	1.53	1.35	0.94	0.89	1.00	1.06	1.14	1.31	MERCOSUR
16.48	22.25	19.04	19.40	25.35	24.07	22.22	21.26	21.30	20.63	19.21	ALENA
0.02	0.03	0.03	0.02	0.02	0.02	0.02	0.02	0.02	0.02	0.02	OECO
											ASIE
2.98	4.62	4.27	6.01	6.81	7.79	8.77	9.58	10.09	10.57	11.09	ACAP
3.17	3.28	4.52	6.79	5.67	5.39	5.10	5.24	5.51	5.53	5.49	ANASE
1.33	1.50	1.36	1.33	1.41	1.52	1.64	1.87	1.85	2.06	2.13	ECO
2.51	2.14	1.32	1.30	1.28	1.49	1.51	1.59	1.82	1.80	2.03	CCG
1.22	1.32	1.06	1.14	1.20	1.27	1.35	1.49	1.80	1.90	2.00	SAARC
											EUROPE
2.62	2.32	2.75	2.20	1.81	1.87	1.84	1.77	1.73	1.71	1.75	AELE
45.50	40.16	44.74	40.62	37.73	38.86	40.20	39.69	38.41	38.37	38.64	UE
34.28	29.61	34.68	31.10	28.11	28.45	29.76	29.22	28.15	27.75	28.00	Zone euro
											OCÉANIE
0.09	0.08	0.06	0.05	0.03	0.03	0.04	0.04	0.03	0.04	0.03	MSG
											INTERRÉGIONAUX
4.27	2.97	2.01	1.80	1.72	1.83	1.92	1.92	2.05	2.08	1.99	ACP
32.30	39.84	39.14	46.59	50.20	48.68	47.25	47.11	47.68	47.30	46.19	CEAP
2.02	2.28	1.59	3.16	2.63	2.96	3.35	3.63	3.71	4.17	4.77	CEMN
..	..	..	1.94	1.29	1.65	1.80	1.93	2.12	2.42	2.84	CEI

Sources :
- Les données dans ce tableau ont été calculées d'après les chiffres du tableau 1.1.1.

1.2.1 Annual average growth rates of exports and imports of countries and geographical regions

Region, country or territory	Exports (f.o.b) - Exportations (f.a.b.) Percentage										
	80-90	80-00	80-05	90-00	90-05	95-05	00-05	2004	2005	2006	2007
WORLD	**6.0**	**7.1**	**7.1**	**6.8**	**6.9**	**6.5**	**11.3**	**21.7**	**14.1**	**15.4**	**14.4**
DEVELOPING ECONOMIES	3.1	7.7	8.2	9.1	9.3	9.1	14.2	27.6	21.9	19.3	15.2
ECONOMIES IN TRANSITION	3.7	1.4	3.6	6.8	9.3	10.1	19.6	36.4	27.4	25.1	18.7
DEVELOPED ECONOMIES	7.2	7.2	6.8	5.9	5.8	5.2	9.5	18.1	9.2	12.5	13.7
Developing economies: Africa	**-1.4**	**2.0**	**3.7**	**3.5**	**6.4**	**9.1**	**15.9**	**30.0**	**30.7**	**18.5**	**10.7**
Eastern Africa	*1.2*	*3.3*	*3.9*	*4.9*	*5.2*	*4.5*	*10.7*	*19.8*	*11.8*	*22.7*	*15.6*
Burundi*	2.5	-2.1	-3.4	-4.3	-5.3	-5.9	4.4	27.5	19.0	2.6	(e)2.7
Comoros*	2.8	-3.1	-0.7	-10.9	-0.6	11.9	0.1	-30.2	-35.5	-17.4	..
Djibouti*	10.9	6.5	6.8	15.1	10.5	8.7	-16.0	2.0	4.0	41.8	..
Eritrea	–	–	–	–	–	-18.5	-15.9	23.9	-4.2	5.6	..
Ethiopia	–	–	–	–	–	4.6	13.2	36.7	33.1	16.3	(e)22.9
Ethiopia (former)	-1.1	–	–	–	–	–	–	–	–	–	–
Kenya	-1.1	3.8	4.4	6.3	6.0	4.2	13.1	11.3	22.7	4.4	(e)19.8
Madagascar*	-1.2	3.8	5.1	9.0	8.6	7.7	1.1	17.6	-14.6	14.2	(e)18.7
Malawi	2.0	3.4	3.0	0.9	1.4	0.8	5.3	-8.0	2.6	25.1	(e)31.1
Mauritius	14.4	9.7	7.8	4.3	3.6	2.6	4.4	5.0	7.3	9.1	-11.9
Mozambique	-9.6	2.7	8.9	10.3	19.7	28.0	34.1	44.1	16.1	36.4	(e)4.7
Rwanda	-0.9	-5.2	-2.8	-3.8	1.4	5.5	14.3	55.1	27.8	18.0	19.9
Seychelles	9.3	12.6	13.6	15.5	15.7	16.2	11.8	6.2	16.8	11.8	(e)-5.2
Somalia	-1.1	3.8	5.8	6.5	9.2	10.0	15.5	8.7	31.4	17.6	..
Uganda	-4.0	2.0	3.2	15.4	10.2	3.3	14.4	26.2	21.7	16.3	60.9
United Republic of Tanzania*	-5.1	3.3	5.5	7.8	10.0	9.4	18.7	21.1	13.8	2.8	16.4
Zambia*	0.9	0.3	1.1	-0.8	1.9	4.1	15.2	60.7	14.9	108.3	28.7
Zimbabwe	2.3	3.0	1.9	3.4	0.7	-2.7	2.3	15.3	-5.5	5.5	(e)3.9
Middle Africa	*2.2*	*3.4*	*5.5*	*3.4*	*8.5*	*13.1*	*24.2*	*43.2*	*56.3*	*26.0*	*20.2*
Angola*	6.4	6.6	8.7	6.1	11.4	16.8	25.2	41.7	78.9	32.2	(e)29.0
Cameroon*(1)	1.4	3.7	4.0	-1.3	2.1	5.7	11.8	10.3	25.3	19.4	(e)-11.3
Central African Republic*(1)	3.5	3.4	2.2	3.6	0.7	-2.6	-4.6	-1.0	1.3	23.9	(e)23.3
Chad*	9.4	6.7	10.1	3.2	14.2	23.9	91.6	264.8	43.7	8.3	(e)12.0
Congo*(1)	2.1	3.7	5.6	7.5	10.0	13.0	15.2	27.3	40.8	41.2	(e)2.5
Dem. Rep. of the Congo*	2.7	-3.2	-2.0	-6.1	-0.9	1.5	23.0	34.6	18.4	5.9	(e)9.1
Equatorial Guinea	19.8	23.6	29.3	41.2	44.3	49.0	41.9	64.2	45.5	22.8	(e)23.4
Gabon*(1)	-3.9	1.9	2.7	1.6	3.4	4.0	15.2	28.1	50.6	11.2	(e)17.0
Sao Tome and Principe*	-8.3	-6.1	-4.7	-6.1	-3.0	-2.2	6.5	-46.9	-3.7	12.7	3.5
Northern Africa	*-2.3*	*0.9*	*3.1*	*2.3*	*6.4*	*10.2*	*16.0*	*26.4*	*37.6*	*22.1*	*11.9*
Algeria*	-3.1	0.6	3.3	2.2	7.4	12.9	17.0	34.1	41.2	16.6	(e)0.9
Egypt*	7.3	0.5	2.4	0.7	5.7	10.6	19.4	19.3	41.7	28.7	17.2
Libyan Arab Jamahiriya	-7.5	-2.7	0.1	-2.3	3.9	10.2	17.7	26.0	66.6	35.9	(e)12.2
Morocco*	6.2	7.6	7.1	8.1	6.5	3.8	7.4	10.1	3.5	15.0	20.6
Sudan*	-2.5	2.1	7.4	14.0	19.8	26.1	24.2	48.6	27.7	17.3	(e)44.0
Tunisia	3.5	7.1	7.3	6.0	6.8	6.7	12.8	20.7	8.4	9.7	30.4
Southern Africa	*0.7*	*3.0*	*4.0*	*4.4*	*5.8*	*7.2*	*13.1*	*26.9*	*12.1*	*12.5*	*17.5*
Botswana*	..	..	..	..	(e)8.4	(e)8.4	10.1	25.0	25.4	2.8	-11.6
Lesotho	..	..	..	..	(e)23.7	(e)23.7	28.0	49.3	-7.3	10.3	(e)10.8
Namibia	..	..	..	..	(e)6.2	(e)6.2	10.6	45.1	8.8	36.7	(e)26.2
South Africa	0.7	2.4	3.2	2.5	4.3	5.3	13.0	26.5	11.9	12.7	20.0
Swaziland	..	..	..	..	(e)13.2	(e)13.2	19.4	19.0	3.4	4.9	(e)2.7
Western Africa	*-4.6*	*1.7*	*3.5*	*4.0*	*6.5*	*9.1*	*15.4*	*35.0*	*29.1*	*11.2*	*-7.3*
Benin*	18.8	14.1	11.1	3.3	3.4	2.5	10.1	4.8	2.0	-1.8	11.0
Burkina Faso	7.9	7.2	7.7	12.6	10.8	5.4	21.0	49.5	-2.4	(e)25.7	(e)15.5
Cape Verde*	5.8	6.8	6.6	11.0	8.2	3.4	12.1	18.7	18.1	16.8	-8.0
Côte d'Ivoire*	1.7	2.8	3.8	6.0	6.5	5.6	15.5	19.5	8.1	8.9	(e)5.4
Gambia	2.7	-5.3	-7.2	-12.5	-11.8	-8.5	-9.6	25.0	-20.0	25.0	(e)6.0
Ghana	-1.2	3.9	4.8	9.0	7.9	5.4	13.1	6.9	2.3	33.0	(e)10.9
Guinea	4.0	2.7	2.3	0.6	1.1	1.0	3.7	19.1	22.7	1.1	(e)7.3
Guinea-Bissau	4.2	8.9	9.3	13.6	11.3	9.5	7.6	16.1	18.2	-11.3	48.8
Liberia*	4.7	0.4	-5.0	-12.6	-16.3	-19.3	-15.0	-4.7	27.0	19.7	(e)29.9
Mali*	6.0	8.1	8.8	6.1	8.5	10.0	13.6	5.3	12.7	40.3	-5.5
Mauritania*	8.0	2.9	1.9	-2.0	-0.8	-0.4	10.3	38.1	42.2	118.6	-1.8
Niger*	-5.4	-1.4	-0.1	0.0	2.2	4.0	13.6	24.1	13.8	2.3	28.2
Nigeria	-8.4	1.0	3.6	4.2	7.7	11.9	16.5	45.8	38.3	8.8	(e)-12.9
Senegal*	3.5	3.6	4.1	4.0	5.0	4.8	12.4	20.1	4.5	-1.4	14.1
Sierra Leone*	-2.4	-12.8	-6.5	-29.5	-4.9	21.6	66.4	50.2	14.4	36.3	(e)25.3
Togo*	1.1	3.8	4.6	6.7	6.6	4.7	14.9	0.3	9.8	(e)16.1	(e)7.3
Developing economies: America	**1.6**	**6.4**	**7.1**	**10.6**	**9.4**	**8.0**	**9.7**	**23.5**	**20.2**	**19.7**	**12.0**

For sources and notes, see end of table.

1.2.1 Taux d'évolution annuels moyens des exportations et importations des pays et des régions géographiques

| Imports (c.i.f.) - Importations (c.a.f.) En pourcentage											Régions, pays ou territoires
80-90	80-00	80-05	90-00	90-05	95-05	00-05	2004	2005	2006	2007	
6.1	7.1	7.1	6.7	6.9	6.7	11.2	21.8	13.9	14.5	13.9	**MONDE**
4.0	8.1	8.3	8.5	8.4	7.5	13.4	27.6	18.1	16.9	16.6	ÉCONOMIES EN DÉVELOPPEMENT
5.0	0.9	2.7	3.7	6.8	7.2	21.7	29.9	22.1	28.3	33.1	ÉCONOMIES EN TRANSITION
6.8	6.9	6.8	6.2	6.4	6.4	10.0	19.0	11.7	12.8	11.8	ÉCONOMIES DÉVELOPPÉES
-0.5	2.3	3.6	4.4	5.9	6.8	15.9	25.4	20.9	14.2	13.5	**Économies en développement : Afrique**
1.6	4.0	4.5	4.5	5.3	5.4	13.6	26.0	20.1	17.6	15.9	*Afrique orientale*
2.2	-1.3	-0.9	-6.9	-2.3	2.3	11.6	12.5	51.6	61.2	(e)-21.5	Burundi*
5.7	3.0	3.1	-1.7	1.7	4.2	18.7	22.9	15.4	16.8	..	Comores*
-1.0	-0.8	0.1	-1.3	1.2	4.5	7.5	9.7	6.1	23.0	..	Djibouti*
–	–	–	–	–	-0.7	1.2	10.9	3.1	(e)13.5	..	Érythrée
–	–	–	–	–	11.3	25.0	45.7	33.7	14.1	(e)11.0	Éthiopie
4.3	–	–	–	–	–	–	–	–	–	–	Éthiopie (anc.)
1.7	3.6	4.5	6.0	6.5	5.5	14.1	22.2	35.1	18.9	(e)25.3	Kenya
-4.3	3.3	5.0	6.3	8.1	10.3	15.3	30.6	0.4	5.3	(e)18.7	Madagascar*
3.3	4.2	4.4	-0.6	2.8	6.2	17.5	18.7	27.0	2.2	(e)-2.1	Malawi
12.9	9.6	7.9	4.1	3.6	3.0	8.8	17.2	13.9	15.0	7.5	Maurice
0.1	2.1	4.1	1.2	6.4	13.5	17.8	16.1	13.4	19.1	(e)3.3	Mozambique
2.7	-1.1	-0.3	-1.6	0.8	2.3	9.7	9.7	41.7	23.3	18.8	Rwanda
7.2	8.8	8.6	9.7	8.4	6.8	10.5	20.5	36.0	11.7	(e)1.5	Seychelles
-19.3	-2.7	2.2	26.6	19.5	7.2	6.8	1.1	14.4	39.4	..	Somalie
4.5	8.5	8.1	21.0	12.6	4.3	5.5	61.9	-6.3	32.1	(e)36.7	Ouganda
-0.5	3.0	3.9	0.1	3.8	7.2	16.3	17.9	28.3	35.6	20.2	République-Unie de Tanzanie*
0.0	0.2	2.7	-0.3	5.9	12.1	24.6	36.7	18.9	20.2	29.8	Zambie*
-0.4	4.7	3.2	2.3	-0.1	-4.4	4.5	23.9	5.7	-9.9	(e)5.0	Zimbabwe
2.3	1.3	3.6	3.4	7.6	10.8	20.2	13.0	29.5	15.9	6.6	*Afrique centrale*
0.7	4.0	6.6	7.8	11.5	16.0	23.0	6.4	43.2	5.1	(e)4.8	Angola*
0.1	-0.2	1.8	2.0	5.5	8.8	12.1	11.2	13.7	15.2	(e)-11.6	Cameroun*(1)
7.9	2.0	1.3	0.2	0.1	-0.9	8.4	25.8	15.8	18.6	(e)12.3	République centrafricaine*(1)
12.6	6.1	8.9	3.9	11.8	15.0	17.9	22.6	-0.3	37.8	(e)15.0	Tchad*
5.3	1.0	1.5	2.9	3.5	1.1	20.2	2.6	65.9	27.2	(e)7.9	Congo*(1)
3.1	-3.7	-0.9	-5.7	2.7	8.3	29.3	24.6	14.3	23.3	(e)2.8	Rép. dém. du Congo*
11.9	16.4	19.9	29.3	29.7	27.1	35.5	27.9	34.3	34.8	(e)21.1	Guinée équatoriale
1.1	1.3	1.8	2.2	2.7	2.6	7.4	16.6	12.7	13.9	(e)23.8	Gabon*(1)
1.6	4.3	4.8	-0.7	3.3	8.7	13.0	1.6	28.2	38.5	8.4	Sao Tomé-et-Principe*
2.7	2.2	2.9	2.7	4.2	5.1	13.6	28.7	22.4	9.3	23.0	*Afrique septentrionale*
-2.7	0.2	1.5	-1.3	2.4	5.1	19.1	46.8	9.3	1.4	(e)15.6	Algérie*
12.6	2.4	1.9	4.7	2.8	1.2	4.8	15.4	54.4	3.8	30.6	Égypte*
-4.4	-1.6	0.2	-1.6	2.6	5.6	23.1	42.2	28.1	18.1	(e)10.0	Jamahiriya arabe libyenne
3.6	6.3	6.6	5.5	6.5	6.9	12.7	23.4	10.6	15.6	34.4	Maroc*
(e)-8.1	(e)1.0	(e)4.7	9.8	13.3	15.3	31.6	39.2	82.6	9.6	(e)4.2	Soudan*
2.7	6.3	6.4	5.2	5.7	5.5	9.5	17.5	2.8	12.8	27.5	Tunisie
-1.3	4.1	5.3	8.0	8.3	7.8	17.7	29.3	14.5	21.5	5.8	*Afrique australe*
..	..	..	..	(e)4.7	(e)4.7	9.7	32.0	-2.6	-2.6	-10.1	Botswana*
..	..	..	..	(e)7.9	(e)7.9	15.6	25.8	2.7	4.5	(e)19.9	Lesotho
..	..	..	..	(e)6.6	(e)6.6	12.3	22.2	1.2	11.4	(e)16.3	Namibie
-1.3	3.5	4.5	5.8	6.7	6.2	18.6	30.1	16.5	24.0	5.8	Afrique du Sud
..	..	..	..	(e)10.7	(e)10.7	17.0	15.7	12.1	5.2	(e)6.7	Swaziland
-8.2	0.2	2.5	3.8	6.5	8.7	18.0	18.6	25.4	10.0	9.6	*Afrique occidentale*
-4.9	4.0	4.4	9.7	6.7	2.5	9.5	0.2	0.0	12.5	(e)5.5	Bénin*
4.3	4.0	5.1	3.6	6.5	9.1	19.7	37.5	8.7	3.1	13.5	Burkina Faso
6.9	7.9	7.6	6.0	6.6	5.9	15.3	10.3	13.4	23.7	36.5	Cap-Vert*
-1.5	1.8	2.5	4.5	4.4	3.8	15.4	32.8	18.7	13.2	(e)9.9	Côte d'Ivoire*
2.5	4.3	2.7	0.2	-1.0	-1.8	8.2	46.8	3.5	3.4	(e)22.4	Gambie
1.8	7.3	7.2	8.3	7.3	8.5	12.8	32.9	24.4	26.3	(e)17.5	Ghana
9.7	4.8	3.6	-3.0	-0.7	0.8	5.4	7.8	18.8	9.8	(e)15.0	Guinée
5.2	2.1	1.4	-4.9	-2.1	-2.0	14.8	26.8	27.4	-7.1	36.5	Guinée-Bissau
-7.2	1.8	-0.7	11.1	-0.6	-9.4	-6.9	98.5	-3.8	44.0	(e)18.9	Libéria*
2.7	5.2	6.0	4.7	6.6	7.4	13.9	3.1	24.8	9.8	(e)14.2	Mali*
-2.1	3.9	5.1	3.1	6.4	9.4	25.7	70.3	54.7	-18.3	2.7	Mauritanie*
-3.5	-0.2	1.7	0.8	4.6	8.0	20.9	20.9	30.4	1.5	(e)34.0	Niger*
-15.0	-2.5	1.4	3.1	8.2	12.4	22.5	12.8	30.9	8.0	(e)2.5	Nigéria
1.4	2.3	4.0	3.9	6.9	8.8	16.3	18.4	12.6	7.4	29.0	Sénégal*
-8.7	-4.4	-0.4	-4.2	4.9	11.9	17.6	-5.6	20.3	13.0	(e)14.5	Sierra Leone*
2.0	2.2	(e)3.4	5.5	(e)6.5	(e)4.5	(e)16.0	(e)13.5	(e)29.3	(e)7.6	(e)20.3	Togo*
-0.2	7.9	7.8	12.0	8.7	5.7	6.0	21.6	18.1	19.1	18.6	**Économies en développement : Amérique**

Pour les sources et les notes, se reporter à la fin du tableau.

Region, country or territory	Exports (f.o.b) - Exportations (f.a.b.) Percentage										
	80-90	80-00	80-05	90-00	90-05	95-05	00-05	2004	2005	2006	2007
Caribbean	*-6.9*	*-2.0*	*0.2*	*7.0*	*6.6*	*6.1*	*6.5*	*19.9*	*21.6*	*25.0*	*-4.2*
Anguilla	..	..	..	..	..	(e)24.6	26.4	34.7	156.8	118.7	(e)-69.2
Antigua and Barbuda*	-4.8	4.8	4.2	0.6	1.2	2.4	4.5	22.8	4.1	4.3	..
Aruba (2)	..	(e)35.0	(e)23.9	16.9	12.0	7.7	6.7	32.7	27.9	5.3	-26.7
Bahamas (3)	-18.2	-17.3	-11.4	8.5	8.6	12.5	0.5	12.3	17.8	20.0	(e)7.4
Barbados	-3.0	-0.2	0.5	3.9	2.9	1.4	4.8	11.4	29.2	7.1	8.7
Cuba*	-0.9	-9.1	-6.5	-1.7	0.7	1.7	7.2	39.1	-7.4	(e)34.5	(e)27.0
Dominica*	15.8	6.2	3.5	0.7	-1.4	-2.3	-4.5	1.5	3.5	-4.6	(e)-6.5
Dominican Republic*	-2.1	11.7	11.1	26.6	15.1	4.2	2.2	8.5	3.5	4.8	12.4
Grenada*	7.0	3.4	3.1	9.0	4.9	4.3	-17.9	-15.6	-14.0	0.9	(e)47.3
Haiti	-1.2	0.4	3.0	12.2	11.4	13.7	9.7	12.9	20.2	10.4	(e)-0.1
Jamaica	1.1	3.6	2.9	2.2	1.1	-0.5	3.4	17.9	7.9	25.0	(e)15.9
Montserrat*	-0.2	1.1	-0.7	5.4	-1.0	-6.9	21.5	138.9	-66.0	-4.3	(e)65.2
Netherlands Antilles*(4)	-15.7	-5.0	-3.3	0.7	0.3	0.5	-7.9	21.4	16.7	14.3	..
Saint Kitts and Nevis*	2.7	3.9	5.0	8.9	8.1	8.6	2.2	-2.0	8.1	(e)0.8	(e)5.7
Saint Lucia*	9.8	1.3	-0.2	-10.2	-6.3	-3.8	9.9	28.4	-19.6	12.7	(e)10.5
Saint Vincent and the Grenadines*	16.2	2.4	0.3	-5.3	-4.6	-2.6	-4.2	-12.7	20.0	-18.3	(e)32.2
Trinidad and Tobago*	-9.4	-0.1	3.5	6.8	10.5	13.8	17.2	23.1	51.5	46.9	(e)-16.7
Turks and Caicos Islands	..	..	..	..	..	(e)10.9	12.8	24.0	20.5	19.7	-7.7
Central America	*4.9*	*10.4*	*10.4*	*15.9*	*12.2*	*8.8*	*5.3*	*13.8*	*12.9*	*16.6*	*9.1*
Belize	-0.6	3.6	3.8	6.9	5.1	3.8	1.9	3.9	-2.3	28.0	0.1
Costa Rica*	4.6	11.2	10.2	17.0	10.7	5.8	5.1	3.3	11.5	16.9	(e)13.7
El Salvador*	-4.3	7.0	8.0	19.7	13.4	7.0	3.5	5.9	2.7	(e)3.8	(e)11.0
Guatemala*	-2.2	4.5	4.8	10.2	7.1	4.1	5.4	11.7	18.3	5.4	(e)23.6
Honduras*	1.6	3.5	3.5	7.2	4.9	1.6	4.2	16.4	9.2	14.9	(e)11.4
Mexico	5.9	11.0	11.0	16.1	12.5	9.2	5.3	14.3	13.1	17.1	8.6
Nicaragua	-5.8	1.7	3.1	10.3	7.8	4.8	6.7	25.0	13.5	19.8	17.0
Panama*	–	–	–	(e)9.4	(e)6.8	(e)4.6	2.8	9.2	7.9	2.1	15.7
South America	*2.3*	*5.5*	*6.2*	*7.2*	*7.7*	*7.4*	*14.4*	*33.4*	*26.0*	*21.5*	*15.5*
Argentina*	2.1	7.6	7.5	10.1	7.9	4.8	9.2	16.9	16.7	15.4	19.5
Bolivia	-1.9	2.3	4.0	4.3	6.8	8.2	18.2	34.3	30.1	38.4	16.2
Brazil	5.1	5.4	6.2	5.9	7.5	8.5	17.2	32.3	22.6	16.3	16.6
Chile*	8.1	10.0	9.7	9.4	9.1	7.8	17.8	50.1	27.0	40.7	17.5
Colombia	7.7	8.1	7.6	7.4	6.6	5.6	10.0	24.0	30.3	15.3	(e)21.8
Ecuador*	-0.4	4.4	5.2	6.8	7.2	6.4	16.4	24.6	30.3	26.0	8.0
Guyana*	-3.3	4.7	4.3	8.7	4.7	0.2	3.2	15.5	-6.8	7.8	(e)14.3
Paraguay	11.6	7.7	7.1	1.7	4.2	5.0	15.7	31.0	4.4	12.3	77.0
Peru*	-1.5	4.2	5.9	9.0	9.9	9.7	19.6	38.8	31.5	43.3	16.5
Suriname	-0.4	1.2	2.2	3.2	4.5	5.2	18.2	40.3	6.2	29.9	..
Uruguay	4.5	5.5	4.7	5.2	3.4	1.6	9.6	32.9	16.2	16.1	(e)12.8
Venezuela (Bolivarian Rep. of)	-4.4	2.3	4.0	6.3	7.4	8.5	11.2	45.7	39.8	17.6	6.1
Developing economies: Asia	**4.6**	**9.0**	**9.3**	**9.5**	**9.7**	**9.4**	**15.0**	**28.3**	**21.4**	**19.3**	**16.3**
Eastern Asia	*14.9*	*13.1*	*12.3*	*10.0*	*10.2*	*9.9*	*16.4*	*28.0*	*19.7*	*20.1*	*18.4*
China	12.8	14.7	15.5	14.5	16.4	17.5	26.7	35.4	28.4	27.2	25.6
China, Hong Kong SAR	16.8	14.5	12.0	8.3	6.7	4.5	8.5	15.9	11.6	11.5	6.8
China, Macao SAR	11.7	7.2	5.9	3.9	3.2	2.6	1.6	9.0	-12.0	3.3	-0.6
China, Taiwan Province of	14.9	10.8	9.2	7.2	6.1	5.0	7.7	20.9	13.7	13.3	10.1
Dem. People's Rep. of Korea	..	(e)-9.2	(e)-2.1	-9.2	-2.1	3.8	13.9	19.9	4.7	36.8	..
Mongolia	5.0	-1.7	0.3	0.7	4.6	7.7	15.8	41.2	22.4	44.9	(e)20.4
Republic of Korea (5)	15.0	12.2	11.1	10.1	9.2	7.8	12.9	31.0	12.0	14.4	14.2
Southern Asia	*3.2*	*6.4*	*7.4*	*6.5*	*8.5*	*10.2*	*16.7*	*26.7*	*28.8*	*14.8*	*18.8*
Afghanistan	-10.5	-9.8	-6.8	-2.0	1.2	5.4	33.0	111.8	25.9	(e)17.7	..
Bangladesh	7.8	12.5	11.9	15.7	12.1	8.5	8.6	15.6	14.0	26.9	4.8
Bhutan	19.6	11.5	10.4	7.0	7.8	7.3	20.6	19.2	41.0	60.3	..
India (6)	7.3	9.4	10.0	9.5	10.9	11.4	19.2	30.0	30.0	21.3	20.3
Iran (Islamic Rep. of)*	-1.2	2.4	4.4	1.2	6.3	11.7	18.0	30.6	35.2	5.4	24.0
Maldives	28.3	13.9	12.0	4.4	6.7	8.3	10.9	19.1	-10.8	39.4	1.2
Nepal	8.1	10.8	9.9	10.7	8.5	8.6	1.1	14.3	9.7	-8.4	(e)20.7
Pakistan	8.1	7.9	7.4	4.3	5.4	5.9	12.7	12.1	20.0	5.5	(e)2.8
Sri Lanka	5.4	9.6	8.5	11.3	7.5	3.9	4.1	12.3	10.2	8.5	(e)11.2
South-Eastern Asia	*6.2*	*11.1*	*10.3*	*11.1*	*9.0*	*6.4*	*10.0*	*25.4*	*14.7*	*17.3*	*13.1*
Brunei Darussalam*	-9.3	-1.7	1.2	2.4	6.2	10.4	10.6	14.4	23.6	24.8	..
Cambodia	18.0	32.1	29.2	26.8	22.3	16.4	16.5	24.1	12.4	26.9	(e)10.1
Indonesia	-1.1	6.3	6.4	8.5	6.8	4.9	6.3	12.0	20.1	14.4	20.5
Lao People's dem. Rep.*	11.0	16.1	13.2	15.4	9.1	2.5	9.2	8.3	52.2	59.5	(e)29.1
Malaysia (7)	8.6	12.7	11.4	12.2	9.3	5.9	8.8	26.5	12.0	14.0	9.6
Myanmar	-7.6	7.4	10.6	14.4	16.4	17.8	12.1	-4.2	60.2	18.2	(e)44.0

For sources and notes, see end of table.

80-90	80-00	80-05	90-00	90-05	95-05	00-05	2004	2005	2006	2007	Régions, pays ou territoires
Imports (c.i.f.) - Importations (c.a.f.) En pourcentage												

80-90	80-00	80-05	90-00	90-05	95-05	00-05	2004	2005	2006	2007	Régions, pays ou territoires
-4.1	*0.2*	*1.7*	*7.1*	*6.4*	*6.0*	*4.8*	*13.1*	*21.7*	*16.2*	*8.4*	**Caraïbes**
..	..	..	..	..	(e)4.3	7.4	33.4	26.8	(e)34.5	(e)43.1	Anguilla
10.9	7.8	6.3	4.5	3.4	2.7	4.5	7.5	9.5	10.6	..	Antigua-et-Barbuda*
..	(e)18.8	(e)13.6	9.4	7.5	5.7	7.1	25.2	16.3	9.8	-25.7	Aruba (2)
-14.3	-8.0	-4.9	7.7	5.7	4.4	2.1	8.1	25.8	18.0	(e)1.2	Bahamas (3)
1.6	3.3	4.0	7.2	6.5	6.0	7.7	18.2	13.6	-1.1	7.8	Barbade
1.5	-4.8	-2.2	2.5	4.8	7.4	7.6	20.3	35.3	(e)25.2	(e)6.1	Cuba*
9.7	6.5	5.1	3.3	2.3	1.7	2.7	12.9	14.6	0.9	(e)18.0	Dominique*
5.4	9.5	8.5	12.0	7.9	5.0	-0.7	3.4	25.2	13.0	23.8	République dominicaine*
8.4	7.8	7.3	8.8	7.2	6.9	4.5	-1.1	14.9	-0.9	(e)33.0	Grenade*
-2.9	3.7	5.7	14.4	12.1	8.7	7.4	10.0	11.3	29.0	(e)-15.7	Haïti
2.8	5.8	5.7	6.9	5.9	3.9	5.5	3.7	18.2	19.1	(e)18.1	Jamaïque
14.6	3.9	2.4	-6.3	-3.1	-1.1	5.5	-11.0	3.6	15.3	(e)-0.6	Montserrat*
-14.6	-3.5	-1.1	1.8	3.2	4.8	3.8	17.0	13.2	13.3	..	Antilles néerlandaises*(4)
10.4	7.1	6.3	3.9	4.1	4.2	1.4	0.1	5.6	(e)17.7	(e)7.8	Saint-Kitts-et-Nevis*
9.0	6.6	5.8	2.3	3.2	4.6	9.7	14.0	19.8	9.1	(e)5.5	Sainte-Lucie*
9.7	6.1	5.4	3.9	3.9	4.6	8.6	12.2	6.6	2.7	(e)28.8	Saint-Vincent-et-les Grenadines*
-12.3	0.0	3.0	12.1	11.3	10.2	11.2	24.8	17.5	13.9	(e)10.0	Trinité-et-Tobago*
..	..	..	..	..	(e)11.4	13.9	30.6	37.7	63.9	16.6	Îles Turques et Caïques
5.1	*12.2*	*11.8*	*13.9*	*11.2*	*10.0*	*5.4*	*15.3*	*12.5*	*15.6*	*11.6*	**Amérique centrale**
4.0	6.3	6.9	5.9	7.2	10.0	2.0	-5.8	14.1	14.0	1.2	Belize
4.4	10.9	10.5	13.9	10.8	8.1	8.6	7.9	18.7	17.4	(e)10.1	Costa Rica*
2.4	9.9	10.0	14.0	11.1	7.9	7.1	10.0	8.0	11.6	(e)12.6	El Salvador*
0.6	7.6	8.6	11.6	11.0	10.6	11.2	16.2	12.8	15.3	(e)16.6	Guatemala*
0.6	6.2	7.4	13.8	11.6	9.4	10.1	19.6	17.8	17.4	(e)24.7	Honduras*
6.4	13.4	12.7	14.2	11.5	10.4	4.9	15.8	12.2	15.7	10.6	Mexique
-3.1	3.1	4.5	11.6	9.4	8.1	7.7	17.7	18.6	13.9	19.8	Nicaragua
–	–	–	8.7	5.4	3.0	4.9	16.5	16.3	15.6	42.2	Panama*
-1.7	*7.1*	*6.4*	*11.0*	*6.5*	*1.5*	*7.1*	*33.7*	*25.1*	*23.9*	*28.5*	**Amérique du Sud**
-6.5	10.3	7.5	17.0	5.6	-3.2	4.0	62.3	27.8	19.1	31.1	Argentine*
-0.3	6.8	6.0	9.7	5.8	2.1	4.0	14.1	27.0	20.4	22.2	Bolivie
-1.9	7.2	6.7	12.7	7.6	1.4	5.2	30.6	16.9	23.5	32.1	Brésil
2.8	9.9	9.0	10.3	7.6	3.9	12.2	28.3	32.0	17.3	22.3	Chili*
0.0	6.9	6.6	9.6	6.9	2.3	11.9	20.6	26.6	22.8	(e)26.9	Colombie
-1.3	5.0	6.6	7.9	9.6	8.4	20.1	22.7	25.0	17.8	(e)9.9	Équateur*
-3.3	5.2	4.7	7.9	4.6	1.6	3.7	13.1	20.8	10.6	(e)19.6	Guyana*
4.2	10.7	8.5	6.8	3.8	-1.3	12.0	39.1	19.9	63.9	(e)23.7	Paraguay
1.3	8.2	7.0	10.8	6.1	0.4	8.3	20.0	23.8	22.5	27.9	Pérou*
-3.1	1.5	2.1	0.9	2.5	3.5	13.9	5.5	23.4	5.4	..	Suriname
-1.2	7.9	5.9	10.1	3.8	-1.6	2.1	42.2	24.6	22.7	(e)17.2	Uruguay
-3.2	2.2	2.5	5.3	4.0	3.7	4.7	59.1	44.1	39.9	35.2	Venezuela (Rép. bolivarienne du)
6.5	*9.4*	*9.3*	*8.2*	*8.6*	*8.0*	*15.0*	*29.2*	*17.8*	*16.8*	*16.5*	**Économies en développement : Asie**
13.3	*12.7*	*11.9*	*9.3*	*9.7*	*9.3*	*15.8*	*28.8*	*14.6*	*16.8*	*15.9*	**Asie orientale**
13.5	13.0	14.3	13.0	16.1	18.5	26.5	36.0	17.6	19.9	20.7	Chine
15.0	14.4	12.0	8.8	6.8	3.8	8.1	16.9	10.5	11.7	9.9	Chine (RAS de Hong Kong)
10.4	7.5	7.0	2.2	4.5	6.6	12.0	26.3	12.5	16.7	17.5	Chine (RAS de Macao)
12.4	11.8	10.1	8.5	6.6	4.9	8.3	32.0	8.6	11.0	8.2	Province chinoise de Taiwan
..	(e)-7.0	(e)0.4	-7.0	0.4	8.0	9.3	11.2	19.3	12.2	..	Rép. populaire dém. de Corée
5.5	-4.2	-1.2	0.5	5.5	10.6	14.8	27.5	16.0	25.4	(e)33.6	Mongolie
11.9	11.1	10.2	7.1	7.5	6.3	12.1	25.5	16.4	18.4	15.3	République de Corée (5)
2.2	*4.8*	*6.2*	*5.2*	*8.2*	*10.8*	*20.6*	*30.6*	*33.5*	*19.7*	*14.9*	**Asie méridionale**
-0.1	-3.2	2.2	5.5	13.6	22.3	14.8	3.6	25.9	4.0	..	Afghanistan
3.6	7.2	7.6	11.3	9.5	6.9	9.9	15.4	15.3	16.6	14.6	Bangladesh
5.6	4.8	6.5	7.9	10.4	13.0	20.4	65.1	-6.0	8.6	..	Bhoutan
4.2	6.9	8.4	10.1	11.7	12.8	23.5	37.5	43.2	22.7	23.0	Inde (6)
-1.1	0.3	2.7	-4.8	3.6	12.3	22.6	21.0	16.4	13.9	-7.4	Iran (Rép. islamique d')*
15.4	15.1	13.5	11.8	10.3	8.7	15.0	36.3	16.1	24.4	18.3	Maldives
6.9	8.6	7.6	9.3	6.5	3.0	5.2	6.6	-0.6	12.9	(e)42.2	Népal
3.0	4.5	4.9	3.1	5.0	5.9	19.0	37.7	41.3	17.6	(e)4.8	Pakistan
2.7	7.8	7.3	8.9	6.7	4.4	7.9	19.5	10.8	16.1	(e)7.3	Sri Lanka
7.2	*10.9*	*9.7*	*8.0*	*6.8*	*4.2*	*10.4*	*25.1*	*19.8*	*14.9*	*13.1*	**Asie du Sud-Est**
3.8	6.9	4.6	1.6	-0.5	-5.0	5.7	7.2	4.9	18.0	..	Brunéi Darussalam*
-3.1	14.8	16.0	25.2	20.5	14.5	15.3	22.5	20.1	20.9	(e)13.8	Cambodge
2.6	6.9	6.6	3.6	4.6	3.8	11.9	27.8	37.3	9.1	22.9	Indonésie
6.6	10.3	8.5	12.7	7.0	0.4	10.6	54.2	23.7	20.1	(e)-4.7	Rép. dém. populaire lao*
7.7	12.9	11.2	9.5	7.3	3.7	8.2	28.5	8.7	14.6	12.0	Malaisie (7)
-4.7	12.9	11.8	22.6	12.5	3.4	-5.6	5.1	-12.3	9.4	(e)45.6	Myanmar

Pour les sources et les notes, se reporter à la fin du tableau.

Region, country or territory	Exports (f.o.b) - Exportations (f.a.b.) Percentage										
	80-90	80-00	80-05	90-00	90-05	95-05	00-05	2004	2005	2006	2007
Philippines	3.9	11.4	11.0	18.8	12.6	7.8	1.7	9.5	0.5	18.9	(e)7.1
Singapore (8)	9.9	12.2	10.8	9.9	8.2	5.5	12.6	37.8	15.6	18.4	10.1
Thailand*	14.0	15.2	13.3	10.5	9.0	6.7	11.1	19.8	14.5	18.7	17.0
Timor-Leste	..	..	..	..	..	..	(e)21.0	0.0	12.5	-11.1	..
Viet Nam	18.9	21.0	20.5	22.7	20.3	17.6	18.5	31.4	22.5	22.1	22.2
Western Asia	***-6.8***	***1.9***	***4.7***	***6.4***	***9.6***	***12.7***	***17.9***	***34.5***	***34.3***	***21.4***	***13.0***
Bahrain	-3.3	2.0	3.6	3.5	6.1	8.6	10.6	14.1	34.5	20.1	11.8
Iraq*	-3.5	-8.6	0.0	31.1	30.0	39.3	2.3	90.4	28.2	28.8	(e)10.7
Jordan	6.2	6.5	7.5	6.6	9.0	9.7	18.0	27.3	9.7	20.3	10.2
Kuwait*	-7.7	-0.1	3.2	16.5	14.2	10.8	19.4	39.0	56.7	27.2	8.7
Lebanon	-5.2	-0.3	3.7	4.1	10.8	15.2	27.1	21.3	6.3	20.4	0.1
Oman	3.3	6.7	7.7	5.7	8.2	10.6	9.3	14.3	40.1	15.5	(e)2.5
Qatar*	-8.1	1.9	6.2	10.1	14.9	22.2	18.6	37.7	37.5	34.4	(e)11.4
Saudi Arabia*	-12.7	-0.1	3.0	3.1	7.6	11.7	19.8	35.1	43.3	19.3	7.0
Syrian Arab Republic*	2.4	4.8	5.6	0.9	4.5	6.9	4.7	-6.1	19.8	69.3	(e)8.2
Turkey*	14.0	10.8	11.0	9.2	11.0	11.8	22.4	32.4	16.6	13.9	30.4
United Arab Emirates	-2.3	5.1	7.2	6.5	10.2	13.9	20.1	35.5	28.9	21.5	(e)17.3
Yemen*	–	–	–	20.6	17.1	11.2	10.0	18.8	37.2	14.1	(e)10.7
Developing economies: Oceania	**4.5**	**5.2**	**4.4**	**3.4**	**2.6**	**1.4**	**9.8**	**14.5**	**14.4**	**21.1**	**16.6**
American Samoa*	8.9	4.3	3.6	1.4	1.8	2.8	4.6	-3.0	-16.1	15.5	..
Cook Islands	1.3	-0.1	2.0	-0.9	4.2	9.5	-2.9	-7.0	-34.1	-32.6	(e)199.7
Fiji	2.1	4.5	4.1	5.5	3.9	1.0	7.0	2.9	1.1	-3.1	(e)14.9
French Polynesia*	15.7	14.0	9.7	9.6	2.9	-2.8	-2.3	22.4	13.5	12.0	-23.5
Guam	-1.8	3.8	1.3	-0.5	-3.9	-6.4	-6.5	21.9	-1.8	2.2	72.4
Kiribati	0.0	2.8	0.6	6.5	-1.0	-8.3	-5.6	-14.8	44.2	77.2	..
Marshall Islands	..	(e)12.5	(e)12.5	4.1	(e)4.1	(e)-21.2	..	..	..	..	..
Micronesia (Federated States of)	..	(e)4.5	(e)4.8	-8.1	-1.0	2.9	-5.2	-23.1	-7.3	(e)-5.3	..
Nauru	-2.3	-6.3	(e)-8.0	-5.3	(e)-9.2	(e)-10.9	(e)-9.5	(e)-6.7	(e)-14.3	(e)25.0	..
New Caledonia*	5.5	4.1	4.7	1.7	4.8	7.9	18.3	30.2	5.7	23.9	52.2
Niue	..	..	..	..	(e)-2.4	(e)-2.4	(e)-11.9	63.6	..	..	..
Palau	..	..	..	(e)-8.9	(e)-2.2	(e)-1.0	(e)-7.1	5.3	(e)44.6	(e)29.7	..
Papua New Guinea	4.9	6.1	4.9	3.7	2.6	0.9	10.7	15.6	28.3	27.3	(e)9.2
Samoa*	-3.3	-1.6	-0.3	12.0	6.5	1.2	-5.3	-28.5	11.1	-10.5	45.0
Solomon Islands*	0.9	4.1	1.5	2.3	-2.4	-7.9	13.8	31.1	8.2	15.9	(e)8.7
Tokelau	..	..	..	..	..	..	..	..	..	..	..
Tonga	2.7	3.3	2.8	-3.8	-0.7	1.7	10.1	-15.3	-33.0	9.6	(e)-35.1
Tuvalu	(e)14.1	(e)-4.2	(e)-6.7	-38.2	-23.5	-1.4	53.7	41.1	-54.5	(e)9.8	..
Vanuatu	-6.3	-0.1	0.3	4.8	2.8	0.4	13.0	39.3	2.6	18.3	..
Wallis and Futuna Islands	..	..	..	..	..	..	(e)-20.0	-74.6	(e)-19.1	(e)-5.3	..
Economies in transition: Asia	**–**	**–**	**–**	**–**	**–**	**11.8**	**21.8**	**40.2**	**29.9**	**37.3**	**16.6**
Armenia*	–	–	–	–	–	14.8	27.0	4.3	32.9	5.6	21.4
Azerbaijan*(9)	–	–	–	–	–	24.0	19.0	39.6	20.2	46.6	(e)-14.4
Georgia (10)	–	–	–	–	–	16.6	23.4	40.2	34.0	14.6	24.9
Kazakhstan*(10)	–	–	–	–	–	16.6	27.8	55.4	38.6	45.3	(e)16.0
Kyrgyzstan	–	–	–	–	–	3.4	8.5	23.6	-6.5	18.4	42.6
Tajikistan (10)	–	–	–	–	–	2.4	5.8	14.8	-0.7	53.9	(e)4.6
Turkmenistan (10)	–	–	–	–	–	9.1	14.4	6.6	27.5	17.0	31.1
Uzbekistan (10)	–	–	–	–	–	0.1	12.8	34.2	11.0	13.0	(e)40.0
Economies in transition: Europe	**–**	**–**	**–**	**–**	**–**	**9.9**	**19.3**	**35.9**	**27.0**	**23.4**	**19.1**
Albania	..	(e)1.8	(e)7.4	8.3	11.7	14.1	22.1	35.1	8.7	21.2	30.8
Belarus	–	–	–	–	–	10.5	18.6	38.5	16.0	23.5	23.3
Bosnia and Herzegovina*(11)	–	–	–	–	–	49.0	17.0	33.6	28.7	48.8	21.1
Croatia*	–	–	–	–	–	6.6	16.3	29.7	9.3	18.3	19.1
Moldova	–	–	–	–	–	2.3	18.8	24.2	11.3	-2.9	26.6
Russian Federation (12)	–	–	–	–	–	10.0	19.2	34.8	33.1	24.7	17.0
Serbia and Montenegro*	–	–	–	–	–	9.2	26.1	61.1	12.9	43.9	(e)37.4
SFR of Yugoslavia (former)	3.8	–	–	–	–	–	–	–	–	–	–
TFYR of Macedonia	–	–	–	–	–	3.8	10.5	22.6	21.8	17.5	37.7
Ukraine (10)	–	–	–	–	–	10.1	20.8	41.6	4.8	12.1	28.4
USSR (former)	3.7	–	–	–	–	–	–	–	–	–	–
Developed economies: America	**6.0**	**7.5**	**6.7**	**7.5**	**5.6**	**3.8**	**3.9**	**12.6**	**12.8**	**12.7**	**10.6**
Bermuda	6.8	3.9	3.0	-0.7	0.3	-0.1	5.9	21.7	-32.9	-49.0	..
Canada	6.8	7.2	6.8	8.3	6.9	5.5	5.5	11.6	18.0	8.4	6.9
Greenland	10.5	2.7	2.5	-3.6	0.1	2.5	12.1	26.5	-15.4	0.1	..
Saint Pierre and Miquelon	(e)46.2	(e)7.9	(e)5.6	-14.9	(e)-5.0	(e)4.6	(e)13.4	(e)16.7	(e)57.1	(e)81.8	..
United States*	5.7	7.6	6.7	7.2	5.2	3.2	3.3	12.9	10.8	14.5	12.0

For sources and notes, see end of table.

1.2.1 Taux d'évolution annuels moyens des exportations et importations des pays et des régions géographiques

Imports (c.i.f.) - Importations (c.a.f.) En pourcentage											Régions, pays ou territoires
80-90	80-00	80-05	90-00	90-05	95-05	00-05	2004	2005	2006	2007	
2.9	10.5	9.6	12.5	8.5	3.6	5.4	7.2	10.9	15.2	(e)4.2	Philippines
8.0	10.6	9.1	7.8	5.9	3.1	9.3	28.1	22.1	19.3	10.2	Singapour (8)
12.7	12.9	11.3	5.0	6.0	4.9	14.2	24.5	25.2	8.9	9.4	Thaïlande*
..	..	..	..	..	(e)-11.8	-11.8	-16.0	-16.0	2.9	..	Timor-Leste
8.7	13.6	14.8	22.7	19.8	15.1	20.8	26.6	15.7	21.4	35.4	Viet Nam
-2.6	**3.2**	**4.9**	**6.8**	**8.3**	**9.6**	**17.3**	**37.9**	**18.8**	**17.9**	**25.8**	**Asie occidentale**
-2.3	1.2	2.7	0.3	4.0	7.7	15.1	16.4	41.9	12.6	9.2	Bahreïn
-6.8	-9.7	-1.0	27.4	28.3	34.7	12.3	100.9	17.9	-11.2	(e)10.5	Iraq*
-1.9	2.4	4.1	5.1	7.5	9.1	18.0	41.5	29.3	9.0	18.2	Jordanie
-4.1	0.9	2.4	5.5	6.4	6.2	19.0	15.0	38.5	-8.6	21.2	Koweït*
-5.5	5.5	5.6	8.7	6.3	2.1	9.2	31.4	0.2	0.1	22.5	Liban
0.7	5.1	5.8	6.1	6.8	7.0	12.6	34.9	-0.4	23.7	(e)33.5	Oman
-1.4	5.2	6.9	7.4	9.8	9.8	23.0	22.6	67.6	63.4	33.8	Qatar*
-6.1	-0.5	1.1	0.8	3.6	6.2	14.1	21.2	32.9	17.4	27.7	Arabie saoudite*
-8.4	0.4	1.9	3.6	4.7	4.5	15.6	37.9	12.0	45.5	(e)12.0	République arabe syrienne*
9.3	10.7	10.4	10.3	9.9	8.9	18.0	46.8	2.7	34.9	26.2	Turquie*
1.0	8.8	10.2	10.7	12.4	14.4	22.0	38.4	26.5	7.4	(e)31.3	Émirats arabes unis
..	..	..	0.6	4.8	10.1	15.7	5.0	22.1	29.8	(e)11.0	Yémen*
4.0	**3.7**	**3.8**	**1.0**	**2.9**	**4.0**	**11.4**	**9.8**	**8.1**	**8.7**	**11.6**	**Économies en développement : Océanie**
10.7	5.9	4.8	3.0	2.6	2.4	2.0	-3.2	-16.0	-32.6	..	Samoa américaines*
9.0	4.9	4.7	-3.8	1.2	7.0	14.8	19.7	3.8	28.3	(e)59.0	Îles Cook
0.3	3.8	4.4	3.0	4.6	5.2	15.1	19.5	11.2	12.1	(e)0.9	Fidji
6.2	3.9	4.3	1.6	4.0	5.7	10.5	-5.6	15.0	-9.1	10.5	Polynésie française*
2.5	3.5	3.9	-0.8	2.4	3.9	3.7	-4.3	5.8	-5.9	37.2	Guam
5.5	6.1	6.4	4.1	5.9	7.1	13.6	15.2	28.7	-17.0	..	Kiribati
..	(e)3.8	(e)3.8	0.9	(e)2.5	(e)3.2	(e)15.3	11.4	(e)43.1	(e)15.0	..	Îles Marshall
..	(e)-1.7	(e)2.0	(e)-4.6	(e)1.5	(e)6.6	4.6	12.5	-1.9	6.0	..	Micronésie (États fédérés de)
4.3	2.6	(e)1.2	-11.0	(e)-6.4	(e)-1.5	(e)-10.2	(e)-25.8	(e)-9.1	(e)20.0	..	Nauru
8.8	6.2	6.1	1.1	4.0	6.3	16.7	7.1	8.6	18.3	32.5	Nouvelle-Calédonie*
..	..	..	..	(e)7.6	(e)7.6	(e)36.7	269.0	(e)-8.9	(e)0.2	..	Nioué
..	..	..	(e)17.0	(e)10.1	9.2	4.6	67.8	4.8	(e)17.5	..	Palaos
0.7	1.2	1.0	-0.8	0.1	0.0	10.5	22.9	2.9	27.8	..	Papouasie-Nouvelle-Guinée
3.8	4.5	5.4	1.7	5.6	9.2	17.0	38.5	13.9	15.1	-3.5	Samoa*
1.9	3.1	1.8	0.7	-0.5	-2.7	14.9	30.1	51.6	17.2	(e)28.3	Îles Salomon*
..	..	..	..	..	(e)-27.8	(e)-38.9	-45.5	..	..	..	Tokélaou
4.7	4.0	4.2	1.9	3.7	4.5	11.8	11.9	14.6	8.3	(e)2.3	Tonga
(e)2.0	(e)4.8	(e)5.2	5.2	5.9	8.0	27.3	-26.9	13.3	-0.4	-57.4	Tuvalu
2.4	2.5	2.7	0.9	2.4	3.3	11.9	21.0	16.7	6.8	..	Vanuatu
..	..	..	..	..	..	(e)18.6	47.7	(e)-2.8	(e)-0.8	..	Îles Wallis-et-Futuna
–	–	–	–	–	**10.4**	**21.7**	**40.1**	**26.0**	**33.4**	**29.0**	**Économies en transition : Asie**
–	–	–	–	–	7.5	15.5	5.6	30.9	24.1	49.6	Arménie*
–	–	–	–	–	19.2	32.0	33.9	23.7	21.1	(e)13.1	Azerbaïdjan*(9)
–	–	–	–	–	13.4	30.6	61.9	34.8	47.8	41.7	Géorgie (10)
–	–	–	–	–	15.1	27.4	52.0	35.8	43.8	(e)31.3	Kazakhstan*(10)
–	–	–	–	–	3.0	17.9	31.2	17.7	66.8	30.8	Kirghizistan
–	–	–	–	–	5.0	16.1	35.2	11.7	29.7	(e)40.0	Tadjikistan (10)
–	–	–	–	–	18.5	15.0	32.2	9.6	11.5	11.4	Turkménistan (10)
–	–	–	–	–	-2.0	6.5	27.4	8.1	6.8	(e)24.8	Ouzbekistan (10)
–	–	–	–	–	**6.8**	**21.7**	**28.5**	**21.6**	**27.5**	**33.7**	**Économies en transition : Europe**
..	(e)10.2	(e)12.0	9.6	12.2	14.2	19.6	23.9	13.4	16.8	32.9	Albanie
–	–	–	–	–	9.7	17.3	42.7	1.3	33.6	28.5	Bélarus
–	–	–	–	–	18.0	15.4	18.5	14.0	-0.2	28.6	Bosnie-Herzégovine*(11)
–	–	–	–	–	9.2	19.9	16.8	11.9	15.9	20.1	Croatie*
–	–	–	–	–	7.6	24.9	26.4	29.3	18.2	36.2	Moldova
–	–	–	–	–	5.1	22.7	28.0	28.8	31.3	35.4	Fédération de Russie (12)
–	–	–	–	–	13.8	28.4	51.1	-1.4	27.0	(e)38.7	Serbie-et-Monténégro*
0.8	–	–	–	–	–	–	–	–	–	–	RSF ce Yougoslavie (anc.)
–	–	–	–	–	5.9	12.0	27.1	10.1	16.2	38.0	LERY de Macédoine
–	–	–	–	–	7.2	21.7	26.0	24.6	24.6	34.7	Ukraine (10)
5.7	–	–	–	–	–	–	–	–	–	–	URSS (anc.)
8.1	**7.9**	**7.8**	**9.1**	**8.1**	**7.4**	**7.1**	**16.6**	**14.3**	**10.3**	**5.6**	**Économies développées : Amérique**
4.7	3.3	3.7	2.7	4.1	6.0	7.8	18.6	-0.3	11.1	..	Bermudes
7.9	7.3	6.8	7.5	6.4	5.7	6.5	14.2	18.4	7.9	8.2	Canada
5.9	1.8	1.8	-1.0	1.2	2.8	13.6	30.7	-0.9	-2.4	..	Groenland
36.8	13.6	(e)8.9	-1.5	(e)-1.4	(e)-1.2	(e)-0.1	(e)0.7	(e)-9.5	(e)-5.3	..	Saint-Pierre-et-Miquelon
8.2	8.1	8.0	9.5	8.4	7.8	7.2	17.1	13.5	10.8	5.1	États-Unis*

Pour les sources et les notes, se reporter à la fin du tableau.

1.2.1 Annual average growth rates of exports and imports of countries and geographical regions

Region, country or territory	Exports (f.o.b) - Exportations (f.a.b.) Percentage										
	80-90	80-00	80-05	90-00	90-05	95-05	00-05	2004	2005	2006	2007
Developed economies: Asia	**8.9**	**7.1**	**6.1**	**4.4**	**3.9**	**3.2**	**6.6**	**20.0**	**5.5**	**9.3**	**9.6**
Israel*	8.3	9.8	9.4	11.1	9.3	7.7	7.3	21.5	10.8	9.4	15.6
Japan	8.9	7.0	5.9	4.1	3.6	3.0	6.5	19.9	5.2	9.2	9.2
Developed economies: Europe	**7.4**	**7.1**	**6.9**	**5.6**	**6.2**	**6.0**	**12.0**	**19.4**	**8.5**	**12.9**	**15.1**
Andorra	..	..	(e)9.6	(e)2.6	(e)9.6	11.6	22.0	36.7	16.2	(e)27.1	..
Austria*	10.2	8.9	8.8	6.1	7.6	8.2	14.8	21.8	6.0	9.0	18.4
Belgium*	–					–	–	20.0	9.2	9.5	16.7
Belgium-Luxembourg*	7.8	8.1	–	6.1	–	–	–	–	–	–	–
Bulgaria*	-0.2	-6.7	-3.3	2.2	5.9	7.0	21.2	31.7	18.2	28.6	21.4
Cyprus*	4.7	4.9	3.5	1.1	0.1	-1.9	6.4	13.4	55.6	-9.5	4.4
Czechoslovakia (former) (13)	0.1	–	–	–	–					–	–
Czech Republic*(14)	–	–	–	–	–	13.9	23.4	41.6	13.4	21.3	28.2
Denmark*(15)	9.0	7.5	7.0	3.7	4.8	5.1	11.7	15.9	10.6	8.6	11.1
Estonia*(10)	–	–	–	–	–	13.7	15.1	5.5	29.8	26.2	12.1
Faeroe Islands	10.8	6.0	5.6	1.6	3.6	5.6	5.2	3.5	-3.0	4.9	15.8
Finland	7.4	7.4	7.0	8.0	6.8	4.5	9.0	15.7	7.5	16.5	15.7
France*	7.5	7.4	6.7	5.0	4.9	4.2	8.7	15.3	2.7	6.8	10.9
Germany*	–	–	–	3.9	5.5	6.3	13.5	21.1	6.9	13.9	19.0
Greece*	5.8	6.0	5.4	3.8	3.9	3.5	9.1	14.4	12.6	20.4	13.0
Hungary*(16)	1.6	5.4	8.0	12.7	14.3	16.2	18.9	30.6	13.5	19.4	24.9
Iceland*	7.9	5.4	5.2	3.1	4.3	5.3	10.1	21.4	1.7	17.3	(e)24.0
Ireland*	12.8	13.2	12.5	13.8	11.7	9.5	7.4	13.0	4.8	-1.0	10.9
Italy*	8.7	7.7	6.9	4.6	4.9	4.1	10.4	18.2	5.7	11.5	17.2
Latvia*	–	–	–	–	–	12.8	23.6	38.4	29.1	19.0	34.1
Lithuania (10)	–	–	–	–	–	13.9	28.0	33.4	27.1	19.5	20.6
Luxembourg*	–	–	–	–	–	–	–	22.2	15.9	21.6	-2.7
Malta	9.2	10.6	8.9	6.3	4.9	3.6	1.4	0.8	-8.3	16.7	9.0
Netherlands*	4.6	6.7	6.9	7.0	7.3	6.6	13.0	20.7	13.9	13.9	18.1
Norway	5.3	6.4	6.9	5.2	7.0	8.0	11.3	21.1	24.7	18.2	14.5
Poland*	1.4	5.2	7.6	9.9	12.7	14.2	24.5	40.1	19.4	23.6	24.5
Portugal*	15.1	11.1	9.5	5.3	5.4	4.6	10.9	12.7	6.8	13.4	17.6
Romania*	-4.0	-2.7	1.3	8.5	11.9	13.6	23.3	33.3	18.1	16.6	23.8
Slovakia*	–	–	–	–	–	14.5	24.7	25.8	16.1	30.4	38.1
Slovenia*	–	–	–	–	–	8.1	18.3	28.1	17.9	20.5	28.6
Spain*	10.8	11.0	10.2	8.4	8.1	6.7	12.5	16.9	5.7	10.7	12.1
Sweden	8.0	6.8	6.3	6.0	5.4	4.0	11.2	20.7	5.9	13.2	13.7
Switzerland*	9.5	7.1	6.6	3.1	4.4	5.0	11.2	17.2	6.4	12.9	15.5
United Kingdom*	5.9	6.6	6.0	5.5	4.7	3.6	6.8	13.7	10.8	16.5	-3.0
Developed economies: Oceania	**6.5**	**6.5**	**6.3**	**4.8**	**5.3**	**5.1**	**10.8**	**21.2**	**19.5**	**14.2**	**15.3**
Australia*	6.6	6.7	6.4	5.0	5.5	5.3	10.7	20.8	22.5	16.5	14.4
New Zealand	6.2	5.8	5.6	3.9	4.7	4.3	11.4	23.1	6.8	3.2	20.1

Sources:
- Data in this table are based on trade figures in table 1.1.1.

Notes:

* Countries which use the Special Trade System as reporting system.

(a) Data refers to South Africa Customs Union (Botswana, Lesotho, Namibia, South Africa and Swaziland)
(b) Including Aruba

(1) Trade with other member countries of CEMAC is excluded.
(2) Prior to 1986, included in Netherlands Antilles. Including exports and imports of crude oil and oil products.
(3) From 1990 onwards, trade statistics exclude certain oil and chemical products.
(4) Prior to 1986, including Aruba.
(5) Excluding imports of goods financed through foreign aid.
(6) Excluding military goods, fissionable materials, bunkers, ships and aircraft.
(7) Inter-trade between the States of Malaysia included. From 1965 onwards, excluding military imports and offshore installations of petroleum industry.
(8) Including trans-shipments to and from peninsular Malaysia.
(9) Excluding military goods, precious metals and goods procured in foreign ports.
(10) Prior to 1994, covers only trade with countries outside the CIS.
(11) Prior to 1998, data refer to the Federation of Bosnia and Herzegovina only. The other entity of Bosnia and Herzegovina, Republika Srpska, is not included.
(12) Prior to 1994, excluding trade with independent states resulting from the former USSR.
(13) From 1985 onwards, data are not comparable to those shown for prior periods due to revisions of the koruna-to-US dollar exchange rate.
(14) From 1995 onward, including goods for processing.
(15) Prior to 1988, excluding ships.
(16) Prior to 1996, excluding customs free zones.

Imports (c.i.f.) - Importations (c.a.f) En pourcentage											Régions, pays ou territoires
80-90	80-00	80-05	90-00	90-05	95-05	00-05	2004	2005	2006	2007	
5.1	**6.2**	**5.8**	**4.8**	**4.7**	**3.8**	**7.3**	**18.6**	**13.0**	**12.1**	**7.4**	**Économies développées : Asie**
5.9	7.7	7.2	7.7	6.4	4.2	7.8	18.1	10.0	6.8	12.5	Israël*
5.1	6.1	5.7	4.6	4.6	3.7	7.2	18.7	13.3	12.6	7.0	Japon
6.6	**6.6**	**6.6**	**5.0**	**6.0**	**6.3**	**11.8**	**20.1**	**10.2**	**14.3**	**14.8**	**Économies développées : Europe**
..	..	(e)6.1	(e)4.5	(e)6.1	6.1	9.1	16.2	2.3	(e)6.9	..	Andorre
8.7	8.0	7.6	4.5	5.9	6.6	13.7	20.4	6.4	7.6	17.6	Autriche*
–	–	–	–	–	–	–	21.6	11.8	10.2	16.6	Belgique*
6.4	7.2	–	5.4	–	–	–	–	–	–	–	Belgique-Luxembourg*
-0.3	-5.6	-1.6	5.3	9.4	11.8	23.9	32.7	25.5	28.1	28.0	Bulgarie*
7.6	7.6	6.9	4.3	4.7	4.3	10.9	28.2	15.2	9.5	23.6	Chypre*
1.7	–	–	–	–	–	–	–	–	–	–	Tchécoslovaquie (anc.) (13)
–	–	–	–	–	11.1	19.1	30.0	9.6	21.6	25.7	République tchèque*(14)
6.8	6.2	5.9	4.2	4.9	4.7	11.8	18.7	11.1	12.9	15.8	Danemark*(15)
–	–	–	–	–	13.5	21.1	28.5	22.8	31.4	12.3	Estonie*(10)
8.0	3.0	4.1	5.5	7.0	8.8	8.2	-15.0	18.8	4.9	23.1	Îles Féroé
6.9	5.3	5.5	5.1	6.0	6.0	13.0	21.0	14.9	16.5	17.6	Finlande
6.6	6.3	6.1	3.9	4.8	5.3	9.8	18.1	7.2	7.3	12.8	France*
–	–	–	3.5	4.5	5.0	10.9	18.4	8.8	16.5	16.0	Allemagne*
6.6	7.5	7.4	5.2	6.3	7.4	12.9	17.6	2.7	17.4	18.0	Grèce*
0.1	6.5	8.6	13.5	14.1	15.2	17.6	27.1	10.1	17.4	20.7	Hongrie*(16)
6.6	5.5	5.6	5.5	6.1	7.3	13.4	27.4	28.3	35.0	(e)-2.4	Islande*
7.0	9.4	9.1	10.7	8.9	7.2	6.2	14.7	11.1	6.5	11.7	Irlande*
6.9	5.8	5.8	3.2	4.9	6.2	11.5	19.4	8.5	14.8	13.3	Italie*
–	–	–	–	–	14.5	23.5	35.2	22.9	32.5	31.4	Lettonie*
–	–	–	–	–	13.2	25.2	28.1	25.8	24.4	24.1	Lituanie (10)
–	–	–	–	–	–	–	24.0	9.4	21.1	2.6	Luxembourg*
8.1	8.7	7.3	4.4	3.6	2.8	4.0	7.9	-1.8	10.5	8.8	Malte
4.4	6.4	6.6	6.7	6.8	6.2	12.2	20.8	14.0	14.4	17.2	Pays-Bas*
6.2	5.2	4.9	4.2	4.2	3.6	10.8	21.8	13.9	15.6	25.9	Norvège
-3.2	8.1	9.6	18.3	15.0	11.2	17.4	31.8	13.5	24.7	27.3	Pologne*
10.3	9.8	8.7	5.3	5.5	5.5	9.8	16.4	11.6	8.8	15.9	Portugal*
-3.8	-0.7	3.1	6.8	11.5	14.1	26.3	36.1	23.9	26.3	35.8	Roumanie*
–	–	–	–	–	13.2	22.6	25.1	19.3	26.4	33.5	Slovaquie*
–	–	–	–	–	7.2	16.7	28.2	14.7	18.5	29.8	Slovénie*
10.6	9.7	9.5	6.0	8.0	9.5	14.9	23.8	12.0	13.6	12.6	Espagne*
6.7	5.5	5.3	4.5	4.8	4.6	11.3	20.2	11.2	14.2	17.9	Suède
8.8	6.1	5.6	2.6	3.9	4.6	9.5	15.6	9.1	11.7	13.1	Suisse*
8.5	7.1	6.8	5.6	5.9	5.9	9.1	17.8	9.3	16.8	2.4	Royaume-Uni*
6.2	**6.5**	**6.5**	**6.2**	**6.5**	**6.2**	**14.3**	**23.2**	**14.3**	**5.6**	**22.6**	**Économies développées : Océanie**
6.4	6.7	6.6	6.4	6.5	6.3	14.1	22.8	14.5	6.7	23.7	Australie*
5.4	5.9	6.0	5.6	6.2	5.6	15.5	25.0	13.1	0.7	16.9	Nouvelle-Zélande

Sources :
- Les données dans ce tableau ont été calculées d'après les chiffres du tableau 1.1.1.

Notes :

* Pays qui utilisent le système du commerce spécial en tant que système d'enregistrement.

(a) Donnée relative à l'Union Douanière d'Afrique du Sud (Afrique du Sud, Botswana, Lesotho, Namibie et Swaziland)
(b) Y compris Aruba

(1) Non-compris le commerce avec les autres pays membres de la CEMAC.
(2) Avant 1986 compris dans Antilles néerlandaises. Les données comprennent les exportations et importations de pétrole brut et produits dérivés.
(3) À partir de 1990, certains produits pétroliers et chimiques ne sont plus inclus dans les statistiques du commerce.
(4) Avant 1986, y compris Aruba.
(5) Non-compris les biens d'importation financés par l'aide à l'étranger.
(6) Non-compris les biens à usage militaire, le matériel fissile, le combustible de soute et l'avitaillement des navires et aéronefs.
(7) Y compris le commerce entre les États de la Malaisie. À partir de 1965, non comprises les importations militaires et l'installation près des côtes de l'industrie pétrolière.
(8) Y compris les transbordements vers et en provenance de la Malaisie péninsulaire.
(9) Non-compris les biens à usage militaire, les métaux précieux et les biens fournis dans les ports étrangers.
(10) Avant 1994, concerne seulement le commerce avec les pays extérieurs à la CEI.
(11) Avant 1998, les données se réfèrent uniquement à la Fédération de la Bosnie-Herzégovine. L'autre entité de la Bosnie-Herzégovine, Republika Srpska, n'est pas incluse.
(12) Avant 1994, non-compris le commerce avec les républiques indépendantes de l'ancienne URSS.
(13) À partir de 1985, les chiffres ne sont pas comparables à ceux des années antérieures à cause des révisions du taux de change de la couronne par rapport au dollar des États-Unis.
(14) À partir de 1995, y compris les biens destinés à subir des transformations.
(15) Avant 1988, non-compris les navires.
(16) Avant 1996, non-compris les zones franches douanières.

1.2.2 Annual average growth rates of exports and imports of economic groupings

Economic grouping	Exports (f.o.b.) - Exportations (f.a.b.) Percentage										
	80-90	80-00	80-05	90-00	90-05	95-05	00-05	2004	2005	2006	2007
DEVELOPING ECONOMIES	**3.1**	**7.7**	**8.2**	**9.1**	**9.3**	**9.1**	**14.2**	**27.6**	**21.9**	**19.3**	**15.2**
Developing economies excluding China	2.6	7.1	7.5	8.5	8.3	7.7	11.9	25.9	20.4	17.3	12.3
Developing economies excluding LDCs	3.1	7.7	8.3	9.1	9.3	9.0	14.1	27.6	21.6	19.2	15.0
High-income developing countries	2.8	7.8	7.9	8.8	8.3	7.4	11.4	26.1	19.9	17.5	10.2
Middle-income developing countries	3.9	6.7	7.1	7.5	7.9	7.8	13.4	26.2	19.3	16.0	16.5
Low-income developing countries	3.1	8.4	9.8	11.4	12.7	13.5	19.7	31.1	26.8	24.1	21.5
Heavily indebted poor countries	0.9	2.4	3.6	3.9	5.9	6.9	15.3	27.6	17.5	22.6	13.6
Landlocked developing countries	1.3	9.8	10.5	15.6	13.3	10.2	18.8	37.6	24.8	31.2	17.1
Small island developing States	-5.2	-0.3	1.4	4.5	5.3	5.8	10.8	15.9	30.2	32.5	-6.9
Least developed countries	*2.2*	*4.7*	*6.5*	*7.3*	*9.9*	*11.7*	*18.1*	*31.6*	*36.0*	*25.2*	*21.2*
Africa and Haiti	2.6	3.0	5.1	3.9	8.4	12.3	22.7	41.3	41.1	26.6	24.2
Asia	0.3	9.1	10.2	16.2	13.8	10.8	10.2	15.2	26.0	21.9	13.8
Islands	3.0	3.9	3.4	2.7	2.2	0.7	10.6	15.0	-3.9	24.9	4.2
Major petroleum exporters	*-6.8*	*1.1*	*3.8*	*4.8*	*8.5*	*12.3*	*16.9*	*35.5*	*40.3*	*20.8*	*9.6*
Africa	-5.4	0.5	3.3	2.6	7.6	12.8	18.6	38.1	48.7	20.7	6.5
America	-4.5	2.3	4.1	6.4	7.7	8.7	12.6	39.3	39.8	22.5	2.8
Asia	-7.6	1.2	4.0	5.2	8.9	12.7	17.1	34.2	37.7	20.6	11.7
Major exporters of manufactured goods	*11.5*	*12.1*	*11.4*	*10.7*	*10.1*	*9.0*	*14.1*	*27.1*	*18.2*	*19.0*	*16.5*
America	5.5	8.8	9.1	12.5	10.7	9.0	8.7	19.8	16.3	16.8	11.5
Asia	13.0	12.8	11.9	10.4	10.0	9.0	15.0	28.2	18.4	19.3	17.2
Emerging economies	*10.0*	*10.9*	*10.1*	*10.3*	*8.8*	*6.9*	*10.5*	*26.4*	*14.8*	*16.9*	*12.4*
America	4.9	8.5	8.8	11.8	10.2	8.4	9.8	22.3	17.8	20.0	13.1
Asia	12.9	12.2	10.8	9.7	8.2	6.2	10.9	28.2	13.5	15.6	12.0
Newly industrialized economies	*11.5*	*11.9*	*10.6*	*9.5*	*7.9*	*5.8*	*9.7*	*23.7*	*13.1*	*14.7*	*11.4*
First tier	14.4	12.5	10.9	8.8	7.5	5.7	10.4	25.5	13.0	14.3	10.3
Second tier	5.2	10.8	10.0	11.5	8.9	6.1	7.9	19.1	13.1	16.0	14.0
Developing economies: Africa	**-1.4**	**2.0**	**3.7**	**3.5**	**6.4**	**9.1**	**15.9**	**30.0**	**30.7**	**18.5**	**10.7**
Northern Africa excluding Sudan	-2.3	0.9	3.0	2.2	6.1	9.8	15.7	25.5	38.1	22.3	10.5
Sub-Saharan Africa	-0.9	2.6	4.1	4.3	6.7	8.8	16.0	32.3	27.0	16.4	10.9
Sub-Saharan Africa excluding South Africa	-1.9	2.7	4.6	5.2	7.9	10.6	17.3	34.9	33.5	17.8	7.8
Developing economies: America	**1.6**	**6.4**	**7.1**	**10.6**	**9.4**	**8.0**	**9.7**	**23.5**	**20.2**	**19.7**	**12.0**
Central America and Greater Carribean Islands excluding Puerto Rico	3.8	9.0	9.3	15.3	11.7	8.5	5.2	13.9	12.4	16.5	9.4
Central America and Greater Carribean Islands excluding Mexico and Puerto Rico	-0.6	3.0	3.7	11.4	7.8	4.3	4.3	10.7	7.3	12.4	15.3
South America and Central America	3.1	7.4	7.8	10.9	9.6	8.1	9.9	23.7	20.1	19.4	12.8
South America excluding Brazil	0.6	5.6	6.2	8.0	7.8	6.8	12.8	34.1	28.2	24.7	14.9
Developing economies: Asia	**4.6**	**9.0**	**9.3**	**9.5**	**9.7**	**9.4**	**15.0**	**28.3**	**21.4**	**19.3**	**16.3**
Eastern and South-Eastern Asia excluding China	11.2	11.8	10.5	9.5	8.0	6.0	9.9	23.7	13.3	15.0	11.6
Southern Asia excluding India	1.1	4.6	5.7	4.3	6.7	9.2	14.4	23.5	27.7	7.9	17.0

Sources:
- Data in this table are based on trade figures in table 1.1.1.

34

80-90	80-00	80-05	90-00	90-05	95-05	00-05	2004	2005	2006	2007	Groupements économiques
4.0	8.1	8.3	8.5	8.4	7.5	13.4	27.6	18.1	16.9	16.6	ÉCONOMIES EN DÉVELOPPEMENT
3.4	7.8	7.6	8.1	7.3	5.9	11.1	25.7	18.2	16.2	15.6	Économies en développement sans la Chine
4.1	8.3	8.4	8.6	8.4	7.5	13.3	27.8	18.0	16.9	16.7	Économies en développement sans les PMA
5.2	9.4	8.7	8.7	7.3	5.6	9.4	24.2	16.6	15.3	14.4	Pays en développement à revenu élevé
3.1	6.9	6.9	7.2	6.7	5.2	12.1	28.1	15.2	18.5	17.0	Pays en développement à revenu intermédiaire
2.7	7.0	8.7	9.8	12.0	13.3	21.2	32.1	22.0	18.0	19.3	Pays en développement à revenu faible
0.0	3.0	4.2	5.7	6.8	7.5	14.5	23.1	23.1	16.7	14.1	Pays pauvres très endettés
2.5	9.0	9.4	13.3	11.3	8.3	16.2	31.4	19.2	23.4	23.0	Pays en développement sans littoral
-4.3	1.1	2.4	6.0	5.7	5.1	8.3	15.6	15.9	15.0	9.2	Petits États insulaires en développement
0.2	3.8	5.2	7.0	8.3	9.1	14.8	19.2	22.1	15.4	13.4	*Pays les moins avancés*
0.0	2.7	4.5	5.0	7.7	9.8	18.5	23.1	27.0	14.3	12.3	Afrique et Haïti
0.4	5.6	6.5	10.3	9.4	8.1	9.7	13.2	14.2	17.4	15.4	Asie
5.1	6.9	7.2	6.1	7.2	8.1	10.5	22.5	16.0	17.0	11.1	Îles
-4.7	0.9	3.0	3.3	6.5	9.6	17.7	31.3	27.2	13.4	19.1	*Principaux exportateurs de pétrole*
-6.9	-0.7	1.8	1.3	5.6	8.9	22.1	26.9	28.6	8.7	8.5	Afrique
-4.3	2.3	3.3	6.5	6.1	5.8	8.9	41.2	34.5	30.5	26.2	Amérique
-3.9	1.2	3.4	3.3	6.9	10.5	18.1	31.4	25.9	12.2	20.9	Asie
9.5	11.7	11.0	9.8	9.2	7.8	13.2	27.8	15.9	17.7	15.7	*Principaux exportateurs d'articles manufacturés*
2.7	10.9	10.4	13.8	10.3	7.5	5.0	19.0	13.3	17.6	16.2	Amérique
10.9	11.9	11.1	9.1	9.0	7.9	14.7	29.2	16.3	17.7	15.6	Asie
7.6	11.2	10.0	9.5	7.5	5.0	8.7	25.9	15.9	16.1	13.6	*Économies émergentes*
1.7	10.6	9.9	13.6	9.5	6.0	5.5	21.9	16.0	17.9	18.3	Amérique
10.6	11.6	10.1	7.7	6.7	4.7	10.3	27.7	15.9	15.3	11.5	Asie
10.4	11.8	10.2	8.0	6.7	4.4	9.6	24.1	15.4	14.1	11.5	*Économies nouvellement industrialisées*
11.9	12.1	10.4	8.1	6.7	4.5	9.4	24.2	14.0	15.1	11.2	Première génération
6.8	11.0	9.8	7.4	6.5	4.0	10.3	23.6	19.3	11.7	12.2	Deuxième génération
-0.5	2.3	3.6	4.4	5.9	6.8	15.9	25.4	20.9	14.2	13.5	Économies en développement : Afrique
3.1	2.3	2.8	2.6	3.9	4.7	12.6	28.2	18.9	9.2	24.7	Afrique septentrionale sans le Soudan
-2.9	2.4	4.0	5.6	7.2	8.0	17.6	24.2	21.8	16.6	8.6	Afrique subsaharienne
-3.7	1.9	3.8	5.4	7.5	9.2	17.1	21.0	24.9	12.6	10.3	Afrique subsaharienne sans l'Afrique du Sud
-0.2	7.9	7.8	12.0	8.7	5.7	6.0	21.6	18.1	19.1	18.6	Économies en développement : Amérique
4.4	10.2	10.2	13.1	10.7	9.6	5.2	14.8	13.5	15.9	11.8	Amérique centrale et Grandes Antilles sans Porto Rico
1.7	4.6	5.3	9.8	8.3	7.1	6.3	11.2	18.8	16.8	16.5	Amérique centrale et Grandes Antilles sans le Mexique et Porto Rico
0.9	9.2	8.8	12.6	9.0	5.7	6.1	22.4	17.8	19.3	19.5	Amérique du Sud et Amérique centrale
-1.6	7.1	6.2	10.2	5.9	1.5	8.3	35.6	30.1	24.2	26.6	Amérique du Sud sans le Brésil
6.5	9.4	9.3	8.2	8.6	8.0	15.0	29.2	17.8	16.8	16.5	Économies en développement : Asie
10.4	11.8	10.3	8.0	6.8	4.6	9.8	24.0	15.3	14.4	12.2	Asie orientale et Asie du Sud-Est sans la Chine
0.9	3.3	4.5	1.4	5.2	8.6	16.9	22.6	21.1	15.2	1.9	Asie méridionale sans l'Inde

Imports (c.i.f.) - Importations (c.a.f.)
En pourcentage

Sources :
- Les données dans ce tableau ont été calculées d'après les chiffres du tableau 1.1.1.

Trade group	Exports (f.o.b) - Exportations (f.a.b.) Percentage										
	80-90	80-00	80-05	90-00	90-05	95-05	00-05	2004	2005	2006	2007
AFRICA											
CEMAC (formerly UDEAC)	-0.3	3.4	5.5	3.5	8.1	12.3	23.4	45.6	42.0	21.5	11.1
CEPGL	2.6	-3.3	-2.1	-5.9	-1.0	1.4	21.7	35.3	18.9	6.4	9.6
COMESA	-1.9	-0.3	1.7	1.1	5.0	8.5	16.1	24.0	39.5	28.5	16.1
ECCAS	2.2	3.2	5.4	3.3	8.4	13.0	24.2	43.2	56.2	25.9	20.2
ECOWAS	-4.7	1.7	3.5	4.1	6.6	9.2	15.5	35.0	29.0	10.2	-7.4
MRU	4.3	0.8	-0.5	-7.5	-5.5	-4.0	2.6	19.4	21.9	7.9	13.2
SADC	1.5	3.1	4.3	4.1	6.2	8.0	15.0	28.7	22.8	19.1	19.8
UEMOA	2.0	3.4	4.3	5.4	6.1	5.6	14.6	17.4	7.6	10.5	7.0
UMA	-3.5	1.0	3.1	2.3	6.0	9.6	15.3	26.3	37.7	22.2	9.5
AMERICA											
ANCOM	2.3	5.7	6.3	7.5	7.6	7.1	14.5	29.2	30.7	27.9	16.8
CACM	-0.4	6.8	6.9	14.1	9.4	5.1	4.8	7.7	10.7	11.7	15.1
CARICOM	-8.1	-2.6	0.1	5.4	6.9	8.3	12.2	21.0	33.3	37.6	-9.4
FTAA	5.1	7.4	6.9	8.2	6.6	4.9	5.5	15.6	15.0	14.9	11.1
LAIA	3.1	7.0	7.5	10.6	9.5	8.2	10.1	24.5	20.4	19.8	12.9
MERCOSUR	4.5	6.0	6.5	7.0	7.5	7.2	14.7	28.0	20.7	16.0	17.8
NAFTA	6.0	7.8	7.1	8.3	6.3	4.5	4.1	12.8	12.8	13.4	10.3
OECS	8.6	3.3	2.1	-1.8	-1.1	0.3	-0.7	7.2	0.3	6.3	3.2
ASIA											
APTA	12.8	12.9	13.1	12.2	13.2	13.4	21.4	33.3	23.9	23.5	22.4
ASEAN	6.2	11.1	10.3	11.1	9.0	6.4	10.0	25.4	14.7	17.3	13.1
ECO	3.9	7.4	8.4	7.5	9.6	11.0	19.9	31.7	25.2	16.1	22.7
GCC	-9.0	1.5	4.3	5.4	9.1	12.5	18.9	34.0	39.3	21.7	10.5
SAARC	7.4	9.4	9.6	9.1	9.8	9.7	16.2	25.0	26.2	19.1	16.8
EUROPE											
EFTA	7.9	6.8	6.7	3.9	5.4	6.1	11.2	18.8	13.6	15.3	15.1
EU	7.3	7.1	7.0	5.7	6.3	6.0	12.0	19.4	8.3	12.7	15.1
Euro zone	8.0	7.4	7.2	5.5	6.1	5.9	11.9	18.8	7.1	11.3	16.3
OCEANIA											
MSG	3.9	5.6	4.6	3.9	2.7	0.6	10.1	13.4	21.8	21.7	9.9
INTERREGIONAL											
ACP	-1.6	1.9	3.4	4.6	6.6	8.3	15.0	30.3	26.1	17.8	9.5
APEC	8.1	9.3	8.6	8.5	7.5	6.2	9.6	21.5	15.5	16.5	13.9
BSEC	3.0	10.4	11.1	17.5	14.6	10.1	19.7	33.6	24.6	21.2	20.1
CIS	..	..	(e)11.3	(e)9.9	(e)11.3	10.2	19.7	36.4	28.2	24.9	18.3

Sources:
- Data in this table are based on trade figures in table 1.1.1.

Imports (c.i.f.) - Importations (c.a.f.) En pourcentage											Groupements commerciaux
80-90	80-00	80-05	90-00	90-05	95-05	00-05	2004	2005	2006	2007	
											AFRIQUE
2.5	1.4	3.3	3.7	6.8	8.4	16.2	16.0	22.6	24.2	8.9	CEMAC (anc. UDEAC)
3.0	-2.9	-0.7	-5.2	1.7	6.6	23.9	21.7	20.1	26.8	2.1	CEPGL
4.3	2.0	2.6	3.8	4.6	4.8	13.4	27.2	34.3	11.5	17.3	COMESA
2.3	1.2	3.3	3.0	7.2	10.4	19.8	13.0	30.0	16.7	6.3	CEEAC
-8.3	0.1	2.4	3.8	6.5	8.7	17.9	17.7	24.7	10.8	9.7	CEDEAO
-0.7	1.9	1.4	1.4	0.4	-0.8	2.9	18.0	13.4	18.0	15.9	UFM
-0.4	3.9	5.0	6.2	7.3	7.7	17.5	26.1	16.7	19.1	6.9	SADC
-0.2	2.4	3.5	4.3	5.5	5.8	15.7	21.1	17.1	9.1	17.1	UEMOA
-1.0	2.4	3.4	2.0	4.4	5.9	15.4	31.9	11.8	10.3	22.6	UMA
											AMÉRIQUE
0.1	6.9	6.7	9.7	7.1	2.8	11.7	20.6	25.5	21.5	23.3	ANCCM
1.4	8.2	8.7	13.1	10.9	8.8	9.1	12.8	14.6	15.4	15.2	MCAC
-7.0	0.0	1.8	7.7	6.9	6.0	7.0	11.8	17.6	14.3	8.4	CARICOM
6.5	8.0	7.8	9.7	8.2	7.1	6.9	17.6	15.0	12.1	8.5	ZLEA
1.0	8.8	8.4	12.3	8.8	5.6	5.9	23.3	18.3	19.8	19.4	ALADI
-2.7	8.1	6.9	13.1	6.7	0.1	4.8	37.5	19.8	23.7	31.0	MERCOSUR
8.0	8.3	8.1	9.6	8.4	7.7	6.9	16.5	14.1	10.9	6.1	ALENA
9.9	7.1	6.2	4.4	4.2	4.7	5.9	8.8	13.3	9.1	14.1	OECO
											ASIE
10.5	11.0	11.6	10.1	12.2	13.2	21.3	32.9	20.0	19.9	19.5	ACAP
7.2	10.9	9.7	8.0	6.8	4.2	10.4	25.1	19.8	14.9	13.1	ANASE
3.4	6.8	7.6	6.0	8.1	9.5	19.3	38.5	12.8	27.7	17.3	ECO
-3.9	2.5	4.3	4.8	7.3	9.7	18.3	28.9	30.1	12.8	28.7	CCG
3.9	6.6	7.7	8.8	9.9	10.3	20.2	33.7	37.9	21.2	19.5	SAARC
											EUROPE
8.0	5.8	5.4	3.1	4.0	4.3	10.0	17.5	10.9	13.4	16.5	AELE
6.5	6.7	6.6	5.2	6.1	6.4	11.9	20.2	10.2	14.4	14.7	UE
6.7	6.7	6.6	4.5	5.6	6.1	11.6	19.6	9.7	12.9	15.0	Zone euro
											OCÉANIE
0.8	2.2	2.3	0.6	1.8	1.9	12.6	21.6	8.7	19.5	1.8	MSG
											INTERRÉGIONAUX
-2.7	1.9	3.5	5.8	6.9	7.5	14.7	21.6	21.7	16.5	9.0	ACP
8.1	9.1	8.7	8.7	8.0	7.0	10.0	21.4	15.3	13.6	11.3	CEAP
3.7	9.6	9.8	12.4	11.0	7.7	20.0	31.8	16.4	28.9	30.4	CEMN
..	..	(e)8.0	(e)5.5	(e)8.0	6.5	22.0	30.6	25.2	30.6	33.8	CEI

Sources :
- Les données dans ce tableau ont été calculées d'après les chiffres du tableau 1.1.1.

1.3.1 Value of trade balance, and as percentage of imports of countries and geographical regions

Region, country or territory	Trade balance - Balance commerciale Millions of dollars - Millions de dollars								
	1979-81	1984-86	1989-91	1994-96	1999-01	2002-04	2003-05	2004-06	2005-07
WORLD	**-40 999**	**-65 239**	**-109 812**	**-68 451**	**-186 671**	**-227 901**	**-268 401**	**-277 267**	**-258 440**
DEVELOPING ECONOMIES	74 285	19 061	17 783	-56 169	105 334	176 366	257 256	377 801	490 139
ECONOMIES IN TRANSITION	1 234	6 281	-8 791	5 842	35 508	40 468	60 063	81 675	84 798
DEVELOPED ECONOMIES	-116 518	-90 580	-118 804	-18 124	-327 512	-444 735	-585 720	-736 742	-833 377
Developing economies: Africa	**11 939**	**1 875**	**3 577**	**-6 581**	**4 867**	**7 382**	**19 819**	**37 716**	**51 767**
Eastern Africa	*-3 155*	*-2 469*	*-4 719*	*-5 998*	*-7 068*	*-8 692*	*-11 557*	*-14 307*	*-16 973*
Burundi*	-79	-69	-143	-106	-87	-115	-153	-237	-287
Comoros*	-15	-24	-30	-48	-37	-48	-65	-86	-96
Djibouti*	-197	-187	-186	-164	-126	-179	-221	-249	-261
Eritrea	–	–	–	-418	-450	-460	-459	-501	-518
Ethiopia	–	–	–	-789	-1 067	-1 725	-2 419	-3 098	-3 608
Ethiopia (former)	-266	-606	-526	–	–	–	–	–	–
Kenya	-742	-429	-1 080	-832	-1 235	-1 437	-2 013	-2 866	-3 924
Madagascar*	-275	-36	-119	-112	-120	-294	-662	-785	-876
Malawi	-129	-6	-211	-121	-162	-333	-466	-576	-550
Mauritius	-201	-65	-376	-503	-472	-534	-754	-1 031	-1 388
Mozambique	-452	-419	-731	-646	-663	-658	-634	-561	-541
Rwanda	-126	-153	-209	-158	-183	-188	-220	-271	-347
Seychelles	-72	-74	-128	-191	-234	-180	-227	-306	-372
Somalia	-263	-214	36	-36	-154	-136	-107	-128	-135
Uganda	63	81	-94	-555	-1 012	-890	-1 011	-1 282	-1 448
United Republic of Tanzania*	-654	-514	-954	-861	-889	-903	-1 209	-1 798	-2 549
Zambia*	301	15	264	309	50	-439	-639	-210	270
Zimbabwe	-48	229	-231	-767	-228	-175	-299	-323	-300
Middle Africa	*2 488*	*1 955*	*4 324*	*5 246*	*7 081*	*11 108*	*18 571*	*28 927*	*40 376*
Angola*	253	646	2 028	2 291	3 428	5 413	9 143	15 495	23 583
Cameroon*(1)	-228	-526	425	452	178	29	174	332	476
Central African Republic*(1)	9	-41	-6	5	31	5	-18	-37	-40
Chad*	-8	-89	-78	-82	-232	-133	1 087	1 846	2 205
Congo*(1)	304	411	338	208	1 359	1 978	2 564	3 599	4 406
Dem. Rep. of the Congo*	774	640	475	550	154	-102	-146	-233	-303
Equatorial Guinea	-6	-11	-14	-41	617	2 065	3 051	4 315	5 535
Gabon*(1)	1 391	930	1 175	1 884	1 574	1 886	2 756	3 661	4 578
Sao Tome and Principe*	-1	-4	-18	-22	-30	-33	-41	-52	-65
Northern Africa	*6 528*	*-4 085*	*-5 201*	*-10 387*	*-1 874*	*2 434*	*9 781*	*19 565*	*26 978*
Algeria*	2 518	1 521	2 734	-183	8 407	10 650	16 489	23 498	28 857
Egypt*	-3 120	-7 861	-9 394	-8 184	-10 137	-6 000	-6 445	-7 129	-8 962
Libyan Arab Jamahiriya	11 029	5 559	5 624	3 824	6 445	6 863	11 305	17 445	24 416
Morocco*	-1 849	-1 598	-2 467	-2 894	-3 519	-5 803	-7 616	-9 454	-12 266
Sudan*	-835	-514	-415	-772	-328	-385	-1 052	-1 739	-1 743
Tunisia	-1 215	-1 191	-1 644	-2 179	-2 742	-2 890	-2 900	-3 056	-3 324
Southern Africa	*4 322*	*3 794*	*4 425*	*-569*	*-100*	*-4 430*	*-8 200*	*-12 516*	*-13 649*
Botswana*	..	..	..	..	487	448	633	1 000	1 323
Lesotho	..	..	..	..	-584	-598	-708	-755	-858
Namibia	..	..	..	..	-324	-516	-590	-354	-71
South Africa	(a)4322	(a)3794	(a)4425	(a)-569	436	-3 822	-7 534	-12 368	-13 915
Swaziland	..	..	..	..	-115	59	-1	-40	-128
Western Africa	*1 756*	*2 679*	*4 748*	*5 126*	*6 828*	*6 961*	*11 223*	*16 047*	*15 035*
Benin*	-351	-195	41	-162	-266	-318	-331	-360	-395
Burkina Faso	-252	-253	-369	-278	-420	-630	-771	-848	-897
Cape Verde*	-61	-82	-125	-223	-226	-325	-377	-438	-554
Côte d'Ivoire*	106	1 243	751	1 081	1 347	2 668	2 522	2 461	2 333
Gambia	-104	-49	-146	-193	-159	-172	-199	-228	-251
Ghana	76	-160	-334	-435	-1 438	-1 029	-1 591	-2 377	-3 126
Guinea	104	145	-45	-35	88	15	25	35	0
Guinea-Bissau	-42	-43	-62	-75	5	-4	-8	-14	-17
Liberia*	59	130	881	225	-164	-99	-162	-245	-284
Mali*	-224	-185	-162	-308	-260	-230	-383	-350	-432
Mauritania*	-69	118	161	61	-79	-269	-504	-362	-153
Niger*	-32	-64	-91	-104	-125	-258	-356	-428	-550
Nigeria	3 471	2 495	5 003	6 145	9 490	9 153	15 212	21 384	22 119
Senegal*	-515	-316	-486	-366	-644	-1 145	-1 363	-1 609	-2 051
Sierra Leone*	-166	-11	-25	-97	-121	-192	-182	-169	-178
Togo*	-245	-95	-244	-111	-200	-206	-311	-405	-528

For sources and notes, see end of table.

1.3.1   Valeur de la balance commerciale et sa part dans les importations des pays et des régions géographiques

Percentage of imports / Part dans les importations en pourcentage									Régions, pays ou territoires
1979-81	1984-86	1989-91	1994-96	1999-01	2002-04	2003-05	2004-06	2005-07	
-2.11	-3.12	-3.17	-1.36	-2.96	-2.86	-2.87	-2.55	-2.09	**MONDE**
15.71	4.01	2.22	-3.90	5.94	7.50	9.05	11.06	12.25	ÉCONOMIES EN DÉVELOPPEMENT
1.52	6.53	-8.03	5.20	33.46	22.90	26.99	28.98	23.38	ÉCONOMIES EN TRANSITION
-8.37	-5.96	-4.65	-0.52	-7.40	-8.18	-9.34	-10.29	-10.38	ÉCONOMIES DÉVELOPPÉES
13.40	2.51	3.84	-5.74	3.72	4.15	9.09	14.49	17.18	**Économies en développement : Afrique**
-32.10	*-30.56*	*-40.01*	*-38.19*	*-41.20*	*-39.91*	*-44.10*	*-45.25*	*-45.63*	*Afrique orientale*
-49.28	-35.84	-63.80	-54.53	-64.75	-74.82	-76.28	-81.33	-83.05	Burundi*
-50.15	-62.45	-59.90	-83.29	-73.62	-68.86	-77.40	-86.45	-89.74	Comores*
-94.66	-92.26	-89.25	-89.97	-63.15	-77.29	-85.23	-84.83	-84.55	Djibouti*
–	–	–	-83.92	-96.08	-95.02	-97.78	-97.84	-97.94	Érythrée
–	–	–	-66.12	-69.44	-75.77	-77.74	-77.93	-76.94	Éthiopie
-39.30	-60.15	-63.00	–	–	–	–	–	–	Éthiopie (anc.)
-39.06	-28.48	-51.19	-31.10	-40.58	-37.42	-41.86	-47.74	-52.04	Kenya
-42.55	-10.44	-26.89	-18.68	-13.32	-24.59	-42.36	-45.45	-46.85	Madagascar*
-32.26	-2.08	-35.42	-22.75	-27.55	-41.34	-48.17	-51.94	-46.10	Malawi
-34.44	-11.61	-25.05	-24.35	-21.97	-21.95	-27.28	-32.37	-38.95	Maurice
-62.38	-83.32	-84.78	-78.06	-59.16	-37.01	-30.71	-23.00	-19.70	Mozambique
-50.97	-49.73	-67.87	-77.10	-73.45	-71.46	-69.78	-68.71	-69.83	Rwanda
-78.27	-75.44	-73.25	-70.08	-55.81	-40.47	-42.94	-47.57	-50.85	Seychelles
-66.06	-74.51	51.07	-17.96	-40.91	-29.63	-22.15	-22.13	-21.24	Somalie
22.52	24.78	-31.05	-53.35	-67.91	-60.91	-58.71	-59.90	-55.51	Ouganda
-55.45	-62.99	-73.38	-56.53	-55.61	-42.46	-45.38	-52.54	-58.60	République-Unie de Tanzanie*
31.09	2.42	26.92	42.20	5.40	-27.25	-30.52	-8.07	8.41	Zambie*
-3.55	23.37	-12.66	-26.38	-11.99	-8.14	-14.19	-14.59	-13.56	Zimbabwe
47.99	*35.07*	*67.38*	*85.35*	*87.34*	*85.45*	*116.49*	*151.96*	*183.13*	*Afrique centrale*
18.44	51.75	142.70	138.49	110.25	107.74	139.47	202.44	268.70	Angola*
-15.89	-39.75	33.25	40.30	11.52	1.37	7.17	12.02	16.48	Cameroun*(1)
11.55	-33.77	-4.27	3.11	26.41	3.94	-12.63	-21.02	-20.10	République centrafricaine*(1)
-9.03	-47.88	-30.34	-28.03	-53.14	-11.83	121.69	172.45	175.76	Tchad*
69.80	68.09	45.10	21.93	201.20	244.27	241.01	257.71	248.85	Congo*(1)
73.96	51.78	28.66	58.89	22.31	-6.56	-7.46	-9.88	-11.44	Rép. dém. du Congo*
-25.99	-37.07	-23.31	-27.21	109.58	186.45	185.43	197.34	196.64	Guinée équatoriale
203.80	114.07	139.90	217.84	169.03	176.75	227.88	264.86	282.39	Gabon*(1)
-5.94	-28.17	-78.11	-80.63	-92.13	-86.62	-89.97	-93.60	-94.58	Sao Tomé-et-Principe*
20.62	*-12.19*	*-12.47*	*-22.26*	*-3.80*	*3.91*	*13.04*	*21.98*	*25.66*	*Afrique septentrionale*
24.96	15.54	27.30	-1.54	89.10	73.79	94.05	116.17	131.17	Algérie*
-53.55	-70.67	-64.62	-70.11	-71.08	-49.25	-44.10	-40.11	-39.89	Égypte*
161.64	115.05	108.00	76.20	152.52	100.99	130.12	157.94	188.13	Jamahiriya arabe libyenne
-44.98	-41.46	-38.38	-31.00	-32.49	-39.84	-44.54	-47.63	-50.97	Maroc*
-59.09	-53.59	-54.99	-57.97	-18.66	-12.27	-22.07	-26.79	-21.92	Soudan*
-35.85	-40.30	-32.69	-29.46	-30.96	-26.07	-23.57	-22.44	-21.22	Tunisie
25.13	*28.00*	*23.82*	*-2.03*	*-0.30*	*-9.18*	*-13.51*	*-17.02*	*-16.37*	*Afrique australe*
..	..	..	..	22.49	17.87	21.53	31.76	44.22	Botswana*
..	..	..	..	-72.45	-54.04	-53.83	-52.26	-54.32	Lesotho
..	..	..	..	-20.68	-27.13	-25.85	-13.96	-2.54	Namibie
(a)25.13	(a)28	(a)23.82	(a)-2.03	1.55	-9.26	-14.41	-19.22	-18.86	Afrique du Sud
..	..	..	..	-10.57	3.98	-0.05	-1.91	-5.75	Swaziland
6.97	*19.22*	*32.52*	*28.40*	*30.38*	*21.33*	*27.99*	*34.11*	*28.01*	*Afrique occidentale*
-88.07	-58.18	17.14	-26.50	-40.16	-38.02	-37.07	-38.68	-39.98	Bénin*
-75.81	-76.57	-75.87	-57.55	-64.83	-64.41	-64.58	-62.36	-60.79	Burkina Faso
-94.88	-95.46	-95.28	-96.18	-95.50	-96.23	-96.14	-96.09	-96.66	Cap-Vert*
4.03	70.37	35.70	41.85	47.79	80.20	59.97	48.73	40.69	Côte d'Ivoire*
-72.11	-49.47	-79.42	-88.83	-92.73	-94.49	-95.82	-96.06	-96.29	Gambie
7.42	-19.06	-28.40	-21.29	-45.80	-30.14	-37.07	-43.48	-46.80	Ghana
34.81	42.34	-6.60	-4.78	14.93	2.32	3.48	4.38	0.04	Guinée
-76.78	-76.79	-77.46	-58.64	9.26	-5.78	-9.25	-14.67	-15.02	Guinée-Bissau
11.93	42.95	333.70	48.33	-34.64	-43.22	-58.52	-65.11	-63.25	Libéria*
-56.92	-54.19	-34.57	-43.32	-29.72	-19.91	-27.65	-22.47	-24.00	Mali*
-25.66	53.44	57.23	14.15	-18.18	-42.55	-52.21	-30.90	-12.10	Mauritanie*
-6.14	-18.66	-24.74	-27.07	-30.84	-42.00	-45.37	-47.10	-49.88	Niger*
20.79	33.19	79.83	86.66	98.53	54.69	73.66	88.90	82.06	Nigéria
-50.56	-34.20	-40.35	-28.37	-39.57	-47.26	-48.49	-50.96	-55.62	Sénégal*
-46.40	-7.34	-14.94	-58.63	-88.28	-67.28	-58.34	-49.73	-45.31	Sierra Leone*
-48.88	-32.72	-48.82	-22.48	-35.00	-27.45	-33.40	-37.45	-41.33	Togo*

Pour les sources et les notes, se reporter à la fin du tableau.

Region, country or territory	Trade balance - Balance commerciale Millions of dollars - Millions de dollars								
	1979-81	1984-86	1989-91	1994-96	1999-01	2002-04	2003-05	2004-06	2005-07
Developing economies: America	**-9 635**	**21 255**	**9 712**	**-25 286**	**-31 471**	**12 653**	**27 218**	**39 261**	**35 952**
Caribbean	*-3 415*	*-4 774*	*-7 922*	*-7 255*	*-13 135*	*-13 381*	*-14 049*	*-15 254*	*-18 149*
Anguilla	..	..	..	..	-85	-78	-95	-118	-166
Antigua and Barbuda*	-53	-151	-219	-306	-362	-379	-405	-443	-465
Aruba (2)	..	-181	-413	-348	-203	-388	-213	-153	-113
Bahamas (3)	-1 120	-547	-796	-1 047	-1 427	-1 349	-1 533	-1 805	-2 042
Barbados	-317	-278	-490	-506	-846	-970	-1 108	-1 194	-1 246
Cuba*	-776	-1 813	-2 397	-1 151	-3 216	-3 006	-3 898	-5 102	-6 141
Dominica*	-27	-24	-60	-67	-87	-86	-104	-117	-135
Dominican Republic*	-703	-1 037	-2 320	-1 505	-3 383	-2 594	-2 613	-3 468	-5 010
Grenada*	-30	-46	-83	-110	-167	-198	-231	-245	-285
Haiti	-182	-240	-184	-429	-716	-869	-913	-1 085	-1 134
Jamaica	-294	-457	-781	-1 328	-1 935	-2 420	-2 601	-2 927	-3 500
Montserrat*	-11	-14	-38	-27	-19	-24	-24	-25	-27
Netherlands Antilles*(4)	(b)-462	(b)-281	-349	-650	-576	-1 249	-1 632	-1 827	-1 920
Saint Kitts and Nevis*	-21	-35	-83	-106	-109	-119	-123	-136	-153
Saint Lucia*	-64	-68	-157	-199	-305	-322	-402	-464	-522
Saint Vincent and the Grenadines*	-36	-21	-60	-86	-133	-165	-185	-202	-230
Trinidad and Tobago*	680	298	509	609	576	1 013	2 250	4 383	5 430
Turks and Caicos Islands	..	..	..	..	-143	-179	-219	-326	-444
Central America	*-6 253*	*5 984*	*-7 901*	*-11 815*	*-25 914*	*-30 169*	*-33 006*	*-37 702*	*-43 946*
Belize	-42	-35	-127	-116	-285	-336	-346	-367	-404
Costa Rica*	-401	-79	-374	-698	-593	-1 817	-2 104	-2 686	-3 146
El Salvador*	36	-230	-717	-1 478	-1 893	-2 585	-2 999	-3 488	-4 038
Guatemala*	-268	-61	-560	-1 208	-2 556	-4 264	-4 765	-5 566	-6 379
Honduras*	-153	-99	-126	-387	-1 535	-1 998	-2 422	-2 934	-3 676
Mexico	-4 124	8 094	-4 565	-5 395	-15 410	-15 524	-16 192	-17 732	-20 060
Nicaragua	-240	-578	-363	-576	-1 221	-1 308	-1 499	-1 728	-2 034
Panama*	–	-1 028	-1 068	-1 958	-2 422	-2 336	-2 678	-3 202	-4 209
South America	*33*	*20 045*	*25 534*	*-6 216*	*7 578*	*56 203*	*74 273*	*92 217*	*98 047*
Argentina*	-567	3 411	5 837	-1 620	1 695	14 841	13 175	12 068	11 645
Bolivia	46	44	110	-333	-576	-63	245	599	847
Brazil	-3 392	9 965	10 688	-3 108	-2 778	21 029	31 116	37 700	38 975
Chile*	-1 783	521	737	-888	907	3 719	6 210	11 999	16 533
Colombia	-1 017	-128	1 333	-3 409	626	-710	-463	-746	-1 686
Ecuador*	312	835	600	422	652	-781	-380	-15	290
Guyana*	-38	-16	-50	-48	-114	-67	-118	-189	-289
Paraguay	-275	-265	-290	-1 962	-1 227	-1 059	-1 491	-2 557	-3 453
Peru*	948	567	-122	-3 217	-1 429	1 138	2 426	5 018	6 879
Suriname	-17	16	-17	-16	-34	21	40	152	152
Uruguay	-489	192	238	-853	-1 097	-90	-214	-487	-799
Venezuela (Bolivarian Rep. of)	6 305	4 904	6 471	8 815	10 953	18 226	23 727	28 676	28 914
Developing economies: Asia	**73 251**	**-2 633**	**6 718**	**-22 939**	**133 779**	**159 458**	**213 515**	**303 991**	**405 415**
Eastern Asia	*-8 025*	*2 057*	*10 834*	*-7 130*	*41 457*	*50 289*	*76 146*	*126 959*	*201 429*
China	-1 286	-9 378	3 421	11 434	25 295	29 328	53 188	103 957	180 658
China, Hong Kong SAR	-2 551	104	-336	-15 748	-9 254	-9 167	-10 048	-11 341	-15 148
China, Macao SAR	27	135	62	-37	120	-338	-759	-1 370	-2 090
China, Taiwan Province of	886	11 511	13 007	9 892	11 206	13 351	12 520	14 103	21 289
Dem. People's Rep. of Korea	..	..	-937	-353	-846	-957	-1 121	-1 200	-1 300
Mongolia	-190	-610	-173	21	-85	-168	-152	-71	-64
Republic of Korea (5)	-4 975	297	-4 524	-12 340	15 020	18 239	22 518	22 882	18 056
Southern Asia	*-8 813*	*-12 001*	*-12 240*	*-5 042*	*-8 042*	*-19 001*	*-30 377*	*-45 265*	*-57 017*
Afghanistan	-105	-745	-514	-326	-1 171	-2 060	-2 062	-2 209	-2 377
Bangladesh	-1 666	-1 701	-2 005	-2 578	-2 763	-3 253	-3 949	-4 280	-5 041
Bhutan	-41	-60	-17	-21	-74	-136	-150	-121	-67
India (6)	-5 141	-6 211	-4 336	-3 578	-9 162	-14 289	-26 648	-40 243	-55 891
Iran (Islamic Rep. of)*	1 592	371	-1 974	6 602	8 815	6 158	11 043	14 946	23 626
Maldives	-20	-26	-64	-184	-291	-346	-454	-582	-718
Nepal	-212	-300	-457	-931	-776	-1 019	-1 079	-1 162	-1 480
Pakistan	-2 494	-2 812	-2 044	-2 601	-1 524	-2 332	-4 994	-8 923	-12 013
Sri Lanka	-740	-517	-828	-1 425	-1 095	-1 723	-2 083	-2 692	-3 070
South-Eastern Asia	*5 266*	*3 848*	*-13 666*	*-28 653*	*52 936*	*59 193*	*62 708*	*71 270*	*78 149*
Brunei Darussalam*	3 240	2 006	1 237	218	2 171	2 958	3 829	4 811	5 400
Cambodia	-159	-127	-67	-338	-508	-617	-760	-918	-1 137
Indonesia	11 132	6 807	4 681	7 316	24 993	23 102	20 855	20 279	21 748
Lao People's dem. Rep.*	-67	-129	-103	-303	-203	-207	-268	-285	-126
Malaysia (7)	1 872	2 793	154	-1 541	16 546	17 088	21 442	25 466	28 402

For sources and notes, see end of table.

Percentage of imports Part dans les importations en pourcentage									Régions, pays ou territoires
1979-81	1984-86	1989-91	1994-96	1999-01	2002-04	2003-05	2004-06	2005-07	
-8.37	**24.68**	**7.48**	**-10.09**	**-8.50**	**3.24**	**6.06**	**7.31**	**5.64**	**Économies en développement : Amérique**
-13.95	*-23.56*	*-41.52*	*-36.42*	*-42.87*	*-41.92*	*-38.98*	*-36.16*	*-37.52*	*Caraïbes*
..	..	..	..	-96.26	-94.25	-92.00	-86.94	-89.65	Anguilla
-60.59	-89.35	-88.40	-87.14	-89.23	-89.08	-88.51	-88.49	-88.77	Antigua-et-Barbuda*
..	-85.96	-52.05	-19.24	-8.78	-15.68	-7.18	-4.45	-3.33	Aruba (2)
-18.31	-15.69	-44.74	-85.73	-74.55	-75.01	-75.86	-75.97	-75.76	Bahamas (3)
-62.29	-44.80	-70.66	-68.40	-76.13	-79.08	-78.93	-77.78	-76.26	Barbade
-12.83	-21.54	-38.75	-41.20	-66.61	-62.41	-65.47	-67.42	-67.79	Cuba*
-67.95	-42.29	-53.85	-58.22	-62.27	-66.61	-71.02	-73.37	-76.58	Dominique*
-41.13	-57.20	-75.02	-28.58	-38.59	-31.95	-30.88	-35.97	-43.13	République dominicaine*
-61.00	-66.38	-75.62	-83.45	-74.57	-84.59	-87.67	-89.38	-89.87	Grenade*
-49.18	-57.47	-53.98	-82.00	-69.87	-71.90	-69.40	-70.22	-69.29	Haïti
-24.25	-42.41	-41.80	-49.76	-60.72	-66.34	-65.72	-64.83	-65.44	Jamaïque
-88.62	-83.70	-96.08	-90.11	-89.12	-90.62	-90.67	-91.35	-94.42	Montserrat*
(b)-8.71	(b)-12.92	-17.78	-31.88	-22.44	-47.26	-53.74	-52.64	-52.15	Antilles néerlandaises*(4)
-50.09	-63.20	-77.06	-80.95	-69.16	-67.77	-68.87	-70.46	-71.93	Saint-Kitts-et-Nevis*
-54.60	-51.40	-56.25	-64.68	-85.84	-82.59	-85.41	-86.56	-87.86	Sainte-Lucie*
-66.62	-25.70	-44.35	-64.94	-74.35	-81.70	-83.29	-85.12	-85.63	Saint-Vincent-et-les Grenadines*
24.28	18.62	38.18	36.62	17.95	24.53	46.69	77.03	84.12	Trinité-et-Tobago*
..	..	..	..	-94.74	-94.57	-94.69	-95.64	-96.48	Îles Turques et Caïques
-22.26	*24.67*	*-15.12*	*-11.85*	*-13.37*	*-13.92*	*-13.83*	*-13.79*	*-14.20*	*Amérique centrale*
-28.67	-27.54	-55.95	-45.14	-60.55	-63.22	-62.39	-61.58	-62.07	Belize
-28.98	-7.08	-20.12	-17.15	-9.21	-23.58	-24.52	-27.22	-27.74	Costa Rica*
3.61	-24.04	-54.62	-48.60	-40.37	-44.92	-47.56	-50.33	-52.54	El Salvador*
-16.76	-5.35	-32.61	-39.29	-49.99	-61.40	-61.24	-62.36	-62.11	Guatemala*
-16.52	-11.18	-13.17	-25.57	-54.34	-58.91	-61.56	-63.10	-65.70	Honduras*
-19.73	45.49	-10.35	-6.41	-9.11	-8.29	-7.87	-7.53	-7.56	Mexique
-32.11	-65.00	-54.40	-57.70	-67.32	-67.13	-66.97	-66.25	-66.41	Nicaragua
_	-76.24	-75.91	-76.33	-73.71	-72.53	-73.98	-76.19	-79.48	Panama*
0.05	*48.16*	*43.62*	*-4.74*	*5.20*	*39.54*	*42.49*	*41.63*	*35.10*	*Amérique du Sud*
-6.38	77.97	106.77	-7.42	7.15	98.35	60.84	42.45	32.46	Argentine*
5.56	7.14	14.50	-23.38	-32.63	-3.59	12.64	25.64	29.53	Bolivie
-14.78	66.29	49.06	-6.34	-4.91	37.77	47.89	47.14	38.97	Brésil
-30.08	15.52	9.53	-5.68	5.24	18.23	24.24	37.52	41.99	Chili*
-22.94	-3.08	25.71	-25.95	5.36	-4.92	-2.68	-3.50	-6.30	Colombie
15.37	48.21	29.43	10.51	16.15	-10.97	-4.52	-0.15	2.44	Équateur*
-9.95	-6.91	-17.04	-8.78	-18.48	-11.19	-17.61	-24.52	-32.14	Guyana*
-47.51	-47.65	-24.37	-67.92	-58.61	-45.42	-49.50	-59.46	-59.75	Paraguay
36.44	24.45	-3.51	-37.93	-17.60	13.12	23.46	39.71	43.55	Pérou*
-3.40	4.90	-3.57	-3.10	-6.84	3.28	5.11	17.36	16.11	Suriname
-32.37	24.47	17.08	-28.51	-33.30	-3.72	-6.99	-12.44	-16.86	Uruguay
53.13	60.33	73.86	83.37	68.03	140.19	139.05	115.75	84.13	Venezuela (Rép. bolivarienne du)
27.59	**-0.85**	**1.17**	**-2.14**	**10.55**	**8.98**	**9.85**	**11.65**	**13.28**	**Économies en développement : Asie**
-9.66	*1.66*	*3.93*	*-1.31*	*6.16*	*5.10*	*6.35*	*8.88*	*12.16*	*Asie orientale*
-6.70	-24.99	5.82	8.87	11.96	6.93	9.77	15.49	22.51	Chine
-11.89	0.33	-0.40	-8.54	-4.68	-3.87	-3.76	-3.76	-4.53	Chine (RAS de Hong Kong)
4.95	16.40	3.85	-1.80	5.38	-11.56	-22.44	-34.39	-45.28	Chine (RAS de Macao)
4.77	52.04	22.90	10.22	9.39	9.81	7.86	7.65	10.56	Province chinoise de Taiwan
..	..	-32.92	-26.72	-53.91	-46.13	-47.74	-44.75	-45.08	Rép. populaire dém. de Corée
-30.36	-46.82	-23.03	5.26	-14.37	-20.03	-15.16	-5.79	-4.11	Mongolie
-21.71	0.95	-6.38	-9.55	10.69	9.85	10.17	8.63	5.84	République de Corée (5)
-23.99	*-29.94*	*-21.86*	*-7.12*	*-8.57*	*-13.41*	*-16.51*	*-19.40*	*-20.15*	*Asie méridionale*
-14.59	-56.07	-70.06	-67.87	-90.42	-91.84	-88.13	-85.31	-85.04	Afghanistan
-69.36	-64.49	-56.32	-42.64	-31.60	-31.42	-32.60	-30.52	-31.14	Bangladesh
-68.98	-71.59	-20.41	-18.60	-40.74	-47.53	-43.14	-29.72	-16.59	Bhoutan
-38.45	-39.96	-20.15	-10.79	-18.46	-18.73	-25.36	-28.89	-31.42	Inde (6)
12.19	2.98	-10.39	49.05	56.47	20.97	31.47	36.51	54.19	Iran (Rép. islamique d')*
-73.98	-52.52	-47.01	-69.63	-73.79	-69.06	-73.37	-75.45	-77.79	Maldives
-65.85	-67.74	-68.86	-71.88	-52.07	-60.63	-59.02	-59.76	-63.91	Népal
-49.75	-49.28	-26.71	-24.02	-14.63	-16.57	-26.59	-36.60	-41.70	Pakistan
-41.49	-27.87	-31.33	-27.81	-18.12	-24.91	-26.62	-29.84	-30.60	Sri Lanka
8.40	*5.55*	*-8.62*	*-8.49*	*15.52*	*14.18*	*12.65*	*12.06*	*11.44*	*Asie du Sud-Est*
622.01	317.26	120.93	10.16	180.54	206.16	270.94	308.88	332.17	Brunéi Darussalam*
-93.73	-86.59	-36.95	-33.76	-27.09	-22.32	-23.10	-23.06	-24.23	Cambodge
106.67	58.58	21.92	19.00	75.71	55.11	39.22	31.09	27.39	Indonésie
-74.26	-71.70	-56.54	-49.29	-38.83	-38.37	-39.13	-32.24	-12.79	Rép. dém. populaire lao*
18.61	22.58	0.52	-2.14	22.44	19.19	21.32	21.78	21.72	Malaisie (7)

Pour les sources et les notes, se reporter à la fin du tableau.

Region, country or territory	Trade balance - Balance commerciale Millions of dollars - Millions de dollars								
	1979-81	1984-86	1989-91	1994-96	1999-01	2002-04	2003-05	2004-06	2005-07
Myanmar	91	22	-51	-398	-813	425	821	1 489	2 567
Philippines	-2 473	-819	-4 117	-11 298	1 502	-2 205	-4 340	-5 471	-6 456
Singapore (8)	-4 882	-3 695	-6 723	-6 136	4 210	19 920	26 876	32 494	32 940
Thailand*	-2 498	-1 803	-8 270	-13 385	6 040	3 267	-547	-1 354	2 136
Timor-Leste	..	..	..	..	-258	-184	-156	-139	-131
Viet Nam	-990	-1 207	-406	-2 789	-836	-4 353	-5 042	-5 102	-7 407
Western Asia	**84 823**	**3 463**	**21 789**	**17 886**	**47 429**	**68 977**	**105 038**	**151 026**	**182 854**
Bahrain	120	-230	-286	229	1 170	905	920	1 159	1 551
Iraq*	7 121	-1 544	2 042	-411	5 037	582	-507	2 779	6 834
Jordan	-1 940	-1 892	-1 311	-2 121	-2 387	-3 058	-4 357	-5 561	-6 769
Kuwait*	11 948	3 837	1 524	5 358	8 390	10 712	17 770	28 299	37 216
Lebanon	-2 375	-2 046	-2 328	-6 296	-5 778	-6 078	-6 736	-7 180	-7 709
Oman	634	179	2 106	2 073	4 706	4 913	6 479	8 337	9 362
Qatar*	3 577	2 127	1 507	729	6 377	9 277	12 061	15 103	16 275
Saudi Arabia*	62 578	2 926	15 378	24 727	35 590	59 252	86 232	116 014	136 081
Syrian Arab Republic*	-2 257	-1 999	1 127	-1 649	381	334	-831	-1 228	-1 023
Turkey*	-4 013	-3 552	-6 988	-13 213	-16 959	-22 949	-26 939	-37 809	-46 806
United Arab Emirates	11 056	6 990	10 207	8 511	9 871	14 495	20 021	29 874	36 442
Yemen (former Arab Republic)	-673	-545	–	–	–	–	–	–	–
Yemen (former Democratic)	-952	-968							
Yemen*	–	–	–	-51	1 030	592	926	1 238	1 401
Developing economies: Oceania	**-1 270**	**-1 437**	**-2 224**	**-1 363**	**-1 841**	**-3 127**	**-3 296**	**-3 168**	**-2 995**
American Samoa*	27	-75	-55	-183	-155	-145	-152	-67	-22
Cook Islands	-20	-20	-46	-55	-39	-59	-73	-89	-120
Fiji	-239	-187	-280	-321	-329	-558	-732	-927	-1 022
French Polynesia*	-494	-571	-768	-742	-796	-1 271	-1 401	-1 366	-1 444
Guam	-251	-219	-321	-298	-346	-452	-471	-460	-508
Kiribati	-4	-10	-22	-27	-35	-51	-59	-62	-65
Marshall Islands	..	..	-47	-51	-53	..	..	..	..
Micronesia (Federated States of)	..	..	-76	-61	-75	-103	-112	-121	-122
Nauru	60	42	33	6	5	-9	-4	-3	-3
New Caledonia*	-34	-156	-305	-414	-448	-625	-686	-692	-736
Niue	..	..	..	-3	-2	-4	-5	-8	..
Palau	..	..	..	-36	-90	-93	-112	-138	-143
Papua New Guinea	-196	-134	-121	1 029	789	706	1 086	1 458	1 751
Samoa*	-49	-34	-74	-85	-102	-151	-188	-230	-247
Solomon Islands*	-13	-2	-29	9	-15	-19	-42	-67	-107
Tonga	-29	-34	-47	-61	-62	-80	-92	-106	-118
Tuvalu	-4	-3	-3	-7	-6	-13	-13	-12	-13
Vanuatu	-28	-35	-64	-66	-68	-79	-93	-105	-112
Wallis and Futuna Islands	..	..	..	..	-32	-46	-54	-60	-59
Economies in transition: Asia	**–**	**–**	**–**	**1 136**	**2 902**	**4 818**	**6 909**	**10 206**	**11 718**
Armenia*	–	–	–	-382	-562	-571	-682	-881	-1 357
Azerbaijan*(9)	–	–	–	-162	450	189	20	400	199
Georgia (10)	–	–	–	-304	-390	-777	-1 168	-1 838	-2 763
Kazakhstan*(10)	–	–	–	928	2 727	4 972	7 442	11 108	13 388
Kyrgyzstan	–	–	–	-141	-62	-153	-264	-570	-924
Tajikistan (10)	–	–	–	-55	32	-144	-260	-341	-566
Turkmenistan (10)	–	–	–	1 260	660	800	989	1 188	2 022
Uzbekistan (10)	–	–	–	-8	46	501	833	1 140	1 720
Economies in transition: Europe	**–**	**–**	**–**	**4 706**	**32 606**	**35 650**	**53 154**	**71 469**	**73 079**
Albania	..	..	-202	-567	-885	-1 428	-1 693	-1 975	-2 414
Belarus	–	–	–	-868	-973	-1 800	-1 686	-2 010	-2 550
Bosnia and Herzegovina*(11)	–	–	–	-1 182	-3 056	-4 181	-4 802	-4 755	-4 991
Croatia*	–	–	–	-2 367	-3 811	-7 469	-8 792	-9 826	-11 461
Moldova	–	–	–	-165	-247	-600	-869	-1 215	-1 733
Russian Federation (12)	–	–	–	14 021	44 172	56 192	78 053	101 558	112 895
Serbia and Montenegro*	–	–	–	-1 700	-2 244	-5 605	-6 532	-7 406	-8 527
SFR of Yugoslavia (former)	-5 753	-1 549	-2 239	–	–	–	–	–	–
TFYR of Macedonia*	–	–	–	-464	-631	-1 025	-1 127	-1 266	-1 472
Ukraine (10)	–	–	–	-2 000	281	1 565	603	-1 636	-6 667
USSR (former)	6 987	7 830	-6 351	–	–	–	–	–	–
Developed economies: America	**-31 185**	**-128 375**	**-110 673**	**-166 822**	**-403 634**	**-572 707**	**-677 853**	**-777 572**	**-825 051**
Bermuda	-286	-390	-494	-505	-671	-793	-875	-973	-1 003
Canada	3 186	9 210	2 935	20 378	27 560	25 761	26 755	28 118	29 764
Greenland	-106	-111	-14	-80	-90	-94	-130	-161	-182
Saint Pierre and Miquelon	-7	-27	-55	-65	-65	-58	-60	-52	-46
United States*	-33 973	-137 057	-113 046	-186 550	-430 368	-597 522	-703 544	-804 504	-853 567

For sources and notes, see end of table.

1979-81	1984-86	1989-91	1994-96	1999-01	2002-04	2003-05	2004-06	2005-07	Régions, pays ou territoires
				Percentage of imports					
				Part dans les importations en pourcentage					
26.01	7.91	-13.78	-33.07	-32.09	19.20	39.63	71.70	108.42	Myanmar
-31.73	-14.33	-33.35	-39.82	4.31	-5.56	-10.11	-11.45	-12.30	Philippines
-21.16	-13.78	-11.42	-5.13	3.49	14.64	16.39	16.18	14.08	Singapour (8)
-28.46	-18.77	-25.74	-20.32	10.40	4.17	-0.57	-1.19	1.65	Thaïlande*
..	..	..		-102.38	-96.17	-94.94	-94.33	-93.88	Timor-Leste
-69.11	-62.88	-15.92	-33.30	-5.75	-17.13	-16.06	-13.45	-15.58	Viet Nam
102.21	*4.47*	*25.87*	*14.98*	*29.73*	*30.08*	*36.56*	*42.66*	*42.59*	*Asie occidentale*
3.56	-7.68	-7.82	5.84	27.79	15.73	12.79	13.16	14.84	Bahreïn
58.21	-14.56	36.37	-42.31	43.36	4.40	-2.85	12.95	30.37	Iraq*
-77.29	-71.40	-54.37	-55.94	-54.30	-48.42	-53.63	-55.46	-57.23	Jordanie
191.64	61.82	30.41	70.31	111.16	98.53	129.69	184.12	211.19	Koweït*
-72.33	-83.46	-82.14	-91.02	-87.46	-77.64	-76.09	-74.56	-74.38	Liban
36.12	6.48	77.68	48.81	91.03	68.74	80.11	87.43	81.83	Oman
244.47	187.68	95.38	26.68	201.20	186.12	172.61	139.39	100.65	Qatar*
209.32	11.48	62.05	93.66	119.47	155.99	183.32	200.02	186.91	Arabie saoudite*
-53.63	-55.46	46.55	-31.80	9.38	6.02	-12.44	-13.93	-9.51	République arabe syrienne*
-54.94	-32.09	-35.45	-38.63	-37.25	-32.53	-30.96	-34.48	-35.01	Turquie*
130.63	105.30	87.60	39.50	28.06	26.07	27.90	34.33	34.43	Émirats arabes unis
-52.20	-53.82	–	–	–	–	–	–	–	Yémen (anc. République arabe du)
-97.06	-79.99	–	–	–	–	–	–	–	Yémen (anc. démocratique)
–	–	–	-2.69	45.45	16.99	22.68	25.28	23.85	Yémen*
-38.17	*-42.65*	*-43.39*	*-22.80*	*-32.50*	*-41.73*	*-38.82*	*-34.28*	*-29.57*	*Économies en développement : Océanie*
22.22	-25.31	-14.77	-39.58	-31.56	-25.11	-26.27	-13.85	-5.07	Samoa américaines*
-82.65	-83.75	-91.25	-93.27	-87.20	-88.36	-91.04	-94.12	-94.99	Îles Cook
-43.17	-42.23	-42.35	-35.53	-36.87	-47.02	-51.49	-57.30	-58.68	Fidji
-94.41	-93.81	-87.55	-76.87	-77.90	-88.33	-88.48	-86.65	-87.37	Polynésie française*
-82.21	-83.78	-81.56	-78.60	-83.10	-90.31	-90.52	-89.74	-88.60	Guam
-29.68	-64.20	-85.69	-82.49	-85.84	-94.52	-95.24	-93.81	-92.94	Kiribati
..	..	-89.78	-70.64	-86.81	..	..	..	..	Îles Marshall
..	..	-93.30	-58.92	-85.78	-86.86	-88.13	-90.28	-90.69	Micronésie (États fédérés de)
476.32	222.81	128.44	23.19	26.23	-40.78	-24.19	-18.18	-18.18	Nauru
-8.27	-40.63	-36.39	-44.25	-47.03	-44.76	-41.50	-37.54	-33.05	Nouvelle-Calédonie*
..	..	..	-93.66	-90.53	-97.11	-84.84	-103.81	..	Nioué
..	..	..	-71.21	-87.78	-88.12	-91.81	-91.50	-90.58	Palaos
-17.61	-12.39	-8.53	65.54	69.36	49.47	68.21	77.86	88.92	Papouasie-Nouvelle-Guinée
-75.95	-68.99	-88.72	-91.86	-85.96	-92.01	-93.73	-95.40	-95.12	Samoa*
-16.21	-2.24	-27.87	6.22	-16.07	-19.80	-31.18	-38.25	-47.26	Îles Salomon*
-79.84	-83.98	-80.67	-82.25	-87.15	-83.64	-86.59	-89.85	-92.68	Tonga
-97.44	-83.00	-75.83	-92.24	-99.16	-99.04	-99.27	-99.85	-124.08	Tuvalu
-43.04	-52.89	-76.43	-70.35	-73.87	-73.61	-72.78	-71.82	-72.44	Vanuatu
..	..	..	..	-99.87	-99.58	-99.55	-99.70	-99.58	Îles Wallis-et-Futuna
–	*–*	*–*	*10.13*	*21.15*	*22.42*	*24.59*	*27.42*	*24.28*	*Économies en transition : Asie*
–	–	–	-59.62	-65.99	-47.32	-46.55	-49.76	-56.19	Arménie*
–	–	–	-20.16	37.11	7.24	0.58	9.14	3.83	Azerbaïdjan*(9)
–	–	–	-64.31	-57.11	-61.57	-63.96	-68.74	-72.78	Géorgie (10)
–	–	–	23.97	54.04	53.71	57.93	60.49	53.49	Kazakhstan*(10)
–	–	–	-25.16	-11.51	-20.43	-28.68	-43.89	-51.58	Kirghizistan
–	–	–	-8.08	4.67	-15.43	-22.95	-24.09	-31.06	Tadjikistan (10)
–	–	–	161.11	35.93	30.18	31.33	32.37	49.67	Turkménistan (10)
–	–	–	-0.23	1.61	17.73	25.70	31.18	41.38	Ouzbékistan (10)
–	*–*	*–*	*4.65*	*35.29*	*22.97*	*27.33*	*29.21*	*23.25*	*Économies en transition : Europe*
..	..	-46.35	-75.37	-74.34	-75.46	-74.80	-74.19	-74.35	Albanie
–	–	–	-16.73	-12.37	-14.54	-11.30	-10.86	-11.30	Bélarus
–	–	–	-96.75	-75.66	-75.20	-72.61	-65.48	-60.24	Bosnie-Herzégovine*(11)
–	–	–	-34.37	-46.04	-53.96	-53.44	-52.03	-52.18	Croatie*
–	–	–	-18.93	-32.88	-42.73	-47.69	-53.78	-59.82	Moldova
–	–	–	21.11	87.27	65.38	71.22	71.48	60.00	Fédération de Russie (12)
–	–	–	-47.97	-56.84	-63.97	-61.61	-57.13	-53.60	Serbie-et-Monténégro*
-39.52	-12.92	-13.86							RSF de Yougoslavie (anc.)
–	–	–	-28.82	-34.01	-42.51	-39.95	-38.31	-36.33	LERY de Macédoine*
–	–	–	-13.69	2.03	6.81	2.05	-4.46	-14.10	Ukraine (10)
10.52	9.30	-6.84	–	–	–	–	–	–	URSS (anc.)
-9.91	*-29.01*	*-17.57*	*-17.98*	*-28.87*	*-35.90*	*-37.50*	*-37.92*	*-36.67*	*Économies développées : Amérique*
-89.77	-90.10	-90.30	-90.66	-93.59	-92.68	-93.51	-95.21	-96.44	Bermudes
5.05	11.33	2.39	12.27	11.94	10.27	9.37	8.70	8.30	Canada
-35.34	-35.59	-3.33	-18.73	-24.54	-19.55	-23.58	-27.25	-30.89	Groenland
-84.90	-84.43	-65.84	-88.60	-92.38	-90.23	-88.17	-80.35	-74.87	Saint-Pierre-et-Miquelon
-13.54	-38.03	-22.34	-24.52	-36.91	-44.49	-46.27	-46.62	-45.17	États-Unis*

Pour les sources et les notes, se reporter à la fin du tableau.

Region, country or territory	Trade balance - Balance commerciale Millions of dollars - Millions de dollars								
	1979-81	1984-86	1989-91	1994-96	1999-01	2002-04	2003-05	2004-06	2005-07
Developed economies: Asia	**-7 533**	**50 709**	**59 551**	**86 952**	**82 837**	**88 206**	**88 956**	**83 104**	**76 560**
Israel*	-4 281	-3 759	-5 188	-9 965	-4 580	-4 978	-4 378	-4 054	-3 491
Japan	-3 253	54 468	64 739	96 918	87 417	93 184	93 334	87 158	80 050
Developed economies: Europe	**-76 223**	**-9 324**	**-64 811**	**68 278**	**1 034**	**57 668**	**26 290**	**-20 913**	**-62 733**
Andorra	..	..	..	-941	-1 143	-1 453	-1 570	-1 676	-1 697
Austria*	-5 643	-3 986	-8 020	-9 661	-4 609	-1 179	-2 019	-1 379	-678
Belgium*						19 896	19 206	17 302	16 055
Belgium-Luxembourg*	-6 059	-1 925	-1 102	10 232	9 473	–	–	–	–
Bulgaria*	322	-416	580	-291	-1 778	-3 379	-4 774	-6 376	-8 680
Cyprus*	-610	-794	-1 587	-2 368	-2 822	-3 700	-4 288	-5 002	-5 877
Czechoslovakia (former) (13)	1 333	368	-16						
Czech Republic*(14)	–	–	–	-4 726	-4 335	-3 454	-1 493	781	2 606
Denmark*(15)	-2 594	-1 127	3 127	5 576	5 557	8 389	9 188	8 512	6 807
Estonia*(10)	–	–	–	-577	-367	-1 244	-1 929	-2 885	-3 488
Faeroe Islands	-47	-86	66	61	-11	-34	-98	-102	-177
Finland	-632	814	-99	9 036	10 804	10 544	9 250	8 418	7 780
France*	-15 280	-8 207	-20 506	5 091	-2 257	-7 721	-22 123	-35 199	-49 350
Germany (former Dem. Rep.)	-1 081	1 349	–	–	–	–	–	–	–
Germany (former Federal Rep.)	9 707	32 204	–	–	–	–	–	–	–
Germany*	–	–	–	56 854	69 905	155 444	178 351	196 502	220 503
Greece*	-5 229	-5 307	-11 062	-14 481	-20 624	-30 006	-35 265	-39 053	-43 774
Hungary*(16)	-586	118	355	-2 946	-3 369	-4 440	-4 552	-3 862	-2 345
Iceland*	-82	-71	-105	-65	-476	-369	-891	-1 657	-2 013
Ireland*	-2 809	447	3 267	11 584	27 720	39 210	40 986	39 900	38 528
Italy*	-15 163	-8 348	-12 382	31 308	8 321	2 566	-3 790	-12 952	-16 735
Latvia*	–	–	–	-550	-1 348	-2 401	-2 990	-4 002	-5 275
Lithuania (10)	–	–	–	-824	-1 775	-2 692	-3 177	-4 022	-5 327
Luxembourg*	–	–	–	–	–	-3 038	-3 260	-3 524	-3 912
Malta	-400	-357	-776	-988	-863	-909	-1 144	-1 273	-1 356
Netherlands*	-1 536	5 111	5 106	15 488	16 506	31 266	37 214	42 373	49 385
Norway	1 341	2 408	6 268	10 146	21 063	28 824	36 268	45 970	54 131
Poland*	-2 225	313	2 389	-7 731	-16 659	-14 405	-13 778	-14 357	-17 380
Portugal*	-4 459	-2 379	-8 402	-9 818	-15 474	-16 275	-19 222	-21 850	-24 254
Romania*	-1 848	237	-1 410	-2 225	-2 915	-6 516	-9 432	-13 561	-20 294
Slovakia*	–	–	–	-1 123	-2 015	-2 288	-2 415	-2 809	-2 789
Slovenia*	–	–	–	-921	-1 272	-1 022	-1 196	-1 139	-1 161
Spain*	-10 802	-6 278	-31 291	-13 931	-36 616	-55 826	-74 793	-95 624	-113 958
Sweden	-1 283	3 145	3 697	14 299	14 340	18 636	20 086	20 649	18 939
Switzerland*	-4 400	-3 584	-5 846	1 785	-1 188	5 442	5 339	5 951	7 194
United Kingdom*	-6 158	-12 970	-36 535	-29 017	-60 739	-100 198	-115 398	-134 965	-154 128
Developed economies: Oceania	**-1 576**	**-3 589**	**-2 871**	**-6 533**	**-7 748**	**-17 902**	**-23 113**	**-21 361**	**-22 153**
Australia*	-1 573	-3 210	-3 278	-6 398	-7 079	-16 053	-19 984	-17 578	-18 006
New Zealand	-3	-380	408	-134	-669	-1 849	-3 129	-3 784	-4 147

Sources:
- Data in this table are based on trade figures in table 1.1.1.

Notes:

* Countries which use the Special Trade System as reporting system.
(a) Data refers to South Africa Customs Union (Botswana, Lesotho, Namibia, South Africa and Swaziland)
(b) Including Aruba

(1) Trade with other member countries of CEMAC is excluded.
(2) Prior to 1986, included in Netherlands Antilles. Including exports and imports of crude oil and oil products.
(3) From 1990 onwards, trade statistics exclude certain oil and chemical products.
(4) Prior to 1986, including Aruba.
(5) Excluding imports of goods financed through foreign aid.
(6) Excluding military goods, fissionable materials, bunkers, ships and aircraft.
(7) Inter-trade between the States of Malaysia included. From 1965 onwards, excluding military imports and offshore installations of petroleum industry.
(8) Including trans-shipments to and from peninsular Malaysia.
(9) Excluding military goods, precious metals and goods procured in foreign ports.
(10) Prior to 1994, covers only trade with countries outside the CIS.
(11) Prior to 1998, data refer to the Federation of Bosnia and Herzegovina only. The other entity of Bosnia and Herzegovina, Republika Srpska, is not included.
(12) Prior to 1994, excluding trade with independent states resulting from the former USSR.
(13) From 1985 onwards, data are not comparable to those shown for prior periods due to revisions of the koruna-to-US dollar exchange rate.
(14) From 1995 onward, including goods for processing.
(15) Prior to 1988, excluding ships.
(16) Prior to 1996, excluding customs free zones.

Percentage of imports Part dans les importations en pourcentage									Régions, pays ou territoires
1979-81	1984-86	1989-91	1994-96	1999-01	2002-04	2003-05	2004-06	2005-07	
-5.35	**35.82**	**24.41**	**24.92**	**21.80**	**20.52**	**18.05**	**14.76**	**12.29**	**Économies développées : Asie**
-44.91	-36.98	-31.25	-34.59	-13.74	-13.02	-10.40	-8.67	-6.80	Israël*
-2.48	41.45	28.47	30.28	25.22	23.80	20.70	16.88	14.01	Japon
-8.39	**-1.03**	**-3.98**	**3.21**	**0.04**	**1.75**	**0.68**	**-0.48**	**-1.26**	**Économies développées : Europe**
..	..	..	-95.22	-95.49	-93.92	-93.02	-91.88	-91.34	Andorre
-25.75	-17.73	-17.33	-15.26	-6.33	-1.19	-1.75	-1.08	-0.48	Autriche*
					8.31	6.86	5.43	4.45	Belgique*
-9.31	-3.20	-0.97	6.29	5.11	–	–	–	–	Belgique-Luxembourg*
3.33	-3.00	7.74	-5.21	-27.75	-30.39	-32.90	-34.22	-36.56	Bulgarie*
-54.20	-61.36	-63.72	-66.42	-74.34	-81.33	-79.84	-80.03	-80.80	Chypre*
10.92	3.03	-0.13							Tchécoslovaquie (anc.) (13)
–	–	–	-19.16	-12.80	-6.22	-2.24	0.98	2.73	République tchèque*(14)
-14.07	-5.85	9.86	13.09	12.20	14.32	13.70	11.14	7.85	Danemark*(15)
–	–	–	-24.87	-9.21	-19.02	-23.11	-27.05	-26.99	Estonie*(10)
-22.46	-30.88	20.15	19.79	-2.26	-5.51	-13.90	-14.16	-21.26	Îles Féroé
-4.60	5.95	-0.41	32.20	32.66	24.69	18.14	14.08	11.17	Finlande
-12.38	-7.04	-9.09	1.81	-0.69	-1.93	-4.83	-6.96	-8.93	France*
-5.85	5.48	–	–	–	–	–	–	–	Allemagne (anc. Rép. dém. d)
5.69	19.23	–	–	–	–	–	–	–	Allemagne (anc. Rép. fédérale d')
			13.09	14.38	25.77	25.50	24.56	24.18	Allemagne*
-54.15	-51.49	-57.70	-57.47	-64.41	-69.73	-69.74	-68.74	-68.13	Grèce*
-6.49	1.36	3.70	-18.52	-10.80	-9.13	-7.81	-5.64	-2.94	Hongrie*(16)
-8.62	-7.42	-6.50	-3.68	-19.45	-12.86	-24.53	-34.85	-36.13	Islande*
-26.63	4.28	16.65	37.69	56.03	70.03	66.71	58.81	51.74	Irlande*
-16.67	-9.16	-7.18	16.11	3.59	0.86	-1.10	-3.29	-3.78	Italie*
–	–	–	-30.60	-41.98	-43.96	-42.64	-43.93	-44.71	Lettonie*
–	–	–	-23.41	-33.48	-27.30	-25.33	-25.50	-27.10	Lituanie (10)
					-18.66	-16.82	-15.43	-15.50	Luxembourg*
-46.97	-45.38	-41.92	-36.23	-28.85	-27.52	-32.18	-33.96	-34.16	Malte
-1.91	7.04	4.28	8.96	7.82	11.68	11.77	11.55	11.67	Pays-Bas*
8.69	14.52	24.60	31.74	62.25	70.61	76.43	82.96	82.05	Norvège
-14.63	2.73	20.58	-26.49	-34.44	-20.31	-15.93	-13.53	-13.36	Pologne*
-52.16	-28.25	-35.62	-31.07	-38.86	-34.33	-35.30	-35.85	-35.46	Portugal*
-14.18	2.10	-17.09	-23.16	-22.42	-26.23	-29.13	-32.75	-37.82	Roumanie*
–	–	–	-12.25	-14.81	-9.68	-8.15	-7.66	-5.97	Slovaquie*
–	–	–	-10.54	-12.57	-7.21	-6.90	-5.49	-4.59	Slovénie*
-35.35	-20.07	-37.33	-12.92	-24.61	-26.52	-29.68	-32.75	-34.61	Espagne*
-4.23	10.76	7.24	23.36	21.01	22.29	20.39	18.25	14.59	Suède
-13.69	-10.57	-9.02	2.37	-1.44	5.38	4.67	4.65	5.04	Suisse*
-5.81	-11.41	-17.30	-11.05	-17.99	-24.37	-25.01	-25.53	-26.72	Royaume-Uni*
-5.73	**-11.20**	**-5.55**	**-8.88**	**-9.45**	**-16.38**	**-17.70**	**-14.43**	**-13.09**	**Économies développées : Océanie**
-7.06	-12.36	-7.65	-10.66	-10.38	-17.76	-18.52	-14.32	-12.73	Australie*
-0.06	-6.24	4.59	-0.99	-4.84	-9.77	-13.81	-14.96	-14.89	Nouvelle-Zélande

Sources :
- Les données dans ce tableau ont été calculées d'après les chiffres du tableau 1.1.1.

Notes :

* Pays qui utilisent le système du commerce spécial en tant que système d'enregistrement.
(a) Donnée relative à l'Union Douanière d'Afrique du Sud (Afrique du Sud, Botswana, Lesotho, Namibie et Swaziland)
(b) Y compris Aruba

(1) Non-compris le commerce avec les autres pays membres de la CEMAC.
(2) Avant 1986 compris dans Antilles néerlandaises. Les données comprennent les exportations et importations de pétrole brut et produits dérivés.
(3) À partir de 1990, certains produits pétroliers et chimiques ne sont plus inclus dans les statistiques du commerce.
(4) Avant 1986, y compris Aruba.
(5) Non-compris les biens d'importation financés par l'aide à l'étranger.
(6) Non-compris les biens à usage militaire, le matériel fissile, le combustible de soute et l'avitaillement des navires et aéronefs.
(7) Y compris le commerce entre les États de la Malaisie. À partir de 1965, non comprises les importations militaires et l'installation près des côtes de l'industrie pétrolière.
(8) Y compris les transbordements vers et en provenance de la Malaisie péninsulaire.
(9) Non-compris les biens à usage militaire, les métaux précieux et les biens fournis dans les ports étrangers.
(10) Avant 1994, concerne seulement le commerce avec les pays extérieurs à la CEI.
(11) Avant 1998, les données se réfèrent uniquement à la Fédération de la Bosnie-Herzégovine. L'autre entité de la Bosnie-Herzégovine, Republika Srpska, n'est pas incluse.
(12) Avant 1994, non-compris le commerce avec les républiques indépendantes de l'ancienne URSS.
(13) À partir de 1985, les chiffres ne sont pas comparables à ceux des années antérieures à cause des révisions du taux de change de la couronne par rapport au dollar des États-Unis.
(14) À partir de 1995, y compris les biens destinés à subir des transformations.
(15) Avant 1988, non-compris les navires.
(16) Avant 1996, non-compris les zones franches douanières.

1.3.2 Value of trade balance, and as percentage of imports of economic groupings

Economic grouping	Trade balance - Balance commerciale Millions of dollars - Millions de dollars								
	79-81	84-86	89-91	94-96	99-01	02-04	03-05	04-06	05-07
DEVELOPING ECONOMIES	**74 285**	**19 061**	**17 783**	**-56 169**	**105 334**	**176 366**	**257 256**	**377 801**	**490 139**
Developing economies excluding China	75 571	28 439	14 362	-67 603	80 039	147 038	204 068	273 843	309 481
Developing economies excluding LDCs	82 096	26 104	23 744	-47 217	116 198	187 996	267 189	382 253	487 319
High-income developing countries	87 432	44 542	41 477	10 510	81 560	159 469	222 912	299 773	345 337
Middle-income developing countries	-12 755	-4 694	-19 778	-60 299	-15 881	-5 504	3 809	3 735	5 431
Low-income developing countries	-392	-20 788	-3 915	-6 380	39 655	22 402	30 535	74 293	139 372
Heavily indebted poor countries	-4 419	-3 735	-3 348	-7 167	-12 246	-14 231	-17 200	-19 990	-23 387
Landlocked developing countries	-1 557	-3 205	-3 300	-5 997	-5 606	-5 945	-4 601	-1 850	-1 077
Small island developing States	-2 150	-1 999	-3 692	-3 986	-6 293	-7 169	-6 969	-6 211	-6 620
Least developed countries	*-7 811*	*-7 044*	*-5 961*	*-8 952*	*-10 864*	*-11 630*	*-9 933*	*-4 452*	*2 820*
Africa and Haiti	-3 908	-2 533	-1 252	-3 578	-4 836	-4 430	-2 299	3 130	10 619
Asia	-3 771	-4 372	-4 405	-4 945	-5 278	-6 276	-6 522	-6 247	-6 246
Islands	-131	-138	-305	-429	-750	-924	-1 111	-1 335	-1 552
Major petroleum exporters	*123 406*	*30 403*	*56 093*	*69 539*	*126 712*	*166 259*	*243 008*	*342 035*	*419 763*
Africa	18 125	11 036	16 834	13 357	30 993	37 623	59 468	87 657	111 752
America	7 298	6 036	7 580	9 847	12 181	18 458	25 597	33 044	34 634
Asia	97 983	13 330	31 680	46 335	83 538	110 179	157 943	221 333	273 377
Major exporters of manufactured goods	*-32 576*	*7 305*	*-12 588*	*-64 415*	*26 257*	*58 088*	*82 946*	*122 651*	*178 095*
America	-7 515	18 059	6 123	-8 503	-18 188	5 505	14 924	19 968	18 914
Asia	-25 060	-10 754	-18 711	-55 912	44 445	52 583	68 021	102 684	159 181
Emerging economies	*-18 516*	*31 660*	*6 220*	*-37 737*	*36 008*	*97 067*	*119 544*	*142 644*	*156 795*
America	-8 918	22 558	12 574	-14 227	-17 015	25 203	36 736	49 053	53 972
Asia	-9 597	9 103	-6 355	-23 510	53 023	71 864	82 808	93 591	102 823
Newly industrialized economies	*-3 489*	*15 194*	*-6 127*	*-43 239*	*70 264*	*83 595*	*89 275*	*97 057*	*102 968*
First tier	-11 522	8 216	1 425	-24 331	21 182	42 343	51 866	58 138	57 137
Second tier	8 033	6 978	-7 552	-18 908	49 081	41 252	37 409	38 919	45 830
Developing economies: Africa	**11 939**	**1 875**	**3 577**	**-6 581**	**4 867**	**7 382**	**19 819**	**37 716**	**51 767**
Northern Africa excluding Sudan	7 363	-3 571	-5 148	-9 615	-1 546	2 819	10 833	21 304	28 721
Sub-Saharan Africa	4 576	5 446	8 725	3 034	6 413	4 563	8 986	16 412	23 046
Sub-Saharan Africa excluding South Africa	254	1 651	4 300	3 603	5 977	8 385	16 519	28 780	36 961
Developing economies: America	**-9 635**	**21 255**	**9 712**	**-25 286**	**-31 471**	**12 653**	**27 218**	**39 261**	**35 952**
Central America and Greater Carribean Islands excluding Puerto Rico	-8 207	2 437	-13 582	-16 229	-35 165	-39 057	-43 031	-50 284	-59 731
Central America and Greater Carribean Islands excluding Mexico and Puerto Rico	-4 083	-5 657	-9 018	-10 834	-19 755	-23 534	-26 839	-32 551	-39 670
South America and Central America	-6 220	26 029	17 633	-18 031	-18 336	26 034	41 267	54 516	54 101
South America excluding Brazil	3 425	10 081	14 846	-3 108	10 356	35 174	43 157	54 517	59 072
Developing economies: Asia	**73 251**	**-2 633**	**6 718**	**-22 939**	**133 779**	**159 458**	**213 515**	**303 991**	**405 415**
Eastern and South-Eastern Asia excluding China	-1 474	15 284	-6 253	-47 217	69 097	80 153	85 666	94 272	98 920
Southern Asia excluding India	-3 672	-5 790	-7 903	-1 464	1 121	-4 712	-3 729	-5 021	-1 126

Sources:
- Data in this table are based on trade figures in table 1.1.1.

46

Percentage of imports Part dans les importations en pourcentage									Groupements économiques
79-81	84-86	89-91	94-96	99-01	02-04	03-05	04-06	05-07	
15.71	4.01	2.22	-3.90	5.94	7.50	9.05	11.06	12.25	ÉCONOMIES EN DÉVELOPPEMENT
16.65	6.50	1.93	-5.15	5.12	7.62	8.88	9.98	9.68	Économies en développement sans la Chine
18.19	5.74	3.05	-3.35	6.72	8.21	9.65	11.49	12.50	Économies en développement sans les PMA
40.87	21.24	10.14	1.38	8.84	14.60	17.37	19.77	19.75	Pays en développement à revenu élevé
-9.30	-3.45	-9.14	-16.24	-3.92	-1.06	0.62	0.51	0.63	Pays en développement à revenu intermédiaire
-0.32	-16.07	-2.21	-2.05	8.88	3.02	3.24	6.40	10.04	Pays en développement à revenu faible
-19.25	-18.38	-14.45	-23.52	-31.66	-28.04	-28.07	-27.06	-26.96	Pays pauvres très endettés
-18.37	-33.52	-29.61	-20.50	-15.17	-11.54	-7.29	-2.36	-1.13	Pays en développement sans littoral
-15.60	-20.01	-32.73	-29.40	-36.91	-36.14	-30.90	-23.85	-22.49	Petits États insulaires en développement
-35.94	*-35.01*	*-25.30*	*-27.77*	*-24.33*	*-19.11*	*-13.56*	*-5.12*	*2.79*	*Pays les moins avancés*
-25.94	-19.76	-8.12	-18.96	-19.55	-12.29	-5.10	5.75	16.69	Afrique et Haïti
-59.25	-62.60	-57.76	-39.08	-27.92	-26.63	-24.37	-20.28	-17.52	Asie
-43.38	-43.85	-59.44	-59.35	-75.19	-74.88	-76.61	-77.89	-79.14	Îles
89.61	*27.23*	*48.16*	*51.37*	*73.03*	*66.83*	*77.82*	*89.45*	*91.99*	*Principaux exportateurs de pétrole*
48.29	42.79	67.17	46.10	102.19	76.60	95.75	117.76	131.68	Afrique
43.69	52.67	62.47	60.57	52.18	76.11	84.51	81.24	65.69	Amérique
117.39	17.92	39.96	51.41	69.72	62.81	71.84	82.82	85.78	Asie
-16.59	*3.10*	*-2.46*	*-6.28*	*2.06*	*3.39*	*4.03*	*4.97*	*6.20*	*Principaux exportateurs d'articles manufacturés*
-17.14	55.01	9.30	-6.38	-8.06	2.27	5.51	6.33	5.17	Amérique
-16.43	-5.30	-4.20	-6.27	4.23	3.57	3.80	4.77	6.35	Asie
-12.80	*21.85*	*1.88*	*-5.70*	*4.58*	*10.65*	*11.18*	*11.24*	*10.73*	*Économies émergentes*
-14.56	52.61	15.23	-7.94	-6.19	8.78	11.19	12.62	11.82	Amérique
-11.51	8.92	-2.56	-4.86	10.35	11.51	11.17	10.62	10.24	Asie
-2.83	*10.09*	*-1.67*	*-5.89*	*9.03*	*8.86*	*8.08*	*7.49*	*7.00*	*Économies nouvellement industrialisées*
-13.39	7.38	0.52	-4.59	3.66	6.10	6.39	6.11	5.30	Première génération
21.67	17.75	-7.92	-9.24	24.58	16.57	12.78	11.32	11.70	Deuxième génération
13.40	**2.51**	**3.84**	**-5.74**	**3.72**	**4.15**	**9.09**	**14.49**	**17.18**	**Économies en développement : Afrique**
24.35	-10.97	-12.49	-21.21	-3.25	4.77	15.42	25.82	29.56	Afrique septentrionale sans le Soudan
7.78	12.93	16.82	4.38	7.70	3.84	6.08	9.23	11.28	Afrique subsaharienne
0.61	5.78	12.91	8.74	10.84	10.81	17.31	25.38	28.33	Afrique subsaharienne sans l'Afrique du Sud
-8.37	**24.68**	**7.48**	**-10.09**	**-8.50**	**3.24**	**6.06**	**7.31**	**5.64**	**Économies en développement : Amérique**
-21.93	6.77	-21.31	-14.62	-16.62	-16.65	-16.66	-16.95	-17.72	Amérique centrale et Grandes Antilles sans Porto Rico
-24.71	-31.11	-45.93	-40.47	-46.55	-49.76	-50.92	-53.32	-55.44	Amérique centrale et Grandes Antilles sans le Mexique et Porto Rico
-6.87	39.52	15.92	-7.81	-5.40	7.25	9.98	11.02	9.19	Amérique du Sud et Amérique centrale
8.66	37.92	40.39	-3.79	11.61	40.67	39.30	38.51	32.94	Amérique du Sud sans le Brésil
27.59	**-0.85**	**1.17**	**-2.14**	**10.55**	**8.98**	**9.85**	**11.65**	**13.28**	**Économies en développement : Asie**
-1.16	9.81	-1.67	-6.28	8.60	8.17	7.44	6.98	6.44	Asie orientale et Asie du Sud-Est sans la Chine
-15.72	-23.59	-22.93	-3.89	2.54	-7.20	-4.72	-5.34	-1.07	Asie méridionale sans l'Inde

Sources :
- Les données dans ce tableau ont été calculées d'après les chiffres du tableau 1.1.1.

1.4 Intra-trade of trade groups

Trade group	Value of intra-trade (exports in millions of dollars) Valeur du commerce interne au groupement (exportations en millions de dollars)						Intra-trade of groups regional exports Commerce interne des exportations régionales		
	1980	1990	1995	2000	2005	2006	1980	1990	1995
AFRICA									
CEPGL	2	7	8	10	20	24	3.6	6.2	6.0
CEMAC (formerly UDEAC)	75	139	120	96	198	245	66.6	28.1	40.3
COMESA	569	1 146	1 367	1 443	2 864	3 489	79.2	61.9	50.5
ECCAS	89	163	163	191	271	334	49.3	26.1	36.3
ECOWAS	661	1 532	1 875	2 715	5 497	5 957	73.5	75.5	77.1
MRU	7	0	1	5	6	8	59.3	0.7	1.6
SADC	106	1 070	4 190	4 383	7 668	8 571	50.9	88.6	84.2
UEMOA	460	621	560	741	1 390	1 545	52.9	49.3	47.2
UMA	109	958	1 109	1 094	1 926	2 400	34.0	69.3	66.9
AMERICA									
ANCOM	468	544	1 788	2 046	4 572	5 458	8.0	6.9	14.8
CACM	1 174	667	1 594	2 586	4 064	5 022	37.2	23.2	33.0
CARICOM	599	453	875	1 074	2 082	2 418	7.7	14.0	21.1
FTAA	167 719	300 694	525 317	855 187	1 103 996	1 239 932	96.4	99.2	99.5
LAIA	11 192	13 350	35 986	44 252	71 711	91 651	25.4	21.3	25.8
MERCOSUR	3 424	4 127	14 199	17 829	21 128	25 775	31.8	22.2	43.1
NAFTA	102 218	226 273	394 472	676 142	824 550	902 086	79.0	88.8	87.4
OECS	4	28	38	36	63	78	23.1	22.0	26.8
ASIA									
APTA	783	2 429	21 728	37 895	127 277	150 545	3.6	3.2	12.7
ASEAN	12 413	27 365	79 544	98 060	165 163	194 321	29.0	34.0	42.0
ECO	392	1 243	4 746	4 518	13 936	19 053	17.1	11.1	25.5
GCC	4 632	6 906	6 832	7 954	16 507	20 050	7.2	14.6	12.1
SAARC	613	863	2 024	2 680	7 266	9 109	12.2	10.8	12.5
EUROPE									
EFTA	524	782	925	831	1 252	1 524	1.4	1.1	1.1
EU	501 402	1 037 044	1 409 714	1 641 252	2 729 376	3 087 605	..	..	..
Euro zone	309 700	675 716	869 215	946 891	1 567 841	1 726 122	70.5	71.8	70.7
OCEANIA									
MSG	11	5	18	22	51	63	3.7	1.1	1.5
INTERREGIONAL									
ACP	2 351	4 565	9 596	11 970	23 042	26 871	..	..	..
APEC	357 697	901 730	1 689 154	2 262 085	3 309 304	3 763 818	..	..	..
BSEC	1 190	1 229	25 505	24 737	65 744	83 504	..	..	..
CIS	..	..	31 529	28 753	59 423	66 583	..	..	..

Sources:
- UNCTAD secretariat calculations based on International Monetary Fund (IMF), *Direction of Trade Statistics*.

as percentage of of each group du groupement en pourcentage de chaque groupement			Intra-trade of groups as percentage of total exports of each group Commerce interne du groupement en pourcentage des exportations totales de chaque groupement						Groupements commerciaux
2000	2005	2006	1980	1990	1995	2000	2005	2006	
									AFRIQUE
25.0	14.6	19.8	0.1	0.5	0.5	0.8	1.2	1.3	CEPGL
30.3	28.4	27.8	1.6	2.3	2.1	1.0	0.9	0.9	CEMAC (anc. UDEAC)
48.3	48.7	48.7	1.8	4.7	6.1	4.6	4.5	4.2	COMESA
51.1	23.7	24.1	1.4	1.4	1.5	1.1	0.6	0.6	CEEAC
74.4	74.6	66.4	9.6	8.0	9.0	7.6	9.3	8.3	CEDEAO
8.2	13.9	3.4	0.8	0.0	0.1	0.4	0.3	0.3	UFM
80.5	75.0	75.2	0.4	3.1	10.7	9.4	9.2	9.1	SADC
46.6	42.1	42.2	9.6	13.0	10.3	13.1	13.4	13.1	UEMOA
67.0	61.6	62.9	0.3	2.9	3.8	2.3	2.0	2.0	UMA
									AMÉRIQUE
11.1	12.5	12.6	4.1	4.0	8.6	7.7	9.0	8.4	ANCOM
31.2	23.0	23.9	24.4	15.3	21.8	19.1	18.9	16.8	MCAC
22.2	15.1	15.9	5.4	8.0	12.1	14.6	11.6	11.3	CARICOM
99.0	98.7	98.6	43.4	46.6	52.5	60.7	60.2	58.4	ZLEA
17.1	19.3	20.9	13.9	11.6	17.3	13.2	13.6	14.3	ALADI
38.7	26.7	28.4	11.6	8.9	20.3	20.0	12.9	13.5	MERCOSUR
91.0	90.7	89.6	33.6	41.4	46.2	55.7	55.8	53.8	ALENA
23.0	29.1	33.3	9.0	8.5	14.5	13.7	15.1	11.2	OECO
									ASIE
15.8	22.1	22.0	1.7	1.6	6.8	8.0	11.0	10.7	ACAP
39.1	39.5	39.3	17.4	18.9	24.5	23.0	25.3	24.9	ANASE
17.9	22.8	24.7	6.3	3.2	7.9	5.6	7.6	8.5	ECO
7.5	7.3	7.1	3.0	8.0	6.8	4.8	4.8	4.8	CCG
12.7	13.1	13.1	4.8	3.2	4.4	4.2	5.6	5.6	SAARC
									EUROPE
0.8	0.7	0.8	1.1	0.8	0.7	0.6	0.5	0.6	AELE
..	..	..	62.3	67.6	66.8	67.7	67.3	67.6	UE
68.8	67.7	66.8	51.9	55.5	52.6	50.8	50.3	49.7	Zone euro
									OCÉANIE
1.9	2.6	2.7	0.7	0.3	0.4	0.6	0.8	0.8	MSG
									INTERRÉGIONAUX
..	..	..	4.0	6.3	11.1	10.4	11.0	10.9	ACP
..	..	..	57.9	68.3	71.7	73.1	70.8	69.4	CEAP
..	..	..	5.9	4.2	18.1	14.2	16.0	16.9	CEMN
..	..	..	..	..	28.6	20.0	18.0	16.5	CEI

Sources :
- Calculs du secrétariat de la CNUCED sur la base de données du Fonds monétaire international (FMI), *Direction of Trade Statistics.*

2 INTERNATIONAL **MERCHANDISE** TRADE BY REGION

COMMERCE INTERNATIONAL DES **MARCHANDISES** PAR RÉGIONS

1
2
3
4
5
6
7
8

Destination / Origin / Origine	Year Année	World (millions of dollars) (1) Monde (millions de dollars) (1)	Developed economies / Économies développées Total	Europe Total	Europe EU UE	USA États-Unis	Japan Japon	Other Autres	Economies in transition Économies en transition	Developing economies / Économies en développement Total	Africa Afrique	America Amérique	Eastern, Southern and South-Eastern Asia / Asie orientale, méridionale et du Sud-Est	Western Asia Asie occidentale	Oceania Océanie
Afghanistan	1990	131	79.4	73.8	69.0	3.4	1.5	0.7	0.1	20.5	0.3	0.6	14.7	4.9	..
	2000	142	38.1	35.5	35.3	1.9	0.3	0.4	5.7	56.2	0.6	4.7	48.6	2.2	0.0
	2006	275	33.5	17.6	17.4	15.2	0.2	0.6	6.8	59.7	3.4	1.6	47.5	7.2	0.0
Albania - Albanie	1990	224	75.1	70.1	68.9	1.0	4.0	0.0	9.6	15.2	4.9	0.2	9.9	0.3	..
	2000	260	94.8	93.9	93.6	0.9	0.1	0.0	4.4	0.7	..	..	0.0	0.7	..
	2006	697	85.4	81.8	81.6	3.3	0.1	0.3	9.1	5.3	0.3	1.1	2.3	1.6	0.0
Algeria - Algérie	1990	11 009	91.0	70.5	70.5	19.2	0.9	0.4	2.0	6.9	2.5	2.1	0.6	1.7	..
	2000	21 871	83.1	63.8	63.4	15.7	0.1	3.6	0.2	16.7	1.4	8.2	0.8	6.3	..
	2006	53 712	87.9	51.7	51.5	27.2	0.2	8.8	0.2	11.9	2.0	3.9	2.6	3.5	0.0
Angola	1990	3 748	90.0	36.4	36.4	50.9	1.3	1.3	5.6	4.4	0.5	3.9	0.0	0.0	..
	2000	7 315	62.8	17.5	17.4	44.9	0.0	0.4	0.0	37.2	0.2	1.8	35.2	0.0	..
	2006	29 059	50.6	8.7	8.4	38.1	1.9	2.0	0.0	49.4	1.3	6.5	41.5	0.1	..
Argentina - Argentine	1990	12 353	52.0	33.3	32.7	13.8	3.2	1.8	4.2	43.8	3.2	27.6	11.2	1.9	0.0
	2000	26 341	33.6	18.5	18.2	12.0	1.4	1.8	0.4	64.2	4.0	48.1	10.1	2.0	0.0
	2006	46 455	29.9	18.7	17.5	8.9	0.9	1.6	2.2	66.3	6.3	42.4	15.0	2.6	0.0
Armenia - Arménie	2000	300	52.8	39.8	36.9	12.6	0.1	0.3	24.0	12.8	0.0	..	10.3	2.5	..
	2006	718	67.6	54.2	54.0	6.1	0.0	7.3	21.9	10.0	0.0	1.0	7.0	2.0	..
Aruba	2000	173	38.2	32.3	32.3	5.8	0.0	0.1	..	61.2	0.1	61.1	0.0	0.0	..
	2006	124	40.1	30.7	30.7	9.4	0.0	0.0	0.0	59.7	..	59.6	0.0	0.0	..
Australia - Australie	1990	38 987	60.3	16.3	14.1	11.0	26.2	6.8	0.9	36.4	1.4	1.0	28.6	2.8	0.1
	2000	63 520	48.0	11.0	10.7	9.8	19.8	7.4	0.3	48.0	2.4	1.3	38.1	4.1	0.6
	2006	121 827	45.2	12.8	12.5	6.2	19.6	6.6	0.5	52.8	2.5	1.6	43.5	3.8	0.1
Austria - Autriche	1990	41 393	87.3	81.1	73.4	3.2	1.6	1.4	4.8	7.8	1.6	0.7	3.9	1.6	0.0
	2000	67 456	89.7	81.9	74.8	5.0	1.3	1.5	3.0	7.3	1.1	1.1	3.8	1.3	0.0
	2006	136 832	85.7	77.1	72.0	5.8	1.1	1.7	5.0	8.6	1.3	1.1	4.2	2.0	0.0
Azerbaijan - Azerbaïdjan	2000	1 747	76.8	68.6	63.6	0.5	0.0	7.8	13.8	8.8	0.6	0.4	1.4	6.4	..
	2006	6 372	70.0	57.7	57.2	1.5	0.0	10.8	14.7	15.2	0.2	0.0	8.2	6.7	..
Bahamas	1990	990	96.4	41.0	29.8	48.3	1.4	5.7	0.0	3.0	0.4	2.1	0.5	..	..
	2000	878	90.8	57.0	51.4	28.8	3.3	1.7	0.3	8.7	0.1	7.7	0.4	0.5	0.0
	2006	2 136	86.7	61.7	58.5	20.2	3.6	1.1	0.4	12.7	0.2	8.7	3.7	0.1	0.0
Bahrain - Bahreïn	1990	3 838	5.4	1.6	1.6	1.8	1.8	0.1	..	10.3	0.1	0.9	3.5	5.8	0.0
	2000	7 719	12.5	5.2	4.9	4.1	2.8	0.5	0.0	25.4	4.4	0.1	14.7	6.2	0.0
	2006	19 787	9.9	3.6	3.2	3.0	2.3	1.0	0.0	22.0	3.7	0.2	8.9	9.1	0.0
Bangladesh	1990	1 671	76.7	38.8	36.9	30.5	3.9	3.5	3.1	19.7	4.1	0.5	11.9	3.1	0.1
	2000	5 590	76.0	40.9	40.3	31.8	1.2	2.1	0.2	9.2	0.7	0.4	6.0	2.1	0.0
	2006	12 740	78.1	48.0	46.8	25.0	1.1	4.0	0.4	9.2	0.7	0.2	6.3	1.9	0.0
Barbados - Barbade	1990	209	35.8	18.8	18.6	13.5	0.3	3.3	..	25.9	0.0	25.6	0.3	..	..
	2000	273	23.1	16.7	16.4	3.8	0.1	2.5	28.5	31.6	0.1	28.7	0.7	1.6	0.1
	2006	324	45.7	15.3	14.1	27.6	0.1	2.8	0.0	53.7	0.1	51.3	1.7	0.5	0.0
Belarus - Bélarus	2000	7 332	30.3	28.8	28.4	1.4	0.1	0.1	60.4	9.0	1.8	1.4	4.8	1.0	..
	2006	19 733	48.9	46.4	46.1	2.3	0.0	0.2	43.9	6.8	0.5	1.3	4.4	0.6	..
Belgium - Belgique	2006	366 926	87.6	78.5	76.7	6.2	0.9	2.1	1.4	10.1	2.0	1.1	4.8	2.2	0.0
Belgium-Luxembourg - Belgique-Luxembourg	1990	117 475	89.7	81.8	79.2	4.3	1.3	2.3	0.6	8.9	2.5	0.7	4.3	1.3	0.0
	2000	194 843	89.3	79.6	77.7	5.8	1.2	2.7	0.8	9.9	1.8	1.2	5.0	1.9	0.0
Belize	1990	131	77.9	27.8	27.8	45.0	0.7	4.4	..	20.6	0.0	19.3	0.1	1.1	..
	2000	184	93.8	38.0	38.0	52.3	2.0	1.6	..	6.1	..	6.0	0.1	..	..
	2006	418	80.7	43.1	43.1	33.9	1.2	2.5	0.2	19.0	6.3	11.0	1.5	0.2	..
Benin - Bénin	1990	122	47.6	24.0	23.8	23.4	0.1	0.2	..	51.9	40.0	5.0	6.9	..	..
	2000	196	20.2	19.5	18.2	0.6	0.1	0.0	0.6	79.2	14.5	10.7	48.1	5.8	..
	2006	390	21.1	20.9	20.9	0.1	0.0	0.0	0.1	78.9	27.6	1.7	46.5	3.0	..
Bermuda - Bermudes	1990	60	98.7	33.2	33.2	54.8	..	10.7	..	0.4	..	0.4	0.0	..	..
	2000	801	91.2	84.3	78.4	4.5	0.1	2.3	0.1	2.5	0.6	1.0	0.6	0.3	..
Bolivia - Bolivie	1990	923	54.2	33.4	31.2	20.0	0.3	0.5	0.0	45.4	..	44.8	0.5	0.1	..
	2000	1 475	53.1	28.2	17.1	24.0	0.2	0.7	0.0	45.7	0.1	44.5	1.0	0.1	..
	2006	3 178	23.0	5.1	5.0	10.8	5.5	1.6	0.1	76.5	0.2	70.3	5.9	0.1	..

For sources and notes, see end of table.　　　　　　　　　　　　　　　　　　　　　　Pour les sources et les notes, se reporter à la fin du tableau.

Destination / Origin	Year / Année	World (millions of dollars) (1) / Monde (millions de dollars) (1)	Developed economies / Économies développées Total	Europe Total	Europe EU / UE	USA États-Unis	Japan Japon	Other Autres	Economies in transition / Économies en transition	Developing economies / Économies en développement Total	Africa Afrique	America Amérique	Eastern, Southern and South-Eastern Asia / Asie orientale, méridionale et du Sud-Est	Western Asia / Asie occidentale	Oceania Océanie
								Percentage / En pourcentage							
Bosnia and Herzegovina - Bosnie-Herzégovine	2000	670	81.3	78.1	77.8	2.6	0.1	0.5	14.4	4.3	2.5	0.1	0.6	1.1	..
	2006	2 759	73.3	72.1	71.4	0.9	0.1	0.2	20.9	5.8	1.2	0.0	4.1	0.4	0.0
Brazil - Brésil	1990	31 414	69.8	35.2	34.1	24.6	7.5	2.5	1.0	27.9	3.2	11.7	10.6	2.4	0.0
	2000	59 643	52.9	24.6	23.0	22.4	4.1	1.7	0.9	35.0	2.3	23.3	7.2	2.3	0.0
	2006	138 365	46.4	23.5	22.5	17.8	2.8	2.3	2.9	48.3	5.4	26.2	13.4	3.3	0.0
Brunei Darussalam - Brunéi Darussalam	1990	2 212	63.1	0.2	0.2	3.4	58.1	1.3	..	33.5	..	..	33.5	0.0	..
	2000	3 162	61.6	3.7	3.6	12.0	40.7	5.3	0.0	38.2	0.1	0.0	38.0	0.1	0.0
	2006	6 699	55.4	2.1	2.0	7.8	30.8	14.6	0.0	44.1	0.0	0.2	43.8	0.0	..
Bulgaria - Bulgarie	1990	2 032	68.8	64.1	62.1	2.4	1.6	0.8	7.2	24.0	5.4	0.7	11.9	6.1	0.0
	2000	4 760	57.5	51.8	50.6	4.0	0.4	1.4	16.8	16.6	1.6	0.9	2.4	11.7	0.0
	2006	15 143	64.4	60.5	59.2	2.8	0.2	0.9	8.7	19.9	1.1	1.0	4.4	13.4	0.0
Burkina Faso	1990	152	53.9	52.5	41.8	0.1	1.3	0.0	..	32.9	17.3	..	15.7	..	..
	2000	171	39.4	35.0	34.9	1.7	2.7	0.1	0.4	57.1	15.5	9.7	30.0	1.9	..
	2006	419	10.7	8.4	8.4	0.2	2.0	0.0	0.0	85.9	16.5	0.4	67.9	1.2	..
Burundi	1990	75	55.6	43.2	43.0	11.8	0.5	0.0	..	10.2	8.7	..	0.7	0.9	..
	2000	49	61.7	60.7	35.8	0.7	0.3	0.0	..	17.2	17.0	..	0.0	0.2	..
	2006	59	51.2	49.8	16.1	0.5	0.5	0.4	1.1	26.8	15.1	..	9.7	2.1	..
Cambodia - Cambodge	1990	42	15.0	7.1	7.1	..	7.6	0.2	0.7	84.3	0.2	0.8	83.3	0.0	..
	2000	1 123	88.4	21.0	20.6	65.9	1.0	0.6	0.0	10.7	0.0	0.1	10.6	0.0	0.0
	2006	3 562	76.3	18.6	18.2	53.3	1.0	3.4	0.2	23.4	0.1	0.5	22.7	0.2	0.0
Cameroon - Cameroun	1990	2 026	84.5	69.0	68.2	14.9	0.4	0.2	0.4	15.1	9.3	0.1	5.7	0.1	..
	2000	1 832	66.0	63.7	62.6	1.5	0.1	0.7	..	28.3	8.1	0.2	19.3	0.6	..
	2006	4 684	72.3	66.1	65.9	5.7	0.4	0.1	0.1	25.7	8.8	2.8	13.3	0.8	0.0
Canada	1990	126 447	91.4	9.5	8.4	75.4	5.6	0.8	0.8	7.8	0.8	1.7	4.8	0.5	0.0
	2000	275 184	94.9	4.9	4.6	87.4	2.2	0.4	0.1	5.0	0.4	1.5	2.9	0.3	0.0
	2006	388 134	91.7	7.3	6.6	81.6	2.1	0.6	0.3	8.0	0.6	2.3	4.6	0.6	0.0
Cape Verde - Cap-Vert	1990	7	93.1	91.2	90.8	..	..	1.9	0.0	3.6	2.9	0.7	..	..	..
	2000	11	97.5	85.2	85.2	12.3	..	0.0	..	1.9	1.8	0.1	0.0	..	..
	2006	37	93.2	88.1	85.8	2.2	..	2.9	0.0	6.5	5.5	0.9	0.1	..	..
Central African Republic - République centrafricaine	1990	283	36.1	35.4	35.1	0.7	0.0	0.0	0.0	63.8	59.8	0.0	4.0	0.0	..
	2000	226	89.4	87.5	87.2	1.0	0.3	0.6	0.0	10.6	1.7	0.4	8.3	0.2	..
	2006	113	67.4	62.4	62.4	3.5	1.3	0.1	0.0	32.6	8.6	0.8	16.0	7.2	..
Chad - Tchad	1990	89	88.8	75.0	73.9	1.3	12.5	0.0	0.7	10.5	1.3	0.2	9.0	0.0	..
	2000	86	77.9	70.7	70.7	6.0	1.2	0.0	0.1	22.0	11.4	4.8	5.5	0.3	..
	2006	2 280	83.0	2.0	1.8	80.6	0.5	0.0	0.0	16.9	0.5	0.0	16.4	0.0	..
Chile - Chili	1990	8 678	72.7	38.5	38.3	17.2	16.0	1.1	0.2	24.1	1.3	12.2	9.5	1.1	0.5
	2000	19 296	56.4	24.7	23.9	16.8	13.2	1.6	0.1	38.5	0.4	21.7	15.0	1.5	0.0
	2006	57 299	55.8	27.1	26.8	15.6	10.5	2.6	0.3	39.8	0.3	16.4	22.1	1.0	0.0
China - Chine	1990	62 760	36.1	11.4	11.1	8.5	14.7	1.5	3.4	59.5	2.0	1.2	54.5	1.7	0.0
	2000	249 208	57.7	17.0	16.5	20.9	16.7	3.1	1.3	40.9	2.0	2.9	33.7	2.3	0.0
	2006	969 284	54.0	20.0	19.6	21.0	9.5	3.5	3.0	42.9	2.7	3.7	33.4	3.1	0.0
China, Hong Kong SAR - Chine (RAS de Hong Kong) (2)	1990	82 272	53.6	20.0	18.8	24.1	5.7	3.7	0.3	45.5	1.7	1.8	40.6	1.4	0.2
	2000	202 249	48.6	16.4	15.7	23.3	5.5	3.4	0.1	51.2	0.9	2.4	46.8	1.1	0.1
	2006	316 819	37.5	14.6	14.0	15.1	4.9	2.8	0.3	62.2	0.6	1.5	59.0	1.1	0.0
China, Macao SAR - Chine (RAS de Macao)	1990	1 690	81.0	38.6	37.4	36.2	3.1	3.1	0.1	18.9	0.3	0.3	18.1	0.2	0.0
	2000	2 540	79.5	28.8	28.1	48.3	0.6	1.8	0.0	19.8	0.0	0.4	19.1	0.1	0.0
	2006	2 557	65.4	19.6	19.5	44.1	0.8	0.9	0.0	29.3	0.0	0.9	28.3	0.1	0.0
China, Taiwan Province of - Province chinoise de Taiwan (3)	1990	66 728	68.4	18.3	17.5	32.7	12.6	4.8	0.1	30.8	1.1	1.9	26.0	1.7	0.0
	2000	148 679	53.6	15.8	15.4	23.5	11.3	3.0	0.2	45.3	0.9	2.5	40.5	1.3	0.1
	2006	221 924	35.9	11.4	11.2	14.6	7.4	2.4	0.4	63.6	1.0	2.1	59.0	1.6	0.1
Colombia - Colombie	1990	6 754	79.6	29.7	29.0	44.5	3.8	1.5	0.5	18.2	0.1	17.2	0.7	0.2	0.0
	2000	13 164	67.7	14.1	13.9	50.4	1.8	1.5	0.5	30.9	0.2	29.4	1.2	0.1	0.0
	2006	24 951	58.7	17.6	16.3	35.8	1.3	4.1	0.5	38.9	0.3	34.8	2.8	0.9	0.0
Comoros - Comores	1990	23	98.3	76.5	76.5	19.1	2.7	0.0	0.0	1.6	0.3	0.7	0.6	..	..
	2000	16	77.7	53.6	53.2	19.3	3.3	1.5	0.1	20.8	0.6	0.5	19.5	0.1	0.1
	2006	32	77.1	72.0	71.8	4.6	0.2	0.3	0.5	21.1	1.2	0.1	11.7	7.9	0.1

For sources and notes, see end of table.

Pour les sources et les notes, se reporter à la fin du tableau.

Destination / Origin / Origine	Year / Année	World (millions of dollars) (1) / Monde (millions de dollars) (1)	Developed economies / Économies développées					Economies in transition / Économies en transition	Developing economies / Économies en développement					
			Total	Europe		USA États-Unis	Japan Japon	Other Autres		Total	Africa Afrique	America Amérique	Eastern, Southern and South-Eastern Asia / Asie orientale, méridionale et du Sud-Est	Western Asia / Asie occidentale	Oceania Océanie
				Total	EU UE										
										Percentage / En pourcentage					
Congo	1990	1 209	94.1	64.5	54.0	29.5	0.1	0.0	0.1	1.7	1.5	0.0	0.0	0.1	..
	2000	2 154	32.0	10.5	7.2	19.9	0.0	1.5	0.0	68.0	3.3	4.8	59.9	0.0	..
	2006	8 053	41.9	5.9	5.6	35.9	0.0	0.0	0.0	57.9	1.0	4.0	52.6	0.3	..
Costa Rica	1990	1 456	81.2	30.3	29.8	45.7	1.0	4.2	0.1	18.0	0.1	16.4	1.3	0.2	0.0
	2000	5 850	25.1	8.7	8.5	15.5	0.4	0.5	0.1	15.4	0.1	14.8	0.4	0.1	0.0
	2006	13 520	58.2	26.0	25.2	27.5	1.9	2.8	0.3	41.5	0.3	20.6	20.2	0.3	0.0
Côte d'Ivoire	1990	2 813	62.1	54.2	54.1	5.9	1.7	0.2	2.3	35.6	31.9	0.0	3.2	0.4	0.0
	2000	3 850	48.6	39.9	39.5	7.8	0.3	0.6	1.6	37.8	29.6	2.7	5.0	0.6	0.0
	2006	8 134	56.4	45.5	45.1	9.1	0.1	1.7	0.2	37.6	29.5	2.8	4.6	0.7	0.0
Croatia - Croatie	2000	4 071	72.7	70.1	69.2	1.8	0.4	0.5	14.8	7.4	5.5	0.2	0.4	1.3	..
	2006	10 304	69.6	65.2	63.8	3.2	0.9	0.3	15.6	6.3	2.1	0.6	0.6	3.0	..
Cuba	1990	1 357	49.7	36.7	35.9	..	6.4	6.6	0.2	50.1	13.7	12.4	21.9	2.2	..
	2000	1 565	59.5	39.3	38.3	0.0	2.3	17.8	22.2	18.3	2.0	8.8	7.0	0.5	..
	2006	2 569	56.2	33.7	32.8	0.0	0.7	21.9	3.5	40.3	2.9	13.6	23.5	0.2	0.0
Cyprus - Chypre	1990	945	57.3	53.8	52.8	1.6	0.5	1.4	5.2	27.5	4.8	0.9	1.8	20.0	..
	2000	917	45.0	40.4	39.7	2.4	0.1	2.2	11.3	31.7	4.9	0.1	3.1	23.6	..
	2006	1 330	59.8	56.5	55.4	0.7	1.2	1.3	2.9	17.0	3.7	0.1	4.1	9.0	0.0
Czech Republic - République tchèque	2000	28 922	91.8	88.0	86.2	2.8	0.4	0.5	3.4	4.6	0.5	0.6	2.2	1.4	0.0
	2006	95 024	91.0	87.5	85.6	2.3	0.4	0.7	4.2	4.5	0.7	0.6	1.8	1.4	0.0
Czechoslovakia (former) - Tchécoslovaquie (anc.)	1990	11 654	58.6	56.3	53.5	0.8	0.8	0.8	29.7	11.6	2.1	1.5	5.1	2.9	0.0
Dem. People's Rep. of Korea - Rép. populaire dém. de Corée	1990	924	45.0	15.6	15.5	..	29.4	0.0	1.4	53.6	10.8	3.6	32.7	6.5	0.0
	2000	976	37.3	13.6	13.4	0.0	23.4	0.4	2.0	60.6	2.7	27.7	21.4	8.6	0.2
	2006	1 436	18.1	12.3	12.3	..	4.7	1.0	5.3	76.7	6.9	11.4	46.7	11.4	0.3
Dem. Rep. of the Congo - Rép. dém. du Congo	1990	1 353	86.5	65.4	65.2	17.8	2.4	0.9	0.3	13.1	7.7	0.2	4.8	0.4	..
	2000	1 133	97.0	76.3	76.0	19.1	1.5	0.0	0.1	2.7	2.2	0.0	0.4	0.0	..
	2006	1 592	50.7	45.6	45.5	4.9	0.1	0.0	0.1	48.9	6.8	20.2	21.8	0.1	0.0
Denmark - Danemark	1990	34 039	88.8	78.5	69.9	5.0	3.3	2.0	1.4	9.4	2.8	1.0	3.8	1.7	0.0
	2000	50 756	89.9	78.2	71.0	5.9	3.5	2.3	1.5	8.5	1.1	1.5	4.4	1.5	0.0
	2006	92 607	88.9	78.1	71.0	6.2	2.0	2.6	2.4	8.6	1.0	1.3	5.0	1.3	0.0
Djibouti	1990	59	7.8	7.6	7.6	..	0.1	0.0	0.0	92.2	58.2	..	0.7	33.4	..
	2000	152	8.4	8.1	8.1	0.2	0.0	0.0	0.1	91.6	67.1	0.1	1.2	23.2	..
	2006	340	3.4	2.5	2.4	0.9	..	0.1	..	96.6	87.8	0.2	2.1	6.4	..
Dominica - Dominique	1990	55	72.5	61.4	61.4	10.9	0.0	0.2	0.2	26.5	..	26.5	..	..	..
	2000	54	39.7	32.1	32.1	7.4	0.0	0.2	..	57.0	0.0	57.0	0.0	..	..
	2006	94	33.5	28.4	28.3	3.3	1.2	0.6	0.1	64.0	0.2	51.9	10.4	1.5	..
Dominican Republic - République dominicaine	1990	744	88.9	19.4	19.4	66.0	2.0	1.6	1.0	8.6	0.5	3.5	4.6	..	0.0
	2000	5 737	94.5	6.3	6.0	87.3	0.2	0.7	0.0	5.3	0.1	4.1	1.1	0.0	0.0
	2006	5 817	89.7	14.2	14.0	72.7	0.8	2.0	0.1	10.2	0.2	5.7	4.2	0.1	0.0
Ecuador - Équateur	1990	2 714	62.3	11.1	11.1	48.5	1.9	0.8	0.6	19.8	0.0	17.4	2.4	..	..
	2000	4 929	54.4	13.0	12.9	38.0	2.7	0.7	2.6	39.5	0.0	31.6	7.2	0.7	0.0
	2006	12 730	66.9	11.9	11.7	53.6	1.0	0.5	2.7	28.3	0.0	27.4	0.6	0.3	0.0
Egypt - Égypte	1990	2 585	62.7	44.6	43.7	8.6	2.7	6.8	16.8	18.9	3.7	0.0	6.9	8.2	..
	2000	6 354	64.0	48.3	48.1	12.8	2.0	0.9	0.4	25.9	4.1	0.9	9.7	11.2	0.0
	2006	20 629	57.6	43.3	43.0	11.3	2.0	1.0	1.1	31.4	6.3	0.8	6.6	17.7	0.0
El Salvador	1990	586	64.8	28.6	28.5	33.9	1.1	1.3	..	34.9	0.0	34.7	0.2	0.0	..
	2000	2 941	70.7	4.7	4.7	65.4	0.3	0.2	0.6	28.2	0.3	27.8	0.1	0.0	0.0
	2006	3 517	57.9	5.8	5.8	49.6	0.7	1.8	1.0	40.1	0.1	37.8	2.2	0.0	0.0
Equatorial Guinea - Guinée équatoriale	1990	35	93.5	93.5	93.4	..	0.0	0.0	4.8	1.7	1.7	0.0	..	0.0	..
	2000	1 079	73.3	56.5	56.5	13.2	3.6	0.0	0.0	26.6	1.9	2.2	22.4	0.1	..
	2006	7 467	56.2	27.3	26.6	22.2	3.9	2.8	0.0	43.8	0.4	1.6	41.5	0.4	..
Estonia - Estonie	2000	3 831	86.9	84.3	81.0	1.8	0.3	0.4	9.6	3.4	0.7	0.6	1.8	0.3	0.0
	2006	9 720	80.8	72.9	65.2	6.6	0.6	0.7	10.5	8.2	2.4	0.8	3.7	1.3	0.0
Ethiopia - Éthiopie	2000	439	71.6	50.3	43.8	4.0	12.9	4.5	0.0	28.3	13.4	0.1	4.6	10.3	..
	2006	1 086	50.2	32.5	30.8	7.2	7.8	2.7	0.4	34.8	9.5	0.1	13.6	11.5	0.0

For sources and notes, see end of table.   Pour les sources et les notes, se reporter à la fin du tableau.

Destination / Origin / Origine	Year / Année	World (millions of dollars) (1) / Monde (millions de dollars) (1)	Developed economies / Économies développées						Economies in transition / Économies en transition	Developing economies / Économies en développement					
			Total	Europe		USA États-Unis	Japan Japon	Other Autres		Total	Africa Afrique	America Amérique	Eastern, Southern and South-Eastern Asia / Asie orientale, méridionale et du Sud-Est	Western Asia / Asie occidentale	Oceania Océanie
				Total	EU UE										
									Percentage / En pourcentage						
Ethiopia (former) - Éthiopie (anc.)	1990	294	67.6	41.5	41.5	10.8	14.9	0.5	4.0	26.0	12.7	2.5	0.7	10.2	0.0
Faeroe Islands - Îles Féroé	1990	381	98.8	94.8	93.4	4.1	..	0.0	1.1	0.0	0.0	0.0	0.0	..	..
	2000	395	98.6	92.9	87.2	5.6	..	0.0	0.0	0.8	0.6	0.0	0.1	0.0	..
	2006	634	83.6	81.6	68.7	0.7	..	1.3	5.2	10.4	9.5	0.0	0.8	..	0.0
Fiji - Fidji	1990	498	69.2	23.3	23.3	8.4	5.9	31.5	..	5.4	..	..	5.4	..	..
	2000	685	70.8	16.6	16.6	21.1	4.1	28.9	0.0	18.0	0.0	0.0	6.4	0.1	1.4
	2006	934	54.7	14.2	14.2	16.8	5.3	18.4	0.0	23.4	0.0	0.5	2.9	0.2	2.9
Finland - Finlande	1990	26 570	78.2	68.5	63.6	5.8	1.4	2.4	13.0	8.8	1.8	1.4	4.3	1.3	0.0
	2000	45 867	78.4	67.1	62.7	7.4	1.7	2.2	4.9	16.2	1.8	2.7	9.0	2.8	0.0
	2006	77 109	71.1	61.0	57.2	6.5	1.7	2.0	11.8	17.0	2.3	2.3	7.4	4.9	0.0
France	1990	217 097	80.1	70.7	66.2	5.9	1.9	1.7	1.2	15.2	6.5	1.4	4.6	2.4	0.0
	2000	323 482	80.7	68.6	64.5	8.7	1.6	1.9	1.0	16.9	5.7	2.5	5.4	3.0	0.0
	2006	495 509	78.1	68.5	65.4	6.6	1.4	1.6	1.8	18.2	5.3	2.1	6.9	3.6	0.0
Gabon	1990	2 483	82.2	47.4	45.8	29.5	4.1	1.2	0.6	16.9	4.7	9.8	2.4	..	..
	2000	3 793	76.0	22.9	22.8	52.4	0.3	0.3	0.0	18.1	1.6	2.3	13.9	0.3	..
	2006	4 667	44.5	15.4	14.9	27.6	1.5	0.1	1.9	40.4	7.2	6.9	26.0	0.3	0.0
Gambia - Gambie	1990	172	89.4	54.8	52.5	..	34.6	0.0	0.7	9.3	6.8	0.1	2.5	0.0	..
	2000	46	69.0	60.7	60.7	0.6	7.1	0.6	0.0	30.9	18.0	6.1	5.7	1.1	..
	2006	37	39.1	35.9	35.7	0.5	1.9	0.9	0.1	60.8	7.0	0.4	53.4	0.0	..
Georgia - Géorgie	2000	326	30.8	28.3	24.2	2.2	0.1	0.2	39.8	29.2	1.4	0.6	2.9	24.3	..
	2006	981	38.5	27.2	26.1	6.0	0.1	5.2	41.1	20.2	0.7	1.0	2.8	15.7	0.0
Germany - Allemagne	1990	409 273	83.8	72.3	65.6	7.1	2.6	1.8	4.2	11.8	2.5	1.8	5.3	2.2	0.0
	2000	548 855	84.2	69.9	64.7	10.3	2.2	1.9	2.0	13.4	1.8	2.5	6.4	2.7	0.0
	2006	1 108 780	80.1	68.2	63.4	8.6	1.5	1.7	4.1	15.2	1.8	2.1	8.0	3.2	0.0
Ghana	1990	1 235	85.0	66.5	64.5	13.1	5.0	0.4	4.3	7.3	2.6	0.5	3.4	0.9	..
	2000	1 492	73.4	55.6	54.2	13.8	3.0	1.0	3.5	14.8	5.6	0.9	5.9	2.3	0.0
	2006	2 841	58.2	46.8	45.2	6.7	2.6	2.1	4.3	25.3	9.4	1.4	11.0	3.4	0.0
Greece - Grèce	1990	8 065	83.9	75.4	73.6	5.6	0.9	2.0	4.0	10.9	3.7	1.0	1.5	4.7	0.0
	2000	10 975	70.8	61.7	59.1	5.3	0.8	2.9	11.7	17.2	3.9	2.0	2.5	8.7	0.1
	2006	20 759	72.7	65.6	64.0	4.4	0.3	2.4	8.0	17.1	4.6	1.1	2.8	8.6	0.0
Greenland - Groenland	1990	391	98.5	97.6	97.5	..	0.9	0.0	..	..	..	..	..	..	..
	2000	332	91.4	57.9	54.7	4.8	26.1	2.6	0.0	7.0	0.1	0.0	6.9	..	..
	2006	480	87.6	73.2	70.4	2.2	12.1	0.1	0.4	8.8	0.3	0.0	8.5	0.0	0.0
Grenada - Grenade	1990	21	68.9	56.2	56.2	7.3	3.2	2.2	..	31.1	..	30.5	..	0.5	..
	2000	77	80.5	30.3	30.3	49.1	..	1.0	..	16.2	..	16.2	..	..	..
	2006	38	25.9	11.9	11.2	11.4	0.2	2.5	0.1	64.8	0.4	63.4	0.7	0.2	..
Guatemala	1990	1 189	56.8	13.6	13.3	38.9	2.9	1.4	0.6	38.3	1.3	33.5	1.9	1.6	..
	2000	2 699	53.1	12.1	11.6	36.1	2.3	2.5	0.8	45.7	0.8	40.8	1.7	2.4	..
	2006	6 784	55.4	6.4	6.0	44.6	1.3	3.1	0.2	42.0	0.3	37.2	3.5	1.0	0.0
Guinea - Guinée	1990	606	85.6	61.4	57.1	21.2	1.1	1.9	2.3	12.2	8.5	0.6	3.1	0.0	..
	2000	617	80.8	65.5	65.5	11.5	0.0	3.8	11.5	7.7	7.6	..	0.1	0.0	..
	2006	1 363	44.1	34.1	34.1	7.7	0.0	2.3	25.4	14.3	2.1	0.0	12.1	0.0	..
Guinea-Bissau - Guinée-Bissau	1990	34	56.1	55.5	55.5	0.3	0.4	0.0	2.0	41.9	4.4	..	37.5	..	..
	2000	112	4.2	3.8	3.8	0.4	0.0	0.0	0.0	95.8	1.5	46.2	48.0	0.0	..
	2006	133	3.0	2.6	2.6	0.3	0.0	0.0	..	97.0	19.3	0.0	77.7	..	..
Guyana	1990	232	83.7	48.7	48.6	20.5	6.3	8.1	2.1	14.0	0.3	13.5	0.2	0.0	..
	2000	596	77.6	29.7	29.7	24.4	0.8	22.7	3.7	18.3	0.3	15.0	3.0	0.0	0.0
	2006	682	68.5	29.1	29.1	18.8	1.0	19.6	0.0	30.7	0.5	22.6	7.5	0.0	0.0
Haiti - Haïti	1990	171	99.3	12.7	12.7	83.0	1.2	2.5	0.0	0.6	..	0.6	0.0	..	..
	2000	324	94.5	5.9	5.4	86.5	0.2	1.9	0.1	5.2	0.6	4.5	0.0	0.1	..
	2006	579	87.4	4.1	3.7	79.8	0.2	3.2	0.0	12.4	0.8	10.1	1.5	0.1	..
Honduras	1990	812	79.6	21.8	21.8	52.8	4.8	0.3	..	3.9	..	3.9	..	..	..
	2000	1 403	68.0	10.0	9.8	53.8	3.8	0.4	..	26.9	0.0	25.2	1.6	0.0	..
	2006	5 017	83.7	10.4	10.1	70.5	0.5	2.3	0.1	16.1	0.0	14.4	1.5	0.1	..

For sources and notes, see end of table.

Pour les sources et les notes, se reporter à la fin du tableau.

Destination / Origin / Origine	Year / Année	World (millions of dollars) (1) / Monde (millions de dollars) (1)	Developed economies / Économies développées Total	Europe Total	Europe EU UE	USA États-Unis	Japan Japon	Other Autres	Economies in transition / Économies en transition	Developing economies / Économies en développement Total	Africa Afrique	America Amérique	Eastern, Southern and South-Eastern Asia / Asie orientale, méridionale et du Sud-Est	Western Asia / Asie occidentale	Oceania / Océanie
Hungary - Hongrie	1990	9 593	61.0	55.5	53.4	3.5	1.2	0.8	25.1	9.7	1.8	0.8	5.0	2.1	..
	2000	28 087	91.3	85.1	83.7	5.3	0.6	0.4	4.6	4.1	0.4	0.6	2.1	1.1	0.0
	2006	75 358	84.6	80.4	79.2	2.7	0.5	0.9	7.2	7.2	1.4	0.5	2.5	2.9	0.0
Iceland - Islande	1990	1 591	95.0	78.4	71.2	9.9	6.0	0.7	2.6	2.2	0.7	0.3	1.1	0.2	..
	2000	1 896	96.1	76.4	68.8	12.4	5.3	2.0	0.5	3.3	1.1	0.2	1.9	0.1	0.0
	2006	3 453	92.5	78.6	71.0	10.8	2.0	1.0	2.4	5.1	1.7	0.3	1.9	1.3	0.0
India - Inde	1990	17 813	57.7	30.9	29.5	15.1	9.3	2.4	16.3	21.5	2.5	0.4	12.6	5.9	0.0
	2000	42 626	54.7	25.5	24.4	21.3	4.1	3.7	2.5	39.4	5.3	2.2	21.4	10.4	0.0
	2006	122 897	45.1	21.7	21.1	17.0	3.0	3.3	1.3	53.3	6.7	3.5	29.7	13.4	0.0
Indonesia - Indonésie	1990	25 683	70.5	12.5	12.3	13.1	42.5	2.4	0.3	29.0	0.7	0.4	25.4	2.5	0.0
	2000	62 118	54.8	14.7	14.4	13.7	23.2	3.3	0.2	45.0	1.8	1.7	38.3	3.1	0.0
	2006	113 534	47.4	12.4	12.2	11.5	19.4	4.1	0.6	52.0	1.8	1.9	45.2	2.9	0.0
Iran (Islamic Rep. of) - Iran (Rép. islamique d')	1990	19 305	73.2	50.8	43.2	1.5	20.7	0.1	1.0	18.3	..	4.4	10.9	3.1	..
	2000	26 998	45.7	26.7	26.3	0.6	18.0	0.4	1.1	40.6	6.0	0.2	29.9	4.6	0.0
	2006	70 639	37.8	23.3	23.3	0.2	14.0	0.2	1.0	46.2	5.2	0.1	30.6	10.2	0.0
Iraq	1990	10 314	64.7	27.3	27.3	28.6	7.9	0.9	2.2	33.1	2.3	10.2	7.3	13.3	..
	2000	14 916	79.5	33.2	33.2	38.7	4.0	3.6	0.6	19.9	3.1	2.1	10.6	4.2	..
	2006	23 759	81.7	24.2	24.2	46.8	4.0	6.7	0.0	18.3	1.0	2.5	10.7	4.1	..
Ireland - Irlande	1990	23 770	92.7	81.0	78.5	8.2	1.8	1.7	0.7	5.6	1.5	1.0	1.9	1.1	0.0
	2000	76 336	87.3	64.7	61.5	17.0	3.8	1.7	0.3	8.9	1.2	0.9	5.3	1.4	0.0
	2006	108 936	89.7	67.0	63.3	18.7	2.3	1.7	0.5	9.4	1.1	1.5	5.5	1.3	0.0
Israel - Israël	1990	12 005	77.6	39.7	37.0	28.8	7.3	1.8	0.3	13.2	1.3	2.6	8.6	0.7	0.0
	2000	31 911	71.6	30.6	28.8	36.8	2.6	1.7	0.9	21.0	1.5	2.8	15.2	1.5	0.0
	2006	46 449	72.4	29.9	27.9	38.4	1.7	2.3	2.0	22.5	1.7	2.9	15.8	2.1	0.0
Italy - Italie	1990	170 466	82.0	69.8	64.8	7.6	2.3	2.2	3.3	14.2	4.4	2.0	4.9	2.8	0.0
	2000	236 597	79.6	64.9	61.1	10.4	1.7	2.6	2.5	17.3	3.5	3.8	5.9	4.0	0.0
	2006	417 098	76.7	65.6	61.1	7.4	1.4	2.3	4.5	18.0	3.8	2.8	6.5	5.0	0.0
Jamaica - Jamaïque	1990	1 133	82.1	42.2	31.9	28.4	0.7	10.9	4.4	12.8	4.7	8.0	0.1	0.0	..
	2000	1 301	90.4	40.4	31.6	38.1	2.3	9.7	0.0	9.0	1.6	6.0	1.0	0.5	..
	2006	1 984	77.3	29.7	24.3	30.2	1.4	15.9	2.2	19.8	0.0	4.2	15.6	0.0	..
Japan - Japon	1990	287 839	59.2	22.1	20.8	31.7	..	5.4	1.0	39.7	1.8	3.3	31.6	2.6	0.1
	2000	478 361	51.6	17.6	16.9	30.1	..	3.9	0.2	48.1	1.0	3.8	41.3	1.9	0.0
	2006	646 779	42.0	15.2	14.5	22.8	..	4.0	1.3	56.6	1.4	4.4	47.8	3.0	0.1
Jordan - Jordanie	1990	922	7.4	4.7	4.7	0.6	2.1	0.0	3.0	89.5	8.1	0.1	40.3	40.9	..
	2000	1 284	16.6	4.3	4.3	4.9	1.0	6.3	0.2	81.0	8.7	0.4	32.9	39.0	0.0
	2006	5 204	37.1	8.5	3.3	25.0	0.8	2.8	0.3	54.3	5.0	0.2	12.3	36.8	..
Kazakhstan	2000	9 878	42.2	27.8	23.0	2.1	0.1	12.2	23.7	12.9	0.2	0.7	11.2	0.9	0.0
	2006	29 959	56.3	52.2	50.6	3.0	1.0	0.1	15.6	20.5	0.1	0.4	16.4	3.6	..
Kenya	1990	1 120	43.8	38.4	37.6	2.5	1.0	1.8	1.4	47.6	38.6	..	8.0	1.0	..
	2000	1 760	36.3	31.4	30.5	2.1	1.1	1.7	0.0	62.4	45.8	0.2	12.6	3.8	0.1
	2006	4 107	39.4	29.4	28.6	8.3	0.6	1.1	1.0	54.3	41.5	0.2	10.5	2.1	1.7
Kuwait - Koweït	1990	8 351	50.4	24.0	23.9	6.8	18.6	1.0	0.0	38.9	1.8	1.9	29.2	6.0	2.0
	2000	18 754	53.0	13.9	13.8	14.4	24.1	0.6	0.0	47.0	1.0	0.5	42.8	2.7	..
	2006	42 183	41.1	11.0	10.8	9.0	20.4	0.7	0.0	58.9	0.8	0.0	54.7	3.4	..
Kyrgyzstan - Kirghizistan	2000	504	45.1	44.3	37.6	0.6	0.1	0.0	41.1	13.8	0.4	..	11.7	1.7	..
	2006	796	31.7	30.4	4.3	1.2	0.1	0.0	47.6	20.7	..	..	16.0	4.6	..
Lao People's dem. Rep. - Rép. dém. populaire lao	1990	64	19.9	11.1	9.9	0.1	7.1	1.6	..	80.1	1.0	0.6	78.4	0.0	..
	2000	391	33.4	27.8	26.2	2.3	2.8	0.5	0.0	45.6	0.2	0.0	45.2	0.3	0.0
	2006	1 130	15.2	10.7	10.5	0.7	1.0	2.8	0.1	64.3	0.1	0.1	64.0	0.1	0.0
Latvia - Lettonie	2000	1 865	87.7	82.2	80.7	3.8	0.4	1.2	8.7	3.3	2.3	0.3	0.4	0.3	0.0
	2006	6 145	80.1	76.9	72.7	1.8	0.7	0.7	16.7	3.0	1.3	0.3	1.0	0.5	0.0
Lebanon - Liban	1990	456	47.2	40.3	29.0	4.9	0.9	1.1	0.1	52.8	9.4	0.1	2.7	40.6	..
	2000	714	39.6	30.4	23.2	6.8	0.8	1.6	0.3	59.1	10.6	0.6	4.8	43.1	0.0
	2006	2 503	20.8	16.4	10.3	3.4	0.3	0.8	0.8	77.5	10.2	0.4	6.3	60.5	0.0

For sources and notes, see end of table.

Pour les sources et les notes, se reporter à la fin du tableau.

2

Destination / Origin / Origine	Year / Année	World (millions of dollars) (1) / Monde (millions de dollars) (1)	Developed economies / Économies développées					Economies in transition / Économies en transition	Developing economies / Économies en développement					
			Total	Europe		USA États-Unis	Japan Japon	Other Autres		Total	Africa Afrique	America Amérique	Eastern, Southern and South-Eastern Asia / Asie orientale, méridionale et du Sud-Est	Western Asia / Asie occiden-tale	Oceania Océanie
				Total	EU UE										
						Percentage / En pourcentage									
Liberia - Libéria	1990	1 943	86.4	83.7	41.8	2.5	0.0	0.3	0.2	13.4	0.2	1.0	12.2	0.0	0.0
	2000	582	77.3	69.8	61.0	7.1	0.0	0.3	1.6	21.1	2.1	2.6	14.3	2.2	0.0
	2006	1 548	77.7	67.5	66.0	8.5	0.6	1.2	0.4	21.8	13.1	0.2	8.4	0.2	0.0
Libyan Arab Jamahiriya - Jamahiriya arabe libyenne	1990	13 878	88.3	88.3	88.2	..	0.0	0.0	4.1	7.6	3.3	0.1	0.3	3.9	..
	2000	12 717	88.4	88.3	85.5	..	0.1	0.0	1.5	10.2	3.4	0.3	0.6	5.9	..
	2006	39 305	85.2	78.9	75.8	6.1	0.0	0.1	0.9	13.9	2.1	1.2	4.2	6.5	..
Lithuania - Lituanie	2000	3 810	80.4	74.8	72.3	4.9	0.3	0.4	16.3	3.2	0.1	0.5	0.7	1.8	0.0
	2006	14 154	73.4	66.9	63.6	4.3	0.1	2.2	21.4	5.1	0.4	0.4	3.1	1.2	0.0
Luxembourg	2006	22 853	92.9	90.1	88.8	2.1	0.1	0.6	1.0	5.3	0.4	0.7	2.2	2.0	0.0
Madagascar	1990	366	87.5	52.4	51.6	29.4	5.5	0.2	0.7	11.7	5.5	0.2	6.1	0.0	0.0
	2000	806	82.5	59.9	59.5	19.2	2.8	0.5	0.0	12.4	3.3	0.1	9.0	0.1	0.0
	2006	1 072	87.0	57.8	57.2	25.3	2.6	1.4	0.1	10.1	2.7	0.1	6.8	0.3	0.1
Malawi	1990	419	76.6	50.6	48.4	11.5	12.8	1.7	..	16.6	15.0	..	1.4	0.2	..
	2000	382	68.9	40.8	39.2	14.1	12.2	1.9	3.6	27.0	18.0	0.8	4.4	3.5	0.4
	2006	612	44.0	29.3	28.9	9.5	3.1	2.1	7.2	48.2	40.6	0.9	3.6	2.5	0.6
Malaysia - Malaisie	1990	29 421	50.8	15.8	15.6	16.9	15.3	2.7	0.8	48.4	0.8	0.7	44.7	2.2	0.0
	2000	98 154	51.5	14.2	14.0	20.5	13.0	3.7	0.1	48.4	0.8	1.5	44.2	1.8	0.0
	2006	160 664	44.6	13.1	12.8	18.8	8.9	3.9	0.5	54.9	1.4	1.3	49.3	2.8	0.0
Maldives	1990	52	61.5	26.5	26.2	24.2	8.5	2.3	..	38.5	..	..	38.5	..	0.0
	2000	76	67.2	18.6	18.6	44.2	4.2	0.2	..	32.8	..	..	32.8	0.0	..
	2006	167	42.4	30.2	30.2	1.3	10.3	0.6	0.0	57.6	8.3	0.0	49.1	0.1	0.0
Mali	1990	252	44.9	37.1	36.2	0.8	1.2	5.7	13.9	40.5	14.4	0.1	26.0	0.0	..
	2000	234	45.4	33.8	33.3	3.8	0.5	7.2	..	52.3	9.6	9.9	32.0	0.8	0.0
	2006	387	39.4	33.6	32.9	1.9	0.1	3.9	0.0	56.6	5.7	1.5	49.1	0.4	0.0
Malta - Malte	1990	1 127	82.1	78.0	77.5	3.8	0.1	0.2	3.0	11.6	6.4	0.1	3.5	1.7	..
	2000	2 442	72.9	40.6	34.1	27.4	3.8	1.1	0.1	21.6	2.3	0.2	18.1	1.0	0.0
	2006	2 668	69.2	50.4	49.7	13.0	4.9	0.9	0.6	29.3	5.4	0.6	21.7	1.7	0.0
Mauritania - Mauritanie	1990	469	81.0	61.3	61.2	..	19.7	0.0	11.8	6.8	5.6	0.5	0.7	0.0	..
	2000	529	70.4	56.6	56.0	0.1	13.8	0.0	2.4	26.0	20.8	1.0	3.8	0.4	0.0
	2006	1 400	54.2	45.3	44.6	3.5	5.4	0.0	3.7	40.9	14.0	0.0	26.5	0.4	0.0
Mauritius - Maurice	1990	1 202	96.2	82.3	81.2	12.7	0.2	1.0	0.1	3.7	2.2	0.1	1.4	0.0	0.0
	2000	1 488	90.4	68.7	67.4	20.2	0.5	1.0	0.0	9.6	7.6	0.3	1.4	0.1	0.0
	2006	2 177	73.6	63.9	62.9	8.3	0.8	0.5	0.1	26.3	8.9	0.2	4.3	11.7	0.0
Mexico - Mexique	1990	27 167	90.8	14.2	13.4	69.3	5.5	1.8	0.1	8.2	0.3	6.6	1.2	0.1	0.0
	2000	166 199	95.1	3.7	3.3	88.7	0.6	2.2	0.0	4.4	0.0	3.7	0.7	0.0	..
	2006	249 997	91.8	4.2	4.1	84.7	0.6	2.3	0.0	6.9	0.1	5.0	1.7	0.1	..
Moldova	2000	472	39.2	35.3	35.0	3.3	0.0	0.6	58.6	2.2	0.2	0.1	0.7	1.2	..
	2006	1 239	52.7	47.8	47.6	2.9	0.2	1.8	42.6	4.5	0.5	0.5	0.2	3.4	0.0
Mongolia - Mongolie	1990	91	61.9	42.3	41.8	2.0	17.6	0.0	2.9	35.2	20.7	0.4	13.9	0.1	0.0
	2000	536	36.9	8.6	7.7	24.3	1.5	2.5	9.0	54.0	0.0	0.1	53.7	0.2	..
	2006	1 449	24.1	3.8	3.6	7.3	0.5	12.5	3.1	72.8	0.0	0.0	72.6	0.2	..
Morocco - Maroc	1990	4 586	69.5	63.5	62.5	1.8	3.6	0.6	0.6	19.7	6.2	1.3	7.3	4.9	0.3
	2000	7 418	82.0	73.6	72.9	3.4	3.8	1.2	1.0	13.9	3.7	1.8	6.3	2.1	0.0
	2006	13 252	70.8	63.5	62.2	3.8	1.3	2.2	1.9	24.9	4.2	4.5	13.0	3.2	0.0
Mozambique	1990	381	34.1	22.3	21.9	6.9	4.0	0.9	0.1	64.5	3.1	0.7	60.3	0.4	..
	2000	364	34.7	25.5	25.5	4.7	4.3	0.1	..	45.0	36.0	0.0	8.9	0.1	..
	2006	2 381	68.9	68.3	66.1	0.3	0.3	0.0	0.4	24.9	20.2	..	4.3	0.5	..
Myanmar	1990	409	17.6	7.6	7.0	2.3	6.9	0.8	2.7	63.6	1.0	0.0	61.6	1.1	..
	2000	1 980	47.2	16.9	16.7	22.4	5.5	2.6	0.0	42.6	0.2	0.2	42.0	0.2	0.0
	2006	4 376	13.2	7.5	7.4	..	5.2	0.6	0.1	79.7	0.5	0.2	78.1	0.9	0.0
Nepal - Népal	1990	211	85.0	60.0	53.8	23.4	0.8	0.7	0.0	15.0	0.1	0.1	14.8	0.0	..
	2000	721	53.7	23.9	23.0	27.5	1.4	0.9	0.0	44.7	0.0	0.0	44.5	0.1	..
	2006	830	26.7	12.7	12.1	11.7	1.0	1.4	0.1	70.8	0.2	0.1	69.8	0.8	..

For sources and notes, see end of table.

Pour les sources et les notes, se reporter à la fin du tableau.

Destination / Origin / Origine	Year / Année	World (millions of dollars) (1) / Monde (millions de dollars) (1)	Developed economies / Économies développées Total	Europe Total	Europe EU UE	USA États-Unis	Japan Japon	Other Autres	Economies in transition / Économies en transition	Developing economies / Économies en développement Total	Africa Afrique	America Amérique	Eastern, Southern and South-Eastern Asia / Asie orientale, méridionale et du Sud-Est	Western Asia / Asie occidentale	Oceania Océanie
									Percentage / En pourcentage						
Netherlands - Pays-Bas	1990	130 715	90.5	84.5	81.7	4.0	0.9	1.2	0.8	7.9	2.1	1.1	3.2	1.5	0.0
	2000	229 742	90.1	83.7	81.4	4.4	0.9	1.1	1.1	8.1	1.4	1.1	3.9	1.7	0.0
	2006	463 829	87.3	81.2	78.9	4.5	0.6	1.1	2.2	9.4	1.8	1.3	4.1	2.3	0.0
Netherlands Antilles - Antilles néerlandaises	1990	1 793	45.0	6.6	6.6	33.5	2.7	2.2	..	52.5	3.2	49.1	0.2	..	0.1
	2000	1 984	29.1	8.7	8.7	16.1	0.1	4.2	0.0	67.3	2.0	61.7	3.5	0.0	0.1
	2006	3 891	39.6	10.5	10.5	27.2	0.2	1.7	0.0	56.4	2.4	48.9	5.1	0.0	0.0
New Caledonia - Nouvelle-Calédonie	1990	405	89.5	55.0	55.0	6.6	25.5	2.4	..	9.0	..	..	8.1	..	0.9
	2000	573	75.8	37.5	37.5	5.2	27.0	6.1	..	24.8	0.0	0.0	23.3	..	0.1
	2006	1 376	64.7	39.2	39.2	3.4	17.4	4.7	1.3	33.9	3.4	0.0	28.5	0.0	2.0
New Zealand - Nouvelle-Zélande	1990	9 457	65.6	16.8	16.4	13.1	15.8	19.9	1.8	26.7	1.6	3.1	16.0	2.4	0.3
	2000	12 742	65.4	15.3	15.0	14.8	13.7	21.7	0.2	31.8	1.4	3.3	22.7	2.0	0.2
	2006	22 441	61.2	15.6	15.3	13.1	10.3	22.1	0.7	36.2	2.8	3.4	24.1	2.9	0.3
Nicaragua	1990	331	69.2	34.9	34.8	10.3	5.4	18.6	..	23.5	..	22.6	0.9	..	..
	2000	643	63.9	19.1	18.5	39.7	0.5	4.6	..	30.6	..	30.5	0.1	..	..
	2006	(e)1 080	54.9	13.2	13.0	34.8	0.9	54.9	1.2	43.8	0.0	42.8	1.0	0.0	..
Niger	1990	283	84.8	64.4	64.4	0.1	20.3	0.0	..	14.2	14.2	..	..	..	..
	2000	196	51.0	34.3	34.2	2.5	13.9	0.3	..	48.9	48.9	..	0.0	0.0	..
	2006	428	64.2	35.5	35.4	26.6	0.0	2.1	11.3	24.5	23.3	0.0	1.0	0.1	..
Nigeria - Nigéria	1990	10 273	92.0	36.6	36.5	54.2	0.0	1.2	0.2	7.6	0.6	0.7	0.3	0.0	..
	2000	27 042	68.2	23.0	23.0	42.5	0.4	2.3	..	31.6	7.0	5.0	19.5	0.0	0.0
	2006	53 910	76.1	24.4	23.0	48.8	1.6	1.2	0.0	22.9	8.9	9.4	3.8	0.8	0.0
Norway - Norvège	1990	33 907	93.3	82.0	80.7	6.5	1.7	3.1	0.6	5.8	1.2	1.2	2.1	1.4	0.0
	2000	57 592	95.0	79.1	78.2	8.0	1.7	6.3	0.6	4.4	0.5	0.8	2.6	0.5	..
	2006	122 123	93.0	82.9	82.2	5.7	1.0	3.4	1.0	5.8	0.5	0.8	3.7	0.7	0.0
Oman	1990	4 584	18.8	13.0	12.4	3.7	2.1	0.1	0.0	81.1	4.4	0.0	15.6	61.2	0.0
	2000	10 667	21.9	1.3	1.3	1.2	18.2	1.1	0.1	78.1	1.7	0.0	64.4	12.0	0.0
	2006	23 620	16.9	2.1	2.0	3.7	10.9	0.2	0.1	83.1	8.9	0.0	65.2	9.0	..
Pakistan	1990	5 587	63.0	39.3	38.1	12.4	8.2	3.1	1.6	31.0	2.2	0.3	19.0	9.5	0.0
	2000	8 876	60.2	28.6	27.9	25.2	2.6	3.7	0.4	38.9	4.0	2.0	20.3	12.7	0.1
	2006	17 182	47.3	22.9	22.2	21.0	1.1	2.3	1.1	50.9	5.6	2.1	27.3	16.0	0.0
Panama	1990	321	78.4	31.6	31.6	45.2	0.6	0.9	0.1	19.8	0.0	19.6	0.2	0.0	..
	2000	779	65.1	17.7	17.7	45.4	1.5	0.4	0.4	27.9	0.1	24.5	3.4	0.0	..
	2006	1 022	70.5	29.8	29.8	39.8	0.4	0.5	0.0	24.1	0.0	18.9	5.2	0.0	..
Papua New Guinea - Papouasie-Nouvelle-Guinée	1990	1 266	82.0	24.7	24.1	2.4	27.8	27.2	..	17.6	0.2	0.0	17.1	0.0	0.3
	2000	2 814	53.5	10.2	10.2	1.3	11.3	30.7	0.0	14.2	0.0	0.0	13.9	0.0	0.0
	2006	6 268	47.7	7.4	7.3	1.3	8.2	30.9	0.0	13.4	0.0	0.0	13.0	0.0	0.0
Paraguay	1990	1 063	39.1	33.4	28.6	3.9	0.2	1.6	0.1	51.1	0.3	47.2	3.3	0.2	0.0
	2000	869	18.3	13.8	13.6	3.9	0.3	0.2	0.0	78.8	0.1	74.5	4.1	0.2	..
	2006	1 906	13.7	7.8	6.0	3.5	1.3	1.1	12.0	64.6	1.7	59.5	2.8	0.5	0.0
Peru - Pérou	1990	3 276	71.0	34.2	33.4	22.3	13.4	1.1	3.4	24.9	0.7	15.7	7.8	0.6	0.0
	2000	6 872	64.5	29.2	20.5	28.1	4.7	2.5	0.3	33.6	0.6	18.6	13.7	0.7	0.0
	2006	23 744	61.4	25.1	17.9	24.1	5.2	7.0	0.3	36.2	0.5	20.1	15.2	0.3	0.0
Philippines	1990	8 195	79.3	18.8	18.5	37.9	19.8	2.8	0.0	20.0	0.3	0.9	17.5	1.1	0.0
	2000	38 216	64.7	18.3	18.1	29.8	14.7	1.9	0.0	34.9	0.1	1.1	33.2	0.4	0.0
	2006	46 976	55.2	18.6	18.5	18.3	16.5	1.8	0.1	44.7	0.3	0.8	42.8	0.7	0.0
Poland - Pologne	1990	13 627	72.0	67.5	61.8	2.8	0.8	0.9	16.9	9.9	2.6	1.5	3.8	2.1	..
	2000	31 645	87.7	83.2	81.3	3.2	0.2	1.1	7.1	5.0	1.2	1.2	1.9	0.8	0.0
	2006	110 890	84.5	81.7	79.0	1.9	0.2	0.7	9.9	5.2	0.9	0.8	1.9	1.7	0.0
Portugal	1990	16 402	91.6	84.4	81.1	4.8	1.0	1.4	0.5	6.9	4.6	0.6	1.2	0.4	0.0
	2000	23 297	91.2	83.3	80.8	6.0	0.5	1.4	0.1	8.0	4.0	1.7	1.4	0.9	0.0
	2006	43 350	83.3	76.0	74.8	6.1	0.3	0.9	0.5	12.5	5.9	1.7	3.7	1.2	0.0
Qatar	1990	3 293	63.9	2.3	2.3	1.6	59.5	0.5	0.0	33.4	0.7	8.9	18.1	5.7	0.0
	2000	11 593	50.8	1.1	1.0	3.1	45.0	1.6	0.0	39.5	0.9	0.1	32.3	6.1	..
	2006	33 376	49.8	6.8	6.2	0.8	41.0	1.3	0.0	43.1	1.2	0.1	37.3	4.5	..

For sources and notes, see end of table.

Pour les sources et les notes, se reporter à la fin du tableau.

Destination / Origin / Origine	Year / Année	World (millions of dollars) (1) / Monde (millions de dollars) (1)	Developed economies / Économies développées — Total	Europe Total	Europe EU UE	USA États-Unis	Japan Japon	Other Autres	Economies in transition / Économies en transition	Developing economies / Économies en développement — Total	Africa Afrique	America Amérique	Eastern, Southern and South-Eastern Asia / Asie orientale, méridionale et du Sud-Est	Western Asia Asie occidentale	Oceania Océanie
Republic of Korea - République de Corée	1990	67 815	67.2	15.7	15.0	28.6	18.6	4.2	..	24.5	1.8	2.9	16.7	2.9	0.0
	2000	172 257	52.4	15.1	14.5	21.9	11.9	3.5	0.8	46.4	1.9	5.3	35.8	3.3	0.3
	2006	296 680	40.7	15.8	15.3	13.3	8.1	3.4	2.3	56.6	3.0	5.9	44.0	3.6	0.3
Romania - Roumanie	1990	5 871	52.7	44.3	42.6	5.8	1.6	1.0	27.9	18.6	3.7	1.9	6.6	6.4	..
	2000	10 367	78.8	73.8	72.7	3.7	0.2	1.1	5.6	15.2	3.6	0.8	2.4	8.3	0.0
	2006	32 479	75.6	72.1	70.4	2.5	0.3	0.7	6.2	16.2	2.1	0.6	2.4	11.1	0.0
Russian Federation - Fédération de Russie	2000	102 999	70.7	59.0	54.3	7.7	2.7	1.2	13.8	15.4	1.1	0.9	9.7	3.7	0.0
	2006	291 881	70.5	65.2	60.7	3.1	1.6	0.7	11.6	16.8	1.1	1.0	9.3	5.5	0.0
Rwanda	1990	100	72.7	64.4	64.3	6.1	1.9	0.3	..	10.4	2.0	..	8.4	..	..
	2000	99	42.2	36.7	36.3	5.1	0.4	0.0	1.5	22.3	7.3	0.0	14.5	0.5	..
	2006	195	29.3	24.7	24.6	4.3	0.0	0.2	1.1	21.0	3.5	0.4	16.7	0.4	..
Saint Kitts and Nevis - Saint-Kitts-et-Nevis	1990	(c)24	96.0	34.4	34.2	61.3	0.2	0.1	..	4.0	0.0	3.7	0.2	..	..
	2000	(c)33	88.2	21.8	21.8	65.9	0.3	0.2	..	8.3	0.0	7.8	0.5	..	..
	2006	(c)84	83.6	10.1	10.1	62.0	1.5	9.9	5.1	6.6	0.1	5.3	0.1	1.0	..
Saint Lucia - Sainte-Lucie	1990	146	91.3	68.9	68.9	16.7	0.1	5.7	..	8.7	0.0	8.7	0.0	..	..
	2000	45	73.3	54.2	54.1	17.8	0.7	0.7	0.0	26.0	0.0	25.6	0.3	0.0	..
	2006	288	89.0	78.7	78.7	10.2	0.0	0.1	..	10.9	0.0	10.1	0.7	0.0	..
Saint Vincent and the Grenadines	1990	83	65.4	54.7	54.7	10.6	0.0	0.1	..	34.1	..	34.1	0.0	..	0.0
	2000	51	49.5	46.3	46.3	2.6	0.0	0.5	1.3	46.9	..	45.9	0.1	1.0	..
	2006	193	77.6	76.5	74.7	0.9	0.0	0.1	7.2	15.1	0.0	14.6	0.1	0.4	..
Samoa	1990	12	71.9	19.2	19.1	6.5	0.9	45.4	..	14.9	0.1	..	4.5	..	6.6
	2000	69	72.9	3.0	3.0	10.6	0.3	59.1	..	20.7	0.1	0.2	17.7	0.0	1.5
	2006	131	50.3	0.8	0.7	3.4	0.7	45.3	..	44.6	0.0	0.2	12.1	0.1	0.4
Sao Tome and Principe - Sao Tomé-et-Principe	1990	29	73.8	73.8	73.5	..	..	0.0	..	26.2	0.0	0.3	25.8	..	..
	2000	18	85.4	75.5	70.3	2.6	2.7	4.7	0.1	14.4	0.3	0.4	4.5	9.2	..
	2006	9	87.2	84.2	84.0	..	0.4	2.6	0.1	12.6	6.1	3.0	3.1	0.4	..
Saudi Arabia - Arabie saoudite	1990	44 417	64.0	19.1	19.0	24.0	19.0	1.9	0.0	35.9	4.0	3.3	19.1	9.4	0.0
	2000	74 746	54.9	17.9	17.7	17.4	17.3	2.3	0.0	45.1	5.5	1.5	31.8	6.3	0.0
	2006	189 481	49.5	14.5	14.3	15.9	17.7	1.4	0.0	50.4	5.3	1.1	35.1	8.9	0.0
Senegal - Sénégal	1990	861	49.8	47.7	47.7	0.0	1.9	0.1	0.0	32.8	19.0	0.0	13.7	0.1	..
	2000	693	48.3	46.3	45.4	0.5	1.2	0.2	0.0	43.7	28.2	0.5	14.5	0.4	..
	2006	1 364	28.5	27.0	23.5	0.5	1.0	0.1	0.0	54.9	44.9	0.5	7.8	1.6	0.1
Serbia and Montenegro - Serbie-et-Monténégro	2000	1 028	88.1	86.8	86.1	0.3	0.3	0.6	0.9	11.0	4.3	0.2	2.0	4.5	0.0
	2006	(b)2 506	..	..	..	..	..	..	..	..	..	..	..	..	..
Seychelles	1990	14	92.4	92.0	92.0	0.1	0.1	0.1	..	7.6	1.2	..	6.3	..	..
	2000	124	93.0	91.7	91.7	0.1	1.0	0.2	..	4.5	4.0	..	0.5	..	..
	2006	350	82.4	69.7	69.6	2.6	8.3	1.8	1.0	13.7	10.0	0.0	3.5	0.1	0.0
SFR of Yugoslavia (former) - RSF de Yougoslavie (anc.)	1990	14 356	67.7	61.6	59.9	4.8	0.3	1.0	19.2	13.1	5.0	0.8	3.1	4.2	0.0
Sierra Leone	1990	137	92.0	66.2	66.1	25.8	..	0.0	..	..	..	..	..	..	..
	2000	126	90.8	86.0	85.9	2.9	0.4	1.6	0.2	6.6	4.0	0.4	2.1	0.1	..
	2006	209	89.3	67.5	67.5	19.1	0.4	2.2	0.5	7.0	2.7	0.2	3.4	0.7	..
Singapore - Singapour (2)	1990	52 804	50.4	16.5	15.7	21.2	8.7	3.9	0.9	46.6	1.5	1.2	40.7	2.2	0.1
	2000	138 046	42.5	14.5	14.0	17.3	7.5	3.2	0.1	57.2	1.2	1.9	52.3	1.3	0.1
	2006	272 057	32.0	11.7	11.3	10.2	5.5	4.7	0.2	67.4	1.3	2.2	61.5	1.8	0.2
Slovakia - Slovaquie	2000	11 874	93.7	91.8	89.7	1.4	0.1	0.3	3.4	2.8	0.5	0.5	1.2	0.6	0.0
	2006	41 957	91.8	87.8	86.8	3.2	0.3	0.5	4.0	3.7	0.6	0.4	1.3	1.5	0.0
Slovenia - Slovénie	2000	8 729	77.5	73.6	72.2	3.1	0.1	0.6	18.4	3.9	0.7	0.5	1.4	1.3	0.0
	2006	23 151	72.6	69.8	68.7	2.2	0.1	0.5	18.6	4.6	1.2	0.4	1.5	1.5	0.0
Solomon Islands - Îles Salomon	1990	75	72.6	21.8	21.8	3.7	41.5	5.6	..	19.6	0.0	..	17.5	0.0	3.8
	2000	101	35.4	10.6	10.6	0.7	20.8	3.3	..	54.5	..	0.0	52.1	0.0	6.2
	2006	237	17.7	5.6	5.6	1.1	8.9	2.0	..	73.0	0.1	0.0	70.2	0.0	7.5
Somalia - Somalie	1990	150	40.4	40.1	37.6	..	0.3	0.0	0.2	59.4	1.3	0.0	1.6	56.5	..
	2000	117	1.8	1.1	1.1	0.4	0.2	0.1	..	98.2	5.9	0.0	2.3	89.9	..
	2006	300	1.0	0.7	0.7	0.1	0.2	0.0	0.0	98.9	4.8	0.0	8.2	86.0	..

For sources and notes, see end of table.

Pour les sources et les notes, se reporter à la fin du tableau.

2.1 Country trade structure by partner: Exports by main region of destination

2.1 Structure du commerce des pays par partenaires : Exportations par principales régions de destination

Destination / Origin / Origine	Year / Année	World (millions of dollars) (1) / Monde (millions de dollars) (1)	Developed economies / Économies développées						Economies in transition / Économies en transition	Developing economies / Économies en développement					
			Total	Europe		USA États-Unis	Japan Japon	Other Autres		Total	Africa Afrique	America Amérique	Eastern, Southern and South-Eastern Asia / Asie orientale, méridionale et du Sud-Est	Western Asia / Asie occidentale	Oceania Océanie
				Total	EU UE										
									Percentage / En pourcentage						
South Africa - Afrique du Sud	1990	(a)24 704	43.9	27.9	25.3	7.4	6.7	1.9	..	5.0	1.7	0.7	2.2	0.4	0.0
	2000	30 429	46.3	29.8	28.7	7.9	4.5	4.1	0.1	26.6	13.2	1.8	10.1	1.5	0.0
	2006	51 564	67.9	39.4	35.9	11.8	12.1	4.6	0.3	31.8	14.9	2.0	12.1	2.8	0.0
Spain - Espagne	1990	55 688	82.5	74.3	72.0	5.8	1.1	1.3	0.8	13.2	4.5	3.7	3.1	1.8	0.0
	2000	108 186	81.3	73.6	71.8	5.0	1.0	1.6	0.8	15.5	3.4	6.0	3.0	3.0	0.0
	2006	212 634	79.8	73.1	70.3	4.4	0.7	1.5	1.3	15.4	4.1	5.3	3.1	3.0	0.1
Sri Lanka	1990	1 895	63.1	28.4	27.5	25.9	5.4	3.4	2.5	30.5	5.5	2.0	13.1	9.8	0.1
	2000	5 459	74.0	26.2	25.4	40.2	4.2	3.5	2.0	17.9	1.7	1.4	9.3	5.5	0.0
	2006	7 492	62.8	29.7	28.9	27.7	2.5	3.0	3.1	26.7	1.4	3.3	15.9	6.1	0.0
Sudan - Soudan	1990	515	48.1	39.3	39.0	2.8	6.0	0.1	8.8	43.0	7.1	0.0	24.9	10.5	0.4
	2000	1 619	27.9	10.6	10.5	0.1	17.2	0.0	0.2	71.8	2.8	0.7	58.5	9.3	0.5
	2006	5 699	52.4	2.3	2.3	0.1	48.0	1.9	0.0	47.3	3.2	0.0	37.6	6.5	0.0
Suriname	1990	456	93.6	75.6	38.7	11.8	6.2	0.0	..	6.4	..	6.4	0.0	..	..
	2000	498	88.2	51.7	29.1	24.9	4.1	7.5	0.0	11.8	1.7	9.4	0.7	0.0	..
	2006	1 234	77.6	48.8	21.6	12.6	0.6	15.5	0.6	21.8	1.7	12.1	1.1	6.9	..
Sweden - Suède	1990	53 069	88.0	72.8	60.9	9.6	2.2	3.4	1.3	10.8	1.6	2.0	5.3	1.8	0.0
	2000	87 867	84.3	68.7	59.8	10.2	2.8	2.7	1.1	14.5	1.7	3.1	7.1	2.6	0.0
	2006	147 413	82.2	68.6	58.2	9.3	1.6	2.8	2.5	13.1	2.1	2.0	6.5	2.4	0.0
Switzerland - Suisse	1990	63 806	82.2	66.2	65.7	8.0	4.8	3.2	1.8	16.0	2.0	2.4	8.7	2.9	0.0
	2000	80 535	82.3	62.1	61.6	13.1	4.2	2.9	0.8	16.8	1.5	2.9	9.4	3.0	0.0
	2006	147 541	79.8	62.1	61.7	11.1	3.6	3.0	1.9	18.2	1.5	2.5	10.4	3.8	0.0
Syrian Arab Republic - République arabe syrienne	1990	4 210	44.4	43.4	43.0	0.9	0.1	0.0	32.8	21.9	2.8	0.0	0.5	18.6	..
	2000	4 759	66.9	62.9	62.9	3.0	0.3	0.7	1.4	28.7	2.7	0.1	1.7	24.1	0.0
	2006	12 225	34.5	32.6	32.5	1.7	0.1	0.2	0.6	64.9	10.4	0.6	1.4	52.4	0.0
Tajikistan - Tadjikistan	2000	770	39.6	39.5	30.2	0.1	..	0.0	48.5	11.8	0.1	..	4.1	7.6	..
	2006	1 399	47.2	47.1	45.4	0.0	0.0	0.0	13.4	39.5	0.0	0.0	7.7	31.8	..
Thailand - Thaïlande	1990	23 072	68.1	24.8	23.4	22.7	17.2	3.4	0.5	30.8	2.4	1.4	22.6	4.3	0.0
	2000	68 963	57.7	17.2	16.3	21.3	14.7	4.4	0.1	41.7	1.8	1.5	36.1	2.2	0.0
	2006	130 555	47.5	14.7	13.8	15.0	12.6	5.2	0.4	51.8	2.6	2.2	43.2	3.7	0.0
TFYR of Macedonia - LERY de Macédoine	2000	1 319	65.4	51.9	48.9	12.6	0.2	0.8	32.5	1.9	0.5	0.1	0.3	1.0	..
	2006	2 400	62.8	61.7	61.2	0.9	0.1	0.2	34.1	3.1	0.2	0.0	0.3	2.6	..
Togo	1990	267	58.6	44.4	43.1	1.1	0.1	13.0	5.1	33.7	17.0	2.2	14.3	0.1	..
	2000	192	22.5	22.0	21.2	0.3	0.0	0.2	..	74.7	41.9	6.5	25.4	0.9	1.5
	2006	568	26.3	24.1	23.8	0.6	0.0	1.6	0.4	71.9	56.8	1.0	13.6	0.6	0.0
Tonga	1990	13	92.4	1.6	1.6	25.9	30.0	34.8	..	5.5	..	..	0.0	..	0.1
	2000	18	92.4	6.6	6.6	30.4	49.2	6.3	..	7.4	0.0	..	3.7	0.1	0.2
	2006	22	79.3	1.4	1.3	39.7	27.8	10.5	..	20.3	..	0.0	10.5	0.1	0.4
Trinidad and Tobago - Trinité-et-Tobago	1990	1 986	71.8	15.1	13.8	53.9	0.8	1.9	..	22.5	0.6	21.1	0.6	0.2	0.0
	2000	3 041	61.8	13.4	13.4	46.8	0.1	1.5	0.0	36.9	0.6	35.9	0.4	0.0	0.0
	2006	13 420	74.5	11.3	11.3	59.8	1.3	2.1	0.0	24.7	0.2	23.3	0.9	0.3	0.0
Tunisia - Tunisie	1990	3 556	79.1	77.9	77.5	0.9	0.3	0.1	2.8	18.0	9.5	0.9	4.1	3.5	0.0
	2000	5 996	80.6	79.5	78.5	0.7	0.2	0.1	0.2	15.4	8.3	1.1	3.4	2.5	0.0
	2006	11 827	79.4	74.1	73.7	4.0	0.6	0.7	0.3	16.3	9.8	1.0	3.3	2.2	0.0
Turkey - Turquie	1990	13 385	69.8	59.7	57.2	7.2	1.8	1.0	5.1	22.4	5.6	0.3	7.7	8.7	0.0
	2000	27 769	72.9	57.6	56.4	11.3	0.5	3.5	7.1	14.4	4.9	1.0	3.7	4.8	0.0
	2006	85 492	66.7	57.7	56.1	6.0	0.3	2.7	9.5	19.1	5.3	0.8	4.0	8.9	0.1
Turkmenistan - Turkménistan	2000	2 505	26.5	25.2	21.5	0.5	..	0.8	52.5	19.5	0.2	..	11.6	7.7	..
	2006	6 339	12.9	10.4	10.4	1.2	0.0	1.3	60.1	25.3	0.0	0.0	19.4	5.8	0.0
Uganda - Ouganda	1990	181	90.5	76.1	75.5	7.9	3.5	2.9	0.7	8.8	6.9	0.0	1.2	0.7	0.0
	2000	402	56.5	50.4	25.3	2.1	2.0	2.0	..	40.5	31.4	0.2	7.8	1.1	..
	2006	693	53.7	48.8	48.1	3.1	0.9	0.9	0.8	36.4	23.7	0.2	7.8	4.7	0.0
Ukraine	2000	14 579	39.2	32.5	31.3	5.0	0.5	1.2	31.3	28.5	5.0	2.3	12.1	9.0	0.0
	2006	39 300	34.5	29.2	28.7	4.1	0.4	0.9	32.2	32.5	7.5	2.3	9.7	13.1	0.0
United Arab Emirates - Émirats arabes unis	1990	21 917	53.8	9.9	9.7	4.0	37.7	2.3	0.0	33.4	2.7	0.5	25.2	5.0	0.0
	2000	40 806	42.4	5.2	5.1	2.2	33.0	1.9	0.6	43.6	3.8	0.2	32.6	7.0	0.0
	2006	111 638	34.5	6.3	5.8	1.2	25.8	1.3	0.7	49.3	3.8	0.3	37.9	7.3	0.0

For sources and notes, see end of table.

Pour les sources et les notes, se reporter à la fin du tableau.

Destination / Origin / Origine	Year / Année	World (millions of dollars) (1) / Monde (millions de dollars) (1)	Developed economies / Économies développées						Economies in transition / Économies en transition	Developing economies / Économies en développement					
			Total	Europe		USA États-Unis	Japan Japon	Other Autres		Total	Africa Afrique	America Amérique	Eastern, Southern and South-Eastern Asia / Asie orientale, méridionale et du Sud-Est	Western Asia / Asie occidentale	Oceania Océanie
				Total	EU UE										
								Percentage / En pourcentage							
United Kingdom - Royaume-Uni	1990	185 127	81.7	62.1	58.5	12.6	2.5	4.4	0.8	16.6	3.5	1.6	7.2	4.2	0.0
	2000	282 838	84.4	62.2	59.2	15.8	2.0	4.5	0.6	14.6	2.4	1.6	7.2	3.4	0.0
	2006	422 685	80.0	60.9	58.0	13.9	1.7	3.5	1.5	15.7	2.7	1.5	7.5	4.0	0.0
United Republic of Tanzania - République-Unie de Tanzanie	1990	416	54.1	43.0	41.2	6.8	3.9	0.5	0.7	42.2	8.2	0.0	32.3	1.7	..
	2000	735	59.3	51.8	50.6	2.1	4.8	0.6	0.5	40.0	19.1	0.2	19.0	1.8	0.0
	2006	1 570	40.9	30.1	24.1	2.1	5.3	3.3	1.7	49.3	18.3	0.1	25.3	5.5	0.0
United States - États-Unis	1990	393 106	65.2	28.4	26.7	..	12.4	24.5	0.9	33.6	2.0	13.5	15.4	2.5	0.1
	2000	772 124	57.1	23.2	21.8	..	8.4	25.5	0.5	42.3	1.4	21.6	17.2	2.0	0.0
	2006	1 037 070	53.5	22.4	20.7	..	5.8	25.3	0.7	45.7	1.8	21.3	19.2	3.3	0.0
Uruguay	1990	1 730	41.8	27.9	27.5	9.5	1.2	3.2	5.2	51.6	1.6	39.8	8.0	2.2	..
	2000	2 295	32.6	17.2	16.3	8.4	1.5	5.6	0.3	66.1	1.8	54.3	9.6	0.4	0.0
	2006	4 109	38.9	21.2	20.0	12.1	2.6	3.0	5.1	52.5	4.1	34.4	12.7	1.2	0.0
USSR (former) - URSS (anc.)	1990	45 924	80.3	70.9	69.4	2.3	6.7	0.4	4.9	14.8	1.7	0.5	9.4	3.2	0.0
Uzbekistan - Ouzbékistan	2000	2 181	32.6	27.2	27.1	1.5	3.3	0.6	51.7	15.7	0.1	1.2	10.8	3.6	..
	2006	4 936	31.6	25.5	25.4	2.8	3.3	0.0	41.4	27.0	0.1	0.0	19.2	7.7	..
Vanuatu	1990	25	89.9	57.9	54.3	3.7	20.6	7.7	0.3	9.5	0.2	0.3	2.2	0.3	6.5
	2000	86	35.6	5.8	5.8	9.8	18.9	1.1	..	64.1	0.1	0.1	60.5	..	3.5
	2006	242	17.1	3.4	3.4	0.9	11.5	1.3	0.0	82.6	0.8	0.1	78.6	..	3.1
Venezuela (Bolivarian Rep. of) - Venezuela (Rép. bolivarienne du)	1990	18 044	71.3	14.2	14.0	51.5	2.8	2.7	0.0	16.2	0.1	14.5	1.6	0.0	..
	2000	33 358	58.9	5.1	5.0	51.9	0.7	1.2	0.1	35.4	0.0	34.6	0.6	0.2	..
	2006	75 494	57.4	9.2	9.2	46.2	0.4	1.5	0.1	30.2	0.4	25.9	3.7	0.1	0.0
Viet Nam	1990	2 525	25.4	11.5	11.3	0.0	13.5	0.4	36.7	28.4	0.2	0.5	27.6	0.2	..
	2000	14 483	54.5	21.9	20.6	5.1	17.8	9.7	1.1	43.8	1.0	0.9	39.2	2.7	0.0
	2006	39 690	65.1	20.5	19.8	21.2	12.3	11.2	0.9	26.6	0.5	0.5	24.3	1.2	..
Yemen - Yémen	1990	1 561	87.5	56.7	56.6	23.3	5.2	2.3	0.4	11.6	1.4	0.0	8.4	1.8	..
	2000	4 076	12.3	2.3	1.2	6.2	2.1	1.7	1.1	83.9	2.0	1.6	76.3	4.0	..
	2006	6 443	14.3	2.4	2.4	6.8	3.5	1.5	0.0	85.2	1.5	0.0	74.1	9.6	0.0
Zambia - Zambie	1990	544	64.1	31.5	30.6	1.6	31.0	0.0	..	35.9	7.8	0.0	22.7	5.4	..
	2000	757	54.4	45.9	36.5	1.6	0.0	6.8	0.0	45.6	41.8	0.1	3.6	0.1	..
	2006	3 695	52.4	51.1	12.7	0.5	0.6	0.1	0.0	47.6	36.3	0.0	11.3	0.0	0.0
Zimbabwe	1990	1 491	59.4	44.2	42.2	7.6	5.5	2.1	0.9	39.4	32.1	0.7	6.2	0.4	0.0
	2000	3 281	27.6	19.7	17.4	3.2	4.0	0.7	0.7	27.4	17.9	0.8	7.7	0.9	0.1
	2006	941	26.3	15.4	13.0	10.4	0.2	0.2	0.7	73.0	67.0	0.1	4.5	1.4	..

Sources:
- International Monetary Fund, *Direction of Trade Statistics*

Notes:
(a) Data refers to South Africa Customs Union (Botswana, Lesotho, Namibia, South Africa and Swaziland)
(b) UNCTAD secretariat estimate
(c) Including Anguilla

(1) Include unspecified destinations.
(2) Exports data include a considerable amount of re-exports.
(3) Estimate. Data are derived by calculating the difference between DOT's aggregate for Asia and the sum of countries classified in Asia by the data source.

Sources :
- Fonds monétaire international, *Direction of Trade Statistics*

Notes :
(a) Donnée relative à l'Union Douanière d'Afrique du Sud (Afrique du Sud, Botswana, Lesotho, Namibie et Swaziland)
(b) Estimation du secrétariat de la UNCTAD
(c) Y compris Anguilla

(1) Y compris des destinations non-spécifiées.
(2) Les données des exportations comprennent une part importante de re-exportations.
(3) Estimation. Les données sont dérivées par différence entre l'agrégat Asie fourni par DOT et la somme des pays classifiés en Asie dans la source.

Origin / Origine (Destination)	Year Année	World (millions of dollars) Monde (millions de dollars)	Developed economies Économies développées						Economies in transition Économies en transition	Developing economies Économies en développement					
			Total	Europe		USA États-Unis	Japan Japon	Other Autres		Total	Africa Afrique	America Amérique	Eastern, Southern and South-Eastern Asia Asie orientale, méridionale et du Sud-Est	Western Asia Asie occidentale	Oceania Océanie
				Total	EU UE										
			Percentage / En pourcentage												
Afghanistan	1990	479	45.9	16.9	16.3	1.0	27.8	0.2	0.2	53.9	0.0	0.5	52.6	0.7	..
	2000	621	21.3	10.2	10.0	2.0	9.2	0.0	21.3	57.4	5.6	0.0	49.6	2.1	..
	2006	3 818	30.1	15.5	15.2	12.0	2.0	0.6	14.0	55.9	1.5	0.1	50.4	3.8	..
Albania - Albanie	1990	423	66.8	63.8	61.6	2.7	0.3	0.1	9.6	23.5	13.7	0.2	8.1	1.5	..
	2000	1 084	85.0	82.9	81.1	1.5	0.4	0.2	6.3	8.4	0.2	0.4	1.9	5.9	..
	2006	2 919	75.9	74.1	73.1	1.0	0.1	0.7	9.3	14.4	0.7	1.2	4.2	8.3	..
Algeria - Algérie	1990	9 679	88.9	68.2	66.9	11.6	4.6	4.4	2.1	8.3	1.8	2.6	1.4	2.5	..
	2000	9 027	79.4	60.2	60.0	11.6	3.0	4.6	4.9	15.7	2.1	2.9	6.3	4.5	0.0
	2006	25 103	64.4	55.7	54.8	4.8	1.9	1.9	6.6	29.0	3.0	5.4	13.4	7.2	..
Angola	1990	1 723	85.0	72.9	70.3	9.6	1.9	0.7	0.2	14.8	2.3	7.3	5.2	..	..
	2000	2 203	63.0	50.4	46.7	10.9	1.3	0.4	2.0	34.9	20.2	6.0	8.3	0.5	..
	2006	11 177	57.6	39.7	37.6	15.3	1.8	0.7	0.9	41.4	7.7	9.9	23.2	0.6	..
Argentina - Argentine	1990	4 078	59.8	32.1	29.5	21.5	3.3	2.9	0.4	39.8	0.5	34.8	4.2	0.3	0.0
	2000	25 281	49.7	24.6	23.6	19.1	4.0	2.0	0.6	47.5	1.8	34.3	11.1	0.3	0.0
	2006	34 151	34.5	18.0	17.1	12.6	2.7	1.3	1.0	60.2	0.7	43.8	15.5	0.2	0.0
Armenia - Arménie	2000	885	52.0	39.4	36.7	11.6	0.4	0.6	19.6	23.0	0.0	2.4	10.7	10.0	..
	2006	1 980	44.1	34.1	33.4	4.5	0.1	5.5	42.4	13.3	0.2	1.1	10.4	1.6	..
Aruba	2000	794	77.4	21.7	21.3	51.4	2.8	1.5	0.0	22.4	1.5	18.8	1.9	0.2	..
	2006	1 054	77.8	21.0	20.6	53.6	2.4	0.8	0.0	22.1	0.1	18.3	3.7	0.1	..
Australia - Australie	1990	43 052	76.8	27.3	25.7	24.1	18.7	6.7	0.2	22.8	0.4	1.2	17.2	3.0	0.0
	2000	74 275	61.7	22.6	21.4	20.1	13.2	5.8	0.1	37.1	0.9	1.2	30.8	2.6	0.0
	2006	146 127	50.5	21.9	20.8	14.1	9.6	4.8	0.1	48.7	1.3	1.4	42.1	2.2	0.3
Austria - Autriche	1990	49 288	88.5	79.6	74.7	3.6	4.5	0.8	3.0	8.5	2.5	1.0	4.2	0.8	0.0
	2000	72 117	91.4	85.0	80.2	4.1	1.5	0.8	2.9	5.7	1.1	0.4	2.9	1.2	0.0
	2006	137 318	88.1	84.4	79.7	2.2	1.0	0.4	3.9	7.8	1.3	0.5	4.4	1.6	0.0
Azerbaijan - Azerbaïdjan	2000	1 172	41.8	28.8	23.5	10.0	1.4	1.5	32.2	25.9	2.1	0.6	10.3	12.9	0.0
	2006	5 266	40.7	32.1	30.8	3.8	3.6	1.2	39.9	19.4	0.9	1.9	8.5	8.1	0.0
Bahamas	1990	2 312	83.9	23.2	19.0	38.1	20.4	2.2	0.2	15.3	1.6	7.7	5.1	1.0	0.0
	2000	3 935	66.9	27.1	24.4	29.4	9.8	0.6	2.5	28.9	1.3	8.5	18.6	0.6	0.0
	2006	10 179	56.2	17.5	14.1	24.7	13.1	0.8	4.3	37.7	0.1	21.4	15.1	1.1	0.0
Bahrain - Bahreïn	1990	3 711	34.5	16.9	16.4	7.1	5.0	5.5	..	59.2	0.1	1.0	4.8	53.3	..
	2000	3 541	46.5	27.8	25.9	12.8	4.0	1.9	0.1	53.0	0.6	2.7	14.0	35.6	0.0
	2006	8 674	39.6	24.9	23.0	6.2	6.8	1.7	0.2	59.6	0.6	1.9	12.2	45.0	0.0
Bangladesh	1990	3 656	44.6	21.3	19.1	5.1	13.2	5.0	0.7	41.3	0.3	1.5	34.6	5.0	..
	2000	9 001	26.3	11.4	9.7	2.4	9.4	3.1	0.9	56.0	1.0	1.4	48.3	5.1	0.1
	2006	17 858	16.9	9.2	8.6	2.0	3.7	1.9	3.3	71.3	0.7	2.6	55.2	12.8	..
Barbados - Barbade	1990	700	68.7	22.1	21.0	33.7	5.3	7.6	0.0	30.3	0.0	27.1	3.2	0.0	..
	2000	1 156	69.0	16.4	15.5	41.5	5.2	5.9	0.1	30.9	0.1	25.2	4.6	0.9	0.0
	2006	1 621	61.4	15.0	13.7	37.7	3.7	4.9	0.0	38.5	0.2	31.7	6.4	0.3	0.0
Belarus - Bélarus	2000	8 646	24.5	22.2	21.4	1.6	0.5	0.2	70.3	4.1	0.3	1.5	2.1	0.2	0.0
	2006	22 351	26.1	23.9	22.5	1.3	0.6	0.3	65.1	6.4	0.2	1.5	4.1	0.5	0.0
Belgium - Belgique	2006	351 919	83.8	74.0	71.8	5.4	2.6	1.8	1.9	14.3	2.6	2.1	7.9	1.6	0.0
Belgium-Luxembourg - Belgique-Luxembourg	1990	119 414	88.5	80.2	77.6	4.4	2.1	1.8	1.4	10.1	4.0	1.6	3.7	0.9	0.0
	2000	186 511	86.2	73.6	71.7	7.3	2.9	2.4	1.1	12.7	3.0	1.9	7.0	0.8	0.0
Belize	1990	211	77.3	15.8	15.6	57.9	1.2	2.3	0.0	22.6	0.0	18.7	3.8	0.1	..
	2000	443	66.7	11.6	11.5	50.3	2.5	2.2	..	33.3	..	31.2	1.9	0.1	..
	2006	735	49.1	10.8	10.3	35.7	1.1	1.4	3.6	47.3	0.6	40.0	6.5	0.1	..
Benin - Bénin	1990	265	50.0	38.1	36.2	8.7	3.1	0.1	0.2	49.6	27.8	1.8	19.6	0.4	..
	2000	563	58.3	50.4	50.1	4.1	3.4	0.5	0.3	40.9	24.1	0.5	14.0	2.2	0.0
	2006	(e)1 594	53.4	43.1	42.2	8.0	1.1	1.2	0.0	46.6	23.4	3.1	18.0	2.1	0.0
Bermuda - Bermudes	1990	595	86.5	16.9	15.7	59.5	5.2	5.0	0.0	12.1	0.0	9.6	2.4	0.0	0.0
	2000	4 156	59.9	43.1	42.8	11.2	5.0	0.7	34.9	5.2	0.0	3.8	1.2	0.2	0.0
	2006	(e)4 365	69.1	47.6	45.0	19.1	0.4	2.0	0.0	30.9	0.1	2.2	28.7	0.0	0.0

For sources and notes, see end of table.

Pour les sources et les notes, se reporter à la fin du tableau.

2.1 Country trade structure by partner: Imports by main region of origin
2.1 Structure du commerce des pays par partenaires : Importations par principales régions d'origine

Origin / Origine — Destination	Year Année	World (millions of dollars) Monde (millions de dollars)	Developed economies / Économies développées Total	Europe Total	EU UE	USA États-Unis	Japan Japon	Other Autres	Economies in transition Économies en transition	Developing economies / Économies en développement Total	Africa Afrique	America Amérique	Eastern, Southern and South-Eastern Asia — Asie orientale, méridionale et du Sud-Est	Western Asia Asie occidentale	Oceania Océanie
										Percentage / En pourcentage					
Bolivia - Bolivie	1990	700	50.0	16.8	16.3	22.3	9.9	1.0	0.5	49.2	0.1	47.2	1.8	0.0	0.0
	2000	2 023	40.8	11.9	11.4	22.5	5.2	1.1	0.1	58.9	0.1	51.3	7.5	0.1	0.0
	2006	2 604	21.7	9.7	9.2	9.1	1.7	1.3	0.1	78.0	0.1	73.6	4.2	0.0	0.0
Bosnia and Herzegovina - Bosnie-Herzégovine	2000	2 644	75.5	73.2	72.3	1.8	0.2	0.4	23.0	1.5	0.0	0.1	0.3	1.1	..
	2006	5 993	68.6	67.4	66.6	0.9	0.0	0.1	27.4	4.0	0.1	0.4	0.7	2.8	..
Brazil - Brésil	1990	24 977	56.6	26.5	24.3	19.8	7.1	3.1	0.6	42.8	2.9	17.6	7.7	14.7	0.0
	2000	61 875	59.7	28.2	25.9	23.1	5.3	3.1	1.3	38.7	5.2	21.0	10.3	2.2	0.0
	2006	101 173	46.9	23.8	22.0	16.2	4.2	2.7	1.6	51.2	9.1	18.3	20.7	3.1	0.0
Brunei Darussalam - Brunéi Darussalam	1990	1 000	51.1	18.5	18.1	15.3	14.6	2.7	0.0	47.2	..	0.2	46.9	0.0	..
	2000	1 427	33.7	16.0	15.8	10.8	4.7	2.2	0.0	66.2	0.1	0.1	65.8	0.2	0.0
	2006	2 000	29.3	15.4	14.6	2.6	5.6	5.7	0.0	70.5	0.1	0.1	69.7	0.6	0.0
Bulgaria - Bulgarie	1990	3 462	73.8	68.2	65.0	2.7	1.7	1.2	3.5	22.7	9.0	2.6	9.6	1.5	0.0
	2000	6 362	58.5	54.0	52.6	3.0	1.0	0.5	29.2	10.5	0.7	2.9	3.2	3.6	0.0
	2006	19 560	67.1	62.1	60.8	2.4	1.6	0.9	8.3	22.2	0.7	6.2	8.1	7.3	0.0
Burkina Faso	1990	536	58.7	46.8	46.1	6.3	4.2	1.4	0.1	30.8	26.6	0.5	3.7	..	0.0
	2000	498	51.5	45.8	45.7	3.5	1.8	0.5	0.5	41.8	37.3	0.3	3.9	0.4	0.0
	2006	1 262	38.9	36.3	36.0	1.6	0.6	0.5	2.1	52.2	45.3	0.6	5.8	0.5	0.0
Burundi	1990	235	55.7	47.2	46.1	1.0	7.3	0.2	..	29.3	10.7	..	18.6	..	..
	2000	147	33.4	24.7	24.1	2.6	5.2	0.9	0.4	44.8	24.2	..	8.6	12.1	..
	2006	430	29.4	18.6	18.4	2.3	7.8	0.7	4.7	43.4	19.6	..	11.2	12.6	0.1
Cambodia - Cambodge	1990	56	40.0	28.5	28.2	..	9.0	2.5	0.0	59.9	0.1	0.5	55.8	3.5	..
	2000	1 424	15.5	8.1	6.6	2.3	4.1	1.0	0.0	83.6	0.0	0.1	83.4	0.1	0.0
	2006	2 985	10.0	4.3	4.1	0.9	4.3	0.5	0.1	89.6	0.1	0.1	89.3	0.2	0.0
Cameroon - Cameroun	1990	1 555	81.9	69.4	67.9	4.7	5.7	2.1	0.9	17.0	8.2	1.9	6.6	0.2	..
	2000	1 490	52.2	40.7	40.1	4.8	4.9	1.8	0.9	37.7	29.3	0.9	6.1	1.5	..
	2006	2 906	52.6	46.4	45.4	4.5	0.7	1.0	0.9	45.9	21.4	5.3	17.8	1.4	..
Canada	1990	131 642	84.7	14.2	12.6	62.9	6.8	0.8	0.2	11.2	0.8	3.3	6.5	0.7	0.0
	2000	262 776	82.1	12.4	10.7	64.3	4.7	0.8	0.2	15.7	0.8	5.0	9.3	0.6	0.0
	2006	384 864	73.8	14.3	12.4	54.9	3.9	0.8	0.5	24.9	2.1	7.3	14.3	1.1	0.0
Cape Verde - Cap-Vert	1990	145	84.9	80.4	80.1	4.5	..	0.1	2.2	9.4	4.1	4.4	0.9	..	..
	2000	237	85.8	75.6	75.4	4.5	5.3	0.4	0.7	12.0	2.0	2.9	5.1	2.0	0.0
	2006	638	75.8	73.4	73.2	2.3	..	0.0	0.2	19.8	10.7	5.9	2.3	0.9	0.1
Central African Republic - République centrafricaine	1990	184	69.5	64.4	63.6	0.8	4.3	0.0	0.2	30.1	24.4	0.8	4.7	0.2	..
	2000	121	56.3	50.1	50.0	2.1	3.6	0.4	2.0	17.9	12.7	0.2	3.9	1.2	..
	2006	298	50.5	40.8	40.3	9.2	0.3	0.2	0.0	22.7	16.5	2.0	2.8	1.5	..
Chad - Tchad	1990	167	75.0	65.9	65.4	5.3	3.8	0.1	0.1	24.9	21.3	0.2	3.1	0.2	..
	2000	139	73.9	64.8	64.3	7.4	1.4	0.2	0.7	25.4	14.0	0.0	4.8	6.5	..
	2006	529	59.3	43.6	41.0	12.5	0.2	3.0	2.4	38.3	25.4	0.3	4.9	7.7	..
Chile - Chili	1990	7 227	58.5	27.7	26.1	19.0	7.9	3.9	..	36.5	7.8	24.1	4.5	..	0.0
	2000	18 535	42.0	16.5	15.7	17.8	3.8	3.9	0.5	46.9	2.8	32.2	11.7	0.3	0.0
	2006	35 892	36.1	15.2	14.6	15.6	3.2	2.2	0.4	54.7	5.7	35.2	13.6	0.2	0.0
China - Chine	1990	53 810	51.8	19.8	18.8	12.2	14.2	5.5	4.2	42.9	0.7	2.8	38.6	0.9	0.0
	2000	225 175	47.3	14.6	13.7	9.9	18.4	4.4	3.3	46.0	2.5	2.4	37.4	3.5	0.0
	2006	791 793	38.0	12.2	11.5	7.5	14.6	3.7	2.9	49.8	3.6	4.3	38.0	3.8	0.0
China, Hong Kong SAR - Chine (RAS de Hong Kong)	1990	82 490	38.6	12.3	10.4	8.1	16.1	2.1	0.1	61.2	0.6	0.7	59.6	0.3	0.0
	2000	213 328	30.8	10.0	8.8	6.8	12.0	2.0	0.2	68.9	0.3	0.6	67.5	0.5	0.0
	2006	334 691	25.2	8.4	7.3	4.8	10.3	1.7	0.1	74.6	0.3	0.7	72.9	0.7	0.0
China, Macao SAR - Chine (RAS de Macao)	1990	1 532	27.6	9.5	9.3	5.1	11.5	1.4	0.4	72.0	0.2	0.2	71.3	0.2	0.0
	2000	2 255	23.3	9.9	9.6	4.5	6.3	2.6	0.0	76.7	0.2	0.3	75.6	0.6	0.0
	2006	4 559	30.7	14.7	13.0	5.5	8.4	2.1	0.0	69.3	0.3	0.4	68.0	0.5	0.0
China, Taiwan Province of - Province chinoise de Taiwan (1)	1990	55 244	76.1	18.0	15.7	23.1	29.7	5.2	0.1	22.8	0.5	2.4	14.3	5.6	0.0
	2000	141 597	61.9	12.5	11.6	17.8	27.3	4.2	1.2	35.7	2.3	1.5	28.1	3.7	0.0
	2006	203 321	47.1	10.0	9.2	10.3	22.9	4.0	1.1	50.2	2.7	2.0	34.8	10.5	0.0
Colombia - Colombie	1990	5 589	76.0	26.4	23.5	35.4	8.9	5.3	0.2	23.0	0.1	21.6	1.3	0.0	0.0
	2000	11 324	62.0	18.6	17.5	35.4	5.5	2.5	0.4	36.3	0.5	28.7	7.1	0.1	0.0
	2006	27 493	48.1	14.7	13.9	26.8	4.1	2.4	0.5	48.0	0.3	34.0	13.5	0.3	0.0

For sources and notes, see end of table.

Pour les sources et les notes, se reporter à la fin du tableau.

Origin / Origine	Year Année	World (millions of dollars) Monde (millions de dollars)	Developed economies / Économies développées						Economies in transition Économies en transition	Developing economies / Économies en développement					
			Total	Europe		USA États-Unis	Japan Japon	Other Autres		Total	Africa Afrique	America Amérique	Eastern, Southern and South-Eastern Asia Asie orientale, méridionale et du Sud-Est	Western Asia Asie occidentale	Oceania Océanie
Destination				Total	EU UE										
			Percentage / En pourcentage												
Comoros - Comores	1990	86	89.8	84.1	84.0	..	5.5	0.2	..	10.2	5.1	0.1	4.9	0.1	..
	2000	70	42.9	36.3	36.3	1.3	0.4	5.0	..	55.8	33.6	0.3	14.5	7.5	..
	2006	143	41.4	39.5	39.3	..	1.4	0.6	0.2	56.7	20.3	2.3	21.3	12.8	..
Congo	1990	598	76.4	66.1	65.0	5.9	4.2	0.3	0.6	9.6	3.9	1.0	3.4	1.4	..
	2000	492	66.2	48.2	47.4	13.6	4.3	0.2	4.2	22.5	13.7	0.4	7.3	1.1	..
	2006	2 009	56.4	47.0	46.3	7.6	0.6	1.3	0.4	40.9	8.8	4.6	26.4	1.1	..
Costa Rica	1990	2 026	65.6	15.0	13.9	40.6	8.4	1.7	0.1	33.6	0.0	28.1	5.4	0.0	0.0
	2000	6 389	37.8	9.7	9.2	23.6	3.1	1.4	0.4	26.8	0.0	22.8	3.8	0.1	0.1
	2006	11 025	61.9	14.2	13.7	41.2	4.9	1.5	0.5	37.1	0.1	26.9	10.0	0.1	0.0
Côte d'Ivoire	1990	2 098	59.7	51.8	50.9	4.8	2.4	0.7	0.7	36.0	29.9	2.2	3.6	0.2	..
	2000	2 734	42.4	35.9	35.1	3.2	2.7	0.6	2.3	42.6	28.6	2.8	8.2	3.0	..
	2006	5 814	43.7	39.2	38.4	2.3	1.8	0.4	0.9	53.0	33.1	4.9	13.3	1.7	0.0
Croatia - Croatie	2000	7 688	77.3	71.9	69.6	2.9	1.7	0.7	10.3	9.5	2.4	1.2	3.6	2.3	..
	2006	21 405	71.7	68.2	66.5	1.7	1.5	0.3	13.8	11.3	0.5	1.3	8.3	1.3	..
Cuba	1990	2 956	51.5	43.0	41.8	0.1	2.7	5.8	0.3	48.1	0.7	36.1	11.4	0.0	..
	2000	3 808	45.3	38.1	38.0	0.1	0.8	6.3	2.8	52.0	1.2	41.5	9.2	0.0	..
	2006	8 917	38.7	26.6	26.3	4.3	1.6	6.2	2.8	58.5	1.0	38.7	18.7	0.1	..
Cyprus - Chypre	1990	2 565	82.1	61.6	59.8	7.1	11.5	1.9	3.7	14.1	1.9	0.8	7.9	3.5	0.0
	2000	3 710	75.7	54.3	53.0	10.8	6.0	4.5	5.6	18.7	1.7	1.1	11.6	4.3	..
	2006	6 932	79.0	68.3	67.5	1.5	2.5	6.7	3.2	16.1	1.8	3.0	8.3	3.0	..
Czech Republic - République tchèque	2000	34 808	85.0	78.1	75.5	4.3	1.9	0.7	8.1	6.7	0.7	0.9	4.7	0.4	0.0
	2006	93 342	85.1	81.4	80.5	1.4	2.0	0.4	7.9	6.9	0.3	0.3	5.9	0.4	0.0
Czechoslovakia (former) - Tchécoslovaquie (anc.)	1990	15 070	65.9	64.0	59.5	0.6	0.5	0.8	24.2	9.9	0.7	2.2	6.5	0.5	..
Dem. People's Rep. of Korea - Rép. populaire dém. de Corée	1990	1 326	39.9	17.8	17.2	..	14.6	7.5	0.0	60.1	1.4	0.9	57.1	0.8	..
	2000	2 104	21.3	9.6	9.3	0.1	10.7	0.9	2.6	76.1	14.4	7.9	49.3	4.6	0.0
	2006	3 181	7.6	5.6	5.5	..	1.5	0.5	7.2	85.1	17.4	5.2	58.3	4.3	0.0
Dem. Rep. of the Congo - Rép. dém. du Congo	1990	1 304	70.9	59.0	57.5	7.0	4.1	0.8	0.5	28.5	11.7	0.9	15.9	0.0	0.0
	2000	669	46.7	42.7	41.5	1.7	1.5	0.8	0.1	52.6	43.5	0.2	8.6	0.2	0.0
	2006	2 262	41.3	35.5	34.6	3.4	1.1	1.3	0.1	58.3	49.7	2.9	5.5	0.3	0.0
Denmark - Danemark	1990	31 372	89.4	77.1	69.6	6.2	4.1	2.0	1.0	9.5	0.9	2.1	5.3	1.2	0.0
	2000	45 530	88.2	81.1	72.3	4.3	1.5	1.4	1.0	10.6	0.4	1.5	7.9	0.8	0.0
	2006	85 557	85.4	80.4	72.3	2.9	0.8	1.2	1.6	13.1	0.4	1.4	9.6	1.5	0.0
Djibouti	1990	215	58.0	49.0	47.6	3.3	5.4	0.3	0.6	36.9	12.2	0.2	14.2	10.4	..
	2000	614	37.1	30.3	30.1	3.0	3.6	0.2	0.1	58.7	11.3	0.3	26.1	21.0	0.0
	2006	1 555	21.3	14.4	14.4	3.4	3.2	0.3	1.2	73.8	6.6	0.6	40.0	26.6	0.0
Dominica - Dominique	1990	118	70.0	28.0	27.0	33.1	6.2	2.6	0.0	29.8	0.1	25.9	3.9	0.0	..
	2000	147	62.9	14.8	14.3	37.5	6.3	4.4	..	36.2	0.0	33.9	2.2	0.2	..
	2006	295	40.4	10.9	10.5	25.3	1.9	2.3	0.1	58.7	0.2	27.0	31.4	0.1	..
Dominican Republic - République dominicaine	1990	2 194	66.0	12.1	11.5	41.4	10.1	2.4	0.0	33.9	0.2	30.9	2.8	0.0	..
	2000	10 426	72.3	8.3	8.0	60.5	3.0	0.6	0.2	27.3	0.3	21.4	5.2	0.3	0.0
	2006	12 542	61.0	10.2	9.7	46.9	2.3	1.6	0.7	38.3	0.5	31.0	6.7	0.1	0.0
Ecuador - Équateur	1990	1 862	69.6	26.7	23.9	31.3	9.2	2.4	0.4	27.9	0.6	25.3	2.1	..	0.0
	2000	3 401	47.9	12.4	11.6	25.0	8.2	2.3	1.8	46.9	1.0	42.1	3.5	0.3	0.0
	2006	11 266	38.6	10.2	9.8	23.1	3.8	1.5	1.6	52.6	1.0	43.5	7.1	1.1	0.0
Egypt - Égypte	1990	9 280	73.2	50.2	47.4	14.0	3.7	5.4	4.9	15.9	1.4	2.9	8.6	2.9	0.7
	2000	22 040	63.5	40.3	38.6	16.9	3.7	2.6	3.7	26.2	1.6	3.1	14.6	6.9	..
	2006	39 607	49.9	32.8	31.8	11.4	3.2	2.5	6.5	36.7	2.7	5.1	18.3	10.6	0.0
El Salvador	1990	1 277	61.4	14.0	12.8	42.4	3.5	1.5	0.0	35.0	0.0	33.2	1.8	0.0	..
	2000	4 948	60.6	6.9	6.6	50.0	2.5	1.1	0.8	35.6	0.1	33.0	2.4	0.1	..
	2006	7 375	48.7	13.6	13.3	32.2	1.8	1.2	1.0	48.0	0.1	38.7	9.2	0.0	0.0
Equatorial Guinea - Guinée équatoriale	1990	102	52.9	52.6	52.0	..	0.2	0.1	2.2	45.0	43.1	0.2	1.6	..	..
	2000	314	82.3	45.7	44.0	32.4	4.1	0.1	0.6	17.1	13.0	1.7	2.3	0.2	..
	2006	1 610	73.9	34.3	33.9	37.7	1.1	0.8	0.8	25.3	10.1	0.9	13.6	0.7	..
Estonia - Estonie	2000	5 334	69.9	62.1	60.1	2.3	5.3	0.3	16.8	13.3	1.3	0.4	5.9	5.6	0.0
	2006	13 459	78.0	75.5	74.5	1.2	1.1	0.2	15.8	6.2	0.0	0.2	5.3	0.6	..

For sources and notes, see end of table.

Pour les sources et les notes, se reporter à la fin du tableau.

Origin / Origine — Destination	Year / Année	World (millions of dollars) / Monde (millions de dollars)	Developed economies / Économies développées — Total	Europe — Total	Europe — EU UE	USA États-Unis	Japan Japon	Other Autres	Economies in transition / Économies en transition	Developing economies / Économies en développement — Total	Africa Afrique	America Amérique	Eastern, Southern and South-Eastern Asia / Asie orientale, méridionale et du Sud-Est	Western Asia / Asie occidentale	Oceania Océanie
			Percentage / En pourcentage												
Ethiopia - Éthiopie	2000	1 226	43.2	31.4	30.5	4.6	6.1	1.1	1.1	45.9	4.9	0.2	17.5	23.3	..
	2006	4 178	28.4	21.0	20.4	3.6	3.0	0.7	1.8	52.2	6.5	1.4	22.9	21.4	..
Ethiopia (former) - Éthiopie (anc.)	1990	1 078	65.8	52.6	50.2	5.4	6.5	1.2	14.2	12.2	3.3	0.2	5.6	3.1	0.1
Faeroe Islands - Îles Féroé	1990	334	97.0	93.2	67.2	1.4	2.0	0.5	1.2	1.3	..	0.2	1.0	0.1	0.1
	2000	455	97.6	96.6	60.0	0.8	..	0.2	0.1	1.6	..	0.5	1.1	0.1	0.0
	2006	752	97.9	96.6	69.7	0.6	..	0.7	0.1	1.0	0.0	0.8	0.2	0.1	0.0
Fiji - Fidji	1990	755	74.1	5.6	5.6	13.1	11.0	44.4	..	19.7	..	..	19.7	..	..
	2000	762	73.1	3.7	3.6	3.4	4.0	62.1	0.0	25.9	0.1	0.3	25.1	0.0	0.0
	2006	1 595	50.1	4.3	4.3	2.2	3.2	40.3	0.0	48.5	1.4	0.3	46.4	0.0	0.0
Finland - Finlande	1990	26 944	82.6	68.1	62.8	6.8	6.4	1.3	10.1	7.2	0.4	1.8	4.0	1.0	0.0
	2000	34 306	79.7	69.8	64.7	4.8	3.7	1.4	9.7	8.4	0.6	1.4	6.1	0.2	0.0
	2006	68 938	73.6	67.4	63.9	2.5	1.8	1.8	14.6	11.8	0.6	2.2	8.6	0.4	0.0
France	1990	240 690	81.2	67.9	64.0	7.9	3.9	1.4	1.8	14.4	5.0	2.1	5.0	2.3	0.0
	2000	331 839	82.5	71.5	66.7	7.4	2.3	1.3	1.6	15.0	3.9	1.8	6.7	2.6	0.0
	2006	541 802	79.9	73.0	69.1	4.6	1.4	0.9	3.1	16.4	4.6	1.8	7.7	2.4	0.0
Gabon	1990	847	83.5	71.5	70.3	6.4	4.9	0.7	0.1	12.4	6.9	1.0	4.6	0.0	..
	2000	1 395	88.8	80.9	80.6	5.1	2.3	0.5	0.0	10.1	5.6	0.7	3.4	0.3	0.0
	2006	1 947	72.6	61.5	61.0	7.6	2.5	1.0	0.1	25.4	12.9	3.3	8.4	0.7	0.0
Gambia - Gambie	1990	231	53.8	49.9	49.2	..	3.8	0.1	3.4	38.9	9.6	0.3	28.9	0.1	..
	2000	334	35.4	30.5	30.2	2.5	2.0	0.5	0.1	64.5	17.1	5.4	38.6	3.4	..
	2006	709	25.0	20.8	20.6	3.3	0.7	0.2	0.6	74.4	24.3	7.2	37.1	5.8	..
Georgia - Géorgie	2000	722	45.0	33.4	30.1	9.6	1.0	1.0	33.3	20.8	0.1	1.0	2.4	17.4	0.8
	2006	3 678	36.9	31.0	30.0	3.5	1.1	1.3	38.8	24.2	0.3	1.6	5.1	17.3	0.0
Germany - Allemagne	1990	346 466	81.9	67.8	62.1	6.6	5.9	1.6	3.4	14.6	3.0	2.7	7.1	1.8	0.0
	2000	500 279	80.5	65.7	60.2	8.6	4.9	1.3	3.4	16.0	2.2	1.9	10.1	1.7	0.0
	2006	907 439	77.7	69.9	63.7	4.7	2.4	0.8	5.0	17.0	2.1	1.9	11.3	1.6	0.0
Ghana	1990	1 614	64.3	47.0	45.5	9.4	4.8	3.1	0.5	35.1	23.1	4.8	7.1	0.1	..
	2000	2 871	57.4	45.7	44.9	7.1	1.6	3.0	0.6	41.2	22.7	3.4	14.2	0.8	0.0
	2006	6 791	39.8	30.3	29.8	4.7	1.5	3.3	1.0	58.2	27.4	4.9	25.0	1.0	0.0
Greece - Grèce	1990	19 764	83.4	72.8	70.4	3.7	5.9	1.1	3.3	13.2	3.5	1.7	5.2	2.7	0.0
	2000	28 324	72.4	64.9	63.1	3.2	3.0	1.3	5.5	22.1	3.4	1.1	11.6	6.0	0.0
	2006	63 621	63.8	58.8	57.3	1.8	2.5	0.7	9.5	24.9	2.8	1.2	14.1	6.8	0.2
Greenland - Groenland	1990	435	98.0	88.9	79.2	4.6	3.9	0.7	0.1	1.8	0.1	0.3	1.4	0.0	..
	2000	413	98.9	97.5	86.3	0.4	0.1	1.0	0.0	0.4	0.0	0.0	0.3	0.0	..
	2006	712	98.8	95.0	90.3	0.5	0.0	3.3	0.0	0.2	0.0	0.0	0.2	0.0	0.0
Grenada - Grenade	1990	109	66.7	22.2	21.6	30.6	7.1	6.8	0.1	33.1	0.0	28.6	4.4	0.0	..
	2000	246	66.5	14.2	14.2	44.8	4.3	3.3	..	26.7	..	25.2	1.4	..	..
	2006	343	42.4	12.8	12.3	24.2	2.7	2.7	..	47.9	0.0	44.7	3.2	0.0	..
Guatemala	1990	1 698	63.1	16.6	14.9	39.1	5.8	1.6	0.0	35.9	0.5	31.5	3.9	0.0	..
	2000	5 171	54.8	8.5	8.0	40.2	3.2	3.0	1.0	43.2	0.1	38.7	4.4	0.1	0.0
	2006	11 640	47.6	9.4	8.2	33.2	2.7	2.2	0.6	48.7	0.1	33.8	14.7	0.2	0.0
Guinea - Guinée	1990	583	75.3	62.5	61.4	8.1	3.6	1.1	0.0	24.7	14.4	2.8	7.4	0.0	..
	2000	533	58.2	45.5	44.5	5.6	5.2	2.0	1.1	40.6	25.0	0.8	13.4	1.4	0.0
	2006	2 250	33.4	26.9	26.5	3.2	2.3	1.0	1.1	29.4	9.7	1.7	16.2	1.9	1.7
Guinea-Bissau - Guinée-Bissau	1990	124	73.3	61.3	61.2	1.1	10.9	0.0	3.2	21.5	12.8	0.8	8.0	0.0	..
	2000	106	47.2	44.8	43.7	0.6	1.6	0.1	0.2	44.6	14.2	2.7	27.6	0.1	..
	2006	200	49.8	46.2	45.6	3.1	0.1	0.4	..	38.4	22.1	6.2	10.0	0.1	..
Guyana	1990	279	64.0	25.2	24.2	29.9	5.1	3.8	0.1	35.8	0.0	31.5	2.9	1.4	..
	2000	651	42.0	11.3	11.3	26.9	2.0	1.8	0.0	58.0	0.1	52.7	5.1	0.2	..
	2006	928	40.8	12.8	12.6	21.3	3.4	3.4	0.0	59.2	0.2	42.4	16.2	0.4	..
Haiti - Haïti	1990	525	77.8	12.6	11.7	58.0	3.8	3.4	..	22.0	0.1	15.9	6.0	0.0	0.1
	2000	737	55.1	9.7	9.1	37.3	4.1	4.0	0.1	43.4	0.4	36.5	5.4	1.1	0.1
	2006	1 911	62.4	12.0	11.6	46.6	1.8	2.1	0.1	37.3	0.1	27.7	9.1	0.4	0.0

For sources and notes, see end of table.

Pour les sources et les notes, se reporter à la fin du tableau.

Origin / Origine / Destination	Year / Année	World (millions of dollars) / Monde (millions de dollars)	Developed economies / Économies développées — Total	Europe — Total	Europe — EU / UE	USA / États-Unis	Japan / Japon	Other / Autres	Economies in transition / Économies en transition	Developing economies / Économies en développement — Total	Africa / Afrique	America / Amérique	Eastern, Southern and South-Eastern Asia / Asie orientale, méridionale et du Sud-Est	Western Asia / Asie occidentale	Oceania / Océanie
Honduras	1990	880	64.6	15.5	15.5	39.5	8.6	0.9	..	24.3	..	24.3	..	..	..
	2000	2 853	57.7	4.9	4.4	47.5	4.1	1.2	0.0	40.5	0.0	35.7	4.7	0.0	0.0
	2006	7 671	60.7	5.5	5.2	53.0	1.5	0.7	0.6	38.3	0.1	29.9	8.1	0.2	0.0
Hungary - Hongrie	1990	8 621	66.1	60.9	57.7	2.6	2.1	0.5	21.4	10.2	3.4	2.5	3.6	0.6	..
	2000	32 187	77.0	67.4	65.9	3.8	5.3	0.5	9.5	13.1	0.4	1.3	11.1	0.4	..
	2006	78 366	75.4	71.1	70.2	1.4	2.6	0.3	10.4	13.9	0.1	0.4	12.8	0.7	0.0
Iceland - Islande	1990	1 678	91.3	68.2	62.0	14.2	5.6	3.3	5.0	3.7	0.3	0.6	2.7	0.1	..
	2000	2 586	90.0	70.1	60.6	11.0	4.9	4.0	1.8	8.2	0.3	2.2	5.3	0.4	0.0
	2006	6 139	87.5	67.4	57.8	12.8	4.1	3.2	0.7	11.7	0.4	1.8	8.2	1.3	0.0
India - Inde	1990	23 991	58.9	35.3	34.3	11.0	7.5	5.1	6.0	34.6	3.1	2.2	13.2	16.0	0.0
	2000	50 336	41.7	27.4	21.3	6.3	4.0	4.0	1.4	33.4	6.4	1.5	18.1	7.3	0.0
	2006	185 095	33.8	19.3	18.2	6.0	2.7	5.8	2.3	36.7	1.7	2.6	26.8	5.5	0.0
Indonesia - Indonésie	1990	22 005	66.2	22.1	20.8	11.4	24.8	7.9	0.3	33.0	0.2	2.3	27.1	2.8	0.0
	2000	33 515	47.2	13.3	12.6	10.1	16.1	7.6	0.7	51.2	2.5	1.8	38.7	8.2	0.0
	2006	92 558	25.6	7.9	7.5	3.7	8.8	5.3	0.8	73.2	2.0	1.3	63.9	5.9	0.0
Iran (Islamic Rep. of) - Iran (Rép. islamique d')	1990	18 722	66.5	53.6	50.5	0.3	10.3	2.2	2.8	21.4	..	3.7	8.0	9.7	..
	2000	14 347	52.7	40.8	38.5	0.7	4.8	6.4	10.8	35.9	1.5	6.7	17.2	10.5	..
	2006	46 817	39.3	34.8	33.3	0.2	2.8	1.6	12.5	47.7	0.8	4.7	26.1	16.2	..
Iraq	1990	6 526	72.0	50.7	49.0	10.8	4.6	5.9	2.0	26.0	2.1	2.3	5.9	15.7	..
	2000	3 414	50.1	35.7	33.6	0.4	1.4	12.7	5.4	44.4	4.6	3.2	30.4	6.2	..
	2006	13 593	29.1	13.7	13.2	12.1	1.6	1.8	1.8	69.0	2.9	1.5	10.2	54.4	..
Ireland - Irlande	1990	20 830	92.9	71.9	70.3	14.4	5.5	1.1	0.5	6.0	1.3	1.0	3.5	0.3	0.0
	2000	50 642	81.5	59.6	57.1	16.2	4.0	1.6	0.1	12.4	0.6	0.6	10.8	0.3	0.0
	2006	72 946	84.3	70.0	66.5	11.5	1.8	1.0	0.2	13.5	0.6	0.7	11.4	0.7	0.0
Israel - Israël	1990	15 338	84.0	61.5	52.1	17.8	3.6	1.2	0.2	6.4	1.8	1.1	3.3	0.2	..
	2000	36 802	70.9	48.3	42.9	18.1	3.2	1.3	1.6	14.4	1.0	0.9	10.8	1.7	0.0
	2006	47 751	59.9	43.8	37.7	12.4	2.7	1.0	2.9	22.0	0.5	2.1	16.6	2.7	..
Italy - Italie	1990	181 773	77.6	68.4	63.5	5.1	2.3	1.7	3.9	18.3	8.4	2.5	4.8	2.6	0.0
	2000	235 280	73.9	64.3	60.7	5.3	2.5	1.8	4.9	21.2	7.8	2.5	7.9	3.0	0.0
	2006	442 579	67.0	61.4	57.6	3.0	1.5	1.1	6.8	25.8	8.9	2.7	10.5	3.7	0.0
Jamaica - Jamaïque	1990	1 867	73.1	12.7	11.4	48.5	4.9	7.0	0.3	24.6	0.0	21.8	2.7	0.0	0.0
	2000	3 307	66.2	9.0	8.2	47.2	5.8	4.2	0.1	30.8	0.1	26.0	4.0	0.8	..
	2006	5 646	56.0	9.7	8.5	39.3	3.7	3.3	0.0	42.5	0.1	35.4	6.6	0.4	0.1
Japan - Japon	1990	235 334	50.9	18.4	16.3	22.5	..	10.1	1.5	47.6	1.6	4.0	30.2	11.5	0.0
	2000	379 577	39.9	13.8	12.6	19.1	..	7.0	1.3	58.8	1.3	2.8	43.1	11.4	0.0
	2006	578 694	30.5	11.4	10.3	12.0	..	7.0	1.3	68.2	2.3	3.2	45.5	17.0	0.0
Jordan - Jordanie	1990	2 581	59.0	36.3	35.0	17.5	3.2	2.0	1.5	39.5	3.0	0.5	9.1	26.9	0.0
	2000	4 597	51.2	33.4	32.1	9.9	3.9	4.0	2.9	43.0	1.9	2.7	14.5	23.9	..
	2006	11 548	34.7	24.4	23.6	4.8	3.1	2.4	3.5	61.6	5.1	1.8	20.9	33.8	..
Kazakhstan	2000	5 048	33.4	24.9	23.8	5.5	2.1	0.9	54.1	12.2	0.5	2.0	6.4	3.3	0.0
	2006	27 082	30.8	26.5	25.7	2.6	1.0	0.7	43.9	25.3	0.2	0.6	21.5	3.0	0.0
Kenya	1990	2 048	67.1	45.5	44.3	8.4	11.9	1.3	0.1	21.3	2.3	0.7	7.7	10.6	0.3
	2000	3 253	43.5	32.0	30.8	4.1	5.1	2.4	1.8	54.4	9.1	1.5	15.4	28.4	0.3
	2006	8 232	34.7	21.0	20.3	7.0	4.7	2.0	1.2	63.1	10.2	1.0	26.5	25.4	0.1
Kuwait - Koweït	1990	4 049	62.2	38.1	36.6	10.9	11.4	1.9	3.0	17.6	0.1	1.0	14.1	2.5	..
	2000	7 358	58.5	34.3	32.9	12.1	8.7	3.4	0.1	41.3	1.4	1.5	20.3	18.1	0.0
	2006	16 672	57.9	32.5	30.4	14.1	7.8	3.5	0.2	41.9	0.8	1.8	21.0	18.4	0.0
Kyrgyzstan - Kirghizistan	2000	555	28.5	14.8	13.9	9.7	1.8	2.1	53.8	17.7	..	0.1	11.4	6.1	0.0
	2006	1 711	21.3	12.6	12.1	5.7	0.8	2.3	58.0	20.7	0.1	0.6	17.1	2.9	..
Lao People's dem. Rep. - Rép. dém. populaire lao	1990	149	25.9	9.7	9.0	0.7	14.5	0.9	0.0	73.7	0.1	0.2	73.3	0.1	..
	2000	690	11.6	6.6	6.5	0.7	3.4	0.9	0.2	86.6	0.0	0.0	86.5	0.0	..
	2006	1 636	5.8	2.6	2.4	0.5	1.4	1.3	0.2	92.1	0.2	0.0	91.9	0.0	..
Latvia - Lettonie	2000	3 184	80.3	77.3	74.3	2.0	0.1	0.8	17.0	2.4	0.1	0.2	1.6	0.5	0.0
	2006	11 581	81.3	79.7	76.6	0.9	0.3	0.4	14.4	4.3	0.1	0.2	3.2	0.6	0.0

For sources and notes, see end of table.

Pour les sources et les notes, se reporter à la fin du tableau.

Origin / Origine (Destination)	Year / Année	World (millions of dollars) / Monde (millions de dollars)	Developed economies / Économies développées						Economies in transition / Économies en transition	Developing economies / Économies en développement					
			Total	Europe Total	Europe EU / UE	USA États-Unis	Japan Japon	Other Autres		Total	Africa Afrique	America Amérique	Eastern, Southern and South-Eastern Asia / Asie orientale, méridionale et du Sud-Est	Western Asia / Asie occidentale	Oceania Océanie
			Percentage / En pourcentage												
Lebanon - Liban	1990	2 515	66.7	58.2	54.4	4.3	3.9	0.3	0.5	32.8	1.4	1.5	12.2	17.8	..
	2000	6 228	65.4	53.7	46.7	7.3	3.4	1.0	5.3	27.9	2.8	1.9	11.2	12.1	0.0
	2006	10 984	54.4	42.6	40.2	9.3	1.7	0.8	3.6	39.7	3.1	2.3	11.3	23.0	0.0
Liberia - Libéria	1990	4 259	68.2	39.0	33.6	1.1	28.0	0.1	5.6	26.2	0.7	1.0	24.6	0.0	..
	2000	5 494	57.5	41.9	40.7	0.9	14.7	0.0	4.2	38.3	2.9	1.0	34.1	0.2	..
	2006	7 143	26.3	12.3	12.0	1.0	12.8	0.1	2.7	71.0	2.5	1.0	67.3	0.3	..
Libyan Arab Jamahiriya - Jamahiriya arabe libyenne	1990	5 663	77.6	70.9	67.0	1.2	4.3	1.2	1.4	19.9	5.3	2.7	6.0	5.9	..
	2000	4 016	71.2	67.2	65.5	0.5	2.6	0.9	1.5	27.2	10.5	2.8	7.8	6.1	..
	2006	10 236	59.4	51.9	49.7	4.7	2.0	0.8	2.1	38.2	7.9	3.5	16.3	10.5	..
Lithuania - Lituanie	2000	5 457	60.7	56.0	54.2	2.4	1.9	0.5	31.7	6.0	0.3	0.9	4.2	0.6	0.0
	2006	19 413	66.0	63.9	62.8	1.6	0.3	0.2	27.9	6.0	0.4	0.9	4.0	0.7	0.0
Luxembourg	2006	26 547	75.9	72.0	70.5	2.8	0.7	0.4	0.7	22.2	0.1	0.2	20.2	1.7	0.0
Madagascar	1990	608	57.6	49.1	47.6	2.2	6.0	0.3	0.6	14.8	2.0	0.9	11.6	0.3	..
	2000	734	34.2	24.2	23.9	5.9	2.9	1.2	0.1	57.5	6.4	3.3	32.4	15.5	0.0
	2006	2 046	27.7	23.7	23.6	2.4	1.1	0.5	0.0	58.7	12.1	1.3	39.4	5.9	0.0
Malawi	1990	627	48.9	38.9	37.6	2.0	7.0	1.0	0.0	45.1	42.1	..	3.0	..	..
	2000	562	16.7	11.0	10.7	2.6	2.3	0.8	0.0	82.0	71.8	1.2	9.1	0.0	..
	2006	798	26.1	17.7	17.6	6.3	1.3	0.7	0.1	73.1	55.7	0.8	16.4	0.2	..
Malaysia - Malaisie	1990	29 173	63.8	17.6	16.1	16.9	24.2	5.1	0.4	35.6	0.5	1.8	32.1	1.1	0.0
	2000	82 204	52.7	12.3	11.0	16.6	21.1	2.8	0.3	45.1	0.5	0.8	41.9	1.9	0.0
	2006	130 477	41.0	12.5	11.5	12.6	13.3	2.6	0.2	58.2	0.9	1.7	51.8	3.8	0.0
Maldives	1990	138	17.4	13.3	13.0	0.5	3.3	0.3	0.0	82.6	..	0.0	82.0	0.5	..
	2000	389	20.5	10.5	9.6	2.2	3.4	4.4	0.0	79.1	0.4	0.1	69.8	8.8	..
	2006	931	19.3	10.4	10.1	2.1	2.6	4.3	0.0	80.5	0.6	0.5	60.8	18.5	..
Mali	1990	714	45.2	41.7	41.0	1.4	1.4	0.8	0.7	35.3	28.7	0.2	4.0	2.4	0.0
	2000	1 286	30.5	26.6	26.5	3.0	0.5	0.5	0.2	35.3	26.8	0.4	7.8	0.3	0.0
	2006	2 357	29.5	26.3	26.2	2.0	0.2	1.0	1.1	37.0	29.5	0.9	6.0	0.5	0.0
Malta - Malte	1990	1 951	87.2	79.6	78.6	3.3	3.7	0.5	2.1	10.7	3.6	1.2	5.1	0.8	..
	2000	3 400	75.9	62.4	60.6	10.6	2.0	0.9	0.4	23.7	1.6	0.5	20.2	1.3	..
	2006	3 980	78.4	69.6	67.7	5.6	2.2	0.9	0.3	21.3	0.8	0.8	18.4	1.3	0.0
Mauritania - Mauritanie	1990	388	78.2	69.3	68.5	6.2	2.3	0.4	0.4	17.0	6.7	1.0	8.9	0.4	..
	2000	651	64.3	58.8	58.6	2.6	2.5	0.4	2.5	24.5	9.0	0.6	13.4	1.5	..
	2006	1 475	51.8	43.3	42.6	6.7	1.2	0.6	1.6	35.7	10.6	5.7	16.5	2.8	..
Mauritius - Maurice	1990	1 620	54.1	39.1	37.2	4.8	5.9	4.4	0.1	45.8	12.9	1.1	26.1	5.7	0.0
	2000	2 088	40.6	28.9	27.3	2.9	4.1	4.7	0.3	59.1	18.6	1.4	33.7	5.4	0.0
	2006	3 646	44.3	35.8	34.6	2.0	2.8	3.7	0.1	55.6	11.1	1.5	34.7	8.3	0.0
Mexico - Mexique	1990	33 022	91.8	19.3	17.8	66.1	4.3	2.1	0.0	7.5	0.3	4.4	2.8	0.0	0.0
	2000	194 749	87.1	8.7	8.2	72.0	3.7	2.7	0.2	10.6	0.2	2.6	7.7	0.2	..
	2006	281 743	71.7	11.3	10.8	50.9	6.0	3.5	0.4	26.6	0.2	5.8	20.4	0.3	..
Moldova	2000	776	61.2	54.2	53.2	6.2	0.3	0.5	33.9	4.9	0.1	0.2	2.2	2.4	0.0
	2006	3 504	48.8	47.5	46.8	1.0	0.1	0.3	43.3	7.8	0.3	1.7	2.3	3.4	..
Mongolia - Mongolie	1990	144	71.2	60.4	57.7	..	10.7	0.1	5.6	23.2	0.7	0.1	22.5	0.0	..
	2000	614	30.5	13.2	12.7	4.6	11.9	0.7	35.8	33.7	0.0	0.0	33.5	0.2	..
	2006	1 769	23.4	7.8	7.7	2.4	11.9	1.4	34.6	41.9	0.0	1.6	39.9	0.4	..
Morocco - Maroc	1990	7 919	62.3	53.2	51.7	5.5	1.6	2.1	2.6	22.5	6.6	2.3	3.2	10.4	0.1
	2000	11 531	68.3	58.7	57.5	5.6	1.7	2.3	3.2	26.9	4.6	3.2	8.7	10.4	0.0
	2006	25 127	64.5	58.6	57.4	3.8	1.1	0.9	2.3	32.8	4.9	3.3	13.9	10.7	..
Mozambique	1990	913	57.7	43.8	42.5	6.1	4.8	3.1	0.0	42.2	11.1	1.6	17.9	11.6	..
	2000	1 046	26.5	16.9	16.7	3.5	4.6	1.5	..	61.2	51.8	0.6	8.2	0.6	..
	2006	2 914	29.1	25.5	25.1	2.2	0.6	0.7	..	54.3	39.5	1.1	11.4	2.3	..
Myanmar	1990	668	43.4	20.0	16.8	2.9	16.6	3.9	3.4	53.2	0.5	0.1	52.6	0.0	..
	2000	3 039	12.4	4.0	4.0	0.6	7.1	0.7	0.6	86.9	0.1	0.0	86.6	0.2	..
	2006	3 788	7.1	3.1	2.9	0.2	3.0	0.9	0.8	91.9	0.1	0.1	91.4	0.2	..

For sources and notes, see end of table.

Pour les sources et les notes, se reporter à la fin du tableau.

Origin / Origine Destination	Year Année	World (millions of dollars) Monde (millions de dollars)	Developed economies Économies développées						Economies in transition Économies en transition	Developing economies Économies en développement					
			Total	Europe		USA États-Unis	Japan Japon	Other Autres		Total	Africa Afrique	America Amérique	Eastern, Southern and South-Eastern Asia Asie orientale, méridionale et du Sud-Est	Western Asia Asie occiden-tale	Oceania Océanie
				Total	EU UE										
						Percentage / En pourcentage									
Nepal - Népal	1990	587	47.2	19.9	18.8	2.4	18.7	6.2	0.2	52.6	0.2	0.5	51.9	0.0	..
	2000	1 570	19.0	12.4	7.3	1.6	2.7	2.3	0.2	73.8	0.1	0.8	67.0	5.9	..
	2006	2 398	7.9	3.9	3.6	1.0	1.1	1.9	0.9	80.1	0.0	1.3	76.2	2.6	..
Netherlands - Pays-Bas	1990	123 383	83.7	71.1	68.2	7.8	3.2	1.5	1.5	14.8	2.8	2.8	5.9	3.3	0.0
	2000	215 716	71.9	55.5	53.1	10.2	4.7	1.5	1.9	24.0	2.1	3.2	15.7	2.9	0.0
	2006	417 098	65.1	52.8	49.7	7.8	3.0	1.5	5.5	29.3	2.6	4.1	19.2	3.4	0.0
Netherlands Antilles - Antilles néerlandaises	1990	2 136	25.0	9.1	8.9	12.8	2.2	0.9	0.0	73.4	..	71.0	1.8	0.6	0.1
	2000	2 853	23.8	8.8	8.7	13.0	1.1	0.9	0.0	75.4	0.9	70.3	0.7	3.4	0.0
	2006	15 743	20.7	9.7	9.5	10.4	0.5	0.2	0.4	77.9	0.1	75.4	2.3	0.0	0.0
New Caledonia - Nouvelle-Calédonie	1990	749	88.4	65.5	65.1	6.0	4.9	12.1	0.0	9.3	0.8	0.1	7.2	..	1.2
	2000	924	83.7	54.7	54.1	3.5	3.3	22.2	0.0	15.5	0.3	0.5	14.1	0.1	0.0
	2006	2 016	73.8	52.7	52.4	2.4	2.3	16.4	0.0	24.9	0.2	0.4	23.7	0.1	0.0
New Zealand - Nouvelle-Zélande	1990	9 566	80.5	24.9	23.1	17.8	15.4	22.4	0.1	18.7	0.3	1.2	11.0	5.2	0.0
	2000	13 953	71.0	18.5	17.6	17.4	11.3	23.9	0.1	28.4	1.2	1.8	19.3	5.6	0.0
	2006	26 363	60.6	17.3	16.6	11.8	9.2	22.4	0.1	39.3	1.2	1.0	32.4	4.3	0.0
Nicaragua	1990	667	41.8	20.3	19.1	11.8	6.7	3.0	..	38.5	..	36.5	2.0	..	..
	2000	1 805	41.1	7.3	6.8	25.0	7.4	1.5	..	47.3	..	45.8	1.5	..	..
	2006	4 131	26.5	3.6	3.5	20.1	1.7	1.1	0.4	60.2	1.4	47.3	11.4	0.0	..
Niger	1990	389	57.7	44.5	44.1	5.8	5.9	1.5	..	35.4	27.8	0.1	7.0	0.5	..
	2000	774	16.1	11.8	11.8	1.8	2.1	0.4	0.1	83.2	13.7	0.2	4.9	64.4	..
	2006	1 012	47.9	32.2	28.7	14.0	0.5	1.2	0.1	52.0	23.7	1.5	16.7	2.5	7.7
Nigeria - Nigéria	1990	4 317	80.8	64.8	61.4	8.7	6.0	1.4	0.8	16.9	0.7	4.3	11.7	0.2	0.0
	2000	5 824	68.5	51.2	48.9	11.3	4.9	1.1	3.7	27.4	4.3	4.2	17.3	1.6	0.0
	2006	29 363	46.3	34.4	33.1	8.4	2.1	1.4	1.6	36.4	5.7	6.4	21.3	3.0	0.0
Norway - Norvège	1990	26 748	84.7	69.8	68.2	7.9	4.4	2.7	1.7	13.4	4.5	4.6	4.0	0.3	0.0
	2000	31 644	85.3	71.6	70.0	6.9	3.7	3.2	2.7	12.0	0.9	2.7	8.0	0.5	..
	2006	64 267	81.6	70.5	69.1	5.3	2.7	3.0	2.9	15.4	1.3	2.5	10.8	0.8	0.0
Oman	1990	2 726	60.2	31.4	29.1	9.2	16.7	2.9	0.4	37.7	0.5	0.4	9.8	27.0	..
	2000	5 039	47.1	20.2	19.3	5.4	18.1	3.4	0.9	51.9	0.6	1.3	15.8	34.2	..
	2006	11 551	49.2	21.8	20.9	8.1	16.5	2.8	0.8	50.1	1.2	1.5	16.8	30.6	..
Pakistan	1990	7 383	56.5	28.2	25.3	12.8	11.9	3.6	1.1	40.8	2.3	1.0	20.3	17.2	0.0
	2000	10 722	33.5	18.1	15.5	6.1	5.7	3.6	0.9	65.3	3.0	1.2	25.3	35.7	0.0
	2006	33 813	32.5	18.2	17.3	6.5	5.7	2.1	2.3	62.7	2.8	1.0	31.9	27.0	0.0
Panama	1990	1 510	49.0	8.4	7.8	34.4	4.9	1.2	0.1	30.8	0.1	26.3	4.4	0.0	..
	2000	3 405	49.1	8.9	8.5	32.9	5.5	1.8	0.2	38.0	0.1	32.6	5.1	0.2	..
	2006	4 831	39.4	6.4	6.2	27.0	4.7	1.2	0.6	43.3	0.0	34.5	8.7	0.1	..
Papua New Guinea - Papouasie-Nouvelle-Guinée	1990	1 315	82.0	6.9	6.7	9.6	13.3	52.1	0.1	17.7	0.3	0.5	16.8	0.0	0.0
	2000	1 228	62.7	3.0	2.8	2.1	4.0	53.5	0.1	36.0	0.9	0.2	34.5	0.0	..
	2006	2 360	65.0	2.8	2.8	2.0	4.3	55.8	0.0	33.3	0.2	0.9	31.6	0.1	0.0
Paraguay	1990	1 341	44.2	16.0	15.3	12.4	15.4	0.3	0.0	53.7	4.8	34.9	14.0	0.0	0.0
	2000	2 255	25.3	13.2	11.4	7.2	4.5	0.5	0.0	74.7	0.2	58.0	16.4	0.1	..
	2006	5 775	24.5	9.1	5.7	6.4	8.3	0.6	0.1	73.6	0.0	40.2	33.3	0.1	0.0
Peru - Pérou	1990	3 172	56.2	22.9	17.5	27.8	2.3	3.4	0.2	29.9	0.3	27.6	2.0	0.0	..
	2000	8 040	48.7	14.2	13.1	24.7	6.0	3.9	0.6	50.0	1.3	38.1	10.4	0.1	0.0
	2006	16 254	34.6	12.0	11.4	16.5	3.5	2.6	0.7	64.2	2.4	44.4	17.3	0.1	0.0
Philippines	1990	12 994	56.6	12.9	12.2	19.5	18.4	5.7	0.3	43.0	0.7	2.6	28.9	10.4	0.0
	2000	34 491	52.2	9.8	9.2	18.6	18.9	4.9	0.9	46.8	0.2	0.8	38.8	6.8	0.0
	2006	51 532	41.6	9.2	8.7	16.3	13.6	2.5	0.5	57.9	0.1	1.2	49.4	6.7	0.0
Poland - Pologne	1990	8 976	69.3	64.7	56.8	1.6	2.3	0.6	21.9	8.2	0.5	0.9	5.2	1.5	..
	2000	48 940	78.6	71.2	69.0	4.4	2.2	0.8	11.1	10.2	0.6	1.3	7.7	0.5	0.0
	2006	127 209	77.4	74.8	73.0	1.3	0.9	0.4	12.3	9.7	0.6	1.3	6.6	1.1	0.0
Portugal	1990	25 105	83.0	75.3	72.0	3.9	2.6	1.2	0.2	16.6	7.4	3.6	3.2	2.4	0.0
	2000	38 224	84.7	78.5	75.5	3.1	2.6	0.5	0.9	14.5	4.6	2.8	4.8	2.1	0.0
	2006	66 684	77.2	74.3	72.3	1.5	1.0	0.4	2.2	17.1	6.2	4.2	4.2	2.5	0.0

For sources and notes, see end of table.   Pour les sources et les notes, se reporter à la fin du tableau.

Origin / Origine Destination	Year Année	World (millions of dollars) Monde (millions de dollars)	Developed economies / Économies développées — Total	Europe Total	Europe EU UE	USA États-Unis	Japan Japon	Other Autres	Economies in transition Économies en transition	Developing economies / Économies en développement — Total	Africa Afrique	America Amérique	Eastern, Southern and South-Eastern Asia Asie orientale, méridionale et du Sud-Est	Western Asia Asie occidentale	Oceania Océanie
Qatar	1990	1 695	71.8	44.8	43.3	9.5	14.6	2.9	0.6	25.6	0.4	2.1	11.4	11.8	..
	2000	3 252	61.6	37.4	35.5	10.3	11.0	2.9	..	37.0	0.4	1.5	18.4	16.8	..
	2006	15 771	68.0	46.8	44.8	9.3	10.2	1.8	0.2	31.9	0.6	1.1	15.8	14.5	..
Republic of Korea - République de Corée	1990	74 405	66.9	13.1	12.2	22.8	25.0	6.1	..	20.6	0.8	2.3	10.3	7.0	0.2
	2000	160 481	54.8	11.0	10.1	18.2	19.8	5.7	1.6	43.5	2.0	2.0	25.3	14.0	0.0
	2006	281 859	43.3	10.4	9.7	11.0	16.8	5.1	1.6	55.0	1.8	3.1	32.0	18.1	0.0
Romania - Roumanie	1990	10 293	42.8	35.8	33.7	4.6	0.8	1.6	26.0	30.6	6.6	2.1	9.5	12.4	..
	2000	13 054	73.2	67.1	65.7	3.0	1.3	1.8	13.6	9.5	0.6	2.3	4.4	2.3	..
	2006	51 330	69.6	64.7	63.4	2.5	1.3	1.1	13.7	15.8	0.6	1.6	8.6	5.0	0.0
Russian Federation - Fédération de Russie	2000	33 853	52.1	40.9	39.6	8.0	1.7	1.5	34.7	13.1	1.1	3.5	7.2	1.1	0.0
	2006	132 517	60.3	48.2	46.3	4.8	5.9	1.4	13.3	26.1	0.9	4.3	18.8	2.2	0.0
Rwanda	1990	288	61.0	52.3	50.7	0.7	6.9	1.2	0.2	33.2	21.1	0.3	10.6	1.2	..
	2000	251	34.5	22.4	22.3	7.9	3.8	0.4	1.6	40.8	33.9	0.0	4.2	2.7	..
	2006	620	30.2	24.4	23.5	2.1	1.2	2.5	0.3	43.3	33.8	0.2	5.5	3.8	..
Saint Kitts and Nevis - Saint-Kitts-et-Nevis	1990	(c)108	87.6	26.2	25.4	52.8	3.8	4.9	..	12.4	..	11.7	0.8	..	..
	2000	(c)196	77.4	9.0	8.8	56.9	3.7	7.8	0.0	21.9	0.1	21.0	0.9	0.0	0.1
	2006	(c)383	73.0	18.0	17.5	48.9	3.6	2.5	2.2	24.1	0.0	22.9	1.0	0.2	0.1
Saint Lucia - Sainte-Lucie	1990	200	84.4	27.3	26.7	45.4	7.6	4.2	0.0	15.6	..	12.5	3.1	..	..
	2000	350	68.4	17.9	17.7	40.9	4.5	5.1	0.0	31.5	0.1	26.3	4.9	0.1	0.0
	2006	765	64.4	37.0	36.7	21.8	3.3	2.3	0.0	35.5	0.1	33.2	2.1	0.2	0.0
Saint Vincent and the Grenadines	1990	136	70.9	27.2	26.8	36.5	3.3	3.9	0.0	28.9	0.0	25.1	3.8	0.0	..
	2000	162	62.1	16.1	15.8	38.2	3.7	4.0	0.0	37.8	0.0	35.9	1.8	0.0	..
	2006	578	54.7	39.2	37.6	11.1	2.5	2.0	0.5	44.7	0.7	18.2	21.3	4.6	..
Samoa	1990	100	58.0	7.5	7.5	8.0	7.3	35.2	0.0	5.8	..	0.0	4.2	..	17.2
	2000	274	76.4	1.1	1.1	25.8	8.7	40.9	..	22.9	0.0	2.1	8.5	0.1	0.1
	2006	324	47.7	2.6	2.6	6.2	8.6	30.3	..	51.1	0.9	1.6	32.2	0.0	0.0
Sao Tome and Principe - Sao Tomé-et-Principe	1990	51	99.2	65.4	59.7	28.2	4.1	1.5	..	0.8	0.2	0.2	0.3	..	..
	2000	40	88.6	83.0	82.3	2.5	3.0	0.1	1.4	10.0	6.5	1.3	2.2	0.1	..
	2006	80	86.5	79.5	79.5	5.1	0.2	1.7	1.0	12.5	5.5	1.3	5.4	0.3	..
Saudi Arabia - Arabie saoudite	1990	24 081	78.0	43.7	37.1	16.7	15.3	2.3	0.4	21.3	2.0	1.6	13.1	4.6	0.0
	2000	30 609	69.3	36.2	32.8	19.0	10.3	3.8	0.7	28.5	2.9	3.7	16.3	5.6	0.0
	2006	70 051	59.9	36.5	34.8	12.3	7.3	3.8	1.5	37.6	2.6	3.6	23.1	8.3	0.0
Senegal - Sénégal	1990	1 387	65.9	55.6	54.9	6.2	2.9	1.2	0.5	32.3	21.1	1.9	8.8	0.6	0.0
	2000	1 463	57.0	48.7	48.1	3.9	2.7	1.7	1.5	38.3	20.9	1.7	14.5	1.2	..
	2006	3 423	57.4	50.4	49.9	3.2	2.8	1.1	2.2	37.8	14.4	6.7	14.7	2.0	0.0
Serbia and Montenegro - Serbie-et-Monténégro	2000	3 275	88.5	86.2	85.7	1.1	1.1	0.1	0.6	10.8	4.8	0.1	2.6	3.3	..
	2006	(b)6 850	..	..	..	..	..	..	..	..	..	..	..	..	..
Seychelles	1990	186	47.6	38.0	37.7	1.8	6.1	1.6	0.1	52.1	17.9	0.2	17.0	17.0	..
	2000	338	44.0	39.4	38.9	1.8	1.1	1.8	..	55.8	15.1	0.1	17.5	23.0	..
	2006	830	37.9	34.2	33.9	1.2	1.5	1.0	4.7	47.1	12.3	0.1	14.2	20.5	..
SFR of Yugoslavia (former) - RSF de Yougoslavie (anc.)	1990	19 227	72.3	64.5	62.1	4.4	2.2	1.1	13.0	14.7	3.9	2.5	5.9	2.4	0.0
Sierra Leone	1990	197	65.7	50.7	49.6	8.6	5.2	1.2	0.2	32.4	24.5	0.5	7.3	0.0	..
	2000	316	76.5	67.8	67.5	6.4	2.0	0.3	0.0	20.0	6.6	0.6	11.9	0.8	..
	2006	559	40.0	30.2	30.1	7.7	0.3	1.7	0.7	53.8	20.0	8.5	22.7	2.5	..
Singapore - Singapour	1990	60 959	54.7	15.6	14.1	16.1	20.1	2.9	0.2	44.3	0.6	1.2	32.5	10.0	0.0
	2000	134 633	48.6	13.8	12.0	15.1	17.2	2.5	0.3	50.7	0.5	0.7	42.6	6.9	0.0
	2006	238 797	35.8	12.4	11.4	12.7	8.3	2.3	0.5	63.3	0.5	1.0	52.9	8.9	0.0
Slovakia - Slovaquie	2000	14 054	75.3	71.2	69.8	2.1	1.7	0.3	19.1	4.8	0.3	0.5	3.7	0.3	0.0
	2006	44 939	77.9	75.9	75.3	0.6	1.2	0.1	13.1	8.8	0.2	0.1	8.1	0.4	0.0
Slovenia - Slovénie	2000	10 090	85.0	79.0	77.0	3.0	1.6	1.3	8.4	6.6	1.0	0.8	4.1	0.6	0.0
	2006	24 174	81.1	79.2	77.8	1.0	0.4	0.5	9.3	8.2	0.8	1.3	3.4	2.7	0.0
Solomon Islands - Îles Salomon	1990	99	74.8	5.8	5.8	6.1	21.0	41.9	..	20.3	0.1	0.0	17.2	..	0.3
	2000	124	45.9	2.6	2.3	5.1	5.3	32.9	..	40.6	0.5	0.1	33.8	..	0.9
	2006	256	45.1	4.1	4.1	2.5	7.8	30.6	..	43.3	0.6	0.3	34.0	0.1	1.2

For sources and notes, see end of table.

Pour les sources et les notes, se reporter à la fin du tableau.

Origin / Origine — Destination	Year Année	World (millions of dollars) Monde (millions de dollars)	Developed economies Économies développées — Total	Europe — Total	Europe — EU UE	USA États-Unis	Japan Japon	Other Autres	Economies in transition Économies en transition	Developing economies Économies en développement — Total	Africa Afrique	America Amérique	Eastern, Southern and South-Eastern Asia Asie orientale, méridionale et du Sud-Est	Western Asia Asie occidentale	Oceania Océanie
Somalia - Somalie	1990	394	68.8	62.6	53.6	3.2	2.3	0.7	0.3	28.2	11.3	0.3	10.2	6.3	0.0
	2000	329	14.8	12.8	12.7	1.6	0.2	0.3	0.2	74.1	40.1	6.3	15.0	12.7	0.0
	2006	798	5.5	2.4	2.4	2.8	0.0	0.3	0.5	81.2	39.1	8.5	15.9	17.7	0.0
South Africa - Afrique du Sud	1990	(a)19 136	71.8	47.1	44.4	12.5	9.7	2.5	..	4.9	0.4	1.9	2.5	0.1	0.0
	2000	29 355	67.4	43.2	40.6	11.9	8.0	4.4	0.4	31.8	2.1	2.4	18.4	8.9	..
	2006	74 781	53.2	35.6	34.6	7.6	6.6	3.5	0.5	46.2	5.0	4.3	26.8	10.1	0.0
Spain - Espagne	1990	87 814	79.1	65.3	63.4	8.3	4.4	1.0	1.7	18.6	6.6	4.6	5.5	1.9	0.0
	2000	144 679	75.7	67.8	66.1	4.6	2.3	1.1	1.8	22.4	7.6	4.1	7.8	2.8	0.0
	2006	328 870	69.4	63.9	61.8	2.7	1.8	1.0	3.4	26.7	8.0	5.1	10.0	3.6	0.0
Sri Lanka	1990	2 636	41.4	17.6	16.7	7.9	12.3	3.7	0.5	57.9	4.4	1.1	48.9	3.5	..
	2000	6 688	32.1	13.9	12.0	3.8	9.7	4.7	0.0	59.4	0.6	0.5	52.9	5.4	..
	2006	11 579	24.8	13.5	12.9	2.2	4.1	5.0	0.8	71.9	0.4	1.1	64.9	5.6	0.0
Sudan - Soudan	1990	1 305	51.9	43.6	42.1	3.6	3.9	0.8	2.7	45.4	16.2	0.1	9.5	19.5	..
	2000	1 453	42.6	33.8	32.4	1.3	2.3	5.2	1.0	56.4	5.6	1.5	31.1	18.2	..
	2006	8 072	29.5	17.7	17.2	1.3	6.6	3.9	1.1	66.9	7.5	3.1	36.9	19.5	..
Suriname	1990	484	73.6	30.7	30.4	40.1	2.8	0.1	..	24.6	..	22.0	2.7	..	..
	2000	480	65.5	26.7	26.3	30.1	7.4	1.3	0.0	34.5	4.2	23.1	7.1	0.1	..
	2006	965	63.4	27.6	27.3	29.4	5.1	1.3	0.0	36.6	0.0	24.8	11.4	0.3	..
Sweden - Suède	1990	49 355	88.8	72.6	62.1	9.4	5.6	1.2	2.1	9.1	0.6	2.0	5.8	0.7	0.0
	2000	72 954	90.3	79.9	70.4	6.7	2.9	0.8	0.9	8.8	0.5	1.2	6.5	0.6	0.0
	2006	127 187	82.6	76.1	66.9	3.5	2.2	0.9	4.1	10.5	0.5	1.4	7.7	0.9	0.0
Switzerland - Suisse	1990	69 705	91.8	79.5	78.8	6.1	4.4	1.8	0.6	7.6	1.7	1.1	3.7	1.0	0.0
	2000	82 543	88.1	76.4	76.1	7.8	2.8	1.0	2.9	9.0	1.7	1.2	5.4	0.7	0.0
	2006	141 254	87.9	79.0	78.7	6.2	1.8	1.0	1.5	10.5	2.7	1.1	5.5	1.3	0.0
Syrian Arab Republic - République arabe syrienne	1990	2 392	65.8	51.4	50.5	10.8	3.3	0.3	4.5	21.7	2.7	2.9	4.3	11.9	..
	2000	5 403	45.6	38.4	37.4	4.3	2.4	0.4	5.8	30.3	2.1	2.3	17.4	8.5	..
	2006	18 953	26.3	22.5	21.9	1.3	2.0	0.5	8.9	64.8	8.7	2.0	20.3	33.8	..
Tajikistan - Tadjikistan	2000	671	12.1	11.9	11.9	..	0.0	0.2	83.5	4.4	0.1	..	3.3	1.0	..
	2006	1 725	15.3	14.4	14.0	0.7	0.1	0.1	63.8	20.9	1.4	3.0	12.5	4.0	..
Thailand - Thaïlande	1990	33 414	63.7	19.1	16.9	10.8	30.4	3.5	0.6	34.8	0.9	2.0	28.4	3.5	0.0
	2000	61 924	51.5	11.7	10.5	11.8	24.7	3.3	1.0	45.4	1.3	1.3	33.6	9.2	0.1
	2006	130 605	41.0	9.9	8.7	7.5	19.9	3.7	1.1	56.4	1.5	1.4	39.6	13.8	0.2
TFYR of Macedonia - LERY de Macédoine	2000	2 085	60.9	55.4	53.9	4.0	1.0	0.5	31.3	7.7	0.6	1.8	2.5	2.7	0.0
	2006	3 762	57.7	54.6	53.0	1.1	0.7	1.3	29.2	13.1	0.4	1.8	7.5	3.4	0.0
Togo	1990	581	69.8	59.0	57.2	5.3	4.3	1.1	0.2	26.1	17.0	0.8	8.1	0.2	..
	2000	324	58.4	50.3	49.9	1.6	3.2	3.4	3.5	34.8	22.7	0.4	9.8	1.8	0.0
	2006	(e)1 276	61.4	49.8	48.3	9.3	1.2	1.1	1.2	37.3	15.6	3.5	15.8	2.5	0.0
Tonga	1990	67	68.1	1.8	1.7	10.3	6.0	50.0	0.0	24.3	..	0.1	11.7	..	0.0
	2000	83	64.4	4.7	4.6	10.2	15.1	34.3	..	35.6	..	0.2	17.0	..	18.4
	2006	139	57.3	12.3	12.3	8.2	1.4	35.3	0.0	42.7	0.1	0.6	9.7	0.0	0.0
Trinidad and Tobago - Trinité-et-Tobago	1990	1 230	69.5	17.5	16.9	40.9	3.6	7.6	0.0	29.1	3.4	21.4	4.2	0.2	0.0
	2000	2 353	53.4	11.6	11.0	34.3	3.5	4.0	0.2	46.1	3.9	37.3	4.9	0.1	0.0
	2006	5 810	51.3	12.7	12.4	30.6	3.8	4.2	0.3	48.2	8.1	30.6	9.3	0.2	0.0
Tunisia - Tunisie	1990	6 128	76.4	68.3	67.1	4.9	1.6	1.6	2.2	16.2	5.4	2.5	4.4	3.8	0.0
	2000	8 601	79.8	72.9	71.8	4.6	2.0	0.4	2.3	16.4	6.5	1.6	4.7	3.6	0.0
	2006	16 436	77.5	74.1	73.4	2.4	0.6	0.4	3.9	17.7	6.4	2.0	5.3	4.0	0.0
Turkey - Turquie	1990	23 147	64.9	48.5	45.9	9.9	4.8	1.7	6.5	26.2	5.8	2.4	7.9	10.1	0.0
	2000	54 503	66.6	54.5	52.3	7.2	3.0	2.0	10.6	19.7	5.0	1.2	10.2	3.3	0.0
	2006	139 480	53.9	45.8	42.5	4.5	2.3	1.3	16.9	28.4	5.3	1.8	18.9	2.5	0.0
Turkmenistan - Turkménistan	2000	1 788	26.0	14.3	14.0	3.5	8.1	0.1	37.9	29.8	..	0.1	7.3	22.5	..
	2006	2 781	28.4	21.1	18.0	4.5	2.1	0.7	26.8	44.6	..	0.4	15.8	28.4	0.0
Uganda - Ouganda	1990	582	50.0	39.9	39.1	4.9	4.6	0.6	0.4	49.6	38.8	0.2	8.7	1.8	..
	2000	958	35.5	22.3	20.4	3.2	7.1	2.9	0.0	64.5	40.6	1.4	16.4	6.0	..
	2006	2 131	29.3	21.7	20.1	2.8	4.2	0.6	1.0	68.7	42.4	0.4	15.4	10.6	0.0
Ukraine	2000	13 955	35.2	30.9	29.0	2.6	0.7	1.0	57.7	6.8	1.0	1.3	3.4	1.2	..
	2006	58 287	47.7	44.4	43.4	1.4	1.3	0.5	37.6	14.6	0.8	0.7	10.8	2.2	0.0

For sources and notes, see end of table.

Pour les sources et les notes, se reporter à la fin du tableau.

Origin / Origine / Destination	Year / Année	World (millions of dollars) / Monde (millions de dollars)	Developed economies / Économies développées						Economies in transition / Économies en transition	Developing economies / Économies en développement					
			Total	Europe		USA États-Unis	Japan Japon	Other Autres		Total	Africa Afrique	America Amérique	Eastern, Southern and South-Eastern Asia / Asie orientale, méridionale et du Sud-Est	Western Asia / Asie occidentale	Oceania Océanie
				Total	EU UE										
									Percentage / En pourcentage						
United Arab Emirates - Émirats arabes unis	1990	11 472	60.8	35.0	33.1	9.1	14.2	2.4	0.5	35.0	0.5	1.0	24.8	8.6	..
	2000	25 464	59.7	39.0	37.4	7.9	9.6	3.3	0.4	39.4	1.0	0.7	30.9	6.9	..
	2006	114 275	50.8	31.3	29.8	11.5	5.8	2.2	1.3	46.8	1.8	1.3	36.8	6.9	..
United Kingdom - Royaume-Uni	1990	223 048	85.2	65.2	58.4	11.2	5.4	3.4	0.9	13.2	2.4	1.8	7.4	1.5	0.0
	2000	334 971	78.7	57.2	51.7	13.4	4.7	3.3	0.8	20.2	2.6	1.9	13.9	1.7	0.0
	2006	546 685	72.1	57.6	50.9	8.9	2.7	3.0	2.5	22.8	3.3	2.0	14.9	2.6	0.0
United Republic of Tanzania - République-Unie de Tanzanie	1990	1 022	73.2	61.1	58.8	1.6	7.7	2.7	0.7	22.9	3.6	0.9	10.5	7.7	..
	2000	1 521	45.6	23.8	22.6	3.9	9.3	8.6	0.5	53.9	20.6	2.0	20.3	11.0	0.0
	2006	4 499	28.6	19.9	19.3	3.9	2.8	2.0	1.3	65.6	25.4	1.1	24.8	14.2	0.0
United States - États-Unis	1990	517 020	59.7	21.7	20.2	..	18.0	20.0	0.4	39.8	3.3	13.0	20.1	3.4	0.0
	2000	1 238 240	52.3	20.0	18.6	..	12.1	20.3	0.8	46.8	2.3	17.0	25.2	2.4	0.0
	2006	1 919 260	44.6	19.0	17.8	..	7.9	17.7	1.3	54.1	4.4	17.8	28.8	3.2	0.0
Uruguay	1990	1 317	35.8	20.5	19.7	10.5	3.3	1.5	3.4	59.2	1.0	50.1	7.0	1.1	0.0
	2000	3 466	32.5	19.7	18.8	9.8	1.7	1.4	3.3	63.8	3.8	51.7	7.5	0.7	0.0
	2006	6 465	29.1	19.0	17.5	8.2	1.2	0.8	0.4	70.2	6.6	52.4	11.1	0.1	0.0
USSR (former) - URSS (anc.)	1990	58 559	76.0	62.7	60.9	5.8	4.8	2.7	5.1	18.9	2.1	1.9	11.4	3.6	..
Uzbekistan - Ouzbékistan	2000	2 072	41.0	30.2	29.5	8.8	1.3	0.6	38.7	20.3	0.0	0.1	15.8	4.4	..
	2006	. 4 291	23.5	21.2	20.2	1.4	0.4	0.5	44.6	31.9	0.0	0.1	27.2	4.6	..
Vanuatu	1990	286	96.6	21.9	21.8	2.3	60.9	11.5	0.0	3.2	..	0.3	1.9	0.0	0.9
	2000	124	59.1	6.7	6.4	1.2	19.1	32.0	..	39.1	0.2	0.4	28.1	..	10.4
	2006	271	56.8	3.8	3.8	3.7	19.7	29.6	..	40.9	0.5	0.2	24.9	0.1	15.2
Venezuela (Bolivarian Rep. of) - Venezuela (Rép. bolivarienne du)	1990	6 682	83.4	28.7	27.1	46.7	3.9	4.2	0.1	15.4	0.0	13.2	2.1	0.1	..
	2000	17 246	54.8	16.3	15.7	33.5	2.7	2.3	0.1	25.6	0.6	21.4	3.6	0.1	..
	2006	30 559	49.3	13.5	12.6	30.6	3.4	1.8	0.2	47.9	0.1	39.8	7.7	0.3	0.1
Viet Nam	1990	2 842	20.3	13.8	13.3	0.0	5.9	0.5	7.5	29.9	0.1	0.2	29.6	..	..
	2000	15 637	29.2	9.6	8.8	2.3	14.7	2.6	2.3	67.7	0.3	0.4	66.0	0.9	0.0
	2006	46 557	23.4	7.4	7.1	2.6	9.8	3.6	1.3	73.3	0.2	1.1	70.4	1.6	..
Yemen - Yémen	1990	2 385	47.8	31.8	31.2	5.1	4.2	6.7	9.6	42.5	5.4	0.8	16.6	19.7	0.0
	2000	2 323	33.9	23.3	18.6	4.4	3.2	3.0	0.3	63.3	5.7	3.6	19.0	35.0	0.0
	2006	6 957	26.2	16.5	15.9	4.0	3.2	2.5	1.9	70.9	4.7	5.7	25.0	35.5	0.0
Zambia - Zambie	1990	1 218	58.0	40.2	39.0	10.1	6.7	1.0	0.0	42.0	31.5	0.2	7.1	3.1	0.0
	2000	1 101	23.8	14.3	13.4	5.0	3.2	1.3	0.0	75.5	69.1	0.3	4.5	1.6	0.0
	2006	3 081	21.9	17.0	12.2	1.9	1.5	1.5	0.0	78.1	59.9	0.3	7.3	10.6	0.0
Zimbabwe	1990	1 849	49.1	33.0	30.9	6.9	4.5	4.7	0.2	39.3	32.9	1.4	4.9	0.1	0.0
	2000	1 842	28.9	17.7	16.5	5.9	4.0	1.4	0.1	59.9	49.8	1.1	7.9	1.1	0.0
	2006	2 812	11.9	5.6	4.9	4.9	0.8	0.7	0.0	84.7	78.1	0.1	3.5	3.0	0.0

Sources:
- International Monetary Fund, *Direction of Trade Statistics*

Sources :
- Fonds monétaire international, *Direction of Trade Statistics*

Notes:
(a) Data refers to South Africa Customs Union (Botswana, Lesotho, Namibia, South Africa and Swaziland)
(b) UNCTAD secretariat estimate
(c) Including Anguilla

(1) Estimate. Data are derived by calculating the difference between DOT's aggregate for Asia and the sum of countries classified in Asia by the data source.

Notes :
(a) Donnée relative à l'Union Douanière d'Afrique du Sud (Afrique du Sud, Botswana, Lesotho, Namibie et Swaziland)
(b) Estimation du secrétariat de la UNCTAD
(c) Y compris Anguilla

(1) Estimation. Les données sont dérivées par différence entre l'agrégat Asie fourni par DOT et la somme des pays classifiés en Asie dans la source.

Destination / Product group	Year / Année	World / Monde	Developed economies / Économies développées Total	Europe Total	Europe EU / UE	Canada	USA / États-Unis	Japan / Japon	Other developed countries / Autres économies développées	Economies in transition / Économies en transition
Millions of dollars										
All products	1995	5 065 268	3 430 428	2 137 657	2 014 714	164 449	744 055	293 536	90 730	98 657
	2000	6 309 659	4 370 229	2 515 979	2 379 963	232 061	1 177 758	332 349	112 082	93 928
	2006	11 921 375	7 713 289	4 853 452	4 590 019	337 348	1 782 644	539 693	200 151	333 242
Share by destination (percentage)										
All products	1995	100.0	67.7	42.2	39.8	3.2	14.7	5.8	1.8	1.9
	2000	100.0	69.3	39.9	37.7	3.7	18.7	5.3	1.8	1.5
	2006	100.0	64.7	40.7	38.5	2.8	15.0	4.5	1.7	2.8
All food items	1995	100.0	68.8	48.5	46.9	2.0	7.5	9.6	1.1	4.6
(SITC 0 + 1 + 22 + 4)	2000	100.0	68.8	44.6	43.1	2.8	10.9	9.2	1.4	3.1
	2006	100.0	67.2	47.4	45.9	2.7	9.9	5.8	1.4	4.7
Agricultural raw materials	1995	100.0	68.4	41.4	39.7	2.1	11.7	12.2	1.0	1.0
(SITC 2 - 22 - 27 - 28)	2000	100.0	67.2	40.4	38.8	2.8	14.2	8.8	1.0	1.3
	2006	100.0	59.0	37.8	36.5	2.1	11.9	6.3	0.8	2.0
Ores, metals, precious stones	1995	100.0	69.8	43.3	38.5	2.5	11.4	9.9	2.8	1.2
and non-monetary gold	2000	100.0	69.1	41.7	36.4	2.6	14.4	6.8	3.6	1.2
(SITC 27 + 28 + 68 + 667 + 971)	2006	100.0	62.0	40.1	35.1	2.3	10.7	6.2	2.6	1.3
Fuels (SITC 3)	1995	100.0	63.8	33.7	31.8	1.3	16.4	11.4	1.0	2.7
	2000	100.0	64.8	31.9	29.6	1.4	21.1	9.2	1.1	1.2
	2006	100.0	63.7	33.8	31.5	1.5	18.1	9.1	1.3	1.2
Manufactured goods	1995	100.0	68.1	42.4	39.9	3.7	15.8	4.4	1.9	1.6
(SITC 5 to 8 less 667 and 68)	2000	100.0	69.6	39.9	37.9	4.2	19.5	4.3	1.8	1.3
	2006	100.0	64.7	41.1	39.1	3.2	15.3	3.4	1.7	2.9
Share by major product group (percentage)										
All products	1995	100.0	100.0	100.0	100.0	100.0	100.0	100.0	100.0	100.0
	2000	100.0	100.0	100.0	100.0	100.0	100.0	100.0	100.0	100.0
	2006	100.0	100.0	100.0	100.0	100.0	100.0	100.0	100.0	100.0
All food items	1995	8.9	9.1	10.3	10.5	5.6	4.6	14.9	5.6	20.9
(SITC 0 + 1 + 22 + 4)	2000	6.7	6.6	7.5	7.6	5.1	3.9	11.7	5.1	13.9
	2006	6.2	6.4	7.2	7.4	5.9	4.1	8.0	5.1	10.3
Agricultural raw materials	1995	2.7	2.7	2.6	2.7	1.7	2.1	5.6	1.5	1.3
(SITC 2 - 22 - 27 - 28)	2000	1.9	1.8	1.9	1.9	1.4	1.4	3.1	1.1	1.7
	2006	1.5	1.4	1.4	1.4	1.1	1.2	2.1	0.7	1.1
Ores, metals, precious stones	1995	4.5	4.6	4.6	4.3	3.5	3.5	7.6	7.0	2.8
and non-monetary gold	2000	4.0	4.0	4.2	3.9	2.8	3.1	5.2	8.2	3.3
(SITC 27 + 28 + 68 + 667 + 971)	2006	5.5	5.2	5.4	5.0	4.5	3.9	7.5	8.6	2.5
Fuels (SITC 3)	1995	7.4	7.0	5.9	5.9	3.0	8.3	14.6	4.1	10.3
	2000	10.5	9.8	8.4	8.2	4.1	11.9	18.4	6.7	8.4
	2006	14.5	14.2	12.0	11.8	7.5	17.5	29.0	11.3	6.4
Manufactured goods	1995	73.7	74.2	74.1	74.1	83.5	79.1	55.8	79.4	60.3
(SITC 5 to 8 less 667 and 68)	2000	73.9	74.3	74.0	74.3	83.9	77.0	59.7	75.0	62.1
	2006	69.3	69.3	70.0	70.5	78.3	71.1	51.4	70.7	72.0

Sources:
- Data and UNCTAD secretariat estimates based on UN DESA Comtrade and IMF *Direction of Trade statistics* databases

2.2.A Structure des exportations par partenaires et groupes de produits
Monde

| | | | Developing economies / Économies en développement | | | | | | | | Destination |
Total	Africa / Afrique	America / Amérique	Asia / Asie — Total	Eastern, Southern and South-Eastern Asia / Asie orientale, méridionale et du Sud-Est	China / Chine	Western Asia / Asie occidentale	Oceania / Océanie	Major petroleum exporters / Principaux exportateurs de pétrole	Major exporters of manufactures / Principaux exportateurs d'articles manufacturés	Year / Année	Groupes de produits
Millions de dollars											
1 408 079	114 187	243 104	1 045 213	926 266	145 984	118 946	5 576	133 418	977 061	1995	Total tous produits
1 771 208	128 907	360 731	1 274 711	1 123 348	208 348	151 362	6 859	151 790	1 279 420	2000	
3 746 523	297 009	595 775	2 841 013	2 435 192	696 374	405 820	12 707	432 154	2 601 766	2006	
Parts par destinations (en pourcentage)											
27.8	**2.3**	**4.8**	**20.6**	**18.3**	**2.9**	**2.3**	**0.1**	**2.6**	**19.3**	**1995**	**Total tous produits**
28.1	**2.0**	**5.7**	**20.2**	**17.8**	**3.3**	**2.4**	**0.1**	**2.4**	**20.3**	**2000**	
31.4	**2.5**	**5.0**	**23.8**	**20.4**	**5.8**	**3.4**	**0.1**	**3.6**	**21.8**	**2006**	
25.4	3.8	4.8	16.5	13.1	2.3	3.4	0.2	4.6	13.0	1995	Produits alimentaires
26.9	4.0	6.0	16.7	12.7	2.2	4.0	0.2	5.2	13.4	2000	(CTCI 0 + 1 + 22 + 4)
27.3	4.5	5.3	17.4	13.0	2.8	4.3	0.2	6.0	12.8	2006	
30.0	2.3	3.7	24.0	22.1	5.4	1.9	0.0	1.6	22.6	1995	Matières premières
30.8	2.2	4.3	24.3	22.1	7.6	2.2	0.0	1.5	23.2	2000	d'origine agricole
38.6	2.3	4.2	32.1	29.2	15.1	2.9	0.1	2.1	29.3	2006	(CTCI 2 - 22 - 27 - 28)
26.9	1.0	2.2	23.7	21.9	2.5	1.8	0.0	1.4	22.7	1995	Minerais, métaux, pierres
27.2	1.2	2.8	23.2	21.3	4.1	1.8	0.0	1.5	22.9	2000	précieuses et or (non monétaire)
35.4	1.5	2.7	31.1	28.2	9.9	3.0	0.0	2.2	29.8	2006	(CTCI 27 + 28 + 68 + 667 + 971)
18.6	1.2	4.6	12.7	11.5	1.5	1.2	0.2	0.7	12.7	1995	Combustibles (CTCI 3)
26.4	2.0	5.1	19.0	17.6	2.3	1.4	0.2	0.7	19.0	2000	
28.7	2.3	4.7	21.6	19.4	3.8	2.2	0.1	1.9	19.1	2006	
29.3	2.3	5.0	21.9	19.5	3.1	2.4	0.1	2.7	20.6	1995	Articles manufacturés
28.6	1.9	6.0	20.6	18.2	3.4	2.4	0.1	2.4	21.1	2000	(CTCI 5 à 8 moins 667 et 68)
32.0	2.4	5.2	24.3	20.7	6.1	3.5	0.1	3.9	22.6	2006	
Parts par principaux groupes de produits (en pourcentage)											
100.0	**100.0**	**100.0**	**100.0**	**100.0**	**100.0**	**100.0**	**100.0**	**100.0**	**100.0**	**1995**	**Total tous produits**
100.0	**100.0**	**100.0**	**100.0**	**100.0**	**100.0**	**100.0**	**100.0**	**100.0**	**100.0**	**2000**	
100.0	**100.0**	**100.0**	**100.0**	**100.0**	**100.0**	**100.0**	**100.0**	**100.0**	**100.0**	**2006**	
8.2	15.2	9.0	7.2	6.4	7.2	13.0	14.3	15.6	6.0	1995	Produits alimentaires
6.4	13.2	7.0	5.5	4.8	4.4	11.0	10.6	14.5	4.4	2000	(CTCI 0 + 1 + 22 + 4)
5.4	11.1	6.6	4.5	3.9	3.0	7.9	9.9	10.3	3.6	2006	
2.9	2.7	2.1	3.1	3.2	5.0	2.2	0.9	1.6	3.1	1995	Matières premières
2.0	2.0	1.4	2.2	2.3	4.3	1.7	0.7	1.1	2.1	2000	d'origine agricole
1.9	1.4	1.3	2.0	2.2	3.9	1.3	0.7	0.9	2.0	2006	(CTCI 2 - 22 - 27 - 28)
4.3	2.0	2.1	5.1	5.4	3.9	3.4	0.6	2.4	5.3	1995	Minerais, métaux, pierres
3.9	2.3	2.0	4.6	4.8	5.0	3.1	0.5	2.5	4.5	2000	précieuses et or (non monétaire)
6.2	3.3	3.0	7.2	7.5	9.3	4.8	0.6	3.3	7.5	2006	(CTCI 27 + 28 + 68 + 667 + 971)
5.0	4.1	7.0	4.6	4.7	3.8	3.7	11.2	2.1	4.9	1995	Combustibles (CTCI 3)
9.9	10.5	9.4	9.9	10.4	7.4	6.0	24.2	3.1	9.8	2000	
13.2	13.5	13.5	13.1	13.7	9.5	9.5	20.1	7.8	12.7	2006	
77.8	73.9	77.3	78.3	78.7	73.4	75.5	70.5	76.5	78.8	1995	Articles manufacturés
75.2	69.1	77.3	75.4	75.6	77.0	73.8	57.6	74.9	76.7	2000	(CTCI 5 à 8 moins 667 et 68)
70.6	66.7	72.7	70.6	70.4	72.2	72.0	61.5	74.3	71.7	2006	

Sources :
- Données et estimations du secrétariat de la CNUCED sur la base de données Comtrade de ONU DAES et *Direction of Trade statistics* du Fonds Monétaire international

Destination / Product group	Year / Année	World / Monde	Developed economies / Économies développées — Total	Europe Total	Europe EU / UE	Canada	USA / États-Unis	Japan / Japon	Other developed countries / Autres économies développées	Economies in transition / Économies en transition
Millions of dollars										
All products	1995	5 098 369	3 519 318	2 130 931	1 992 826	197 267	628 359	474 804	87 957	120 459
	2000	6 473 204	4 150 855	2 419 228	2 259 385	285 221	816 874	514 190	115 341	156 434
	2006	12 125 083	6 846 758	4 525 378	4 179 467	388 117	1 024 403	707 540	201 320	441 162
Share by destination (percentage)										
All products	1995	100.0	69.0	41.8	39.1	3.9	12.3	9.3	1.7	2.4
	2000	100.0	64.1	37.4	34.9	4.4	12.6	7.9	1.8	2.4
	2006	100.0	56.5	37.3	34.5	3.2	8.4	5.8	1.7	3.6
All food items	1995	100.0	66.5	44.3	42.5	3.6	13.9	0.5	4.1	1.8
(SITC 0 + 1 + 22 + 4)	2000	100.0	64.6	41.2	39.4	4.5	13.3	0.5	5.0	1.9
	2006	100.0	62.2	44.0	42.2	3.7	9.6	0.5	4.5	2.5
Agricultural raw materials	1995	100.0	66.0	30.0	28.9	12.3	16.6	1.6	5.4	5.4
(SITC 2 - 22 - 27 - 28)	2000	100.0	66.2	30.7	29.7	14.0	14.4	1.8	5.4	5.1
	2006	100.0	60.4	32.8	32.0	9.3	12.4	1.8	4.1	6.5
Ores, metals, precious stones	1995	100.0	61.6	35.8	30.0	6.4	8.6	2.4	8.4	7.4
and non-monetary gold	2000	100.0	59.5	34.8	27.6	5.5	7.0	2.6	9.6	9.4
(SITC 27 + 28 + 68 + 667 + 971)	2006	100.0	52.3	29.5	24.7	4.9	5.8	2.7	9.3	7.3
Fuels (SITC 3)	1995	100.0	29.8	19.0	13.7	4.3	3.1	0.5	2.8	9.1
	2000	100.0	27.9	18.1	12.9	5.0	2.1	0.3	2.5	8.3
	2006	100.0	26.9	18.1	13.9	4.4	2.1	0.4	2.0	11.9
Manufactured goods	1995	100.0	73.9	44.5	42.1	3.3	13.2	12.2	0.7	1.2
(SITC 5 to 8 less 667 and 68)	2000	100.0	68.9	39.5	37.7	3.8	14.5	10.4	0.8	1.0
	2006	100.0	62.1	40.9	39.1	2.6	10.0	8.0	0.7	1.3
Share by major product group (percentage)										
All products	1995	100.0	100.0	100.0	100.0	100.0	100.0	100.0	100.0	100.0
	2000	100.0	100.0	100.0	100.0	100.0	100.0	100.0	100.0	100.0
	2006	100.0	100.0	100.0	100.0	100.0	100.0	100.0	100.0	100.0
All food items	1995	9.1	8.7	9.6	9.9	8.5	10.2	0.5	21.5	7.1
(SITC 0 + 1 + 22 + 4)	2000	6.9	7.0	7.6	7.8	7.1	7.3	0.5	19.6	5.5
	2006	6.3	6.9	7.4	7.7	7.2	7.1	0.5	17.0	4.4
Agricultural raw materials	1995	2.9	2.8	2.1	2.2	9.3	3.9	0.5	9.2	6.6
(SITC 2 - 22 - 27 - 28)	2000	2.0	2.1	1.7	1.7	6.5	2.3	0.5	6.2	4.3
	2006	1.6	1.7	1.4	1.5	4.6	2.3	0.5	3.9	2.8
Ores, metals, precious stones	1995	5.0	4.5	4.3	3.8	8.3	3.5	1.3	24.3	15.6
and non-monetary gold	2000	4.5	4.1	4.2	3.5	5.5	2.5	1.5	24.2	17.4
(SITC 27 + 28 + 68 + 667 + 971)	2006	5.6	5.1	4.4	4.0	8.5	3.8	2.6	31.1	11.2
Fuels (SITC 3)	1995	7.5	3.2	3.4	2.6	8.4	1.9	0.4	12.2	28.7
	2000	10.3	4.5	5.0	3.8	11.8	1.7	0.3	14.3	35.3
	2006	14.6	7.0	7.1	5.9	20.1	3.6	0.9	17.6	47.9
Manufactured goods	1995	73.0	78.1	77.6	78.6	61.5	78.1	95.6	31.4	36.1
(SITC 5 to 8 less 667 and 68)	2000	73.3	78.8	77.4	79.1	63.3	84.0	95.8	33.7	29.6
	2006	68.5	75.4	75.1	77.7	54.9	80.8	93.9	28.5	24.5

Sources:
- Data and UNCTAD secretariat estimates based on UN DESA Comtrade and IMF *Direction of Trade statistics* databases

2.2.A Structure des importations par partenaires et groupes de produits
Monde

			Developing economies / Économies en développement							Destination	
				Asia / Asie						Year	
Total	Africa / Afrique	America / Amérique	Total	Eastern, Southern and South-Eastern Asia / Asie orientale, méridionale et du Sud-Est	China / Chine	Western Asia / Asie occidentale	Oceania / Océanie	Major petroleum exporters / Principaux exportateurs de pétrole	Major exporters of manufactures / Principaux exportateurs d'articles manufacturés	Année	Groupes de produits
Millions de dollars											
1 398 031	110 698	242 597	1 039 792	909 335	230 725	130 457	4 944	197 440	962 527	1995	**Total tous produits**
2 107 495	157 940	379 573	1 565 673	1 346 392	412 968	219 281	4 309	336 520	1 457 063	2000	
4 710 553	391 144	728 179	3 582 569	3 015 261	1 282 020	567 308	8 620	868 013	3 195 521	2006	
Parts par destinations (en pourcentage)											
27.4	2.2	4.8	20.4	17.8	4.5	2.6	0.1	3.9	18.9	1995	**Total tous produits**
32.6	2.4	5.9	24.2	20.8	6.4	3.4	0.1	5.2	22.5	2000	
38.8	3.2	6.0	29.5	24.9	10.6	4.7	0.1	7.2	26.4	2006	
31.4	3.8	12.5	14.8	13.4	2.7	1.4	0.3	1.8	15.9	1995	Produits alimentaires
33.4	3.9	13.8	15.5	14.0	3.6	1.5	0.2	2.0	16.6	2000	(CTCI 0 + 1 + 22 + 4)
34.9	3.8	15.2	15.7	13.9	3.8	1.8	0.2	2.0	17.5	2006	
28.1	4.3	6.4	16.9	16.2	2.3	0.7	0.5	1.6	15.1	1995	Matières premières
28.5	4.5	7.0	16.8	16.1	3.0	0.7	0.3	1.7	15.2	2000	d'origine agricole
32.9	4.4	8.0	20.1	19.4	3.2	0.7	0.4	1.5	17.9	2006	(CTCI 2 - 22 - 27 - 28)
29.1	6.0	9.9	12.6	10.9	1.9	1.7	0.6	2.4	13.6	1995	Minerais, métaux, pierres
30.6	7.0	9.1	14.1	12.3	2.3	1.8	0.4	2.4	14.5	2000	précieuses et or (non monétaire)
39.7	7.0	13.8	18.5	15.9	3.7	2.7	0.4	3.2	18.0	2006	(CTCI 27 + 28 + 68 + 667 + 971)
57.4	11.6	8.2	37.4	14.6	1.6	22.8	0.2	41.0	8.9	1995	Combustibles (CTCI 3)
59.2	11.7	9.7	37.6	13.2	1.3	24.5	0.1	43.1	8.8	2000	
58.3	13.1	8.7	36.4	13.3	1.0	23.1	0.1	42.2	10.1	2006	
24.2	0.7	3.1	20.5	19.6	5.4	0.8	0.0	0.6	21.1	1995	Articles manufacturés
29.7	0.7	4.4	24.6	23.7	7.9	0.9	0.0	0.6	26.1	2000	(CTCI 5 à 8 moins 667 et 68)
36.2	0.8	4.0	31.4	29.9	14.4	1.4	0.0	0.8	32.3	2006	
Parts par principaux groupes de produits (en pourcentage)											
100.0	100.0	100.0	100.0	100.0	100.0	100.0	100.0	100.0	100.0	1995	**Total tous produits**
100.0	100.0	100.0	100.0	100.0	100.0	100.0	100.0	100.0	100.0	2000	
100.0	100.0	100.0	100.0	100.0	100.0	100.0	100.0	100.0	100.0	2006	
10.4	15.7	23.9	6.6	6.8	5.5	5.1	26.2	4.1	7.7	1995	Produits alimentaires
7.1	11.1	16.4	4.4	4.7	3.9	3.1	23.7	2.6	5.1	2000	(CTCI 0 + 1 + 22 + 4)
5.7	7.4	15.9	3.3	3.5	2.2	2.5	18.2	1.8	4.2	2006	
3.0	5.8	4.0	2.4	2.7	1.5	0.7	14.7	1.2	2.3	1995	Matières premières
1.8	3.8	2.4	1.4	1.6	0.9	0.4	9.1	0.7	1.4	2000	d'origine agricole
1.3	2.2	2.1	1.1	1.2	0.5	0.2	8.3	0.3	1.1	2006	(CTCI 2 - 22 - 27 - 28)
5.3	13.9	10.4	3.1	3.0	2.1	3.3	28.9	3.1	3.6	1995	Minerais, métaux, pierres
4.2	12.8	7.0	2.6	2.6	1.6	2.3	26.1	2.1	2.9	2000	précieuses et or (non monétaire)
5.7	12.1	12.7	3.5	3.5	2.0	3.2	31.1	2.5	3.8	2006	(CTCI 27 + 28 + 68 + 667 + 971)
15.7	40.0	13.0	13.7	6.1	2.6	66.8	13.3	79.2	3.6	1995	Combustibles (CTCI 3)
18.8	49.6	17.1	16.1	6.5	2.0	74.7	17.6	85.8	4.1	2000	
21.9	59.2	21.3	18.0	7.8	1.3	72.0	15.2	86.1	5.6	2006	
64.4	22.3	47.2	73.2	80.3	87.7	23.5	15.9	11.2	81.5	1995	Articles manufacturés
66.8	21.3	54.7	74.4	83.2	91.0	18.9	22.1	8.2	85.0	2000	(CTCI 5 à 8 moins 667 et 68)
63.9	17.3	45.9	72.7	82.5	93.3	21.0	26.6	7.7	83.9	2006	

Sources :
- Données et estimations du secrétariat de la CNUCED sur la base de données Comtrade de ONU DAES et *Direction of Trade statistics* du Fonds Monétaire international

2.2.B Export structure by partner and product group
Developed economies

Destination / Product group	Year / Année	World / Monde	Developed economies / Économies développées Total	Europe Total	Europe EU / UE	Canada	USA / États-Unis	Japan / Japon	Other developed countries / Autres économies développées	Economies in transition / Économies en transition
Millions of dollars										
All products	1995	3 528 995	2 597 088	1 819 060	1 711 831	148 277	427 229	134 120	68 402	52 200
	2000	4 133 153	3 110 058	2 056 946	1 946 505	208 346	636 299	132 214	76 255	49 240
	2006	7 013 671	5 177 096	3 766 185	3 563 766	282 083	855 688	157 730	115 410	186 360
Share by destination (percentage)										
All products	1995	100.0	73.6	51.5	48.5	4.2	12.1	3.8	1.9	1.5
	2000	100.0	75.2	49.8	47.1	5.0	15.4	3.2	1.8	1.2
	2006	100.0	73.8	53.7	50.8	4.0	12.2	2.2	1.6	2.7
All food items	1995	100.0	75.4	58.7	56.8	2.6	5.2	7.7	1.1	3.9
(SITC 0 + 1 + 22 + 4)	2000	100.0	75.9	54.8	53.0	3.7	8.3	7.8	1.4	2.4
	2006	100.0	77.8	60.6	58.5	3.5	7.7	4.7	1.4	3.3
Agricultural raw materials	1995	100.0	75.6	48.2	45.9	2.9	12.1	11.4	1.1	0.5
(SITC 2 - 22 - 27 - 28)	2000	100.0	74.3	46.2	44.3	3.8	15.5	7.7	1.1	0.8
	2006	100.0	67.5	46.7	44.8	2.9	12.2	4.9	0.8	1.6
Ores, metals, precious stones	1995	100.0	74.1	49.1	44.2	3.4	11.4	6.7	3.5	0.5
and non-monetary gold	2000	100.0	73.4	45.4	39.8	3.4	15.6	4.8	4.2	0.6
(SITC 27 + 28 + 68 + 667 + 971)	2006	100.0	68.9	48.0	43.6	2.7	11.5	3.9	2.8	0.9
Fuels (SITC 3)	1995	100.0	81.6	55.3	51.7	2.8	18.3	4.5	0.7	1.5
	2000	100.0	85.0	53.0	50.3	3.3	25.3	2.6	0.7	0.8
	2006	100.0	83.1	56.1	53.0	3.0	21.3	2.1	0.6	0.9
Manufactured goods	1995	100.0	73.1	50.9	47.9	4.5	12.6	3.0	2.0	1.3
(SITC 5 to 8 less 667 and 68)	2000	100.0	74.4	49.3	46.6	5.4	15.2	2.6	1.8	1.2
	2006	100.0	72.9	53.4	50.6	4.3	11.7	1.8	1.7	2.9
Share by major product group (percentage)										
All products	1995	100.0	100.0	100.0	100.0	100.0	100.0	100.0	100.0	100.0
	2000	100.0	100.0	100.0	100.0	100.0	100.0	100.0	100.0	100.0
	2006	100.0	100.0	100.0	100.0	100.0	100.0	100.0	100.0	100.0
All food items	1995	8.7	8.9	9.9	10.2	5.4	3.7	17.6	5.0	22.9
(SITC 0 + 1 + 22 + 4)	2000	6.8	6.8	7.5	7.6	4.9	3.7	16.5	5.0	13.9
	2006	6.7	7.1	7.6	7.8	5.9	4.2	13.9	5.6	8.4
Agricultural raw materials	1995	2.6	2.6	2.4	2.4	1.8	2.6	7.7	1.4	0.9
(SITC 2 - 22 - 27 - 28)	2000	1.9	1.9	1.8	1.8	1.5	1.9	4.7	1.1	1.3
	2006	1.6	1.5	1.4	1.4	1.1	1.6	3.5	0.8	0.9
Ores, metals, precious stones	1995	4.1	4.2	4.0	3.8	3.3	3.9	7.3	7.4	1.5
and non-monetary gold	2000	3.9	3.8	3.5	3.3	2.6	3.9	5.8	8.9	2.1
(SITC 27 + 28 + 68 + 667 + 971)	2006	5.1	4.8	4.6	4.4	3.5	4.8	8.9	8.8	1.8
Fuels (SITC 3)	1995	3.3	3.7	3.6	3.6	2.2	5.1	4.0	1.2	3.3
	2000	4.7	5.3	5.0	5.1	3.1	7.8	3.9	1.9	3.0
	2006	7.0	7.8	7.3	7.3	5.3	12.1	6.5	2.5	2.3
Manufactured goods	1995	78.3	77.8	77.4	77.3	84.3	81.5	61.6	82.1	69.1
(SITC 5 to 8 less 667 and 68)	2000	78.9	78.0	78.1	78.1	84.9	78.1	65.2	78.4	76.5
	2006	76.3	75.4	75.9	75.9	81.1	73.3	61.8	78.3	84.5

Sources:
- Data and UNCTAD secretariat estimates based on UN DESA Comtrade and IMF *Direction of Trade statistics* databases

Developing economies / Économies en développement										Destination	
			Asia / Asie							Year	
Total	Africa / Afrique	America / Amérique	Total	Eastern, Southern and South-Eastern Asia / Asie orientale, méridionale et du Sud-Est	China / Chine	Western Asia / Asie occidentale	Oceania / Océanie	Major petroleum exporters / Principaux exportateurs de pétrole	Major exporters of manufactures / Principaux exportateurs d'articles manufacturés	Année	Groupes de produits
Millions de dollars											
823 689	80 135	167 776	571 529	493 335	58 877	78 194	4 250	86 125	560 787	1995	Total tous produits
942 030	80 045	252 904	605 214	511 304	77 566	93 910	3 867	91 062	676 751	2000	
1 610 858	153 671	356 752	1 093 987	880 384	257 488	213 603	6 447	213 258	1 109 583	2006	
Parts par destinations (en pourcentage)											
23.3	2.3	4.8	16.2	14.0	1.7	2.2	0.1	2.4	15.9	1995	Total tous produits
22.8	1.9	6.1	14.6	12.4	1.9	2.3	0.1	2.2	16.4	2000	
23.0	2.2	5.1	15.6	12.6	3.7	3.0	0.1	3.0	15.8	2006	
19.1	3.6	4.1	11.2	8.6	1.3	2.7	0.2	3.7	9.7	1995	Produits alimentaires
20.3	3.5	5.3	11.2	8.3	1.2	2.9	0.2	4.0	10.4	2000	(CTCI 0 + 1 + 22 + 4)
17.9	3.0	4.8	9.9	7.5	1.6	2.4	0.2	3.5	9.4	2006	
23.2	2.0	3.4	17.8	16.1	3.7	1.6	0.0	1.4	17.1	1995	Matières premières
24.2	1.9	4.4	17.8	15.8	4.4	1.9	0.1	1.2	18.0	2000	d'origine agricole
30.5	2.2	4.4	23.8	21.2	11.0	2.6	0.1	1.6	23.7	2006	(CTCI 2 - 22 - 27 - 28)
22.5	0.9	1.7	20.0	18.2	1.3	1.7	0.0	1.0	19.4	1995	Minerais, métaux, pierres
22.8	1.0	2.4	19.4	18.1	2.7	1.3	0.0	0.9	19.9	2000	précieuses et or (non monétaire)
28.0	1.1	2.1	24.9	22.7	8.3	2.1	0.0	1.2	24.6	2006	(CTCI 27 + 28 + 68 + 667 + 971)
12.9	1.5	3.7	7.4	6.5	0.4	1.0	0.3	1.0	8.5	1995	Combustibles (CTCI 3)
10.5	1.4	3.8	5.1	4.2	0.5	0.9	0.2	0.8	7.3	2000	
11.7	2.0	4.2	5.5	4.2	0.7	1.2	0.1	1.5	6.5	2006	
24.4	2.3	5.1	17.0	14.7	1.7	2.3	0.1	2.5	16.8	1995	Articles manufacturés
23.7	1.9	6.6	15.2	12.8	1.9	2.3	0.1	2.2	17.3	2000	(CTCI 5 à 8 moins 667 et 68)
23.7	2.2	5.4	16.0	12.7	3.6	3.3	0.1	3.3	16.3	2006	
Parts par principaux groupes de produits (en pourcentage)											
100.0	100.0	100.0	100.0	100.0	100.0	100.0	100.0	100.0	100.0	1995	Total tous produits
100.0	100.0	100.0	100.0	100.0	100.0	100.0	100.0	100.0	100.0	2000	
100.0	100.0	100.0	100.0	100.0	100.0	100.0	100.0	100.0	100.0	2006	
7.1	13.8	7.5	6.0	5.3	6.5	10.4	16.2	13.2	5.3	1995	Produits alimentaires
6.0	12.4	5.8	5.2	4.5	4.3	8.8	15.0	12.4	4.3	2000	(CTCI 0 + 1 + 22 + 4)
5.2	9.3	6.3	4.3	4.0	3.0	5.4	13.9	7.8	4.0	2006	
2.6	2.3	1.8	2.8	3.0	5.7	1.9	1.0	1.4	2.8	1995	Matières premières
2.0	1.9	1.4	2.3	2.5	4.6	1.7	1.1	1.0	2.1	2000	d'origine agricole
2.1	1.6	1.4	2.4	2.7	4.8	1.4	1.2	0.9	2.4	2006	(CTCI 2 - 22 - 27 - 28)
4.0	1.7	1.5	5.1	5.4	3.1	3.2	0.6	1.7	5.1	1995	Minerais, métaux, pierres
3.9	1.9	1.5	5.1	5.7	5.5	2.2	0.7	1.6	4.7	2000	précieuses et or (non monétaire)
6.2	2.5	2.1	8.2	9.3	11.5	3.6	0.8	2.0	8.0	2006	(CTCI 27 + 28 + 68 + 667 + 971)
1.8	2.2	2.6	1.5	1.5	0.7	1.5	7.0	1.3	1.8	1995	Combustibles (CTCI 3)
2.2	3.4	2.9	1.7	1.6	1.1	1.9	11.1	1.6	2.1	2000	
3.5	6.2	5.7	2.4	2.3	1.2	2.8	8.3	3.4	2.9	2006	
81.9	77.6	83.4	82.2	82.5	80.7	79.9	72.8	79.9	82.5	1995	Articles manufacturés
82.0	76.6	84.7	81.7	81.9	80.7	80.6	62.9	78.0	83.1	2000	(CTCI 5 à 8 moins 667 et 68)
78.7	76.4	80.8	78.5	77.2	75.1	83.7	69.4	82.5	78.7	2006	

Sources :
- Données et estimations du secrétariat de la CNUCED sur la base de données Comtrade de ONU DAES et *Direction of Trade statistics* du Fonds Monétaire international

Destination / Product group	Year / Année	World / Monde	Developed economies / Économies développées				Canada	USA / États-Unis	Japan / Japon	Other developed countries / Autres économies développées	Economies in transition / Économies en transition
			Total	Europe							
				Total	Total	EU / UE					
Millions of dollars											
All products	1995	3 524 933	2 591 050	1 772 403	1 658 890	177 182	357 691	230 485	53 289	64 255
	2000	4 525 440	3 103 128	2 044 752	1 911 347	262 387	457 260	269 056	69 672	92 238
	2006	7 928 314	5 071 092	3 760 826	3 470 018	350 863	551 860	297 932	109 611	267 193
Share by destination (percentage)											
All products	1995	100.0	73.5	50.3	47.1	5.0	10.1	6.5	1.5	1.8
	2000	100.0	68.6	45.2	42.2	5.8	10.1	5.9	1.5	2.0
	2006	100.0	64.0	47.4	43.8	4.4	7.0	3.8	1.4	3.4
All food items	1995	100.0	70.8	53.0	50.9	3.6	10.7	0.2	3.3	1.1
(SITC 0 + 1 + 22 + 4)	2000	100.0	69.5	50.4	48.2	4.8	10.2	0.2	3.9	1.2
	2006	100.0	70.6	55.9	53.8	4.1	6.8	0.2	3.7	1.2
Agricultural raw materials	1995	100.0	71.9	37.8	36.4	15.9	13.3	0.5	4.5	4.8
(SITC 2 - 22 - 27 - 28)	2000	100.0	72.3	38.3	37.1	18.1	11.1	0.7	4.0	4.2
	2006	100.0	67.7	44.3	43.2	12.3	7.5	0.7	2.8	4.6
Ores, metals, precious stones	1995	100.0	64.3	41.4	35.6	8.0	7.2	0.6	7.2	7.9
and non-monetary gold	2000	100.0	62.3	39.4	32.2	7.3	6.2	0.9	8.5	10.1
(SITC 27 + 28 + 68 + 667 + 971)	2006	100.0	58.4	38.3	34.2	7.1	5.5	0.7	6.8	8.0
Fuels (SITC 3)	1995	100.0	36.2	25.2	17.7	6.0	2.3	0.1	2.6	7.8
	2000	100.0	35.5	24.8	17.4	7.2	1.3	0.1	2.0	8.7
	2006	100.0	35.2	25.4	19.3	6.5	1.4	0.2	1.7	13.2
Manufactured goods	1995	100.0	78.0	53.2	50.4	4.3	11.1	8.8	0.7	0.6
(SITC 5 to 8 less 667 and 68)	2000	100.0	72.7	47.4	45.3	5.1	11.6	7.9	0.8	0.6
	2006	100.0	69.0	51.3	49.1	3.5	8.3	5.2	0.7	0.9
Share by major product group (percentage)											
All products	1995	100.0	100.0	100.0	100.0	100.0	100.0	100.0	100.0	100.0
	2000	100.0	100.0	100.0	100.0	100.0	100.0	100.0	100.0	100.0
	2006	100.0	100.0	100.0	100.0	100.0	100.0	100.0	100.0	100.0
All food items	1995	9.3	9.0	9.9	10.1	6.8	9.9	0.3	20.1	5.7
(SITC 0 + 1 + 22 + 4)	2000	6.9	7.0	7.7	7.9	5.8	6.9	0.3	17.5	4.1
	2006	6.6	7.3	7.8	8.1	6.1	6.5	0.3	17.5	2.4
Agricultural raw materials	1995	2.9	2.9	2.2	2.3	9.2	3.8	0.2	8.6	7.8
(SITC 2 - 22 - 27 - 28)	2000	2.0	2.1	1.7	1.7	6.1	2.1	0.2	5.1	4.0
	2006	1.5	1.6	1.4	1.4	4.1	1.6	0.3	3.0	2.0
Ores, metals, precious stones	1995	5.1	4.4	4.2	3.8	8.1	3.6	0.5	24.1	22.0
and non-monetary gold	2000	4.4	4.0	3.8	3.4	5.5	2.7	0.7	24.4	21.8
(SITC 27 + 28 + 68 + 667 + 971)	2006	5.1	4.7	4.1	4.0	8.2	4.0	0.9	25.3	12.1
Fuels (SITC 3)	1995	7.5	3.7	3.8	2.8	8.9	1.7	0.2	12.7	32.3
	2000	10.1	5.2	5.5	4.1	12.6	1.3	0.2	13.4	43.0
	2006	14.8	8.2	7.9	6.5	21.8	2.9	0.8	18.3	58.2
Manufactured goods	1995	72.6	77.1	76.8	77.8	62.7	79.2	97.8	32.8	25.3
(SITC 5 to 8 less 667 and 68)	2000	73.1	77.5	76.6	78.4	63.7	83.7	96.8	37.1	20.4
	2006	68.6	74.0	74.1	76.9	54.8	81.8	95.9	33.9	17.4

Sources:
- Data and UNCTAD secretariat estimates based on UN DESA Comtrade and IMF *Direction of Trade statistics* databases

2.2.B Structure des importations par partenaires et groupes de produits
Économies développées

	Developing economies / Économies en développement									Year	Destination
Total	Africa Afrique	America Amérique	Asia / Asie Total	Eastern, Southern and South-Eastern Asia Asie orientale, méridionale et du Sud-Est	China Chine	Western Asia Asie occidentale	Oceania Océanie	Major petroleum exporters Principaux exportateurs de pétrole	Major exporters of manufactures Principaux exportateurs d'articles manufacturés	Année	Groupes de produits
Millions de dollars											
836 708	82 800	172 863	577 010	504 066	126 345	72 945	4 035	123 009	559 192	1995	Total tous produits
1 298 724	112 041	290 341	893 119	768 295	250 527	124 823	3 224	204 138	893 935	2000	
2 546 052	261 080	505 403	1 773 581	1 494 198	750 005	279 382	5 987	465 958	1 709 999	2006	
Parts par destinations (en pourcentage)											
23.7	**2.3**	**4.9**	**16.4**	**14.3**	**3.6**	**2.1**	**0.1**	**3.5**	**15.9**	**1995**	**Total tous produits**
28.7	**2.5**	**6.4**	**19.7**	**17.0**	**5.5**	**2.8**	**0.1**	**4.5**	**19.8**	**2000**	
32.1	**3.3**	**6.4**	**22.4**	**18.8**	**9.5**	**3.5**	**0.1**	**5.9**	**21.6**	**2006**	
27.9	4.2	12.1	11.3	10.4	2.1	0.9	0.3	1.3	13.7	1995	Produits alimentaires
29.3	3.8	13.3	11.9	11.1	3.0	0.8	0.2	1.2	14.9	2000	(CTCI 0 + 1 + 22 + 4)
28.1	3.5	13.4	11.0	10.0	3.3	1.1	0.2	1.1	14.5	2006	
22.6	3.9	6.0	12.3	11.7	1.9	0.5	0.4	1.4	11.8	1995	Matières premières
23.3	3.9	7.4	11.8	11.3	2.8	0.5	0.2	1.3	12.6	2000	d'origine agricole
27.5	3.8	8.6	15.0	14.5	3.7	0.5	0.1	1.1	15.1	2006	(CTCI 2 - 22 - 27 - 28)
25.1	6.1	9.9	8.4	7.5	1.3	0.8	0.7	1.7	10.8	1995	Minerais, métaux, pierres
27.0	7.8	9.1	9.6	8.6	1.6	1.0	0.5	1.7	11.3	2000	précieuses et or (non monétaire)
32.9	7.5	13.8	11.1	9.4	2.5	1.7	0.5	1.8	12.6	2006	(CTCI 27 + 28 + 68 + 667 + 971)
52.4	13.5	8.8	29.9	10.5	1.2	19.3	0.2	39.2	6.2	1995	Combustibles (CTCI 3)
52.9	12.8	10.6	29.4	8.8	0.8	20.6	0.1	40.2	6.8	2000	
47.9	14.1	9.8	23.9	7.2	0.5	16.7	0.1	36.4	6.8	2006	
20.5	0.6	3.2	16.7	16.1	4.3	0.6	0.0	0.3	17.9	1995	Articles manufacturés
26.3	0.7	5.0	20.6	19.8	7.0	0.7	0.0	0.3	23.1	2000	(CTCI 5 à 8 moins 667 et 68)
30.0	0.8	4.4	24.8	23.6	13.0	1.2	0.0	0.4	26.8	2006	
Parts par principaux groupes de produits (en pourcentage)											
100.0	**100.0**	**100.0**	**100.0**	**100.0**	**100.0**	**100.0**	**100.0**	**100.0**	**100.0**	**1995**	**Total tous produits**
100.0	**100.0**	**100.0**	**100.0**	**100.0**	**100.0**	**100.0**	**100.0**	**100.0**	**100.0**	**2000**	
100.0	**100.0**	**100.0**	**100.0**	**100.0**	**100.0**	**100.0**	**100.0**	**100.0**	**100.0**	**2006**	
11.0	16.5	23.0	6.5	6.8	5.6	4.0	26.1	3.5	8.1	1995	Produits alimentaires
7.0	10.6	14.3	4.2	4.5	3.7	2.0	23.9	1.8	5.2	2000	(CTCI 0 + 1 + 22 + 4)
5.8	7.1	13.9	3.3	3.5	2.3	2.0	17.9	1.3	4.4	2006	
2.8	4.9	3.6	2.2	2.4	1.5	0.7	10.9	1.2	2.2	1995	Matières premières
1.6	3.0	2.3	1.2	1.3	1.0	0.4	5.1	0.6	1.2	2000	d'origine agricole
1.3	1.7	2.0	1.0	1.1	0.6	0.2	2.0	0.3	1.0	2006	(CTCI 2 - 22 - 27 - 28)
5.4	13.2	10.3	2.6	2.7	1.8	2.0	31.0	2.5	3.4	1995	Minerais, métaux, pierres
4.1	13.9	6.2	2.2	2.2	1.3	1.6	30.2	1.6	2.5	2000	précieuses et or (non monétaire)
5.2	11.7	11.1	2.5	2.6	1.3	2.4	34.0	1.6	3.0	2006	(CTCI 27 + 28 + 68 + 667 + 971)
16.6	43.2	13.5	13.7	5.5	2.5	70.1	14.5	84.3	2.9	1995	Combustibles (CTCI 3)
18.6	52.2	16.7	15.0	5.2	1.4	75.4	18.7	89.9	3.5	2000	
22.1	63.4	22.8	15.9	5.7	0.7	70.5	18.4	91.9	4.7	2006	
62.9	19.6	47.4	74.0	81.5	88.1	22.2	16.3	6.9	81.9	1995	Articles manufacturés
67.0	19.4	57.5	76.2	85.3	91.9	19.7	20.3	5.5	85.6	2000	(CTCI 5 à 8 moins 667 et 68)
64.1	15.7	47.9	76.0	85.7	94.3	24.1	26.4	4.5	85.2	2006	

Sources :
- Données et estimations du secrétariat de la CNUCED sur la base de données Comtrade de ONU DAES et *Direction of Trade statistics* du Fonds Monétaire international

Destination / Product group	Year / Année	World / Monde	Developed economies / Économies développées							Economies in transition / Économies en transition
			Total	Europe		Canada	USA / États-Unis	Japan / Japon	Other developed countries / Autres économies développées	
				Total	EU / UE					
Millions of dollars										
All products	1995	118 704	55 346	48 182	43 977	117	4 160	2 517	371	32 903
	2000	152 380	91 790	79 865	73 884	210	6 081	2 977	2 657	32 194
	2006	441 120	279 052	257 650	236 955	874	11 912	5 168	3 447	84 726
Share by destination (percentage)										
All products	1995	100.0	46.6	40.6	37.0	0.1	3.5	2.1	0.3	27.7
	2000	100.0	60.2	52.4	48.5	0.1	4.0	2.0	1.7	21.1
	2006	100.0	63.3	58.4	53.7	0.2	2.7	1.2	0.8	19.2
All food items	1995	100.0	30.3	25.7	24.9	0.1	1.6	2.0	0.9	63.1
(SITC 0 + 1 + 22 + 4)	2000	100.0	30.0	24.7	22.7	0.1	1.2	2.9	1.2	57.7
	2006	100.0	26.6	23.3	23.0	0.1	0.7	1.3	1.2	50.0
Agricultural raw materials	1995	100.0	61.4	51.7	49.8	0.0	0.9	8.6	0.1	12.1
(SITC 2 - 22 - 27 - 28)	2000	100.0	60.2	50.0	47.1	0.0	0.7	9.3	0.3	14.1
	2006	100.0	47.2	39.8	39.6	0.1	0.6	6.3	0.3	11.8
Ores, metals, precious stones	1995	100.0	78.7	56.6	48.8	0.0	10.7	11.3	0.1	11.5
and non-monetary gold	2000	100.0	74.9	58.5	53.2	0.1	8.2	8.0	0.2	11.1
(SITC 27 + 28 + 68 + 667 + 971)	2006	100.0	72.5	60.7	49.5	0.3	4.9	5.6	1.1	10.0
Fuels (SITC 3)	1995	100.0	64.5	62.5	56.5	0.0	0.8	0.6	0.5	20.8
	2000	100.0	54.8	51.2	47.0	0.0	0.4	0.5	2.8	9.1
	2006	100.0	65.4	62.9	57.7	0.2	1.1	0.6	0.7	6.9
Manufactured goods	1995	100.0	35.6	28.6	26.7	0.2	5.8	0.7	0.2	35.9
(SITC 5 to 8 less 667 and 68)	2000	100.0	45.5	37.0	35.7	0.4	7.3	0.4	0.3	25.4
	2006	100.0	40.4	34.1	33.0	0.3	5.3	0.4	0.3	33.3
Share by major product group (percentage)										
All products	1995	100.0	100.0	100.0	100.0	100.0	100.0	100.0	100.0	100.0
	2000	100.0	100.0	100.0	100.0	100.0	100.0	100.0	100.0	100.0
	2006	100.0	100.0	100.0	100.0	100.0	100.0	100.0	100.0	100.0
All food items	1995	6.1	4.0	3.8	4.1	5.5	2.9	5.6	17.7	13.8
(SITC 0 + 1 + 22 + 4)	2000	3.6	1.8	1.7	1.7	2.7	1.1	5.4	2.5	9.9
	2006	3.8	1.6	1.5	1.6	1.6	0.9	4.3	5.7	9.8
Agricultural raw materials	1995	5.1	6.7	6.5	6.9	0.8	1.3	20.6	2.4	2.2
(SITC 2 - 22 - 27 - 28)	2000	4.0	4.0	3.8	3.9	1.3	0.7	19.1	0.6	2.7
	2006	2.5	1.9	1.7	1.8	1.0	0.6	13.5	1.1	1.5
Ores, metals, precious stones	1995	9.8	16.5	13.7	12.9	2.2	29.8	52.2	3.3	4.1
and non-monetary gold	2000	10.2	12.7	11.4	11.2	6.3	21.0	41.9	1.3	5.4
(SITC 27 + 28 + 68 + 667 + 971)	2006	8.6	9.9	9.0	8.0	11.1	15.7	40.9	12.0	4.5
Fuels (SITC 3)	1995	32.8	45.4	50.5	50.1	14.3	7.4	9.6	52.2	24.6
	2000	42.0	38.2	41.0	40.7	0.3	3.7	10.1	67.3	18.1
	2006	54.0	55.8	58.1	57.9	48.2	21.6	25.7	51.1	19.5
Manufactured goods	1995	35.5	27.1	25.1	25.6	76.6	58.5	11.9	24.3	46.0
(SITC 5 to 8 less 667 and 68)	2000	31.6	23.9	22.3	23.3	88.7	58.0	6.5	6.1	38.0
	2006	24.9	15.9	14.5	15.3	37.8	48.7	9.3	11.0	43.2

Sources:
- Data and UNCTAD secretariat estimates based on UN DESA Comtrade and IMF *Direction of Trade statistics* databases

Total	Africa Afrique	America Amérique	Asia Asie Total	Eastern, Southern and South-Eastern Asia / Asie orientale, méridionale et du Sud-Est	China Chine	Western Asia Asie occidentale	Oceania Océanie	Major petroleum exporters Principaux exportateurs de pétrole	Major exporters of manufactures Principaux exportateurs d'articles manufacturés	Year Année	Destination Groupes de produits
Developing economies / Économies en développement											
Millions de dollars											
17 929	1 131	3 025	13 772	10 736	4 811	3 036	1	1 818	11 508	1995	Total tous produits
28 193	2 273	6 063	19 852	13 900	6 733	5 952	6	3 037	16 762	2000	
76 848	6 085	6 683	63 921	40 443	20 796	23 478	160	12 302	51 633	2006	
Parts par destinations (en pourcentage)											
15.1	1.0	2.5	11.6	9.0	4.1	2.6	0.0	1.5	9.7	1995	Total tous produits
18.5	1.5	4.0	13.0	9.1	4.4	3.9	0.0	2.0	11.0	2000	
17.4	1.4	1.5	14.5	9.2	4.7	5.3	0.0	2.8	11.7	2006	
6.1	1.1	0.2	4.8	1.4	0.5	3.4	0.0	0.8	3.6	1995	Produits alimentaires
11.9	2.4	0.2	9.4	5.4	1.3	4.0	0.0	2.7	5.4	2000	(CTCI 0 + 1 + 22 + 4)
22.3	5.7	0.3	16.3	8.2	1.3	8.1	0.0	6.9	6.9	2006	
22.4	1.1	1.2	20.1	14.6	6.6	5.4	0.0	1.0	19.4	1995	Matières premières
25.6	2.2	0.7	22.7	17.5	10.6	5.2	0.0	1.9	20.5	2000	d'origine agricole
41.0	2.8	0.1	38.1	33.1	25.8	5.0	0.0	2.0	33.2	2006	(CTCI 2 - 22 - 27 - 28)
7.3	0.2	0.1	7.1	5.6	1.1	1.5	0.0	0.6	6.3	1995	Minerais, métaux, pierres
13.9	0.7	0.7	12.6	9.0	5.6	3.6	0.0	0.4	12.1	2000	précieuses et or (non monétaire)
17.3	0.4	0.2	16.7	9.7	6.1	7.0	0.0	0.8	15.9	2006	(CTCI 27 + 28 + 68 + 667 + 971)
10.4	0.1	5.4	4.9	3.0	0.1	1.9	0.0	1.3	3.2	1995	Combustibles (CTCI 3)
10.9	0.1	7.2	3.6	2.2	0.7	1.3	0.0	0.4	2.6	2000	
9.6	0.2	1.2	8.2	5.7	3.4	2.5	0.0	1.3	6.6	2006	
26.5	2.2	1.9	22.5	18.8	10.0	3.6	0.0	2.6	19.2	1995	Articles manufacturés
29.1	3.4	2.6	23.1	17.7	7.9	5.5	0.0	4.4	19.2	2000	(CTCI 5 à 8 moins 667 et 68)
26.1	3.2	3.0	19.8	13.1	4.9	6.7	0.1	5.3	15.2	2006	
Parts par principaux groupes de produits (en pourcentage)											
100.0	100.0	100.0	100.0	100.0	100.0	100.0	100.0	100.0	100.0	1995	Total tous produits
100.0	100.0	100.0	100.0	100.0	100.0	100.0	100.0	100.0	100.0	2000	
100.0	100.0	100.0	100.0	100.0	100.0	100.0	100.0	100.0	100.0	2006	
2.4	7.0	0.5	2.5	0.9	0.7	8.1	15.8	3.4	2.3	1995	Produits alimentaires
2.3	5.7	0.2	2.6	2.1	1.1	3.7	9.7	5.0	1.8	2000	(CTCI 0 + 1 + 22 + 4)
4.8	15.7	0.6	4.2	3.4	1.0	5.8	0.0	9.3	2.2	2006	
7.6	5.6	2.5	8.8	8.3	8.3	10.8	14.8	3.4	10.2	1995	Matières premières
5.5	5.9	0.7	7.0	7.7	9.6	5.3	3.7	3.7	7.5	2000	d'origine agricole
5.9	5.1	0.2	6.5	9.0	13.6	2.3	0.0	1.8	7.1	2006	(CTCI 2 - 22 - 27 - 28)
4.8	1.8	0.3	6.0	6.0	2.6	5.8	0.4	4.1	6.4	1995	Minerais, métaux, pierres
7.7	4.5	1.8	9.9	10.1	13.1	9.4	4.1	2.0	11.3	2000	précieuses et or (non monétaire)
8.6	2.5	1.0	10.0	9.2	11.1	11.3	0.1	2.5	11.7	2006	(CTCI 27 + 28 + 68 + 667 + 971)
22.7	2.5	70.1	13.9	10.9	0.7	24.6	9.0	28.7	10.9	1995	Combustibles (CTCI 3)
24.7	2.8	76.4	11.5	10.2	6.8	14.5	22.8	8.5	10.1	2000	
29.8	6.1	43.3	30.7	33.8	38.6	25.3	0.4	25.5	30.2	2006	
62.4	80.8	26.4	68.8	73.9	87.7	50.7	60.0	59.5	70.2	1995	Articles manufacturés
49.7	71.2	20.8	56.1	61.2	56.7	44.3	59.8	70.3	55.1	2000	(CTCI 5 à 8 moins 667 et 68)
37.3	57.3	48.8	34.0	35.6	25.7	31.3	99.5	47.3	32.3	2006	

Sources :
- Données et estimations du secrétariat de la CNUCED sur la base de données Comtrade de ONU DAES et *Direction of Trade statistics* du Fonds Monétaire international

Destination / Product group	Year / Année	World / Monde	Developed economies / Économies développées							Economies in transition / Économies en transition
			Total	Europe		Canada	USA / États-Unis	Japan / Japon	Other developed countries / Autres économies développées	
				Total	EU / UE					
Millions of dollars										
All products	**1995**	**93 920**	**38 184**	**32 661**	**31 434**	**352**	**3 565**	**1 129**	**478**	**33 508**
	2000	**88 808**	**42 940**	**36 195**	**34 928**	**321**	**4 627**	**1 252**	**544**	**35 517**
	2006	**301 456**	**152 126**	**128 242**	**123 731**	**1 375**	**10 266**	**10 615**	**1 628**	**89 388**
Share by destination (percentage)										
All products	**1995**	**100.0**	**40.7**	**34.8**	**33.5**	**0.4**	**3.8**	**1.2**	**0.5**	**35.7**
	2000	**100.0**	**48.4**	**40.8**	**39.3**	**0.4**	**5.2**	**1.4**	**0.6**	**40.0**
	2006	**100.0**	**50.5**	**42.5**	**41.0**	**0.5**	**3.4**	**3.5**	**0.5**	**29.7**
All food items	1995	100.0	49.5	39.1	37.3	0.5	8.4	0.0	1.4	27.1
(SITC 0 + 1 + 22 + 4)	2000	100.0	47.0	38.1	36.4	0.3	8.0	0.0	0.6	26.9
	2006	100.0	43.3	37.1	34.2	0.9	4.2	0.1	1.1	22.1
Agricultural raw materials	1995	100.0	34.3	29.3	28.5	0.3	2.8	0.3	1.6	58.4
(SITC 2 - 22 - 27 - 28)	2000	100.0	38.1	31.7	30.2	0.5	4.4	0.5	1.1	53.5
	2006	100.0	44.1	38.2	37.7	0.3	3.4	0.3	1.9	39.9
Ores, metals, precious stones	1995	100.0	25.3	21.2	20.0	0.4	1.4	0.0	2.3	53.0
and non-monetary gold	2000	100.0	26.7	19.8	18.9	0.2	1.1	0.3	5.3	55.7
(SITC 27 + 28 + 68 + 667 + 971)	2006	100.0	31.1	24.8	23.1	0.3	0.8	0.2	5.1	53.2
Fuels (SITC 3)	1995	100.0	12.6	11.7	11.0	0.0	0.6	0.2	0.0	83.2
	2000	100.0	10.9	10.3	9.9	0.0	0.4	0.1	0.0	82.4
	2006	100.0	11.5	11.1	10.7	0.0	0.3	0.1	0.0	86.5
Manufactured goods	1995	100.0	60.0	52.0	50.2	0.6	4.7	2.4	0.4	28.5
(SITC 5 to 8 less 667 and 68)	2000	100.0	64.9	54.9	53.1	0.5	6.6	2.4	0.4	25.0
	2006	100.0	61.5	51.5	50.1	0.5	4.1	5.1	0.3	17.2
Share by major product group (percentage)										
All products	**1995**	**100.0**	**100.0**	**100.0**	**100.0**	**100.0**	**100.0**	**100.0**	**100.0**	**100.0**
	2000	**100.0**	**100.0**	**100.0**	**100.0**	**100.0**	**100.0**	**100.0**	**100.0**	**100.0**
	2006	**100.0**	**100.0**	**100.0**	**100.0**	**100.0**	**100.0**	**100.0**	**100.0**	**100.0**
All food items	1995	15.4	18.8	17.3	17.2	20.5	34.3	0.5	43.1	11.7
(SITC 0 + 1 + 22 + 4)	2000	14.3	13.9	13.4	13.3	13.2	21.9	0.2	13.3	9.6
	2006	11.3	9.7	9.8	9.4	22.0	14.0	0.2	22.4	8.4
Agricultural raw materials	1995	1.5	1.3	1.3	1.3	1.1	1.1	0.3	5.0	2.5
(SITC 2 - 22 - 27 - 28)	2000	1.8	1.4	1.4	1.4	2.3	1.5	0.6	3.2	2.4
	2006	1.1	1.0	1.0	1.0	0.8	1.1	0.1	3.8	1.5
Ores, metals, precious stones	1995	3.4	2.1	2.1	2.0	3.4	1.3	0.0	15.5	5.0
and non-monetary gold	2000	4.6	2.6	2.3	2.2	2.1	1.0	1.0	40.3	6.5
(SITC 27 + 28 + 68 + 667 + 971)	2006	3.2	2.0	1.8	1.8	1.7	0.7	0.2	30.0	5.7
Fuels (SITC 3)	1995	15.1	4.7	5.1	5.0	0.9	2.5	2.5	0.9	35.2
	2000	16.1	3.6	4.1	4.0	1.5	1.3	0.9	0.9	33.2
	2006	12.0	2.7	3.2	3.1	0.4	0.9	0.3	0.2	35.1
Manufactured goods	1995	48.3	71.3	72.2	72.4	73.9	60.0	96.4	35.2	38.5
(SITC 5 to 8 less 667 and 68)	2000	57.0	76.5	76.8	77.0	78.2	72.7	96.6	41.7	35.6
	2006	69.1	84.2	83.7	84.3	75.0	82.3	99.2	43.0	40.1

Sources:
- Data and UNCTAD secretariat estimates based on UN DESA Comtrade and IMF *Direction of Trade statistics* databases

2.2.C Structure des importations par partenaires et groupes de produits
Économies en transition

Total	Africa Afrique	America Amérique	Total	Eastern, Southern and South-Eastern Asia / Asie orientale, méridionale et du Sud-Est	China Chine	Western Asia / Asie occidentale	Oceania Océanie	Major petroleum exporters / Principaux exportateurs de pétrole	Major exporters of manufactures / Principaux exportateurs d'articles manufacturés	Year Année	Groupes de produits
											Millions de dollars
8 559	752	1 641	6 156	4 457	1 087	1 699	9	1 226	5 254	1995	Total tous produits
9 957	844	1 955	7 148	4 977	1 619	2 171	10	1 411	6 471	2000	
57 797	2 030	7 886	47 870	39 820	21 705	8 050	13	2 815	48 507	2006	
											Parts par destinations (en pourcentage)
9.1	0.8	1.7	6.6	4.7	1.2	1.8	0.0	1.3	5.6	1995	Total tous produits
11.2	1.0	2.2	8.0	5.6	1.8	2.4	0.0	1.6	7.3	2000	
19.2	0.7	2.6	15.9	13.2	7.2	2.7	0.0	0.9	16.1	2006	
22.1	1.6	8.9	11.6	8.0	2.6	3.6	0.0	3.0	10.6	1995	Produits alimentaires
26.1	2.6	12.1	11.5	8.6	1.6	2.9	0.0	3.0	13.2	2000	(CTCI 0 + 1 + 22 + 4)
34.4	3.1	18.5	12.8	9.8	2.9	3.0	0.0	2.9	19.7	2006	
6.3	0.4	1.4	4.6	4.3	0.8	0.3	0.0	0.8	2.8	1995	Matières premières
8.4	0.8	1.8	5.8	5.4	1.0	0.4	0.0	0.6	4.4	2000	d'origine agricole
15.6	1.3	5.3	9.0	8.2	1.6	0.8	0.0	3.0	8.1	2006	(CTCI 2 - 22 - 27 - 28)
20.9	5.3	6.4	9.2	7.4	1.3	1.8	0.0	1.5	6.3	1995	Minerais, métaux, pierres
17.6	5.4	5.6	6.6	4.3	1.5	2.3	0.0	2.0	6.5	2000	précieuses et or (non monétaire)
15.6	5.3	2.2	8.0	5.5	2.8	2.5	0.1	1.5	6.9	2006	(CTCI 27 + 28 + 68 + 667 + 971)
3.5	1.8	0.1	1.6	1.1	0.2	0.4	0.0	2.6	0.7	1995	Combustibles (CTCI 3)
3.6	1.1	0.3	2.3	0.8	0.5	1.4	0.0	2.5	0.7	2000	
1.6	0.1	0.1	1.4	0.9	0.5	0.5	0.0	0.3	1.1	2006	
8.9	0.1	0.2	8.5	6.2	1.4	2.3	0.0	0.7	7.4	1995	Articles manufacturés
10.1	0.2	0.2	9.7	6.8	2.5	2.9	0.0	1.1	8.5	2000	(CTCI 5 à 8 moins 667 et 68)
20.6	0.2	0.5	20.0	17.0	9.7	3.0	0.0	0.7	19.3	2006	
											Parts par principaux groupes de produits (en pourcentage)
100.0	100.0	100.0	100.0	100.0	100.0	100.0	100.0	100.0	100.0	1995	Total tous produits
100.0	100.0	100.0	100.0	100.0	100.0	100.0	100.0	100.0	100.0	2000	
100.0	100.0	100.0	100.0	100.0	100.0	100.0	100.0	100.0	100.0	2006	
37.4	31.4	78.2	27.3	25.8	33.9	31.1	14.6	35.4	29.1	1995	Produits alimentaires
33.4	39.2	78.5	20.4	22.0	12.4	16.9	20.4	27.1	26.1	2000	(CTCI 0 + 1 + 22 + 4)
20.2	52.6	79.6	9.0	8.3	4.6	12.6	31.8	35.1	13.8	2006	
1.1	0.7	1.2	1.1	1.4	1.1	0.2	0.0	1.0	0.8	1995	Matières premières
1.3	1.5	1.4	1.3	1.7	1.0	0.3	1.4	0.7	1.1	2000	d'origine agricole
0.9	2.1	2.2	0.6	0.7	0.2	0.3	0.2	3.5	0.6	2006	(CTCI 2 - 22 - 27 - 28)
7.8	22.6	12.4	4.8	5.3	3.8	3.3	0.1	3.8	3.9	1995	Minerais, métaux, pierres
7.3	26.2	11.8	3.8	3.6	3.9	4.4	0.8	5.9	4.2	2000	précieuses et or (non monétaire)
2.6	24.9	2.7	1.6	1.3	1.2	3.0	58.5	5.1	1.4	2006	(CTCI 27 + 28 + 68 + 667 + 971)
5.8	34.3	1.1	3.6	3.6	3.0	3.6	0.0	30.3	2.0	1995	Combustibles (CTCI 3)
5.2	18.3	2.2	4.5	2.4	4.5	9.4	0.0	25.1	1.6	2000	
1.0	2.7	0.5	1.0	0.8	0.8	2.3	0.1	3.6	0.8	2006	
46.9	8.4	6.5	62.3	62.7	58.1	61.4	84.8	24.6	64.0	1995	Articles manufacturés
51.3	9.8	5.0	68.8	69.6	77.8	67.0	77.3	39.5	66.2	2000	(CTCI 5 à 8 moins 667 et 68)
74.3	15.9	12.5	86.9	88.7	93.0	78.2	5.1	50.9	82.6	2006	

Note: column group headers — Developing economies / Économies en développement (covering Africa, America, Asia, Oceania); Asia / Asie (covering Total, Eastern Southern and South-Eastern Asia, China, Western Asia); Destination (covering Year and Groupes de produits).

Sources :
- Données et estimations du secrétariat de la CNUCED sur la base de données Comtrade de ONU DAES et *Direction of Trade statistics* du Fonds Monétaire international

Destination / Product group	Year / Année	World / Monde	Developed economies / Économies développées								Economies in transition / Économies en transition
			Total	Europe		Canada	USA / États-Unis	Japan / Japon	Other developed countries / Autres économies développées		
				Total	EU / UE						

						Millions of dollars					
All products	1995	1 417 569	777 994	270 416	258 906	16 055	312 666	156 899	21 958		13 554
	2000	2 024 127	1 168 381	379 169	359 575	23 505	535 379	197 158	33 170		12 494
	2006	4 466 584	2 257 141	829 618	789 299	54 391	915 044	376 795	81 293		62 155

						Share by destination (percentage)					
All products	1995	100.0	54.9	19.1	18.3	1.1	22.1	11.1	1.5		1.0
	2000	100.0	57.7	18.7	17.8	1.2	26.4	9.7	1.6		0.6
	2006	100.0	50.5	18.6	17.7	1.2	20.5	8.4	1.8		1.4
All food items	1995	100.0	56.3	26.9	26.0	0.8	13.0	14.3	1.2		3.0
(SITC 0 + 1 + 22 + 4)	2000	100.0	55.8	24.2	23.4	1.2	16.6	12.5	1.4		2.2
	2006	100.0	49.7	24.0	23.4	1.2	14.7	8.4	1.4		4.2
Agricultural raw materials	1995	100.0	52.1	23.8	23.1	0.6	12.2	14.5	1.0		0.3
(SITC 2 - 22 - 27 - 28)	2000	100.0	50.5	23.7	23.0	0.6	13.8	11.4	1.0		0.3
	2006	100.0	44.9	20.4	19.9	1.0	13.7	9.0	0.9		0.9
Ores, metals, precious stones	1995	100.0	59.3	28.6	24.6	1.2	11.4	16.3	1.8		0.9
and non-monetary gold	2000	100.0	59.3	30.9	26.2	1.4	13.3	10.7	3.0		0.4
(SITC 27 + 28 + 68 + 667 + 971)	2006	100.0	50.6	26.0	20.9	2.1	10.4	9.4	2.6		0.5
Fuels (SITC 3)	1995	100.0	54.1	17.1	16.7	0.7	18.1	17.0	1.2		0.2
	2000	100.0	56.5	18.6	16.8	0.7	22.4	13.8	1.1		0.1
	2006	100.0	53.8	15.9	14.7	1.0	20.5	14.5	1.8		0.0
Manufactured goods	1995	100.0	54.9	17.6	17.0	1.3	25.6	8.7	1.7		0.9
(SITC 5 to 8 less 667 and 68)	2000	100.0	58.8	17.5	17.0	1.3	30.0	8.3	1.8		0.6
	2006	100.0	50.0	18.0	17.5	1.2	22.6	6.4	1.8		1.6

						Share by major product group (percentage)					
All products	1995	100.0	100.0	100.0	100.0	100.0	100.0	100.0	100.0		100.0
	2000	100.0	100.0	100.0	100.0	100.0	100.0	100.0	100.0		100.0
	2006	100.0	100.0	100.0	100.0	100.0	100.0	100.0	100.0		100.0
All food items	1995	9.8	10.0	13.8	13.9	7.3	5.7	12.7	7.4		30.5
(SITC 0 + 1 + 22 + 4)	2000	6.7	6.5	8.6	8.8	6.6	4.2	8.5	5.6		24.3
	2006	5.6	5.5	7.2	7.4	5.7	4.0	5.5	4.4		16.9
Agricultural raw materials	1995	2.7	2.6	3.4	3.4	1.5	1.5	3.5	1.7		0.8
(SITC 2 - 22 - 27 - 28)	2000	1.6	1.4	2.0	2.0	0.8	0.8	1.8	0.9		0.8
	2006	1.3	1.2	1.4	1.5	1.1	0.9	1.4	0.6		0.8
Ores, metals, precious stones	1995	4.9	5.3	7.3	6.6	5.1	2.5	7.2	5.7		4.5
and non-monetary gold	2000	3.9	4.0	6.4	5.7	4.7	2.0	4.3	7.0		2.5
(SITC 27 + 28 + 68 + 667 + 971)	2006	5.7	5.7	8.0	6.8	9.9	2.9	6.4	8.2		1.9
Fuels (SITC 3)	1995	15.5	15.3	13.8	14.1	10.1	12.7	23.8	12.4		2.6
	2000	19.9	19.5	19.7	18.8	12.8	16.9	28.2	12.9		4.6
	2006	22.3	23.8	19.2	18.6	18.3	22.4	38.5	22.0		0.7
Manufactured goods	1995	65.6	65.6	60.6	61.0	75.3	76.0	51.6	72.0		61.2
(SITC 5 to 8 less 667 and 68)	2000	66.9	68.2	62.5	63.9	74.7	75.9	56.8	72.7		67.2
	2006	62.8	62.2	60.8	62.3	64.4	69.3	47.7	62.4		73.7

Sources:
- Data and UNCTAD secretariat estimates based on UN DESA Comtrade and IMF *Direction of Trade statistics* databases

2.2.D Structure des exportations par partenaires et groupes de produits
Économies en développement

			Developing economies / Économies en développement							Destination	
				Asia / Asie				Major petroleum exporters	Major exporters of manufactures	Year	
Total	Africa / Afrique	America / Amérique	Total	Eastern, Southern and South-Eastern Asia / Asie orientale, méridionale et du Sud-Est	China / Chine	Western Asia / Asie occidentale	Oceania / Océanie	Principaux exportateurs de pétrole	Principaux exportateurs d'articles manufacturés	Année	Groupes de produits
Millions de dollars											
566 461	32 921	72 303	459 912	422 195	82 296	37 716	1 325	45 475	404 765	1995	**Total tous produits**
800 984	46 589	101 764	649 644	598 145	124 050	51 500	2 987	57 690	585 906	2000	
2 058 816	137 253	232 340	1 683 104	1 514 365	418 090	168 739	6 100	206 593	1 440 550	2006	
Parts par destinations (en pourcentage)											
40.0	2.3	5.1	32.4	29.8	5.8	2.7	0.1	3.2	28.6	1995	**Total tous produits**
39.6	2.3	5.0	32.1	29.6	6.1	2.5	0.1	2.9	28.9	2000	
46.1	3.1	5.2	37.7	33.9	9.4	3.8	0.1	4.6	32.3	2006	
40.3	4.5	6.8	29.0	23.8	4.8	5.1	0.1	6.8	20.7	1995	Produits alimentaires
41.2	5.1	7.8	28.2	22.1	4.2	6.1	0.1	7.8	19.9	2000	(CTCI 0 + 1 + 22 + 4)
45.6	7.1	6.7	31.6	23.9	5.2	7.7	0.1	10.7	19.7	2006	
47.5	3.2	4.9	39.5	37.5	9.5	2.0	0.0	2.2	36.2	1995	Matières premières
48.9	3.1	4.6	41.2	38.9	15.0	2.3	0.0	2.0	37.0	2000	d'origine agricole
53.8	2.5	4.5	46.8	43.7	21.0	3.1	0.0	2.9	39.3	2006	(CTCI 2 - 22 - 27 - 28)
39.4	1.3	3.8	34.3	32.3	5.3	2.0	0.0	2.5	32.2	1995	Minerais, métaux, pierres
38.8	1.7	4.0	33.0	30.3	6.7	2.7	0.0	2.9	31.2	2000	précieuses et or (non monétaire)
48.5	2.3	4.0	42.1	38.6	12.8	3.6	0.0	3.8	39.1	2006	(CTCI 27 + 28 + 68 + 667 + 971)
23.1	1.3	4.8	16.8	15.7	2.3	1.1	0.2	0.5	16.7	1995	Combustibles (CTCI 3)
36.5	2.6	5.4	28.1	26.5	3.5	1.6	0.3	0.8	27.3	2000	
41.6	3.0	5.7	32.7	30.0	5.5	2.6	0.2	2.3	28.3	2006	
44.0	2.3	5.1	36.5	33.7	6.7	2.8	0.1	3.5	32.2	1995	Articles manufacturés
40.3	1.9	4.7	33.6	31.1	6.9	2.5	0.1	3.0	30.3	2000	(CTCI 5 à 8 moins 667 et 68)
48.0	2.7	5.0	40.2	36.4	10.8	3.8	0.1	5.0	34.8	2006	
Parts par principaux groupes de produits (en pourcentage)											
100.0	100.0	100.0	100.0	100.0	100.0	100.0	100.0	100.0	100.0	1995	**Total tous produits**
100.0	100.0	100.0	100.0	100.0	100.0	100.0	100.0	100.0	100.0	2000	
100.0	100.0	100.0	100.0	100.0	100.0	100.0	100.0	100.0	100.0	2006	
9.9	19.1	12.9	8.7	7.8	8.0	18.8	8.1	20.7	7.1	1995	Produits alimentaires
7.0	14.9	10.4	5.9	5.0	4.6	16.0	4.9	18.3	4.6	2000	(CTCI 0 + 1 + 22 + 4)
5.5	12.9	7.2	4.7	3.9	3.1	11.3	6.0	12.9	3.4	2006	
3.2	3.7	2.6	3.3	3.4	4.4	2.0	0.4	1.9	3.4	1995	Matières premières
1.9	2.1	1.4	2.0	2.0	3.8	1.4	0.2	1.1	2.0	2000	d'origine agricole
1.5	1.1	1.1	1.6	1.7	2.9	1.1	0.2	0.8	1.6	2006	(CTCI 2 - 22 - 27 - 28)
4.8	2.7	3.6	5.2	5.3	4.5	3.7	0.5	3.7	5.5	1995	Minerais, métaux, pierres
3.8	2.9	3.1	4.0	4.0	4.2	4.1	0.3	3.9	4.2	2000	précieuses et or (non monétaire)
6.0	4.4	4.4	6.4	6.5	7.8	5.4	0.3	4.7	6.9	2006	(CTCI 27 + 28 + 68 + 667 + 971)
9.0	8.8	14.7	8.0	8.1	6.2	6.7	24.9	2.5	9.0	1995	Combustibles (CTCI 3)
18.4	22.9	21.6	17.5	17.9	11.4	12.5	41.1	5.3	18.8	2000	
20.2	22.0	24.6	19.4	19.8	13.1	15.6	33.0	11.3	19.6	2006	
72.2	64.8	65.3	73.8	74.3	76.2	68.3	63.0	70.7	74.0	1995	Articles manufacturés
68.2	56.1	62.3	70.1	70.6	75.7	64.8	50.6	70.2	70.0	2000	(CTCI 5 à 8 moins 667 et 68)
65.5	56.2	60.8	66.9	67.4	72.8	62.9	52.2	67.5	67.8	2006	

Sources :
- Données et estimations du secrétariat de la CNUCED sur la base de données Comtrade de ONU DAES et *Direction of Trade statistics* du Fonds Monétaire international

Destination / Product group	Year Année	World Monde	Developed economies / Économies développées Total	Europe Total	EU UE	Canada	USA États-Unis	Japan Japon	Other developed countries Autres économies développées	Economies in transition Économies en transition
Millions of dollars										
All products	1995	1 479 516	890 084	325 867	302 502	19 733	267 103	243 190	34 191	22 696
	2000	1 858 955	1 004 787	338 280	313 110	22 514	354 987	243 881	45 125	28 679
	2006	3 895 312	1 623 540	636 309	585 718	35 880	462 276	398 994	90 081	84 580
Share by destination (percentage)										
All products	1995	100.0	60.2	22.0	20.4	1.3	18.1	16.4	2.3	1.5
	2000	100.0	54.1	18.2	16.8	1.2	19.1	13.1	2.4	1.5
	2006	100.0	41.7	16.3	15.0	0.9	11.9	10.2	2.3	2.2
All food items	1995	100.0	56.5	20.8	19.9	3.9	23.5	1.6	6.7	0.8
(SITC 0 + 1 + 22 + 4)	2000	100.0	54.0	18.5	17.7	4.1	21.8	1.4	8.3	1.1
	2006	100.0	43.7	14.5	13.6	3.1	17.6	1.3	7.2	2.6
Agricultural raw materials	1995	100.0	53.5	12.3	12.0	4.5	24.6	4.2	7.8	4.8
(SITC 2 - 22 - 27 - 28)	2000	100.0	54.7	14.8	14.4	5.9	21.4	4.2	8.3	5.0
	2006	100.0	49.3	13.9	13.6	4.9	20.6	3.8	6.1	7.9
Ores, metals, precious stones	1995	100.0	56.5	22.9	16.8	2.9	12.2	7.0	11.6	4.1
and non-monetary gold	2000	100.0	54.6	24.7	17.3	1.6	9.0	6.8	12.5	5.6
(SITC 27 + 28 + 68 + 667 + 971)	2006	100.0	43.5	16.0	9.9	1.7	6.4	6.1	13.3	4.6
Fuels (SITC 3)	1995	100.0	15.7	4.0	3.9	0.7	5.7	1.6	3.9	2.0
	2000	100.0	11.5	3.3	2.7	0.3	3.8	0.6	3.6	1.9
	2006	100.0	10.5	3.1	2.8	0.3	3.7	0.7	2.8	4.4
Manufactured goods	1995	100.0	64.8	24.2	22.7	0.9	18.4	20.4	0.9	1.3
(SITC 5 to 8 less 667 and 68)	2000	100.0	60.1	20.0	18.8	0.9	21.6	16.6	0.9	1.1
	2006	100.0	48.1	19.0	17.8	0.7	13.8	13.9	0.7	1.0
Share by major product group (percentage)										
All products	1995	100.0	100.0	100.0	100.0	100.0	100.0	100.0	100.0	100.0
	2000	100.0	100.0	100.0	100.0	100.0	100.0	100.0	100.0	100.0
	2006	100.0	100.0	100.0	100.0	100.0	100.0	100.0	100.0	100.0
All food items	1995	8.0	7.5	7.6	7.8	23.6	10.4	0.8	23.2	4.3
(SITC 0 + 1 + 22 + 4)	2000	6.7	6.7	6.8	7.0	22.4	7.6	0.7	22.9	4.6
	2006	5.2	5.5	4.6	4.7	17.5	7.8	0.6	16.2	6.3
Agricultural raw materials	1995	3.0	2.7	1.7	1.8	10.3	4.2	0.8	10.3	9.6
(SITC 2 - 22 - 27 - 28)	2000	2.3	2.3	1.9	2.0	11.2	2.6	0.7	7.8	7.4
	2006	1.8	2.2	1.6	1.7	9.7	3.2	0.7	4.9	6.7
Ores, metals, precious stones	1995	4.9	4.6	5.1	4.0	10.6	3.3	2.1	24.7	13.2
and non-monetary gold	2000	4.6	4.6	6.2	4.7	5.9	2.2	2.4	23.7	16.7
(SITC 27 + 28 + 68 + 667 + 971)	2006	6.6	6.9	6.5	4.4	12.0	3.6	3.9	38.3	14.0
Fuels (SITC 3)	1995	7.0	1.8	1.3	1.3	3.6	2.2	0.7	11.6	9.0
	2000	10.7	2.3	1.9	1.7	2.3	2.1	0.5	15.8	13.3
	2006	14.3	3.6	2.7	2.6	4.3	4.4	1.0	17.1	28.8
Manufactured goods	1995	75.3	81.2	82.8	83.5	50.6	76.8	93.6	29.1	63.1
(SITC 5 to 8 less 667 and 68)	2000	74.7	83.0	82.0	83.4	57.8	84.4	94.7	28.3	52.0
	2006	68.3	78.8	79.2	81.0	54.9	79.6	92.4	21.7	30.6

Sources:
- Data and UNCTAD secretariat estimates based on UN DESA Comtrade and IMF *Direction of Trade statistics* databases

2.2.D Structure des importations par partenaires et groupes de produits
Économies en développement

			Developing economies / Économies en développement								Destination
				Asia / Asie				Major petroleum exporters / Principaux exportateurs de pétrole	Major exporters of manufactures / Principaux exportateurs d'articles manufacturés	Year / Année	
Total	Africa / Afrique	America / Amérique	Total	Eastern, Southern and South-Eastern Asia / Asie orientale, méridionale et du Sud-Est	China / Chine	Western Asia / Asie occidentale	Oceania / Océanie				Groupes de produits
Millions de dollars											
552 764	27 146	68 093	456 625	400 812	103 293	55 813	900	73 205	398 082	1995	Total tous produits
798 814	45 055	87 276	665 406	573 119	160 823	92 287	1 076	130 971	556 656	2000	
2 106 704	128 034	214 890	1 761 118	1 481 242	510 310	279 876	2 620	399 240	1 437 014	2006	
Parts par destinations (en pourcentage)											
37.4	1.8	4.6	30.9	27.1	7.0	3.8	0.1	4.9	26.9	1995	Total tous produits
43.0	2.4	4.7	35.8	30.8	8.7	5.0	0.1	7.0	29.9	2000	
54.1	3.3	5.5	45.2	38.0	13.1	7.2	0.1	10.2	36.9	2006	
42.1	2.9	14.2	24.9	22.2	4.4	2.7	0.2	2.8	22.7	1995	Produits alimentaires
44.6	4.3	15.4	24.7	21.6	5.4	3.1	0.2	3.9	21.2	2000	(CTCI 0 + 1 + 22 + 4)
52.7	4.7	19.3	28.4	24.7	5.0	3.6	0.2	4.1	25.1	2006	
41.2	5.2	7.5	27.9	26.9	3.4	1.0	0.6	2.0	23.1	1995	Matières premières
40.2	5.9	6.2	27.6	26.6	3.4	1.0	0.5	2.4	21.0	2000	d'origine agricole
42.4	5.5	7.1	29.0	28.1	2.5	0.9	0.8	2.0	23.0	2006	(CTCI 2 - 22 - 27 - 28)
39.1	5.9	10.0	23.0	19.2	3.5	3.8	0.2	4.2	21.0	1995	Minerais, métaux, pierres
39.7	5.2	9.5	24.8	21.3	3.8	3.5	0.2	4.2	22.4	2000	précieuses et or (non monétaire)
51.3	6.3	14.1	30.6	26.4	5.8	4.2	0.2	5.4	27.0	2006	(CTCI 27 + 28 + 68 + 667 + 971)
77.7	8.1	7.8	61.8	27.0	2.8	34.9	0.1	50.8	17.2	1995	Combustibles (CTCI 3)
77.5	10.0	8.3	59.1	24.2	2.4	35.0	0.1	52.9	14.1	2000	
83.9	11.8	7.1	64.9	27.1	2.1	37.8	0.0	57.2	17.6	2006	
33.3	0.8	2.9	29.6	28.4	8.1	1.2	0.0	1.2	29.0	1995	Articles manufacturés
38.4	0.9	2.9	34.6	33.5	10.4	1.1	0.0	1.1	33.8	2000	(CTCI 5 à 8 moins 667 et 68)
50.2	1.0	3.4	45.7	44.0	17.6	1.7	0.0	1.7	44.6	2006	
Parts par principaux groupes de produits (en pourcentage)											
100.0	100.0	100.0	100.0	100.0	100.0	100.0	100.0	100.0	100.0	1995	Total tous produits
100.0	100.0	100.0	100.0	100.0	100.0	100.0	100.0	100.0	100.0	2000	
100.0	100.0	100.0	100.0	100.0	100.0	100.0	100.0	100.0	100.0	2006	
9.1	12.7	24.7	6.5	6.6	5.1	5.7	26.7	4.6	6.8	1995	Produits alimentaires
6.9	11.8	22.0	4.6	4.7	4.2	4.1	23.2	3.7	4.7	2000	(CTCI 0 + 1 + 22 + 4)
5.1	7.5	18.2	3.3	3.4	2.0	2.6	18.8	2.1	3.5	2006	
3.4	8.6	5.0	2.8	3.0	1.5	0.8	31.8	1.2	2.6	1995	Matières premières
2.1	5.6	3.0	1.8	2.0	0.9	0.5	21.3	0.8	1.6	2000	d'origine agricole
1.4	3.1	2.4	1.2	1.4	0.4	0.2	22.6	0.4	1.1	2006	(CTCI 2 - 22 - 27 - 28)
5.1	15.7	10.7	3.7	3.5	2.5	5.0	19.5	4.2	3.8	1995	Minerais, métaux, pierres
4.2	9.8	9.3	3.2	3.2	2.0	3.2	13.9	2.8	3.5	2000	précieuses et or (non monétaire)
6.3	12.8	17.0	4.5	4.6	2.9	3.9	24.3	3.5	4.9	2006	(CTCI 27 + 28 + 68 + 667 + 971)
14.5	30.7	11.8	14.0	6.9	2.8	64.4	8.0	71.6	4.4	1995	Combustibles (CTCI 3)
19.3	43.9	18.9	17.6	8.4	3.0	75.3	14.2	80.2	5.0	2000	
22.2	51.6	18.4	20.6	10.2	2.2	75.5	7.8	80.0	6.8	2006	
67.1	31.0	47.5	72.2	78.9	87.6	24.1	13.6	18.3	81.3	1995	Articles manufacturés
66.7	26.3	46.5	72.1	81.0	89.6	16.7	27.2	12.0	84.4	2000	(CTCI 5 à 8 moins 667 et 68)
63.3	20.7	42.4	69.0	79.0	91.9	16.3	26.9	11.1	82.5	2006	

Sources :
- Données et estimations du secrétariat de la CNUCED sur la base de données Comtrade de ONU DAES et *Direction of Trade statistics* du Fonds Monétaire international

2.2.E Export structure by partner and product group
Developing economies: Africa

Destination / Product group	Year Année	World Monde	Developed economies / Économies développées — Total	Europe Total	Europe EU UE	Canada	USA États-Unis	Japan Japon	Other developed countries Autres économies développées	Economies in transition Économies en transition
Millions of dollars										
All products	1995	103 373	71 468	51 189	48 048	971	14 919	3 341	1 049	689
	2000	149 949	99 240	67 638	65 216	1 802	25 837	2 464	1 500	537
	2006	335 652	226 612	137 643	129 999	5 891	71 277	9 256	2 545	1 271
Share by destination (percentage)										
All products	1995	100.0	69.1	49.5	46.5	0.9	14.4	3.2	1.0	0.7
	2000	100.0	66.2	45.1	43.5	1.2	17.2	1.6	1.0	0.4
	2006	100.0	67.5	41.0	38.7	1.8	21.2	2.8	0.8	0.4
All food items	1995	100.0	72.6	61.4	58.7	0.5	3.5	6.4	0.8	1.9
(SITC 0 + 1 + 22 + 4)	2000	100.0	63.0	51.3	49.7	0.7	4.5	5.5	1.0	1.4
	2006	100.0	59.7	49.8	48.2	1.1	4.2	3.7	0.8	1.9
Agricultural raw materials	1995	100.0	60.8	49.8	48.7	0.2	3.9	6.3	0.6	0.1
(SITC 2 - 22 - 27 - 28)	2000	100.0	54.0	43.6	41.3	0.2	4.3	5.4	0.5	0.1
	2006	100.0	47.3	37.9	37.1	0.4	4.0	4.8	0.3	0.5
Ores, metals, precious stones	1995	100.0	78.8	65.2	50.8	1.0	5.5	5.8	1.4	0.5
and non-monetary gold	2000	100.0	80.7	68.0	58.1	0.5	5.3	4.0	2.9	0.3
(SITC 27 + 28 + 68 + 667 + 971)	2006	100.0	70.2	49.0	37.4	0.7	9.0	10.0	1.5	0.9
Fuels (SITC 3)	1995	100.0	80.4	50.5	48.5	1.5	26.7	1.0	0.7	0.5
	2000	100.0	71.0	41.7	41.2	1.8	26.7	0.4	0.5	0.3
	2006	100.0	72.5	38.1	37.0	2.5	30.8	1.0	0.1	0.0
Manufactured goods	1995	100.0	59.9	47.2	46.7	0.6	7.5	2.7	1.9	0.6
(SITC 5 to 8 less 667 and 68)	2000	100.0	66.6	52.2	51.0	0.6	9.8	2.1	1.8	0.3
	2006	100.0	58.8	44.6	44.0	0.6	7.7	3.3	2.6	0.7
Share by major product group (percentage)										
All products	1995	100.0	100.0	100.0	100.0	100.0	100.0	100.0	100.0	100.0
	2000	100.0	100.0	100.0	100.0	100.0	100.0	100.0	100.0	100.0
	2006	100.0	100.0	100.0	100.0	100.0	100.0	100.0	100.0	100.0
All food items	1995	13.9	14.6	17.2	17.5	8.0	3.3	27.6	11.5	40.3
(SITC 0 + 1 + 22 + 4)	2000	9.1	8.7	10.4	10.4	5.5	2.4	30.7	9.0	34.5
	2006	7.0	6.2	8.5	8.7	4.3	1.4	9.5	7.5	35.3
Agricultural raw materials	1995	5.3	4.6	5.3	5.5	1.1	1.4	10.4	3.3	0.8
(SITC 2 - 22 - 27 - 28)	2000	3.0	2.4	2.9	2.8	0.6	0.7	9.6	1.6	1.2
	2006	2.2	1.6	2.1	2.2	0.5	0.4	3.9	0.9	2.7
Ores, metals, precious stones	1995	10.9	12.4	14.4	11.9	11.0	4.2	19.5	14.6	7.7
and non-monetary gold	2000	9.1	11.1	13.7	12.2	4.0	2.8	22.2	26.1	7.3
(SITC 27 + 28 + 68 + 667 + 971)	2006	12.0	12.5	14.4	11.6	5.1	5.1	43.7	23.3	27.0
Fuels (SITC 3)	1995	40.0	46.5	40.8	41.8	64.0	74.0	12.2	28.9	30.2
	2000	53.2	57.0	49.1	50.4	79.5	82.4	11.7	26.3	37.4
	2006	59.7	64.0	55.4	57.1	84.2	86.5	21.9	7.6	0.9
Manufactured goods	1995	22.5	19.5	21.4	22.5	15.2	11.6	18.7	41.1	20.9
(SITC 5 to 8 less 667 and 68)	2000	20.3	20.4	23.5	23.8	10.3	11.6	25.4	37.0	17.8
	2006	17.8	15.5	19.4	20.2	5.8	6.5	21.0	60.4	31.0

Sources:
- Data and UNCTAD secretariat estimates based on UN DESA Comtrade and IMF *Direction of Trade statistics* databases

2.2.E Structure des exportations par partenaires et groupes de produits
Économies en développement : Afrique

| | | | Developing economies — Économies en développement | | | | | | | Destination | |
| | Africa / Afrique | America / Amérique | Asia / Asie | | | | | Major petroleum exporters / Principaux exportateurs de pétrole | Major exporters of manufactures / Principaux exportateurs d'articles manufacturés | Year / Année | |
Total			Total	Eastern, Southern and South-Eastern Asia / Asie orientale, méridionale et du Sud-Est	China / Chine	Western Asia / Asie occidentale	Oceania / Océanie				Groupes de produits
Millions de dollars											
24 244	10 728	2 307	11 200	8 610	910	2 590	9	2 716	10 137	1995	Total tous produits
41 146	14 649	4 723	21 183	16 886	4 235	4 297	592	3 881	20 708	2000	
100 217	32 969	12 072	55 133	44 589	25 034	10 544	42	10 355	54 446	2006	
Parts par destinations (en pourcentage)											
23.5	10.4	2.2	10.8	8.3	0.9	2.5	0.0	2.6	9.8	1995	Total tous produits
27.4	9.8	3.1	14.1	11.3	2.8	2.9	0.4	2.6	13.8	2000	
29.9	9.8	3.6	16.4	13.3	7.5	3.1	0.0	3.1	16.2	2006	
23.8	14.2	0.5	9.1	4.8	0.5	4.4	0.0	6.4	4.0	1995	Produits alimentaires
35.0	20.3	0.7	13.9	7.2	0.8	6.7	0.1	10.5	5.9	2000	(CTCI 0 + 1 + 22 + 4)
36.6	21.8	0.5	14.2	8.0	1.2	6.3	0.0	9.5	6.5	2006	
38.9	12.7	1.5	24.7	22.0	3.9	2.7	0.0	1.8	20.9	1995	Matières premières
45.3	15.1	1.7	28.5	25.5	6.2	3.0	0.0	1.8	24.4	2000	d'origine agricole
50.7	9.7	0.6	40.4	37.8	14.4	2.5	0.0	1.7	24.3	2006	(CTCI 2 - 22 - 27 - 28)
20.4	4.9	0.7	14.8	13.0	1.3	1.8	0.0	1.8	12.6	1995	Minerais, métaux, pierres
18.1	6.3	1.4	10.4	9.5	1.7	0.9	0.0	1.1	10.3	2000	précieuses et or (non monétaire)
27.9	9.8	1.1	17.0	14.7	6.1	2.3	0.0	2.3	14.6	2006	(CTCI 27 + 28 + 68 + 667 + 971)
17.9	5.3	3.5	9.1	6.7	0.7	2.4	0.0	0.5	10.5	1995	Combustibles (CTCI 3)
27.5	5.3	4.7	16.7	14.0	4.2	2.7	0.7	0.7	18.6	2000	
26.3	4.9	5.0	16.4	14.7	10.2	1.7	0.0	1.1	19.2	2006	
38.6	22.6	2.7	13.2	10.6	0.8	2.6	0.0	5.6	11.3	1995	Articles manufacturés
32.5	19.7	2.0	10.7	7.6	0.7	3.1	0.0	5.2	8.3	2000	(CTCI 5 à 8 moins 667 et 68)
36.2	22.1	2.3	11.8	7.1	1.3	4.6	0.0	8.1	8.3	2006	
Parts par principaux groupes de produits (en pourcentage)											
100.0	100.0	100.0	100.0	100.0	100.0	100.0	100.0	100.0	100.0	1995	Total tous produits
100.0	100.0	100.0	100.0	100.0	100.0	100.0	100.0	100.0	100.0	2000	
100.0	100.0	100.0	100.0	100.0	100.0	100.0	100.0	100.0	100.0	2006	
14.1	19.0	3.0	11.7	7.9	8.3	24.2	17.0	33.6	5.6	1995	Produits alimentaires
11.6	18.9	2.0	9.0	5.8	2.7	21.4	2.2	37.1	3.9	2000	(CTCI 0 + 1 + 22 + 4)
8.6	15.5	0.9	6.1	4.2	1.1	13.9	25.7	21.6	2.8	2006	
8.8	6.5	3.5	12.0	14.0	23.1	5.6	8.4	3.5	11.3	1995	Matières premières
4.9	4.6	1.6	6.0	6.7	6.5	3.1	0.1	2.0	5.2	2000	d'origine agricole
3.8	2.2	0.4	5.5	6.4	4.3	1.8	7.2	1.2	3.4	2006	(CTCI 2 - 22 - 27 - 28)
9.5	5.1	3.4	14.9	17.0	16.4	7.7	17.0	7.5	14.1	1995	Minerais, métaux, pierres
6.0	5.9	4.2	6.7	7.7	5.4	2.9	0.0	3.9	6.8	2000	précieuses et or (non monétaire)
11.2	12.0	3.6	12.5	13.4	9.9	8.7	0.4	9.0	10.8	2006	(CTCI 27 + 28 + 68 + 667 + 971)
30.5	20.4	62.2	33.7	32.2	30.8	38.7	18.3	6.9	42.9	1995	Combustibles (CTCI 3)
53.2	29.1	79.2	62.9	65.9	79.8	50.7	95.8	15.3	71.8	2000	
52.6	29.6	83.7	59.7	66.2	81.5	32.1	7.0	20.5	70.7	2006	
36.9	48.9	27.6	27.4	28.5	21.3	23.5	39.3	48.2	25.8	1995	Articles manufacturés
24.0	41.0	13.0	15.3	13.7	5.2	21.9	1.8	40.9	12.1	2000	(CTCI 5 à 8 moins 667 et 68)
21.7	40.2	11.3	12.8	9.6	3.1	26.3	59.1	46.8	9.1	2006	

Sources :
- Données et estimations du secrétariat de la CNUCED sur la base de données Comtrade de ONU DAES et *Direction of Trade statistics* du Fonds Monétaire international

Product group / Destination	Year / Année	World / Monde	Developed economies / Économies développées							Economies in transition / Économies en transition
			Total	Europe Total	EU / UE	Canada	USA / États-Unis	Japan / Japon	Other developed countries / Autres économies développées	
Millions of dollars										
All products	1995	114 358	80 128	58 562	56 311	1 444	10 544	8 253	1 326	1 630
	2000	126 809	77 029	57 387	55 291	1 329	10 146	5 917	2 250	2 531
	2006	282 661	136 160	103 611	100 207	1 872	16 041	10 922	3 714	6 164
Share by destination (percentage)										
All products	1995	100.0	70.1	51.2	49.2	1.3	9.2	7.2	1.2	1.4
	2000	100.0	60.7	45.3	43.6	1.0	8.0	4.7	1.8	2.0
	2006	100.0	48.2	36.7	35.5	0.7	5.7	3.9	1.3	2.2
All food items	1995	100.0	65.5	41.2	39.4	4.3	17.6	0.2	2.3	0.6
(SITC 0 + 1 + 22 + 4)	2000	100.0	60.3	37.6	36.4	4.0	13.8	0.1	4.8	1.3
	2006	100.0	43.4	28.5	27.4	2.3	8.9	0.1	3.5	3.1
Agricultural raw materials	1995	100.0	62.7	48.9	48.3	1.8	8.6	0.9	2.5	6.9
(SITC 2 - 22 - 27 - 28)	2000	100.0	64.6	50.4	49.8	3.0	7.7	1.2	2.3	6.8
	2006	100.0	53.9	44.2	43.8	2.3	4.1	1.6	1.6	8.5
Ores, metals, precious stones	1995	100.0	67.4	49.3	45.4	4.3	3.9	1.0	9.0	3.7
and non-monetary gold	2000	100.0	67.4	46.0	39.6	1.4	2.1	0.7	17.1	5.9
(SITC 27 + 28 + 68 + 667 + 971)	2006	100.0	39.9	25.3	23.9	1.0	3.3	0.4	10.0	4.3
Fuels (SITC 3)	1995	100.0	20.4	15.2	15.1	0.3	4.4	0.0	0.5	1.6
	2000	100.0	13.6	11.8	11.6	0.1	1.3	0.0	0.5	1.2
	2006	100.0	15.6	13.5	13.2	0.1	1.1	0.1	0.8	2.6
Manufactured goods	1995	100.0	76.4	57.4	55.2	0.6	8.1	9.8	0.6	1.3
(SITC 5 to 8 less 667 and 68)	2000	100.0	69.2	53.7	51.7	0.5	8.4	5.8	0.8	2.0
	2006	100.0	57.0	44.2	42.7	0.5	6.5	5.1	0.7	1.8
Share by major product group (percentage)										
All products	1995	100.0	100.0	100.0	100.0	100.0	100.0	100.0	100.0	100.0
	2000	100.0	100.0	100.0	100.0	100.0	100.0	100.0	100.0	100.0
	2006	100.0	100.0	100.0	100.0	100.0	100.0	100.0	100.0	100.0
All food items	1995	16.3	15.2	13.1	13.0	54.9	31.0	0.4	32.8	6.8
(SITC 0 + 1 + 22 + 4)	2000	15.1	15.0	12.5	12.6	57.6	26.0	0.4	40.4	9.5
	2006	11.7	10.5	9.1	9.0	41.4	18.4	0.5	31.1	16.7
Agricultural raw materials	1995	2.9	2.6	2.8	2.9	4.3	2.7	0.4	6.3	14.2
(SITC 2 - 22 - 27 - 28)	2000	2.2	2.3	2.4	2.5	6.3	2.1	0.5	2.8	7.4
	2006	1.6	1.7	1.9	1.9	5.4	1.1	0.7	1.9	6.1
Ores, metals, precious stones	1995	2.4	2.3	2.3	2.2	8.2	1.0	0.3	18.4	6.2
and non-monetary gold	2000	2.4	2.7	2.5	2.2	3.3	0.6	0.4	23.4	7.2
(SITC 27 + 28 + 68 + 667 + 971)	2006	2.8	2.3	1.9	1.9	4.0	1.6	0.3	21.3	5.5
Fuels (SITC 3)	1995	6.9	2.0	2.1	2.1	1.4	3.3	0.0	3.2	8.0
	2000	12.0	2.7	3.1	3.2	1.4	1.9	0.0	3.1	7.5
	2006	15.0	4.8	5.5	5.6	1.4	3.0	0.4	9.4	17.9
Manufactured goods	1995	70.3	76.7	78.8	78.8	30.9	61.4	95.3	38.9	64.6
(SITC 5 to 8 less 667 and 68)	2000	65.2	74.3	77.3	77.3	31.2	68.3	81.4	30.0	66.9
	2006	64.7	76.5	78.1	77.9	45.4	74.1	84.9	35.2	52.9

Sources:
- Data and UNCTAD secretariat estimates based on UN DESA Comtrade and IMF *Direction of Trade statistics* databases

			Developing economies Économies en développement							Year	Destination
				Asia Asie						Année	
Total	Africa Afrique	America Amérique	Total	Eastern, Southern and South-Eastern Asia Asie orientale, méridionale et du Sud-Est	China Chine	Western Asia Asie occidentale	Oceania Océanie	Major petroleum exporters Principaux exportateurs de pétrole	Major exporters of manufactures Principaux exportateurs d'articles manufacturés		Groupes de produits
Millions de dollars											
30 727	9 117	3 023	18 576	14 732	2 258	3 845	12	5 979	14 705	1995	**Total tous produits**
45 271	16 398	2 940	25 883	17 216	4 021	8 667	50	12 100	16 505	2000	
131 927	38 436	10 950	82 476	58 409	22 328	24 067	89	32 194	61 727	2006	
Parts par destinations (en pourcentage)											
26.9	**8.0**	**2.6**	**16.2**	**12.9**	**2.0**	**3.4**	**0.0**	**5.2**	**12.9**	1995	**Total tous produits**
35.7	**12.9**	**2.3**	**20.4**	**13.6**	**3.2**	**6.8**	**0.0**	**9.5**	**13.0**	2000	
46.7	**13.6**	**3.9**	**29.2**	**20.7**	**7.9**	**8.5**	**0.0**	**11.4**	**21.8**	2006	
33.0	8.5	9.8	14.6	12.6	1.9	2.1	0.0	1.3	15.4	1995	Produits alimentaires
37.9	14.5	8.9	14.3	11.9	2.7	2.4	0.2	1.9	13.5	2000	(CTCI 0 + 1 + 22 + 4)
52.2	16.5	16.7	18.9	15.9	2.1	3.1	0.0	2.6	20.8	2006	
29.2	13.4	3.8	12.1	9.2	0.3	2.8	0.0	4.0	10.0	1995	Matières premières
28.5	15.8	3.1	9.6	7.0	0.5	2.6	0.0	3.7	7.5	2000	d'origine agricole
34.5	16.4	3.0	15.1	12.1	1.8	2.9	0.0	3.3	11.5	2006	(CTCI 2 - 22 - 27 - 28)
28.6	15.5	2.6	10.6	3.3	1.3	7.3	0.0	6.3	5.9	1995	Minerais, métaux, pierres
26.5	13.8	2.8	9.8	4.3	1.3	5.5	0.1	5.4	6.3	2000	précieuses et or (non monétaire)
53.8	33.5	6.4	13.9	8.9	3.7	5.0	0.0	5.7	14.4	2006	(CTCI 27 + 28 + 68 + 667 + 971)
69.6	28.4	1.7	39.6	19.6	0.2	20.0	0.0	54.7	1.5	1995	Combustibles (CTCI 3)
81.5	33.8	0.5	47.3	11.8	0.5	35.5	0.0	62.8	1.1	2000	
78.7	29.7	2.7	46.3	14.9	0.4	31.4	0.0	57.5	8.4	2006	
21.1	5.4	1.1	14.6	12.6	2.3	2.0	0.0	1.4	13.6	1995	Articles manufacturés
28.2	9.1	1.1	18.0	15.0	4.0	3.0	0.0	2.3	15.5	2000	(CTCI 5 à 8 moins 667 et 68)
39.4	9.0	1.7	28.7	23.9	11.5	4.8	0.0	3.4	25.7	2006	
Parts par principaux groupes de produits (en pourcentage)											
100.0	**100.0**	**100.0**	**100.0**	**100.0**	**100.0**	**100.0**	**100.0**	**100.0**	**100.0**	1995	**Total tous produits**
100.0	**100.0**	**100.0**	**100.0**	**100.0**	**100.0**	**100.0**	**100.0**	**100.0**	**100.0**	2000	
100.0	**100.0**	**100.0**	**100.0**	**100.0**	**100.0**	**100.0**	**100.0**	**100.0**	**100.0**	2006	
20.0	17.3	60.7	14.7	15.9	15.9	10.0	17.4	3.9	19.5	1995	Produits alimentaires
16.0	16.9	57.7	10.6	13.2	13.0	5.3	75.6	2.9	15.6	2000	(CTCI 0 + 1 + 22 + 4)
13.1	14.2	50.6	7.6	9.0	3.0	4.2	6.4	2.6	11.2	2006	
3.2	4.9	4.2	2.2	2.1	0.4	2.5	0.3	2.2	2.3	1995	Matières premières
1.7	2.6	2.9	1.0	1.1	0.4	0.8	0.2	0.9	1.2	2000	d'origine agricole
1.2	1.9	1.2	0.8	0.9	0.4	0.5	0.8	0.4	0.8	2006	(CTCI 2 - 22 - 27 - 28)
2.5	4.6	2.3	1.5	0.6	1.5	5.1	1.1	2.9	1.1	1995	Minerais, métaux, pierres
1.8	2.6	2.9	1.2	0.8	1.0	2.0	3.8	1.4	1.2	2000	précieuses et or (non monétaire)
3.2	6.9	4.6	1.3	1.2	1.3	1.6	0.1	1.4	1.8	2006	(CTCI 27 + 28 + 68 + 667 + 971)
18.0	24.7	4.4	16.9	10.6	0.8	41.1	0.0	72.5	0.8	1995	Combustibles (CTCI 3)
27.5	31.4	2.4	27.9	10.4	2.0	62.6	0.0	79.2	1.1	2000	
25.3	32.7	10.5	23.8	10.8	0.7	55.2	1.4	75.7	5.7	2006	
55.2	47.9	28.1	63.2	68.9	81.1	41.2	80.9	18.4	74.3	1995	Articles manufacturés
51.6	45.8	31.8	57.6	72.0	83.3	29.1	20.2	15.6	77.9	2000	(CTCI 5 à 8 moins 667 et 68)
54.6	42.7	28.5	63.6	75.0	94.4	36.2	64.1	19.6	76.0	2006	

Sources :
- Données et estimations du secrétariat de la CNUCED sur la base de données Comtrade de ONU DAES et *Direction of Trade statistics* du Fonds Monétaire international

Destination / Product group	Year / Année	World / Monde	Developed economies / Économies développées Total	Europe Total	Europe EU / UE	Canada	USA / États-Unis	Japan / Japon	Other developed countries / Autres économies développées	Economies in transition / Économies en transition
Millions of dollars										
All products	1995	225 708	157 632	40 338	38 088	3 895	103 433	8 971	996	1 583
	2000	352 408	267 262	44 397	41 669	6 036	207 639	7 552	1 639	1 319
	2006	667 959	450 721	98 449	90 979	13 558	321 744	14 539	2 431	6 700
Share by destination (percentage)										
All products	1995	100.0	69.8	17.9	16.9	1.7	45.8	4.0	0.4	0.7
	2000	100.0	75.8	12.6	11.8	1.7	58.9	2.1	0.5	0.4
	2006	100.0	67.5	14.7	13.6	2.0	48.2	2.2	0.4	1.0
All food items	1995	100.0	64.5	33.8	32.9	0.9	23.7	5.3	0.8	2.7
(SITC 0 + 1 + 22 + 4)	2000	100.0	63.9	29.8	28.8	1.4	27.4	4.4	0.9	2.2
	2006	100.0	56.0	27.8	27.2	1.5	22.5	3.5	0.8	5.6
Agricultural raw materials	1995	100.0	66.4	30.5	29.0	0.4	25.2	10.1	0.2	0.1
(SITC 2 - 22 - 27 - 28)	2000	100.0	71.8	30.2	29.0	0.6	32.4	8.3	0.3	0.2
	2006	100.0	65.8	26.3	24.9	0.8	32.4	5.7	0.5	1.0
Ores, metals, precious stones	1995	100.0	73.9	34.9	31.0	2.7	19.9	16.1	0.3	0.4
and non-monetary gold	2000	100.0	72.2	34.9	29.3	3.6	21.5	12.0	0.2	0.3
(SITC 27 + 28 + 68 + 667 + 971)	2006	100.0	63.9	30.6	25.6	5.1	18.3	9.8	0.1	0.2
Fuels (SITC 3)	1995	100.0	70.5	8.7	8.7	1.2	58.8	1.5	0.3	0.0
	2000	100.0	71.2	6.4	6.4	1.3	62.7	0.6	0.2	0.0
	2006	100.0	67.2	9.2	7.9	1.0	56.6	0.1	0.2	0.0
Manufactured goods	1995	100.0	71.9	8.7	8.1	2.2	59.5	1.1	0.4	0.1
(SITC 5 to 8 less 667 and 68)	2000	100.0	81.7	6.6	6.2	1.8	72.3	0.6	0.5	0.0
	2006	100.0	73.2	8.5	8.3	1.9	62.0	0.5	0.4	0.2
Share by major product group (percentage)										
All products	1995	100.0	100.0	100.0	100.0	100.0	100.0	100.0	100.0	100.0
	2000	100.0	100.0	100.0	100.0	100.0	100.0	100.0	100.0	100.0
	2006	100.0	100.0	100.0	100.0	100.0	100.0	100.0	100.0	100.0
All food items	1995	22.5	20.7	42.5	43.8	12.3	11.6	29.8	39.4	88.0
(SITC 0 + 1 + 22 + 4)	2000	15.1	12.8	35.8	36.9	12.0	7.0	31.3	30.7	88.8
	2006	15.2	12.6	28.7	30.4	10.9	7.1	24.6	32.3	85.2
Agricultural raw materials	1995	3.7	3.6	6.4	6.4	0.9	2.1	9.5	1.7	0.3
(SITC 2 - 22 - 27 - 28)	2000	2.2	2.1	5.3	5.5	0.8	1.2	8.6	1.5	1.3
	2006	1.9	1.9	3.4	3.5	0.7	1.3	5.1	2.5	2.0
Ores, metals, precious stones	1995	10.3	10.9	20.0	18.9	16.0	4.5	41.6	6.5	6.3
and non-monetary gold	2000	7.1	6.8	19.8	17.7	14.8	2.6	39.8	3.1	6.3
(SITC 27 + 28 + 68 + 667 + 971)	2006	13.0	12.3	27.0	24.4	32.8	4.9	58.7	3.9	2.9
Fuels (SITC 3)	1995	14.6	14.7	7.1	7.5	10.1	18.7	5.4	9.3	0.5
	2000	18.0	16.9	9.2	9.7	14.1	19.2	4.7	8.6	0.3
	2006	22.4	22.3	13.9	13.0	10.9	26.3	1.1	14.6	0.6
Manufactured goods	1995	48.4	49.8	23.6	23.1	60.6	62.8	13.5	42.8	4.8
(SITC 5 to 8 less 667 and 68)	2000	56.9	61.3	29.7	30.1	58.2	69.9	15.4	55.9	3.3
	2006	46.6	50.6	26.8	28.5	44.5	60.0	10.5	46.1	9.4

Sources:
- Data and UNCTAD secretariat estimates based on UN DESA Comtrade and IMF *Direction of Trade statistics* databases

Total	Africa / Afrique	America / Amérique	Asia / Asie Total	Eastern, Southern and South-Eastern Asia / Asie orientale, méridionale et du Sud-Est	China / Chine	Western Asia / Asie occidentale	Oceania / Océanie	Major petroleum exporters / Principaux exportateurs de pétrole	Major exporters of manufactures / Principaux exportateurs d'articles manufacturés	Year / Année	Destination / Groupes de produits
Millions de dollars											
65 157	2 966	46 507	15 655	13 825	2 621	1 830	29	6 974	24 158	1995	**Total tous produits**
79 852	2 867	61 098	15 872	13 507	3 776	2 365	15	9 218	27 611	2000	
205 380	14 164	133 333	57 819	50 577	22 888	7 243	63	27 809	75 892	2006	
Parts par destinations (en pourcentage)											
28.9	1.3	20.6	6.9	6.1	1.2	0.8	0.0	3.1	10.7	1995	**Total tous produits**
22.7	0.8	17.3	4.5	3.8	1.1	0.7	0.0	2.6	7.8	2000	
30.7	2.1	20.0	8.7	7.6	3.4	1.1	0.0	4.2	11.4	2006	
32.5	3.6	17.4	11.6	9.6	2.9	1.9	0.0	5.1	13.5	1995	Produits alimentaires
33.3	3.0	18.6	11.7	9.3	3.1	2.5	0.0	5.5	13.4	2000	(CTCI 0 + 1 + 22 + 4)
38.0	5.7	14.7	17.6	13.9	5.8	3.7	0.0	9.0	15.3	2006	
33.4	1.1	15.3	17.1	16.0	3.3	1.1	0.0	3.1	18.7	1995	Matières premières
27.9	0.8	13.5	13.5	12.5	4.6	1.0	0.0	2.3	15.9	2000	d'origine agricole
33.1	0.8	12.2	20.1	18.7	9.7	1.4	0.0	2.4	20.8	2006	(CTCI 2 - 22 - 27 - 28)
24.9	0.7	10.7	13.5	12.7	2.0	0.8	0.0	2.1	16.9	1995	Minerais, métaux, pierres
27.3	1.1	11.3	14.9	13.1	4.4	1.8	0.0	2.8	18.4	2000	précieuses et or (non monétaire)
35.6	0.9	10.8	24.0	22.9	11.5	1.1	0.0	1.9	28.8	2006	(CTCI 27 + 28 + 68 + 667 + 971)
28.4	0.3	26.8	1.3	1.3	0.0	0.0	0.0	0.8	9.2	1995	Combustibles (CTCI 3)
26.1	0.1	24.7	1.3	1.2	0.1	0.1	0.0	1.9	6.1	2000	
32.5	2.3	27.5	2.7	2.6	1.4	0.1	0.0	1.0	6.1	2006	
28.0	0.7	22.9	4.4	3.9	0.4	0.5	0.0	3.1	8.0	1995	Articles manufacturés
18.1	0.4	15.7	2.0	1.7	0.3	0.2	0.0	2.1	5.4	2000	(CTCI 5 à 8 moins 667 et 68)
26.5	1.2	21.2	4.0	3.3	1.2	0.7	0.0	4.9	7.5	2006	
Parts par principaux groupes de produits (en pourcentage)											
100.0	100.0	100.0	100.0	100.0	100.0	100.0	100.0	100.0	100.0	1995	**Total tous produits**
100.0	100.0	100.0	100.0	100.0	100.0	100.0	100.0	100.0	100.0	2000	
100.0	100.0	100.0	100.0	100.0	100.0	100.0	100.0	100.0	100.0	2006	
25.3	60.7	19.0	37.4	35.3	55.6	53.3	30.0	37.3	28.2	1995	Produits alimentaires
22.2	54.9	16.2	39.5	36.6	43.1	56.2	73.7	31.8	25.8	2000	(CTCI 0 + 1 + 22 + 4)
18.8	41.3	11.2	30.9	28.0	25.9	51.6	30.2	33.0	20.6	2006	
4.3	3.0	2.8	9.2	9.8	10.6	5.1	0.3	3.7	6.6	1995	Matières premières
2.7	2.2	1.7	6.7	7.3	9.5	3.4	0.3	1.9	4.5	2000	d'origine agricole
2.1	0.7	1.2	4.4	4.7	5.4	2.5	1.3	1.1	3.5	2006	(CTCI 2 - 22 - 27 - 28)
8.9	5.3	5.3	20.1	21.4	17.8	10.1	0.1	7.1	16.2	1995	Minerais, métaux, pierres
8.6	9.3	4.6	23.6	24.3	29.2	19.2	0.0	7.5	16.7	2000	précieuses et or (non monétaire)
15.1	5.7	7.0	36.0	39.3	43.6	12.9	0.0	6.0	33.0	2006	(CTCI 27 + 28 + 68 + 667 + 971)
14.4	3.5	19.0	2.7	3.0	0.1	0.8	3.1	3.8	12.6	1995	Combustibles (CTCI 3)
20.7	3.2	25.6	5.2	5.8	1.3	1.8	0.6	13.2	14.0	2000	
23.7	24.8	30.8	7.1	7.8	9.1	2.1	23.1	5.3	12.0	2006	
46.9	27.4	53.7	30.5	30.4	15.9	30.6	66.5	48.0	36.3	1995	Articles manufacturés
45.6	30.1	51.7	25.0	26.0	16.9	19.4	25.3	45.3	38.9	2000	(CTCI 5 à 8 moins 667 et 68)
40.2	27.5	49.6	21.6	20.2	15.9	30.9	44.8	54.4	30.9	2006	

Sources :
- Données et estimations du secrétariat de la CNUCED sur la base de données Comtrade de ONU DAES et *Direction of Trade statistics* du Fonds Monétaire international

Destination / Product group	Year / Année	World / Monde	Developed economies / Économies développées								Economies in transition / Économies en transition
			Total	Europe		Canada	USA / États-Unis	Japan / Japon	Other developed countries / Autres économies développées		
				Total	EU / UE						

Millions of dollars

All products	1995	238 185	169 428	47 359	44 389	5 245	102 469	12 737	1 618	1 231
	2000	367 616	262 517	55 180	52 202	8 021	182 032	14 831	2 453	1 940
	2006	611 054	340 274	89 576	84 307	12 187	206 320	27 685	4 506	7 286

Share by destination (percentage)

All products	1995	100.0	71.1	19.9	18.6	2.2	43.0	5.3	0.7	0.5
	2000	100.0	71.4	15.0	14.2	2.2	49.5	4.0	0.7	0.5
	2006	100.0	55.7	14.7	13.8	2.0	33.8	4.5	0.7	1.2
All food items	1995	100.0	58.0	15.1	13.9	5.2	35.6	0.1	2.0	0.1
(SITC 0 + 1 + 22 + 4)	2000	100.0	59.5	11.6	10.9	5.8	40.1	0.0	2.0	0.1
	2006	100.0	56.8	8.9	8.2	5.2	40.9	0.0	1.8	0.1
Agricultural raw materials	1995	100.0	60.6	7.7	7.4	3.5	46.9	0.5	2.1	1.7
(SITC 2 - 22 - 27 - 28)	2000	100.0	68.1	8.3	8.0	2.4	55.3	0.7	1.4	0.7
	2006	100.0	61.5	8.9	8.7	2.9	48.3	0.5	0.9	0.6
Ores, metals, precious stones	1995	100.0	53.9	11.4	10.3	5.6	34.5	0.8	1.6	0.3
and non-monetary gold	2000	100.0	55.8	9.0	8.7	3.9	41.2	0.6	1.1	2.3
(SITC 27 + 28 + 68 + 667 + 971)	2006	100.0	41.2	7.3	6.9	2.8	30.0	0.4	0.6	0.9
Fuels (SITC 3)	1995	100.0	30.1	6.6	6.4	1.4	20.0	0.3	1.8	2.7
	2000	100.0	25.6	3.9	3.5	0.5	19.8	0.2	1.1	0.7
	2006	100.0	30.9	5.8	5.1	1.0	22.1	0.3	1.8	4.0
Manufactured goods	1995	100.0	76.7	22.7	21.3	1.7	45.7	6.2	0.4	0.4
(SITC 5 to 8 less 667 and 68)	2000	100.0	77.9	16.8	15.9	2.0	53.7	4.9	0.5	0.5
	2006	100.0	61.0	17.3	16.3	1.9	35.5	5.9	0.5	0.8

Share by major product group (percentage)

All products	1995	100.0	100.0	100.0	100.0	100.0	100.0	100.0	100.0	100.0
	2000	100.0	100.0	100.0	100.0	100.0	100.0	100.0	100.0	100.0
	2006	100.0	100.0	100.0	100.0	100.0	100.0	100.0	100.0	100.0
All food items	1995	9.5	7.7	7.2	7.1	22.5	7.8	0.1	27.9	1.3
(SITC 0 + 1 + 22 + 4)	2000	7.3	6.1	5.7	5.6	19.5	5.9	0.1	21.9	1.2
	2006	6.7	6.9	4.1	4.0	17.6	8.1	0.1	16.4	0.6
Agricultural raw materials	1995	2.3	2.0	0.9	0.9	3.7	2.5	0.2	7.2	7.5
(SITC 2 - 22 - 27 - 28)	2000	1.6	1.5	0.9	0.9	1.8	1.8	0.3	3.2	2.2
	2006	1.3	1.4	0.8	0.8	1.9	1.8	0.1	1.5	0.6
Ores, metals, precious stones	1995	2.5	1.9	1.4	1.4	6.3	2.0	0.4	5.9	1.3
and non-monetary gold	2000	2.2	1.7	1.3	1.3	3.9	1.8	0.4	3.5	9.6
(SITC 27 + 28 + 68 + 667 + 971)	2006	3.1	2.3	1.5	1.6	4.4	2.8	0.3	2.7	2.3
Fuels (SITC 3)	1995	7.0	2.9	2.3	2.4	4.5	3.2	0.4	18.5	35.8
	2000	8.0	2.9	2.1	2.0	1.9	3.2	0.4	13.8	11.4
	2006	12.2	6.8	4.8	4.5	5.9	8.0	0.8	30.4	41.2
Manufactured goods	1995	76.2	82.1	86.9	86.9	59.2	80.9	88.6	40.4	54.1
(SITC 5 to 8 less 667 and 68)	2000	79.4	86.7	89.1	89.2	72.7	86.2	95.6	57.3	75.2
	2006	74.7	81.8	88.1	88.3	70.0	78.5	97.1	47.3	52.4

Sources:
- Data and UNCTAD secretariat estimates based on UN DESA Comtrade and IMF *Direction of Trade statistics* databases

2.2.F Structure des importations par partenaires et groupes de produits
Économies en développement : Amérique

Total	Africa / Afrique	America / Amérique	Asia / Asie — Total	Eastern, Southern and South-Eastern Asia / Asie orientale, méridionale et du Sud-Est	China / Chine	Western Asia / Asie occidentale	Oceania / Océanie	Major petroleum exporters / Principaux exportateurs de pétrole	Major exporters of manufactures / Principaux exportateurs d'articles manufacturés	Year / Année	Destination / Groupes de produits
Millions de dollars											
65 890	2 525	45 110	18 230	16 253	2 691	1 977	24	10 761	29 514	1995	**Total tous produits**
100 434	5 031	63 405	31 990	29 968	8 443	2 022	8	17 274	48 270	2000	
252 672	13 383	129 111	110 137	105 951	51 400	4 186	41	35 437	150 062	2006	
Parts par destinations (en pourcentage)											
27.7	1.1	18.9	7.7	6.8	1.1	0.8	0.0	4.5	12.4	1995	**Total tous produits**
27.3	1.4	17.2	8.7	8.2	2.3	0.6	0.0	4.7	13.1	2000	
41.4	2.2	21.1	18.0	17.3	8.4	0.7	0.0	5.8	24.6	2006	
41.5	0.4	38.8	2.3	2.1	0.4	0.2	0.0	3.3	6.5	1995	Produits alimentaires
40.0	0.4	37.2	2.4	2.2	0.7	0.2	0.0	3.1	7.1	2000	(CTCI 0 + 1 + 22 + 4)
40.7	0.4	36.4	3.9	3.6	1.3	0.2	0.1	2.4	7.6	2006	
37.2	2.5	25.6	9.2	9.1	0.4	0.1	0.0	0.9	11.9	1995	Matières premières
30.9	3.2	20.7	7.0	6.9	1.1	0.1	0.0	1.0	10.6	2000	d'origine agricole
37.6	1.2	22.8	13.6	13.4	1.6	0.2	0.0	0.9	16.6	2006	(CTCI 2 - 22 - 27 - 28)
45.7	2.9	41.1	1.6	1.5	0.4	0.1	0.0	5.0	10.6	1995	Minerais, métaux, pierres
41.3	2.7	36.4	2.2	2.1	0.9	0.1	0.0	3.9	12.2	2000	précieuses et or (non monétaire)
57.8	1.8	52.0	3.9	3.5	1.8	0.4	0.0	4.1	14.2	2006	(CTCI 27 + 28 + 68 + 667 + 971)
66.9	8.8	44.5	13.6	3.0	0.9	10.6	0.0	42.3	5.0	1995	Combustibles (CTCI 3)
73.2	13.0	52.8	7.5	1.9	0.7	5.5	0.0	45.7	3.7	2000	
64.6	15.3	41.4	7.8	3.6	0.4	4.2	0.0	37.9	8.4	2006	
22.3	0.4	13.8	8.1	8.0	1.3	0.1	0.0	1.4	14.2	1995	Articles manufacturés
20.8	0.2	11.4	9.2	9.1	2.7	0.1	0.0	0.9	14.3	2000	(CTCI 5 à 8 moins 667 et 68)
37.5	0.3	15.5	21.8	21.6	10.8	0.1	0.0	1.1	29.5	2006	
Parts par principaux groupes de produits (en pourcentage)											
100.0	100.0	100.0	100.0	100.0	100.0	100.0	100.0	100.0	100.0	1995	**Total tous produits**
100.0	100.0	100.0	100.0	100.0	100.0	100.0	100.0	100.0	100.0	2000	
100.0	100.0	100.0	100.0	100.0	100.0	100.0	100.0	100.0	100.0	2006	
14.2	3.3	19.4	2.9	2.9	3.2	2.4	4.1	7.0	5.0	1995	Produits alimentaires
10.8	2.3	15.8	2.0	1.9	2.2	3.2	13.5	4.8	4.0	2000	(CTCI 0 + 1 + 22 + 4)
6.6	1.1	11.6	1.4	1.4	1.0	2.3	52.3	2.8	2.1	2006	
3.1	5.4	3.1	2.8	3.1	0.8	0.2	0.3	0.5	2.2	1995	Matières premières
1.8	3.8	1.9	1.3	1.3	0.8	0.1	1.2	0.3	1.3	2000	d'origine agricole
1.2	0.7	1.4	1.0	1.0	0.2	0.4	1.0	0.2	0.9	2006	(CTCI 2 - 22 - 27 - 28)
4.1	6.9	5.4	0.5	0.6	0.9	0.3	0.1	2.7	2.1	1995	Minerais, métaux, pierres
3.3	4.3	4.6	0.6	0.6	0.8	0.6	0.0	1.8	2.0	2000	précieuses et or (non monétaire)
4.3	2.6	7.6	0.7	0.6	0.7	1.8	0.1	2.2	1.8	2006	(CTCI 27 + 28 + 68 + 667 + 971)
16.8	57.9	16.3	12.3	3.0	5.5	88.6	0.0	65.1	2.8	1995	Combustibles (CTCI 3)
21.5	76.2	24.6	6.9	1.9	2.6	80.8	0.0	78.1	2.3	2000	
19.0	85.1	23.9	5.3	2.5	0.6	75.2	0.0	79.6	4.2	2006	
61.3	26.5	55.4	80.7	89.5	89.3	8.4	95.4	24.1	87.2	1995	Articles manufacturés
60.6	13.4	52.7	83.6	88.2	92.1	15.2	85.2	14.8	86.7	2000	(CTCI 5 à 8 moins 667 et 68)
67.8	10.5	54.6	90.2	93.1	96.2	16.3	41.6	14.8	89.8	2006	

Sources :
- Données et estimations du secrétariat de la CNUCED sur la base de données Comtrade de ONU DAES et *Direction of Trade statistics* du Fonds Monétaire international

Destination / Product group	Year / Année	World / Monde	Developed economies / Économies développées							Economies in transition / Économies en transition
			Total	Europe Total	Europe EU / UE (Total)	Canada	USA / États-Unis	Japan / Japon	Other developed countries / Autres économies développées	
Millions of dollars										
All products	1995	1 083 149	544 419	177 754	171 637	11 157	194 080	142 673	18 755	11 279
	2000	1 517 430	800 258	266 571	252 131	15 664	301 674	186 620	29 730	10 632
	2006	3 455 153	1 574 073	591 653	566 477	34 931	521 747	351 958	73 784	54 172
Share by destination (percentage)										
All products	1995	100.0	50.3	16.4	15.8	1.0	17.9	13.2	1.7	1.0
	2000	100.0	52.7	17.6	16.6	1.0	19.9	12.3	2.0	0.7
	2006	100.0	45.6	17.1	16.4	1.0	15.1	10.2	2.1	1.6
All food items (SITC 0 + 1 + 22 + 4)	1995	100.0	46.9	14.9	14.2	0.8	7.5	22.3	1.4	3.4
	2000	100.0	48.0	14.4	13.8	1.1	10.6	20.2	1.7	2.5
	2006	100.0	42.3	15.7	15.3	1.1	10.2	13.3	2.0	3.6
Agricultural raw materials (SITC 2 - 22 - 27 - 28)	1995	100.0	44.7	15.9	15.7	0.9	9.9	16.7	1.3	0.4
	2000	100.0	40.9	16.5	16.3	0.7	8.4	14.0	1.3	0.4
	2006	100.0	37.8	15.1	15.0	1.2	9.4	10.9	1.1	0.9
Ores, metals, precious stones and non-monetary gold (SITC 27 + 28 + 68 + 667 + 971)	1995	100.0	41.3	12.4	11.5	0.3	7.8	18.9	1.9	1.4
	2000	100.0	44.6	16.0	13.5	0.4	11.3	12.2	4.8	0.5
	2006	100.0	34.6	15.8	12.6	0.5	5.7	8.7	3.9	0.5
Fuels (SITC 3)	1995	100.0	42.7	9.5	9.5	0.4	6.4	25.2	1.3	0.1
	2000	100.0	48.7	14.5	11.9	0.3	11.3	21.2	1.4	0.1
	2006	100.0	44.9	10.7	9.5	0.5	9.1	22.1	2.5	0.1
Manufactured goods (SITC 5 to 8 less 667 and 68)	1995	100.0	52.4	18.0	17.3	1.2	21.5	9.9	1.9	1.0
	2000	100.0	54.5	18.5	18.0	1.2	23.0	9.8	2.0	0.7
	2006	100.0	46.8	18.5	18.0	1.2	17.9	7.2	2.0	1.8
Share by major product group (percentage)										
All products	1995	100.0	100.0	100.0	100.0	100.0	100.0	100.0	100.0	100.0
	2000	100.0	100.0	100.0	100.0	100.0	100.0	100.0	100.0	100.0
	2006	100.0	100.0	100.0	100.0	100.0	100.0	100.0	100.0	100.0
All food items (SITC 0 + 1 + 22 + 4)	1995	6.7	6.2	6.1	6.0	5.2	2.8	11.3	5.5	21.8
	2000	4.5	4.1	3.6	3.7	4.7	2.4	7.3	4.0	15.8
	2006	3.5	3.3	3.2	3.3	3.9	2.4	4.6	3.4	8.0
Agricultural raw materials (SITC 2 - 22 - 27 - 28)	1995	2.2	1.9	2.1	2.2	1.8	1.2	2.8	1.6	0.8
	2000	1.2	1.0	1.2	1.2	0.9	0.5	1.4	0.8	0.7
	2006	1.1	0.9	1.0	1.0	1.3	0.7	1.2	0.6	0.6
Ores, metals, precious stones and non-monetary gold (SITC 27 + 28 + 68 + 667 + 971)	1995	3.1	2.5	2.3	2.2	0.8	1.3	4.4	3.4	4.1
	2000	2.5	2.1	2.3	2.0	1.0	1.4	2.5	6.1	1.7
	2006	3.6	2.8	3.4	2.8	1.8	1.4	3.1	6.7	1.2
Fuels (SITC 3)	1995	13.3	11.3	7.7	8.0	5.5	4.7	25.5	9.7	1.2
	2000	17.1	15.8	14.1	12.2	4.6	9.7	29.5	12.5	3.5
	2006	18.7	18.4	11.7	10.8	10.1	11.2	40.6	21.9	0.7
Manufactured goods (SITC 5 to 8 less 667 and 68)	1995	73.5	76.6	80.5	80.4	85.8	88.1	55.2	78.9	71.6
	2000	74.0	76.5	77.9	80.0	88.5	85.6	59.0	75.7	77.6
	2006	70.4	72.3	76.0	77.4	82.1	83.6	50.0	64.9	82.6

Sources:
- Data and UNCTAD secretariat estimates based on UN DESA Comtrade and IMF *Direction of Trade statistics* databases

2.2.G Structure des exportations par partenaires et groupes de produits
Économies en développement : Asie

Total	Africa / Afrique	America / Amérique	Asia / Asie Total	Eastern, Southern and South-Eastern Asia / Asie orientale, méridionale et du Sud-Est	China / Chine	Western Asia / Asie occidentale	Oceania / Océanie	Major petroleum exporters / Principaux exportateurs de pétrole	Major exporters of manufactures / Principaux exportateurs d'articles manufacturés	Year / Année	Destination / Groupes de produits
Millions de dollars											
476 212	19 220	23 478	432 247	398 956	78 677	33 291	1 267	35 780	369 665	1995	Total tous produits
679 165	29 062	35 812	611 979	567 143	116 016	44 836	2 311	44 585	536 871	2000	
1 751 341	90 053	86 917	1 568 525	1 417 575	369 575	150 950	5 845	168 411	1 308 662	2006	
Parts par destinations (en pourcentage)											
44.0	1.8	2.2	39.9	36.8	7.3	3.1	0.1	3.3	34.1	1995	Total tous produits
44.8	1.9	2.4	40.3	37.4	7.6	3.0	0.2	2.9	35.4	2000	
50.7	2.6	2.5	45.4	41.0	10.7	4.4	0.2	4.9	37.9	2006	
49.4	3.4	0.6	45.2	37.7	7.0	7.6	0.1	8.1	29.1	1995	Produits alimentaires
49.0	3.8	0.8	44.2	35.3	5.9	8.9	0.1	9.1	28.0	2000	(CTCI 0 + 1 + 22 + 4)
53.7	5.5	1.3	46.7	35.4	5.6	11.3	0.2	12.5	25.8	2006	
54.8	1.8	2.0	51.0	48.7	13.2	2.3	0.0	2.1	45.9	1995	Matières premières
58.4	1.3	1.6	55.5	52.8	21.3	2.7	0.0	2.0	48.6	2000	d'origine agricole
61.1	1.6	2.7	56.7	52.9	25.4	3.8	0.0	3.3	48.0	2006	(CTCI 2 - 22 - 27 - 28)
57.1	0.5	0.2	56.3	53.2	9.2	3.1	0.0	3.0	50.4	1995	Minerais, métaux, pierres
54.8	0.6	0.4	53.7	49.7	10.3	4.0	0.0	3.8	47.7	2000	précieuses et or (non monétaire)
64.5	1.0	0.4	63.1	57.4	16.1	5.8	0.0	5.6	54.5	2006	(CTCI 27 + 28 + 68 + 667 + 971)
23.5	0.4	0.2	22.6	21.6	3.3	1.0	0.2	0.5	20.2	1995	Combustibles (CTCI 3)
41.9	2.4	1.0	38.3	36.6	4.1	1.6	0.3	0.5	35.1	2000	
48.6	2.6	0.9	44.7	41.2	5.0	3.5	0.3	3.0	36.4	2006	
46.4	1.9	2.7	41.6	38.5	7.8	3.1	0.1	3.5	36.2	1995	Articles manufacturés
44.5	1.7	2.8	39.9	37.0	8.3	2.8	0.1	3.1	35.3	2000	(CTCI 5 à 8 moins 667 et 68)
51.1	2.5	3.0	45.5	41.3	12.3	4.2	0.1	4.9	38.9	2006	
Parts par principaux groupes de produits (en pourcentage)											
100.0	100.0	100.0	100.0	100.0	100.0	100.0	100.0	100.0	100.0	1995	Total tous produits
100.0	100.0	100.0	100.0	100.0	100.0	100.0	100.0	100.0	100.0	2000	
100.0	100.0	100.0	100.0	100.0	100.0	100.0	100.0	100.0	100.0	2006	
7.5	12.7	2.0	7.6	6.8	6.5	16.4	7.4	16.5	5.7	1995	Produits alimentaires
4.9	8.9	1.6	4.9	4.2	3.5	13.4	4.3	13.9	3.5	2000	(CTCI 0 + 1 + 22 + 4)
3.7	7.4	1.9	3.6	3.0	1.8	9.2	4.4	9.1	2.4	2006	
2.7	2.2	2.0	2.8	2.9	4.0	1.6	0.3	1.4	2.9	1995	Matières premières
1.6	0.8	0.8	1.7	1.8	3.5	1.1	0.2	0.9	1.7	2000	d'origine agricole
1.3	0.7	1.1	1.4	1.4	2.6	1.0	0.1	0.7	1.4	2006	(CTCI 2 - 22 - 27 - 28)
4.0	0.9	0.3	4.3	4.4	3.9	3.1	0.3	2.8	4.5	1995	Minerais, métaux, pierres
3.1	0.8	0.4	3.3	3.3	3.4	3.4	0.3	3.2	3.4	2000	précieuses et or (non monétaire)
4.6	1.3	0.6	5.1	5.1	5.5	4.8	0.2	4.2	5.2	2006	(CTCI 27 + 28 + 68 + 667 + 971)
7.1	3.1	1.5	7.6	7.8	6.0	4.5	25.6	1.9	7.9	1995	Combustibles (CTCI 3)
16.0	21.7	7.2	16.2	16.8	9.2	9.4	28.6	2.8	17.0	2000	
17.9	18.7	6.9	18.4	18.8	8.7	15.1	34.0	11.7	18.0	2006	
77.5	79.4	92.1	76.7	76.9	78.9	73.9	63.3	76.8	77.9	1995	Articles manufacturés
73.6	66.3	86.9	73.2	73.4	80.2	71.3	63.1	77.9	73.9	2000	(CTCI 5 à 8 moins 667 et 68)
71.0	66.6	84.8	70.6	70.9	81.1	67.0	52.3	70.9	72.4	2006	

Sources :
- Données et estimations du secrétariat de la CNUCED sur la base de données Comtrade de ONU DAES et *Direction of Trade statistics* du Fonds Monétaire international

Destination / Product group	Year / Année	World / Monde	Developed economies / Économies développées Total	Europe Total	Europe EU / UE	Canada	USA / États-Unis	Japan / Japon	Other developed countries / Autres économies développées	Economies in transition / Économies en transition
Millions of dollars										
All products	1995	1 121 160	635 920	218 504	200 372	13 030	153 717	221 395	29 273	19 834
	2000	1 359 101	661 643	224 478	204 400	13 147	162 427	222 738	38 853	24 194
	2006	2 990 994	1 141 082	441 033	399 165	21 780	239 485	359 791	78 994	71 127
Share by destination (percentage)										
All products	1995	100.0	56.7	19.5	17.9	1.2	13.7	19.7	2.6	1.8
	2000	100.0	48.7	16.5	15.0	1.0	12.0	16.4	2.9	1.8
	2006	100.0	38.2	14.7	13.3	0.7	8.0	12.0	2.6	2.4
All food items	1995	100.0	53.4	17.5	16.9	3.5	21.5	2.3	8.6	1.1
(SITC 0 + 1 + 22 + 4)	2000	100.0	50.3	16.1	15.4	3.5	17.4	2.2	11.0	1.4
	2006	100.0	39.2	12.6	11.7	2.6	12.6	1.9	9.5	3.3
Agricultural raw materials	1995	100.0	51.5	9.7	9.3	4.9	22.7	5.1	9.1	5.1
(SITC 2 - 22 - 27 - 28)	2000	100.0	51.5	13.1	12.7	6.8	16.7	5.0	9.9	5.6
	2006	100.0	47.3	12.3	12.1	5.3	18.2	4.4	7.1	8.8
Ores, metals, precious stones	1995	100.0	56.3	22.8	16.1	2.6	10.5	7.8	12.6	4.5
and non-monetary gold	2000	100.0	53.9	25.5	17.3	1.3	5.9	7.8	13.5	5.9
(SITC 27 + 28 + 68 + 667 + 971)	2006	100.0	43.8	16.4	9.7	1.6	4.6	6.7	14.5	4.9
Fuels (SITC 3)	1995	100.0	11.9	2.3	2.2	0.6	2.8	2.0	4.2	1.9
	2000	100.0	8.4	2.3	1.7	0.2	1.0	0.7	4.1	2.2
	2006	100.0	6.4	1.6	1.4	0.2	0.8	0.8	3.0	4.6
Manufactured goods	1995	100.0	61.1	21.4	19.8	0.8	13.6	24.5	0.9	1.5
(SITC 5 to 8 less 667 and 68)	2000	100.0	54.1	18.1	16.9	0.7	13.4	21.0	1.0	1.2
	2006	100.0	44.4	17.0	15.9	0.5	9.6	16.5	0.7	0.9
Share by major product group (percentage)										
All products	1995	100.0	100.0	100.0	100.0	100.0	100.0	100.0	100.0	100.0
	2000	100.0	100.0	100.0	100.0	100.0	100.0	100.0	100.0	100.0
	2006	100.0	100.0	100.0	100.0	100.0	100.0	100.0	100.0	100.0
All food items	1995	6.8	6.4	6.1	6.5	20.6	10.7	0.8	22.6	4.3
(SITC 0 + 1 + 22 + 4)	2000	5.7	5.9	5.6	5.8	20.6	8.3	0.8	21.9	4.4
	2006	4.3	4.4	3.6	3.7	15.4	6.7	0.7	15.3	6.0
Agricultural raw materials	1995	3.2	2.9	1.6	1.7	13.7	5.4	0.8	11.2	9.3
(SITC 2 - 22 - 27 - 28)	2000	2.5	2.6	2.0	2.1	17.5	3.5	0.8	8.7	7.9
	2006	2.0	2.5	1.7	1.8	14.4	4.5	0.7	5.3	7.4
Ores, metals, precious stones	1995	5.7	5.7	6.7	5.2	12.6	4.4	2.3	27.6	14.5
and non-monetary gold	2000	5.5	6.1	8.4	6.3	7.5	2.7	2.6	25.9	18.3
(SITC 27 + 28 + 68 + 667 + 971)	2006	7.8	8.9	8.6	5.6	16.9	4.5	4.3	42.5	15.9
Fuels (SITC 3)	1995	7.0	1.5	0.8	0.9	3.4	1.4	0.7	11.2	7.4
	2000	11.2	1.9	1.6	1.3	2.7	1.0	0.5	16.2	14.0
	2006	14.7	2.5	1.6	1.5	3.6	1.5	1.0	16.7	28.4
Manufactured goods	1995	75.7	81.6	83.0	84.1	49.2	75.2	93.9	26.2	63.5
(SITC 5 to 8 less 667 and 68)	2000	74.3	82.6	81.5	83.6	51.4	83.4	95.0	25.7	48.6
	2006	67.3	78.3	77.7	80.2	47.3	80.9	92.3	18.5	26.5

Sources:
- Data and UNCTAD secretariat estimates based on UN DESA Comtrade and IMF *Direction of Trade statistics* databases

Total	Africa / Afrique	America / Amérique	Total (Asia)	Eastern, Southern and South-Eastern Asia / Asie orientale, méridionale et du Sud-Est	China / Chine	Western Asia / Asie occidentale	Oceania / Océanie	Major petroleum exporters / Principaux exportateurs de pétrole	Major exporters of manufactures / Principaux exportateurs d'articles manufacturés	Year / Année	Destination / Groupes de produits
Millions de dollars											
454 948	15 494	19 927	418 682	368 692	98 273	49 990	845	56 463	352 769	1995	Total tous produits
651 357	23 596	20 635	606 184	524 589	148 259	81 594	943	101 577	490 619	2000	
1 717 600	76 171	74 747	1 564 315	1 312 708	436 127	251 607	2 367	331 589	1 221 180	2006	
Parts par destinations (en pourcentage)											
40.6	1.4	1.8	37.3	32.9	8.8	4.5	0.1	5.0	31.5	1995	Total tous produits
47.9	1.7	1.5	44.6	38.6	10.9	6.0	0.1	7.5	36.1	2000	
57.4	2.5	2.5	52.3	43.9	14.6	8.4	0.1	11.1	40.8	2006	
44.9	2.3	8.1	34.1	30.6	6.3	3.6	0.3	3.1	29.4	1995	Produits alimentaires
48.2	3.1	9.6	35.3	31.0	7.8	4.3	0.2	4.7	28.1	2000	(CTCI 0 + 1 + 22 + 4)
56.9	3.1	14.6	38.8	33.9	7.0	4.9	0.3	5.0	31.9	2006	
43.0	4.9	5.1	32.2	31.3	4.1	0.9	0.8	1.9	26.1	1995	Matières premières
42.8	5.6	4.0	32.6	31.5	4.1	1.1	0.7	2.6	24.0	2000	d'origine agricole
43.7	5.3	5.3	32.1	31.2	2.7	0.9	1.0	2.1	24.7	2006	(CTCI 2 - 22 - 27 - 28)
38.9	5.7	7.4	25.5	21.5	3.9	4.0	0.3	4.0	22.5	1995	Minerais, métaux, pierres
40.0	5.1	6.9	27.9	24.1	4.3	3.8	0.2	4.2	24.2	2000	précieuses et or (non monétaire)
50.7	5.8	11.3	33.4	28.8	6.2	4.5	0.3	5.5	28.5	2006	(CTCI 27 + 28 + 68 + 667 + 971)
81.2	5.9	0.6	74.5	32.7	3.5	41.8	0.1	52.6	21.2	1995	Combustibles (CTCI 3)
78.0	7.1	0.5	70.4	29.6	2.9	40.9	0.1	53.6	17.2	2000	
87.7	9.6	1.7	76.3	31.9	2.5	44.4	0.0	60.8	19.7	2006	
36.8	0.4	0.8	35.7	34.3	10.1	1.4	0.0	1.1	33.7	1995	Articles manufacturés
44.3	0.4	0.6	43.3	42.1	13.2	1.2	0.0	1.1	41.0	2000	(CTCI 5 à 8 moins 667 et 68)
54.1	0.4	0.9	52.7	51.0	19.8	1.8	0.0	1.6	49.8	2006	
Parts par principaux groupes de produits (en pourcentage)											
100.0	100.0	100.0	100.0	100.0	100.0	100.0	100.0	100.0	100.0	1995	Total tous produits
100.0	100.0	100.0	100.0	100.0	100.0	100.0	100.0	100.0	100.0	2000	
100.0	100.0	100.0	100.0	100.0	100.0	100.0	100.0	100.0	100.0	2006	
7.6	11.5	31.3	6.3	6.4	4.9	5.5	27.8	4.2	6.4	1995	Produits alimentaires
5.7	10.2	35.9	4.5	4.6	4.1	4.0	20.0	3.6	4.4	2000	(CTCI 0 + 1 + 22 + 4)
4.2	5.3	25.0	3.2	3.3	2.1	2.5	16.1	1.9	3.3	2006	
3.4	11.3	9.3	2.8	3.1	1.5	0.7	33.7	1.2	2.7	1995	Matières premières
2.2	8.0	6.5	1.8	2.0	0.9	0.5	23.6	0.9	1.7	2000	d'origine agricole
1.5	4.1	4.2	1.2	1.4	0.4	0.2	24.7	0.4	1.2	2006	(CTCI 2 - 22 - 27 - 28)
5.5	23.7	23.9	3.9	3.7	2.5	5.1	20.7	4.6	4.1	1995	Minerais, métaux, pierres
4.6	16.0	24.8	3.4	3.4	2.1	3.5	15.4	3.1	3.7	2000	précieuses et or (non monétaire)
6.8	17.6	35.0	4.9	5.1	3.3	4.2	26.7	3.8	5.4	2006	(CTCI 27 + 28 + 68 + 667 + 971)
13.9	29.8	2.5	13.9	6.9	2.8	65.2	8.2	72.7	4.7	1995	Combustibles (CTCI 3)
18.3	45.7	3.6	17.7	8.6	3.0	76.5	14.6	80.6	5.4	2000	
22.4	55.3	10.0	21.4	10.7	2.5	77.4	7.8	80.4	7.1	2006	
68.7	21.7	32.5	72.3	78.9	87.7	23.4	9.4	17.1	81.1	1995	Articles manufacturés
68.7	15.6	29.0	72.1	81.0	89.7	15.4	26.2	11.1	84.5	2000	(CTCI 5 à 8 moins 667 et 68)
63.4	11.3	23.3	67.9	78.2	91.2	14.3	23.6	9.9	82.1	2006	

Sources :
- Données et estimations du secrétariat de la CNUCED sur la base de données Comtrade de ONU DAES et *Direction of Trade statistics* du Fonds Monétaire international

Destination / Product group	Year Année	World Monde	Developed economies — Économies développées : Total	Europe Total	Europe EU UE	Canada	USA États-Unis	Japan Japon	Other developed countries Autres économies développées	Economies in transition Économies en transition
Millions of dollars										
All products	1995	950 005	485 570	152 628	146 858	10 630	183 440	121 285	17 586	8 638
	2000	1 297 727	690 242	221 690	207 753	14 742	270 513	155 277	28 019	7 908
	2006	2 841 169	1 299 154	483 756	462 224	31 077	463 466	251 728	69 128	44 725
Share by destination (percentage)										
All products	1995	100.0	51.1	16.1	15.5	1.1	19.3	12.8	1.9	0.9
	2000	100.0	53.2	17.1	16.0	1.1	20.8	12.0	2.2	0.6
	2006	100.0	45.7	17.0	16.3	1.1	16.3	8.9	2.4	1.6
All food items	1995	100.0	47.8	13.0	12.4	0.9	7.8	24.6	1.5	2.7
(SITC 0 + 1 + 22 + 4)	2000	100.0	49.2	12.9	12.4	1.2	11.3	22.3	1.6	2.0
	2006	100.0	44.1	14.4	14.1	1.2	11.3	15.0	2.2	3.3
Agricultural raw materials	1995	100.0	44.5	14.9	14.7	0.9	10.2	17.3	1.3	0.4
(SITC 2 - 22 - 27 - 28)	2000	100.0	40.8	15.6	15.4	0.8	8.6	14.5	1.3	0.4
	2006	100.0	38.4	15.1	15.0	1.3	9.6	11.2	1.1	0.9
Ores, metals, precious stones	1995	100.0	42.4	11.7	10.7	0.3	8.5	19.9	2.1	1.4
and non-monetary gold	2000	100.0	44.9	15.0	12.5	0.4	11.9	12.6	5.0	0.3
(SITC 27 + 28 + 68 + 667 + 971)	2006	100.0	36.2	14.5	12.3	0.6	6.6	9.9	4.6	0.5
Fuels (SITC 3)	1995	100.0	40.8	6.8	6.8	0.4	2.5	29.0	2.1	0.2
	2000	100.0	45.8	12.4	5.2	0.1	3.4	26.2	3.7	0.1
	2006	100.0	38.7	10.4	7.1	0.1	3.6	18.5	6.1	0.1
Manufactured goods	1995	100.0	52.6	17.2	16.5	1.2	22.1	10.2	1.9	0.8
(SITC 5 to 8 less 667 and 68)	2000	100.0	54.6	17.8	17.2	1.3	23.4	10.2	2.0	0.6
	2006	100.0	47.2	18.0	17.5	1.2	18.5	7.5	2.0	1.7
Share by major product group (percentage)										
All products	1995	100.0	100.0	100.0	100.0	100.0	100.0	100.0	100.0	100.0
	2000	100.0	100.0	100.0	100.0	100.0	100.0	100.0	100.0	100.0
	2006	100.0	100.0	100.0	100.0	100.0	100.0	100.0	100.0	100.0
All food items	1995	6.9	6.4	5.6	5.5	5.2	2.8	13.2	5.5	20.5
(SITC 0 + 1 + 22 + 4)	2000	4.7	4.4	3.5	3.6	4.8	2.6	8.8	3.6	15.3
	2006	3.8	3.6	3.2	3.3	4.2	2.6	6.4	3.4	7.8
Agricultural raw materials	1995	2.4	2.1	2.2	2.3	1.9	1.3	3.2	1.6	1.0
(SITC 2 - 22 - 27 - 28)	2000	1.4	1.1	1.3	1.4	1.0	0.6	1.7	0.8	0.8
	2006	1.3	1.1	1.1	1.2	1.5	0.8	1.6	0.6	0.8
Ores, metals, precious stones	1995	3.1	2.6	2.2	2.1	0.8	1.4	4.8	3.5	4.8
and non-monetary gold	2000	2.7	2.2	2.3	2.1	1.0	1.5	2.8	6.2	1.5
(SITC 27 + 28 + 68 + 667 + 971)	2006	3.8	3.0	3.2	2.8	2.1	1.5	4.2	7.1	1.1
Fuels (SITC 3)	1995	5.8	4.6	2.5	2.5	1.9	0.8	13.2	6.6	1.1
	2000	7.1	6.1	5.2	2.3	0.6	1.2	15.6	12.3	1.4
	2006	8.3	7.0	5.1	3.6	0.6	1.8	17.3	20.9	0.7
Manufactured goods	1995	80.5	82.8	86.0	86.1	89.2	91.9	64.6	81.9	71.8
(SITC 5 to 8 less 667 and 68)	2000	83.4	85.6	86.7	89.7	92.4	93.8	70.8	76.1	80.4
	2006	82.1	84.8	86.7	88.4	91.5	93.0	69.8	67.1	89.3

Sources:
- Data and UNCTAD secretariat estimates based on UN DESA Comtrade and IMF *Direction of Trade statistics* databases

Total	Africa / Afrique	America / Amérique	Asia / Asie Total	Eastern, Southern and South-Eastern Asia / Asie orientale, méridionale et du Sud-Est	China / Chine	Western Asia / Asie occidentale	Oceania / Océanie	Major petroleum exporters / Principaux exportateurs de pétrole	Major exporters of manufactures / Principaux exportateurs d'articles manufacturés	Year / Année	Destination / Groupes de produits
Millions de dollars											
443 678	16 122	23 092	403 197	380 738	77 083	22 459	1 267	24 831	353 621	1995	**Total tous produits**
595 774	21 619	33 941	537 911	507 276	110 802	30 635	2 303	34 093	478 738	2000	
1 490 213	67 138	83 086	1 334 251	1 239 225	349 066	95 026	5 737	108 490	1 150 198	2006	
Parts par destinations (en pourcentage)											
46.7	1.7	2.4	42.4	40.1	8.1	2.4	0.1	2.6	37.2	1995	**Total tous produits**
45.9	1.7	2.6	41.5	39.1	8.5	2.4	0.2	2.6	36.9	2000	
52.5	2.4	2.9	47.0	43.6	12.3	3.3	0.2	3.8	40.5	2006	
49.3	3.2	0.6	45.4	41.0	7.8	4.4	0.1	4.8	32.0	1995	Produits alimentaires
48.6	3.6	0.9	44.0	38.0	6.5	5.9	0.2	6.7	30.6	2000	(CTCI 0 + 1 + 22 + 4)
52.4	5.1	1.5	45.6	38.8	6.3	6.8	0.2	8.0	29.0	2006	
55.1	1.5	2.1	51.5	49.7	13.6	1.8	0.0	1.7	46.9	1995	Matières premières
58.9	1.1	1.6	56.1	54.1	22.1	2.0	0.0	1.7	49.7	2000	d'origine agricole
60.6	1.4	2.8	56.4	53.6	26.0	2.8	0.0	2.3	48.8	2006	(CTCI 2 - 22 - 27 - 28)
56.2	0.3	0.2	55.7	54.8	10.2	0.9	0.0	1.1	52.3	1995	Minerais, métaux, pierres
54.8	0.4	0.4	54.0	51.3	11.2	2.7	0.0	2.6	49.5	2000	précieuses et or (non monétaire)
63.3	0.8	0.4	62.0	57.7	18.4	4.3	0.0	4.3	55.0	2006	(CTCI 27 + 28 + 68 + 667 + 971)
39.8	0.1	0.3	38.9	38.6	6.6	0.3	0.6	0.3	35.2	1995	Combustibles (CTCI 3)
50.8	2.3	1.1	46.7	46.3	6.3	0.4	0.7	0.6	41.4	2000	
59.9	3.1	1.4	54.6	51.7	6.4	2.9	0.8	3.3	42.5	2006	
46.4	1.7	2.8	41.8	39.4	8.1	2.4	0.1	2.7	37.1	1995	Articles manufacturés
44.8	1.5	2.9	40.3	38.0	8.6	2.3	0.1	2.6	36.3	2000	(CTCI 5 à 8 moins 667 et 68)
51.0	2.2	3.2	45.5	42.3	12.7	3.2	0.1	3.7	40.1	2006	
Parts par principaux groupes de produits (en pourcentage)											
100.0	100.0	100.0	100.0	100.0	100.0	100.0	100.0	100.0	100.0	1995	**Total tous produits**
100.0	100.0	100.0	100.0	100.0	100.0	100.0	100.0	100.0	100.0	2000	
100.0	100.0	100.0	100.0	100.0	100.0	100.0	100.0	100.0	100.0	2006	
7.2	12.8	1.8	7.3	7.0	6.6	12.7	7.4	12.7	5.9	1995	Produits alimentaires
5.0	10.1	1.5	5.0	4.6	3.6	11.8	4.3	12.0	3.9	2000	(CTCI 0 + 1 + 22 + 4)
3.8	8.2	1.9	3.7	3.4	1.9	7.6	4.4	7.9	2.7	2006	
2.8	2.1	2.1	2.9	3.0	4.0	1.8	0.3	1.6	3.0	1995	Matières premières
1.8	0.9	0.9	1.9	1.9	3.6	1.2	0.2	0.9	1.9	2000	d'origine agricole
1.5	0.7	1.2	1.5	1.6	2.7	1.1	0.1	0.8	1.5	2006	(CTCI 2 - 22 - 27 - 28)
3.7	0.5	0.3	4.1	4.2	3.9	1.2	0.3	1.3	4.3	1995	Minerais, métaux, pierres
3.2	0.6	0.4	3.5	3.5	3.5	3.0	0.3	2.7	3.6	2000	précieuses et or (non monétaire)
4.5	1.3	0.6	5.0	5.0	5.6	4.9	0.2	4.3	5.1	2006	(CTCI 27 + 28 + 68 + 667 + 971)
5.0	0.4	0.7	5.3	5.6	4.7	0.7	25.6	0.7	5.5	1995	Combustibles (CTCI 3)
7.9	9.8	3.1	8.0	8.4	5.2	1.3	28.7	1.7	8.0	2000	
9.5	10.9	3.8	9.6	9.8	4.3	7.2	34.7	7.1	8.7	2006	
80.0	82.4	93.0	79.2	79.0	80.0	82.8	63.3	82.8	80.1	1995	Articles manufacturés
81.3	76.8	90.9	81.0	81.0	83.8	81.1	62.9	81.3	82.1	2000	(CTCI 5 à 8 moins 667 et 68)
79.8	76.6	88.5	79.6	79.7	85.2	78.2	53.2	78.7	81.4	2006	

Sources :
- Données et estimations du secrétariat de la CNUCED sur la base de données Comtrade de ONU DAES et *Direction of Trade statistics* du Fonds Monétaire international

Destination / Product group	Year / Année	World / Monde	Developed economies / Économies développées							Economies in transition / Économies en transition
			Total	Europe		Canada	USA / États-Unis	Japan / Japon	Other developed countries / Autres économies développées	
				Total	EU UE					
Millions of dollars										
All products	1995	1 001 117	558 665	166 907	152 270	12 063	138 844	213 131	27 719	15 378
	2000	1 205 985	566 302	159 944	143 443	11 987	147 806	212 720	33 845	17 073
	2006	2 601 990	952 030	304 712	273 340	19 597	216 105	339 228	72 389	42 288
Share by destination (percentage)										
All products	1995	100.0	55.8	16.7	15.2	1.2	13.9	21.3	2.8	1.5
	2000	100.0	47.0	13.3	11.9	1.0	12.3	17.6	2.8	1.4
	2006	100.0	36.6	11.7	10.5	0.8	8.3	13.0	2.8	1.6
All food items	1995	100.0	53.9	13.7	13.2	4.2	23.4	2.9	9.7	0.7
(SITC 0 + 1 + 22 + 4)	2000	100.0	50.3	12.3	11.6	4.2	19.0	2.9	11.9	1.3
	2006	100.0	40.1	10.0	9.4	3.1	14.2	2.5	10.3	3.0
Agricultural raw materials	1995	100.0	51.2	7.5	7.2	5.1	23.8	5.5	9.3	4.1
(SITC 2 - 22 - 27 - 28)	2000	100.0	50.7	10.8	10.4	7.3	16.9	5.4	10.4	4.8
	2006	100.0	46.4	10.2	9.9	5.6	18.4	4.8	7.5	8.5
Ores, metals, precious stones	1995	100.0	55.1	19.8	14.1	2.6	10.7	8.6	13.5	4.5
and non-monetary gold	2000	100.0	54.2	23.9	16.5	1.4	6.2	8.5	14.2	5.1
(SITC 27 + 28 + 68 + 667 + 971)	2006	100.0	44.9	14.8	8.9	1.7	4.7	7.6	16.1	3.5
Fuels (SITC 3)	1995	100.0	11.7	1.6	1.5	0.6	2.7	2.2	4.5	0.8
	2000	100.0	7.3	1.3	0.8	0.2	0.9	0.8	4.0	1.3
	2006	100.0	5.8	0.8	0.7	0.2	0.7	0.9	3.1	3.6
Manufactured goods	1995	100.0	60.0	18.4	17.0	0.8	13.7	26.2	1.0	1.3
(SITC 5 to 8 less 667 and 68)	2000	100.0	52.1	14.4	13.3	0.7	13.8	22.4	0.9	1.0
	2006	100.0	42.9	14.1	13.2	0.5	9.9	17.6	0.7	0.7
Share by major product group (percentage)										
All products	1995	100.0	100.0	100.0	100.0	100.0	100.0	100.0	100.0	100.0
	2000	100.0	100.0	100.0	100.0	100.0	100.0	100.0	100.0	100.0
	2006	100.0	100.0	100.0	100.0	100.0	100.0	100.0	100.0	100.0
All food items	1995	6.1	5.9	5.0	5.3	21.5	10.3	0.8	21.4	2.9
(SITC 0 + 1 + 22 + 4)	2000	4.9	5.2	4.5	4.7	20.5	7.5	0.8	20.6	4.6
	2006	3.8	4.1	3.2	3.4	15.7	6.5	0.7	14.0	6.9
Agricultural raw materials	1995	3.3	3.0	1.5	1.6	14.1	5.7	0.9	11.1	8.8
(SITC 2 - 22 - 27 - 28)	2000	2.6	2.8	2.1	2.2	18.8	3.5	0.8	9.5	8.7
	2006	2.1	2.7	1.8	2.0	15.6	4.6	0.8	5.7	11.0
Ores, metals, precious stones	1995	5.8	5.7	6.9	5.4	12.4	4.5	2.3	28.4	16.9
and non-monetary gold	2000	5.6	6.5	10.1	7.8	8.0	2.8	2.7	28.4	20.1
(SITC 27 + 28 + 68 + 667 + 971)	2006	7.9	9.6	9.9	6.7	18.0	4.5	4.6	45.4	16.9
Fuels (SITC 3)	1995	7.0	1.5	0.7	0.7	3.6	1.4	0.7	11.5	3.9
	2000	11.7	1.8	1.2	0.8	2.6	0.9	0.5	16.8	11.1
	2006	16.0	2.5	1.1	1.1	4.0	1.4	1.1	18.0	35.6
Manufactured goods	1995	76.1	81.8	83.8	84.9	48.0	74.9	93.7	26.5	66.4
(SITC 5 to 8 less 667 and 68)	2000	74.7	82.9	81.1	83.5	49.8	84.0	94.9	22.9	53.3
	2006	68.5	80.2	82.7	85.8	46.5	82.0	92.4	16.6	29.3

Sources:
- Data and UNCTAD secretariat estimates based on UN DESA Comtrade and IMF *Direction of Trade statistics* databases

2.2.H Structure des importations par partenaires et groupes de produits
Économies en développement : Asie orientale, méridionale et du Sud-Est

Total	Africa / Afrique	America / Amérique	Asia / Asie — Total	Eastern, Southern and South-Eastern Asia / Asie orientale, méridionale et du Sud-Est	China / Chine	Western Asia / Asie occidentale	Oceania / Océanie	Major petroleum exporters / Principaux exportateurs de pétrole	Major exporters of manufactures / Principaux exportateurs d'articles manufacturés	Year / Année	Destination / Groupes de produits
Millions de dollars											
417 542	12 495	17 656	386 550	348 785	95 204	37 765	840	44 165	333 657	1995	**Total tous produits**
603 008	18 835	17 691	565 543	498 028	141 935	67 515	939	85 314	466 036	2000	
1 571 702	63 079	66 549	1 439 715	1 224 325	406 695	215 390	2 358	289 679	1 136 298	2006	
Parts par destinations (en pourcentage)											
41.7	**1.2**	**1.8**	**38.6**	**34.8**	**9.5**	**3.8**	**0.1**	**4.4**	**33.3**	1995	**Total tous produits**
50.0	**1.6**	**1.5**	**46.9**	**41.3**	**11.8**	**5.6**	**0.1**	**7.1**	**38.6**	2000	
60.4	**2.4**	**2.6**	**55.3**	**47.1**	**15.6**	**8.3**	**0.1**	**11.1**	**43.7**	2006	
44.8	1.7	8.3	34.4	33.7	7.6	0.7	0.4	0.7	31.8	1995	Produits alimentaires
48.3	2.3	10.3	35.4	34.3	9.9	1.1	0.3	1.3	31.5	2000	(CTCI 0 + 1 + 22 + 4)
56.9	2.2	15.3	39.0	38.1	8.5	0.8	0.4	1.2	34.6	2006	
44.3	4.8	5.3	33.4	32.8	4.4	0.6	0.9	1.5	27.4	1995	Matières premières
44.4	5.6	4.0	34.1	33.3	4.4	0.7	0.7	2.3	25.2	2000	d'origine agricole
45.0	5.3	5.4	33.2	32.6	2.7	0.6	1.1	1.9	25.8	2006	(CTCI 2 - 22 - 27 - 28)
40.2	5.8	7.7	26.3	23.1	4.2	3.2	0.3	3.2	24.1	1995	Minerais, métaux, pierres
40.6	5.0	6.7	28.6	25.6	4.6	3.0	0.2	3.4	25.3	2000	précieuses et or (non monétaire)
51.4	5.2	12.6	33.3	29.5	6.8	3.8	0.3	4.6	29.0	2006	(CTCI 27 + 28 + 68 + 667 + 971)
81.8	5.1	0.7	76.0	35.1	3.9	40.9	0.1	50.7	23.3	1995	Combustibles (CTCI 3)
79.9	6.6	0.5	72.8	31.5	3.2	41.3	0.1	53.6	18.6	2000	
90.6	9.8	1.8	79.0	33.4	2.6	45.6	0.0	62.7	20.5	2006	
38.1	0.3	0.7	37.0	36.2	10.9	0.9	0.0	0.7	35.6	1995	Articles manufacturés
46.5	0.3	0.6	45.6	44.9	14.1	0.7	0.0	0.7	43.8	2000	(CTCI 5 à 8 moins 667 et 68)
56.2	0.3	0.9	55.0	54.0	20.8	0.9	0.0	1.0	52.7	2006	
Parts par principaux groupes de produits (en pourcentage)											
100.0	**100.0**	**100.0**	**100.0**	**100.0**	**100.0**	**100.0**	**100.0**	**100.0**	**100.0**	1995	**Total tous produits**
100.0	**100.0**	**100.0**	**100.0**	**100.0**	**100.0**	**100.0**	**100.0**	**100.0**	**100.0**	2000	
100.0	**100.0**	**100.0**	**100.0**	**100.0**	**100.0**	**100.0**	**100.0**	**100.0**	**100.0**	2006	
6.6	8.1	28.9	5.4	5.9	4.9	1.1	27.5	0.9	5.8	1995	Produits alimentaires
4.7	7.3	34.0	3.7	4.0	4.1	0.9	20.1	0.9	4.0	2000	(CTCI 0 + 1 + 22 + 4)
3.6	3.4	22.7	2.7	3.1	2.1	0.4	16.2	0.4	3.0	2006	
3.5	12.7	9.9	2.9	3.1	1.5	0.6	33.9	1.2	2.7	1995	Matières premières
2.3	9.2	7.1	1.9	2.1	1.0	0.3	23.7	0.8	1.7	2000	d'origine agricole
1.6	4.6	4.4	1.3	1.4	0.4	0.1	24.8	0.4	1.2	2006	(CTCI 2 - 22 - 27 - 28)
5.6	27.3	25.6	4.0	3.9	2.6	4.9	20.8	4.2	4.2	1995	Minerais, métaux, pierres
4.5	18.1	25.7	3.4	3.5	2.2	3.0	15.5	2.7	3.7	2000	précieuses et or (non monétaire)
6.7	17.0	38.6	4.7	4.9	3.4	3.6	26.8	3.3	5.2	2006	(CTCI 27 + 28 + 68 + 667 + 971)
13.8	28.5	2.8	13.8	7.1	2.9	76.2	8.3	80.8	4.9	1995	Combustibles (CTCI 3)
18.6	49.0	4.0	18.1	8.9	3.1	86.1	14.7	88.4	5.6	2000	
24.0	64.7	11.1	22.8	11.4	2.6	88.1	7.8	90.1	7.5	2006	
69.5	21.1	32.3	72.9	79.0	87.5	17.2	9.4	12.8	81.3	1995	Articles manufacturés
69.4	14.7	29.1	72.6	81.1	89.5	9.6	26.0	7.1	84.7	2000	(CTCI 5 à 8 moins 667 et 68)
63.7	9.3	23.1	68.0	78.6	91.2	7.7	23.6	5.9	82.6	2006	

Sources :
- Données et estimations du secrétariat de la CNUCED sur la base de données Comtrade de ONU DAES et *Direction of Trade statistics* du Fonds Monétaire international

Destination / Product group	Year Année	World Monde	Developed economies — Économies développées Total	Europe Total	EU UE	Canada	USA États-Unis	Japan Japon	Other developed countries Autres économies développées	Economies in transition Économies en transition
Millions of dollars										
All products	1995	133 143	58 849	25 126	24 780	526	10 640	21 388	1 169	2 640
	2000	219 703	110 016	44 881	44 378	922	31 161	31 342	1 710	2 724
	2006	613 984	274 919	107 897	104 254	3 854	58 282	100 230	4 656	9 447
Share by destination (percentage)										
All products	1995	100.0	44.2	18.9	18.6	0.4	8.0	16.1	0.9	2.0
	2000	100.0	50.1	20.4	20.2	0.4	14.2	14.3	0.8	1.2
	2006	100.0	44.8	17.6	17.0	0.6	9.5	16.3	0.8	1.5
All food items	1995	100.0	39.5	32.5	31.3	0.4	4.7	1.0	0.9	9.6
(SITC 0 + 1 + 22 + 4)	2000	100.0	36.6	28.2	27.1	0.4	3.9	1.3	2.7	7.2
	2006	100.0	29.7	24.9	23.9	0.4	2.5	0.8	1.1	5.8
Agricultural raw materials	1995	100.0	50.1	44.7	43.8	0.1	2.0	1.5	1.8	0.5
(SITC 2 - 22 - 27 - 28)	2000	100.0	44.5	38.8	37.9	0.2	1.6	2.1	1.8	0.9
	2006	100.0	18.7	16.9	16.6	0.1	0.6	0.7	0.3	1.1
Ores, metals, precious stones	1995	100.0	33.0	18.1	17.5	0.1	2.3	11.9	0.6	1.1
and non-monetary gold	2000	100.0	42.0	25.5	23.1	0.3	6.1	8.1	2.0	1.8
(SITC 27 + 28 + 68 + 667 + 971)	2006	100.0	25.7	22.6	13.9	0.0	0.9	2.0	0.2	0.8
Fuels (SITC 3)	1995	..	..	..	..	..	..	..	..	..
	2000	100.0	50.2	15.6	15.6	0.4	15.7	18.4	0.2	0.2
	2006	100.0	48.4	10.8	10.8	0.8	12.2	24.1	0.4	0.0
Manufactured goods	1995	100.0	46.9	36.9	36.2	0.3	7.1	1.4	1.2	5.9
(SITC 5 to 8 less 667 and 68)	2000	100.0	52.4	37.9	37.3	0.6	10.8	0.2	2.8	4.7
	2006	100.0	38.0	30.7	30.0	0.2	5.2	0.4	1.5	4.9
Share by major product group (percentage)										
All products	1995	100.0	100.0	100.0	100.0	100.0	100.0	100.0	100.0	100.0
	2000	100.0	100.0	100.0	100.0	100.0	100.0	100.0	100.0	100.0
	2006	100.0	100.0	100.0	100.0	100.0	100.0	100.0	100.0	100.0
All food items	1995	5.4	4.8	9.2	9.0	5.2	3.1	0.3	5.7	26.0
(SITC 0 + 1 + 22 + 4)	2000	3.0	2.2	4.1	4.0	2.6	0.8	0.3	10.5	17.3
	2006	2.4	1.6	3.4	3.4	1.4	0.6	0.1	3.6	9.2
Agricultural raw materials	1995	0.6	0.7	1.4	1.4	0.2	0.1	0.1	1.2	0.2
(SITC 2 - 22 - 27 - 28)	2000	0.3	0.3	0.6	0.6	0.1	0.0	0.0	0.7	0.2
	2006	0.2	0.1	0.2	0.2	0.0	0.0	0.0	0.1	0.1
Ores, metals, precious stones	1995	2.9	2.2	2.8	2.8	0.5	0.8	2.2	2.2	1.7
and non-monetary gold	2000	1.6	1.4	2.0	1.9	1.0	0.7	0.9	4.1	2.4
(SITC 27 + 28 + 68 + 667 + 971)	2006	3.1	1.8	4.0	2.6	0.1	0.3	0.4	0.9	1.6
Fuels (SITC 3)	1995	66.9	66.6	39.5	40.0	77.8	73.3	95.3	57.0	1.3
	2000	76.2	76.4	58.2	58.7	69.3	84.1	98.4	16.3	9.3
	2006	66.9	72.3	41.3	42.5	86.9	86.0	98.9	36.0	0.3
Manufactured goods	1995	24.0	25.5	47.0	46.7	16.2	21.3	2.1	33.9	70.9
(SITC 5 to 8 less 667 and 68)	2000	18.6	19.4	34.5	34.3	26.4	14.2	0.3	68.0	69.7
	2006	16.1	13.7	28.1	28.5	5.8	8.8	0.4	32.5	50.8

Sources:
- Data and UNCTAD secretariat estimates based on UN DESA Comtrade and IMF *Direction of Trade statistics* databases

			Developing economies / Économies en développement							Year	Destination
			Asia / Asie					Major petroleum exporters	Major exporters of manufactures	Année	
Total	Africa / Afrique	America / Amérique	Total	Eastern, Southern and South-Eastern Asia / Asie orientale, méridionale et du Sud-Est	China / Chine	Western Asia / Asie occidentale	Oceania / Océanie	Principaux exportateurs de pétrole	Principaux exportateurs d'articles manufacturés		Groupes de produits
Millions de dollars											
32 535	3 098	386	29 050	18 218	1 594	10 832	1	10 950	16 044	1995	Total tous produits
83 391	7 443	1 871	74 068	59 867	5 213	14 202	8	10 492	58 133	2000	
261 127	22 915	3 831	234 274	178 350	20 509	55 924	107	59 920	158 464	2006	
Parts par destinations (en pourcentage)											
24.4	2.3	0.3	21.8	13.7	1.2	8.1	0.0	8.2	12.1	1995	Total tous produits
38.0	3.4	0.9	33.7	27.2	2.4	6.5	0.0	4.8	26.5	2000	
42.5	3.7	0.6	38.2	29.0	3.3	9.1	0.0	9.8	25.8	2006	
49.7	5.3	0.6	43.8	7.1	0.1	36.7	0.0	38.4	2.7	1995	Produits alimentaires
52.7	6.0	0.8	45.9	9.9	0.3	36.0	0.0	32.1	4.0	2000	(CTCI 0 + 1 + 22 + 4)
63.6	7.9	0.4	55.3	11.0	0.3	44.3	0.0	45.3	3.1	2006	
48.1	12.0	0.3	35.8	21.2	2.8	14.5	0.0	12.7	19.3	1995	Matières premières
47.1	6.8	0.3	40.0	19.2	1.3	20.8	0.0	10.5	20.3	2000	d'origine agricole
76.4	9.6	0.0	66.7	30.1	6.3	36.7	0.0	34.8	23.8	2006	(CTCI 2 - 22 - 27 - 28)
63.4	2.5	0.2	60.6	41.4	1.9	19.3	0.0	17.4	36.1	1995	Minerais, métaux, pierres
54.6	3.0	0.2	51.4	34.2	1.8	17.2	0.0	14.7	30.4	2000	précieuses et or (non monétaire)
71.4	1.9	0.1	69.5	55.8	3.0	13.7	0.0	12.4	51.7	2006	(CTCI 27 + 28 + 68 + 667 + 971)
..	..	..	..	..	..	..	..	..	..	1995	Combustibles (CTCI 3)
37.0	2.5	0.9	33.6	31.3	2.9	2.3	0.0	0.4	31.7	2000	
42.1	2.3	0.7	39.1	35.2	4.2	3.9	0.0	2.9	32.9	2006	
44.3	6.2	0.4	37.7	19.0	1.3	18.8	0.0	21.6	14.3	1995	Articles manufacturés
37.6	6.5	0.7	30.4	13.0	0.5	17.4	0.0	17.2	8.6	2000	(CTCI 5 à 8 moins 667 et 68)
54.5	8.7	0.2	45.6	18.5	2.3	27.1	0.0	34.4	10.5	2006	
Parts par principaux groupes de produits (en pourcentage)											
100.0	100.0	100.0	100.0	100.0	100.0	100.0	100.0	100.0	100.0	1995	Total tous produits
100.0	100.0	100.0	100.0	100.0	100.0	100.0	100.0	100.0	100.0	2000	
100.0	100.0	100.0	100.0	100.0	100.0	100.0	100.0	100.0	100.0	2006	
10.9	12.3	11.9	10.7	2.8	0.5	24.1	5.2	25.0	1.2	1995	Produits alimentaires
4.2	5.3	2.7	4.1	1.1	0.4	16.7	0.3	20.1	0.5	2000	(CTCI 0 + 1 + 22 + 4)
3.6	5.1	1.7	3.5	0.9	0.2	11.7	0.7	11.2	0.3	2006	
1.2	3.1	0.6	1.0	0.9	1.4	1.1	4.5	0.9	1.0	1995	Matières premières
0.4	0.6	0.1	0.4	0.2	0.2	1.0	0.0	0.7	0.2	2000	d'origine agricole
0.3	0.5	0.0	0.3	0.2	0.4	0.8	0.0	0.7	0.2	2006	(CTCI 2 - 22 - 27 - 28)
7.6	3.2	2.3	8.1	8.8	4.7	6.9	7.6	6.2	8.8	1995	Minerais, métaux, pierres
2.3	1.4	0.4	2.5	2.0	1.2	4.3	0.1	5.0	1.9	2000	précieuses et or (non monétaire)
5.3	1.6	0.4	5.7	6.0	2.8	4.7	0.5	4.0	6.3	2006	(CTCI 27 + 28 + 68 + 667 + 971)
36.6	17.7	49.6	38.4	54.0	68.2	12.4	0.0	4.7	60.4	1995	Combustibles (CTCI 3)
74.4	56.3	82.4	76.0	87.6	94.5	27.0	0.0	6.1	91.3	2000	
66.2	41.8	72.6	68.6	81.1	83.4	28.7	0.0	20.0	85.3	2006	
43.5	63.5	35.6	41.5	33.3	25.2	55.4	82.7	63.2	28.4	1995	Articles manufacturés
18.4	35.9	14.3	16.7	8.8	3.7	50.0	99.6	66.9	6.0	2000	(CTCI 5 à 8 moins 667 et 68)
20.6	37.4	5.3	19.3	10.3	11.2	47.9	2.1	56.8	6.6	2006	

Sources :
- Données et estimations du secrétariat de la CNUCED sur la base de données Comtrade de ONU DAES et *Direction of Trade statistics* du Fonds Monétaire international

Product group	Year / Année	World / Monde	Developed economies / Économies développées							Economies in transition / Économies en transition
			Total	Europe Total	EU / UE	Canada	USA / États-Unis	Japan / Japon	Other developed countries / Autres économies développées	
Millions of dollars										
All products	1995	120 042	77 255	51 597	48 102	967	14 873	8 264	1 554	4 456
	2000	153 116	95 341	64 535	60 958	1 160	14 621	10 017	5 009	7 122
	2006	389 004	189 052	136 321	125 824	2 183	23 380	20 563	6 605	28 840
Share by destination (percentage)										
All products	1995	100.0	64.4	43.0	40.1	0.8	12.4	6.9	1.3	3.7
	2000	100.0	62.3	42.1	39.8	0.8	9.5	6.5	3.3	4.7
	2006	100.0	48.6	35.0	32.3	0.6	6.0	5.3	1.7	7.4
All food items	1995	100.0	51.6	32.5	31.6	0.6	13.9	0.2	4.5	2.7
(SITC 0 + 1 + 22 + 4)	2000	100.0	50.1	28.0	27.1	1.3	12.5	0.1	8.1	1.5
	2006	100.0	36.0	21.1	19.5	1.0	6.9	0.1	6.9	4.5
Agricultural raw materials	1995	100.0	54.5	33.2	32.5	2.7	10.8	0.9	6.9	16.4
(SITC 2 - 22 - 27 - 28)	2000	100.0	59.2	36.6	36.2	1.7	14.9	0.6	5.4	13.8
	2006	100.0	57.0	36.9	36.5	1.8	15.9	0.4	2.1	12.4
Ores, metals, precious stones	1995	100.0	67.7	52.9	35.7	2.4	8.5	0.3	3.5	4.9
and non-monetary gold	2000	100.0	50.8	40.4	25.6	0.4	2.6	0.9	6.6	14.4
(SITC 27 + 28 + 68 + 667 + 971)	2006	100.0	35.7	28.4	15.1	0.6	3.6	0.5	2.6	15.2
Fuels (SITC 3)	1995	100.0	13.3	8.7	8.7	0.2	3.1	0.0	1.3	11.4
	2000	100.0	21.4	14.0	12.1	0.3	1.9	0.0	5.1	12.3
	2006	100.0	18.8	15.7	13.1	0.1	2.5	0.1	0.5	22.8
Manufactured goods	1995	100.0	71.1	47.4	44.8	0.7	13.3	9.3	0.4	2.7
(SITC 5 to 8 less 667 and 68)	2000	100.0	70.8	48.6	46.7	0.7	10.3	9.0	2.0	2.4
	2006	100.0	55.8	39.1	37.0	0.5	7.2	7.9	1.1	2.8
Share by major product group (percentage)										
All products	1995	100.0	100.0	100.0	100.0	100.0	100.0	100.0	100.0	100.0
	2000	100.0	100.0	100.0	100.0	100.0	100.0	100.0	100.0	100.0
	2006	100.0	100.0	100.0	100.0	100.0	100.0	100.0	100.0	100.0
All food items	1995	12.8	10.3	9.7	10.1	9.9	14.3	0.3	44.5	9.2
(SITC 0 + 1 + 22 + 4)	2000	12.3	9.9	8.2	8.3	21.6	16.1	0.2	30.3	3.9
	2006	7.5	5.6	4.5	4.5	12.9	8.6	0.2	30.4	4.5
Agricultural raw materials	1995	2.5	2.2	2.0	2.1	8.7	2.2	0.3	13.7	11.3
(SITC 2 - 22 - 27 - 28)	2000	2.0	1.9	1.7	1.8	4.5	3.1	0.2	3.3	5.9
	2006	1.3	1.5	1.3	1.4	3.9	3.3	0.1	1.5	2.1
Ores, metals, precious stones	1995	4.9	5.2	6.1	4.4	14.7	3.4	0.2	13.5	6.5
and non-monetary gold	2000	4.5	3.7	4.3	2.9	2.2	1.2	0.6	9.1	14.0
(SITC 27 + 28 + 68 + 667 + 971)	2006	7.0	5.2	5.7	3.3	7.3	4.3	0.7	10.6	14.5
Fuels (SITC 3)	1995	6.3	1.3	1.3	1.4	1.2	1.6	0.0	6.5	19.4
	2000	7.9	2.7	2.6	2.4	3.6	1.6	0.1	12.3	20.9
	2006	5.8	2.3	2.6	2.4	0.9	2.4	0.1	1.8	17.9
Manufactured goods	1995	72.7	80.4	80.3	81.3	65.1	78.0	98.7	20.7	53.5
(SITC 5 to 8 less 667 and 68)	2000	71.5	81.3	82.5	83.9	67.6	77.4	98.7	44.8	37.1
	2006	59.6	68.4	66.5	68.2	54.2	71.0	89.0	39.0	22.3

Sources:
- Data and UNCTAD secretariat estimates based on UN DESA Comtrade and IMF *Direction of Trade statistics* databases

2.2.I Structure des importations par partenaires et groupes de produits
Économies en développement : Asie occidentale

Total	Africa / Afrique	America / Amérique	Asia / Asie — Total	Eastern, Southern and South-Eastern Asia / Asie orientale, méridionale et du Sud-Est	China / Chine	Western Asia / Asie occidentale	Oceania / Océanie	Major petroleum exporters / Principaux exportateurs de pétrole	Major exporters of manufactures / Principaux exportateurs d'articles manufacturés	Year / Année	Destination / Groupes de produits
Millions de dollars											
37 406	2 999	2 270	32 132	19 907	3 069	12 225	5	12 298	19 112	1995	Total tous produits
48 349	4 761	2 944	40 640	26 561	6 324	14 079	4	16 263	24 583	2000	
145 898	13 091	8 198	124 600	88 383	29 432	36 217	9	41 910	84 881	2006	
Parts par destinations (en pourcentage)											
31.2	2.5	1.9	26.8	16.6	2.6	10.2	0.0	10.2	15.9	1995	Total tous produits
31.6	3.1	1.9	26.5	17.3	4.1	9.2	0.0	10.6	16.1	2000	
37.5	3.4	2.1	32.0	22.7	7.6	9.3	0.0	10.8	21.8	2006	
45.5	4.9	7.3	33.2	18.1	1.1	15.1	0.0	12.8	20.2	1995	Produits alimentaires
47.9	5.5	7.5	34.9	20.7	1.4	14.2	0.0	15.1	17.4	2000	(CTCI 0 + 1 + 22 + 4)
56.9	6.3	12.2	38.4	19.6	1.9	18.8	0.0	17.8	22.9	2006	
28.5	5.7	3.5	19.4	15.2	0.5	4.2	0.0	6.2	12.1	1995	Matières premières
26.3	5.3	3.0	18.1	13.2	0.8	4.8	0.0	5.6	11.1	2000	d'origine agricole
28.8	4.2	4.2	20.5	15.9	3.1	4.6	0.0	4.5	13.1	2006	(CTCI 2 - 22 - 27 - 28)
26.5	4.5	4.2	17.8	5.5	0.4	12.4	0.0	12.3	7.7	1995	Minerais, métaux, pierres
34.2	5.5	8.3	20.4	9.2	0.9	11.1	0.0	11.8	13.4	2000	précieuses et or (non monétaire)
45.6	9.8	1.9	33.9	24.1	1.6	9.8	0.0	11.6	24.3	2006	(CTCI 27 + 28 + 68 + 667 + 971)
75.1	13.9	0.1	61.0	10.9	0.3	50.1	0.0	70.4	1.5	1995	Combustibles (CTCI 3)
56.0	12.9	0.3	42.8	7.2	0.3	35.6	0.0	53.6	1.0	2000	
33.6	5.8	0.6	27.2	5.0	1.2	22.2	0.0	25.8	5.0	2006	
25.4	0.8	0.9	23.7	17.7	3.2	6.0	0.0	4.6	17.2	1995	Articles manufacturés
26.0	0.8	0.8	24.4	18.9	5.4	5.6	0.0	4.7	18.1	2000	(CTCI 5 à 8 moins 667 et 68)
37.8	1.2	0.9	35.8	27.3	11.7	8.5	0.0	6.8	27.3	2006	
Parts par principaux groupes de produits (en pourcentage)											
100.0	100.0	100.0	100.0	100.0	100.0	100.0	100.0	100.0	100.0	1995	Total tous produits
100.0	100.0	100.0	100.0	100.0	100.0	100.0	100.0	100.0	100.0	2000	
100.0	100.0	100.0	100.0	100.0	100.0	100.0	100.0	100.0	100.0	2006	
18.7	25.4	49.8	15.9	14.0	5.4	19.0	84.7	16.1	16.3	1995	Produits alimentaires
18.6	21.8	47.6	16.1	14.6	4.3	18.9	3.0	17.5	13.3	2000	(CTCI 0 + 1 + 22 + 4)
11.4	14.0	43.6	9.0	6.5	1.9	15.1	0.8	12.4	7.9	2006	
2.3	5.8	4.7	1.8	2.3	0.5	1.0	0.0	1.6	1.9	1995	Matières premières
1.7	3.4	3.1	1.4	1.5	0.4	1.0	6.8	1.1	1.4	2000	d'origine agricole
1.0	1.6	2.5	0.8	0.9	0.5	0.6	0.1	0.5	0.7	2006	(CTCI 2 - 22 - 27 - 28)
4.2	8.8	11.0	3.3	1.6	0.8	6.0	3.7	5.9	2.4	1995	Minerais, métaux, pierres
4.9	8.0	19.7	3.5	2.4	1.0	5.5	9.1	5.0	3.8	2000	précieuses et or (non monétaire)
8.6	20.5	6.3	7.5	7.5	1.5	7.4	0.0	7.6	7.8	2006	(CTCI 27 + 28 + 68 + 667 + 971)
15.3	35.3	0.4	14.4	4.2	0.8	31.2	0.0	43.5	0.6	1995	Combustibles (CTCI 3)
14.0	32.9	1.3	12.8	3.3	0.5	30.6	0.0	39.9	0.5	2000	
5.2	10.1	1.6	5.0	1.3	0.9	13.9	0.0	14.0	1.3	2006	
59.3	24.4	34.1	64.3	77.5	92.3	42.8	11.7	32.8	78.5	1995	Articles manufacturés
59.0	18.9	28.1	65.9	77.8	93.4	43.4	81.1	31.9	80.6	2000	(CTCI 5 à 8 moins 667 et 68)
60.1	21.1	24.9	66.6	71.7	92.0	54.1	31.0	37.7	74.6	2006	

Sources :
- Données et estimations du secrétariat de la CNUCED sur la base de données Comtrade de ONU DAES et *Direction of Trade statistics* du Fonds Monétaire international

2.2.J Export structure by partner and product group
Developing economies: Oceania

Product group	Year / Année	World / Monde	Developed economies — Économies développées Total	Europe Total	Europe EU / UE	Canada	USA / États-Unis	Japan / Japon	Other developed countries / Autres économies développées	Economies in transition / Économies en transition
Millions of dollars										
All products	1995	5 339	4 474	1 135	1 132	32	234	1 914	1 158	2
	2000	4 339	1 621	564	558	4	229	522	302	6
	2006	7 820	5 734	1 871	1 843	11	276	1 042	2 534	12
Share by destination (percentage)										
All products	1995	100.0	83.8	21.3	21.2	0.6	4.4	35.9	21.7	0.0
	2000	..	..	..	..	..	..	..	..	..
	2006	100.0	73.3	23.9	23.6	0.1	3.5	13.3	32.4	0.1
All food items	1995	100.0	80.1	51.2	51.2	2.5	5.1	13.4	7.8	0.1
(SITC 0 + 1 + 22 + 4)	2000	100.0	52.2	27.4	27.3	0.2	10.4	8.2	6.0	0.1
	2006	100.0	74.5	37.9	37.7	0.6	14.6	13.3	8.1	0.3
Agricultural raw materials	1995	100.0	61.8	1.9	1.9	0.0	0.3	58.0	1.6	0.0
(SITC 2 - 22 - 27 - 28)	2000	100.0	45.6	6.0	5.9	0.0	2.2	29.7	7.7	0.0
	2006	100.0	17.2	2.3	2.3	0.1	1.9	9.5	3.4	0.0
Ores, metals, precious stones	1995	100.0	87.3	16.0	16.0	0.0	2.4	40.6	28.3	0.0
and non-monetary gold	2000	..	..	..	..	..	..	..	..	..
(SITC 27 + 28 + 68 + 667 + 971)	2006	100.0	79.8	14.8	14.8	0.0	0.2	22.9	41.8	0.2
Fuels (SITC 3)	1995	100.0	88.9	0.0	0.0	0.0	3.5	1.9	83.4	0.0
	2000	..	..	..	..	..	..	..	..	..
	2006	100.0	84.6	0.1	0.1	0.0	1.3	6.4	76.8	0.0
Manufactured goods	1995	100.0	86.6	30.6	30.5	0.4	10.6	31.1	13.9	0.1
(SITC 5 to 8 less 667 and 68)	2000	100.0	66.0	20.7	20.7	0.2	12.1	17.8	15.2	0.2
	2006	100.0	71.5	54.6	53.3	0.2	2.7	6.6	7.4	0.0
Share by major product group (percentage)										
All products	1995	100.0	100.0	100.0	100.0	100.0	100.0	100.0	100.0	100.0
	2000	100.0	100.0	100.0	100.0	100.0	100.0	100.0	100.0	100.0
	2006	100.0	100.0	100.0	100.0	100.0	100.0	100.0	100.0	100.0
All food items	1995	20.4	19.5	49.3	49.4	86.0	23.8	7.7	7.4	42.1
(SITC 0 + 1 + 22 + 4)	2000	15.6	21.8	32.9	33.1	28.8	30.6	10.7	13.5	7.2
	2006	15.6	15.9	24.8	25.0	62.8	64.5	15.6	3.9	34.6
Agricultural raw materials	1995	12.5	9.2	1.1	1.1	0.2	0.8	20.2	0.9	0.0
(SITC 2 - 22 - 27 - 28)	2000	2.9	3.6	1.4	1.4	0.6	1.2	7.3	3.3	0.9
	2006	7.4	1.7	0.7	0.7	3.0	3.9	5.3	0.8	0.7
Ores, metals, precious stones	1995	26.4	27.5	19.9	19.9	0.4	14.3	29.9	34.5	0.4
and non-monetary gold	2000	39.3	30.2	26.0	25.5	20.1	10.6	45.4	26.8	46.6
(SITC 27 + 28 + 68 + 667 + 971)	2006	32.1	34.9	19.9	20.2	2.4	1.9	55.1	41.4	53.9
Fuels (SITC 3)	1995	11.6	12.2	0.0	0.0	0.1	9.3	0.6	44.4	0.0
	2000	16.5	0.2	0.0	0.0	0.0	0.0	0.0	1.2	0.0
	2006	20.4	23.5	0.1	0.1	0.7	7.6	9.9	48.2	3.4
Manufactured goods	1995	19.9	20.6	28.7	28.6	13.1	48.0	17.3	12.8	57.5
(SITC 5 to 8 less 667 and 68)	2000	24.7	43.7	39.4	39.8	44.1	56.6	36.6	54.1	45.2
	2006	23.9	23.3	54.4	53.9	30.2	17.9	11.9	5.5	7.1

Sources:
- Data and UNCTAD secretariat estimates based on UN DESA Comtrade and IMF *Direction of Trade statistics* databases

2.2.J Structure des exportations par partenaires et groupes de produits
Économies en développement : Océanie

Total	Africa / Afrique	America / Amérique	Asia Asie — Total	Eastern, Southern and South-Eastern Asia / Asie orientale, méridionale et du Sud-Est	China / Chine	Western Asia / Asie occidentale	Oceania / Océanie	Major petroleum exporters / Principaux exportateurs de pétrole	Major exporters of manufactures / Principaux exportateurs d'articles manufacturés	Year / Année	Destination / Groupes de produits
Millions de dollars											
848	7	11	810	805	87	6	19	4	806	1995	**Total tous produits**
821	12	130	610	609	24	1	69	6	717	2000	
1 880	67	18	1 627	1 625	593	2	150	19	1 550	2006	
Parts par destinations (en pourcentage)											
15.9	0.1	0.2	15.2	15.1	1.6	0.1	0.4	0.1	15.1	1995	**Total tous produits**
..	..	..	..	..	..	..	..	..	..	2000	
24.0	0.9	0.2	20.8	20.8	7.6	0.0	1.9	0.2	19.8	2006	
18.6	0.1	0.1	18.2	17.9	1.1	0.3	0.3	0.1	17.5	1995	Produits alimentaires
14.1	0.3	0.0	10.2	10.1	0.0	0.1	3.6	0.3	8.1	2000	(CTCI 0 + 1 + 22 + 4)
25.2	1.9	0.0	16.8	16.8	2.2	0.0	6.5	1.1	16.3	2006	
38.2	0.0	0.0	38.0	38.0	4.3	0.0	0.2	0.0	38.0	1995	Matières premières
53.5	0.1	0.1	51.8	51.8	16.6	0.0	1.5	0.1	49.9	2000	d'origine agricole
82.8	0.1	0.4	81.6	81.6	72.1	0.0	0.7	0.0	81.3	2006	(CTCI 2 - 22 - 27 - 28)
12.7	0.0	0.0	12.7	12.7	0.0	0.0	0.0	0.0	12.7	1995	Minerais, métaux, pierres
..	..	..	..	..	..	..	..	..	..	2000	précieuses et or (non monétaire)
20.0	0.0	0.0	19.8	19.8	1.9	0.0	0.1	0.0	19.8	2006	(CTCI 27 + 28 + 68 + 667 + 971)
11.1	0.0	0.0	10.7	10.7	7.5	0.0	0.4	0.0	10.7	1995	Combustibles (CTCI 3)
..	..	..	..	..	..	..	..	..	..	2000	
5.0	0.0	0.0	4.5	4.5	0.0	0.0	0.5	0.0	0.6	2006	
13.0	0.6	1.0	10.4	10.2	0.0	0.2	1.0	0.3	10.8	1995	Articles manufacturés
32.6	0.4	12.1	16.5	16.4	0.2	0.0	3.6	0.3	28.1	2000	(CTCI 5 à 8 moins 667 et 68)
27.3	2.3	0.8	20.4	20.3	5.6	0.1	3.8	0.3	20.1	2006	
Parts par principaux groupes de produits (en pourcentage)											
100.0	100.0	100.0	100.0	100.0	100.0	100.0	100.0	100.0	100.0	1995	**Total tous produits**
100.0	100.0	100.0	100.0	100.0	100.0	100.0	100.0	100.0	100.0	2000	
100.0	100.0	100.0	100.0	100.0	100.0	100.0	100.0	100.0	100.0	2006	
24.0	10.4	7.8	24.5	24.3	14.1	62.2	14.3	21.3	23.7	1995	Produits alimentaires
11.6	16.4	0.1	11.3	11.2	1.4	55.7	35.3	33.3	7.7	2000	(CTCI 0 + 1 + 22 + 4)
16.4	34.1	2.1	12.6	12.6	4.5	0.9	52.8	68.9	12.9	2006	
30.0	0.1	0.4	31.3	31.5	32.7	0.0	5.8	0.0	31.4	1995	Matières premières
8.3	1.2	0.1	10.9	10.9	90.1	0.0	2.8	2.0	8.9	2000	d'origine agricole
25.3	0.8	13.2	28.9	28.9	69.9	3.9	2.5	1.0	30.2	2006	(CTCI 2 - 22 - 27 - 28)
21.2	0.3	0.1	22.1	22.3	0.0	0.4	2.0	0.0	22.3	1995	Minerais, métaux, pierres
35.1	47.8	0.0	45.9	46.0	0.4	12.4	3.2	3.3	38.9	2000	précieuses et or (non monétaire)
26.7	0.1	0.4	30.6	30.7	8.0	3.4	2.2	0.3	32.1	2006	(CTCI 27 + 28 + 68 + 667 + 971)
8.1	0.0	0.0	8.1	8.2	53.0	0.0	14.3	0.0	8.2	1995	Combustibles (CTCI 3)
2.2	0.0	0.0	2.9	2.9	0.0	0.0	1.0	0.0	2.4	2000	
4.2	0.3	0.0	4.4	4.4	0.0	0.0	5.1	0.2	0.6	2006	
16.3	88.8	91.7	13.7	13.5	0.1	37.4	54.6	78.6	14.2	1995	Articles manufacturés
42.6	33.5	99.8	28.9	28.9	7.9	31.9	56.7	61.1	42.0	2000	(CTCI 5 à 8 moins 667 et 68)
27.1	64.2	81.6	23.4	23.4	17.6	70.8	47.5	28.7	24.1	2006	

Sources :
- Données et estimations du secrétariat de la CNUCED sur la base de données Comtrade de ONU DAES et *Direction of Trade statistics* du Fonds Monétaire international

Destination / Product group	Year Année	World Monde	Developed economies / Économies développées							Economies in transition / Économies en transition
			Total	Europe		Canada	USA États-Unis	Japan Japon	Other developed countries Autres économies développées	
				Total	EU UE					

Millions of dollars										
All products	1995	5 814	4 608	1 441	1 430	13	374	805	1 974	1
	2000	5 429	3 598	1 234	1 218	17	383	396	1 569	14
	2006	10 604	6 023	2 089	2 039	41	430	596	2 867	2

Share by destination (percentage)										
All products	1995	100.0	79.3	24.8	24.6	0.2	6.4	13.9	34.0	0.0
	2000	100.0	66.3	22.7	22.4	0.3	7.0	7.3	28.9	0.3
	2006	100.0	56.8	19.7	19.2	0.4	4.1	5.6	27.0	0.0
All food items	1995	100.0	86.5	23.6	23.6	0.2	10.6	5.1	46.9	0.0
(SITC 0 + 1 + 22 + 4)	2000	100.0	84.2	20.8	20.7	0.4	13.9	1.5	47.6	0.1
	2006	100.0	70.4	19.4	19.3	0.4	5.8	3.6	41.2	0.0
Agricultural raw materials	1995	100.0	89.3	7.2	7.2	0.0	27.8	3.0	51.3	0.3
(SITC 2 - 22 - 27 - 28)	2000	100.0	81.1	8.1	8.1	1.2	33.1	0.9	37.8	0.1
	2006	100.0	80.3	5.0	5.0	6.3	23.1	0.8	45.2	0.0
Ores, metals, precious stones	1995	100.0	86.9	32.2	32.2	0.0	3.6	1.8	49.3	0.0
and non-monetary gold	2000	100.0	71.9	31.4	31.3	0.0	7.0	2.1	31.4	0.5
(SITC 27 + 28 + 68 + 667 + 971)	2006	100.0	80.9	41.6	41.5	1.3	1.7	3.0	33.3	0.1
Fuels (SITC 3)	1995	100.0	61.8	0.9	0.9	0.0	1.7	0.0	59.1	0.0
	2000	100.0	44.5	0.5	0.5	0.0	0.5	0.0	43.4	1.2
	2006	100.0	20.7	0.6	0.5	0.0	0.0	1.1	19.0	0.0
Manufactured goods	1995	100.0	80.0	29.3	29.0	0.3	5.3	18.2	26.9	0.0
(SITC 5 to 8 less 667 and 68)	2000	100.0	68.3	30.2	29.7	0.4	6.5	11.1	20.1	0.0
	2006	100.0	67.8	29.1	28.4	0.4	5.1	8.3	24.7	0.0

Share by major product group (percentage)										
All products	1995	100.0	100.0	100.0	100.0	100.0	100.0	100.0	100.0	100.0
	2000	100.0	100.0	100.0	100.0	100.0	100.0	100.0	100.0	100.0
	2006	100.0	100.0	100.0	100.0	100.0	100.0	100.0	100.0	100.0
All food items	1995	16.1	17.5	15.3	15.4	12.3	26.6	6.0	22.2	18.4
(SITC 0 + 1 + 22 + 4)	2000	15.9	20.2	14.6	14.7	20.1	31.3	3.3	26.2	4.9
	2006	13.7	16.9	13.5	13.7	14.3	19.4	8.7	20.8	5.0
Agricultural raw materials	1995	1.0	1.1	0.3	0.3	0.1	4.3	0.2	1.5	14.9
(SITC 2 - 22 - 27 - 28)	2000	1.0	1.3	0.4	0.4	4.0	4.8	0.1	1.4	0.2
	2006	0.9	1.3	0.2	0.2	15.2	5.4	0.1	1.6	0.7
Ores, metals, precious stones	1995	0.7	0.7	0.9	0.9	0.0	0.4	0.1	1.0	1.3
and non-monetary gold	2000	0.8	0.9	1.1	1.1	0.0	0.8	0.2	0.9	1.5
(SITC 27 + 28 + 68 + 667 + 971)	2006	0.8	1.1	1.7	1.7	2.7	0.3	0.4	1.0	5.5
Fuels (SITC 3)	1995	10.1	7.9	0.4	0.4	0.2	2.7	0.0	17.5	5.2
	2000	17.7	11.9	0.4	0.4	0.0	1.3	0.1	26.6	86.8
	2006	25.3	9.2	0.8	0.7	0.1	0.2	4.7	17.8	0.2
Manufactured goods	1995	69.9	70.5	82.5	82.4	85.7	57.9	91.9	55.3	60.2
(SITC 5 to 8 less 667 and 68)	2000	62.8	64.7	83.3	83.2	75.6	58.2	96.0	43.7	6.4
	2006	56.1	66.9	83.0	82.8	63.3	70.7	83.3	51.3	85.9

Sources:
- Data and UNCTAD secretariat estimates based on UN DESA Comtrade and IMF *Direction of Trade statistics* databases

2.2.J Structure des importations par partenaires et groupes de produits
Économies en développement : Océanie

| | | | Developing economies / Économies en développement | | | | | | | Year | Destination |
Total	Africa / Afrique	America / Amérique	Asia / Asie — Total	Eastern, Southern and South-Eastern Asia / Asie orientale, méridionale et du Sud-Est	China / Chine	Western Asia / Asie occidentale	Oceania / Océanie	Major petroleum exporters / Principaux exportateurs de pétrole	Major exporters of manufactures / Principaux exportateurs d'articles manufacturés	Année	Groupes de produits
Millions de dollars											
1 199	9	34	1 137	1 136	71	1	19	1	1 094	1995	Total tous produits
1 751	30	297	1 349	1 346	100	3	75	20	1 262	2000	
4 506	44	82	4 190	4 174	456	16	124	20	4 046	2006	
Parts par destinations (en pourcentage)											
20.6	0.2	0.6	19.6	19.5	1.2	0.0	0.3	0.0	18.8	1995	Total tous produits
32.3	0.6	5.5	24.8	24.8	1.8	0.1	1.4	0.4	23.2	2000	
42.5	0.4	0.8	39.5	39.4	4.3	0.1	1.2	0.2	38.2	2006	
13.4	0.4	1.4	11.3	11.3	0.8	0.0	0.3	0.0	10.3	1995	Produits alimentaires
15.2	0.7	3.5	8.4	8.3	0.7	0.0	2.5	0.0	7.1	2000	(CTCI 0 + 1 + 22 + 4)
26.9	0.7	2.1	18.3	18.2	3.6	0.1	5.8	0.1	17.3	2006	
10.3	1.0	0.2	7.3	7.1	0.0	0.2	1.8	0.2	6.7	1995	Matières premières
18.7	0.2	2.0	6.0	6.0	0.2	0.0	10.5	0.1	4.9	2000	d'origine agricole
17.9	0.7	0.9	9.4	9.4	0.6	0.0	6.9	0.0	6.0	2006	(CTCI 2 - 22 - 27 - 28)
12.6	1.0	0.1	10.6	10.5	0.1	0.1	0.8	0.1	10.4	1995	Minerais, métaux, pierres
25.9	0.1	4.6	16.7	16.7	0.3	0.0	4.5	0.0	14.3	2000	précieuses et or (non monétaire)
18.1	0.2	0.2	14.0	14.0	3.4	0.1	3.7	0.1	13.1	2006	(CTCI 27 + 28 + 68 + 667 + 971)
38.2	0.2	0.1	37.4	37.4	0.0	0.0	0.4	0.0	37.2	1995	Combustibles (CTCI 3)
54.1	1.8	4.7	45.9	45.9	0.0	0.0	1.6	1.8	45.7	2000	
79.3	0.0	0.6	78.0	78.0	0.1	0.0	0.8	0.6	77.7	2006	
19.9	0.1	0.5	19.0	19.0	1.6	0.0	0.3	0.0	18.3	1995	Articles manufacturés
31.4	0.2	6.4	24.0	24.0	2.7	0.1	0.9	0.1	21.9	2000	(CTCI 5 à 8 moins 667 et 68)
31.7	0.5	0.6	29.4	29.2	6.6	0.2	1.2	0.1	27.5	2006	
Parts par principaux groupes de produits (en pourcentage)											
100.0	100.0	100.0	100.0	100.0	100.0	100.0	100.0	100.0	100.0	1995	Total tous produits
100.0	100.0	100.0	100.0	100.0	100.0	100.0	100.0	100.0	100.0	2000	
100.0	100.0	100.0	100.0	100.0	100.0	100.0	100.0	100.0	100.0	2006	
10.5	39.0	40.2	9.3	9.3	10.0	11.1	13.4	28.6	8.8	1995	Produits alimentaires
7.5	19.9	10.2	5.4	5.4	6.4	13.6	29.2	2.0	4.9	2000	(CTCI 0 + 1 + 22 + 4)
8.6	22.3	37.4	6.3	6.3	11.5	12.6	67.5	6.9	6.2	2006	
0.5	6.3	0.3	0.4	0.4	0.0	7.2	5.6	14.0	0.4	1995	Matières premières
0.6	0.5	0.4	0.3	0.3	0.1	0.0	7.8	0.3	0.2	2000	d'origine agricole
0.4	1.6	1.1	0.2	0.2	0.1	0.0	5.6	0.0	0.1	2006	(CTCI 2 - 22 - 27 - 28)
0.4	4.2	0.1	0.4	0.4	0.0	4.1	1.6	6.3	0.4	1995	Minerais, métaux, pierres
0.6	0.1	0.7	0.5	0.5	0.1	0.6	2.5	0.0	0.5	2000	précieuses et or (non monétaire)
0.3	0.4	0.2	0.3	0.3	0.6	0.5	2.5	0.4	0.3	2006	(CTCI 27 + 28 + 68 + 667 + 971)
18.6	13.7	2.2	19.3	19.3	0.1	0.0	13.6	0.6	19.9	1995	Combustibles (CTCI 3)
29.7	58.2	15.4	32.8	32.9	0.1	0.0	20.3	87.2	34.9	2000	
47.3	2.1	18.0	50.0	50.2	0.8	0.5	16.3	75.2	51.6	2006	
67.3	36.8	57.1	68.0	68.0	89.8	77.6	55.5	50.6	67.8	1995	Articles manufacturés
61.2	21.1	73.0	60.8	60.7	92.7	85.1	38.8	10.4	59.3	2000	(CTCI 5 à 8 moins 667 et 68)
41.9	70.4	43.0	41.8	41.7	86.0	59.6	58.3	17.5	40.4	2006	

Sources :
- Données et estimations du secrétariat de la CNUCED sur la base de données Comtrade de ONU DAES et *Direction of Trade statistics* du Fonds Monétaire international

2.2.K **Export structure by partner and product group**
Developing economies:
Major petroleum exporters

Destination / Product group	Year Année	World Monde	Developed economies — Économies développées							Economies in transition Économies en transition
			Total	Europe		Canada	USA États-Unis	Japan Japon	Other developed countries Autres économies développées	
				Total	EU UE					
Millions of dollars										
All products	1995	194 681	100 443	39 397	38 480	1 574	32 395	26 072	1 005	1 534
	2000	337 109	188 628	74 863	67 702	2 757	71 640	38 580	788	1 800
	2006	865 978	445 729	156 807	143 454	9 222	156 137	119 590	3 972	3 325
Share by destination (percentage)										
All products	1995	100.0	51.6	20.2	19.8	0.8	16.6	13.4	0.5	0.8
	2000	100.0	56.0	22.2	20.1	0.8	21.3	11.4	0.2	0.5
	2006	100.0	51.5	18.1	16.6	1.1	18.0	13.8	0.5	0.4
All food items	1995	100.0	41.0	22.5	22.1	0.4	15.1	2.5	0.4	6.7
(SITC 0 + 1 + 22 + 4)	2000	100.0	32.1	17.2	17.0	0.4	11.3	2.9	0.4	5.8
	2006	100.0	26.7	17.8	17.4	0.4	7.1	1.1	0.3	5.0
Agricultural raw materials	1995	100.0	58.2	44.8	43.9	0.3	7.3	5.1	0.8	0.6
(SITC 2 - 22 - 27 - 28)	2000	100.0	50.2	37.1	35.5	0.4	10.0	2.2	0.5	1.4
	2006	100.0	31.3	20.8	20.4	0.6	9.3	0.6	0.1	3.0
Ores, metals, precious stones	1995	100.0	42.1	19.9	19.3	0.0	7.5	14.5	0.2	1.0
and non-monetary gold	2000	100.0	50.9	30.3	28.7	0.2	9.8	10.3	0.3	1.3
(SITC 27 + 28 + 68 + 667 + 971)	2006	100.0	26.4	20.1	14.7	0.9	2.7	2.5	0.1	0.4
Fuels (SITC 3)	1995	100.0	55.0	20.3	19.9	0.9	17.8	15.5	0.5	0.1
	2000	100.0	58.8	22.8	20.5	0.8	22.3	12.6	0.2	0.1
	2006	100.0	57.7	19.0	17.3	1.2	20.7	16.4	0.4	0.0
Manufactured goods	1995	100.0	31.0	17.0	16.4	0.6	10.5	2.0	1.0	3.7
(SITC 5 to 8 less 667 and 68)	2000	100.0	30.0	13.8	13.4	0.9	14.1	0.4	0.9	3.6
	2006	100.0	23.3	16.0	15.3	0.4	5.3	0.5	1.0	3.0
Share by major product group (percentage)										
All products	1995	100.0	100.0	100.0	100.0	100.0	100.0	100.0	100.0	100.0
	2000	100.0	100.0	100.0	100.0	100.0	100.0	100.0	100.0	100.0
	2006	100.0	100.0	100.0	100.0	100.0	100.0	100.0	100.0	100.0
All food items	1995	3.5	2.8	3.9	3.9	1.9	3.2	0.7	2.8	30.1
(SITC 0 + 1 + 22 + 4)	2000	1.9	1.1	1.5	1.6	1.0	1.0	0.5	3.3	20.9
	2006	1.8	0.9	1.8	1.9	0.7	0.7	0.1	1.4	23.8
Agricultural raw materials	1995	1.0	1.1	2.1	2.1	0.3	0.4	0.4	1.5	0.7
(SITC 2 - 22 - 27 - 28)	2000	0.4	0.4	0.7	0.7	0.2	0.2	0.1	0.9	1.0
	2006	0.4	0.2	0.4	0.5	0.2	0.2	0.0	0.1	3.0
Ores, metals, precious stones	1995	2.4	2.0	2.4	2.3	0.1	1.1	2.6	0.7	3.1
and non-monetary gold	2000	1.5	1.3	2.0	2.1	0.4	0.7	1.3	2.0	3.5
(SITC 27 + 28 + 68 + 667 + 971)	2006	2.5	1.3	2.8	2.2	2.1	0.4	0.5	0.8	2.7
Fuels (SITC 3)	1995	81.9	87.3	82.3	82.3	89.5	87.9	94.7	74.4	14.9
	2000	88.7	93.2	91.2	90.6	90.5	93.2	97.9	65.5	23.6
	2006	83.4	93.4	87.3	87.3	93.7	95.8	99.0	73.6	2.2
Manufactured goods	1995	11.0	6.6	9.2	9.2	8.1	7.0	1.6	20.4	51.1
(SITC 5 to 8 less 667 and 68)	2000	7.4	4.0	4.6	4.9	7.9	4.9	0.2	28.1	49.8
	2006	8.6	3.9	7.6	8.0	3.2	2.5	0.3	19.4	66.4

Sources:
- Data and UNCTAD secretariat estimates based on UN DESA Comtrade and IMF *Direction of Trade statistics* databases

2.2.K Structure des exportations par partenaires et groupes de produits
Économies en développement : Principaux exportateurs de pétrole

Total	Africa Afrique	America Amérique	Asia Asie Total	Eastern, Southern and South-Eastern Asia / Asie orientale, méridionale et du Sud-Est	China Chine	Western Asia / Asie occidentale	Oceania Océanie	Major petroleum exporters / Principaux exportateurs de pétrole	Major exporters of manufactures / Principaux exportateurs d'articles manufacturés	Year Année	Destination / Groupes de produits
Millions de dollars											
44 276	3 421	10 039	30 815	20 880	2 008	9 935	1	8 891	22 709	1995	**Total tous produits**
123 122	11 299	17 052	94 740	79 305	9 031	15 434	31	10 130	83 124	2000	
351 492	30 687	40 660	280 128	224 999	41 758	55 129	17	53 408	216 051	2006	
Parts par destinations (en pourcentage)											
22.7	1.8	5.2	15.8	10.7	1.0	5.1	0.0	4.6	11.7	1995	**Total tous produits**
36.5	3.4	5.1	28.1	23.5	2.7	4.6	0.0	3.0	24.7	2000	
40.6	3.5	4.7	32.3	26.0	4.8	6.4	0.0	6.2	24.9	2006	
51.1	2.9	12.3	35.9	6.1	0.3	29.8	0.0	28.4	4.0	1995	Produits alimentaires
61.2	4.4	11.1	45.7	11.7	1.2	34.0	0.1	29.8	7.5	2000	(CTCI 0 + 1 + 22 + 4)
67.7	6.8	6.1	54.9	14.0	0.6	40.8	0.0	41.7	5.6	2006	
40.7	6.6	2.2	31.9	23.1	8.9	8.7	0.0	6.5	25.0	1995	Matières premières
46.6	5.0	2.6	39.0	26.9	14.8	12.1	0.0	4.5	29.8	2000	d'origine agricole
65.4	5.7	1.0	58.7	44.8	12.2	13.8	0.0	12.7	21.4	2006	(CTCI 2 - 22 - 27 - 28)
52.7	1.6	5.7	45.5	29.8	1.1	15.7	0.0	14.0	29.6	1995	Minerais, métaux, pierres
47.5	1.9	5.2	40.5	27.3	2.8	13.2	0.0	10.9	28.1	2000	précieuses et or (non monétaire)
71.4	2.2	2.4	66.7	52.9	4.0	13.8	0.0	12.3	50.8	2006	(CTCI 27 + 28 + 68 + 667 + 971)
14.9	1.0	4.1	9.7	8.3	0.9	1.5	0.0	0.5	10.1	1995	Combustibles (CTCI 3)
33.5	3.0	4.6	25.9	23.9	2.8	2.0	0.0	0.6	25.7	2000	
36.9	3.0	4.9	29.0	26.3	5.2	2.7	0.0	1.9	26.1	2006	
64.1	6.4	10.9	46.9	25.2	1.9	21.7	0.0	25.1	20.4	1995	Articles manufacturés
63.0	7.9	8.7	46.4	21.1	0.8	25.3	0.0	23.5	16.0	2000	(CTCI 5 à 8 moins 667 et 68)
71.9	10.0	4.6	57.3	25.8	3.6	31.5	0.0	40.0	16.5	2006	
Parts par principaux groupes de produits (en pourcentage)											
100.0	100.0	100.0	100.0	100.0	100.0	100.0	100.0	100.0	100.0	1995	**Total tous produits**
100.0	100.0	100.0	100.0	100.0	100.0	100.0	100.0	100.0	100.0	2000	
100.0	100.0	100.0	100.0	100.0	100.0	100.0	100.0	100.0	100.0	2006	
7.9	5.8	8.4	8.0	2.0	1.2	20.6	22.8	21.9	1.2	1995	Produits alimentaires
3.2	2.5	4.2	3.1	1.0	0.8	14.2	11.9	19.0	0.6	2000	(CTCI 0 + 1 + 22 + 4)
3.0	3.5	2.4	3.1	1.0	0.2	11.7	4.9	12.3	0.4	2006	
1.7	3.6	0.4	1.9	2.1	8.3	1.7	8.2	1.4	2.1	1995	Matières premières
0.5	0.6	0.2	0.6	0.5	2.2	1.1	0.3	0.6	0.5	2000	d'origine agricole
0.6	0.6	0.1	0.7	0.7	1.0	0.8	0.0	0.8	0.3	2006	(CTCI 2 - 22 - 27 - 28)
5.6	2.1	2.7	6.9	6.7	2.6	7.4	4.8	7.4	6.1	1995	Minerais, métaux, pierres
1.9	0.8	1.5	2.1	1.7	1.5	4.2	0.0	5.3	1.7	2000	précieuses et or (non monétaire)
4.4	1.6	1.3	5.2	5.1	2.1	5.4	2.9	5.0	5.1	2006	(CTCI 27 + 28 + 68 + 667 + 971)
53.5	47.9	65.3	50.3	63.1	67.7	23.3	0.5	8.6	71.1	1995	Combustibles (CTCI 3)
81.5	78.5	81.4	81.8	90.2	93.2	39.1	85.0	16.5	92.4	2000	
75.8	69.7	87.8	74.7	84.5	90.3	34.8	77.6	25.2	87.4	2006	
31.1	40.3	23.2	32.7	25.9	20.2	46.9	63.7	60.6	19.3	1995	Articles manufacturés
12.7	17.3	12.7	12.2	6.6	2.2	40.7	2.8	57.7	4.8	2000	(CTCI 5 à 8 moins 667 et 68)
15.3	24.4	8.4	15.2	8.6	6.4	42.6	13.8	55.8	5.7	2006	

Sources :
- Données et estimations du secrétariat de la CNUCED sur la base de données Comtrade de ONU DAES et *Direction of Trade statistics* du Fonds Monétaire international

2.2.K **Import structure by partner and product group**
Developing economies:
Major petroleum exporters

Destination / Product group	Year Année	World Monde	Developed economies / Économies développées							Economies in transition / Économies en transition
			Total	Europe Total	EU UE	Canada	USA États-Unis	Japan Japon	Other developed countries Autres économies développées	
Millions of dollars										
All products	1995	133 287	86 831	52 839	49 467	2 482	19 940	9 672	1 898	2 125
	2000	147 871	89 566	53 422	50 489	2 553	19 987	10 417	3 187	3 097
	2006	390 915	171 506	106 944	99 870	3 076	33 393	21 929	6 164	6 961
Share by destination (percentage)										
All products	1995	100.0	65.1	39.6	37.1	1.9	15.0	7.3	1.4	1.6
	2000	100.0	60.6	36.1	34.1	1.7	13.5	7.0	2.2	2.1
	2006	100.0	43.9	27.4	25.5	0.8	8.5	5.6	1.6	1.8
All food items	1995	100.0	55.3	31.0	30.2	5.6	12.6	0.1	6.0	0.9
(SITC 0 + 1 + 22 + 4)	2000	100.0	52.7	30.3	29.6	5.4	10.5	0.1	6.4	0.9
	2006	100.0	41.1	24.5	22.9	2.4	7.5	0.1	6.6	2.6
Agricultural raw materials	1995	100.0	56.4	30.5	30.2	4.1	17.9	2.5	1.6	5.8
(SITC 2 - 22 - 27 - 28)	2000	100.0	58.1	35.5	34.6	3.3	15.0	1.5	2.7	5.0
	2006	100.0	55.4	38.3	37.6	3.1	8.5	3.3	2.2	3.1
Ores, metals, precious stones	1995	100.0	57.5	42.2	22.5	2.6	8.3	0.5	3.9	2.0
and non-monetary gold	2000	100.0	49.5	35.4	23.1	0.4	5.2	1.0	7.5	3.2
(SITC 27 + 28 + 68 + 667 + 971)	2006	100.0	28.0	21.2	15.5	1.0	1.7	0.7	3.3	4.4
Fuels (SITC 3)	1995	100.0	28.9	16.1	16.0	0.4	10.7	0.1	1.6	3.5
	2000	100.0	15.0	9.6	7.9	0.1	4.2	0.1	1.0	0.8
	2006	100.0	27.2	20.7	19.0	0.2	5.7	0.2	0.5	5.4
Manufactured goods	1995	100.0	69.1	42.3	40.1	1.0	16.0	9.6	0.3	1.6
(SITC 5 to 8 less 667 and 68)	2000	100.0	65.3	38.8	37.0	1.0	15.1	9.4	1.0	2.3
	2006	100.0	53.9	33.2	31.3	0.7	11.0	8.1	0.9	1.5
Share by major product group (percentage)										
All products	1995	100.0	100.0	100.0	100.0	100.0	100.0	100.0	100.0	100.0
	2000	100.0	100.0	100.0	100.0	100.0	100.0	100.0	100.0	100.0
	2006	100.0	100.0	100.0	100.0	100.0	100.0	100.0	100.0	100.0
All food items	1995	16.7	14.2	13.1	13.6	50.6	14.0	0.3	70.2	9.8
(SITC 0 + 1 + 22 + 4)	2000	17.3	15.0	14.5	15.0	53.6	13.5	0.2	51.1	7.4
	2006	9.9	9.2	8.8	8.8	29.7	8.7	0.2	41.1	14.6
Agricultural raw materials	1995	1.7	1.5	1.3	1.4	3.8	2.1	0.6	1.9	6.3
(SITC 2 - 22 - 27 - 28)	2000	1.3	1.3	1.3	1.4	2.6	1.5	0.3	1.7	3.2
	2006	0.8	1.0	1.1	1.1	3.0	0.8	0.4	1.1	1.3
Ores, metals, precious stones	1995	3.7	3.3	3.9	2.2	5.2	2.0	0.2	10.1	4.6
and non-monetary gold	2000	3.5	2.9	3.4	2.4	0.8	1.3	0.5	12.2	5.3
(SITC 27 + 28 + 68 + 667 + 971)	2006	4.7	3.0	3.7	2.8	6.3	0.9	0.6	9.9	11.6
Fuels (SITC 3)	1995	2.6	1.1	1.0	1.1	0.6	1.8	0.0	2.9	5.5
	2000	3.9	1.0	1.0	0.9	0.3	1.2	0.1	1.8	1.5
	2006	5.7	3.6	4.3	4.3	1.4	3.8	0.2	1.7	17.4
Manufactured goods	1995	74.7	79.2	79.8	80.8	39.7	79.6	98.5	14.0	73.8
(SITC 5 to 8 less 667 and 68)	2000	73.6	79.3	79.1	79.7	42.6	82.3	98.3	33.2	81.2
	2006	65.9	80.9	80.0	80.6	58.8	84.6	94.7	39.1	53.8

Sources:
- Data and UNCTAD secretariat estimates based on UN DESA Comtrade and IMF *Direction of Trade statistics* databases

2.2.K Structure des importations par partenaires et groupes de produits
Économies en développement :
Principaux exportateurs de pétrole

Total	Africa / Afrique	America / Amérique	Asia / Asie — Total	Eastern, Southern and South-Eastern Asia / Asie orientale, méridionale et du Sud-Est	China / Chine	Western Asia / Asie occidentale	Oceania / Océanie	Major petroleum exporters / Principaux exportateurs de pétrole	Major exporters of manufactures / Principaux exportateurs d'articles manufacturés	Year / Année	Destination / Groupes de produits
Millions de dollars											
43 350	3 101	7 683	32 562	21 753	3 310	10 808	5	9 160	23 732	1995	**Total tous produits**
54 641	3 909	10 488	40 202	26 861	6 154	13 342	42	13 515	28 357	2000	
151 655	10 281	25 672	115 696	84 134	30 847	31 562	9	28 086	96 030	2006	
Parts par destinations (en pourcentage)											
32.5	2.3	5.8	24.4	16.3	2.5	8.1	0.0	6.9	17.8	1995	**Total tous produits**
37.0	2.6	7.1	27.2	18.2	4.2	9.0	0.0	9.1	19.2	2000	
38.8	2.6	6.6	29.6	21.5	7.9	8.1	0.0	7.2	24.6	2006	
43.3	4.8	13.9	24.5	14.6	1.2	9.9	0.0	8.0	17.5	1995	Produits alimentaires
46.1	5.8	12.3	27.9	17.2	1.2	10.7	0.1	11.2	17.2	2000	(CTCI 0 + 1 + 22 + 4)
54.1	5.8	18.5	29.9	17.2	1.8	12.7	0.0	11.8	22.9	2006	
36.8	3.9	11.1	21.8	17.4	0.5	4.3	0.0	4.9	18.6	1995	Matières premières
36.8	5.0	9.8	22.0	16.9	0.8	5.1	0.0	4.1	18.7	2000	d'origine agricole
38.7	4.1	9.9	24.7	18.8	2.2	6.0	0.0	5.1	18.6	2006	(CTCI 2 - 22 - 27 - 28)
40.3	6.1	11.2	23.0	8.6	0.6	14.3	0.0	14.5	14.0	1995	Minerais, métaux, pierres
47.1	7.8	13.2	26.1	13.0	1.1	13.1	0.0	14.1	20.2	2000	précieuses et or (non monétaire)
62.5	7.3	7.3	47.9	36.7	2.7	11.2	0.0	13.4	39.7	2006	(CTCI 27 + 28 + 68 + 667 + 971)
64.3	4.2	5.1	55.0	5.5	0.3	49.5	0.0	55.7	4.0	1995	Combustibles (CTCI 3)
82.1	7.5	25.3	49.3	5.3	2.3	44.0	0.0	61.6	5.4	2000	
42.3	9.3	12.3	20.6	10.2	0.7	10.4	0.0	17.5	14.8	2006	
28.7	1.5	3.6	23.6	17.5	3.0	6.1	0.0	4.7	18.6	1995	Articles manufacturés
32.0	1.4	4.6	26.0	19.4	5.2	6.7	0.0	5.8	20.3	2000	(CTCI 5 à 8 moins 667 et 68)
41.5	1.7	5.5	34.3	26.2	11.4	8.1	0.0	6.4	29.0	2006	
Parts par principaux groupes de produits (en pourcentage)											
100.0	100.0	100.0	100.0	100.0	100.0	100.0	100.0	100.0	100.0	1995	**Total tous produits**
100.0	100.0	100.0	100.0	100.0	100.0	100.0	100.0	100.0	100.0	2000	
100.0	100.0	100.0	100.0	100.0	100.0	100.0	100.0	100.0	100.0	2006	
22.3	34.8	40.4	16.8	15.0	7.8	20.5	37.4	19.4	16.4	1995	Produits alimentaires
21.5	38.1	29.9	17.7	16.3	5.2	20.4	83.7	21.2	15.5	2000	(CTCI 0 + 1 + 22 + 4)
13.8	21.6	27.7	10.0	7.9	2.2	15.5	22.4	16.2	9.2	2006	
2.0	3.0	3.4	1.6	1.9	0.4	0.9	0.0	1.2	1.8	1995	Matières premières
1.3	2.5	1.8	1.1	1.2	0.3	0.8	0.8	0.6	1.3	2000	d'origine agricole
0.8	1.2	1.1	0.6	0.7	0.2	0.6	1.0	0.5	0.6	2006	(CTCI 2 - 22 - 27 - 28)
4.6	9.6	7.2	3.5	2.0	0.9	6.5	0.5	7.8	2.9	1995	Minerais, métaux, pierres
4.5	10.3	6.5	3.4	2.5	0.9	5.1	0.8	5.4	3.7	2000	précieuses et or (non monétaire)
7.6	13.1	5.2	7.6	8.0	1.6	6.5	0.1	8.8	7.6	2006	(CTCI 27 + 28 + 68 + 667 + 971)
5.1	4.6	2.3	5.8	0.9	0.4	15.6	0.0	20.7	0.6	1995	Combustibles (CTCI 3)
8.6	10.9	13.8	7.0	1.1	2.1	18.8	0.0	26.0	1.1	2000	
6.3	20.4	10.7	4.0	2.7	0.5	7.4	0.0	14.0	3.5	2006	
65.9	47.8	46.7	72.1	80.0	90.4	56.4	62.1	50.7	78.0	1995	Articles manufacturés
63.8	37.8	47.9	70.5	78.4	91.1	54.5	14.6	46.5	78.0	2000	(CTCI 5 à 8 moins 667 et 68)
70.4	42.8	54.8	76.3	80.1	95.3	66.3	41.4	59.0	77.8	2006	

Sources :
- Données et estimations du secrétariat de la CNUCED sur la base de données Comtrade de ONU DAES et *Direction of Trade statistics* du Fonds Monétaire international

2.2.L Export structure by partner and product group
Developing economies:
Major exporters of manufactured goods

Destination / Product group	Year / Année	World / Monde	Developed economies / Économies développées								Economies in transition / Économies en transition
			Total	Europe		Canada	USA / États-Unis	Japan / Japon	Other developed countries / Autres économies développées		
				Total	EU / UE						

Millions of dollars

All products	1995	1 004 321	548 598	164 221	157 558	12 216	248 698	106 502	16 960		10 043
	2000	1 409 447	821 562	228 040	219 677	17 746	415 130	134 246	26 401		9 173
	2006	3 050 952	1 510 190	522 868	506 688	36 728	674 429	212 163	64 002		54 135

Share by destination (percentage)

All products	1995	100.0	54.6	16.4	15.7	1.2	24.8	10.6	1.7		1.0
	2000	100.0	58.3	16.2	15.6	1.3	29.5	9.5	1.9		0.7
	2006	100.0	49.5	17.1	16.6	1.2	22.1	7.0	2.1		1.8
All food items	1995	100.0	53.9	18.8	18.1	0.8	13.9	19.0	1.3		3.3
(SITC 0 + 1 + 22 + 4)	2000	100.0	58.4	19.2	18.5	1.1	18.9	17.5	1.6		2.2
	2006	100.0	52.1	19.8	19.3	1.4	17.4	11.7	1.8		5.0
Agricultural raw materials	1995	100.0	49.7	17.8	17.4	0.6	12.2	17.8	1.2		0.2
(SITC 2 - 22 - 27 - 28)	2000	100.0	49.4	19.5	19.0	0.6	13.9	14.4	1.1		0.2
	2006	100.0	44.2	18.8	18.3	1.1	13.0	10.3	1.0		0.8
Ores, metals, precious stones and non-monetary gold	1995	100.0	49.9	16.2	14.5	0.4	14.5	17.0	1.8		0.6
	2000	100.0	51.4	19.1	16.3	0.6	17.2	10.2	4.4		0.4
(SITC 27 + 28 + 68 + 667 + 971)	2006	100.0	41.7	17.7	14.9	0.9	11.3	7.7	4.1		0.5
Fuels (SITC 3)	1995	100.0	46.5	4.7	4.6	0.2	21.4	18.4	1.8		0.3
	2000	100.0	48.1	4.0	3.8	0.7	24.9	16.1	2.5		0.2
	2006	100.0	40.4	5.2	5.2	0.5	21.9	7.9	4.9		0.2
Manufactured goods	1995	100.0	55.3	16.5	15.9	1.4	26.6	9.1	1.7		0.9
(SITC 5 to 8 less 667 and 68)	2000	100.0	59.3	16.4	15.9	1.3	31.1	8.7	1.8		0.6
	2006	100.0	50.3	17.2	16.7	1.3	23.4	6.7	1.8		1.7

Share by major product group (percentage)

All products	1995	100.0	100.0	100.0	100.0	100.0	100.0	100.0	100.0		100.0
	2000	100.0	100.0	100.0	100.0	100.0	100.0	100.0	100.0		100.0
	2006	100.0	100.0	100.0	100.0	100.0	100.0	100.0	100.0		100.0
All food items	1995	7.8	7.7	9.0	9.0	5.3	4.4	14.0	6.2		25.6
(SITC 0 + 1 + 22 + 4)	2000	5.1	5.1	6.1	6.1	4.7	3.3	9.4	4.5		17.7
	2006	4.4	4.6	5.0	5.1	5.1	3.4	7.3	3.7		12.3
Agricultural raw materials	1995	2.2	2.0	2.4	2.4	1.1	1.1	3.6	1.5		0.4
(SITC 2 - 22 - 27 - 28)	2000	1.3	1.1	1.6	1.6	0.6	0.6	2.0	0.8		0.4
	2006	1.1	1.0	1.2	1.2	1.0	0.6	1.6	0.5		0.5
Ores, metals, precious stones and non-monetary gold	1995	3.4	3.1	3.4	3.1	1.2	2.0	5.4	3.6		2.0
	2000	2.8	2.5	3.3	2.9	1.3	1.6	3.0	6.5		1.7
(SITC 27 + 28 + 68 + 667 + 971)	2006	3.8	3.2	4.0	3.4	2.9	2.0	4.2	7.4		1.1
Fuels (SITC 3)	1995	3.3	2.8	1.0	1.0	0.6	2.9	5.8	3.5		0.9
	2000	4.3	3.6	1.1	1.1	2.2	3.7	7.3	5.9		1.5
	2006	6.0	4.9	1.8	1.9	2.5	6.0	6.8	14.1		0.5
Manufactured goods	1995	82.0	83.1	82.9	83.1	91.0	88.2	70.1	84.1		70.5
(SITC 5 to 8 less 667 and 68)	2000	85.7	87.2	87.0	87.5	90.9	90.5	77.9	81.4		78.4
	2006	82.5	84.0	82.6	83.2	87.8	87.4	79.2	71.7		78.9

Sources:
- Data and UNCTAD secretariat estimates based on UN DESA Comtrade and IMF *Direction of Trade statistics* databases

2.2.L   Structure des exportations par partenaires et groupes de produits
Économies en développement :
Principaux exportateurs d'articles manufacturés

Total	Africa Afrique	America Amérique	Asia Asie Total	Eastern, Southern and South-Eastern Asia Asie orientale, méridionale et du Sud-Est	China Chine	Western Asia Asie occidentale	Oceania Océanie	Major petroleum exporters Principaux exportateurs de pétrole	Major exporters of manufactures Principaux exportateurs d'articles manufacturés	Year Année	Destination Groupes de produits
Millions de dollars											
442 404	17 472	37 445	386 237	364 149	75 602	22 088	1 250	26 544	338 034	1995	**Total tous produits**
572 559	20 435	51 980	497 946	469 642	106 636	28 304	2 197	34 331	444 219	2000	
1 477 508	72 386	131 030	1 268 417	1 172 788	344 371	95 630	5 675	123 011	1 093 002	2006	
Parts par destinations (en pourcentage)											
44.1	1.7	3.7	38.5	36.3	7.5	2.2	0.1	2.6	33.7	1995	**Total tous produits**
40.6	1.4	3.7	35.3	33.3	7.6	2.0	0.2	2.4	31.5	2000	
48.4	2.4	4.3	41.6	38.4	11.3	3.1	0.2	4.0	35.8	2006	
42.7	3.5	2.1	36.9	32.8	6.9	4.1	0.1	5.0	25.4	1995	Produits alimentaires
39.0	3.5	2.7	32.7	28.2	5.1	4.5	0.1	5.8	22.1	2000	(CTCI 0 + 1 + 22 + 4)
42.8	5.7	2.6	34.3	28.5	5.8	5.8	0.2	8.9	20.7	2006	
50.1	1.5	2.9	45.7	44.1	12.6	1.6	0.0	1.8	41.1	1995	Matières premières
50.1	1.1	2.8	46.2	44.6	18.3	1.6	0.0	1.8	40.7	2000	d'origine agricole
54.8	1.3	3.5	50.0	47.3	22.5	2.7	0.0	2.3	42.4	2006	(CTCI 2 - 22 - 27 - 28)
49.3	0.5	1.7	47.1	45.9	8.9	1.2	0.0	1.7	43.7	1995	Minerais, métaux, pierres
48.0	0.8	2.1	45.1	42.4	9.9	2.7	0.0	3.1	40.7	2000	précieuses et or (non monétaire)
57.7	1.2	1.9	54.5	50.4	18.2	4.2	0.0	4.6	48.2	2006	(CTCI 27 + 28 + 68 + 667 + 971)
50.0	0.3	2.5	46.2	46.0	8.2	0.2	1.0	0.3	40.7	1995	Combustibles (CTCI 3)
46.8	0.2	3.4	42.1	41.8	6.2	0.3	1.1	0.7	35.0	2000	
58.1	2.6	5.4	49.0	46.0	6.0	3.0	1.1	4.0	35.9	2006	
43.6	1.7	4.0	37.8	35.7	7.4	2.2	0.1	2.6	33.6	1995	Articles manufacturés
40.0	1.4	3.8	34.7	32.8	7.6	1.9	0.1	2.3	31.5	2000	(CTCI 5 à 8 moins 667 et 68)
47.9	2.1	4.4	41.3	38.4	11.8	2.9	0.1	3.7	36.6	2006	
Parts par principaux groupes de produits (en pourcentage)											
100.0	100.0	100.0	100.0	100.0	100.0	100.0	100.0	100.0	100.0	1995	**Total tous produits**
100.0	100.0	100.0	100.0	100.0	100.0	100.0	100.0	100.0	100.0	2000	
100.0	100.0	100.0	100.0	100.0	100.0	100.0	100.0	100.0	100.0	2006	
7.6	15.9	4.5	7.5	7.1	7.1	14.7	7.3	14.9	5.9	1995	Produits alimentaires
4.9	12.3	3.7	4.8	4.3	3.5	11.6	3.8	12.3	3.6	2000	(CTCI 0 + 1 + 22 + 4)
3.8	10.4	2.7	3.6	3.2	2.3	8.1	4.0	9.6	2.5	2006	
2.5	1.9	1.7	2.6	2.6	3.6	1.6	0.3	1.5	2.6	1995	Matières premières
1.6	1.0	1.0	1.7	1.7	3.2	1.1	0.1	1.0	1.7	2000	d'origine agricole
1.2	0.6	0.9	1.3	1.3	2.1	0.9	0.1	0.6	1.3	2006	(CTCI 2 - 22 - 27 - 28)
3.8	1.1	1.5	4.2	4.3	4.0	1.8	0.3	2.2	4.4	1995	Minerais, métaux, pierres
3.3	1.6	1.6	3.6	3.5	3.6	3.8	0.2	3.5	3.6	2000	précieuses et or (non monétaire)
4.6	2.0	1.7	5.0	5.0	6.2	5.1	0.2	4.4	5.1	2006	(CTCI 27 + 28 + 68 + 667 + 971)
3.8	0.5	2.3	4.0	4.2	3.6	0.3	25.9	0.4	4.0	1995	Combustibles (CTCI 3)
5.0	0.7	4.0	5.2	5.4	3.5	0.6	29.8	1.3	4.8	2000	
7.2	6.6	7.6	7.1	7.2	3.2	5.8	34.6	5.9	6.0	2006	
81.2	79.0	88.6	80.6	80.6	80.8	80.9	63.1	80.3	81.9	1995	Articles manufacturés
84.4	82.6	87.6	84.2	84.4	86.0	81.2	62.3	80.5	85.8	2000	(CTCI 5 à 8 moins 667 et 68)
81.6	74.0	84.0	82.0	82.4	85.9	76.4	51.8	75.1	84.4	2006	

Sources :
- Données et estimations du secrétariat de la CNUCED sur la base de données Comtrade de ONU DAES et *Direction of Trade statistics* du Fonds Monétaire international

2.2.L Import structure by partner and product group
Developing economies:
Major exporters of manufactured goods

Product group / Destination	Year / Année	World / Monde	Developed economies / Économies développées — Total	Europe — Total	Europe — EU / UE	Canada	USA / États-Unis	Japan / Japon	Other developed countries / Autres économies développées	Economies in transition / Économies en transition
Millions of dollars										
All products	1995	1 066 078	634 356	186 895	171 264	13 271	202 204	206 557	25 428	16 878
	2000	1 390 160	752 660	204 437	186 284	15 740	287 096	213 017	32 371	21 164
	2006	2 863 168	1 199 373	395 702	359 315	26 906	359 685	346 316	70 765	63 662
Share by destination (percentage)										
All products	1995	100.0	59.5	17.5	16.1	1.2	19.0	19.4	2.4	1.6
	2000	100.0	54.1	14.7	13.4	1.1	20.7	15.3	2.3	1.5
	2006	100.0	41.9	13.8	12.5	0.9	12.6	12.1	2.5	2.2
All food items	1995	100.0	58.4	15.7	14.8	3.8	28.4	2.7	7.7	1.0
(SITC 0 + 1 + 22 + 4)	2000	100.0	56.7	12.6	11.7	3.9	28.6	2.7	9.0	1.4
	2006	100.0	47.9	10.1	9.3	3.4	23.9	2.3	8.2	2.8
Agricultural raw materials	1995	100.0	52.7	8.4	8.1	5.0	25.9	4.7	8.8	4.9
(SITC 2 - 22 - 27 - 28)	2000	100.0	54.0	11.7	11.4	6.3	22.5	4.7	8.8	5.3
	2006	100.0	50.3	11.4	11.2	5.3	22.5	4.2	6.8	8.5
Ores, metals, precious stones	1995	100.0	56.6	20.0	15.1	2.8	13.2	8.2	12.5	4.5
and non-monetary gold	2000	100.0	55.2	23.2	16.5	1.7	9.8	7.8	12.7	6.1
(SITC 27 + 28 + 68 + 667 + 971)	2006	100.0	45.3	15.2	9.2	1.8	7.0	6.9	14.4	4.8
Fuels (SITC 3)	1995	100.0	14.5	2.1	2.0	0.8	5.4	2.0	4.2	1.6
	2000	100.0	11.3	2.2	1.7	0.3	4.0	0.7	4.1	2.0
	2006	100.0	9.3	1.6	1.4	0.3	3.1	0.9	3.4	4.4
Manufactured goods	1995	100.0	63.8	19.3	17.8	0.8	19.2	23.7	0.8	1.3
(SITC 5 to 8 less 667 and 68)	2000	100.0	59.9	16.1	15.0	0.9	23.1	19.0	0.8	0.9
	2006	100.0	47.5	15.6	14.6	0.7	14.5	16.0	0.6	0.8
Share by major product group (percentage)										
All products	1995	100.0	100.0	100.0	100.0	100.0	100.0	100.0	100.0	100.0
	2000	100.0	100.0	100.0	100.0	100.0	100.0	100.0	100.0	100.0
	2006	100.0	100.0	100.0	100.0	100.0	100.0	100.0	100.0	100.0
All food items	1995	5.8	5.7	5.2	5.3	17.7	8.7	0.8	18.6	3.8
(SITC 0 + 1 + 22 + 4)	2000	4.4	4.6	3.7	3.8	15.0	6.0	0.8	16.8	3.9
	2006	3.5	4.0	2.6	2.6	12.7	6.7	0.7	11.7	4.4
Agricultural raw materials	1995	3.2	2.8	1.5	1.6	12.8	4.4	0.8	11.7	9.8
(SITC 2 - 22 - 27 - 28)	2000	2.3	2.3	1.8	2.0	13.0	2.5	0.7	8.8	8.1
	2006	2.0	2.4	1.6	1.8	11.1	3.5	0.7	5.4	7.5
Ores, metals, precious stones	1995	5.6	5.3	6.4	5.3	12.7	3.9	2.4	29.3	16.0
and non-monetary gold	2000	5.2	5.3	8.2	6.4	7.6	2.5	2.6	28.4	20.7
(SITC 27 + 28 + 68 + 667 + 971)	2006	7.6	8.3	8.4	5.6	14.5	4.3	4.4	44.5	16.5
Fuels (SITC 3)	1995	7.1	1.7	0.8	0.9	4.5	2.0	0.7	12.4	7.3
	2000	10.6	2.2	1.6	1.3	2.8	2.1	0.5	18.4	14.1
	2006	14.4	3.2	1.7	1.6	4.5	3.6	1.1	19.7	28.7
Manufactured goods	1995	76.4	81.9	84.0	84.8	50.7	77.3	93.4	26.8	62.1
(SITC 5 to 8 less 667 and 68)	2000	76.6	84.7	83.6	85.6	61.2	85.7	94.9	25.7	45.3
	2006	69.7	79.0	78.5	81.0	55.4	80.6	92.3	17.2	24.9

Sources:
- Data and UNCTAD secretariat estimates based on UN DESA Comtrade and IMF *Direction of Trade statistics* databases

2.2.L Structure des importations par partenaires et groupes de produits
Économies en développement :
Principaux exportateurs d'articles manufacturés

			Developing economies — Économies en développement							Destination	
				Asia / Asie				Major petroleum exporters	Major exporters of manufactures	Year	
Total	Africa / Afrique	America / Amérique	Total	Eastern, Southern and South-Eastern Asia / Asie orientale, méridionale et du Sud-Est	China / Chine	Western Asia / Asie occidentale	Oceania / Océanie	Principaux exportateurs de pétrole	Principaux exportateurs d'articles manufacturés	Année	Groupes de produits
Millions de dollars											
406 035	14 124	28 419	362 638	326 181	91 035	36 457	854	46 767	311 595	1995	**Total tous produits**
594 854	23 212	32 665	538 093	476 432	139 513	61 661	884	85 919	447 586	2000	
1 594 226	76 603	97 826	1 417 637	1 213 793	420 368	203 844	2 160	293 575	1 133 588	2006	
Parts par destinations (en pourcentage)											
38.1	1.3	2.7	34.0	30.6	8.5	3.4	0.1	4.4	29.2	1995	**Total tous produits**
42.8	1.7	2.3	38.7	34.3	10.0	4.4	0.1	6.2	32.2	2000	
55.7	2.7	3.4	49.5	42.4	14.7	7.1	0.1	10.3	39.6	2006	
40.4	1.3	12.1	26.7	26.3	6.5	0.4	0.4	0.6	25.0	1995	Produits alimentaires
41.9	1.9	13.1	26.5	26.1	8.3	0.4	0.3	0.9	23.7	2000	(CTCI 0 + 1 + 22 + 4)
49.3	2.0	17.7	29.2	28.8	7.2	0.4	0.4	0.8	26.6	2006	
42.3	4.7	6.0	30.8	30.3	4.2	0.5	0.8	1.6	24.8	1995	Matières premières
40.6	5.3	4.8	29.7	29.1	3.8	0.7	0.7	2.2	21.7	2000	d'origine agricole
41.2	4.6	6.0	29.5	29.0	2.6	0.5	1.0	1.8	22.8	2006	(CTCI 2 - 22 - 27 - 28)
38.5	5.7	9.0	23.5	20.9	3.9	2.6	0.3	2.9	21.7	1995	Minerais, métaux, pierres
38.7	4.9	8.4	25.2	22.8	4.2	2.5	0.2	3.1	22.6	2000	précieuses et or (non monétaire)
49.6	5.6	14.1	29.7	26.3	6.2	3.4	0.3	4.3	26.1	2006	(CTCI 27 + 28 + 68 + 667 + 971)
78.8	7.0	3.2	68.6	29.5	2.9	39.1	0.1	52.0	18.0	1995	Combustibles (CTCI 3)
75.0	8.7	2.9	63.3	25.9	2.7	37.4	0.1	52.4	13.7	2000	
86.2	11.7	3.0	71.5	28.2	2.1	43.3	0.0	61.8	16.1	2006	
34.4	0.3	1.4	32.7	32.1	9.9	0.6	0.0	0.6	31.7	1995	Articles manufacturés
38.9	0.3	1.2	37.4	37.0	11.8	0.4	0.0	0.4	36.3	2000	(CTCI 5 à 8 moins 667 et 68)
51.5	0.3	1.5	49.6	48.9	19.4	0.7	0.0	0.8	48.0	2006	
Parts par principaux groupes de produits (en pourcentage)											
100.0	100.0	100.0	100.0	100.0	100.0	100.0	100.0	100.0	100.0	1995	**Total tous produits**
100.0	100.0	100.0	100.0	100.0	100.0	100.0	100.0	100.0	100.0	2000	
100.0	100.0	100.0	100.0	100.0	100.0	100.0	100.0	100.0	100.0	2006	
6.1	5.7	26.2	4.5	5.0	4.4	0.6	27.1	0.8	4.9	1995	Produits alimentaires
4.3	5.0	24.4	3.0	3.3	3.6	0.4	18.7	0.6	3.2	2000	(CTCI 0 + 1 + 22 + 4)
3.1	2.7	18.3	2.1	2.4	1.7	0.2	17.5	0.3	2.4	2006	
3.5	11.3	7.1	2.9	3.2	1.6	0.5	33.4	1.1	2.7	1995	Matières premières
2.2	7.4	4.8	1.8	2.0	0.9	0.3	24.3	0.8	1.6	2000	d'origine agricole
1.4	3.4	3.5	1.2	1.3	0.3	0.1	26.4	0.3	1.1	2006	(CTCI 2 - 22 - 27 - 28)
5.7	24.3	18.9	3.9	3.8	2.5	4.3	20.4	3.7	4.2	1995	Minerais, métaux, pierres
4.7	15.1	18.5	3.4	3.4	2.2	2.9	16.4	2.6	3.6	2000	précieuses et or (non monétaire)
6.8	15.9	31.6	4.6	4.7	3.2	3.6	29.2	3.2	5.0	2006	(CTCI 27 + 28 + 68 + 667 + 971)
14.6	37.1	8.4	14.3	6.8	2.4	80.8	8.1	83.8	4.3	1995	Combustibles (CTCI 3)
18.5	55.0	13.2	17.3	8.0	2.8	89.0	15.6	89.7	4.5	2000	
22.3	63.2	12.7	20.8	9.6	2.0	87.7	0.4	86.9	5.8	2006	
69.1	19.5	38.9	73.5	80.2	88.6	13.7	10.8	10.4	82.8	1995	Articles manufacturés
69.6	13.1	38.8	73.9	82.6	90.4	7.3	24.9	5.4	86.3	2000	(CTCI 5 à 8 moins 667 et 68)
64.6	8.7	31.5	69.9	80.5	92.0	7.2	25.3	5.4	84.6	2006	

Sources :
- Données et estimations du secrétariat de la CNUCED sur la base de données Comtrade de ONU DAES et *Direction of Trade statistics* du Fonds Monétaire international

3

INTERNATIONAL **MERCHANDISE** TRADE BY PRODUCT

COMMERCE INTERNATIONAL DES **MARCHANDISES** PAR PRODUITS

Country or territory / Pays ou territoires	Year / Année	Total value (millions of dollars) / Valeur totale (millions de dollars)	All food items / Produits alimentaires	Agricultural raw materials / Matières premières agricoles	Fuels / Combustibles	Ores, metals, precious stones and non monetary gold / Minerais, métaux, pierres précieuses et or (non monétaire)	Manu-factured goods / Articles manu-facturés	Of which: / dont : Chemical products / Produits chimiques	Of which: / dont : Machinery and transport equipment / Machines et matériel de transport	Of which: / dont : Other manu-factured goods / Articles manu-facturés divers
			0 + 1 + 22 + 4	2 - (22 + 27 + 28)	3	27 + 28 + 68 + 667 + 971	5 + 6 +7 + 8- (667 + 68)	5	7	6 + 8 - (667 + 68)
Albania - Albanie	1995	211	11.1	9.0	3.0	11.6	3.0	1.4	1.7	62.2
	2000	261	6.6	6.0	1.9	3.7	1.9	0.7	1.9	79.2
	2006	793	5.7	4.1	4.1	11.7	4.1	0.3	3.9	70.1
Algeria - Algérie	1995	9 357	1.2	0.1	95.2	0.5	95.2	1.2	0.4	1.4
	2000	22 031	0.2	0.0	98.1	0.3	98.1	0.7	0.2	0.5
	2006	54 613	0.2	0.0	98.1	0.7	98.1	0.6	0.0	0.4
Andorra - Andorre	1995	48	6.5	1.6	0.2	2.3	0.2	3.6	33.8	52.0
	2000	45	8.2	1.3	0.1	4.6	0.1	8.2	25.4	49.5
	2006	181	27.2	0.5	0.0	1.8	0.0	3.5	39.4	27.1
Angola	1995	3 723	1.0	0.0	93.8	4.6	93.8	0.0	0.2	0.1
	2000	7 702	0.6	0.0	91.1	8.1	91.1	0.0	0.1	0.0
	2006	30 678	0.1	0.0	97.5	1.8	97.5	0.0	0.1	0.2
Argentina - Argentine	1995	20 963	49.8	4.3	10.3	1.6	10.3	6.4	10.9	16.6
	2000	26 341	43.6	1.8	17.6	3.3	17.6	7.3	12.8	12.4
	2006	46 423	44.5	1.3	14.6	6.5	14.6	8.1	12.7	10.8
Armenia - Arménie	1995	271	10.8	4.6	0.7	48.5	0.7	1.9	13.0	17.7
	2000	294	9.4	3.4	7.0	54.7	7.0	1.2	10.5	13.8
	2006	1 004	11.9	2.6	1.9	48.7	1.9	0.5	2.2	30.2
Australia - Australie	1995	53 001	19.6	8.1	16.7	27.1	16.7	4.1	12.8	9.6
	2000	63 766	19.7	6.1	20.9	25.5	20.9	4.3	11.3	7.6
	2006	123 323	14.5	3.4	24.0	33.2	24.0	4.2	8.0	5.6
Austria - Autriche	1995	57 583	3.8	3.3	1.0	3.4	1.0	9.2	39.1	39.6
	2000	63 675	4.7	2.4	1.3	3.3	1.3	6.8	40.9	31.6
	2006	134 053	6.0	1.8	5.3	3.5	5.3	9.1	40.8	30.2
Azerbaijan - Azerbaïdjan	1995	631	4.4	8.3	66.4	1.2	66.4	6.5	7.6	5.6
	2000	1 745	3.2	2.4	85.1	2.9	85.1	2.0	3.6	0.9
	2006	6 372	5.0	0.7	84.6	3.8	84.6	2.1	1.9	1.7
Bahamas	1995	176	38.8	5.1	0.0	12.6	0.0	9.5	26.6	7.1
	2000	555	22.0	2.2	15.0	3.2	15.0	21.3	25.9	10.5
	2006	509	20.8	1.1	18.3	2.6	18.3	41.1	11.6	4.6
Bahrain - Bahreïn	1995	3 475	2.8	0.0	52.3	25.9	52.3	6.4	1.7	10.9
	2000	6 195	0.9	0.1	72.5	16.0	72.5	2.4	1.0	7.1
	2006	11 662	0.5	0.0	79.1	13.6	79.1	2.6	1.6	2.6
Bangladesh	1995	3 407	10.4	2.7	0.4	0.0	0.4	3.0	1.6	80.5
	2000	5 493	7.6	1.4	0.2	0.0	0.2	1.3	1.3	87.8
	2006	11 963	5.2	1.3	0.4	0.3	0.4	1.3	1.0	90.2
Barbados - Barbade	1995	238	29.0	0.9	14.4	1.7	14.4	13.9	19.8	20.2
	2000	273	27.8	0.1	22.1	0.2	22.1	13.7	14.0	21.0
	2006	441	18.0	0.6	31.2	1.5	31.2	10.2	12.7	25.3
Belarus - Bélarus	1995	5 652	8.5	3.1	7.8	1.0	7.8	14.0	28.3	35.5
	2000	7 331	6.8	3.6	19.8	1.0	19.8	11.5	23.9	29.3
	2006	19 739	7.5	1.9	38.3	0.5	38.3	9.6	18.6	22.0
Belgium - Belgique	2006	369 256	7.9	1.3	7.7	7.9	7.7	27.7	23.9	21.3
Belgium-Luxembourg - Belgique-Luxembourg	1995	168 154	10.3	1.2	2.6	10.2	2.6	16.2	27.3	26.5
	2000	187 577	8.8	1.5	3.9	10.1	3.9	18.4	28.9	24.4
Belize	1995	162	79.7	1.3	3.2	0.2	3.2	1.2	3.0	11.6
	2000	200	81.7	1.3	2.0	0.0	2.0	0.3	1.3	12.9
	2006	274	72.8	0.3	16.4	0.0	16.4	1.1	0.6	1.7
Benin - Bénin	1995	333	11.8	38.9	2.8	40.0	2.8	0.2	1.5	4.9
	2000	188	20.1	69.7	0.0	3.2	0.0	0.7	1.3	5.1
	2006	283	20.5	64.5	0.4	1.8	0.4	1.2	2.2	8.7

For sources and notes, see end of table.

Pour les sources et les notes, se reporter à la fin du tableau.

Country or territory / Pays ou territoires	Year / Année	Total value (millions of dollars) / Valeur totale (millions de dollars)	By main SITC Revision 3 procuct group (percentage) / Par principaux groupes de produits de la CTCI Révision 3 (en pourcentage)					Of which: / dont :		
			All food items / Produits alimentaires	Agricultural raw materials / Matières premières agricoles	Fuels / Combustibles	Ores, metals, precious stones and non monetary gold / Minerais, métaux, pierres précieuses et or (non monétaire)	Manufactured goods / Articles manufacturés	Chemical products / Produits chimiques	Machinery and transport equipment / Machines et matériel de transport	Other manufactured goods / Articles manufacturés divers
			0 + 1 + 22 + 4	2 - (22 + 27 + 28)	3	27 + 28 + 68 + 667 + 971	5 + 6 +7 + 8- (667 + 68)	5	7	6 + 8 - (667 + 68)
Bolivia - Bolivie	1995	1 181	19.1	8.7	12.9	42.6	12.9	1.1	3.2	12.1
	2000	1 457	28.4	3.0	12.2	29.2	12.2	0.8	13.3	12.9
	2006	4 223	14.2	1.6	48.8	25.1	48.8	1.2	3.1	6.0
Bosnia and Herzegovina - Bosnie-Herzégovine	1995	86	17.1	21.3	4.0	6.0	4.0	2.7	14.8	33.4
	2000	1 067	3.6	19.9	5.9	23.2	5.9	3.8	6.4	36.2
	2006	3 428	4.9	8.3	8.2	20.4	8.2	3.8	14.2	40.1
Botswana	2000	2 763	2.8	0.3	0.1	88.9	0.1	1.0	3.6	3.1
	2006	4 506	2.7	0.2	0.1	89.8	0.1	0.8	1.7	4.4
Brazil - Brésil	1995	46 505	28.5	5.2	0.9	11.3	0.9	6.6	19.0	27.2
	2000	55 119	23.2	4.8	1.6	11.0	1.6	6.5	28.0	22.9
	2006	137 806	24.9	3.8	7.7	12.1	7.7	6.7	24.2	18.7
Brunei Darussalam - Brunéi Darussalam	1995	2 379	0.1	0.0	91.1	0.0	91.1	0.1	4.5	3.6
	2000	3 877	0.0	0.0	89.3	0.0	89.3	0.1	4.0	6.4
	2006	7 636	0.1	0.0	96.3	0.1	96.3	0.0	1.2	2.1
Bulgaria - Bulgarie	1995	5 353	18.1	3.0	6.5	9.7	6.5	18.3	12.4	29.4
	2000	4 822	9.8	2.7	11.7	12.7	11.7	10.1	9.6	37.1
	2006	15 101	8.6	1.7	13.3	20.2	13.3	6.3	13.5	33.5
Burkina Faso	1995	171	22.1	59.1	1.6	8.7	1.6	0.4	3.1	5.0
	2000	184	18.8	58.0	3.2	2.0	3.2	1.7	4.6	11.8
	2006	483	31.1	58.4	0.1	1.4	0.1	0.7	0.8	5.5
Burundi	1995	179	59.8	2.7	0.0	35.2	0.0	0.5	0.1	1.6
	2000	43	85.8	7.1	0.0	6.4	0.0	0.0	0.3	0.2
	2006	120	44.7	1.5	0.0	50.8	0.0	0.1	1.7	1.0
Cambodia - Cambodge	1995	304	3.5	72.1	0.0	0.3	0.0	0.3	0.7	22.4
	2000	1 389	1.0	2.9	0.0	0.4	0.0	0.0	0.7	94.9
	2006	3 991	5.7	2.5	0.0	1.7	0.0	0.2	4.7	85.0
Cameroon - Cameroun	1995	1 539	27.0	27.5	29.2	8.4	29.2	1.0	1.1	5.8
	2000	1 823	14.9	9.1	54.2	5.6	54.2	0.4	0.5	2.4
	2006	3 576	12.0	16.3	61.6	4.9	61.6	0.3	0.4	2.3
Canada	1995	191 118	7.6	9.2	9.1	7.8	9.1	5.9	38.5	17.6
	2000	277 113	6.4	6.2	13.1	5.1	13.1	5.3	40.2	17.7
	2006	388 091	7.0	4.4	20.0	9.1	20.0	7.6	31.8	15.9
Cape Verde - Cap-Vert	1995	32	6.1	0.3	34.1	0.1	34.1	0.8	38.3	20.2
	2000	49	4.0	0.1	48.5	0.0	48.5	0.5	25.1	21.9
	2006	110	14.2	0.0	47.6	0.3	47.6	0.5	26.9	10.5
Central African Republic - République centrafricaine	1995	120	4.2	19.8	0.8	64.1	0.8	0.4	8.8	1.9
	2000	79	10.6	13.1	0.5	72.1	0.5	0.1	2.5	1.2
	2006	144	1.1	33.7	0.2	60.7	0.2	0.1	0.8	0.8
Chad - Tchad	1995	116	1.3	93.3	0.0	0.0	0.0	0.0	4.8	0.4
	2000	90	4.6	87.7	0.0	0.3	0.0	0.1	6.5	0.7
	2006	2 280	0.0	4.5	94.6	0.0	94.6	0.1	0.4	0.1
Chile - Chili	1995	15 901	23.7	13.6	0.2	49.5	0.2	3.5	1.8	6.5
	2000	18 214	24.3	10.8	1.1	46.1	1.1	5.6	2.7	7.0
	2006	55 881	15.3	5.3	1.9	64.7	1.9	4.4	1.4	4.9
China - Chine	1995	148 779	8.3	1.8	3.6	2.4	3.6	6.1	21.1	56.5
	2000	249 203	5.4	1.1	3.2	2.1	3.2	4.9	33.1	50.0
	2006	968 936	2.9	0.5	1.8	2.4	1.8	4.6	47.1	40.5
China, Hong Kong SAR - Chine (RAS de Hong Kong)	1995	173 871	3.0	1.3	1.0	2.6	1.0	6.2	32.4	53.1
	2000	202 683	1.8	1.0	0.3	3.1	0.3	5.1	38.3	50.2
	2006	322 669	0.9	0.5	0.3	5.6	0.3	4.8	53.8	33.9
China, Macao SAR - Chine (RAS de Macao)	1995	2 025	1.7	2.4	0.0	0.0	0.0	1.1	4.4	90.5
	2000	2 547	1.0	0.8	0.7	0.1	0.7	0.9	5.7	91.0
	2006	2 557	1.8	0.2	5.3	2.4	5.3	1.1	8.3	80.9

For sources and notes, see end of table.

Pour les sources et les notes, se reporter à la fin du tableau.

Country or territory / Pays ou territcires	Year / Année	Total value (millions of dollars) / Valeur totale (millions de dollars)	By main SITC Revision 3 product group (percentage) / Par principaux groupes de produits de la CTCI Révision 3 (en pourcentage)					Of which: / dont :		
			All food items / Produits alimentaires	Agricultural raw materials / Matières premières agricoles	Fuels / Combustibles	Ores, metals, precious stones and non monetary gold / Minerais, métaux, pierres précieuses et or (non monétaire)	Manufactured goods / Articles manufacturés	Chemical products / Produits chimiques	Machinery and transport equipment / Machines et matériel de transport	Other manufactured goods / Articles manufacturés divers
			0 + 1 + 22 + 4	2 - (22 + 27 + 28)	3	27 + 28 + 68 + 667 + 971	5 + 6 +7 + 8- (667 + 68)	5	7	6 + 8 - (667 + 68)
China, Taiwan Province of - Province chinoise de Taiwan	1995	111 343	3.4	1.6	0.7	1.5	0.7	6.8	48.1	37.8
	2000	148 316	1.2	1.1	1.1	1.3	1.1	6.2	58.4	30.5
	2006	224 012	0.9	1.1	4.8	2.5	4.8	10.0	50.9	29.4
Colombia - Colombie	1995	10 201	30.8	5.4	27.2	6.8	27.2	7.9	2.6	19.3
	2000	13 158	19.0	4.7	43.1	1.5	43.1	10.2	4.3	17.3
	2006	24 391	15.8	4.4	38.4	6.2	38.4	8.3	6.2	20.7
Congo	1995	1 090	1.0	8.3	87.6	0.3	87.6	0.3	0.4	2.1
	2000	2 477	1.6	5.2	82.7	9.3	82.7	0.1	0.3	0.5
	2006	8 135	0.3	3.1	90.3	4.2	90.3	0.1	0.2	0.3
Costa Rica	1995	2 702	63.4	5.0	0.8	1.1	0.8	6.5	3.2	15.4
	2000	5 487	30.0	3.0	0.6	0.8	0.6	5.4	39.4	20.7
	2006	7 255	29.6	3.1	0.6	2.2	0.6	5.8	35.2	23.4
Côte d'Ivoire	1995	3 737	58.7	16.0	9.8	0.8	9.8	4.2	1.4	8.6
	2000	3 628	49.8	13.8	20.3	1.1	20.3	4.2	1.0	9.2
	2006	8 148	35.1	8.0	36.9	0.5	36.9	3.5	7.1	8.8
Croatia - Croatie	1995	4 633	10.8	4.6	8.4	2.3	8.4	17.6	16.8	39.5
	2000	4 432	8.9	4.5	11.0	3.0	11.0	12.5	27.0	33.1
	2006	10 377	11.4	3.3	15.1	4.4	15.1	9.2	28.8	27.9
Cuba	1995	1 625	78.7	0.2	0.3	14.0	0.3	3.8	0.5	2.3
	2000	1 676	50.0	0.2	3.1	37.3	3.1	2.5	0.7	6.2
	2006	2 905	27.4	0.1	0.7	47.8	0.7	9.7	3.3	11.0
Cyprus - Chypre	1995	1 231	50.5	0.4	3.7	1.4	3.7	6.4	12.2	25.4
	2000	981	42.3	0.6	10.4	3.1	10.4	7.2	15.6	18.2
	2006	1 415	20.3	0.6	18.2	5.5	18.2	12.7	30.8	11.9
Czech Republic - République tchèque	1995	21 686	6.0	3.7	4.3	2.9	4.3	9.2	29.3	43.0
	2000	29 053	4.1	2.4	3.1	2.0	3.1	7.1	44.5	36.9
	2006	95 141	3.5	1.3	2.8	2.0	2.8	5.8	52.6	30.2
Dem. Rep. of the Congo - Rép. dém. du Congo	1995	1 563	14.0	6.7	9.4	67.9	9.4	0.2	0.3	1.4
	2000	824	3.1	1.8	22.3	68.1	22.3	1.8	0.4	0.4
	2006	2 319	2.0	8.4	12.6	73.0	12.6	1.0	0.6	1.2
Denmark - Danemark	1995	48 789	24.0	2.9	2.6	1.2	2.6	9.7	25.1	25.0
	2000	49 210	19.7	2.5	7.0	1.0	7.0	10.9	26.5	26.8
	2006	90 118	17.8	2.6	10.3	1.6	10.3	12.2	27.6	24.9
Dominican Republic - République dominicaine	1995	2 603	14.5	0.3	0.0	2.2	0.0	1.6	6.0	73.2
	2000	895	11.8	0.4	0.0	1.0	0.0	1.2	8.7	74.6
	2006	1 377	16.4	0.4	0.1	3.9	0.1	3.0	13.8	59.9
Ecuador - Équateur	1995	4 361	51.8	3.0	35.1	2.5	35.1	1.2	2.0	4.4
	2000	4 822	36.5	3.9	50.7	0.4	50.7	1.6	1.9	5.1
	2006	12 728	27.0	4.0	59.3	1.0	59.3	1.4	3.7	3.6
Egypt - Égypte	1995	3 444	9.9	6.1	37.3	6.4	37.3	5.8	0.6	33.8
	2000	4 713	8.0	5.0	41.9	3.9	41.9	6.6	1.0	30.8
	2006	13 756	6.5	1.5	55.5	4.1	55.5	5.2	0.7	14.8
El Salvador	1995	985	57.1	1.2	0.1	2.9	0.1	11.5	2.8	24.6
	2000	1 341	42.4	0.6	4.9	2.4	4.9	13.0	3.9	31.5
	2006	1 451	35.9	0.9	3.0	5.0	3.0	20.8	5.7	28.5
Equatorial Guinea - Guinée équatoriale	1995	86	7.6	51.9	33.0	0.0	33.0	0.0	0.6	6.4
	2000	1 097	3.3	8.1	87.8	0.0	87.8	0.0	0.1	0.6
	2006	3 375	0.0	1.4	94.5	0.0	94.5	2.7	0.7	0.3
Estonia - Estonie	1995	1 840	16.1	9.6	7.1	3.1	7.1	8.3	19.9	35.9
	2000	3 830	8.0	9.6	4.5	5.6	4.5	5.6	36.0	30.7
	2006	9 608	6.7	5.6	15.8	3.2	15.8	4.7	30.4	28.7

For sources and notes, see end of table.

Pour les sources et les notes, se reporter à la fin du tableau.

Country or territory / Pays ou territoires	Year / Année	Total value (millions of dollars) / Valeur totale (millions de dollars)	All food items / Produits alimentaires	Agricultural raw materials / Matières premières agricoles	Fuels / Combus-tibles	Ores, metals, precious stones and non monetary gold / Minerais, métaux, pierres précieuses et or (non monétaire)	Manu-factured goods / Articles manu-facturés	Of which: / dont :		
								Chemical products / Produits chimiques	Machinery and transport equipment / Machines et matériel de transport	Other manu-factured goods / Articles manu-facturés divers
			0 + 1 + 22 + 4	2 - (22 + 27 + 28)	3	27 + 28 + 68 + 667 + 971	5 + 6 +7 + 8- (667 + 68)	5	7	6 + 8 - (667 + 68)
Ethiopia - Éthiopie	1995	422	72.5	13.4	2.9	0.1	2.9	0.3	0.0	10.8
	2000	482	66.5	17.6	0.0	6.6	0.0	0.0	0.1	9.1
	2006	1 043	70.5	16.6	0.0	6.8	0.0	0.1	0.1	5.7
Faeroe Islands - Îles Féroé	1995	362	91.1	2.2	0.0	0.0	0.0	0.1	4.8	1.8
	2000	472	93.4	1.3	0.0	0.0	0.0	0.1	3.8	1.4
	2006	631	91.8	2.2	2.0	0.2	2.0	0.1	2.6	1.1
Fiji - Fidji	1995	619	51.5	7.0	0.4	7.6	0.4	0.3	1.0	31.8
	2000	469	34.9	4.6	0.0	7.2	0.0	0.8	0.2	45.1
	2006	679	46.2	3.9	24.7	4.9	24.7	1.8	2.5	15.2
Finland - Finlande	1995	40 409	2.4	8.4	1.9	3.1	1.9	6.0	35.4	42.0
	2000	45 475	1.7	6.3	3.4	3.2	3.4	6.0	45.3	33.6
	2006	77 279	1.8	5.5	5.2	5.0	5.2	7.4	42.0	31.8
France	1995	277 845	14.4	1.5	2.4	2.8	2.4	14.9	39.4	24.6
	2000	295 345	11.0	1.1	2.8	2.0	2.8	13.7	45.0	22.2
	2006	479 013	10.5	0.9	4.3	3.0	4.3	15.7	41.3	22.3
French Polynesia - Polynésie française	1995	196	2.7	1.0	0.0	61.8	0.0	0.8	20.8	7.1
	2000	244	5.9	0.8	0.0	72.3	0.0	0.6	14.1	5.9
	2006	186	12.4	2.7	0.0	59.7	0.0	1.5	13.6	10.0
Gabon	1995	2 718	0.2	13.1	82.7	2.0	82.7	0.4	0.4	1.1
	2000	2 602	0.8	11.8	83.3	1.7	83.3	0.1	0.4	1.9
	2006	6 015	0.8	6.7	85.6	3.1	85.6	0.0	1.5	2.2
Gambia - Gambie	1995	19	58.8	0.5	0.2	1.1	0.2	2.4	7.0	27.5
	2000	16	80.8	1.2	0.1	0.3	0.1	9.6	4.7	2.6
	2006	11	81.1	3.9	0.0	0.9	0.0	0.5	9.8	3.8
Georgia - Géorgie	1995	158	29.3	3.3	18.8	8.0	18.8	11.1	5.7	23.8
	2000	323	28.0	3.0	8.1	29.0	8.1	10.6	12.0	8.8
	2006	992	23.5	2.1	3.0	25.3	3.0	7.9	20.8	17.3
Germany - Allemagne	1995	523 697	5.1	1.1	1.0	2.8	1.0	13.2	46.9	24.3
	2000	549 607	4.2	0.9	1.4	2.6	1.4	12.7	49.6	21.3
	2006	1 121 963	4.4	0.9	2.5	3.4	2.5	14.0	49.1	21.8
Ghana	1995	1 754	40.9	10.3	3.4	36.1	3.4	0.1	0.5	8.7
	2000	1 671	30.7	6.5	4.9	48.6	4.9	0.6	1.2	7.5
	2006	3 614	41.9	2.8	0.4	34.1	0.4	1.1	0.4	19.1
Greece - Grèce	1995	10 955	29.5	4.4	6.5	7.9	6.5	4.9	8.0	36.9
	2000	10 964	21.8	3.3	14.7	7.7	14.7	8.0	12.0	29.6
	2006	20 943	20.3	2.4	13.0	10.8	13.0	13.1	12.6	25.2
Greenland - Groenland	1995	364	95.1	0.6	0.8	0.0	0.8	0.0	0.3	1.2
	2000	271	95.5	0.4	0.0	0.0	0.0	0.0	0.7	0.6
	2006	408	84.4	0.0	0.0	7.3	0.0	0.0	1.1	2.9
Grenada - Grenade	1995	22	79.5	0.1	0.0	0.2	0.0	2.6	3.8	13.8
	2000	76	33.1	0.0	0.0	0.1	0.0	1.4	58.6	6.9
	2006	25	54.8	0.0	0.1	0.1	0.1	4.7	11.9	28.4
Guatemala	1995	1 936	65.2	4.1	2.0	0.5	2.0	10.9	1.8	15.5
	2000	2 699	56.2	3.8	6.0	1.9	6.0	11.7	2.4	18.0
	2006	3 198	49.8	5.4	8.8	1.1	8.8	12.3	4.2	18.4
Guinea - Guinée	1995	702	7.4	1.1	0.5	70.3	0.5	18.2	2.1	0.4
	2000	522	2.5	2.4	0.0	70.2	0.0	10.9	0.9	12.9
	2006	976	8.8	2.5	5.5	78.0	5.5	0.1	2.3	0.8
Guinea-Bissau - Guinée-Bissau	1995	28	81.9	6.3	4.6	0.1	4.6	0.0	6.6	0.6
	2000	62	51.1	4.1	43.7	0.0	43.7	0.0	0.1	0.6
	2006	84	81.3	0.4	0.5	0.6	0.5	0.4	11.5	5.0

For sources and notes, see end of table.　　　　　　　　　　　　　Pour les sources et les notes, se reporter à la fin du tableau.

Country or territory / Pays ou territoires	Year / Année	Total value (millions of dollars) / Valeur totale (millions de dollars)	By main SITC Revision 3 product group (percentage) / Par principaux groupes de produits de la CTCI Révision 3 (en pourcentage)					Of which: / dont :		
			All food items / Produits alimentaires	Agricultural raw materials / Matières premières agricoles	Fuels / Combus-tibles	Ores, metals, precious stones and non monetary gold / Minerais, métaux, pierres précieuses et or (non monétaire)	Manu-factured goods / Articles manu-facturés	Chemical products / Produits chimiques	Machinery and transport equipment / Machines et matériel de transport	Other manu-factured goods / Articles manu-facturés divers
			0 + 1 + 22 + 4	2 - (22 + 27 + 28)	3	27 + 28 + 68 + 667 + 971	5 + 6 +7 + 8- (667 + 68)	5	7	6 + 8 - (667 + 68)
Guyana	1995	455	44.9	2.2	0.0	42.1	0.0	0.7	1.1	9.0
	2000	520	43.4	2.9	0.0	42.6	0.0	0.8	1.8	8.5
	2006	567	51.0	8.7	0.0	29.2	0.0	0.7	2.4	7.3
Haiti - Haïti	1995	35	37.5	0.3	0.0	0.0	0.0	7.1	1.4	53.6
	2000	313	9.9	0.5	0.4	0.2	0.4	1.5	0.8	85.6
	2006	523	4.8	0.1	0.0	1.7	0.0	2.3	0.6	79.5
Honduras	1995	656	86.9	3.3	0.0	0.6	0.0	1.7	0.7	6.7
	2000	1 076	67.8	4.9	2.3	5.8	2.3	6.5	0.6	12.1
	2006	1 880	57.4	2.9	0.3	10.0	0.3	2.0	17.4	10.0
Hungary - Hongrie	1995	12 452	21.4	2.3	3.1	5.0	3.1	11.5	26.1	30.5
	2000	28 092	7.3	1.0	1.6	2.3	1.6	6.1	59.7	20.4
	2006	74 055	5.7	0.5	2.3	2.0	2.3	7.7	59.8	16.3
Iceland - Islande	1995	1 803	75.5	0.5	0.0	12.0	0.0	0.7	5.1	5.8
	2000	1 901	65.2	0.9	0.4	19.3	0.4	1.4	5.5	6.4
	2006	3 453	53.0	0.8	2.3	24.1	2.3	2.8	10.1	6.2
India - Inde	1995	31 699	18.7	1.3	1.7	18.6	1.7	8.1	7.5	42.5
	2000	45 250	12.9	1.2	4.3	17.2	4.3	10.5	7.9	43.8
	2006	126 126	8.6	2.0	15.0	16.9	15.0	11.4	11.1	33.8
Indonesia - Indonésie	1995	45 418	11.4	6.7	25.3	6.1	25.3	3.4	8.4	38.7
	2000	62 124	8.9	3.6	25.2	5.6	25.2	5.1	17.3	34.3
	2006	100 799	11.6	6.4	27.4	10.5	27.4	5.1	14.0	25.0
Iran (Islamic Rep. of) - Iran (Rép. islamique d')	1995	18 360	3.6	1.0	85.8	0.6	85.8	1.9	0.3	6.9
	2000	28 345	2.9	0.4	88.9	0.8	88.9	1.2	0.5	5.4
	2006	63 247	4.3	0.3	83.3	2.4	83.3	3.2	1.2	5.2
Ireland - Irlande	1995	43 789	19.4	1.1	0.4	1.2	0.4	18.4	34.5	18.0
	2000	76 262	8.3	0.5	0.3	0.8	0.3	32.8	40.2	12.8
	2006	108 763	9.7	0.5	0.6	1.4	0.6	45.7	26.7	11.8
Israel - Israël	1995	19 047	5.4	1.8	0.0	31.6	0.0	14.7	26.8	17.4
	2000	31 407	2.6	1.1	0.7	31.9	0.7	12.9	35.6	15.0
	2006	46 792	2.4	0.7	0.1	35.8	0.1	16.2	18.7	12.9
Italy - Italie	1995	230 441	6.6	0.7	1.2	1.5	1.2	8.0	37.7	43.6
	2000	240 516	6.1	0.7	2.0	1.5	2.0	9.4	38.3	40.7
	2006	417 153	6.3	0.6	3.6	2.3	3.6	10.4	36.8	37.4
Jamaica - Jamaïque	1995	1 424	21.7	0.3	0.5	49.4	0.5	2.7	3.1	22.4
	2000	1 308	22.0	0.2	0.3	56.9	0.3	5.4	2.1	13.2
	2006	1 989	16.6	0.1	13.5	63.2	13.5	3.7	1.1	1.8
Japan - Japon	1995	442 937	0.5	0.6	0.6	1.2	0.6	6.8	70.3	18.0
	2000	479 248	0.5	0.5	0.3	1.5	0.3	7.3	68.8	17.6
	2006	646 725	0.5	0.5	0.9	2.8	0.9	8.9	63.7	18.0
Jordan - Jordanie	1995	1 769	22.3	1.8	0.0	19.8	0.0	27.0	13.1	14.9
	2000	1 293	14.0	0.6	0.0	11.3	0.0	22.2	19.1	32.5
	2006	5 167	13.4	0.3	0.8	15.8	0.8	18.7	13.0	37.9
Kazakhstan	1995	5 227	9.9	2.8	25.0	24.1	25.0	10.3	6.0	21.9
	2000	8 789	6.8	1.4	52.0	21.7	52.0	1.1	2.1	13.2
	2006	38 244	2.8	0.6	68.7	16.8	68.7	2.7	1.7	6.6
Kenya	1995	1 826	56.1	7.4	6.1	3.1	6.1	6.6	1.6	19.1
	2000	1 571	59.0	8.6	8.1	3.8	8.1	5.6	0.5	14.4
	2006	3 480	42.6	11.9	7.3	2.8	7.3	7.3	3.9	24.1
Kuwait - Koweït	1995	12 944	0.3	0.0	94.7	0.3	94.7	2.0	1.4	1.3
	2000	19 401	0.3	0.1	93.5	0.2	93.5	4.3	0.8	0.8
	2006	57 266	0.2	0.0	94.3	0.5	94.3	3.0	0.4	1.0

For sources and notes, see end of table.

Pour les sources et les notes, se reporter à la fin du tableau.

Country or territory / Pays ou territoires	Year / Année	Total value (millions of dollars) / Valeur totale (millions de dollars)	By main SITC Revision 3 product group (percentage) / Par principaux groupes de produits de la CTCI Révision 3 (en pourcentage)					Of which: / dont :		
			All food items / Produits alimentaires	Agricultural raw materials / Matières premières agricoles	Fuels / Combustibles	Ores, metals, precious stones and non monetary gold / Minerais, métaux, pierres précieuses et or (non monétaire)	Manufactured goods / Articles manufacturés	Chemical products / Produits chimiques	Machinery and transport equipment / Machines et matériel de transport	Other manufactured goods / Articles manufacturés divers
			0 + 1 + 22 + 4	2 - (22 + 27 + 28)	3	27 + 28 + 68 + 667 + 971	5 + 6 +7 + 8- (667 + 68)	5	7	6 + 8 - (667 + 68)
Kyrgyzstan - Kirghizistan	1995	412	22.8	12.7	11.1	11.7	11.1	11.8	9.3	19.9
	2000	504	10.4	8.7	16.4	45.6	16.4	2.9	9.7	6.3
	2006	794	12.1	6.5	18.7	29.7	18.7	1.6	9.4	21.0
Latvia - Lettonie	1995	1 305	14.4	23.0	1.7	1.0	1.7	6.9	16.3	34.9
	2000	1 869	5.7	30.0	2.5	6.1	2.5	6.4	7.1	42.0
	2006	5 891	12.3	15.4	5.2	4.0	5.2	7.4	15.0	36.9
Lebanon - Liban	1995	656	19.5	1.5	0.1	10.6	0.1	12.5	14.4	41.4
	2000	714	18.4	1.8	0.2	14.0	0.2	13.5	12.3	39.9
	2006	2 234	16.5	1.6	0.3	11.7	0.3	10.9	16.0	40.8
Lesotho	2000	336	5.0	0.1	0.0	0.0	0.0	0.3	7.7	86.9
	2006	990	0.0	0.0	0.0	10.2	0.0	0.2	0.1	89.3
Libyan Arab Jamahiriya - Jamahiriya arabe libyenne	1995	9 364	0.3	0.1	94.8	0.0	94.8	3.3	0.0	1.6
	2000	10 415	0.5	0.2	92.6	0.0	92.6	4.2	0.1	2.3
	2006	30 763	0.1	0.0	90.6	0.5	90.6	2.8	0.2	0.8
Lithuania - Lituanie	1995	2 706	18.1	7.8	11.4	5.0	11.4	14.3	15.7	27.7
	2000	3 809	11.6	5.2	20.9	2.1	20.9	9.5	17.3	33.2
	2006	14 135	13.7	2.8	23.5	1.7	23.5	9.1	22.4	26.1
Luxembourg	2006	14 183	6.2	0.8	0.8	7.1	0.8	6.3	24.7	49.8
Madagascar	1995	360	67.6	5.8	4.0	7.9	4.0	2.1	0.9	9.9
	2000	862	31.7	3.4	5.1	3.7	5.1	1.5	1.5	52.9
	2006	1 008	32.7	4.0	8.0	6.0	8.0	1.5	2.5	35.4
Malawi	1995	433	88.0	2.1	0.1	0.1	0.1	0.4	2.0	7.3
	2000	379	87.3	2.9	0.2	0.3	0.2	0.7	2.8	6.0
	2006	668	82.5	3.3	0.1	0.1	0.1	0.6	2.5	10.8
Malaysia - Malaisie	1995	73 778	9.5	6.2	7.0	1.5	7.0	3.0	55.1	16.4
	2000	98 230	5.5	2.6	9.6	1.2	9.6	3.8	62.5	14.0
	2006	160 669	7.0	2.7	13.7	1.7	13.7	5.4	52.6	15.4
Maldives	1995	50	73.8	0.7	0.0	0.2	0.0	0.0	0.0	25.3
	2000	76	53.7	0.0	0.0	0.1	0.0	0.0	0.0	46.1
	2006	136	98.5	0.0	0.0	1.0	0.0	0.0	0.5	0.0
Mali	1995	443	18.2	58.1	1.0	17.1	1.0	0.3	1.1	3.9
	2000	473	1.7	34.4	1.0	57.7	1.0	0.5	2.8	1.5
	2006	1 526	5.8	16.7	0.6	74.2	0.6	0.5	1.3	0.7
Malta - Malte	1995	1 913	2.1	0.1	1.5	0.6	1.5	2.2	66.3	27.1
	2000	2 438	2.6	0.1	4.4	0.4	4.4	1.6	70.9	20.0
	2006	2 780	6.0	0.1	1.3	0.5	1.3	6.3	63.3	21.8
Mauritania - Mauritanie	1995	509	52.9	0.1	3.9	41.0	3.9	0.0	1.3	0.5
	2000	343	20.8	0.0	0.0	45.7	0.0	0.0	0.0	0.0
	2006	1 216	28.3	0.0	0.0	64.7	0.0	0.0	0.0	0.0
Mauritius - Maurice	1995	1 538	28.9	0.7	0.0	2.0	0.0	0.8	2.3	65.3
	2000	1 490	18.5	0.5	0.0	2.7	0.0	0.9	1.3	76.2
	2006	2 174	29.7	0.5	0.1	3.2	0.1	1.3	17.5	47.8
Mayotte	2000	3	7.4	0.0	0.1	0.0	0.1	49.0	31.4	5.6
	2006	7	14.6	0.0	0.5	0.3	0.5	15.1	48.3	21.2
Mexico - Mexique	1995	79 541	7.7	1.3	10.3	3.1	10.3	5.0	52.3	20.2
	2000	166 192	4.9	0.6	9.7	1.4	9.7	3.2	59.2	21.0
	2006	249 961	5.4	0.4	15.5	2.8	15.5	3.5	54.1	18.0
Moldova	1995	746	71.7	1.8	0.9	3.0	0.9	1.4	7.9	13.4
	2000	472	59.8	3.1	0.1	1.8	0.1	1.8	6.2	26.9
	2006	1 052	43.9	0.8	0.2	3.4	0.2	2.2	6.5	42.9

For sources and notes, see end of table.

Pour les sources et les notes, se reporter à la fin du tableau.

Country or territory / Pays ou territoires	Year / Année	Total value (millions of dollars) / Valeur totale (millions de dollars)	All food items / Produits alimentaires	Agricultural raw materials / Matières premières agricoles	Fuels / Combustibles	Ores, metals, precious stones and non monetary gold / Minerais, métaux, pierres précieuses et or (non monétaire)	Manufactured goods / Articles manufacturés	Of which: / dont : Chemical products / Produits chimiques	Of which: / dont : Machinery and transport equipment / Machines et matériel de transport	Of which: / dont : Other manufactured goods / Articles manufacturés divers
			0 + 1 + 22 + 4	2 - (22 + 27 + 28)	3	27 + 28 + 68 + 667 + 971	5 + 6 +7 + 8- (667 + 68)	5	7	6 + 8 - (667 + 68)
Mongolia - Mongolie	1995	473	2.2	27.7	0.0	59.9	0.0	0.6	1.7	7.8
	2000	466	3.8	27.9	0.5	42.2	0.5	0.3	0.4	24.9
	2006	1 542	1.9	10.9	4.6	72.2	4.6	0.1	1.1	9.2
Morocco - Maroc	1995	4 719	31.4	3.4	2.2	11.5	2.2	20.8	3.2	27.4
	2000	7 432	21.5	2.0	3.7	8.8	3.7	12.0	11.0	41.0
	2006	12 531	19.3	1.7	3.8	9.5	3.8	13.4	17.2	35.2
Mozambique	1995	174	65.5	15.8	2.0	3.5	2.0	0.4	4.8	7.9
	2000	364	42.9	11.3	21.0	17.3	21.0	0.2	3.0	3.5
	2006	2 381	15.8	3.5	14.7	60.0	14.7	0.1	3.4	1.6
Myanmar	1995	860	41.9	38.5	0.2	7.4	0.2	1.0	0.9	10.0
	2000	1 647	20.0	22.2	6.1	4.6	6.1	0.5	1.3	44.9
	2006	4 869	19.2	16.0	47.2	4.4	47.2	0.1	0.4	11.1
Namibia - Namibie	2000	1 327	28.8	1.0	2.1	51.7	2.1	0.7	3.1	12.1
	2006	3 375	25.6	0.6	0.5	53.7	0.5	3.1	3.6	12.6
Nepal - Népal	1995	359	7.8	1.1	0.0	0.1	0.0	1.2	0.1	82.4
	2000	709	10.0	0.5	0.0	0.2	0.0	8.5	0.5	57.7
	2006	760	20.1	1.2	0.0	6.2	0.0	15.1	1.9	55.1
Netherlands - Pays-Bas	1995	177 626	19.8	3.9	7.1	2.8	7.1	16.4	26.6	19.5
	2000	180 072	15.0	3.2	9.9	2.3	9.9	13.9	36.7	18.8
	2006	370 209	13.3	3.0	13.6	3.9	13.6	17.0	31.1	17.8
Netherlands Antilles - Antilles néerlandaises	1995	1 522	11.9	0.1	61.6	10.0	61.6	1.6	6.3	4.5
	2000	1 588	4.1	0.4	84.8	3.9	84.8	0.8	2.4	3.4
	2006	3 336	1.1	0.1	83.8	1.6	83.8	0.9	5.6	1.5
New Caledonia - Nouvelle-Calédonie	1995	570	2.7	0.4	0.0	41.0	0.0	0.1	0.6	54.7
	2000	635	4.0	0.1	0.9	34.4	0.9	0.2	1.8	58.6
	2006	1 135	2.6	0.1	0.4	35.3	0.4	0.2	2.1	59.1
New Zealand - Nouvelle-Zélande	1995	13 745	42.4	18.0	1.6	6.3	1.6	7.6	8.6	14.3
	2000	13 272	43.9	13.7	2.6	5.4	2.6	6.9	10.4	12.7
	2006	22 409	48.8	10.3	1.6	6.0	1.6	5.1	12.0	12.9
Nicaragua	1995	509	73.5	2.9	0.6	2.7	0.6	1.2	6.1	13.0
	2000	629	84.9	2.0	1.7	4.0	1.7	1.9	0.7	4.8
	2006	759	79.3	1.7	0.5	9.7	0.5	2.5	1.2	5.0
Niger	1995	273	27.1	2.4	0.6	55.5	0.6	0.6	5.9	7.9
	2000	330	38.7	2.8	1.1	27.7	1.1	1.1	12.8	15.9
	2006	356	24.5	2.9	1.5	60.1	1.5	0.3	5.4	4.2
Nigeria - Nigéria	1995	11 877	2.7	2.4	92.5	0.3	92.5	0.4	0.2	1.4
	2000	27 079	0.1	0.0	99.6	0.0	99.6	0.0	0.1	0.1
	2006	46 896	1.5	1.8	95.0	0.3	95.0	0.0	0.2	0.6
Norway - Norvège	1995	41 740	8.3	1.5	47.3	8.8	47.3	3.1	13.3	10.4
	2000	59 899	6.4	0.7	63.9	6.1	63.9	2.6	9.2	6.7
	2006	121 624	5.0	0.5	67.8	7.2	67.8	2.4	8.2	5.5
Oman	1995	5 917	5.1	0.0	78.6	1.9	78.6	0.4	9.6	3.9
	2000	10 852	3.7	0.0	82.5	0.9	82.5	0.9	8.3	3.2
	2006	19 821	2.0	0.0	94.7	0.6	94.7	0.6	0.4	1.8
Pakistan	1995	8 158	11.8	3.8	1.0	0.2	1.0	0.7	0.5	81.8
	2000	9 201	10.5	2.9	1.4	0.2	1.4	1.6	1.0	82.1
	2006	16 933	11.8	1.2	5.0	0.6	5.0	2.6	1.9	76.8
Panama	1995	577	74.3	0.5	3.1	1.9	3.1	5.1	0.2	14.9
	2000	772	73.7	1.5	6.7	2.1	6.7	5.0	0.1	10.8
	2006	1 086	78.7	0.9	0.8	4.6	0.8	3.6	2.3	9.2

For sources and notes, see end of table.

Pour les sources et les notes, se reporter à la fin du tableau.

Country or territory Pays ou territoires	Year Année	Total value (millions of dollars) Valeur totale (millions de dollars)	By main SITC Revision 3 product group (percentage) Par principaux groupes de produits de la CTCI Révision 3 (en pourcentage)						Of which: / dont :		
			All food items Produits alimentaires	Agricultural raw materials Matières premières agricoles	Fuels Combustibles	Ores, metals, precious stones and non monetary gold Minerais, métaux, pierres précieuses et or (non monétaire)	Manu-factured goods Articles manu-facturés	Chemical products Produits chimiques	Machinery and transport equipment Machines et matériel de transport	Other manu-factured goods Articles manu-facturés divers
			0 + 1 + 22 + 4	2 - (22 + 27 + 28)	3	27 + 28 + 68 + 667 + 971	5 + 6 +7 + 8-(667 + 68)	5	7	6 + 8 - (667 + 68)
Papua New Guinea - Papouasie-Nouvelle-Guinée	1995	2 654	20.8	19.2	23.1	36.0	23.1	0.1	0.6	0.1
	2000	2 407	15.3	2.3	28.8	51.3	28.8	0.0	2.0	0.2
	2006	4 444	14.6	10.4	31.7	41.9	31.7	0.1	0.3	0.8
Paraguay	1995	919	43.9	36.4	0.2	0.3	0.2	2.6	0.8	15.9
	2000	871	64.8	15.5	0.1	0.4	0.1	2.6	0.5	16.2
	2006	1 906	75.8	7.2	0.0	1.1	0.0	3.1	1.2	11.7
Peru - Pérou	1995	5 440	28.8	2.5	4.9	50.2	4.9	2.2	0.6	10.8
	2000	6 856	25.3	2.5	5.9	49.4	5.9	2.4	1.1	13.4
	2006	23 765	14.7	1.4	8.0	64.3	8.0	2.0	0.5	9.2
Philippines	1995	17 447	12.8	1.2	1.5	5.4	1.5	2.0	22.2	16.7
	2000	38 078	4.8	0.6	1.3	2.0	1.3	0.9	76.1	14.3
	2006	47 410	5.5	0.5	2.3	5.1	2.3	1.6	69.5	15.0
Poland - Pologne	1995	22 862	10.4	2.8	8.2	7.3	8.2	7.7	21.1	42.4
	2000	31 613	7.9	1.8	5.1	5.0	5.1	6.8	34.2	39.2
	2006	109 584	9.3	1.1	4.5	5.3	4.5	7.1	40.0	31.6
Portugal	1995	23 370	7.2	4.6	3.2	2.1	3.2	4.9	26.8	51.1
	2000	24 365	6.8	3.5	2.6	2.1	2.6	5.7	34.4	44.8
	2006	43 358	8.0	1.9	5.5	3.6	5.5	6.5	31.5	35.3
Qatar	1995	3 557	0.4	0.0	80.2	0.2	80.2	11.2	1.3	6.6
	2000	8 847	0.1	0.0	89.5	0.1	89.5	5.3	1.2	3.7
	2006	34 051	0.1	0.0	89.7	0.1	89.7	6.3	0.8	1.0
Republic of Korea - République de Corée	1995	125 056	2.3	1.3	2.0	3.0	2.0	7.2	52.5	31.8
	2000	172 267	1.5	0.9	5.4	2.1	5.4	8.0	58.2	23.7
	2006	325 457	0.9	0.7	6.4	2.7	6.4	9.8	59.1	20.3
Romania - Roumanie	1995	7 910	6.6	3.3	7.9	3.5	7.9	10.7	13.1	54.4
	2000	10 367	3.1	4.9	7.2	7.5	7.2	5.8	18.8	52.1
	2006	32 336	3.3	2.2	10.0	5.6	10.0	5.7	29.9	43.3
Russian Federation - Fédération de Russie	1995	78 217	1.8	3.3	43.1	9.9	43.1	5.9	7.0	13.1
	2000	103 093	1.2	3.1	50.6	9.1	50.6	6.0	6.2	11.9
	2006	301 551	1.6	2.6	62.9	7.9	62.9	3.8	4.1	8.5
Rwanda	1995	52	57.0	15.9	0.2	12.9	0.2	0.6	6.8	6.6
	2000	52	57.0	3.2	0.0	37.7	0.0	0.5	0.0	1.6
	2006	138	54.8	3.6	0.7	34.0	0.7	0.7	4.7	1.1
Saint Kitts and Nevis - Saint-Kitts-et-Nevis	1995	19	54.3	0.3	0.2	0.1	0.2	0.8	36.6	7.7
	2000	33	24.6	0.0	0.0	0.0	0.0	0.2	66.3	8.9
	2006	40	7.9	0.0	0.2	0.1	0.2	0.0	87.3	4.5
Saint Lucia - Sainte-Lucie	1995	109	58.5	0.4	0.0	0.0	0.0	0.8	11.2	28.9
	2000	43	72.3	0.4	0.0	0.0	0.0	1.3	11.4	14.6
	2006	72	43.7	0.3	19.7	1.2	19.7	2.5	16.8	14.6
Saint Vincent and the Grenadines - Saint-Vincent-et-les Grenadines	1995	59	81.0	0.2	0.0	0.1	0.0	1.0	4.0	13.8
	2000	51	74.6	0.2	0.0	0.1	0.0	1.9	13.7	9.6
	2006	38	77.0	0.2	0.1	0.4	0.1	0.6	9.2	12.7
Samoa	1995	9	12.8	1.1	0.0	2.1	0.0	0.1	72.7	10.7
	2000	14	32.1	0.5	0.2	0.1	0.2	0.2	63.1	3.9
	2006	78	22.3	0.5	0.4	0.1	0.4	0.3	72.9	2.8
Sao Tome and Principe - Sao Tomé-et-Principe	1995	5	58.6	2.2	0.0	0.1	0.0	5.0	18.4	14.8
	2000	3	96.9	0.1	0.0	0.0	0.0	0.0	1.7	0.8
	2006	4	94.5	0.6	0.0	0.0	0.0	0.0	3.7	1.2
Saudi Arabia - Arabie saoudite	1995	49 030	0.9	0.1	86.8	0.6	86.8	8.4	1.0	2.2
	2000	77 480	0.6	0.1	91.5	0.2	91.5	5.4	0.8	1.5
	2006	211 306	0.7	0.1	89.2	0.5	89.2	5.7	2.0	1.9

For sources and notes, see end of table.

Pour les sources et les notes, se reporter à la fin du tableau.

Country or territory / Pays ou territoires	Year / Année	Total value (millions of dollars) / Valeur totale (millions de dollars)	By main SITC Revision 3 product group (percentage) / Par principaux groupes de produits de la CTCI Révision 3 (en pourcentage)					Of which: / dont :		
			All food items / Produits alimentaires	Agricultural raw materials / Matières premières agricoles	Fuels / Combustibles	Ores, metals, precious stones and non monetary gold / Minerais, métaux, pierres précieuses et or (non monétaire)	Manufactured goods / Articles manufacturés	Chemical products / Produits chimiques	Machinery and transport equipment / Machines et matériel de transport	Other manufactured goods / Articles manufacturés divers
			0 + 1 + 22 + 4	2 - (22 + 27 + 28)	3	27 + 28 + 68 + 667 + 971	5 + 6 + 7 + 8 - (667 + 68)	5	7	6 + 8 - (667 + 68)
Senegal - Sénégal	1995	531	15.4	8.5	15.1	11.3	15.1	39.5	2.5	7.7
	2000	693	52.4	1.7	14.0	4.8	14.0	17.4	3.5	6.2
	2006	1 492	33.2	2.5	28.2	4.4	28.2	12.7	6.2	12.8
Serbia and Montenegro - Serbie-et-Monténégro	1995	1 531	28.2	4.0	2.1	14.8	2.1	9.0	12.1	27.9
	2000	1 711	17.0	5.7	0.3	15.6	0.3	8.5	12.6	40.4
	2006	6 428	19.0	2.3	3.5	11.4	3.5	10.1	11.0	42.5
Seychelles	1995	53	45.9	0.0	46.7	0.1	46.7	0.5	3.0	3.9
	2000	194	75.6	0.1	21.9	0.0	21.9	0.4	1.2	0.7
	2006	380	53.1	0.0	42.4	0.0	42.4	0.2	0.1	4.0
Singapore - Singapour	1995	118 263	3.9	1.1	6.8	2.3	6.8	6.0	65.6	12.0
	2000	137 806	2.2	0.5	7.4	1.5	7.4	7.0	67.4	10.9
	2006	271 801	1.6	0.3	13.1	2.1	13.1	11.3	57.7	9.6
Slovakia - Slovaquie	1995	8 374	6.2	3.6	4.2	3.6	4.2	12.6	19.0	50.8
	2000	11 885	3.2	2.2	7.0	3.4	7.0	7.9	39.5	36.7
	2006	41 719	4.2	1.2	5.4	3.3	5.4	5.3	48.7	30.7
Slovenia - Slovénie	1995	8 316	3.9	1.8	1.2	3.4	1.2	10.5	31.4	47.6
	2000	8 732	3.7	1.6	0.7	4.2	0.7	11.0	36.0	42.8
	2006	20 983	3.0	1.1	2.7	5.9	2.7	13.6	38.2	35.3
South Africa - Afrique du Sud	1995	28 226	7.9	4.4	8.9	16.9	8.9	7.0	8.8	18.8
	2000	30 209	7.4	3.3	8.8	15.2	8.8	6.8	15.1	18.6
	2006	53 170	7.1	2.3	9.5	33.6	9.5	7.5	21.5	18.5
Spain - Espagne	1995	89 616	15.4	1.6	1.7	2.6	1.7	8.5	42.4	27.1
	2000	113 343	13.5	1.3	3.7	2.4	3.7	9.4	42.5	25.6
	2006	214 061	13.5	1.1	4.6	3.3	4.6	11.9	39.6	24.1
Sri Lanka	1995	3 798	18.7	4.3	0.4	6.9	0.4	0.9	3.6	64.5
	2000	5 433	21.1	1.6	0.4	3.6	0.4	0.7	6.2	66.5
	2006	6 683	21.5	2.1	0.1	7.9	0.1	1.2	5.3	60.9
Sudan - Soudan	1995	685	44.4	46.1	0.3	3.1	0.3	0.0	0.0	6.1
	2000	1 631	16.7	4.7	66.7	4.3	66.7	0.1	5.4	2.1
	2006	5 479	5.5	2.3	87.5	3.1	87.5	0.1	1.1	0.0
Suriname	1995	483	18.3	0.3	2.2	77.2	2.2	0.0	1.1	0.9
	2000	514	14.4	0.7	6.7	73.5	6.7	0.9	2.6	1.0
	2006	993	9.1	1.2	3.3	80.5	3.3	0.6	0.7	4.1
Swaziland	2000	891	33.6	10.7	0.7	0.4	0.7	20.1	9.7	24.5
	2006	1 647	16.3	7.2	0.7	0.4	0.7	47.2	5.3	21.8
Sweden - Suède	1995	77 436	2.2	6.5	1.9	3.2	1.9	6.6	42.1	29.9
	2000	86 937	2.5	4.7	3.3	2.5	3.3	8.9	47.5	25.3
	2006	147 370	3.5	4.0	5.6	4.1	5.6	10.9	41.1	25.3
Switzerland - Suisse	1995	81 641	3.0	0.7	0.1	5.3	0.1	26.0	31.4	33.5
	2000	81 534	2.5	0.6	0.4	7.4	0.4	27.3	30.6	31.1
	2006	147 856	2.8	0.4	2.5	4.8	2.5	35.0	24.7	29.7
Syrian Arab Republic - République arabe syrienne	1995	3 970	12.3	7.0	62.5	0.8	62.5	0.6	0.8	16.0
	2000	4 633	8.8	4.6	76.4	0.7	76.4	0.3	0.1	7.4
	2006	10 919	17.4	2.1	40.3	1.2	40.3	4.9	4.7	22.4
Tajikistan - Tadjikistan	1995	749	11.4	44.9	1.3	26.2	1.3	2.5	2.4	11.3
	2000	692	4.2	12.2	13.3	57.4	13.3	1.4	7.8	3.6
	2006	1 373	3.0	7.7	0.5	74.3	0.5	3.3	0.5	4.0
Thailand - Thaïlande	1995	56 439	19.3	5.4	0.7	2.9	0.7	4.4	33.7	32.9
	2000	68 819	14.4	3.3	3.2	2.1	3.2	5.9	43.6	24.7
	2006	130 580	11.2	5.3	5.0	2.8	5.0	8.0	44.7	21.7
TFYR of Macedonia - L'ERY de Macédoine	1995	1 204	18.3	5.2	0.4	17.9	0.4	5.5	12.9	39.7
	2000	1 323	15.0	1.7	4.8	8.8	4.8	4.5	6.3	58.6
	2006	2 401	16.1	0.8	9.4	4.3	9.4	4.2	4.9	60.3

For sources and notes, see end of table.   Pour les sources et les notes, se reporter à la fin du tableau.

Country or territory / Pays ou territoires	Year / Année	Total value (millions of dollars) / Valeur totale (millions de dollars)	By main SITC Revision 3 product group (percentage) / Par principaux groupes de produits de la CTCI Révision 3 (en pourcentage)					Of which: / dont :		
			All food items / Produits alimentaires	Agricultural raw materials / Matières premières agricoles	Fuels / Combustibles	Ores, metals, precious stones and non monetary gold / Minerais, métaux, pierres précieuses et or (non monétaire)	Manufactured goods / Articles manufacturés	Chemical products / Produits chimiques	Machinery and transport equipment / Machines et matériel de transport	Other manufactured goods / Articles manufacturés divers
			0 + 1 + 22 + 4	2 - (22 + 27 + 28)	3	27 + 28 + 68 + 667 + 971	5 + 6 +7 + 8- (667 + 68)	5	7	6 + 8 - (667 + 68)
Togo	1995	383	14.1	24.7	18.7	27.4	18.7	1.2	5.1	8.8
	2000	192	19.6	23.4	0.6	25.5	0.6	0.7	3.9	26.3
	2006	418	22.2	12.1	0.8	11.2	0.8	3.7	1.6	45.9
Trinidad and Tobago - Trinité-et-Tobago	1995	2 467	8.4	0.2	47.9	0.2	47.9	25.0	2.3	16.1
	2000	4 273	5.7	0.1	65.3	0.1	65.3	17.3	1.2	10.3
	2006	14 019	2.3	0.0	76.5	0.3	76.5	14.6	1.1	5.2
Tunisia - Tunisie	1995	5 475	9.8	0.6	8.5	1.8	8.5	11.9	9.4	57.9
	2000	5 850	8.7	0.7	12.1	1.6	12.1	10.6	14.0	52.3
	2006	11 513	10.7	0.7	11.3	1.2	11.3	9.4	18.6	48.1
Turkey - Turquie	1995	21 599	19.6	1.5	1.3	3.3	1.3	4.1	11.1	59.1
	2000	27 485	12.8	1.1	1.1	2.6	1.1	3.9	20.6	56.8
	2006	85 526	6.7	0.3	0.2	1.8	0.2	1.7	8.0	31.7
Turkmenistan - Turkménistan	1995	1 939	0.8	13.0	76.5	1.3	76.5	0.6	0.1	7.7
	2000	2 506	0.3	9.9	81.0	0.4	81.0	0.4	0.6	5.8
	2006	4 436	0.2	2.1	79.7	0.4	79.7	2.0	4.2	5.5
Turks and Caicos Islands - Îles Turques et Caïques	1995	5	56.9	0.2	13.9	21.6	13.9	2.9	0.7	2.3
	2000	9	46.8	1.3	0.3	0.1	0.3	0.2	33.2	16.3
	2006	18	38.5	1.1	0.0	0.4	0.0	0.1	34.0	20.2
Uganda - Ouganda	1995	575	86.0	4.4	0.1	5.4	0.1	1.0	1.2	2.0
	2000	403	60.2	12.5	7.0	14.9	7.0	1.1	2.5	1.8
	2006	962	54.4	7.8	4.4	15.0	4.4	1.6	9.3	7.5
Ukraine	1995	13 317	19.0	1.0	4.3	8.2	4.3	12.8	14.1	39.4
	2000	14 573	9.2	1.7	5.5	14.1	5.5	9.0	12.3	45.7
	2006	38 368	12.0	1.4	6.7	7.1	6.7	9.4	14.1	48.4
United Arab Emirates - Émirats arabes unis	1995	27 753	3.4	0.3	71.8	5.0	71.8	2.9	6.9	9.1
	2000	37 720	3.0	0.2	76.2	3.4	76.2	1.2	6.6	9.0
	2006	140 316	2.5	0.2	51.3	9.5	51.3	2.3	10.2	7.1
United Kingdom - Royaume-Uni	1995	234 372	7.6	0.7	6.2	4.8	6.2	12.4	43.8	23.8
	2000	282 854	5.4	0.5	8.5	4.6	8.5	12.1	43.6	19.1
	2006	444 439	4.7	0.6	9.7	5.1	9.7	14.4	42.8	18.2
United Republic of Tanzania - République-Unie de Tanzanie	1995	685	65.2	23.1	0.3	3.9	0.3	0.7	1.3	5.0
	2000	656	54.8	11.1	0.1	26.8	0.1	0.8	1.0	5.3
	2006	1 690	34.6	7.0	0.1	48.4	0.1	3.1	1.1	5.6
United States - États-Unis	1995	582 965	10.1	3.7	1.8	3.8	1.8	10.6	48.3	18.7
	2000	780 332	7.0	2.2	1.7	3.2	1.7	10.6	52.8	19.5
	2006	1 037 029	6.7	2.3	3.4	5.3	3.4	13.1	47.7	18.6
Uruguay	1995	2 106	44.2	14.9	1.0	0.9	1.0	5.6	6.0	27.1
	2000	2 299	46.3	9.3	1.5	1.4	1.5	6.2	8.5	26.8
	2006	3 952	55.2	9.7	3.5	2.2	3.5	5.7	3.7	19.9
Uzbekistan - Ouzbékistan	1995	3 720	7.9	52.0	12.9	11.8	12.9	3.5	2.9	9.0
	2000	3 265	9.1	38.8	19.2	12.8	19.2	3.1	5.0	10.7
	2006	3 771	10.5	20.0	13.7	13.6	13.7	7.8	10.7	7.4
Venezuela (Bolivarian Rep. of) - Venezuela (Rép. bolivarienne du)	1995	19 093	2.8	0.1	76.3	7.2	76.3	4.1	2.8	6.7
	2000	30 948	1.5	0.2	86.1	3.4	86.1	2.8	1.1	4.9
	2006	61 385	0.2	0.0	92.6	2.1	92.6	1.1	0.8	3.2
Viet Nam	1995	5 449	30.2	3.1	18.0	0.8	18.0	1.1	7.0	35.6
	2000	14 483	25.3	2.0	26.4	0.7	26.4	1.0	8.7	32.8
	2006	39 826	19.3	4.1	24.4	0.8	24.4	2.0	10.5	38.6
Yemen - Yémen	1995	1 917	2.7	0.6	94.3	0.5	94.3	0.1	0.9	0.8
	2000	4 078	2.1	0.4	96.5	0.1	96.5	0.3	0.3	0.3
	2006	6 264	4.4	0.2	91.8	0.2	91.8	0.3	2.3	0.8

For sources and notes, see end of table.

Pour les sources et les notes, se reporter à la fin du tableau.

3

Country or territory Pays ou territoires	Year Année	Total value (millions of dollars) Valeur totale (millions de dollars)	By main SITC Revision 3 product group (percentage) Par principaux groupes de produits de la CTCI Révision 3 (en pourcentage)					Of which: / dont :		
			All food items Produits alimentaires	Agricultural raw materials Matières premières agricoles	Fuels Combustibles	Ores, metals, precious stones and non monetary gold Minerais, métaux, pierres précieuses et or (non monétaire)	Manufactured goods Articles manufacturés	Chemical products Produits chimiques	Machinery and transport equipment Machines et matériel de transport	Other manufactured goods Articles manufacturés divers
			0 + 1 + 22 + 4	2 - (22 + 27 + 28)	3	27 + 28 + 68 + 667 + 971	5 + 6 +7 + 8- (667 + 68)	5	7	6 + 8 - (667 + 68)
Zambia - Zambie	1995	1 055	2.7	0.6	3.3	87.1	3.3	0.2	1.6	4.7
	2000	892	9.4	4.4	1.1	67.8	1.1	0.5	1.5	15.1
	2006	3 770	6.0	2.8	0.6	81.5	0.6	0.6	2.8	5.7
Zimbabwe	1995	1 846	43.4	6.8	1.3	12.1	1.3	2.6	2.7	31.1
	2000	1 925	47.1	12.5	1.1	11.3	1.1	2.8	2.4	22.8
	2006	1 470	28.4	11.9	1.1	29.5	1.1	1.6	2.2	25.3

Sources:
- Data and UNCTAD secretariat estimates based on UN DESA Comtrade and IMF Direction of Trade statistics databases

Sources :
- Données et estimations du secrétariat de la CNUCED sur la base de données Comtrade de ONU DAES et Direction of Trade statistics du Fonds Monétaire international

3.1 Country trade structure by product group
Imports

3.1 Structure du commerce des pays par groupes de produits
Importations

Country or territory / Pays ou territoires	Year / Année	Total value (millions of dollars) / Valeur totale (millions de dollars)	By main SITC Revision 3 product group (percentage) / Par principaux groupes de produits de la CTCI Révision 3 (en pourcentage)					Of which: / dont :		
			All food items / Produits alimentaires	Agricultural raw materials / Matières premières agricoles	Fuels / Combustibles	Ores, metals, precious stones and non monetary gold / Minerais, métaux, pierres précieuses et or (non monétaire)	Manufactured goods / Articles manufacturés	Chemical products / Produits chimiques	Machinery and transport equipment / Machines et matériel de transport	Other manufactured goods / Articles manufacturés divers
			0 + 1 + 22 + 4	2 - (22 + 27 + 28)	3	27 + 28 + 68 + 667 + 971	5 + 6 +7 + 8 - (667 + 68)	5	7	6 + 8 - (667 + 68)
Albania - Albanie	1995	938	34.3	0.9	2.6	1.0	2.6	5.9	22.8	32.5
	2000	1 039	21.8	0.9	9.0	1.5	9.0	7.0	21.6	38.1
	2006	3 057	17.7	1.1	10.5	2.3	10.5	9.3	19.9	39.2
Algeria - Algérie	1995	10 782	29.5	3.2	1.1	1.6	1.1	11.3	30.5	22.9
	2000	9 152	28.2	2.6	1.4	1.2	1.4	11.6	34.5	20.6
	2006	21 456	19.2	2.1	1.1	1.8	1.1	12.0	37.5	26.2
Andorra - Andorre	1995	1 025	29.7	0.7	3.6	1.0	3.6	9.2	20.0	35.9
	2000	1 012	19.9	0.5	4.4	1.3	4.4	10.3	23.1	40.3
	2006	1 930	17.3	0.4	6.5	0.7	6.5	8.9	26.6	39.0
Angola	1995	1 468	25.5	0.9	0.7	0.4	0.7	6.0	43.3	22.0
	2000	3 040	27.2	0.8	4.5	0.5	4.5	6.1	35.5	22.8
	2006	5 378	15.0	0.6	1.4	0.4	1.4	5.1	53.3	23.0
Argentina - Argentine	1995	20 122	5.5	2.0	4.2	2.7	4.2	17.8	44.5	23.1
	2000	25 280	5.0	1.5	3.7	2.5	3.7	18.5	44.4	23.9
	2006	34 160	2.6	1.5	4.7	3.9	4.7	18.8	48.2	19.6
Armenia - Arménie	1995	674	31.1	0.5	27.3	6.6	27.3	10.0	11.4	11.3
	2000	840	25.0	0.9	20.8	14.4	20.8	10.8	14.7	13.5
	2006	2 194	15.3	0.8	16.0	16.1	16.0	8.6	18.8	19.8
Australia - Australie	1995	57 423	5.0	1.7	5.0	2.5	5.0	11.1	47.0	27.7
	2000	71 263	4.6	1.4	8.3	2.7	8.3	11.5	46.1	25.3
	2006	132 651	4.7	0.8	13.2	4.9	13.2	10.6	42.5	23.0
Austria - Autriche	1995	66 406	5.7	3.2	4.4	4.3	4.4	10.7	36.8	34.2
	2000	68 374	5.4	2.6	5.4	3.1	5.4	10.1	41.1	30.1
	2006	134 248	5.9	2.3	13.8	4.8	13.8	10.8	35.2	26.6
Azerbaijan - Azerbaïdjan	1995	961	39.1	1.0	4.5	2.3	4.5	7.5	23.6	22.0
	2000	1 172	18.6	1.7	4.9	3.6	4.9	7.9	40.0	23.3
	2006	5 267	10.5	1.0	11.6	2.3	11.6	5.9	46.2	22.3
Bahamas	1995	1 243	18.8	1.9	12.6	0.5	12.6	8.1	25.8	30.6
	2000	2 002	16.7	2.7	10.4	0.6	10.4	9.1	26.3	32.4
	2006	2 984	14.9	2.4	20.3	0.7	20.3	8.8	22.3	26.6
Bahrain - Bahreïn	1995	3 679	12.3	1.0	36.7	4.9	36.7	5.7	16.8	22.4
	2000	4 633	9.7	0.8	45.5	6.9	45.5	4.7	16.1	16.4
	2006	8 957	5.7	0.4	55.6	5.4	55.6	3.6	16.8	12.5
Bangladesh	1995	5 438	17.3	3.4	7.7	2.3	7.7	10.2	14.7	44.3
	2000	7 611	16.5	6.1	7.3	2.4	7.3	11.3	19.6	36.9
	2006	15 279	14.6	4.1	13.0	2.8	13.0	10.0	22.8	30.6
Barbados - Barbade	1995	766	18.3	2.4	8.5	1.2	8.5	12.2	26.8	30.5
	2000	1 156	15.4	2.3	11.5	1.2	11.5	9.7	27.8	31.8
	2006	1 629	15.3	2.0	18.4	1.1	18.4	9.5	26.4	26.7
Belarus - Bélarus	1995	6 939	11.1	2.4	23.8	3.1	23.8	11.8	22.7	23.4
	2000	8 646	11.9	2.3	29.9	3.8	29.9	10.5	16.5	20.5
	2006	22 323	8.5	1.5	32.8	3.7	32.8	9.9	20.1	18.1
Belgium - Belgique	2006	353 790	7.4	1.2	13.5	8.7	13.5	24.8	24.3	19.1
Belgium-Luxembourg - Belgique-Luxembourg	1995	153 388	11.2	2.1	6.1	11.6	6.1	13.7	26.3	23.9
	2000	176 812	8.6	1.9	8.5	10.8	8.5	15.9	30.7	22.6
Belize	1995	259	19.1	0.3	11.5	0.7	11.5	10.7	25.8	31.9
	2000	447	14.0	0.6	17.0	0.5	17.0	10.3	28.7	28.4
	2006	660	12.2	0.7	16.1	0.6	16.1	7.1	16.6	19.7
Benin - Bénin	1995	719	27.3	2.7	9.4	1.0	9.4	13.7	18.0	27.7
	2000	547	21.9	5.3	19.2	1.0	19.2	10.3	15.1	27.3
	2006	1 011	27.1	3.9	21.7	1.0	21.7	8.0	14.1	23.5

For sources and notes, see end of table.

Pour les sources et les notes, se reporter à la fin du tableau.

Country or territory / Pays ou territoires	Year / Année	Total value (millions of dollars) / Valeur totale (millions de dollars)	By main SITC Revision 3 product group (percentage) / Par principaux groupes de produits de la CTCI Révision 3 (en pourcentage)					Of which: / dont :		
			All food items / Produits alimentaires	Agricultural raw materials / Matières premières agricoles	Fuels / Combustibles	Ores, metals, precious stones and non monetary gold / Minerais, métaux, pierres précieuses et or (non monétaire)	Manufactured goods / Articles manufacturés	Chemical products / Produits chimiques	Machinery and transport equipment / Machines et matériel de transport	Other manufactured goods / Articles manufacturés divers
			0 + 1 + 22 + 4	2 - (22 + 27 + 28)	3	27 + 28 + 68 + 667 + 971	5 + 6 +7 + 8- (667 + 68)	5	7	6 + 8 - (667 + 68)
Bolivia - Bolivie	1995	1 396	9.5	1.7	4.5	3.2	4.5	13.7	46.3	21.1
	2000	1 849	13.5	1.6	4.8	1.1	4.8	14.3	36.9	27.6
	2006	2 825	9.3	1.3	9.7	1.4	9.7	17.6	33.6	26.8
Bosnia and Herzegovina - Bosnie-Herzégovine	1995	101	42.2	0.9	7.3	1.0	7.3	9.9	12.6	24.8
	2000	3 083	21.2	1.0	7.7	1.9	7.7	10.9	22.7	33.6
	2006	7 559	16.8	1.4	15.4	4.1	15.4	10.7	22.6	28.9
Botswana	2000	2 072	14.0	0.8	4.9	5.1	4.9	6.8	34.6	30.7
	2006	3 053	13.7	0.8	17.2	4.9	17.2	10.1	26.5	25.5
Brazil - Brésil	1995	53 734	10.7	2.7	12.1	3.4	12.1	15.2	39.2	16.7
	2000	55 851	6.6	2.0	14.8	3.1	14.8	17.9	41.8	13.8
	2006	91 343	4.5	1.5	18.8	5.0	18.8	18.0	37.4	14.7
Brunei Darussalam - Brunéi Darussalam	1995	2 078	13.6	0.6	0.2	3.3	0.2	6.4	39.0	36.5
	2000	1 098	17.9	0.3	0.2	1.2	0.2	7.7	30.8	41.8
	2006	1 676	17.0	0.2	1.6	1.4	1.6	10.5	35.1	33.7
Bulgaria - Bulgarie	1995	5 651	7.6	2.6	33.7	4.4	33.7	11.1	16.0	20.8
	2000	6 505	5.2	1.3	25.8	5.7	25.8	9.4	24.9	24.7
	2006	23 269	4.6	1.2	5.3	8.8	5.3	8.8	28.7	24.5
Burkina Faso	1995	484	21.2	1.5	14.0	1.2	14.0	14.7	19.7	27.7
	2000	724	12.6	0.6	25.2	0.9	25.2	8.4	37.1	15.2
	2006	1 417	18.2	0.6	17.3	0.5	17.3	19.7	19.0	23.4
Burundi	1995	270	20.9	1.9	11.3	1.2	11.3	14.1	29.3	20.7
	2000	150	22.9	2.4	11.8	2.3	11.8	13.3	22.9	23.8
	2006	434	22.2	1.0	0.9	4.5	0.9	10.5	34.1	26.7
Cambodia - Cambodge	1995	218	24.9	1.6	7.8	7.7	7.8	6.1	34.2	16.3
	2000	1 439	9.5	3.3	12.7	2.8	12.7	6.7	16.2	48.1
	2006	2 996	7.8	1.3	8.2	0.7	8.2	5.5	20.5	55.0
Cameroon - Cameroun	1995	1 079	17.4	2.5	2.4	5.6	2.4	16.5	30.5	24.9
	2000	1 484	18.2	1.6	23.2	3.6	23.2	11.9	23.0	18.7
	2006	3 150	17.6	1.6	32.1	3.1	32.1	11.1	17.1	17.3
Canada	1995	164 371	5.7	1.7	3.6	3.7	3.6	8.1	51.6	23.1
	2000	240 091	5.0	1.4	5.2	2.9	5.2	8.4	52.0	23.2
	2006	349 906	5.7	1.1	9.1	4.4	9.1	10.3	44.8	23.1
Cape Verde - Cap-Vert	1995	327	31.1	2.6	14.3	0.2	14.3	5.4	22.8	23.4
	2000	237	31.0	2.2	6.1	0.3	6.1	6.6	28.5	25.4
	2006	538	29.2	1.4	8.9	0.6	8.9	6.4	25.6	27.9
Central African Republic - République centrafricaine	1995	265	15.6	9.8	8.7	1.6	8.7	8.0	42.2	14.0
	2000	70	29.3	4.3	7.5	4.5	7.5	12.8	23.2	18.2
	2006	221	20.0	17.2	14.2	5.2	14.2	11.8	17.9	13.4
Chad - Tchad	1995	147	16.6	0.7	4.0	0.3	4.0	15.0	37.3	25.0
	2000	137	16.7	1.2	3.2	0.6	3.2	17.2	41.9	18.7
	2006	444	15.4	0.6	2.3	1.1	2.3	10.4	47.4	19.7
Chile - Chili	1995	14 903	6.7	1.7	9.0	2.2	9.0	12.2	42.3	24.7
	2000	16 620	7.4	1.2	18.1	1.1	18.1	12.7	35.0	23.7
	2006	34 726	6.8	0.9	24.3	3.2	24.3	11.3	33.6	19.9
China - Chine	1995	132 083	7.0	5.2	3.9	4.6	3.9	13.1	39.9	25.7
	2000	225 094	4.0	4.7	9.2	6.3	9.2	13.4	40.8	20.9
	2006	791 461	2.9	3.6	11.2	9.1	11.2	11.0	45.1	16.8
China, Hong Kong SAR - Chine (RAS de Hong Kong)	1995	196 072	5.4	1.6	1.9	5.6	1.9	7.4	36.5	41.3
	2000	214 042	4.3	1.2	2.1	4.4	2.1	6.3	42.4	39.3
	2006	335 754	2.8	0.7	2.9	5.6	2.9	6.0	53.7	28.2
China, Macao SAR - Chine (RAS de Macao)	1995	2 025	14.0	2.7	5.1	0.8	5.1	4.5	18.9	53.9
	2000	2 261	11.5	1.4	7.7	0.6	7.7	3.8	15.8	59.3
	2006	5 236	10.0	0.3	9.6	1.1	9.6	4.1	22.4	52.5

For sources and notes, see end of table.

Pour les sources et les notes, se reporter à la fin du tableau.

Country or territory / Pays ou territoires	Year / Année	Total value (millions of dollars) / Valeur totale (millions de dollars)	All food items / Produits alimentaires	Agricultural raw materials / Matières premières agricoles	Fuels / Combustibles	Ores, metals, precious stones and non monetary gold / Minerais, métaux, pierres précieuses et or (non monétaire)	Manufactured goods / Articles manufacturés	Of which: / dont : Chemical products / Produits chimiques	Machinery and transport equipment / Machines et matériel de transport	Other manufactured goods / Articles manufacturés divers
			0 + 1 + 22 + 4	2 - (22 + 27 + 28)	3	27 + 28 + 68 + 667 + 971	5 + 6 +7 + 8- (667 + 68)	5	7	6 + 8 - (667 + 68)
China, Taiwan Province of - Province chinoise de Taiwan	1995	103 506	5.4	4.2	6.9	7.4	6.9	13.3	40.2	20.7
	2000	139 991	3.6	2.1	9.3	5.2	9.3	11.1	50.2	17.5
	2006	202 686	3.3	1.5	18.1	8.6	18.1	12.9	37.9	17.1
Colombia - Colombie	1995	13 883	9.4	2.5	2.8	2.5	2.8	18.1	37.3	22.6
	2000	11 757	11.9	2.8	2.1	2.4	2.1	23.2	32.9	24.5
	2006	26 162	8.7	1.6	2.6	3.4	2.6	20.0	40.2	22.5
Congo	1995	556	20.8	0.9	19.5	0.8	19.5	14.0	20.3	23.8
	2000	665	24.5	2.6	2.0	1.1	2.0	13.1	29.4	26.0
	2006	1 612	15.6	2.3	3.2	0.7	3.2	11.6	35.9	27.9
Costa Rica	1995	3 205	10.2	1.2	8.5	2.6	8.5	19.8	26.6	31.0
	2000	6 029	7.4	0.8	8.1	2.2	8.1	14.7	37.9	28.9
	2006	11 070	6.3	1.0	11.8	2.6	11.8	13.9	40.5	23.8
Côte d'Ivoire	1995	2 472	20.9	0.9	19.2	1.5	19.2	13.0	24.5	19.2
	2000	2 432	17.2	1.1	33.7	1.4	33.7	14.3	16.4	15.4
	2006	5 820	17.3	0.6	31.8	1.1	31.8	11.6	19.1	17.5
Croatia - Croatie	1995	7 509	11.8	1.8	11.6	2.5	11.6	10.8	26.7	29.0
	2000	7 887	8.3	1.6	14.5	2.3	14.5	12.7	32.6	28.0
	2006	21 502	8.3	1.2	15.9	2.7	15.9	10.8	32.2	28.9
Cuba	1995	2 805	21.0	1.6	22.7	1.6	22.7	12.2	20.0	20.1
	2000	4 843	15.8	1.3	23.9	1.3	23.9	8.8	25.1	23.8
	2006	9 503	20.7	0.8	24.7	1.2	24.7	8.8	22.9	21.0
Cyprus - Chypre	1995	3 694	20.4	1.3	7.7	2.3	7.7	8.8	27.6	31.9
	2000	3 846	18.6	1.0	12.8	1.6	12.8	8.6	28.0	29.4
	2006	7 046	12.6	1.0	18.0	1.5	18.0	9.1	28.4	28.1
Czech Republic - République tchèque	1995	25 303	6.7	2.7	7.8	4.3	7.8	11.8	36.1	29.4
	2000	32 243	4.9	2.1	9.6	3.7	9.6	11.2	40.1	28.4
	2006	93 429	5.1	1.4	9.0	4.3	9.0	10.3	41.1	27.4
Dem. Rep. of the Congo - Rép. dém. du Congo	1995	871	23.2	3.1	10.4	1.2	10.4	9.4	20.8	30.9
	2000	697	27.6	2.3	14.1	2.5	14.1	11.6	21.7	19.7
	2006	2 799	26.6	2.0	9.8	1.0	9.8	10.3	27.8	20.7
Denmark - Danemark	1995	43 142	12.0	3.0	3.3	2.1	3.3	11.2	32.0	29.5
	2000	44 587	11.4	2.7	5.7	1.8	5.7	9.8	35.9	30.2
	2006	84 511	11.2	2.3	5.9	2.2	5.9	10.8	36.3	29.9
Dominican Republic - République dominicaine	1995	3 164	13.2	1.7	9.0	0.7	9.0	7.8	21.0	44.3
	2000	6 281	10.2	1.3	16.3	0.7	16.3	5.8	26.4	37.6
	2006	7 070	11.3	1.4	14.5	1.5	14.5	8.4	25.4	34.1
Ecuador - Équateur	1995	4 195	7.6	2.8	5.9	1.9	5.9	17.6	40.1	24.1
	2000	3 446	9.0	3.3	8.1	1.8	8.1	23.9	26.6	26.0
	2006	12 114	7.1	1.1	21.2	1.3	21.2	15.3	32.3	21.8
Egypt - Égypte	1995	11 739	28.4	7.1	1.2	2.7	1.2	13.2	25.3	22.1
	2000	14 010	25.2	4.8	7.6	2.5	7.6	11.6	25.3	18.5
	2006	20 667	19.0	3.9	16.3	3.8	16.3	9.5	19.1	14.2
El Salvador	1995	2 628	14.8	2.0	9.2	1.6	9.2	17.2	30.1	25.2
	2000	3 795	16.2	2.1	15.7	1.2	15.7	14.9	26.5	23.4
	2006	5 945	13.0	1.6	18.3	1.2	18.3	17.9	23.8	23.9
Equatorial Guinea - Guinée équatoriale	1995	50	24.2	2.4	3.2	0.6	3.2	10.1	26.4	32.5
	2000	451	9.8	0.6	9.4	0.3	9.4	5.3	49.8	19.7
	2006	1 527	7.8	0.7	8.2	0.4	8.2	3.4	57.0	19.5
Estonia - Estonie	1995	2 546	13.8	2.9	10.9	1.4	10.9	9.6	29.8	31.4
	2000	5 052	9.9	3.3	7.2	3.6	7.2	9.2	41.3	25.6
	2006	13 285	6.7	2.7	16.0	1.5	16.0	8.3	35.7	22.7

For sources and notes, see end of table.

Pour les sources et les notes, se reporter à la fin du tableau.

Country or territory Pays ou territoires	Year Année	Total value (millions of dollars) Valeur totale (millions de dollars)	By main SITC Revision 3 product group (percentage) Par principaux groupes de produits de la CTCI Révision 3 (en pourcentage)					Of which: / dont :		
			All food items Produits alimentaires	Agricultural raw materials Matières premières agricoles	Fuels Combus-tibles	Ores, metals, precious stones and non monetary gold Minerais, métaux, pierres précieuses et or (non monétaire)	Manu-factured goods Articles manu-facturés	Chemical products Produits chimiques	Machinery and transport equipment Machines et matériel de transport	Other manu-factured goods Articles manu-facturés divers
			0 + 1 + 22 + 4	2 - (22 + 27 + 28)	3	27 + 28 + 68 + 667 + 971	5 + 6 +7 + 8- (667 + 68)	5	7	6 + 8 - (667 + 68)
Ethiopia - Éthiopie	1995	1 141	13.8	1.9	11.1	0.8	11.1	14.1	35.5	22.7
	2000	1 260	7.0	1.2	20.1	0.7	20.1	11.5	31.9	27.6
	2006	5 207	8.5	1.6	19.9	0.8	19.9	11.0	35.6	22.6
Faeroe Islands - Îles Féroé	1995	314	22.3	3.5	11.7	1.2	11.7	7.4	27.5	23.0
	2000	532	20.3	2.4	8.1	0.9	8.1	7.0	36.6	22.5
	2006	783	13.6	3.1	18.8	1.2	18.8	6.9	28.3	26.8
Fiji - Fidji	1995	892	14.1	0.6	13.3	0.9	13.3	6.9	23.6	38.3
	2000	776	13.7	0.6	6.8	0.9	6.8	7.0	20.4	43.5
	2006	1 804	14.0	0.3	32.7	1.1	32.7	7.3	21.8	22.2
Finland - Finlande	1995	29 520	6.0	3.6	8.8	5.7	8.8	12.2	38.7	23.3
	2000	33 886	5.2	2.4	11.9	5.6	11.9	10.5	42.1	20.0
	2006	69 427	4.8	2.6	15.3	9.1	15.3	10.8	36.6	18.5
France	1995	275 510	10.7	2.5	6.9	3.9	6.9	12.5	35.4	28.1
	2000	303 758	7.9	1.9	9.9	3.2	9.9	12.2	39.2	25.7
	2006	529 902	7.4	1.4	14.8	3.6	14.8	12.7	35.2	24.9
French Polynesia - Polynésie française	1995	1 019	21.6	1.5	5.5	0.9	5.5	8.5	34.7	27.4
	2000	1 072	20.0	1.9	7.2	1.0	7.2	8.6	33.3	28.0
	2006	1 547	19.7	1.7	12.9	0.8	12.9	9.5	29.5	26.0
Gabon	1995	884	19.1	0.7	3.4	1.1	3.4	10.7	39.3	25.7
	2000	952	18.2	0.5	4.1	1.0	4.1	8.6	48.0	19.5
	2006	1 725	16.6	0.4	3.9	1.1	3.9	9.2	42.8	25.6
Gambia - Gambie	1995	215	36.4	0.7	14.1	0.3	14.1	5.9	22.0	17.9
	2000	189	34.5	0.7	11.9	0.8	11.9	5.6	21.9	23.7
	2006	259	31.2	2.2	17.4	0.6	17.4	4.6	25.2	18.9
Georgia - Géorgie	1995	412	36.1	0.2	38.8	0.5	38.8	4.8	9.7	9.9
	2000	709	23.3	0.7	19.6	0.7	19.6	11.1	24.8	19.2
	2006	3 675	16.4	0.5	19.4	0.7	19.4	9.0	28.9	23.0
Germany - Allemagne	1995	464 145	9.8	2.6	6.2	4.4	6.2	9.1	31.8	28.9
	2000	500 830	6.6	1.7	8.6	3.8	8.6	8.9	35.8	22.6
	2006	922 213	6.6	1.4	12.1	5.4	12.1	11.5	37.1	21.3
Ghana	1995	1 896	7.9	1.0	5.8	2.6	5.8	9.3	43.7	21.9
	2000	2 933	12.8	2.4	21.4	2.9	21.4	9.8	30.4	19.3
	2006	5 329	13.4	1.2	13.8	1.5	13.8	10.8	34.0	25.2
Greece - Grèce	1995	25 927	16.0	2.5	7.2	3.2	7.2	13.2	27.4	30.5
	2000	29 816	11.3	1.5	13.4	2.7	13.4	11.6	34.6	24.8
	2006	63 739	10.7	1.2	19.1	3.9	19.1	13.7	28.5	22.6
Greenland - Groenland	1995	421	14.2	1.2	5.8	0.4	5.8	4.3	24.6	30.4
	2000	364	15.2	0.8	18.7	0.4	18.7	3.5	26.6	21.8
	2006	581	19.6	0.7	21.9	0.5	21.9	5.2	22.0	29.5
Grenada - Grenade	1995	129	27.5	2.5	7.8	0.4	7.8	8.8	21.3	31.7
	2000	239	18.4	2.2	8.8	0.8	8.8	6.6	32.9	30.4
	2006	299	18.7	3.3	5.9	0.7	5.9	9.6	22.1	39.8
Guatemala	1995	3 292	11.9	1.5	12.4	1.2	12.4	17.2	31.5	24.3
	2000	4 882	12.1	1.7	12.7	1.3	12.7	16.4	32.6	23.3
	2006	9 540	10.1	1.0	19.5	1.3	19.5	16.0	28.9	23.3
Guinea - Guinée	1995	819	31.0	1.0	19.1	0.8	19.1	6.6	20.9	19.9
	2000	612	24.2	1.2	24.9	0.8	24.9	8.7	19.0	21.0
	2006	807	17.1	1.2	11.7	0.5	11.7	11.2	28.0	23.9
Guinea-Bissau - Guinée-Bissau	1995	57	43.6	0.5	16.2	0.2	16.2	4.9	22.9	11.8
	2000	49	24.7	0.8	5.0	0.5	5.0	9.6	18.2	38.9
	2006	97	28.8	0.4	18.8	0.5	18.8	5.8	21.3	22.3

For sources and notes, see end of table.

Pour les sources et les notes, se reporter à la fin du tableau.

Country or territory / Pays ou territoires	Year / Année	Total value (millions of dollars) / Valeur totale (millions de dollars)	By main SITC Revision 3 product group (percentage) / Par principaux groupes de produits de la CTCI Révision 3 (en pourcentage)					Of which: / dont :		
			All food items / Produits alimentaires	Agricultural raw materials / Matières premières agricoles	Fuels / Combustibles	Ores, metals, precious stones and non monetary gold / Minerais, métaux, pierres précieuses et or (non monétaire)	Manufactured goods / Articles manufacturés	Chemical products / Produits chimiques	Machinery and transport equipment / Machines et matériel de transport	Other manufactured goods / Articles manufacturés divers
			0 + 1 + 22 + 4	2 - (22 + 27 + 28)	3	27 + 28 + 68 + 667 + 971	5 + 6 +7 + 8- (667 + 68)	5	7	6 + 8 - (667 - 68)
Guyana	1995	528	14.1	0.4	5.6	0.5	5.6	11.1	34.8	22.8
	2000	573	13.9	0.5	22.3	0.4	22.3	11.4	27.0	24.2
	2006	893	12.7	0.2	30.3	0.5	30.3	10.2	27.0	18.9
Haiti - Haïti	1995	654	38.5	1.8	3.8	0.6	3.8	5.6	21.7	20.8
	2000	1 040	33.7	1.5	6.2	0.8	6.2	5.6	14.0	32.6
	2006	1 891	28.6	0.9	2.0	0.3	2.0	4.2	20.8	22.8
Honduras	1995	1 728	12.6	1.1	11.5	1.2	11.5	17.3	29.1	27.2
	2000	2 482	22.2	2.4	18.3	1.0	18.3	20.7	6.3	23.0
	2006	4 921	13.4	1.0	21.7	1.2	21.7	14.9	24.9	23.0
Hungary - Hongrie	1995	15 186	5.7	3.0	11.9	4.3	11.9	14.5	30.1	30.6
	2000	32 079	2.9	1.5	4.7	2.7	4.7	8.9	51.0	24.1
	2006	76 979	3.9	0.9	7.4	2.6	7.4	9.1	47.7	18.2
Iceland - Islande	1995	1 751	11.8	1.6	7.2	4.6	7.2	9.3	32.4	32.9
	2000	2 380	9.1	1.2	9.4	4.8	9.4	7.9	39.7	27.8
	2006	5 991	6.8	1.2	8.9	6.1	8.9	7.0	44.8	25.2
India - Inde	1995	36 592	4.2	4.0	23.7	14.1	23.7	15.4	20.2	11.5
	2000	51 377	4.4	3.2	34.7	22.6	34.7	9.0	15.1	9.2
	2006	185 385	3.3	1.7	33.3	18.3	33.3	9.0	22.5	10.5
Indonesia - Indonésie	1995	40 629	8.8	6.2	7.4	4.6	7.4	15.4	40.1	17.4
	2000	33 515	10.0	7.1	18.1	3.6	18.1	17.6	27.5	16.1
	2006	61 065	8.8	3.5	31.2	3.9	31.2	14.3	25.2	13.2
Iran (Islamic Rep. of) - Iran (Rép. islamique d')	1995	13 882	20.9	2.4	1.8	5.1	1.8	13.3	35.6	20.9
	2000	13 626	19.0	2.6	2.3	2.5	2.3	14.5	35.3	23.9
	2006	40 686	1.9	0.6	4.0	0.4	4.0	2.7	8.1	5.5
Ireland - Irlande	1995	32 321	8.5	1.2	3.3	2.2	3.3	12.8	42.3	20.7
	2000	50 649	6.3	1.0	4.1	1.2	4.1	11.0	53.1	17.7
	2006	76 621	8.3	1.0	7.8	1.7	7.8	13.1	42.0	20.3
Israel - Israël	1995	28 344	6.6	1.6	5.9	19.3	5.9	9.3	34.0	21.9
	2000	35 742	5.4	1.0	10.0	21.0	10.0	8.9	34.8	18.6
	2006	47 834	5.7	1.1	15.6	21.3	15.6	11.2	27.5	17.0
Italy - Italie	1995	200 320	11.5	5.6	7.3	6.3	7.3	13.1	29.8	23.8
	2000	238 257	8.5	4.0	9.7	6.1	9.7	12.2	33.3	22.4
	2006	442 565	8.1	2.5	12.2	6.5	12.2	12.5	28.0	22.8
Jamaica - Jamaïque	1995	2 773	14.3	1.6	12.7	0.9	12.7	9.9	27.5	30.3
	2000	3 192	15.5	1.5	18.4	0.6	18.4	10.7	23.3	27.3
	2006	5 041	14.4	1.5	24.5	0.6	24.5	11.3	22.6	23.6
Japan - Japon	1995	336 094	16.1	6.2	16.0	8.5	16.0	7.1	22.6	22.3
	2000	379 663	12.8	3.6	20.4	6.2	20.4	6.9	27.9	20.8
	2006	579 064	9.0	2.3	27.9	8.1	27.9	7.1	24.5	19.6
Jordan - Jordanie	1995	3 696	20.6	2.1	12.9	3.4	12.9	12.3	24.5	23.7
	2000	4 013	21.2	2.3	4.8	3.0	4.8	12.0	32.3	21.6
	2006	11 447	13.3	1.3	23.8	2.8	23.8	8.7	24.6	23.8
Kazakhstan	1995	3 805	9.8	2.1	25.0	4.6	25.0	9.4	27.8	21.3
	2000	5 033	9.1	0.9	11.2	3.1	11.2	10.0	38.9	24.4
	2006	23 663	6.9	0.9	12.9	1.5	12.9	8.6	43.0	26.2
Kenya	1995	2 818	10.1	1.9	14.7	2.0	14.7	17.6	33.5	20.2
	2000	2 891	14.0	2.5	22.2	1.5	22.2	14.7	27.8	17.4
	2006	7 234	9.2	1.9	24.1	2.0	24.1	13.9	31.2	17.6
Kuwait - Koweït	1995	7 790	15.5	1.1	0.5	2.0	0.5	7.3	41.2	32.3
	2000	7 157	17.5	0.9	0.6	3.5	0.6	8.5	37.4	31.8
	2006	15 199	12.2	0.6	1.3	2.3	1.3	7.2	44.4	29.2

For sources and notes, see end of table.

Pour les sources et les notes, se reporter à la fin du tableau.

Country or territory / Pays ou territoires	Year / Année	Total value (millions of dollars) / Valeur totale (millions de dollars)	All food items / Produits alimentaires 0 + 1 + 22 + 4	Agricultural raw materials / Matières premières agricoles 2 - (22 + 27 + 28)	Fuels / Combustibles 3	Ores, metals, precious stones and non monetary gold / Minerais, métaux, pierres précieuses et or (non monétaire) 27 + 28 + 68 + 667 + 971	Manufactured goods / Articles manufacturés 5 + 6 +7 + 8- (667 + 68)	Chemical products / Produits chimiques 5	Machinery and transport equipment / Machines et matériel de transport 7	Other manufactured goods / Articles manufacturés divers 6 + 8 - (667 + 68)
Kyrgyzstan - Kirghizistan	1995	522	18.3	2.7	35.9	2.6	35.9	6.3	18.4	15.9
	2000	554	14.6	1.8	23.2	1.3	23.2	12.0	25.6	21.4
	2006	1 718	14.4	1.2	29.2	2.0	29.2	10.4	23.7	19.0
Latvia - Lettonie	1995	1 818	10.5	1.7	21.2	1.1	21.2	12.7	25.4	27.5
	2000	3 191	12.3	2.0	12.3	2.0	12.3	12.5	28.2	30.7
	2006	11 427	10.4	2.1	12.7	1.7	12.7	10.2	31.9	27.8
Lebanon - Liban	1995	5 480	19.4	1.8	8.2	8.2	8.2	8.9	25.7	27.8
	2000	6 227	17.8	1.7	16.5	8.4	16.5	10.2	21.8	23.6
	2006	9 434	17.1	1.2	20.3	4.4	20.3	12.4	18.6	23.4
Lesotho	2000	613	17.6	0.9	18.9	2.3	18.9	5.9	7.7	34.8
	2006	1 501	16.9	0.8	6.4	0.4	6.4	5.3	12.8	35.4
Libyan Arab Jamahiriya - Jamahiriya arabe libyenne	1995	5 033	22.8	0.9	0.2	1.2	0.2	7.5	36.0	31.4
	2000	3 731	27.4	0.9	0.3	1.6	0.3	7.4	33.3	29.2
	2006	9 556	13.8	0.7	8.6	2.5	8.6	6.7	37.7	24.6
Lithuania - Lituanie	1995	3 649	13.1	3.9	19.4	3.9	19.4	12.5	21.7	23.6
	2000	5 456	9.7	3.0	21.7	2.2	21.7	12.3	24.3	24.1
	2006	19 388	8.8	2.0	22.4	1.7	22.4	11.5	31.2	21.8
Luxembourg	2006	19 640	9.4	1.2	9.6	8.4	9.6	9.4	29.3	27.6
Madagascar	1995	550	16.3	1.8	14.0	0.6	14.0	13.0	25.7	26.4
	2000	991	13.2	0.3	22.7	0.3	22.7	7.9	18.7	36.4
	2006	1 760	14.5	1.0	18.7	0.7	18.7	8.6	19.1	37.0
Malawi	1995	500	13.9	0.6	11.1	0.9	11.1	22.6	27.6	23.2
	2000	532	9.8	1.5	15.7	0.7	15.7	12.7	33.1	26.4
	2006	1 209	15.1	1.0	11.4	0.7	11.4	18.6	29.5	23.6
Malaysia - Malaisie	1995	77 046	4.8	1.2	2.3	5.9	2.3	7.1	60.0	16.3
	2000	81 290	4.3	1.3	4.8	4.2	4.8	7.2	62.6	13.9
	2006	131 127	5.2	1.3	9.0	5.8	9.0	7.8	55.2	14.0
Maldives	1995	268	24.0	2.1	11.4	1.9	11.4	5.9	26.5	28.4
	2000	389	23.6	1.8	11.7	1.9	11.7	5.4	25.1	30.5
	2006	927	16.0	3.4	19.6	2.3	19.6	5.4	27.8	25.6
Mali	1995	774	19.9	0.8	15.6	1.1	15.6	14.9	21.6	26.0
	2000	806	15.1	0.9	23.6	0.7	23.6	13.8	25.2	20.6
	2006	1 820	17.3	0.4	23.9	0.5	23.9	13.9	22.4	21.1
Malta - Malte	1995	2 942	10.1	0.8	3.9	1.8	3.9	6.9	51.9	24.5
	2000	3 399	8.4	0.5	7.1	1.4	7.1	6.2	57.1	19.2
	2006	4 260	11.1	0.7	9.0	1.6	9.0	8.6	46.8	21.8
Mauritania - Mauritanie	1995	455	23.6	0.6	22.0	0.3	22.0	4.3	33.3	15.8
	2000	354	18.7	0.4	22.9	0.3	22.9	3.1	25.3	12.6
	2006	1 073	25.0	0.6	26.9	0.3	26.9	4.5	24.0	18.6
Mauritius - Maurice	1995	2 000	16.6	3.1	6.9	3.1	6.9	7.7	19.2	43.4
	2000	2 081	14.2	2.4	11.7	2.9	11.7	7.7	22.6	38.4
	2006	3 643	16.5	2.1	16.8	2.9	16.8	7.1	31.1	23.6
Mayotte	2000	139	23.4	1.9	1.1	0.4	1.1	9.1	27.1	28.5
	2006	365	19.9	1.3	13.9	0.4	13.9	8.4	30.4	25.5
Mexico - Mexique	1995	72 453	6.3	2.3	2.1	2.3	2.1	9.8	43.2	27.1
	2000	174 412	4.9	1.4	3.0	2.3	3.0	8.7	51.2	26.0
	2006	256 086	5.9	1.4	5.7	3.4	5.7	10.7	47.7	24.1
Moldova	1995	841	8.1	2.6	45.9	1.7	45.9	9.2	15.2	17.2
	2000	777	13.1	2.4	32.4	1.1	32.4	11.3	14.3	25.4
	2006	2 693	11.2	1.8	24.1	0.9	24.1	11.9	19.5	30.6

For sources and notes, see end of table.

Pour les sources et les notes, se reporter à la fin du tableau.

Country or territory / Pays ou territoires	Year / Année	Total value (millions of dollars) / Valeur totale (millions de dollars)	All food items / Produits alimentaires	Agricultural raw materials / Matières premières agricoles	Fuels / Combustibles	Ores, metals, precious stones and non monetary gold / Minerais, métaux, pierres précieuses et or (non monétaire)	Manufactured goods / Articles manufacturés	Chemical products / Produits chimiques	Machinery and transport equipment / Machines et matériel de transport	Other manufactured goods / Articles manufacturés divers
			0 + 1 + 22 + 4	2 - (22 + 27 + 28)	3	27 + 28 + 68 + 667 + 971	5 + 6 +7 + 8- (667 + 68)	5	7	6 + 8 - (667 + 68)
Mongolia - Mongolie	1995	415	14.3	0.7	19.3	0.7	19.3	5.0	39.7	20.3
	2000	615	16.6	0.6	19.1	0.4	19.1	4.9	33.7	24.8
	2006	1 486	12.1	0.4	29.3	0.4	29.3	5.5	28.3	24.2
Morocco - Maroc	1995	8 540	19.5	6.3	13.7	4.0	13.7	11.9	23.3	21.2
	2000	11 533	13.7	3.1	17.7	2.6	17.7	8.7	27.5	26.7
	2006	23 298	9.3	2.9	21.6	3.6	21.6	9.7	27.7	25.3
Mozambique	1995	727	22.3	3.3	9.9	0.6	9.9	10.7	35.8	15.7
	2000	1 162	14.0	0.4	13.3	0.8	13.3	6.5	38.9	23.7
	2006	2 869	13.9	1.0	16.9	0.4	16.9	6.6	24.8	16.8
Myanmar	1995	1 348	21.7	0.7	4.0	1.8	4.0	9.5	32.8	28.7
	2000	2 401	11.6	0.4	15.0	0.7	15.0	11.6	27.1	32.9
	2006	2 163	14.1	0.6	10.1	1.1	10.1	14.0	23.7	32.7
Namibia - Namibie	2000	1 435	16.9	0.7	3.1	1.4	3.1	8.6	37.7	31.5
	2006	2 797	16.2	0.6	3.1	1.0	3.1	10.5	38.7	29.4
Nepal - Népal	1995	1 292	9.8	2.3	9.5	22.3	9.5	8.6	15.0	13.4
	2000	1 558	11.9	3.5	15.2	9.9	15.2	10.7	17.2	17.7
	2006	2 099	15.3	2.0	29.1	1.7	29.1	11.9	17.0	21.3
Netherlands - Pays-Bas	1995	157 929	13.9	2.4	7.7	3.7	7.7	13.1	32.9	25.9
	2000	174 671	9.8	2.0	11.5	3.0	11.5	10.6	41.4	21.8
	2006	331 496	9.2	1.6	17.8	4.4	17.8	12.6	34.7	19.6
Netherlands Antilles - Antilles néerlandaises	1995	1 841	9.6	0.5	50.2	0.5	50.2	2.9	16.7	17.6
	2000	2 019	9.1	0.7	58.5	6.1	58.5	4.3	10.3	10.9
	2006	8 385	3.6	0.2	63.4	1.7	63.4	3.8	13.8	11.7
New Caledonia - Nouvelle-Calédonie	1995	967	15.4	1.0	11.2	0.8	11.2	9.0	33.7	27.2
	2000	1 017	15.1	1.0	14.7	0.9	14.7	9.1	33.2	25.9
	2006	1 998	12.0	0.8	15.1	1.0	15.1	8.6	37.5	24.8
New Zealand - Nouvelle-Zélande	1995	13 958	7.4	1.2	5.3	3.7	5.3	13.1	42.2	27.1
	2000	13 904	7.7	0.9	10.4	3.2	10.4	12.3	39.4	26.0
	2006	26 424	8.0	0.8	14.8	2.9	14.8	10.8	37.4	24.7
Nicaragua	1995	1 009	17.9	0.9	17.9	0.6	17.9	17.5	23.1	22.0
	2000	1 721	15.9	0.6	17.8	0.8	17.8	14.7	24.8	25.3
	2006	2 741	11.6	0.5	25.2	0.4	25.2	16.7	22.9	21.2
Niger	1995	345	32.4	0.7	12 9	3.1	12.9	11.4	17.3	22.3
	2000	385	35.1	3.6	21 4	1.7	21.4	9.8	13.0	15.4
	2006	747	32.7	3.5	14 6	1.3	14.6	8.4	20.2	19.3
Nigeria - Nigéria	1995	5 499	11.1	0.9	5 0	1.0	5.0	17.5	35.6	27.3
	2000	5 817	19.9	0.9	1 7	2.4	1.7	20.2	33.6	21.2
	2006	20 020	11.6	0.5	13 4	1.6	13.4	11.4	40.0	19.2
Norway - Norvège	1995	32 706	6.8	2.7	2 9	6.8	2.9	9.6	37.7	32.7
	2000	34 358	6.5	2.1	3 5	6.7	3.5	8.7	44.6	27.0
	2006	64 183	6.6	1.5	4 5	8.5	4.5	9.1	40.1	29.2
Oman	1995	4 249	19.8	0.8	1 5	5.3	1.5	6.8	39.4	22.0
	2000	5 039	22.3	0.7	1 6	4.2	1.6	6.4	43.3	19.0
	2006	10 898	10.7	0.6	3 3	5.4	3.3	6.6	49.8	22.0
Pakistan	1995	11 704	17.5	5.5	16.1	4.0	16.1	17.0	28.9	10.8
	2000	11 070	13.8	3.2	32.5	4.2	32.5	18.1	18.5	9.3
	2006	29 826	10.3	3.6	25.7	4.6	25.7	13.3	29.7	12.7
Panama	1995	2 511	10.7	0.8	13.6	1.7	13.6	13.5	29.0	30.6
	2000	3 378	11.7	0.5	18.6	0.9	18.6	11.6	29.6	27.2
	2006	4 828	11.2	0.5	18.0	1.1	18.0	12.8	29.1	27.3

For sources and notes, see end of table.

Pour les sources et les notes, se reporter à la fin du tableau.

Country or territory / Pays ou territoires	Year / Année	Total value (millions of dollars) / Valeur totale (millions de dollars)	All food items / Produits alimentaires 0+1+22+4	Agricultural raw materials / Matières premières agricoles 2-(22+27+28)	Fuels / Combustibles 3	Ores, metals, precious stones and non monetary gold / Minerais, métaux, pierres précieuses et or (non monétaire) 27+28+68+667+971	Manufactured goods / Articles manufacturés 5+6+7+8-(667+68)	Chemical products / Produits chimiques 5	Machinery and transport equipment / Machines et matériel de transport 7	Other manufactured goods / Articles manufacturés divers 6+8-(667+68)
Papua New Guinea - Papouasie-Nouvelle-Guinée	1995	1 452	14.3	0.8	10.8	0.6	10.8	6.4	39.4	24.0
	2000	1 035	18.3	0.7	22.1	0.9	22.1	7.1	29.5	21.0
	2006	2 061	10.2	0.5	27.1	0.4	27.1	5.9	31.9	16.8
Paraguay	1995	3 136	18.5	0.2	6.5	0.7	6.5	9.0	42.3	22.7
	2000	2 193	17.2	0.5	13.5	0.7	13.5	14.2	29.1	24.6
	2006	5 879	6.0	0.8	12.7	0.7	12.7	12.2	46.9	20.6
Peru - Pérou	1995	7 584	13.5	1.9	8.8	0.8	8.8	13.2	39.2	22.6
	2000	7 415	11.6	1.8	15.6	0.6	15.6	15.5	32.8	22.1
	2006	15 312	10.2	1.5	19.3	1.0	19.3	15.2	30.9	21.8
Philippines	1995	28 487	8.3	2.2	9.2	3.2	9.2	9.2	32.5	16.2
	2000	37 007	7.0	1.4	11.1	2.6	11.1	8.0	56.5	13.3
	2006	54 078	6.7	0.8	15.3	2.8	15.3	7.4	56.2	10.8
Poland - Pologne	1995	29 019	9.6	3.2	9.1	3.3	9.1	14.9	29.9	29.5
	2000	48 834	6.1	2.0	10.8	2.9	10.8	14.1	37.1	27.0
	2006	125 645	5.9	1.7	10.4	3.8	10.4	13.3	35.6	25.6
Portugal	1995	33 565	13.6	3.6	8.1	2.8	8.1	10.4	33.8	27.7
	2000	39 947	11.2	2.6	10.3	3.0	10.3	9.4	37.3	26.2
	2006	66 694	11.1	1.5	15.1	3.5	15.1	10.9	29.6	23.5
Qatar	1995	3 398	9.4	0.6	0.4	2.5	0.4	5.0	48.3	33.7
	2000	3 252	11.7	0.6	0.4	2.6	0.4	6.4	44.8	33.2
	2006	16 440	5.2	0.6	0.6	2.6	0.6	5.1	44.0	33.9
Republic of Korea - République de Corée	1995	135 113	5.4	5.5	14.1	8.4	14.1	9.7	36.6	20.3
	2000	160 479	4.8	3.2	23.7	7.0	23.7	8.4	36.8	16.1
	2006	309 379	4.2	1.8	28.0	8.5	28.0	8.9	30.0	18.6
Romania - Roumanie	1995	10 278	8.5	2.3	21.4	3.6	21.4	10.6	24.8	28.0
	2000	13 054	7.0	1.4	12.1	3.8	12.1	10.0	29.2	36.1
	2006	51 106	5.7	1.1	13.5	2.9	13.5	10.6	35.4	30.8
Russian Federation - Fédération de Russie	1995	46 301	18.0	0.8	2.7	3.4	2.7	7.2	19.9	16.9
	2000	33 880	20.2	2.1	4.1	6.4	4.1	11.8	24.5	19.7
	2006	137 728	14.4	0.9	1.3	2.8	1.3	12.2	43.4	19.6
Rwanda	1995	241	18.9	2.5	11.5	2.8	11.5	9.3	31.7	23.2
	2000	211	20.8	2.9	14.4	1.9	14.4	8.9	21.7	29.3
	2006	557	13.4	1.9	16.7	2.3	16.7	12.5	25.7	27.5
Saint Kitts and Nevis - Saint-Kitts-et-Nevis	1995	132	21.1	2.5	4.3	0.9	4.3	8.3	27.8	35.1
	2000	196	19.0	2.5	7.6	0.7	7.6	7.5	28.1	34.6
	2006	250	18.6	1.8	7.9	1.3	7.9	7.2	29.6	33.6
Saint Lucia - Sainte-Lucie	1995	306	26.7	2.4	7.6	1.0	7.6	9.4	19.1	33.7
	2000	355	23.6	2.4	9.3	0.9	9.3	8.2	24.6	31.0
	2006	530	22.5	1.9	13.4	1.2	13.4	7.6	21.2	31.6
Saint Vincent and the Grenadines - Saint-Vincent-et-les Grenadines	1995	134	22.5	2.6	6.0	0.5	6.0	12.9	17.7	37.7
	2000	162	26.7	2.4	9.6	0.7	9.6	10.1	19.0	31.6
	2006	271	20.2	2.3	14.6	0.5	14.6	7.9	23.0	31.4
Samoa	1995	95	16.6	0.9	7.1	0.4	7.1	5.0	46.7	22.2
	2000	106	24.4	1.4	12.5	0.5	12.5	7.7	26.8	26.7
	2006	275	22.3	2.0	14.9	0.7	14.9	5.3	12.8	30.1
Sao Tome and Principe - Sao Tomé-et-Principe	1995	29	25.4	0.4	1.9	0.5	1.9	6.6	39.0	25.9
	2000	30	30.8	0.4	10.8	0.7	10.8	4.0	30.4	22.4
	2006	71	30.6	0.8	20.2	1.4	20.2	4.4	20.2	22.4
Saudi Arabia - Arabie saoudite	1995	28 085	16.1	1.2	0.2	7.0	0.2	9.6	35.6	29.7
	2000	30 237	17.8	1.0	0.2	6.9	0.2	9.6	39.2	25.4
	2006	69 800	13.4	0.7	0.2	5.6	0.2	9.5	45.0	25.6

For sources and notes, see end of table.

Pour les sources et les notes, se reporter à la fin du tableau.

Country or territory / Pays ou territoires	Year / Année	Total value (millions of dollars) / Valeur totale (millions de dollars)	By main SITC Revision 3 product group (percentage) / Par principaux groupes de produits de la CTCI Révision 3 (en pourcentage)					Of which: / dont :		
			All food items / Produits alimentaires	Agricultural raw materials / Matières premières agricoles	Fuels / Combustibles	Ores, metals, precious stones and non monetary gold / Minerais, métaux, pierres précieuses et or (non monétaire)	Manu-factured goods / Articles manu-facturés	Chemical products / Produits chimiques	Machinery and transport equipment / Machines et matériel de transport	Other manu-factured goods / Articles manu-facturés divers
			0 + 1 + 22 + 4	2 - (22 + 27 + 28)	3	27 + 28 + 68 + 667 + 971	5 + 6 + 7 + 8 - (667 + 68)	5	7	6 + 8 - (667 + 68)
Senegal - Sénégal	1995	1 224	32.5	2.2	10.0	1.6	10.0	13.9	18.1	21.7
	2000	1 553	23.3	2.1	22.5	1.3	22.5	10.6	22.8	17.3
	2006	3 671	23.4	1.6	25.9	1.1	25.9	9.4	22.6	16.0
Serbia and Montenegro - Serbie-et-Monténégro	1995	2 666	14.2	4.1	13.9	7.1	13.9	14.3	19.4	26.1
	2000	3 711	9.3	3.6	20.1	3.7	20.1	15.0	22.1	26.3
	2006	13 172	6.6	1.5	19.7	7.0	19.7	14.2	25.6	25.3
Seychelles	1995	255	21.2	1.4	17.4	0.7	17.4	6.5	27.0	25.5
	2000	342	22.2	1.1	10.0	0.7	10.0	5.6	28.9	31.6
	2006	757	24.0	1.3	26.6	0.7	26.6	4.3	16.2	19.8
Singapore - Singapour	1995	124 503	4.6	0.9	8.1	2.9	8.1	6.5	57.9	18.3
	2000	134 546	3.2	0.4	12.1	2.2	12.1	5.7	60.7	14.8
	2006	238 704	2.6	0.4	18.8	3.3	18.8	6.0	54.7	12.4
Slovakia - Slovaquie	1995	8 162	8.9	2.8	12.7	6.0	12.7	14.5	30.2	24.9
	2000	12 774	5.6	1.8	17.5	3.8	17.5	11.0	35.7	24.6
	2006	44 383	5.1	1.2	13.6	3.5	13.6	8.9	38.8	28.5
Slovenia - Slovénie	1995	9 492	7.8	4.6	6.6	4.4	6.6	12.1	33.8	28.0
	2000	10 115	6.0	3.6	9.1	5.4	9.1	12.4	34.2	29.3
	2006	23 013	6.1	2.5	11.1	7.1	11.1	12.2	32.5	28.4
South Africa - Afrique du Sud	1995	26 745	6.7	2.3	8.3	3.5	8.3	12.4	44.9	19.4
	2000	26 785	4.7	1.5	14.3	4.4	14.3	11.6	36.4	17.9
	2006	69 185	4.3	1.0	18.3	4.6	18.3	8.9	37.8	17.3
Spain - Espagne	1995	113 399	13.6	3.0	8.3	4.3	8.3	12.1	35.6	23.1
	2000	152 898	9.1	2.0	12.1	3.5	12.1	10.7	40.7	21.4
	2006	329 976	8.4	1.3	15.7	4.4	15.7	11.0	36.7	22.0
Sri Lanka	1995	5 185	14.8	1.6	2.2	5.2	2.2	9.2	24.9	38.9
	2000	6 281	14.2	1.3	9.4	5.3	9.4	9.1	18.5	42.3
	2006	9 647	12.3	1.2	13.9	7.4	13.9	9.5	20.3	35.4
Sudan - Soudan	1995	1 185	24.4	1.8	13.9	0.5	13.9	10.8	27.8	20.8
	2000	1 657	21.7	1.0	7.4	0.9	7.4	12.1	33.9	23.1
	2006	8 844	11.9	0.4	5.0	1.1	5.0	7.3	49.6	23.7
Suriname	1995	583	14.0	0.1	11.8	1.2	11.8	16.0	35.7	21.3
	2000	526	18.1	0.4	6.7	0.9	6.7	10.6	36.3	26.4
	2006	1 009	12.8	0.1	19.2	0.7	19.2	7.7	26.7	32.7
Swaziland	2000	1 099	18.7	2.3	12.6	0.8	12.6	11.2	27.3	25.7
	2006	1 740	18.9	1.2	10.2	0.8	10.2	13.9	21.1	30.7
Sweden - Suède	1995	61 647	6.7	2.2	5.8	3.8	5.8	10.7	41.8	27.5
	2000	72 767	5.9	1.9	9.0	3.2	9.0	9.1	42.6	22.6
	2006	127 101	7.4	1.4	12.4	4.3	12.4	10.1	38.0	23.4
Switzerland - Suisse	1995	80 152	6.4	2.0	2.9	5.6	2.9	14.6	33.4	35.0
	2000	83 584	5.5	1.4	4.6	8.6	4.6	16.4	33.2	30.2
	2006	141 400	5.2	1.1	7.9	8.0	7.9	21.2	27.4	29.2
Syrian Arab Republic - République arabe syrienne	1995	4 709	16.7	3.3	1.1	1.3	1.1	10.2	31.6	33.9
	2000	3 815	19.0	3.3	3.7	1.8	3.7	13.0	20.9	30.8
	2006	11 488	13.2	2.5	27.1	3.1	27.1	10.7	21.2	20.2
Tajikistan - Tadjikistan	1995	810	29.7	0.8	18.6	11.2	18.6	6.6	19.7	12.7
	2000	644	10.2	0.7	37.5	0.1	37.5	36.4	9.6	5.3
	2006	2 096	13.0	3.0	10.2	13.9	10.2	6.2	14.7	18.5
Thailand - Thaïlande	1995	70 781	3.8	4.1	6.7	5.4	6.7	10.5	47.5	20.7
	2000	61 921	4.3	2.9	12.2	5.5	12.2	11.0	45.0	18.3
	2006	128 584	3.9	1.8	19.9	7.7	19.9	10.3	36.4	19.0
TFYR of Macedonia - LERY de Macédoine	1995	1 719	17.4	3.3	11.6	3.0	11.6	11.9	19.5	22.8
	2000	2 094	12.1	1.8	13.8	1.9	13.8	9.0	19.6	16.5
	2006	3 763	11.7	1.2	20.2	3.9	20.2	9.7	18.3	34.9

For sources and notes, see end of table.

Pour les sources et les notes, se reporter à la fin du tableau.

Country or territory / Pays ou territoires	Year / Année	Total value (millions of dollars) / Valeur totale (millions de dollars)	All food items / Produits alimentaires	Agricultural raw materials / Matières premières agricoles	Fuels / Combustibles	Ores, metals, precious stones and non monetary gold / Minerais, métaux, pierres précieuses et or (non monétaire)	Manufactured goods / Articles manufacturés	Chemical products / Produits chimiques	Machinery and transport equipment / Machines et matériel de transport	Other manufactured goods / Articles manufacturés divers
			0 + 1 + 22 + 4	2 - (22 + 27 + 28)	3	27 + 28 + 68 + 667 + 971	5 + 6 +7 + 8- (667 + 68)	5	7	6 + 8 - (667 + 68)
Togo	1995	556	18.4	1.9	29.9	1.3	29.9	8.5	17.2	22.8
	2000	324	18.4	1.7	18.8	1.6	18.8	10.7	18.6	30.3
	2006	637	15.6	0.8	26.1	2.2	26.1	8.8	14.9	30.0
Trinidad and Tobago - Trinité-et-Tobago	1995	1 724	15.7	0.7	0.5	5.7	0.5	13.1	36.7	27.2
	2000	3 308	8.3	1.0	32.3	2.0	32.3	7.9	30.6	17.6
	2006	6 478	7.8	0.6	35.0	4.8	35.0	8.1	26.7	16.8
Tunisia - Tunisie	1995	7 903	12.5	4.2	7.2	3.3	7.2	9.1	25.9	37.8
	2000	8 566	8.2	3.1	10.5	2.7	10.5	8.9	32.5	34.0
	2006	14 862	8.5	2.7	12.0	3.0	12.0	10.2	29.8	33.7
Turkey - Turquie	1995	35 707	7.0	5.6	12.9	5.9	12.9	15.0	32.2	21.5
	2000	54 150	3.9	3.7	13.9	4.0	13.9	13.6	37.6	19.6
	2006	138 581	1.8	2.2	4.9	7.5	4.9	9.0	17.3	14.0
Turkmenistan - Turkménistan	1995	777	24.4	0.4	2.7	1.7	2.7	11.3	36.6	22.7
	2000	1 786	11.7	0.4	1.2	1.0	1.2	8.9	43.8	27.1
	2006	2 668	7.1	0.4	0.8	1.2	0.8	7.8	42.6	28.0
Turks and Caicos Islands - Îles Turques et Caïques	1995	51	11.8	1.7	0.9	0.3	0.9	20.8	16.9	22.0
	2000	149	21.4	2.2	10.4	0.9	10.4	6.0	29.4	29.6
	2006	498	13.3	2.6	10.2	1.5	10.2	4.9	27.4	37.2
Uganda - Ouganda	1995	1 038	15.8	2.6	1.8	2.0	1.8	10.7	34.8	32.4
	2000	954	14.1	2.1	17.2	1.9	17.2	11.4	27.1	26.3
	2006	2 557	13.6	1.4	21.1	1.1	21.1	13.2	25.9	23.5
Ukraine	1995	16 052	7.9	2.4	47.8	3.1	47.8	6.7	17.0	14.2
	2000	13 956	6.3	1.5	43.0	5.4	43.0	8.8	17.5	14.8
	2006	45 022	6.8	1.2	28.2	3.5	28.2	12.1	28.8	18.6
United Arab Emirates - Émirats arabes unis	1995	20 984	10.0	0.9	1.6	2.6	1.6	6.3	36.9	40.3
	2000	27 192	11.1	0.8	0.8	3.8	0.8	7.9	39.8	35.4
	2006	86 766	6.8	0.5	1.5	11.6	1.5	5.4	34.9	28.0
United Kingdom - Royaume-Uni	1995	261 456	10.1	2.4	3.5	5.2	3.5	10.3	41.3	26.6
	2000	339 445	7.8	1.6	4.3	5.0	4.3	8.9	42.5	24.2
	2006	606 428	7.8	1.2	8.9	4.5	8.9	9.6	33.7	22.1
United Republic of Tanzania - République-Unie de Tanzanie	1995	1 653	10.0	1.2	0.5	3.8	0.5	19.6	38.4	26.4
	2000	1 586	14.6	2.5	18.5	1.2	18.5	10.2	32.7	20.2
	2006	4 440	12.2	0.8	24.2	1.2	24.2	11.5	31.1	18.9
United States - États-Unis	1995	770 821	4.8	2.1	8.2	3.8	8.2	5.5	46.4	26.2
	2000	1 258 080	4.1	1.4	11.1	3.5	11.1	6.0	44.8	25.1
	2006	1 918 997	4.2	1.2	18.0	4.0	18.0	7.6	37.7	24.1
Uruguay	1995	2 866	10.4	4.0	10.1	1.2	10.1	15.3	34.5	24.5
	2000	3 466	11.5	2.6	15.3	1.1	15.3	16.9	28.0	24.5
	2006	4 775	8.1	2.9	27.5	1.4	27.5	17.5	23.4	19.2
Uzbekistan - Ouzbékistan	1995	2 893	16.0	1.7	1.5	3.0	1.5	9.5	37.3	30.2
	2000	2 947	11.1	0.9	8.6	3.2	8.6	11.0	40.2	23.9
	2006	3 355	5.8	3.6	2.8	3.5	2.8	11.5	41.8	25.2
Venezuela (Bolivarian Rep. of) - Venezuela (Rép. bolivarienne du)	1995	10 791	14.3	4.5	1.1	3.7	1.1	16.4	37.0	23.1
	2000	14 584	11.7	1.8	3.6	1.8	3.6	14.1	41.7	25.3
	2006	30 559	7.5	0.9	0.5	1.4	0.5	11.0	41.5	17.2
Viet Nam	1995	8 155	4.9	2.4	10.3	2.4	10.3	16.7	28.3	30.9
	2000	15 637	5.2	2.9	13.5	2.6	13.5	15.3	30.0	27.2
	2006	44 891	6.0	3.8	14.9	8.5	14.9	14.0	24.0	28.4
Yemen - Yémen	1995	1 817	28.9	2.4	7.9	1.4	7.9	8.2	23.1	28.1
	2000	2 326	35.6	1.5	12.0	1.1	12.0	9.7	20.8	18.4
	2006	4 935	21.2	0.8	21.9	0.7	21.9	8.7	23.4	23.1

For sources and notes, see end of table.

Pour les sources et les notes, se reporter à la fin du tableau.

Country or territory / Pays ou territoires	Year / Année	Total value (millions of dollars) / Valeur totale (millions de dollars)	By main SITC Revision 3 product group (percentage) / Par principaux groupes de produits de la CTCI Révision 3 (en pourcentage)					Of which: / dont :		
			All food items / Produits alimentaires	Agricultural raw materials / Matières premières agricoles	Fuels / Combustibles	Ores, metals, precious stones and non monetary gold / Minerais, métaux, pierres précieuses et or (non monétaire)	Manufactured goods / Articles manufacturés	Chemical products / Produits chimiques	Machinery and transport equipment / Machines et matériel de transport	Other manufactured goods / Articles manufacturés divers
			0 + 1 + 22 + 4	2 - (22 + 27 + 28)	3	27 + 28 + 68 + 667 + 971	5 + 6 +7 + 8 - (667 + 68)	5	7	6 + 8 - (667 + 68)
Zambia - Zambie	1995	708	9.9	2.3	13.2	2.1	13.2	13.5	38.0	20.9
	2000	888	8.1	2.8	12.2	3.1	12.2	15.0	29.8	27.9
	2006	3 074	7.6	0.8	15.1	2.5	15.1	14.6	40.2	19.3
Zimbabwe	1995	2 659	6.0	1.9	9.0	2.6	9.0	13.8	42.4	22.0
	2000	1 888	3.9	1.5	42.5	2.6	42.5	14.9	19.8	13.7
	2006	1 868	14.3	2.1	14.4	22.5	14.4	9.7	21.3	14.7

Sources:
- Data and UNCTAD secretariat estimates based on UN DESA Comtrade and IMF Direction of Trade statistics databases

Sources :
- Données et estimations du secrétariat de la CNUCED sur la base de données Comtrade de ONU DAES et Direction of Trade statistics du Fonds Monétaire international

3

Products ranked by average 2005-2006 values SITC Revision 3 (3-digit level) / Produits classés d'après la moyenne des valeurs de 2005-2006 CTCI révision 3 (positions à 3 chiffres)	1995 Value (millions of dollars) / Valeur (millions de dollars)	1995 % of the country grouping exports / En % des exportations du groupe de pays	1995 % of world product exports / En % des exportations mondiales des produits	2006 Value (millions of dollars) / Valeur (millions de dollars)	2006 % of the country grouping exports / En % des exportations du groupe de pays	2006 % of world product exports / En % des exportations mondiales des produits	Growth rates (percentage) Taux d'accroissement (en pourcentage) 1995-2006 Value / Valeur	Difference from world / Différence par rapport au monde
All commodity groups	**5 065 268**	**100.00**	**100.00**	**11 921 375**	**100.00**	**100.00**	**7.57**	..
333 Crude petroleum & bituminous oil	204 919	4.05	100.00	916 778	7.69	100.00	14.17	..
781 Passenger cars and race cars	232 456	4.59	100.00	529 962	4.45	100.00	7.72	..
334 Heavy petroleum & bituminous oil	92 078	1.82	100.00	461 585	3.87	100.00	14.55	..
776 Valves tubes; diodes, transistors	189 020	3.73	100.00	424 098	3.56	100.00	7.15	..
764 Telecommunicate equipment part nes	121 666	2.40	100.00	426 065	3.57	100.00	11.25	..
752 Computer equipment nes	131 913	2.60	100.00	298 661	2.51	100.00	6.47	..
784 Motor vehicle parts and accessories	112 773	2.23	100.00	256 981	2.16	100.00	7.67	..
542 Medicines including veterinary	45 350	0.90	100.00	236 668	1.99	100.00	17.21	..
759 Office equipment part & accessories	98 970	1.95	100.00	222 022	1.86	100.00	7.09	..
343 Natural gas, liquefied or not	34 754	0.69	100.00	194 666	1.63	100.00	15.76	..
778 Electrical machinery apparatus nes	80 376	1.59	100.00	166 556	1.40	100.00	6.76	..
772 Electrical circuit equipment	66 464	1.31	100.00	163 619	1.37	100.00	7.94	..
792 Aircraft, spacecraft & equipment	68 236	1.35	100.00	162 325	1.36	100.00	5.72	..
713 Internal combustion engine part nes	55 429	1.09	100.00	123 719	1.04	100.00	7.36	..
874 Measure analyze control device nes	52 695	1.04	100.00	125 703	1.05	100.00	7.84	..
728 Special industrial machine part nes	60 139	1.19	100.00	110 426	0.93	100.00	5.15	..
821 Furniture part; bedding furnishing	45 231	0.89	100.00	107 686	0.90	100.00	7.97	..
845 Articles of apparel nes	45 142	0.89	100.00	107 558	0.90	100.00	7.43	..
641 Paper and paperboard	72 235	1.43	100.00	103 285	0.87	100.00	3.91	..
699 Base metal manufactures nes	41 850	0.83	100.00	106 585	0.89	100.00	8.01	..
782 Goods and service vehicles	45 291	0.89	100.00	99 774	0.84	100.00	6.59	..
667 Pearls, precious semiprecious stone	40 409	0.80	100.00	93 507	0.78	100.00	8.64	..
893 Articles of plastic nes	42 200	0.83	100.00	94 988	0.80	100.00	7.51	..
684 Aluminium	45 507	0.90	100.00	100 676	0.84	100.00	6.64	..
682 Copper	35 261	0.70	100.00	110 833	0.93	100.00	8.11	..
515 Organo-inorganic compound acid salt	26 793	0.53	100.00	86 312	0.72	100.00	11.21	..
793 Ships boats floating structures	36 788	0.73	100.00	88 291	0.74	100.00	7.54	..
723 Civil engineering plant & equipment	29 640	0.59	100.00	84 127	0.71	100.00	8.78	..
743 Gas pump, compressor, fan, filter	34 723	0.69	100.00	79 653	0.67	100.00	7.64	..
741 Heating cooling equipment parts nes	38 308	0.76	100.00	79 809	0.67	100.00	6.22	..
714 Non-electric engines excluding 712 713 718	26 245	0.52	100.00	78 299	0.66	100.00	9.42	..
541 Pharmaceuticals excluding medicines	26 369	0.52	100.00	74 390	0.62	100.00	10.46	..
575 Other plastics, in primary forms	29 753	0.59	100.00	75 254	0.63	100.00	8.68	..
598 Miscellaneous chemical products nes	29 576	0.58	100.00	75 542	0.63	100.00	8.26	..
851 Footwear	46 988	0.93	100.00	72 562	0.61	100.00	3.43	..
773 Electrical distribute equipment nes	29 835	0.59	100.00	76 545	0.64	100.00	7.23	..
673 Flat iron non-alloy steel products	35 760	0.71	100.00	71 932	0.60	100.00	7.01	..
894 Baby carriage toy game sport good	41 065	0.81	100.00	71 074	0.60	100.00	4.28	..
842 Female clothing, woven	37 027	0.73	100.00	69 891	0.59	100.00	5.82	..
761 Television video receive project	24 020	0.47	100.00	76 159	0.64	100.00	10.53	..
775 Household equipment nes	31 717	0.63	100.00	69 791	0.59	100.00	7.40	..
763 Sound TV recorder or reproducer	21 475	0.42	100.00	62 020	0.52	100.00	12.41	..
679 Iron steel pipe tube fittings etc	24 264	0.48	100.00	69 289	0.58	100.00	8.27	..
582 Plastic sheet film foil & strips	29 390	0.58	100.00	65 639	0.55	100.00	7.45	..
676 Iron steel bar rod section piling	27 544	0.54	100.00	63 126	0.53	100.00	7.60	..
744 Mechanical handling equipment nes	28 092	0.55	100.00	62 015	0.52	100.00	6.28	..
716 Rotating electric plant parts nes	25 675	0.51	100.00	60 729	0.51	100.00	7.64	..
872 Medical instruments appliances nes	19 088	0.38	100.00	56 143	0.47	100.00	10.49	..
841 Male clothing, woven	36 943	0.73	100.00	55 598	0.47	100.00	3.15	..
511 Hydrocarbons nes; derivatives	20 884	0.41	100.00	56 784	0.48	100.00	10.70	..
898 Music instrument device recording	30 075	0.59	100.00	52 689	0.44	100.00	4.73	..
871 Optical instruments apparatus nes	5 594	0.11	100.00	57 303	0.48	100.00	22.01	..
771 Electric power machine part excluding 716	23 652	0.47	100.00	55 574	0.47	100.00	6.34	..
675 Flat rolled products of alloy steel	20 377	0.40	100.00	56 965	0.48	100.00	9.89	..
971 Gold non-monetary excluding ores	21 659	0.43	100.00	59 848	0.50	100.00	6.16	..
057 Fruit nut (exc oil), fresh or dried	26 564	0.52	100.00	49 730	0.42	100.00	5.32	..
112 Alcoholic beverages	27 696	0.55	100.00	50 629	0.42	100.00	5.49	..
321 Coal excluding non-agglomomerated	18 735	0.37	100.00	49 429	0.41	100.00	8.35	..
899 Manufactured articles nes	19 856	0.39	100.00	49 489	0.42	100.00	8.88	..
625 Rubber for wheels, incl inner tube	23 234	0.46	100.00	49 195	0.41	100.00	6.18	..

For sources and notes, see end of table.

Pour les sources et les notes, se reporter à la fin du tableau

Products ranked by average 2005-2006 values SITC Revision 3 (3-digit level) / Produits classés d'après la moyenne des valeurs de 2005-2006 CTCI révision 3 (positions à 3 chiffres)	1995			2006			Growth rates (percentage) Taux d'accroissement (en pourcentage) 1995-2006	
	Value (millions of dollars) / Valeur (millions de dollars)	% of the country grouping exports / En % des exportations du groupe de pays	% of world product exports / En % des exportations mondiales des produits	Value (millions of dollars) / Valeur (millions de dollars)	% of the country grouping exports / En % des exportations du groupe de pays	% of world product exports / En % des exportations mondiales des produits	Value / Valeur	Difference from world / Différence par rapport au monde
553 Perfume toilet cosmetics, excluding soap	18 761	0.37	100.00	48 768	0.41	100.00	9.08	..
747 Pipe, boiler, tank & vat appliances	19 497	0.38	100.00	49 945	0.42	100.00	8.01	..
897 Jewellery nes (667)	19 410	0.38	100.00	48 347	0.41	100.00	8.05	..
571 Primary form ethylene polymers	16 329	0.32	100.00	46 406	0.39	100.00	9.56	..
651 Textile yarn	33 214	0.66	100.00	43 953	0.37	100.00	2.35	..
745 Non-electrical machinery tool nes	21 830	0.43	100.00	43 963	0.37	100.00	6.14	..
533 Pigment, paint, varnish & related	20 047	0.40	100.00	43 508	0.36	100.00	7.15	..
892 Printed matter	25 459	0.50	100.00	41 530	0.35	100.00	4.57	..
012 Meat nes, fresh chilled frozen	24 154	0.48	100.00	39 997	0.34	100.00	4.50	..
574 Polyacetals and polyesters, etc	15 890	0.31	100.00	39 986	0.34	100.00	9.04	..
642 Cut paper and paperboard articles	25 489	0.50	100.00	38 985	0.33	100.00	3.60	..
674 Flat plated iron non-alloy steel	18 216	0.36	100.00	40 037	0.34	100.00	7.30	..
248 Wood simply worked, railway sleeper	26 204	0.52	100.00	38 567	0.32	100.00	3.07	..
742 Liquid pump; liquid elevator parts	17 759	0.35	100.00	37 902	0.32	100.00	6.89	..
034 Fish, fresh live chilled frozen	19 002	0.38	100.00	37 696	0.32	100.00	6.26	..
513 Carboxylic acid and compounds	16 905	0.33	100.00	37 223	0.31	100.00	8.07	..
054 Vegetable & vegetable products nes	20 920	0.41	100.00	36 751	0.31	100.00	5.41	..
514 Nitrogen function compounds	18 857	0.37	100.00	35 037	0.29	100.00	6.02	..
098 Edible products & preparations nes	17 456	0.34	100.00	35 381	0.30	100.00	6.83	..
785 Motorcycles, mopeds and cycles	18 422	0.36	100.00	35 323	0.30	100.00	6.18	..
884 Optical goods fibres nes	10 141	0.20	100.00	35 143	0.29	100.00	11.22	..
658 Made-up textile articles nes	13 305	0.26	100.00	33 656	0.28	100.00	8.92	..
653 Man-made woven fabrics	35 675	0.70	100.00	32 671	0.27	100.00	-1.02	..
695 Tools for use in hand or in machine	17 414	0.34	100.00	34 266	0.29	100.00	5.87	..
783 Road motor vehicles nes	16 818	0.33	100.00	33 696	0.28	100.00	6.38	..
081 Animal feed excluding unmilled cereal	20 509	0.40	100.00	33 059	0.28	100.00	3.67	..
748 Mechanical transmission equipment	14 745	0.29	100.00	33 439	0.28	100.00	7.48	..
634 Veneer, plywood & other wood nes	17 168	0.34	100.00	32 436	0.27	100.00	5.84	..
512 Alcohols, phenols; derivatives	13 624	0.27	100.00	32 731	0.27	100.00	8.76	..
657 Special yarn and textile fabric etc	21 114	0.42	100.00	31 923	0.27	100.00	3.51	..
522 Inorganic chemical elem oxide salt	16 270	0.32	100.00	32 644	0.27	100.00	5.95	..
691 Iron steel aluminium structures nes	13 725	0.27	100.00	34 359	0.29	100.00	7.87	..
281 Iron ore and concentrates	8 536	0.17	100.00	33 410	0.28	100.00	11.25	..
731 Machine tools for material removal	16 299	0.32	100.00	32 048	0.27	100.00	4.73	..
672 Ingots, Iron steel primary products	12 734	0.25	100.00	30 585	0.26	100.00	9.26	..
652 Woven cotton fabrics	22 207	0.44	100.00	28 877	0.24	100.00	2.83	..
681 Silver, platinum, platinum metals	6 211	0.12	100.00	35 020	0.29	100.00	13.96	..
844 Female clothing, knitted crocheted	13 461	0.27	100.00	31 116	0.26	100.00	6.44	..
342 Liquefied propane and butane	5 798	0.11	100.00	31 177	0.26	100.00	16.65	..
251 Pulp and waste paper	27 474	0.54	100.00	29 721	0.25	100.00	2.79	..
774 Electrodiagnostic equipment	12 420	0.25	100.00	29 309	0.25	100.00	8.01	..
282 Ferrous iron & steel, waste & scrap	7 875	0.16	100.00	30 883	0.26	100.00	14.38	..
351 Electric current	7 772	0.15	100.00	30 441	0.26	100.00	13.06	..
664 Glass	14 036	0.28	100.00	27 784	0.23	100.00	6.69	..
724 Textile leather machinery parts nes	25 255	0.50	100.00	27 263	0.23	100.00	0.83	..
048 Cereal & preparation flour starch	12 658	0.25	100.00	27 368	0.23	100.00	6.96	..
885 Watches and clocks	22 901	0.45	100.00	27 197	0.23	100.00	1.41	..
671 Pig & sponge iron, ferro alloys etc	10 482	0.21	100.00	25 164	0.21	100.00	9.76	..
831 Case bag: storage travel shopping	14 993	0.30	100.00	26 822	0.22	100.00	4.85	..
516 Other organic chemicals	11 118	0.22	100.00	26 358	0.22	100.00	7.88	..
786 Trailer caravan transport container	9 855	0.19	100.00	26 643	0.22	100.00	9.48	..
283 Copper ores and concentrates	6 854	0.14	100.00	32 056	0.27	100.00	13.03	..
562 Manufactured fertilizer excluding crude	17 730	0.35	100.00	24 439	0.20	100.00	3.16	..
288 Non ferrous base metal waste nes	9 203	0.18	100.00	29 698	0.25	100.00	8.90	..
554 Soaps cleansers polishes	11 434	0.23	100.00	24 725	0.21	100.00	7.33	..
663 Mineral manufactures nes	13 087	0.26	100.00	24 937	0.21	100.00	5.20	..
292 Crude vegetable materials nes	15 044	0.30	100.00	23 895	0.20	100.00	4.61	..
022 Milk products, excluding butter & cheese	15 441	0.30	100.00	23 770	0.20	100.00	4.27	..
749 Non-electric machinery part nes	12 852	0.25	100.00	24 184	0.20	100.00	5.49	..
694 Nails screws nuts bolts rivets	10 828	0.21	100.00	24 489	0.21	100.00	7.33	..
011 Beef, fresh chilled frozen	15 851	0.31	100.00	24 236	0.20	100.00	4.37	..

For sources and notes, see end of table.

Pour les sources et les notes, se reporter à la fin du tableau

Products ranked by average 2005-2006 values SITC Revision 3 (3-digit level) / Produits classés d'après la moyenne des valeurs de 2005-2006 CTCI révision 3 (positions à 3 chiffres)	1995			2006			Growth rates (percentage) Taux d'accroissement (en pourcentage) 1995-2006	
	Value (millions of dollars) Valeur (millions de dollars)	% of the country grouping exports En % des exportations du groupe de pays	% of world product exports En % des exportations mondiales des produits	Value (millions of dollars) Valeur (millions de dollars)	% of the country grouping exports En % des exportations du groupe de pays	% of world product exports En % des exportations mondiales des produits	Value Valeur	Difference from world Différence par rapport au monde
635 Wood manufactures nes	11 271	0.22	100.00	23 908	0.20	100.00	6.65	..
222 Oil seed etc for soft oil	12 242	0.24	100.00	22 818	0.19	100.00	5.28	..
611 Leather	15 877	0.31	100.00	22 930	0.19	100.00	3.46	..
721 Agricultural machine nes excluding tractor	10 484	0.21	100.00	22 475	0.19	100.00	6.36	..
848 Headgear, non-textile clothing	12 722	0.25	100.00	20 655	0.17	100.00	5.20	..
746 Ball or roller bearings	12 173	0.24	100.00	21 785	0.18	100.00	5.21	..
655 Knitted or crocheted fabrics nes	12 056	0.24	100.00	21 546	0.18	100.00	4.90	..
661 Lime cement construction material	11 030	0.22	100.00	22 073	0.19	100.00	5.43	..
036 Crustacean mollusc aquat invertebra	16 419	0.32	100.00	21 169	0.18	100.00	2.38	..
287 Base metal ores & concentrates nes	5 842	0.12	100.00	22 858	0.19	100.00	10.94	..
335 Residual petroleum products nes	6 039	0.12	100.00	22 569	0.19	100.00	11.27	..
061 Sugar, mollasses and honey	15 731	0.31	100.00	22 708	0.19	100.00	1.70	..
572 Primary form styrene polymers	11 046	0.22	100.00	21 001	0.18	100.00	6.82	..
813 Lighting fixtures and fittings nes	9 840	0.19	100.00	20 994	0.18	100.00	6.75	..
882 Photo cinematographic supply excluding 883	17 652	0.35	100.00	19 846	0.17	100.00	1.06	..
697 Base metal household equipment nes	9 981	0.20	100.00	21 007	0.18	100.00	6.79	..
726 Printing bookbinding machines parts	13 977	0.28	100.00	20 427	0.17	100.00	2.55	..
629 Articles of rubber nes	9 192	0.18	100.00	20 239	0.17	100.00	7.29	..
041 Wheat meslin, incl spelt, unmilled	17 321	0.34	100.00	20 571	0.17	100.00	0.46	..
762 Radio broadcast receivers	22 482	0.44	100.00	18 831	0.16	100.00	-1.25	..
122 Manufactured tabacco	18 937	0.37	100.00	18 822	0.16	100.00	-1.09	..
665 Glassware	10 130	0.20	100.00	19 454	0.16	100.00	5.96	..
421 Fixed veg fat and oil, "soft"	12 158	0.24	100.00	19 573	0.16	100.00	3.67	..
662 Clay and refractory materials	10 865	0.21	100.00	19 115	0.16	100.00	5.22	..
846 Clothing accessory excluding 831 848 851	10 577	0.21	100.00	18 369	0.15	100.00	4.34	..
024 Cheese and curd	11 071	0.22	100.00	18 485	0.16	100.00	4.78	..
683 Nickel	5 144	0.10	100.00	21 900	0.18	100.00	12.21	..
737 Metalwork machinery nes excluding tools	10 069	0.20	100.00	18 994	0.16	100.00	4.50	..
791 Railway vehicles and equipment	7 071	0.14	100.00	18 283	0.15	100.00	8.82	..
881 Photographic device nes	12 794	0.25	100.00	17 425	0.15	100.00	2.56	..
071 Coffee and coffee substitutes	15 552	0.31	100.00	18 406	0.15	100.00	-1.20	..
056 Vegetables roots tubers nes	10 760	0.21	100.00	17 691	0.15	100.00	4.92	..
751 Office machines	15 990	0.32	100.00	18 303	0.15	100.00	-0.70	..
551 Essential oils, perfumes & flavours	5 657	0.11	100.00	16 944	0.14	100.00	10.65	..
591 Household and garden chemicals	10 684	0.21	100.00	16 342	0.14	100.00	3.77	..
037 Fish shellfish, prepared preserved	8 774	0.17	100.00	17 117	0.14	100.00	5.51	..
896 Work of art & collections; antiques	6 483	0.13	100.00	17 066	0.14	100.00	8.77	..
843 Male clothing, knitted crocheted	7 992	0.16	100.00	17 500	0.15	100.00	5.46	..
722 Tractors	8 592	0.17	100.00	15 482	0.13	100.00	4.39	..
592 Starches, glutenes, glues, etc	7 667	0.15	100.00	15 311	0.13	100.00	6.25	..
422 Fixed veg fat and oil, excluding "soft"	7 747	0.15	100.00	15 532	0.13	100.00	5.94	..
621 Rubber material e.g. paste tube rod	6 586	0.13	100.00	15 243	0.13	100.00	7.53	..
001 Live animal excluding fish & crustacean	10 490	0.21	100.00	14 441	0.12	100.00	2.85	..
073 Chocolate & cocoa preparations nes	7 988	0.16	100.00	13 940	0.12	100.00	5.25	..
523 Inorganic acid metal salt peroxy	7 553	0.15	100.00	14 123	0.12	100.00	5.08	..
232 Synthetic & reclaimed rubber; waste	5 878	0.12	100.00	14 052	0.12	100.00	7.69	..
581 Plastic tube pipe hose & fittings	5 467	0.11	100.00	13 930	0.12	100.00	8.38	..
573 Vinyl chloride etc polymers	7 677	0.15	100.00	13 463	0.11	100.00	5.55	..
231 Natural rubber, latex, gum, etc	7 750	0.15	100.00	15 110	0.13	100.00	5.63	..
735 Machine part accessory for 731 733	6 522	0.13	100.00	13 183	0.11	100.00	5.47	..
692 Metal storage transport container	6 986	0.14	100.00	13 528	0.11	100.00	4.93	..
812 Sanitary plumb heat fixtures nes	5 428	0.11	100.00	13 278	0.11	100.00	7.96	..
044 Maize unmilled, excluding sweet corn	10 915	0.22	100.00	13 208	0.11	100.00	1.14	..
718 Power generating machinery part nes	5 206	0.10	100.00	13 058	0.11	100.00	8.66	..
659 Floor coverings etc	9 533	0.19	100.00	12 673	0.11	100.00	1.61	..
597 Additive e.g. lubricate, antifreeze	7 285	0.14	100.00	13 067	0.11	100.00	4.62	..
285 Aluminium ore concentrate alumina	5 228	0.10	100.00	13 323	0.11	100.00	7.49	..
111 Non alcoholic beverage nes	4 501	0.09	100.00	12 621	0.11	100.00	10.49	..
686 Zinc	4 126	0.08	100.00	15 779	0.13	100.00	6.73	..
017 Meat offal preserved nes	5 872	0.12	100.00	11 785	0.10	100.00	5.99	..
654 Other woven textile fabrics nes	10 978	0.22	100.00	11 328	0.10	100.00	0.27	..

For sources and notes, see end of table.

Pour les sources et les notes, se reporter à la fin du tableau

Products ranked by average 2005-2006 values SITC Revision 3 (3-digit level) Produits classés d'après la moyenne des valeurs de 2005-2006 CTCI révision 3 (positions à 3 chiffres)	1995			2006			Growth rates (percentage) Taux d'accroissement (en pourcentage) 1995-2006	
	Value (millions of dollars) Valeur (millions de dollars)	% of the country grouping exports En % des exportations du groupe de pays	% of world product exports En % des exportations mondiales des produits	Value (millions of dollars) Valeur (millions de dollars)	% of the country grouping exports En % des exportations du groupe de pays	% of world product exports En % des exportations mondiales des produits	Value Valeur	Difference from world Différence par rapport au monde
247 Wood in rough or roughly squared	9 236	0.18	100.00	11 431	0.10	100.00	2.30	..
263 Cotton	11 058	0.22	100.00	11 798	0.10	100.00	0.05	..
895 Office and stationery supplies nes	6 986	0.14	100.00	11 498	0.10	100.00	4.13	..
278 Other crude minerals	7 437	0.15	100.00	11 237	0.09	100.00	3.73	..
531 Synthetic organic colour agents	9 850	0.19	100.00	11 074	0.09	100.00	0.51	..
058 Fruit preserve preparation excluding juice	6 059	0.12	100.00	11 176	0.09	100.00	5.37	..
042 Rice	7 465	0.15	100.00	10 661	0.09	100.00	2.01	..
059 Fruit & vegetable juice unferment	5 890	0.12	100.00	10 919	0.09	100.00	4.47	..
344 Petroleum and hydrocarbon gas nes	2 680	0.05	100.00	10 292	0.09	100.00	12.91	..
727 Food processing machine excluding domestic	6 461	0.13	100.00	10 374	0.09	100.00	3.60	..
693 Wire products and fencing grills	4 809	0.09	100.00	10 406	0.09	100.00	6.81	..
725 Paper & pulp mill, cut manufacture	8 076	0.16	100.00	9 962	0.08	100.00	1.19	..
733 Metal work tool no material removal	6 985	0.14	100.00	10 057	0.08	100.00	2.09	..
072 Cocoa	5 196	0.10	100.00	9 225	0.08	100.00	5.69	..
656 Tulle lace embroidery trim etc	4 539	0.09	100.00	8 830	0.07	100.00	6.00	..
525 Radio active & associated materials	4 574	0.09	100.00	9 360	0.08	100.00	5.23	..
689 Misc non-ferrous base metals	3 279	0.06	100.00	8 449	0.07	100.00	7.35	..
891 Arms and ammunition	7 811	0.15	100.00	8 255	0.07	100.00	-0.26	..
678 Wire of iron or steel	4 281	0.08	100.00	8 243	0.07	100.00	6.28	..
696 Cutlery	4 169	0.08	100.00	7 878	0.07	100.00	6.06	..
524 Other inorganic chemicals	3 127	0.06	100.00	8 140	0.07	100.00	7.84	..
121 Unmanufactured tabacco and refuse	5 228	0.10	100.00	7 414	0.06	100.00	1.06	..
062 Sugar confectionery	4 483	0.09	100.00	7 058	0.06	100.00	4.20	..
873 Meters and counters nes	3 579	0.07	100.00	7 058	0.06	100.00	6.64	..
284 Nickel ores, concentrates, etc	2 041	0.04	100.00	7 686	0.06	100.00	11.96	..
666 Pottery	5 799	0.11	100.00	6 556	0.05	100.00	0.85	..
273 Stone, sand and gravel	3 688	0.07	100.00	6 898	0.06	100.00	5.39	..
211 Raw hides & skins, excluding furskins	5 961	0.12	100.00	6 200	0.05	100.00	0.78	..
266 Synthetic fibres for spinning	5 925	0.12	100.00	5 952	0.05	100.00	0.48	..
431 Processed animal & veg fats & oils	4 701	0.09	100.00	6 190	0.05	100.00	4.18	..
811 Prefabricated buildings	2 708	0.05	100.00	6 341	0.05	100.00	6.88	..
325 Coke, semi coke, retort carbon	2 320	0.05	100.00	5 353	0.04	100.00	11.99	..
291 Crude animal materials nes	3 669	0.07	100.00	5 292	0.04	100.00	3.13	..
289 Prec metal ore concentrate excluding gold	1 224	0.02	100.00	6 344	0.05	100.00	9.44	..
268 Wool & animal hair, incl wool tops	7 241	0.14	100.00	5 194	0.04	100.00	-2.97	..
074 Tea and maté	2 504	0.05	100.00	4 774	0.04	100.00	4.35	..
712 Steam vapour turbines & parts nes	2 709	0.05	100.00	4 253	0.04	100.00	3.40	..
023 Butter fats oils derived from milk	4 011	0.08	100.00	4 043	0.03	100.00	0.59	..
579 Plastic waste, parings and scrap	1 250	0.02	100.00	4 377	0.04	100.00	13.53	..
583 Plastic rod stick & profile shapes	1 475	0.03	100.00	4 256	0.04	100.00	9.92	..
711 Steam generating boilers & parts	3 094	0.06	100.00	4 005	0.03	100.00	0.55	..
035 Fish, dried salted smoked	2 769	0.05	100.00	3 965	0.03	100.00	3.09	..
043 Barley grain unmilled	2 788	0.06	100.00	3 469	0.03	100.00	1.36	..
685 Lead	1 446	0.03	100.00	3 874	0.03	100.00	6.10	..
267 Man made fibre for spinning; waste	2 971	0.06	100.00	3 472	0.03	100.00	1.85	..
687 Tin	1 583	0.03	100.00	3 408	0.03	100.00	5.86	..
612 Leather manufactures nes	1 030	0.02	100.00	3 406	0.03	100.00	12.26	..
075 Spices	1 884	0.04	100.00	3 468	0.03	100.00	4.56	..
246 Wood chips, particles and waste	2 099	0.04	100.00	3 270	0.03	100.00	3.69	..
091 Margarine and shortening	1 659	0.03	100.00	2 953	0.02	100.00	4.43	..
016 Meat offal preserved	1 641	0.03	100.00	3 004	0.03	100.00	5.11	..
212 Raw furskins and furskin pieces	1 265	0.02	100.00	3 082	0.03	100.00	6.35	..
411 Animals oils and fats	2 260	0.04	100.00	2 749	0.02	100.00	2.25	..
046 Wheat meal & flour, meslin flour	2 808	0.06	100.00	2 443	0.02	100.00	-2.04	..
677 Iron steel rail railway materials	1 252	0.02	100.00	2 459	0.02	100.00	5.87	..
025 Eggs, yolks and albumin	1 443	0.03	100.00	2 417	0.02	100.00	3.85	..
269 Worn clothing, textile article; rag	1 501	0.03	100.00	2 282	0.02	100.00	2.52	..
593 Explosives and pyrotechnic products	1 154	0.02	100.00	2 260	0.02	100.00	5.28	..
272 Crude fertilizer, excluding manufactured	1 297	0.03	100.00	1 816	0.02	100.00	1.70	..
045 Grain, excluding wheat rice barley maize	1 733	0.03	100.00	1 792	0.02	100.00	-0.35	..
613 Furskin tanned dressed etc	1 324	0.03	100.00	1 796	0.02	100.00	1.16	..

Sources:
- Data and UNCTAD secretariat estimates based on UN DESA Comtrade and IMF Direction of Trade statistics databases

Sources :
- Données et estimations du secrétariat de la CNUCED sur la base de données Comtrade de ONU DAES et Direction of Trade statistics du Fonds Monétaire international

Products ranked by average 2005-2006 values SITC Revision 3 (3-digit level) Produits classés d'après la moyenne des valeurs de 2005-2006 CTCI révision 3 (positions à 3 chiffres)	1995			2006			Growth rates (percentage) Taux d'accroissement (en pourcentage) 1995-2006	
	Value (millions of dollars) Valeur (millions de dollars)	% of the country grouping exports En % des exportations du groupe de pays	% of world product exports En % des exportations mondiales des produits	Value (millions of dollars) Valeur (millions de dollars)	% of the country grouping exports En % des exportations du groupe de pays	% of world product exports En % des exportations mondiales des produits	Value Valeur	Difference from world Différence par rapport au monde
All commodity groups	**3 528 995**	**100.00**	**69.67**	**7 013 671**	**100.00**	**58.83**	**6.02**	**-1.56**
781 Passenger cars and race cars	213 671	6.05	91.92	460 456	6.57	86.88	7.24	-0.48
542 Medicines including veterinary	42 078	1.19	92.79	223 209	3.18	94.31	17.52	0.31
784 Motor vehicle parts and accessories	102 718	2.91	91.08	206 180	2.94	80.23	6.54	-1.13
764 Telecommunicate equipment part nes	83 001	2.35	68.22	210 165	3.00	49.33	7.11	-4.14
334 Heavy petroleum & bituminous oil	40 133	1.14	43.59	195 808	2.79	42.42	14.11	-0.44
776 Valves tubes; diodes, transistors	113 795	3.22	60.20	159 021	2.27	37.50	3.19	-3.97
792 Aircraft, spacecraft & equipment	63 973	1.81	93.75	146 973	2.10	90.54	5.25	-0.47
752 Computer equipment nes	88 518	2.51	67.10	123 962	1.77	41.51	1.86	-4.62
333 Crude petroleum & bituminous oil	34 903	0.99	17.03	122 642	1.75	13.38	11.87	-2.30
713 Internal combustion engine part nes	48 771	1.38	87.99	104 640	1.49	84.58	7.01	-0.34
874 Measure analyze control device nes	48 554	1.38	92.14	104 700	1.49	83.29	6.80	-1.04
772 Electrical circuit equipment	51 045	1.45	76.80	98 933	1.41	60.47	5.61	-2.33
759 Office equipment part & accessories	64 514	1.83	65.18	95 629	1.36	43.07	2.84	-4.25
778 Electrical machinery apparatus nes	58 140	1.65	72.34	94 432	1.35	56.70	4.16	-2.60
728 Special industrial machine part nes	53 717	1.52	89.32	91 628	1.31	82.98	4.44	-0.71
641 Paper and paperboard	64 759	1.84	89.65	87 524	1.25	84.74	3.46	-0.45
343 Natural gas, liquefied or not	11 717	0.33	33.71	79 630	1.14	40.91	18.93	3.17
782 Goods and service vehicles	39 871	1.13	88.03	75 946	1.08	76.12	5.24	-1.35
515 Organo-inorganic compound acid salt	24 058	0.68	89.79	73 972	1.05	85.70	10.65	-0.57
699 Base metal manufactures nes	32 158	0.91	76.84	73 521	1.05	68.98	7.02	-1.00
714 Non-electric engines excluding 712 713 718	24 509	0.69	93.39	70 729	1.01	90.33	8.95	-0.47
821 Furniture part; bedding furnishing	35 116	1.00	77.64	66 873	0.95	62.10	5.74	-2.23
541 Pharmaceuticals excluding medicines	23 016	0.65	87.28	66 276	0.94	89.09	10.81	0.35
723 Civil engineering plant & equipment	26 019	0.74	87.78	65 671	0.94	78.06	7.69	-1.09
893 Articles of plastic nes	28 738	0.81	68.10	62 959	0.90	66.28	7.24	-0.27
684 Aluminium	32 931	0.93	72.36	66 098	0.94	65.65	5.80	-0.84
598 Miscellaneous chemical products nes	25 798	0.73	87.23	61 721	0.88	81.70	7.82	-0.44
743 Gas pump, compressor, fan, filter	28 353	0.80	81.66	60 477	0.86	75.93	6.83	-0.81
667 Pearls, precious semiprecious stone	26 843	0.76	66.43	55 684	0.79	59.55	7.22	-1.42
575 Other plastics, in primary forms	25 776	0.73	86.63	58 521	0.83	77.76	7.49	-1.19
741 Heating cooling equipment parts nes	31 363	0.89	81.87	56 588	0.81	70.90	4.47	-1.75
582 Plastic sheet film foil & strips	24 572	0.70	83.61	51 368	0.73	78.26	6.89	-0.57
744 Mechanical handling equipment nes	25 043	0.71	89.15	52 073	0.74	83.97	5.81	-0.47
872 Medical instruments appliances nes	16 691	0.47	87.44	45 669	0.65	81.34	9.66	-0.83
793 Ships boats floating structures	26 603	0.75	72.31	44 918	0.64	50.88	4.87	-2.67
679 Iron steel pipe tube fittings etc	19 321	0.55	79.63	44 934	0.64	64.85	6.41	-1.86
773 Electrical distribute equipment nes	20 190	0.57	67.67	44 967	0.64	58.75	6.04	-1.19
112 Alcoholic beverages	24 204	0.69	87.39	42 159	0.60	83.27	4.97	-0.52
682 Copper	20 221	0.57	57.35	48 656	0.69	43.90	5.86	-2.25
553 Perfume toilet cosmetics, excluding soap	16 758	0.47	89.33	40 452	0.58	82.95	8.32	-0.76
673 Flat iron non-alloy steel products	24 037	0.68	67.22	40 063	0.57	55.70	5.54	-1.47
716 Rotating electric plant parts nes	18 936	0.54	73.75	41 119	0.59	67.71	6.86	-0.78
675 Flat rolled products of alloy steel	17 630	0.50	86.52	41 765	0.60	73.32	8.56	-1.33
775 Household equipment nes	22 667	0.64	71.47	37 678	0.54	53.99	4.60	-2.80
676 Iron steel bar rod section piling	20 129	0.57	73.08	38 697	0.55	61.30	6.12	-1.48
745 Non-electrical machinery tool nes	20 125	0.57	92.19	36 876	0.53	83.88	5.22	-0.92
747 Pipe, boiler, tank & vat appliances	17 497	0.50	89.74	37 989	0.54	76.06	6.39	-1.62
898 Music instrument device recording	23 716	0.67	78.86	34 670	0.49	65.80	2.87	-1.85
511 Hydrocarbons nes; derivatives	16 722	0.47	80.07	36 965	0.53	65.10	8.67	-2.03
533 Pigment, paint, varnish & related	16 808	0.48	83.84	35 587	0.51	81.80	6.84	-0.30
899 Manufactured articles nes	10 672	0.30	53.75	34 289	0.49	69.29	11.81	2.93
012 Meat nes, fresh chilled frozen	19 243	0.55	79.67	32 781	0.47	81.96	4.64	0.13
892 Printed matter	21 868	0.62	85.89	32 507	0.46	78.27	3.74	-0.83
845 Articles of apparel nes	19 302	0.55	42.76	32 662	0.47	30.37	4.52	-2.91
625 Rubber for wheels, incl inner tube	17 744	0.50	76.37	32 323	0.46	65.70	4.84	-1.34
742 Liquid pump; liquid elevator parts	16 339	0.46	92.00	31 881	0.45	84.12	6.11	-0.78
851 Footwear	20 196	0.57	42.98	30 354	0.43	41.83	3.16	-0.27
761 Television video receive project	9 448	0.27	39.33	33 778	0.48	44.35	10.65	0.11
642 Cut paper and paperboard articles	20 868	0.59	81.87	29 558	0.42	75.82	2.93	-0.67
894 Baby carriage toy game sport good	16 405	0.46	39.95	28 785	0.41	40.50	4.43	0.15

For sources and notes, see end of table.

Pour les sources et les notes, se reporter à la fin du tableau

Products ranked by average 2005-2006 values SITC Revision 3 (3-digit level) Produits classés d'après la moyenne des valeurs de 2005-2006 CTCI révision 3 (positions à 3 chiffres)	1995			2006			Growth rates (percentage) Taux d'accroissement (en pourcentage) 1995-2006	
	Value (millions of dollars) Valeur (millions de dollars)	% of the country grouping exports En % des exportations du groupe de pays	% of world product exports En % des exportations mondiales des produits	Value (millions of dollars) Valeur (millions de dollars)	% of the country grouping exports En % des exportations du groupe de pays	% of world product exports En % des exportations mondiales des produits	Value Valeur	Difference from world Différence par rapport au monde
057 Fruit nut (exc oil), fresh or dried	15 458	0.44	58.19	27 534	0.39	55.37	5.08	-0.24
748 Mechanical transmission equipment	13 366	0.38	90.65	28 252	0.40	84.49	6.74	-0.74
783 Road motor vehicles nes	15 577	0.44	92.62	28 444	0.41	84.41	5.45	-0.92
571 Primary form ethylene polymers	11 979	0.34	73.36	28 904	0.41	62.29	7.79	-1.77
321 Coal excluding non-agglomomerated	12 933	0.37	69.03	27 306	0.39	55.24	5.44	-2.90
098 Edible products & preparations nes	14 515	0.41	83.16	27 682	0.39	78.24	6.34	-0.49
248 Wood simply worked, railway sleeper	20 402	0.58	77.86	26 993	0.38	69.99	2.01	-1.05
514 Nitrogen function compounds	16 143	0.46	85.60	25 786	0.37	73.60	4.86	-1.16
763 Sound TV recorder or reproducer	9 807	0.28	45.67	25 518	0.36	41.14	10.29	-2.12
774 Electrodiagnostic equipment	11 990	0.34	96.54	26 427	0.38	90.17	7.42	-0.59
674 Flat plated iron non-alloy steel	14 755	0.42	81.00	26 253	0.37	65.57	5.34	-1.97
731 Machine tools for material removal	14 304	0.41	87.76	26 104	0.37	81.45	3.99	-0.74
351 Electric current	6 423	0.18	82.65	26 898	0.38	88.36	13.84	0.77
771 Electric power machine part excluding 716	13 608	0.39	57.53	25 876	0.37	46.56	4.23	-2.11
574 Polyacetals and polyesters, etc	11 835	0.34	74.48	24 606	0.35	61.54	6.75	-2.29
897 Jewellery nes (667)	12 427	0.35	64.02	26 016	0.37	53.81	6.18	-1.87
971 Gold non-monetary excluding ores	14 544	0.41	67.15	28 670	0.41	47.90	2.82	-3.34
695 Tools for use in hand or in machine	13 897	0.39	79.81	24 452	0.35	71.36	4.77	-1.10
842 Female clothing, woven	14 774	0.42	39.90	23 372	0.33	33.44	3.93	-1.89
054 Vegetable & vegetable products nes	14 064	0.40	67.23	23 372	0.33	63.59	5.15	-0.26
884 Optical goods fibres nes	7 888	0.22	77.78	23 022	0.33	65.51	9.60	-1.63
048 Cereal & preparation flour starch	10 796	0.31	85.29	22 965	0.33	83.91	6.85	-0.11
282 Ferrous iron & steel, waste & scrap	6 648	0.19	84.41	24 916	0.36	80.68	14.27	-0.11
691 Iron steel aluminium structures nes	10 647	0.30	77.57	23 132	0.33	67.32	6.37	-1.50
251 Pulp and waste paper	22 563	0.64	82.12	22 466	0.32	75.59	2.14	-0.65
513 Carboxylic acid and compounds	12 906	0.37	76.34	22 188	0.32	59.61	5.30	-2.77
034 Fish, fresh live chilled frozen	11 674	0.33	61.43	21 778	0.31	57.77	5.52	-0.74
657 Special yarn and textile fabric etc	13 999	0.40	66.30	21 475	0.31	67.27	3.88	0.37
785 Motorcycles, mopeds and cycles	11 387	0.32	61.81	21 247	0.30	60.15	5.72	-0.46
022 Milk products, excluding butter & cheese	14 277	0.40	92.46	20 027	0.29	84.25	3.45	-0.82
634 Veneer, plywood & other wood nes	9 067	0.26	52.81	19 739	0.28	60.85	7.91	2.07
664 Glass	11 526	0.33	82.12	20 285	0.29	73.01	5.55	-1.14
721 Agricultural machine nes excluding tractor	9 835	0.28	93.81	20 241	0.29	90.06	5.90	-0.46
663 Mineral manufactures nes	11 338	0.32	86.64	20 215	0.29	81.07	4.50	-0.70
724 Textile leather machinery parts nes	21 210	0.60	83.99	19 267	0.27	70.67	-0.69	-1.52
081 Animal feed excluding unmilled cereal	13 219	0.37	64.45	19 568	0.28	59.19	2.84	-0.83
554 Soaps cleansers polishes	9 367	0.27	81.92	19 348	0.28	78.25	7.03	-0.30
288 Non ferrous base metal waste nes	6 756	0.19	73.42	23 348	0.33	78.62	10.12	1.23
841 Male clothing, woven	13 473	0.38	36.47	18 489	0.26	33.25	2.40	-0.75
651 Textile yarn	16 380	0.46	49.32	18 685	0.27	42.51	0.92	-1.42
726 Printing bookbinding machines parts	13 368	0.38	95.64	18 437	0.26	90.26	1.94	-0.62
516 Other organic chemicals	9 017	0.26	81.11	18 499	0.26	70.19	6.28	-1.61
522 Inorganic chemical elem oxide salt	9 804	0.28	60.26	18 212	0.26	55.79	5.16	-0.79
749 Non-electric machinery part nes	10 735	0.30	83.53	17 897	0.26	74.01	4.27	-1.22
292 Crude vegetable materials nes	10 899	0.31	72.45	17 453	0.25	73.04	4.87	0.26
024 Cheese and curd	10 843	0.31	97.95	17 302	0.25	93.60	4.34	-0.44
882 Photo cinematographic supply excluding 883	15 767	0.45	89.32	16 502	0.24	83.15	0.28	-0.78
512 Alcohols, phenols; derivatives	9 601	0.27	70.47	16 950	0.24	51.79	5.59	-3.17
011 Beef, fresh chilled frozen	13 903	0.39	87.71	17 007	0.24	70.17	2.48	-1.89
885 Watches and clocks	11 976	0.34	52.29	17 031	0.24	62.62	3.42	2.00
746 Ball or roller bearings	10 082	0.29	82.82	16 730	0.24	76.80	4.45	-0.76
681 Silver, platinum, platinum metals	4 997	0.14	80.44	19 788	0.28	56.51	10.31	-3.65
786 Trailer caravan transport container	6 309	0.18	64.02	17 112	0.24	64.23	8.75	-0.74
694 Nails screws nuts bolts rivets	7 953	0.23	73.45	16 078	0.23	65.65	6.12	-1.21
629 Articles of rubber nes	7 803	0.22	84.89	15 722	0.22	77.68	6.56	-0.74
041 Wheat meslin, incl spelt, unmilled	15 371	0.44	88.74	15 912	0.23	77.35	-1.01	-1.47
635 Wood manufactures nes	7 316	0.21	64.92	15 363	0.22	64.26	6.50	-0.16
896 Work of art & collections; antiques	6 151	0.17	94.88	15 557	0.22	91.16	8.38	-0.40
551 Essential oils, perfumes & flavours	4 775	0.14	84.41	14 271	0.20	84.23	10.58	-0.07
737 Metalwork machinery nes excluding tools	9 045	0.26	89.84	14 986	0.21	78.89	3.05	-1.45
791 Railway vehicles and equipment	6 332	0.18	89.54	14 452	0.21	79.05	7.81	-1.00

For sources and notes, see end of table.

Pour les sources et les notes, se reporter à la fin du tableau

Products ranked by average 2005-2006 values SITC Revision 3 (3-digit level) / Produits classés d'après la moyenne des valeurs de 2005-2006 CTCI révision 3 (positions à 3 chiffres)	1995			2006			Growth rates (percentage) Taux d'accroissement (en pourcentage) 1995-2006	
	Value (millions of dollars) Valeur (millions de dollars)	% of the country grouping exports En % des exportations du groupe de pays	% of world product exports En % des exportations mondiales des produits	Value (millions of dollars) Valeur (millions de dollars)	% of the country grouping exports En % des exportations du groupe de pays	% of world product exports En % des exportations mondiales des produits	Value Valeur	Difference from world Différence par rapport au monde
122 Manufactured tabacco	13 778	0.39	72.76	13 888	0.20	73.79	-0.80	0.29
281 Iron ore and concentrates	3 682	0.10	42.88	14 790	0.21	44.27	10.61	-0.64
665 Glassware	8 129	0.23	80.25	13 860	0.20	71.25	4.75	-1.21
335 Residual petroleum products nes	4 589	0.13	75.99	14 444	0.21	64.00	10.49	-0.78
881 Photographic device nes	8 745	0.25	68.35	13 280	0.19	76.21	3.45	0.89
662 Clay and refractory materials	9 529	0.27	87.71	13 445	0.19	70.34	3.16	-2.06
722 Tractors	8 035	0.23	93.51	13 324	0.19	86.06	3.48	-0.92
591 Household and garden chemicals	9 200	0.26	86.11	12 762	0.18	78.09	2.68	-1.09
653 Man-made woven fabrics	15 646	0.44	43.86	12 316	0.18	37.70	-2.20	-1.18
222 Oil seed etc for soft oil	8 716	0.25	71.20	12 386	0.18	54.28	2.11	-3.17
056 Vegetables roots tubers nes	7 527	0.21	69.95	12 162	0.17	68.75	4.74	-0.19
621 Rubber material e.g. paste tube rod	5 787	0.16	87.87	12 129	0.17	79.57	6.77	-0.76
592 Starches, glutenes, glues, etc	6 326	0.18	82.51	11 787	0.17	76.98	5.66	-0.59
562 Manufactured fertilizer excluding crude	11 023	0.31	62.17	11 393	0.16	46.62	0.55	-2.61
073 Chocolate & cocoa preparations nes	7 387	0.21	92.47	11 835	0.17	84.90	4.31	-0.94
683 Nickel	3 549	0.10	68.98	13 775	0.20	62.90	10.92	-1.30
672 Ingots, Iron steel primary products	5 803	0.16	45.57	11 333	0.16	37.05	7.41	-1.85
001 Live animal excluding fish & crustacean	8 211	0.23	78.27	11 753	0.17	81.39	2.78	-0.08
871 Optical instruments apparatus nes	3 949	0.11	70.59	11 146	0.16	19.45	10.01	-12.00
813 Lighting fixtures and fittings nes	6 186	0.18	62.86	11 381	0.16	54.21	4.96	-1.78
652 Woven cotton fabrics	9 902	0.28	44.59	10 502	0.15	36.37	1.26	-1.57
581 Plastic tube pipe hose & fittings	4 641	0.13	84.90	11 351	0.16	81.49	7.64	-0.74
597 Additive e.g. lubricate, antifreeze	6 629	0.19	90.99	11 277	0.16	86.30	4.02	-0.60
735 Machine part accessory for 731 733	6 069	0.17	93.05	11 043	0.16	83.77	4.48	-0.99
718 Power generating machinery part nes	4 651	0.13	89.35	11 014	0.16	84.34	8.05	-0.62
831 Case bag: storage travel shopping	4 774	0.14	31.84	10 770	0.15	40.15	7.54	2.69
421 Fixed veg fat and oil, "soft"	7 247	0.21	59.61	10 711	0.15	54.72	2.40	-1.27
812 Sanitary plumb heat fixtures nes	4 741	0.13	87.34	10 521	0.15	79.24	6.78	-1.17
573 Vinyl chloride etc polymers	5 849	0.17	76.19	9 911	0.14	73.62	5.33	-0.22
658 Made-up textile articles nes	5 601	0.16	42.10	9 716	0.14	28.87	4.92	-4.01
697 Base metal household equipment nes	5 740	0.16	57.51	9 994	0.14	47.57	4.58	-2.21
111 Non alcoholic beverage nes	3 457	0.10	76.82	10 279	0.15	81.44	11.01	0.53
661 Lime cement construction material	7 416	0.21	67.23	9 859	0.14	44.67	1.80	-3.63
692 Metal storage transport container	5 760	0.16	82.45	9 845	0.14	72.78	3.94	-0.99
572 Primary form styrene polymers	6 285	0.18	56.90	9 676	0.14	46.08	4.45	-2.37
611 Leather	7 618	0.22	47.98	9 465	0.13	41.28	2.02	-1.43
342 Liquefied propane and butane	2 799	0.08	48.28	9 677	0.14	31.04	11.33	-5.33
287 Base metal ores & concentrates nes	3 000	0.09	51.36	10 587	0.15	46.32	8.39	-2.55
727 Food processing machine excluding domestic	5 933	0.17	91.83	9 297	0.13	89.61	3.49	-0.11
044 Maize unmilled, excluding sweet corn	9 686	0.27	88.74	9 850	0.14	74.57	-0.54	-1.68
725 Paper & pulp mill, cut manufacture	7 546	0.21	93.44	8 948	0.13	89.82	0.79	-0.41
232 Synthetic & reclaimed rubber; waste	4 422	0.13	75.24	9 380	0.13	66.75	6.33	-1.36
751 Office machines	11 366	0.32	71.08	8 966	0.13	48.99	-3.77	-3.06
523 Inorganic acid metal salt peroxy	5 554	0.16	73.53	8 647	0.12	61.23	3.32	-1.76
846 Clothing accessory excluding 831 848 851	6 200	0.18	58.62	8 102	0.12	44.11	1.31	-3.03
061 Sugar, mollasses and honey	7 179	0.20	45.63	8 671	0.12	38.19	0.45	-1.26
036 Crustacean mollusc aquat invertebra	5 074	0.14	30.90	7 910	0.11	37.36	4.63	2.25
733 Metal work tool no material removal	6 034	0.17	86.38	8 080	0.12	80.34	1.19	-0.89
659 Floor coverings etc	6 516	0.18	68.35	7 896	0.11	62.31	0.78	-0.83
017 Meat offal preserved nes	4 373	0.12	74.47	7 569	0.11	64.23	4.26	-1.72
844 Female clothing, knitted crocheted	4 901	0.14	36.41	7 536	0.11	24.22	2.47	-3.98
525 Radio active & associated materials	3 879	0.11	84.81	7 906	0.11	84.47	5.62	0.39
895 Office and stationery supplies nes	4 989	0.14	71.41	7 407	0.11	64.42	2.90	-1.23
344 Petroleum and hydrocarbon gas nes	1 965	0.06	73.33	7 268	0.10	70.61	12.54	-0.36
655 Knitted or crocheted fabrics nes	4 722	0.13	39.17	7 025	0.10	32.61	3.59	-1.31
531 Synthetic organic colour agents	7 751	0.22	78.70	7 088	0.10	64.00	-1.19	-1.70
278 Other crude minerals	5 027	0.14	67.59	7 357	0.10	65.47	3.05	-0.68
285 Aluminium ore concentrate alumina	3 053	0.09	58.40	7 669	0.11	57.56	7.02	-0.47
891 Arms and ammunition	7 519	0.21	96.27	7 289	0.10	88.29	-1.36	-1.11
654 Other woven textile fabrics nes	7 623	0.22	69.44	6 910	0.10	61.00	-1.11	-1.38
671 Pig & sponge iron, ferro alloys etc	2 953	0.08	28.18	6 603	0.09	26.24	6.82	-2.94

For sources and notes, see end of table.

Pour les sources et les notes, se reporter à la fin du tableau

Products ranked by average 2005-2006 values SITC Revision 3 (3-digit level) / Produits classés d'après la moyenne des valeurs de 2005-2006 CTCI révision 3 (positions à 3 chiffres)	1995			2006			Growth rates (percentage) Taux d'accroissement (en pourcentage) 1995-2006	
	Value (millions of dollars) / Valeur (millions de dollars)	% of the country grouping exports / En % des exportations du groupe de pays	% of world product exports / En % des exportations mondiales des produits	Value (millions of dollars) / Valeur (millions de dollars)	% of the country grouping exports / En % des exportations du groupe de pays	% of world product exports / En % des exportations mondiales des produits	Value / Valeur	Difference from world / Différence par rapport au monde
686 Zinc	2 706	0.08	65.58	8 924	0.13	56.55	5.78	-0.95
762 Radio broadcast receivers	6 553	0.19	29.15	6 440	0.09	34.20	0.44	1.70
848 Headgear, non-textile clothing	3 715	0.11	29.20	6 792	0.10	32.88	4.95	-0.25
693 Wire products and fencing grills	3 528	0.10	73.36	6 737	0.10	64.74	5.56	-1.25
071 Coffee and coffee substitutes	3 392	0.10	21.81	6 522	0.09	35.44	4.64	5.84
059 Fruit & vegetable juice unferment	3 538	0.10	60.08	6 439	0.09	58.98	4.72	0.25
263 Cotton	5 142	0.15	46.50	6 157	0.09	52.19	2.49	2.44
058 Fruit preserve preparation excluding juice	3 740	0.11	61.72	6 027	0.09	53.93	4.02	-1.34
037 Fish shellfish, prepared preserved	3 853	0.11	43.91	5 757	0.08	33.64	3.54	-1.97
283 Copper ores and concentrates	1 853	0.05	27.04	6 636	0.09	20.70	9.05	-3.98
873 Meters and counters nes	3 231	0.09	90.27	5 258	0.07	74.50	5.06	-1.58
247 Wood in rough or roughly squared	5 167	0.15	55.94	5 113	0.07	44.73	0.46	-1.84
678 Wire of iron or steel	3 180	0.09	74.29	5 117	0.07	62.07	4.55	-1.73
211 Raw hides & skins, excluding furskins	4 808	0.14	80.65	5 020	0.07	80.97	0.82	0.04
811 Prefabricated buildings	2 521	0.07	93.09	4 903	0.07	77.32	5.51	-1.37
524 Other inorganic chemicals	2 277	0.06	72.83	5 363	0.08	65.88	6.52	-1.32
689 Misc non-ferrous base metals	1 952	0.06	59.53	4 693	0.07	55.54	6.59	-0.77
062 Sugar confectionery	3 069	0.09	68.46	4 285	0.06	60.72	3.40	-0.80
273 Stone, sand and gravel	2 666	0.08	72.29	4 251	0.06	61.63	3.93	-1.46
696 Cutlery	2 381	0.07	57.11	4 084	0.06	51.84	5.20	-0.86
023 Butter fats oils derived from milk	3 806	0.11	94.88	3 757	0.05	92.92	0.44	-0.15
712 Steam vapour turbines & parts nes	2 521	0.07	93.06	3 581	0.05	84.22	2.42	-0.98
583 Plastic rod stick & profile shapes	1 409	0.04	95.58	3 791	0.05	89.06	9.30	-0.62
656 Tulle lace embroidery trim etc	2 607	0.07	57.43	3 551	0.05	40.21	3.24	-2.76
284 Nickel ores, concentrates, etc	1 139	0.03	55.81	3 995	0.06	51.98	12.02	0.06
289 Prec metal ore concentrate excluding gold	866	0.02	70.73	4 324	0.06	68.16	13.99	4.55
268 Wool & animal hair, incl wool tops	5 334	0.15	73.66	3 459	0.05	66.61	-3.57	-0.59
291 Crude animal materials nes	2 090	0.06	56.97	3 250	0.05	61.41	3.71	0.57
843 Male clothing, knitted crocheted	2 356	0.07	29.48	3 271	0.05	18.69	0.81	-4.65
072 Cocoa	1 673	0.05	32.20	3 051	0.04	33.07	6.38	0.69
666 Pottery	3 387	0.10	58.41	2 858	0.04	43.60	-1.53	-2.38
035 Fish, dried salted smoked	2 085	0.06	75.29	2 975	0.04	75.03	2.79	-0.30
325 Coke, semi coke, retort carbon	1 445	0.04	62.26	2 783	0.04	51.99	8.15	-3.83
043 Barley grain unmilled	2 472	0.07	88.66	2 627	0.04	75.73	-0.38	-1.73
711 Steam generating boilers & parts	2 726	0.08	88.10	2 627	0.04	65.58	-1.87	-2.42
016 Meat offal preserved	1 598	0.05	97.41	2 930	0.04	97.53	5.14	0.03
121 Unmanufactured tabacco and refuse	2 481	0.07	47.44	2 716	0.04	36.64	0.01	-1.04
431 Processed animal & veg fats & oils	2 266	0.06	48.19	2 737	0.04	44.22	3.85	-0.33
267 Man made fibre for spinning; waste	2 555	0.07	85.98	2 647	0.04	76.24	1.23	-0.62
042 Rice	2 242	0.06	30.03	2 514	0.04	23.58	-0.19	-2.19
266 Synthetic fibres for spinning	2 787	0.08	47.04	2 420	0.03	40.66	-1.23	-1.71
579 Plastic waste, parings and scrap	621	0.02	49.73	2 588	0.04	59.14	15.67	2.14
411 Animals oils and fats	2 019	0.06	89.35	2 308	0.03	83.93	1.71	-0.53
212 Raw furskins and furskin pieces	1 040	0.03	82.19	2 398	0.03	77.81	5.06	-1.29
246 Wood chips, particles and waste	1 449	0.04	69.06	2 190	0.03	66.98	2.84	-0.85
677 Iron steel rail railway materials	1 017	0.03	81.21	2 017	0.03	82.01	6.43	0.56
685 Lead	973	0.03	67.32	2 164	0.03	55.87	4.39	-1.70
422 Fixed veg fat and oil, excluding "soft"	782	0.02	10.09	2 092	0.03	13.47	8.36	2.42
091 Margarine and shortening	1 221	0.03	73.60	2 035	0.03	68.79	3.65	-0.78
025 Eggs, yolks and albumin	1 208	0.03	83.71	1 989	0.03	82.29	3.85	0.00
269 Worn clothing, textile article; rag	1 188	0.03	79.16	1 743	0.02	76.37	2.32	-0.20
612 Leather manufactures nes	508	0.01	49.35	1 635	0.02	48.00	11.95	-0.30
045 Grain, excluding wheat rice barley maize	1 537	0.04	88.69	1 590	0.02	88.75	-0.61	-0.26
633 Cork manufactures	953	0.03	97.11	1 441	0.02	93.02	4.07	-0.46
046 Wheat meal & flour, meslin flour	1 964	0.06	69.94	1 307	0.02	53.47	-3.97	-1.93
593 Explosives and pyrotechnic products	669	0.02	57.95	1 344	0.02	59.50	5.61	0.34
074 Tea and maté	577	0.02	23.03	1 217	0.02	25.50	6.32	1.97
223 Oil seed for non soft oil	415	0.01	57.67	991	0.01	68.88	7.77	1.67
322 Briquettes, lignite and peat	831	0.02	92.32	1 008	0.01	91.85	1.49	-0.17
532 Dyeing and tanning extracts	546	0.02	64.03	876	0.01	61.16	3.89	-0.52
613 Furskin tanned dressed etc	965	0.03	72.89	913	0.01	50.83	-2.98	-4.15

Sources:
- Data and UNCTAD secretariat estimates based on UN DESA Comtrade and IMF Direction of Trade statistics databases

Sources :
- Données et estimations du secrétariat de la CNUCED sur la base de données Comtrade de ONU DAES et Direction of Trade statistics du Fonds Monétaire international

Products ranked by average 2005-2006 values SITC Revision 3 (3-digit level) Produits classés d'après la moyenne des valeurs de 2005-2006 CTCI révision 3 (positions à 3 chiffres)	1995			2006			Growth rates (percentage) Taux d'accroissement (en pourcentage) 1995-2006	
	Value (millions of dollars) Valeur (millions de dollars)	% of the country grouping exports En % des exportations du groupe de pays	% of world product exports En % des exportations mondiales des produits	Value (millions of dollars) Valeur (millions de dollars)	% of the country grouping exports En % des exportations du groupe de pays	% of world product exports En % des exportations mondiales des produits	Value Valeur	Difference from world Différence par rapport au monde
All commodity groups	**1 417 569**	**100.00**	**27.99**	**4 466 584**	**100.00**	**37.47**	**10.40**	**2.83**
333 Crude petroleum & bituminous oil	155 854	10.99	76.06	669 309	14.98	73.01	13.54	-0.63
776 Valves tubes; diodes, transistors	75 105	5.30	39.73	264 786	5.93	62.44	11.19	4.04
764 Telecommunicate equipment part nes	38 243	2.70	31.43	214 825	4.81	50.42	17.94	6.69
334 Heavy petroleum & bituminous oil	43 219	3.05	46.94	208 027	4.66	45.07	14.07	-0.48
752 Computer equipment nes	43 321	3.06	32.84	174 507	3.91	58.43	12.19	5.72
759 Office equipment part & accessories	34 423	2.43	34.78	126 312	2.83	56.89	12.17	5.08
845 Articles of apparel nes	25 551	1.80	56.60	74 168	1.66	68.96	9.20	1.77
778 Electrical machinery apparatus nes	21 857	1.54	27.19	71 272	1.60	42.79	12.17	5.41
781 Passenger cars and race cars	18 157	1.28	7.81	68 151	1.53	12.86	11.95	4.23
343 Natural gas, liquefied or not	9 652	0.68	27.77	68 358	1.53	35.12	17.22	1.46
772 Electrical circuit equipment	15 169	1.07	22.82	63 973	1.43	39.10	13.38	5.44
784 Motor vehicle parts and accessories	9 530	0.67	8.45	49 614	1.11	19.31	15.53	7.86
842 Female clothing, woven	21 610	1.52	58.36	45 497	1.02	65.10	7.04	1.22
682 Copper	12 939	0.91	36.70	53 981	1.21	48.70	10.66	2.55
894 Baby carriage toy game sport good	24 604	1.74	59.92	42 095	0.94	59.23	4.16	-0.12
871 Optical instruments apparatus nes	1 599	0.11	28.59	45 997	1.03	80.27	33.17	11.16
851 Footwear	26 177	1.85	55.71	41 166	0.92	56.73	3.65	0.22
761 Television video receive project	14 470	1.02	60.24	42 303	0.95	55.55	10.60	0.07
821 Furniture part; bedding furnishing	9 628	0.68	21.29	39 314	0.88	36.51	13.73	5.76
763 Sound TV recorder or reproducer	11 642	0.82	54.21	36 484	0.82	58.83	14.42	2.01
793 Ships boats floating structures	8 800	0.62	23.92	40 568	0.91	45.95	12.66	5.12
667 Pearls, precious semiprecious stone	13 506	0.95	33.42	35 830	0.80	38.32	10.83	2.20
841 Male clothing, woven	22 912	1.62	62.02	36 233	0.81	65.17	3.58	0.43
893 Articles of plastic nes	13 356	0.94	31.65	31 345	0.70	33.00	7.96	0.45
775 Household equipment nes	8 787	0.62	27.71	31 362	0.70	44.94	12.42	5.02
699 Base metal manufactures nes	9 235	0.65	22.07	31 359	0.70	29.42	10.80	2.79
773 Electrical distribute equipment nes	9 273	0.65	31.08	30 530	0.68	39.89	9.28	2.05
771 Electric power machine part excluding 716	9 840	0.69	41.60	28 966	0.65	52.12	8.75	2.41
971 Gold non-monetary excluding ores	6 825	0.48	31.51	30 337	0.68	50.69	10.37	4.21
651 Textile yarn	16 329	1.15	49.16	24 599	0.55	55.97	3.63	1.28
658 Made-up textile articles nes	7 582	0.53	56.99	23 698	0.53	70.41	11.30	2.38
684 Aluminium	8 321	0.59	18.28	24 843	0.56	24.68	10.33	3.69
782 Goods and service vehicles	4 720	0.33	10.42	22 065	0.49	22.12	13.35	6.76
741 Heating cooling equipment parts nes	6 795	0.48	17.74	22 672	0.51	28.41	12.36	6.14
844 Female clothing, knitted crocheted	8 456	0.60	62.81	23 340	0.52	75.01	8.33	1.88
673 Flat iron non-alloy steel products	8 159	0.58	22.82	22 857	0.51	31.78	9.50	2.48
057 Fruit nut (exc oil), fresh or dried	10 873	0.77	40.93	21 410	0.48	43.05	5.52	0.20
897 Jewellery nes (667)	6 966	0.49	35.89	22 136	0.50	45.79	10.62	2.57
653 Man-made woven fabrics	19 918	1.41	55.83	20 279	0.45	62.07	-0.15	0.87
283 Copper ores and concentrates	4 955	0.35	72.29	25 121	0.56	78.37	14.08	1.05
874 Measure analyze control device nes	3 904	0.28	7.41	20 191	0.45	16.06	16.25	8.41
342 Liquefied propane and butane	2 929	0.21	50.51	20 587	0.46	66.03	20.34	3.68
652 Woven cotton fabrics	11 978	0.84	53.94	18 124	0.41	62.76	4.07	1.24
679 Iron steel pipe tube fittings etc	3 824	0.27	15.76	20 820	0.47	30.05	14.15	5.88
716 Rotating electric plant parts nes	6 514	0.46	25.37	19 067	0.43	31.40	9.54	1.91
713 Internal combustion engine part nes	6 282	0.44	11.33	18 316	0.41	14.80	9.81	2.46
743 Gas pump, compressor, fan filter	6 210	0.44	17.89	18 677	0.42	23.45	10.83	3.19
728 Special industrial machine part nes	6 181	0.44	10.28	18 197	0.41	16.48	9.96	4.81
511 Hydrocarbons nes; derivatives	3 747	0.26	17.94	18 392	0.41	32.39	16.82	6.13
898 Music instrument device recording	6 274	0.44	20.86	17 893	0.40	33.96	10.24	5.52
676 Iron steel bar rod section piling	5 010	0.35	18.19	18 802	0.42	29.79	11.97	4.38
321 Coal excluding non-agglomomerated	4 483	0.32	23.93	17 098	0.38	34.59	12.98	4.63
571 Primary form ethylene polymers	3 937	0.28	24.11	16 639	0.37	35.86	13.80	4.25
723 Civil engineering plant & equipment	3 389	0.24	11.43	17 661	0.40	20.99	14.76	5.98
831 Case bag: storage travel shopping	10 205	0.72	68.06	16 007	0.36	59.68	3.38	-1.47
575 Other plastics, in primary forms	3 830	0.27	12.87	16 296	0.36	21.65	14.84	6.16
281 Iron ore and concentrates	4 208	0.30	49.01	16 159	0.36	48.37	11.88	0.63
625 Rubber for wheels, incl inner tube	4 790	0.34	20.62	15 522	0.35	31.55	10.40	4.22
848 Headgear, non-textile clothing	8 956	0.63	70.40	13 779	0.31	66.71	5.30	0.10
034 Fish, fresh live chilled frozen	7 117	0.50	37.46	15 273	0.34	40.52	7.33	1.07

For sources and notes, see end of table.

Pour les sources et les notes, se reporter à la fin du tableau

Products ranked by average 2005-2006 values SITC Revision 3 (3-digit level) / Produits classés d'après la moyenne des valeurs de 2005-2006 CTCI révision 3 (positions à 3 chiffres)	1995			2006			Growth rates (percentage) Taux d'accroissement (en pourcentage) 1995-2006	
	Value (millions of dollars) / Valeur (millions de dollars)	% of the country grouping exports / En % des exportations du groupe de pays	% of world product exports / En % des exportations mondiales des produits	Value (millions of dollars) / Valeur (millions de dollars)	% of the country grouping exports / En % des exportations du groupe de pays	% of world product exports / En % des exportations mondiales des produits	Value / Valeur	Difference from world / Différence par rapport au monde
574 Polyacetals and polyesters, etc	4 002	0.28	25.19	15 204	0.34	38.02	14.72	5.67
899 Manufactured articles nes	9 110	0.64	45.88	15 094	0.34	30.50	4.22	-4.66
655 Knitted or crocheted fabrics nes	7 292	0.51	60.49	14 474	0.32	67.18	5.68	0.78
512 Alcohols, phenols; derivatives	3 380	0.24	24.81	14 806	0.33	45.23	15.29	6.53
513 Carboxylic acid and compounds	3 858	0.27	22.82	14 478	0.32	38.90	14.91	6.84
785 Motorcycles, mopeds and cycles	6 991	0.49	37.95	14 036	0.31	39.74	7.01	0.83
671 Pig & sponge iron, ferro alloys etc	5 866	0.41	55.96	13 209	0.30	52.49	10.24	0.48
582 Plastic sheet film foil & strips	4 724	0.33	16.07	13 929	0.31	21.22	9.89	2.44
641 Paper and paperboard	6 670	0.47	9.23	13 669	0.31	13.23	6.82	2.91
081 Animal feed excluding unmilled cereal	7 156	0.50	34.89	13 085	0.29	39.58	4.91	1.23
036 Crustacean mollusc aquat invertebra	11 278	0.80	68.69	13 211	0.30	62.41	1.25	-1.13
843 Male clothing, knitted crocheted	5 592	0.39	69.97	14 155	0.32	80.89	7.17	1.71
422 Fixed veg fat and oil, excluding "soft"	6 963	0.49	89.89	13 425	0.30	86.44	5.61	-0.33
681 Silver, platinum, platinum metals	1 188	0.08	19.13	14 925	0.33	42.62	24.41	10.45
231 Natural rubber, latex, gum, etc	7 557	0.53	97.51	14 744	0.33	97.58	5.69	0.05
762 Radio broadcast receivers	15 924	1.12	70.83	12 383	0.28	65.76	-2.04	-0.79
792 Aircraft, spacecraft & equipment	3 928	0.28	5.76	13 760	0.31	8.48	10.07	4.35
054 Vegetable & vegetable products nes	6 568	0.46	31.40	12 888	0.29	35.07	5.96	0.55
611 Leather	8 132	0.57	51.22	12 640	0.28	55.12	4.24	0.78
675 Flat rolled products of alloy steel	2 486	0.18	12.20	13 429	0.30	23.57	14.73	4.83
598 Miscellaneous chemical products nes	3 631	0.26	12.28	13 303	0.30	17.61	10.78	2.52
522 Inorganic chemical elem oxide salt	5 173	0.36	31.80	12 245	0.27	37.51	7.70	1.75
674 Flat plated iron non-alloy steel	3 212	0.23	17.63	12 683	0.28	31.68	12.87	5.56
061 Sugar, mollasses and honey	7 684	0.54	48.85	13 285	0.30	58.50	2.78	1.08
542 Medicines including veterinary	2 962	0.21	6.53	12 718	0.28	5.37	12.67	-4.54
071 Coffee and coffee substitutes	12 129	0.86	77.99	11 828	0.26	64.26	-3.55	-2.35
287 Base metal ores & concentrates nes	2 633	0.19	45.06	11 686	0.26	51.12	13.67	2.73
884 Optical goods fibres nes	2 233	0.16	22.02	12 066	0.27	34.34	15.83	4.60
572 Primary form styrene polymers	4 572	0.32	41.40	11 157	0.25	53.13	9.53	2.71
634 Veneer, plywood & other wood nes	7 767	0.55	45.24	11 588	0.26	35.73	2.46	-3.39
515 Organo-inorganic compound acid salt	2 471	0.17	9.22	11 663	0.26	13.51	16.24	5.03
661 Lime cement construction material	3 401	0.24	30.83	11 345	0.25	51.40	10.25	4.82
037 Fish shellfish, prepared preserved	4 819	0.34	54.93	11 155	0.25	65.17	6.81	1.30
222 Oil seed etc for soft oil	2 939	0.21	24.01	10 022	0.22	43.92	12.24	6.96
747 Pipe, boiler, tank & vat appliances	1 876	0.13	9.62	11 604	0.26	23.23	17.18	9.16
697 Base metal household equipment nes	4 150	0.29	41.58	10 660	0.24	50.74	9.19	2.40
885 Watches and clocks	10 896	0.77	47.58	10 129	0.23	37.24	-1.09	-2.50
657 Special yarn and textile fabric etc	6 895	0.49	32.65	10 172	0.23	31.87	2.82	-0.70
872 Medical instruments appliances nes	2 334	0.16	12.23	10 327	0.23	18.39	15.43	4.94
846 Clothing accessory excluding 831 848 851	4 310	0.30	40.75	10 039	0.22	54.65	7.74	3.40
813 Lighting fixtures and fittings nes	3 596	0.25	36.54	9 475	0.21	45.13	9.37	2.62
672 Ingots, Iron steel primary products	4 286	0.30	33.66	9 032	0.20	29.53	8.73	-0.53
786 Trailer caravan transport container	3 450	0.24	35.00	9 299	0.21	34.90	10.98	1.50
695 Tools for use in hand or in machine	3 408	0.24	19.57	9 567	0.21	27.92	9.55	3.68
691 Iron steel aluminium structures nes	2 960	0.21	21.56	10 434	0.23	30.37	12.29	4.43
642 Cut paper and paperboard articles	4 451	0.31	17.46	9 054	0.20	23.23	6.09	2.49
514 Nitrogen function compounds	2 660	0.19	14.11	9 041	0.20	25.80	10.88	4.86
744 Mechanical handling equipment nes	2 851	0.20	10.15	9 411	0.21	15.17	9.63	3.35
751 Office machines	4 601	0.32	28.77	9 306	0.21	50.84	4.37	5.07
892 Printed matter	3 157	0.22	12.40	8 412	0.19	20.26	9.47	4.90
042 Rice	5 197	0.37	69.62	8 132	0.18	76.28	2.84	0.84
248 Wood simply worked, railway sleeper	4 971	0.35	18.97	8 356	0.19	21.67	4.73	1.67
694 Nails screws nuts bolts rivets	2 798	0.20	25.84	8 173	0.18	33.38	10.25	2.92
635 Wood manufactures nes	3 872	0.27	34.36	8 074	0.18	33.77	6.79	0.13
724 Textile leather machinery parts nes	3 977	0.28	15.75	7 943	0.18	29.14	6.60	5.77
553 Perfume toilet cosmetics, excluding soap	1 947	0.14	10.38	7 962	0.18	16.33	13.92	4.83
541 Pharmaceuticals excluding medicines	3 180	0.22	12.06	7 953	0.18	10.69	8.12	-2.35
516 Other organic chemicals	2 050	0.14	18.44	7 489	0.17	28.41	12.61	4.72
012 Meat nes, fresh chilled frozen	4 784	0.34	19.81	7 075	0.16	17.69	4.08	-0.42
533 Pigment, paint, varnish & related	3 007	0.21	15.00	7 369	0.16	16.94	8.88	1.73
421 Fixed veg fat and oil, "soft"	4 684	0.33	38.52	7 360	0.16	37.60	4.26	0.59

For sources and notes, see end of table.   Pour les sources et les notes, se reporter à la fin du tableau

Products ranked by average 2005-2006 values SITC Revision 3 (3-digit level) / Produits classés d'après la moyenne des valeurs de 2005-2006 CTCI révision 3 (positions à 3 chiffres)	1995			2006			Growth rates (percentage) Taux d'accroissement (en pourcentage) 1995-2006	
	Value (millions of dollars) / Valeur (millions de dollars)	% of the country grouping exports / En % des exportations du groupe de pays	% of world product exports / En % des exportations mondiales des produits	Value (millions of dollars) / Valeur (millions de dollars)	% of the country grouping exports / En % des exportations du groupe de pays	% of world product exports / En % des exportations mondiales des produits	Value / Valeur	Difference from world / Différence par rapport au monde
112 Alcoholic beverages	2 819	0.20	10.18	7 364	0.16	14.54	9.07	3.59
098 Edible products & preparations nes	2 754	0.19	15.78	7 084	0.16	20.02	8.60	1.77
664 Glass	2 404	0.17	17.13	7 187	0.16	25.87	10.90	4.21
335 Residual petroleum products nes	1 242	0.09	20.56	7 434	0.17	32.94	13.86	2.59
562 Manufactured fertilizer excluding crude	3 819	0.27	21.54	6 531	0.15	26.73	5.81	2.65
745 Non-electrical machinery tool nes	1 650	0.12	7.56	6 928	0.16	15.76	13.82	7.68
011 Beef, fresh chilled frozen	1 591	0.11	10.04	6 972	0.16	28.77	13.99	9.62
292 Crude vegetable materials nes	4 055	0.29	26.95	6 336	0.14	26.52	3.89	-0.71
072 Cocoa	3 520	0.25	67.74	6 161	0.14	66.79	5.34	-0.34
251 Pulp and waste paper	4 496	0.32	16.36	6 375	0.14	21.45	4.96	2.16
749 Non-electric machinery part nes	2 082	0.15	16.20	6 181	0.14	25.56	10.27	4.77
714 Non-electric engines excluding 712 713 718	1 330	0.09	5.07	6 158	0.14	7.86	18.64	9.22
731 Machine tools for material removal	1 889	0.13	11.59	5 800	0.13	18.10	9.32	4.60
288 Non ferrous base metal waste nes	1 932	0.14	20.99	5 921	0.13	19.94	9.51	0.61
056 Vegetables roots tubers nes	3 104	0.22	28.85	5 319	0.12	30.07	5.43	0.50
742 Liquid pump; liquid elevator parts	1 112	0.08	6.26	5 546	0.12	14.63	15.22	8.33
665 Glassware	1 870	0.13	18.46	5 271	0.12	27.09	9.96	4.00
656 Tulle lace embroidery trim etc	1 924	0.14	42.39	5 255	0.12	59.52	8.77	2.78
662 Clay and refractory materials	1 164	0.08	10.71	5 202	0.12	27.22	14.57	9.36
783 Road motor vehicles nes	1 098	0.08	6.53	4 698	0.11	13.94	13.23	6.85
554 Soaps cleansers polishes	1 988	0.14	17.39	4 894	0.11	19.79	7.99	0.67
523 Inorganic acid metal salt peroxy	1 749	0.12	23.15	5 025	0.11	35.58	9.54	4.46
058 Fruit preserve preparation excluding juice	2 189	0.15	36.12	4 753	0.11	42.53	7.04	1.67
748 Mechanical transmission equipment	1 297	0.09	8.80	4 894	0.11	14.64	13.07	5.60
659 Floor coverings etc	2 945	0.21	30.90	4 668	0.10	36.83	3.22	1.61
746 Ball or roller bearings	1 838	0.13	15.09	4 719	0.11	21.66	8.88	3.67
881 Photographic device nes	4 032	0.28	31.51	4 140	0.09	23.76	0.40	-2.17
121 Unmanufactured tabacco and refuse	2 613	0.18	49.98	4 533	0.10	61.14	1.92	0.86
654 Other woven textile fabrics nes	3 218	0.23	29.32	4 205	0.09	37.12	2.91	2.63
122 Manufactured tabacco	4 968	0.35	26.23	4 370	0.10	23.22	-2.61	-1.52
629 Articles of rubber nes	1 267	0.09	13.78	4 340	0.10	21.44	11.14	3.85
285 Aluminium ore concentrate alumina	1 936	0.14	37.04	4 503	0.10	33.80	7.24	-0.25
263 Cotton	3 388	0.24	30.64	4 468	0.10	37.87	1.32	1.27
686 Zinc	1 072	0.08	25.98	5 763	0.13	36.52	9.83	3.10
895 Office and stationery supplies nes	1 984	0.14	28.40	4 076	0.09	35.45	6.76	2.63
663 Mineral manufactures nes	1 543	0.11	11.79	4 320	0.10	17.33	9.60	4.40
059 Fruit & vegetable juice unferment	2 214	0.16	37.59	4 268	0.10	39.09	4.16	-0.31
048 Cereal & preparation flour starch	1 755	0.12	13.86	3 921	0.09	14.33	7.04	0.08
017 Meat offal preserved nes	1 368	0.10	23.30	3 988	0.09	33.84	11.10	5.12
531 Synthetic organic colour agents	2 074	0.15	21.06	3 975	0.09	35.89	5.09	4.58
591 Household and garden chemicals	1 439	0.10	13.47	3 527	0.08	21.58	8.80	5.03
696 Cutlery	1 777	0.13	42.62	3 744	0.08	47.53	7.04	0.98
666 Pottery	2 376	0.17	40.96	3 656	0.08	55.76	3.49	2.65
882 Photo cinematographic supply excluding 883	1 872	0.13	10.61	3 328	0.07	16.77	5.99	4.94
737 Metalwork machinery nes excluding tools	904	0.06	8.98	3 775	0.08	19.87	14.09	9.59
266 Synthetic fibres for spinning	3 013	0.21	50.85	3 351	0.08	56.29	1.76	1.28
278 Other crude minerals	2 171	0.15	29.19	3 291	0.07	29.29	4.77	1.03
074 Tea and maté	1 895	0.13	75.70	3 478	0.08	72.86	3.75	-0.60
573 Vinyl chloride etc polymers	1 663	0.12	21.66	3 443	0.08	25.57	6.82	1.27
232 Synthetic & reclaimed rubber; waste	1 018	0.07	17.31	3 433	0.08	24.43	11.78	4.09
693 Wire products and fencing grills	1 126	0.08	23.42	3 339	0.07	32.09	10.06	3.25
284 Nickel ores, concentrates, etc	898	0.06	44.01	3 691	0.08	48.02	11.91	-0.04
431 Processed animal & veg fats & oils	2 414	0.17	51.34	3 398	0.08	54.90	4.34	0.16
592 Starches, glutenes, glues, etc	1 172	0.08	15.28	3 356	0.08	21.92	9.64	3.39
044 Maize unmilled, excluding sweet corn	1 137	0.08	10.42	2 944	0.07	22.29	6.96	5.82
692 Metal storage transport container	1 171	0.08	16.77	3 467	0.08	25.63	8.43	3.50
022 Milk products, excluding butter & cheese	970	0.07	6.28	3 035	0.07	12.77	10.47	6.19
689 Misc non-ferrous base metals	888	0.06	27.09	3 082	0.07	36.48	11.55	4.20
247 Wood in rough or roughly squared	3 171	0.22	34.33	2 793	0.06	24.43	-1.25	-3.54
687 Tin	1 255	0.09	79.32	2 740	0.06	80.39	6.25	0.39
282 Ferrous iron & steel, waste & scrap	768	0.05	9.75	3 107	0.07	10.06	14.21	-0.18

For sources and notes, see end of table.   Pour les sources et les notes, se reporter à la fin du tableau

Products ranked by average 2005-2006 values SITC Revision 3 (3-digit level) Produits classés d'après la moyenne des valeurs de 2005-2006 CTCI révision 3 (positions à 3 chiffres)	1995			2006			Growth rates (percentage) Taux d'accroissement (en pourcentage) 1995-2006	
	Value (millions of dollars) Valeur (millions de dollars)	% of the country grouping exports En % des exportations du groupe de pays	% of world product exports En % des exportations mondiales des produits	Value (millions of dollars) Valeur (millions de dollars)	% of the country grouping exports En % des exportations du groupe de pays	% of world product exports En % des exportations mondiales des produits	Value Valeur	Difference from world Différence par rapport au monde
344 Petroleum and hydrocarbon gas nes	510	0.04	19.01	2 818	0.06	27.38	16.17	3.26
621 Rubber material e.g. paste tube rod	738	0.05	11.21	2 992	0.07	19.63	12.25	4.71
001 Live animal excluding fish & crustacean	2 210	0.16	21.07	2 660	0.06	18.42	3.43	0.57
774 Electrodiagnostic equipment	414	0.03	3.33	2 837	0.06	9.68	17.38	9.37
551 Essential oils, perfumes & flavours	870	0.06	15.38	2 648	0.06	15.63	11.25	0.60
678 Wire of iron or steel	977	0.07	22.81	2 680	0.06	32.52	9.97	3.69
812 Sanitary plumb heat fixtures nes	609	0.04	11.22	2 591	0.06	19.51	14.87	6.92
062 Sugar confectionery	1 322	0.09	29.49	2 603	0.06	36.88	5.84	1.64
325 Coke, semi coke, retort carbon	763	0.05	32.90	2 203	0.05	41.15	14.95	2.96
075 Spices	1 451	0.10	77.02	2 598	0.06	74.91	3.99	-0.57
524 Other inorganic chemicals	759	0.05	24.27	2 129	0.05	26.15	9.63	1.79
581 Plastic tube pipe hose & fittings	806	0.06	14.75	2 369	0.05	17.01	12.45	4.07
273 Stone, sand and gravel	945	0.07	25.62	2 380	0.05	34.50	8.39	3.00
351 Electric current	622	0.04	8.00	2 069	0.05	6.80	13.99	0.93
111 Non alcoholic beverage nes	994	0.07	22.08	2 052	0.05	16.26	8.19	-2.30
291 Crude animal materials nes	1 551	0.11	42.27	1 994	0.04	37.68	2.20	-0.94
041 Wheat meslin, incl spelt, unmilled	1 367	0.10	7.89	2 115	0.05	10.28	4.31	3.85
735 Machine part accessory for 731 733	408	0.03	6.25	2 047	0.05	15.53	14.62	9.15
733 Metal work tool no material removal	917	0.06	13.13	1 894	0.04	18.83	6.73	4.65
726 Printing bookbinding machines parts	601	0.04	4.30	1 963	0.04	9.61	11.34	8.79
791 Railway vehicles and equipment	319	0.02	4.52	2 107	0.05	11.52	12.86	4.04
721 Agricultural machine nes excluding tractor	487	0.03	4.65	1 876	0.04	8.35	12.63	6.27
873 Meters and counters nes	331	0.02	9.24	1 735	0.04	24.58	14.45	7.81
683 Nickel	333	0.02	6.48	2 105	0.05	9.61	18.70	6.49
579 Plastic waste, parings and scrap	624	0.04	49.93	1 775	0.04	40.57	11.16	-2.37
612 Leather manufactures nes	519	0.04	50.44	1 694	0.04	49.73	12.08	-0.18
268 Wool & animal hair, incl wool tops	1 771	0.12	24.46	1 661	0.04	31.97	-1.27	1.71
073 Chocolate & cocoa preparations nes	491	0.03	6.15	1 405	0.03	10.08	10.75	5.49
597 Additive e.g. lubricate, antifreeze	575	0.04	7.89	1 639	0.04	12.54	10.07	5.44
289 Prec metal ore concentrate excluding gold	341	0.02	27.82	1 931	0.04	30.44	3.98	-5.45
722 Tractors	319	0.02	3.71	1 455	0.03	9.40	16.04	11.65
272 Crude fertilizer, excluding manufactured	931	0.07	71.76	1 341	0.03	73.83	1.80	0.11
896 Work of art & collections; antiques	293	0.02	4.52	1 502	0.03	8.80	15.49	6.71
685 Lead	402	0.03	27.79	1 526	0.03	39.40	9.78	3.69
711 Steam generating boilers & parts	275	0.02	8.89	1 241	0.03	30.97	12.93	12.38
811 Prefabricated buildings	146	0.01	5.38	1 323	0.03	20.86	19.21	12.33
718 Power generating machinery part nes	235	0.02	4.52	1 103	0.02	8.44	13.22	4.55
246 Wood chips, particles and waste	632	0.04	30.11	989	0.02	30.25	5.08	1.39
211 Raw hides & skins, excluding furskins	761	0.05	12.76	1 020	0.02	16.45	4.10	3.32
046 Wheat meal & flour, meslin flour	590	0.04	21.01	893	0.02	36.55	1.97	4.00
725 Paper & pulp mill, cut manufacture	511	0.04	6.33	965	0.02	9.68	5.80	4.60
727 Food processing machine excluding domestic	478	0.03	7.39	1 005	0.02	9.68	5.13	1.54
035 Fish, dried salted smoked	674	0.05	24.34	937	0.02	23.63	3.75	0.66
613 Furskin tanned dressed etc	345	0.02	26.07	862	0.02	48.01	8.47	7.31
891 Arms and ammunition	244	0.02	3.12	834	0.02	10.10	13.63	13.89
091 Margarine and shortening	417	0.03	25.11	809	0.02	27.36	5.77	1.34
593 Explosives and pyrotechnic products	397	0.03	34.37	821	0.02	36.34	6.30	1.02
024 Cheese and curd	154	0.01	1.39	756	0.02	4.09	13.51	8.74
267 Man made fibre for spinning; waste	380	0.03	12.78	783	0.02	22.56	4.87	3.01
277 Natural abrasives nes	381	0.03	38.08	625	0.01	56.98	9.61	7.18
532 Dyeing and tanning extracts	305	0.02	35.78	554	0.01	38.69	5.30	0.90
269 Worn clothing, textile article; rag	310	0.02	20.69	531	0.01	23.26	3.00	0.49
212 Raw furskins and furskin pieces	154	0.01	12.18	553	0.01	17.95	12.98	6.63
712 Steam vapour turbines & parts nes	127	0.01	4.67	578	0.01	13.58	13.78	10.38
525 Radio active & associated materials	321	0.02	7.03	580	0.01	6.19	3.15	-2.09
223 Oil seed for non soft oil	267	0.02	37.04	416	0.01	28.93	4.24	-1.86
411 Animals oils and fats	232	0.02	10.27	434	0.01	15.80	6.58	4.34
274 Sulphur and unroasted iron pyrites	142	0.01	16.81	469	0.01	36.67	15.33	9.79
025 Eggs, yolks and albumin	175	0.01	12.13	380	0.01	15.73	5.68	1.83
583 Plastic rod stick & profile shapes	46	0.00	3.11	425	0.01	9.99	21.91	11.99
931 Transaction commodity unclassified	26	0.00	5.90	288	0.01	24.85	35.74	24.70

Sources:
- Data and UNCTAD secretariat estimates based on UN DESA Comtrade and IMF Direction of Trade statistics databases

Sources :
- Données et estimations du secrétariat de la CNUCED sur la base de données Comtrade de ONU DAES et Direction of Trade statistics du Fonds Monétaire international

3.2.D Export structure by product
Individual countries and territories

3.2.D Structure des exportations par produits
Pays et territoires individuels

Leading products exported based on average 2005-2006 values SITC Revision 3 (3-digit level) / Principaux produits exportés d'après la moyenne des valeurs de 2005-2006 CTCI révision 3 (positions à 3 chiffres)	2005-2006 Value (f.o.b., thousands of dollars) / Valeur (f.a.b., milliers de dollars)	of country total / du total du pays	of ** (1) / des ** (1)	of world / du monde
Albania - Albanie (**=Transition)				
All commodity groups	725 431	100.0	0.18	0.01
851 Footwear	192 187	26.5	20.74	0.28
841 Male clothing, woven	93 803	12.9	10.92	0.17
845 Articles of apparel nes	42 835	5.9	5.92	0.04
844 Female clothing, knitted crocheted	31 301	4.3	13.62	0.11
699 Base metal manufactures nes	30 212	4.2	2.06	0.03
288 Non ferrous base metal waste nes	28 705	4.0	8.96	0.12
671 Pig & sponge iron, ferro alloys etc	20 157	2.8	0.37	0.08
037 Fish shellfish, prepared preserved	18 869	2.6	9.45	0.12
842 Female clothing, woven	17 633	2.4	1.75	0.03
292 Crude vegetable materials nes	16 500	2.3	17.27	0.07
Remainder	233 228	32.2		
Algeria - Algérie (**=Developing)				
All commodity groups	50 307 229	100.0	1.22	0.45
333 Crude petroleum & bituminous oil	27 451 194	54.6	4.47	3.27
343 Natural gas, liquefied or not	14 323 714	28.5	23.79	8.12
342 Liquefied propane and butane	3 848 497	7.6	21.21	13.69
334 Heavy petroleum & bituminous oil	3 657 407	7.3	1.92	0.88
522 Inorganic chemical elem oxide salt	188 525	0.4	1.63	0.61
335 Residual petroleum products nes	126 049	0.3	1.90	0.63
282 Ferrous iron & steel, waste & scrap	120 047	0.2	4.46	0.44
288 Non ferrous base metal waste nes	92 632	0.2	1.81	0.39
686 Zinc	60 337	0.1	1.52	0.54
673 Flat iron non-alloy steel products	51 443	0.1	0.25	0.07
Remainder	387 384	0.8		
Andorra - Andorre (**=Developed)				
All commodity groups	162 062	100.0	0.00	0.00
061 Sugar, mollasses and honey	38 818	24.0	0.49	0.19
781 Passenger cars and race cars	21 713	13.4	0.00	0.00
763 Sound TV recorder or reproducer	20 581	12.7	0.08	0.03
892 Printed matter	6 610	4.1	0.02	0.02
899 Manufactured articles nes	6 239	3.8	0.02	0.01
898 Music instrument device recording	5 749	3.5	0.02	0.01
553 Perfume toilet cosmetics, excl. soap	4 332	2.7	0.01	0.01
744 Mechanical handling equipment nes	4 227	2.6	0.01	0.01
896 Work of art & collections; antiques	3 504	2.2	0.02	0.02
845 Articles of apparel nes	2 396	1.5	0.01	0.00
Remainder	47 892	29.6		
Angola (**=Developing)				
All commodity groups	26 945 281	100.0	0.66	0.24
333 Crude petroleum & bituminous oil	25 656 849	95.2	4.18	3.06
667 Pearls, precious semiprecious stone	615 274	2.3	1.75	0.66
334 Heavy petroleum & bituminous oil	294 629	1.1	0.15	0.07
342 Liquefied propane and butane	120 260	0.4	0.66	0.43
763 Sound TV recorder or reproducer	42 896	0.2	0.12	0.07
344 Petroleum and hydrocarbon gas nes	33 105	0.1	1.27	0.34
036 Crustacean mollusc aquat invertebra	25 525	0.1	0.20	0.12
893 Articles of plastic nes	25 313	0.1	0.09	0.03
273 Stone, sand and gravel	20 463	0.1	0.95	0.32
874 Measure analyze control device nes	9 193	0.0	0.05	0.01
Remainder	101 774	0.4		
Antigua and Barbuda - Antigua-et-Barbuda (**=Developing)				
All commodity groups	123 210	100.0	0.00	0.00
334 Heavy petroleum & bituminous oil	74 426	60.4	0.04	0.02
793 Ships boats floating structures	24 006	19.5	0.07	0.03
764 Telecommunicate equipment part nes	5 377	4.4	0.00	0.00
574 Polyacetals and polyesters, etc	2 170	1.8	0.02	0.01
658 Made-up textile articles nes	1 759	1.4	0.01	0.01
892 Printed matter	1 702	1.4	0.02	0.00
674 Flat plated iron non-alloy steel	1 626	1.3	0.01	0.00
533 Pigment, paint, varnish & related	750	0.6	0.01	0.00
744 Mechanical handling equipment nes	669	0.5	0.01	0.00
034 Fish, fresh live chilled frozen	653	0.5	0.00	0.00
Remainder	10 073	8.2		
Argentina - Argentine (**=Developing)				
All commodity groups	43 264 778	100.0	1.05	0.39
081 Animal feed excluding unmilled cereal	4 342 509	10.0	34.14	13.68
421 Fixed veg fat and oil, "soft"	3 372 715	7.8	48.53	18.64
334 Heavy petroleum & bituminous oil	2 593 292	6.0	1.36	0.62
333 Crude petroleum & bituminous oil	2 456 189	5.7	0.40	0.29
222 Oil seed etc for soft oil	2 178 806	5.0	21.35	9.83
041 Wheat meslin, incl spelt, unmilled	1 375 577	3.2	70.66	7.19
283 Copper ores and concentrates	1 316 098	3.0	6.75	5.29
044 Maize unmilled, excluding sweet corn	1 314 004	3.0	42.64	10.75
782 Goods and service vehicles	1 246 547	2.9	5.88	1.32
011 Beef, fresh chilled frozen	1 142 183	2.6	17.91	4.99
Remainder	21 926 860	50.7		
Armenia - Arménie (**=Transition)				
All commodity groups	970 469	100.0	0.24	0.01
667 Pearls, precious semiprecious stone	255 363	26.3	12.90	0.28
671 Pig & sponge iron, ferro alloys etc	198 186	20.4	3.63	0.78
112 Alcoholic beverages	78 356	8.1	6.77	0.16
682 Copper	57 393	5.9	0.89	0.07
283 Copper ores and concentrates	44 705	4.6	18.08	0.18
971 Gold non-monetary excluding ores	36 578	3.8	4.73	0.08
897 Jewellery nes (667)	35 280	3.6	18.00	0.08
287 Base metal ores & concentrates nes	24 619	2.5	4.74	0.12
845 Articles of apparel nes	21 181	2.2	2.93	0.02
661 Lime cement construction material	20 594	2.1	2.70	0.10
Remainder	198 214	20.4		
Australia - Australie (**=Developed)				
All commodity groups	114 537 134	100.0	1.73	1.03
321 Coal excluding non-agglomerated	17 100 522	14.9	64.27	35.88
281 Iron ore and concentrates	9 641 053	8.4	73.14	31.56
971 Gold non-monetary excluding ores	5 672 151	5.0	24.11	11.67
333 Crude petroleum & bituminous oil	4 934 526	4.3	4.33	0.59
285 Aluminium ore concentrate alumina	4 066 074	3.6	59.03	34.12
684 Aluminium	3 926 244	3.4	6.73	4.47
011 Beef, fresh chilled frozen	3 614 403	3.2	22.28	15.81
343 Natural gas, liquefied or not	3 277 930	2.9	4.32	1.86
283 Copper ores and concentrates	2 503 599	2.2	48.64	10.06
041 Wheat meslin, incl spelt, unmilled	2 407 306	2.1	16.18	12.59
Remainder	57 393 327	50.1		
Austria - Autriche (**=Developed)				
All commodity groups	125 896 542	100.0	1.90	1.13
781 Passenger cars and race cars	8 214 163	6.5	1.86	1.62
351 Electric current	4 493 367	3.6	18.81	16.43
713 Internal combustion engine part nes	4 343 622	3.5	4.32	3.67
784 Motor vehicle parts and accessories	3 503 905	2.8	1.77	1.43
542 Medicines including veterinary	3 306 252	2.6	1.58	1.49
641 Paper and paperboard	3 283 140	2.6	3.87	3.30
728 Special industrial machine part nes	3 013 263	2.4	3.47	2.89
699 Base metal manufactures nes	2 787 521	2.2	4.07	2.83
764 Telecommunicate equipment part nes	2 172 521	1.7	1.13	0.56
772 Electrical circuit equipment	2 023 179	1.6	2.17	1.32
Remainder	88 755 609	70.5		
Azerbaijan - Azerbaïdjan (**=Transition)				
All commodity groups	5 359 658	100.0	1.35	0.05
333 Crude petroleum & bituminous oil	3 033 655	56.6	2.70	0.36
334 Heavy petroleum & bituminous oil	1 297 632	24.2	2.53	0.31
793 Ships boats floating structures	169 034	3.2	7.11	0.21
285 Aluminium ore concentrate alumina	126 834	2.4	12.62	1.06
057 Fruit nut (exc oil), fresh or dried	122 568	2.3	16.59	0.25
684 Aluminium	61 966	1.2	0.76	0.07
571 Primary form ethylene polymers	50 010	0.9	6.29	0.12
263 Cotton	39 870	0.7	3.37	0.36
054 Vegetable & vegetable products nes	31 379	0.6	7.04	0.09
431 Processed animal & veg fats & oils	29 228	0.5	52.91	0.50
Remainder	397 483	7.4		

For sources and notes, see end of table.

Pour les sources et les notes, se reporter à la fin du tableau.

156

Leading products exported based on average 2005-2006 values SITC Revision 3 (3-digit level) / Principaux produits exportés d'après la moyenne des valeurs de 2005-2006 CTCI révision 3 (positions à 3 chiffres)	Value (f.o.b., thousands of dollars) Valeur (f.a.b., milliers de dollars)	2005-2006 As percentage En pourcentage		
		of country total du total du pays	of ** (1) des ** (1)	of world du monde
Bahamas (=Developing)**				
All commodity groups	465 994	100.0	0.01	0.00
572 Primary form styrene polymers	108 200	23.2	1.00	0.54
334 Heavy petroleum & bituminous oil	88 911	19.1	0.05	0.02
036 Crustacean mollusc aquat invertebra	74 126	15.9	0.58	0.36
793 Ships boats floating structures	34 911	7.5	0.10	0.04
515 Organo-inorganic compound acid salt	33 611	7.2	0.32	0.04
112 Alcoholic beverages	21 139	4.5	0.30	0.04
278 Other crude minerals	9 849	2.1	0.30	0.09
542 Medicines including veterinary	9 303	2.0	0.08	0.00
553 Perfume toilet cosmetics, excl. soap	8 490	1.8	0.11	0.02
713 Internal combustion engine part nes	5 476	1.2	0.03	0.00
Remainder	71 978	15.4		
Bahrain - Bahreïn (=Developing)**				
All commodity groups	10 950 096	100.0	0.27	0.10
334 Heavy petroleum & bituminous oil	8 502 802	77.7	4.47	2.04
684 Aluminium	1 357 141	12.4	6.40	1.55
281 Iron ore and concentrates	166 192	1.5	1.12	0.54
562 Manufactured fertilizer excl. crude	131 990	1.2	2.04	0.55
781 Passenger cars and race cars	93 224	0.9	0.14	0.02
512 Alcohols, phenols; derivatives	76 569	0.7	0.56	0.25
842 Female clothing, woven	47 348	0.4	0.11	0.07
652 Woven cotton fabrics	39 578	0.4	0.22	0.14
741 Heating cooling equipment parts nes	38 923	0.4	0.18	0.05
893 Articles of plastic nes	27 838	0.3	0.09	0.03
Remainder	468 490	4.3		
Bangladesh (=Developing)**				
All commodity groups	10 694 795	100.0	0.26	0.10
845 Articles of apparel nes	3 631 956	34.0	5.38	3.64
841 Male clothing, woven	2 318 018	21.7	6.69	4.32
842 Female clothing, woven	1 458 782	13.6	3.32	2.16
843 Male clothing, knitted crocheted	478 355	4.5	3.79	3.02
844 Female clothing, knitted crocheted	415 225	3.9	1.99	1.47
036 Crustacean mollusc aquat invertebra	404 925	3.8	3.19	1.98
658 Made-up textile articles nes	389 272	3.6	1.70	1.20
611 Leather	254 953	2.4	2.13	1.17
651 Textile yarn	204 668	1.9	0.86	0.48
848 Headgear, non-textile clothing	129 429	1.2	0.90	0.62
Remainder	1 009 214	9.4		
Barbados - Barbade (=Developing)**				
All commodity groups	401 228	100.0	0.01	0.00
334 Heavy petroleum & bituminous oil	105 893	26.4	0.06	0.03
112 Alcoholic beverages	29 995	7.5	0.43	0.06
061 Sugar, mollasses and honey	20 952	5.2	0.18	0.10
542 Medicines including veterinary	20 272	5.1	0.18	0.01
333 Crude petroleum & bituminous oil	19 905	5.0	0.00	0.00
764 Telecommunicate equipment part nes	17 386	4.3	0.01	0.00
661 Lime cement construction material	16 964	4.2	0.16	0.08
772 Electrical circuit equipment	15 950	4.0	0.03	0.01
591 Household and garden chemicals	12 507	3.1	0.34	0.08
897 Jewellery nes (667)	11 776	2.9	0.06	0.03
Remainder	129 629	32.3		
Belarus - Bélarus (=Transition)**				
All commodity groups	17 857 882	100.0	4.49	0.16
334 Heavy petroleum & bituminous oil	5 791 238	32.4	11.30	1.39
562 Manufactured fertilizer excl. crude	1 124 848	6.3	17.62	4.65
782 Goods and service vehicles	700 006	3.9	43.29	0.74
722 Tractors	509 514	2.9	81.04	3.44
333 Crude petroleum & bituminous oil	490 901	2.7	0.44	0.06
676 Iron steel bar rod section piling	387 190	2.2	7.50	0.67
775 Household equipment nes	312 966	1.8	45.87	0.47
625 Rubber for wheels, incl inner tube	298 305	1.7	26.05	0.64
821 Furniture part; bedding furnishing	283 361	1.6	21.51	0.28
783 Road motor vehicles nes	263 118	1.5	52.07	0.82
Remainder	7 696 434	43.1		

Leading products exported based on average 2005-2006 values SITC Revision 3 (3-digit level) / Principaux produits exportés d'après la moyenne des valeurs de 2005-2006 CTCI révision 3 (positions à 3 chiffres)	Value (f.o.b., thousands of dollars) Valeur (f.a.b., milliers de dollars)	2005-2006 As percentage En pourcentage		
		of country total du total du pays	of ** (1) des ** (1)	of world du monde
Belgium - Belgique (=Developed)**				
All commodity groups	351 681 184	100.0	5.32	3.16
542 Medicines including veterinary	31 103 103	8.8	14.83	14.03
781 Passenger cars and race cars	29 510 296	8.4	6.68	5.81
667 Pearls, precious semiprecious stone	15 905 627	4.5	28.56	17.13
334 Heavy petroleum & bituminous oil	14 561 136	4.1	8.33	3.50
515 Organo-inorganic compound acid salt	12 674 059	3.6	17.70	15.29
575 Other plastics, in primary forms	7 797 411	2.2	14.17	11.07
784 Motor vehicle parts and accessories	7 141 090	2.0	3.60	2.91
343 Natural gas, liquefied or not	6 982 077	2.0	9.20	3.96
541 Pharmaceuticals excluding medicines	5 487 103	1.6	8.71	7.79
673 Flat iron non-alloy steel products	5 282 995	1.5	13.72	7.69
Remainder	215 236 287	61.2		
Belize (=Developing)**				
All commodity groups	240 975	100.0	0.01	0.00
059 Fruit & vegetable juice unferment	55 019	22.8	1.43	0.55
061 Sugar, mollasses and honey	43 954	18.2	0.39	0.22
036 Crustacean mollusc aquat invertebra	42 303	17.6	0.33	0.21
057 Fruit nut (exc oil), fresh or dried	39 783	16.5	0.19	0.08
333 Crude petroleum & bituminous oil	22 193	9.2	0.00	0.00
843 Male clothing, knitted crocheted	16 809	7.0	0.13	0.11
054 Vegetable & vegetable products nes	3 692	1.5	0.03	0.01
551 Essential oils, perfumes & flavours	3 638	1.5	0.15	0.02
634 Veneer, plywood & other wood nes	1 043	0.4	0.01	0.00
642 Cut paper and paperboard articles	1 036	0.4	0.01	0.00
Remainder	11 506	4.8		
Benin - Bénin (=Developing)**				
All commodity groups	285 644	100.0	0.01	0.00
263 Cotton	173 084	60.6	4.30	1.57
057 Fruit nut (exc oil), fresh or dried	19 215	6.7	0.09	0.04
122 Manufactured tabacco	19 022	6.7	0.46	0.10
661 Lime cement construction material	11 603	4.1	0.11	0.06
421 Fixed veg fat and oil, "soft"	6 123	2.1	0.09	0.03
676 Iron steel bar rod section piling	5 952	2.1	0.04	0.01
971 Gold non-monetary excluding ores	5 360	1.9	0.02	0.01
081 Animal feed excluding unmilled cereal	5 092	1.8	0.04	0.02
248 Wood simply worked, railway sleeper	3 914	1.4	0.05	0.01
223 Oil seed for non soft oil	3 578	1.3	0.85	0.25
Remainder	32 701	11.4		
Bolivia - Bolivie (=Developing)**				
All commodity groups	3 510 357	100.0	0.09	0.03
343 Natural gas, liquefied or not	1 326 526	37.8	2.20	0.75
287 Base metal ores & concentrates nes	435 047	12.4	4.00	2.13
333 Crude petroleum & bituminous oil	327 293	9.3	0.05	0.04
081 Animal feed excluding unmilled cereal	216 039	6.2	1.70	0.68
421 Fixed veg fat and oil, "soft"	140 196	4.0	2.02	0.77
289 Prec metal ore concentrate excl. gold	126 025	3.6	8.30	2.49
687 Tin	109 605	3.1	4.01	3.33
971 Gold non-monetary excluding ores	102 828	2.9	0.42	0.21
057 Fruit nut (exc oil), fresh or dried	81 936	2.3	0.40	0.17
897 Jewellery nes (667)	71 040	2.0	0.34	0.16
Remainder	573 822	16.3		
Bosnia and Herzegovina - Bosnie-Herzégovine (=Transition)**				
All commodity groups	2 908 132	100.0	0.73	0.03
684 Aluminium	308 050	10.6	3.77	0.35
713 Internal combustion engine part nes	198 186	6.8	28.39	0.17
821 Furniture part; bedding furnishing	191 063	6.6	14.50	0.19
248 Wood simply worked, railway sleeper	174 168	6.0	5.82	0.47
676 Iron steel bar rod section piling	139 520	4.8	2.70	0.24
851 Footwear	135 435	4.7	14.62	0.20
351 Electric current	130 173	4.5	10.03	0.48
285 Aluminium ore concentrate alumina	125 466	4.3	12.48	1.05
325 Coke, semi coke, retort carbon	79 700	2.7	13.74	1.39
691 Iron steel aluminium structures nes	75 051	2.6	10.61	0.24
Remainder	1 351 320	46.5		

For sources and notes, see end of table.

Pour les sources et les notes, se reporter à la fin du tableau.

157

3.2.D Export structure by product
Individual countries and territories

3.2.D Structure des exportations par produits
Pays et territoires individuels

Leading products exported based on average 2005-2006 values SITC Revision 3 (3-digit level)

Principaux produits exportés d'après la moyenne des valeurs de 2005-2006 CTCI révision 3 (positions à 3 chiffres)

Columns: Value (f.o.b., thousands of dollars) / Valeur (f.a.b., milliers de dollars); As percentage / En pourcentage — of country total (du total du pays); of ** (1) (des ** (1)); of world (du monde). Period: 2005-2006.

Botswana (**=Developing)

Product	Value	of country total	of ** (1)	of world
All commodity groups	4 468 405	100.0	0.11	0.04
667 Pearls, precious semiprecious stone	3 280 365	73.4	9.33	3.53
283 Copper ores and concentrates	565 969	12.7	2.90	2.27
011 Beef, fresh chilled frozen	77 056	1.7	1.21	0.34
845 Articles of apparel nes	76 848	1.7	0.11	0.08
842 Female clothing, woven	42 559	1.0	0.10	0.06
783 Road motor vehicles nes	41 057	0.9	0.86	0.13
277 Natural abrasives nes	38 297	0.9	5.50	3.32
971 Gold non-monetary excluding ores	30 879	0.7	0.13	0.06
841 Male clothing, woven	24 422	0.5	0.07	0.05
523 Inorganic acid metal salt peroxy	21 159	0.5	0.45	0.16
Remainder	269 794	6.0		

Brazil - Brésil (**=Developing)

Product	Value	of country total	of ** (1)	of world
All commodity groups	128 167 439	100.0	3.12	1.15
281 Iron ore and concentrates	8 122 756	6.3	54.62	26.59
222 Oil seed etc for soft oil	5 536 533	4.3	54.24	24.98
333 Crude petroleum & bituminous oil	5 529 640	4.3	0.90	0.66
061 Sugar, mollasses and honey	5 079 542	4.0	44.64	25.32
781 Passenger cars and race cars	4 496 330	3.5	6.89	0.88
012 Meat nes, fresh chilled frozen	4 460 184	3.5	62.30	11.26
784 Motor vehicle parts and accessories	3 696 813	2.9	7.99	1.50
792 Aircraft, spacecraft & equipment	3 373 399	2.6	27.61	2.32
334 Heavy petroleum & bituminous oil	3 202 122	2.5	1.68	0.77
071 Coffee and coffee substitutes	3 146 419	2.5	28.69	18.41
Remainder	81 523 702	63.6		

Brunei Darussalam - Brunéi Darussalam (**=Developing)

Product	Value	of country total	of ** (1)	of world
All commodity groups	6 770 863	100.0	0.16	0.06
333 Crude petroleum & bituminous oil	4 352 437	64.3	0.71	0.52
343 Natural gas, liquefied or not	2 068 944	30.6	3.44	1.17
845 Articles of apparel nes	94 449	1.4	0.14	0.09
844 Female clothing, knitted crocheted	36 452	0.5	0.17	0.13
793 Ships boats floating structures	36 109	0.5	0.10	0.05
792 Aircraft, spacecraft & equipment	19 328	0.3	0.16	0.01
731 Machine tools for material removal	16 705	0.2	0.32	0.06
843 Male clothing, knitted crocheted	13 594	0.2	0.11	0.09
695 Tools for use in hand or in machine	13 491	0.2	0.15	0.04
728 Special industrial machine part nes	10 979	0.2	0.06	0.01
Remainder	108 375	1.6		

Bulgaria - Bulgarie (**=Developed)

Product	Value	of country total	of ** (1)	of world
All commodity groups	13 420 469	100.0	0.20	0.12
334 Heavy petroleum & bituminous oil	1 602 644	11.9	0.92	0.38
682 Copper	1 436 379	10.7	3.71	1.65
673 Flat iron non-alloy steel products	572 289	4.3	1.49	0.83
842 Female clothing, woven	487 700	3.6	2.16	0.72
841 Male clothing, woven	468 615	3.5	2.58	0.87
845 Articles of apparel nes	431 946	3.2	1.36	0.43
844 Female clothing, knitted crocheted	266 181	2.0	3.70	0.94
851 Footwear	253 465	1.9	0.87	0.37
793 Ships boats floating structures	215 932	1.6	0.52	0.27
821 Furniture part; bedding furnishing	207 977	1.5	0.32	0.20
Remainder	7 477 341	55.7		

Burkina Faso (**=Developing)

Product	Value	of country total	of ** (1)	of world
All commodity groups	433 528	100.0	0.01	0.00
263 Cotton	253 269	58.4	6.29	2.30
057 Fruit nut (exc oil), fresh or dried	63 255	14.6	0.30	0.13
222 Oil seed etc for soft oil	14 328	3.3	0.14	0.06
054 Vegetable & vegetable products nes	7 316	1.7	0.06	0.02
122 Manufactured tabacco	5 830	1.3	0.14	0.03
611 Leather	4 919	1.1	0.04	0.02
022 Milk products, excl. butter & cheese	4 610	1.1	0.16	0.02
061 Sugar, mollasses and honey	4 316	1.0	0.04	0.02
001 Live animal excl. fish & crustacean	3 956	0.9	0.16	0.03
971 Gold non-monetary excluding ores	3 954	0.9	0.02	0.01
Remainder	67 774	15.6		

Burundi (**=Developing)

Product	Value	of country total	of ** (1)	of world
All commodity groups	118 626	100.0	0.00	0.00
971 Gold non-monetary excluding ores	57 990	48.9	0.24	0.12
071 Coffee and coffee substitutes	47 130	39.7	0.43	0.28
061 Sugar, mollasses and honey	1 911	1.6	0.02	0.01
112 Alcoholic beverages	1 641	1.4	0.02	0.00
263 Cotton	1 439	1.2	0.04	0.01
782 Goods and service vehicles	1 247	1.1	0.01	0.00
287 Base metal ores & concentrates nes	894	0.8	0.01	0.00
122 Manufactured tabacco	892	0.8	0.02	0.00
074 Tea and maté	846	0.7	0.03	0.02
211 Raw hides & skins, excluding furskins	387	0.3	0.04	0.01
Remainder	4 251	3.6		

Cambodia - Cambodge (**=Developing)

Product	Value	of country total	of ** (1)	of world
All commodity groups	3 567 432	100.0	0.09	0.03
845 Articles of apparel nes	1 073 877	30.1	1.59	1.07
842 Female clothing, woven	608 309	17.1	1.39	0.90
844 Female clothing, knitted crocheted	451 891	12.7	2.17	1.60
841 Male clothing, woven	366 648	10.3	1.06	0.68
843 Male clothing, knitted crocheted	244 493	6.9	1.94	1.54
036 Crustacean mollusc aquat invertebra	151 751	4.3	1.20	0.74
851 Footwear	119 576	3.4	0.31	0.17
764 Telecommunicate equipment part nes	52 452	1.5	0.03	0.01
651 Textile yarn	47 061	1.3	0.20	0.11
655 Knitted or crocheted fabrics nes	43 710	1.2	0.32	0.21
Remainder	407 663	11.4		

Cameroon - Cameroun (**=Developing)

Product	Value	of country total	of ** (1)	of world
All commodity groups	3 008 518	100.0	0.07	0.03
333 Crude petroleum & bituminous oil	1 310 658	43.6	0.21	0.16
334 Heavy petroleum & bituminous oil	396 653	13.2	0.21	0.10
072 Cocoa	252 870	8.4	4.27	2.82
248 Wood simply worked, railway sleeper	229 037	7.6	2.98	0.62
684 Aluminium	142 549	4.7	0.67	0.16
263 Cotton	118 169	3.9	2.94	1.07
057 Fruit nut (exc oil), fresh or dried	67 444	2.2	0.33	0.14
071 Coffee and coffee substitutes	64 586	2.1	0.59	0.38
231 Natural rubber, latex, gum, etc	54 865	1.8	0.45	0.44
247 Wood in rough or roughly squared	42 850	1.4	1.56	0.39
Remainder	328 837	10.9		

Canada (**=Developed)

Product	Value	of country total	of ** (1)	of world
All commodity groups	374 283 349	100.0	5.66	3.37
781 Passenger cars and race cars	37 556 693	10.0	8.50	7.39
333 Crude petroleum & bituminous oil	29 121 583	7.8	25.56	3.47
343 Natural gas, liquefied or not	27 095 047	7.2	35.72	15.36
784 Motor vehicle parts and accessories	13 677 802	3.7	6.90	5.57
641 Paper and paperboard	10 687 705	2.9	12.60	10.74
334 Heavy petroleum & bituminous oil	10 223 111	2.7	5.85	2.46
782 Goods and service vehicles	9 644 146	2.6	13.40	10.18
248 Wood simply worked, railway sleeper	8 780 581	2.3	33.52	23.82
792 Aircraft, spacecraft & equipment	8 403 769	2.2	6.36	5.77
684 Aluminium	7 869 815	2.1	13.48	8.97
Remainder	211 223 096	56.4		

Cape Verde - Cap-Vert (**=Developing)

Product	Value	of country total	of ** (1)	of world
All commodity groups	99 853	100.0	0.00	0.00
334 Heavy petroleum & bituminous oil	47 198	47.3	0.02	0.01
786 Trailer caravan transport container	12 894	12.9	0.14	0.05
034 Fish, fresh live chilled frozen	10 823	10.8	0.08	0.03
793 Ships boats floating structures	3 962	4.0	0.01	0.00
851 Footwear	2 897	2.9	0.01	0.00
841 Male clothing, woven	2 549	2.6	0.01	0.00
874 Measure analyze control device nes	2 325	2.3	0.01	0.00
713 Internal combustion engine part nes	2 142	2.1	0.01	0.00
843 Male clothing, knitted crocheted	1 538	1.5	0.01	0.01
716 Rotating electric plant parts nes	990	1.0	0.01	0.00
Remainder	12 536	12.6		

For sources and notes, see end of table.

Pour les sources et les notes, se reporter à la fin du tableau.

Leading products exported based on average 2005-2006 values SITC Revision 3 (3-digit level) / Principaux produits exportés d'après la moyenne des valeurs de 2005-2006 CTCI révision 3 (positions à 3 chiffres)	Value (f.o.b., thousands of dollars) Valeur (f.a.b., milliers de dollars)	of country total du total du pays	of ** (1) des ** (1)	of world du monde
Central African Republic - République centrafricaine (**=Developing)				
All commodity groups	130 279	100.0	0.00	0.00
667 Pearls, precious semiprecious stone	44 785	34.4	0.13	0.05
247 Wood in rough or roughly squared	32 009	24.6	1.17	0.29
277 Natural abrasives nes	28 472	21.9	4.09	2.47
248 Wood simply worked, railway sleeper	15 536	11.9	0.20	0.04
071 Coffee and coffee substitutes	1 066	0.8	0.01	0.01
782 Goods and service vehicles	657	0.5	0.00	0.00
263 Cotton	526	0.4	0.01	0.00
334 Heavy petroleum & bituminous oil	394	0.3	0.00	0.00
781 Passenger cars and race cars	254	0.2	0.00	0.00
658 Made-up textile articles nes	247	0.2	0.00	0.00
Remainder	6 333	4.9		
Chile - Chili (**=Developing)				
All commodity groups	47 238 294	100.0	1.15	0.42
682 Copper	16 001 722	33.9	38.23	18.39
283 Copper ores and concentrates	8 855 066	18.7	45.44	35.59
287 Base metal ores & concentrates nes	2 561 354	5.4	23.57	12.56
034 Fish, fresh live chilled frozen	2 212 058	4.7	15.38	6.17
057 Fruit nut (exc oil), fresh or dried	1 970 308	4.2	9.50	4.08
251 Pulp and waste paper	1 273 323	2.7	21.67	4.58
248 Wood simply worked, railway sleeper	1 026 686	2.2	13.36	2.78
112 Alcoholic beverages	932 569	2.0	13.45	1.94
334 Heavy petroleum & bituminous oil	889 212	1.9	0.47	0.21
512 Alcohols, phenols; derivatives	707 925	1.5	5.19	2.29
Remainder	10 808 070	22.9		
China - Chine (**=Developing)				
All commodity groups	865 444 505	100.0	21.06	7.78
752 Computer equipment nes	84 658 352	9.8	51.55	29.67
764 Telecommunicate equipment part nes	73 579 514	8.5	37.36	18.85
759 Office equipment part & accessories	32 194 220	3.7	26.95	15.22
845 Articles of apparel nes	28 141 977	3.3	41.72	28.17
776 Valves tubes; diodes, transistors	24 811 060	2.9	10.38	6.28
894 Baby carriage toy game sport good	22 470 512	2.6	55.94	33.20
763 Sound TV recorder or reproducer	20 860 730	2.4	56.80	33.54
851 Footwear	20 432 940	2.4	52.14	29.54
778 Electrical machinery apparatus nes	18 818 781	2.2	28.52	11.97
821 Furniture part; bedding furnishing	18 731 461	2.2	50.96	18.26
Remainder	520 744 959	60.2		
China, Hong Kong SAR - Chine (RAS de Hong Kong) (**=Developing)				
All commodity groups	307 393 733	100.0	7.48	2.77
776 Valves tubes; diodes, transistors	34 235 364	11.1	14.32	8.67
764 Telecommunicate equipment part nes	32 002 599	10.4	16.25	8.20
759 Office equipment part & accessories	28 072 903	9.1	23.50	13.27
894 Baby carriage toy game sport good	11 812 081	3.8	29.41	17.45
772 Electrical circuit equipment	11 457 080	3.7	19.35	7.49
845 Articles of apparel nes	10 923 499	3.6	16.19	10.93
752 Computer equipment nes	10 091 659	3.3	6.15	3.54
763 Sound TV recorder or reproducer	8 465 411	2.8	23.05	13.61
778 Electrical machinery apparatus nes	8 176 825	2.7	12.39	5.20
842 Female clothing, woven	7 235 877	2.4	16.48	10.71
Remainder	144 920 433	47.1		
China, Macao SAR - Chine (RAS de Macao) (**=Developing)				
All commodity groups	2 516 381	100.0	0.06	0.02
845 Articles of apparel nes	654 848	26.0	0.97	0.66
842 Female clothing, woven	339 947	13.5	0.77	0.50
844 Female clothing, knitted crocheted	296 422	11.8	1.42	1.05
841 Male clothing, woven	238 065	9.5	0.69	0.44
334 Heavy petroleum & bituminous oil	115 343	4.6	0.06	0.03
843 Male clothing, knitted crocheted	89 495	3.6	0.71	0.56
655 Knitted or crocheted fabrics nes	81 024	3.2	0.59	0.39
652 Woven cotton fabrics	64 128	2.5	0.36	0.22
851 Footwear	60 420	2.4	0.15	0.09
651 Textile yarn	57 380	2.3	0.24	0.14
Remainder	519 309	20.6		
China, Taiwan Province of - Province chinoise de Taiwan (**=Developing)				
All commodity groups	206 702 508	100.0	5.03	1.86
776 Valves tubes; diodes, transistors	37 383 341	18.1	15.64	9.47
871 Optical instruments apparatus nes	12 815 875	6.2	32.08	25.12
759 Office equipment part & accessories	10 185 026	4.9	8.52	4.81
334 Heavy petroleum & bituminous oil	9 430 310	4.6	4.95	2.27
764 Telecommunicate equipment part nes	8 821 087	4.3	4.48	2.26
778 Electrical machinery apparatus nes	8 785 730	4.3	13.32	5.59
772 Electrical circuit equipment	7 265 690	3.5	12.27	4.75
898 Music instrument device recording	4 671 825	2.3	27.72	9.04
752 Computer equipment nes	4 024 927	1.9	2.45	1.41
699 Base metal manufactures nes	3 325 320	1.6	11.62	3.37
Remainder	99 993 376	48.4		
Colombia - Colombie (**=Developing)				
All commodity groups	22 790 707	100.0	0.55	0.21
333 Crude petroleum & bituminous oil	4 283 622	18.8	0.70	0.51
321 Coal excluding non-agglomomerated	2 623 581	11.5	16.08	5.50
334 Heavy petroleum & bituminous oil	1 637 038	7.2	0.86	0.39
071 Coffee and coffee substitutes	1 632 593	7.2	14.89	9.55
292 Crude vegetable materials nes	948 513	4.2	15.64	4.09
671 Pig & sponge iron, ferro alloys etc	923 056	4.1	6.95	3.63
971 Gold non-monetary excluding ores	727 808	3.2	3.00	1.50
057 Fruit nut (exc oil), fresh or dried	554 034	2.4	2.67	1.15
781 Passenger cars and race cars	493 121	2.2	0.76	0.10
061 Sugar, mollasses and honey	329 118	1.4	2.89	1.64
Remainder	8 638 223	37.9		
Congo (**=Developing)				
All commodity groups	6 946 974	100.0	0.17	0.06
333 Crude petroleum & bituminous oil	5 915 302	85.1	0.96	0.70
334 Heavy petroleum & bituminous oil	206 960	3.0	0.11	0.05
247 Wood in rough or roughly squared	200 520	2.9	7.30	1.81
287 Base metal ores & concentrates nes	97 461	1.4	0.90	0.48
342 Liquefied propane and butane	71 018	1.0	0.39	0.25
682 Copper	58 791	0.8	0.14	0.07
248 Wood simply worked, railway sleeper	58 329	0.8	0.76	0.16
689 Misc non-ferrous base metals	52 920	0.8	1.90	0.68
283 Copper ores and concentrates	40 023	0.6	0.21	0.16
344 Petroleum and hydrocarbon gas nes	17 214	0.2	0.66	0.18
Remainder	228 436	3.3		
Cook Islands - Îles Cook (**=Developing)				
All commodity groups	4 386	100.0	0.00	0.00
034 Fish, fresh live chilled frozen	1 875	42.7	0.01	0.01
059 Fruit & vegetable juice unferment	1 135	25.9	0.03	0.01
667 Pearls, precious semiprecious stone	1 046	23.9	0.00	0.00
841 Male clothing, woven	77	1.8	0.00	0.00
291 Crude animal materials nes	70	1.6	0.00	0.00
897 Jewellery nes (667)	58	1.3	0.00	0.00
057 Fruit nut (exc oil), fresh or dried	52	1.2	0.00	0.00
843 Male clothing, knitted crocheted	22	0.5	0.00	0.00
658 Made-up textile articles nes	17	0.4	0.00	0.00
292 Crude vegetable materials nes	12	0.3	0.00	0.00
Remainder	23	0.5		
Costa Rica (**=Developing)				
All commodity groups	7 202 777	100.0	0.18	0.06
057 Fruit nut (exc oil), fresh or dried	1 050 734	14.6	5.07	2.18
776 Valves tubes; diodes, transistors	1 019 826	14.2	0.43	0.26
759 Office equipment part & accessories	655 795	9.1	0.55	0.31
872 Medical instruments appliances nes	545 951	7.6	5.55	1.00
071 Coffee and coffee substitutes	247 550	3.4	2.26	1.45
292 Crude vegetable materials nes	192 915	2.7	3.18	0.83
542 Medicines including veterinary	183 486	2.5	1.63	0.08
772 Electrical circuit equipment	172 092	2.4	0.29	0.11
764 Telecommunicate equipment part nes	160 181	2.2	0.08	0.04
841 Male clothing, woven	144 003	2.0	0.42	0.27
Remainder	2 830 244	39.3		

For sources and notes, see end of table.

Pour les sources et les notes, se reporter à la fin du tableau.

159

Leading products exported based on average 2005-2006 values SITC Revision 3 (3-digit level) / Principaux produits exportés d'après la moyenne des valeurs de 2005-2006 CTCI révision 3 (positions à 3 chiffres)	2005-2006 Value (f.o.b., thousands of dollars) / Valeur (f.a.b., milliers de dollars)	As percentage / En pourcentage — of country total / du total du pays	of ** (1) / des ** (1)	of world / du monde
Côte d'Ivoire (=Developing)**				
All commodity groups	7 697 836	100.0	0.19	0.07
072 Cocoa	1 967 488	25.6	33.20	21.91
334 Heavy petroleum & bituminous oil	1 564 187	20.3	0.82	0.38
333 Crude petroleum & bituminous oil	908 168	11.8	0.15	0.11
891 Arms and ammunition	405 795	5.3	46.37	5.19
057 Fruit nut (exc oil), fresh or dried	273 953	3.6	1.32	0.57
793 Ships boats floating structures	258 768	3.4	0.72	0.33
231 Natural rubber, latex, gum, etc	257 513	3.3	2.11	2.06
248 Wood simply worked, railway sleeper	200 365	2.6	2.61	0.54
071 Coffee and coffee substitutes	139 776	1.8	1.27	0.82
263 Cotton	127 123	1.7	3.16	1.15
Remainder	1 594 700	20.7		
Croatia - Croatie (=Transition)**				
All commodity groups	9 574 759	100.0	2.41	0.09
793 Ships boats floating structures	1 045 965	10.9	44.02	1.31
334 Heavy petroleum & bituminous oil	839 312	8.8	1.64	0.20
343 Natural gas, liquefied or not	299 051	3.1	0.74	0.17
821 Furniture part; bedding furnishing	272 386	2.8	20.67	0.27
248 Wood simply worked, railway sleeper	210 506	2.2	7.04	0.57
845 Articles of apparel nes	208 927	2.2	28.88	0.21
542 Medicines including veterinary	188 413	2.0	28.26	0.09
684 Aluminium	174 394	1.8	2.14	0.20
851 Footwear	174 203	1.8	18.80	0.25
771 Electric power machine part excl. 716	173 821	1.8	28.70	0.34
Remainder	5 987 782	62.5		
Cuba (=Developing)**				
All commodity groups	2 532 372	100.0	0.06	0.02
284 Nickel ores, concentrates, etc	1 159 030	45.8	36.02	17.16
122 Manufactured tabacco	243 352	9.6	5.87	1.33
061 Sugar, mollasses and honey	217 643	8.6	1.91	1.08
542 Medicines including veterinary	210 531	8.3	1.87	0.09
036 Crustacean mollusc aquat invertebra	85 215	3.4	0.67	0.42
898 Music instrument device recording	56 792	2.2	0.34	0.11
059 Fruit & vegetable juice unferment	47 234	1.9	1.22	0.48
288 Non ferrous base metal waste nes	42 950	1.7	0.84	0.18
661 Lime cement construction material	42 854	1.7	0.41	0.21
672 Ingots, Iron steel primary products	42 486	1.7	0.47	0.14
Remainder	384 285	15.2		
Cyprus - Chypre (=Developed)**				
All commodity groups	1 480 614	100.0	0.02	0.01
334 Heavy petroleum & bituminous oil	244 475	16.5	0.14	0.06
764 Telecommunicate equipment part nes	234 794	15.9	0.12	0.06
542 Medicines including veterinary	115 946	7.8	0.06	0.05
781 Passenger cars and race cars	114 926	7.8	0.03	0.02
122 Manufactured tabacco	60 138	4.1	0.44	0.33
054 Vegetable & vegetable products nes	54 985	3.7	0.25	0.16
057 Fruit nut (exc oil), fresh or dried	45 158	3.0	0.17	0.09
782 Goods and service vehicles	41 270	2.8	0.06	0.04
024 Cheese and curd	36 271	2.4	0.22	0.20
776 Valves tubes; diodes, transistors	33 256	2.2	0.02	0.01
Remainder	499 396	33.7		
Czech Republic - République tchèque (=Developed)**				
All commodity groups	86 674 767	100.0	1.31	0.78
781 Passenger cars and race cars	7 371 413	8.5	1.67	1.45
784 Motor vehicle parts and accessories	6 013 599	6.9	3.03	2.45
752 Computer equipment nes	4 832 870	5.6	4.00	1.69
699 Base metal manufactures nes	2 756 834	3.2	4.02	2.80
772 Electrical circuit equipment	2 272 176	2.6	2.44	1.49
778 Electrical machinery apparatus nes	2 046 632	2.4	2.26	1.30
773 Electrical distribute equipment nes	1 964 775	2.3	4.83	2.85
821 Furniture part; bedding furnishing	1 898 759	2.2	2.94	1.85
741 Heating cooling equipment parts nes	1 704 699	2.0	3.24	2.30
761 Television video receive project	1 582 458	1.8	5.47	2.37
Remainder	54 230 553	62.6		
Dem. Rep. of the Congo - Rép. dém. du Congo (=Developing)**				
All commodity groups	2 254 685	100.0	0.05	0.02
667 Pearls, precious semiprecious stone	853 122	37.8	2.43	0.92
287 Base metal ores & concentrates nes	378 494	16.8	3.48	1.86
333 Crude petroleum & bituminous oil	296 468	13.1	0.05	0.04
283 Copper ores and concentrates	150 540	6.7	0.77	0.61
689 Misc non-ferrous base metals	110 105	4.9	3.96	1.41
247 Wood in rough or roughly squared	84 864	3.8	3.09	0.77
277 Natural abrasives nes	70 811	3.1	10.18	6.14
248 Wood simply worked, railway sleeper	70 391	3.1	0.92	0.19
682 Copper	57 692	2.6	0.14	0.07
071 Coffee and coffee substitutes	15 791	0.7	0.14	0.09
Remainder	166 406	7.4		
Denmark - Danemark (=Developed)**				
All commodity groups	86 266 795	100.0	1.31	0.78
333 Crude petroleum & bituminous oil	5 434 269	6.3	4.77	0.65
542 Medicines including veterinary	4 544 749	5.3	2.17	2.05
012 Meat nes, fresh chilled frozen	3 632 951	4.2	11.24	9.17
764 Telecommunicate equipment part nes	2 980 252	3.5	1.55	0.76
716 Rotating electric plant parts nes	2 799 818	3.2	7.38	4.99
821 Furniture part; bedding furnishing	2 679 303	3.1	4.16	2.61
334 Heavy petroleum & bituminous oil	2 365 307	2.7	1.35	0.57
541 Pharmaceuticals excluding medicines	1 925 971	2.2	3.06	2.73
893 Articles of plastic nes	1 454 909	1.7	2.42	1.61
034 Fish, fresh live chilled frozen	1 377 278	1.6	6.60	3.84
Remainder	57 071 989	66.2		
Dominican Republic - République dominicaine (=Developing)**				
All commodity groups	1 345 206	100.0	0.03	0.01
845 Articles of apparel nes	134 871	10.0	0.20	0.14
841 Male clothing, woven	131 028	9.7	0.38	0.24
872 Medical instruments appliances nes	112 014	8.3	1.14	0.21
671 Pig & sponge iron, ferro alloys etc	93 105	6.9	0.70	0.37
122 Manufactured tabacco	63 039	4.7	1.52	0.34
772 Electrical circuit equipment	62 103	4.6	0.10	0.04
897 Jewellery nes (667)	58 370	4.3	0.28	0.13
057 Fruit nut (exc oil), fresh or dried	46 893	3.5	0.23	0.10
843 Male clothing, knitted crocheted	46 450	3.5	0.37	0.29
759 Office equipment part & accessories	44 196	3.3	0.04	0.02
Remainder	553 135	41.1		
Ecuador - Équateur (=Developing)**				
All commodity groups	11 298 577	100.0	0.27	0.10
333 Crude petroleum & bituminous oil	6 165 425	54.6	1.01	0.73
057 Fruit nut (exc oil), fresh or dried	1 208 263	10.7	5.83	2.50
036 Crustacean mollusc aquat invertebra	521 602	4.6	4.12	2.55
037 Fish shellfish, prepared preserved	504 329	4.5	4.90	3.14
334 Heavy petroleum & bituminous oil	426 954	3.8	0.22	0.10
292 Crude vegetable materials nes	407 102	3.6	6.71	1.76
072 Cocoa	165 174	1.5	2.79	1.84
782 Goods and service vehicles	148 098	1.3	0.70	0.16
335 Residual petroleum products nes	114 412	1.0	1.72	0.57
034 Fish, fresh live chilled frozen	106 004	0.9	0.74	0.30
Remainder	1 531 214	13.6		
Egypt - Égypte (=Developing)**				
All commodity groups	12 201 676	100.0	0.30	0.11
334 Heavy petroleum & bituminous oil	3 405 158	27.9	1.79	0.82
343 Natural gas, liquefied or not	2 232 050	18.3	3.71	1.27
333 Crude petroleum & bituminous oil	700 644	5.7	0.11	0.08
661 Lime cement construction material	352 146	2.9	3.37	1.71
042 Rice	306 635	2.5	3.93	2.99
676 Iron steel bar rod section piling	274 567	2.3	1.65	0.48
571 Primary form ethylene polymers	225 013	1.8	1.45	0.52
054 Vegetable & vegetable products nes	181 344	1.5	1.50	0.52
263 Cotton	156 769	1.3	3.90	1.42
673 Flat iron non-alloy steel products	146 387	1.2	0.71	0.21
Remainder	4 220 962	34.6		

For sources and notes, see end of table.

Pour les sources et les notes, se reporter à la fin du tableau.

Left panel

Leading products exported based on average 2005-2006 values SITC Revision 3 (3-digit level) / Principaux produits exportés d'après la moyenne des valeurs de 2005-2006 CTCI révision 3 (positions à 3 chiffres)	Value (f.o.b., thousands of dollars) Valeur (f.a.b., milliers de dollars)	of country total du total du pays	of ** (1) des ** (1)	of world du monde
El Salvador (=Developing)**				
All commodity groups	1 554 405	100.0	0.04	0.01
071 Coffee and coffee substitutes	176 507	11.4	1.61	1.03
512 Alcohols, phenols; derivatives	92 923	6.0	0.68	0.30
061 Sugar, mollasses and honey	81 363	5.2	0.71	0.41
642 Cut paper and paperboard articles	70 223	4.5	0.81	0.19
542 Medicines including veterinary	55 961	3.6	0.50	0.03
048 Cereal & preparation flour starch	53 172	3.4	1.39	0.20
893 Articles of plastic nes	52 527	3.4	0.18	0.06
037 Fish shellfish, prepared preserved	50 637	3.3	0.49	0.32
334 Heavy petroleum & bituminous oil	45 108	2.9	0.02	0.01
673 Flat iron non-alloy steel products	40 693	2.6	0.20	0.06
Remainder	835 292	53.7		
Equatorial Guinea - Guinée équatoriale (=Developing)**				
All commodity groups	3 061 560	100.0	0.07	0.03
333 Crude petroleum & bituminous oil	2 802 057	91.5	0.46	0.33
512 Alcohols, phenols; derivatives	97 050	3.2	0.71	0.31
342 Liquefied propane and butane	72 377	2.4	0.40	0.26
247 Wood in rough or roughly squared	42 587	1.4	1.55	0.38
634 Veneer, plywood & other wood nes	9 275	0.3	0.09	0.03
344 Petroleum and hydrocarbon gas nes	7 331	0.2	0.28	0.07
742 Liquid pump; liquid elevator parts	6 435	0.2	0.13	0.02
747 Pipe, boiler, tank & vat appliances	2 818	0.1	0.03	0.01
334 Heavy petroleum & bituminous oil	1 839	0.1	0.00	0.00
772 Electrical circuit equipment	1 777	0.1	0.00	0.00
Remainder	18 013	0.6		
Estonia - Estonie (=Developed)**				
All commodity groups	8 658 916	100.0	0.13	0.08
764 Telecommunicate equipment part nes	1 093 296	12.6	0.57	0.28
334 Heavy petroleum & bituminous oil	926 819	10.7	0.53	0.22
821 Furniture part; bedding furnishing	364 774	4.2	0.57	0.36
248 Wood simply worked, railway sleeper	305 539	3.5	1.17	0.83
781 Passenger cars and race cars	247 728	2.9	0.06	0.05
635 Wood manufactures nes	203 537	2.4	1.40	0.90
674 Flat plated iron non-alloy steel	183 400	2.1	0.74	0.49
773 Electrical distribute equipment nes	170 397	2.0	0.42	0.25
691 Iron steel aluminium structures nes	135 239	1.6	0.64	0.44
811 Prefabricated buildings	134 759	1.6	2.87	2.30
Remainder	4 893 428	56.5		
Ethiopia - Éthiopie (=Developing)**				
All commodity groups	984 583	100.0	0.02	0.01
071 Coffee and coffee substitutes	380 720	38.7	3.47	2.23
222 Oil seed etc for soft oil	170 890	17.4	1.67	0.77
292 Crude vegetable materials nes	117 472	11.9	1.94	0.51
971 Gold non-monetary excluding ores	54 425	5.5	0.22	0.11
054 Vegetable & vegetable products nes	47 450	4.8	0.39	0.14
611 Leather	38 391	3.9	0.32	0.18
211 Raw hides & skins, excluding furskins	31 907	3.2	3.26	0.54
001 Live animal excl. fish & crustacean	28 706	2.9	1.13	0.21
012 Meat nes, fresh chilled frozen	17 168	1.7	0.24	0.04
223 Oil seed for non soft oil	13 694	1.4	3.27	0.94
Remainder	83 761	8.5		
Faeroe Islands - Îles Féroé (=Developed)**				
All commodity groups	616 366	100.0	0.01	0.01
034 Fish, fresh live chilled frozen	379 374	61.6	1.82	1.06
035 Fish, dried salted smoked	97 685	15.8	3.44	2.57
081 Animal feed excluding unmilled cereal	61 673	10.0	0.33	0.19
793 Ships boats floating structures	22 605	3.7	0.05	0.03
036 Crustacean mollusc aquat invertebra	14 191	2.3	0.18	0.07
334 Heavy petroleum & bituminous oil	12 312	2.0	0.01	0.00
291 Crude animal materials nes	11 309	1.8	0.36	0.22
037 Fish shellfish, prepared preserved	10 366	1.7	0.19	0.06
657 Special yarn and textile fabric etc	2 782	0.5	0.01	0.01
892 Printed matter	2 597	0.4	0.01	0.01
Remainder	1 472	0.2		

Right panel

Leading products exported based on average 2005-2006 values SITC Revision 3 (3-digit level) / Principaux produits exportés d'après la moyenne des valeurs de 2005-2006 CTCI révision 3 (positions à 3 chiffres)	Value (f.o.b., thousands of dollars) Valeur (f.a.b., milliers de dollars)	of country total du total du pays	of ** (1) des ** (1)	of world du monde
Fiji - Fidji (=Developing)**				
All commodity groups	690 305	100.0	0.02	0.01
334 Heavy petroleum & bituminous oil	165 926	24.0	0.09	0.04
061 Sugar, mollasses and honey	128 505	18.6	1.13	0.64
111 Non alcoholic beverage nes	55 541	8.0	2.62	0.47
034 Fish, fresh live chilled frozen	46 977	6.8	0.33	0.13
971 Gold non-monetary excluding ores	32 616	4.7	0.13	0.07
845 Articles of apparel nes	26 157	3.8	0.04	0.03
048 Cereal & preparation flour starch	22 298	3.2	0.58	0.09
841 Male clothing, woven	20 922	3.0	0.06	0.04
054 Vegetable & vegetable products nes	17 752	2.6	0.15	0.05
843 Male clothing, knitted crocheted	10 867	1.6	0.09	0.07
Remainder	162 743	23.6		
Finland - Finlande (=Developed)**				
All commodity groups	71 258 710	100.0	1.08	0.64
764 Telecommunicate equipment part nes	11 733 948	16.5	6.09	3.01
641 Paper and paperboard	9 501 545	13.3	11.20	9.54
334 Heavy petroleum & bituminous oil	3 267 463	4.6	1.87	0.78
675 Flat rolled products of alloy steel	2 974 396	4.2	7.99	5.89
781 Passenger cars and race cars	1 992 766	2.8	0.45	0.39
248 Wood simply worked, railway sleeper	1 785 411	2.5	6.82	4.84
251 Pulp and waste paper	1 315 131	1.8	6.24	4.73
744 Mechanical handling equipment nes	1 236 460	1.7	2.56	2.17
728 Special industrial machine part nes	1 212 321	1.7	1.40	1.16
716 Rotating electric plant parts nes	1 108 852	1.6	2.92	1.98
Remainder	35 130 418	49.3		
France (=Developed)**				
All commodity groups	456 683 549	100.0	6.91	4.11
781 Passenger cars and race cars	32 327 879	7.1	7.31	6.36
792 Aircraft, spacecraft & equipment	26 709 190	5.8	20.23	18.35
542 Medicines including veterinary	19 897 804	4.4	9.49	8.98
784 Motor vehicle parts and accessories	16 536 739	3.6	8.34	6.73
334 Heavy petroleum & bituminous oil	11 207 527	2.5	6.41	2.69
764 Telecommunicate equipment part nes	10 834 999	2.4	5.63	2.78
112 Alcoholic beverages	10 704 023	2.3	26.73	22.23
553 Perfume toilet cosmetics, excl. soap	10 447 476	2.3	27.09	22.56
776 Valves tubes; diodes, transistors	8 370 493	1.8	5.38	2.12
772 Electrical circuit equipment	7 804 394	1.7	8.39	5.10
Remainder	301 843 025	66.1		
French Polynesia - Polynesie française (=Developing)**				
All commodity groups	198 301	100.0	0.00	0.00
667 Pearls, precious semiprecious stone	119 849	60.4	0.34	0.13
792 Aircraft, spacecraft & equipment	17 385	8.8	0.14	0.01
897 Jewellery nes (667)	14 903	7.5	0.07	0.03
058 Fruit preserve preparation excl. juice	10 727	5.4	0.23	0.10
291 Crude animal materials nes	4 317	2.2	0.22	0.08
034 Fish, fresh live chilled frozen	3 943	2.0	0.03	0.01
714 Non-electric engines excl. 712 713 718	3 788	1.9	0.07	0.01
422 Fixed veg fat and oil, excl. "soft"	3 001	1.5	0.02	0.02
059 Fruit & vegetable juice unferment	2 578	1.3	0.07	0.03
793 Ships boats floating structures	2 253	1.1	0.01	0.00
Remainder	15 558	7.8		
Gabon (=Developing)**				
All commodity groups	5 541 864	100.0	0.13	0.05
333 Crude petroleum & bituminous oil	4 631 494	83.6	0.75	0.55
247 Wood in rough or roughly squared	304 353	5.5	11.08	2.75
287 Base metal ores & concentrates nes	182 735	3.3	1.68	0.90
634 Veneer, plywood & other wood nes	111 690	2.0	1.04	0.36
334 Heavy petroleum & bituminous oil	72 543	1.3	0.04	0.02
248 Wood simply worked, railway sleeper	72 302	1.3	0.94	0.20
792 Aircraft, spacecraft & equipment	41 983	0.8	0.34	0.03
122 Manufactured tabacco	25 375	0.5	0.61	0.14
036 Crustacean mollusc aquat invertebra	17 752	0.3	0.14	0.09
231 Natural rubber, latex, gum, etc	16 066	0.3	0.13	0.13
Remainder	65 570	1.2		

For sources and notes, see end of table.   Pour les sources et les notes, se reporter à la fin du tableau.

161

3

3.2.D Export structure by product
Individual countries and territories

3.2.D Structure des exportations par produits
Pays et territoires individuels

Leading products exported based on average 2005-2006 values SITC Revision 3 (3-digit level) / Principaux produits exportés d'après la moyenne des valeurs de 2005-2006 CTCI révision 3 (positions à 3 chiffres)	Value (f.o.b., thousands of dollars) Valeur (f.a.b., milliers de dollars)	of country total du total du pays	of ** (1) des ** (1)	of world du monde
Gambia - Gambie (=Developing)**				
All commodity groups	8 279	100.0	0.00	0.00
222 Oil seed etc for soft oil	2 751	33.2	0.03	0.01
111 Non alcoholic beverage nes	2 257	27.3	0.11	0.02
054 Vegetable & vegetable products nes	1 487	18.0	0.01	0.00
057 Fruit nut (exc oil), fresh or dried	497	6.0	0.00	0.00
781 Passenger cars and race cars	424	5.1	0.00	0.00
036 Crustacean mollusc aquat invertebra	275	3.3	0.00	0.00
034 Fish, fresh live chilled frozen	245	3.0	0.00	0.00
269 Worn clothing, textile article; rag	178	2.1	0.03	0.01
724 Textile leather machinery parts nes	176	2.1	0.00	0.00
778 Electrical machinery apparatus nes	116	1.4	0.00	0.00
Remainder	-128	-1.5		
Georgia - Géorgie (=Transition)**				
All commodity groups	928 867	100.0	0.23	0.01
112 Alcoholic beverages	91 950	9.9	7.94	0.19
671 Pig & sponge iron, ferro alloys etc	84 987	9.1	1.56	0.33
282 Ferrous iron & steel, waste & scrap	78 325	8.4	2.66	0.29
057 Fruit nut (exc oil), fresh or dried	69 274	7.5	9.38	0.14
792 Aircraft, spacecraft & equipment	65 612	7.1	0.52	0.05
283 Copper ores and concentrates	57 961	6.2	23.45	0.23
111 Non alcoholic beverage nes	50 008	5.4	19.71	0.43
971 Gold non-monetary excluding ores	41 541	4.5	5.37	0.09
562 Manufactured fertilizer excl. crude	41 235	4.4	0.65	0.17
781 Passenger cars and race cars	34 275	3.7	2.94	0.01
Remainder	313 700	33.8		
Germany - Allemagne (=Developed)**				
All commodity groups	1 049 547 430	100.0	15.88	9.44
781 Passenger cars and race cars	112 333 523	10.7	25.42	22.10
784 Motor vehicle parts and accessories	36 236 762	3.5	18.27	14.75
542 Medicines including veterinary	31 349 457	3.0	14.95	14.14
764 Telecommunicate equipment part nes	25 749 695	2.5	13.37	6.60
792 Aircraft, spacecraft & equipment	22 235 211	2.1	16.84	15.27
772 Electrical circuit equipment	21 454 466	2.0	23.06	14.03
713 Internal combustion engine part nes	21 330 288	2.0	21.22	18.00
874 Measure analyze control device nes	21 194 371	2.0	21.36	17.91
728 Special industrial machine part nes	18 706 185	1.8	21.57	17.96
752 Computer equipment nes	17 584 207	1.7	14.54	6.16
Remainder	721 373 269	68.7		
Ghana (=Developing)**				
All commodity groups	4 589 914	100.0	0.11	0.04
072 Cocoa	1 085 204	23.6	18.31	12.09
971 Gold non-monetary excluding ores	999 133	21.8	4.11	2.06
634 Veneer, plywood & other wood nes	307 214	6.7	2.87	0.98
057 Fruit nut (exc oil), fresh or dried	246 434	5.4	1.19	0.51
037 Fish shellfish, prepared preserved	195 256	4.3	1.90	1.22
073 Chocolate & cocoa preparations nes	139 920	3.0	9.07	1.05
334 Heavy petroleum & bituminous oil	139 834	3.0	0.07	0.03
652 Woven cotton fabrics	115 795	2.5	0.65	0.40
056 Vegetables roots tubers nes	113 983	2.5	2.23	0.67
054 Vegetable & vegetable products nes	99 082	2.2	0.82	0.29
Remainder	1 148 060	25.0		
Greece - Grèce (=Developed)**				
All commodity groups	19 188 604	100.0	0.29	0.17
334 Heavy petroleum & bituminous oil	2 068 271	10.8	1.18	0.50
542 Medicines including veterinary	1 133 210	5.9	0.54	0.51
684 Aluminium	838 475	4.4	1.44	0.96
844 Female clothing, knitted crocheted	604 879	3.2	8.40	2.14
057 Fruit nut (exc oil), fresh or dried	547 630	2.9	2.05	1.14
421 Fixed veg fat and oil, "soft"	533 033	2.8	5.36	2.95
682 Copper	426 240	2.2	1.10	0.49
034 Fish, fresh live chilled frozen	390 238	2.0	1.87	1.09
263 Cotton	379 770	2.0	6.54	3.45
056 Vegetables roots tubers nes	366 061	1.9	3.15	2.16
Remainder	11 900 798	62.0		

Leading products exported based on average 2005-2006 values SITC Revision 3 (3-digit level) / Principaux produits exportés d'après la moyenne des valeurs de 2005-2006 CTCI révision 3 (positions à 3 chiffres)	Value (f.o.b., thousands of dollars) Valeur (f.a.b., milliers de dollars)	of country total du total du pays	of ** (1) des ** (1)	of world du monde
Greenland - Groenland (=Developed)**				
All commodity groups	405 466	100.0	0.01	0.00
036 Crustacean mollusc aquat invertebra	115 587	28.5	1.50	0.57
037 Fish shellfish, prepared preserved	115 235	28.4	2.08	0.72
034 Fish, fresh live chilled frozen	106 677	26.3	0.51	0.30
289 Prec metal ore concentrate excl. gold	26 066	6.4	0.76	0.52
035 Fish, dried salted smoked	10 030	2.5	0.35	0.26
613 Furskin tanned dressed etc	5 507	1.4	0.65	0.31
896 Work of art & collections; antiques	2 046	0.5	0.01	0.01
273 Stone, sand and gravel	1 569	0.4	0.04	0.02
848 Headgear, non-textile clothing	1 017	0.3	0.02	0.00
764 Telecommunicate equipment part nes	832	0.2	0.00	0.00
Remainder	20 899	5.2		
Grenada - Grenade (=Developing)**				
All commodity groups	26 508	100.0	0.00	0.00
075 Spices	5 501	20.8	0.23	0.17
046 Wheat meal & flour, meslin flour	3 921	14.8	0.40	0.16
034 Fish, fresh live chilled frozen	3 494	13.2	0.02	0.01
642 Cut paper and paperboard articles	2 392	9.0	0.03	0.01
081 Animal feed excluding unmilled cereal	1 531	5.8	0.01	0.00
897 Jewellery nes (667)	1 031	3.9	0.00	0.00
782 Goods and service vehicles	759	2.9	0.00	0.00
533 Pigment, paint, varnish & related	699	2.6	0.01	0.00
845 Articles of apparel nes	655	2.5	0.00	0.00
674 Flat plated iron non-alloy steel	595	2.2	0.01	0.00
Remainder	5 930	22.4		
Guatemala (=Developing)**				
All commodity groups	4 289 450	100.0	0.10	0.04
071 Coffee and coffee substitutes	470 784	11.0	4.29	2.75
844 Female clothing, knitted crocheted	362 879	8.5	1.74	1.28
057 Fruit nut (exc oil), fresh or dried	313 957	7.3	1.51	0.65
061 Sugar, mollasses and honey	299 040	7.0	2.63	1.49
333 Crude petroleum & bituminous oil	229 731	5.4	0.04	0.03
842 Female clothing, woven	185 659	4.3	0.42	0.27
553 Perfume toilet cosmetics, excl. soap	90 104	2.1	1.21	0.19
843 Male clothing, knitted crocheted	89 728	2.1	0.71	0.57
542 Medicines including veterinary	89 537	2.1	0.79	0.04
231 Natural rubber, latex, gum, etc	87 530	2.0	0.72	0.70
Remainder	2 070 500	48.3		
Guinea - Guinée (=Developing)**				
All commodity groups	970 784	100.0	0.02	0.01
285 Aluminium ore concentrate alumina	642 174	66.2	15.96	5.39
283 Copper ores and concentrates	66 375	6.8	0.34	0.27
333 Crude petroleum & bituminous oil	57 111	5.9	0.01	0.01
667 Pearls, precious semiprecious stone	44 741	4.6	0.13	0.05
034 Fish, fresh live chilled frozen	23 557	2.4	0.16	0.07
072 Cocoa	21 413	2.2	0.36	0.24
071 Coffee and coffee substitutes	17 623	1.8	0.16	0.10
231 Natural rubber, latex, gum, etc	11 320	1.2	0.09	0.09
792 Aircraft, spacecraft & equipment	9 697	1.0	0.08	0.01
036 Crustacean mollusc aquat invertebra	9 239	1.0	0.07	0.05
Remainder	67 535	7.0		
Guyana (=Developing)**				
All commodity groups	553 018	100.0	0.01	0.00
061 Sugar, mollasses and honey	147 902	26.7	1.30	0.74
971 Gold non-monetary excluding ores	80 082	14.5	0.33	0.16
042 Rice	48 015	8.7	0.62	0.47
667 Pearls, precious semiprecious stone	40 324	7.3	0.11	0.04
036 Crustacean mollusc aquat invertebra	39 069	7.1	0.31	0.19
248 Wood simply worked, railway sleeper	34 383	6.2	0.45	0.09
285 Aluminium ore concentrate alumina	31 628	5.7	0.79	0.27
034 Fish, fresh live chilled frozen	23 099	4.2	0.16	0.06
112 Alcoholic beverages	17 238	3.1	0.25	0.04
634 Veneer, plywood & other wood nes	12 497	2.3	0.12	0.04
Remainder	78 780	14.2		

For sources and notes, see end of table.

Pour les sources et les notes, se reporter à la fin du tableau.

Leading products exported based on average 2005-2006 values SITC Revision 3 (3-digit level) / Principaux produits exportés d'après la moyenne des valeurs de 2005-2006 CTCI révision 3 (positions à 3 chiffres)	2005-2006 Value (f.o.b., thousands of dollars) / Valeur (f.a.b., milliers de dollars)	As percentage / En pourcentage: of country total / du total du pays	of ** (1) / des ** (1)	of world / du monde
Haiti - Haïti (=Developing)**				
All commodity groups	498 033	100.0	0.01	0.00
845 Articles of apparel nes	322 781	64.8	0.48	0.32
841 Male clothing, woven	35 442	7.1	0.10	0.07
843 Male clothing, knitted crocheted	18 576	3.7	0.15	0.12
551 Essential oils, perfumes & flavours	9 789	2.0	0.39	0.06
057 Fruit nut (exc oil), fresh or dried	9 339	1.9	0.05	0.02
282 Ferrous iron & steel, waste & scrap	5 472	1.1	0.20	0.02
844 Female clothing, knitted crocheted	5 316	1.1	0.03	0.02
036 Crustacean mollusc aquat invertebra	3 679	0.7	0.03	0.02
072 Cocoa	3 642	0.7	0.06	0.04
071 Coffee and coffee substitutes	3 268	0.7	0.03	0.02
Remainder	80 729	16.2		
Honduras (=Developing)**				
All commodity groups	1 587 043	100.0	0.04	0.01
071 Coffee and coffee substitutes	360 030	22.7	3.28	2.11
057 Fruit nut (exc oil), fresh or dried	191 995	12.1	0.93	0.40
773 Electrical distribute equipment nes	133 503	8.4	0.49	0.19
036 Crustacean mollusc aquat invertebra	104 510	6.6	0.82	0.51
422 Fixed veg fat and oil, excl. "soft"	55 585	3.5	0.44	0.38
287 Base metal ores & concentrates nes	46 453	2.9	0.43	0.23
122 Manufactured tabacco	45 960	2.9	1.11	0.25
289 Prec metal ore concentrate excl. gold	45 352	2.9	2.99	0.90
971 Gold non-monetary excluding ores	41 376	2.6	0.17	0.09
054 Vegetable & vegetable products nes	34 918	2.2	0.29	0.10
Remainder	527 363	33.2		
Hungary - Hongrie (=Developed)**				
All commodity groups	68 163 709	100.0	1.03	0.61
764 Telecommunicate equipment part nes	7 940 801	11.6	4.12	2.03
713 Internal combustion engine part nes	6 342 750	9.3	6.31	5.35
752 Computer equipment nes	3 540 591	5.2	2.93	1.24
781 Passenger cars and race cars	2 757 242	4.0	0.62	0.54
784 Motor vehicle parts and accessories	2 619 581	3.8	1.32	1.07
761 Television video receive project	2 309 521	3.4	7.99	3.46
772 Electrical circuit equipment	1 731 736	2.5	1.86	1.13
773 Electrical distribute equipment nes	1 713 198	2.5	4.22	2.49
778 Electrical machinery apparatus nes	1 675 181	2.5	1.85	1.07
542 Medicines including veterinary	1 349 969	2.0	0.64	0.61
Remainder	36 183 142	53.1		
Iceland - Islande (=Developed)**				
All commodity groups	3 271 836	100.0	0.05	0.03
034 Fish, fresh live chilled frozen	1 126 298	34.4	5.40	3.14
684 Aluminium	692 738	21.2	1.19	0.79
035 Fish, dried salted smoked	336 535	10.3	11.85	8.86
792 Aircraft, spacecraft & equipment	167 760	5.1	0.13	0.12
081 Animal feed excluding unmilled cereal	140 742	4.3	0.75	0.44
037 Fish shellfish, prepared preserved	124 023	3.8	2.23	0.77
671 Pig & sponge iron, ferro alloys etc	90 151	2.8	1.35	0.35
542 Medicines including veterinary	85 842	2.6	0.04	0.04
899 Manufactured articles nes	65 844	2.0	0.20	0.14
334 Heavy petroleum & bituminous oil	57 100	1.7	0.03	0.01
Remainder	384 803	11.8		
India - Inde (=Developing)**				
All commodity groups	114 764 835	100.0	2.79	1.03
334 Heavy petroleum & bituminous oil	14 877 721	13.0	7.82	3.57
667 Pearls, precious semiprecious stone	11 384 736	9.9	32.37	12.26
897 Jewellery nes (667)	4 440 121	3.9	21.49	10.00
281 Iron ore and concentrates	3 855 310	3.4	25.92	12.62
842 Female clothing, woven	3 217 867	2.8	7.33	4.76
542 Medicines including veterinary	2 620 444	2.3	23.23	1.18
651 Textile yarn	2 460 751	2.1	10.39	5.79
658 Made-up textile articles nes	2 337 615	2.0	10.22	7.18
845 Articles of apparel nes	2 070 360	1.8	3.07	2.07
682 Copper	2 037 977	1.8	4.87	2.34
Remainder	65 461 934	57.0		

Leading products exported based on average 2005-2006 values SITC Revision 3 (3-digit level) / Principaux produits exportés d'après la moyenne des valeurs de 2005-2006 CTCI révision 3 (positions à 3 chiffres)	2005-2006 Value (f.o.b., thousands of dollars) / Valeur (f.a.b., milliers de dollars)	As percentage / En pourcentage: of country total / du total du pays	of ** (1) / des ** (1)	of world / du monde
Indonesia - Indonésie (=Developing)**				
All commodity groups	93 229 282	100.0	2.27	0.84
343 Natural gas, liquefied or not	9 298 610	10.0	15.45	5.27
333 Crude petroleum & bituminous oil	8 157 333	8.7	1.33	0.97
422 Fixed veg fat and oil, excl. "soft"	5 235 271	5.6	41.89	36.22
321 Coal excluding non-agglomomerated	5 218 144	5.6	31.98	10.95
283 Copper ores and concentrates	3 978 537	4.3	20.42	15.99
231 Natural rubber, latex, gum, etc	3 453 129	3.7	28.25	27.58
334 Heavy petroleum & bituminous oil	2 359 560	2.5	1.24	0.57
641 Paper and paperboard	2 232 812	2.4	17.53	2.24
821 Furniture part; bedding furnishing	1 866 029	2.0	5.08	1.82
634 Veneer, plywood & other wood nes	1 842 418	2.0	17.19	5.90
Remainder	49 587 437	53.2		
Iran (Islamic Rep. of) - Iran (Rép. islamique d') (=Developing)**				
All commodity groups	61 629 500	100.0	1.50	0.55
333 Crude petroleum & bituminous oil	49 254 965	79.9	8.03	5.87
057 Fruit nut (exc oil), fresh or dried	1 373 270	2.2	6.62	2.85
342 Liquefied propane and butane	742 556	1.2	4.09	2.64
659 Floor coverings etc	617 827	1.0	13.57	5.06
335 Residual petroleum products nes	561 431	0.9	8.45	2.79
673 Flat iron non-alloy steel products	468 396	0.8	2.26	0.68
511 Hydrocarbons nes; derivatives	371 478	0.6	2.20	0.70
682 Copper	336 472	0.5	0.80	0.39
334 Heavy petroleum & bituminous oil	315 954	0.5	0.17	0.08
672 Ingots, Iron steel primary products	292 953	0.5	3.23	0.99
Remainder	7 294 198	11.8		
Ireland - Irlande (=Developed)**				
All commodity groups	109 382 956	100.0	1.65	0.98
515 Organo-inorganic compound acid salt	18 828 338	17.2	26.29	22.71
542 Medicines including veterinary	14 875 707	13.6	7.09	6.71
752 Computer equipment nes	12 327 319	11.3	10.19	4.32
551 Essential oils, perfumes & flavours	5 851 436	5.3	42.20	35.72
759 Office equipment part & accessories	5 170 877	4.7	5.62	2.44
776 Valves tubes; diodes, transistors	4 689 864	4.3	3.01	1.19
872 Medical instruments appliances nes	3 245 686	3.0	7.30	5.96
541 Pharmaceuticals excluding medicines	3 026 726	2.8	4.80	4.29
899 Manufactured articles nes	2 950 747	2.7	9.06	6.29
598 Miscellaneous chemical products nes	2 516 644	2.3	4.37	3.62
Remainder	35 899 612	32.8		
Israel - Israël (=Developed)**				
All commodity groups	44 781 287	100.0	0.68	0.40
667 Pearls, precious semiprecious stone	16 117 807	36.0	28.94	17.36
542 Medicines including veterinary	2 509 811	5.6	1.20	1.13
764 Telecommunicate equipment part nes	2 326 347	5.2	1.21	0.60
792 Aircraft, spacecraft & equipment	949 394	2.1	0.72	0.65
893 Articles of plastic nes	847 893	1.9	1.41	0.94
562 Manufactured fertilizer excl. crude	721 526	1.6	6.37	2.98
774 Electrodiagnostic equipment	698 097	1.6	2.79	2.53
874 Measure analyze control device nes	656 442	1.5	0.66	0.55
695 Tools for use in hand or in machine	641 264	1.4	2.78	1.98
759 Office equipment part & accessories	502 742	1.1	0.55	0.24
Remainder	18 809 966	42.0		
Italy - Italie (=Developed)**				
All commodity groups	395 055 071	100.0	5.98	3.55
784 Motor vehicle parts and accessories	13 015 899	3.3	6.56	5.30
334 Heavy petroleum & bituminous oil	12 527 849	3.2	7.17	3.01
542 Medicines including veterinary	11 256 395	2.8	5.37	5.08
821 Furniture part; bedding furnishing	11 076 616	2.8	17.18	10.80
728 Special industrial machine part nes	10 862 964	2.7	12.53	10.43
851 Footwear	9 291 036	2.4	31.97	13.43
699 Base metal manufactures nes	8 732 901	2.2	12.74	8.86
781 Passenger cars and race cars	8 718 993	2.2	1.97	1.72
741 Heating cooling equipment parts nes	7 068 720	1.8	13.45	9.53
775 Household equipment nes	6 788 064	1.7	18.56	10.17
Remainder	295 715 635	74.9		

For sources and notes, see end of table.

Pour les sources et les notes, se reporter à la fin du tableau.

Leading products exported based on average 2005-2006 values SITC Revision 3 (3-digit level) / Principaux produits exportés d'après la moyenne des valeurs de 2005-2006 CTCI révision 3 (positions à 3 chiffres)	2005-2006			
	Value (f.o.b., thousands of dollars) / Valeur (f.a.b., milliers de dollars)	As percentage / En pourcentage		
		of country total / du total du pays	of ** (1) / des ** (1)	of world / du monde
Jamaica - Jamaïque (=Developing)**				
All commodity groups	1 751 638	100.0	0.04	0.02
285 Aluminium ore concentrate alumina	1 086 393	62.0	27.00	9.12
334 Heavy petroleum & bituminous oil	189 665	10.8	0.10	0.05
061 Sugar, mollasses and honey	83 293	4.8	0.73	0.42
112 Alcoholic beverages	75 351	4.3	1.09	0.16
282 Ferrous iron & steel, waste & scrap	54 750	3.1	2.03	0.20
512 Alcohols, phenols; derivatives	40 671	2.3	0.30	0.13
071 Coffee and coffee substitutes	24 456	1.4	0.22	0.14
054 Vegetable & vegetable products nes	19 427	1.1	0.16	0.06
098 Edible products & preparations nes	19 240	1.1	0.28	0.06
057 Fruit nut (exc oil), fresh or dried	14 977	0.9	0.07	0.03
Remainder	143 413	8.2		
Japan - Japon (=Developed)**				
All commodity groups	620 832 962	100.0	9.39	5.58
781 Passenger cars and race cars	87 127 262	14.0	19.71	17.14
776 Valves tubes; diodes, transistors	40 805 288	6.6	26.23	10.33
784 Motor vehicle parts and accessories	26 173 060	4.2	13.20	10.65
778 Electrical machinery apparatus nes	19 350 927	3.1	21.40	12.31
728 Special industrial machine part nes	18 589 739	3.0	21.43	17.84
764 Telecommunicate equipment part nes	18 071 498	2.9	9.39	4.63
759 Office equipment part & accessories	16 583 758	2.7	18.03	7.84
772 Electrical circuit equipment	15 878 627	2.6	17.06	10.38
713 Internal combustion engine part nes	14 789 292	2.4	14.72	12.48
874 Measure analyze control device nes	13 071 199	2.1	13.17	11.05
Remainder	350 392 311	56.4		
Jordan - Jordanie (=Developing)**				
All commodity groups	4 722 652	100.0	0.11	0.04
272 Crude fertilizer, excl. manufactured	429 619	9.1	32.00	23.55
845 Articles of apparel nes	426 360	9.0	0.63	0.43
842 Female clothing, woven	321 589	6.8	0.73	0.48
542 Medicines including veterinary	294 500	6.2	2.61	0.13
844 Female clothing, knitted crocheted	241 378	5.1	1.16	0.85
054 Vegetable & vegetable products nes	217 230	4.6	1.80	0.63
562 Manufactured fertilizer excl. crude	197 720	4.2	3.05	0.82
897 Jewellery nes (667)	185 645	3.9	0.90	0.42
971 Gold non-monetary excluding ores	140 726	3.0	0.58	0.29
764 Telecommunicate equipment part nes	115 317	2.4	0.06	0.03
Remainder	2 152 567	45.6		
Kazakhstan (=Transition)**				
All commodity groups	33 046 736	100.0	8.31	0.30
333 Crude petroleum & bituminous oil	20 503 623	62.0	18.25	2.44
682 Copper	2 062 811	6.2	31.96	2.37
334 Heavy petroleum & bituminous oil	1 053 067	3.2	2.06	0.25
671 Pig & sponge iron, ferro alloys etc	958 839	2.9	17.55	3.77
281 Iron ore and concentrates	656 319	2.0	26.37	2.15
686 Zinc	558 268	1.7	74.24	4.95
673 Flat iron non-alloy steel products	525 547	1.6	5.56	0.76
343 Natural gas, liquefied or not	475 876	1.4	1.18	0.27
321 Coal excluding non-agglomomerated	462 945	1.4	9.76	0.97
285 Aluminium ore concentrate alumina	448 861	1.4	44.65	3.77
Remainder	5 340 578	16.2		
Kenya (=Developing)**				
All commodity groups	3 523 856	100.0	0.09	0.03
074 Tea and maté	603 553	17.1	18.51	13.57
334 Heavy petroleum & bituminous oil	415 062	11.8	0.22	0.10
292 Crude vegetable materials nes	331 421	9.4	5.47	1.43
054 Vegetable & vegetable products nes	194 952	5.5	1.61	0.56
071 Coffee and coffee substitutes	128 929	3.7	1.18	0.75
842 Female clothing, woven	96 459	2.7	0.22	0.14
674 Flat plated iron non-alloy steel	79 965	2.3	0.70	0.22
523 Inorganic acid metal salt peroxy	73 763	2.1	1.58	0.56
122 Manufactured tabacco	72 510	2.1	1.75	0.39
893 Articles of plastic nes	66 455	1.9	0.22	0.07
Remainder	1 460 788	41.5		

Leading products exported based on average 2005-2006 values SITC Revision 3 (3-digit level) / Principaux produits exportés d'après la moyenne des valeurs de 2005-2006 CTCI révision 3 (positions à 3 chiffres)	2005-2006			
	Value (f.o.b., thousands of dollars) / Valeur (f.a.b., milliers de dollars)	As percentage / En pourcentage		
		of country total / du total du pays	of ** (1) / des ** (1)	of world / du monde
Kuwait - Koweït (=Developing)**				
All commodity groups	51 138 491	100.0	1.24	0.46
333 Crude petroleum & bituminous oil	31 728 442	62.0	5.17	3.78
334 Heavy petroleum & bituminous oil	14 175 499	27.7	7.45	3.41
342 Liquefied propane and butane	1 909 447	3.7	10.52	6.79
571 Primary form ethylene polymers	759 431	1.5	4.88	1.77
512 Alcohols, phenols; derivatives	336 194	0.7	2.46	1.09
562 Manufactured fertilizer excl. crude	255 528	0.5	3.95	1.06
575 Other plastics, in primary forms	193 961	0.4	1.29	0.28
897 Jewellery nes (667)	93 505	0.2	0.45	0.21
971 Gold non-monetary excluding ores	75 777	0.1	0.31	0.16
274 Sulphur and unroasted iron pyrites	70 518	0.1	18.47	5.79
Remainder	1 540 188	3.0		
Kyrgyzstan - Kirghizistan (=Transition)**				
All commodity groups	733 041	100.0	0.18	0.01
971 Gold non-monetary excluding ores	218 339	29.8	28.23	0.45
334 Heavy petroleum & bituminous oil	89 310	12.2	0.17	0.02
263 Cotton	38 886	5.3	3.29	0.35
664 Glass	30 246	4.1	11.06	0.11
661 Lime cement construction material	27 112	3.7	3.56	0.13
842 Female clothing, woven	26 907	3.7	2.66	0.04
351 Electric current	22 762	3.1	1.75	0.08
054 Vegetable & vegetable products nes	18 746	2.6	4.21	0.05
778 Electrical machinery apparatus nes	16 985	2.3	2.05	0.01
893 Articles of plastic nes	15 719	2.1	2.66	0.02
Remainder	228 030	31.1		
Latvia - Lettonie (=Developed)**				
All commodity groups	5 597 109	100.0	0.08	0.05
248 Wood simply worked, railway sleeper	581 918	10.4	2.22	1.58
676 Iron steel bar rod section piling	349 445	6.2	0.98	0.61
334 Heavy petroleum & bituminous oil	314 207	5.6	0.18	0.08
635 Wood manufactures nes	185 076	3.3	1.27	0.82
634 Veneer, plywood & other wood nes	182 577	3.3	0.94	0.59
821 Furniture part; bedding furnishing	166 731	3.0	0.26	0.16
247 Wood in rough or roughly squared	166 453	3.0	3.32	1.50
542 Medicines including veterinary	140 828	2.5	0.07	0.06
781 Passenger cars and race cars	122 481	2.2	0.03	0.02
246 Wood chips, particles and waste	118 813	2.1	5.89	3.85
Remainder	3 268 580	58.4		
Lebanon - Liban (=Developing)**				
All commodity groups	2 044 476	100.0	0.05	0.02
661 Lime cement construction material	200 259	9.8	1.91	0.97
897 Jewellery nes (667)	196 581	9.6	0.95	0.44
282 Ferrous iron & steel, waste & scrap	86 214	4.2	3.20	0.31
716 Rotating electric plant parts nes	80 341	3.9	0.45	0.14
667 Pearls, precious semiprecious stone	77 959	3.8	0.22	0.08
562 Manufactured fertilizer excl. crude	66 982	3.3	1.03	0.28
057 Fruit nut (exc oil), fresh or dried	65 235	3.2	0.31	0.14
892 Printed matter	62 308	3.0	0.79	0.15
642 Cut paper and paperboard articles	56 881	2.8	0.66	0.15
054 Vegetable & vegetable products nes	43 475	2.1	0.36	0.13
Remainder	1 108 241	54.2		
Libyan Arab Jamahiriya - Jamahiriya arabe libyenne (=Developing)**				
All commodity groups	26 700 166	100.0	0.65	0.24
333 Crude petroleum & bituminous oil	21 879 688	81.9	3.57	2.61
334 Heavy petroleum & bituminous oil	2 225 924	8.3	1.17	0.53
571 Primary form ethylene polymers	299 623	1.1	1.92	0.70
342 Liquefied propane and butane	243 731	0.9	1.34	0.87
344 Petroleum and hydrocarbon gas nes	169 981	0.6	6.50	1.73
562 Manufactured fertilizer excl. crude	155 135	0.6	2.40	0.64
511 Hydrocarbons nes; derivatives	150 526	0.6	0.89	0.29
512 Alcohols, phenols; derivatives	135 726	0.5	1.00	0.44
673 Flat iron non-alloy steel products	127 853	0.5	0.62	0.19
343 Natural gas, liquefied or not	123 084	0.5	0.20	0.07
Remainder	1 188 894	4.5		

For sources and notes, see end of table.

Pour les sources et les notes, se reporter à la fin du tableau.

3

Leading products exported based on average 2005-2006 values SITC Revision 3 (3-digit level) / Principaux produits exportés d'après la moyenne des valeurs de 2005-2006 CTCI révision 3 (positions à 3 chiffres)	Value (f.o.b., thousands of dollars) Valeur (f.a.b., milliers de dollars)	As percentage / En pourcentage — of country total / du total du pays	of ** (1) / des ** (1)	of world / du monde
Lithuania - Lituanie (=Developed)**				
All commodity groups	13 102 817	100.0	0.20	0.12
334 Heavy petroleum & bituminous oil	2 986 949	22.8	1.71	0.72
821 Furniture part; bedding furnishing	618 461	4.7	0.96	0.60
562 Manufactured fertilizer excl. crude	521 698	4.0	4.60	2.16
781 Passenger cars and race cars	499 132	3.8	0.11	0.10
842 Female clothing, woven	261 263	2.0	1.16	0.39
793 Ships boats floating structures	260 055	2.0	0.63	0.33
893 Articles of plastic nes	244 877	1.9	0.41	0.27
248 Wood simply worked, railway sleeper	226 265	1.7	0.86	0.61
773 Electrical distribute equipment nes	220 358	1.7	0.54	0.32
024 Cheese and curd	189 921	1.4	1.14	1.06
Remainder	7 073 838	54.0		
Luxembourg (=Developed)**				
All commodity groups	13 449 009	100.0	0.20	0.12
676 Iron steel bar rod section piling	1 916 819	14.3	5.37	3.34
674 Flat plated iron non-alloy steel	655 092	4.9	2.65	1.76
684 Aluminium	538 130	4.0	0.92	0.61
657 Special yarn and textile fabric etc	507 140	3.8	2.46	1.65
893 Articles of plastic nes	472 402	3.5	0.79	0.52
625 Rubber for wheels, incl inner tube	454 086	3.4	1.48	0.98
641 Paper and paperboard	426 460	3.2	0.50	0.43
781 Passenger cars and race cars	411 514	3.1	0.09	0.08
898 Music instrument device recording	410 384	3.1	1.18	0.79
772 Electrical circuit equipment	389 945	2.9	0.42	0.25
Remainder	7 267 037	54.0		
Madagascar (=Developing)**				
All commodity groups	922 024	100.0	0.02	0.01
036 Crustacean mollusc aquat invertebra	122 205	13.3	0.96	0.60
845 Articles of apparel nes	80 694	8.8	0.12	0.08
842 Female clothing, woven	73 302	8.0	0.17	0.11
075 Spices	71 919	7.8	3.01	2.23
334 Heavy petroleum & bituminous oil	61 548	6.7	0.03	0.01
841 Male clothing, woven	55 928	6.1	0.16	0.10
037 Fish shellfish, prepared preserved	32 785	3.6	0.32	0.20
248 Wood simply worked, railway sleeper	24 919	2.7	0.32	0.07
667 Pearls, precious semiprecious stone	22 458	2.4	0.06	0.02
892 Printed matter	21 317	2.3	0.27	0.05
Remainder	354 948	38.5		
Malawi (=Developing)**				
All commodity groups	581 953	100.0	0.01	0.01
121 Unmanufactured tabacco and refuse	337 618	58.0	7.83	4.73
074 Tea and maté	49 629	8.5	1.52	1.12
061 Sugar, mollasses and honey	43 727	7.5	0.38	0.22
263 Cotton	15 257	2.6	0.38	0.14
841 Male clothing, woven	14 846	2.6	0.04	0.03
845 Articles of apparel nes	14 798	2.5	0.02	0.01
057 Fruit nut (exc oil), fresh or dried	8 957	1.5	0.04	0.02
222 Oil seed etc for soft oil	7 524	1.3	0.07	0.03
843 Male clothing, knitted crocheted	7 411	1.3	0.06	0.05
891 Arms and ammunition	6 241	1.1	0.71	0.08
Remainder	75 947	13.1		
Malaysia - Malaisie (=Developing)**				
All commodity groups	150 816 079	100.0	3 67	1.36
776 Valves tubes; diodes, transistors	24 635 746	16.3	10.31	6.24
752 Computer equipment nes	15 283 577	10.1	9.31	5.36
759 Office equipment part & accessories	9 981 732	6.6	8.35	4.72
333 Crude petroleum & bituminous oil	8 434 133	5.6	1.37	1.00
764 Telecommunicate equipment part nes	8 298 508	5.5	4.21	2.13
343 Natural gas, liquefied or not	5 921 748	3.9	9.84	3.36
422 Fixed veg fat and oil, excl. "soft"	5 165 709	3.4	41.33	35.74
772 Electrical circuit equipment	5 143 788	3.4	8.69	3.36
334 Heavy petroleum & bituminous oil	4 622 685	3.1	2.43	1.11
874 Measure analyze control device nes	2 207 743	1.5	12.06	1.87
Remainder	61 120 711	40.5		

Leading products exported based on average 2005-2006 values SITC Revision 3 (3-digit level) / Principaux produits exportés d'après la moyenne des valeurs de 2005-2006 CTCI révision 3 (positions à 3 chiffres)	Value (f.o.b., thousands of dollars) Valeur (f.a.b., milliers de dollars)	As percentage / En pourcentage — of country total / du total du pays	of ** (1) / des ** (1)	of world / du monde
Maldives (=Developing)**				
All commodity groups	144 889	100.0	0.00	0.00
034 Fish, fresh live chilled frozen	86 895	60.0	0.60	0.24
334 Heavy petroleum & bituminous oil	37 250	25.7	0.02	0.01
037 Fish shellfish, prepared preserved	16 160	11.2	0.16	0.10
035 Fish, dried salted smoked	12 153	8.4	1.33	0.32
892 Printed matter	5 867	4.0	0.07	0.01
081 Animal feed excluding unmilled cereal	1 431	1.0	0.01	0.00
036 Crustacean mollusc aquat invertebra	1 404	1.0	0.01	0.01
793 Ships boats floating structures	1 205	0.8	0.00	0.00
723 Civil engineering plant & equipment	670	0.5	0.00	0.00
288 Non ferrous base metal waste nes	628	0.4	0.01	0.00
Remainder	-18 772	-13.0		
Mali (=Developing)**				
All commodity groups	1 300 616	100.0	0.03	0.01
971 Gold non-monetary excluding ores	912 586	70.2	3.76	1.88
263 Cotton	258 388	19.9	6.42	2.35
001 Live animal excl fish & crustacean	51 901	4.0	2.04	0.38
045 Grain, excl. wheat rice barley maize	9 041	0.7	3.55	0.51
723 Civil engineering plant & equipment	7 928	0.6	0.05	0.01
334 Heavy petroleum & bituminous oil	7 435	0.6	0.00	0.00
222 Oil seed etc for soft oil	3 090	0.2	0.03	0.01
781 Passenger cars and race cars	2 843	0.2	0.00	0.00
057 Fruit nut (exc oil), fresh or dried	2 633	0.2	0.01	0.01
782 Goods and service vehicles	2 624	0.2	0.01	0.00
Remainder	42 148	3.2		
Malta - Malte (=Developed)**				
All commodity groups	2 602 882	100.0	0.04	0.02
776 Valves tubes; diodes, transistors	1 169 759	44.9	0.75	0.30
772 Electrical circuit equipment	129 143	5.0	0.14	0.08
892 Printed matter	101 573	3.9	0.32	0.25
542 Medicines including veterinary	99 200	3.8	0.05	0.04
894 Baby carriage toy game sport good	85 565	3.3	0.31	0.13
034 Fish, fresh live chilled frozen	74 540	2.9	0.36	0.21
781 Passenger cars and race cars	60 691	2.3	0.01	0.01
872 Medical instruments appliances nes	60 629	2.3	0.14	0.11
098 Edible products & preparations nes	56 728	2.2	0.21	0.17
841 Male clothing, woven	56 084	2.2	0.31	0.10
Remainder	708 970	27.2		
Mauritius - Maurice (=Developing)**				
All commodity groups	2 089 095	100.0	0.05	0.02
845 Articles of apparel nes	480 462	23.0	0.71	0.48
061 Sugar, mollasses and honey	353 220	16.9	3.10	1.76
764 Telecommunicate equipment part nes	265 207	12.7	0.13	0.07
841 Male clothing, woven	169 899	8.1	0.49	0.32
037 Fish shellfish, prepared preserved	133 209	6.4	1.29	0.83
034 Fish, fresh live chilled frozen	59 184	2.8	0.41	0.17
667 Pearls, precious semiprecious stone	48 016	2.3	0.14	0.05
843 Male clothing, knitted crocheted	45 414	2.2	0.36	0.29
897 Jewellery nes (667)	36 699	1.8	0.18	0.08
842 Female clothing, woven	28 136	1.3	0.06	0.04
Remainder	469 648	22.5		
Mexico - Mexique (=Developing)**				
All commodity groups	232 083 926	100.0	5.65	2.09
333 Crude petroleum & bituminous oil	31 518 313	13.6	5.14	3.75
781 Passenger cars and race cars	15 405 937	6.6	23.62	3.03
761 Television video receive project	13 480 019	5.8	35.70	20.19
764 Telecommunicate equipment part nes	12 715 498	5.5	6.46	3.26
784 Motor vehicle parts and accessories	10 695 837	4.6	23.12	4.35
752 Computer equipment nes	9 370 138	4.0	5.71	3.28
782 Goods and service vehicles	7 845 851	3.4	37.03	8.28
773 Electrical distribute equipment nes	7 780 200	3.4	28.41	11.29
778 Electrical machinery apparatus nes	7 281 572	3.1	11.04	4.63
772 Electrical circuit equipment	5 838 989	2.5	9.86	3.82
Remainder	110 151 572	47 5		

For sources and notes, see end of table.

Pour les sources et les notes, se reporter à la fin du tableau.

Leading products exported based on average 2005-2006 values SITC Revision 3 (3-digit level) / Principaux produits exportés d'après la moyenne des valeurs de 2005-2006 CTCI révision 3 (positions à 3 chiffres)	2005-2006			
	Value (f.o.b., thousands of dollars) Valeur (f.a.b., milliers de dollars)	As percentage / En pourcentage		
		of country total du total du pays	of ** (1) des ** (1)	of world du monde
Moldova (**=Transition)				
All commodity groups	1 071 428	100.0	0.27	0.01
112 Alcoholic beverages	250 211	23.4	21.61	0.52
057 Fruit nut (exc oil), fresh or dried	62 467	5.8	8.45	0.13
845 Articles of apparel nes	56 928	5.3	7.87	0.06
842 Female clothing, woven	52 404	4.9	5.19	0.08
841 Male clothing, woven	46 051	4.3	5.36	0.09
421 Fixed veg fat and oil, "soft"	36 253	3.4	3.02	0.20
211 Raw hides & skins, excluding furskins	30 582	2.9	15.55	0.51
851 Footwear	28 597	2.7	3.09	0.04
676 Iron steel bar rod section piling	23 442	2.2	0.45	0.04
665 Glassware	21 272	2.0	7.72	0.12
Remainder	463 220	43.2		
Mongolia - Mongolie (**=Developing)				
All commodity groups	1 303 353	100.0	0.03	0.01
283 Copper ores and concentrates	480 822	36.9	2.47	1.93
971 Gold non-monetary excluding ores	300 758	23.1	1.24	0.62
268 Wool & animal hair, incl wool tops	122 508	9.4	7.89	2.43
287 Base metal ores & concentrates nes	99 205	7.6	0.91	0.49
321 Coal excluding non-agglomerated	35 848	2.8	0.22	0.08
611 Leather	31 850	2.4	0.27	0.15
278 Other crude minerals	30 397	2.3	0.92	0.28
845 Articles of apparel nes	29 797	2.3	0.04	0.03
842 Female clothing, woven	24 892	1.9	0.06	0.04
841 Male clothing, woven	21 128	1.6	0.06	0.04
Remainder	126 149	9.7		
Morocco - Maroc (**=Developing)				
All commodity groups	11 857 735	100.0	0.29	0.11
842 Female clothing, woven	1 093 355	9.2	2.49	1.62
522 Inorganic chemical elem oxide salt	946 498	8.0	8.18	3.08
845 Articles of apparel nes	935 043	7.9	1.39	0.94
773 Electrical distribute equipment nes	781 325	6.6	2.85	1.13
776 Valves tubes; diodes, transistors	679 287	5.7	0.28	0.17
841 Male clothing, woven	678 490	5.7	1.96	1.26
272 Crude fertilizer, excl. manufactured	531 390	4.5	39.58	29.13
562 Manufactured fertilizer excl. crude	479 342	4.0	7.40	1.98
036 Crustacean mollusc aquat invertebra	452 261	3.8	3.57	2.21
037 Fish shellfish, prepared preserved	447 979	3.8	4.35	2.79
Remainder	4 832 766	40.8		
Mozambique (**=Developing)				
All commodity groups	2 082 066	100.0	0.05	0.02
684 Aluminium	700 807	33.7	3.30	0.80
288 Non ferrous base metal waste nes	513 388	24.7	10.03	2.16
351 Electric current	159 815	7.7	7.43	0.58
343 Natural gas, liquefied or not	110 174	5.3	0.18	0.06
036 Crustacean mollusc aquat invertebra	85 402	4.1	0.67	0.42
121 Unmanufactured tabacco and refuse	76 776	3.7	1.78	1.08
061 Sugar, mollasses and honey	45 697	2.2	0.40	0.23
263 Cotton	40 948	2.0	1.02	0.37
334 Heavy petroleum & bituminous oil	37 459	1.8	0.02	0.01
057 Fruit nut (exc oil), fresh or dried	33 363	1.6	0.16	0.07
Remainder	278 237	13.4		
Myanmar (**=Developing)				
All commodity groups	4 495 377	100.0	0.11	0.04
343 Natural gas, liquefied or not	1 920 599	42.7	3.19	1.09
247 Wood in rough or roughly squared	591 707	13.2	21.55	5.34
054 Vegetable & vegetable products nes	460 759	10.2	3.81	1.33
841 Male clothing, woven	187 558	4.2	0.54	0.35
036 Crustacean mollusc aquat invertebra	168 938	3.8	1.33	0.83
248 Wood simply worked, railway sleeper	154 516	3.4	2.01	0.42
682 Copper	110 049	2.4	0.26	0.13
034 Fish, fresh live chilled frozen	101 662	2.3	0.71	0.28
845 Articles of apparel nes	93 224	2.1	0.14	0.09
333 Crude petroleum & bituminous oil	80 706	1.8	0.01	0.01
Remainder	625 659	13.9		

Leading products exported based on average 2005-2006 values SITC Revision 3 (3-digit level) / Principaux produits exportés d'après la moyenne des valeurs de 2005-2006 CTCI révision 3 (positions à 3 chiffres)	2005-2006			
	Value (f.o.b., thousands of dollars) Valeur (f.a.b., milliers de dollars)	As percentage / En pourcentage		
		of country total du total du pays	of ** (1) des ** (1)	of world du monde
Namibia - Namibie (**=Developing)				
All commodity groups	2 908 152	100.0	0.07	0.03
667 Pearls, precious semiprecious stone	792 753	27.3	2.25	0.85
034 Fish, fresh live chilled frozen	362 985	12.5	2.52	1.01
686 Zinc	254 978	8.8	6.44	2.26
892 Printed matter	200 106	6.9	2.53	0.50
278 Other crude minerals	133 882	4.6	4.07	1.24
682 Copper	110 384	3.8	0.26	0.13
286 Uranium & thorium ore concentrates	106 517	3.7	40.74	15.47
112 Alcoholic beverages	87 712	3.0	1.27	0.18
001 Live animal excl. fish & crustacean	83 645	2.9	3.29	0.61
011 Beef, fresh chilled frozen	71 431	2.5	1.12	0.31
Remainder	703 760	24.2		
Nepal - Népal (**=Developing)				
All commodity groups	794 671	100.0	0.02	0.01
659 Floor coverings etc	89 345	11.2	1.96	0.73
431 Processed animal & veg fats & oils	68 414	8.6	2.16	1.16
651 Textile yarn	38 027	4.8	0.16	0.09
842 Female clothing, woven	31 857	4.0	0.07	0.05
553 Perfume toilet cosmetics, excl. soap	29 858	3.8	0.40	0.06
841 Male clothing, woven	29 491	3.7	0.09	0.05
674 Flat plated iron non-alloy steel	28 528	3.6	0.25	0.08
893 Articles of plastic nes	27 899	3.5	0.09	0.03
111 Non alcoholic beverage nes	26 631	3.4	1.26	0.23
598 Miscellaneous chemical products nes	24 939	3.1	0.21	0.04
Remainder	399 684	50.3		
Netherlands - Pays-Bas (**=Developed)				
All commodity groups	345 137 249	100.0	5.22	3.10
334 Heavy petroleum & bituminous oil	28 156 657	8.2	16.11	6.76
752 Computer equipment nes	21 391 865	6.2	17.69	7.50
759 Office equipment part & accessories	15 644 865	4.5	17.01	7.40
343 Natural gas, liquefied or not	12 352 547	3.6	16.28	7.00
776 Valves tubes; diodes, transistors	8 505 966	2.5	5.47	2.15
542 Medicines including veterinary	8 341 906	2.4	3.98	3.76
764 Telecommunicate equipment part nes	8 275 961	2.4	4.30	2.12
292 Crude vegetable materials nes	7 876 764	2.3	46.30	33.99
511 Hydrocarbons nes; derivatives	6 197 689	1.8	17.94	11.76
054 Vegetable & vegetable products nes	4 650 484	1.3	21.01	13.42
Remainder	223 742 547	64.8		
Netherlands Antilles - Antilles néerlandaises (**=Developing)				
All commodity groups	3 049 085	100.0	0.07	0.03
334 Heavy petroleum & bituminous oil	2 464 955	80.8	1.30	0.59
931 Transaction commodity unclassified	178 811	5.9	54.49	17.91
793 Ships boats floating structures	119 752	3.9	0.33	0.15
333 Crude petroleum & bituminous oil	33 683	1.1	0.01	0.00
335 Residual petroleum products nes	30 224	1.0	0.45	0.15
278 Other crude minerals	22 781	0.7	0.69	0.21
591 Household and garden chemicals	14 821	0.5	0.40	0.09
073 Chocolate & cocoa preparations nes	10 827	0.4	0.70	0.08
723 Civil engineering plant & equipment	10 544	0.3	0.07	0.01
897 Jewellery nes (667)	9 009	0.3	0.04	0.02
Remainder	153 678	5.0		
New Caledonia - Nouvelle-Calédonie (**=Developing)				
All commodity groups	1 124 631	100.0	0.03	0.01
671 Pig & sponge iron, ferro alloys etc	682 025	60.6	5.14	2.68
284 Nickel ores, concentrates, etc	352 762	31.4	10.96	5.22
036 Crustacean mollusc aquat invertebra	25 170	2.2	0.20	0.12
334 Heavy petroleum & bituminous oil	10 124	0.9	0.01	0.00
679 Iron steel pipe tube fittings etc	6 535	0.6	0.04	0.01
741 Heating cooling equipment parts nes	5 312	0.5	0.03	0.01
792 Aircraft, spacecraft & equipment	4 914	0.4	0.04	0.00
892 Printed matter	3 954	0.4	0.05	0.01
034 Fish, fresh live chilled frozen	2 916	0.3	0.02	0.01
713 Internal combustion engine part nes	2 149	0.2	0.01	0.00
Remainder	28 771	2.6		

For sources and notes, see end of table.

Pour les sources et les notes, se reporter à la fin du tableau.

3.2.D Export structure by product
Individual countries and territories

3.2.D Structure des exportations par produits
Pays et territoires individuels

Leading products exported based on average 2005-2006 values SITC Revision 3 (3-digit level) / Principaux produits exportés d'après la moyenne des valeurs de 2005-2006 CTCI révision 3 (positions à 3 chiffres)	Value (f.o.b., thousands of dollars) Valeur (f.a.b., milliers de dollars)	of country total du total du pays	of ** (1) des ** (1)	of world du monde
New Zealand - Nouvelle-Zélande (**=Developed)				
All commodity groups	22 069 639	100.0	0.33	0.20
022 Milk products, excl. butter & cheese	2 393 831	10.8	12.27	10.39
012 Meat nes, fresh chilled frozen	1 929 280	8.7	5.97	4.87
011 Beef, fresh chilled frozen	1 218 662	5.5	7.51	5.33
057 Fruit nut (exc oil), fresh or dried	786 714	3.6	2.94	1.63
024 Cheese and curd	780 793	3.5	4.69	4.38
684 Aluminium	764 847	3.5	1.31	0.87
023 Butter fats oils derived from milk	680 526	3.1	17.70	16.45
098 Edible products & preparations nes	676 800	3.1	2.55	1.99
248 Wood simply worked, railway sleeper	595 831	2.7	2.27	1.62
592 Starches, glutenes, glues, etc	595 565	2.7	5.24	4.06
Remainder	11 646 789	52.8		
Nicaragua (**=Developing)				
All commodity groups	812 288	100.0	0.02	0.01
071 Coffee and coffee substitutes	169 857	20.9	1.55	0.99
011 Beef, fresh chilled frozen	98 839	12.2	1.55	0.43
036 Crustacean mollusc aquat invertebra	81 120	10.0	0.64	0.40
061 Sugar, mollasses and honey	61 826	7.6	0.54	0.31
971 Gold non-monetary excluding ores	51 135	6.3	0.21	0.11
222 Oil seed etc for soft oil	47 701	5.9	0.47	0.22
001 Live animal excl. fish & crustacean	27 898	3.4	1.10	0.20
054 Vegetable & vegetable products nes	25 170	3.1	0.21	0.07
057 Fruit nut (exc oil), fresh or dried	20 915	2.6	0.10	0.04
034 Fish, fresh live chilled frozen	16 147	2.0	0.11	0.05
Remainder	211 681	26.1		
Niger (**=Developing)				
All commodity groups	351 693	100.0	0.01	0.00
286 Uranium & thorium ore concentrates	154 730	44.0	59.18	22.47
971 Gold non-monetary excluding ores	61 101	17.4	0.25	0.13
001 Live animal excl. fish & crustacean	36 765	10.5	1.45	0.27
054 Vegetable & vegetable products nes	28 279	8.0	0.23	0.08
652 Woven cotton fabrics	10 183	2.9	0.06	0.04
269 Worn clothing, textile article; rag	9 658	2.7	1.83	0.44
723 Civil engineering plant & equipment	8 502	2.4	0.05	0.01
122 Manufactured tabacco	5 445	1.5	0.13	0.03
334 Heavy petroleum & bituminous oil	5 320	1.5	0.00	0.00
781 Passenger cars and race cars	4 823	1.4	0.01	0.00
Remainder	26 886	7.6		
Nigeria - Nigéria (**=Developing)				
All commodity groups	44 993 965	100.0	1.09	0.40
333 Crude petroleum & bituminous oil	39 271 595	87.3	6.40	4.68
343 Natural gas, liquefied or not	1 893 722	4.2	3.15	1.07
334 Heavy petroleum & bituminous oil	1 175 229	2.6	0.62	0.28
342 Liquefied propane and butane	571 467	1.3	3.15	2.03
072 Cocoa	439 979	1.0	7.42	4.90
263 Cotton	206 132	0.5	5.12	1.87
248 Wood simply worked, railway sleeper	184 958	0.4	2.41	0.50
611 Leather	160 643	0.4	1.34	0.74
344 Petroleum and hydrocarbon gas nes	123 459	0.3	4.72	1.26
222 Oil seed etc for soft oil	92 244	0.2	0.90	0.42
Remainder	874 576	1.9		
Norway - Norvège (**=Developed)				
All commodity groups	112 691 382	100.0	1.70	1.01
333 Crude petroleum & bituminous oil	49 469 803	43.9	43.42	5.89
343 Natural gas, liquefied or not	18 919 708	16.8	24.94	10.72
334 Heavy petroleum & bituminous oil	4 956 252	4.4	2.84	1.19
684 Aluminium	4 466 058	4.0	7.65	5.09
034 Fish, fresh live chilled frozen	4 126 990	3.7	19.77	11.52
342 Liquefied propane and butane	2 123 311	1.9	23.33	7.55
683 Nickel	1 565 199	1.4	13.98	8.86
793 Ships boats floating structures	1 549 962	1.4	3.77	1.95
874 Measure analyze control device nes	859 458	0.8	0.87	0.73
641 Paper and paperboard	825 058	0.7	0.97	0.83
Remainder	23 829 584	21.1		

Leading products exported based on average 2005-2006 values SITC Revision 3 (3-digit level) / Principaux produits exportés d'après la moyenne des valeurs de 2005-2006 CTCI révision 3 (positions à 3 chiffres)	Value (f.o.b., thousands of dollars) Valeur (f.a.b., milliers de dollars)	of country total du total du pays	of ** (1) des ** (1)	of world du monde
Oman (**=Developing)				
All commodity groups	20 095 488	100.0	0.49	0.18
333 Crude petroleum & bituminous oil	13 922 098	69.3	2.27	1.66
343 Natural gas, liquefied or not	3 902 953	19.4	6.48	2.21
334 Heavy petroleum & bituminous oil	281 017	1.4	0.15	0.07
022 Milk products, excl. butter & cheese	120 072	0.6	4.19	0.52
034 Fish, fresh live chilled frozen	83 475	0.4	0.58	0.23
661 Lime cement construction material	78 374	0.4	0.75	0.38
562 Manufactured fertilizer excl. crude	76 966	0.4	1.19	0.32
679 Iron steel pipe tube fittings etc	75 921	0.4	0.43	0.12
773 Electrical distribute equipment nes	75 212	0.4	0.27	0.11
723 Civil engineering plant & equipment	67 670	0.3	0.44	0.09
Remainder	1 411 728	7.0		
Pakistan (**=Developing)				
All commodity groups	16 491 537	100.0	0.40	0.15
658 Made-up textile articles nes	3 142 691	19.1	13.74	9.65
652 Woven cotton fabrics	2 071 793	12.6	11.60	7.19
651 Textile yarn	1 378 514	8.4	5.82	3.24
042 Rice	1 125 573	6.8	14.43	10.99
843 Male clothing, knitted crocheted	849 085	5.1	6.72	5.35
841 Male clothing, woven	787 157	4.8	2.27	1.47
334 Heavy petroleum & bituminous oil	732 720	4.4	0.38	0.18
848 Headgear, non-textile clothing	637 595	3.9	4.43	3.05
845 Articles of apparel nes	575 313	3.5	0.85	0.58
842 Female clothing, woven	386 935	2.3	0.88	0.57
Remainder	4 804 162	29.1		
Panama (**=Developing)				
All commodity groups	1 024 917	100.0	0.02	0.01
034 Fish, fresh live chilled frozen	296 061	28.9	2.06	0.83
057 Fruit nut (exc oil), fresh or dried	274 979	26.8	1.33	0.57
036 Crustacean mollusc aquat invertebra	81 367	7.9	0.64	0.40
001 Live animal excl. fish & crustacean	26 038	2.5	1.02	0.19
054 Vegetable & vegetable products nes	24 776	2.4	0.21	0.07
061 Sugar, mollasses and honey	22 500	2.2	0.20	0.11
282 Ferrous iron & steel, waste & scrap	18 979	1.9	0.71	0.07
035 Fish, dried salted smoked	18 901	1.8	2.06	0.50
542 Medicines including veterinary	18 700	1.8	0.17	0.01
642 Cut paper and paperboard articles	17 623	1.7	0.20	0.05
Remainder	224 993	22.0		
Papua New Guinea - Papouasie-Nouvelle-Guinée (**=Developing)				
All commodity groups	3 967 962	100.0	0.10	0.04
333 Crude petroleum & bituminous oil	1 116 078	28.1	0.18	0.13
971 Gold non-monetary excluding ores	851 078	21.4	3.50	1.75
283 Copper ores and concentrates	703 149	17.7	3.61	2.83
247 Wood in rough or roughly squared	376 961	9.5	13.73	3.40
422 Fixed veg fat and oil, excl. "soft"	240 037	6.0	1.92	1.66
071 Coffee and coffee substitutes	148 139	3.7	1.35	0.87
334 Heavy petroleum & bituminous oil	131 355	3.3	0.07	0.03
072 Cocoa	84 902	2.1	1.43	0.95
037 Fish shellfish, prepared preserved	53 773	1.4	0.52	0.33
034 Fish, fresh live chilled frozen	45 059	1.1	0.31	0.13
Remainder	217 432	5.5		
Paraguay (**=Developing)				
All commodity groups	1 797 095	100.0	0.04	0.02
222 Oil seed etc for soft oil	539 763	30.0	5.29	2.43
011 Beef, fresh chilled frozen	327 322	18.2	5.13	1.43
081 Animal feed excluding unmilled cereal	141 796	7.9	1.11	0.45
421 Fixed veg fat and oil, "soft"	104 407	5.8	1.50	0.58
044 Maize unmilled, excluding sweet corn	104 301	5.8	3.38	0.85
611 Leather	62 340	3.5	0.52	0.29
263 Cotton	61 455	3.4	1.53	0.56
248 Wood simply worked, railway sleeper	57 244	3.2	0.75	0.16
041 Wheat meslin, incl spelt, unmilled	53 630	3.0	2.75	0.28
061 Sugar, mollasses and honey	23 326	1.3	0.20	0.12
Remainder	321 512	17.9		

For sources and notes, see end of table.

Pour les sources et les notes, se reporter à la fin du tableau.

3.2.D Export structure by product
Individual countries and territories

3.2.D Structure des exportations par produits
Pays et territoires individuels

Leading products exported based on average 2005-2006 values SITC Revision 3 (3-digit level) / Principaux produits exportés d'après la moyenne des valeurs de 2005-2006 CTCI révision 3 (positions à 3 chiffres)	2005-2006 Value (f.o.b., thousands of dollars) Valeur (f.a.b., milliers de dollars)	of country total du total du pays	of ** (1) des ** (1)	of world du monde
Peru - Pérou (=Developing)**				
All commodity groups	20 439 593	100.0	0.50	0.18
971 Gold non-monetary excluding ores	3 537 338	17.3	14.56	7.28
682 Copper	2 835 245	13.9	6.77	3.26
287 Base metal ores & concentrates nes	2 603 086	12.7	23.96	12.77
283 Copper ores and concentrates	2 139 919	10.5	10.98	8.60
334 Heavy petroleum & bituminous oil	1 352 563	6.6	0.71	0.32
081 Animal feed excluding unmilled cereal	1 190 831	5.8	9.36	3.75
845 Articles of apparel nes	603 570	3.0	0.89	0.60
071 Coffee and coffee substitutes	410 602	2.0	3.74	2.40
681 Silver, platinum, platinum metals	382 587	1.9	3.12	1.35
333 Crude petroleum & bituminous oil	337 522	1.7	0.06	0.04
Remainder	5 046 330	24.7		
Philippines (=Developing)**				
All commodity groups	44 332 400	100.0	1.08	0.40
776 Valves tubes; diodes, transistors	15 989 221	36.1	6.69	4.05
752 Computer equipment nes	4 373 366	9.9	2.66	1.53
759 Office equipment part & accessories	3 533 390	8.0	2.96	1.67
778 Electrical machinery apparatus nes	2 004 229	4.5	3.04	1.27
784 Motor vehicle parts and accessories	1 377 877	3.1	2.98	0.56
772 Electrical circuit equipment	970 255	2.2	1.64	0.63
682 Copper	865 031	2.0	2.07	0.99
773 Electrical distribute equipment nes	861 856	1.9	3.15	1.25
764 Telecommunicate equipment part nes	848 697	1.9	0.43	0.22
334 Heavy petroleum & bituminous oil	752 023	1.7	0.40	0.18
Remainder	12 756 456	28.8		
Poland - Pologne (=Developed)**				
All commodity groups	99 481 091	100.0	1.50	0.89
781 Passenger cars and race cars	6 194 873	6.2	1.40	1.22
821 Furniture part; bedding furnishing	5 878 602	5.9	9.12	5.73
784 Motor vehicle parts and accessories	4 324 448	4.3	2.18	1.76
713 Internal combustion engine part nes	4 068 049	4.1	4.05	3.43
793 Ships boats floating structures	3 083 855	3.1	7.49	3.87
761 Television video receive project	2 591 054	2.6	8.96	3.88
682 Copper	2 363 465	2.4	6.11	2.72
773 Electrical distribute equipment nes	2 331 741	2.3	5.74	3.38
699 Base metal manufactures nes	2 244 835	2.3	3.28	2.28
775 Household equipment nes	2 046 183	2.1	5.60	3.07
Remainder	64 353 984	64.7		
Portugal (=Developed)**				
All commodity groups	40 722 078	100.0	0.62	0.37
781 Passenger cars and race cars	2 852 663	7.0	0.65	0.56
334 Heavy petroleum & bituminous oil	1 605 024	3.9	0.92	0.39
784 Motor vehicle parts and accessories	1 587 540	3.9	0.80	0.65
851 Footwear	1 508 322	3.7	5.19	2.18
845 Articles of apparel nes	1 397 584	3.4	4.41	1.40
776 Valves tubes; diodes, transistors	1 152 707	2.8	0.74	0.29
762 Radio broadcast receivers	1 005 120	2.5	15.62	5.39
633 Cork manufactures	924 385	2.3	65.47	60.81
821 Furniture part; bedding furnishing	919 076	2.3	1.43	0.90
112 Alcoholic beverages	818 811	2.0	2.04	1.70
Remainder	26 950 845	66.2		
Qatar (=Developing)**				
All commodity groups	29 906 902	100.0	0.73	0.27
333 Crude petroleum & bituminous oil	14 412 315	48.2	2.35	1.72
343 Natural gas, liquefied or not	9 892 953	33.1	16.43	5.61
342 Liquefied propane and butane	963 497	3.2	5.31	3.43
571 Primary form ethylene polymers	862 402	2.9	5.54	2.01
334 Heavy petroleum & bituminous oil	784 070	2.6	0.41	0.19
562 Manufactured fertilizer excl. crude	679 576	2.3	10.50	2.81
511 Hydrocarbons nes; derivatives	125 874	0.4	0.75	0.24
781 Passenger cars and race cars	98 726	0.3	0.15	0.02
676 Iron steel bar rod section piling	61 089	0.2	0.37	0.11
673 Flat iron non-alloy steel products	60 546	0.2	0.29	0.09
Remainder	1 965 854	6.6		

Leading products exported based on average 2005-2006 values SITC Revision 3 (3-digit level) / Principaux produits exportés d'après la moyenne des valeurs de 2005-2006 CTCI révision 3 (positions à 3 chiffres)	2005-2006 Value (f.o.b., thousands of dollars) Valeur (f.a.b., milliers de dollars)	of country total du total du pays	of ** (1) des ** (1)	of world du monde
Republic of Korea - République de Corée (=Developing)**				
All commodity groups	304 937 707	100.0	7.42	2.74
764 Telecommunicate equipment part nes	33 592 775	11.0	17.06	8.61
781 Passenger cars and race cars	28 926 648	9.5	44.35	5.69
776 Valves tubes; diodes, transistors	27 987 334	9.2	11.71	7.09
793 Ships boats floating structures	19 362 182	6.3	53.69	24.32
334 Heavy petroleum & bituminous oil	17 521 826	5.7	9.21	4.21
871 Optical instruments apparatus nes	11 519 753	3.8	28.83	22.58
752 Computer equipment nes	8 875 949	2.9	5.41	3.11
784 Motor vehicle parts and accessories	8 642 813	2.8	18.68	3.52
759 Office equipment part & accessories	8 576 442	2.8	7.18	4.05
778 Electrical machinery apparatus nes	7 623 514	2.5	11.55	4.85
Remainder	132 308 472	43.4		
Romania - Roumanie (=Developed)**				
All commodity groups	30 032 813	100.0	0.45	0.27
334 Heavy petroleum & bituminous oil	2 779 950	9.3	1.59	0.67
842 Female clothing, woven	1 776 396	5.9	7.86	2.63
773 Electrical distribute equipment nes	1 696 159	5.6	4.17	2.46
851 Footwear	1 646 107	5.5	5.66	2.38
841 Male clothing, woven	1 372 925	4.6	7.55	2.56
673 Flat iron non-alloy steel products	1 339 485	4.5	3.48	1.95
821 Furniture part; bedding furnishing	1 171 463	3.9	1.82	1.14
784 Motor vehicle parts and accessories	1 067 408	3.6	0.54	0.43
845 Articles of apparel nes	775 272	2.6	2.44	0.78
793 Ships boats floating structures	669 471	2.2	1.63	0.84
Remainder	15 738 178	52.4		
Russian Federation - Fédération de Russie (=Transition)**				
All commodity groups	271 501 161	100.0	68.31	2.44
333 Crude petroleum & bituminous oil	88 129 524	32.5	78.44	10.49
334 Heavy petroleum & bituminous oil	39 029 482	14.4	76.18	9.38
343 Natural gas, liquefied or not	36 623 198	13.5	90.77	20.76
684 Aluminium	6 467 752	2.4	79.24	7.37
672 Ingots, Iron steel primary products	5 194 580	1.9	55.61	17.59
683 Nickel	4 803 562	1.8	99.90	27.19
673 Flat iron non-alloy steel products	4 347 739	1.6	45.99	6.33
321 Coal excluding non-agglomomerated	4 048 580	1.5	85.36	8.49
562 Manufactured fertilizer excl. crude	3 978 036	1.5	62.33	16.45
682 Copper	3 494 940	1.3	54.14	4.02
Remainder	75 383 768	27.8		
Rwanda (=Developing)**				
All commodity groups	142 280	100.0	0.00	0.00
287 Base metal ores & concentrates nes	51 811	36.4	0.48	0.25
071 Coffee and coffee substitutes	42 487	29.9	0.39	0.25
074 Tea and maté	24 292	17.1	0.74	0.55
211 Raw hides & skins, excluding furskins	2 797	2.0	0.29	0.05
334 Heavy petroleum & bituminous oil	2 340	1.6	0.00	0.00
723 Civil engineering plant & equipment	2 181	1.5	0.01	0.00
781 Passenger cars and race cars	2 071	1.5	0.00	0.00
292 Crude vegetable materials nes	1 474	1.0	0.02	0.01
782 Goods and service vehicles	1 116	0.8	0.01	0.00
764 Telecommunicate equipment part nes	1 007	0.7	0.00	0.00
Remainder	10 703	7.5		
Saint Kitts and Nevis - Saint-Kitts-et-Nevis (=Developing)**				
All commodity groups	37 006	100.0	0.00	0.00
772 Electrical circuit equipment	18 098	48.9	0.03	0.01
764 Telecommunicate equipment part nes	5 371	14.5	0.00	0.00
778 Electrical machinery apparatus nes	4 776	12.9	0.01	0.00
716 Rotating electric plant parts nes	2 746	7.4	0.02	0.00
112 Alcoholic beverages	917	2.5	0.01	0.00
111 Non alcoholic beverage nes	744	2.0	0.04	0.01
723 Civil engineering plant & equipment	628	1.7	0.01	0.00
892 Printed matter	532	1.4	0.01	0.00
692 Metal storage transport container	256	0.7	0.01	0.00
771 Electric power machine part excl. 716	234	0.6	0.00	0.00
Remainder	2 705	7.3		

For sources and notes, see end of table.

Pour les sources et les notes, se reporter à la fin du tableau.

168

3.2.D Export structure by product
Individual countries and territories

3.2.D Structure des exportations par produits
Pays et territoires individuels

Leading products exported based on average 2005-2006 values SITC Revision 3 (3-digit level) / Principaux produits exportés d'après la moyenne des valeurs de 2005-2006 CTCI révision 3 (positions à 3 chiffres)	Value (f.o.b., thousands of dollars) Valeur (f.a.b., milliers de dollars)	2005-2006 As percentage En pourcentage of country total du total du pays	of ** (1) des ** (1)	of world du monde
Saint Lucia - Sainte-Lucie (**=Developing)				
All commodity groups	68 300	100.0	0.00	0.00
057 Fruit nut (exc oil), fresh or dried	16 996	24.9	0.08	0.04
334 Heavy petroleum & bituminous oil	12 106	17.7	0.01	0.00
112 Alcoholic beverages	11 059	16.2	0.16	0.02
642 Cut paper and paperboard articles	3 434	5.0	0.04	0.01
764 Telecommunicate equipment part nes	2 006	2.9	0.00	0.00
772 Electrical circuit equipment	1 675	2.5	0.00	0.00
723 Civil engineering plant & equipment	1 550	2.3	0.01	0.00
897 Jewellery nes (667)	1 375	2.0	0.01	0.00
111 Non alcoholic beverage nes	1 121	1.6	0.05	0.01
781 Passenger cars and race cars	768	1.1	0.00	0.00
Remainder	16 211	23.7		
Saint Vincent and the Grenadines - Saint-Vincent-et-les Grenadines (**=Developing)				
All commodity groups	38 994	100.0	0.00	0.00
057 Fruit nut (exc oil), fresh or dried	12 620	32.4	0.06	0.03
046 Wheat meal & flour, meslin flour	5 017	12.9	0.52	0.20
054 Vegetable & vegetable products nes	3 971	10.2	0.03	0.01
042 Rice	3 408	8.7	0.04	0.03
081 Animal feed excluding unmilled cereal	1 933	5.0	0.02	0.01
111 Non alcoholic beverage nes	1 478	3.8	0.07	0.01
674 Flat plated iron non-alloy steel	1 265	3.2	0.01	0.00
691 Iron steel aluminium structures nes	874	2.2	0.01	0.00
642 Cut paper and paperboard articles	839	2.2	0.01	0.00
845 Articles of apparel nes	710	1.8	0.00	0.00
Remainder	6 879	17.6		
Samoa (**=Developing)				
All commodity groups	82 594	100.0	0.00	0.00
773 Electrical distribute equipment nes	59 777	72.4	0.22	0.09
034 Fish, fresh live chilled frozen	9 198	11.1	0.06	0.03
059 Fruit & vegetable juice unferment	2 987	3.6	0.08	0.03
112 Alcoholic beverages	2 327	2.8	0.03	0.00
422 Fixed veg fat and oil, excl. "soft"	1 451	1.8	0.01	0.01
054 Vegetable & vegetable products nes	574	0.7	0.00	0.00
057 Fruit nut (exc oil), fresh or dried	544	0.7	0.00	0.00
269 Worn clothing, textile article; rag	431	0.5	0.08	0.02
334 Heavy petroleum & bituminous oil	349	0.4	0.00	0.00
699 Base metal manufactures nes	318	0.4	0.00	0.00
Remainder	4 639	5.6		
Sao Tome and Principe - Sao Tomé-et-Principe (**=Developing)				
All commodity groups	3 645	100.0	0.00	0.00
072 Cocoa	3 214	88.2	0.05	0.04
057 Fruit nut (exc oil), fresh or dried	73	2.0	0.00	0.00
112 Alcoholic beverages	57	1.6	0.00	0.00
784 Motor vehicle parts and accessories	56	1.5	0.00	0.00
073 Chocolate & cocoa preparations nes	53	1.5	0.00	0.00
781 Passenger cars and race cars	48	1.3	0.00	0.00
421 Fixed veg fat and oil, "soft"	26	0.7	0.00	0.00
422 Fixed veg fat and oil, excl. "soft"	24	0.7	0.00	0.00
292 Crude vegetable materials nes	18	0.5	0.00	0.00
716 Rotating electric plant parts nes	13	0.4	0.00	0.00
Remainder	63	1.7		
Saudi Arabia - Arabie saoudite (**=Developing)				
All commodity groups	196 021 531	100.0	4.77	1.76
333 Crude petroleum & bituminous oil	149 697 352	76.4	24 40	17.83
334 Heavy petroleum & bituminous oil	18 149 617	9.3	9 54	4.36
342 Liquefied propane and butane	6 024 671	3.1	33 21	21.43
571 Primary form ethylene polymers	3 403 685	1.7	21.86	7.92
512 Alcohols, phenols; derivatives	2 286 429	1.2	16.76	7.39
511 Hydrocarbons nes; derivatives	1 449 198	0.7	8.60	2.75
516 Other organic chemicals	948 660	0.5	13.03	3.80
343 Natural gas, liquefied or not	857 942	0.4	1.43	0.49
575 Other plastics, in primary forms	808 108	0.4	5.39	1.15
562 Manufactured fertilizer excl. crude	652 575	0.3	10.08	2.70
Remainder	11 743 293	6.0		

Leading products exported based on average 2005-2006 values SITC Revision 3 (3-digit level) / Principaux produits exportés d'après la moyenne des valeurs de 2005-2006 CTCI révision 3 (positions à 3 chiffres)	Value (f.o.b., thousands of dollars) Valeur (f.a.b., milliers de dollars)	2005-2006 As percentage En pourcentage of country total du total du pays	of ** (1) des ** (1)	of world du monde
Senegal - Sénégal (**=Developing)				
All commodity groups	1 481 187	100.0	0.04	0.01
334 Heavy petroleum & bituminous oil	295 879	20.0	0.16	0.07
034 Fish, fresh live chilled frozen	139 960	9.4	0.97	0.39
522 Inorganic chemical elem oxide salt	132 556	8.9	1.15	0.43
036 Crustacean mollusc aquat invertebra	100 953	6.8	0.80	0.49
661 Lime cement construction material	67 294	4.5	0.64	0.33
333 Crude petroleum & bituminous oil	63 935	4.3	0.01	0.01
421 Fixed veg fat and oil, "soft"	39 887	2.7	0.57	0.22
098 Edible products & preparations nes	39 292	2.7	0.57	0.12
042 Rice	34 190	2.3	0.44	0.33
553 Perfume toilet cosmetics, excl. soap	32 343	2.2	0.43	0.07
Remainder	534 897	36.1		
Serbia and Montenegro - Serbie-et-Monténégro (**=Transition)				
All commodity groups	5 454 837	100.0	1.37	0.05
673 Flat iron non-alloy steel products	573 540	10.5	6.07	0.83
682 Copper	318 105	5.8	4.93	0.37
625 Rubber for wheels, incl inner tube	188 393	3.5	16.45	0.41
061 Sugar, mollasses and honey	164 036	3.0	22.04	0.82
058 Fruit preserve preparation excl. juice	157 844	2.9	45.98	1.49
684 Aluminium	141 934	2.6	1.74	0.16
044 Maize unmilled, excluding sweet corn	141 489	2.6	34.04	1.16
851 Footwear	140 453	2.6	15.16	0.20
893 Articles of plastic nes	139 142	2.6	23.53	0.15
674 Flat plated iron non-alloy steel	139 107	2.6	13.11	0.37
Remainder	3 350 794	61.4		
Seychelles (**=Developing)				
All commodity groups	359 829	100.0	0.01	0.00
037 Fish shellfish, prepared preserved	182 608	50.7	1.77	1.14
334 Heavy petroleum & bituminous oil	142 008	39.5	0.07	0.03
872 Medical instruments appliances nes	7 837	2.2	0.08	0.01
542 Medicines including veterinary	6 275	1.7	0.06	0.00
036 Crustacean mollusc aquat invertebra	5 227	1.5	0.04	0.03
081 Animal feed excluding unmilled cereal	4 720	1.3	0.04	0.01
034 Fish, fresh live chilled frozen	2 861	0.8	0.02	0.01
899 Manufactured articles nes	2 153	0.6	0.02	0.00
342 Liquefied propane and butane	774	0.2	0.00	0.00
112 Alcoholic beverages	669	0.2	0.01	0.00
Remainder	4 698	1.3		
Singapore - Singapour (**=Developing)				
All commodity groups	250 726 617	100.0	6.10	2.26
776 Valves tubes; diodes, transistors	60 863 356	24.3	25.46	15.41
334 Heavy petroleum & bituminous oil	30 204 358	12.0	15.87	7.26
759 Office equipment part & accessories	17 731 720	7.1	14.84	8.38
764 Telecommunicate equipment part nes	14 418 065	5.8	7.32	3.69
752 Computer equipment nes	14 275 329	5.7	8.69	5.00
772 Electrical circuit equipment	5 328 186	2.1	9.00	3.48
515 Organo-inorganic compound acid salt	5 083 396	2.0	47.80	6.13
778 Electrical machinery apparatus nes	5 032 482	2.0	7.63	3.20
723 Civil engineering plant & equipment	3 446 420	1.4	22.19	4.49
898 Music instrument device recording	3 410 286	1.4	20.23	6.60
Remainder	90 933 019	36.3		
Slovakia - Slovaquie (**=Developed)				
All commodity groups	36 858 236	100.0	0.56	0.33
781 Passenger cars and race cars	5 159 357	14.0	1.17	1.01
761 Television video receive project	2 164 924	5.9	7.49	3.24
334 Heavy petroleum & bituminous oil	2 036 154	5.5	1.17	0.49
784 Motor vehicle parts and accessories	1 800 633	4.9	0.91	0.73
673 Flat iron non-alloy steel products	1 522 700	4.1	3.95	2.22
773 Electrical distribute equipment nes	1 080 966	2.9	2.66	1.57
752 Computer equipment nes	817 373	2.2	0.68	0.29
821 Furniture part; bedding furnishing	715 078	1.9	1.11	0.70
699 Base metal manufactures nes	664 405	1.8	0.97	0.67
674 Flat plated iron non-alloy steel	621 772	1.7	2.52	1.67
Remainder	20 274 874	55.0		

For sources and notes, see end of table.

Pour les sources et les notes, se reporter à la fin du tableau.

Leading products exported based on average 2005-2006 values SITC Revision 3 (3-digit level) / Principaux produits exportés d'après la moyenne des valeurs de 2005-2006 CTCI révision 3 (positions à 3 chiffres)	2005-2006			
	Value (f.o.b., thousands of dollars) / Valeur (f.a.b., milliers de dollars)	As percentage / En pourcentage		
		of country total / du total du pays	of ** (1) / des ** (1)	of world / du monde
Slovenia - Slovénie (=Developed)**				
All commodity groups	19 439 368	100.0	0.29	0.17
781 Passenger cars and race cars	1 927 724	9.9	0.44	0.38
542 Medicines including veterinary	1 226 342	6.3	0.58	0.55
821 Furniture part; bedding furnishing	1 064 533	5.5	1.65	1.04
775 Household equipment nes	1 060 776	5.5	2.90	1.59
684 Aluminium	692 576	3.6	1.19	0.79
784 Motor vehicle parts and accessories	564 189	2.9	0.28	0.23
778 Electrical machinery apparatus nes	474 155	2.4	0.52	0.30
641 Paper and paperboard	430 379	2.2	0.51	0.43
743 Gas pump, compressor, fan, filter	429 559	2.2	0.76	0.58
699 Base metal manufactures nes	409 880	2.1	0.60	0.42
Remainder	11 159 256	57.4		
South Africa - Afrique du Sud (=Developing)**				
All commodity groups	50 080 466	100.0	1.22	0.45
681 Silver, platinum, platinum metals	6 759 701	13.5	55.18	23.84
321 Coal excluding non-agglomomerated	3 220 680	6.4	19.74	6.76
781 Passenger cars and race cars	2 807 600	5.6	4.30	0.55
671 Pig & sponge iron, ferro alloys etc	2 730 088	5.5	20.57	10.74
667 Pearls, precious semiprecious stone	2 539 040	5.1	7.22	2.73
743 Gas pump, compressor, fan, filter	2 095 597	4.2	12.15	2.81
684 Aluminium	1 846 578	3.7	8.70	2.10
334 Heavy petroleum & bituminous oil	1 279 578	2.6	0.67	0.31
057 Fruit nut (exc oil), fresh or dried	1 203 408	2.4	5.80	2.49
287 Base metal ores & concentrates nes	1 155 089	2.3	10.63	5.66
Remainder	24 443 105	48.8		
Spain - Espagne (=Developed)**				
All commodity groups	203 429 814	100.0	3.08	1.83
781 Passenger cars and race cars	24 237 028	11.9	5.48	4.77
784 Motor vehicle parts and accessories	11 151 946	5.5	5.62	4.54
334 Heavy petroleum & bituminous oil	7 563 050	3.7	4.33	1.82
542 Medicines including veterinary	5 833 242	2.9	2.78	2.63
782 Goods and service vehicles	5 734 304	2.8	7.97	6.05
057 Fruit nut (exc oil), fresh or dried	5 550 502	2.7	20.74	11.51
054 Vegetable & vegetable products nes	4 351 424	2.1	19.66	12.56
793 Ships boats floating structures	4 319 665	2.1	10.50	5.43
676 Iron steel bar rod section piling	2 852 549	1.4	8.00	4.96
662 Clay and refractory materials	2 828 295	1.4	22.12	15.72
Remainder	129 007 808	63.4		
Sri Lanka (=Developing)**				
All commodity groups	6 421 291	100.0	0.16	0.06
842 Female clothing, woven	937 413	14.6	2.13	1.39
074 Tea and maté	850 225	13.2	26.07	19.12
845 Articles of apparel nes	709 824	11.1	1.05	0.71
841 Male clothing, woven	539 171	8.4	1.56	1.00
844 Female clothing, knitted crocheted	425 340	6.6	2.04	1.50
667 Pearls, precious semiprecious stone	304 474	4.7	0.87	0.33
625 Rubber for wheels, incl inner tube	250 035	3.9	1.72	0.54
843 Male clothing, knitted crocheted	180 107	2.8	1.43	1.14
682 Copper	137 826	2.1	0.33	0.16
848 Headgear, non-textile clothing	134 728	2.1	0.94	0.65
Remainder	1 952 147	30.4		
Sudan - Soudan (=Developing)**				
All commodity groups	4 992 260	100.0	0.12	0.04
334 Heavy petroleum & bituminous oil	4 264 473	85.4	2.24	1.02
971 Gold non-monetary excluding ores	128 160	2.6	0.53	0.26
222 Oil seed etc for soft oil	123 246	2.5	1.21	0.56
001 Live animal excl. fish & crustacean	108 172	2.2	4.25	0.79
263 Cotton	87 382	1.8	2.17	0.79
292 Crude vegetable materials nes	78 208	1.6	1.29	0.34
786 Trailer caravan transport container	47 524	1.0	0.52	0.19
061 Sugar, mollasses and honey	24 162	0.5	0.21	0.12
054 Vegetable & vegetable products nes	19 112	0.4	0.16	0.06
012 Meat nes, fresh chilled frozen	13 048	0.3	0.18	0.03
Remainder	98 773	2.0		

For sources and notes, see end of table.

Leading products exported based on average 2005-2006 values SITC Revision 3 (3-digit level) / Principaux produits exportés d'après la moyenne des valeurs de 2005-2006 CTCI révision 3 (positions à 3 chiffres)	2005-2006			
	Value (f.o.b., thousands of dollars) / Valeur (f.a.b., milliers de dollars)	As percentage / En pourcentage		
		of country total / du total du pays	of ** (1) / des ** (1)	of world / du monde
Suriname (=Developing)**				
All commodity groups	878 587	100.0	0.02	0.01
285 Aluminium ore concentrate alumina	414 252	47.1	10.29	3.48
971 Gold non-monetary excluding ores	284 255	32.4	1.17	0.59
034 Fish, fresh live chilled frozen	28 540	3.2	0.20	0.08
036 Crustacean mollusc aquat invertebra	24 247	2.8	0.19	0.12
334 Heavy petroleum & bituminous oil	23 770	2.7	0.01	0.01
811 Prefabricated buildings	19 096	2.2	1.79	0.33
057 Fruit nut (exc oil), fresh or dried	14 757	1.7	0.07	0.03
333 Crude petroleum & bituminous oil	14 065	1.6	0.00	0.00
892 Printed matter	10 708	1.2	0.14	0.03
042 Rice	7 768	0.9	0.10	0.08
Remainder	37 129	4.2		
Swaziland (=Developing)**				
All commodity groups	1 608 242	100.0	0.04	0.01
551 Essential oils, perfumes & flavours	649 002	40.4	26.06	3.96
061 Sugar, mollasses and honey	166 733	10.4	1.47	0.83
845 Articles of apparel nes	97 466	6.1	0.14	0.10
598 Miscellaneous chemical products nes	78 307	4.9	0.68	0.11
251 Pulp and waste paper	70 251	4.4	1.20	0.25
842 Female clothing, woven	49 830	3.1	0.11	0.07
841 Male clothing, woven	36 827	2.3	0.11	0.07
892 Printed matter	22 697	1.4	0.29	0.06
843 Male clothing, knitted crocheted	22 459	1.4	0.18	0.14
775 Household equipment nes	19 355	1.2	0.07	0.03
Remainder	395 315	24.6		
Sweden - Suède (=Developed)**				
All commodity groups	138 817 064	100.0	2.10	1.25
764 Telecommunicate equipment part nes	11 183 819	8.1	5.81	2.87
781 Passenger cars and race cars	8 683 522	6.3	1.96	1.71
641 Paper and paperboard	8 567 641	6.2	10.10	8.61
542 Medicines including veterinary	7 241 430	5.2	3.45	3.27
334 Heavy petroleum & bituminous oil	6 015 698	4.3	3.44	1.45
784 Motor vehicle parts and accessories	5 773 568	4.2	2.91	2.35
675 Flat rolled products of alloy steel	3 605 762	2.6	9.68	7.14
248 Wood simply worked, railway sleeper	3 164 283	2.3	12.08	8.58
713 Internal combustion engine part nes	2 429 369	1.8	2.42	2.05
744 Mechanical handling equipment nes	2 298 933	1.7	4.77	4.03
Remainder	79 853 038	57.5		
Switzerland - Suisse (=Developed)**				
All commodity groups	139 392 959	100.0	2.11	1.25
542 Medicines including veterinary	18 115 133	13.0	8.64	8.17
885 Watches and clocks	10 461 837	7.5	64.64	39.96
541 Pharmaceuticals excluding medicines	10 427 040	7.5	16.55	14.80
515 Organo-inorganic compound acid salt	6 066 222	4.4	8.47	7.32
899 Manufactured articles nes	4 171 278	3.0	12.81	8.89
897 Jewellery nes (667)	3 356 028	2.4	14.26	7.56
874 Measure analyze control device nes	3 291 982	2.4	3.32	2.78
772 Electrical circuit equipment	3 031 058	2.2	3.26	1.98
728 Special industrial machine part nes	2 921 045	2.1	3.37	2.80
514 Nitrogen function compounds	2 885 371	2.1	11.22	8.37
Remainder	74 665 966	53.6		
Syrian Arab Republic - République arabe syrienne (=Developing)**				
All commodity groups	8 684 626	100.0	0.21	0.08
333 Crude petroleum & bituminous oil	3 765 432	43.4	0.61	0.45
334 Heavy petroleum & bituminous oil	611 267	7.0	0.32	0.15
054 Vegetable & vegetable products nes	259 477	3.0	2.15	0.75
001 Live animal excl. fish & crustacean	246 393	2.8	9.69	1.80
653 Man-made woven fabrics	207 107	2.4	1.04	0.64
263 Cotton	200 579	2.3	4.98	1.82
844 Female clothing, knitted crocheted	175 102	2.0	0.84	0.62
554 Soaps cleansers polishes	151 704	1.7	3.24	0.64
421 Fixed veg fat and oil, "soft"	151 537	1.7	2.18	0.84
041 Wheat meslin, incl spelt, unmilled	143 375	1.7	7.37	0.75
Remainder	2 772 653	31.9		

Pour les sources et les notes, se reporter à la fin du tableau.

3.2.D Export structure by product
Individual countries and territories

3.2.D Structure des exportations par produits
Pays et territoires individuels

Leading products exported based on average 2005-2006 values SITC Revision 3 (3-digit level) / Principaux produits exportés d'après la moyenne des valeurs de 2005-2006 CTCI révision 3 (positions à 3 chiffres)	2005-2006			
	Value (f.o.b., thousands of dollars) Valeur (f.a.b., milliers de dollars)	As percentage / En pourcentage		
		of country total / du total du pays	of ** (1) / des ** (1)	of world / du monde
Tajikistan - Tadjikistan (=Transition)**				
All commodity groups	1 132 555	100.0	0.28	0.01
684 Aluminium	643 485	56.8	7.88	0.73
671 Pig & sponge iron, ferro alloys etc	123 311	10.9	2.26	0.49
263 Cotton	105 340	9.3	8.91	0.96
562 Manufactured fertilizer excl. crude	31 762	2.8	0.50	0.13
057 Fruit nut (exc oil), fresh or dried	25 895	2.3	3.50	0.05
759 Office equipment part & accessories	21 184	1.9	23.54	0.01
651 Textile yarn	19 344	1.7	2.93	0.05
652 Woven cotton fabrics	17 010	1.5	6.54	0.06
288 Non ferrous base metal waste nes	11 559	1.0	3.61	0.05
054 Vegetable & vegetable products nes	8 116	0.7	1.82	0.02
Remainder	125 489	11.1		
Thailand - Thaïlande (=Developing)**				
All commodity groups	120 345 040	100.0	2.93	1.08
752 Computer equipment nes	9 596 512	8.0	5.84	3.36
776 Valves tubes; diodes, transistors	7 424 362	6.2	3.11	1.88
231 Natural rubber, latex, gum, etc	4 562 498	3.8	37.33	36.43
759 Office equipment part & accessories	3 481 216	2.9	2.91	1.65
782 Goods and service vehicles	3 354 493	2.8	15.83	3.54
334 Heavy petroleum & bituminous oil	3 305 362	2.7	1.74	0.79
037 Fish shellfish, prepared preserved	2 745 279	2.3	26.66	17.10
764 Telecommunicate equipment part nes	2 735 601	2.3	1.39	0.70
741 Heating cooling equipment parts nes	2 554 285	2.1	12.12	3.44
772 Electrical circuit equipment	2 551 883	2.1	4.31	1.67
Remainder	78 033 548	64.8		
TFYR of Macedonia - LERY de Macédoine (=Transition)**				
All commodity groups	2 220 990	100.0	0.56	0.02
842 Female clothing, woven	239 054	10.8	23.66	0.35
673 Flat iron non-alloy steel products	220 052	9.9	2.33	0.32
671 Pig & sponge iron, ferro alloys etc	207 170	9.3	3.79	0.81
334 Heavy petroleum & bituminous oil	179 369	8.1	0.35	0.04
841 Male clothing, woven	165 949	7.5	19.33	0.31
121 Unmanufactured tabacco and refuse	91 687	4.1	55.90	1.28
679 Iron steel pipe tube fittings etc	77 058	3.5	2.40	0.12
674 Flat plated iron non-alloy steel	68 189	3.1	6.42	0.18
851 Footwear	57 573	2.6	6.21	0.08
112 Alcoholic beverages	45 254	2.0	3.91	0.09
Remainder	869 635	39.2		
Togo (=Developing)**				
All commodity groups	388 955	100.0	0.01	0.00
661 Lime cement construction material	102 974	26.5	0.98	0.50
272 Crude fertilizer, excl. manufactured	40 023	10.3	2.98	2.19
263 Cotton	39 345	10.1	0.98	0.36
893 Articles of plastic nes	28 164	7.2	0.10	0.03
072 Cocoa	22 428	5.8	0.38	0.25
676 Iron steel bar rod section piling	19 013	4.9	0.11	0.03
553 Perfume toilet cosmetics, excl. soap	11 423	2.9	0.15	0.02
091 Margarine and shortening	10 966	2.8	1.38	0.39
674 Flat plated iron non-alloy steel	10 675	2.7	0.09	0.03
046 Wheat meal & flour, meslin flour	8 356	2.1	0.86	0.34
Remainder	95 588	24.6		
Trinidad and Tobago - Trinité-et-Tobago (=Developing)**				
All commodity groups	11 815 107	100.0	0.29	0.11
334 Heavy petroleum & bituminous oil	3 384 076	28.6	1.78	0.81
343 Natural gas, liquefied or not	3 207 205	27.1	5.33	1.82
333 Crude petroleum & bituminous oil	1 776 851	15.0	0.29	0.21
522 Inorganic chemical elem oxide salt	896 526	7.6	7.75	2.92
512 Alcohols, phenols; derivatives	823 272	7.0	6.04	2.66
342 Liquefied propane and butane	245 861	2.1	1.36	0.87
676 Iron steel bar rod section piling	207 501	1.8	1.25	0.36
671 Pig & sponge iron, ferro alloys etc	163 954	1.4	1.24	0.64
562 Manufactured fertilizer excl. crude	148 031	1.3	2.29	0.61
344 Petroleum and hydrocarbon gas nes	117 783	1.0	4.51	1.20
Remainder	844 048	7.1		
Tunisia - Tunisie (=Developing)**				
All commodity groups	11 003 321	100.0	0.27	0.10
845 Articles of apparel nes	1 524 591	13.9	2.26	1.53
333 Crude petroleum & bituminous oil	1 072 025	9.7	0.17	0.13
841 Male clothing, woven	1 043 028	9.5	3.01	1.94
842 Female clothing, woven	631 189	5.7	1.44	0.93
773 Electrical distribute equipment nes	617 115	5.6	2.25	0.90
772 Electrical circuit equipment	534 237	4.9	0.90	0.35
421 Fixed veg fat and oil, "soft"	498 047	4.5	7.17	2.75
851 Footwear	470 373	4.3	1.20	0.68
562 Manufactured fertilizer excl. crude	454 552	4.1	7.02	1.88
334 Heavy petroleum & bituminous oil	258 312	2.3	0.14	0.06
Remainder	3 899 851	35.4		
Turkey - Turquie (=Developing)**				
All commodity groups	79 501 183	100.0	1.93	0.72
845 Articles of apparel nes	4 346 882	5.5	6.44	4.35
676 Iron steel bar rod section piling	3 280 288	4.1	19.71	5.71
842 Female clothing, woven	2 720 737	3.4	6.20	4.03
781 Passenger cars and race cars	2 387 233	3.0	3.66	0.47
057 Fruit nut (exc oil), fresh or dried	2 346 827	3.0	11.31	4.86
761 Television video receive project	2 262 456	2.8	5.99	3.39
658 Made-up textile articles nes	1 706 739	2.1	7.46	5.24
841 Male clothing, woven	1 672 854	2.1	4.83	3.12
844 Female clothing, knitted crocheted	1 356 507	1.7	6.50	4.79
775 Household equipment nes	1 297 923	1.6	4.41	1.95
Remainder	56 122 737	70.6		
Turkmenistan - Turkménistan (=Transition)**				
All commodity groups	4 113 451	100.0	1.03	0.04
343 Natural gas, liquefied or not	2 296 102	55.8	5.69	1.30
334 Heavy petroleum & bituminous oil	910 180	22.1	1.78	0.22
651 Textile yarn	160 059	3.9	24.24	0.38
333 Crude petroleum & bituminous oil	105 492	2.6	0.09	0.01
793 Ships boats floating structures	86 630	2.1	3.65	0.11
263 Cotton	70 644	1.7	5.97	0.64
575 Other plastics, in primary forms	69 727	1.7	17.56	0.10
342 Liquefied propane and butane	33 216	0.8	3.79	0.12
652 Woven cotton fabrics	21 307	0.5	8.17	0.07
658 Made-up textile articles nes	21 213	0.5	8.93	0.07
Remainder	338 882	8.2		
Turks and Caicos Islands - Îles Turques et Caïques (=Developing)**				
All commodity groups	16 163	100.0	0.00	0.00
037 Fish shellfish, prepared preserved	3 864	23.9	0.04	0.02
036 Crustacean mollusc aquat invertebra	2 940	18.2	0.02	0.01
723 Civil engineering plant & equipment	1 272	7.9	0.01	0.00
291 Crude animal materials nes	948	5.9	0.05	0.02
716 Rotating electric plant parts nes	765	4.7	0.00	0.00
699 Base metal manufactures nes	600	3.7	0.00	0.00
793 Ships boats floating structures	570	3.5	0.00	0.00
764 Telecommunicate equipment part nes	567	3.5	0.00	0.00
781 Passenger cars and race cars	496	3.1	0.00	0.00
813 Lighting fixtures and fittings nes	478	3.0	0.01	0.00
Remainder	3 663	22.7		
Uganda - Ouganda (=Developing)**				
All commodity groups	887 501	100.0	0.02	0.01
071 Coffee and coffee substitutes	181 391	20.4	1.65	1.06
034 Fish, fresh live chilled frozen	137 801	15.5	0.96	0.38
971 Gold non-monetary excluding ores	97 802	11.0	0.40	0.20
074 Tea and maté	42 574	4.8	1.31	0.96
764 Telecommunicate equipment part nes	35 139	4.0	0.02	0.01
334 Heavy petroleum & bituminous oil	34 737	3.9	0.02	0.01
292 Crude vegetable materials nes	34 001	3.8	0.56	0.15
263 Cotton	29 794	3.4	0.74	0.27
121 Unmanufactured tabacco and refuse	29 159	3.3	0.68	0.41
287 Base metal ores & concentrates nes	17 109	1.9	0.16	0.08
Remainder	247 993	27.9		

For sources and notes, see end of table.

Pour les sources et les notes, se reporter à la fin du tableau.

Leading products exported based on average 2005-2006 values SITC Revision 3 (3-digit level) / Principaux produits exportés d'après la moyenne des valeurs de 2005-2006 CTCI révision 3 (positions à 3 chiffres)	2005-2006 Value (f.o.b., thousands of dollars) / Valeur (f.a.b., milliers de dollars)	As percentage / En pourcentage: of country total / du total du pays	of ** (1) / des ** (1)	of world / du monde
Ukraine (**=Transition)				
All commodity groups	36 297 792	100.0	9.13	0.33
672 Ingots, Iron steel primary products	3 795 215	10.5	40.63	12.85
673 Flat iron non-alloy steel products	3 775 846	10.4	39.94	5.49
676 Iron steel bar rod section piling	2 727 250	7.5	52.83	4.75
334 Heavy petroleum & bituminous oil	1 852 305	5.1	3.62	0.44
679 Iron steel pipe tube fittings etc	1 665 260	4.6	51.79	2.70
671 Pig & sponge iron, ferro alloys etc	1 077 353	3.0	19.72	4.24
791 Railway vehicles and equipment	1 002 111	2.8	61.98	5.80
562 Manufactured fertilizer excl. crude	981 202	2.7	15.37	4.06
281 Iron ore and concentrates	870 434	2.4	34.97	2.85
421 Fixed veg fat and oil, "soft"	749 012	2.1	62.36	4.14
Remainder	17 801 802	49.0		
United Arab Emirates - Émirats arabes unis (**=Developing)				
All commodity groups	127 884 590	100.0	3.11	1.15
333 Crude petroleum & bituminous oil	47 444 371	37.1	7.73	5.65
334 Heavy petroleum & bituminous oil	11 177 663	8.7	5.87	2.69
667 Pearls, precious semiprecious stone	4 391 892	3.4	12.49	4.73
971 Gold non-monetary excluding ores	3 618 954	2.8	14.90	7.45
764 Telecommunicate equipment part nes	3 615 748	2.8	1.84	0.93
343 Natural gas, liquefied or not	1 957 551	1.5	3.25	1.11
781 Passenger cars and race cars	1 168 032	0.9	1.79	0.23
684 Aluminium	1 118 114	0.9	5.27	1.27
342 Liquefied propane and butane	1 090 894	0.9	6.01	3.88
784 Motor vehicle parts and accessories	1 020 447	0.8	2.21	0.42
Remainder	51 280 923	40.1		
United Kingdom - Royaume-Uni (**=Developed)				
All commodity groups	414 402 081	100.0	6.27	3.73
764 Telecommunicate equipment part nes	37 685 527	9.1	19.57	9.65
781 Passenger cars and race cars	23 783 329	5.7	5.38	4.68
333 Crude petroleum & bituminous oil	21 559 705	5.2	18.92	2.57
542 Medicines including veterinary	20 530 264	5.0	9.79	9.26
714 Non-electric engines excl. 712 713 718	14 417 563	3.5	21.63	19.70
334 Heavy petroleum & bituminous oil	14 133 234	3.4	8.09	3.39
752 Computer equipment nes	10 239 196	2.5	8.47	3.59
667 Pearls, precious semiprecious stone	8 999 092	2.2	16.16	9.69
759 Office equipment part & accessories	8 234 076	2.0	8.95	3.89
784 Motor vehicle parts and accessories	7 767 871	1.9	3.92	3.16
Remainder	247 052 225	59.6		
United Republic of Tanzania - République-Unie de Tanzanie (**=Developing)				
All commodity groups	1 617 191	100.0	0.04	0.01
971 Gold non-monetary excluding ores	570 325	35.3	2.35	1.17
034 Fish, fresh live chilled frozen	152 511	9.4	1.06	0.43
289 Prec metal ore concentrate excl. gold	140 780	8.7	9.27	2.78
121 Unmanufactured tabacco and refuse	118 772	7.3	2.75	1.66
263 Cotton	90 096	5.6	2.24	0.82
071 Coffee and coffee substitutes	79 827	4.9	0.73	0.47
057 Fruit nut (exc oil), fresh or dried	50 266	3.1	0.24	0.10
667 Pearls, precious semiprecious stone	34 963	2.2	0.10	0.04
054 Vegetable & vegetable products nes	33 400	2.1	0.28	0.10
074 Tea and maté	30 205	1.9	0.93	0.68
Remainder	316 045	19.5		
United States - États-Unis (**=Developed)				
All commodity groups	970 684 366	100.0	14.68	8.73
792 Aircraft, spacecraft & equipment	58 256 709	6.0	44.12	40.02
776 Valves tubes; diodes, transistors	50 642 278	5.2	32.56	12.83
781 Passenger cars and race cars	33 339 176	3.4	7.54	6.56
784 Motor vehicle parts and accessories	32 781 317	3.4	16.53	13.34
764 Telecommunicate equipment part nes	27 226 534	2.8	14.14	6.97
752 Computer equipment nes	25 978 176	2.7	21.48	9.10
874 Measure analyze control device nes	25 798 838	2.7	26.00	21.81
714 Non-electric engines excl. 712 713 718	22 245 206	2.3	33.37	30.40
759 Office equipment part & accessories	20 918 725	2.2	22.75	9.89
334 Heavy petroleum & bituminous oil	18 444 431	1.9	10.56	4.43
Remainder	655 052 976	67.5		
Uruguay (**=Developing)				
All commodity groups	3 678 411	100.0	0.09	0.03
011 Beef, fresh chilled frozen	836 080	22.7	13.11	3.66
611 Leather	269 983	7.3	2.26	1.24
042 Rice	209 181	5.7	2.68	2.04
268 Wool & animal hair, incl wool tops	151 937	4.1	9.78	3.01
222 Oil seed etc for soft oil	142 537	3.9	1.40	0.64
334 Heavy petroleum & bituminous oil	141 628	3.9	0.07	0.03
022 Milk products, excl. butter & cheese	134 734	3.7	4.70	0.58
034 Fish, fresh live chilled frozen	113 251	3.1	0.79	0.32
893 Articles of plastic nes	93 972	2.6	0.32	0.10
024 Cheese and curd	88 618	2.4	12.37	0.50
Remainder	1 496 490	40.7		
Uzbekistan - Ouzbékistan (**=Transition)				
All commodity groups	3 554 083	100.0	0.89	0.03
263 Cotton	748 923	21.1	63.32	6.80
343 Natural gas, liquefied or not	455 870	12.8	1.13	0.26
781 Passenger cars and race cars	296 851	8.4	25.46	0.06
682 Copper	273 839	7.7	4.24	0.31
057 Fruit nut (exc oil), fresh or dried	227 400	6.4	30.78	0.47
971 Gold non-monetary excluding ores	152 017	4.3	19.66	0.31
525 Radio active & associated materials	129 950	3.7	19.06	1.56
651 Textile yarn	121 689	3.4	18.43	0.29
054 Vegetable & vegetable products nes	91 364	2.6	20.49	0.26
571 Primary form ethylene polymers	67 833	1.9	8.53	0.16
Remainder	988 345	27.8		
Venezuela (Bolivarian Rep. of) - Venezuela (Rép. bolivarienne du) (**=Developing)				
All commodity groups	58 436 120	100.0	1.42	0.53
333 Crude petroleum & bituminous oil	52 452 994	89.8	8.55	6.25
684 Aluminium	1 020 259	1.7	4.81	1.16
671 Pig & sponge iron, ferro alloys etc	988 824	1.7	7.45	3.89
673 Flat iron non-alloy steel products	419 815	0.7	2.02	0.61
672 Ingots, Iron steel primary products	281 397	0.5	3.11	0.95
321 Coal excluding non-agglomerated	246 930	0.4	1.51	0.52
512 Alcohols, phenols; derivatives	175 402	0.3	1.29	0.57
285 Aluminium ore concentrate alumina	168 288	0.3	4.18	1.41
676 Iron steel bar rod section piling	160 151	0.3	0.96	0.28
334 Heavy petroleum & bituminous oil	150 362	0.3	0.08	0.04
Remainder	2 371 697	4.1		
Viet Nam (**=Developing)				
All commodity groups	36 136 676	100.0	0.88	0.33
333 Crude petroleum & bituminous oil	7 842 767	21.7	1.28	0.93
851 Footwear	3 366 683	9.3	8.59	4.87
036 Crustacean mollusc aquat invertebra	1 767 636	4.9	13.95	8.66
821 Furniture part; bedding furnishing	1 591 869	4.4	4.33	1.55
841 Male clothing, woven	1 517 666	4.2	4.38	2.83
042 Rice	1 342 137	3.7	17.20	13.10
842 Female clothing, woven	1 255 887	3.5	2.86	1.86
845 Articles of apparel nes	1 097 702	3.0	1.63	1.10
071 Coffee and coffee substitutes	989 880	2.7	9.03	5.79
231 Natural rubber, latex, gum, etc	925 839	2.6	7.57	7.39
Remainder	14 438 611	40.0		
Yemen - Yémen (**=Developing)				
All commodity groups	5 936 442	100.0	0.14	0.05
333 Crude petroleum & bituminous oil	5 065 476	85.3	0.83	0.60
334 Heavy petroleum & bituminous oil	341 537	5.8	0.18	0.08
034 Fish, fresh live chilled frozen	84 117	1.4	0.59	0.23
335 Residual petroleum products nes	34 062	0.6	0.51	0.17
781 Passenger cars and race cars	34 022	0.6	0.05	0.01
036 Crustacean mollusc aquat invertebra	32 037	0.5	0.25	0.16
723 Civil engineering plant & equipment	28 059	0.5	0.18	0.04
057 Fruit nut (exc oil), fresh or dried	24 340	0.4	0.12	0.05
122 Manufactured tabacco	23 979	0.4	0.58	0.13
971 Gold non-monetary excluding ores	20 499	0.3	0.08	0.04
Remainder	248 315	4.2		

For sources and notes, see end of table.

Pour les sources et les notes, se reporter à la fin du tableau.

3.2.D Export structure by product
Individual countries and territories

3.2.D Structure des exportations par produits
Pays et territoires individuels

Leading products exported based on average 2005-2006 values SITC Revision 3 (3-digit level) Principaux produits exportés d'après la moyenne des valeurs de 2005-2006 CTCI révision 3 (positions à 3 chiffres)	2005-2006			
	Value (f.o.b., thousands of dollars) Valeur (f.a.b., milliers de dollars)	As percentage En pourcentage		
		of country total du total du pays	of ** (1) des ** (1)	of world du monde
Zambia - Zambie (**=Developing)				
All commodity groups	2 790 067	100.0	0.07	0.03
682 Copper	1 806 983	64.8	4.32	2.08
283 Copper ores and concentrates	251 511	9.0	1.29	1.01
699 Base metal manufactures nes	154 458	5.5	0.54	0.16
121 Unmanufactured tabacco and refuse	68 694	2.5	1.59	0.96
061 Sugar, mollasses and honey	67 466	2.4	0.59	0.34
263 Cotton	60 010	2.2	1.49	0.54
054 Vegetable & vegetable products nes	25 711	0.9	0.21	0.07
292 Crude vegetable materials nes	25 644	0.9	0.42	0.11
773 Electrical distribute equipment nes	24 542	0.9	0.09	0.04
723 Civil engineering plant & equipment	22 029	0.8	0.14	0.03
Remainder	283 018	10.1		

Leading products exported based on average 2005-2006 values SITC Revision 3 (3-digit level) Principaux produits exportés d'après la moyenne des valeurs de 2005-2006 CTCI révision 3 (positions à 3 chiffres)	2005-2006			
	Value (f.o.b., thousands of dollars) Valeur (f.a.b., milliers de dollars)	As percentage En pourcentage		
		of country total du total du pays	of ** (1) des ** (1)	of world du monde
Zimbabwe (**=Developing)				
All commodity groups	1 431 888	100.0	0.03	0.01
121 Unmanufactured tabacco and refuse	224 595	15.7	5.21	3.15
284 Nickel ores, concentrates, etc	163 751	11.4	5.09	2.42
971 Gold non-monetary excluding ores	156 317	10.9	0.64	0.32
671 Pig & sponge iron, ferro alloys etc	123 035	8.6	0.93	0.48
263 Cotton	89 277	6.2	2.22	0.81
892 Printed matter	86 388	6.0	1.09	0.21
683 Nickel	80 791	5.6	4.86	0.46
061 Sugar, mollasses and honey	50 709	3.5	0.45	0.25
676 Iron steel bar rod section piling	38 438	2.7	0.23	0.07
292 Crude vegetable materials nes	32 908	2.3	0.54	0.14
Remainder	385 679	26.9		

Sources:
- Data and UNCTAD secretariat estimates based on UN DESA Comtrade and IMF Direction of Trade statistics databases

Notes:

(1) The symbol ** indicates the grouping to which the country belongs and the percentage share shown applies. The percentage is the share of exports of each commodity shown by the country in the relevant grouping total exports for that commodity (i.e. "developed", which refers to developed economies; "developing", which refers to developing economies; or "Economies in transition", which refers to economies in transition).

Sources :
- Données et estimations du secrétariat de la CNUCED sur la base de données Comtrade de ONU DAES et Direction of Trade statistics du Fonds Monétaire international

Notes :

(1) Le symbole ** indique le groupement auquel le pays appartient et par rapport auquel est calculé le pourcentage. Ce pourcentage est la part que représentent les exportations du produit par le pays par rapport aux exportations du même produit par le groupement auquel le pays appartient («developed» se réfère aux économies développées, «developing» aux économies en développement et " Economies in transition " aux économies en transition).

3

3.2.E   Exports structure by product
Major exporters for leading products among
developing economies

3.2.E   Structure des exportations par produits
Principaux exportateurs de produits majeurs
parmi les économies en développement

Left panel

Leading exporting developing economies (1) based on average 2005-2006 exports (2) SITC Revision 3 (3-digit level) / Principales économies en dévelopement exportatrices (1) d'après la moyenne des exportations de 2005-2006 (2) CTCI révision 3 (positions à 3	2005-2006			
	Value (f.o.b., thousands of dollars) Valeur (f.a.b., milliers de dollars)	As percentage / En pourcentage		
		of country total / du total du pays	of developing economies / des économies en déve-loppement	of world / du monde
034 - Fish, fresh live chilled frozen				
World	35 833 816	0.32	_	100.0
Developed economies	20 876 480	0.32	_	58.26
Economies in transition	578 687	0.15	_	1.61
Developing economies	14 378 649	0.35	100.00	40.13
China	3 246 267	0.38	22.58	9.06
Chile	2 212 058	4.68	15.38	6.17
China, Taiwan Province of	1 204 654	0.58	8.38	3.36
Viet Nam	865 968	2.40	6.02	2.42
Republic of Korea	562 751	0.18	3.91	1.57
Argentina	511 097	1.18	3.55	1.43
Thailand	481 219	0.40	3.35	1.34
Indonesia	463 980	0.50	3.23	1.29
Namibia	362 985	12.48	2.52	1.01
India	343 450	0.30	2.39	0.96
057 - Fruit nut (exc oil), fresh or dried				
World	48 242 950	0.43	_	100.0
Developed economies	26 761 939	0.40	_	55.47
Economies in transition	738 907	0.19	_	1.53
Developing economies	20 742 104	0.50	100.00	43.00
Turkey	2 346 827	2.95	11.31	4.86
Chile	1 970 308	4.17	9.50	4.08
Mexico	1 460 414	0.63	7.04	3.03
Iran (Islamic Rep. of)	1 373 270	2.23	6.62	2.85
Ecuador	1 208 263	10.69	5.83	2.50
South Africa	1 203 408	2.40	5.80	2.49
Costa Rica	1 050 734	14.59	5.07	2.18
China	1 001 423	0.12	4.83	2.08
India	857 636	0.75	4.13	1.78
Argentina	796 932	1.84	3.84	1.65
081 - Animal feed excluding unmilled cereal				
World	31 753 169	0.29	_	100.0
Developed economies	18 673 035	0.28	_	58.81
Economies in transition	362 118	0.09	_	1.14
Developing economies	12 718 016	0.31	100.00	40.05
Argentina	4 342 509	10.04	34.14	13.68
Brazil	2 794 032	2.18	21.97	8.80
Peru	1 190 831	5.83	9.36	3.75
India	1 183 720	1.03	9.31	3.73
Thailand	550 825	0.46	4.33	1.73
Chile	525 129	1.11	4.13	1.65
China	515 821	0.06	4.06	1.62
Bolivia	216 039	6.15	1.70	0.68
Malaysia	164 054	0.11	1.29	0.52
Indonesia	158 656	0.17	1.25	0.50
281 - Iron ore and concentrates				
World	30 543 665	0.27	_	100.0
Developed economies	13 182 394	0.20	_	43.16
Economies in transition	2 489 203	0.63	_	8.15
Developing economies	14 872 068	0.36	100.00	48.69
Brazil	8 122 756	6.34	54.62	26.59
India	3 855 310	3.36	25.92	12.62
South Africa	1 061 205	2.12	7.14	3.47
Mauritania	584 535	65.94	3.93	1.91
Chile	315 003	0.67	2.12	1.03
Peru	236 034	1.15	1.59	0.77
Bahrain	166 192	1.52	1.12	0.54
Philippines	136 039	0.31	0.91	0.45
Iran (Islamic Rep. of)	97 547	0.16	0.66	0.32
Mexico	80 870	0.03	0.54	0.26

Right panel

Leading exporting developing economies (1) based on average 2005-2006 exports (2) SITC Revision 3 (3-digit level) / Principales économies en dévelopement exportatrices (1) d'après la moyenne des exportations de 2005-2006 (2) CTCI révision 3 (positions à 3	2005-2006			
	Value (f.o.b., thousands of dollars) Valeur (f.a.b., milliers de dollars)	As percentage / En pourcentage		
		of country total / du total du pays	of developing economies / des économies en déve-loppement	of world / du monde
283 - Copper ores and concentrates				
World	24 879 742	0.22	_	100.0
Developed economies	5 146 847	0.08	_	20.69
Economies in transition	247 194	0.06	_	0.99
Developing economies	19 485 702	0.47	100.00	78.32
Chile	8 855 066	18.75	45.44	35.59
Indonesia	3 978 537	4.27	20.42	15.99
Peru	2 139 919	10.47	10.98	8.60
Argentina	1 316 098	3.04	6.75	5.29
Papua New Guinea	703 149	17.73	3.61	2.83
Botswana	565 969	12.68	2.90	2.27
Mongolia	480 822	36.89	2.47	1.93
Brazil	424 045	0.33	2.18	1.70
Zambia	251 511	9.01	1.29	1.01
Dem. Rep. of the Congo	150 540	6.69	0.77	0.61
321 - Coal excluding non-agglomomerated				
World	47 665 467	0.43	_	100.0
Developed economies	26 608 139	0.40	_	55.82
Economies in transition	4 742 911	1.19	_	9.95
Developing economies	16 314 417	0.40	100.00	34.23
Indonesia	5 218 144	5.60	31.98	10.95
China	3 970 965	0.46	24.34	8.33
South Africa	3 220 680	6.43	19.74	6.76
Colombia	2 623 581	11.51	16.08	5.50
Viet Nam	792 273	2.19	4.86	1.66
Venezuela (Bolivarian Rep. of)	246 930	0.42	1.51	0.52
Dem. People's Rep. of Korea	72 658	7.89	0.45	0.15
India	64 723	0.06	0.40	0.14
Mongolia	35 848	2.75	0.22	0.08
United Arab Emirates	11 116	0.01	0.07	0.02
333 - Crude petroleum & bituminous oil				
World	839 742 047	7.55	_	100.0
Developed economies	113 940 925	1.72	_	13.57
Economies in transition	112 348 556	28.30	_	13.38
Developing economies	613 452 566	14.93	100.00	73.05
Saudi Arabia	149 697 352	76.37	24.40	17.83
Venezuela (Bolivarian Rep. of)	52 452 994	89.76	8.55	6.25
Iran (Islamic Rep. of)	49 254 965	79.92	8.03	5.87
United Arab Emirates	47 444 371	37.10	7.73	5.65
Nigeria	39 271 595	87.28	6.40	4.68
Kuwait	31 728 442	62.05	5.17	3.78
Mexico	31 518 313	13.58	5.14	3.75
Algeria	27 451 194	54.57	4.47	3.27
Angola	25 656 849	95.27	4.18	3.06
Iraq	24 405 843	93.46	3.98	2.91
334 - Heavy petroleum & bituminous oil				
World	416 296 537	3.74	_	100.0
Developed economies	174 738 568	2.64	_	41.97
Economies in transition	51 231 142	12.90	_	12.31
Developing economies	190 326 827	4.63	100.00	45.72
Singapore	30 204 358	12.05	15.87	7.26
Saudi Arabia	18 149 617	9.26	9.54	4.36
Republic of Korea	17 521 826	5.75	9.21	4.21
India	14 877 721	12.96	7.82	3.57
Kuwait	14 175 499	27.72	7.45	3.41
United Arab Emirates	11 177 663	8.74	5.87	2.69
China, Taiwan Province of	9 430 310	4.56	4.95	2.27
Bahrain	8 502 802	77.65	4.47	2.04
China	6 729 811	0.78	3.54	1.62
Malaysia	4 622 685	3.07	2.43	1.11

For sources and notes, see end of table.   Pour les sources et les notes, se reporter à la fin du tableau.

3.2.E Exports structure by product
Major exporters for leading products among
developing economies

3.2.E Structure des exportations par produits
Principaux exportateurs de produits majeurs
parmi les économies en développement

Leading exporting developing economies (1) based on average 2005-2006 exports (2) SITC Revision 3 (3-digit level) Principales économies en dévelopement exportatrices (1) d'après la moyenne des exportations de 2005-2006 (2) CTCI révision 3 (positions à 3	2005-2006		
	Value (f.o.b., thousands of dollars) Valeur (f.a.b., milliers de dollars)	As percentage En pourcentage		
		of country total du total du pays	of developing economies des économies en déve-loppement	of world du monde

342 - Liquefied propane and butane

	Value	of country total	of developing economies	of world
World	28 117 981	0.25	_	100.0
Developed economies	9 099 974	0.14	_	32.36
Economies in transition	875 853	0.22	_	3.11
Developing economies	18 142 154	0.44	100.00	64.52
Saudi Arabia	6 024 671	3.07	33.21	21.43
Algeria	3 848 497	7.65	21.21	13.69
Kuwait	1 909 447	3.73	10.52	6.79
United Arab Emirates	1 090 894	0.85	6.01	3.88
Qatar	963 497	3.22	5.31	3.43
Iran (Islamic Rep. of)	742 556	1.20	4.09	2.64
Argentina	660 974	1.53	3.64	2.35
Nigeria	571 467	1.27	3.15	2.03
Malaysia	507 553	0.34	2.80	1.81
Singapore	324 267	0.13	1.79	1.15

343 - Natural gas, liquefied or not

	Value	of country total	of developing economies	of world
World	176 408 836	1.59	_	100.0
Developed economies	75 858 973	1.15	_	43.00
Economies in transition	40 346 527	10.16	_	22.87
Developing economies	60 203 336	1.47	100.00	34.13
Algeria	14 323 714	28.47	23.79	8.12
Qatar	9 892 953	33.08	16.43	5.61
Indonesia	9 298 610	9.97	15.45	5.27
Malaysia	5 921 748	3.93	9.84	3.36
Oman	3 902 953	19.42	6.48	2.21
Trinidad and Tobago	3 207 205	27.14	5.33	1.82
Egypt	2 232 050	18.29	3.71	1.27
Brunei Darussalam	2 068 944	30.56	3.44	1.17
United Arab Emirates	1 957 551	1.53	3.25	1.11
Myanmar	1 920 599	43.17	3.19	1.09

511 - Hydrocarbons nes; derivatives

	Value	of country total	of developing economies	of world
World	52 719 845	0.47	_	100.0
Developed economies	34 547 375	0.52	_	65.53
Economies in transition	1 311 727	0.33	_	2.49
Developing economies	16 860 743	0.41	100.00	31.98
Republic of Korea	5 287 640	1.73	31.36	10.03
Singapore	2 320 160	0.93	13.76	4.40
Saudi Arabia	1 449 198	0.74	8.60	2.75
India	1 379 636	1.20	8.18	2.62
China	1 207 103	0.14	7.16	2.29
Thailand	1 001 313	0.83	5.94	1.90
Malaysia	753 471	0.50	4.47	1.43
China, Taiwan Province of	675 530	0.33	4.01	1.28
Brazil	625 631	0.49	3.71	1.19
Iran (Islamic Rep. of)	371 478	0.60	2.20	0.70

512 - Alcohols, phenols; derivatives

	Value	of country total	of developing economies	of world
World	30 938 830	0.28	_	100.0
Developed economies	16 415 896	0.25	_	53.06
Economies in transition	883 498	0.22	_	2.86
Developing economies	13 639 436	0.33	100.00	44.09
Saudi Arabia	2 286 429	1.17	16.76	7.39
Brazil	1 364 418	1.06	10.00	4.41
China, Taiwan Province of	1 267 235	0.61	9.29	4.10
Singapore	1 190 293	0.47	8.73	3.85
China	949 636	0.11	6.96	3.07
Malaysia	841 804	0.56	6.17	2.72
Trinidad and Tobago	823 272	6.97	6.04	2.66
Republic of Korea	750 698	0.25	5.50	2.43
Chile	707 925	1.50	5.19	2.29
Indonesia	480 279	0.52	3.52	1.55

513 - Carboxylic acid and compounds

	Value	of country total	of developing economies	of world
World	34 922 523	0.31	_	100.0
Developed economies	21 053 143	0.32	_	60.29
Economies in transition	502 359	0.13	_	1.44
Developing economies	13 367 021	0.33	100.00	38.28
Republic of Korea	3 402 264	1.12	25.45	9.74
China, Taiwan Province of	2 646 245	1.28	19.80	7.58
China	2 047 663	0.24	15.32	5.86
Singapore	1 041 986	0.42	7.80	2.98
Thailand	847 509	0.70	6.34	2.43
Malaysia	736 631	0.49	5.51	2.11
Mexico	686 132	0.30	5.13	1.96
Indonesia	541 914	0.58	4.05	1.55
India	296 468	0.26	2.22	0.85
Brazil	257 787	0.20	1.93	0.74

571 - Primary form ethylene polymers

	Value	of country total	of developing economies	of world
World	42 973 015	0.39	_	100.0
Developed economies	26 610 034	0.40	_	61.92
Economies in transition	795 066	0.20	_	1.85
Developing economies	15 567 914	0.38	100.00	36.23
Saudi Arabia	3 403 685	1.74	21.86	7.92
Republic of Korea	2 339 726	0.77	15.03	5.44
Singapore	1 568 974	0.63	10.08	3.65
Thailand	1 004 200	0.83	6.45	2.34
Qatar	862 402	2.88	5.54	2.01
China, Taiwan Province of	859 935	0.42	5.52	2.00
Brazil	857 259	0.67	5.51	1.99
China, Hong Kong SAR	786 382	0.26	5.05	1.83
Kuwait	759 431	1.49	4.88	1.77
Malaysia	658 429	0.44	4.23	1.53

574 - Polyacetals and polyesters, etc

	Value	of country total	of developing economies	of world
World	37 973 763	0.34	_	100.0
Developed economies	23 543 072	0.36	_	62.00
Economies in transition	139 982	0.04	_	0.37
Developing economies	14 290 709	0.35	100.00	37.63
Republic of Korea	2 693 666	0.88	18.85	7.09
China, Taiwan Province of	2 287 579	1.11	16.01	6.02
China	1 790 478	0.21	12.53	4.72
Singapore	1 679 349	0.67	11.75	4.42
Thailand	1 507 783	1.25	10.55	3.97
China, Hong Kong SAR	1 438 612	0.47	10.07	3.79
Mexico	591 976	0.26	4.14	1.56
Malaysia	468 095	0.31	3.28	1.23
Indonesia	427 279	0.46	2.99	1.13
India	411 097	0.36	2.88	1.08

575 - Other plastics, in primary forms

	Value	of country total	of developing economies	of world
World	70 408 992	0.63	_	100.0
Developed economies	55 009 535	0.83	_	78.13
Economies in transition	397 100	0.10	_	0.56
Developing economies	15 002 357	0.37	100.00	21.31
Republic of Korea	2 779 983	0.91	18.53	3.95
China, Taiwan Province of	2 218 147	1.07	14.79	3.15
China, Hong Kong SAR	2 026 091	0.66	13.51	2.88
Singapore	1 881 811	0.75	12.54	2.67
China	1 195 298	0.14	7.97	1.70
Thailand	998 968	0.83	6.66	1.42
Saudi Arabia	808 108	0.41	5.39	1.15
India	516 090	0.45	3.44	0.73
Malaysia	489 576	0.32	3.26	0.70
Brazil	482 829	0.38	3.22	0.69

For sources and notes, see end of table.

Pour les sources et les notes, se reporter à la fin du tableau.

3.2.E **Exports structure by product**
Major exporters for leading products among developing economies

3.2.E **Structure des exportations par produits**
Principaux exportateurs de produits majeurs parmi les économies en développement

Left panel

Leading exporting developing economies (1) based on average 2005-2006 exports (2) SITC Revision 3 (3-digit level) / Principales économies en développement exportatrices (1) d'après la moyenne des exportations de 2005-2006 (2) CTCI révision 3 (positions à 3	2005-2006			
	Value (f.o.b., thousands of dollars) Valeur (f.a.b., milliers de dollars)	of country total du total du pays	of developing economies des économies en déve-loppement	of world du monde
582 - Plastic sheet film foil & strips				
World	61 525 753	0.55	–	100.0
Developed economies	48 233 009	0.73	–	78.39
Economies in transition	289 401	0.07	–	0.47
Developing economies	13 003 343	0.32	100.00	21.13
China	2 394 178	0.28	18.41	3.89
Republic of Korea	2 147 424	0.70	16.51	3.49
China, Taiwan Province of	2 041 157	0.99	15.70	3.32
China, Hong Kong SAR	1 227 757	0.40	9.44	2.00
Malaysia	690 128	0.46	5.31	1.12
Thailand	548 947	0.46	4.22	0.89
Singapore	492 327	0.20	3.79	0.80
Mexico	460 764	0.20	3.54	0.75
Indonesia	431 378	0.46	3.32	0.70
India	403 214	0.35	3.10	0.66
625 - Rubber for wheels, incl inner tube				
World	46 366 380	0.42	–	100.0
Developed economies	30 670 792	0.46	–	66.15
Economies in transition	1 145 120	0.29	–	2.47
Developing economies	14 550 468	0.35	100.00	31.38
China	4 718 130	0.55	32.43	10.18
Republic of Korea	2 500 844	0.82	17.19	5.39
Thailand	1 052 654	0.87	7.23	2.27
Brazil	937 266	0.73	6.44	2.02
China, Taiwan Province of	747 637	0.36	5.14	1.61
Indonesia	723 188	0.78	4.97	1.56
India	638 640	0.56	4.39	1.38
United Arab Emirates	508 079	0.40	3.49	1.10
Turkey	365 312	0.46	2.51	0.79
Singapore	325 483	0.13	2.24	0.70
641 - Paper and paperboard				
World	99 545 827	0.90	–	100.0
Developed economies	84 820 710	1.28	–	85.21
Economies in transition	1 987 174	0.50	–	2.00
Developing economies	12 737 943	0.31	100.00	12.80
Indonesia	2 232 812	2.39	17.53	2.24
China	2 167 869	0.25	17.02	2.18
Republic of Korea	1 864 307	0.61	14.64	1.87
Brazil	1 244 982	0.97	9.77	1.25
China, Hong Kong SAR	753 460	0.25	5.92	0.76
China, Taiwan Province of	696 530	0.34	5.47	0.70
Thailand	631 464	0.52	4.96	0.63
South Africa	440 887	0.88	3.46	0.44
Singapore	374 332	0.15	2.94	0.38
Chile	360 590	0.76	2.83	0.36
651 - Textile yarn				
World	42 496 286	0.38	–	100.0
Developed economies	18 160 050	0.27	–	42.73
Economies in transition	660 186	0.17	–	1.55
Developing economies	23 676 050	0.58	100.00	55.71
China	5 911 554	0.68	24.97	13.91
China, Hong Kong SAR	3 578 752	1.16	15.12	8.42
India	2 460 751	2.14	10.39	5.79
China, Taiwan Province of	2 321 201	1.12	9.80	5.46
Indonesia	1 707 358	1.83	7.21	4.02
Republic of Korea	1 437 482	0.47	6.07	3.38
Pakistan	1 378 514	8.36	5.82	3.24
Thailand	807 384	0.67	3.41	1.90
Turkey	807 162	1.02	3.41	1.90
Malaysia	665 661	0.44	2.81	1.57

Right panel

Leading exporting developing economies (1) based on average 2005-2006 exports (2) SITC Revision 3 (3-digit level) / Principales économies en développement exportatrices (1) d'après la moyenne des exportations de 2005-2006 (2) CTCI révision 3 (positions à 3	2005-2006			
	Value (f.o.b., thousands of dollars) Valeur (f.a.b., milliers de dollars)	of country total du total du pays	of developing economies des économies en déve-loppement	of world du monde
652 - Woven cotton fabrics				
World	28 834 895	0.26	–	100.0
Developed economies	10 721 095	0.16	–	37.18
Economies in transition	260 835	0.07	–	0.90
Developing economies	17 852 965	0.43	100.00	61.91
China	7 455 075	0.86	41.76	25.85
China, Hong Kong SAR	3 299 210	1.07	18.48	11.44
Pakistan	2 071 793	12.56	11.60	7.19
India	881 321	0.77	4.94	3.06
Turkey	677 535	0.85	3.80	2.35
Republic of Korea	663 811	0.22	3.72	2.30
China, Taiwan Province of	493 748	0.24	2.77	1.71
Indonesia	405 341	0.43	2.27	1.41
Thailand	366 567	0.30	2.05	1.27
Brazil	293 703	0.23	1.65	1.02
653 - Man-made woven fabrics				
World	32 392 772	0.29	–	100.0
Developed economies	12 335 198	0.19	–	38.08
Economies in transition	73 466	0.02	–	0.23
Developing economies	19 984 108	0.49	100.00	61.69
China	8 552 257	0.99	42.80	26.40
Republic of Korea	2 221 228	0.73	11.11	6.86
China, Taiwan Province of	2 154 599	1.04	10.78	6.65
China, Hong Kong SAR	1 387 187	0.45	6.94	4.28
India	999 997	0.87	5.00	3.09
Turkey	917 940	1.15	4.59	2.83
United Arab Emirates	834 650	0.65	4.18	2.58
Indonesia	824 859	0.88	4.13	2.55
Thailand	533 932	0.44	2.67	1.65
Pakistan	280 907	1.70	1.41	0.87
655 - Knitted or crocheted fabrics nes				
World	20 716 154	0.19	–	100.0
Developed economies	7 006 471	0.11	–	33.82
Economies in transition	45 546	0.01	–	0.22
Developing economies	13 664 137	0.33	100.00	65.96
China	4 146 053	0.48	30.34	20.01
China, Hong Kong SAR	2 994 636	0.97	21.92	14.46
Republic of Korea	2 793 901	0.92	20.45	13.49
China, Taiwan Province of	1 918 717	0.93	14.04	9.26
Turkey	589 058	0.74	4.31	2.84
Thailand	157 703	0.13	1.15	0.76
Singapore	120 690	0.05	0.88	0.58
Malaysia	108 341	0.07	0.79	0.52
Mexico	101 336	0.04	0.74	0.49
Indonesia	81 701	0.09	0.60	0.39
658 - Made-up textile articles nes				
World	32 551 427	0.29	–	100.0
Developed economies	9 439 329	0.14	–	29.00
Economies in transition	237 538	0.06	–	0.73
Developing economies	22 874 560	0.56	100.00	70.27
China	11 114 273	1.28	48.59	34.14
Pakistan	3 142 691	19.06	13.74	9.65
India	2 337 615	2.04	10.22	7.18
Turkey	1 706 739	2.15	7.46	5.24
Mexico	781 967	0.34	3.42	2.40
China, Hong Kong SAR	406 631	0.13	1.78	1.25
Bangladesh	389 272	3.64	1.70	1.20
Republic of Korea	377 167	0.12	1.65	1.16
Brazil	373 048	0.29	1.63	1.15
Viet Nam	320 167	0.89	1.40	0.98

For sources and notes, see end of table.

Pour les sources et les notes, se reporter à la fin du tableau.

3.2.E **Exports structure by product**
Major exporters for leading products among
developing economies

3.2.E **Structure des exportations par produits**
Principaux exportateurs de produits majeurs
parmi les économies en développement

Left Table

Leading exporting developing economies (1) based on average 2005-2006 exports (2) SITC Revision 3 (3-digit level) / Principales économies en dévelopement exportatrices (1) d'après la moyenne des exportations de 2005-2006 (2) CTCI révision 3 (positions à 3	Value (f.o.b., thousands of dollars) Valeur (f.a.b., milliers de dollars)	2005-2006 As percentage En pourcentage — of country total du total du pays	of developing economies des économies en déve-loppement	of world du monde
667 - Pearls, precious semiprecious stone				
World	92 849 961	0.84	_	100.0
Developed economies	55 700 003	0.84	_	59.99
Economies in transition	1 980 066	0.50	_	2.13
Developing economies	35 169 892	0.86	100.00	37.88
India	11 384 736	9.92	32.37	12.26
China, Hong Kong SAR	5 733 740	1.87	16.30	6.18
United Arab Emirates	4 391 892	3.43	12.49	4.73
Botswana	3 280 365	73.52	9.33	3.53
South Africa	2 539 040	5.07	7.22	2.73
China	1 806 406	0.21	5.14	1.95
Thailand	1 089 288	0.91	3.10	1.17
Singapore	1 034 434	0.41	2.94	1.11
Dem. Rep. of the Congo	853 122	37.91	2.43	0.92
Namibia	792 753	27.26	2.25	0.85
671 - Pig & sponge iron, ferro alloys etc				
World	25 422 189	0.23	_	100.0
Developed economies	6 683 862	0.10	_	26.29
Economies in transition	5 464 553	1.38	_	21.50
Developing economies	13 273 774	0.32	100.00	52.21
China	3 164 302	0.37	23.84	12.45
South Africa	2 730 088	5.45	20.57	10.74
Brazil	2 507 440	1.96	18.89	9.86
Venezuela (Bolivarian Rep. of)	988 824	1.69	7.45	3.89
Colombia	923 056	4.05	6.95	3.63
New Caledonia	682 025	60.64	5.14	2.68
Chile	502 773	1.06	3.79	1.98
India	490 000	0.43	3.69	1.93
Indonesia	195 779	0.21	1.47	0.77
Republic of Korea	170 022	0.06	1.28	0.67
673 - Flat iron non-alloy steel products				
World	68 716 909	0.62	_	100.0
Developed economies	38 503 439	0.58	_	56.03
Economies in transition	9 452 835	2.38	_	13.76
Developing economies	20 760 635	0.51	100.00	30.21
China	5 712 067	0.66	27.51	8.31
Republic of Korea	4 311 992	1.41	20.77	6.28
China, Taiwan Province of	2 487 521	1.20	11.98	3.62
Brazil	1 392 693	1.09	6.71	2.03
India	1 053 009	0.92	5.07	1.53
South Africa	793 149	1.58	3.82	1.15
Thailand	623 304	0.52	3.00	0.91
China, Hong Kong SAR	576 559	0.19	2.78	0.84
Indonesia	480 035	0.51	2.31	0.70
Iran (Islamic Rep. of)	468 396	0.76	2.26	0.68
676 - Iron steel bar rod section piling				
World	57 469 201	0.52	_	100.0
Developed economies	35 664 027	0.54	_	62.06
Economies in transition	5 162 702	1.30	_	8.98
Developing economies	16 642 472	0.41	100.00	28.96
China	4 617 805	0.53	27.75	8.04
Turkey	3 280 288	4.13	19.71	5.71
Republic of Korea	1 670 722	0.55	10.04	2.91
Brazil	1 217 192	0.95	7.31	2.12
China, Taiwan Province of	1 026 021	0.50	6.17	1.79
India	637 036	0.56	3.83	1.11
South Africa	386 375	0.77	2.32	0.67
Singapore	385 357	0.15	2.32	0.67
Saudi Arabia	335 233	0.17	2.01	0.58
Mexico	332 771	0.14	2.00	0.58

Right Table

Leading exporting developing economies (1) based on average 2005-2006 exports (2) SITC Revision 3 (3-digit level) / Principales économies en dévelopement exportatrices (1) d'après la moyenne des exportations de 2005-2006 (2) CTCI révision 3 (positions à 3	Value (f.o.b., thousands of dollars) Valeur (f.a.b., milliers de dollars)	2005-2006 As percentage En pourcentage — of country total du total du pays	of developing economies des économies en déve-loppement	of world du monde
679 - Iron steel pipe tube fittings etc				
World	61 771 365	0.56	_	100.0
Developed economies	40 723 567	0.62	_	65.93
Economies in transition	3 215 629	0.81	_	5.21
Developing economies	17 832 169	0.43	100.00	28.87
China	5 637 973	0.65	31.62	9.13
Republic of Korea	1 876 025	0.62	10.52	3.04
India	1 293 453	1.13	7.25	2.09
Mexico	1 281 210	0.55	7.18	2.07
Singapore	1 085 125	0.43	6.09	1.76
Argentina	1 024 458	2.37	5.75	1.66
Malaysia	937 103	0.62	5.26	1.52
China, Taiwan Province of	876 082	0.42	4.91	1.42
Turkey	758 664	0.95	4.25	1.23
Brazil	604 352	0.47	3.39	0.98
682 - Copper				
World	86 992 871	0.78	_	100.0
Developed economies	38 682 099	0.59	_	44.47
Economies in transition	6 455 082	1.63	_	7.42
Developing economies	41 855 690	1.02	100.00	48.11
Chile	16 001 722	33.87	38.23	18.39
China	3 907 228	0.45	9.33	4.49
Peru	2 835 245	13.87	6.77	3.26
Republic of Korea	2 762 840	0.91	6.60	3.18
China, Taiwan Province of	2 524 192	1.22	6.03	2.90
India	2 037 977	1.78	4.87	2.34
China, Hong Kong SAR	1 900 313	0.62	4.54	2.18
Zambia	1 806 983	64.77	4.32	2.08
Indonesia	1 457 808	1.56	3.48	1.68
Mexico	1 109 681	0.48	2.65	1.28
684 - Aluminium				
World	87 741 358	0.79	_	100.0
Developed economies	58 360 317	0.88	_	66.51
Economies in transition	8 162 656	2.06	_	9.30
Developing economies	21 218 385	0.52	100.00	24.18
China	5 515 519	0.64	25.99	6.29
Brazil	2 269 910	1.77	10.70	2.59
South Africa	1 846 578	3.69	8.70	2.10
Republic of Korea	1 473 764	0.48	6.95	1.68
Bahrain	1 357 141	12.39	6.40	1.55
United Arab Emirates	1 118 114	0.87	5.27	1.27
Venezuela (Bolivarian Rep. of)	1 020 259	1.75	4.81	1.16
China, Taiwan Province of	735 040	0.36	3.46	0.84
Mozambique	700 807	33.66	3.30	0.80
China, Hong Kong SAR	688 339	0.22	3.24	0.78
699 - Base metal manufactures nes				
World	98 613 437	0.89	_	100.0
Developed economies	68 523 551	1.04	_	69.49
Economies in transition	1 464 181	0.37	_	1.48
Developing economies	28 625 706	0.70	100.00	29.03
China	11 538 369	1.33	40.31	11.70
Mexico	3 649 994	1.57	12.75	3.70
China, Taiwan Province of	3 325 320	1.61	11.62	3.37
Republic of Korea	1 667 815	0.55	5.83	1.69
China, Hong Kong SAR	1 635 802	0.53	5.71	1.66
India	1 193 917	1.04	4.17	1.21
Singapore	945 502	0.38	3.30	0.96
Thailand	932 243	0.77	3.26	0.95
Malaysia	700 152	0.46	2.45	0.71
Turkey	589 764	0.74	2.06	0.60

For sources and notes, see end of table.

Pour les sources et les notes, se reporter à la fin du tableau.

3.2.E   **Exports structure by product**
Major exporters for leading products among developing economies

3.2.E   **Structure des exportations par produits**
Principaux exportateurs de produits majeurs parmi les économies en développement

Left table

Leading exporting developing economies (1) based on average 2005-2006 exports (2) SITC Revision 3 (3-digit level) / Principales économies en dévelopement exportatrices (1) d'après la moyenne des exportations de 2005-2006 (2) CTCI révision 3 (positions à 3	Value (f.o.b., thousands of dollars) Valeur (f.a.b., milliers de dollars)	2005-2006 As percentage / En pourcentage		
		of country total / du total du pays	of developing economies / des économies en déve-loppement	of world / du monde
713 - Internal combustion engine part nes				
World	118 471 672	1.07	_	100.0
Developed economies	100 496 398	1.52	_	84.83
Economies in transition	698 006	0.18	_	0.59
Developing economies	17 277 268	0.42	100.00	14.58
Mexico	4 878 814	2.10	28.24	4.12
Brazil	2 721 923	2.12	15.75	2.30
China	2 145 943	0.25	12.42	1.81
Thailand	1 474 126	1.22	8.53	1.24
Republic of Korea	1 325 327	0.43	7.67	1.12
Singapore	1 240 689	0.49	7.18	1.05
India	579 030	0.50	3.35	0.49
South Africa	504 278	1.01	2.92	0.43
Turkey	480 595	0.60	2.78	0.41
Malaysia	340 008	0.23	1.97	0.29
716 - Rotating electric plant parts nes				
World	56 112 768	0.50	_	100.0
Developed economies	37 919 261	0.57	_	67.58
Economies in transition	477 843	0.12	_	0.85
Developing economies	17 715 664	0.43	100.00	31.57
China	5 811 751	0.67	32.81	10.36
Mexico	2 707 750	1.17	15.28	4.83
China, Hong Kong SAR	2 498 280	0.81	14.10	4.45
Singapore	1 364 998	0.54	7.71	2.43
Brazil	889 296	0.69	5.02	1.58
Thailand	865 258	0.72	4.88	1.54
Republic of Korea	823 649	0.27	4.65	1.47
China, Taiwan Province of	557 036	0.27	3.14	0.99
India	446 765	0.39	2.52	0.80
Indonesia	355 946	0.38	2.01	0.63
723 - Civil engineering plant & equipment				
World	76 741 647	0.69	_	100.0
Developed economies	60 491 660	0.92	_	78.83
Economies in transition	718 048	0.18	_	0.94
Developing economies	15 531 939	0.38	100.00	20.24
Singapore	3 446 420	1.37	22.19	4.49
Republic of Korea	3 168 555	1.04	20.40	4.13
China	2 985 787	0.35	19.22	3.89
Brazil	1 521 133	1.19	9.79	1.98
Mexico	955 252	0.41	6.15	1.24
United Arab Emirates	675 155	0.53	4.35	0.88
China, Hong Kong SAR	633 907	0.21	4.08	0.83
Indonesia	344 067	0.37	2.22	0.45
Thailand	248 294	0.21	1.60	0.32
South Africa	180 733	0.36	1.16	0.24
728 - Special industrial machine part nes				
World	104 175 925	0.94	_	100.0
Developed economies	86 727 481	1.31	_	83.25
Economies in transition	540 144	0.14	_	0.52
Developing economies	16 908 299	0.41	100.00	16.23
Republic of Korea	3 653 057	1.20	21.61	3.51
China	3 068 556	0.35	18.15	2.95
China, Taiwan Province of	2 876 435	1.39	17.01	2.76
Singapore	1 677 126	0.67	9.92	1.61
China, Hong Kong SAR	1 661 095	0.54	9.82	1.59
Mexico	724 915	0.31	4.29	0.70
Malaysia	720 373	0.48	4.26	0.69
Brazil	498 785	0.39	2.95	0.48
India	484 171	0.42	2.86	0.46
South Africa	288 575	0.58	1.71	0.28

Right table

Leading exporting developing economies (1) based on average 2005-2006 exports (2) SITC Revision 3 (3-digit level) / Principales économies en dévelopement exportatrices (1) d'après la moyenne des exportations de 2005-2006 (2) CTCI révision 3 (positions à 3	Value (f.o.b., thousands of dollars) Valeur (f.a.b., milliers de dollars)	2005-2006 As percentage / En pourcentage		
		of country total / du total du pays	of developing economies / des économies en déve-loppement	of world / du monde
741 - Heating cooling equipment parts nes				
World	74 148 737	0.67	_	100.0
Developed economies	52 567 218	0.80	_	70.89
Economies in transition	507 193	0.13	_	0.68
Developing economies	21 074 326	0.51	100.00	28.42
China	7 829 823	0.90	37.15	10.56
Thailand	2 554 285	2.12	12.12	3.44
Republic of Korea	2 538 724	0.83	12.05	3.42
Mexico	2 383 194	1.03	11.31	3.21
Malaysia	1 082 942	0.72	5.14	1.46
China, Hong Kong SAR	813 291	0.26	3.86	1.10
China, Taiwan Province of	778 834	0.38	3.70	1.05
Singapore	712 190	0.28	3.38	0.96
Brazil	367 042	0.29	1.74	0.50
India	365 533	0.32	1.73	0.49
743 - Gas pump, compressor, fan, filter				
World	74 564 109	0.67	_	100.0
Developed economies	56 829 278	0.86	_	76.22
Economies in transition	486 097	0.12	_	0.65
Developing economies	17 248 733	0.42	100.00	23.13
China	5 013 209	0.58	29.06	6.72
South Africa	2 095 597	4.18	12.15	2.81
Mexico	2 036 324	0.88	11.81	2.73
Republic of Korea	1 265 873	0.42	7.34	1.70
Singapore	1 006 548	0.40	5.84	1.35
China, Taiwan Province of	980 277	0.47	5.68	1.31
Thailand	972 540	0.81	5.64	1.30
Brazil	971 877	0.76	5.63	1.30
China, Hong Kong SAR	933 552	0.30	5.41	1.25
Malaysia	619 535	0.41	3.59	0.83
752 - Computer equipment nes				
World	285 331 419	2.57	_	100.0
Developed economies	120 932 374	1.83	_	42.38
Economies in transition	187 115	0.05	_	0.07
Developing economies	164 211 929	4.00	100.00	57.55
China	84 658 352	9.78	51.55	29.67
Malaysia	15 283 577	10.13	9.31	5.36
Singapore	14 275 329	5.69	8.69	5.00
China, Hong Kong SAR	10 091 659	3.28	6.15	3.54
Thailand	9 596 512	7.97	5.84	3.36
Mexico	9 370 138	4.04	5.71	3.28
Republic of Korea	8 875 949	2.91	5.41	3.11
Philippines	4 373 366	9.86	2.66	1.53
China, Taiwan Province of	4 024 927	1.95	2.45	1.41
Indonesia	1 818 003	1.95	1.11	0.64
759 - Office equipment part & accessories				
World	211 531 026	1.90	_	100.0
Developed economies	91 965 342	1.39	_	43.48
Economies in transition	89 991	0.02	_	0.04
Developing economies	119 475 693	2.91	100.00	56.48
China	32 194 220	3.72	26.95	15.22
China, Hong Kong SAR	28 072 903	9.13	23.50	13.27
Singapore	17 731 720	7.07	14.84	8.38
China, Taiwan Province of	10 185 026	4.93	8.52	4.81
Malaysia	9 981 732	6.62	8.35	4.72
Republic of Korea	8 576 442	2.81	7.18	4.05
Philippines	3 533 390	7.97	2.96	1.67
Thailand	3 481 216	2.89	2.91	1.65
Mexico	2 476 867	1.07	2.07	1.17
Indonesia	794 400	0.85	0.66	0.38

For sources and notes, see end of table.

Pour les sources et les notes, se reporter à la fin du tableau.

Exports structure by product
Major exporters for leading products among
developing economies

Structure des exportations par produits
Principaux exportateurs de produits majeurs
parmi les économies en développement

Left panel

Leading exporting developing economies (1) based on average 2005-2006 exports (2) SITC Revision 3 (3-digit level) / Principales économies en dévelopement exportatrices (1) d'après la moyenne des exportations de 2005-2006 (2) CTCI révision 3 (positions à 3	2005-2006		
	Value (f.o.b., thousands of dollars) / Valeur (f.a.b., milliers de dollars)	As percentage / En pourcentage	
		of country total / du total du pays	of developing economies / des économies en déve-loppement	of world / du monde
761 - Television video receive project				
World	66 764 869	0.60	_	100.0
Developed economies	28 906 650	0.44	_	43.30
Economies in transition	97 718	0.02	_	0.15
Developing economies	37 760 501	0.92	100.00	56.56
Mexico	13 480 019	5.81	35.70	20.19
China	10 689 560	1.24	28.31	16.01
Republic of Korea	2 616 328	0.86	6.93	3.92
China, Taiwan Province of	2 557 783	1.24	6.77	3.83
Turkey	2 262 456	2.85	5.99	3.39
Thailand	1 821 668	1.51	4.82	2.73
Malaysia	1 580 081	1.05	4.18	2.37
China, Hong Kong SAR	1 318 011	0.43	3.49	1.97
Singapore	496 311	0.20	1.31	0.74
Indonesia	302 230	0.32	0.80	0.45
763 - Sound TV recorder or reproducer				
World	62 199 744	0.56	_	100.0
Developed economies	25 456 551	0.39	_	40.93
Economies in transition	17 359	0.00	_	0.03
Developing economies	36 725 834	0.89	100.00	59.04
China	20 860 730	2.41	56.80	33.54
China, Hong Kong SAR	8 465 411	2.75	23.05	13.61
Malaysia	2 146 632	1.42	5.85	3.45
Singapore	1 196 527	0.48	3.26	1.92
Indonesia	1 144 756	1.23	3.12	1.84
Republic of Korea	1 089 694	0.36	2.97	1.75
Thailand	788 440	0.66	2.15	1.27
Mexico	357 112	0.15	0.97	0.57
China, Taiwan Province of	287 955	0.14	0.78	0.46
United Arab Emirates	174 884	0.14	0.48	0.28
764 - Telecommunicate equipment part nes				
World	390 357 341	3.51	_	100.0
Developed economies	192 528 572	2.91	_	49.32
Economies in transition	868 648	0.22	_	0.22
Developing economies	196 960 121	4.79	100.00	50.46
China	73 579 514	8.50	37.36	18.85
Republic of Korea	33 592 775	11.02	17.06	8.61
China, Hong Kong SAR	32 002 599	10.41	16.25	8.20
Singapore	14 418 065	5.75	7.32	3.69
Mexico	12 715 498	5.48	6.46	3.26
China, Taiwan Province of	8 821 087	4.27	4.48	2.26
Malaysia	8 298 508	5.50	4.21	2.13
United Arab Emirates	3 615 748	2.83	1.84	0.93
Brazil	3 042 027	2.37	1.54	0.78
Thailand	2 735 601	2.27	1.39	0.70
771 - Electric power machine part excl. 716				
World	50 630 054	0.46	_	100.0
Developed economies	23 887 189	0.36	_	47.18
Economies in transition	605 694	0.15	_	1.20
Developing economies	26 137 171	0.64	100.00	51.62
China	9 761 678	1.13	37.35	19.28
China, Hong Kong SAR	6 667 832	2.17	25.51	13.17
Mexico	2 097 162	0.90	8.02	4.14
China, Taiwan Province of	1 374 308	0.66	5.26	2.71
Republic of Korea	1 322 134	0.43	5.06	2.61
Singapore	1 257 129	0.50	4.81	2.48
Thailand	798 611	0.66	3.06	1.58
India	508 296	0.44	1.94	1.00
Malaysia	480 771	0.32	1.84	0.95
Indonesia	360 546	0.39	1.38	0.71

Right panel

Leading exporting developing economies (1) based on average 2005-2006 exports (2) SITC Revision 3 (3-digit level) / Principales économies en dévelopement exportatrices (1) d'après la moyenne des exportations de 2005-2006 (2) CTCI révision 3 (positions à 3	2005-2006		
	Value (f.o.b., thousands of dollars) / Valeur (f.a.b., milliers de dollars)	As percentage / En pourcentage	
		of country total / du total du pays	of developing economies / des économies en déve-loppement	of world / du monde
772 - Electrical circuit equipment				
World	152 933 107	1.38	_	100.0
Developed economies	93 053 907	1.41	_	60.85
Economies in transition	682 971	0.17	_	0.45
Developing economies	59 196 228	1.44	100.00	38.71
China	13 448 440	1.55	22.72	8.79
China, Hong Kong SAR	11 457 080	3.73	19.35	7.49
China, Taiwan Province of	7 265 690	3.52	12.27	4.75
Mexico	5 838 989	2.52	9.86	3.82
Singapore	5 328 186	2.13	9.00	3.48
Malaysia	5 143 788	3.41	8.69	3.36
Republic of Korea	3 213 028	1.05	5.43	2.10
Thailand	2 551 883	2.12	4.31	1.67
Philippines	970 255	2.19	1.64	0.63
Indonesia	966 799	1.04	1.63	0.63
773 - Electrical distribute equipment nes				
World	68 914 486	0.62	_	100.0
Developed economies	40 639 084	0.61	_	58.97
Economies in transition	894 274	0.23	_	1.30
Developing economies	27 381 129	0.67	100.00	39.73
Mexico	7 780 200	3.35	28.41	11.29
China	6 379 814	0.74	23.30	9.26
China, Hong Kong SAR	2 044 057	0.66	7.47	2.97
Republic of Korea	1 857 639	0.61	6.78	2.70
China, Taiwan Province of	869 800	0.42	3.18	1.26
Philippines	861 856	1.94	3.15	1.25
Thailand	793 578	0.66	2.90	1.15
Morocco	781 325	6.59	2.85	1.13
Malaysia	649 166	0.43	2.37	0.94
Indonesia	635 005	0.68	2.32	0.92
775 - Household equipment nes				
World	66 717 483	0.60	_	100.0
Developed economies	36 570 660	0.55	_	54.81
Economies in transition	682 303	0.17	_	1.02
Developing economies	29 464 520	0.72	100.00	44.16
China	14 637 015	1.69	49.68	21.94
Republic of Korea	3 321 791	1.09	11.27	4.98
China, Hong Kong SAR	2 560 815	0.83	8.69	3.84
Mexico	2 225 977	0.96	7.55	3.34
Thailand	1 896 915	1.58	6.44	2.84
Turkey	1 297 923	1.63	4.41	1.95
Singapore	869 415	0.35	2.95	1.30
Malaysia	806 535	0.53	2.74	1.21
Brazil	419 924	0.33	1.43	0.63
United Arab Emirates	313 069	0.24	1.06	0.47
776 - Valves tubes; diodes, transistors				
World	394 833 244	3.55	_	100.0
Developed economies	155 555 005	2.35	_	39.40
Economies in transition	261 755	0.07	_	0.07
Developing economies	239 016 484	5.82	100.00	60.54
Singapore	60 863 356	24.27	25.46	15.41
China, Taiwan Province of	37 383 341	18.09	15.64	9.47
China, Hong Kong SAR	34 235 364	11.14	14.32	8.67
Republic of Korea	27 987 334	9.18	11.71	7.09
China	24 811 060	2.87	10.38	6.28
Malaysia	24 635 746	16.33	10.31	6.24
Philippines	15 989 221	36.07	6.69	4.05
Thailand	7 424 362	6.17	3.11	1.88
Mexico	2 195 859	0.95	0.92	0.56
Costa Rica	1 019 826	14.16	0.43	0.26

For sources and notes, see end of table.

Pour les sources et les notes, se reporter à la fin du tableau.

3.2.E Exports structure by product
Major exporters for leading products among developing economies

3.2.E Structure des exportations par produits
Principaux exportateurs de produits majeurs parmi les économies en développement

Leading exporting developing economies (1) based on average 2005-2006 exports (2) SITC Revision 3 (3-digit level) / Principales économies en dévelopement exportatrices (1) d'après la moyenne des exportations de 2005-2006 (2) CTCI révision 3 (positions à 3	2005-2006			
	Value (f.o.b., thousands of dollars) Valeur (f.a.b., milliers de dollars)	As percentage En pourcentage		
		of country total du total du pays	of developing economies des économies en déve-loppement	of world du monde
778 - Electrical machinery apparatus nes				
World	157 226 171	1.41	_	100.0
Developed economies	90 418 035	1.37	_	57.51
Economies in transition	828 976	0.21	_	0.53
Developing economies	65 979 159	1.61	100.00	41.96
China	18 818 781	2.17	28.52	11.97
China, Taiwan Province of	8 785 730	4.25	13.32	5.59
China, Hong Kong SAR	8 176 825	2.66	12.39	5.20
Republic of Korea	7 623 514	2.50	11.55	4.85
Mexico	7 281 572	3.14	11.04	4.63
Singapore	5 032 482	2.01	7.63	3.20
Thailand	2 271 807	1.89	3.44	1.44
Malaysia	2 153 986	1.43	3.26	1.37
Philippines	2 004 229	4.52	3.04	1.27
Indonesia	1 184 516	1.27	1.80	0.75
781 - Passenger cars and race cars				
World	508 357 589	4.57	_	100.0
Developed economies	441 965 807	6.69	_	86.94
Economies in transition	1 165 941	0.29	_	0.23
Developing economies	65 225 841	1.59	100.00	12.83
Republic of Korea	28 926 648	9.49	44.35	5.69
Mexico	15 405 937	6.64	23.62	3.03
Brazil	4 496 330	3.51	6.89	0.88
South Africa	2 807 600	5.61	4.30	0.55
Thailand	2 541 186	2.11	3.90	0.50
Turkey	2 387 233	3.00	3.66	0.47
China	1 193 312	0.14	1.83	0.23
United Arab Emirates	1 168 032	0.91	1.79	0.23
Argentina	1 115 097	2.58	1.71	0.22
China, Hong Kong SAR	1 071 785	0.35	1.64	0.21
782 - Goods and service vehicles				
World	94 758 147	0.85	_	100.0
Developed economies	71 951 399	1.09	_	75.93
Economies in transition	1 617 159	0.41	_	1.71
Developing economies	21 189 588	0.52	100.00	22.36
Mexico	7 845 851	3.38	37.03	8.28
Thailand	3 354 493	2.79	15.83	3.54
Brazil	1 786 359	1.39	8.43	1.89
Republic of Korea	1 536 626	0.50	7.25	1.62
Turkey	1 276 114	1.61	6.02	1.35
Argentina	1 246 547	2.88	5.88	1.32
China	1 160 471	0.13	5.48	1.22
South Africa	812 453	1.62	3.83	0.86
United Arab Emirates	495 667	0.39	2.34	0.52
Saudi Arabia	306 158	0.16	1.44	0.32
784 - Motor vehicle parts and accessories				
World	245 662 118	2.21	_	100.0
Developed economies	198 300 316	3.00	_	80.72
Economies in transition	1 098 891	0.28	_	0.45
Developing economies	46 262 911	1.13	100.00	18.83
Mexico	10 695 837	4.61	23.12	4.35
Republic of Korea	8 642 813	2.83	18.68	3.52
China	7 781 771	0.90	16.82	3.17
Brazil	3 696 813	2.88	7.99	1.50
China, Taiwan Province of	2 702 174	1.31	5.84	1.10
Thailand	2 321 118	1.93	5.02	0.94
Singapore	1 501 514	0.60	3.25	0.61
Philippines	1 377 877	3.11	2.98	0.56
India	1 315 692	1.15	2.84	0.54
Turkey	1 143 991	1.44	2.47	0.47

Leading exporting developing economies (1) based on average 2005-2006 exports (2) SITC Revision 3 (3-digit level) / Principales économies en dévelopement exportatrices (1) d'après la moyenne des exportations de 2005-2006 (2) CTCI révision 3 (positions à 3	2005-2006			
	Value (f.o.b., thousands of dollars) Valeur (f.a.b., milliers de dollars)	As percentage En pourcentage		
		of country total du total du pays	of developing economies des économies en déve-loppement	of world du monde
785 - Motorcycles, mopeds and cycles				
World	33 896 987	0.30	_	100.0
Developed economies	20 565 321	0.31	_	60.67
Economies in transition	43 274	0.01	_	0.13
Developing economies	13 288 393	0.32	100.00	39.20
China	6 590 472	0.76	49.60	19.44
China, Taiwan Province of	3 008 903	1.46	22.64	8.88
Thailand	833 239	0.69	6.27	2.46
India	497 492	0.43	3.74	1.47
Singapore	456 565	0.18	3.44	1.35
Indonesia	295 897	0.32	2.23	0.87
Brazil	287 750	0.22	2.17	0.85
China, Hong Kong SAR	269 430	0.09	2.03	0.79
Malaysia	237 114	0.16	1.78	0.70
Viet Nam	189 747	0.53	1.43	0.56
793 - Ships boats floating structures				
World	79 600 576	0.72	_	100.0
Developed economies	41 159 026	0.62	_	51.71
Economies in transition	2 376 014	0.60	_	2.98
Developing economies	36 065 536	0.88	100.00	45.31
Republic of Korea	19 362 182	6.35	53.69	24.32
China	6 386 576	0.74	17.71	8.02
Cayman Islands	1 225 171	89.68	3.40	1.54
Liberia	1 113 168	76.14	3.09	1.40
India	983 609	0.86	2.73	1.24
Singapore	929 223	0.37	2.58	1.17
Malaysia	763 484	0.51	2.12	0.96
China, Taiwan Province of	750 408	0.36	2.08	0.94
Turkey	710 471	0.89	1.97	0.89
Marshall Islands	693 881	92.29	1.92	0.87
821 - Furniture part; bedding furnishing				
World	102 554 838	0.92	_	100.0
Developed economies	64 477 093	0.98	_	62.87
Economies in transition	1 317 486	0.33	_	1.28
Developing economies	36 760 260	0.89	100.00	35.84
China	18 731 461	2.16	50.96	18.26
Mexico	4 630 131	2.00	12.60	4.51
Malaysia	2 140 466	1.42	5.82	2.09
Indonesia	1 866 029	2.00	5.08	1.82
Viet Nam	1 591 869	4.41	4.33	1.55
Thailand	1 254 616	1.04	3.41	1.22
China, Taiwan Province of	1 221 920	0.59	3.32	1.19
Brazil	984 763	0.77	2.68	0.96
Turkey	630 091	0.79	1.71	0.61
China, Hong Kong SAR	535 975	0.17	1.46	0.52
831 - Case bag: storage travel shopping				
World	25 259 105	0.23	_	100.0
Developed economies	10 074 544	0.15	_	39.88
Economies in transition	41 123	0.01	_	0.16
Developing economies	15 143 438	0.37	100.00	59.95
China	8 087 902	0.93	53.41	32.02
China, Hong Kong SAR	4 968 154	1.62	32.81	19.67
India	560 071	0.49	3.70	2.22
Viet Nam	323 818	0.90	2.14	1.28
Thailand	209 423	0.17	1.38	0.83
Singapore	192 463	0.08	1.27	0.76
Philippines	88 189	0.20	0.58	0.35
Republic of Korea	82 761	0.03	0.55	0.33
Mexico	80 807	0.08	0.53	0.32
Indonesia	76 257	0.08	0.50	0.30

For sources and notes, see end of table. Pour les sources et les notes, se reporter à la fin du tableau.

3.2.E Exports structure by product
Major exporters for leading products among developing economies

3.2.E Structure des exportations par produits
Principaux exportateurs de produits majeurs parmi les économies en développement

Leading exporting developing economies (1) based on average 2005-2006 exports (2) SITC Revision 3 (3-digit level) Principales économies en dévelopement exportatrices (1) d'après la moyenne des exportations de 2005-2006 (2) CTCI révision 3 (positions à 3	2005-2006		
	Value (f.o.b., thousands of dollars) Valeur (f.a.b., milliers de dollars)	As percentage / En pourcentage		
		of country total du total du pays	of developing economies des économies en déve-loppement	of world du monde
841 - Male clothing, woven				
World	53 698 716	0.48	_	100.0
Developed economies	18 188 537	0.28	_	33.87
Economies in transition	858 676	0.22	_	1.60
Developing economies	34 651 503	0.84	100.00	64.53
China	13 287 552	1.54	38.35	24.74
China, Hong Kong SAR	3 107 140	1.01	8.97	5.79
Bangladesh	2 318 018	21.67	6.69	4.32
Mexico	2 293 463	0.99	6.62	4.27
Turkey	1 672 854	2.10	4.83	3.12
India	1 519 769	1.32	4.39	2.83
Viet Nam	1 517 666	4.20	4.38	2.83
Indonesia	1 337 094	1.43	3.86	2.49
Tunisia	1 043 028	9.48	3.01	1.94
Pakistan	787 157	4.77	2.27	1.47
842 - Female clothing, woven				
World	67 534 179	0.61	_	100.0
Developed economies	22 610 137	0.34	_	33.48
Economies in transition	1 010 201	0.25	_	1.50
Developing economies	43 913 841	1.07	100.00	65.02
China	17 229 974	1.99	39.24	25.51
China, Hong Kong SAR	7 235 877	2.35	16.48	10.71
India	3 217 867	2.80	7.33	4.76
Turkey	2 720 737	3.42	6.20	4.03
Bangladesh	1 458 782	13.64	3.32	2.16
Indonesia	1 407 886	1.51	3.21	2.08
Mexico	1 313 881	0.57	2.99	1.95
Viet Nam	1 255 887	3.48	2.86	1.86
Morocco	1 093 355	9.22	2.49	1.62
Sri Lanka	937 413	14.60	2.13	1.39
844 - Female clothing, knitted crocheted				
World	28 293 776	0.25	_	100.0
Developed economies	7 199 495	0.11	_	25.45
Economies in transition	229 821	0.06	_	0.81
Developing economies	20 864 459	0.51	100.00	73.74
China	8 625 192	1.00	41.34	30.48
China, Hong Kong SAR	2 992 937	0.97	14.34	10.58
Turkey	1 356 507	1.71	6.50	4.79
India	769 345	0.67	3.69	2.72
Viet Nam	620 066	1.72	2.97	2.19
Indonesia	554 347	0.59	2.66	1.96
Mexico	517 421	0.22	2.48	1.83
Cambodia	451 891	12.67	2.17	1.60
Sri Lanka	425 340	6.62	2.04	1.50
Bangladesh	415 225	3.88	1.99	1.47
845 - Articles of apparel nes				
World	99 901 197	0.90	_	100.0
Developed economies	31 724 572	0.48	_	31.76
Economies in transition	723 435	0.18	_	0.72
Developing economies	67 453 190	1.64	100.00	67.52
China	28 141 977	3.25	41.72	28.17
China, Hong Kong SAR	10 923 499	3.55	16.19	10.93
Turkey	4 346 882	5.47	6.44	4.35
Bangladesh	3 631 956	33.96	5.38	3.64
India	2 070 360	1.80	3.07	2.07
Mexico	2 054 320	0.89	3.05	2.06
Tunisia	1 524 591	13.86	2.26	1.53
Thailand	1 426 515	1.19	2.11	1.43
Indonesia	1 338 350	1.44	1.98	1.34
Viet Nam	1 097 702	3.04	1.63	1.10

Leading exporting developing economies (1) based on average 2005-2006 exports (2) SITC Revision 3 (3-digit level) Principales économies en dévelopement exportatrices (1) d'après la moyenne des exportations de 2005-2006 (2) CTCI révision 3 (positions à 3	2005-2006		
	Value (f.o.b., thousands of dollars) Valeur (f.a.b., milliers de dollars)	As percentage / En pourcentage		
		of country total du total du pays	of developing economies des économies en déve-loppement	of world du monde
848 - Headgear non-textile clothing				
World	20 877 865	0.19	_	100.0
Developed economies	6 394 869	0.10	_	30.63
Economies in transition	89 487	0.02	_	0.43
Developing economies	14 393 508	0.35	100.00	68.94
China	7 513 973	0.87	52.20	35.99
China, Hong Kong SAR	1 689 746	0.55	11.74	8.09
Malaysia	1 394 504	0.92	9.69	6.68
Pakistan	637 595	3.87	4.43	3.05
Thailand	622 072	0.52	4.32	2.98
India	543 543	0.47	3.78	2.60
Turkey	369 650	0.46	2.57	1.77
China, Taiwan Province of	245 317	0.12	1.70	1.18
Republic of Korea	226 011	0.07	1.57	1.08
Indonesia	216 673	0.23	1.51	1.04
851 - Footwear				
World	69 179 196	0.62	_	100.0
Developed economies	29 064 203	0.44	_	42.01
Economies in transition	926 604	0.23	_	1.34
Developing economies	39 188 389	0.95	100.00	56.65
China	20 432 940	2.36	52.14	29.54
China, Hong Kong SAR	6 084 351	1.98	15.53	8.80
Viet Nam	3 366 683	9.32	8.59	4.87
Brazil	1 975 522	1.54	5.04	2.86
Indonesia	1 514 142	1.62	3.86	2.19
India	1 141 965	1.00	2.91	1.65
Thailand	912 558	0.76	2.33	1.32
Republic of Korea	474 370	0.16	1.21	0.69
Tunisia	470 373	4.27	1.20	0.68
China, Taiwan Province of	358 639	0.17	0.92	0.52
871 - Optical instruments apparatus nes				
World	51 022 047	0.46	_	100.0
Developed economies	10 924 589	0.17	_	21.41
Economies in transition	142 370	0.04	_	0.28
Developing economies	39 955 089	0.97	100.00	78.31
China	12 958 455	1.50	32.43	25.40
China, Taiwan Province of	12 815 875	6.20	32.08	25.12
Republic of Korea	11 519 753	3.78	28.83	22.58
China, Hong Kong SAR	1 871 038	0.61	4.68	3.67
Singapore	501 539	0.20	1.26	0.98
Thailand	132 248	0.11	0.33	0.26
Mexico	38 896	0.02	0.10	0.08
Malaysia	32 797	0.02	0.08	0.06
Philippines	17 509	0.04	0.04	0.03
Brazil	15 173	0.01	0.04	0.03
874 - Measure analyze control device nes				
World	118 314 735	1.06	_	100.0
Developed economies	99 224 668	1.50	_	83.87
Economies in transition	784 435	0.20	_	0.66
Developing economies	18 305 632	0.45	100.00	15.47
China	3 546 628	0.41	19.37	3.00
Mexico	3 459 337	1.49	18.90	2.92
China, Hong Kong SAR	2 561 727	0.83	13.99	2.17
Singapore	2 515 478	1.00	13.74	2.13
Malaysia	2 207 743	1.46	12.06	1.87
Republic of Korea	1 141 182	0.37	6.23	0.96
China, Taiwan Province of	1 124 318	0.54	6.14	0.95
Thailand	364 302	0.30	1.99	0.31
Brazil	238 274	0.19	1.30	0.20
India	213 090	0.19	1.16	0.18

For sources and notes, see end of table.

Pour les sources et les notes, se reporter à la fin du tableau.

3.2.E **Exports structure by product**
Major exporters for leading products among developing economies

3.2.E **Structure des exportations par produits**
Principaux exportateurs de produits majeurs parmi les économies en développement

Leading exporting developing economies (1) based on average 2005-2006 exports (2) SITC Revision 3 (3-digit level) Principales économies en développement exportatrices (1) d'après la moyenne des exportations de 2005-2006 (2) CTCI révision 3 (positions à 3	2005-2006			
	Value (f.o.b., thousands of dollars) Valeur (f.a.b., milliers de dollars)	As percentage En pourcentage		
		of country total du total du pays	of developing economies des économies en déve-loppement	of world du monde
893 - Articles of plastic nes				
World	90 251 085	0.81	_	100.0
Developed economies	60 034 933	0.91	_	66.52
Economies in transition	591 254	0.15	_	0.66
Developing economies	29 624 898	0.72	100.00	32.82
China	12 289 122	1.42	41.48	13.62
China, Hong Kong SAR	3 029 126	0.99	10.22	3.36
Mexico	2 418 287	1.04	8.16	2.68
China, Taiwan Province of	2 384 653	1.15	8.05	2.64
Republic of Korea	1 359 610	0.45	4.59	1.51
Thailand	1 270 797	1.06	4.29	1.41
Malaysia	1 194 732	0.79	4.03	1.32
Singapore	841 576	0.34	2.84	0.93
Turkey	649 245	0.82	2.19	0.72
India	504 193	0.44	1.70	0.56
894 - Baby carriage toy game sport good				
World	67 672 978	0.61	_	100.0
Developed economies	27 328 247	0.41	_	40.38
Economies in transition	178 622	0.04	_	0.26
Developing economies	40 166 109	0.98	100.00	59.35
China	22 470 512	2.60	55.94	33.20
China, Hong Kong SAR	11 812 081	3.84	29.41	17.45
China, Taiwan Province of	1 824 793	0.88	4.54	2.70
Mexico	719 136	0.31	1.79	1.06
Thailand	681 892	0.57	1.70	1.01
Republic of Korea	414 735	0.14	1.03	0.61
Singapore	414 534	0.17	1.03	0.61
Pakistan	328 639	1.99	0.82	0.49
Malaysia	278 477	0.18	0.69	0.41
Indonesia	268 307	0.29	0.67	0.40
897 - Jewellery nes (667)				
World	44 391 003	0.40	_	100.0
Developed economies	23 530 102	0.36	_	53.01
Economies in transition	196 027	0.05	_	0.44
Developing economies	20 664 874	0.50	100.00	46.55
China, Hong Kong SAR	4 531 733	1.47	21.93	10.21
India	4 440 121	3.87	21.49	10.00
China	3 019 970	0.35	14.61	6.80
Thailand	1 853 730	1.54	8.97	4.18
Turkey	1 151 012	1.45	5.57	2.59
Malaysia	1 005 547	0.67	4.87	2.27
United Arab Emirates	751 893	0.59	3.64	1.69
Singapore	656 412	0.26	3.18	1.48
Mexico	604 590	0.26	2.93	1.36
Republic of Korea	512 680	0.17	2.48	1.15

Leading exporting developing economies (1) based on average 2005-2006 exports (2) SITC Revision 3 (3-digit level) Principales économies en développement exportatrices (1) d'après la moyenne des exportations de 2005-2006 (2) CTCI révision 3 (positions à 3	2005-2006			
	Value (f.o.b., thousands of dollars) Valeur (f.a.b., milliers de dollars)	As percentage En pourcentage		
		of country total du total du pays	of developing economies des économies en déve-loppement	of world du monde
898 - Music instrument device recording				
World	51 663 707	0.46	_	100.0
Developed economies	34 693 346	0.52	_	67.15
Economies in transition	115 670	0.03	_	0.22
Developing economies	16 854 692	0.41	100.00	32.62
China, Taiwan Province of	4 671 825	2.26	27.72	9.04
Singapore	3 410 286	1.36	20.23	6.60
China	2 998 293	0.35	17.79	5.80
Republic of Korea	1 473 983	0.48	8.75	2.85
Malaysia	1 086 916	0.72	6.45	2.10
China, Hong Kong SAR	957 088	0.31	5.68	1.85
Mexico	632 489	0.27	3.75	1.22
Thailand	419 036	0.35	2.49	0.81
Indonesia	366 074	0.39	2.17	0.71
India	360 188	0.31	2.14	0.70
899 - Manufactured articles nes				
World	46 933 466	0.42	_	100.0
Developed economies	32 557 980	0.49	_	69.37
Economies in transition	101 778	0.03	_	0.22
Developing economies	14 273 708	0.35	100.00	30.41
China	7 397 782	0.85	51.83	15.76
China, Hong Kong SAR	2 340 744	0.76	16.40	4.99
Singapore	655 862	0.26	4.59	1.40
Mexico	652 655	0.28	4.57	1.39
China, Taiwan Province of	526 728	0.25	3.69	1.12
Republic of Korea	448 922	0.15	3.15	0.96
Indonesia	310 398	0.33	2.17	0.66
Viet Nam	282 361	0.78	1.98	0.60
India	270 850	0.24	1.90	0.58
Thailand	265 164	0.22	1.86	0.56
971 - Gold non-monetary excluding ores				
World	48 590 498	0.44	_	100.0
Developed economies	23 525 247	0.36	_	48.42
Economies in transition	773 424	0.19	_	1.59
Developing economies	24 291 827	0.59	100.00	49.99
China, Hong Kong SAR	4 321 837	1.41	17.79	8.89
United Arab Emirates	3 618 954	2.83	14.90	7.45
Peru	3 537 338	17.31	14.56	7.28
Singapore	1 222 060	0.49	5.03	2.52
Ghana	999 133	21.77	4.11	2.06
Mali	912 586	70.17	3.76	1.88
Papua New Guinea	851 078	21.46	3.50	1.75
Colombia	727 808	3.19	3.00	1.50
Mexico	702 595	0.30	2.89	1.45
United Republic of Tanzania	570 325	35.27	2.35	1.17

Sources:
- Data and UNCTAD secretariat estimates based on UN DESA Comtrade and IMF Direction of Trade statistics databases

Notes:

(1) In addition, are presented for each product group the world total exports, the exports from developed, economies in transition and developing economies.
(2) Commodity groups are selected on the basis of ranking by value.

Sources :
- Données et estimations du secrétariat de la CNUCED sur la base de données Comtrade de ONU DAES et Direction of Trade statistics du Fonds Monétaire international

Notes :

(1) Les exportations mondiales totales, les exportations des économies développées, en transition et en développement sont également présentées pour chaque groupe de produits.
(2) Les groupes de produits sont sélectionnés d'après le classement par valeur.

SITC group Revision 3 (3-digit level) ranked according to the concentration index in 2006 Groupes de la CTCI Révision 3 (positions à 3 chiffres) classés d'après l'indice de concentration en 2006	Concentration index (1) Indice de concentration (1)			Structural change index (2) Indice de changement structurel (2) 1995=0	
	1995	2000	2006	2000	2006
264 Jute, other textile bast fibres n.e.s., raw, processed, not spun; waste of	0.830	0.862	0.903	0.062	0.106
261 Silk	0.593	0.745	0.688	0.233	0.298
286 Uranium or thorium ores and concentrates	0.617	0.691	0.603	0.248	0.199
633 Cork manufactures	0.645	0.613	0.592	0.056	0.078
244 Cork, natural, raw and waste (including natural cork in blocks or sheets)	0.588	0.519	0.592	0.111	0.052
044 Maize (not including sweet corn), unmilled	0.688	0.549	0.543	0.199	0.206
883 Cinematographic film, exposed developed, whether or not incorporating soundtrack	0.323	0.308	0.502	0.311	0.555
422 Fixed vegetable fats and oils, crude, refined or fractionated, other than "soft"	0.493	0.452	0.486	0.194	0.310
345 Coal gas, water gas, producer gas, similar gas (exclude other gas hydrocarbons)	0.526	0.554	0.463	0.394	0.288
231 Natural rubber, balata, gutta-percha, guayule, chicle, natural gums	0.427	0.449	0.454	0.140	0.173
792 Aircraft, associated equipment; spacecraft, satellites, launch vehicles; parts	0.405	0.433	0.442	0.135	0.163
891 Arms and ammunition	0.547	0.500	0.442	0.227	0.240
885 Watches & clocks	0.377	0.398	0.437	0.081	0.191
896 Works of art, collectors' pieces and antiques	0.399	0.446	0.422	0.119	0.160
281 Iron ore and concentrates	0.374	0.410	0.407	0.076	0.146
871 Optical instruments and apparatus, n.e.s.	0.321	0.317	0.407	0.235	0.605
325 Coke, semi-coke of coal, lignite, peat, agglomerated or not; retort carbon	0.334	0.419	0.406	0.200	0.245
045 Cereals, unmilled (excluding wheat, rice, barley, maize)	0.437	0.485	0.406	0.139	0.183
666 Pottery	0.228	0.284	0.396	0.168	0.293
344 Petroleum gases and other gaseous hydrocarbons, n.e.s.	0.367	0.390	0.393	0.346	0.406
222 Oil-seed, oleaginous fruit for soft fixed vegetable oils (exclude flours, meals)	0.472	0.429	0.390	0.158	0.266
212 Furskins, raw, other than hides and skins of group 211	0.349	0.365	0.389	0.186	0.226
263 Cotton	0.350	0.290	0.386	0.219	0.292
267 Other man-made fibres suitable for spinning; waste of man-made fibres	0.410	0.390	0.385	0.091	0.176
283 Copper ores and concentrates; copper mattes; cement copper	0.356	0.421	0.383	0.210	0.291
763 Sound or television image recorder reproducer; prepared unrecorded media	0.297	0.365	0.378	0.210	0.420
583 Plastic monofilament, cross-section > 1 mm, rods, sticks, profile shapes	0.379	0.355	0.376	0.129	0.177
831 Cases bags(storage hand executive equipment instrument gun travel shopping back)	0.351	0.354	0.375	0.100	0.231
751 Office machines	0.279	0.282	0.373	0.129	0.410
321 Coal, whether or not pulverized, excluding agglomerated	0.345	0.348	0.373	0.146	0.246
265 Vegetable textile fibre (exclu cotton, jute), raw, processed, not spun; waste of	0.383	0.433	0.372	0.133	0.182
284 Nickel ores, concentrates; mattes, oxide sinters, intermediate product of	0.392	0.378	0.369	0.232	0.193
881 Photographic apparatus and equipment, n.e.s.	0.353	0.328	0.361	0.151	0.317
894 Baby carriages, toys, games and sporting goods	0.296	0.331	0.359	0.112	0.271
272 Fertilizers, crude (excluding those of division 56)	0.325	0.339	0.357	0.235	0.218
551 Essential oils, perfume and flavour materials	0.239	0.269	0.355	0.179	0.321
726 Printing and bookbinding machinery, and parts thereof	0.339	0.330	0.354	0.052	0.128
268 Wool and other animal hair (including wool tops)	0.365	0.399	0.347	0.143	0.195
843 Men's textile, knitted (coat suit trouser short shirt underwear nightwear)	0.171	0.188	0.345	0.194	0.400
714 Engines, motors, non-electric (exclude group 712, 713 and 718); parts of, n.e.s.	0.367	0.380	0.344	0.085	0.141
285 Aluminium ores and concentrates (including alumina)	0.356	0.371	0.343	0.119	0.173
658 Made-up articles, wholly or chiefly of textile materials, n.e.s.	0.195	0.208	0.342	0.130	0.263
786 Trailers semi-trailers vehicles not mechanically-propelled; transport containers	0.232	0.291	0.334	0.193	0.259
844 Women's textiles, knitted (articles as code 841, plus dresses skirts)	0.185	0.201	0.334	0.189	0.398
525 Radio-actives and associated materials	0.354	0.381	0.330	0.253	0.305
774 Electrodiagnostic apparatus, medical surgical dental veterinary radiological	0.351	0.348	0.328	0.119	0.106
712 Steam turbines and other vapour turbines, and parts thereof, n.e.s.	0.340	0.336	0.327	0.220	0.290
292 Crude vegetable materials, n.e.s.	0.325	0.299	0.325	0.093	0.099
322 Briquettes, lignites and peat	0.357	0.373	0.323	0.213	0.244
848 Apparel articles accessories other than textile fabrics; headgear (all material)	0.240	0.280	0.321	0.102	0.188
731 Machine tools working by removing metal or other material	0.357	0.347	0.316	0.059	0.112
593 Explosives and pyrotechnic products	0.269	0.325	0.314	0.233	0.228
752 Automatic data-processing transcibing machines; magnetic optical readers, n.e.s.	0.257	0.217	0.312	0.202	0.467
696 Cutlery	0.232	0.250	0.311	0.215	0.352
851 Footwear	0.251	0.265	0.309	0.152	0.284
042 Rice	0.322	0.301	0.308	0.163	0.177
016 Meat, edible meat offal (salted dried); flours, meals	0.343	0.330	0.305	0.116	0.200
662 Clay construction materials and refractory construction materials	0.340	0.352	0.303	0.121	0.236
683 Nickel	0.280	0.280	0.302	0.147	0.189
043 Barley, unmilled	0.283	0.329	0.302	0.175	0.359
813 Lighting fixtures and fittings, n.e.s.	0.216	0.233	0.300	0.140	0.270
687 Tin	0.269	0.303	0.299	0.256	0.362
845 Articles of apparel, textile fabrics, knitted or crocheted or not, n.e.s.	0.204	0.209	0.296	0.146	0.286
289 Ores and concentrates of precious metals; waste of (excluding gold)	0.325	0.332	0.295	0.391	0.327

For sources and notes, see end of table 3.3 Imports.

Pour les sources et les notes, se reporter à la fin du tableau 3.3 Importations.

SITC group Revision 3 (3-digit level) ranked according to the concentration index in 2006 Groupes de la CTCI Révision 3 (positions à 3 chiffres) classés d'après l'indice de concentration en 2006	Concentration index (1) Indice de concentration (1)			Structural change index (2) Indice de changement structurel (2) 1995=0	
	1995	2000	2006	2000	2006
961 Coin (other than gold coin), not being legal tender	0.585	0.887	0.294	0.899	0.429
785 Motor cycles, mopeds, cycles, motorized and non-motorized; invalid carriages	0.345	0.334	0.294	0.118	0.261
697 Household equipment of base metal, n.e.s.	0.190	0.202	0.294	0.132	0.314
247 Wood in the rough or roughly squared	0.269	0.242	0.292	0.237	0.327
846 Clothing accessories of textiles, knitted or crocheted or not (exluding babies)	0.217	0.223	0.292	0.161	0.274
882 Photographic and cinematographic supplies	0.298	0.290	0.291	0.108	0.152
223 Oil-seed, oleaginous fruit to extract other vegetable oil; flour, meal of n.e.s.	0.281	0.187	0.291	0.313	0.456
041 Wheat (including spelt) and meslin, unmilled	0.371	0.336	0.290	0.159	0.211
431 Animal, vegetable fats, oils, processed; waxes; inedible preparations of, n.e.s.	0.275	0.265	0.289	0.193	0.180
597 Prepared additives: mineral oil; transmission; anti-freeze, de-ice; lubricating	0.311	0.311	0.289	0.100	0.130
745 Non-electrical machinery, tools and mechanical apparatus, parts thereof, n.e.s.	0.303	0.283	0.288	0.097	0.105
072 Cocoa	0.300	0.323	0.287	0.164	0.120
211 Hides and skins (except furskins), raw	0.270	0.288	0.287	0.134	0.184
654 Other textile fabrics, woven n.e.s.	0.299	0.255	0.287	0.144	0.192
652 Cotton fabrics, woven (not including narrow or special fabrics)	0.203	0.206	0.287	0.107	0.195
748 Transmission shaft camshaft crankshaft; bearing housing; gearbox speed changer	0.318	0.286	0.285	0.094	0.160
681 Silver, platinum, other metals of the platinum group	0.251	0.315	0.282	0.230	0.326
655 Knitted, crocheted fabric (include tubular knit, pile, openwork fabric), n.e.s.	0.257	0.266	0.280	0.120	0.264
613 Furskin, tanned, dressed, unassembled, assembled (without other materials)	0.223	0.251	0.279	0.226	0.352
515 Organo-inorganic and heterocyclic compounds, nucleic acids-salts, sulphonamides	0.239	0.325	0.279	0.230	0.214
274 Sulphur and unroasted iron pyrites	0.389	0.354	0.278	0.223	0.322
781 Vehicles to transport less than 10 persons, including station-wagons race cars	0.290	0.283	0.277	0.081	0.114
689 Miscellaneous non-ferrous base metals employed in metallurgy, and cermets	0.215	0.199	0.277	0.196	0.306
793 Ships, boats (including hovercraft) and floating structures	0.312	0.303	0.277	0.162	0.313
874 Measuring, checking, analysing and controlling instruments and apparatus, n.e.s.	0.309	0.330	0.275	0.100	0.138
653 Fabrics, woven, of man-made textiles (excluding narrow or special fabrics)	0.230	0.204	0.274	0.138	0.308
722 Tractors (excluding headings 714.14 & 744.15)	0.302	0.294	0.274	0.111	0.142
667 Pearls and precious or semiprecious stones, unworked or worked	0.315	0.314	0.272	0.126	0.184
037 Fish, crustaceans, molluscs, aquatic invertebrates (prepared preserved) n.e.s.	0.188	0.239	0.272	0.173	0.280
251 Pulp and waste paper	0.350	0.321	0.270	0.073	0.160
579 Waste, parings and scrap, of plastics	0.413	0.316	0.269	0.203	0.249
025 Eggs, birds', yolks, fresh, dried, preserved, sweetened or not; albumin	0.336	0.309	0.268	0.128	0.204
725 Paper mill pulp mill paper-cutting other paper manufacture machines; parts of	0.263	0.257	0.268	0.076	0.159
842 Women's textiles not knitted (articles as code 841, plus dresses skirts)	0.209	0.200	0.267	0.156	0.246
343 Natural gas, whether or not liquefied	0.378	0.316	0.267	0.206	0.259
762 Radio-broadcast receivers, with without sound-recording reproducing or clock	0.276	0.255	0.265	0.170	0.357
884 Optical goods, n.e.s.	0.260	0.286	0.265	0.166	0.158
728 Other machinery or specialized industrial equipment; parts thereof, n.e.s.	0.285	0.303	0.263	0.114	0.104
733 Machine tool to work metal sintered metal carbide cermet, not removing material	0.289	0.260	0.260	0.089	0.158
724 Textile and leather machinery, and parts thereof, n.e.s.	0.318	0.275	0.259	0.108	0.181
761 Television receiver, video monitor projector, w wo radio video-record reproduce	0.206	0.226	0.259	0.263	0.440
121 Tobacco, unmanufactured; tobacco refuse	0.292	0.263	0.258	0.125	0.250
727 Food-processing machines (excluding domestic); parts thereof	0.259	0.248	0.258	0.081	0.123
541 Medicinal and pharmaceutical products, excluding medicines of group 542	0.237	0.245	0.256	0.107	0.118
112 Alcoholic beverages	0.290	0.280	0.256	0.107	0.135
775 Household-type electrical and non-electrical equipment, n.e.s.	0.225	0.212	0.256	0.133	0.306
061 Sugar, molasses and honey	0.197	0.173	0.255	0.199	0.353
872 Instruments and appliances, n.e.s., (medical, surgical, dental or veterinary)	0.276	0.278	0.255	0.116	0.147
553 Perfumery, cosmetic or toilet preparations (excluding soaps)	0.320	0.276	0.254	0.112	0.161
122 Tobacco, manufactured (whether or not containing tobacco substitutes)	0.309	0.294	0.252	0.162	0.427
783 Road motor vehicles, n.e.s.	0.302	0.262	0.252	0.154	0.192
742 Liquid pump, with without a fitted measuring device; liquid elevator; parts for	0.301	0.289	0.251	0.101	0.167
656 Tulles, lace, embroidery, ribbons, trimmings and other smallwares	0.197	0.204	0.251	0.145	0.255
735 Parts, n.e.s. and accessories for machines of groups 731, 733; tool holder	0.280	0.299	0.250	0.124	0.141
721 Agricultural machinery (excluding tractors), and parts thereof	0.271	0.274	0.250	0.062	0.121
351 Electric current	0.484	0.367	0.250	0.301	0.420
024 Cheese and curd	0.304	0.268	0.249	0.099	0.161
023 Butter and other fats and oils derived from milk	0.256	0.259	0.249	0.142	0.158
841 Men's textile, not knitted (coat suit trouser short shirt underwear nightwear)	0.187	0.189	0.248	0.149	0.247
776 Thermionic cold cathode photo-cathode valves tubes; diodes, transistors	0.295	0.261	0.246	0.138	0.286
074 Tea and maté	0.253	0.289	0.246	0.158	0.192
524 Other inorganic chemicals; organic and inorganic compounds of precious metals	0.221	0.230	0.245	0.245	0.177
612 Manufactures of leather or of composition leather, n.e.s.; saddlery and harness	0.196	0.207	0.244	0.185	0.382
342 Liquefied propane and butane	0.234	0.250	0.244	0.198	0.373

For sources and notes, see end of table 3.3 Imports.

Pour les sources et les notes, se reporter à la fin du tableau 3.3 Importations.

SITC group Revision 3 (3-digit level) ranked according to the concentration index in 2006 / Groupes de la CTCI Révision 3 (positions à 3 chiffres) classés d'après l'indice de concentration en 2006	Concentration index (1) / Indice de concentration (1)			Structural change index (2) / Indice de changement structurel (2) 1995=0	
	1995	2000	2006	2000	2006
791 Railway vehicles (including hovertrains) and associated equipment	0.246	0.234	0.244	0.183	0.213
672 Ingots, other primary forms of iron or steel; semi-finished products of	0.210	0.232	0.243	0.162	0.223
659 Floor coverings, etc.	0.287	0.250	0.241	0.095	0.129
764 Telecommunications equipment and parts, n.e.s.; accessories within division 76	0.218	0.185	0.240	0.177	0.326
723 Civil engineering and contractors' plant and equipment; parts thereof	0.294	0.288	0.239	0.076	0.135
266 Synthetic fibres suitable for spinning	0.246	0.267	0.238	0.130	0.231
718 Power-generating machinery, and parts thereof, n.e.s.	0.280	0.219	0.238	0.224	0.166
737 Metalworking machinery (other than machine tools), and parts thereof, n.e.s.	0.263	0.250	0.236	0.130	0.168
232 Synthetic rubber; reclaimed rubber; waste, parings, scrap of unhardened rubber	0.259	0.266	0.236	0.141	0.180
531 Synthetic organic colouring matter and colour lakes, preparations based thereon	0.298	0.247	0.236	0.148	0.232
713 Internal combustion piston engines, and parts thereof, n.e.s.	0.294	0.272	0.235	0.138	0.217
759 Parts, accessories for machines of groups 751, 752	0.254	0.213	0.235	0.190	0.330
873 Meters and counters, n.e.s.	0.260	0.260	0.234	0.186	0.268
598 Miscellaneous chemical products, n.e.s.	0.265	0.259	0.234	0.109	0.126
771 Electric power machinery parts (excluding rotating electric plant, group 716)	0.192	0.201	0.234	0.146	0.237
575 Other plastics, in primary forms	0.277	0.266	0.233	0.097	0.145
694 Nails, screws, nuts, bolts, rivets, of iron, steel, copper or aluminium	0.231	0.237	0.233	0.085	0.151
611 Leather	0.216	0.236	0.232	0.101	0.211
047 Other cereal meals and flours	0.240	0.284	0.232	0.204	0.203
572 Polymers of styrene, in primary forms	0.237	0.235	0.231	0.129	0.172
248 Wood, simply worked, and railway sleepers of wood	0.318	0.316	0.231	0.111	0.233
542 Medicines (including veterinary medicines)	0.228	0.221	0.230	0.109	0.143
516 Other organic chemicals	0.227	0.217	0.229	0.110	0.180
747 Appliances for pipes boiler shells tanks vats; pressure and temperature valves	0.259	0.239	0.229	0.139	0.187
291 Crude animal materials, nes	0.220	0.239	0.227	0.105	0.168
287 Ores and concentrates of base metals, n.e.s.	0.226	0.231	0.227	0.154	0.191
246 Wood in chips or particles and wood waste	0.333	0.314	0.227	0.150	0.355
899 Miscellaneous manufactured articles, n.e.s.	0.227	0.222	0.227	0.125	0.238
421 Fixed vegetable fats and oils, "soft", crude, refined or fractionated	0.225	0.238	0.226	0.176	0.228
746 Ball or roller bearings	0.270	0.248	0.226	0.103	0.147
591 Insecticide, rodenticide, fungicide, herbicide, plant-growth reg, disinfectant	0.256	0.245	0.223	0.123	0.168
685 Lead	0.219	0.221	0.223	0.206	0.233
035 Fish (dried, salted, in brine, smoked); flours, meals, pellets for human consump	0.274	0.233	0.223	0.172	0.263
411 Animals oils and fats	0.357	0.270	0.222	0.155	0.237
743 Pump (non liquid), air gas compressor, fan ventilation filter; centrifuge; parts	0.244	0.241	0.221	0.105	0.174
011 Meat of bovine animals (fresh chilled frozen)	0.241	0.267	0.220	0.195	0.275
782 Motor vehicles for the transport of goods and special-purpose motor vehicles	0.276	0.250	0.219	0.148	0.206
523 Metallic salts and peroxysalts, of inorganic acids	0.233	0.244	0.219	0.115	0.221
821 Furniture and parts; bedding, mattresses, mattress supports, cushions	0.204	0.186	0.218	0.152	0.264
621 Materials of rubber (e.g., pastes, plates, sheets, rods, thread, tubes, of rubber)	0.243	0.232	0.217	0.118	0.154
812 Sanitary, plumbing and heating fixtures and fittings, n.e.s.	0.253	0.231	0.217	0.153	0.207
695 Tools for use in the hand or in machine	0.224	0.202	0.217	0.112	0.146
269 Worn clothing and other worn textile articles; rags	0.259	0.227	0.216	0.139	0.262
744 Mechanical handling equipment, and parts thereof, n.e.s.	0.239	0.229	0.216	0.119	0.149
784 Parts and accessories of the motor vehicles of groups 722, 781, 782 and 783	0.283	0.268	0.215	0.088	0.231
511 Hydrocarbons, n.e.s., halogenated, sulphonated, nitrated, nitrosated derivatives	0.247	0.230	0.215	0.119	0.171
081 Feeding stuff for animals (excluding unmilled cereals)	0.232	0.240	0.214	0.134	0.156
897 Jewellery, articles of goldsmiths' silversmiths' B2 semiprecious, n.e.s.	0.256	0.258	0.214	0.163	0.246
749 Non-electric parts and accessories of machinery, n.e.s.	0.253	0.236	0.213	0.093	0.143
898 Musical instrument, parts accessory; tape, sound recording (excluding 763 & 883)	0.258	0.229	0.212	0.138	0.267
111 Non-alcoholic beverages, n.e.s.	0.213	0.206	0.212	0.161	0.268
895 Office and stationery supplies, n.e.s.	0.236	0.224	0.212	0.122	0.242
073 Chocolate and other food preparations containing cocoa, n.e.s.	0.241	0.216	0.211	0.140	0.174
892 Printed matter	0.238	0.229	0.210	0.104	0.134
533 Pigments, paints, varnishes and related materials	0.223	0.218	0.210	0.106	0.103
581 Tubes, pipes and hoses, and fittings therefor, of plastics	0.225	0.228	0.209	0.164	0.202
056 Vegetables, roots and tubers (prepared preserved) n.e.s.	0.221	0.209	0.209	0.123	0.169
582 Plates, sheets, film, foil and strip, of plastics	0.224	0.220	0.209	0.093	0.121
012 Other meat and edible meat offal (fresh chilled frozen)	0.224	0.222	0.209	0.149	0.270
333 Petroleum oils and oils obtained from bituminous minerals, crude	0.212	0.200	0.208	0.128	0.181
971 Gold, non-monetary (excluding gold ores and concentrates)	0.293	0.293	0.208	0.220	0.384
001 Live animals other than animals of division 03	0.223	0.220	0.208	0.154	0.147
772 Electrical apparatus to switch protect circuits or make circuit connections	0.246	0.222	0.207	0.144	0.195
071 Coffee and coffee substitutes	0.190	0.186	0.207	0.139	0.243

For sources and notes, see end of table 3.3 Imports.   Pour les sources et les notes, se reporter à la fin du tableau 3.3 Importations.

SITC group Revision 3 (3-digit level) ranked according to the concentration index in 2006 Groupes de la CTCI Révision 3 (positions à 3 chiffres) classés d'après l'indice de concentration en 2006	Concentration index (1) Indice de concentration (1)			Structural change index (2) Indice de changement structurel (2) 1995=0	
	1995	2000	2006	2000	2006
778 Electrical machinery and apparatus, n.e.s.	0.239	0.241	0.206	0.138	0.206
641 Paper and paperboard	0.227	0.220	0.206	0.066	0.132
282 Ferrous waste and scrap; remelting scrap ingots of iron or steel	0.272	0.201	0.206	0.222	0.201
677 Rails or railway track construction material, of iron or steel	0.217	0.226	0.205	0.186	0.232
054 Vegetables and veg products (fresh chilled frozen preserved dried edible) n.e.s.	0.219	0.215	0.204	0.122	0.141
022 Milk, cream and milk products (excluding butter, cheese)	0.268	0.236	0.204	0.125	0.213
514 Nitrogen-function compounds	0.243	0.225	0.204	0.097	0.208
663 Mineral manufactures, n.e.s.	0.224	0.222	0.204	0.100	0.155
288 Non-ferrous base metal waste and scrap, n.e.s.	0.210	0.188	0.203	0.152	0.205
017 Meat, edible meat offal (prepared preserved) n.e.s.	0.192	0.188	0.203	0.160	0.266
592 Starches, inulin and wheat gluten; albuminoidal substances; glues	0.212	0.208	0.203	0.126	0.129
562 Fertilizers (excluding group 272)	0.207	0.220	0.203	0.140	0.196
573 Polymers of vinyl chloride or of other halogenated olefins, in primary forms	0.217	0.196	0.203	0.187	0.178
699 Manufactures of base metal, n.e.s.	0.203	0.211	0.201	0.133	0.167
513 Carboxylic acid, anhydrides, halides, peroxides, peroxyacids; halogenate, derivatives	0.241	0.216	0.198	0.142	0.285
059 Fruit and vegetable juice (unfermented, no added spirit, sweetened or not)	0.232	0.219	0.198	0.140	0.199
741 Heating and cooling equipment, and parts thereof, n.e.s.	0.232	0.221	0.198	0.140	0.228
675 Flat-rolled products of alloy steel	0.272	0.227	0.196	0.157	0.245
532 Dyeing and tanning extracts, and synthetic tanning materials	0.225	0.203	0.195	0.140	0.205
661 Lime, cement, fabricated construction material (excluding glass, clay material)	0.203	0.194	0.195	0.161	0.308
629 Articles of rubber, n.e.s.	0.233	0.223	0.194	0.130	0.172
048 Cereal preparations and preparations of flour or starch of fruits or vegetables	0.205	0.200	0.194	0.106	0.157
893 Articles, n.e.s., of plastics	0.184	0.197	0.193	0.145	0.184
691 Structures and parts of structures, n.e.s., of iron, steel or aluminium	0.186	0.177	0.193	0.194	0.269
335 Residual petroleum products, n.e.s., related mater.	0.274	0.226	0.192	0.147	0.224
682 Copper	0.175	0.182	0.192	0.122	0.186
716 Rotating electric plant, and parts thereof, n.e.s.	0.213	0.188	0.192	0.126	0.203
671 Pig-iron, spiegeleisen, sponge iron, iron steel granules, powders, ferro-alloys	0.203	0.206	0.192	0.178	0.238
657 Special yarns, special textile fabrics and related products	0.212	0.207	0.191	0.102	0.179
693 Wire products (excluding insulated electrical wiring) and fencing grills	0.173	0.173	0.191	0.155	0.201
665 Glassware	0.210	0.185	0.191	0.127	0.244
674 Flat-rolled products of iron or non-alloy steel, clad, plated or coated	0.225	0.208	0.190	0.153	0.231
574 Polyacetal, polyether, epoxide resin; polycarbonate, alkyd resin, polyester	0.229	0.219	0.190	0.119	0.187
091 Margarine and shortening	0.233	0.171	0.190	0.265	0.260
571 Polymers of ethylene, in primary forms	0.218	0.213	0.189	0.118	0.183
711 Steam vapour superheated water boiler, auxiliary plant for use with; parts of	0.247	0.219	0.189	0.207	0.320
664 Glass	0.217	0.213	0.188	0.112	0.169
642 Paper and paperboard, cut to size or shape, and articles of paper or paperboard	0.202	0.183	0.187	0.120	0.174
679 Tubes, pipes and hollow profiles, and tube or pipe fittings, of iron or steel	0.208	0.186	0.187	0.104	0.180
634 Veneers, plywood, particle board, and other wood, worked, n.e.s.	0.240	0.212	0.186	0.160	0.296
635 Wood manufactures, n.e.s.	0.146	0.167	0.185	0.150	0.264
554 Soaps, cleansing and polishing preparations	0.212	0.195	0.184	0.124	0.139
651 Textile yarn	0.158	0.161	0.184	0.127	0.190
522 Inorganic chemical elements, oxides and halogen salts	0.171	0.179	0.184	0.119	0.170
625 Rubber tyres, interchangeable tyre treads, tyre flaps, inner tubes for wheels	0.200	0.194	0.180	0.101	0.205
075 Spices	0.192	0.181	0.179	0.139	0.255
278 Other crude minerals	0.193	0.215	0.174	0.112	0.152
057 Fruits and nuts (excluding oil nuts), fresh or dried	0.191	0.179	0.174	0.110	0.133
673 Flat-rolled products of iron or non-alloy steel, not clad, plated or coated	0.182	0.182	0.173	0.122	0.177
277 Natural abrasives, n.e.s. (including industrial diamonds)	0.237	0.252	0.173	0.353	0.280
098 Edible products and preparations, n.e.s.	0.222	0.193	0.172	0.187	0.217
686 Zinc	0.193	0.196	0.170	0.187	0.214
692 Metal containers for storage or transport	0.200	0.171	0.169	0.130	0.189
773 Equipment for distributing electricity, n.e.s.	0.198	0.210	0.167	0.134	0.255
512 Alcohol, phenol, phenol-alcohol;halogenate, sulphonate, nitrate, nitrosate deriv	0.209	0.198	0.166	0.156	0.244
046 Meal and flour of wheat and flour of meslin	0.203	0.175	0.165	0.237	0.366
678 Wire of iron or steel	0.170	0.172	0.162	0.126	0.211
058 Fruit, preserved, and fruit preparations (excluding fruit juices)	0.147	0.149	0.158	0.138	0.195
676 Iron and steel bars, rods, angles, shapes and sections (including sheet piling)	0.166	0.162	0.157	0.111	0.192
811 Prefabricated buildings	0.200	0.190	0.157	0.145	0.263
034 Fish, fresh (live dead chilled frozen)	0.159	0.155	0.155	0.134	0.218
684 Aluminium	0.167	0.161	0.155	0.092	0.148
273 Stone, sand and gravel	0.158	0.160	0.152	0.163	0.239
062 Sugar confectionery	0.151	0.148	0.141	0.188	0.229
036 Crustaceans, mollusks and aquatic invertebrates	0.166	0.152	0.141	0.141	0.225
334 Petroleum oil, oil from bituminous (excl crude); preparations, n.e.s., > 70% oil	0.142	0.126	0.136	0.151	0.226
245 Fuel wood (excluding wood waste) and wood charcoal	0.167	0.175	0.114	0.263	0.346

For sources and notes, see end of table 3.3 Imports.

Pour les sources et les notes, se reporter à la fin du tableau 3.3 Importations.

SITC group Revision 3 (3-digit level) ranked according to the concentration index in 2006 Groupes de la CTCI Révision 3 (positions à 3 chiffres) classés d'après l'indice de concentration en 2006	Concentration index (1) Indice de concentration (1)			Structural change index (2) Indice de changement structurel (2) 1995=0	
	1995	2000	2006	2000	2006
286 Uranium or thorium ores and concentrates	0.551	0.733	0.914	0.304	0.294
871 Optical instruments and apparatus, n.e.s.	0.243	0.270	0.558	0.289	0.658
883 Cinematographic film, exposed developed, whether or not incorporating soundtrack	0.317	0.367	0.511	0.213	0.370
579 Waste, parings and scrap, of plastics	0.473	0.425	0.500	0.256	0.362
244 Cork, natural, raw and waste (including natural cork in blocks or sheets)	0.359	0.464	0.499	0.238	0.291
246 Wood in chips or particles and wood waste	0.735	0.723	0.491	0.055	0.274
896 Works of art, collectors' pieces and antiques	0.441	0.533	0.473	0.145	0.114
281 Iron ore and concentrates	0.275	0.276	0.442	0.116	0.351
289 Ores and concentrates of precious metals; waste of (excluding gold)	0.390	0.402	0.410	0.138	0.223
345 Coal gas, water gas, producer gas, similar gas (exclude other gas hydrocarbons)	0.722	0.251	0.399	0.764	0.515
265 Vegetable textile fibre (exclu cotton, jute), raw, processed, not spun; waste of	0.211	0.242	0.392	0.224	0.422
263 Cotton	0.167	0.154	0.391	0.245	0.430
212 Furskins, raw, other than hides and skins of group 211	0.292	0.358	0.386	0.190	0.257
264 Jute, other textile bast fibres n.e.s., raw, processed, not spun; waste of	0.253	0.324	0.380	0.282	0.349
613 Furskin, tanned, dressed, unassembled, assembled (without other materials)	0.297	0.308	0.376	0.311	0.380
016 Meat, edible meat offal (salted dried); flours, meals	0.519	0.408	0.367	0.167	0.206
261 Silk	0.308	0.324	0.364	0.198	0.313
274 Sulphur and unroasted iron pyrites	0.209	0.205	0.357	0.229	0.414
283 Copper ores and concentrates; copper mattes; cement copper	0.451	0.391	0.347	0.191	0.375
761 Television receiver, video monitor projector, w wo radio video-record reproduce	0.226	0.275	0.343	0.244	0.320
843 Men's textile, knitted (coat suit trouser short shirt underwear nightwear)	0.301	0.346	0.332	0.143	0.170
284 Nickel ores, concentrates; mattes, oxide sinters, intermediate product of	0.376	0.387	0.328	0.179	0.275
525 Radio-actives and associated materials	0.343	0.362	0.327	0.223	0.220
268 Wool and other animal hair (including wool tops)	0.236	0.295	0.313	0.178	0.272
043 Barley, unmilled	0.199	0.232	0.313	0.257	0.239
894 Baby carriages, toys, games and sporting goods	0.317	0.361	0.312	0.091	0.093
222 Oil-seed, oleaginous fruit for soft fixed vegetable oils (exclude flours, meals)	0.217	0.231	0.311	0.259	0.386
658 Made-up articles, wholly or chiefly of textile materials, n.e.s.	0.228	0.285	0.306	0.143	0.198
821 Furniture and parts; bedding, mattresses, mattress supports, cushions	0.252	0.319	0.301	0.168	0.210
891 Arms and ammunition	0.200	0.248	0.301	0.269	0.328
667 Pearls and precious or semiprecious stones, unworked or worked	0.315	0.326	0.299	0.136	0.161
036 Crustaceans, mollusks and aquatic invertebrates	0.423	0.371	0.294	0.127	0.242
211 Hides and skins (except furskins), raw	0.268	0.273	0.293	0.140	0.312
844 Women's textiles, knitted (articles as code 841, plus dresses skirts)	0.294	0.312	0.291	0.148	0.154
247 Wood in the rough or roughly squared	0.357	0.256	0.287	0.257	0.409
848 Apparel articles accessories other than textile fabrics; headgear (all material)	0.294	0.358	0.286	0.139	0.137
681 Silver, platinum, other metals of the platinum group	0.301	0.345	0.282	0.200	0.215
897 Jewellery, articles of goldsmiths' silversmiths' B2 semiprecious, n.e.s.	0.292	0.330	0.279	0.144	0.160
762 Radio-broadcast receivers, with without sound-recording reproducing or clock	0.290	0.334	0.277	0.147	0.166
842 Women's textiles not knitted (articles as code 841, plus dresses skirts)	0.299	0.342	0.275	0.126	0.168
776 Thermionic cold cathode photo-cathode valves tubes; diodes, transistors	0.246	0.207	0.274	0.128	0.325
697 Household equipment of base metal, n.e.s.	0.214	0.278	0.274	0.141	0.173
813 Lighting fixtures and fittings, n.e.s.	0.222	0.308	0.274	0.158	0.196
841 Men's textile, not knitted (coat suit trouser short shirt underwear nightwear)	0.285	0.336	0.274	0.119	0.134
515 Organo-inorganic and heterocyclic compounds, nucleic acids-salts, sulphonamides	0.194	0.315	0.272	0.198	0.189
845 Articles of apparel, textile fabrics, knitted or crocheted or not, n.e.s.	0.280	0.319	0.271	0.126	0.160
971 Gold, non-monetary (excluding gold ores and concentrates)	0.220	0.246	0.268	0.327	0.552
342 Liquefied propane and butane	0.355	0.308	0.265	0.135	0.237
831 Cases bags(storage hand executive equipment instrument gun travel shopping back)	0.317	0.313	0.264	0.090	0.177
045 Cereals, unmilled (excluding wheat, rice, barley, maize)	0.271	0.339	0.263	0.277	0.242
763 Sound or television image recorder reproducer; prepared unrecorded media	0.307	0.390	0.263	0.140	0.128
635 Wood manufactures, n.e.s.	0.259	0.295	0.262	0.182	0.217
112 Alcoholic beverages	0.216	0.276	0.262	0.142	0.168
689 Miscellaneous non-ferrous base metals employed in metallurgy, and cermets	0.281	0.269	0.261	0.094	0.139
248 Wood, simply worked, and railway sleepers of wood	0.264	0.289	0.261	0.156	0.200
781 Vehicles to transport less than 10 persons, including station-wagons race cars	0.288	0.348	0.257	0.141	0.164
666 Pottery	0.299	0.318	0.256	0.090	0.161
851 Footwear	0.291	0.309	0.256	0.104	0.150
231 Natural rubber, balata, gutta-percha, guayule, chicle, natural gums	0.247	0.241	0.256	0.147	0.218
633 Cork manufactures	0.260	0.260	0.255	0.125	0.184
572 Polymers of styrene, in primary forms	0.229	0.266	0.251	0.151	0.211
285 Aluminium ores and concentrates (including alumina)	0.241	0.225	0.251	0.131	0.277
343 Natural gas, whether or not liquefied	0.296	0.294	0.250	0.194	0.264
037 Fish, crustaceans, molluscs, aquatic invertebrates (prepared preserved) n.e.s.	0.275	0.296	0.249	0.109	0.188

For sources and notes, see end of table.

Pour les sources et les notes, se reporter à la fin du tableau.

SITC group Revision 3 (3-digit level) ranked according to the concentration index in 2006 Groupes de la CTCI Révision 3 (positions à 3 chiffres) classés d'après l'indice de concentration en 2006	Concentration index (1) Indice de concentration (1)			Structural change index (2) Indice de changement structurel (2) 1995=0	
	1995	2000	2006	2000	2006
611 Leather	0.211	0.222	0.246	0.134	0.224
333 Petroleum oils and oils obtained from bituminous minerals, crude	0.247	0.250	0.245	0.102	0.133
881 Photographic apparatus and equipment, n.e.s.	0.237	0.263	0.245	0.145	0.291
251 Pulp and waste paper	0.206	0.198	0.242	0.114	0.234
661 Lime, cement, fabricated construction material (excluding glass, clay material)	0.164	0.224	0.241	0.251	0.360
961 Coin (other than gold coin), not being legal tender	0.363	0.912	0.241	0.896	0.554
774 Electrodiagnostic apparatus, medical surgical dental veterinary radiological	0.203	0.233	0.239	0.132	0.154
321 Coal, whether or not pulverized, excluding agglomerated	0.285	0.261	0.239	0.114	0.160
017 Meat, edible meat offal (prepared preserved) n.e.s.	0.221	0.231	0.235	0.147	0.173
751 Office machines	0.263	0.224	0.235	0.118	0.128
792 Aircraft, associated equipment; spacecraft, satellites, launch vehicles; parts	0.162	0.246	0.235	0.271	0.333
288 Non-ferrous base metal waste and scrap, n.e.s.	0.207	0.219	0.234	0.153	0.222
752 Automatic data-processing transcibing machines; magnetic optical readers, n.e.s.	0.265	0.266	0.234	0.091	0.164
714 Engines, motors, non-electric (exclude group 712, 713 and 718); parts of, n.e.s.	0.258	0.292	0.233	0.135	0.176
344 Petroleum gases and other gaseous hydrocarbons, n.e.s.	0.353	0.275	0.229	0.378	0.508
025 Eggs, birds', yolks, fresh, dried, preserved, sweetened or not; albumin	0.256	0.195	0.228	0.160	0.206
513 Carboxylic acid, anhydrides, halides, peroxides, peroxyacids; halogenate, derivatives	0.142	0.171	0.226	0.151	0.242
325 Coke, semi-coke of coal, lignite, peat, agglomerated or not; retort carbon	0.180	0.207	0.226	0.254	0.295
659 Floor coverings, etc.	0.244	0.234	0.224	0.195	0.251
287 Ores and concentrates of base metals, n.e.s.	0.190	0.180	0.224	0.141	0.254
322 Briquettes, lignites and peat	0.208	0.257	0.224	0.231	0.252
885 Watches & clocks	0.270	0.260	0.224	0.099	0.136
001 Live animals other than animals of division 03	0.216	0.234	0.222	0.166	0.224
634 Veneers, plywood, particle board, and other wood, worked, n.e.s.	0.206	0.224	0.221	0.162	0.265
071 Coffee and coffee substitutes	0.243	0.249	0.221	0.103	0.103
593 Explosives and pyrotechnic products	0.176	0.205	0.219	0.174	0.290
058 Fruit, preserved, and fruit preparations (excluding fruit juices)	0.230	0.227	0.219	0.104	0.175
884 Optical goods, n.e.s.	0.235	0.241	0.218	0.125	0.301
351 Electric current	0.232	0.295	0.215	0.320	0.349
023 Butter and other fats and oils derived from milk	0.259	0.223	0.215	0.156	0.191
612 Manufactures of leather or of composition leather, n.e.s.; saddlery and harness	0.269	0.244	0.215	0.202	0.260
072 Cocoa	0.241	0.229	0.214	0.127	0.150
759 Parts, accessories for machines of groups 751, 752	0.259	0.238	0.214	0.133	0.262
731 Machine tools working by removing metal or other material	0.209	0.221	0.211	0.139	0.222
687 Tin	0.226	0.214	0.211	0.128	0.309
683 Nickel	0.240	0.225	0.211	0.111	0.198
784 Parts and accessories of the motor vehicles of groups 722, 781, 782 and 783	0.228	0.239	0.210	0.117	0.170
512 Alcohol, phenol, phenol-alcohol;halogenate, sulphonate, nitrate, nitrosate derivatives	0.162	0.170	0.208	0.160	0.260
872 Instruments and appliances, n.e.s., (medical, surgical, dental or veterinary)	0.177	0.201	0.206	0.121	0.159
713 Internal combustion piston engines, and parts thereof, n.e.s.	0.235	0.249	0.204	0.132	0.193
846 Clothing accessories of textiles, knitted or crocheted or not (exluding babies)	0.191	0.207	0.202	0.185	0.194
771 Electric power machinery parts (excluding rotating electric plant, group 716)	0.186	0.227	0.201	0.140	0.179
775 Household-type electrical and non-electrical equipment, n.e.s.	0.176	0.198	0.201	0.133	0.193
722 Tractors (excluding headings 714.14 & 744.15)	0.234	0.247	0.201	0.128	0.180
671 Pig-iron, spiegeleisen, sponge iron, iron steel granules, powders, ferro-alloys	0.223	0.225	0.201	0.148	0.162
899 Miscellaneous manufactured articles, n.e.s.	0.200	0.212	0.200	0.097	0.155
024 Cheese and curd	0.269	0.213	0.200	0.147	0.162
542 Medicines (including veterinary medicines)	0.135	0.156	0.200	0.149	0.177
511 Hydrocarbons, n.e.s., halogenated, sulphonated, nitrated, nitrosated derivatives	0.168	0.170	0.200	0.159	0.184
541 Medicinal and pharmaceutical products, excluding medicines of group 542	0.165	0.188	0.199	0.131	0.169
696 Cutlery	0.199	0.226	0.199	0.138	0.188
034 Fish, fresh (live dead chilled frozen)	0.312	0.283	0.199	0.104	0.206
785 Motor cycles, mopeds, cycles, motorized and non-motorized; invalid carriages	0.194	0.218	0.198	0.211	0.229
873 Meters and counters, n.e.s.	0.233	0.254	0.195	0.120	0.155
122 Tobacco, manufactured (whether or not containing tobacco substitutes)	0.196	0.193	0.194	0.183	0.249
292 Crude vegetable materials, n.e.s.	0.218	0.204	0.193	0.115	0.138
277 Natural abrasives, n.e.s. (including industrial diamonds)	0.206	0.203	0.193	0.193	0.288
625 Rubber tyres, interchangeable tyre treads, tyre flaps, inner tubes for wheels	0.177	0.202	0.192	0.134	0.152
718 Power-generating machinery, and parts thereof, n.e.s.	0.167	0.181	0.191	0.260	0.232
694 Nails, screws, nuts, bolts, rivets, of iron, steel, copper or aluminium	0.209	0.218	0.190	0.127	0.161
059 Fruit and vegetable juice (unfermented, no added spirit, sweetened or not)	0.221	0.207	0.189	0.125	0.135
782 Motor vehicles for the transport of goods and special-purpose motor vehicles	0.211	0.254	0.189	0.169	0.179
551 Essential oils, perfume and flavour materials	0.139	0.154	0.189	0.153	0.238
655 Knitted, crocheted fabric (include tubular knit, pile, openwork fabric), n.e.s.	0.216	0.186	0.188	0.198	0.290

For sources and notes, see end of table.

Pour les sources et les notes, se reporter à la fin du tableau.

SITC group Revision 3 (3-digit level) ranked according to the concentration index in 2006 Groupes de la CTCI Révision 3 (positions à 3 chiffres) classés d'après l'indice de concentration en 2006	Concentration index (1) Indice de concentration (1)			Structural change index (2) Indice de changement structurel (2) 1995=0	
	1995	2000	2006	2000	2006
011 Meat of bovine animals (fresh chilled frozen)	0.239	0.236	0.188	0.188	0.235
764 Telecommunications equipment and parts, n.e.s.; accessories within division 76	0.181	0.206	0.187	0.149	0.163
291 Crude animal materials, nes	0.228	0.223	0.186	0.142	0.211
054 Vegetables and veg products (fresh chilled frozen preserved dried edible) n.e.s.	0.210	0.197	0.186	0.131	0.182
812 Sanitary, plumbing and heating fixtures and fittings, n.e.s.	0.214	0.179	0.185	0.189	0.226
682 Copper	0.162	0.184	0.184	0.162	0.200
111 Non-alcoholic beverages, n.e.s.	0.177	0.186	0.184	0.196	0.240
737 Metalworking machinery (other than machine tools), and parts thereof, n.e.s.	0.164	0.165	0.184	0.167	0.219
056 Vegetables, roots and tubers (prepared preserved) n.e.s.	0.213	0.204	0.183	0.123	0.159
266 Synthetic fibres suitable for spinning	0.193	0.197	0.183	0.093	0.208
035 Fish (dried, salted, in brine, smoked); flours, meals, pellets for human consump	0.228	0.223	0.183	0.145	0.202
747 Appliances for pipes boiler shells tanks vats; pressure and temperature valves	0.166	0.206	0.183	0.137	0.159
245 Fuel wood (excluding wood waste) and wood charcoal	0.198	0.222	0.182	0.225	0.232
772 Electrical apparatus to switch protect circuits or make circuit connections	0.167	0.182	0.182	0.123	0.237
724 Textile and leather machinery, and parts thereof, n.e.s.	0.159	0.152	0.182	0.133	0.250
686 Zinc	0.212	0.214	0.181	0.132	0.195
773 Equipment for distributing electricity, n.e.s.	0.197	0.223	0.181	0.112	0.167
044 Maize (not including sweet corn), unmilled	0.211	0.193	0.181	0.195	0.222
684 Aluminium	0.190	0.183	0.181	0.109	0.136
062 Sugar confectionery	0.153	0.193	0.181	0.167	0.202
895 Office and stationery supplies, n.e.s.	0.188	0.202	0.180	0.112	0.149
748 Transmission shaft camshaft crankshaft; bearing housing; gearbox speed changer	0.195	0.204	0.180	0.114	0.186
793 Ships, boats (including hovercraft) and floating structures	0.241	0.223	0.179	0.370	0.507
057 Fruits and nuts (excluding oil nuts), fresh or dried	0.212	0.193	0.178	0.125	0.161
778 Electrical machinery and apparatus, n.e.s.	0.178	0.185	0.177	0.120	0.174
232 Synthetic rubber; reclaimed rubber; waste, parings, scrap of unhardened rubber	0.145	0.167	0.177	0.137	0.179
733 Machine tool to work metal sintered metal carbide cermet, not removing material	0.172	0.203	0.177	0.212	0.243
422 Fixed vegetable fats and oils, crude, refined or fractionated, other than "soft"	0.170	0.166	0.176	0.187	0.220
735 Parts, n.e.s. and accessories for machines of groups 731, 733; tool holder	0.204	0.212	0.175	0.092	0.150
893 Articles, n.e.s., of plastics	0.173	0.185	0.175	0.115	0.142
716 Rotating electric plant, and parts thereof, n.e.s.	0.155	0.189	0.175	0.157	0.192
874 Measuring, checking, analysing and controlling instruments and apparatus, n.e.s.	0.167	0.190	0.175	0.120	0.131
672 Ingots, other primary forms of iron or steel; semi-finished products of	0.202	0.223	0.174	0.234	0.260
675 Flat-rolled products of alloy steel	0.161	0.176	0.174	0.155	0.211
282 Ferrous waste and scrap; remelting scrap ingots of iron or steel	0.206	0.187	0.174	0.193	0.234
522 Inorganic chemical elements, oxides and halogen salts	0.159	0.162	0.174	0.097	0.137
223 Oil-seed, oleaginous fruit to extract other vegetable oil; flour, meal of n.e.s.	0.193	0.190	0.173	0.209	0.351
272 Fertilizers, crude (excluding those of division 56)	0.139	0.155	0.173	0.173	0.261
335 Residual petroleum products, n.e.s., related mater.	0.152	0.157	0.170	0.203	0.258
629 Articles of rubber, n.e.s.	0.170	0.186	0.169	0.120	0.141
699 Manufactures of base metal, n.e.s.	0.163	0.195	0.169	0.142	0.128
012 Other meat and edible meat offal (fresh chilled frozen)	0.284	0.231	0.169	0.157	0.264
898 Musical instrument, parts accessory; tape, sound recording (excluding 763 & 883)	0.181	0.182	0.168	0.121	0.172
695 Tools for use in the hand or in machine	0.168	0.185	0.168	0.113	0.147
677 Rails or railway track construction material, of iron or steel	0.153	0.173	0.166	0.332	0.335
641 Paper and paperboard	0.184	0.185	0.165	0.099	0.126
075 Spices	0.184	0.196	0.165	0.119	0.147
712 Steam turbines and other vapour turbines, and parts thereof, n.e.s.	0.167	0.192	0.165	0.467	0.431
514 Nitrogen-function compounds	0.171	0.172	0.164	0.106	0.136
746 Ball or roller bearings	0.168	0.168	0.164	0.090	0.160
786 Trailers semi-trailers vehicles not mechanically-propelled; transport containers	0.166	0.204	0.164	0.160	0.193
524 Other inorganic chemicals; organic and inorganic compounds of precious metals	0.172	0.214	0.164	0.207	0.192
743 Pump (non liquid), air gas compressor, fan ventilation filter; centrifuge; parts	0.151	0.175	0.163	0.109	0.149
663 Mineral manufactures, n.e.s.	0.173	0.203	0.163	0.148	0.165
621 Materials of rubber (e.g., pastes, plates, sheets, rods, thread, tubes, of rubber)	0.157	0.167	0.163	0.140	0.199
728 Other machinery or specialized industrial equipment; parts thereof, n.e.s.	0.162	0.174	0.162	0.167	0.158
421 Fixed vegetable fats and oils, "soft", crude, refined or fractionated	0.144	0.126	0.162	0.230	0.283
571 Polymers of ethylene, in primary forms	0.151	0.157	0.161	0.139	0.190
685 Lead	0.176	0.169	0.160	0.196	0.251
742 Liquid pump, with without a fitted measuring device; liquid elevator; parts for	0.149	0.159	0.160	0.120	0.173
516 Other organic chemicals	0.180	0.208	0.158	0.095	0.176
745 Non-electrical machinery, tools and mechanical apparatus, parts thereof, n.e.s.	0.138	0.167	0.158	0.118	0.143
273 Stone, sand and gravel	0.184	0.167	0.158	0.201	0.268
665 Glassware	0.171	0.188	0.157	0.137	0.171

For sources and notes, see end of table.   Pour les sources et les notes, se reporter à la fin du tableau.

SITC group Revision 3 (3-digit level) ranked according to the concentration index in 2006 Groupes de la CTCI Révision 3 (positions à 3 chiffres) classés d'après l'indice de concentration en 2006	Concentration index (1) Indice de concentration (1)			Structural change index (2) Indice de changement structurel (2) 1995=0	
	1995	2000	2006	2000	2006
744 Mechanical handling equipment, and parts thereof, n.e.s.	0.142	0.193	0.157	0.205	0.188
574 Polyacetal, polyether, epoxide resin; polycarbonate, alkyd resin, polyester	0.141	0.142	0.156	0.145	0.224
048 Cereal preparations and preparations of flour or starch of fruits or vegetables	0.169	0.163	0.156	0.170	0.212
121 Tobacco, unmanufactured; tobacco refuse	0.170	0.158	0.156	0.178	0.268
892 Printed matter	0.160	0.168	0.156	0.112	0.133
791 Railway vehicles (including hovertrains) and associated equipment	0.176	0.223	0.156	0.249	0.319
678 Wire of iron or steel	0.177	0.173	0.155	0.136	0.165
651 Textile yarn	0.159	0.154	0.154	0.115	0.190
575 Other plastics, in primary forms	0.151	0.143	0.154	0.112	0.171
334 Petroleum oil, oil from bituminous (excl crude); preparations, n.e.s., > 70% oil	0.138	0.174	0.153	0.171	0.236
725 Paper mill pulp mill paper-cutting other paper manufacture machines; parts of	0.151	0.177	0.153	0.201	0.210
598 Miscellaneous chemical products, n.e.s.	0.142	0.146	0.152	0.133	0.161
073 Chocolate and other food preparations containing cocoa, n.e.s.	0.186	0.174	0.152	0.124	0.177
642 Paper and paperboard, cut to size or shape, and articles of paper or paperboard	0.145	0.158	0.152	0.117	0.135
267 Other man-made fibres suitable for spinning; waste of man-made fibres	0.144	0.165	0.151	0.182	0.234
882 Photographic and cinematographic supplies	0.176	0.172	0.151	0.104	0.203
693 Wire products (excluding insulated electrical wiring) and fencing grills	0.162	0.171	0.151	0.144	0.162
726 Printing and bookbinding machinery, and parts thereof	0.164	0.171	0.150	0.139	0.180
664 Glass	0.159	0.168	0.150	0.141	0.168
573 Polymers of vinyl chloride or of other halogenated olefins, in primary forms	0.151	0.181	0.149	0.214	0.248
721 Agricultural machinery (excluding tractors), and parts thereof	0.163	0.172	0.149	0.114	0.146
749 Non-electric parts and accessories of machinery, n.e.s.	0.165	0.157	0.149	0.125	0.166
654 Other textile fabrics, woven n.e.s.	0.177	0.163	0.147	0.160	0.235
723 Civil engineering and contractors' plant and equipment; parts thereof	0.145	0.165	0.147	0.176	0.198
532 Dyeing and tanning extracts, and synthetic tanning materials	0.130	0.136	0.146	0.126	0.210
562 Fertilizers (excluding group 272)	0.191	0.144	0.146	0.200	0.221
783 Road motor vehicles, n.e.s.	0.212	0.188	0.145	0.247	0.283
074 Tea and maté	0.152	0.144	0.144	0.142	0.216
674 Flat-rolled products of iron or non-alloy steel, clad, plated or coated	0.139	0.146	0.143	0.144	0.208
662 Clay construction materials and refractory construction materials	0.173	0.171	0.143	0.201	0.254
278 Other crude minerals	0.164	0.166	0.141	0.104	0.140
652 Cotton fabrics, woven (not including narrow or special fabrics)	0.156	0.157	0.141	0.149	0.240
583 Plastic monofilament, cross-section > 1 mm, rods, sticks, profile shapes	0.180	0.196	0.141	0.219	0.317
592 Starches, inulin and wheat gluten; albuminoidal substances; glues	0.158	0.153	0.140	0.107	0.147
679 Tubes, pipes and hollow profiles, and tube or pipe fittings, of iron or steel	0.121	0.149	0.140	0.170	0.208
657 Special yarns, special textile fabrics and related products	0.137	0.135	0.140	0.115	0.160
582 Plates, sheets, film, foil and strip, of plastics	0.153	0.146	0.139	0.115	0.171
673 Flat-rolled products of iron or non-alloy steel, not clad, plated or coated	0.144	0.154	0.137	0.171	0.217
411 Animals oils and fats	0.141	0.127	0.135	0.228	0.271
741 Heating and cooling equipment, and parts thereof, n.e.s.	0.117	0.133	0.134	0.155	0.197
553 Perfumery, cosmetic or toilet preparations (excluding soaps)	0.143	0.142	0.133	0.117	0.147
531 Synthetic organic colouring matter and colour lakes, preparations based thereon	0.143	0.140	0.133	0.090	0.164
656 Tulles, lace, embroidery, ribbons, trimmings and other smallwares	0.148	0.156	0.129	0.178	0.225
653 Fabrics, woven, of man-made textiles (excluding narrow or special fabrics)	0.174	0.151	0.129	0.171	0.246
691 Structures and parts of structures, n.e.s., of iron, steel or aluminium	0.157	0.153	0.129	0.214	0.271
676 Iron and steel bars, rods, angles, shapes and sections (including sheet piling)	0.155	0.167	0.128	0.188	0.216
811 Prefabricated buildings	0.243	0.192	0.128	0.307	0.437
581 Tubes, pipes and hoses, and fittings therefor, of plastics	0.140	0.141	0.128	0.151	0.167
711 Steam vapour superheated water boiler, auxiliary plant for use with; parts of	0.148	0.180	0.128	0.326	0.335
022 Milk, cream and milk products (excluding butter, cheese)	0.176	0.134	0.125	0.154	0.230
081 Feeding stuff for animals (excluding unmilled cereals)	0.152	0.128	0.120	0.111	0.149
597 Prepared additives: mineral oil; transmission; anti-freeze, de-ice; lubricating	0.110	0.111	0.119	0.121	0.172
431 Animal, vegetable fats, oils, processed; waxes; inedible preparations of, n.e.s.	0.155	0.115	0.118	0.225	0.238
692 Metal containers for storage or transport	0.127	0.130	0.118	0.148	0.165
554 Soaps, cleansing and polishing preparations	0.126	0.117	0.116	0.104	0.142
091 Margarine and shortening	0.142	0.111	0.114	0.325	0.370
533 Pigments, paints, varnishes and related materials	0.116	0.117	0.112	0.104	0.137
098 Edible products and preparations, n.e.s.	0.138	0.114	0.112	0.152	0.162
523 Metallic salts and peroxysalts, of inorganic acids	0.113	0.120	0.111	0.101	0.125
047 Other cereal meals and flours	0.096	0.093	0.111	0.267	0.353
041 Wheat (including spelt) and meslin, unmilled	0.140	0.111	0.109	0.207	0.283
591 Insecticide, rodenticide, fungicide, herbicide, plant-growth reg, disinfectant	0.140	0.126	0.108	0.116	0.166
727 Food-processing machines (excluding domestic); parts thereof	0.117	0.108	0.105	0.180	0.206
061 Sugar, molasses and honey	0.116	0.114	0.104	0.152	0.218
046 Meal and flour of wheat and flour of meslin	0.137	0.087	0.101	0.399	0.466
042 Rice	0.104	0.093	0.084	0.269	0.321
269 Worn clothing and other worn textile articles; rags	0.118	0.087	0.074	0.310	0.351

For sources and notes, see end of table.

Pour les sources et les notes, se reporter à la fin du tableau.

Sources:
- Data and UNCTAD secretariat estimates based on UN DESA Comtrade and IMF Direction of Trade statistics databases

Notes:

(1) Concentration index:

The Herfindahl-Hirschmann index is a measure of the degree of market concentration. It has been normalized to obtain values ranking from 0 to 1 (maximum concentration), according to the following formula:

$$H_i = \frac{\sqrt{\sum_{j=1}^{n}(\frac{x_{ij}}{X_i})^2} - \sqrt{\frac{1}{n}}}{1 - \sqrt{\frac{1}{n}}}$$

where

H_i = value of concentration index for product i

x_{ij} = value of exports or imports for country j and product i

$$X_i = \sum_{j=1}^{n} x_{ij} \text{ and}$$

n = maximum number of individual economies over the period from 1995 to 2006.

An index value that is close to 1 indicates a very concentrated market. On the contrary, values closer to 0 reflect a more equal distribution of market shares among exporters or importers.

(2) Structural change index:

This index, ranging from 0 to 1 reveals the structural change in trade for a particular product as compared to the reference year (1995 = 0).

An index value close to 1 indicates a significant change in the composition of exporters (importers). On the contrary, values closer to 0 would demonstrate a higher degree of "traditionality" in the markets over the period concerned.

The value is calculated as follows:

$$I_i = \frac{\sum_{j=1}^{} |S^1_{ij} - S^0_{ij}|}{2}$$

where

I_i = Value of structure index for product i

S^0_{ij} = Share of trade of product i for country j in 1995

S^1_{ij} = Share of trade of product i for the country j in the concerned year

Sources :
- Données et estimations du secrétariat de la CNUCED sur la base de données Comtrade de ONU DAES et Direction of Trade statistics du Fonds Monétaire international

Notes :

(1) Indice de concentration :

L'indice Herfindahl-Hirschmann mesure le degré de concentration des marchés. Il a été normalisé afin d'obtenir des valeurs comprises entre 0 et 1 (concentration maximale), d'après la formule suivante:

$$H_i = \frac{\sqrt{\sum_{j=1}^{n}(\frac{x_{ij}}{X_i})^2} - \sqrt{\frac{1}{n}}}{1 - \sqrt{\frac{1}{n}}}$$

où

H_i = Valeur de l'indice de concentration pour le produit i

x_{ij} = Valeur des exportations ou des importations du pays j pour le produit i

$$X_i = \sum_{j=1}^{n} x_{ij} \text{ et}$$

n = nombre maximum d'économies individuelles sur la période allant de 1995 à 2006.

Un indice proche de 1 indique une concentration très forte du marché pour ce produit en particulier. En revanche, une valeur proche de 0 démontre une répartition plus homogène du commerce entre les exportateurs ou les importateurs.

(2) Indice de changement structurel :

Cet indice, dont la valeur est comprise entre 0 et 1, représente les changements de structure du commerce par rapport à une année de référence(1995 = 0).

Une valeur proche de 1 indique un important changement structurel du commerce de ce produit, c'est à dire, une grande variation des parts de marché au sein des exportateurs ou importateurs, par rapport à l'année de référence. Plus la valeur de l'indice est proche de 0, plus la structure du commerce de ce produit est stable.

Il est calculé comme suit :

$$I_i = \frac{\sum_{j=1}^{} |S^1_{ij} - S^0_{ij}|}{2}$$

où

I_i = Valeur de l'indice de changement structurel, pour le produit i

S^0_{ij} = Part du commerce du produit i pour le pays j par rapport au commerce total de ce produit pour l'année 1995

S^1_{ij} = Part du commerce du produit i pour le pays j, par rapport au commerce total de ce produit pour l'année concernée

3

4

INTERNATIONAL **MERCHANDISE** TRADE INDICATORS

INDICATEURS DU COMMERCE INTERNATIONAL DES **MARCHANDISES**

1

2

3

4

5

6

7

8

Region, country or territory	Exports - Exportations					
	1995			2006		
	Number of products exported	Diversification index	Concentration index	Number of products exported	Diversification index	Concentration index
	Nombre de produits exportés (1)	Indice de diversification (2)	Indice de concentration (3)	Nombre de produits exportés (1)	Indice de diversification (2)	Indice de concentration (3)
WORLD	**261**	**0.000**	**0.053**	**260**	**0.000**	**0.079**
DEVELOPING ECONOMIES	261	0.280	0.098	260	0.234	0.142
ECONOMIES IN TRANSITION	256	0.559	0.169	255	0.584	0.314
DEVELOPED ECONOMIES	261	0.120	0.055	260	0.165	0.063
Developing economies: Africa	**259**	**0.618**	**0.288**	**260**	**0.589**	**0.424**
Eastern Africa	*242*	*0.711*	*0.173*	*248*	*0.690*	*0.152*
Burundi	18	0.632	0.631	24	0.782	0.607
Ethiopia	25	0.535	0.647	62	0.714	0.432
Kenya	185	0.708	0.232	216	0.697	0.203
Madagascar	66	0.769	0.285	120	0.728	0.200
Malawi	70	0.818	0.663	89	0.808	0.599
Mauritius	109	0.800	0.363	165	0.696	0.283
Mozambique	63	0.716	0.448	107	0.805	0.581
Rwanda	16	0.571	0.464	31	0.761	0.485
Seychelles	18	0.699	0.557	17	0.719	0.628
Uganda	81	0.863	0.650	133	0.758	0.251
United Republic of Tanzania	80	0.749	0.276	135	0.791	0.353
Zambia	85	0.855	0.829	139	0.882	0.684
Zimbabwe	190	0.723	0.252	155	0.752	0.223
Middle Africa	*162*	*0.845*	*0.636*	*177*	*0.843*	*0.857*
Angola	35	0.758	0.897	70	0.817	0.956
Cameroon	77	0.795	0.326	92	0.778	0.512
Central African Republic	28	0.690	0.450	15	0.742	0.482
Congo	34	0.781	0.854	82	0.823	0.870
Dem. Rep. of the Congo	60	0.807	0.499	90	0.801	0.388
Equatorial Guinea	10	0.626	0.559	20	0.720	0.906
Gabon	61	0.796	0.812	60	0.792	0.837
Sao Tome and Principe	6	0.547	0.524	3	0.582	0.869
Northern Africa	*229*	*0.722*	*0.374*	*244*	*0.695*	*0.462*
Algeria	99	0.821	0.530	108	0.797	0.606
Egypt	164	0.669	0.247	196	0.684	0.356
Libyan Arab Jamahiriya	29	0.522	0.768	94	0.795	0.843
Morocco	168	0.746	0.179	199	0.678	0.159
Sudan	19	0.559	0.351	57	0.747	0.872
Tunisia	193	0.670	0.216	209	0.608	0.187
Southern Africa	*252*	*0.570*	*0.124*	*255*	*0.570*	*0.150*
Botswana	..	..	..	139	0.903	0.725
Namibia	..	..	..	187	0.844	0.300
South Africa	252	0.570	0.124	253	0.569	0.156
Swaziland	..	..	..	162	0.812	0.415
Western Africa	*233*	*0.804*	*0.458*	*237*	*0.755*	*0.609*
Benin	53	0.751	0.517	53	0.740	0.623
Burkina Faso	40	0.776	0.573	62	0.825	0.585
Cape Verde	17	0.670	0.392	41	0.705	0.475
Côte d'Ivoire	150	0.821	0.347	147	0.725	0.322
Gambia	22	0.596	0.323	9	0.593	0.506
Ghana	95	0.848	0.444	117	0.823	0.441
Guinea	39	0.800	0.644	57	0.834	0.660
Mali	41	0.756	0.587	74	0.836	0.747
Niger	32	0.756	0.552	53	0.834	0.472
Nigeria	149	0.892	0.853	174	0.855	0.857
Senegal	104	0.766	0.288	168	0.682	0.247
Togo	92	0.720	0.327	74	0.738	0.289
Developing economies: America	**258**	**0.361**	**0.090**	**256**	**0.350**	**0.150**
Caribbean	*231*	*0.682*	*0.221*	*253*	*0.675*	*0.292*
Antigua and Barbuda	41	0.686	0.358	39	0.715	0.562
Bahamas	67	0.662	0.339	85	0.701	0.351
Barbados	100	0.647	0.184	113	0.612	0.252
Cuba	89	0.827	0.616	138	0.835	0.453
Dominican Republic	121	0.748	0.223	130	0.683	0.165

For sources and notes, see end of table.

Imports - Importations						Régions, pays ou territoires
1995			2006			
Number of products exported Nombre de produits exportés (1)	Diversification index Indice de diversification (2)	Concentration index Indice de concentration (3)	Number of products exported Nombre de produits exportés (1)	Diversification index Indice de diversification (2)	Concentration index Indice de concentration (3)	
261	**0.000**	**0.052**	**260**	**0.000**	**0.081**	**MONDE**
261	0.174	0.056	260	0.181	0.104	ÉCONOMIES EN DÉVELOPPEMENT
258	0.353	0.068	258	0.264	0.070	ÉCONOMIES EN TRANSITION
261	0.074	0.058	260	0.087	0.083	ÉCONOMIES DÉVELOPPÉES
261	**0.291**	**0.053**	**260**	**0.270**	**0.080**	**Économies en développement : Afrique**
255	*0.365*	*0.060*	*254*	*0.408*	*0.129*	*Afrique orientale*
144	0.507	0.120	147	0.584	0.143	Burundi
192	0.491	0.126	212	0.493	0.181	Éthiopie
216	0.406	0.099	233	0.416	0.153	Kenya
181	0.447	0.107	199	0.537	0.159	Madagascar
171	0.526	0.131	194	0.508	0.138	Malawi
216	0.451	0.089	218	0.414	0.150	Maurice
187	0.530	0.102	208	0.502	0.147	Mozambique
140	0.496	0.123	166	0.511	0.143	Rwanda
169	0.440	0.143	179	0.588	0.277	Seychelles
186	0.476	0.072	204	0.511	0.181	Ouganda
202	0.510	0.097	218	0.524	0.213	République-Unie de Tanzanie
201	0.464	0.100	223	0.432	0.100	Zambie
227	0.407	0.086	223	0.551	0.138	Zimbabwe
234	*0.431*	*0.063*	*245*	*0.421*	*0.084*	*Afrique centrale*
202	0.523	0.143	214	0.545	0.123	Angola
195	0.485	0.071	205	0.503	0.264	Cameroun
129	0.525	0.141	121	0.550	0.164	République centrafricaine
160	0.569	0.173	203	0.443	0.072	Congo
204	0.477	0.094	223	0.496	0.086	Rép. dém. du Congo
75	0.556	0.126	174	0.625	0.275	Guinée equatoriale
193	0.421	0.064	204	0.445	0.078	Gabon
66	0.461	0.100	93	0.523	0.189	Sao Tomé-et-Principe
256	*0.360*	*0.052*	*254*	*0.329*	*0.063*	*Afrique septentrionale*
231	0.463	0.084	234	0.467	0.096	Algérie
237	0.436	0.076	241	0.428	0.099	Égypte
188	0.397	0.080	224	0.397	0.096	Jamahiriya arabe libyenne
236	0.414	0.082	246	0.338	0.105	Maroc
185	0.497	0.133	214	0.475	0.095	Soudan
242	0.392	0.076	241	0.397	0.084	Tunisie
247	*0.257*	*0.077*	*256*	*0.219*	*0.121*	*Afrique australe*
..	..	..	226	0.448	0.128	Botswana
..	..	..	229	0.395	0.077	Namibie
247	0.257	0.077	251	0.225	0.137	Afrique du Sud
..	..	..	230	0.462	0.076	Swaziland
261	*0.484*	*0.216*	*260*	*0.433*	*0.136*	*Afrique occidentale*
147	0.554	0.141	174	0.567	0.167	Bénin
167	0.537	0.129	188	0.519	0.171	Burkina Faso
145	0.518	0.125	179	0.474	0.089	Cap-Vert
218	0.454	0.147	213	0.499	0.280	Côte d'Ivoire
127	0.609	0.179	135	0.532	0.180	Gambie
198	0.460	0.103	216	0.439	0.132	Ghana
178	0.557	0.196	182	0.508	0.115	Guinée
168	0.583	0.151	183	0.563	0.213	Mali
152	0.587	0.135	173	0.586	0.145	Niger
246	0.423	0.059	232	0.452	0.123	Nigéria
181	0.473	0.115	213	0.464	0.165	Sénégal
166	0.564	0.269	168	0.622	0.243	Togo
258	**0.203**	**0.048**	**259**	**0.192**	**0.071**	**Économies en développement : Amérique**
253	*0.344*	*0.082*	*258*	*0.392*	*0.184*	*Caraïbes*
168	0.489	0.172	168	0.523	0.278	Antigua-et-Barbuda
165	0.469	0.113	213	0.499	0.172	Bahamas
205	0.347	0.072	207	0.380	0.147	Barbade
235	0.475	0.140	233	0.399	0.135	Cuba
230	0.445	0.081	238	0.404	0.088	République dominicaine

Pour les sources et les notes, se reporter à la fin du tableau.

Region, country or territory	Exports - Exportations					
	1995			2006		
	Number of products exported / Nombre de produits exportés (1)	Diversification index / Indice de diversification (2)	Concentration index / Indice de concentration (3)	Number of products exported / Nombre de produits exportés (1)	Diversification index / Indice de diversification (2)	Concentration index / Indice de concentration (3)
Grenada	18	0.683	0.299	27	0.671	0.241
Haiti	24	0.547	0.326	47	0.730	0.726
Jamaica	107	0.769	0.481	114	0.796	0.576
Netherlands Antilles	134	0.792	0.529	228	0.849	0.808
Saint Kitts and Nevis	15	0.717	0.439	21	0.678	0.499
Saint Lucia	50	0.700	0.511	53	0.620	0.324
Saint Vincent and the Grenadines	36	0.710	0.445	28	0.716	0.337
Trinidad and Tobago	125	0.737	0.398	166	0.775	0.415
Turks and Caicos Islands	5	0.608	0.445	19	0.591	0.303
Central America	*248*	*0.371*	*0.113*	*250*	*0.369*	*0.144*
Belize	34	0.730	0.376	26	0.734	0.382
Costa Rica	162	0.698	0.319	203	0.630	0.226
El Salvador	130	0.682	0.354	181	0.600	0.150
Guatemala	162	0.704	0.284	210	0.598	0.174
Honduras	95	0.818	0.536	171	0.734	0.249
Mexico	248	0.380	0.123	249	0.386	0.154
Nicaragua	93	0.767	0.272	121	0.785	0.288
Panama	78	0.557	0.364	124	0.739	0.360
South America	*255*	*0.507*	*0.110*	*256*	*0.511*	*0.192*
Argentina	239	0.565	0.126	243	0.561	0.132
Bolivia	104	0.728	0.218	145	0.760	0.403
Brazil	240	0.524	0.089	248	0.475	0.092
Chile	216	0.788	0.311	228	0.782	0.402
Colombia	216	0.654	0.244	230	0.571	0.207
Ecuador	160	0.781	0.376	184	0.736	0.532
Guyana	58	0.768	0.383	62	0.829	0.293
Paraguay	98	0.710	0.337	123	0.771	0.320
Peru	175	0.799	0.245	216	0.787	0.256
Suriname	33	0.793	0.631	57	0.855	0.555
Uruguay	162	0.638	0.166	185	0.671	0.228
Venezuela (Bolivarian Rep. of)	209	0.767	0.517	174	0.844	0.911
Developing economies: Asia	**261**	**0.321**	**0.099**	**260**	**0.270**	**0.131**
Eastern Asia	*257*	*0.372*	*0.075*	*257*	*0.382*	*0.109*
China	254	0.472	0.070	255	0.442	0.110
China, Hong Kong SAR	246	0.443	0.094	245	0.512	0.159
China, Macao SAR	143	0.756	0.293	136	0.703	0.299
China, Taiwan Province of	235	0.435	0.111	243	0.462	0.191
Mongolia	47	0.737	0.496	82	0.834	0.437
Republic of Korea	240	0.399	0.149	241	0.387	0.156
Southern Asia	*252*	*0.634*	*0.225*	*258*	*0.528*	*0.211*
Bangladesh	73	0.674	0.357	149	0.832	0.400
India	240	0.589	0.142	254	0.538	0.142
Iran (Islamic Rep. of)	175	0.827	0.835	220	0.768	0.782
Maldives	9	0.483	0.410	8	0.509	0.767
Nepal	35	0.496	0.473	109	0.670	0.146
Pakistan	138	0.781	0.245	204	0.733	0.230
Sri Lanka	172	0.751	0.221	181	0.766	0.223
South-Eastern Asia	*256*	*0.397*	*0.127*	*258*	*0.342*	*0.156*
Brunei Darussalam	87	0.815	0.606	86	0.838	0.717
Cambodia	150	0.791	0.400	97	0.761	0.365
Indonesia	230	0.596	0.144	245	0.489	0.129
Malaysia	247	0.520	0.182	254	0.454	0.186
Myanmar	88	0.815	0.308	105	0.821	0.461
Philippines	203	0.566	0.156	225	0.611	0.348
Singapore	249	0.499	0.218	247	0.491	0.271
Thailand	241	0.478	0.091	244	0.390	0.095
Viet Nam	198	0.683	0.211	237	0.621	0.210
Western Asia	*252*	*0.673*	*0.552*	*257*	*0.645*	*0.572*
Bahrain	137	0.763	0.481	138	0.815	0.787
Jordan	191	0.641	0.217	202	0.597	0.145
Kuwait	135	0.840	0.940	190	0.833	0.670
Lebanon	180	0.600	0.102	200	0.658	0.125
Oman	129	0.709	0.770	118	0.647	0.749

For sources and notes, see end of table.

Imports - Importations						Régions, pays ou territoires
1995			2006			
Number of products exported	Diversification index	Concentration index	Number of products exported	Diversification index	Concentration index	
Nombre de produits exportés (1)	Indice de diversification (2)	Indice de concentration (3)	Nombre de produits exportés (1)	Indice de diversification (2)	Indice de concentration (3)	
137	0.445	0.075	161	0.482	0.091	Grenade
191	0.480	0.106	189	0.541	0.139	Haïti
216	0.401	0.099	213	0.373	0.142	Jamaïque
206	0.612	0.364	248	0.664	0.477	Antilles néerlandaises
142	0.463	0.072	158	0.463	0.077	Saint-Kitts-et-Nevis
166	0.451	0.073	177	0.442	0.106	Sainte-Lucie
137	0.476	0.070	154	0.506	0.113	Saint-Vincent-et-les Grenadines
192	0.443	0.117	229	0.436	0.300	Trinité-et-Tobago
73	0.512	0.148	158	0.495	0.114	Îles Turques et Caïques
256	*0.285*	*0.066*	*256*	*0.259*	*0.080*	*Amérique centrale*
158	0.457	0.090	173	0.456	0.170	Belize
221	0.349	0.069	236	0.361	0.158	Costa Rica
226	0.347	0.069	231	0.347	0.096	El Salvador
228	0.382	0.088	234	0.402	0.146	Guatemala
218	0.480	0.108	223	0.438	0.171	Honduras
252	0.318	0.081	253	0.273	0.082	Mexique
201	0.449	0.119	206	0.393	0.149	Nicaragua
224	0.325	0.086	221	0.360	0.146	Panama
258	*0.218*	*0.053*	*258*	*0.194*	*0.073*	*Amérique du Sud*
245	0.285	0.057	241	0.325	0.077	Argentine
210	0.410	0.090	219	0.450	0.096	Bolivie
250	0.279	0.072	253	0.245	0.097	Brésil
241	0.288	0.067	249	0.282	0.126	Chili
242	0.326	0.062	240	0.335	0.070	Colombie
226	0.382	0.076	234	0.394	0.111	Équateur
176	0.456	0.074	185	0.503	0.259	Guyana
206	0.448	0.095	211	0.433	0.150	Paraguay
239	0.318	0.063	240	0.330	0.120	Pérou
158	0.453	0.121	187	0.455	0.180	Suriname
224	0.305	0.074	236	0.352	0.155	Uruguay
238	0.327	0.053	234	0.353	0.088	Venezuela (Rép. bolivarienne du)
261	**0.206**	**0.066**	**260**	**0.229**	**0.124**	**Économies en développement : Asie**
259	*0.242*	*0.062*	*258*	*0.294*	*0.138*	*Asie orientale*
257	0.409	0.068	257	0.366	0.152	Chine
252	0.354	0.076	248	0.439	0.164	Chine (RAS de Hong Kong)
206	0.528	0.141	207	0.495	0.117	Chine (RAS de Macao)
252	0.323	0.117	255	0.385	0.167	Province chinoise de Taiwan
165	0.510	0.151	198	0.496	0.256	Mongolie
255	0.340	0.087	256	0.330	0.165	République de Corée
257	*0.383*	*0.081*	*258*	*0.403*	*0.186*	*Asie méridionale*
218	0.566	0.136	239	0.526	0.117	Bangladesh
233	0.482	0.137	251	0.458	0.238	Inde
215	0.468	0.083	218	0.411	0.150	Iran (Rép. islamique d')
151	0.490	0.098	173	0.506	0.148	Maldives
123	0.484	0.243	223	0.482	0.213	Népal
225	0.499	0.113	245	0.422	0.153	Pakistan
236	0.455	0.086	234	0.436	0.096	Sri Lanka
258	*0.266*	*0.110*	*258*	*0.282*	*0.171*	*Asie du Sud-Est*
212	0.455	0.083	204	0.452	0.083	Brunéi Darussalam
128	0.590	0.170	200	0.544	0.195	Cambodge
254	0.423	0.062	249	0.427	0.184	Indonésie
254	0.394	0.183	256	0.373	0.221	Malaisie
201	0.485	0.078	214	0.501	0.085	Myanmar
247	0.315	0.090	245	0.442	0.319	Philippines
248	0.365	0.163	250	0.366	0.224	Singapour
247	0.309	0.081	255	0.312	0.147	Thaïlande
234	0.472	0.096	250	0.415	0.118	Viet Nam
256	*0.237*	*0.045*	*259*	*0.277*	*0.062*	*Asie occidentale*
207	0.496	0.318	226	0.573	0.524	Bahreïn
228	0.385	0.084	234	0.343	0.159	Jordanie
204	0.383	0.110	239	0.412	0.117	Koweït
236	0.364	0.086	244	0.437	0.162	Liban
215	0.466	0.100	237	0.466	0.154	Oman

Pour les sources et les notes, se reporter à la fin du tableau.

4.1.1 Export and import concentration and diversification indices of countries and geographical regions

Region, country or territory	Exports - Exportations					
	1995			2006		
	Number of products exported	Diversification index	Concentration index	Number of products exported	Diversification index	Concentration index
	Nombre de produits exportés (1)	Indice de diversification (2)	Indice de concentration (3)	Nombre de produits exportés (1)	Indice de diversification (2)	Indice de concentration (3)
Qatar	102	0.831	0.641	164	0.808	0.574
Saudi Arabia	220	0.857	0.736	239	0.786	0.758
Syrian Arab Republic	130	0.691	0.539	186	0.693	0.340
Turkey	233	0.629	0.112	213	0.619	0.129
United Arab Emirates	242	0.693	0.562	252	0.580	0.452
Yemen	70	0.756	0.891	124	0.770	0.852
Developing economies: Oceania	**155**	**0.779**	**0.215**	**251**	**0.758**	**0.249**
Cook Islands	7	0.560	0.325	3	0.500	0.500
Fiji	70	0.799	0.385	133	0.764	0.295
French Polynesia	52	0.716	0.640	47	0.783	0.584
New Caledonia	36	0.789	0.618	74	0.863	0.659
Papua New Guinea	57	0.841	0.376	83	0.791	0.392
Samoa	6	0.578	0.716	20	0.833	0.715
Economies in transition: Asia	**243**	**0.697**	**0.205**	**236**	**0.692**	**0.475**
Armenia	102	0.670	0.246	119	0.787	0.292
Azerbaijan	104	0.691	0.609	129	0.747	0.628
Georgia	91	0.653	0.168	136	0.689	0.167
Kazakhstan	206	0.740	0.206	199	0.760	0.600
Kyrgyzstan	135	0.659	0.138	139	0.699	0.279
Tajikistan	110	0.777	0.469	52	0.797	0.773
Turkmenistan	58	0.566	0.454	59	0.759	0.612
Uzbekistan	171	0.801	0.487	131	0.771	0.285
Economies in transition: Europe	**255**	**0.557**	**0.179**	**254**	**0.579**	**0.296**
Albania	78	0.722	0.241	119	0.750	0.267
Belarus	224	0.487	0.099	213	0.588	0.319
Bosnia and Herzegovina	105	0.563	0.164	208	0.676	0.142
Croatia	225	0.527	0.103	232	0.504	0.119
Moldova	160	0.736	0.229	155	0.674	0.177
Russian Federation	250	0.667	0.260	248	0.665	0.381
Serbia and Montenegro	216	0.555	0.091	241	0.578	0.106
TFYR of Macedonia	170	0.600	0.126	180	0.640	0.173
Ukraine	233	0.576	0.109	247	0.596	0.145
Developed economies: America	**258**	**0.242**	**0.074**	**259**	**0.226**	**0.071**
Canada	255	0.411	0.135	256	0.355	0.124
Greenland	15	0.795	0.562	22	0.812	0.468
United States	257	0.277	0.075	256	0.278	0.076
Developed economies: Asia	**252**	**0.394**	**0.122**	**249**	**0.408**	**0.137**
Israel	219	0.568	0.283	216	0.609	0.377
Japan	243	0.388	0.127	246	0.389	0.147
Developed economies: Europe	**261**	**0.155**	**0.048**	**260**	**0.183**	**0.063**
Andorra	50	0.561	0.226	86	0.641	0.282
Austria	247	0.371	0.062	250	0.340	0.071
Belgium	–	–	–	256	0.367	0.105
Belgium-Luxembourg	255	0.367	0.100	–	–	–
Bulgaria	228	0.498	0.091	230	0.502	0.158
Cyprus	161	0.633	0.280	159	0.518	0.208
Czech Republic	248	0.369	0.045	249	0.406	0.102
Denmark	244	0.466	0.069	248	0.397	0.079
Estonia	221	0.512	0.082	222	0.508	0.170
Faeroe Islands	14	0.531	0.617	24	0.692	0.618
Finland	256	0.532	0.204	253	0.461	0.175
France	258	0.251	0.059	257	0.295	0.079
Germany	256	0.276	0.078	256	0.291	0.090
Greece	237	0.603	0.108	240	0.503	0.120
Hungary	228	0.403	0.061	233	0.363	0.141
Iceland	84	0.774	0.408	127	0.778	0.395
Ireland	238	0.557	0.175	243	0.670	0.233
Italy	255	0.348	0.056	256	0.380	0.054
Latvia	207	0.633	0.142	224	0.495	0.108
Lithuania	225	0.528	0.089	236	0.502	0.191
Luxembourg	–	–	–	221	0.583	0.155

For sources and notes, see end of table.

Imports - Importations						Régions, pays ou territoires
1995			2006			
Number of products exported	Diversification index	Concentration index	Number of products exported	Diversification index	Concentration index	
Nombre de produits exportés (1)	Indice de diversification (2)	Indice de concentration (3)	Nombre de produits exportés (1)	Indice de diversification (2)	Indice de concentration (3)	
211	0.456	0.113	247	0.482	0.103	Qatar
250	0.361	0.062	250	0.345	0.093	Arabie saoudite
190	0.499	0.090	225	0.517	0.220	République arabe syrienne
249	0.376	0.077	237	0.345	0.072	Turquie
249	0.354	0.061	256	0.381	0.092	Émirats arabes unis
180	0.472	0.087	217	0.540	0.196	Yémen
237	**0.402**	**0.088**	**257**	**0.407**	**0.185**	**Économies en développement : Océanie**
93	0.497	0.127	131	0.503	0.080	Îles Cook
209	0.433	0.113	209	0.501	0.287	Fidji
189	0.379	0.072	196	0.404	0.112	Polynésie française
199	0.383	0.105	208	0.415	0.125	Nouvelle-Calédonie
203	0.462	0.119	206	0.442	0.183	Papouasie-Nouvelle-Guinée
98	0.565	0.253	156	0.597	0.155	Samoa
251	**0.445**	**0.064**	**253**	**0.358**	**0.071**	**Économies en transition : Asie**
180	0.639	0.181	217	0.424	0.126	Arménie
194	0.516	0.099	216	0.454	0.117	Azerbaïdjan
150	0.678	0.256	227	0.393	0.126	Géorgie
230	0.491	0.099	245	0.381	0.081	Kazakhstan
159	0.570	0.201	212	0.516	0.221	Kirghizistan
177	0.605	0.161	196	0.507	0.178	Tadjikistan
177	0.541	0.108	206	0.455	0.118	Turkménistan
225	0.440	0.062	218	0.439	0.109	Ouzbékistan
257	**0.348**	**0.073**	**257**	**0.264**	**0.073**	**Économies en transition : Europe**
215	0.515	0.095	224	0.462	0.075	Albanie
240	0.385	0.105	242	0.378	0.231	Bélarus
137	0.509	0.073	239	0.399	0.086	Bosnie-Herzégovine
246	0.294	0.074	250	0.248	0.078	Croatie
212	0.581	0.219	227	0.463	0.114	Moldova
250	0.414	0.045	252	0.364	0.088	Fédération de Russie
242	0.366	0.068	248	0.287	0.080	Serbie-et-Monténégro
228	0.408	0.092	235	0.391	0.121	LERY de Macédoine
243	0.512	0.302	250	0.323	0.126	Ukraine
258	**0.190**	**0.093**	**258**	**0.169**	**0.112**	**Économies développées : Amérique**
257	0.223	0.092	256	0.219	0.082	Canada
160	0.450	0.084	169	0.533	0.187	Groenland
258	0.211	0.099	258	0.184	0.121	États-Unis
256	**0.286**	**0.076**	**257**	**0.276**	**0.143**	**Économies développées : Asie**
246	0.261	0.146	245	0.265	0.182	Israël
255	0.305	0.079	257	0.293	0.149	Japon
261	**0.093**	**0.047**	**260**	**0.108**	**0.069**	**Économies développées : Europe**
176	0.523	0.094	191	0.503	0.098	Andorre
256	0.216	0.052	257	0.230	0.064	Autriche
			257	0.281	0.099	Belgique
258	0.236	0.067	–	–	–	Belgique-Luxembourg
235	0.443	0.181	244	0.312	0.071	Bulgarie
229	0.351	0.095	226	0.355	0.159	Chypre
254	0.245	0.043	255	0.254	0.063	République tchèque
252	0.230	0.046	253	0.246	0.055	Danemark
236	0.371	0.077	243	0.341	0.138	Estonie
169	0.422	0.122	191	0.441	0.162	Îles Féroé
258	0.199	0.054	258	0.211	0.091	Finlande
259	0.135	0.048	258	0.145	0.076	France
257	0.155	0.050	257	0.147	0.070	Allemagne
252	0.252	0.055	253	0.274	0.123	Grèce
244	0.269	0.052	251	0.267	0.103	Hongrie
220	0.320	0.069	228	0.412	0.106	Islande
253	0.305	0.113	253	0.313	0.117	Irlande
255	0.198	0.059	257	0.207	0.092	Italie
230	0.414	0.108	245	0.354	0.091	Lettonie
239	0.372	0.085	250	0.317	0.157	Lituanie
–	–	–	240	0.400	0.108	Luxembourg

Pour les sources et les notes, se reporter à la fin du tableau.

Region, country or territory	Exports - Exportations					
	1995			2006		
	Number of products exported	Diversification index	Concentration index	Number of products exported	Diversification index	Concentration index
	Nombre de produits exportés (1)	Indice de diversification (2)	Indice de concentration (3)	Nombre de produits exportés (1)	Indice de diversification (2)	Indice de concentration (3)
Malta	137	0.703	0.507	143	0.618	0.456
Netherlands	254	0.345	0.055	256	0.373	0.088
Norway	238	0.647	0.377	232	0.663	0.452
Poland	248	0.486	0.082	252	0.431	0.083
Portugal	240	0.474	0.105	245	0.420	0.088
Romania	214	0.579	0.128	242	0.480	0.115
Slovakia	228	0.457	0.094	239	0.416	0.152
Slovenia	223	0.453	0.096	237	0.488	0.109
Spain	254	0.358	0.143	256	0.357	0.106
Sweden	249	0.430	0.124	250	0.379	0.112
Switzerland	241	0.510	0.091	244	0.561	0.143
United Kingdom	256	0.224	0.071	257	0.280	0.124
Developed economies: Oceania	**256**	**0.555**	**0.103**	**256**	**0.602**	**0.141**
Australia	256	0.566	0.123	254	0.618	0.169
New Zealand	234	0.653	0.119	235	0.655	0.137

Sources:
- Data and UNCTAD secretariat estimates based on UN DESA Comtrade and IMF Direction of Trade statistics databases

Notes:

(1)   Number of products (at SITC, Revision 3, 3-digit group level) exported or imported by country or country grouping; this figure includes only those products that are greater than 100,000 dollars or more than 0.3 per cent of the country's or country group's total exports or imports.

(2)   Diversification index that ranges from 0 to 1, reveals the extent of the differences between the structure of trade of the country or country group and the world average. The index value closer to 1 indicates a bigger difference from the world average.

Diversification index is computed by measuring absolute deviation of the country share from world structure, as follows:

$$S_j = \frac{\sum_i \left| h_{ij} - h_i \right|}{2}$$

where h_{ij} = share of product i in total exports or imports of country or country group j
h_i = share of product i in total world exports or imports.

This index is a modified Finger-Kreinin measure of similarity in trade. For more information, please consult the article of Finger, J. M. and M. E. Kreinin (1979), "A measure of 'export similarity' and its possible uses" in *Economic Journal*, 89: 905-12.

(3)   The Herfindahl-Hirschmann index is a measure of the degree of market concentration. It has been normalized to obtain values ranking from 0 to 1 (maximum concentration), according to the following formula:

$$H_j = \frac{\sqrt{\sum_{i=1}^{n} \left(\frac{x_i}{X} \right)^2} - \sqrt{1/n}}{1 - \sqrt{1/n}}$$

where H_j = country or country group index
x_i = value of exports of product i

$$X = \sum_{i=1}^{n} x_i$$

and   n = number of products (at SITC Revision 3, 3-digit group level) .

Imports - Importations						Régions, pays ou territoires
1995			2006			
Number of products exported	Diversification index	Concentration index	Number of products exported	Diversification index	Concentration index	
Nombre de produits exportés (1)	Indice de diversification (2)	Indice de concentration (3)	Nombre de produits exportés (1)	Indice de diversification (2)	Indice de concentration (3)	
228	0.393	0.254	224	0.373	0.233	Malte
255	0.190	0.058	257	0.219	0.098	Pays-Bas
253	0.261	0.047	253	0.311	0.061	Norvège
251	0.284	0.050	255	0.236	0.069	Pologne
252	0.208	0.059	253	0.191	0.090	Portugal
239	0.394	0.093	252	0.286	0.075	Roumanie
248	0.295	0.061	250	0.286	0.088	Slovaquie
251	0.247	0.057	250	0.307	0.064	Slovénie
257	0.187	0.064	257	0.168	0.093	Espagne
254	0.203	0.056	254	0.182	0.077	Suède
252	0.246	0.055	252	0.298	0.076	Suisse
257	0.163	0.064	256	0.215	0.082	Royaume-Uni
252	**0.209**	**0.065**	**255**	**0.223**	**0.096**	**Économies développées : Océanie**
251	0.214	0.065	251	0.227	0.097	Australie
244	0.242	0.073	247	0.257	0.099	Nouvelle-Zélande

Sources :
- Données et estimations du secrétariat de la CNUCED sur la base de données Comtrade de ONU DAES et Direction of Trade statistics du Fonds Monétaire international

Notes :

(1) Nombre de produits (au niveau de la CTCI révision 3, position à 3 chiffres) exportés ou importés par chaque pays ou groupes de pays; cependant, seuls les produits ayant une valeur supérieure à 100 000 dollars ou comptant pour plus de 0,3 pour cent des exportations ou des importations totales du pays ou groupe de pays sont inclus.

(2) L'indice de diversification, dont la valeur est comprise entre 0 et 1, indique si la structure par produits des exportations d'un pays ou groupe de pays diverge peu ou beaucoup de la structure par produits des exportations totales dans le monde. Plus l'indice est proche de 1, plus la divergence est forte.

L'indice de diversification mesure la déviation absolue de la structure du pays par rapport à la structure mondiale comme ci-dessous :

$$S_j = \frac{\sum_i |h_{ij} - h_i|}{2}$$

où h_{ij} = part du produit i dans le total des exportations (ou importations) du pays j
   h_i = part du produit i dans le total des exportations (ou importations) mondiales.

Cet indice est une variante de l'indicateur de Finger-Kreinin sur la similarité de la structure du commerce. Pour plus d'information, veuillez consulter l'article de Finger, J. M. et M. E. Kreinin (1979), "A measure of 'export similarity' and its possible uses", dans l'*Economic Journal*, 89: 905-12.

(3) L'indice Herfindahl-Hirschmann mesure le degré de concentration des marchés. Il a été normalisé afin d'obtenir des valeurs comprises entre 0 et 1 (concentration maximale), d'après la formule suivante:

$$H_j = \frac{\sqrt{\sum_{i=1}^{n} \left(\frac{x_i}{X}\right)^2} - \sqrt{1/n}}{1 - \sqrt{1/n}}$$

où H_j = indice du pays
    x_i = valeur des exportations du produit i

$$X = \sum_{i=1}^{n} x_i$$

et n = nombre de groupes de produits (de la CTCI révision 3, position à 3 chiffres).

4.1.2 Export and import concentration and diversification indices of economic groupings

Region, country or territory	Exports - Exportations					
	1995			2006		
	Number of products exported Nombre de produits exportés (1)	Diversification index Indice de diversification (2)	Concentration index Indice de concentration (3)	Number of products exported Nombre de produits exportés (1)	Diversification index Indice de diversification (2)	Concentration index Indice de concentration (3)
DEVELOPING ECONOMIES	**261**	**0.280**	**0.098**	**260**	**0.234**	**0.142**
Developing economies excluding China	261	0.283	0.109	260	0.256	0.180
Developing economies excluding LDCs	261	0.278	0.097	260	0.231	0.138
High-income developing countries	260	0.304	0.123	259	0.299	0.196
Middle-income developing countries	259	0.351	0.091	260	0.291	0.133
Low-income developing countries	260	0.440	0.079	260	0.308	0.100
Heavily indebted poor countries	250	0.714	0.153	254	0.648	0.224
Landlocked developing countries	256	0.633	0.144	257	0.623	0.321
Small island developing States	221	0.714	0.174	232	0.682	0.252
Least developed countries	*250*	*0.727*	*0.232*	*254*	*0.680*	*0.406*
Africa and Haiti	240	0.778	0.260	246	0.722	0.516
Asia	191	0.761	0.275	225	0.732	0.273
Islands	69	0.738	0.340	90	0.829	0.405
Major petroleum exporters	*257*	*0.774*	*0.665*	*258*	*0.729*	*0.681*
Africa	204	0.865	0.718	221	0.822	0.756
America	226	0.750	0.456	231	0.763	0.728
Asia	250	0.779	0.701	256	0.709	0.651
Major exporters of manufactured goods	*258*	*0.300*	*0.075*	*259*	*0.289*	*0.101*
America	251	0.320	0.079	253	0.317	0.111
Asia	258	0.343	0.084	259	0.332	0.113
Emerging economies	*258*	*0.275*	*0.094*	*259*	*0.262*	*0.113*
America	254	0.336	0.070	255	0.332	0.095
Asia	257	0.357	0.129	258	0.362	0.159
Newly industrialized economies	*258*	*0.351*	*0.100*	*259*	*0.337*	*0.145*
First tier	257	0.376	0.108	256	0.384	0.162
Second tier	254	0.414	0.101	257	0.362	0.126
Developing economies: Africa	**259**	**0.618**	**0.288**	**260**	**0.589**	**0.424**
Northern Africa excluding Sudan	228	0.726	0.383	244	0.695	0.478
Sub-Saharan Africa	258	0.626	0.252	259	0.593	0.404
Sub-Saharan Africa excluding South Africa	252	0.738	0.383	256	0.688	0.551
Developing economies: America	**258**	**0.361**	**0.090**	**256**	**0.350**	**0.150**
Central America and Greater Carribean Islands excluding Puerto Rico	250	0.370	0.105	252	0.364	0.139
Central America and Greater Carribean Islands excluding Mexico and Puerto Rico	228	0.696	0.197	238	0.572	0.124
South America and Central America	256	0.360	0.091	256	0.363	0.154
South America excluding Brazil	255	0.600	0.172	256	0.613	0.292
Developing economies: Asia	**261**	**0.321**	**0.099**	**260**	**0.270**	**0.131**
Eastern and South-Eastern Asia excluding China	259	0.349	0.098	259	0.326	0.139
Southern Asia excluding India	230	0.757	0.433	249	0.706	0.479

For sources and notes, see end of table 4.1.1.

Imports - Importations						Régions, pays ou territoires
1995			2006			
Number of products exported	Diversification index	Concentration index	Number of products exported	Diversification index	Concentration index	
Nombre de produits exportés (1)	Indice de diversification (2)	Indice de concentration (3)	Nombre de produits exportés (1)	Indice de diversification (2)	Indice de concentration (3)	
261	0.174	0.056	260	0.181	0.104	**ÉCONOMIES EN DÉVELOPPEMENT**
261	0.160	0.058	260	0.158	0.097	Économies en développement sans la Chine
261	0.173	0.057	260	0.183	0.107	Économies en développement sans les PMA
259	0.174	0.068	259	0.173	0.105	Pays en développement à revenu élevé
260	0.199	0.059	259	0.183	0.085	Pays en développement à revenu intermédiaire
261	0.311	0.054	260	0.280	0.123	Pays en développement à revenu faible
261	0.453	0.134	260	0.409	0.109	Pays pauvres très endettés
258	0.361	0.057	258	0.329	0.078	Pays en développement sans littoral
248	0.368	0.065	250	0.344	0.135	Petits États insulaires en développement
261	*0.473*	*0.138*	260	*0.446*	*0.108*	*Pays les moins avancés*
261	0.518	0.204	260	0.464	0.123	Afrique et Haïti
245	0.467	0.079	254	0.458	0.110	Asie
196	0.467	0.090	258	0.509	0.145	Îles
260	*0.275*	*0.042*	259	*0.296*	*0.068*	*Principaux exportateurs de pétrole*
259	0.369	0.055	250	0.391	0.078	Afrique
246	0.311	0.052	246	0.280	0.078	Amérique
257	0.293	0.045	258	0.317	0.073	Asie
259	*0.205*	*0.073*	259	*0.239*	*0.130*	*Principaux exportateurs d'articles manufacturés*
255	0.260	0.061	256	0.234	0.075	Amérique
259	0.224	0.078	259	0.270	0.143	Asie
258	*0.215*	*0.091*	259	*0.202*	*0.126*	*Économies émergentes*
257	0.225	0.054	257	0.211	0.071	Amérique
257	0.266	0.112	259	0.278	0.164	Asie
258	*0.220*	*0.087*	259	*0.249*	*0.151*	*Économies nouvellement industrialisées*
257	0.229	0.087	258	0.264	0.149	Première génération
256	0.294	0.093	257	0.295	0.164	Deuxième génération
261	0.291	0.053	260	0.270	0.080	**Économies en développement : Afrique**
255	0.363	0.052	254	0.326	0.064	Afrique septentrionale sans le Soudan
261	0.291	0.075	260	0.277	0.095	Afrique subsaharienne
261	0.412	0.111	260	0.385	0.099	Afrique subsaharienne sans l'Afrique du Sud
258	0.203	0.048	259	0.192	0.071	**Économies en développement : Amérique**
257	0.267	0.061	257	0.250	0.077	Amérique centrale et Grandes Antilles sans Porto Rico
254	0.322	0.068	253	0.306	0.107	Amérique centrale et Grandes Antilles sans le Mexique et Porto Rico
258	0.214	0.049	259	0.202	0.068	Amérique du Sud et Amérique centrale
258	0.235	0.049	257	0.229	0.069	Amérique du Sud sans le Brésil
261	0.206	0.066	260	0.229	0.124	**Économies en développement : Asie**
259	0.217	0.085	259	0.242	0.146	Asie orientale et Asie du Sud-Est sans la Chine
255	0.403	0.062	256	0.382	0.111	Asie méridionale sans l'Inde

Pour les sources et les notes, se reporter à la fin du tableau 4.1.1.

4.2.1 Volume indices of exports and imports of countries and geographical regions
2000 = 100

Region, country or territory	Exports (1) - Exportations (1)										
	1995	1996	1997	1998	1999	2001	2002	2003	2004	2005	2006
WORLD	70	74	80	84	90	99	103	110	122	129	139
DEVELOPING ECONOMIES	63	68	75	76	85	98	106	120	140	149	163
ECONOMIES IN TRANSITION	..	..	..	..	..	104	113	123	139	137	151
DEVELOPED ECONOMIES	69	73	80	84	87	99	101	105	113	119	128
Developing economies: Africa	67	76	82	75	84	95	100	110	120	120	122
Eastern Africa	69	82	78	88	94	108	127	125	133	130	125
Burundi	48	30	66	63	83	93	74	79	90	87	72
Ethiopia	55	69	92	79	80	108	114	108	129	147	161
Kenya	101	114	97	95	99	123	137	146	145	153	152
Madagascar	75	74	75	73	81	131	127	117	135	109	117
Malawi	95	107	115	114	115	120	118	151	134	130	148
Mauritius	99	108	96	109	107	89	102	107	111	110	109
Mozambique	32	52	52	56	64	212	251	303	374	365	395
Rwanda	91	120	130	119	138	168	145	130	181	152	162
Seychelles	25	66	56	61	68	117	125	150	143	137	143
Uganda	48	73	77	78	96	109	106	125	147	151	158
United Republic of Tanzania	106	117	76	72	76	120	134	152	162	169	140
Zambia	71	92	84	136	181	118	118	113	142	135	169
Zimbabwe	74	77	71	82	98	66	126	85	84	73	64
Middle Africa	54	60	75	65	94	103	118	125	141	159	167
Angola	75	71	92	104	103	94	118	117	127	163	180
Cameroon	94	103	109	132	128	103	97	109	101	100	102
Central African Republic	43	42	61	67	76	92	98	78	70	69	80
Congo	74	70	96	112	94	91	102	103	103	104	122
Dem. Rep. of the Congo	81	87	74	56	111	110	144	166	204	191	170
Equatorial Guinea	16	26	65	77	82	180	215	246	313	326	339
Gabon	77	77	82	74	93	109	103	105	107	116	109
Northern Africa	72	77	82	72	81	97	101	110	115	116	129
Algeria	78	84	90	93	92	90	100	97	105	107	118
Egypt	74	75	80	67	82	92	108	128	129	142	175
Libyan Arab Jamahiriya	..	..	..	..	..	101	88	105	102	121	138
Morocco	87	83	93	95	99	97	109	122	126	121	131
Sudan	28	39	31	31	47	103	122	133	159	144	144
Tunisia	82	79	87	91	94	114	118	135	154	155	162
Southern Africa	76	85	92	85	90	96	99	118	130	129	123
Botswana	72	89	97	71	96	91	95	102	118	143	130
Lesotho	59	74	78	84	75	133	168	224	333	306	335
Namibia	94	95	89	90	94	91	84	96	128	130	139
South Africa	76	85	92	85	89	96	99	118	127	125	119
Swaziland	83	87	94	104	102	117	116	182	206	196	191
Western Africa	70	80	86	78	81	83	84	93	106	102	98
Benin	83	119	97	91	96	101	130	129	133	139	124
Burkina Faso	89	79	86	125	112	117	134	141	209	210	237
Cape Verde	62	96	111	83	92	92	100	119	140	133	140
Côte d'Ivoire	80	89	100	100	102	95	99	106	121	114	111
Ghana	92	88	86	91	100	100	85	112	124	118	135
Guinea	76	83	79	90	87	117	107	80	72	74	47
Mali	59	59	89	89	102	138	153	133	132	143	155
Mauritania	100	102	81	79	95	98	94	85	107	100	186
Nigeria	96	104	113	125	106	77	80	89	100	99	92
Senegal	62	65	82	88	96	114	122	134	146	132	118
Togo	92	111	110	100	95	100	120	160	155	163	181
Developing economies: America	60	68	76	81	89	102	103	107	117	123	128
Caribbean	64	70	73	74	81	102	90	92	94	90	101
Aruba	..	..	..	..	..	105	68	79	82	71	74
Barbados	..	..	..	..	..	96	91	88	94	102	99
Cuba	..	..	..	..	..	102	92	100	108	88	85
Dominican Republic	85	93	99	91	84	94	92	96	100	100	101
Haiti	34	29	68	94	103	88	90	109	117	135	146
Montserrat	..	..	..	..	..	66	134	154	351	102	91
Netherlands Antilles	..	..	..	..	..	134	96	59	58	48	46
Saint Kitts and Nevis	..	..	..	..	..	105	130	115	112	121	120
Saint Lucia	..	..	..	..	..	79	115	122	133	96	97
Saint Vincent and the Grenadines	..	..	..	..	..	77	74	78	56	64	48
Trinidad and Tobago	..	..	..	..	..	104	100	110	117	133	191

For sources and notes, see end of table 4.2.2.

Imports (1) - Importations (1)											Régions, pays ou territoires
1995	1996	1997	1998	1999	2001	2002	2003	2004	2005	2006	
71	74	81	85	89	100	104	112	125	134	144	**MONDE**
72	77	85	81	86	98	105	118	140	152	165	ÉCONOMIES EN DÉVELOPPEMENT
..	..	..	..	..	116	132	160	192	214	261	ÉCONOMIES EN TRANSITION
67	70	77	83	89	100	103	108	118	125	132	ÉCONOMIES DÉVELOPPÉES
85	87	94	98	97	105	111	129	150	165	176	**Économies en développement : Afrique**
80	87	84	96	99	107	110	119	137	146	159	*Afrique orientale*
59	38	34	63	71	96	89	101	106	149	230	Burundi
87	103	85	123	127	146	130	161	218	262	280	Éthiopie
94	98	99	93	88	106	106	113	123	144	158	Kenya
61	61	71	72	75	99	62	127	155	138	136	Madagascar
84	112	140	100	129	108	132	141	155	181	176	Malawi
84	93	90	96	110	90	99	104	114	117	126	Maurice
65	66	63	71	102	94	136	146	156	175	195	Mozambique
114	117	144	155	133	135	120	119	119	153	178	Rwanda
64	103	93	119	116	136	119	110	120	142	147	Seychelles
65	70	86	92	90	106	74	78	118	98	121	Ouganda
111	86	58	76	94	115	110	135	146	162	204	République-Unie de Tanzanie
61	76	72	108	82	123	124	170	215	233	263	Zambie
95	93	111	129	114	95	136	93	104	92	68	Zimbabwe
52	60	78	62	95	122	142	172	184	223	244	*Afrique centrale*
62	65	85	71	97	105	124	176	184	254	255	Angola
58	65	87	92	80	128	129	142	143	140	145	Cameroun
116	93	109	110	100	92	103	95	112	117	129	République centrafricaine
76	181	118	76	110	147	146	173	168	262	321	Congo
30	29	35	28	100	117	159	221	256	267	310	Rép. dém. du Congo
20	39	42	50	94	180	112	274	333	409	527	Guinée équatoriale
81	88	114	114	89	105	99	108	118	125	133	Gabon
91	92	94	104	98	103	110	114	137	153	157	*Afrique septentrionale*
121	106	108	106	94	107	123	134	187	194	187	Algérie
98	103	96	114	119	92	90	75	79	111	106	Égypte
129	142	146	143	91	109	135	146	195	227	253	Jamahiriya arabe libyenne
68	65	72	87	84	97	105	118	134	132	142	Maroc
73	113	95	114	100	149	161	182	241	411	427	Soudan
78	75	82	87	90	113	113	124	137	128	136	Tunisie
89	95	105	99	92	96	98	134	160	168	189	*Afrique australe*
63	62	83	96	88	73	76	98	121	106	96	Botswana
110	121	123	111	101	92	100	133	157	152	152	Lesotho
76	86	91	98	99	101	86	125	146	141	151	Namibie
89	95	105	99	92	98	101	137	164	175	201	Afrique du Sud
84	94	91	101	101	109	91	149	161	165	165	Swaziland
84	85	95	100	103	114	126	148	162	182	187	*Afrique occidentale*
101	89	100	104	109	103	122	140	125	109	116	Bénin
66	92	91	122	114	110	125	147	183	181	176	Burkina Faso
87	82	86	84	92	101	121	144	149	156	184	Cap-Vert
122	112	118	137	116	91	92	116	140	143	148	Côte d'Ivoire
61	68	78	91	125	103	94	106	134	154	183	Ghana
87	64	68	60	63	100	112	101	99	104	108	Guinée
77	79	86	93	101	125	119	151	142	151	155	Mali
112	99	99	92	89	104	99	116	197	293	219	Mauritanie
87	88	103	108	99	135	160	190	198	232	233	Nigéria
83	95	92	104	102	114	135	148	158	154	154	Sénégal
93	100	108	104	107	100	106	132	135	149	149	Togo
60	67	81	89	88	100	93	94	108	119	134	**Économies en développement : Amérique**
59	66	76	83	88	101	96	93	97	105	113	*Caraïbes*
..	..	..	..	..	91	78	90	106	117	120	Aruba
..	..	..	..	..	93	94	101	115	117	110	Barbade
..	..	..	..	..	111	89	93	101	118	137	Cuba
51	55	66	81	87	96	97	79	78	93	100	République dominicaine
69	66	68	79	105	100	111	113	115	118	144	Haïti
..	..	..	..	..	89	120	128	104	93	101	Montserrat
..	..	..	..	..	111	88	89	95	89	88	Antilles néerlandaises
..	..	..	..	..	96	104	99	93	91	103	Saint-Kitts-et-Nevis
..	..	..	..	..	100	89	112	118	128	133	Sainte-Lucie
..	..	..	..	..	106	112	121	126	122	119	Saint-Vincent-et-les Grenadines
..	..	..	..	..	112	113	114	128	125	129	Trinité-et-Tobago

Pour les sources et les notes, se reporter à la fin du tableau 4.2.2.

Region, country or territory	Exports (1) - Exportations (1)										
	1995	1996	1997	1998	1999	2001	2002	2003	2004	2005	2006
Central America	*49*	*59*	*68*	*76*	*87*	*100*	*100*	*101*	*106*	*112*	*125*
Belize	..	..	..	..	..	72	84	107	100	87	96
Costa Rica	52	59	66	86	108	91	98	112	114	127	148
El Salvador	69	73	95	87	87	101	106	112	114	111	112
Guatemala	64	68	78	89	90	99	99	106	109	120	120
Honduras	84	100	93	101	84	118	122	123	134	134	148
Mexico	49	58	67	75	86	100	100	100	106	112	125
Nicaragua	62	68	82	83	87	106	102	110	130	136	156
Panama	76	86	85	91	95	106	99	103	109	114	114
South America	*71*	*78*	*86*	*87*	*92*	*105*	*108*	*116*	*133*	*142*	*142*
Argentina	73	78	92	101	97	104	105	111	118	136	145
Bolivia	89	83	86	90	89	111	111	129	154	174	185
Brazil	72	74	81	83	89	110	119	138	164	179	186
Chile	59	71	82	90	98	107	107	117	136	141	144
Colombia	84	84	90	98	101	104	104	107	116	131	139
Ecuador	100	106	112	105	109	113	119	139	162	173	186
Guyana	91	62	133	106	..	103	105	102	108	86	75
Paraguay	96	109	114	107	84	121	121	146	173	183	201
Peru	60	66	75	76	89	110	117	127	150	167	176
Suriname	..	..	..	..	..	90	101	118	119	110	96
Uruguay	75	88	102	103	95	92	90	100	124	140	152
Venezuela (Bolivarian Rep. of)	82	91	93	104	93	97	92	81	93	95	91
Developing economies: Asia	**63**	**67**	**74**	**75**	**84**	**97**	**108**	**124**	**148**	**160**	**178**
Eastern Asia	*64*	*67*	*75*	*77*	*83*	*98*	*113*	*138*	*171*	*200*	*236*
China	57	57	68	71	77	108	133	180	240	303	377
China, Hong Kong SAR	78	81	86	83	85	96	104	118	135	149	164
China, Macao SAR	..	..	..	..	..	90	92	100	108	92	92
China, Taiwan Province of	94	90	93	81	88	84	92	101	118	128	141
Mongolia	..	..	..	..	..	101	95	99	113	119	123
Republic of Korea	45	53	62	75	83	100	113	132	161	178	204
Southern Asia	*66*	*76*	*69*	*66*	*80*	*99*	*113*	*126*	*141*	*150*	*155*
Bangladesh	69	69	79	81	85	96	97	113	129	145	181
India	67	76	71	74	83	104	122	139	165	190	210
Iran (Islamic Rep. of)	..	..	..	..	..	94	110	117	119	117	105
Maldives	..	..	..	..	..	100	120	138	153	114	143
Nepal	..	..	..	..	..	93	72	82	89	92	80
Pakistan	75	91	84	80	86	104	111	131	141	161	164
Sri Lanka	71	74	81	81	84	92	91	98	106	113	115
South-Eastern Asia	*64*	*66*	*73*	*78*	*88*	*95*	*101*	*109*	*129*	*138*	*153*
Brunei Darussalam	..	..	..	..	..	96	108	100	96	87	101
Cambodia	..	..	..	..	..	113	126	146	180	200	248
Indonesia	71	74	83	97	121	90	93	91	91	95	98
Malaysia	59	61	67	70	84	92	99	103	124	131	148
Myanmar	35	32	42	55	63	144	198	137	121	162	206
Philippines	54	60	70	76	86	84	96	98	106	107	125
Singapore	72	76	81	82	87	95	100	117	156	174	192
Thailand	70	64	68	74	83	102	106	118	133	142	160
Viet Nam	..	..	..	..	..	111	122	143	170	182	206
Western Asia	*70*	*77*	*84*	*79*	*90*	*97*	*103*	*111*	*123*	*123*	*129*
Bahrain	..	..	..	..	..	97	106	105	96	92	93
Jordan	84	82	85	89	92	122	147	160	192	202	229
Kuwait	..	..	..	..	..	94	90	102	111	123	133
Lebanon	..	..	..	..	..	152	170	235	259	260	288
Oman	88	89	96	108	98	107	110	97	89	90	94
Qatar	..	..	..	..	..	93	115	108	123	123	162
Saudi Arabia	104	106	112	111	101	84	91	103	114	113	112
Syrian Arab Republic	78	83	103	104	100	128	158	122	94	87	132
Turkey	60	68	81	87	91	116	130	159	182	200	220
United Arab Emirates	..	..	..	..	..	106	115	130	147	148	157
Yemen	..	..	..	..	..	95	100	95	88	87	83
Developing economies: Oceania	**161**	**170**	**141**	**103**	**97**	**90**	**86**	**100**	**93**	**90**	**83**
Fiji	..	..	..	..	..	99	101	127	126	105	87
French Polynesia	..	..	..	..	..	76	70	64	75	82	91
New Caledonia	..	..	..	..	..	78	85	123	113	106	102
Papua New Guinea	183	176	136	98	92	94	78	90	83	88	86
Samoa	76	95	119	98	117	111	99	108	75	77	65

For sources and notes, see end of table 4.2.2.

					Imports (1) - Importations (1)						Régions, pays ou territoires
1995	1996	1997	1998	1999	2001	2002	2003	2004	2005	2006	
42	*52*	*64*	*74*	*83*	*100*	*100*	*100*	*109*	*117*	*129*	**Amérique centrale**
..	..	..	..	..	100	103	102	88	89	96	Belize
59	62	73	97	101	107	119	123	126	143	163	Costa Rica
84	76	83	84	86	107	111	119	125	128	137	El Salvador
65	61	81	100	95	114	127	132	140	145	156	Guatemala
53	61	74	92	99	120	122	130	143	155	167	Honduras
39	50	62	72	81	99	98	97	107	114	126	Mexique
60	69	80	87	111	100	99	103	112	121	128	Nicaragua
77	86	93	104	110	90	90	91	101	111	123	Panama
84	*89*	*107*	*111*	*94*	*100*	*84*	*88*	*108*	*125*	*147*	**Amérique du Sud**
67	81	111	119	101	83	38	58	87	108	125	Argentine
69	81	95	106	98	95	98	87	92	110	122	Bolivie
87	90	107	106	93	103	90	87	103	108	125	Brésil
83	99	113	114	95	99	102	112	134	162	181	Chili
113	110	122	123	93	115	115	122	138	165	193	Colombie
103	100	127	150	84	145	175	178	208	239	258	Équateur
..	..	..	..	..	91	91	85	86	88	91	Guyana
154	152	167	132	90	106	81	105	136	154	243	Paraguay
98	98	112	114	97	86	87	94	105	118	134	Pérou
..	..	..	..	..	89	96	130	128	142	141	Suriname
79	90	102	112	104	94	64	68	87	96	108	Uruguay
70	56	87	96	87	112	74	64	95	132	179	Venezuela (Rép. bolivarienne du)
75	**79**	**85**	**78**	**84**	**97**	**107**	**124**	**148**	**160**	**173**	**Économies en développement : Asie**
72	*76*	*82*	*75*	*83*	*98*	*111*	*132*	*158*	*167*	*182*	**Asie orientale**
57	61	65	66	76	111	136	184	231	249	277	Chine
82	85	92	85	84	98	105	117	133	143	156	Chine (RAS de Hong Kong)
..	..	..	..	..	106	113	119	145	154	173	Chine (RAS de Macao)
83	80	91	82	88	78	83	92	111	110	112	Province chinoise de Taiwan
..	..	..	..	..	105	115	126	147	148	172	Mongolie
72	84	86	67	86	97	108	117	130	139	153	République de Corée
78	*84*	*87*	*95*	*96*	*105*	*118*	*135*	*157*	*180*	*191*	**Asie méridionale**
102	97	98	96	100	103	97	109	118	123	132	Bangladesh
67	71	78	92	95	103	114	135	161	194	207	Inde
..	..	..	..	..	120	155	181	201	211	225	Iran (Rép. islamique d')
..	..	..	..	..	101	103	119	151	158	186	Maldives
..	..	..	..	..	97	93	106	102	87	91	Népal
107	118	110	100	101	99	108	115	141	174	185	Pakistan
83	85	93	..	..	96	99	103	113	113	121	Sri Lanka
85	*88*	*92*	*76*	*83*	*93*	*98*	*105*	*124*	*136*	*146*	**Asie du Sud-Est**
..	..	..	..	..	104	139	117	119	119	136	Brunéi Darussalam
..	..	..	..	..	110	125	136	159	179	208	Cambodge
106	114	118	82	73	89	92	95	109	126	123	Indonésie
81	82	90	71	81	92	101	103	125	129	140	Malaisie
80	66	84	110	98	122	100	85	82	65	68	Myanmar
76	87	97	77	85	97	105	111	112	117	130	Philippines
80	86	92	84	89	89	90	96	118	134	149	Singapour
114	105	96	71	86	100	103	117	140	164	168	Thaïlande
..	..	..	..	..	106	125	158	181	186	206	Viet Nam
59	*69*	*82*	*84*	*89*	*97*	*105*	*121*	*154*	*172*	*188*	**Asie occidentale**
..	..	..	..	..	97	113	118	117	135	131	Bahreïn
84	91	88	83	82	108	113	120	153	174	176	Jordanie
..	..	..	..	..	109	126	151	166	219	192	Koweït
..	..	..	..	..	120	108	114	136	122	115	Liban
..	..	..	..	..	115	120	127	160	148	172	Oman
..	..	..	..	..	115	124	147	167	266	418	Qatar
..	..	..	..	..	103	107	120	137	172	190	Arabie saoudite
..	..	..	..	..	121	120	130	164	170	224	République arabe syrienne
54	70	85	83	78	76	93	113	148	142	176	Turquie
..	..	..	..	..	106	121	145	192	231	233	Émirats arabes unis
42	54	49	106	96	107	128	152	147	155	187	Yémen
..	**..**	**..**	**..**	**..**	**103**	**112**	**134**	**136**	**129**	**131**	**Économies en développement : Océanie**
..	..	..	..	..	105	109	138	152	144	149	Fidji
..	..	..	..	..	100	120	144	128	136	119	Polynésie française
..	..	..	..	..	102	112	163	163	160	180	Nouvelle-Calédonie
..	..	..	..	..	95	110	116	130	115	136	Papouasie-Nouvelle-Guinée
..	..	..	..	..	128	129	139	176	175	190	Samoa

Pour les sources et les notes, se reporter à la fin du tableau 4.2.2.

4.2.1 Unit value indices of exports and imports of countries and geographical regions
2000 = 100

Region, country or territory	Exports - Exportations										
	1995	1996	1997	1998	1999	2001	2002	2003	2004	2005	2006
WORLD	114	113	108	101	99	97	97	106	116	126	134
DEVELOPING ECONOMIES	110	110	107	98	95	95	94	98	107	123	135
ECONOMIES IN TRANSITION	..	..	..	..	..	97	93	109	131	170	193
DEVELOPED ECONOMIES	123	120	112	108	106	98	98	110	119	124	130
Developing economies: Africa	109	108	103	93	90	95	95	106	126	165	192
Eastern Africa	137	129	135	114	101	94	92	98	110	125	160
Burundi	440	270	264	206	131	83	83	95	106	131	162
Ethiopia	157	124	132	147	120	87	87	95	108	127	134
Kenya	107	105	122	122	102	91	89	95	107	124	130
Madagascar	82	84	83	90	88	86	82	88	90	95	101
Malawi	112	118	123	100	104	99	91	91	95	101	110
Mauritius	100	107	106	97	95	101	97	98	99	107	118
Mozambique	142	114	117	112	113	94	89	95	111	131	165
Rwanda	109	96	128	96	83	95	85	92	102	155	172
Seychelles	110	110	104	103	111	96	94	95	105	128	138
Uganda	209	175	156	139	117	91	91	98	105	124	138
United Republic of Tanzania	97	101	150	123	108	96	99	109	124	135	168
Zambia	220	169	163	114	88	93	91	97	124	150	250
Zimbabwe	149	163	158	109	100	95	96	102	119	129	156
Middle Africa	123	129	108	97	79	90	91	104	132	183	219
Angola	63	90	69	43	63	88	89	103	134	187	224
Cameroon	113	102	101	91	78	93	101	113	134	170	198
Central African Republic	247	217	165	141	120	96	94	102	112	115	123
Congo	64	77	70	49	67	90	90	104	132	185	223
Dem. Rep. of the Congo	268	250	212	276	111	99	95	100	110	139	166
Equatorial Guinea	50	62	69	52	79	88	90	104	134	187	221
Gabon	143	168	149	105	104	89	90	103	130	180	215
Northern Africa	93	97	93	86	87	95	91	106	128	175	193
Algeria	66	77	75	55	63	97	86	114	140	196	206
Egypt	100	100	105	99	93	95	93	105	124	160	168
Libyan Arab Jamahiriya	..	..	..	..	..	88	88	103	134	188	223
Morocco	114	119	109	108	107	99	97	97	103	111	118
Sudan	108	88	107	108	91	91	88	106	131	185	217
Tunisia	114	119	109	108	107	99	99	102	107	116	121
Southern Africa	123	115	113	103	100	101	100	102	119	134	158
Botswana	109	105	108	101	102	99	96	98	106	110	124
Lesotho	124	115	115	105	105	100	100	99	100	100	101
Namibia	114	113	114	104	99	98	97	99	108	116	148
South Africa	123	115	113	103	100	101	100	103	121	138	163
Swaziland	115	108	112	103	101	100	97	98	104	113	121
Western Africa	90	94	87	79	82	92	100	111	133	177	206
Benin	129	113	110	114	112	94	88	107	109	106	117
Burkina Faso	148	141	129	122	109	93	89	111	111	108	121
Cape Verde	126	124	119	118	117	100	99	100	101	126	139
Côte d'Ivoire	122	128	115	119	117	106	137	140	146	169	189
Ghana	112	114	114	118	103	102	130	137	132	142	165
Guinea	138	129	130	116	110	94	99	115	152	181	285
Mali	137	134	114	114	102	97	105	128	135	141	182
Mauritania	139	135	140	124	110	102	100	105	116	176	208
Nigeria	60	73	69	43	59	87	88	102	132	185	217
Senegal	175	164	120	120	116	96	95	102	112	130	144
Togo	113	109	106	116	113	98	98	103	106	111	116
Developing economies: America	105	105	104	96	93	94	94	99	111	127	146
Caribbean	107	104	105	99	98	95	93	104	121	154	172
Aruba	..	..	..	..	..	91	86	103	131	194	197
Barbados	..	..	..	..	..	99	97	104	109	130	143
Cuba	..	..	..	..	..	97	92	100	129	146	205
Dominican Republic	106	105	106	100	99	98	98	99	103	107	111
Haiti	103	99	99	107	102	98	98	100	105	110	112
Montserrat	..	..	..	..	..	97	94	103	108	127	135
Netherlands Antilles	..	..	..	..	..	90	85	99	122	174	204
Saint Kitts and Nevis	..	..	..	..	..	102	96	97	97	98	99
Saint Lucia	..	..	..	..	..	119	115	108	127	142	158
Saint Vincent and the Grenadines	..	..	..	..	..	115	112	103	125	133	145
Trinidad and Tobago	..	..	..	..	..	96	91	110	127	170	174

For sources and notes, see end of table 4.2.2.

4.2.1 Indices de la valeur unitaire des exportations et importations des pays et des régions géographiques
2000 = 100

	Imports - Importations											Régions, pays ou territoires
1995	1996	1997	1998	1999	2001	2002	2003	2004	2005	2006	
112	**111**	**105**	**100**	**98**	**97**	**96**	**104**	**113**	**120**	**129**	**MONDE**
108	108	104	98	96	97	96	100	108	117	126	ÉCONOMIES EN DÉVELOPPEMENT
..	..	..	..	..	100	98	103	111	122	128	ÉCONOMIES EN TRANSITION
117	116	108	103	101	97	96	106	116	122	130	ÉCONOMIES DÉVELOPPÉES
114	**113**	**109**	**105**	**101**	**98**	**99**	**103**	**111**	**122**	**131**	**Économies en développement : Afrique**
117	*121*	*122*	*107*	*101*	*98*	*98*	*104*	*114*	*128*	*138*	*Afrique orientale*
269	227	241	170	113	98	98	105	112	121	127	Burundi
104	108	104	98	96	98	99	104	112	125	133	Éthiopie
103	97	107	111	104	97	98	106	119	137	149	Kenya
103	103	98	96	99	97	97	103	110	123	132	Madagascar
106	105	105	97	98	98	99	105	113	123	129	Malawi
113	118	116	103	98	100	98	103	111	123	130	Maurice
94	99	101	96	96	98	98	104	112	118	126	Mozambique
99	104	98	87	89	98	97	102	112	123	131	Rwanda
107	107	107	94	109	103	103	109	121	139	150	Seychelles
106	111	100	100	97	98	98	104	112	125	134	Ouganda
99	106	152	125	109	98	99	105	115	132	143	République-Unie de Tanzanie
116	111	115	101	101	99	100	104	113	123	132	Zambie
154	167	163	112	103	97	98	103	114	135	166	Zimbabwe
149	*167*	*131*	*155*	*106*	*99*	*99*	*102*	*108*	*115*	*122*	*Afrique centrale*
78	104	101	97	105	100	100	102	104	108	113	Angola
125	124	116	109	111	97	98	103	114	131	146	Cameroun
128	130	110	114	112	100	100	105	113	125	135	République centrafricaine
123	120	110	125	104	100	100	103	109	116	121	Congo
336	465	315	421	107	99	98	103	111	122	129	Rép. dém. du Congo
136	166	187	140	100	100	100	100	105	115	120	Guinée équatoriale
114	114	102	102	99	100	100	101	108	115	119	Gabon
109	*109*	*105*	*104*	*103*	*99*	*100*	*104*	*112*	*122*	*131*	*Afrique septentrionale*
114	114	106	108	106	101	101	104	110	116	122	Algérie
86	90	98	101	96	99	99	106	116	128	139	Égypte
98	96	93	96	114	101	101	105	111	123	130	Jamahiriya arabe libyenne
128	130	115	102	103	98	98	104	114	128	137	Maroc
108	88	107	108	91	99	100	103	108	115	122	Soudan
119	120	113	112	110	99	99	103	110	120	128	Tunisie
116	*107*	*106*	*100*	*99*	*98*	*98*	*101*	*110*	*120*	*129*	*Afrique australe*
122	112	110	101	102	100	99	101	108	120	129	Botswana
124	115	115	105	106	100	100	104	110	117	122	Lesotho
138	125	124	109	105	99	98	102	107	112	117	Namibie
116	107	106	99	98	97	97	101	110	120	129	Afrique du Sud
115	108	112	103	101	99	99	104	111	122	128	Swaziland
110	*102*	*105*	*101*	*101*	*98*	*97*	*103*	*112*	*125*	*134*	*Afrique occidentale*
121	120	111	115	112	99	97	104	116	133	142	Bénin
113	115	106	98	97	97	97	103	114	125	133	Burkina Faso
126	124	119	118	117	100	99	106	113	122	128	Cap-Vert
100	108	98	102	99	95	95	100	110	128	140	Côte d'Ivoire
105	105	100	95	94	97	97	102	107	116	124	Ghana
154	165	149	145	143	98	97	104	114	129	136	Guinée
125	121	107	102	101	98	97	103	113	132	142	Mali
136	144	136	120	106	98	96	103	103	107	117	Mauritanie
108	84	106	98	99	98	98	104	112	125	135	Nigéria
112	99	95	92	101	97	97	104	116	134	143	Sénégal
114	118	106	101	99	98	99	104	116	136	146	Togo
107	**106**	**103**	**100**	**98**	**97**	**97**	**100**	**106**	**114**	**120**	**Économies en développement : Amérique**
106	*108*	*105*	*99*	*97*	*97*	*97*	*102*	*111*	*125*	*135*	*Caraïbes*
..	..	..	..	..	101	101	104	110	115	123	Aruba
..	..	..	..	..	99	98	102	106	118	125	Barbade
..	..	..	..	..	98	97	103	115	133	143	Cuba
108	109	106	99	97	97	96	101	107	112	117	République dominicaine
91	97	92	97	94	97	98	102	110	119	126	Haïti
..	..	..	..	..	100	98	103	113	130	139	Montserrat
..	..	..	..	..	89	90	102	112	135	156	Antilles néerlandaises
..	..	..	..	..	100	99	102	109	118	122	Saint-Kitts-et-Nevis
..	..	..	..	..	100	98	102	110	121	127	Sainte-Lucie
..	..	..	..	..	100	98	103	110	121	128	Saint-Vincent-et-les Grenadines
..	..	..	..	..	97	97	103	115	138	153	Trinité-et-Tobago

Pour les sources et les notes, se reporter à la fin du tableau 4.2.2.

4.2.1 Unit value indices of exports and imports of countries and geographical regions
2000 = 100

Region, country or territory	Exports - Exportations										
	1995	1996	1997	1998	1999	2001	2002	2003	2004	2005	2006
Central America	*100*	*100*	*100*	*96*	*96*	*95*	*96*	*99*	*107*	*114*	*119*
Belize	..	..	..	..	..	107	92	88	98	110	128
Costa Rica	114	108	112	110	105	94	92	93	95	95	95
El Salvador	109	106	108	109	101	97	96	95	99	104	107
Guatemala	125	111	111	108	99	92	92	92	99	107	112
Honduras	105	95	113	110	101	81	79	78	83	91	95
Mexico	98	99	99	94	95	95	97	100	108	115	121
Nicaragua	116	106	109	108	98	87	85	85	90	98	102
Panama	96	98	99	100	101	100	100	98	101	104	106
South America	*109*	*109*	*107*	*96*	*90*	*92*	*91*	*98*	*114*	*134*	*162*
Argentina	109	116	109	99	91	97	93	101	111	113	122
Bolivia	101	111	110	100	96	94	95	100	113	130	170
Brazil	117	117	119	112	98	97	92	96	107	120	135
Chile	141	115	113	94	91	89	88	96	125	152	210
Colombia	92	97	98	85	88	91	88	94	108	124	135
Ecuador	87	94	95	81	83	84	86	91	97	119	139
Guyana	100	167	97	92	..	95	94	100	109	128	159
Paraguay	110	110	110	109	101	94	91	98	108	107	109
Peru	132	129	131	109	98	92	95	103	121	143	194
Suriname	..	..	..	..	..	88	91	107	149	171	253
Uruguay	122	119	117	117	103	98	91	97	103	106	113
Venezuela (Bolivarian Rep. of)	71	80	73	52	68	82	87	100	128	174	214
Developing economies: Asia	**112**	**111**	**108**	**99**	**96**	**96**	**94**	**97**	**105**	**118**	**126**
Eastern Asia	*114*	*112*	*108*	*101*	*99*	*96*	*94*	*94*	*97*	*99*	*101*
China	105	107	108	104	101	99	98	97	99	101	103
China, Hong Kong SAR	110	110	108	104	101	98	95	94	95	96	97
China, Macao SAR	..	..	..	..	..	100	100	101	103	106	110
China, Taiwan Province of	80	87	88	92	93	98	96	97	100	105	108
Mongolia	..	..	..	..	..	97	103	116	144	167	234
Republic of Korea	162	141	128	102	100	87	83	85	92	93	92
Southern Asia	*107*	*104*	*114*	*108*	*102*	*96*	*96*	*101*	*115*	*138*	*154*
Bangladesh	85	91	96	99	100	99	98	98	99	100	102
India	108	103	117	107	101	98	97	100	109	124	136
Iran (Islamic Rep. of)	..	..	..	..	..	90	91	103	132	180	213
Maldives	..	..	..	..	..	101	102	102	109	130	145
Nepal	..	..	..	..	..	98	99	101	106	113	118
Pakistan	118	114	115	117	109	99	99	101	105	110	114
Sri Lanka	99	102	105	110	101	96	95	97	100	103	110
South-Eastern Asia	*116*	*119*	*112*	*98*	*95*	*95*	*94*	*97*	*102*	*110*	*116*
Brunei Darussalam	..	..	..	..	..	97	88	114	135	185	198
Cambodia	..	..	..	..	..	100	100	102	103	104	106
Indonesia	103	109	104	81	65	97	97	108	121	139	153
Malaysia	127	130	119	107	103	97	95	99	103	109	111
Myanmar	150	142	128	118	109	100	94	110	120	143	133
Philippines	81	86	89	97	107	98	95	93	94	94	95
Singapore	120	119	112	97	96	93	91	90	93	96	103
Thailand	116	127	122	106	102	93	93	99	105	113	118
Viet Nam	..	..	..	..	..	94	94	97	108	123	133
Western Asia	*82*	*88*	*84*	*71*	*78*	*96*	*95*	*109*	*132*	*177*	*205*
Bahrain	..	..	..	..	..	93	88	102	127	178	212
Jordan	111	117	114	107	105	99	99	101	107	112	119
Kuwait	..	..	..	..	..	89	87	104	133	188	221
Lebanon	..	..	..	..	..	100	102	108	119	126	137
Oman	61	73	70	45	65	92	90	106	133	183	204
Qatar	..	..	..	..	..	96	84	109	132	181	184
Saudi Arabia	62	74	70	45	65	104	103	117	143	206	248
Syrian Arab Republic	99	104	82	60	75	89	89	101	124	160	179
Turkey	129	123	117	112	105	97	96	105	122	129	134
United Arab Emirates	..	..	..	..	..	92	91	103	124	159	181
Yemen	..	..	..	..	..	87	89	101	130	181	216
Developing economies: Oceania	**69**	**68**	**75**	**86**	**97**	**95**	**98**	**111**	**136**	**161**	**210**
Fiji	..	..	..	..	..	100	95	98	102	124	145
French Polynesia	..	..	..	..	..	99	97	98	101	105	106
New Caledonia	..	..	..	..	..	94	97	106	150	168	217
Palau	..	..	..	..	..	98	96	97	107	119	128
Papua New Guinea	69	68	75	86	97	92	100	118	147	178	231
Samoa	82	75	89	105	123	98	98	97	100	108	115

For sources and notes, see end of table 4.2.2.

4.2.1 Indices de la valeur unitaire des exportations et importations des pays et des régions géographiques
2000 = 100

				Imports - Importations							Régions, pays ou territoires
1995	1996	1997	1998	1999	2001	2002	2003	2004	2005	2006	
105	*103*	*102*	*100*	*99*	*97*	*98*	*100*	*106*	*111*	*116*	***Amérique centrale***
..	..	..	..	..	99	97	103	112	127	135	Belize
109	109	106	101	98	96	95	97	103	107	110	Costa Rica
90	93	95	98	96	95	95	98	102	108	112	El Salvador
106	107	99	97	96	95	96	99	108	117	126	Guatemala
109	106	102	97	95	86	86	89	96	104	114	Honduras
106	103	102	100	100	97	99	101	106	111	116	Mexique
90	93	100	95	93	98	98	101	110	120	129	Nicaragua
96	96	96	97	95	97	98	101	106	111	117	Panama
108	*109*	*105*	*100*	*96*	*97*	*94*	*98*	*106*	*115*	*121*	***Amérique du Sud***
119	116	109	104	100	97	94	94	102	106	108	Argentine
113	111	106	102	98	99	99	102	109	117	126	Bolivie
106	108	104	98	95	97	94	99	109	121	130	Brésil
104	105	100	94	91	95	91	93	100	109	114	Chili
106	108	109	103	99	96	95	98	105	112	117	Colombie
108	106	105	100	97	99	99	101	106	116	126	Équateur
..	..	..	..	..	98	96	104	116	136	146	Guyana
93	93	93	100	97	94	94	97	104	110	114	Paraguay
107	108	103	98	95	96	97	101	109	119	128	Pérou
..	..	..	..	..	99	97	103	111	123	130	Suriname
105	106	105	98	93	94	88	93	103	117	128	Uruguay
112	109	103	102	100	100	99	101	108	113	116	Venezuela (Rép. bolivarienne du)
108	**108**	**103**	**96**	**95**	**97**	**96**	**99**	**107**	**117**	**126**	**Économies en développement : Asie**
107	*105*	*101*	*95*	*95*	*96*	*94*	*97*	*105*	*114*	*122*	***Asie orientale***
103	101	98	94	97	98	97	100	108	118	127	Chine
111	110	107	102	100	97	93	93	96	98	101	Chine (RAS de Hong Kong)
..	..	..	..	..	100	99	102	106	113	117	Chine (RAS de Macao)
89	90	89	91	90	98	97	99	108	119	129	Province chinoise de Taiwan
..	..	..	..	..	99	98	103	113	131	141	Mongolie
117	112	105	87	87	91	88	96	107	117	126	République de Corée
97	*100*	*100*	*90*	*95*	*97*	*98*	*105*	*118*	*137*	*155*	***Asie méridionale***
76	82	84	87	92	98	100	107	114	127	138	Bangladesh
100	104	103	91	96	95	97	105	120	143	164	Inde
..	..	..	..	..	99	101	105	115	127	136	Iran (Rép. islamique d')
..	..	..	..	..	100	98	102	110	121	128	Maldives
..	..	..	..	..	97	97	105	117	136	146	Népal
99	95	97	86	93	95	95	104	117	134	148	Pakistan
100	102	100	..	..	99	98	103	113	125	135	Sri Lanka
111	*113*	*107*	*98*	*96*	*98*	*97*	*100*	*106*	*115*	*124*	***Asie du Sud-Est***
..	..	..	..	..	101	101	103	108	113	117	Brunéi Darussalam
..	..	..	..	..	98	97	101	106	113	118	Cambodge
114	112	105	99	98	96	96	103	115	137	153	Indonésie
117	116	107	100	98	98	97	97	102	108	114	Malaisie
70	86	102	102	99	98	98	102	111	123	129	Myanmar
101	106	108	111	104	98	95	96	102	109	113	Philippines
115	114	107	93	93	96	96	99	104	111	119	Singapour
100	111	106	98	95	100	101	105	109	116	124	Thaïlande
..	..	..	..	..	98	97	102	113	127	139	Viet Nam
121	*116*	*107*	*100*	*96*	*100*	*99*	*104*	*113*	*120*	*129*	***Asie occidentale***
..	..	..	..	..	95	96	103	121	150	173	Bahreïn
96	103	101	100	98	98	98	104	115	131	141	Jordanie
..	..	..	..	..	100	100	102	106	112	116	Koweït
..	..	..	..	..	98	97	103	113	127	135	Liban
..	..	..	..	..	100	99	102	110	118	126	Oman
..	..	..	..	..	101	100	102	110	116	121	Qatar
..	..	..	..	..	100	100	102	108	114	121	Arabie saoudite
..	..	..	..	..	99	98	103	113	122	134	République arabe syrienne
122	115	105	101	96	100	98	106	120	128	139	Turquie
..	..	..	..	..	100	100	103	107	113	120	Émirats arabes unis
161	161	176	88	90	99	98	104	113	130	141	Yémen
..	**..**	**..**	**..**	**..**	**98**	**97**	**101**	**109**	**124**	**134**	**Économies en développement : Océanie**
..	..	..	..	..	99	97	102	111	130	142	Fidji
..	..	..	..	..	100	99	101	108	117	122	Polynésie française
..	..	..	..	..	100	98	102	109	122	127	Nouvelle-Calédonie
..	..	..	..	..	100	100	101	105	111	116	Palaos
..	..	..	..	..	98	98	102	112	131	141	Papouasie-Nouvelle-Guinée
..	..	..	..	..	100	97	103	112	129	137	Samoa

Pour les sources et les notes, se reporter à la fin du tableau 4.2.2.

4.2.1 Terms of trade indices and purchasing power indices of exports of countries and geographical regions
2000 = 100

Region, country or territory	Terms of trade (2) - Termes de l'échange (2)										
	1995	1996	1997	1998	1999	2001	2002	2003	2004	2005	2006
WORLD	103	102	103	101	100	100	101	102	102	104	104
DEVELOPING ECONOMIES	102	102	103	100	99	98	98	98	100	105	107
ECONOMIES IN TRANSITION	..	..	..	..	..	97	95	106	118	140	150
DEVELOPED ECONOMIES	105	103	104	105	105	101	102	103	103	102	100
Developing economies: Africa	95	96	94	89	89	97	97	102	114	135	146
Eastern Africa	118	107	110	107	100	96	94	94	97	98	115
Burundi	164	119	110	121	116	84	85	90	95	108	128
Ethiopia	151	115	127	150	125	88	88	91	96	101	101
Kenya	104	108	114	110	98	94	91	90	90	90	87
Madagascar	80	82	85	94	89	89	85	86	82	77	77
Malawi	106	112	117	103	106	101	92	87	84	82	85
Mauritius	88	91	91	94	97	101	99	95	90	87	90
Mozambique	151	115	116	117	118	97	91	91	98	111	131
Rwanda	110	92	131	110	93	98	88	90	91	126	131
Seychelles	103	103	97	110	102	94	91	87	87	93	92
Uganda	197	158	156	139	121	93	93	94	94	99	103
United Republic of Tanzania	98	95	99	98	99	98	101	104	108	102	117
Zambia	190	152	142	113	87	94	91	94	110	122	190
Zimbabwe	97	98	97	97	97	97	98	100	104	95	94
Middle Africa	82	77	82	62	75	90	91	102	122	158	179
Angola	81	87	68	44	60	88	89	101	128	173	198
Cameroon	90	82	87	83	70	96	104	109	118	129	136
Central African Republic	193	167	150	124	107	96	94	97	100	92	92
Congo	52	64	64	39	64	90	90	101	121	159	185
Dem. Rep. of the Congo	80	54	67	66	104	100	97	97	99	114	128
Equatorial Guinea	37	37	37	37	79	88	90	104	128	163	184
Gabon	125	147	146	103	105	89	90	102	120	157	180
Northern Africa	85	89	88	82	84	96	91	102	115	143	147
Algeria	58	68	71	51	59	96	86	109	127	169	168
Egypt	116	111	107	98	97	96	94	99	107	125	120
Libyan Arab Jamahiriya	..	..	..	..	..	87	87	98	120	153	172
Morocco	89	92	95	106	104	101	99	93	91	87	86
Sudan	100	100	100	100	100	92	88	103	122	160	179
Tunisia	96	99	96	96	97	100	101	99	98	96	95
Southern Africa	106	107	107	103	101	104	102	101	108	112	123
Botswana	89	94	98	100	100	99	97	97	98	92	96
Lesotho	100	100	100	100	99	100	100	96	90	86	83
Namibia	83	90	92	95	94	99	99	97	101	104	127
South Africa	106	107	107	104	102	104	103	102	110	115	126
Swaziland	100	100	100	100	100	100	98	95	93	93	95
Western Africa	82	92	82	79	82	94	103	108	119	141	153
Benin	107	94	99	99	100	95	90	103	94	80	82
Burkina Faso	131	123	122	124	112	96	92	107	98	87	91
Cape Verde	100	100	100	100	100	100	100	94	89	103	109
Côte d'Ivoire	122	119	117	117	118	112	143	141	133	132	135
Ghana	107	109	114	124	110	106	134	134	123	122	133
Guinea	90	78	87	80	77	96	102	111	133	141	210
Mali	110	111	107	112	101	98	108	124	120	107	128
Mauritania	102	94	103	103	104	103	104	102	113	164	177
Nigeria	56	87	65	44	60	89	90	98	118	148	161
Senegal	156	166	126	130	115	99	98	98	97	97	100
Togo	99	92	100	115	114	100	99	98	92	82	79
Developing economies: America	99	99	101	96	95	96	97	99	105	112	122
Caribbean	101	96	100	100	102	98	96	101	109	124	128
Aruba	..	..	..	..	..	90	85	99	119	168	160
Barbados	..	..	..	..	..	100	99	102	102	110	115
Cuba	..	..	..	..	..	100	95	97	112	110	143
Dominican Republic	98	96	100	101	102	101	101	98	97	96	95
Haiti	113	102	108	110	109	101	100	99	96	92	89
Montserrat	..	..	..	..	..	97	96	100	96	98	97
Netherlands Antilles	..	..	..	..	..	101	94	97	109	128	131
Saint Kitts and Nevis	..	..	..	..	..	101	97	94	89	83	81
Saint Lucia	..	..	..	..	..	119	117	107	116	118	125
Saint Vincent and the Grenadines	..	..	..	..	..	115	114	101	114	109	114
Trinidad and Tobago	..	..	..	..	..	99	94	107	111	123	114

For sources and notes, see end of table 4.2.2.

Purchasing power (3) - Pouvoir d'achat (3)											Régions, pays ou territoires
1995	1996	1997	1998	1999	2001	2002	2003	2004	2005	2006	
72	76	82	85	90	99	104	112	125	134	145	**MONDE**
64	69	77	76	84	96	104	118	140	157	174	ÉCONOMIES EN DÉVELOPPEMENT
..	..	..	..	..	100	107	130	164	191	227	ÉCONOMIES EN TRANSITION
73	76	83	88	92	100	104	108	117	121	128	ÉCONOMIES DÉVELOPPÉES
64	73	77	67	75	92	97	113	136	162	179	**Économies en développement : Afrique**
82	88	86	94	94	104	119	117	128	128	145	*Afrique orientale*
79	35	72	76	96	78	63	72	85	94	92	Burundi
84	80	116	118	100	95	100	98	124	149	162	Éthiopie
105	123	111	104	97	115	124	131	130	138	133	Kenya
60	60	64	68	72	116	108	100	111	84	90	Madagascar
101	121	135	117	122	121	108	132	113	106	127	Malawi
87	98	88	103	104	90	101	102	100	96	99	Maurice
49	60	60	66	75	204	227	277	367	405	518	Mozambique
100	111	169	131	128	164	127	116	165	191	213	Rwanda
26	67	55	67	69	109	114	130	125	127	131	Seychelles
94	115	121	109	116	102	98	118	138	150	162	Ouganda
104	112	75	71	75	119	135	157	175	172	164	République-Unie de Tanzanie
135	140	120	154	158	112	107	105	156	164	321	Zambie
71	75	68	80	95	64	124	84	88	70	60	Zimbabwe
45	47	61	41	70	93	108	126	172	251	298	*Afrique centrale*
60	62	63	46	62	82	105	117	163	282	355	Angola
85	84	95	110	90	98	101	119	119	129	138	Cameroun
83	70	92	83	81	89	92	75	70	64	73	République centrafricaine
38	45	61	44	60	83	92	104	125	166	226	Congo
65	47	50	37	115	111	141	161	202	218	217	Rép. dém. du Congo
6	10	24	29	65	158	193	256	399	531	623	Guinée équatoriale
97	113	120	76	98	97	93	107	129	182	195	Gabon
61	69	72	60	68	93	93	112	132	166	190	*Afrique septentrionale*
45	57	64	47	55	87	85	106	134	180	199	Algérie
86	84	85	66	79	89	101	127	138	178	210	Égypte
69	83	81	50	55	89	77	103	123	185	238	Jamahiriya arabe libyenne
77	76	88	101	103	98	108	113	115	106	113	Maroc
28	39	31	31	47	95	108	137	194	231	257	Soudan
79	79	84	88	91	115	119	133	151	149	154	Tunisie
80	91	98	88	91	100	101	119	140	144	150	*Afrique australe*
65	83	95	71	96	90	92	99	116	131	125	Botswana
59	74	78	84	74	133	168	214	301	262	273	Lesotho
77	86	82	86	89	90	82	93	129	135	177	Namibie
80	91	98	89	91	100	102	120	140	143	150	Afrique du Sud
83	87	94	104	102	118	115	173	192	181	181	Swaziland
57	74	71	61	66	78	86	101	125	145	150	*Afrique occidentale*
88	112	96	90	96	96	118	133	124	111	102	Bénin
117	97	105	156	126	112	123	151	204	182	216	Burkina Faso
62	96	111	83	92	92	100	112	125	136	152	Cap-Vert
98	106	117	116	121	107	142	149	161	150	150	Côte d'Ivoire
98	95	98	113	110	106	114	150	153	144	180	Ghana
68	65	69	72	67	112	109	88	95	104	99	Guinée
64	65	95	100	103	136	165	165	159	153	200	Mali
102	95	83	81	98	102	98	87	120	164	329	Mauritanie
54	91	74	55	63	68	72	87	118	146	148	Nigéria
96	108	104	114	111	112	120	131	141	128	118	Sénégal
91	103	110	115	109	100	119	158	142	134	144	Togo
59	67	76	78	85	99	99	106	123	138	156	**Économies en développement : Amérique**
64	67	73	74	82	100	87	93	103	111	128	*Caraïbes*
..	..	..	..	..	95	58	78	98	120	118	Aruba
..	..	..	..	..	96	90	90	96	112	113	Barbade
..	..	..	..	..	102	88	97	121	97	121	Cuba
84	90	99	92	86	95	93	94	97	96	96	République dominicaine
38	29	73	104	112	89	90	107	112	125	130	Haïti
..	..	..	..	..	64	128	154	336	99	89	Montserrat
..	..	..	..	..	135	90	57	63	61	61	Antilles néerlandaises
..	..	..	..	..	106	126	108	100	100	97	Saint-Kitts-et-Nevis
..	..	..	..	..	94	135	130	154	112	121	Sainte-Lucie
..	..	..	..	..	88	85	79	64	70	54	Saint-Vincent-et-les Grenadines
..	..	..	..	..	103	93	118	130	164	217	Trinité-et-Tobago

Pour les sources et les notes, se reporter à la fin du tableau 4.2.2.

Region, country or territory	Terms of trade (2) - Termes de l'échange (2)										
	1995	1996	1997	1998	1999	2001	2002	2003	2004	2005	2006
Central America	*95*	*97*	*98*	*96*	*96*	*98*	*98*	*99*	*101*	*103*	*103*
Belize	..	..	..	..	..	108	95	85	87	86	95
Costa Rica	105	99	106	109	107	98	97	95	92	88	86
El Salvador	121	114	114	111	105	102	102	98	97	97	95
Guatemala	118	104	112	111	103	97	96	93	92	91	90
Honduras	96	90	111	113	106	95	92	88	87	87	83
Mexico	92	96	97	94	95	97	98	99	102	104	104
Nicaragua	129	114	109	114	105	88	87	84	82	81	79
Panama	100	102	103	103	106	103	102	97	95	94	91
South America	*101*	*100*	*102*	*97*	*93*	*95*	*96*	*100*	*107*	*117*	*134*
Argentina	92	100	100	95	91	99	99	107	109	107	113
Bolivia	89	100	104	98	98	96	96	99	104	112	135
Brazil	110	108	114	114	103	100	98	97	98	99	104
Chile	136	110	113	100	100	93	97	103	125	140	184
Colombia	87	90	90	83	89	94	92	95	102	111	115
Ecuador	81	89	90	81	86	85	87	90	91	102	110
Guyana	..	..	..	..	..	97	98	97	94	94	109
Paraguay	118	118	118	109	104	100	97	101	104	97	96
Peru	123	119	127	111	103	96	98	102	111	119	151
Suriname	..	..	..	..	..	90	94	105	134	139	195
Uruguay	116	112	111	119	111	104	103	103	100	91	89
Venezuela (Bolivarian Rep. of)	63	73	71	51	68	82	88	99	118	154	184
Developing economies: Asia	**104**	**103**	**104**	**103**	**101**	**99**	**98**	**98**	**98**	**101**	**100**
Eastern Asia	*107*	*106*	*107*	*107*	*105*	*100*	*100*	*97*	*92*	*87*	*83*
China	102	106	110	111	104	102	101	98	92	86	81
China, Hong Kong SAR	99	100	101	102	101	101	102	101	99	98	97
China, Macao SAR	..	..	..	..	..	100	101	99	97	94	94
China, Taiwan Province of	90	97	99	101	103	100	100	97	92	88	83
Mongolia	..	..	..	..	..	98	105	112	128	128	167
Republic of Korea	138	126	122	117	115	95	95	89	85	79	73
Southern Asia	*110*	*104*	*114*	*121*	*107*	*100*	*98*	*96*	*97*	*101*	*99*
Bangladesh	112	111	114	114	109	101	98	91	87	79	74
India	108	99	114	118	105	104	101	96	91	87	83
Iran (Islamic Rep. of)	..	..	..	..	..	90	90	98	114	141	157
Maldives	..	..	..	..	..	101	104	100	100	107	113
Nepal	..	..	..	..	..	102	101	96	91	83	81
Pakistan	119	120	119	136	117	104	104	97	89	82	77
Sri Lanka	99	100	105	..	..	98	96	93	88	83	81
South-Eastern Asia	*105*	*106*	*105*	*100*	*99*	*97*	*96*	*97*	*96*	*95*	*94*
Brunei Darussalam	..	..	..	..	..	97	87	110	125	164	170
Cambodia	..	..	..	..	..	102	103	101	97	92	90
Indonesia	90	97	99	82	66	101	101	105	105	102	100
Malaysia	109	112	111	107	105	99	99	101	101	101	97
Myanmar	214	165	125	116	110	102	95	108	108	117	104
Philippines	80	81	82	87	103	101	100	96	92	86	85
Singapore	104	104	105	104	103	96	94	91	89	87	86
Thailand	116	114	115	108	107	92	92	94	96	97	96
Viet Nam	..	..	..	..	..	96	96	95	95	97	96
Western Asia	*68*	*76*	*78*	*71*	*81*	*96*	*95*	*105*	*117*	*148*	*158*
Bahrain	..	..	..	..	..	97	92	99	105	119	123
Jordan	116	114	113	107	107	101	101	98	93	86	84
Kuwait	..	..	..	..	..	89	87	102	125	169	190
Lebanon	..	..	..	..	..	102	105	105	105	99	102
Oman	..	..	..	..	..	92	91	104	121	155	162
Qatar	..	..	..	..	..	95	84	106	119	156	152
Saudi Arabia	..	..	..	..	..	104	103	115	132	180	204
Syrian Arab Republic	..	..	..	..	..	90	91	98	110	132	133
Turkey	106	107	111	111	109	98	97	99	102	101	96
United Arab Emirates	..	..	..	..	..	92	91	101	116	141	151
Yemen	..	..	..	..	..	88	90	98	115	139	153
Developing economies: Oceania	**..**	**..**	**..**	**..**	**..**	**96**	**101**	**110**	**125**	**130**	**157**
Fiji	..	..	..	..	..	102	98	96	92	95	103
French Polynesia	..	..	..	..	..	100	98	96	94	90	88
New Caledonia	..	..	..	..	..	95	99	104	138	140	171
Palau	..	..	..	..	..	98	96	96	101	108	111
Papua New Guinea	..	..	..	..	..	94	103	115	131	136	163
Samoa	..	..	..	..	..	98	101	95	89	84	84

For sources and notes, see end of table 4.2.2.

	Purchasing power (3) - Pouvoir d'achat (3)										Régions, pays ou territoires
1995	1996	1997	1998	1999	2001	2002	2003	2004	2005	2006	
47	*57*	*67*	*73*	*84*	*98*	*98*	*99*	*107*	*115*	*128*	**Amérique centrale**
..	..	..	..	..	78	80	91	87	75	91	Belize
55	59	70	94	116	90	95	107	104	112	127	Costa Rica
83	83	108	96	92	103	108	109	110	108	107	El Salvador
75	70	88	99	93	95	95	98	101	109	108	Guatemala
81	90	103	115	89	112	112	108	116	117	123	Honduras
45	56	65	71	82	98	98	99	107	116	130	Mexique
81	78	90	94	91	94	89	93	107	111	124	Nicaragua
76	88	88	94	101	109	100	100	104	107	104	Panama
72	*78*	*88*	*84*	*86*	*100*	*103*	*115*	*142*	*166*	*191*	**Amérique du Sud**
67	78	92	96	88	104	103	119	129	145	164	Argentine
79	83	90	88	87	106	107	128	160	195	250	Bolivie
80	80	93	95	92	109	117	134	161	177	193	Brésil
80	78	93	90	98	100	104	121	169	197	264	Chili
73	75	81	81	90	98	96	102	118	145	160	Colombie
81	94	102	85	93	96	104	125	148	177	205	Équateur
..	..	..	..	..	99	102	99	102	81	81	Guyana
114	129	135	117	88	121	117	148	181	178	192	Paraguay
74	78	95	84	92	105	115	130	167	200	266	Pérou
..	..	..	..	..	81	95	123	160	153	188	Suriname
87	99	113	123	105	96	92	103	124	127	135	Uruguay
52	67	66	53	63	80	81	80	109	147	168	Venezuela (Rép. bolivarienne du)
66	**70**	**77**	**77**	**85**	**96**	**106**	**122**	**145**	**161**	**178**	**Économies en développement : Asie**
68	*71*	*81*	*82*	*87*	*98*	*113*	*133*	*158*	*174*	*196*	**Asie orientale**
58	60	75	78	81	109	135	176	221	259	307	Chine
78	81	87	85	86	97	107	119	134	146	159	Chine (RAS de Hong Kong)
..	..	..	..	..	91	93	99	104	86	86	Chine (RAS de Macao)
85	87	92	82	91	85	91	98	109	113	117	Province chinoise de Taiwan
..	..	..	..	..	99	100	111	144	152	205	Mongolie
62	67	75	88	96	96	108	118	137	141	150	République de Corée
72	*80*	*78*	*79*	*86*	*99*	*110*	*122*	*137*	*152*	*154*	**Asie méridionale**
77	76	90	92	93	97	96	103	111	114	134	Bangladesh
72	75	80	87	88	108	123	133	150	165	174	Inde
..	..	..	..	..	85	98	114	136	166	164	Iran (Rép. islamique d')
..	..	..	..	..	102	124	138	152	122	162	Maldives
..	..	..	..	..	95	73	78	81	76	65	Népal
89	109	100	109	100	108	115	127	126	133	126	Pakistan
70	74	85	..	..	90	88	91	94	94	94	Sri Lanka
68	*70*	*77*	*78*	*87*	*92*	*97*	*105*	*124*	*131*	*143*	**Asie du Sud-Est**
..	..	..	..	..	93	94	110	120	142	171	Brunéi Darussalam
..	..	..	..	..	114	130	147	175	184	224	Cambodge
64	72	82	79	80	91	94	95	95	96	99	Indonésie
64	69	75	75	88	91	98	104	125	132	143	Malaisie
75	53	52	64	70	148	189	148	130	189	213	Myanmar
44	48	58	67	88	84	96	94	98	92	106	Philippines
75	80	85	86	89	92	95	106	139	151	165	Singapour
82	73	78	80	89	94	98	111	128	138	153	Thaïlande
..	..	..	..	..	107	118	136	162	177	197	Viet Nam
48	*58*	*65*	*56*	*74*	*94*	*98*	*116*	*144*	*181*	*204*	**Asie occidentale**
..	..	..	..	..	95	98	104	101	110	114	Bahreïn
97	93	96	95	98	123	149	156	179	173	193	Jordanie
..	..	..	..	..	83	79	105	139	207	254	Koweït
..	..	..	..	..	156	178	247	272	258	292	Liban
..	..	..	..	..	98	99	101	107	140	152	Oman
..	..	..	..	..	88	96	114	146	191	246	Qatar
..	..	..	..	..	87	94	118	150	204	229	Arabie saoudite
..	..	..	..	..	115	144	120	103	114	176	République arabe syrienne
64	73	90	96	100	113	126	158	186	202	212	Turquie
..	..	..	..	..	98	104	131	170	208	238	Émirats arabes unis
30	41	35	42	66	83	90	93	101	121	127	Yémen
..	**..**	**..**	**..**	**..**	**87**	**86**	**109**	**115**	**116**	**131**	**Économies en développement : Océanie**
..	..	..	..	..	100	99	122	116	100	89	Fidji
..	..	..	..	..	75	69	61	70	74	79	Polynésie française
..	..	..	..	..	74	84	128	155	149	175	Nouvelle-Calédonie
..	..	..	..	..	..	..	..	..	..	..	Palaos
..	..	..	..	..	88	80	103	108	119	141	Papouasie-Nouvelle-Guinée
..	..	..	..	..	109	99	103	67	65	55	Samoa

Pour les sources et les notes, se reporter à la fin du tableau 4.2.2.

4

4.2.2 Volume indices of exports and imports of economic groupings
2000 = 100

Economic grouping	Exports (1) - Exportations (1)										
	1995	1996	1997	1998	1999	2001	2002	2003	2004	2005	2006
DEVELOPING ECONOMIES	63	68	75	76	85	98	106	120	140	149	163
Developing economies excluding China	64	70	76	77	86	97	103	112	127	129	137
Developing economies excluding LDCs	63	68	75	76	85	98	106	120	140	149	163
High-income developing countries	64	72	78	78	85	96	101	111	127	130	137
Middle-income developing countries	67	69	75	76	86	100	108	119	133	137	145
Low-income developing countries	58	61	70	73	83	100	116	140	173	200	233
Heavily indebted poor countries	66	73	80	81	91	106	107	117	134	129	130
Landlocked developing countries	55	64	70	77	86	105	114	124	144	142	150
Small island developing States	95	98	88	81	86	97	94	101	100	103	120
Least developed countries	*52*	*60*	*68*	*64*	*84*	*106*	*120*	*124*	*139*	*145*	*153*
Africa and Haiti	53	64	71	66	89	110	127	133	155	162	168
Asia	57	61	66	63	75	102	110	112	118	126	144
Islands	117	116	124	108	99	95	107	125	134	114	131
Major petroleum exporters	*82*	*84*	*91*	*99*	*98*	*94*	*99*	*102*	*112*	*113*	*117*
Africa	74	78	87	89	88	90	95	101	109	116	122
America	81	88	96	98	94	99	96	91	102	106	109
Asia	87	88	94	109	103	94	100	105	114	114	117
Major exporters of manufactured goods	*62*	*66*	*74*	*77*	*84*	*99*	*109*	*127*	*154*	*175*	*201*
America	54	62	70	77	87	103	105	109	120	128	139
Asia	64	67	74	77	84	98	110	130	161	184	213
Emerging economies	*61*	*66*	*73*	*78*	*86*	*97*	*103*	*113*	*134*	*145*	*158*
America	56	64	73	80	89	103	105	110	122	130	137
Asia	64	67	74	77	85	94	102	115	140	153	172
Newly industrialized economies	*66*	*70*	*77*	*79*	*87*	*94*	*102*	*113*	*134*	*145*	*161*
First tier	68	73	79	80	86	94	103	117	142	157	175
Second tier	63	63	71	77	89	93	99	103	115	120	133
Developing economies: Africa	67	76	82	75	84	95	100	110	120	120	122
Northern Africa excluding Sudan	73	79	84	74	82	97	101	109	114	116	128
Sub-Saharan Africa	66	76	82	77	86	94	100	111	123	122	119
Sub-Saharan Africa excluding South Africa	62	72	78	74	85	93	100	108	122	122	121
Developing economies: America	60	68	76	81	89	102	103	107	117	123	128
Central America and Greater Carribean Islands excluding Puerto Rico	51	60	68	77	87	100	100	100	106	111	122
Central America and Greater Carribean Islands excluding Mexico and Puerto Rico	63	71	78	87	95	97	98	105	107	108	107
South America and Central America	59	68	76	81	89	102	104	108	119	125	130
South America excluding Brazil	70	80	89	92	95	103	102	105	117	124	124
Developing economies: Asia	63	67	74	75	84	97	108	124	148	160	178
Eastern and South-Eastern Asia excluding China	66	69	76	79	87	94	102	113	134	145	161
Southern Asia excluding India	65	76	69	58	77	95	105	116	121	120	114

For sources and notes, see end of table 4.2.2.

	Imports (1) - Importations (1)										Groupements économiques
1995	1996	1997	1998	1999	2001	2002	2003	2004	2005	2006	
72	**77**	**85**	**81**	**86**	**98**	**105**	**118**	**140**	**152**	**165**	**ÉCONOMIES EN DÉVELOPPEMENT**
74	79	88	83	87	96	100	109	128	139	150	Économies en développement sans la Chine
72	77	85	81	86	98	104	118	140	151	165	Économies en développement sans les PMA
71	77	86	82	87	95	98	106	123	134	146	Pays en développement à revenu élevé
84	87	94	89	88	97	102	112	132	141	156	Pays en développement à revenu intermédiaire
65	70	75	74	81	106	122	150	182	199	216	Pays en développement à revenu faible
69	75	81	85	101	110	117	128	145	161	176	Pays pauvres très endettés
75	87	91	98	93	109	115	129	157	169	196	Pays en développement sans littoral
68	75	83	89	92	101	104	108	114	115	123	Petits États insulaires en développement
69	*71*	*77*	*83*	*97*	*111*	*116*	*132*	*147*	*163*	*176*	*Pays les moins avancés*
68	71	77	80	97	112	121	144	166	193	207	Afrique et Haïti
77	77	79	93	98	109	111	118	124	127	139	Asie
65	68	81	85	98	106	104	114	129	133	146	Îles
73	*77*	*87*	*90*	*89*	*111*	*117*	*132*	*163*	*193*	*205*	*Principaux exportateurs de pétrole*
99	101	108	108	97	120	138	162	194	231	236	Afrique
72	65	94	103	86	117	96	89	118	147	183	Amérique
46	50	49	96	100	107	117	133	164	193	202	Asie
70	*75*	*82*	*77*	*84*	*96*	*105*	*119*	*141*	*150*	*165*	*Principaux exportateurs d'articles manufacturés*
51	59	72	80	84	100	96	94	106	113	126	Amérique
75	79	85	76	84	96	106	124	148	158	173	Asie
73	*78*	*86*	*79*	*86*	*93*	*94*	*100*	*117*	*126*	*137*	*Économies émergentes*
55	65	79	86	87	98	91	92	106	115	129	Amérique
81	85	90	75	86	90	96	104	123	132	142	Asie
82	*85*	*91*	*77*	*84*	*92*	*99*	*107*	*124*	*133*	*142*	*Économies nouvellement industrialisées*
79	83	90	79	86	91	98	107	124	132	143	Première génération
90	92	94	71	79	94	101	107	124	135	141	Deuxième génération
85	**87**	**94**	**98**	**97**	**105**	**111**	**129**	**150**	**165**	**176**	**Économies en développement : Afrique**
92	91	94	104	98	101	108	112	134	145	148	Afrique septentrionale sans le Soudan
81	85	94	94	97	106	113	139	160	176	192	Afrique subsaharienne
76	80	87	92	100	111	120	140	157	178	186	Afrique subsaharienne sans l'Afrique du Sud
60	**67**	**81**	**89**	**88**	**100**	**93**	**94**	**108**	**119**	**134**	**Économies en développement : Amérique**
43	53	64	75	84	100	99	99	107	115	127	Amérique centrale et Grandes Antilles sans Porto Rico
62	65	76	89	95	105	107	106	110	120	132	Amérique centrale et Grandes Antilles sans le Mexique et Porto Rico
60	67	82	90	88	100	93	95	109	120	137	Amérique du Sud et Amérique centrale
83	88	110	115	95	99	81	89	112	137	162	Amérique du Sud sans le Brésil
75	**79**	**85**	**78**	**84**	**97**	**107**	**124**	**148**	**160**	**173**	**Économies en développement : Asie**
81	85	91	77	84	93	99	108	125	134	143	Asie orientale et Asie du Sud-Est sans la Chine
92	102	99	102	99	108	123	136	153	165	176	Asie méridionale sans l'Inde

Pour les sources et les notes, se reporter à la fin du tableau 4.2.2.

4

4.2.2 Unit value indices of exports and imports of economic groupings
2000 = 100

Economic grouping	Exports - Exportations										
	1995	1996	1997	1998	1999	2001	2002	2003	2004	2005	2006
DEVELOPING ECONOMIES	**110**	**110**	**107**	**98**	**95**	**95**	**94**	**98**	**107**	**123**	**135**
Developing economies excluding China	111	110	106	97	95	95	93	98	109	129	143
Developing economies excluding LDCs	110	110	106	98	95	95	94	98	107	122	133
High-income developing countries	111	108	104	94	94	94	93	97	106	125	139
Middle-income developing countries	117	119	115	104	99	96	94	100	113	131	143
Low-income developing countries	104	105	106	99	95	97	97	99	106	116	123
Heavily indebted poor countries	136	129	121	119	102	95	103	111	124	151	183
Landlocked developing countries	152	142	137	111	102	95	94	106	125	158	196
Small island developing States	89	89	93	92	96	96	95	108	126	159	182
Least developed countries	*129*	*122*	*112*	*110*	*94*	*94*	*93*	*102*	*121*	*157*	*186*
Africa and Haiti	139	128	115	113	91	92	91	103	125	169	206
Asia	97	99	101	102	102	97	95	101	111	131	139
Islands	113	108	107	109	120	95	99	102	111	124	136
Major petroleum exporters	*68*	*79*	*74*	*51*	*67*	*93*	*92*	*107*	*133*	*184*	*215*
Africa	71	84	77	53	65	91	88	106	135	189	217
America	74	83	77	58	71	84	87	100	123	166	197
Asia	64	76	71	46	66	95	94	109	134	185	217
Major exporters of manufactured goods	*114*	*113*	*110*	*102*	*99*	*96*	*94*	*95*	*100*	*104*	*108*
America	105	105	105	99	96	95	96	99	107	117	126
Asia	116	115	111	102	100	96	94	95	99	102	105
Emerging economies	*119*	*117*	*111*	*100*	*97*	*94*	*92*	*94*	*101*	*107*	*115*
America	110	108	107	99	95	95	95	99	110	121	138
Asia	122	120	113	100	98	93	91	92	97	101	104
Newly industrialized economies	*117*	*116*	*110*	*99*	*97*	*95*	*92*	*94*	*98*	*102*	*105*
First tier	118	115	109	100	98	94	91	91	94	97	99
Second tier	114	120	112	99	95	96	95	100	107	116	121
Developing economies: Africa	**109**	**108**	**103**	**93**	**90**	**95**	**95**	**106**	**126**	**165**	**192**
Northern Africa excluding Sudan	92	97	93	85	87	95	91	107	128	174	192
Sub-Saharan Africa	115	112	106	96	91	95	97	105	125	161	191
Sub-Saharan Africa excluding South Africa	109	111	102	93	87	92	96	106	127	169	201
Developing economies: America	**105**	**105**	**104**	**96**	**93**	**94**	**94**	**99**	**111**	**127**	**146**
Central America and Greater Carribean Islands excluding Puerto Rico	100	100	100	96	96	95	96	99	107	115	121
Central America and Greater Carribean Islands excluding Mexico and Puerto Rico	111	105	108	106	101	95	93	95	103	110	124
South America and Central America	105	105	104	96	93	93	94	98	111	126	145
South America excluding Brazil	105	104	101	87	86	90	90	98	118	143	178
Developing economies: Asia	**112**	**111**	**108**	**99**	**96**	**96**	**94**	**97**	**105**	**118**	**126**
Eastern and South-Eastern Asia excluding China	117	116	110	99	97	95	92	94	98	103	107
Southern Asia excluding India	105	106	107	110	104	94	94	101	120	154	175

For sources and notes, see end of table 4.2.2.

218

Imports - Importations											Groupements économiques
1995	1996	1997	1998	1999	2001	2002	2003	2004	2005	2006	
108	**108**	**104**	**98**	**96**	**97**	**96**	**100**	**108**	**117**	**126**	**ÉCONOMIES EN DÉVELOPPEMENT**
109	109	104	98	96	97	96	100	107	117	125	Économies en développement sans la Chine
108	108	103	97	96	97	96	100	107	117	126	Économies en développement sans les PMA
109	107	103	96	95	97	95	98	104	111	118	Pays en développement à revenu élevé
110	111	106	100	97	98	98	102	110	119	127	Pays en développement à revenu intermédiaire
105	105	103	98	98	97	97	101	110	123	134	Pays en développement à revenu faible
119	123	113	114	100	97	97	102	110	122	131	Pays pauvres très endettés
118	123	116	103	100	99	98	103	111	123	130	Pays en développement sans littoral
115	118	115	103	102	99	98	103	111	128	139	Petits États insulaires en développement
112	*119*	*113*	*110*	*99*	*98*	*99*	*104*	*111*	*122*	*131*	*Pays les moins avancés*
123	129	119	121	102	99	99	103	111	121	128	Afrique et Haïti
89	98	104	90	93	98	99	105	112	125	134	Asie
144	144	127	117	112	99	97	101	110	124	132	Îles
111	*107*	*107*	*102*	*102*	*100*	*100*	*103*	*110*	*118*	*126*	*Principaux exportateurs de pétrole*
108	103	104	103	104	100	100	104	110	119	126	Afrique
111	108	104	101	99	99	99	101	109	117	123	Amérique
161	161	176	88	90	100	100	103	110	118	126	Asie
108	*108*	*103*	*97*	*96*	*97*	*95*	*99*	*107*	*116*	*124*	*Principaux exportateurs d'articles manufacturés*
106	105	103	99	99	97	98	100	107	114	120	Amérique
108	108	103	96	95	97	95	99	107	116	125	Asie
108	*108*	*103*	*95*	*94*	*96*	*95*	*99*	*106*	*114*	*122*	*Économies émergentes*
107	106	103	99	98	97	97	100	106	113	119	Amérique
108	109	102	93	92	96	94	99	106	115	123	Asie
109	*109*	*104*	*96*	*95*	*96*	*94*	*97*	*104*	*112*	*119*	*Économies nouvellement industrialisées*
109	108	103	95	93	96	93	96	103	110	117	Première génération
109	112	107	101	98	98	98	100	107	117	125	Deuxième génération
114	**113**	**109**	**105**	**101**	**98**	**99**	**103**	**111**	**122**	**131**	**Économies en développement : Afrique**
109	110	105	104	103	99	100	105	112	123	132	Afrique septentrionale sans le Soudan
117	115	112	106	100	98	98	103	111	122	131	Afrique subsaharienne
118	120	116	111	101	98	98	103	111	123	132	Afrique subsaharienne sans l'Afrique du Sud
107	**106**	**103**	**100**	**98**	**97**	**97**	**100**	**106**	**114**	**120**	**Économies en développement : Amérique**
105	103	102	100	99	97	98	100	106	112	118	Amérique centrale et Grandes Antilles sans Porto Rico
102	103	101	98	96	96	95	99	106	116	123	Amérique centrale et Grandes Antilles sans le Mexique et Porto Rico
107	106	103	100	98	97	97	99	106	113	119	Amérique du Sud et Amérique centrale
109	109	105	101	97	97	95	97	104	111	117	Amérique du Sud sans le Brésil
108	**108**	**103**	**96**	**95**	**97**	**96**	**99**	**107**	**117**	**126**	**Économies en développement : Asie**
109	109	104	96	95	96	94	97	104	112	120	Asie orientale et Asie du Sud-Est sans la Chine
93	93	94	86	93	98	99	105	115	129	139	Asie méridionale sans l'Inde

Pour les sources et les notes, se reporter à la fin du tableau 4.2.2.

4.2.2 Terms of trade indices and purchasing power indices
of exports of economic groupings
2000 = 100

Economic grouping	Terms of trade (2) - Termes de l'échange (2)										
	1995	1996	1997	1998	1999	2001	2002	2003	2004	2005	2006
DEVELOPING ECONOMIES	**102**	**102**	**103**	**100**	**99**	**98**	**98**	**98**	**100**	**105**	**107**
Developing economies excluding China	102	102	102	99	98	98	97	99	102	110	114
Developing economies excluding LDCs	102	102	103	100	99	98	98	99	100	105	106
High-income developing countries	101	101	101	98	99	98	98	99	102	112	118
Middle-income developing countries	107	107	108	104	102	97	96	98	102	110	112
Low-income developing countries	99	100	103	102	97	100	100	98	96	94	92
Heavily indebted poor countries	114	105	107	104	102	98	106	109	112	124	140
Landlocked developing countries	128	116	118	108	102	96	95	103	113	129	150
Small island developing States	77	76	80	89	95	98	97	105	113	124	131
Least developed countries	*116*	*102*	*98*	*100*	*95*	*95*	*94*	*99*	*109*	*129*	*143*
Africa and Haiti	113	99	97	93	89	93	93	100	114	140	160
Asia	109	101	97	113	109	98	97	97	99	104	104
Islands	78	75	84	93	107	96	101	101	101	100	103
Major petroleum exporters	*61*	*74*	*69*	*50*	*65*	*93*	*92*	*104*	*121*	*156*	*171*
Africa	65	82	74	52	63	91	88	102	122	159	172
America	67	76	74	57	71	85	88	98	113	142	161
Asia	40	47	40	52	73	95	94	105	122	157	172
Major exporters of manufactured goods	*106*	*105*	*107*	*105*	*104*	*99*	*99*	*96*	*94*	*90*	*87*
America	99	100	103	100	97	98	98	98	101	103	105
Asia	107	106	107	106	105	99	99	96	93	88	84
Emerging economies	*110*	*108*	*108*	*105*	*103*	*97*	*97*	*95*	*95*	*94*	*94*
America	102	102	104	100	97	98	98	99	104	107	116
Asia	113	110	110	108	107	97	96	94	91	88	84
Newly industrialized economies	*107*	*106*	*106*	*103*	*103*	*98*	*98*	*96*	*94*	*91*	*88*
First tier	108	106	106	105	105	98	98	95	92	88	85
Second tier	105	107	106	98	97	98	98	99	100	99	97
Developing economies: Africa	**95**	**96**	**94**	**89**	**89**	**97**	**97**	**102**	**114**	**135**	**146**
Northern Africa excluding Sudan	85	89	88	82	84	96	91	102	114	141	146
Sub-Saharan Africa	98	98	95	91	91	97	99	102	113	132	146
Sub-Saharan Africa excluding South Africa	93	92	89	84	86	94	98	103	114	138	152
Developing economies: America	**99**	**99**	**101**	**96**	**95**	**96**	**97**	**99**	**105**	**112**	**122**
Central America and Greater Carribean Islands excluding Puerto Rico	95	97	98	96	96	98	98	99	101	102	103
Central America and Greater Carribean Islands excluding Mexico and Puerto Rico	108	102	107	107	105	99	98	96	97	95	101
South America and Central America	99	99	101	96	95	96	97	99	104	111	122
South America excluding Brazil	96	96	96	87	88	92	94	101	113	129	153
Developing economies: Asia	**104**	**103**	**104**	**103**	**101**	**99**	**98**	**98**	**98**	**101**	**100**
Eastern and South-Eastern Asia excluding China	107	106	106	103	103	98	98	96	94	92	89
Southern Asia excluding India	114	114	114	127	113	96	95	96	104	120	126

Sources:
- UN, Economic Commission for Latin America and the Caribbean (ECLAC)
- IMF, *International Financial Statistics (IFS)*
- USA BLS external trade prices indices
- Unit value indices of Japan Customs
- UNCTAD *Commodity Price Statistics* on line

Notes:

(1) The volume index is the percentage ratio of the export or import value index to the corresponding unit value index.

(2) The terms of trade or "net barter" terms of trade is the percentage ratio of the export unit value index to the import unit value index.
(3) The purchasing power index of exports is the value index of exports deflated by the import unit value index.

Purchasing power (3) - Pouvoir d'achat (3)											Groupements économiques
1995	1996	1997	1998	1999	2001	2002	2003	2004	2005	2006	
64	**69**	**77**	**76**	**84**	**96**	**104**	**118**	**140**	**157**	**174**	**ÉCONOMIES EN DÉVELOPPEMENT**
65	71	78	76	84	94	100	110	129	143	156	Économies en développement sans la Chine
64	70	77	76	84	96	104	118	140	156	174	Économies en développement sans les PMA
65	72	78	76	84	94	99	110	130	146	162	Pays en développement à revenu élevé
71	74	81	79	88	97	104	117	136	150	163	Pays en développement à revenu intermédiaire
57	61	72	74	81	101	117	138	166	188	215	Pays en développement à revenu faible
75	77	85	84	93	104	114	127	150	159	182	Pays pauvres très endettés
70	74	82	83	87	101	108	127	162	183	226	Pays en développement sans littoral
73	74	71	73	81	95	92	106	113	128	157	Petits États insulaires en développement
60	*62*	*67*	*64*	*80*	*101*	*113*	*123*	*151*	*187*	*219*	*Pays les moins avancés*
60	63	69	62	79	102	118	133	176	227	270	Afrique et Haïti
62	62	65	71	82	100	106	108	116	131	149	Asie
92	87	104	100	106	92	109	126	134	114	135	Îles
50	*63*	*63*	*49*	*64*	*87*	*91*	*106*	*135*	*177*	*201*	*Principaux exportateurs de pétrole*
48	64	64	46	55	82	84	103	134	185	210	Afrique
54	67	72	56	66	84	85	89	116	151	175	Amérique
35	41	38	57	75	90	94	111	139	179	202	Asie
66	*70*	*78*	*81*	*87*	*97*	*108*	*122*	*144*	*157*	*174*	*Principaux exportateurs d'articles manufacturés*
54	62	72	77	84	101	102	107	121	132	146	Amérique
68	71	80	82	88	97	109	125	149	162	179	Asie
67	*71*	*79*	*81*	*89*	*94*	*99*	*108*	*127*	*136*	*149*	*Économies émergentes*
57	65	76	80	86	101	102	109	126	139	159	Amérique
72	74	81	83	91	91	98	107	128	134	144	Asie
71	*74*	*81*	*82*	*89*	*92*	*100*	*109*	*126*	*132*	*142*	*Économies nouvellement industrialisées*
73	77	84	84	90	93	101	111	130	138	148	Première génération
66	67	75	75	86	91	97	102	115	119	129	Deuxième génération
64	**73**	**77**	**67**	**75**	**92**	**97**	**113**	**136**	**162**	**179**	**Économies en développement : Afrique**
62	70	74	61	69	93	92	111	130	163	187	Afrique septentrionale sans le Soudan
65	74	78	70	78	91	99	114	140	161	174	Afrique subsaharienne
58	66	69	62	73	87	98	111	139	168	184	Afrique subsaharienne sans l'Afrique du Sud
59	**67**	**76**	**78**	**85**	**99**	**99**	**106**	**123**	**138**	**156**	**Économies en développement : Amérique**
48	58	67	73	84	98	98	99	107	114	126	Amérique centrale et Grandes Antilles sans Porto Rico
68	72	84	93	99	96	96	100	104	102	108	Amérique centrale et Grandes Antilles sans le Mexique et Porto Rico
59	67	77	78	85	99	100	107	124	140	159	Amérique du Sud et Amérique centrale
67	77	85	79	83	95	96	106	133	160	190	Amérique du Sud sans le Brésil
66	**70**	**77**	**77**	**85**	**96**	**106**	**122**	**145**	**161**	**178**	**Économies en développement : Asie**
71	74	81	81	89	93	100	109	126	133	143	Asie orientale et Asie du Sud-Est sans la Chine
74	87	79	74	87	91	100	112	126	144	143	Asie méridionale sans l'Inde

Sources :
- ONU, Commission Économique pour l'Amérique latine et les Caraïbes (CEPALC)
- FMI, *International Financial Statistics (IFS)*
- USA BLS external trade prices indices
- Unit value indices of Japan Customs
- CNUCED, *Statistiques des prix des produits de base* en ligne

Notes :

(1) L'Indice de volume des exportations ou des importations est le rapport de l'indice de la valeur des exportations ou des importations à l'indice de la valeur unitaire correspondant exprimé en pourcentage.
(2) Le terme de l'échange, appelé aussi "troc net", est le rapport de l'indice de la valeur unitaire des exportations à l'indice de la valeur unitaire des importations exprimé en pourcentage.
(3) Le pouvoir d'achat des exportations est l'indice de la valeur des exportations corrigé par l'indice de la valeur unitaire des importations.

Market / Marchés	Year / Année	MFN rate - Simple average (2) / Droit NPF - Moyenne simple (2)						MFN rate - Weighted average (3) / Droit NPF - Moyenne pondérée (3)					
		Total of non-agricultural and non-fuel products / Total des produits non-agricoles et non-pétroliers	Ores and metals / Minérais et métaux	Manufactured products / Produits manufacturés	Chemical products / Produits chimiques	Machinery and transport equipment / Machines et matériel de transport	Other manufactured products / Produits manufacturés divers	Total of non-agricultural and non-fuel products / Total des produits non-agricoles et non-pétroliers	Ores and metals / Minérais et métaux	Manufactured products / Produits manufacturés	Chemical products / Produits chimiques	Machinery and transport equipment / Machines et matériel de transport	Other manufactured products / Produits manufacturés divers
SITC Rev.2 (1) / CTCI Rév.2 (1)		5+6+7+8 +27+28	27+28+68	(5+6+7+8) - 68	5	7	(6+8) - 68	5+6+7+8 +27+28	27+28+68	(5+6+7+8) - 68	5	7	(6+8) - 68
Albania - Albanie	1997	16.1	12.2	16.3	12.4	8.9	21.0	15.2	15.1	15.2	12.3	9.8	18.7
	2001	10.5	8.3	10.6	7.6	6.0	13.7	11.6	9.5	11.6	8.1	7.2	15.0
	2002	7.2	5.1	7.3	3.8	3.5	10.2	8.6	7.9	8.7	4.8	3.9	11.8
	2005	5.8	2.5	6.1	2.0	2.5	9.1	7.4	0.9	7.6	2.9	4.2	10.7
Algeria - Algérie	1993	24.4	12.1	25.2	13.2	16.8	33.2	18.7	11.5	18.9	13.7	16.5	24.3
	1997	23.5	11.5	24.3	15.5	17.3	30.6	19.4	12.1	19.5	10.0	18.3	25.7
	1998	23.3	11.4	24.1	15.1	17.1	30.4	18.6	12.1	18.7	9.0	17.2	26.0
	2001	21.7	11.4	22.4	13.8	16.8	28.0	17.2	12.7	17.3	9.2	17.0	21.9
	2002	18.6	12.3	19.1	15.7	12.2	23.2	13.1	13.8	13.1	11.6	11.5	16.2
	2003	18.1	11.9	18.6	14.3	11.9	23.0	12.5	10.9	12.5	8.5	11.3	16.5
	2005	18.1	11.9	18.6	14.3	11.8	23.0	12.5	9.6	12.5	8.6	11.7	16.4
	2006	18.1	11.9	18.6	14.3	11.8	23.0	12.5	9.6	12.5	8.6	11.7	16.4
Angola	2002	8.0	9.5	7.9	4.8	3.8	10.9	5.8	6.4	5.8	7.0	4.1	8.7
	2005	6.4	7.2	6.3	4.7	3.0	8.4	5.0	6.5	5.0	7.6	2.8	9.9
	2006	6.4	7.2	6.3	4.7	3.0	8.4	5.0	6.5	5.0	7.6	2.8	9.9
Antigua and Barbuda - Antigua-et-Barbuda	1996	20.6	16.0	20.7	14.5	20.6	21.6	25.0	13.6	25.1	19.1	31.0	20.7
	1999	17.2	12.8	17.2	11.3	17.9	18.0	22.1	11.4	22.2	14.7	29.8	16.4
	2000	10.1	4.3	10.4	6.3	8.9	12.7	15.3	10.0	15.4	16.0	13.6	17.2
	2001	8.6	3.9	8.9	5.7	8.0	10.5	12.4	7.8	12.5	12.4	12.0	13.1
	2002	8.6	3.9	8.9	5.7	8.0	10.5	12.4	7.8	12.5	12.4	12.0	13.1
	2003	8.6	3.9	8.9	5.7	8.0	10.5	13.9	6.4	13.9	12.7	14.5	13.6
	2006	8.6	3.9	9.0	5.7	7.9	10.6	13.5	6.4	13.5	8.8	14.5	13.6
Argentina - Argentine	1992	13.8	8.1	14.2	9.4	13.6	16.3	13.5	6.5	13.7	8.5	14.5	15.2
	1993	12.5	6.0	12.9	7.6	14.6	14.2	13.4	5.2	13.6	7.7	14.7	14.5
	1995	12.7	6.5	13.1	8.3	9.9	16.3	12.0	5.9	12.2	8.9	11.3	16.1
	1996	13.5	6.3	13.9	8.3	13.4	16.3	14.2	5.8	14.4	8.8	15.5	16.5
	1997	13.6	6.3	14.1	8.3	14.5	16.1	14.7	6.0	14.9	9.3	16.1	16.2
	1998	15.9	9.1	16.4	11.3	15.2	18.8	16.3	8.5	16.5	12.4	16.8	18.5
	1999	15.8	9.1	16.2	11.4	14.9	18.6	15.3	8.6	15.4	12.5	15.2	17.9
	2000	15.7	9.0	16.1	11.4	14.7	18.5	15.1	8.2	15.3	12.4	15.0	17.9
	2001	13.0	8.5	13.3	11.0	14.5	13.6	14.1	7.3	14.3	12.1	15.4	14.3
	2002	14.5	7.3	15.0	9.7	15.0	16.9	12.7	5.1	13.1	10.9	13.9	15.3
	2003	15.2	5.9	15.8	8.3	14.0	19.5	13.6	4.0	14.1	9.5	16.1	16.2
	2004	12.7	7.0	13.1	9.0	8.8	16.5	12.9	4.8	13.2	9.5	14.2	15.0
	2005	11.6	5.8	12.0	8.0	8.5	15.1	12.5	4.0	12.8	8.5	14.3	13.6
	2006	11.6	5.8	12.0	7.9	8.4	15.0	12.5	4.0	12.8	8.4	14.3	13.6
Armenia - Arménie	2001	2.2	0.0	2.4	0.1	1.4	3.7	1.5	0.0	1.6	0.0	2.1	1.8
	2006	2.1	0.4	2.3	0.0	1.9	3.3	2.3	0.1	2.4	0.0	3.4	2.5
Australia - Australie	1991	13.6	2.6	14.4	5.0	11.5	19.1	11.7	5.1	11.8	5.5	9.9	16.8
	1993	10.1	2.4	10.7	4.4	9.3	13.6	10.0	4.9	10.1	5.0	9.4	13.0
	1996	6.5	1.2	6.8	1.9	4.0	9.9	5.4	2.2	5.5	1.8	4.5	8.6
	1997	6.1	1.2	6.5	1.9	4.0	9.3	5.4	2.2	5.4	1.9	4.6	8.1
	1998	5.8	1.2	6.1	1.9	3.9	8.6	5.2	2.1	5.2	1.8	4.5	7.7
	1999	5.5	1.2	5.8	1.9	3.9	8.0	4.9	2.4	4.9	1.8	4.2	7.4
	2000	5.2	1.2	5.4	1.9	3.9	7.5	4.7	2.4	4.7	1.7	4.2	7.1
	2001	4.8	1.1	5.1	1.5	3.2	7.2	4.5	2.3	4.5	1.7	3.9	6.8
	2002	4.9	1.0	5.1	1.5	3.2	7.3	4.6	2.2	4.6	1.7	4.0	6.9
	2003	4.9	1.0	5.1	1.5	3.2	7.3	4.7	2.2	4.7	1.7	4.2	6.9
	2004	4.9	1.0	5.1	1.5	3.2	7.3	4.7	2.5	4.7	1.6	4.2	6.9
	2005	4.0	1.0	4.2	1.5	3.0	5.8	3.8	2.6	3.8	1.5	3.4	5.6
	2006	4.0	1.0	4.2	1.4	3.0	5.7	3.8	2.6	3.8	1.5	3.4	5.6
Azerbaijan - Azerbaïdjan	2002	8.3	4.4	8.5	3.9	5.2	11.7	6.9	3.4	7.0	6.0	4.0	10.6
	2005	8.6	4.3	8.9	4.0	6.0	11.8	5.8	2.1	6.0	5.5	2.8	10.8
Bahamas	1999	32.1	34.3	32.0	34.0	35.6	29.7	32.1	28.7	32.1	26.9	38.5	27.6
	2002	31.6	33.3	31.5	33.5	34.6	29.5	30.3	26.9	30.4	24.6	36.8	26.1
	2006	31.3	33.1	31.1	33.5	34.1	29.0	15.0	31.3	15.0	27.5	13.2	23.4

For sources and notes, see end of table.   Pour les sources et les notes, se reporter à la fin du tableau.

222

Market / Marchés	Year / Année	MFN rate - Simple average (2) / Droit NPF - Moyenne simple (2)						MFN rate - Weighted average (3) / Droit NPF - Moyenne pondérée (3)					
		Total of non-agricultural and non-fuel products / Total des produits non-agricoles et non-pétroliers	Ores and metals / Minérais et métaux	Manufactured products / Produits manufacturés	of which: Chemical products / Produits chimiques	Machinery and transport equipment / Machines et matériel de transport	Other manufactured products / Produits manufacturés divers	Total of non-agricultural and non-fuel products / Total des produits non-agricoles et non-pétroliers	Ores and metals / Minérais et métaux	Manufactured products / Produits manufacturés	of which: Chemical products / Produits chimiques	Machinery and transport equipment / Machines et matériel de transport	Other manufactured products / Produits manufacturés divers
SITC Rev.2 (1) / CTCI Rév.2 (1)		5+6+7+8 +27+28	27+28+68	(5+6+7+8) - 68	5	7	(6+8) - 68	5+6+7+8 +27+28	27+28+68	(5+6+7+8) - 68	5	7	(6+8) - 68
Bahrain - Bahreïn	1999	7.7	5.4	7.9	5.3	9.5	8.2	9.0	5.4	9.6	6.2	12.4	7.9
	2001	7.7	5.4	7.9	5.3	9.5	8.2	9.3	5.3	10.0	6.2	13.0	8.0
	2005	4.9	4.8	4.9	4.9	4.9	5.0	4.9	5.0	4.9	4.3	5.0	5.0
	2006	4.9	4.8	4.9	4.6	4.9	5.0	4.9	5.0	4.9	4.3	5.0	5.0
Bangladesh	1989	118.1	45.0	123.5	62.7	69.2	166.5	108.8	57.5	112.1	52.5	74.7	149.7
	1994	82.7	61.2	84.1	68.6	77.3	92.8	86.3	67.5	86.9	70.1	78.0	93.5
	1999	21.6	14.4	22.1	16.7	13.4	27.8	19.1	11.7	19.4	11.4	11.7	26.1
	2000	21.6	14.4	22.1	16.7	13.3	27.8	18.5	11.7	18.7	11.4	10.8	26.1
	2002	20.4	12.8	20.9	14.9	12.4	26.8	19.2	8.2	19.6	10.5	12.0	27.2
	2003	19.2	13.0	19.6	14.6	12.9	24.3	19.2	11.5	19.5	10.9	12.8	26.0
	2004	18.1	13.0	18.5	14.2	12.5	22.7	16.7	12.1	16.8	9.3	12.4	24.0
	2005	15.0	9.9	15.3	11.5	10.6	18.8	25.6	9.5	26.1	8.6	14.7	42.4
	2006	15.0	9.9	15.3	11.5	10.6	18.8	25.6	9.5	26.1	8.6	14.7	42.4
Barbados - Barbade	1996	21.2	19.4	21.2	14.5	18.9	22.8	23.5	43.6	23.3	15.9	24.9	24.6
	1999	17.9	16.2	17.9	11.4	16.4	19.2	22.4	19.1	22.4	14.2	27.8	21.6
	2000	17.9	16.2	17.9	11.4	16.4	19.2	21.6	18.2	21.6	14.3	26.1	21.2
	2001	9.5	5.8	9.8	6.5	8.0	11.7	14.8	8.9	14.8	13.8	11.3	18.2
	2002	9.5	5.8	9.8	6.5	8.0	11.7	14.3	9.6	14.3	14.0	11.2	17.2
	2003	9.5	5.8	9.8	6.5	8.0	11.7	14.9	9.0	14.9	14.1	12.0	17.8
	2006	10.5	5.6	10.8	6.1	7.8	13.9	15.6	7.1	15.8	11.9	11.4	21.3
Belarus - Bélarus	1996	12.4	9.9	12.6	6.0	11.9	15.4	10.3	5.0	10.5	7.0	11.1	11.8
	1997	13.0	8.9	13.2	7.0	12.7	15.8	11.0	7.0	11.2	8.6	11.6	12.2
	2002	11.1	8.2	11.3	6.7	10.6	13.3	10.2	8.1	10.3	8.0	10.6	11.3
Belize	1996	21.2	19.6	21.2	14.5	18.8	22.8	18.9	22.8	18.8	12.6	21.0	20.2
	1999	17.8	16.4	17.8	11.1	16.1	19.2	17.1	21.6	16.6	14.2	27.4	14.5
	2001	8.9	4.4	9.2	5.6	7.5	11.4	11.2	15.8	11.2	9.7	10.4	12.4
	2002	8.9	4.4	9.2	5.6	7.5	11.4	11.0	15.0	10.9	9.3	10.2	12.3
	2003	8.9	4.4	9.2	5.6	7.5	11.4	10.8	11.8	10.8	9.3	10.7	11.3
	2006	8.7	4.0	9.0	5.5	7.5	11.0	13.0	8.6	13.0	9.2	11.0	15.9
Benin - Bénin	2001	11.8	7.5	12.0	6.3	8.5	15.7	12.3	6.6	12.4	4.8	10.3	16.5
	2002	11.7	7.5	12.0	6.3	8.5	15.7	12.4	7.1	12.5	5.2	11.7	16.6
	2003	11.7	7.3	12.0	6.3	8.6	15.7	12.2	6.2	12.4	5.4	10.6	16.2
	2004	11.7	7.4	12.0	6.3	8.6	15.7	12.1	6.5	12.2	4.6	11.0	16.1
	2005	11.7	7.4	12.0	6.3	8.6	15.7	12.7	6.9	12.8	4.3	11.6	15.6
	2006	11.7	7.4	12.0	6.3	8.6	15.7	12.8	6.9	12.9	4.3	11.8	15.6
Bermuda - Bermudes	2001	19.3	19.9	19.3	20.1	23.9	16.9	26.5	20.2	26.5	1.8	32.4	19.3
	2005	19.3	20.0	19.2	20.2	23.7	17.0	28.2	21.9	28.2	13.1	31.0	14.9
Bhutan - Bhoutan	1996	15.5	17.8	15.5	9.2	12.0	19.4	16.7	12.3	16.8	28.8	14.3	19.0
	2002	16.5	17.4	16.4	12.7	11.3	20.1	15.0	16.3	15.0	26.3	11.2	19.2
	2004	19.0	24.0	18.6	13.5	11.6	23.6	14.7	26.0	14.5	26.8	9.1	21.5
	2005	19.0	24.0	18.6	13.5	11.6	23.6	14.7	26.0	14.5	26.8	9.1	21.5
Bolivia - Bolivie	1993	9.8	10.0	9.8	10.0	9.0	10.0	9.3	10.0	9.3	10.0	8.8	9.9
	1994	10.0	10.0	10.0	10.0	10.0	10.0	9.9	10.0	9.9	10.0	10.0	9.8
	1995	9.7	10.0	9.7	10.0	8.6	10.0	9.4	10.0	9.4	10.0	8.9	9.9
	1996	9.7	10.0	9.6	10.0	8.6	10.0	9.1	10.0	9.1	10.0	8.7	9.6
	1997	9.7	10.0	9.6	10.0	8.6	10.0	9.1	10.0	9.1	10.0	8.7	9.6
	1998	9.7	10.0	9.6	10.0	8.6	10.0	8.9	10.0	8.9	10.0	8.3	9.6
	1999	9.7	10.0	9.6	10.0	8.6	10.0	9.0	10.0	9.0	10.0	8.2	9.8
	2000	9.2	9.9	9.1	9.9	6.7	9.9	8.2	10.0	8.2	9.7	6.4	9.7
	2001	9.2	9.9	9.1	9.9	6.7	9.9	8.6	10.0	8.6	9.7	6.8	9.8
	2002	9.6	10.0	9.6	10.7	7.1	10.2	9.0	10.0	9.0	10.3	6.3	10.6
	2004	9.3	10.0	9.2	10.0	6.7	9.9	8.7	10.0	8.7	10.0	6.8	9.8
	2005	8.1	8.2	8.1	7.4	5.6	9.4	8.4	9.5	8.4	9.5	6.6	9.5
	2006	8.0	8.1	8.0	7.2	5.5	9.4	8.1	9.5	8.1	9.4	6.3	9.5

For sources and notes, see end of table.

Pour les sources et les notes, se reporter à la fin du tableau.

Market / Marchés	Year / Année	MFN rate - Simple average (2) / Droit NPF - Moyenne simple (2)						MFN rate - Weighted average (3) / Droit NPF - Moyenne pondérée (3)					
		Total of non-agricultural and non-fuel products / Total des produits non-agricoles et non-pétroliers	Ores and metals / Minérais et métaux	Manufactured products / Produits manufacturés	Chemical products / Produits chimiques	Machinery and transport equipment / Machines et matériel de transport	Other manufactured products / Produits manufacturés divers	Total of non-agricultural and non-fuel products / Total des produits non-agricoles et non-pétroliers	Ores and metals / Minérais et métaux	Manufactured products / Produits manufacturés	Chemical products / Produits chimiques	Machinery and transport equipment / Machines et matériel de transport	Other manufactured products / Produits manufacturés divers
SITC Rev.2 (1) / CTCI Rév.2 (1)		5+6+7+8 +27+28	27+28+68	(5+6+7+8) - 68	5	7	(6+8) - 68	5+6+7+8 +27+28	27+28+68	(5+6+7+8) - 68	5	7	(6+8) - 68
Bosnia and Herzegovina - Bosnie-Herzégovine	2001	6.4	1.8	6.7	2.8	6.2	8.4	7.8	5.0	7.9	6.5	7.6	8.5
	2006	6.4	1.8	6.7	2.8	6.2	8.5	7.3	3.7	7.6	5.7	7.4	8.3
Botswana	2001	7.9	1.4	8.4	2.5	3.2	13.0	9.7	0.5	10.0	7.5	9.4	11.0
	2004	8.1	1.3	8.5	2.4	3.0	13.2	13.5	1.1	13.6	0.9	12.6	18.5
	2005	8.0	1.2	8.5	2.5	3.0	13.1	11.3	0.1	12.7	0.9	10.6	18.8
	2006	8.0	1.2	8.5	2.4	3.0	13.1	11.1	0.1	12.5	0.9	10.3	18.8
Brazil - Brésil	1989	46.7	22.6	48.3	38.7	44.5	53.5	35.3	12.8	38.0	33.9	40.9	36.7
	1990	34.0	10.7	35.5	25.0	38.5	38.3	27.0	6.9	28.7	21.5	32.9	28.0
	1991	27.6	6.9	29.0	18.4	31.2	32.1	22.2	5.0	23.6	16.3	28.4	22.5
	1992	22.7	5.4	23.9	15.1	26.8	26.0	19.8	3.4	21.1	13.4	25.9	18.9
	1993	15.0	2.9	15.9	11.3	19.6	16.0	15.8	1.6	16.6	10.7	20.4	14.1
	1994	13.7	3.3	14.4	7.9	19.5	14.7	15.5	2.8	16.2	6.9	21.1	13.5
	1995	13.8	6.0	14.4	8.4	16.8	15.6	13.7	5.4	14.1	8.1	16.2	14.5
	1996	14.2	6.3	14.8	8.3	17.7	15.9	16.0	5.3	16.4	8.0	20.3	15.2
	1997	13.9	6.2	14.4	8.5	16.9	15.6	16.1	5.8	16.5	8.5	20.1	14.5
	1998	16.8	9.2	17.3	11.5	19.3	18.6	17.8	9.2	18.0	11.3	20.9	17.0
	1999	16.5	9.1	17.0	11.5	18.4	18.5	15.4	8.6	15.7	11.4	17.2	16.8
	2000	16.3	9.0	16.8	11.4	17.6	18.5	14.7	8.2	15.0	11.0	16.1	16.4
	2001	14.7	8.6	15.1	10.9	12.8	17.8	12.2	7.8	12.4	10.1	12.5	15.1
	2002	14.4	7.5	14.9	9.8	14.8	16.9	11.9	6.8	12.1	8.7	12.8	14.9
	2003	14.0	7.4	14.5	9.7	14.6	16.2	11.4	6.4	11.6	8.4	12.5	14.4
	2004	14.0	7.4	14.4	9.5	14.7	16.2	11.1	6.0	11.4	8.1	12.2	14.4
	2005	13.0	5.8	13.5	8.1	13.9	15.4	10.5	4.7	10.8	7.3	11.6	13.5
	2006	12.9	5.8	13.4	8.0	13.8	15.4	10.4	4.7	10.9	7.3	11.6	13.2
Brunei Darussalam - Brunéi Darussalam	1992	2.5	0.0	2.7	0.6	2.5	3.5	4.4	0.0	4.5	2.3	6.2	2.6
	2001	3.1	0.0	3.3	0.3	9.6	1.7	10.6	0.0	10.7	1.1	19.0	0.9
	2002	3.1	0.0	3.3	0.3	9.6	1.7	10.6	0.0	10.7	1.1	19.0	0.9
	2003	3.1	0.0	3.3	0.3	9.6	1.7	12.3	0.0	12.5	1.0	27.1	1.0
	2004	3.1	0.0	3.3	0.2	9.5	1.8	6.9	0.0	7.0	1.1	11.4	2.7
	2005	3.1	0.0	3.3	0.2	9.5	1.8	6.5	0.0	6.6	1.0	11.4	2.5
	2006	3.1	0.0	3.3	0.2	9.5	1.8	6.5	0.0	6.6	1.0	11.4	2.5
Bulgaria - Bulgarie	2001	11.4	3.9	11.9	8.2	7.9	15.0	10.3	1.6	11.0	8.5	7.4	15.5
	2003	9.0	2.7	9.4	7.4	5.8	11.7	8.8	1.8	9.3	7.4	6.6	12.6
	2004	9.0	2.7	9.4	7.4	5.8	11.7	8.6	1.6	9.2	6.8	7.1	12.2
	2005	9.0	2.7	9.4	7.4	5.8	11.7	8.2	1.5	8.9	7.2	6.8	11.8
	2006	9.1	2.8	9.5	7.2	6.3	11.8	8.3	1.5	9.0	6.8	7.0	12.0
Burkina Faso	1993	24.6	20.1	24.9	28.3	17.0	26.9	20.2	10.3	20.4	16.5	21.1	21.9
	2001	11.8	7.5	12.0	6.3	8.5	15.7	11.4	8.0	11.5	5.3	11.2	15.4
	2002	11.7	7.5	12.0	6.3	8.5	15.7	11.5	8.7	11.5	5.0	12.1	15.5
	2003	11.7	7.3	12.0	6.3	8.6	15.7	12.1	7.9	12.2	4.9	13.4	14.2
	2004	11.7	7.4	12.0	6.3	8.6	15.7	12.6	8.4	12.6	5.5	13.9	14.8
	2005	11.7	7.4	12.0	6.3	8.6	15.7	12.6	8.4	12.6	5.5	13.9	14.8
	2006	11.7	7.4	12.0	6.3	8.6	15.7	12.7	8.4	12.7	5.5	14.1	14.8
Burundi	2002	21.8	11.9	22.4	12.3	17.0	28.5	20.1	14.6	20.2	14.2	22.8	21.0
	2005	18.1	11.3	18.6	12.0	14.8	22.7	18.5	14.9	18.5	15.4	16.5	22.3
	2006	13.3	6.0	13.8	8.0	10.2	17.5	13.8	9.3	13.8	14.2	12.2	15.4
Cambodia - Cambodge	2001	16.2	11.6	16.5	10.7	17.9	18.1	16.8	11.4	16.8	6.8	18.9	17.5
	2002	16.2	11.6	16.5	10.7	17.9	18.1	16.7	11.4	16.8	6.2	18.8	17.3
	2003	16.2	11.6	16.5	10.7	17.9	18.1	16.9	9.8	16.9	5.9	18.8	17.5
	2005	13.9	8.9	14.3	10.1	17.3	14.6	10.9	9.9	10.9	5.9	16.4	10.2
Cameroon - Cameroun	1994	18.0	15.4	18.1	11.3	14.1	22.3	13.6	11.3	13.8	7.3	15.2	16.3
	1995	17.5	12.1	17.9	10.6	14.0	22.2	13.3	10.8	13.5	8.1	14.9	15.3
	2001	17.3	11.7	17.7	10.6	14.0	21.9	13.3	10.4	13.5	8.7	14.8	14.2
	2002	17.3	11.7	17.7	10.6	14.0	21.9	13.4	11.0	13.6	8.9	14.5	15.1
	2005	17.3	11.8	17.7	10.8	14.1	21.9	14.8	10.7	15.1	7.7	16.6	17.7

For sources and notes, see end of table.

Pour les sources et les notes, se reporter à la fin du tableau.

Market / Marchés	Year / Année	MFN rate - Simple average (2) / Droit NPF - Moyenne simple (2)						MFN rate - Weighted average (3) / Droit NPF - Moyenne pondérée (3)					
		Total of non-agricultural and non-fuel products / Total des produits non-agricoles et non-pétroliers	Ores and metals / Minérais et métaux	of which: / dont :				Total of non-agricultural and non-fuel products / Total des produits non-agricoles et non-pétroliers	Ores and metals / Minérais et métaux	of which: / dont :			
				Manu-factured products / Produits manu-facturés	Of which: / dont :					Manu-factured products / Produits manu-facturés	Of which: / dont :		
					Chemical products / Produits chimiques	Machinery and transport equipment / Machines et matériel de transport	Other manu-factured products / Produits manu-facturés divers				Chemical products / Produits chimiques	Machinery and transport equipment / Machines et matériel de transport	Other manu-factured products / Produits manu-facturés divers
SITC Rev.2 (1) / CTCI Rév.2 (1)		5+6+7+8 +27+28	27+28+68	(5+6+7+8) - 68	5	7	(6+8) - 68	5+6+7+8 +27+28	27+28+68	(5+6+7+8) - 68	5	7	(6+8) - 68
Canada	1989	10.2	3.8	10.6	8.5	7.3	12.9	7.6	2.3	7.8	8.7	6.4	10.7
	1993	10.0	3.8	10.4	8.4	7.1	12.5	7.5	2.0	7.7	8.8	6.3	10.4
	1995	9.1	3.4	9.5	7.4	6.5	11.5	6.6	2.0	6.8	7.6	5.6	9.4
	1996	7.4	1.4	7.7	4.4	4.9	10.2	5.4	0.9	5.5	5.7	4.4	8.0
	1997	6.9	1.3	7.2	4.2	4.4	9.6	4.9	0.9	5.1	5.4	4.0	7.4
	1998	5.1	0.7	5.4	3.1	2.3	7.5	3.5	0.6	3.6	3.7	2.8	5.3
	1999	4.8	0.7	5.1	2.9	2.2	7.2	3.2	0.6	3.3	3.3	2.6	4.9
	2000	4.7	0.7	5.0	2.8	2.2	6.9	3.1	0.6	3.2	3.2	2.5	4.7
	2001	4.6	0.7	4.8	2.7	2.2	6.7	3.2	0.6	3.3	3.0	2.6	4.7
	2002	4.4	0.7	4.7	2.7	2.2	6.5	3.2	0.7	3.3	2.9	2.8	4.5
	2003	4.3	0.7	4.5	2.6	2.2	6.2	3.2	0.6	3.3	2.7	2.9	4.3
	2004	4.2	0.7	4.4	2.6	2.2	6.0	3.1	0.6	3.2	2.6	2.9	4.2
	2005	4.1	0.7	4.4	2.6	2.2	6.0	3.1	0.6	3.2	2.6	2.8	4.2
	2006	3.9	0.7	4.1	2.5	2.2	5.5	3.1	0.6	3.2	2.6	2.8	4.1
Central African Republic - République centrafricaine	1995	17.5	12.1	17.9	10.6	14.0	22.2	14.6	19.0	14.5	7.8	14.4	18.5
	1997	17.5	12.1	17.9	10.6	14.0	22.2	14.6	16.7	14.5	7.0	14.9	19.0
	2001	17.3	11.7	17.7	10.6	14.0	21.9	15.9	21.0	15.6	9.3	17.1	17.8
	2002	17.3	11.7	17.7	10.6	14.0	21.9	15.1	18.3	15.0	9.7	16.4	16.5
	2005	17.3	11.8	17.7	10.8	14.1	21.9	15.3	22.2	15.2	7.4	15.7	18.8
Chad - Tchad	1995	17.5	12.1	17.9	10.6	14.0	22.2	15.1	12.4	15.1	7.5	14.8	17.7
	1997	17.5	12.1	17.9	10.6	14.0	22.2	15.1	12.4	15.1	7.5	14.8	17.7
	2001	17.3	11.7	17.7	10.6	14.0	21.9	12.0	10.4	12.0	7.9	11.5	14.8
	2002	17.3	11.7	17.7	10.6	14.0	21.9	13.5	8.7	13.5	10.8	12.0	16.2
	2005	17.3	11.8	17.7	10.8	14.1	21.9	11.4	14.5	11.4	8.2	10.6	16.5
Chile - Chili	1992	11.0	11.0	11.0	11.0	10.9	11.0	10.9	11.0	10.9	11.0	10.9	11.0
	1993	11.0	11.0	11.0	11.0	10.9	11.0	10.9	11.0	10.9	11.0	10.9	11.0
	1994	11.0	11.0	11.0	11.0	10.9	11.0	10.9	11.0	10.9	11.0	10.9	11.0
	1995	11.0	11.0	11.0	11.0	10.9	11.0	10.9	11.0	10.9	11.0	10.9	11.0
	1997	11.0	11.0	11.0	11.0	10.9	11.0	11.0	11.0	11.0	11.0	10.9	11.0
	1998	11.0	11.0	11.0	11.0	10.9	11.0	10.9	11.0	10.9	11.0	10.9	11.0
	1999	10.0	10.0	10.0	10.0	9.9	10.0	10.0	10.0	9.9	10.0	9.9	10.0
	2000	9.0	9.0	9.0	9.0	9.0	9.0	9.0	9.0	9.0	9.0	9.0	9.0
	2001	8.0	8.0	8.0	8.0	8.0	8.0	8.0	8.0	8.0	8.0	8.0	8.0
	2002	7.0	7.0	7.0	7.0	6.9	7.0	6.9	7.0	6.9	7.0	6.9	7.0
	2004	6.0	6.0	6.0	6.0	5.9	6.0	6.0	6.0	6.0	6.0	6.0	6.0
	2005	6.0	6.0	6.0	6.0	5.9	6.0	6.0	6.0	6.0	6.0	6.0	6.0
	2006	6.0	6.0	6.0	6.0	5.9	6.0	6.0	6.0	6.0	6.0	6.0	6.0
China - Chine	1992	42.2	17.7	43.9	27.2	32.6	54.8	34.8	7.7	36.4	22.2	34.0	46.4
	1993	39.3	16.8	40.8	26.1	31.3	50.1	32.1	7.4	33.3	24.1	34.1	34.9
	1994	35.2	15.4	36.6	23.3	27.9	45.1	29.8	7.8	30.7	21.5	29.8	35.4
	1996	22.0	7.5	23.0	14.1	19.7	27.8	17.8	5.8	18.4	14.6	16.1	23.7
	1997	16.5	5.3	17.3	11.1	16.2	20.1	14.3	4.8	14.9	12.8	13.2	18.2
	1998	16.5	5.3	17.3	11.1	16.3	20.0	14.2	5.2	14.8	12.9	13.5	17.9
	1999	16.1	5.3	16.8	11.1	16.2	19.3	13.5	5.3	14.0	12.8	12.8	17.0
	2000	15.8	5.3	16.5	11.1	16.2	18.7	13.1	5.2	13.7	13.0	12.8	16.0
	2001	14.7	4.5	15.4	10.2	15.4	17.3	12.4	4.2	13.0	12.5	12.5	14.6
	2003	10.6	3.8	11.0	7.4	10.0	12.9	6.4	2.7	6.7	8.9	5.3	8.5
	2004	9.8	3.7	10.2	7.1	9.4	11.7	5.6	2.0	5.9	8.2	4.5	7.8
	2005	9.2	3.7	9.6	6.9	9.1	10.8	5.0	1.8	5.4	7.3	4.0	7.4
	2006	9.1	3.6	9.5	6.7	8.9	10.7	4.3	1.4	4.7	6.2	3.3	7.1

For sources and notes, see end of table.

Pour les sources et les notes, se reporter à la fin du tableau.

Market / Marchés	Year / Année	MFN rate - Simple average (2) / Droit NPF - Moyenne simple (2)						MFN rate - Weighted average (3) / Droit NPF - Moyenne pondérée (3)					
		Total of non-agricultural and non-fuel products / Total des produits non-agricoles et non-pétroliers	Ores and metals / Minérais et métaux	Manu-factured products / Produits manu-facturés	Chemical products / Produits chimiques	Machinery and transport equipment / Machines et matériel de transport	Other manu-factured products / Produits manu-facturés divers	Total of non-agricultural and non-fuel products / Total des produits non-agricoles et non-pétroliers	Ores and metals / Minérais et métaux	Manu-factured products / Produits manu-facturés	Chemical products / Produits chimiques	Machinery and transport equipment / Machines et matériel de transport	Other manu-factured products / Produits manu-facturés divers
SITC Rev.2 (1) / CTCI Rév.2 (1)		5+6+7+8 +27+28	27+28+68	(5+6+7+8) - 68	5	7	(6+8) - 68	5+6+7+8 +27+28	27+28+68	(5+6+7+8) - 68	5	7	(6+8) - 68
China, Taiwan Province of - Province chinoise de Taiwan	1989	10.2	4.0	10.6	9.0	11.6	10.7	10.2	4.5	10.8	6.5	12.8	9.7
	1992	6.5	1.7	6.8	4.1	6.8	7.8	6.3	1.8	6.6	3.7	7.8	6.0
	1996	6.3	1.5	6.6	4.0	6.5	7.6	4.2	1.4	4.4	3.5	4.3	5.1
	1999	6.3	1.5	6.6	4.0	6.6	7.7	4.5	1.4	4.7	3.8	4.7	5.2
	2000	6.1	1.5	6.4	3.9	6.0	7.5	2.9	1.4	3.0	3.3	2.5	4.1
	2001	6.0	1.5	6.3	3.9	6.0	7.4	2.9	1.3	3.0	3.6	2.4	4.3
	2002	5.9	1.4	6.2	3.8	5.7	7.3	3.0	1.2	3.1	3.4	2.8	4.0
	2003	5.2	1.1	5.5	3.4	5.1	6.4	2.8	1.1	2.9	2.8	2.8	3.3
	2005	4.4	0.8	4.6	2.8	4.4	5.5	2.3	0.6	2.4	1.9	2.7	2.3
	2006	4.4	0.8	4.6	2.9	4.3	5.4	2.3	0.6	2.4	2.0	2.6	2.2
Colombia - Colombie	1991	6.3	2.2	6.6	3.4	5.1	8.4	6.0	1.1	6.2	3.9	8.7	5.1
	1992	12.0	6.7	12.4	8.2	10.2	14.9	10.3	7.7	10.5	7.7	11.2	12.3
	1994	12.0	6.7	12.4	8.1	10.3	14.8	11.4	7.9	11.5	7.7	12.5	12.6
	1995	13.5	7.2	14.0	10.6	12.7	15.8	12.0	5.5	12.2	9.4	12.8	13.5
	1996	11.7	6.4	12.0	7.7	9.8	14.6	10.7	6.1	10.9	7.3	11.5	12.7
	1997	11.7	6.4	12.0	7.7	9.8	14.6	10.9	6.0	11.1	7.6	11.7	12.7
	1999	11.8	6.4	12.1	7.8	9.9	14.7	9.9	6.4	10.0	7.9	9.4	13.0
	2000	11.8	6.4	12.1	7.8	9.9	14.7	10.4	6.6	10.6	7.9	10.7	12.9
	2001	11.8	6.4	12.1	7.8	9.9	14.7	10.2	7.0	10.3	8.1	9.8	13.2
	2002	11.8	6.4	12.1	7.8	9.9	14.8	10.6	6.9	10.6	7.9	11.0	13.3
	2004	11.8	6.3	12.1	7.8	9.9	14.8	10.9	6.8	11.0	7.9	11.6	13.0
	2005	11.8	6.3	12.1	7.8	9.8	14.8	11.0	6.4	11.2	8.1	11.7	13.1
	2006	11.8	6.3	12.1	7.8	9.8	14.8	11.5	6.2	11.7	8.3	12.6	13.2
Congo	1994	17.4	13.6	17.7	10.9	14.1	21.8	14.6	16.1	14.6	9.6	14.4	17.2
	1997	15.3	10.9	15.6	6.6	13.0	20.1	17.0	10.8	17.0	16.0	13.5	20.1
	2001	17.3	11.7	17.7	10.6	14.0	21.9	16.1	16.6	16.1	12.2	13.5	22.3
	2002	17.3	11.7	17.7	10.6	14.0	21.9	16.5	16.4	16.5	11.4	14.4	21.3
	2005	17.3	11.8	17.7	10.8	14.1	21.9	15.9	17.0	15.9	9.1	14.3	20.6
Costa Rica	1995	9.5	5.8	9.7	5.8	4.6	13.3	8.3	6.1	8.3	6.4	7.7	10.1
	1999	5.4	1.3	5.7	1.3	2.5	8.7	4.5	2.5	4.5	3.6	2.6	7.4
	2000	4.6	1.4	4.8	1.2	2.1	7.3	3.8	1.6	3.9	2.9	1.9	6.9
	2001	4.5	1.3	4.7	1.2	2.0	7.2	3.7	2.0	3.7	3.1	1.6	7.0
	2002	4.8	1.0	5.1	1.3	2.2	7.7	3.6	1.5	3.6	3.0	2.1	6.3
	2004	4.8	1.0	5.1	1.3	2.3	7.7	3.9	1.3	3.9	2.9	2.7	6.2
	2005	4.8	1.0	5.1	1.3	2.2	7.7	3.6	1.3	3.7	2.8	1.9	6.8
Côte d'Ivoire	1993	21.7	16.4	22.0	13.0	19.3	26.5	22.4	17.0	22.6	8.6	28.9	24.0
	1996	18.6	12.8	18.9	12.4	12.0	24.4	12.9	12.7	13.0	9.6	11.8	17.3
	2001	11.8	7.5	12.0	6.3	8.5	15.7	8.7	7.3	8.8	5.1	9.5	11.7
	2002	11.7	7.5	12.0	6.3	8.5	15.7	8.7	7.4	8.8	5.1	9.5	11.7
	2003	11.7	7.3	12.0	6.3	8.6	15.7	9.1	6.8	9.2	5.0	9.5	12.0
	2004	11.7	7.4	12.0	6.3	8.6	15.7	9.2	6.9	9.3	5.0	9.5	12.3
	2005	11.7	7.4	12.0	6.3	8.6	15.7	8.8	7.0	8.8	5.1	8.2	12.5
	2006	11.7	7.4	12.0	6.3	8.6	15.7	9.4	7.0	9.5	5.3	9.9	12.6
Croatia - Croatie	2001	10.1	5.6	10.4	7.0	8.8	12.3	10.9	5.9	11.0	10.1	9.5	13.1
	2004	4.0	1.5	4.1	1.3	3.1	5.7	4.0	2.2	4.1	2.6	3.7	5.0
	2005	3.9	1.5	4.0	1.2	3.1	5.5	3.8	2.0	3.9	2.2	3.6	4.9
	2006	4.0	1.5	4.1	1.2	3.3	5.6	4.0	1.7	4.1	2.2	3.7	5.1
Cuba	1993	12.8	5.6	13.3	11.1	11.0	15.1	12.9	5.1	13.1	10.0	12.3	15.1
	1997	11.1	5.4	11.5	9.3	9.8	13.0	10.3	3.7	10.4	7.2	9.9	12.2
	2002	11.2	5.3	11.6	9.1	9.9	13.2	10.8	3.7	10.9	7.2	11.1	12.3
	2003	11.3	5.1	11.7	9.0	10.0	13.5	11.0	3.8	11.2	7.8	10.9	12.6
	2004	11.2	5.1	11.6	9.0	9.9	13.4	10.5	4.6	10.6	8.0	10.4	12.0
	2005	11.2	5.1	11.6	9.0	9.9	13.4	10.5	4.6	10.6	8.0	10.4	11.9
	2006	11.2	5.1	11.6	8.9	9.9	13.4	10.4	4.5	10.6	8.0	10.4	11.9
Cyprus - Chypre (4)	2002	4.2	1.6	4.4	4.7	2.3	5.1	5.0	4.8	5.0	2.8	5.6	5.0

For sources and notes, see end of table.

Pour les sources et les notes, se reporter à la fin du tableau.

Market Marchés	Year Année	MFN rate - Simple average (2) / Droit NPF - Moyenne simple (2)						MFN rate - Weighted average (3) / Droit NPF - Moyenne pondérée (3)					
				of which: / dont :						of which: / dont :			
		Total of non-agricultural and non-fuel products Total des produits non-agricoles et non-pétroliers	Ores and metals Minérais et métaux	Manu-factured products Produits manu-facturés	Of which: / dont :			Total of non-agricultural and non-fuel products Total des produits non-agricoles et non-pétroliers	Ores and metals Minérais et métaux	Manu-factured products Produits manu-facturés	Of which: / dont :		
					Chemical products Produits chimiques	Machinery and transport equipment Machines et matériel de transport	Other manu-factured products Produits manu-facturés divers				Chemical products Produits chimiques	Machinery and transport equipment Machines et matériel de transport	Other manu-factured products Produits manu-facturés divers
SITC Rev.2 (1) / CTCI Rév.2 (1)		5+6+7+8 +27+28	27+28+68	(5+6+7+8) - 68	5	7	(6+8) - 68	5+6+7+8 +27+28	27+28+68	(5+6+7+8) - 68	5	7	(6+8) - 68
Czech Republic - (4) République tchèque	1996	5.9	1.6	6.2	5.3	5.6	6.8	6.1	1.9	6.3	5.0	6.2	7.0
	1999	5.2	2.2	5.4	4.5	5.9	5.6	5.8	2.8	5.9	4.0	6.2	6.1
	2002	4.5	1.2	4.7	4.1	3.8	5.3	4.3	1.6	4.4	3.5	3.8	5.5
	2003	4.5	1.2	4.7	4.1	3.8	5.3	4.3	1.7	4.4	3.4	3.9	5.5
Czechoslovakia (former) - Tchécoslovaquie (anc.)	1992	8.9	1.6	9.4	5.2	11.4	10.1	8.7	2.2	8.8	5.0	9.3	9.2
Dem. Rep. of the Congo - Rép. dém. du Congo	2003	11.8	8.8	12.0	7.7	8.3	15.2	12.9	13.5	12.9	13.6	8.8	16.4
	2006	11.8	8.8	12.0	7.7	8.3	15.2	11.4	8.4	11.5	14.5	8.0	14.7
Djibouti	2002	32.9	32.5	32.9	31.2	33.3	33.3	32.3	31.8	32.3	27.1	34.5	31.8
	2006	32.2	30.9	32.3	31.0	33.0	32.5	31.3	31.1	31.3	24.7	33.0	32.0
Dominica - Dominique	1996	20.3	17.1	20.3	14.5	18.5	21.6	18.7	22.3	18.7	14.1	23.5	18.4
	1999	16.9	13.8	16.9	11.3	16.0	18.0	16.5	16.9	16.5	11.6	22.0	15.0
	2000	13.2	13.7	13.2	8.7	12.4	14.7	15.0	14.4	15.0	9.0	21.8	12.6
	2001	8.0	3.7	8.2	6.1	5.8	10.1	11.2	5.2	11.2	10.1	10.1	12.4
	2002	8.0	3.7	8.3	6.2	5.8	10.1	12.5	5.0	12.5	11.0	10.7	14.4
	2003	8.0	3.7	8.3	6.2	5.8	10.1	12.0	4.8	12.0	10.7	10.4	13.8
	2006	7.9	3.5	8.2	6.2	5.8	9.9	11.9	4.7	11.9	9.8	9.9	14.6
Dominican Republic - République dominicaine	1997	14.1	7.6	14.6	8.3	10.2	18.7	13.7	11.0	13.8	8.6	14.3	15.6
	2000	17.5	9.2	18.1	9.9	13.1	23.2	17.5	13.6	17.6	9.5	17.8	21.3
	2001	7.7	4.5	7.9	4.4	5.5	10.4	8.6	5.1	8.7	4.0	8.6	11.2
	2002	7.8	4.5	8.0	4.4	5.4	10.4	9.3	4.2	9.4	4.7	9.6	11.1
	2003	7.8	4.5	8.0	4.4	5.4	10.4	8.6	5.2	8.7	3.9	8.6	11.2
	2004	7.7	4.6	7.9	4.3	5.5	10.4	8.7	5.3	8.7	3.9	8.6	11.4
	2005	7.7	4.5	7.9	4.5	5.4	10.3	9.2	5.1	9.2	6.0	8.1	10.8
	2006	7.7	4.4	7.9	4.5	5.4	10.3	9.2	4.6	9.2	5.9	8.2	10.8
Ecuador - Équateur	1993	9.4	3.7	9.8	6.0	6.7	12.5	8.3	4.3	8.4	4.7	9.8	7.8
	1994	12.0	6.5	12.4	7.5	9.5	15.4	11.6	7.3	11.7	6.9	13.7	11.1
	1995	12.6	6.5	13.1	9.4	11.0	15.3	11.3	5.7	11.4	6.5	12.9	12.3
	1996	11.5	5.9	11.8	7.1	8.9	14.9	11.3	5.7	11.4	5.8	14.2	11.6
	1997	11.5	5.9	11.8	7.1	8.9	14.9	10.9	5.6	11.0	6.0	13.2	11.9
	1998	11.5	5.9	11.8	7.1	9.0	14.9	10.8	5.8	10.9	6.2	12.2	12.1
	1999	13.4	7.9	13.7	8.5	10.8	17.0	11.3	7.5	11.3	7.5	12.0	14.1
	2002	11.4	5.9	11.8	7.2	8.7	14.9	10.8	6.2	10.8	7.0	10.9	13.0
	2004	11.4	5.9	11.8	7.2	8.7	14.9	10.5	6.1	10.6	6.8	10.8	12.8
	2005	11.2	5.9	11.6	7.0	8.3	14.8	10.3	6.6	10.4	7.0	10.5	12.5
	2006	11.2	5.9	11.6	7.0	8.3	14.8	10.3	6.9	10.4	7.1	10.5	12.4
Egypt - Égypte	1995	28.4	13.8	29.3	14.1	19.1	39.2	21.9	11.2	22.4	11.4	27.2	23.4
	1998	21.7	12.8	22.3	13.0	12.6	29.2	17.2	9.6	17.6	10.9	19.4	19.1
	2002	19.9	12.6	20.5	12.7	14.0	26.9	16.5	10.9	16.7	11.0	15.9	21.2
	2004	13.2	6.0	13.7	6.7	8.2	18.7	11.1	4.5	11.4	15.7	8.3	14.4
	2005	12.9	5.1	13.4	6.3	8.0	18.4	11.8	2.3	12.3	16.5	10.0	13.5
El Salvador	1995	9.5	5.9	9.7	6.0	4.0	13.5	8.7	6.0	8.7	7.6	7.1	11.4
	1997	7.4	1.7	7.8	1.9	2.8	12.1	6.7	2.8	6.8	5.2	5.4	9.5
	1998	3.8	1.7	4.0	1.8	2.7	5.3	5.6	3.0	5.6	5.5	4.7	6.7
	2000	6.6	1.1	6.9	1.4	2.2	11.0	5.4	1.6	5.5	4.5	3.5	8.3
	2001	6.6	1.1	6.9	1.4	2.2	11.0	5.9	1.7	6.0	4.6	3.9	8.7
	2002	6.3	1.0	6.7	1.5	2.2	10.6	6.5	1.3	6.6	5.3	4.8	9.0
	2004	6.6	1.0	7.0	1.5	2.2	11.2	6.4	1.4	6.4	5.1	4.7	8.9
	2005	5.0	1.0	5.2	1.5	2.2	7.9	5.7	1.4	5.8	5.1	4.7	7.3
	2006	6.6	1.0	7.0	1.5	2.2	11.1	7.8	1.3	7.9	10.2	5.0	8.4
Equatorial Guinea - Guinée équatoriale	1998	17.4	12.0	17.7	10.3	13.8	22.1	13.5	7.1	13.6	15.0	11.7	17.7
	2001	17.3	11.7	17.7	10.6	14.0	21.9	12.8	9.8	12.9	14.9	10.4	17.4
	2002	17.3	11.7	17.7	10.6	14.0	21.9	14.0	8.3	14.1	15.7	12.5	17.0
	2005	17.3	11.8	17.7	10.8	14.1	21.9	14.3	9.9	14.3	14.8	12.9	18.5

For sources and notes, see end of table.

Pour les sources et les notes, se reporter à la fin du tableau.

4.3 Average applied import MFN tariff rates on non-agricultural and non-fuel products

4.3 Droits de douane moyens NPF appliqués à l'importation des produits non-agricoles et non-pétroliers

Market / Marchés	Year / Année	MFN rate - Simple average (2) / Droit NPF - Moyenne simple (2)						MFN rate - Weighted average (3) / Droit NPF - Moyenne pondérée (3)					
		Total of non-agricultural and non-fuel products / Total des produits non-agricoles et non-pétroliers	Ores and metals / Minérais et métaux	Manu-factured products / Produits manu-facturés	Chemical products / Produits chimiques	Machinery and transport equipment / Machines et matériel de transport	Other manu-factured products / Produits manu-facturés divers	Total of non-agricultural and non-fuel products / Total des produits non-agricoles et non-pétroliers	Ores and metals / Minérais et métaux	Manu-factured products / Produits manu-facturés	Chemical products / Produits chimiques	Machinery and transport equipment / Machines et matériel de transport	Other manu-factured products / Produits manu-facturés divers
SITC Rev.2 (1) / CTCI Rév.2 (1)		5+6+7+8 +27+28	27+28+68	(5+6+7+8) - 68	5	7	(6+8) - 68	5+6+7+8 +27+28	27+28+68	(5+6+7+8) - 68	5	7	(6+8) - 68
Estonia - Estonie (4)	1995	0.1	0.0	0.1	0.0	0.1	0.1	0.5	0.0	0.6	0.0	1.3	0.0
	2000	0.1	0.0	0.1	0.4	0.0	0.0	0.0	0.0	0.0	0.1	0.0	0.0
	2001	0.1	0.0	0.1	0.4	0.0	0.0	0.0	0.0	0.0	0.1	0.0	0.0
	2002	0.1	0.0	0.1	0.4	0.0	0.0	0.0	0.0	0.0	0.1	0.0	0.0
	2003	0.1	0.0	0.1	0.4	0.0	0.0	0.0	0.0	0.0	0.1	0.0	0.0
Ethiopia - Éthiopie	1995	27.4	13.6	28.3	16.5	14.6	38.4	18.0	11.0	18.1	9.5	19.3	21.4
	2001	18.6	10.0	19.1	10.8	12.4	25.2	15.1	9.1	15.2	8.8	13.9	19.4
	2002	18.6	10.0	19.1	10.8	12.4	25.2	15.6	8.6	15.7	7.9	14.8	20.1
	2006	17.3	9.3	17.9	10.7	11.6	23.2	10.4	7.5	10.4	6.7	7.9	19.3
EU - UE (5)	1988	5.8	2.5	6.1	7.6	4.9	6.0	5.4	1.7	5.8	7.8	5.7	5.3
	1989	5.8	2.5	6.1	7.6	4.9	6.0	5.3	1.7	5.8	7.7	5.6	5.4
	1990	8.1	2.5	8.5	7.5	5.0	10.3	7.1	1.7	7.6	7.4	5.9	9.6
	1991	6.7	2.5	7.0	7.5	5.0	7.6	6.4	1.7	6.8	7.6	5.9	7.7
	1992	6.8	2.5	7.1	7.7	5.1	7.7	6.8	1.7	7.1	7.7	6.3	7.9
	1993	6.7	2.5	7.0	7.5	5.1	7.6	6.7	1.7	7.0	7.5	6.0	7.9
	1994	6.7	2.5	7.0	7.5	5.0	7.6	6.5	1.9	6.8	7.6	5.9	7.6
	1995	6.1	2.3	6.4	6.6	4.5	7.0	6.1	2.0	6.4	5.9	5.8	7.2
	1996	5.2	2.0	5.4	5.0	3.5	6.4	4.8	1.8	5.0	4.0	4.2	6.3
	1997	5.3	1.9	5.5	5.7	3.5	6.4	4.8	1.8	5.1	4.7	4.2	6.2
	1998	4.8	1.8	5.0	4.8	2.8	5.9	4.0	1.9	4.1	3.7	2.9	5.8
	1999	4.4	1.6	4.5	4.4	2.3	5.5	3.4	1.8	3.5	3.0	2.4	5.3
	2000	4.2	1.6	4.4	4.1	2.3	5.3	3.1	1.7	3.1	2.7	2.0	5.0
	2001	4.3	1.6	4.4	4.9	2.3	5.2	3.2	1.8	3.3	3.4	2.1	5.0
	2002	4.4	1.6	4.6	4.7	2.3	5.6	3.4	1.9	3.5	3.1	2.3	5.3
	2003	4.2	1.6	4.4	4.6	2.3	5.1	3.4	1.9	3.5	3.2	2.4	5.2
	2004	3.9	1.6	4.1	4.5	2.3	4.7	3.3	1.8	3.4	3.0	2.5	4.8
	2005	3.9	1.6	4.1	4.5	2.3	4.7	3.2	1.7	3.3	3.2	2.4	4.7
	2006	3.9	1.6	4.1	4.5	2.2	4.7	3.2	1.7	3.3	3.1	2.3	4.7
Gabon	1995	17.5	12.1	17.9	10.6	14.0	22.2	15.1	16.5	15.1	9.9	14.8	17.7
	1998	17.4	12.0	17.7	10.3	13.8	22.1	14.2	16.7	14.2	7.9	13.6	18.0
	2001	17.3	11.7	17.7	10.6	14.0	21.9	15.1	17.9	15.1	11.1	14.4	17.7
	2002	17.3	11.7	17.7	10.6	14.0	21.9	13.4	10.6	13.5	9.9	12.8	16.1
	2005	17.3	11.8	17.7	10.8	14.1	21.9	15.6	16.4	15.6	9.3	15.3	18.3
Georgia - Géorgie	1999	10.3	11.8	10.2	11.7	5.8	11.5	8.3	10.6	8.3	6.9	6.7	11.0
	2002	10.2	11.8	10.1	11.7	5.9	11.3	8.4	11.4	8.4	7.2	7.3	10.8
	2003	7.6	8.7	7.6	7.7	4.4	8.9	6.9	9.9	6.8	4.6	5.4	9.2
	2004	7.0	7.9	6.9	6.6	4.2	8.2	6.3	8.8	6.3	4.3	5.2	8.5
	2006	6.5	7.1	6.4	5.7	4.0	7.7	6.0	7.4	6.0	4.3	5.4	7.2
Ghana	1993	14.0	11.0	14.2	11.1	10.1	17.1	9.2	9.8	9.2	9.7	8.4	10.4
	2000	13.8	11.7	13.9	11.7	5.3	18.3	8.9	10.2	8.9	11.2	5.2	13.3
	2004	12.5	11.5	12.5	10.9	5.7	16.1	8.9	11.1	8.8	10.1	5.9	13.4
Grenada - Grenade	1996	20.4	16.5	20.4	14.5	19.2	21.6	21.5	14.3	21.6	18.4	28.0	19.4
	1999	17.0	13.3	17.0	11.4	16.8	18.0	16.7	10.5	16.8	14.2	21.2	15.4
	2001	17.0	13.3	17.1	11.5	16.8	18.0	16.2	12.4	16.3	14.3	20.3	15.1
	2002	9.0	5.6	9.2	6.3	7.8	10.7	11.3	7.7	11.3	13.2	9.8	12.0
	2003	9.0	5.6	9.2	6.3	7.8	10.7	10.3	6.2	10.4	12.7	10.0	10.3
	2006	8.8	5.6	9.0	6.1	7.6	10.7	11.6	6.5	11.6	13.1	10.3	12.3
Guatemala	1995	9.5	5.9	9.7	6.0	4.2	13.4	8.0	6.4	8.1	6.3	7.4	10.1
	1997	7.9	2.5	8.2	2.6	3.6	12.3	6.5	3.2	6.6	4.4	5.7	9.2
	1998	7.8	1.4	8.2	1.6	2.8	13.1	6.0	2.9	6.0	3.8	5.5	8.1
	2000	6.6	1.1	7.0	1.4	2.5	11.0	5.1	2.0	5.1	3.4	4.7	7.0
	2001	6.3	1.1	6.6	1.4	2.5	10.3	5.8	2.1	5.9	3.7	5.6	7.7
	2002	5.6	1.0	5.9	1.5	2.5	9.1	5.7	2.0	5.7	3.6	5.4	7.6
	2004	5.0	1.0	5.3	1.5	2.4	7.9	5.9	1.4	6.0	3.7	6.0	7.5
	2005	4.9	1.0	5.2	1.5	2.5	7.8	5.9	1.7	6.0	3.2	5.5	7.6

For sources and notes, see end of table.

Pour les sources et les notes, se reporter à la fin du tableau.

4.3 Average applied import MFN tariff rates on non-agricultural and non-fuel products

4.3 Droits de douane moyens NPF appliqués à l'importation des produits non-agricoles et non-pétroliers

Market / Marchés	Year / Année	MFN rate - Simple average (2) / Droit NPF - Moyenne simple (2)						MFN rate - Weighted average (3) / Droit NPF - Moyenne pondérée (3)					
		Total of non-agricultural and non-fuel products / Total des produits non-agricoles et non-pétroliers	Ores and metals / Minérais et métaux	Manufactured products / Produits manufacturés	Chemical products / Produits chimiques	Machinery and transport equipment / Machines et matériel de transport	Other manufactured products / Produits manufacturés divers	Total of non-agricultural and non-fuel products / Total des produits non-agricoles et non-pétroliers	Ores and metals / Minérais et métaux	Manufactured products / Produits manufacturés	Chemical products / Produits chimiques	Machinery and transport equipment / Machines et matériel de transport	Other manufactured products / Produits manufacturés divers
SITC Rev.2 (1) / CTCI Rév.2 (1)		5+6+7+8 +27+28	27+28+68	(5+6+7+8) - 68	5	7	(6+8) - 68	5+6+7+8 +27+28	27+28+68	(5+6+7+8) - 68	5	7	(6+8) - 68
Guinea - Guinée	2005	11.6	7.5	11.9	6.3	8.4	15.5	11.2	8.8	11.2	3.8	11.8	15.1
Guinea-Bissau - Guinée-Bissau	2001	11.8	7.5	12.0	6.3	8.5	15.7	12.9	9.1	12.9	9.9	10.0	16.2
	2002	11.7	7.5	12.0	6.3	8.5	15.7	13.0	9.4	13.1	8.7	10.9	16.5
	2003	11.7	7.3	12.0	6.3	8.6	15.7	12.9	11.8	12.9	7.2	9.7	16.9
	2004	11.7	7.4	12.0	6.3	8.6	15.7	14.8	10.5	14.9	14.1	11.3	17.3
	2005	11.7	7.4	12.0	6.3	8.6	15.7	13.5	13.4	13.5	10.8	10.2	17.0
	2006	11.7	7.4	12.0	6.3	8.6	15.7	13.5	13.4	13.5	10.8	10.2	17.1
Guyana	1996	21.4	19.0	21.4	15.6	18.9	22.9	18.4	21.2	18.4	13.9	20.4	18.9
	1999	18.0	15.8	18.0	12.5	16.4	19.3	15.6	16.5	15.6	10.7	19.7	14.7
	2000	18.0	15.8	18.0	12.5	16.4	19.3	16.1	16.2	16.1	12.1	20.3	14.9
	2001	9.2	5.7	9.4	6.3	7.7	11.4	9.7	6.6	9.8	8.7	9.6	10.5
	2002	9.2	5.7	9.4	6.3	7.7	11.4	10.0	9.2	10.1	9.1	9.7	10.8
	2003	9.2	5.7	9.4	6.3	7.7	11.4	9.7	10.6	9.6	9.7	9.1	10.1
	2006	9.1	5.6	9.3	6.2	7.7	11.2	9.5	7.5	9.5	10.2	8.8	10.1
Honduras	1995	9.4	5.8	9.6	5.7	4.0	13.4	7.5	6.6	7.6	5.0	4.7	12.2
	1999	6.9	2.0	7.2	2.3	3.4	10.7	5.9	3.3	6.0	3.9	4.1	9.5
	2000	6.7	2.0	7.0	2.2	3.5	10.4	6.0	3.8	6.0	2.4	8.0	8.7
	2001	6.4	2.0	6.7	2.1	3.3	9.8	5.4	3.9	5.5	2.2	8.0	7.8
	2002	5.2	1.0	5.5	1.3	2.4	8.5	5.6	3.0	5.6	2.9	5.0	7.9
	2004	5.2	1.0	5.5	1.3	2.4	8.5	4.9	2.9	5.0	2.7	4.0	7.6
	2005	4.9	1.0	5.2	1.3	2.4	7.8	5.3	2.6	5.3	2.5	5.0	7.5
Hungary - Hongrie (4)	1991	11.5	3.9	12.0	9.6	16.4	11.0	11.7	4.1	12.0	6.8	15.2	10.8
	1993	9.7	4.0	10.1	8.5	10.7	10.4	10.4	2.8	10.7	6.3	12.9	10.2
	1996	8.7	3.2	9.0	7.1	9.9	9.4	9.1	2.4	9.5	6.1	11.1	9.3
	1997	8.3	3.0	8.6	6.6	9.6	8.9	8.7	2.7	8.9	5.6	9.8	8.9
	2002	7.0	2.5	7.3	5.2	8.8	7.4	8.0	2.8	8.1	4.2	9.0	7.6
Iceland - Islande	1993	3.4	0.0	3.6	0.8	3.9	4.6	4.9	0.0	5.1	3.4	4.6	6.0
	1996	2.5	0.0	2.7	0.7	1.3	4.0	2.8	0.0	2.9	3.1	0.8	5.2
	2001	2.5	0.0	2.7	1.0	1.3	4.0	2.9	0.0	3.1	3.3	0.8	5.6
	2003	2.5	0.0	2.6	0.7	1.3	4.0	2.8	0.0	3.0	3.1	0.7	5.7
	2006	2.5	0.0	2.6	0.7	1.3	4.0	2.2	0.0	2.4	3.2	0.5	5.3
India - Inde	1990	83.0	67.8	84.1	77.5	75.8	90.0	70.5	74.1	69.9	78.7	74.0	60.9
	1992	59.1	55.4	59.4	62.0	51.3	61.8	41.5	25.8	43.6	60.0	51.6	27.3
	1997	30.8	24.0	31.2	29.7	26.1	34.0	21.0	25.2	20.5	25.2	21.4	16.5
	1999	33.7	27.1	34.1	34.6	29.2	36.1	31.1	28.1	31.4	28.7	26.9	36.2
	2001	31.3	26.4	31.7	34.1	28.2	32.2	28.0	25.1	28.3	30.3	22.8	31.8
	2004	28.1	22.2	28.5	29.4	26.7	29.0	24.9	22.8	25.1	26.3	21.2	28.8
	2005	15.3	13.7	15.4	15.9	15.1	15.2	12.3	13.6	12.2	14.5	9.4	14.9
Indonesia - Indonésie	1989	22.5	7.1	23.6	9.4	18.1	31.2	14.7	4.2	15.6	6.3	19.3	16.5
	1990	18.6	6.9	19.4	9.4	16.9	24.1	15.1	3.9	15.8	7.1	19.5	14.5
	1993	17.9	6.9	18.6	8.9	16.1	23.3	14.0	4.2	14.5	8.5	16.3	14.9
	1995	15.6	6.4	16.2	7.5	13.1	20.8	12.6	3.6	13.2	6.7	15.8	12.6
	1996	11.9	5.4	12.4	7.1	8.4	16.1	9.0	2.9	9.4	8.1	9.3	10.7
	1999	10.8	5.0	11.2	6.8	8.1	14.2	7.8	3.0	8.1	6.9	7.6	10.3
	2000	8.7	4.9	9.0	5.9	5.4	11.7	6.5	2.9	6.7	5.5	6.1	9.0
	2001	6.8	4.3	7.0	4.9	4.6	8.8	5.3	2.5	5.5	4.2	5.3	7.2
	2002	6.9	4.3	7.0	4.9	4.7	8.8	6.1	3.0	6.3	5.3	5.4	8.5
	2003	6.9	4.3	7.0	4.9	4.7	8.9	5.6	3.2	5.7	5.1	4.7	8.5
	2004	7.0	4.4	7.1	5.0	4.7	9.0	6.4	3.5	6.5	5.7	5.6	9.1
	2005	7.0	4.4	7.1	5.0	4.7	9.0	6.4	3.4	6.5	5.7	5.5	9.1
	2006	7.0	4.4	7.1	5.0	4.7	9.0	6.4	3.4	6.5	5.7	5.5	9.1
Iran (Islamic Rep. of) - Iran (Rép. islamique d')	2000	64.7	18.9	67.6	19.1	43.9	96.2	28.1	13.3	28.6	11.9	34.8	29.6
	2003	27.0	8.5	28.3	11.4	16.1	39.9	17.9	9.9	18.1	20.7	18.6	15.7
	2004	20.9	7.9	21.8	11.6	16.4	28.0	14.4	7.5	14.6	14.1	14.9	14.5

For sources and notes, see end of table.

Pour les sources et les notes, se reporter à la fin du tableau.

4

Market / Marchés	Year / Année	MFN rate - Simple average (2) / Droit NPF - Moyenne simple (2)						MFN rate - Weighted average (3) / Droit NPF - Moyenne pondérée (3)					
		Total of non-agricultural and non-fuel products / Total des produits non-agricoles et non-pétroliers	Ores and metals / Minérais et métaux	Manufactured products / Produits manufacturés	Chemical products / Produits chimiques	Machinery and transport equipment / Machines et matériel de transport	Other manufactured products / Produits manufacturés divers	Total of non-agricultural and non-fuel products / Total des produits non-agricoles et non-pétroliers	Ores and metals / Minérais et métaux	Manufactured products / Produits manufacturés	Chemical products / Produits chimiques	Machinery and transport equipment / Machines et matériel de transport	Other manufactured products / Produits manufacturés divers
SITC Rev.2 (1) / CTCI Rév.2 (1)		5+6+7+8 +27+28	27+28+68	(5+6+7+8) - 68	5	7	(6+8) - 68	5+6+7+8 +27+28	27+28+68	(5+6+7+8) - 68	5	7	(6+8) - 68
Israel - Israël	1993	8.4	1.0	8.9	3.4	5.1	12.5	5.4	2.0	5.5	5.2	4.7	6.2
	2004	4.5	0.6	4.8	1.8	3.6	6.4	2.7	0.5	2.8	3.0	2.7	2.7
	2005	4.4	0.6	4.7	1.8	3.6	6.3	2.7	0.5	2.7	2.9	2.6	2.8
	2006	4.4	0.5	4.7	1.8	3.6	6.3	2.7	0.5	2.7	2.9	2.7	2.8
Jamaica - Jamaïque	1996	20.1	16.5	20.1	14.6	17.9	21.5	20.8	17.2	20.9	16.9	22.3	20.9
	1999	16.7	13.2	16.7	11.5	15.4	17.9	18.4	14.7	18.4	14.1	21.2	18.1
	2000	5.4	1.4	5.6	1.9	3.8	7.9	9.9	1.1	10.0	6.6	10.5	10.9
	2001	5.4	1.4	5.7	1.9	3.8	7.9	9.1	0.7	9.2	5.7	9.5	10.3
	2002	5.4	1.4	5.7	1.9	3.8	7.9	9.3	0.7	9.3	6.0	9.1	10.9
	2003	5.4	1.4	5.7	1.9	3.8	7.9	9.5	1.8	9.6	6.9	9.8	10.7
	2006	5.3	1.3	5.5	1.9	3.9	7.6	9.1	2.2	9.2	5.4	10.6	10.0
Japan - Japon	1988	4.5	2.0	4.7	4.4	1.9	6.0	3.4	0.4	4.1	4.1	1.2	6.0
	1989	4.5	2.0	4.7	4.4	1.8	6.0	3.4	0.4	4.1	4.2	1.0	6.0
	1990	3.7	1.8	3.9	4.3	0.2	5.2	2.7	0.4	3.2	3.9	0.1	5.2
	1991	3.7	1.8	3.8	4.2	0.1	5.2	2.8	0.4	3.3	3.7	0.1	5.6
	1992	3.7	1.8	3.8	4.2	0.1	5.2	3.1	0.4	3.5	3.6	0.1	6.1
	1993	3.7	1.8	3.8	4.2	0.1	5.2	3.2	0.4	3.6	3.6	0.1	6.3
	1994	3.7	1.8	3.8	4.2	0.1	5.2	3.1	0.4	3.5	3.7	0.1	6.2
	1995	3.5	1.8	3.6	3.6	0.0	5.0	2.7	0.2	3.0	2.8	0.0	6.1
	1996	3.3	1.7	3.4	3.3	0.1	4.8	2.7	0.2	2.9	2.5	0.1	6.0
	1997	3.1	1.5	3.2	3.2	0.1	4.7	2.4	0.2	2.6	2.2	0.1	5.4
	1998	3.0	1.3	3.1	3.0	0.1	4.5	2.2	0.2	2.4	2.1	0.1	5.2
	1999	2.9	1.1	3.0	2.8	0.1	4.3	2.1	0.2	2.3	1.9	0.1	5.1
	2000	2.8	1.1	2.9	2.8	0.1	4.2	2.0	0.1	2.1	1.8	0.1	5.0
	2001	2.7	1.1	2.8	2.8	0.1	4.0	2.0	0.2	2.2	1.9	0.1	4.9
	2002	2.6	1.1	2.7	2.7	0.1	3.9	1.9	0.2	2.1	1.8	0.1	4.7
	2003	2.5	1.1	2.6	2.7	0.1	3.7	1.8	0.2	2.0	1.7	0.1	4.5
	2004	2.4	1.1	2.5	2.8	0.1	3.5	1.7	0.2	1.9	1.8	0.1	4.2
	2005	2.4	1.1	2.5	2.7	0.1	3.5	1.6	0.2	1.8	1.7	0.1	4.0
	2006	2.4	1.1	2.5	2.7	0.1	3.5	1.6	0.2	1.8	1.7	0.1	4.0
Jordan - Jordanie	2000	21.8	16.0	22.1	18.0	14.4	27.0	19.8	14.3	19.9	13.9	18.7	24.9
	2001	14.0	11.0	14.2	7.5	11.5	18.0	12.8	9.3	12.9	7.3	12.9	15.4
	2002	14.1	11.0	14.3	7.5	11.5	18.0	13.0	8.7	13.2	7.7	12.9	15.9
	2003	12.0	6.6	12.4	2.7	10.4	16.9	10.9	4.8	11.1	4.5	11.4	13.8
	2005	12.4	7.4	12.8	2.5	10.9	17.6	12.1	6.6	12.3	4.1	12.4	15.1
	2006	10.2	6.4	10.5	1.6	9.3	14.4	8.3	6.4	8.4	3.2	8.7	9.9
Kazakhstan	1996	9.2	8.5	9.3	3.7	1.1	14.7	8.4	3.6	8.6	17.8	1.0	13.6
	2004	2.8	4.1	2.7	3.5	0.3	3.4	1.5	1.7	1.5	1.7	0.2	3.3
Kenya	1994	34.4	28.3	34.8	30.0	25.5	40.4	23.7	26.3	23.6	18.1	24.5	28.0
	2000	17.7	12.7	18.1	11.7	13.4	23.8	12.9	7.7	13.0	7.1	12.3	19.8
	2001	18.9	12.0	19.4	10.9	11.8	25.9	11.5	6.3	11.6	6.1	9.6	20.1
	2004	16.0	12.2	16.3	9.2	9.6	21.8	10.2	4.0	10.4	3.8	11.2	14.2
	2005	11.6	6.6	11.9	3.1	6.2	17.7	7.2	3.8	7.2	3.3	6.8	10.6
	2006	11.6	6.5	11.9	3.0	6.2	17.7	6.9	3.7	7.0	2.4	6.9	10.5
Kuwait - Koweït	2002	4.0	4.0	4.0	4.0	4.0	4.0	4.0	4.0	4.0	4.0	4.0	4.0
	2005	4.9	4.8	4.9	4.8	4.9	5.0	4.8	5.0	4.8	3.1	4.8	5.0
	2006	4.9	4.8	4.9	4.5	4.9	5.0	4.8	5.0	4.8	3.1	4.8	5.0
Kyrgyzstan - Kirghizistan	2002	8.4	7.0	8.5	7.6	7.0	9.5	7.1	5.4	7.2	4.8	6.9	9.0
	2003	4.8	3.6	4.9	2.8	4.6	5.7	2.9	3.2	2.9	0.8	3.3	3.9
	2006	4.2	3.6	4.2	2.7	3.4	5.2	1.9	3.0	1.9	0.8	1.4	3.0
Lao People's dem. Rep. - Rép. dém. populaire lao	2000	7.9	5.8	8.0	6.3	7.2	9.0	12.6	5.0	12.7	9.2	16.7	8.6
	2001	8.0	5.9	8.1	6.3	7.5	9.0	12.0	5.0	12.0	10.6	14.9	8.4
	2004	8.0	5.9	8.1	6.3	7.5	9.0	11.0	5.1	11.0	10.9	13.6	8.2
	2005	8.0	6.0	8.2	6.3	7.6	9.2	12.3	5.0	12.3	11.4	15.4	8.6
	2006	8.0	6.0	8.2	6.3	7.6	9.2	12.3	5.0	12.3	11.4	15.4	8.6

For sources and notes, see end of table.

Pour les sources et les notes, se reporter à la fin du tableau.

Market / Marchés	Year / Année	MFN rate - Simple average (2) / Droit NPF - Moyenne simple (2)						MFN rate - Weighted average (3) / Droit NPF - Moyenne pondérée (3)					
		Total of non-agricultural and non-fuel products / Total des produits non-agricoles et non-pétroliers	Ores and metals / Minérais et métaux	Manufactured products / Produits manufacturés	of which: Chemical products / Produits chimiques	of which: Machinery and transport equipment / Machines et matériel de transport	of which: Other manufactured products / Produits manufacturés divers	Total of non-agricultural and non-fuel products / Total des produits non-agricoles et non-pétroliers	Ores and metals / Minérais et métaux	Manufactured products / Produits manufacturés	of which: Chemical products / Produits chimiques	of which: Machinery and transport equipment / Machines et matériel de transport	of which: Other manufactured products / Produits manufacturés divers
SITC Rev.2 (1) / CTCI Rév.2 (1)		5+6+7+8 +27+28	27+28+68	(5+6+7+8) - 68	5	7	(6+8) - 68	5+6+7+8 +27+28	27+28+68	(5+6+7+8) - 68	5	7	(6+8) - 68
Latvia - Lettonie (4)	1996	2.7	0.5	2.8	1.1	1.7	3.9	2.6	0.5	2.6	1.8	0.9	4.3
	1997	3.6	0.5	3.8	1.1	1.4	5.7	2.8	0.5	2.9	1.9	0.9	5.0
	2001	2.1	0.5	2.2	0.8	0.4	3.5	1.5	0.5	1.6	0.6	0.1	3.3
Lebanon - Liban	1999	9.8	4.1	10.1	4.7	7.7	13.3	12.6	4.6	12.9	6.7	13.5	14.8
	2000	13.6	6.5	14.1	7.4	11.5	17.7	16.0	6.4	16.5	10.6	15.7	19.3
	2001	4.7	2.0	4.9	2.3	3.8	6.4	6.7	2.1	6.8	5.6	5.3	8.4
	2002	4.1	1.9	4.2	2.3	3.6	5.3	6.2	2.0	6.3	5.7	5.1	7.6
	2004	4.1	1.9	4.2	2.3	3.6	5.3	6.0	1.6	6.1	5.5	4.9	7.5
	2005	4.1	1.8	4.2	2.3	3.6	5.2	6.0	1.5	6.1	5.5	4.9	7.5
	2006	4.1	1.8	4.2	2.3	3.6	5.2	6.0	1.6	6.1	5.5	4.9	7.5
Lesotho	2001	7.9	1.4	8.4	2.5	3.2	13.0	17.6	0.0	17.6	1.4	5.9	21.5
	2004	8.1	1.3	8.5	2.4	3.0	13.2	17.4	4.4	17.4	3.6	7.5	20.2
	2005	8.0	1.2	8.5	2.5	3.0	13.1	17.3	2.4	17.3	2.1	8.0	20.1
	2006	8.0	1.2	8.5	2.4	3.0	13.1	17.3	2.4	17.3	2.1	7.9	20.1
Libyan Arab Jamahiriya - Jamahiriya arabe libyenne	1996	18.6	8.3	19.2	6.9	21.3	23.0	25.1	3.4	25.7	10.2	35.1	18.0
	2002	16.8	7.7	17.4	6.5	19.3	20.7	28.5	7.3	28.7	8.7	38.9	16.4
Lithuania - Lituanie (4)	1995	2.8	0.0	2.9	0.7	0.5	4.8	2.0	0.0	2.1	0.4	0.7	4.2
	1997	2.7	0.0	2.9	0.6	0.4	4.8	2.0	0.0	2.0	0.7	0.6	4.4
	2002	2.6	0.0	2.7	0.5	0.4	4.6	1.9	0.0	1.9	0.5	0.6	4.3
	2003	2.4	0.0	2.6	0.5	0.4	4.3	1.9	0.0	1.9	0.6	0.7	4.2
Madagascar	1995	7.3	2.1	7.6	0.9	7.7	10.1	6.3	0.7	6.3	0.8	9.0	6.4
	2001	4.6	1.5	4.8	0.6	4.5	6.5	4.6	0.7	4.6	0.9	5.3	5.4
	2005	11.1	11.0	11.1	9.9	6.7	13.4	6.2	7.9	6.2	6.6	3.5	9.6
	2006	13.1	8.2	13.4	9.8	11.0	15.8	12.6	8.3	12.6	6.4	12.4	15.3
Malawi	1994	31.8	15.4	33.0	25.0	26.8	37.5	26.3	10.9	26.6	13.4	26.7	34.1
	1996	27.4	14.8	28.3	20.1	23.2	33.5	19.4	13.3	19.5	6.8	19.9	31.1
	1997	25.7	13.9	26.5	19.8	22.1	30.8	21.0	4.1	21.2	11.9	20.1	27.4
	1998	20.3	10.4	20.9	11.1	17.2	26.1	16.4	2.4	16.6	8.2	14.8	23.4
	2001	13.0	8.0	13.3	6.1	9.4	17.7	11.6	5.7	11.7	5.5	11.8	14.6
	2006	13.0	7.8	13.4	6.2	9.4	17.8	10.1	2.7	10.2	3.8	10.4	15.1
Malaysia - Malaisie	1988	14.1	5.9	14.7	5.5	11.1	19.6	10.8	4.8	11.2	4.7	10.9	14.5
	1991	14.3	6.0	14.8	6.9	10.4	19.6	10.9	5.7	11.1	9.9	10.3	13.8
	1993	11.8	5.4	12.3	6.0	9.2	15.9	9.3	5.5	9.5	9.3	8.9	11.3
	1996	9.0	2.4	9.4	2.7	5.9	13.5	6.2	4.2	6.3	4.7	5.6	9.3
	1997	9.4	2.4	9.9	3.7	6.5	13.7	5.7	4.4	5.8	4.8	5.2	8.4
	2001	9.3	2.4	9.7	3.0	7.0	13.4	5.2	4.3	5.2	4.4	4.3	9.6
	2002	9.3	2.4	9.7	3.0	7.0	13.4	5.1	4.6	5.1	4.4	4.2	9.4
	2003	9.3	2.4	9.7	3.0	7.0	13.5	5.1	4.4	5.1	4.5	4.2	9.6
	2005	8.3	2.3	8.7	2.6	5.6	12.4	4.8	4.0	4.8	4.9	2.8	13.2
	2006	8.2	2.3	8.6	2.6	5.1	12.3	4.4	3.7	4.5	4.5	2.2	13.5
Maldives	2000	20.6	24.3	20.3	14.7	23.9	20.9	21.4	19.2	21.5	19.8	23.8	19.9
	2001	20.6	24.3	20.3	14.7	23.9	20.9	21.4	18.3	21.5	20.5	23.8	19.8
	2002	20.6	24.2	20.3	14.7	23.9	20.9	21.5	18.1	21.7	20.1	23.4	20.7
	2003	20.6	24.3	20.3	14.7	23.9	21.0	21.9	19.8	21.9	20.7	24.0	20.3
	2004	20.6	24.3	20.3	14.7	24.1	20.9	21.5	19.7	21.5	21.2	23.8	19.8
	2005	20.6	24.3	20.3	14.7	23.9	21.0	21.9	20.1	22.0	20.9	23.7	20.2
	2006	20.6	24.3	20.3	14.7	23.9	21.0	21.9	20.1	22.0	20.9	23.7	20.2
Mali	1995	14.8	16.9	14.7	3.3	8.4	21.5	8.6	12.0	8.5	2.0	9.0	11.7
	2001	11.8	7.5	12.0	6.3	8.5	15.7	10.6	8.9	10.6	5.1	9.2	15.5
	2002	11.7	7.5	12.0	6.3	8.5	15.7	10.6	8.8	10.6	5.3	9.7	16.0
	2003	11.7	7.3	12.0	6.3	8.6	15.7	11.2	8.2	11.2	4.7	10.8	16.2
	2004	11.7	7.4	12.0	6.3	8.6	15.7	11.2	8.4	11.2	4.7	10.7	16.2
	2005	11.7	7.4	12.0	6.3	8.6	15.7	11.2	8.4	11.2	4.7	10.7	16.3
	2006	11.7	7.4	12.0	6.3	8.6	15.7	11.2	8.4	11.3	4.7	10.8	16.3

For sources and notes, see end of table.

Pour les sources et les notes, se reporter à la fin du tableau.

4

Market / Marchés	Year / Année	MFN rate - Simple average (2) / Droit NPF - Moyenne simple (2)						MFN rate - Weighted average (3) / Droit NPF - Moyenne pondérée (3)					
		Total of non-agricultural and non-fuel products / Total des produits non-agricoles et non-pétroliers	Ores and metals / Minérais et métaux	Manufactured products / Produits manufacturés	Chemical products / Produits chimiques	Machinery and transport equipment / Machines et matériel de transport	Other manufactured products / Produits manufacturés divers	Total of non-agricultural and non-fuel products / Total des produits non-agricoles et non-pétroliers	Ores and metals / Minérais et métaux	Manufactured products / Produits manufacturés	Chemical products / Produits chimiques	Machinery and transport equipment / Machines et matériel de transport	Other manufactured products / Produits manufacturés divers
SITC Rev.2 (1) / CTCI Rév.2 (1)		5+6+7+8 +27+28	27+28+68	(5+6+7+8) - 68	5	7	(6+8) - 68	5+6+7+8 +27+28	27+28+68	(5+6+7+8) - 68	5	7	(6+8) - 68
Malta - Malte (4)	1997	7.9	7.9	7.9	7.3	7.2	8.4	9.3	4.6	9.3	4.4	10.9	7.9
	2000	7.8	7.9	7.8	7.3	7.1	8.4	10.3	4.5	10.3	4.2	11.7	8.1
	2002	6.2	2.5	6.4	6.5	4.7	7.1	6.4	5.0	6.4	4.7	6.3	7.2
	2003	6.2	2.5	6.4	6.5	4.7	7.1	6.0	6.0	6.0	4.8	5.6	7.1
Mauritania - Mauritanie	2001	10.5	5.6	10.8	4.9	8.4	14.2	9.9	5.1	9.9	9.4	8.9	12.1
	2006	10.4	5.6	10.7	5.0	8.2	13.9	6.6	5.0	6.6	7.6	5.8	11.7
Mauritius - Maurice	1995	31.7	15.9	32.7	22.0	31.5	37.2	23.0	16.4	23.1	20.6	38.6	16.9
	1997	30.6	16.1	31.6	22.0	30.7	35.5	19.0	12.3	19.1	19.8	25.5	15.0
	1998	30.6	22.6	31.2	24.9	30.0	34.0	27.0	23.8	27.1	36.6	27.9	24.9
	2002	18.7	1.0	19.9	6.1	14.2	27.6	14.2	2.2	14.5	14.1	13.5	15.0
	2005	5.5	1.1	5.8	3.3	5.3	6.9	4.7	1.7	4.8	5.2	3.6	5.8
	2006	2.5	0.3	2.6	1.4	2.6	3.2	1.8	0.3	1.9	2.8	1.2	2.4
Mexico - Mexique	1991	13.7	10.0	14.0	11.2	13.7	15.2	12.9	8.1	13.0	9.8	13.7	13.4
	1995	13.1	9.8	13.3	10.8	11.3	15.0	11.7	8.9	11.8	9.5	11.1	13.7
	1997	13.9	9.6	14.2	9.9	11.1	17.1	12.4	8.3	12.5	8.8	11.3	15.6
	1998	13.8	9.4	14.1	9.6	10.9	17.1	12.1	8.8	12.2	8.7	10.8	15.7
	1999	17.0	12.4	17.3	12.3	14.3	20.6	15.1	12.0	15.2	11.5	14.0	18.5
	2000	17.0	12.4	17.3	12.3	14.1	20.5	14.6	11.9	14.6	11.4	13.2	18.3
	2001	17.0	12.4	17.3	12.3	14.0	20.5	14.5	12.2	14.5	11.6	12.9	18.6
	2002	17.1	12.4	17.4	12.6	14.0	20.7	14.5	12.3	14.6	11.9	12.8	18.9
	2003	17.1	12.3	17.4	12.4	14.0	20.8	14.5	12.2	14.5	11.7	12.6	19.1
	2004	16.4	12.3	16.7	12.3	13.5	19.7	12.8	11.8	12.8	11.4	10.8	17.1
	2005	13.5	9.4	13.8	9.4	10.4	16.9	11.8	9.4	11.9	8.7	11.1	14.6
	2006	13.4	9.4	13.7	9.2	10.4	16.8	11.7	9.6	11.8	8.6	11.2	14.0
Moldova	1996	4.9	2.9	5.1	3.4	1.0	7.4	2.3	1.9	2.3	1.4	1.1	3.7
	2000	4.3	2.0	4.4	3.5	1.5	5.9	2.8	1.8	2.8	1.5	1.3	4.1
	2001	4.1	1.3	4.3	3.4	1.5	5.8	2.9	1.6	2.9	1.7	1.1	4.3
	2006	4.2	0.9	4.4	2.9	1.6	6.2	3.3	0.6	3.3	2.1	1.6	4.7
Mongolia - Mongolie	2005	4.4	5.0	4.3	5.0	2.1	5.0	3.8	5.0	3.7	5.0	2.6	5.0
	2006	4.4	5.0	4.3	5.0	2.1	5.0	3.9	5.0	3.9	5.0	2.8	5.0
Montserrat	1996	19.8	15.8	19.8	14.5	16.7	21.3	15.4	7.0	15.6	19.8	10.7	18.7
	1999	16.4	12.9	16.4	11.2	14.3	17.7	12.1	6.9	12.2	15.1	9.1	14.4
Morocco - Maroc	1993	64.5	28.0	67.0	49.5	55.3	78.3	53.6	17.8	55.7	45.9	51.9	66.4
	1997	18.4	9.3	19.0	12.5	10.7	25.0	17.7	3.9	18.3	12.2	10.9	26.6
	2000	27.9	23.8	28.2	26.2	13.1	35.4	25.9	12.8	26.4	25.6	15.5	36.2
	2001	27.7	23.7	28.0	25.8	13.0	35.1	25.6	12.9	26.1	25.3	14.4	36.4
	2002	27.5	24.1	27.8	24.6	13.0	35.2	25.4	12.7	25.9	24.1	15.2	35.7
	2003	27.1	23.9	27.3	23.2	12.7	35.0	24.1	10.7	24.7	21.1	14.5	35.1
	2005	23.0	12.8	23.7	16.8	10.8	31.8	21.2	7.5	21.8	18.8	14.3	30.3
	2006	20.9	12.8	21.5	16.6	10.8	27.9	18.8	7.5	19.3	18.0	14.3	24.7
Mozambique	1994	5.0	5.0	5.0	5.0	5.0	5.0	5.0	5.0	5.0	5.0	5.0	5.0
	1997	14.5	4.4	15.2	4.9	9.4	21.5	15.4	4.3	15.5	12.0	10.6	21.4
	2001	12.9	4.4	13.4	4.7	8.8	18.7	11.9	6.8	12.0	5.5	8.8	17.6
	2002	11.2	4.3	11.7	4.4	8.1	16.0	9.5	6.7	9.5	9.4	8.2	11.6
	2003	11.2	4.3	11.7	4.4	8.1	16.0	9.5	6.7	9.5	9.4	8.2	11.6
	2005	11.2	4.3	11.7	4.4	8.1	16.0	8.8	6.2	8.8	5.6	8.1	11.0
	2006	11.2	4.3	11.7	4.4	8.1	16.0	8.8	6.2	8.8	5.6	8.1	11.1
Myanmar	2001	5.0	3.2	5.1	1.9	2.9	7.3	4.8	2.9	4.8	2.5	2.8	6.9
	2002	5.0	3.2	5.1	1.9	2.9	7.3	4.7	3.0	4.7	2.5	2.9	6.8
	2003	5.0	3.2	5.1	1.9	2.9	7.3	4.0	2.7	4.1	2.4	2.6	6.2
	2004	5.0	3.2	5.1	1.9	2.9	7.3	4.0	2.5	4.0	2.4	3.1	5.5
	2005	5.1	3.1	5.2	1.8	3.0	7.4	4.0	2.8	4.1	2.6	3.0	5.5
	2006	5.1	3.1	5.2	1.8	3.0	7.4	4.1	2.8	4.1	2.6	3.0	5.6

For sources and notes, see end of table.

Pour les sources et les notes, se reporter à la fin du tableau.

Market / Marchés	Year / Année	MFN rate - Simple average (2) / Droit NPF - Moyenne simple (2)						MFN rate - Weighted average (3) / Droit NPF - Moyenne pondérée (3)					
		Total of non-agricultural and non-fuel products / Total des produits non-agricoles et non-pétroliers	Ores and metals / Minérais et métaux	Manufactured products / Produits manufacturés	Chemical products / Produits chimiques	Machinery and transport equipment / Machines et matériel de transport	Other manufactured products / Produits manufactures divers	Total of non-agricultural and non-fuel products / Total des produits non-agricoles et non-pétroliers	Ores and metals / Minérais et métaux	Manufactured products / Produits manufacturés	Chemical products / Produits chimiques	Machinery and transport equipment / Machines et matériel de transport	Other manufactured products / Produits manufacturés divers
SITC Rev.2 (1) / CTCI Rév.2 (1)		5+6+7+8 +27+28	27+28+68	(5+6+7+8) - 68	5	7	(6+8) - 68	5+6+7+8 +27+28	27+28+68	(5+6+7+8) - 68	5	7	(6+8) - 68
Namibia - Namibie	2001	7.9	1.4	8.4	2.5	3.2	13.0	11.3	0.7	11.5	10.4	10.2	13.5
	2004	8.1	1.3	8.5	2.4	3.0	13.2	10.9	1.8	11.1	6.1	10.2	14.0
	2005	8.0	1.2	8.5	2.5	3.0	13.1	11.0	1.9	11.1	5.9	10.6	13.6
	2006	8.0	1.2	8.5	2.4	3.0	13.1	10.9	1.9	11.0	5.9	10.3	13.6
Nepal - Népal	1993	18.0	7.4	18.7	8.9	18.0	22.6	20.8	5.2	22.1	8.5	25.6	24.9
	1998	17.5	7.5	18.1	8.8	17.4	22.1	29.2	5.1	30.4	9.2	44.9	23.7
	1999	12.9	7.2	13.3	9.7	12.1	15.2	15.1	7.2	15.5	10.9	21.9	12.5
	2000	13.4	9.5	13.6	12.1	11.8	15.0	19.5	5.4	20.3	12.0	33.2	12.4
	2002	13.6	10.2	13.9	12.2	11.9	15.3	16.8	7.3	17.5	13.9	22.7	15.9
	2003	13.7	10.2	14.0	12.3	12.0	15.5	17.0	7.3	17.7	14.1	23.0	16.1
	2004	13.8	10.4	14.1	12.5	11.4	15.8	16.1	7.2	16.8	14.5	18.8	16.5
	2005	13.8	10.4	14.1	12.5	11.4	15.8	16.4	7.2	17.0	14.5	19.6	16.4
	2006	12.3	10.0	12.5	11.4	10.3	13.8	14.9	7.0	15.5	12.6	17.1	15.6
New Zealand - Nouvelle-Zélande	1992	8.9	2.4	9.3	2.4	10.9	11.3	9.3	3.5	9.6	5.5	9.5	11.5
	1993	8.4	2.4	8.8	2.1	9.7	11.0	9.0	3.4	9.3	4.4	9.7	11.0
	1996	6.1	1.7	6.4	1.4	6.6	8.2	7.3	2.2	7.5	2.9	8.1	8.8
	1997	5.3	1.3	5.6	1.2	5.8	7.2	6.2	2.4	6.4	2.3	6.4	8.1
	1998	4.5	1.0	4.7	0.9	4.9	6.0	5.3	1.8	5.5	1.8	5.4	7.3
	1999	3.7	0.8	3.9	0.8	4.1	5.1	4.6	1.7	4.7	1.7	4.8	5.9
	2000	2.9	0.6	3.1	0.6	3.1	4.0	3.6	1.3	3.7	1.3	3.8	4.6
	2002	3.6	0.8	3.8	0.8	3.9	5.0	4.6	1.8	4.7	1.8	4.8	5.8
	2003	3.6	0.8	3.8	0.8	3.9	4.9	4.6	1.9	4.7	1.9	4.9	5.5
	2004	3.5	0.8	3.7	0.8	3.9	4.7	4.5	2.0	4.6	1.7	4.8	5.4
	2005	3.5	0.8	3.7	0.8	3.9	4.7	4.3	2.2	4.4	1.7	4.6	5.2
	2006	3.3	0.8	3.5	0.8	3.9	4.4	4.2	2.2	4.3	1.7	4.5	5.0
Nicaragua	1995	9.4	5.8	9.6	5.8	4.1	13.3	7.6	6.3	7.6	6.5	5.1	10.9
	1998	4.8	1.2	5.0	1.3	1.9	7.7	5.1	3.8	5.1	3.9	4.0	7.3
	1999	9.7	6.2	9.9	6.2	6.9	12.6	9.6	10.0	9.6	8.0	8.2	12.1
	2000	3.1	0.9	3.3	0.9	1.5	5.0	3.9	2.3	3.9	3.0	3.5	4.8
	2001	3.9	0.9	4.1	1.1	1.8	6.3	4.5	2.2	4.5	3.8	3.6	5.7
	2002	3.9	0.9	4.1	1.1	1.8	6.3	4.5	2.2	4.5	3.9	3.7	5.5
	2004	4.3	1.0	4.6	1.4	2.2	6.8	5.5	4.5	5.5	3.7	5.3	6.8
	2005	4.8	1.0	5.1	1.4	2.2	7.7	5.4	4.7	5.4	3.3	4.2	7.9
Niger	2001	11.8	7.5	12.0	6.3	8.5	15.7	13.0	5.5	13.3	6.2	12.9	16.8
	2002	11.7	7.5	12.0	6.3	8.5	15.7	12.4	5.4	12.6	6.0	11.5	16.8
	2003	11.7	7.3	12.0	6.3	8.6	15.7	11.3	5.5	11.5	4.0	10.7	15.7
	2004	11.7	7.4	12.0	6.3	8.6	15.7	11.4	5.6	11.5	4.0	10.7	15.8
	2005	11.7	7.4	12.0	6.3	8.6	15.7	11.8	5.6	12.0	5.1	11.0	15.6
	2006	11.7	7.4	12.0	6.3	8.6	15.7	11.9	5.6	12.1	5.1	11.1	15.6
Nigeria - Nigéria	1988	33.6	22.5	34.4	18.5	18.2	47.0	21.3	18.7	21.4	18.5	18.9	27.4
	1989	35.6	29.9	36.0	19.1	19.5	49.2	22.3	15.8	22.5	19.0	19.8	29.1
	1990	35.8	30.0	36.2	19.0	20.2	49.2	22.5	16.6	22.7	18.9	20.6	28.6
	1992	34.5	23.2	35.2	22.6	20.2	46.2	23.1	16.6	23.3	22.3	20.6	28.2
	1995	27.0	11.4	28.5	11.5	12.3	36.4	19.5	10.3	19.8	12.4	17.8	24.6
	1996	23.4	16.6	23.9	13.2	12.7	32.7	14.9	9.8	15.1	14.4	12.9	18.3
	1997	23.4	16.6	23.9	13.2	12.7	32.7	15.1	10.0	15.3	15.1	12.9	18.4
	1998	23.4	16.6	23.9	13.2	12.7	32.7	15.1	10.0	15.3	15.1	12.9	18.4
	1999	25.3	18.8	25.7	17.6	16.3	32.9	18.5	14.6	18.7	18.9	16.7	20.8
	2000	25.3	18.8	25.7	17.6	16.3	32.9	18.2	15.4	18.2	17.0	17.5	20.6
	2001	25.3	18.8	25.8	17.6	16.3	32.9	18.6	16.9	18.7	17.5	17.4	21.3
	2002	26.7	17.4	27.3	16.1	15.4	36.6	15.7	10.0	15.8	12.4	14.6	20.3
	2005	11.4	6.9	11.7	6.8	5.9	16.0	9.8	10.1	9.8	10.1	6.6	14.8
	2006	11.4	6.9	11.8	6.8	6.0	16.1	10.2	10.1	10.2	10.1	7.3	14.9

For sources and notes, see end of table.

Pour les sources et les notes, se reporter à la fin du tableau.

Market / Marchés	Year / Année	MFN rate - Simple average (2) / Droit NPF - Moyenne simple (2)						MFN rate - Weighted average (3) / Droit NPF - Moyenne pondérée (3)					
		Total of non-agricultural and non-fuel products / Total des produits non-agricoles et non-pétroliers	Ores and metals / Minérais et métaux	Manu-factured products / Produits manu-facturés	Chemical products / Produits chimiques	Machinery and transport equipment / Machines et matériel de transport	Other manu-factured products / Produits manu-facturés divers	Total of non-agricultural and non-fuel products / Total des produits non-agricoles et non-pétroliers	Ores and metals / Minérais et métaux	Manu-factured products / Produits manu-facturés	Chemical products / Produits chimiques	Machinery and transport equipment / Machines et matériel de transport	Other manu-factured products / Produits manu-facturés divers
SITC Rev.2 (1) / CTCI Rév.2 (1)		5+6+7+8 +27+28	27+28+68	(5+6+7+8) - 68	5	7	(6+8) - 68	5+6+7+8 +27+28	27+28+68	(5+6+7+8) - 68	5	7	(6+8) - 68
Norway - Norvège	1988	6.5	0.5	7.0	5.0	5.1	8.6	5.5	0.4	5.9	6.2	3.6	9.0
	1993	6.6	0.4	7.0	5.0	5.2	8.6	5.7	0.3	6.2	6.0	4.2	8.8
	1995	6.2	0.4	6.6	4.7	4.8	8.1	5.4	0.4	5.8	5.8	4.3	7.8
	1996	5.7	0.4	6.1	4.8	4.0	7.6	4.6	0.3	5.0	6.7	3.1	7.2
	1998	3.6	0.3	3.8	3.5	0.7	5.3	2.3	0.3	2.4	5.2	0.7	4.3
	2000	2.4	0.3	2.6	1.4	0.3	4.0	1.6	0.3	1.7	3.2	0.2	3.9
	2001	2.3	0.3	2.4	1.0	0.3	3.8	1.5	0.3	1.6	2.1	0.2	3.6
	2002	1.8	0.2	1.9	0.7	0.2	3.2	1.3	0.2	1.4	1.4	0.1	3.0
	2003	0.8	0.0	0.9	0.3	0.0	1.4	0.6	0.0	0.7	0.7	0.0	1.6
	2006	0.7	0.0	0.7	0.3	0.0	1.2	0.4	0.0	0.5	0.5	0.0	1.1
Oman	1992	5.1	5.0	5.1	5.0	5.0	5.2	5.4	5.7	5.4	4.5	5.0	6.5
	1997	4.9	4.9	4.9	4.8	4.8	5.0	4.9	4.9	4.9	4.7	5.0	4.9
	2002	7.1	5.4	7.2	5.6	7.0	7.9	6.5	5.2	6.5	7.4	6.1	7.2
	2005	4.9	4.8	4.9	4.8	4.9	5.0	4.7	5.0	4.7	3.7	4.8	5.0
	2006	4.9	4.8	4.9	4.6	4.9	5.0	4.7	5.0	4.7	3.7	4.8	5.0
Pakistan	1995	51.9	37.2	52.9	43.3	45.6	59.6	48.8	29.3	49.5	41.6	51.1	58.4
	1998	47.7	36.8	48.5	42.0	38.7	54.8	43.5	28.7	44.1	38.9	43.8	52.4
	2001	20.4	12.1	20.9	14.9	19.6	23.7	20.8	9.6	21.3	13.8	25.7	22.7
	2002	17.4	10.6	17.8	13.9	16.4	19.9	17.5	8.9	17.9	13.2	20.5	19.2
	2003	17.1	9.9	17.6	13.6	16.1	19.7	17.2	8.6	17.6	13.0	20.0	19.0
	2004	16.6	9.7	17.1	12.7	15.4	19.5	15.6	8.3	15.9	10.8	18.2	18.6
	2005	14.3	8.4	14.7	9.7	13.5	17.2	14.4	9.4	14.7	8.4	18.0	14.9
	2006	14.3	8.4	14.7	9.7	13.5	17.2	14.3	8.7	14.6	8.6	17.0	15.4
Panama	1997	10.9	12.9	10.8	6.4	9.5	12.9	11.0	11.5	11.0	6.7	9.6	14.4
	1998	7.6	8.9	7.6	4.9	7.0	8.9	8.5	5.6	8.5	5.4	9.1	8.8
	2000	7.1	8.7	7.0	4.1	6.9	8.2	7.7	6.9	7.7	4.9	7.8	8.6
	2001	6.8	8.4	6.7	3.4	6.9	7.9	7.4	6.5	7.4	4.7	7.8	8.2
	2005	6.2	8.3	6.1	1.9	6.8	7.4	6.7	4.3	6.7	2.7	7.5	7.7
	2006	6.2	8.3	6.1	1.9	6.8	7.4	6.7	4.3	6.7	2.7	7.5	7.7
Papua New Guinea - Papouasie-Nouvelle-Guinée	1997	16.7	13.3	17.0	9.5	9.9	22.8	13.2	20.1	13.2	10.5	11.9	15.9
	2002	4.9	0.0	5.2	1.1	0.3	8.9	2.5	0.0	2.5	2.2	0.1	5.4
	2003	4.1	0.0	4.4	0.9	0.3	7.5	1.7	0.0	1.8	2.5	0.1	3.8
	2004	4.1	0.0	4.4	0.9	0.3	7.5	1.7	0.0	1.8	2.5	0.1	3.8
	2005	4.1	0.0	4.4	0.9	0.3	7.5	1.7	0.0	1.8	2.5	0.1	3.8
	2006	3.3	0.0	3.5	0.7	0.2	6.0	1.3	0.0	1.3	1.8	0.1	2.9
Paraguay	1991	15.0	5.6	15.6	5.4	11.8	21.0	14.4	3.1	14.5	8.8	14.0	17.6
	1994	7.7	2.1	8.0	1.1	7.1	11.0	8.1	0.8	8.2	3.1	9.0	9.1
	1995	11.1	6.0	11.4	8.0	6.6	14.7	10.4	6.9	10.4	9.3	9.5	12.5
	1996	11.2	6.0	11.5	7.8	6.1	15.2	9.4	8.1	9.4	8.2	8.7	11.4
	1997	11.4	6.0	11.7	7.9	7.1	15.1	10.4	7.6	10.4	8.8	9.7	12.3
	1998	11.4	6.0	11.8	7.9	7.6	15.1	10.2	8.2	10.2	8.8	9.6	12.1
	1999	13.4	8.8	13.6	10.6	8.1	17.2	10.5	10.7	10.5	10.3	9.1	12.8
	2000	13.4	8.8	13.7	10.7	8.7	17.1	11.7	8.8	11.7	11.1	10.0	14.1
	2001	13.1	7.9	13.5	9.8	9.8	16.4	11.9	8.5	11.9	10.3	10.8	14.2
	2002	12.8	7.3	13.2	9.2	9.8	16.2	11.3	7.2	11.4	9.7	9.9	14.3
	2003	12.9	7.3	13.2	9.3	9.8	16.2	11.9	7.4	12.0	9.4	11.4	14.7
	2004	12.1	7.3	12.4	9.4	6.4	16.1	12.3	7.6	12.4	9.8	11.5	15.3
	2005	10.9	5.8	11.2	7.7	5.9	14.8	10.1	6.2	10.1	7.4	9.0	13.6
	2006	10.1	5.7	10.4	7.1	5.1	13.9	6.0	4.4	6.0	4.9	4.5	10.2

For sources and notes, see end of table.

Pour les sources et les notes, se reporter à la fin du tableau.

Market / Marchés	Year / Année	MFN rate - Simple average (2) / Droit NPF - Moyenne simple (2)						MFN rate - Weighted average (3) / Droit NPF - Moyenne pondérée (3)					
		Total of non-agricultural and non-fuel products / Total des produits non-agricoles et non-pétroliers	Ores and metals / Minérais et métaux	Manufactured products / Produits manu-facturés	Chemical products / Produits chimiques	Machinery and transport equipment / Machines et matériel de transport	Other manufactured products / Produits manu-facturés divers	Total of non-agricultural and non-fuel products / Total des produits non-agricoles et non-pétroliers	Ores and metals / Minérais et métaux	Manufactured products / Produits manu-facturés	Chemical products / Produits chimiques	Machinery and transport equipment / Machines et matériel de transport	Other manufactured products / Produits manu-facturés divers
SITC Rev.2 (1) / CTCI Rév.2 (1)		5+6+7+8 +27+28	27+28+68	(5+6+7+8) - 68	5	7	(6+8) - 68	5+6+7+8 +27+28	27+28+68	(5+6+7+8) - 68	5	7	(6+8) - 68
Peru - Pérou	1993	17.9	15.4	18.1	15.5	16.0	20.0	16.6	15.0	16.6	15.7	16.0	18.3
	1995	16.5	15.0	16.6	15.0	15.3	17.8	15.4	15.0	15.4	15.0	15.2	15.8
	1997	13.2	12.0	13.3	12.0	12.3	14.2	12.3	12.0	12.3	12.0	12.2	12.7
	1998	13.2	12.0	13.3	12.0	12.3	14.2	12.3	12.0	12.3	12.0	12.2	12.7
	1999	13.2	12.0	13.3	12.0	12.3	14.2	12.3	12.0	12.3	12.0	12.2	12.8
	2000	13.2	12.0	13.3	12.0	12.3	14.2	12.3	12.0	12.4	12.0	12.2	12.8
	2004	10.2	8.8	10.3	6.7	7.7	12.7	8.9	9.4	8.9	7.2	8.4	10.8
	2005	9.6	8.7	9.7	6.6	6.1	12.4	8.2	9.4	8.1	6.8	7.3	10.2
	2006	9.6	8.5	9.7	6.6	6.1	12.4	7.9	9.2	7.9	6.9	6.6	10.3
Philippines	1988	27.5	17.2	28.2	16.9	23.7	34.4	23.1	12.8	23.5	19.6	22.5	28.3
	1989	27.6	17.2	28.3	16.9	23.7	34.4	23.1	12.8	23.5	19.6	22.5	28.3
	1990	19.2	13.8	19.6	12.5	15.1	24.0	14.8	10.8	15.0	12.7	13.4	20.6
	1992	19.2	13.8	19.6	12.5	15.1	24.0	14.8	10.8	14.9	12.7	13.4	20.6
	1993	21.8	11.4	22.5	12.7	15.2	29.2	15.1	9.5	15.3	12.2	13.3	22.5
	1994	21.3	11.3	21.9	12.7	14.8	28.4	14.8	9.5	15.0	12.2	13.2	21.8
	1995	19.4	12.9	19.9	12.5	14.1	25.0	14.1	9.5	14.3	12.1	12.4	20.9
	1998	10.0	3.9	10.4	4.6	7.0	14.1	5.6	3.9	5.7	5.9	4.3	10.9
	1999	9.1	3.8	9.4	4.5	6.9	12.3	5.7	3.9	5.8	5.8	4.5	10.0
	2000	7.2	3.3	7.4	3.9	5.0	9.8	3.5	3.4	3.5	5.1	2.1	7.6
	2001	6.8	3.3	7.1	3.8	4.6	9.4	3.2	3.7	3.2	4.9	1.8	7.0
	2002	5.2	2.7	5.4	3.2	3.5	7.0	2.1	2.9	2.1	4.3	1.1	5.5
	2003	4.3	2.7	4.4	3.1	3.1	5.4	2.0	2.9	2.0	4.3	1.2	4.4
	2004	5.8	2.5	6.0	3.5	3.5	8.0	3.1	2.5	3.1	5.1	1.8	6.2
	2005	5.8	2.5	6.0	3.4	3.5	8.0	3.3	2.5	3.3	5.2	2.0	6.3
	2006	5.8	2.5	6.0	3.4	3.5	8.0	3.3	2.5	3.3	5.2	2.0	6.3
Poland - Pologne (4)	1991	11.8	6.7	12.1	11.4	9.3	13.5	10.6	3.9	10.9	12.2	9.4	11.8
	1992	11.8	6.7	12.1	11.3	9.3	13.5	10.6	3.9	10.9	12.2	9.4	11.8
	1995	9.6	6.5	9.8	12.7	13.1	7.4	10.2	5.5	10.4	11.4	12.2	8.1
	1996	13.7	6.8	14.1	11.8	12.5	15.7	12.9	5.1	13.2	10.5	13.9	13.5
	1997	12.0	5.8	12.4	11.3	9.9	13.8	10.2	4.6	10.4	9.1	9.7	11.8
	1998	11.4	5.7	11.8	11.0	9.2	13.1	9.6	5.1	9.8	8.8	8.5	11.4
	1999	10.9	5.5	11.3	10.7	8.8	12.5	9.1	5.8	9.2	8.5	7.9	11.0
	2000	10.5	5.4	10.9	9.7	9.2	12.0	10.0	5.6	10.1	7.8	10.7	10.6
	2001	10.0	5.1	10.4	10.3	8.1	11.3	8.1	5.5	8.2	7.5	6.5	10.2
	2002	9.9	4.7	10.3	9.3	8.8	11.3	10.1	4.7	10.2	7.1	11.4	10.3
	2003	10.0	5.1	10.3	10.2	8.1	11.3	8.2	5.9	8.3	7.5	6.6	10.4
Qatar	2002	4.1	4.0	4.1	4.0	4.0	4.1	4.0	4.0	4.0	4.0	4.0	4.0
	2005	4.9	4.8	4.9	4.9	4.9	5.0	4.9	5.0	4.9	4.1	5.0	5.0
	2006	4.9	4.8	4.9	4.6	4.9	5.0	4.9	5.0	4.9	4.0	5.0	5.0
Republic of Korea - République de Corée	1988	18.2	13.4	18.6	18.6	18.2	18.7	16.1	8.5	16.9	17.3	16.4	17.5
	1989	14.3	7.4	14.7	14.3	14.8	14.9	12.5	4.5	13.6	12.4	14.4	13.2
	1990	12.3	7.0	12.7	12.4	12.6	12.9	10.9	4.7	11.5	11.4	11.5	11.7
	1992	10.5	6.0	10.8	10.6	10.7	10.9	9.4	4.4	9.9	10.1	9.7	10.1
	1995	7.6	4.5	7.8	7.8	7.7	7.8	7.1	3.7	7.4	7.5	7.4	7.5
	1996	8.3	4.4	8.6	11.8	7.6	7.8	7.3	3.6	7.6	9.6	7.3	7.4
	1999	7.8	4.3	8.0	7.6	7.2	8.6	5.9	2.9	6.2	7.1	5.5	7.5
	2002	7.9	4.2	8.1	11.0	5.9	8.0	4.9	2.8	5.0	8.5	3.3	6.5
	2004	7.2	4.1	7.5	9.4	5.9	7.3	4.3	2.7	4.5	7.4	3.5	5.0
	2006	7.2	4.1	7.4	9.4	5.9	7.3	4.2	2.5	4.5	7.2	3.5	4.8
Romania - Roumanie	1991	17.3	6.8	18.0	16.5	16.3	19.3	15.8	2.8	18.2	15.4	20.1	17.2
	1999	16.0	6.7	16.7	15.9	14.6	17.8	14.1	5.6	14.4	13.9	12.1	16.0
	2001	16.1	6.6	16.7	14.5	14.0	18.7	14.7	3.9	15.1	10.9	12.6	18.0
	2004	16.0	6.5	16.6	15.2	13.3	18.6	14.8	4.4	15.2	12.0	13.9	17.2
	2005	15.3	6.3	16.0	14.2	12.8	18.0	13.9	4.3	14.3	9.8	14.0	15.8

For sources and notes, see end of table.

Pour les sources et les notes, se reporter à la fin du tableau.

Market / Marchés	Year / Année	MFN rate - Simple average (2) / Droit NPF - Moyenne simple (2)						MFN rate - Weighted average (3) / Droit NPF - Moyenne pondérée (3)					
		Total of non-agricultural and non-fuel products / Total des produits non-agricoles et non-pétroliers	Ores and metals / Minérais et métaux	Manu-factured products / Produits manu-facturés	Chemical products / Produits chimiques	Machinery and transport equipment / Machines et matériel de transport	Other manu-factured products / Produits manu-facturés divers	Total of non-agricultural and non-fuel products / Total des produits non-agricoles et non-pétroliers	Ores and metals / Minérais et métaux	Manu-factured products / Produits manu-facturés	Chemical products / Produits chimiques	Machinery and transport equipment / Machines et matériel de transport	Other manu-factured products / Produits manu-facturés divers
SITC Rev.2 (1) / CTCI Rév.2 (1)		5+6+7+8 +27+28	27+28+68	(5+6+7+8) - 68	5	7	(6+8) - 68	5+6+7+8 +27+28	27+28+68	(5+6+7+8) - 68	5	7	(6+8) - 68
Russian Federation - Fédération de Russie	1993	8.7	7.1	8.8	5.3	6.3	11.1	7.2	3.7	7.5	7.6	6.4	8.8
	1994	12.1	6.9	12.5	5.7	12.1	15.2	9.2	3.5	9.6	5.8	8.8	12.1
	1996	11.4	10.0	11.5	5.7	11.4	13.9	9.1	5.4	9.4	7.7	8.1	12.1
	1997	13.0	9.0	13.3	7.1	12.8	15.8	11.5	5.7	11.9	9.3	11.2	14.1
	2001	10.0	8.2	10.2	6.5	10.2	11.9	9.0	6.4	9.2	8.5	8.6	10.7
	2002	9.7	8.6	9.8	6.6	8.9	11.7	8.8	6.8	8.9	8.7	7.9	10.9
	2005	9.6	8.6	9.6	6.6	8.5	11.7	8.4	5.6	8.5	9.0	7.5	10.4
Rwanda	1993	33.1	24.9	33.7	17.8	24.8	43.3	25.2	17.2	25.6	15.2	25.2	29.6
	2001	9.5	6.7	9.7	5.7	7.2	12.3	7.0	5.4	7.1	4.8	8.2	6.9
	2003	9.5	6.7	9.7	5.7	7.2	12.3	8.8	5.5	8.9	4.7	9.1	10.6
	2005	19.6	10.9	20.2	14.8	18.4	23.0	16.2	15.2	16.2	7.8	15.5	22.8
	2006	19.6	10.9	20.2	14.8	18.4	23.0	16.2	15.2	16.2	7.8	15.5	22.8
Saint Kitts and Nevis - Saint-Kitts-et-Nevis	1996	20.8	16.0	20.8	14.5	21.3	21.7	23.7	15.7	23.8	17.6	34.2	19.9
	1999	17.3	12.8	17.4	11.0	18.5	18.1	19.1	10.9	19.1	14.4	32.6	15.7
	2000	8.8	2.4	9.2	5.1	7.8	11.4	13.3	4.4	13.4	13.1	12.5	14.2
	2001	8.8	2.4	9.2	5.1	7.8	11.4	12.1	5.6	12.2	12.0	11.2	13.0
	2002	8.8	2.4	9.2	5.1	7.8	11.4	13.4	2.7	13.6	12.0	11.9	15.2
	2003	8.8	2.4	9.2	5.1	7.8	11.4	13.4	3.9	13.5	12.1	12.2	14.7
	2006	8.6	2.4	9.0	5.1	7.2	11.3	13.7	7.6	13.8	12.7	12.2	15.3
Saint Lucia - Sainte-Lucie	1996	20.5	16.5	20.6	14.5	20.5	21.5	20.8	14.1	20.9	15.8	25.7	20.1
	1999	17.1	13.3	17.1	11.3	17.3	18.0	17.6	13.1	17.6	13.5	24.3	15.5
	2000	17.1	13.3	17.2	11.5	17.3	18.0	17.7	13.1	17.7	14.2	24.3	15.6
	2001	7.5	2.2	7.9	5.6	5.2	9.9	11.6	1.5	11.7	13.2	11.6	11.5
	2002	7.5	2.2	7.9	5.6	5.2	9.9	12.4	1.4	12.5	13.3	10.7	13.6
	2003	7.5	2.2	7.9	5.6	5.2	9.9	12.4	1.6	12.5	12.8	10.5	14.2
	2005	7.5	2.2	7.8	5.6	5.0	9.9	13.5	2.8	13.7	12.8	12.8	14.5
	2006	7.5	2.2	7.8	5.6	5.0	9.9	13.5	2.8	13.7	12.8	12.8	14.5
Saint Vincent and the Grenadines - Saint-Vincent-et-les Grenadines	1996	20.1	15.5	20.1	14.5	18.4	21.4	20.2	18.8	20.2	16.0	23.3	19.9
	1999	16.7	12.2	16.7	11.3	15.9	17.8	16.5	13.0	16.5	12.0	20.1	16.4
	2000	16.7	12.2	16.7	11.5	15.9	17.7	16.5	14.5	16.6	12.6	22.3	15.5
	2001	8.5	4.4	8.8	5.7	7.4	10.6	12.2	6.9	12.3	10.1	11.4	13.3
	2002	8.5	4.4	8.8	5.7	7.4	10.6	11.3	7.0	11.3	11.2	10.5	12.0
	2003	8.5	4.4	8.8	5.7	7.4	10.6	11.2	5.5	11.2	11.2	10.6	11.7
	2006	1.8	2.4	1.7	4.8	0.6	1.0	3.5	3.5	3.5	9.7	3.5	2.1
Saudi Arabia - Arabie saoudite	1994	12.2	12.2	12.2	11.8	11.8	12.5	11.5	13.4	11.5	9.0	11.0	12.8
	1999	12.1	12.2	12.1	11.8	11.8	12.4	11.5	13.3	11.4	8.3	11.3	12.9
	2000	12.1	12.2	12.1	11.8	11.8	12.3	11.4	13.1	11.3	8.4	11.4	12.5
	2003	6.1	5.5	6.1	6.0	5.4	6.5	6.6	7.9	6.5	5.2	5.8	8.2
	2004	6.1	5.5	6.1	6.0	5.4	6.5	6.3	7.5	6.3	5.5	5.6	7.8
	2005	4.9	4.8	4.9	4.8	4.9	5.0	4.7	5.0	4.7	3.4	4.8	5.0
	2006	4.9	4.8	4.9	4.5	4.9	5.0	4.7	5.0	4.7	3.4	4.8	5.0
Senegal - Sénégal	2001	11.8	7.5	12.0	6.3	8.5	15.7	10.3	6.8	10.4	5.7	10.5	13.2
	2002	11.7	7.5	12.0	6.3	8.5	15.7	10.9	8.5	11.0	5.6	12.4	13.4
	2003	11.7	7.3	12.0	6.3	8.6	15.7	10.2	6.4	10.5	5.7	10.4	13.5
	2004	11.7	7.4	12.0	6.3	8.6	15.7	10.3	6.2	10.5	5.5	10.5	13.5
	2005	11.7	7.4	12.0	6.3	8.6	15.7	10.2	6.0	10.4	5.6	10.1	13.6
	2006	11.7	7.4	12.0	6.3	8.6	15.7	10.5	7.7	10.6	5.6	10.2	13.9
Seychelles	2000	25.1	22.5	25.2	28.7	20.8	25.8	18.5	21.3	18.5	22.7	17.3	21.1
	2001	24.8	22.5	25.0	28.7	20.8	25.3	18.5	21.3	18.5	22.7	17.3	21.1
	2005	6.5	2.7	6.7	1.2	7.6	8.4	11.3	1.4	11.3	4.2	17.2	5.4
	2006	4.1	0.0	4.4	0.8	3.5	6.0	6.6	0.0	6.7	2.6	13.5	2.1
Singapore - Singapour	1989	0.4	0.0	0.5	0.0	0.6	0.6	0.6	0.0	0.6	0.0	0.9	0.4
Slovakia - Slovaquie (4)	2002	4.5	1.2	4.7	4.1	3.8	5.3	4.7	1.2	4.9	3.6	4.7	5.6

For sources and notes, see end of table.

Pour les sources et les notes, se reporter à la fin du tableau.

Market / Marchés	Year / Année	MFN rate - Simple average (2) / Droit NPF - Moyenne simple (2)						MFN rate - Weighted average (3) / Droit NPF - Moyenne pondérée (3)					
		Total of non-agricultural and non-fuel products / Total des produits non-agricoles et non-pétroliers	Ores and metals / Minérais et métaux	Manufactured products / Produits manufacturés	Chemical products / Produits chimiques	Machinery and transport equipment / Machines et matériel de transport	Other manufactured products / Produits manufacturés divers	Total of non-agricultural and non-fuel products / Total des produits non-agricoles et non-pétroliers	Ores and metals / Minérais et métaux	Manufactured products / Produits manufacturés	Chemical products / Produits chimiques	Machinery and transport equipment / Machines et matériel de transport	Other manufactured products / Produits manufacturés divers
SITC Rev.2 (1) / CTCI Rév.2 (1)		5+6+7+8 +27+28	27+28+68	(5+6+7+8) - 68	5	7	(6+8) - 68	5+6+7+8 +27+28	27+28+68	(5+6+7+8) - 68	5	7	(6+8) - 68
Slovenia - Slovénie (4)	1999	10.0	3.2	10.4	7.5	10.7	11.4	11.9	4.4	12.4	9.0	13.6	12.1
	2001	9.7	3.0	10.1	7.5	9.5	11.3	10.4	4.8	10.8	9.0	10.4	11.9
	2002	9.6	3.0	10.1	7.5	9.4	11.3	10.3	4.9	10.6	9.0	10.1	11.8
	2003	9.6	3.0	10.1	7.5	9.4	11.3	10.3	4.7	10.7	9.0	10.5	11.6
Solomon Islands - Îles Salomon	1995	39.1	7.9	41.3	16.3	20.4	59.1	34.0	10.9	34.2	24.8	27.4	42.8
	2006	13.8	11.0	14.0	9.4	13.0	16.1	12.8	14.3	12.8	11.7	12.2	13.5
South Africa - Afrique du Sud	1988	(a)11.9	(a)3.9	(a)12.4	(a)8.8	(a)7.6	(a)16.1	(a)12.2	(a)4.4	(a)12.4	(a)7.0	(a)14.6	(a)10.0
	1990	(a)10.8	(a)3.8	(a)11.3	(a)8.6	(a)7.7	(a)14.2	(a)10.9	(a)5.9	(a)11.0	(a)7.1	(a)12.3	(a)10.6
	1991	(a)10.5	(a)3.5	(a)11.0	(a)8.4	(a)7.9	(a)13.7	(a)11.8	(a)5.7	(a)11.9	(a)6.9	(a)14.2	(a)10.1
	1993	(a)17.2	(a)3.9	(a)18.1	(a)8.9	(a)8.2	(a)25.6	(a)14.0	(a)5.7	(a)14.1	(a)7.8	(a)15.2	(a)15.5
	1996	(a)15.0	(a)1.8	(a)16.2	(a)3.2	(a)4.6	(a)26.1	(a)8.8	(a)1.1	(a)9.2	(a)3.5	(a)7.4	(a)15.5
	1997	(a)7.0	(a)2.0	(a)7.4	(a)3.0	(a)5.7	(a)10.3	(a)6.0	(a)1.8	(a)6.2	(a)2.9	(a)5.6	(a)9.2
	1999	(a)5.7	(a)1.7	(a)6.0	(a)2.9	(a)3.4	(a)8.9	(a)4.9	(a)1.4	(a)5.1	(a)3.0	(a)4.7	(a)7.2
	2001	7.9	1.4	8.4	2.5	3.2	13.0	5.9	0.9	6.0	2.6	5.4	9.4
	2004	8.1	1.3	8.5	2.4	3.0	13.2	6.5	0.5	6.7	2.8	6.1	10.0
	2005	8.0	1.2	8.5	2.5	3.0	13.1	7.0	0.6	7.2	3.0	7.0	9.9
	2006	8.0	1.2	8.5	2.4	3.0	13.1	7.0	0.6	7.3	3.0	6.7	10.3
Sri Lanka	1990	26.0	11.4	27.0	12.3	14.1	38.2	24.1	7.4	24.5	7.8	14.4	36.7
	1993	22.5	12.0	23.2	12.2	15.7	30.4	26.4	11.8	26.6	9.5	18.4	34.6
	1994	22.5	12.0	23.2	12.2	15.7	30.4	26.9	11.6	27.2	9.8	20.2	34.5
	1997	18.2	11.7	18.6	11.6	14.4	23.0	21.5	10.7	21.6	9.9	20.2	24.5
	2000	7.9	5.5	8.0	6.1	6.1	9.6	5.5	5.3	5.5	5.3	7.0	4.8
	2001	7.9	5.5	8.0	6.1	6.1	9.6	5.2	6.3	5.1	5.4	6.5	4.5
	2004	8.3	5.1	8.5	5.1	6.8	10.5	6.4	4.2	6.5	5.2	9.3	5.2
	2005	9.4	5.3	9.6	4.9	7.8	12.3	6.5	4.4	6.6	4.7	9.8	5.5
	2006	9.1	5.2	9.4	4.7	7.5	12.0	6.2	4.1	6.3	4.2	9.5	5.1
Sudan - Soudan	1996	4.3	1.8	4.5	2.3	1.6	6.5	4.0	3.9	4.0	3.2	1.8	7.6
	2002	22.6	16.9	23.0	14.5	14.5	29.8	19.0	11.2	19.1	15.3	15.6	30.0
	2006	18.1	13.9	18.4	6.7	11.1	26.1	15.0	10.3	15.0	9.5	11.4	23.7
Suriname	1996	20.0	17.1	20.1	14.9	16.9	21.6	18.5	17.1	18.5	18.8	17.4	20.0
	1999	16.6	13.8	16.7	11.9	14.2	18.0	15.3	14.8	15.3	14.7	14.6	15.9
	2000	12.5	13.7	12.5	9.3	8.7	14.6	11.7	14.1	11.6	8.9	10.9	13.0
Swaziland	2001	7.9	1.4	8.4	2.5	3.2	13.0	11.3	3.3	11.4	4.9	10.6	14.9
	2004	8.1	1.3	8.5	2.4	3.0	13.2	10.8	2.1	10.9	1.9	3.9	15.5
	2005	8.0	1.2	8.5	2.5	3.0	13.1	9.7	1.9	9.8	2.1	5.2	15.2
	2006	8.0	1.2	8.5	2.4	3.0	13.1	9.7	1.9	9.7	2.1	5.2	15.1
Syrian Arab Republic - République arabe syrienne	2002	19.8	6.9	20.7	5.5	15.1	28.8	16.6	5.6	17.1	3.6	30.6	11.4
Tajikistan - Tadjikistan	2002	8.1	8.7	8.0	5.2	5.3	10.3	7.5	6.1	8.0	5.1	5.0	11.3
	2006	7.3	7.7	7.3	5.6	5.0	8.9	7.0	5.1	7.4	5.6	5.0	9.8
Thailand - Thaïlande	1989	39.9	17.8	41.7	32.0	35.2	50.7	34.1	10.7	35.9	31.0	39.7	28.4
	1991	39.9	17.8	41.8	32.2	35.2	50.8	33.8	12.2	34.9	31.4	37.9	28.5
	1993	45.4	18.8	47.3	36.7	34.0	57.1	36.1	14.1	37.1	38.4	34.9	41.2
	1995	20.2	10.3	20.9	14.0	13.3	26.9	15.6	8.7	15.8	15.2	15.6	16.7
	2000	15.5	6.5	16.1	11.1	12.1	19.7	9.9	5.4	10.1	10.5	8.8	13.0
	2001	14.6	6.1	15.1	6.2	12.4	19.6	10.5	4.2	10.7	9.7	8.7	15.9
	2003	13.7	4.7	14.3	5.6	12.3	18.5	10.7	3.7	11.1	9.6	10.0	13.9
	2005	10.2	2.4	10.7	4.6	8.0	14.2	6.4	2.0	6.6	6.7	6.1	7.5
	2006	10.2	2.4	10.7	4.6	8.0	14.2	6.2	2.1	6.5	6.7	5.7	8.0
TFYR of Macedonia - LERY de Macédoine	2001	13.6	7.6	14.0	7.3	11.5	17.6	12.9	8.4	13.0	10.8	11.6	15.7
	2004	8.8	3.9	9.2	3.8	6.6	12.3	7.1	3.3	7.2	6.0	7.1	7.8
	2005	8.0	3.0	8.3	3.5	6.1	11.0	7.0	1.9	7.3	5.6	5.9	8.4
	2006	7.6	2.8	7.9	3.4	6.5	10.3	6.4	1.7	6.7	5.1	6.0	7.5

For sources and notes, see end of table.

Pour les sources et les notes, se reporter à la fin du tableau.

Market / Marchés	Year / Année	MFN rate - Simple average (2) / Droit NPF - Moyenne simple (2)						MFN rate - Weighted average (3) / Droit NPF - Moyenne pondérée (3)					
		Total of non-agricultural and non-fuel products / Total des produits non-agricoles et non-pétroliers	Ores and metals / Minérais et métaux	Manufactured products / Produits manufacturés	Chemical products / Produits chimiques	Machinery and transport equipment / Machines et matériel de transport	Other manufactured products / Produits manufacturés divers	Total of non-agricultural and non-fuel products / Total des produits non-agricoles et non-pétroliers	Ores and metals / Minérais et métaux	Manufactured products / Produits manufacturés	Chemical products / Produits chimiques	Machinery and transport equipment / Machines et matériel de transport	Other manufactured products / Produits manufacturés divers
SITC Rev.2 (1) / CTCI Rév.2 (1)		5+6+7+8 +27+28	27+28+68	(5+6+7+8) - 68	5	7	(6+8) - 68	5+6+7+8 +27+28	27+28+68	(5+6+7+8) - 68	5	7	(6+8) - 68
Togo	2001	11.8	7.5	12.0	6.3	8.5	15.7	11.1	5.9	11.2	6.1	11.2	12.9
	2002	11.7	7.5	12.0	6.3	8.5	15.7	10.1	5.8	10.3	5.4	9.7	12.3
	2003	11.7	7.3	12.0	6.3	8.6	15.7	11.1	5.6	11.4	5.4	11.0	13.3
	2004	11.7	7.4	12.0	6.3	8.6	15.7	11.2	5.6	11.4	5.4	11.0	13.4
	2005	11.7	7.4	12.0	6.3	8.6	15.7	10.8	5.6	11.0	4.1	10.7	13.1
	2006	11.7	7.4	12.0	6.3	8.6	15.7	10.8	5.6	11.0	4.1	10.8	13.1
Trinidad and Tobago - Trinité-et-Tobago	1991	16.4	8.0	16.9	11.3	12.7	20.8	13.7	6.8	14.2	13.0	14.0	15.0
	1992	16.4	8.0	16.9	11.3	12.7	20.8	13.9	7.7	14.3	13.2	14.3	14.9
	1996	8.3	3.6	8.6	4.5	6.3	11.1	7.0	3.4	7.2	8.0	6.7	7.7
	1999	17.3	15.5	17.4	11.4	17.0	18.4	16.7	15.6	16.7	13.4	19.0	15.7
	2001	6.2	1.4	6.5	2.1	4.9	8.9	4.5	3.2	4.5	6.3	3.3	6.6
	2002	6.3	1.4	6.6	2.1	5.1	8.9	5.4	1.4	5.5	7.2	4.5	6.9
	2003	6.3	1.4	6.6	2.1	5.1	8.9	5.6	0.8	5.9	7.4	4.8	7.2
	2006	6.1	1.3	6.4	2.0	5.0	8.7	6.3	0.7	6.8	6.4	6.4	7.6
Tunisia - Tunisie	1990	28.5	21.4	29.0	24.2	25.0	32.5	28.1	19.7	28.6	22.6	24.8	33.3
	1992	28.6	21.5	29.0	23.6	25.3	32.6	28.3	20.0	28.6	22.6	24.7	33.0
	1995	28.9	21.5	29.4	21.2	26.4	33.7	30.2	20.2	30.6	20.6	26.4	35.7
	1998	28.4	24.2	28.7	23.5	19.8	34.4	27.8	21.9	28.0	22.3	21.0	35.9
	2002	27.4	24.3	27.6	23.3	18.7	33.0	25.5	22.9	25.6	21.1	18.2	32.7
	2003	22.1	15.8	22.6	14.5	14.5	29.1	22.2	13.8	22.5	12.4	16.9	29.8
	2004	22.4	15.6	22.9	14.3	14.1	29.9	23.2	9.9	23.6	12.4	17.4	31.9
	2005	21.3	15.6	21.7	14.2	14.0	27.8	20.2	9.3	20.7	12.3	16.7	26.5
	2006	20.9	15.1	21.3	13.8	13.6	27.5	20.0	9.2	20.4	12.4	16.2	26.4
Turkey - Turquie	1993	9.3	6.1	9.5	8.0	7.9	10.8	7.4	1.9	7.8	8.1	7.4	8.4
	1995	8.4	4.0	8.7	7.8	6.3	10.0	6.9	2.3	7.3	8.3	6.1	8.5
	1997	5.6	1.9	5.9	5.7	3.7	6.9	5.6	1.6	5.8	5.8	5.3	6.8
	1999	6.3	1.6	6.6	5.4	2.5	8.9	5.1	1.9	5.3	5.1	4.0	8.0
	2003	4.3	1.6	4.5	4.7	2.2	5.4	4.5	1.4	4.8	4.1	4.1	6.2
	2005	4.1	1.6	4.3	4.6	2.3	5.0	4.0	1.5	4.2	4.1	3.9	4.7
	2006	4.1	1.6	4.3	4.7	2.3	5.0	3.7	1.6	3.9	4.6	3.1	4.6
Turkmenistan - Turkménistan	2002	4.0	1.4	4.2	0.7	1.2	6.7	1.1	2.9	1.1	0.5	0.9	1.6
Uganda - Ouganda	1994	16.1	11.8	16.3	11.0	13.7	19.4	14.9	15.3	14.9	6.2	15.2	17.2
	2000	8.5	8.0	8.5	7.1	3.8	11.1	7.0	7.2	7.0	4.7	6.3	8.6
	2001	8.4	8.0	8.4	7.1	3.6	10.9	6.8	7.1	6.8	4.2	5.9	9.0
	2002	8.3	8.0	8.3	7.0	3.5	10.8	6.7	6.9	6.7	4.2	6.2	8.4
	2003	7.9	7.7	7.9	5.9	3.2	10.7	6.2	5.7	6.2	2.8	5.8	8.1
	2004	7.0	7.5	7.0	1.9	3.2	10.6	5.5	5.1	5.5	1.7	4.8	8.0
	2005	11.6	6.6	11.9	3.1	6.2	17.7	11.6	12.5	11.6	5.9	8.1	18.0
	2006	11.6	6.5	11.9	3.0	6.2	17.7	10.5	12.4	10.5	4.1	6.8	18.1
Ukraine	1995	6.6	1.9	6.9	5.3	4.7	8.4	4.3	3.0	4.4	2.5	3.9	5.9
	1997	7.4	1.9	7.7	6.0	5.4	9.4	5.1	1.6	5.4	4.2	4.8	6.8
	2002	7.0	3.6	7.2	5.3	5.8	8.6	6.2	2.2	6.5	5.5	5.6	7.9
	2006	4.6	2.4	4.7	3.3	4.2	5.5	5.7	2.2	5.9	2.2	8.4	4.4
United Arab Emirates - Émirats arabes unis	2005	4.9	4.8	4.9	4.8	4.9	5.0	4.7	4.8	4.7	4.3	4.5	5.0
	2006	4.9	4.8	4.9	4.6	4.9	5.0	4.7	4.8	4.6	4.2	4.5	5.0
United Republic of Tanzania - République-Unie de Tanzanie	1993	19.0	19.2	19.0	17.2	11.1	23.0	15.0	18.1	14.8	22.2	10.1	16.2
	1997	22.6	28.9	22.2	27.0	17.7	22.2	18.3	24.3	18.1	16.2	16.2	22.3
	1998	22.9	29.3	22.5	27.2	18.0	22.6	19.7	26.6	19.6	19.6	17.9	22.4
	2000	15.9	12.0	16.2	7.9	13.1	20.6	13.0	10.4	13.0	8.4	11.0	18.5
	2003	12.9	7.0	13.3	3.7	8.9	18.8	9.1	7.0	9.1	4.8	7.0	14.7
	2005	11.6	6.6	11.9	3.1	6.2	17.7	8.6	8.5	8.6	3.9	7.9	13.1
	2006	11.6	6.5	11.9	3.0	6.2	17.7	8.3	4.0	8.4	2.7	7.4	13.2

For sources and notes, see end of table.

Pour les sources et les notes, se reporter à la fin du tableau.

Market / Marchés	Year / Année	MFN rate - Simple average (2) / Droit NPF - Moyenne simple (2)						MFN rate - Weighted average (3) / Droit NPF - Moyenne pondérée (3)					
		Total of non-agricultural and non-fuel products / Total des produits non-agricoles et non-pétroliers	Ores and metals / Minérais et métaux	Manufactured products / Produits manufacturés	of which: / dont :			Total of non-agricultural and non-fuel products / Total des produits non-agricoles et non-pétroliers	Ores and metals / Minérais et métaux	Manufactured products / Produits manufacturés	of which: / dont :		
					Chemical products / Produits chimiques	Machinery and transport equipment / Machines et matériel de transport	Other manufactured products / Produits manufacturés divers				Chemical products / Produits chimiques	Machinery and transport equipment / Machines et matériel de transport	Other manufactured products / Produits manufacturés divers
SITC Rev.2 (1) / CTCI Rév.2 (1)		5+6+7+8 +27+28	27+28+68	(5+6+7+8) - 68	5	7	(6+8) - 68	5+6+7+8 +27+28	27+28+68	(5+6+7+8) - 68	5	7	(6+8) - 68
United States - États-Unis	1989	5.9	2.3	6.1	5.0	3.7	7.6	4.5	1.4	4.7	5.2	3.1	7.1
	1990	5.9	2.3	6.1	5.0	3.7	7.6	4.6	1.3	4.8	5.2	3.1	7.3
	1991	5.9	2.3	6.1	5.0	3.7	7.6	4.7	1.2	4.8	5.3	3.1	7.4
	1992	5.9	2.3	6.1	5.0	3.7	7.6	4.8	1.4	4.9	5.3	3.1	7.5
	1993	5.9	2.3	6.1	5.0	3.7	7.6	4.7	1.4	4.8	5.2	3.1	7.4
	1995	5.3	2.1	5.5	4.0	3.4	7.0	4.1	1.4	4.2	3.8	3.0	6.5
	1996	5.0	1.9	5.2	4.0	3.0	6.7	4.0	1.4	4.1	3.7	2.8	6.2
	1997	4.9	1.6	5.2	4.3	2.7	6.5	3.9	1.4	4.0	4.0	2.6	6.2
	1998	4.4	1.5	4.5	3.6	2.2	5.9	3.4	1.3	3.4	3.2	2.2	5.6
	1999	4.0	1.3	4.2	3.5	1.8	5.5	3.1	1.2	3.2	3.1	2.1	5.2
	2000	3.9	1.3	4.0	3.4	1.7	5.3	2.9	1.1	3.0	3.0	1.8	5.0
	2001	3.8	1.3	3.9	3.3	1.7	5.2	3.1	1.1	3.1	2.8	2.0	4.9
	2002	3.7	1.3	3.8	3.1	1.7	5.0	3.0	1.4	3.1	2.6	2.1	4.8
	2003	3.6	1.3	3.7	3.0	1.7	4.9	3.0	1.4	3.0	2.3	2.0	4.6
	2004	3.5	1.3	3.6	3.0	1.7	4.7	2.8	1.3	2.8	2.3	1.9	4.3
	2005	3.5	1.3	3.6	3.0	1.7	4.7	2.7	1.4	2.8	2.2	1.9	4.3
	2006	3.5	1.3	3.6	3.0	1.7	4.7	2.7	1.4	2.7	2.2	1.9	4.2
Uruguay	1992	5.6	4.9	5.7	4.2	5.4	6.3	5.8	5.4	5.8	4.7	5.1	7.5
	1995	11.3	6.1	11.6	8.1	6.3	15.1	11.9	7.7	11.9	8.7	11.3	14.7
	1996	11.6	6.1	12.0	8.1	6.5	15.8	11.2	6.7	11.3	8.6	9.5	15.6
	1997	11.8	6.1	12.2	8.1	7.6	15.7	11.5	6.7	11.6	8.7	10.2	15.5
	1998	14.0	8.8	14.4	10.7	9.1	18.1	13.6	3.9	13.6	11.0	12.1	17.4
	1999	14.2	8.8	14.5	10.8	9.7	18.0	13.7	3.8	13.8	11.8	11.6	17.7
	2000	14.4	9.0	14.7	10.9	10.4	18.1	14.4	3.6	14.4	12.5	12.8	17.6
	2001	14.2	8.4	14.6	10.7	11.1	17.6	14.1	3.3	14.2	12.4	12.7	17.0
	2002	13.3	7.3	13.7	9.4	10.7	16.7	12.7	3.4	12.8	10.7	11.7	15.6
	2004	13.3	7.3	13.7	9.4	10.7	16.7	12.3	5.4	12.5	10.1	11.6	15.7
	2005	11.1	5.8	11.5	7.9	6.3	15.0	10.5	4.5	10.6	9.1	8.7	14.2
	2006	10.9	5.5	11.2	7.5	6.3	14.8	9.7	2.9	9.9	7.3	8.6	13.6
Uzbekistan - Ouzbékistan	2001	11.7	9.3	11.8	8.9	4.9	15.8	6.2	7.0	6.2	8.0	3.0	10.9
	2006	15.0	14.1	15.1	8.3	11.0	19.7	11.1	10.2	11.1	11.0	9.8	13.5
Vanuatu	2002	13.3	9.5	13.5	10.5	12.5	15.0	6.8	11.9	6.8	5.0	4.6	16.1
	2006	13.1	10.1	13.3	10.2	12.3	14.9	7.0	10.3	7.0	7.0	4.9	13.3
Venezuela (Bolivarian Rep. of) - Venezuela (Rép. bolivarienne du)	1992	16.4	8.2	17.0	10.2	12.7	21.4	16.4	6.9	16.7	9.5	18.1	17.6
	1995	13.5	7.4	13.9	10.6	12.6	15.8	13.2	7.5	13.4	10.7	13.6	15.1
	1997	12.0	6.7	12.3	8.1	10.2	14.8	13.4	7.3	13.6	8.8	14.9	13.5
	1998	12.0	6.6	12.3	8.1	10.3	14.8	13.2	7.0	13.4	8.9	14.3	13.6
	1999	12.0	6.7	12.4	8.1	10.4	14.9	12.7	7.2	12.8	9.1	12.6	14.8
	2000	12.0	6.7	12.3	8.1	10.3	14.8	13.2	8.5	13.4	9.3	14.0	14.4
	2002	12.4	6.7	12.7	8.2	10.4	15.5	13.5	8.5	13.6	10.0	13.9	15.5
	2004	12.0	6.7	12.4	8.1	10.4	14.9	12.9	8.3	13.0	9.7	13.9	14.0
	2005	12.0	6.7	12.4	8.1	10.4	14.9	13.5	8.7	13.5	9.9	14.4	13.8
	2006	12.7	6.6	13.1	8.0	10.4	16.2	13.7	8.7	13.8	10.0	14.0	15.9
Viet Nam	1994	13.5	1.2	14.4	3.8	6.4	21.6	12.5	0.5	12.7	2.5	12.0	19.7
	1999	15.4	1.7	16.3	3.8	9.4	24.0	14.2	1.6	14.6	4.6	13.4	21.7
	2001	15.4	1.8	16.3	3.7	9.9	23.9	16.0	1.5	16.5	3.9	19.9	19.0
	2002	15.4	1.8	16.3	3.7	9.7	23.8	15.1	1.2	15.5	4.2	16.0	19.9
	2003	15.7	1.9	16.6	4.2	9.9	24.3	13.6	1.3	14.0	4.1	11.8	20.8
	2004	15.7	1.9	16.6	4.1	9.9	24.3	13.8	1.2	14.2	3.8	13.2	19.6
	2005	15.7	1.9	16.6	4.2	9.9	24.3	13.8	1.1	14.3	4.1	13.2	19.6
	2006	15.7	1.9	16.6	4.2	9.9	24.3	13.8	1.1	14.3	4.1	13.2	19.6
Yemen - Yémen	2000	12.2	12.7	12.2	9.5	11.2	13.6	12.4	10.5	12.4	8.2	13.2	13.0
	2006	6.2	6.7	6.1	5.7	4.9	6.8	5.6	5.5	5.6	5.1	4.7	6.7

For sources and notes, see end of table.　　　　Pour les sources et les notes, se reporter à la fin du tableau.

Market / Marchés	Year / Année	MFN rate - Simple average (2) / Droit NPF - Moyenne simple (2)						MFN rate - Weighted average (3) / Droit NPF - Moyenne pondérée (3)					
		Total of non-agricultural and non-fuel products / Total des produits non-agricoles et non-pétroliers	Ores and metals / Minérais et métaux	Manufactured products / Produits manu-facturés	Chemical products / Produits chimiques	Machinery and transport equipment / Machines et matériel de transport	Other manu-factured products / Produits manu-facturés divers	Total of non-agricultural and non-fuel products / Total des produits non-agricoles et non-pétroliers	Ores and metals / Minérais et métaux	Manufactured products / Produits manu-facturés	Chemical products / Produits chimiques	Machinery and transport equipment / Machines et matériel de transport	Other manu-factured products / Produits manu-facturés divers
SITC Rev.2 (1) / CTCI Rév.2 (1)		5+6+7+8 +27+28	27+28+68	(5+6+7+8) - 68	5	7	(6+8) - 68	5+6+7+8 +27+28	27+28+68	(5+6+7+8) - 68	5	7	(6+8) - 68
Zambia - Zambie	1993	25.6	20.6	26.0	20.5	22.9	29.3	20.0	20.1	20.0	11.3	21.2	23.2
	1997	13.4	9.6	13.6	7.0	10.8	17.4	11.6	6.6	11.9	6.5	11.9	15.5
	2002	11.4	6.8	11.7	6.2	6.5	15.8	8.3	4.8	8.3	5.5	7.8	10.3
	2003	13.0	9.3	13.3	6.3	10.5	17.1	10.6	4.6	10.8	5.6	10.7	14.3
	2005	12.9	9.1	13.2	6.2	10.3	17.1	9.9	3.6	10.1	3.7	11.2	12.9
Zimbabwe	1996	41.9	30.5	42.7	33.0	37.9	48.3	39.2	31.9	39.4	32.1	39.6	43.5
	1997	24.0	9.4	24.9	8.3	15.7	35.2	17.4	8.3	17.6	9.8	16.8	23.7
	1998	21.2	9.6	22.0	8.4	15.2	30.0	16.1	9.7	16.3	9.2	15.8	21.9
	1999	18.6	9.6	19.2	9.3	14.1	26.0	16.9	8.8	17.2	9.6	18.0	22.1
	2001	19.1	8.6	19.8	7.9	13.3	27.0	13.9	7.8	14.2	7.4	16.2	18.6
	2002	15.3	8.5	15.8	7.9	11.9	21.1	18.9	7.3	19.4	7.0	26.9	18.7
	2003	15.0	8.2	15.5	7.7	11.6	20.7	14.0	6.2	15.1	8.4	16.7	17.2

Sources:
- UNCTAD TRAINS database

Notes:
(a) Data refers to South Africa Customs Union (Botswana, Lesotho, Namibia, South Africa and Swaziland)
(1) Product categories are defined in terms of SITC Revision 2, and all corresponding Harmonized System (HS) 6-digit codes have been aggregated for each category.
(2) Simple average for each product group calculated from simple average at HS 6-digit level.
(3) Weighted average for each product group calculated from simple average at HS 6-digit level. Country's own imports at HS 6-digit level for corresponding years are used as weights. Where imports are not reported, mirror imports have been compiled using exports of partner countries.
(4) From 2004 onwards, member of the European Union.
(5) For the union, data refer to the composition of the group during that year. Excluding Bulgaria and Romania.

Sources :
- Base de données TRAINS de la CNUCED

Notes :
(a) Donnée relative à l'Union Douanière d'Afrique du Sud (Afrique du Sud, Botswana, Lesotho, Namibie et Swaziland)
(1) Les catégories de produits sont définies sur la base de la CTCI, révision 2, et pour chaque catégorie, les codes à 6 chiffres du Système harmonisé (SH) correspondants ont été agrégés.
(2) Moyenne arithmétique, pour chaque catégorie de produits, calculée à partir des moyennes arithmétiques au niveau du code à 6 chiffres du SH.
(3) Moyenne arithmétique pondérée, pour chaque catégorie de produits, calculée à partir des moyennes simples au niveau du code à 6 chiffres du SH. Pour chaque année, les coefficients de pondération sont les importations de chaque marché au niveau du code à 6 chiffres du SH. Lorsque les importations n'étaient pas disponibles, elles ont été évaluées par les données miroir basées sur les exportations des pays partenaires.
(4) À partir de 2004, membre de l'Union européenne.
(5) Pour une année donnée, les tarifs de l'union se réfèrent à la composition du groupe durant cette année. Non-compris la Bulagrie et la Roumanie.

5

INTERNATIONAL TRADE IN SERVICES

COMMERCE INTERNATIONAL DES SERVICES

5.1.1 Value of exports and imports of services of countries and geographical regions

Region, country or territory	Exports - Exportations Millions of dollars							
	1980	1990	2000	2003	2004	2005	2006	2007 (1)
WORLD	387 979	830 188	1 526 612	1 896 403	2 285 210	2 537 920	2 826 007	3 337 492
DEVELOPING ECONOMIES	71 147	150 159	348 081	427 605	534 728	622 463	718 136	848 071
ECONOMIES IN TRANSITION (2)	4 552	6 406	23 381	39 130	49 183	57 296	69 237	90 386
DEVELOPED ECONOMIES	312 280	673 624	1 155 150	1 429 668	1 701 299	1 858 160	2 038 634	2 399 036
Developing economies: Africa	13 558	21 624	33 187	45 321	54 353	61 764	70 395	84 330
Eastern Africa	*1 832*	*3 118*	*5 170*	*6 204*	*7 530*	*8 626*	*9 962*	*11 799*
Burundi	..	17	4	7	16	35	35	..
Comoros	2	17	17	29	41	45	47	..
Djibouti	..	..	162	216	213	248	257	..
Eritrea	–	–	61	..	..	..	..	..
Ethiopia	–	–	506	762	1 005	1 012	1 174	(e)1 436
Ethiopia (former)	125	305	–	–	–	–	–	–
Kenya	577	1 138	993	1 198	1 557	1 880	2 461	(e)2 709
Madagascar	79	153	364	322	425	498	(e)698	
Malawi	32	37	34	40	41	54	52	..
Mauritius	140	484	1 070	1 280	1 456	1 618	1 671	2 162
Mozambique	118	103	325	304	256	342	386	(e)628
Rwanda	34	42	59	76	103	129	131	(e)144
Seychelles	91	172	287	330	327	369	431	..
Somalia	66	..	..	..	..	..	..	..
Uganda	10	..	213	266	358	508	490	(e)544
United Republic of Tanzania	165	131	627	948	1 134	1 269	1 483	(e)1 571
Zambia	151	107	115	165	232	272	305	..
Zimbabwe	169	264	(e)331	(e)185	(e)317	(e)298	(e)292	(e)277
Middle Africa	*1 152*	*1 180*	*1 356*	*1 497*	*1 967*	*2 231*	*3 790*	*3 412*
Angola	..	109	267	201	323	177	1 484	..
Cameroon	401	382	590	645	921	..	..	..
Central African Republic	54	69	..	..	..	..	..	..
Chad	0	41	51	71	90	126	..	..
Congo	111	99	137	194	197	235	..	..
Equatorial Guinea	..	5	18	34	50	71	..	..
Gabon	325	242	178	172	156	(e)188	(e)208	..
Sao Tome and Principe	3	4	14	9	17	18	..	..
Northern Africa	*5 175*	*10 455*	*16 779*	*21 536*	*26 867*	*29 870*	*33 635*	*42 475*
Algeria	476	497	(e)976	(e)1 570	(e)1 850	(e)2 460	(e)2 676	(e)3 284
Egypt	2 393	5 971	9 803	11 073	14 197	14 643	16 135	(e)19 997
Libyan Arab Jamahiriya	165	117	172	442	437	534	489	..
Morocco	783	2 009	3 034	5 478	6 710	8 098	9 835	(e)13 442
Sudan	292	173	27	36	44	114	206	(e)245
Tunisia	1 067	1 688	2 767	2 937	3 629	4 021	4 295	4 907
Southern Africa	*2 759*	*3 897*	*5 908*	*9 611*	*11 251*	*12 766*	*13 657*	*15 458*
Botswana	101	210	325	643	780	854	771	(e)963
Lesotho	32	41	43	50	64	56	60	(e)57
Namibia	..	132	222	414	475	414	529	..
South Africa	2 463	3 407	5 046	8 298	9 682	11 157	12 014	13 518
Swaziland	36	108	273	205	250	284	283	..
Western Africa	*2 639*	*2 975*	*3 973*	*6 473*	*6 739*	*8 271*	*9 351*	*11 186*
Benin	62	126	136	172	216	194	(e)232	(e)255
Burkina Faso	49	69	31	46	47	68	80	75
Cape Verde	10	35	108	202	239	277	397	542
Côte d'Ivoire	564	590	482	664	763	832	819	..
Gambia	18	57	130	84	73	80	92	..
Ghana	107	86	504	630	702	1 106	1 399	(e)1 501
Guinea	..	157	68	134	85	(e)88	(e)92	(e)82
Guinea-Bissau	..	7	6	6	8	5	..	..
Liberia	13	..	..	..	3	3	4	..
Mali	58	85	99	224	241	274	..	..
Mauritania	56	27	47	44	52	63	..	..
Niger	41	44	38	63	93	88	..	..
Nigeria	1 127	965	1 833	3 473	3 336	4 164	..	..
Senegal	337	515	387	569	670	774	..	..
Sierra Leone	49	61	42	66	61	78	40	..
Togo	74	149	62	95	150	177	(e)212	..
Developing economies: America	18 615	31 561	62 590	64 224	73 500	86 564	96 940	109 500

For sources and notes, see end of table.

	Imports - Importations Millions de dollars							Régions, pays ou territoires
1980	1990	2000	2003	2004	2005	2006	2007 (1)	
442 680	870 896	1 536 564	1 872 796	2 227 426	2 459 922	2 716 233	3 102 922	**MONDE**
142 065	197 681	418 998	485 693	596 793	699 008	812 372	916 063	ÉCONOMIES EN DÉVELOPPEMENT
5 229	15 041	27 475	47 209	60 092	70 322	81 424	104 691	ÉCONOMIES EN TRANSITION (2)
295 387	658 173	1 090 091	1 339 894	1 570 540	1 690 592	1 822 437	2 082 168	ÉCONOMIES DÉVELOPPÉES
29 358	30 016	39 983	51 799	63 598	77 301	88 615	101 093	Économies en développement : Afrique
3 358	*4 000*	*5 632*	*6 335*	*7 413*	*8 769*	*9 807*	*11 781*	*Afrique orientale*
..	129	43	45	74	113	199	..	Burundi
12	44	23	37	38	42	45	..	Comores
..	..	71	67	77	84	96	..	Djibouti
–	–	28	..	..	..	..	..	Érythrée
–	–	490	709	958	1 194	1 171	(e)1 795	Éthiopie
208	359	–	–	–	–	–	..	Éthiopie (anc.)
502	700	719	691	939	1 138	1 431	(e)1 632	Kenya
311	242	522	619	637	615	(e)718	..	Madagascar
179	268	167	189	209	280	265	..	Malawi
174	421	763	906	1 023	1 198	1 324	1 518	Maurice
124	206	446	574	531	649	758	(e)894	Mozambique
133	129	200	204	240	304	243	(e)277	Rwanda
40	80	190	220	216	256	312	..	Seychelles
133	..	..	..	..	..	..	..	Somalie
123	195	459	502	651	787	990	(e)1 118	Ouganda
295	288	682	726	975	1 207	1 249	..	République-Unie de Tanzanie
651	386	335	408	384	471	587	..	Zambie
395	496	(e)495	(e)401	(e)424	(e)395	(e)380	(e)385	Zimbabwe
3 318	*5 828*	*6 425*	*8 595*	*11 478*	*14 897*	*16 887*	*20 359*	*Afrique centrale*
..	1 807	2 699	3 321	4 803	6 791	7 511	..	Angola
717	1 045	957	1 222	1 497	..	..	..	Cameroun
142	169	..	..	..	..	..	..	République centrafricaine
24	228	241	828	1 366	1 522	..	..	Tchad
480	769	738	875	1 016	1 560	..	..	Congo
..	36	567	1 017	1 243	1 518	..	..	Guinée équatoriale
789	1 007	858	840	939	(e)1 141	(e)1 360	..	Gabon
6	9	11	14	21	23	..	..	Sao Tomé-et-Principe
9 733	*9 013*	*13 652*	*16 295*	*20 296*	*25 358*	*29 316*	*31 395*	*Afrique septentrionale*
2 697	1 321	(e)1 486	(e)2 920	(e)3 860	(e)4 620	(e)5 460	(e)5 988	Algérie
2 343	3 788	7 513	6 474	8 020	10 508	11 569	10 580	Égypte
2 303	1 385	895	1 597	1 914	2 349	2 564	..	Jamahiriya arabe libyenne
1 436	1 445	1 892	2 861	3 451	3 845	4 479	(e)5 972	Maroc
353	228	648	830	1 065	1 844	2 789	(e)3 208	Soudan
600	846	1 218	1 612	1 986	2 191	2 455	2 836	Tunisie
3 998	*4 728*	*7 056*	*9 408*	*12 039*	*13 891*	*16 019*	*18 596*	*Afrique australe*
216	376	547	652	793	857	835	(e)997	Botswana
50	81	43	85	96	103	95	(e)121	Lesotho
..	354	333	276	420	369	430	..	Namibie
3 295	3 738	5 823	8 045	10 328	12 155	14 291	16 573	Afrique du Sud
80	179	310	349	402	407	368	..	Swaziland
8 951	*6 448*	*7 218*	*11 167*	*12 373*	*14 385*	*16 585*	*18 962*	*Afrique occidentale*
109	131	192	254	287	279	..	..	Bénin
209	216	140	196	275	363	291	221	Burkina Faso
7	28	100	189	207	208	245	293	Cap-Vert
1 531	1 626	1 227	1 780	2 033	2 124	2 217	..	Côte d'Ivoire
42	52	100	36	46	45	94	..	Gambie
270	301	584	900	1 058	1 273	1 533	(e)2 050	Ghana
..	367	285	307	275	(e)244	(e)272	(e)329	Guinée
..	20	40	36	44	42	..	..	Guinée-Bissau
73	..	..	..	55	54	74	..	Libéria
212	374	335	482	532	588	..	..	Mali
128	137	149	189	296	390	..	..	Mauritanie
279	227	132	193	262	279	..	..	Niger
5 285	1 976	3 300	5 715	5 973	7 321	..	..	Nigéria
340	676	405	591	698	805	..	..	Sénégal
85	74	113	94	92	91	83	..	Sierra Leone
167	244	118	204	239	279	(e)327	..	Togo
29 679	37 164	74 638	71 775	80 855	95 958	107 985	125 042	Économies en développement : Amérique

Pour les sources et les notes, se reporter à la fin du tableau.

Region, country or territory	Exports - Exportations Millions of dollars							
	1980	1990	2000	2003	2004	2005	2006	2007 (1)
Caribbean	*3 511*	*7 474*	*16 068*	*16 642*	*18 211*	*21 216*	*23 352*	*24 457*
Anguilla	..	41	65	69	78	99	124	..
Antigua and Barbuda	45	312	415	418	477	488	477	(e)473
Aruba	..	411	1 009	1 046	1 248	1 304	1 314	(e)1 447
Bahamas	746	1 500	1 973	2 055	2 244	2 485	2 449	(e)2 426
Barbados	345	654	1 090	1 165	1 224	1 457	(e)1 444	(e)1 430
Cuba	..	526	3 114	2 979	3 450	(e)5 326	(e)6 472	(e)6 611
Dominica	6	33	90	77	88	83	97	(e)96
Dominican Republic	309	1 097	3 228	3 469	3 504	3 913	4 224	4 690
Grenada	21	64	153	134	157	117	130	..
Haiti	90	52	172	136	133	138	204	(e)225
Jamaica	401	1 027	2 026	2 138	2 297	2 330	2 649	(e)2 619
Montserrat	..	18	16	12	15	15	15	..
Netherlands Antilles	878	1 161	1 614	1 701	1 799	1 847	(e)1 981	(e)2 105
Saint Kitts and Nevis	8	54	99	108	135	148	168	..
Saint Lucia	41	151	324	318	367	410	440	512
Saint Vincent and the Grenadines	18	45	128	133	145	159	171	..
Trinidad and Tobago	411	329	554	685	851	897	..	..
Central America	*6 196*	*10 793*	*20 015*	*20 214*	*22 549*	*25 677*	*27 635*	*29 584*
Belize	..	115	153	212	235	292	355	(e)371
Costa Rica	194	609	1 936	2 021	2 242	2 621	2 955	(e)3 161
El Salvador	139	329	698	948	1 090	1 128	1 503	(e)1 526
Guatemala	211	356	777	1 059	1 178	1 230	1 395	(e)1 491
Honduras	82	137	479	589	683	744	753	..
Mexico	4 591	8 094	13 756	12 617	14 047	16 137	16 393	17 257
Nicaragua	44	60	221	258	286	309	342	(e)365
Panama, excl. Canal Zone (former)	902	–	–	–	–	–	–	–
Panama	–	1 092	1 994	2 510	2 788	3 217	3 940	(e)4 608
South America	*8 908*	*13 294*	*26 507*	*27 369*	*32 740*	*39 671*	*45 953*	*55 459*
Argentina	1 876	2 446	4 936	4 500	5 289	6 453	7 666	(e)9 795
Bolivia	88	146	224	364	416	489	434	468
Brazil	1 737	3 762	9 498	10 447	12 584	16 048	19 462	23 772
Chile	1 263	1 848	4 083	5 070	6 034	7 020	7 504	8 786
Colombia	1 342	1 600	2 049	1 921	2 255	2 664	3 373	(e)3 735
Ecuador	367	538	849	881	1 014	1 012	1 016	(e)1 131
Guyana	20	..	169	157	161	148	148	(e)176
Paraguay	164	418	595	574	628	693	807	(e)811
Peru	715	798	1 555	1 716	1 993	2 289	2 451	3 343
Suriname	176	37	91	59	141	204	234	..
Uruguay	468	466	1 276	803	1 112	1 311	1 285	(e)1 453
Venezuela (Bolivarian Rep. of)	693	1 183	1 182	878	1 114	1 341	1 572	(e)1 707
Developing economies: Asia	**38 670**	**96 196**	**251 373**	**315 591**	**404 186**	**471 130**	**547 676**	**650 918**
Eastern Asia	*12 937*	*42 149*	*125 068*	*155 224*	*193 664*	*218 149*	*256 452*	*306 491*
China	..	5 855	30 431	46 734	62 434	74 404	91 999	(p)117 153
China, Hong Kong SAR	5 763	18 128	40 430	46 555	55 157	63 761	72 283	82 710
China, Macao SAR	379	1 473	3 586	5 605	8 063	8 612	10 538	(e)12 281
China, Taiwan Province of	(e)2 133	7 008	20 010	23 166	25 789	25 827	29 272	30 642
Mongolia	..	48	78	208	338	414	486	(e)502
Republic of Korea	2 570	9 637	30 534	32 957	41 882	45 129	51 873	(e)63 204
Southern Asia	*5 060*	*7 655*	*22 072*	*35 152*	*51 317*	*69 902*	*90 328*	*104 467*
Afghanistan	36	..	..	..	..	..	..	..
Bangladesh	211	392	815	1 012	1 083	1 249	1 334	(e)1 602
Bhutan	..	..	..	31	46	62	(e)66	(e)89
India (3)	2 971	4 625	16 684	23 902	38 281	55 831	75 354	(e)84 838
Iran (Islamic Rep. of)	731	436	1 382	5 025	6 663	(e)6 839	..	..
Maldives	52	101	348	432	508	323	473	548
Nepal	155	204	506	372	461	380	386	(e)477
Pakistan	652	1 429	1 380	2 968	2 749	3 678	3 506	(e)5 839
Sri Lanka	231	440	939	1 411	1 527	1 540	1 625	(e)1 766
South-Eastern Asia	*9 393*	*29 369*	*68 717*	*78 977*	*104 574*	*116 285*	*130 188*	*157 303*
Brunei Darussalam	..	..	..	437	544	617	744	..
Cambodia	..	..	428	548	805	1 118	1 296	(e)1 747
Indonesia (4)	(e)381	2 488	5 214	5 293	12 045	12 927	11 518	(e)12 069
Lao People's dem. Rep.	..	24	176	..	..	..	..	..
Malaysia	1 135	3 859	13 941	13 578	17 111	19 576	21 831	(e)27 630
Myanmar	53	94	478	249	255	259	280	(e)226
Philippines	1 447	3 244	3 377	3 389	4 043	4 525	6 453	8 448

For sources and notes, see end of table.

	Imports - Importations Millions de dollars							Régions, pays ou territoires
1980	1990	2000	2003	2004	2005	2006	2007 (1)	
2 600	*4 108*	*7 872*	*7 939*	*8 477*	*9 510*	*11 093*	*11 798*	**Caraïbes**
..	15	41	44	47	56	101	..	Anguilla
17	105	156	182	190	208	257	(e)270	Antigua-et-Barbuda
..	135	644	727	794	904	985	(e)926	Aruba
226	573	1 026	1 092	1 231	1 373	1 916	(e)2 020	Bahamas
129	250	487	519	556	680	(e)883	(e)931	Barbade
..	600	891	650	740	(e)776	(e)793	(e)816	Cuba
6	30	53	44	46	52	52	(e)55	Dominique
399	440	1 373	1 219	1 213	1 467	1 558	1 722	République dominicaine
11	33	89	83	93	93	99	..	Grenade
162	72	282	301	336	452	538	(e)607	Haïti
370	697	1 423	1 586	1 725	1 722	2 021	(e)2 136	Jamaïque
..	12	23	18	23	26	17	..	Montserrat
529	518	732	812	801	813	(e)834	(e)962	Antilles néerlandaises
6	35	76	80	83	92	102	..	Saint-Kitts-et-Nevis
22	81	133	145	154	171	205	217	Sainte-Lucie
11	32	56	65	73	85	88	..	Saint-Vincent-et-les Grenadines
645	479	388	371	371	541	..	..	Trinité-et-Tobago
8 460	*12 652*	*22 604*	*24 083*	*26 423*	*28 897*	*30 990*	*33 362*	**Amérique centrale**
..	60	123	141	147	159	151	(e)175	Belize
286	550	1 273	1 245	1 384	1 505	1 612	(e)1 798	Costa Rica
273	315	933	1 055	1 154	1 210	1 484	(e)1 867	El Salvador
487	384	825	1 126	1 308	1 479	1 681	(e)1 875	Guatemala
174	220	597	686	784	875	1 019	..	Honduras
6 514	10 323	17 360	18 141	19 779	21 440	22 833	23 896	Mexique
104	112	351	377	409	448	483	(e)539	Nicaragua
588								Panama, sans la zone du canal (anc.)
–	689	1 141	1 312	1 457	1 781	1 726	(e)2 076	Panama
18 620	*20 404*	*44 162*	*39 753*	*45 955*	*57 550*	*65 903*	*79 882*	**Amérique du Sud**
3 788	3 120	9 219	5 693	6 618	7 640	8 503	(e)10 349	Argentine
259	311	468	551	607	683	805	628	Bolivie
4 871	7 523	16 660	15 378	17 260	24 356	29 116	36 432	Brésil
1 583	2 076	4 802	5 688	6 780	7 656	8 426	9 947	Chili
1 170	1 750	3 307	3 360	3 935	4 766	5 493	(e)6 364	Colombie
704	804	1 269	1 624	1 968	2 142	2 341	(e)2 626	Équateur
107	(e)124	193	172	208	201	218	(e)252	Guyana
165	434	420	329	301	344	425	(e)457	Paraguay
880	1 164	2 290	2 616	2 725	3 123	3 400	4 270	Pérou
364	171	216	195	271	352	269	..	Suriname
476	393	882	636	786	939	902	(e)1 086	Uruguay
4 253	2 534	4 435	3 512	4 497	5 349	6 005	(e)7 150	Venezuela (Rép. bolivarienne du)
82 532	*129 671*	*303 059*	*359 500*	*449 360*	*522 166*	*611 544*	*684 742*	**Économies en développement : Asie**
12 908	*42 592*	*121 824*	*148 880*	*185 796*	*211 095*	*244 053*	*289 119*	**Asie orientale**
..	4 352	36 031	55 306	72 133	83 796	100 833	(p)123 256	Chine
4 373	12 937	24 698	26 126	31 138	33 979	36 533	41 028	Chine (RAS de Hong Kong)
22	238	904	1 175	1 364	1 576	1 866	(e)2 016	Chine (RAS de Macao)
(e)2 962	14 658	26 647	25 635	30 731	32 480	33 661	36 068	Province chinoise de Taiwan
..	155	163	257	504	476	523	(e)636	Mongolie
3 293	10 252	33 381	40 381	49 928	58 788	70 637	(e)86 115	République de Corée
10 219	*13 697*	*27 315*	*40 515*	*57 240*	*73 421*	*92 901*	*80 447*	**Asie méridionale**
144	..	..	..	..	..	..	..	Afghanistan
481	700	1 620	1 711	1 931	2 207	2 340	(e)2 849	Bangladesh
..	..	..	38	56	63	(e)71	(e)81	Bhoutan
2 981	6 090	19 187	24 878	35 641	47 989	63 537	(e)48 073	Inde (3)
5 223	3 962	2 296	(e)8 528	(e)11 828	(e)12 927	..	..	Iran (Rép. islamique d')
43	38	110	120	157	204	233	272	Maldives
88	167	200	266	385	435	493	(e)657	Népal
877	2 073	2 252	3 294	5 333	7 508	8 418	(e)8 999	Pakistan
351	639	1 621	1 679	1 908	2 089	2 394	(e)2 612	Sri Lanka
13 748	*29 025*	*87 591*	*104 354*	*126 054*	*139 661*	*154 459*	*170 313*	**Asie du Sud-Est**
..	..	..	1 032	1 075	1 110	1 213	..	Brunéi Darussalam
..	..	328	434	514	647	790	(e)898	Cambodge
(e)4 597	6 056	15 637	17 400	20 856	22 049	21 625	(e)23 251	Indonésie (4)
..	26	43	..	..	..	..	..	Rép. dém. populaire lao
2 957	5 485	16 747	17 532	19 269	21 956	23 720	(e)27 481	Malaisie
74	73	328	420	460	502	563	(e)986	Myanmar
1 439	1 761	5 247	5 352	5 815	5 865	6 120	7 371	Philippines

Pour les sources et les notes, se reporter à la fin du tableau.

5

Region, country or territory	Exports - Exportations Millions of dollars							
	1980	1990	2000	2003	2004	2005	2006	2007 (1)
Singapore	4 856	12 811	28 171	36 288	46 688	52 742	59 076	(p)69 747
Thailand	1 490	6 419	13 868	15 798	19 040	20 163	24 130	(e)30 033
Viet Nam	..	398	2 702	3 272	3 867	4 176	(e)4 668	(e)6 291
Western Asia	*11 280*	*17 024*	*35 517*	*46 237*	*54 632*	*66 794*	*70 708*	*82 657*
Bahrain	333	359	933	1 260	1 558	1 662	1 849	(e)1 962
Jordan	1 003	1 447	1 640	1 748	2 073	2 334	2 489	(e)2 921
Kuwait	1 225	1 279	1 823	3 144	3 743	4 723	6 972	..
Lebanon	..	..	..	9 462	9 704	10 858	11 625	..
Occupied Palestinian territory	..	..	462	214	181	265		
Oman	9	68	452	645	726	741	913	(e)1 120
Qatar	..	..	364	1 138	1 679	3 221	(e)4 193	(e)4 644
Saudi Arabia	5 191	3 027	4 779	5 713	5 852	6 677	7 297	(p)7 662
Syrian Arab Republic	365	874	1 699	1 331	2 613	2 910	2 924	(e)3 588
Turkey	711	8 016	19 528	18 013	22 960	26 648	24 547	28 662
United Arab Emirates	..	..	2 170	(e)2 783	(e)3 024	(e)6 027	(e)6 700	..
Yemen (former Arab Republic)	87	–	–	–	–	–	–	–
Yemen (former Democratic)	164	–	–	–	–	–	–	–
Yemen	–	106	211	318	370	372	549	..
Developing economies: Oceania	**305**	**778**	**931**	**2 469**	**2 688**	**3 005**	**3 125**	**3 322**
Fiji	201	417	423	614	688	810	774	(e)726
French Polynesia	..	..	..	954	1 028	1 072	1 102	..
Kiribati	4	8	..	..	..	..	..	..
New Caledonia	..	..	..	429	487	483	554	..
Papua New Guinea	43	206	243	233	203	302	315	(e)374
Samoa	8	36	..	(e)68	95	112	134	(e)172
Solomon Islands	12	25	52	25	31	41	60	(e)72
Tonga	9	26	(e)16	26	27	37	31	(e)39
Vanuatu	..	60	130	111	122	139	146	169
Economies in transition: Asia	**–**	**–**	**2 943**	**4 369**	**5 206**	**6 097**	**7 584**	**9 560**
Armenia	–	–	137	207	333	411	485	(e)560
Azerbaijan	–	–	260	432	492	683	940	(e)1 257
Georgia	–	–	206	456	552	711	901	(e)1 120
Kazakhstan	–	–	1 053	1 712	2 009	2 228	2 808	3 552
Kyrgyzstan	–	–	62	158	210	256	374	(e)608
Tajikistan	–	–	..	89	123	146	134	(e)167
Economies in transition: Europe	**–**	**–**	**20 439**	**34 761**	**43 978**	**51 200**	**61 653**	**80 826**
Albania	11	32	448	720	1 003	1 165	1 504	(e)2 001
Belarus	–	–	1 000	1 500	1 747	1 959	2 299	(e)3 211
Bosnia and Herzegovina	–	–	450	721	864	950	1 115	(e)1 418
Croatia	–	–	4 071	8 569	9 373	9 921	10 809	(e)16 178
Moldova	–	–	165	250	332	399	489	(e)665
Russian Federation	–	–	9 565	16 229	20 595	24 970	30 927	(e)38 600
Serbia and Montenegro	–	–	624	1 232	1 797	2 010	(e)2 619	..
SFR of Yugoslavia (former)	4 541	6 374	–	–	–	–	–	–
TFYR of Macedonia	–	–	317	327	408	472	601	(e)827
Ukraine	–	–	3 800	5 214	7 859	9 354	11 290	14 161
Developed economies: America	**54 987**	**165 642**	**336 176**	**344 687**	**395 327**	**438 227**	**478 180**	**542 054**
Canada	7 437	19 182	40 211	43 634	49 087	53 615	59 332	62 904
United States	(b)47 550	(b)146 460	(b)295 965	(b)301 053	(b)346 240	(b)384 612	(b)418 848	(b)479 150
Developed economies: Asia	**22 962**	**45 953**	**84 320**	**91 015**	**113 640**	**127 657**	**136 565**	**150 286**
Israel	2 722	4 569	15 082	13 394	16 029	17 447	19 267	(e)21 133
Japan	20 240	41 384	69 238	77 621	97 611	110 210	117 298	(e)129 153
Developed economies: Europe	**229 352**	**449 333**	**710 384**	**963 527**	**1 155 989**	**1 252 934**	**1 382 927**	**1 657 805**
Austria (5)	9 423	23 279	31 342	42 964	49 153	53 921	46 373	(e)55 571
Belgium	–	–	–	44 708	52 708	56 144	59 592	(e)78 340
Belgium-Luxembourg	12 925	28 417	49 789	–	–	–	–	–
Bulgaria	1 211	837	2 175	2 961	4 029	4 404	5 044	6 166
Cyprus	482	2 004	4 068	5 372	6 235	6 502	7 274	(e)9 117
Czechoslovakia (former)	..	2 673	–	–	–	–	–	–
Czech Republic	–	–	6 839	7 789	9 643	11 748	13 331	16 899
Denmark	(e)4 779	13 136	23 961	31 195	36 200	42 506	52 578	61 255
Estonia	–	–	1 486	2 224	2 830	3 156	3 493	(e)4 505
Faeroe Islands	..	..	54	78	..	..	..	..
Finland	2 733	4 649	7 728	11 471	15 169	17 010	16 102	(e)18 721
France	43 506	75 174	80 603	98 567	109 365	116 042	118 478	130 438

For sources and notes, see end of table.

Imports - Importations Millions de dollars								Régions, pays ou territoires
1980	1990	2000	2003	2004	2005	2006	2007 (1)	
2 912	8 642	29 506	39 926	50 206	55 083	61 929	(p)72 354	Singapour
1 644	6 309	15 460	18 169	23 077	27 120	32 415	(e)29 732	Thaïlande
..	343	3 252	4 050	4 739	5 282	(e)6 032	(e)6 855	Viet Nam
45 657	*44 357*	*66 329*	*65 752*	*80 270*	*97 989*	*120 131*	*144 864*	*Asie occidentale*
474	474	738	886	933	977	1 153	(e)1 221	Bahreïn
1 094	1 268	1 722	1 889	2 146	2 542	2 712	(e)3 066	Jordanie
3 067	3 359	4 921	6 615	7 586	8 604	10 192	..	Koweït
..	..	..	6 488	8 230	7 895	8 706	..	Liban
..	..	566	516	489	487			Territoire palestinien occupé
518	719	1 759	2 180	2 756	3 052	3 740	(e)4 101	Oman
..	..	1 640	2 341	2 906	4 144	(e)6 957	(e)7 578	Qatar
30 231	22 384	25 228	20 857	25 696	28 639	40 552	(p)54 279	Arabie saoudite
521	892	1 667	1 806	2 235	2 359	2 520	(e)2 764	République arabe syrienne
569	3 071	8 153	7 502	10 163	11 376	11 186	14 609	Turquie
..	..	8 587	(e)11 858	(e)15 098	(e)20 578	(e)24 487	..	Émirats arabes unis
130	–	–	–	–	–	–	–	Yémen (anc. République arabe du)
375	–	–	–	–	–	–	–	Yémen (anc. démocratique)
–	683	809	1 004	1 059	1 241	1 855	..	Yémen
495	**830**	**1 319**	**2 619**	**2 980**	**3 583**	**4 229**	**5 185**	**Économies en développement : Océanie**
124	257	333	397	486	525	543	(e)503	Fidji
..	..	..	599	666	728	718	..	Polynésie française
9	19	..	..	..	..	..	..	Kiribati
..	..	..	538	599	890	1 174	..	Nouvelle-Calédonie
302	403	772	868	998	1 167	1 475	(e)1 981	Papouasie-Nouvelle-Guinée
15	25	..	(e)25	42	53	57	(e)58	Samoa
28	79	73	62	41	58	95	(e)158	Îles Salomon
6	23	(e)27	44	52	50	58	(e)56	Tonga
..	24	70	61	66	74	71	68	Vanuatu
–	**–**	**4 402**	**9 131**	**12 049**	**14 736**	**16 877**	**21 516**	**Économies en transition : Asie**
–	–	193	276	432	531	615	(e)731	Arménie
–	–	485	2 047	2 730	2 653	2 863	(e)3 533	Azerbaïdjan
–	–	216	397	485	632	727	(e)880	Géorgie
–	–	1 850	3 753	5 108	7 496	8 720	11 523	Kazakhstan
–	–	148	160	223	291	461	(e)692	Kirghizistan
–	–	..	122	213	252	394	(e)421	Tadjikistan
–	**–**	**23 073**	**38 078**	**48 043**	**55 586**	**64 546**	**83 175**	**Économies en transition : Europe**
18	29	429	803	1 055	1 383	1 585	(e)2 202	Albanie
–	–	563	915	1 058	1 250	1 487	(e)2 074	Bélarus
–	–	263	384	432	459	508	(e)613	Bosnie-Herzégovine
–	–	1 822	2 982	3 565	3 400	3 548	(e)3 864	Croatie
–	–	202	294	353	420	484	(e)664	Moldova
–	–	16 230	27 122	33 287	38 865	44 739	(e)58 300	Fédération de Russie
–	–	293	798	1 208	1 756	(e)2 456	..	Serbie-et-Monténégro
5 211	15 012	–	–	–	–	–	–	RSF de Yougoslavie (anc.)
–	–	268	337	462	505	576	(e)784	LERY de Macédoine
–	–	3 004	4 444	6 622	7 548	9 164	11 465	Ukraine
51 631	**145 348**	**267 843**	**302 418**	**351 076**	**380 567**	**415 466**	**453 339**	**Économies développées : Amérique**
10 661	28 298	44 104	52 090	58 862	64 935	72 649	81 043	Canada
(b)40 970	(b)117 050	(b)223 739	(b)250 328	(b)292 214	(b)315 632	(b)342 817	(b)372 296	États-Unis
34 670	**89 203**	**128 769**	**122 733**	**148 339**	**147 967**	**150 490**	**168 760**	**Économies développées : Asie**
2 310	4 921	11 905	11 205	12 825	13 711	14 934	(e)18 078	Israël
32 360	84 281	116 864	111 528	135 514	134 256	135 556	(e)150 682	Japon
200 638	**406 528**	**670 046**	**887 074**	**1 035 980**	**1 123 341**	**1 216 457**	**1 413 044**	**Économies développées : Europe**
6 204	14 197	29 653	41 261	46 737	49 107	32 637	(e)38 632	Autriche (5)
			42 862	49 023	51 172	53 148	(e)68 556	Belgique
12 827	26 581	41 868						Belgique-Luxembourg
549	600	1 670	2 447	3 238	3 404	4 112	4 785	Bulgarie
268	674	1 585	2 237	2 644	2 706	2 987	(e)3 614	Chypre
..	2 472	–	–	–	–	–	–	Tchécoslovaquie (anc.)
–	–	5 436	7 320	9 008	10 217	11 801	14 182	République tchèque
(e)3 555	10 408	21 083	27 816	33 349	37 844	45 438	53 739	Danemark
–	–	886	1 393	1 756	2 156	2 460	(e)3 231	Estonie
..	..	97	147	..	..	..	..	Îles Féroé
2 555	7 627	8 440	10 007	12 284	15 202	15 604	(e)16 801	Finlande
32 148	60 194	60 802	82 765	98 427	106 024	107 995	120 506	France

Pour les sources et les notes, se reporter à la fin du tableau.

Region, country or territory	Exports - Exportations Millions of dollars							
	1980	1990	2000	2003	2004	2005	2006	2007 (1)
Germany (former Federal Rep.)	32 817	–	–	–	–	–	–	–
Germany	–	62 662	83 150	122 560	144 345	155 894	173 115	208 618
Greece	3 947	10 483	19 337	24 153	33 203	34 270	35 762	(e)42 203
Hungary	..	2 884	5 901	9 211	10 890	12 778	13 295	(e)16 640
Iceland	280	560	1 044	1 378	1 623	2 041	1 834	2 263
Ireland	1 381	3 400	16 885	41 911	52 677	57 349	68 960	88 182
Italy	19 192	49 666	56 556	71 767	84 524	89 205	98 581	113 598
Latvia	–	–	1 150	1 506	1 779	2 163	2 642	3 570
Lithuania	–	–	1 059	1 878	2 444	3 104	3 623	4 028
Luxembourg	–	–	–	25 283	33 684	40 833	51 007	62 194
Malta	481	752	1 092	1 379	1 701	2 004	2 660	3 192
Netherlands	17 150	29 302	49 319	63 227	73 772	80 092	82 271	(e)85 255
Norway	8 615	12 727	17 292	20 894	25 417	29 318	33 328	42 717
Poland	2 018	3 200	10 398	11 174	13 471	16 258	20 584	28 839
Portugal	2 006	5 192	9 047	12 317	14 856	15 149	17 809	22 324
Romania	1 063	610	1 747	3 028	3 614	5 083	7 032	(e)10 938
Slovakia	–	–	2 258	3 185	3 635	4 299	5 404	7 016
Slovenia	–	–	1 888	2 791	3 455	3 976	4 344	5 576
Spain	11 593	27 681	52 582	74 138	86 116	93 780	106 278	127 167
Sweden	7 489	13 726	21 624	30 690	38 906	43 664	50 374	62 214
Switzerland	6 888	19 622	29 862	35 228	43 050	47 110	51 968	62 892
United Kingdom	36 452	56 696	120 150	158 500	197 402	203 031	229 681	277 236
Developed economies: Oceania	**4 978**	**12 696**	**24 270**	**30 438**	**36 344**	**39 342**	**40 962**	**48 890**
Australia	3 862	10 204	19 894	23 747	28 485	31 047	33 089	39 723
New Zealand	1 116	2 492	4 376	6 691	7 859	8 296	7 874	9 167

Sources:
UNCTAD secretariat calculations based on IMF *Balance of Payments Statistics* on CD-ROM and other international and national sources

Notes:
(1)   Year 2007 data are provisional.
(2)   Year 1990: the breaks in series result from the data reporting of the former SFR of Yugoslavia and the countries that succeeded from it, as well as from the inclusion of the figures of the Russian Federation, while the former USSR data are not available.
(3)   Years 2004 and 2005: break in series.
(4)   Year 2004: break in series.
(5)   Year 2006: break in series.

Imports - Importations Millions de dollars								Régions, pays ou territoires
1980	1990	2000	2003	2004	2005	2006	2007 (1)	
45 110	–	–	–	–	–	–	–	Allemagne (anc. Rép. fédérale d')
–	85 052	137 254	169 162	191 257	202 684	215 020	236 547	Allemagne
1 428	3 859	11 292	11 173	14 001	14 749	16 367	(e)20 037	Grèce
(e)550	2 400	4 775	9 150	10 605	11 466	11 674	(e)15 209	Hongrie
263	556	1 164	1 503	1 838	2 560	2 553	2 937	Islande
1 593	5 274	28 922	54 426	65 349	69 898	78 378	93 578	Irlande
16 249	46 795	55 601	74 332	83 246	90 046	100 409	121 852	Italie
–	–	690	929	1 178	1 557	1 980	2 634	Lettonie
–	–	679	1 264	1 632	2 055	2 540	3 208	Lituanie
–	–	–	15 377	20 789	24 572	30 207	35 770	Luxembourg
243	514	761	894	1 045	1 211	1 696	2 061	Malte
18 148	29 708	51 339	63 897	69 444	73 313	79 539	(e)85 324	Pays-Bas
6 996	9 544	14 486	19 186	23 004	29 568	31 957	35 758	Norvège
2 023	2 847	8 993	10 647	12 457	14 312	18 367	23 770	Pologne
1 525	3 810	7 046	8 279	9 674	10 058	11 612	13 775	Portugal
1 045	787	1 993	2 958	3 879	5 518	7 027	(e)10 427	Roumanie
–	–	1 808	2 962	3 349	3 980	4 740	6 487	Slovaquie
–	–	1 438	2 183	2 603	2 915	3 254	4 180	Slovénie
5 732	15 959	33 207	47 841	59 106	65 632	78 315	96 711	Espagne
7 018	17 058	23 977	28 560	33 048	35 342	39 774	47 958	Suède
4 885	9 501	13 720	16 882	21 889	23 360	28 774	30 318	Suisse
27 933	50 112	99 382	127 214	149 949	160 527	175 894	200 228	Royaume-Uni
8 448	**17 095**	**23 433**	**27 669**	**35 146**	**38 718**	**40 025**	**47 025**	**Économies développées : Océanie**
6 568	13 772	18 934	21 941	27 943	30 505	32 251	38 121	Australie
1 880	3 323	4 499	5 729	7 204	8 213	7 774	8 904	Nouvelle-Zélande

Sources :
Calculs du secrétariat de la CNUCED basés sur les *Statistiques de la balance des paiements* sur CD-ROM du FMI et autres sources internationales et nationales

Notes :
(1) Les données de l'année 2007 sont provisoires.
(2) Année 1990 : la rupture de série est due aux chiffres reportés par l'ex RSF de Yougoslavie et les pays qui lui ont succédé, ainsi que à l'inclusion des données de la Fédération de Russie, tandis que les statistiques de l'ancienne URSS ne sont pas disponibles.
(3) Années 2004 et 2005 : rupture de série.
(4) Année 2004 : rupture de série.
(5) Année 2006 : rupture de série.

5.1.2 Value of exports and imports of services of economic groupings

Economic grouping	Exports - Exportations Millions of dollars							
	1980	1990	2000	2003	2004	2005	2006	2007
DEVELOPING ECONOMIES	**71 147**	**150 159**	**348 081**	**427 605**	**534 728**	**622 463**	**718 136**	**848 071**
Developing economies excluding China	69 087	144 304	317 650	380 872	472 294	548 059	626 137	730 918
Developing economies excluding LDCs	67 868	145 999	340 623	418 882	524 263	610 776	703 347	831 595
High-income developing countries	34 552	74 098	167 792	202 884	242 875	274 584	309 868	357 471
Middle-income developing countries	20 460	49 006	106 321	120 772	147 603	167 938	185 791	223 106
Low-income developing countries	16 135	27 055	73 967	103 949	144 249	179 941	222 476	267 494
Heavily indebted poor countries	3 791	4 570	7 114	8 952	10 657	12 416	14 046	16 621
Landlocked developing countries	1 408	2 341	6 967	8 993	11 138	12 580	14 432	17 471
Small island developing States	2 643	5 758	9 624	10 600	11 745	12 672	13 528	14 675
Least developed countries	*3 279*	*4 160*	*7 457*	*8 723*	*10 464*	*11 687*	*14 789*	*16 476*
Africa and Haiti	2 412	3 059	4 198	5 385	6 449	7 377	9 796	10 409
Asia	757	850	2 632	2 656	3 195	3 625	4 102	5 014
Islands	109	251	628	683	820	686	890	1 053
Major petroleum exporters	*14 401*	*12 164*	*20 648*	*30 830*	*36 293*	*45 337*	*53 690*	*64 650*
Africa	2 634	2 205	3 608	6 123	6 393	7 942	10 024	11 028
America	1 471	2 050	2 585	2 444	2 979	3 250	3 583	4 059
Asia	10 297	7 910	14 455	22 262	26 921	34 145	40 083	49 563
Major exporters of manufactured goods	*31 464*	*91 457*	*240 226*	*283 443*	*360 015*	*420 790*	*492 673*	*584 095*
America	6 328	11 856	23 254	23 064	26 630	32 184	35 855	41 029
Asia	25 136	79 601	216 972	260 379	333 385	388 606	456 818	543 067
Emerging economies	*22 365*	*56 682*	*140 351*	*156 135*	*190 455*	*211 382*	*239 658*	*284 208*
America	10 182	16 948	33 828	34 349	39 946	47 946	53 476	62 952
Asia	12 183	39 734	106 523	121 786	150 510	163 436	186 182	221 256
Newly industrialized economies	*19 775*	*63 593*	*155 544*	*177 023*	*221 755*	*244 649*	*276 436*	*324 483*
First tier	15 322	47 583	119 144	138 966	169 515	187 459	212 504	246 303
Second tier	4 453	16 010	36 400	38 058	52 240	57 190	63 932	78 180
Developing economies: Africa	**13 558**	**21 624**	**33 187**	**45 321**	**54 353**	**61 764**	**70 395**	**84 330**
Northern Africa excluding Sudan	4 883	10 283	16 752	21 500	26 823	29 756	33 430	42 230
Sub-Saharan Africa	8 675	11 341	16 435	23 821	27 530	32 008	36 965	42 100
Sub-Saharan Africa excluding South Africa	6 212	7 934	11 389	15 523	17 848	20 851	24 951	28 582
Developing economies: America	**18 615**	**31 561**	**62 590**	**64 224**	**73 500**	**86 564**	**96 940**	**109 500**
Central America and Greater Carribean Islands excluding Puerto Rico	6 996	13 495	28 554	28 935	31 932	37 385	41 183	43 729
Central America and Greater Carribean Islands excluding Mexico and Puerto Rico	2 405	5 401	14 798	16 318	17 885	21 248	24 791	26 472
South America and Central America	15 104	24 087	46 522	47 582	55 289	65 348	73 588	85 043
South America excluding Brazil	7 171	9 532	17 009	16 922	20 157	23 623	26 491	31 687
Developing economies: Asia	**38 670**	**96 196**	**251 373**	**315 591**	**404 186**	**471 130**	**547 676**	**650 918**
Eastern and South-Eastern Asia excluding China	20 270	65 662	163 354	187 468	235 803	260 030	294 640	346 641
Southern Asia excluding India	2 089	3 030	5 388	11 250	13 036	14 071	14 974	19 629

Sources:
UNCTAD secretariat calculations based on IMF *Balance of Payments Statistics* on CD-ROM and other international and national sources

Imports - Importations Millions de dollars								Groupements économiques
1980	1990	2000	2003	2004	2005	2006	2007	
142 065	**197 681**	**418 998**	**485 693**	**596 793**	**699 008**	**812 372**	**916 063**	**ÉCONOMIES EN DÉVELOPPEMENT**
139 835	193 329	382 968	430 387	524 661	615 212	711 539	792 807	Économies en développement sans la Chine
134 508	187 592	405 028	467 914	574 572	671 055	780 176	876 835	Économies en développement sans les PMA
72 049	101 142	201 019	226 198	273 844	309 108	359 104	418 931	Pays en développement à revenu élevé
35 128	50 845	101 304	115 225	138 997	164 691	186 989	208 629	Pays en développement à revenu intermédiaire
34 888	45 693	116 676	144 269	183 953	225 209	266 279	288 503	Pays en développement à revenu faible
9 182	10 903	12 400	16 074	19 436	23 231	27 021	31 761	Pays pauvres très endettés
3 692	4 933	10 028	16 178	21 039	24 858	27 837	34 461	Pays en développement sans littoral
2 223	3 765	6 402	7 135	7 900	8 914	10 789	12 040	Petits États insulaires en développement
7 557	*10 089*	*13 970*	*17 779*	*22 221*	*27 952*	*32 197*	*39 228*	*Pays les moins avancés*
5 984	8 156	10 283	13 523	17 377	22 318	25 467	30 991	Afrique et Haïti
1 447	1 696	3 357	3 912	4 449	5 142	6 164	7 560	Asie
125	237	330	343	396	492	566	677	Îles
67 322	*55 253*	*76 120*	*81 539*	*99 794*	*124 903*	*154 547*	*181 103*	*Principaux exportateurs de pétrole*
12 502	8 529	11 190	17 115	20 813	27 145	31 952	36 765	Afrique
5 602	3 817	6 092	5 508	6 836	8 032	8 991	10 483	Amérique
49 217	42 907	58 837	58 916	72 145	89 727	113 603	133 855	Asie
36 745	*91 402*	*249 077*	*294 326*	*365 139*	*424 227*	*492 520*	*546 414*	*Principaux exportateurs d'articles manufacturés*
11 385	17 846	34 020	33 519	37 039	45 796	51 949	60 328	Amérique
25 360	73 556	215 057	260 806	328 100	378 431	440 571	486 087	Asie
31 403	*69 551*	*172 073*	*189 158*	*226 373*	*259 642*	*294 640*	*336 644*	*Économies émergentes*
17 636	24 206	50 332	47 515	53 162	64 215	72 278	84 894	Amérique
13 768	45 345	121 742	141 643	173 210	195 426	222 362	251 750	Asie
24 176	*66 099*	*167 324*	*190 521*	*231 019*	*257 319*	*286 640*	*323 400*	*Économies nouvellement industrialisées*
13 539	46 489	114 232	132 068	162 002	180 330	202 760	235 565	Première génération
10 636	19 611	53 092	58 453	69 017	76 989	83 881	87 835	Deuxième génération
29 358	**30 016**	**39 983**	**51 799**	**63 598**	**77 301**	**88 615**	**101 093**	**Économies en développement : Afrique**
9 380	8 785	13 004	15 464	19 231	23 514	26 527	28 187	Afrique septentrionale sans le Soudan
19 979	21 231	26 978	36 335	44 367	53 737	62 088	72 906	Afrique subsaharienne
16 684	17 494	21 156	28 290	34 039	41 632	47 797	56 333	Afrique subsaharienne sans l'Afrique du Sud
29 679	**37 164**	**74 638**	**71 775**	**80 855**	**95 958**	**107 985**	**125 042**	**Économies en développement : Amérique**
9 391	14 462	26 573	27 839	30 438	33 314	35 899	38 643	Amérique centrale et Grandes Antilles sans Porto Rico
2 877	4 139	9 213	9 698	10 659	11 874	13 067	14 747	Amérique centrale et Grandes Antilles sans le Mexique et Porto Rico
27 079	33 056	66 766	63 836	72 378	86 448	96 893	113 244	Amérique du Sud et Amérique centrale
13 749	12 881	27 501	24 375	28 695	33 194	36 787	43 450	Amérique du Sud sans le Brésil
82 532	**129 671**	**303 059**	**359 500**	**449 360**	**522 166**	**611 544**	**684 742**	**Économies en développement : Asie**
24 426	67 264	173 384	197 927	239 718	266 960	297 679	336 175	Asie orientale et Asie du Sud-Est sans la Chine
7 238	7 608	8 128	15 637	21 599	25 432	29 364	32 374	Asie méridionale sans l'Inde

Sources :
Calculs du secrétariat de la CNUCED basés sur les *Statistiques de la balance des paiements* sur CD-ROM du FMI et autres sources internationales et nationales

5.1.3 Value of exports and imports of services of trade groups

Trade group	Exports - Exportations Millions of dollars							
	1980	1990	2000	2003	2004	2005	2006	2007
AFRICA								
CEPGL	164	289	135	228	290	507	556	670
CEMAC (formerly UDEAC)	897	837	1 004	1 142	1 456	1 694	1 894	2 336
COMESA	4 489	9 483	14 564	16 853	21 239	22 933	25 595	31 241
ECCAS	1 196	1 238	1 419	1 581	2 085	2 395	3 955	3 595
ECOWAS	2 583	2 948	3 926	6 429	6 687	8 208	9 281	11 098
MRU	130	219	110	200	149	169	136	130
SADC	3 865	5 514	9 114	13 200	15 605	17 637	20 418	22 455
UEMOA	1 191	1 585	1 241	1 839	2 187	2 413	2 640	3 158
UMA	2 547	4 339	6 996	10 471	12 678	15 176	17 365	22 320
AMERICA								
ANCOM	2 511	3 082	4 677	4 882	5 679	6 454	7 275	8 677
CACM	670	1 491	4 112	4 875	5 478	6 031	6 947	7 349
CARICOM	2 367	4 442	7 451	7 807	8 670	9 371	9 974	10 310
FTAA	72 530	195 046	392 948	403 106	462 238	516 200	565 215	641 254
LAIA	13 303	21 825	43 117	42 749	49 935	60 782	68 436	78 868
MERCOSUR	4 245	7 092	16 305	16 324	19 611	24 504	29 221	35 831
NAFTA	59 578	173 736	349 932	357 304	409 374	454 363	494 573	559 311
OECS	146	717	1 288	1 269	1 462	1 518	1 622	1 683
ASIA								
APTA	8 056	20 972	79 577	106 140	145 382	178 338	222 378	268 762
ASEAN	9 393	29 369	68 717	78 977	104 574	116 285	130 188	157 303
ECO	2 130	9 881	24 889	29 711	36 693	42 139	41 835	51 688
GCC	7 016	5 876	10 521	14 682	16 581	23 052	27 925	34 643
SAARC	4 293	7 219	20 690	30 127	44 654	63 063	82 744	95 160
EUROPE								
EFTA	15 783	32 909	48 197	57 500	70 090	78 470	87 130	107 872
EU	213 569	416 424	662 133	905 949	1 085 806	1 174 363	1 295 687	1 549 802
Euro zone	156 672	319 907	456 338	633 066	749 573	809 688	874 328	1 032 612
OCEANIA								
MSG	283	708	848	983	1 044	1 292	1 294	1 341
INTERREGIONAL								
ACP	11 647	18 167	31 142	39 150	44 313	52 053	59 089	65 259
APEC	108 652	300 544	647 924	716 075	860 753	962 343	1 067 878	1 237 296
BSEC	6 943	19 978	57 367	71 663	94 972	108 098	118 921	146 333
CIS	..	..	17 472	27 561	35 738	42 779	52 589	66 197

Sources:
UNCTAD secretariat calculations based on IMF *Balance of Payments Statistics* on CD-ROM and other international and national sources

Imports - Importations Millions de dollars								Groupements commerciaux
1980	1990	2000	2003	2004	2005	2006	2007	
AFRIQUE								
729	1 017	482	639	808	1 187	1 292	1 519	CEPGL
2 209	3 253	3 475	4 870	6 160	7 313	8 499	9 293	CEMAC (anc. UDEAC)
8 451	9 844	14 109	14 676	17 801	22 792	25 941	27 431	COMESA
3 483	6 086	6 668	8 844	11 792	15 314	17 328	20 862	CEEAC
8 823	6 311	7 069	10 977	12 077	13 995	16 148	18 440	CEDEAO
356	442	398	401	422	388	429	508	UFM
7 228	9 600	13 404	16 942	21 519	26 267	29 662	35 750	SADC
2 863	3 513	2 588	3 737	4 371	4 759	5 117	5 908	UEMOA
7 164	5 134	5 640	9 180	11 507	13 396	15 395	18 129	UMA
AMÉRIQUE								
3 013	4 029	7 335	8 151	9 234	10 714	12 039	13 888	ANCOM
1 325	1 580	3 980	4 489	5 039	5 518	6 279	7 215	MCAC
2 119	2 755	4 723	4 995	5 508	6 206	7 460	8 014	CARICOM
80 716	181 232	340 151	371 942	429 526	473 950	520 721	575 553	ZLEA
24 662	31 032	62 004	58 178	65 995	79 214	89 042	104 021	ALADI
9 300	11 470	27 182	22 036	24 966	33 279	38 946	48 324	MERCOSUR
58 145	155 671	285 203	320 559	370 854	402 007	438 298	477 235	ALENA
82	343	627	661	709	783	920	972	OECO
ASIE								
9 382	22 059	91 883	123 994	161 583	194 914	239 793	262 960	ACAP
13 748	29 025	87 591	104 354	126 054	139 661	154 459	170 313	ANASE
6 813	9 106	16 694	27 783	38 456	45 385	50 555	60 418	ECO
37 880	30 571	42 872	44 738	54 975	65 994	87 080	104 768	CCG
4 852	9 735	25 019	31 987	45 412	60 494	77 486	63 542	SAARC
EUROPE								
12 144	19 601	29 370	37 571	46 732	55 488	63 285	69 013	AELE
188 494	386 927	640 578	849 356	989 077	1 067 667	1 152 974	1 343 802	UE
143 519	299 055	465 423	621 382	719 338	772 457	819 230	948 089	Zone euro
OCÉANIE								
466	763	1 248	1 387	1 590	1 824	2 184	2 709	MSG
INTERRÉGIONAUX								
22 984	25 844	35 262	44 662	53 520	64 176	74 217	86 300	ACP
128 123	331 797	657 243	746 957	894 270	973 299	1 066 637	1 204 281	CEAP
3 609	8 347	43 865	59 462	76 246	87 077	98 869	127 633	CEMN
..	..	24 400	41 907	53 369	62 818	72 751	94 019	CEI

Sources :
Calculs du secrétariat de la CNUCED basés sur les *Statistiques de la balance des paiements* sur CD-ROM du FMI et autres sources internationales et nationales

5.2 Trade in services by category: Leading exporters among developing economies

5.2 Commerce des services par catégories : Principaux exportateurs parmi les économies en développement

Ranking based on 2005 exports Classement d'après les exportations de 2005	2004			2005			2006		
	Millions of dollars Millions de dollars	As % of country's total En % du total du pays	Annual change in % Variation annuelle en %	Millions of dollars Millions de dollars	As % of country's total En % du total du pays	Annual change in % Variation annuelle en %	Millions of dollars Millions de dollars	As % of country's total En % du total du pays	Annual change in % Variation annuelle en %
TRANSPORT (1) - TRANSPORTS (1)									
Republic of Korea - République de Corée	22 529	53.8	31.1	23 877	52.9	6.0	25 858	49.8	8.3
China, Hong Kong SAR - Chine (RAS de Hong Kong)	17 358	31.5	25.5	20 319	31.9	17.1	(e)22 298	(e)30.8	(e)9.7
Singapore - Singapour	17 180	36.8	26.7	19 292	36.6	12.3	20 975	35.5	8.7
China - Chine	12 068	19.3	52.6	15 427	20.7	27.8	21 015	22.8	36.2
China, Taiwan Province of - Province chinoise de Taiwan	5 294	20.5	20.7	5 924	22.9	11.9	6 259	21.4	5.7
India - Inde (5)	4 373	11.4	44.7	5 720	10.2	30.8	7 629	10.1	33.4
Turkey - Turquie	3 267	14.2	49.6	4 797	18.0	46.8	4 230	17.2	-11.8
Egypt - Égypte	4 016	28.3	21.7	4 746	32.4	18.2	5 489	34.0	15.7
Thailand - Thaïlande	4 350	22.8	24.2	4 626	22.9	6.3	5 377	22.3	16.2
Chile - Chili	3 457	57.3	24.8	4 272	60.9	23.6	4 469	59.6	4.6
Malaysia - Malaisie	3 196	18.7	15.5	4 056	20.7	26.9	4 228	19.4	4.3
Brazil - Brésil	2 467	19.6	35.4	3 139	19.6	27.2	3 439	17.7	9.6
Indonesia - Indonésie (6)	2 279	18.9	166.3	2 842	22.0	24.7	2 102	18.2	-26.0
Kuwait - Koweït	1 683	45.0	11.0	2 211	46.8	31.3	2 323	33.3	5.1
Panama	1 519	54.5	12.2	1 779	55.3	17.1	2 218	56.3	24.7
Mexico - Mexique	1 362	9.7	22.4	1 753	10.9	28.7	1 913	11.7	9.1
Qatar	1 130	67.3	80.0	1 723	53.5	52.5	..	..	..
South Africa - Afrique du Sud	1 417	14.6	12.4	1 534	13.7	8.2	1 488	12.4	-3.0
Morocco - Maroc	1 025	15.3	12.6	1 300	16.1	26.8	1 486	15.1	14.3
Argentina - Argentine	1 140	21.6	22.3	1 274	19.7	11.7	1 422	18.6	11.7
TRAVEL (2) - VOYAGES (2)									
China - Chine	25 739	41.2	47.9	29 296	39.4	13.8	33 949	36.9	15.9
Turkey - Turquie	15 888	69.2	20.3	18 152	68.1	14.2	16 853	68.7	-7.2
Mexico - Mexique	10 796	76.9	15.3	11 803	73.1	9.3	12 177	74.3	3.2
China, Hong Kong SAR - Chine (RAS de Hong Kong)	8 999	16.3	26.0	10 296	16.1	14.4	(e)11 475	(e)15.9	(e)11.5
Thailand - Thaïlande	10 043	52.7	27.8	9 577	47.5	-4.6	12 432	51.5	29.8
Malaysia - Malaisie	8 203	47.9	39.0	8 846	45.2	7.8	10 427	47.8	17.9
China, Macao SAR - Chine (RAS de Macao)	7 479	92.8	45.1	7 979	92.6	6.7	9 828	93.3	23.2
India - Inde (5)	6 170	16.1	38.3	7 493	13.4	21.4	8 934	11.9	19.2
South Africa - Afrique du Sud	6 322	65.3	13.5	7 335	65.7	16.0	7 876	65.6	7.4
Egypt - Égypte	6 125	43.1	33.6	6 851	46.8	11.8	7 591	47.0	10.8
Singapore - Singapour	5 226	11.2	38.1	5 903	11.2	13.0	7 069	12.0	19.7
Republic of Korea - République de Corée	6 069	14.5	13.3	5 806	12.9	-4.3	5 322	10.3	-8.3
Lebanon - Liban	5 411	55.8	-15.1	5 532	50.9	2.2	5 015	43.1	-9.3
China, Taiwan Province of - Province chinoise de Taiwan	4 054	15.7	36.2	4 977	19.3	22.8	5 136	17.5	3.2
Morocco - Maroc	3 922	58.5	21.8	4 610	56.9	17.5	5 984	60.8	29.8
Indonesia - Indonésie (6)	4 798	39.8	18.8	4 522	35.0	-5.8	4 448	38.6	-1.6
Brazil - Brésil	3 222	25.6	30.0	3 861	24.1	19.8	4 316	22.2	11.8
Dominican Republic - République dominicaine	3 152	89.9	0.8	3 518	89.9	11.6	3 792	89.8	7.8
Argentina - Argentine	2 235	42.3	11.4	2 729	42.3	22.1	3 308	43.2	21.2
Philippines	2 017	49.9	30.6	2 265	50.1	12.3	3 501	54.3	54.6
COMMUNICATIONS (3)									
India - Inde (5)	1 094	2.9	12.9	1 973	3.5	80.4	2 191	2.9	11.1
Kuwait - Koweït	506	13.5	..	1 295	27.4	156.0	3 398	48.7	162.5
Indonesia - Indonésie (6)	835	6.9	>200.0	998	7.7	19.5	1 103	9.6	10.5
China, Hong Kong SAR - Chine (RAS de Hong Kong)	852	1.5	12.8	942	1.5	10.5	(e)1 375	(e)1.9	(e)46
Malaysia - Malaisie	395	2.3	96.1	615	3.1	55.8	641	2.9	4.3
Singapore - Singapour	495	1.1	19.8	558	1.1	12.8	614	1.0	10.0
Mexico - Mexique	423	3.0	0.0	548	3.4	29.6	466	2.8	-14.9
Philippines	487	12.0	12.5	522	11.5	7.2	575	8.9	10.2
China - Chine	440	0.7	-31.0	485	0.7	10.2	738	0.8	52.1
Morocco - Maroc	342	5.1	36.9	446	5.5	30.6	387	3.9	-13.2
Republic of Korea - République de Corée	446	1.1	30.6	443	1.0	-0.6	466	0.9	5.3
Turkey - Turquie	346	1.5	54.5	412	1.5	19.1	416	1.7	1.0
Egypt - Égypte	405	2.9	31.0	362	2.5	-10.6	496	3.1	36.9
China, Taiwan Province of - Province chinoise de Taiwan	333	1.3	-1.5	320	1.2	-3.9	264	0.9	-17.5
Pakistan	233	8.5	22.6	284	7.7	21.9	157	4.5	-44.7
Thailand - Thaïlande	201	1.1	35.7	258	1.3	28.1	244	1.0	-5.3
Lebanon - Liban	229	2.4	41.0	241	2.2	4.8	305	2.6	26.7
Brazil - Brésil	243	1.9	-45.8	239	1.5	-1.7	205	1.1	-14.1
South Africa - Afrique du Sud	189	1.9	38.4	231	2.1	22.4	305	2.5	32.0
Colombia - Colombie	183	8.1	37.1	217	8.2	18.8	252	7.5	16.1

For sources and notes, see end of table.

Pour les sources et les notes, se reporter à la fin du tableau.

Ranking based on 2005 exports Classement d'après les exportations de 2005	2004			2005			2006		
	Millions of dollars Millions de dollars	As % of country's total En % du total du pays	Annual change in % Variation annuelle en %	Millions of dollars Millions de dollars	As % of country's total En % du total du pays	Annual change in % Variation annuelle en %	Millions of dollars Millions de dollars	As % of country's total En % du total du pays	Annual change in % Variation annuelle en %

CONSTRUCTION - BÂTIMENTS ET TRAVAUX PUBLICS									
China - Chine	1 467	2.4	13.8	2 593	3.5	76.7	2 753	3.0	6.2
India - Inde (5)	516	1.3	87.1	1 009	1.8	95.4	403	0.5	-60.1
Turkey - Turquie	743	3.2	0.0	882	3.3	18.7	936	3.8	6.1
Malaysia - Malaisie	453	2.6	72.7	811	4.1	79.0	1 041	4.8	28.3
Singapore - Singapour	647	1.4	51.8	619	1.2	-4.4	666	1.1	7.6
Egypt - Égypte	406	2.9	83.1	503	3.4	23.7	430	2.7	-14.5
Indonesia - Indonésie (6)	463	3.8	..	484	3.7	4.6	456	4.0	-5.7
China, Hong Kong SAR - Chine (RAS de Hong Kong)	378	0.7	-25.9	313	0.5	-17.1	(e)533	(e)0.7	(e)70.3
Thailand - Thaïlande	236	1.2	25.7	255	1.3	8.2	336	1.4	31.7
Tunisia - Tunisie	148	4.1	21.2	143	3.6	-3.0	143	3.3	0.0
China, Taiwan Province of - Province chinoise de Taiwan	152	0.6	28.8	121	0.5	-20.4	152	0.5	25.6
Republic of Korea - République de Corée	99	0.2	166.7	111	0.2	11.4	126	0.2	14.1
Philippines	71	1.8	47.9	66	1.5	-7.0	69	1.1	4.5
Argentina - Argentine	61	1.2	50.6	46	0.7	-25.4	20	0.3	-56.0
South Africa - Afrique du Sud	28	0.3	31.4	35	0.3	23.5	40	0.3	15.7
Sri Lanka	26	1.7	-32.5	29	1.9	13.4	29	1.8	-0.5
El Salvador	19	1.7	86.0	24	2.1	29.6	45	3.0	88.4
Mauritius - Maurice	5	0.3	37.5	24	1.5	>200.0	18	1.1	-26.3
Netherlands Antilles - Antilles néerlandaises	16	0.9	-11.4	23	1.2	46.3	(e)36	(e)1.8	(e)54.4
Mozambique	11	4.3	-6.1	22	6.5	98.9	25	6.4	12.5
COMPUTER AND INFORMATION SERVICES - INFORMATIQUE ET INFORMATION									
India - Inde (5)	16 344	42.7	37.6	22 005	39.4	34.6	29 186	38.7	32.6
China - Chine	1 637	2.6	48.5	1 840	2.5	12.4	2 958	3.2	60.7
Singapore - Singapour	527	1.1	31.5	571	1.1	8.2	633	1.1	10.9
Malaysia - Malaisie	348	2.0	61.3	435	2.2	24.9	572	2.6	31.3
China, Hong Kong SAR - Chine (RAS de Hong Kong)	245	0.4	-0.3	265	0.4	8.2	(e)391	(e)0.5	(e)47.5
Costa Rica	200	8.9	20.1	255	9.7	27.2	351	11.9	37.6
Argentina - Argentine	194	3.7	17.0	237	3.7	21.9	349	4.6	47.6
Indonesia - Indonésie (6)	138	1.1	..	147	1.1	7.0	118	1.0	-20.1
South Africa - Afrique du Sud	89	0.9	34.0	109	1.0	22.9	129	1.1	17.7
China, Taiwan Province of - Province chinoise de Taiwan	110	0.4	0.0	105	0.4	-4.5	186	0.6	77.1
Philippines	33	0.8	17.9	89	2.0	169.7	95	1.5	6.7
Brazil - Brésil	53	0.4	83.6	88	0.5	64.4	102	0.5	15.7
Uruguay	72	6.5	>200.0	83	6.3	14.4	83	6.4	0.0
Sri Lanka	72	4.7	10.8	82	5.4	14.5	98	6.0	18.8
Chile - Chili	71	1.2	-13.4	74	1.1	5.2	72	1.0	-3.3
Syrian Arab Republic - République arabe syrienne	50	1.9	0.0	60	2.1	20.0	50	1.7	-16.7
Pakistan	38	1.4	11.8	59	1.6	55.3	87	2.5	47.5
Republic of Korea - République de Corée	25	0.1	-14.8	57	0.1	125.7	240	0.5	>200.0
Jamaica - Jamaïque	33	1.4	-8.1	34	1.5	4.1	29	1.1	-16.5
Uganda - Ouganda	8	2.2	>200.0	33	6.5	>200.0	31	6.4	-4.1
INSURANCE - ASSURANCES									
Mexico - Mexique	864	6.2	-25.7	1 550	9.6	79.4	1 263	7.7	-18.5
Singapore - Singapour	1 321	2.8	7.5	1 208	2.3	-8.5	1 466	2.5	21.3
India - Inde (5)	842	2.2	106.4	929	1.7	10.3	1 116	1.5	20.1
China - Chine	381	0.6	21.7	549	0.7	44.3	548	0.6	-0.2
China, Hong Kong SAR - Chine (RAS de Hong Kong)	411	0.7	4.3	414	0.6	0.8	(e)412	(e)0.6	(e)-0.4
China, Taiwan Province of - Province chinoise de Taiwan	382	1.5	-15.3	365	1.4	-4.5	532	1.8	45.8
Turkey - Turquie	274	1.2	29.9	323	1.2	17.9	229	0.9	-29.1
Thailand - Thaïlande	135	0.7	0.8	280	1.4	106.9	253	1.0	-9.6
Malaysia - Malaisie	280	1.6	25.7	278	1.4	-0.7	292	1.3	5.1
Lebanon - Liban	141	1.5	13.8	209	1.9	48.7	200	1.7	-4.6
Republic of Korea - République de Corée	139	0.3	>200.0	169	0.4	21.6	366	0.7	116.7
Chile - Chili	136	2.3	9.8	158	2.3	16.2	166	2.2	5.1
Barbados - Barbade	91	7.4	1.0	143	9.8	57.4	..	..	..
Trinidad and Tobago - Trinité-et-Tobago	113	13.3	4.6	135	15.1	19.4	..	..	..
Brazil - Brésil	105	0.8	-14.9	134	0.8	27.5	324	1.7	141.9
South Africa - Afrique du Sud	106	1.1	37.3	124	1.1	17.6	152	1.3	22.2
Peru - Pérou	82	4.1	-8.0	118	5.2	44.6	103	4.2	-13.5
Kuwait - Koweït	79	2.1	-5.4	83	1.8	5.7	64	0.9	-23.4
Sri Lanka	50	3.3	4.9	73	4.7	45.0	57	3.5	-21.6
Morocco - Maroc	95	1.4	24.3	72	0.9	-24.1	76	0.8	5.2

For sources and notes, see end of table.

Pour les sources et les notes, se reporter à la fin du tableau.

5

5.2   Trade in services by category:
Leading exporters among developing
economies

5.2   Commerce des services par catégories :
Principaux exportateurs parmi les économies
en développement

	2004			2005			2006		
Ranking based on 2005 exports Classement d'après les exportations de 2005	Millions of dollars Millions de dollars	As % of country's total En % du total du pays	Annual change in % Variation annuelle en %	Millions of dollars Millions de dollars	As % of country's total En % du total du pays	Annual change in % Variation annuelle en %	Millions of dollars Millions de dollars	As % of country's total En % du total du pays	Annual change in % Variation annuelle en %
FINANCIAL SERVICES - SERVICES FINANCIERS									
China, Hong Kong SAR - Chine (RAS de Hong Kong)	4 553	8.3	21.0	6 322	9.9	38.8	(e)9 269	(e)12.8	(e)46.6
Singapore - Singapour	2 452	5.3	33.4	3 042	5.8	24.1	4 064	6.9	33.6
Republic of Korea - République de Corée	1 083	2.6	55.1	1 651	3.7	52.4	2 557	4.9	54.9
China, Taiwan Province of - Province chinoise de Taiwan	1 142	4.4	32.3	1 517	5.9	32.8	1 232	4.2	-18.8
India - Inde (5)	341	0.9	-6.9	1 469	2.6	>200.0	2 071	2.7	41.0
South Africa - Afrique du Sud	426	4.4	44.4	534	4.8	25.5	706	5.9	32.0
Brazil - Brésil	423	3.4	16.5	507	3.2	20.0	738	3.8	45.5
Indonesia - Indonésie (6)	297	2.5	..	367	2.8	23.8	181	1.6	-50.7
Turkey - Turquie	288	1.3	-1.0	345	1.3	19.8	277	1.1	-19.7
Panama	240	8.6	-18.0	198	6.1	-17.6	268	6.8	35.4
Swaziland	105	42.2	7.8	151	53.2	43.7	33	11.6	-78.3
China - Chine	94	0.2	-38.2	145	0.2	54.6	145	0.2	0.1
Egypt - Égypte	74	0.5	-7.3	137	0.9	85.6	149	0.9	8.7
Barbados - Barbade	80	6.5	8.4	117	8.0	46.9	..	..	..
Uruguay	53	4.8	-7.9	66	5.0	22.9	64	5.0	-3.1
Malaysia - Malaisie	97	0.6	-11.0	60	0.3	-38.5	71	0.3	19.3
Lebanon - Liban	40	0.4	48.5	58	0.5	46.2	58	0.5	-0.1
Tunisia - Tunisie	55	1.5	0.5	58	1.4	4.1	66	1.5	13.9
Côte d'Ivoire	53	6.9	11.6	54	6.5	2.0	..	..	..
Philippines	42	1.0	10.5	53	1.2	26.2	101	1.6	90.6
ROYALTIES AND LICENSE FEES - REDEVANCES ET DROITS DE LICENCE									
Republic of Korea - République de Corée	1 861	4.4	41.9	1 908	4.2	2.5	2 011	3.9	5.4
Singapore - Singapour	495	1.1	152.1	624	1.2	25.9	730	1.2	17.1
Indonesia - Indonésie (6)	221	1.8	..	263	2.0	19.1	14	0.1	-94.9
China, Hong Kong SAR - Chine (RAS de Hong Kong)	218	0.4	-36.0	245	0.4	12.5	(e)355	(e)0.5	(e)44.7
China, Taiwan Province of - Province chinoise de Taiwan	290	1.1	34.9	234	0.9	-19.3	244	0.8	4.3
Paraguay	208	33.1	7.5	219	31.6	5.2	236	29.3	8.1
China - Chine	236	0.4	120.9	157	0.2	-33.4	205	0.2	29.9
Egypt - Égypte	100	0.7	-17.2	136	0.9	36.0	138	0.9	1.5
India - Inde (5)	53	0.1	119.2	131	0.2	148.4	112	0.1	-14.9
Brazil - Brésil	114	0.9	5.9	102	0.6	-11.2	150	0.8	47.9
Mexico - Mexique	92	0.7	8.9	70	0.4	-23.1	171	1.0	142.8
Chile - Chili	48	0.8	6.6	54	0.8	11.5	55	0.7	2.2
Argentina - Argentine	61	1.2	18.8	51	0.8	-16.7	71	0.9	39.9
Angola	227	70.3	..	49	28.0	-78.2	1 340	90.3	>200.0
South Africa - Afrique du Sud	37	0.4	40.8	45	0.4	21.2	46	0.4	1.1
Guyana	34	20.9	5.0	35	24.0	5.0	37	25.2	5.1
Malaysia - Malaisie	42	0.2	104.6	27	0.1	-34.9	26	0.1	-3.2
Lesotho	17	26.6	14.3	18	32.1	6.2	18	30.8	2.1
Kenya	17	1.1	42.9	18	0.9	5.2	10	0.4	-43.5
Thailand - Thaïlande	14	0.1	90.4	17	0.1	17.7	46	0.2	175.5
OTHER BUSINESS SERVICES (4) - AUTRES SERVICES AUX ENTREPRISES (4)									
China, Hong Kong SAR - Chine (RAS de Hong Kong)	21 798	39.5	12.5	24 318	38.1	11.6	(e)35 337	(e)48.9	(e)45.3
China - Chine	19 952	32.0	14.5	23 283	31.3	16.7	28 973	31.5	24.4
Singapore - Singapour	18 056	38.7	27.2	20 636	39.1	14.3	22 544	38.2	9.2
India - Inde (5)	8 153	21.3	>200.0	14 634	26.2	79.5	23 198	30.8	58.5
China, Taiwan Province of - Province chinoise de Taiwan	13 739	53.3	1.6	11 950	46.3	-13.0	14 779	50.5	23.7
Republic of Korea - République de Corée	8 125	19.4	21.5	9 422	20.9	16.0	13 071	25.2	38.7
Brazil - Brésil	4 938	39.2	19.5	6 722	41.9	36.1	8 568	44.0	27.5
Saudi Arabia - Arabie saoudite	5 852	100.0	2.4	6 677	100.0	14.1	7 297	100.0	9.3
Thailand - Thaïlande	3 952	20.8	2.5	4 998	24.8	26.5	5 255	21.8	5.1
Lebanon - Liban	3 340	34.4	42.1	4 362	40.2	30.6	5 555	47.8	27.4
Nigeria - Nigéria	2 637	79.0	-14.3	3 407	81.8	29.2	..	..	..
Indonesia - Indonésie (6)	2 669	22.2	..	2 876	22.2	7.7	2 564	22.3	-10.8
Malaysia - Malaisie	2 315	13.5	20.3	2 773	14.2	19.8	3 559	16.3	28.3
Argentina - Argentine	1 194	22.6	25.2	1 593	24.7	33.5	1 860	24.3	16.7
Egypt - Égypte	2 780	19.6	32.9	1 549	10.6	-44.3	1 337	8.3	-13.6
Morocco - Maroc	904	13.5	40.6	1 129	13.9	24.9	1 380	14.0	22.3
Chile - Chili	890	14.7	7.2	1 060	15.1	19.1	1 188	15.8	12.1
South Africa - Afrique du Sud	742	7.7	22.7	837	7.5	12.8	868	7.2	3.7
Netherlands Antilles - Antilles néerlandaises	644	35.8	3.4	647	35.0	0.6	..	..	..
Philippines	361	8.9	12.1	525	11.6	45.4	898	13.9	71.0

For sources and notes, see end of table.   Pour les sources et les notes, se reporter à la fin du tableau.

Ranking based on 2005 exports Classement d'après les exportations de 2005	2004			2005			2006		
	Millions of dollars Millions de dollars	As % of country's total En % du total du pays	Annual change in % Variation annuelle en %	Millions of dollars Millions de dollars	As % of country's total En % du total du pays	Annual change in % Variation annuelle en %	Millions of dollars Millions de dollars	As % of country's total En % du total du pays	Annual change in % Variation annuelle en %
PERSONAL, CULTURAL AND RECREATIONAL SERVICES - SERVICES PERSONNELS, CULTURELS ET RELATIFS AUX LOISIRS									
Malaysia - Malaisie	1 670	9.8	-9.0	1 562	8.0	-6.5	864	4.0	-44.7
Turkey - Turquie	1 418	6.2	81.6	1 079	4.0	-23.9	992	4.0	-8.1
Mexico - Mexique	358	2.5	22.1	373	2.3	4.3	383	2.3	2.6
China, Hong Kong SAR - Chine (RAS de Hong Kong)	290	0.5	110.8	270	0.4	-6.7	(e)431	(e)0.6	(e)59.5
Republic of Korea - République de Corée	128	0.3	68.0	268	0.6	109.2	369	0.7	37.6
Argentina - Argentine	153	2.9	25.0	194	3.0	27.3	231	3.0	19.1
Singapore - Singapour	185	0.4	20.1	180	0.3	-3.0	196	0.3	9.4
India - Inde (5)	46	0.1	..	146	0.3	>200.0	218	0.3	49.3
China - Chine	41	0.1	22.6	134	0.2	>200.0	137	0.1	2.7
South Africa - Afrique du Sud	88	0.9	46.1	114	1.0	29.5	103	0.9	-9.2
Syrian Arab Republic - République arabe syrienne	62	2.4	..	85	2.9	37.1	92	3.1	8.2
Egypt - Égypte	69	0.5	-4.0	83	0.6	19.8	116	0.7	40.1
Chile - Chili	58	1.0	-13.8	69	1.0	18.7	78	1.0	13.4
China, Taiwan Province of - Province chinoise de Taiwan	49	0.2	22.5	61	0.2	24.5	76	0.3	24.6
Indonesia - Indonésie (6)	47	0.4	..	57	0.4	20.9	74	0.6	29.3
Brazil - Brésil	47	0.4	-13.2	56	0.3	20.0	81	0.4	45.6
Colombia - Colombie	39	1.7	24.3	41	1.6	7.1	46	1.4	10.0
Ecuador - Équateur	36	3.6	6.7	39	3.8	6.7	41	4.0	6.7
Jamaica - Jamaïque	28	1.2	39.4	30	1.3	4.3	31	1.2	5.2
Philippines	7	0.2	-22.2	20	0.4	185.7	27	0.4	35.0

Sources:
- International Monetary Fund (IMF), *Balance of Payments Statistics* on CD-ROM and other international and national sources

Sources :
- Fonds monétaire international (FMI), *Statistiques de la balance des paiements* sur CD-ROM et autres sources internationales et nationales

Notes:

(1) Excludes freight insurance, which is included with insurance services.
(2) Includes goods and services acquired from an economy by non-resident travelers during visits shorter than one year.
(3) Postal, courier and telecommunications services between residents and non-residents.
(4) Includes merchanting and other trade-related services, operational leasing services, and miscellaneous business, professional and technical services.
(5) Years 2004 and 2005: break in series.
(6) Year 2004: break in series.

Notes :

(1) Non-comprise l'assurance du fret, incluse dans la rubrique des services d'assurance.
(2) Comprend les biens et services acquis dans une économie par les voyageurs non-résidents, au cours d'un séjour inférieur à un an.
(3) Services postaux (y compris les messageries) et les services de télécommunication, entre résidents et non-résidents.
(4) Y compris le négoce international et les autres services liés au commerce, la location-exploitation et divers services aux entreprises, spécialisés et techniques.
(5) Années 2004 et 2005 : rupture de série.
(6) Année 2004 : rupture de série.

5

5.2 Trade in services by category:
Leading importers among
developing economies

5.2 Commerce des services par catégories :
Principaux importateurs parmi les économies en
développement

	2004			2005			2006		
Ranking based on 2005 imports Classement d'après les importations de 2005	Millions of dollars Millions de dollars	As % of country's total En % du total du pays	Annual change in % Variation annuelle en %	Millions of dollars Millions de dollars	As % of country's total En % du total du pays	Annual change in % Variation annuelle en %	Millions of dollars Millions de dollars	As % of country's total En % du total du pays	Annual change in % Variation annuelle en %
TRANSPORT (1) - TRANSPORTS (1)									
China - Chine	24 544	34.0	34.6	28 448	33.9	15.9	34 369	34.1	20.8
Singapore - Singapour	18 112	36.1	34.4	20 588	37.4	13.7	22 947	37.1	11.5
Republic of Korea - République de Corée	17 655	35.4	29.7	20 144	34.3	14.1	23 394	33.1	16.1
India - Inde (5)	13 233	37.1	42.1	20 140	42.0	52.2	25 198	39.7	25.1
Thailand - Thaïlande	10 830	46.9	27.7	14 536	53.6	34.2	16 222	50.0	11.6
China, Hong Kong SAR - Chine (RAS de Hong Kong)	8 687	27.9	29.3	10 462	30.8	20.4	(e)11 299	(e)30.9	(e)8.0
United Arab Emirates - Émirats arabes unis	(e)8 743	(e)57.9	(e)35.7	(e)10 392	(e)50.5	(e)18.9	..	..	..
China, Taiwan Province of - Province chinoise de Taiwan	8 132	26.5	21.1	8 439	26.0	3.8	9 030	26.8	7.0
Malaysia - Malaisie	7 814	40.6	24.8	8 396	38.2	7.5	9 577	40.4	14.1
Indonesia - Indonésie (6)	5 474	26.2	13.5	7 451	33.8	36.1	8 179	37.8	9.8
South Africa - Afrique du Sud	4 401	42.6	38.6	5 328	43.8	21.1	6 628	46.4	24.4
Brazil - Brésil	4 452	25.8	30.5	5 089	20.9	14.3	6 565	22.5	29.0
Turkey - Turquie	4 331	42.6	60.0	4 732	41.6	9.3	4 308	38.5	-9.0
Saudi Arabia - Arabie saoudite	3 325	12.9	21.2	4 422	15.4	33.0	5 297	13.1	19.8
Chile - Chili	3 354	49.5	29.7	4 125	53.9	23.0	4 551	54.0	10.3
Egypt - Égypte	2 986	37.2	48.4	3 731	35.5	24.9	4 525	39.1	21.3
Philippines	3 095	53.2	27.9	3 125	53.3	1.0	3 389	55.4	8.4
Kuwait - Koweït	2 297	30.3	13.4	2 789	32.4	21.4	2 840	27.9	1.8
Mexico - Mexique	2 127	10.8	10.2	2 716	12.7	27.7	2 684	11.8	-1.2
Pakistan	2 076	38.9	31.0	2 614	34.8	25.9	3 027	36.0	15.8
TRAVEL (2) - VOYAGES (2)									
China - Chine	19 149	26.5	26.1	21 759	26.0	13.6	24 322	24.1	11.8
Republic of Korea - République de Corée	12 350	24.7	22.2	15 406	26.2	24.7	18 241	25.8	18.4
China, Hong Kong SAR - Chine (RAS de Hong Kong)	13 269	42.6	15.9	13 305	39.2	0.3	(e)13 982	(e)38.3	(e)5.1
Singapore - Singapour	9 242	18.4	16.7	9 947	18.1	7.6	10 384	16.8	4.4
China, Taiwan Province of - Province chinoise de Taiwan	8 170	26.6	26.1	8 682	26.7	6.3	8 746	26.0	0.7
Mexico - Mexique	6 959	35.2	11.3	7 600	35.4	9.2	8 108	35.5	6.7
India - Inde (5)	4 816	13.5	34.3	6 013	12.5	24.9	7 352	11.6	22.3
United Arab Emirates - Émirats arabes unis	(e)4 472	(e)29.6	(e)13.0	(e)5 266	(e)25.6	(e)17.7	..	..	..
Brazil - Brésil	2 871	16.6	27.0	4 720	19.4	64.4	5 764	19.8	22.1
Kuwait - Koweït	3 701	48.8	10.6	4 277	49.7	15.6	5 253	51.5	22.8
Thailand - Thaïlande	4 514	19.6	54.6	3 800	14.0	-15.8	4 632	14.3	21.9
Malaysia - Malaisie	3 178	16.5	11.6	3 711	16.9	16.8	4 020	16.9	8.3
Indonesia - Indonésie (6)	3 507	16.8	13.8	3 584	16.3	2.2	3 600	16.6	0.4
South Africa - Afrique du Sud	3 157	30.6	9.3	3 373	27.8	6.9	3 384	23.7	0.3
Lebanon - Liban	3 170	38.5	7.7	2 908	36.8	-8.3	3 006	34.5	3.4
Turkey - Turquie	2 524	24.8	19.5	2 872	25.2	13.8	2 743	24.5	-4.5
Argentina - Argentine	2 604	39.3	3.7	2 790	36.5	7.1	3 131	36.8	12.2
Qatar	691	23.8	46.8	1 759	42.4	154.6	..	..	..
Egypt - Égypte	1 257	15.7	-4.8	1 629	15.5	29.5	1 784	15.4	9.5
Pakistan	1 268	23.8	37.1	1 280	17.0	0.9	1 545	18.4	20.7
COMMUNICATIONS (3)									
China, Hong Kong SAR - Chine (RAS de Hong Kong)	1 124	3.6	19.4	1 141	3.4	1.5	(e)1 637	(e)4.5	(e)43.5
Singapore - Singapour	769	1.5	7.2	889	1.6	15.6	979	1.6	10.1
Republic of Korea - République de Corée	636	1.3	-8.3	773	1.3	21.6	778	1.1	0.7
Malaysia - Malaisie	504	2.6	100.0	680	3.1	35.0	653	2.8	-4.0
India - Inde (5)	579	1.6	-5.3	667	1.4	15.3	899	1.4	34.8
China - Chine	472	0.7	10.5	603	0.7	27.8	764	0.8	26.6
China, Taiwan Province of - Province chinoise de Taiwan	496	1.6	7.8	505	1.6	1.8	393	1.2	-22.2
Indonesia - Indonésie (6)	359	1.7	173.5	495	2.2	37.7	571	2.6	15.5
Egypt - Égypte	224	2.8	51.3	406	3.9	80.9	309	2.7	-23.9
Argentina - Argentine	223	3.4	-1.9	269	3.5	20.4	307	3.6	14.3
Turkey - Turquie	207	2.0	-10.4	228	2.0	10.1	296	2.6	29.8
Thailand - Thaïlande	141	0.6	-21.2	214	0.8	51.1	159	0.5	-25.7
South Africa - Afrique du Sud	147	1.4	47.7	198	1.6	34.4	246	1.7	24.1
Colombia - Colombie	144	3.7	33.8	152	3.2	5.0	199	3.6	31.1
Lebanon - Liban	203	2.5	110.4	138	1.8	-31.9	217	2.5	56.5
Mexico - Mexique	176	0.9	-43.4	119	0.6	-32.4	107	0.5	-9.6
Chile - Chili	160	2.4	2.8	115	1.5	-28.0	131	1.6	13.9
Philippines	128	2.2	58.0	115	2.0	-10.2	98	1.6	-14.8
Brazil - Brésil	70	0.4	-81.0	112	0.5	60.8	102	0.3	-9.0
Kenya	108	11.5	>200.0	108	9.4	-0.8	130	9.1	21.3

For sources and notes, see end of table.

Pour les sources et les notes, se reporter à la fin du tableau.

5.2 Trade in services by category:
Leading importers among
developing economies

5.2 Commerce des services par catégories :
Principaux importateurs parmi les économies en
développement

Ranking based on 2005 imports / Classement d'après les importations de 2005	2004			2005			2006		
	Millions of dollars / Millions de dollars	As % of country's total / En % du total du pays	Annual change in % / Variation annuelle en %	Millions of dollars / Millions de dollars	As % of country's total / En % du total du pays	Annual change in % / Variation annuelle en %	Millions of dollars / Millions de dollars	As % of country's total / En % du total du pays	Annual change in % / Variation annuelle en %
CONSTRUCTION - BÂTIMENTS ET TRAVAUX PUBLICS									
China - Chine	1 339	1.9	13.1	1 619	1.9	21.0	2 050	2.0	26.6
Angola	866	18.0	>200.0	1 323	19.5	52.7	1 476	19.6	11.5
Malaysia - Malaisie	518	2.7	26.5	1 087	5.0	109.8	1 314	5.5	20.8
Indonesia - Indonésie (6)	708	3.4	..	726	3.3	2.5	984	4.6	35.6
India - Inde (5)	829	2.3	-31.5	665	1.4	-19.7	906	1.4	36.1
China, Taiwan Province of - Province chinoise de Taiwan	558	1.8	22.1	376	1.2	-32.6	295	0.9	-21.5
Thailand - Thaïlande	229	1.0	51.2	314	1.2	37.2	581	1.8	84.8
China, Hong Kong SAR - Chine (RAS de Hong Kong)	346	1.1	-13.3	273	0.8	-21.2	(e)450	(e)1.2	(e)65.0
Singapore - Singapour	325	0.6	129.4	243	0.4	-25.1	262	0.4	7.6
Egypt - Égypte	171	2.1	59.3	231	2.2	34.8	166	1.4	-28.1
Tunisia - Tunisie	183	9.2	14.5	197	9.0	7.4	227	9.2	15.3
Libyan Arab Jamahiriya - Jamahiriya arabe libyenne	183	9.6	8.9	149	6.3	-18.6	160	6.2	7.4
United Republic of Tanzania - République-Unie de Tanzanie	93	9.5	>200.0	143	11.8	53.8	132	10.6	-7.8
Pakistan	8	0.2	-33.3	132	1.8	>200.0	58	0.7	-56.1
Ethiopia - Éthiopie	78	8.1	15.3	121	10.1	55.7	179	15.3	47.9
Yemen - Yémen	108	10.2	>200.0	108	8.7	0.0	106	5.7	-1.5
New Caledonia - Nouvelle-Calédonie	11	1.9	-66.5	93	10.4	>200.0	118	10.1	27.8
Mozambique	52	9.8	-14.3	79	12.1	50.6	94	12.4	19.1
Papua New Guinea - Papouasie-Nouvelle-Guinée	38	3.8	-5.0	58	5.0	54.0	..	..	..
Cambodia - Cambodge	42	8.1	-3.9	43	6.6	2.2	48	6.1	13.1
COMPUTER AND INFORMATION SERVICES - INFORMATIQUE ET INFORMATION									
Brazil - Brésil	1 281	7.4	20.6	1 713	7.0	33.7	2 005	6.9	17.0
China - Chine	1 253	1.7	20.9	1 623	1.9	29.5	1 739	1.7	7.2
India - Inde (5)	932	2.6	36.0	1 566	3.3	68.0	2 199	3.5	40.4
Indonesia - Indonésie (6)	468	2.2	..	561	2.5	19.9	596	2.8	6.2
China, Hong Kong SAR - Chine (RAS de Hong Kong)	395	1.3	40.0	427	1.3	8.0	(e)593	(e)1.6	(e)38.9
Singapore - Singapour	315	0.6	-4.6	385	0.7	22.1	426	0.7	10.9
Malaysia - Malaisie	325	1.7	64.8	379	1.7	16.6	518	2.2	36.7
China, Taiwan Province of - Province chinoise de Taiwan	238	0.8	-4.0	315	1.0	32.4	313	0.9	-0.6
Argentina - Argentine	160	2.4	14.9	187	2.4	16.5	208	2.4	11.3
Republic of Korea - République de Corée	157	0.3	17.3	183	0.3	16.6	773	1.1	>200.0
Colombia - Colombie	66	1.7	-8.3	119	2.5	79.3	143	2.6	20.6
South Africa - Afrique du Sud	84	0.8	41.9	114	0.9	35.1	127	0.9	11.5
Syrian Arab Republic - République arabe syrienne	100	4.5	-9.1	100	4.2	0.0	95	3.8	-5.0
Venezuela (Bolivarian Rep. of) - Venezuela (Rép. bolivarienne du)	69	1.5	19.0	85	1.6	23.2	94	1.6	10.6
Chile - Chili	74	1.1	-2.3	71	0.9	-3.4	73	0.9	2.0
Philippines	49	0.8	6.5	62	1.1	26.5	67	1.1	8.1
Pakistan	18	0.3	200.0	34	0.5	88.9	65	0.8	91.2
Egypt - Égypte	24	0.3	-10.9	27	0.3	15.2	30	0.3	10.3
China, Macao SAR - Chine (RAS de Macao)	25	1.8	48.3	25	1.6	3.0	33	1.8	32.7
Libyan Arab Jamahiriya - Jamahiriya arabe libyenne	15	0.8	25.0	25	1.1	66.7	30	1.2	20.0
INSURANCE - ASSURANCES									
Mexico - Mexique	7 666	38.8	13.5	8 714	40.6	13.7	9 278	40.6	6.5
China - Chine	6 124	8.5	34.2	7 200	8.6	17.6	8 831	8.8	22.7
Singapore - Singapour	2 196	4.4	22.0	2 552	4.6	16.2	3 082	5.0	20.8
India - Inde (5)	1 748	4.9	50.1	2 237	4.7	28.0	2 664	4.2	19.1
Thailand - Thaïlande	1 290	5.6	14.7	1 656	6.1	28.3	1 791	5.5	8.1
China, Taiwan Province of - Province chinoise de Taiwan	1 205	3.9	-2.5	967	3.0	-19.8	1 002	3.0	3.6
Turkey - Turquie	839	8.3	34.9	891	7.8	6.2	850	7.6	-4.6
Egypt - Égypte	588	7.3	39.1	781	7.4	32.9	978	8.5	25.1
Republic of Korea - République de Corée	461	0.9	18.2	733	1.2	58.9	909	1.3	24.0
Brazil - Brésil	649	3.3	16.0	702	2.9	8.1	755	2.6	7.5
China, Hong Kong SAR - Chine (RAS de Hong Kong)	611	2.0	-1.7	606	1.8	-0.9	(e)618	(e)1.7	(e)2.0
Malaysia - Malaisie	494	2.6	2.9	518	2.4	4.8	612	2.6	18.2
Saudi Arabia - Arabie saoudite	369	1.4	21.2	491	1.7	33.0	589	1.5	19.8
South Africa - Afrique du Sud	391	3.8	31.8	478	3.9	22.3	587	4.1	22.8
Chile - Chili	451	6.7	3.7	468	6.1	3.6	515	6.1	10.2
Indonesia - Indonésie (6)	353	1.7	17.7	338	1.5	-4.1	384	1.8	13.4
Oman	257	9.3	16.5	299	9.8	16.2	343	9.2	14.8
Colombia - Colombie	249	6.3	4.8	290	6.1	16.2	318	5.8	9.5
Lebanon - Liban	176	2.1	-18.9	248	3.1	40.9	262	3.0	5.8
Peru - Pérou	209	7.7	-21.8	233	7.5	11.6	265	7.8	13.7

For sources and notes, see end of table.

Pour les sources et les notes, se reporter à la fin du tableau.

5

5.2   Trade in services by category:
Leading importers among
developing economies

5.2   Commerce des services par catégories :
Principaux importateurs parmi les économies en
développement

	2004			2005			2006		
Ranking based on 2005 imports Classement d'après les importations de 2005	Millions of dollars Millions de dollars	As % of country's total En % du total du pays	Annual change in % Variation annuelle en %	Millions of dollars Millions de dollars	As % of country's total En % du total du pays	Annual change in % Variation annuelle en %	Millions of dollars Millions de dollars	As % of country's total En % du total du pays	Annual change in % Variation annuelle en %
FINANCIAL SERVICES - SERVICES FINANCIERS									
China, Hong Kong SAR - Chine (RAS de Hong Kong)	1 165	3.7	32.7	1 406	4.1	20.7	(e)2 021	(e)5.5	(e)43.8
China, Taiwan Province of - Province chinoise de Taiwan	884	2.9	-20.5	1 370	4.2	55.0	1 390	4.1	1.5
India - Inde (5)	791	2.2	62.1	1 144	2.4	44.7	1 316	2.1	15.0
Brazil - Brésil	499	2.9	-33.0	737	3.0	47.5	861	3.0	16.8
Singapore - Singapour	666	1.3	32.6	725	1.3	8.7	972	1.6	34.1
Mexico - Mexique	412	2.1	3.1	550	2.6	33.3	374	1.6	-32.0
Indonesia - Indonésie (6)	594	2.8	..	539	2.4	-9.2	363	1.7	-32.7
Turkey - Turquie	377	3.7	0.8	386	3.4	2.4	524	4.7	35.8
Chile - Chili	283	4.2	32.2	257	3.4	-9.3	287	3.4	11.7
Venezuela (Bolivarian Rep. of) - Venezuela (Rép. bolivarienne du)	110	2.4	-29.9	243	4.5	120.9	197	3.3	-18.9
Republic of Korea - République de Corée	127	0.3	25.1	235	0.4	85.8	616	0.9	162.0
Argentina - Argentine	105	1.6	-6.9	210	2.7	99.1	78	0.9	-62.8
Egypt - Égypte	27	0.3	6.3	198	1.9	>200.0	67	0.6	-66.1
South Africa - Afrique du Sud	149	1.4	45.2	184	1.5	23.3	177	1.2	-3.3
China - Chine	138	0.2	-40.6	159	0.2	15.5	891	0.9	>200.0
Panama	138	9.5	-18.4	157	8.8	14.0	142	8.2	-9.7
Colombia - Colombie	95	2.4	-5.4	145	3.0	52.1	162	3.0	12.1
Pakistan	75	1.4	2.7	124	1.7	65.3	132	1.6	6.5
Swaziland	96	23.8	169.7	123	30.2	28.7	56	15.2	-54.4
Côte d'Ivoire	125	6.1	12.7	120	5.6	-3.9	..	..	..
ROYALTIES AND LICENSE FEES - REDEVANCES ET DROITS DE LICENCE									
Singapore - Singapour	7 917	15.8	19.3	8 941	16.2	12.9	10 470	16.9	17.1
China - Chine	4 497	6.2	26.7	5 321	6.4	18.3	6 634	6.6	24.7
Republic of Korea - République de Corée	4 446	8.9	24.5	4 561	7.8	2.6	4 487	6.4	-1.6
China, Taiwan Province of - Province chinoise de Taiwan	1 677	5.5	-0.7	1 796	5.5	7.1	2 321	6.9	29.2
Thailand - Thaïlande	1 584	6.9	24.9	1 674	6.2	5.7	2 046	6.3	22.2
Brazil - Brésil	1 197	6.9	-2.5	1 404	5.8	17.3	1 664	5.7	18.5
Malaysia - Malaisie	896	4.6	14.5	1 370	6.2	52.9	1 052	4.4	-23.2
China, Hong Kong SAR - Chine (RAS de Hong Kong)	1 111	3.6	28.6	1 289	3.8	16.0	(e)1 729	(e)4.7	(e)34.1
South Africa - Afrique du Sud	891	8.6	44.5	1 071	8.8	20.2	1 282	9.0	19.7
Indonesia - Indonésie (6)	990	4.7	..	961	4.4	-3.0	870	4.0	-9.5
India - Inde (5)	611	1.7	11.2	767	1.6	25.4	949	1.5	23.7
Argentina - Argentine	520	7.9	29.1	654	8.6	25.8	807	9.5	23.4
Turkey - Turquie	362	3.6	116.9	439	3.9	21.3	531	4.7	21.0
Chile - Chili	307	4.5	19.5	348	4.5	13.1	381	4.5	9.7
Philippines	273	4.7	-1.8	265	4.5	-2.9	349	5.7	31.7
Venezuela (Bolivarian Rep. of) - Venezuela (Rép. bolivarienne du)	219	4.9	19.7	239	4.5	9.1	257	4.3	7.5
Egypt - Égypte	108	1.3	-34.5	182	1.7	68.4	159	1.4	-12.5
Colombia - Colombie	82	2.1	8.9	118	2.5	43.5	127	2.3	7.4
Mexico - Mexique	805	4.1	32.4	111	0.5	-86.2	503	2.2	>200.0
Pakistan	86	1.6	138.9	109	1.5	26.7	106	1.3	-2.8
OTHER BUSINESS SERVICES (4) - AUTRES SERVICES AUX ENTREPRISES (4)									
China - Chine	13 911	19.3	34.1	16 287	19.4	17.1	20 605	20.4	26.5
Republic of Korea - République de Corée	13 163	26.4	19.1	15 538	26.4	18.0	19 905	28.2	28.1
India - Inde (5)	11 693	32.8	65.3	14 231	29.7	21.7	21 453	33.8	50.8
Singapore - Singapour	10 218	20.4	27.3	10 350	18.8	1.3	11 919	19.2	15.2
Saudi Arabia - Arabie saoudite	7 363	28.7	50.6	9 606	33.5	30.5	13 504	33.3	40.6
China, Taiwan Province of - Province chinoise de Taiwan	8 261	26.9	33.2	8 669	26.7	4.9	8 909	26.5	2.8
Brazil - Brésil	4 682	27.1	6.9	7 480	30.7	59.8	8 898	30.6	19.0
Indonesia - Indonésie (6)	7 984	38.3	-9.6	7 017	31.8	-12.1	5 736	26.5	-18.3
China, Hong Kong SAR - Chine (RAS de Hong Kong)	4 223	13.6	12.0	4 878	14.4	15.5	(e)6 555	(e)17.9	(e)34.4
Thailand - Thaïlande	4 320	18.7	11.6	4 779	17.6	10.6	6 811	21.0	42.5
Malaysia - Malaisie	3 219	16.7	5.3	3 636	16.6	12.9	4 196	17.7	15.4
Angola	2 213	46.1	32.9	3 265	48.1	47.5	3 092	41.2	-5.3
Lebanon - Liban	3 426	41.6	48.3	3 242	41.1	-5.4	3 718	42.7	14.7
Pakistan	1 431	26.8	>200.0	2 695	35.9	88.3	2 944	35.0	9.3
Egypt - Égypte	2 069	25.8	15.4	2 301	21.9	11.2	2 232	19.3	-3.0
Congo	607	59.8	12.8	1 138	73.0	87.5	..	..	..
South Africa - Afrique du Sud	833	8.1	38.2	1 104	9.1	32.5	1 503	10.5	36.2
Chile - Chili	999	14.7	6.7	1 036	13.5	3.7	1 044	12.4	0.8
Oman	832	30.2	56.1	1 017	33.3	22.2	1 428	38.2	40.4
Argentina - Argentine	827	12.5	27.6	897	11.7	8.5	938	11.0	4.5

For sources and notes, see end of table.

Pour les sources et les notes, se reporter à la fin du tableau.

5.2 Trade in services by category:
Leading importers among
developing economies

5.2 Commerce des services par catégories :
Principaux importateurs parmi les économies en
développement

	2004			2005			2006		
Ranking based on 2005 imports Classement d'après les importations de 2005	Millions of dollars Millions de dollars	As % of country's total En % du total du pays	Annual change in % Variation annuelle en %	Millions of dollars Millions de dollars	As % of country's total En % du total du pays	Annual change n % Variation annuelle en %	Millions of dollars Millions de dollars	As % of country's total En % du total du pays	Annual change in % Variation annuelle en %
PERSONAL, CULTURAL AND RECREATIONAL SERVICES - SERVICES PERSONNELS, CULTURELS ET RELATIFS AUX LOISIRS									
Malaysia - Malaisie	1 899	9.9	-35.0	1 855	8.4	-2.3	1 428	6.0	-23.0
Republic of Korea - République de Corée	376	0.8	43.9	477	0.8	26.8	680	1.0	42.6
Brazil - Brésil	409	2.4	21.5	451	1.9	10.4	533	1.8	18.1
China, Taiwan Province of - Province chinoise de Taiwan	238	0.8	15.5	301	0.9	26.5	199	0.6	-33.9
Singapore - Singapour	268	0.5	11.2	278	0.5	3.8	304	0.5	9.4
Mexico - Mexique	225	1.1	2.1	275	1.3	22.2	326	1.4	18.3
Venezuela (Bolivarian Rep. of) - Venezuela (Rép. bolivarienne du)	165	3.7	>200.0	181	3.4	9.7	254	4.2	40.3
Argentina - Argentine	143	2.2	32.5	173	2.3	20.7	182	2.1	5.1
Indonesia - Indonésie (6)	184	0.9	..	166	0.8	-9.8	124	0.6	-25.3
China - Chine	176	0.2	152.8	154	0.2	-12.4	121	0.1	-21.1
India - Inde (5)	61	0.2	..	115	0.2	88.2	118	0.2	2.4
Ecuador - Équateur	98	5.0	6.6	106	5.0	8.2	116	4.9	9.0
Turkey - Turquie	176	1.7	50.4	88	0.8	-50.0	106	0.9	20.5
Chile - Chili	48	0.7	2.6	53	0.7	8.8	55	0.7	4.3
China, Hong Kong SAR - Chine (RAS de Hong Kong)	52	0.2	-24.6	52	0.2	0.4	(e)75	(e)0.2	(e)44.3
Angola	28	0.6	163.9	45	0.7	57.6	65	0.9	44.2
Colombia - Colombie	31	0.8	6.1	44	0.9	40.5	58	1.1	32.7
New Caledonia - Nouvelle-Calédonie	11	1.8	42.1	38	4.3	>200.0	41	3.5	8.6
Mauritius - Maurice	21	2.1	54.4	31	2.6	43.4	33	2.5	9.2
Egypt - Égypte	15	0.2	0.0	22	0.2	45.4	39	0.3	76.0

Sources:
- International Monetary Fund (IMF), *Balance of Payments Statistics* on CD-ROM and
other international and national sources

Notes:

(1) Excludes freight insurance, which is included with insurance services.
(2) Includes goods and services acquired from an economy by non-resident travelers during visits shorter than one year.
(3) Postal, courier and telecommunications services between residents and non-residents.
(4) Includes merchanting and other trade-related services, operational leasing services, and miscellaneous business, professional and technical services.
(5) Years 2004 and 2005: break in series.
(6) Year 2004: break in series.

Sources :
- Fonds monétaire international (FMI), *Statistiques de la balance des paiements* sur CD-ROM et autres sources internationales et nationales

Notes :

(1) Non-comprise l'assurance du fret, incluse dans la rubrique des services d'assurance.
(2) Comprend les biens et services acquis dans une économie par les voyageurs non-résidents, au cours d'un séjour inférieur à un an.
(3) Services postaux (y compris les messageries) et les services de télécommunication, entre résidents et non-résidents.
(4) Y compris le négoce international et les autres services liés au commerce, la location-exploitation et divers services aux entreprises, spécialisés et techniques.
(5) Années 2004 et 2005 : rupture de série.
(6) Année 2004 : rupture de série.

5

	1990	2000	2001	2002	2003	2004	2005	2006
				Afghanistan				
Arrivées des visiteurs (milliers)	8	..	..	..	..	..	..	..
Nuitées des touristes (milliers)	..	..	..	..	..	..	..	..
Dépenses totales des visiteurs (millions de dollars)	..	..	..	..	..	..	..	..
Dépenses sans transport (millions de dollars)	..	..	..	..	..	..	..	..
				Albania - Albanie (1)				
Arrivals of visitors (thousands)	30	(d)317	(d)354	(d)470	(d)557	(d)645	(d)748	(d)937
Tourists' overnight stays (thousands)	..	..	..	..	..	..	..	..
Total expenditure of visitors (millions of dollars)	..	398	451	492	537	756	880	1 057
Expenditure excluding transport (millions of dollars)	4	389	446	487	522	735	854	1 012
				Algeria - Algérie				
Arrivées des visiteurs (milliers)	1 137	(d)866	(d)901	(d)988	(d)1 166	(d)1 234	(d)1 443	(d)1 638
Nuitées des touristes (milliers)	..	..	..	..	..	..	..	..
Dépenses totales des visiteurs (millions de dollars)	150	102	100	111	112	178	184	215
Dépenses sans transport (millions de dollars)	64	..	..	..	..	..	..	..
				American Samoa - Samoa américaines				
Arrivals of visitors (thousands)	26	(a)44	(a)36	..	..	..	(a)25	(a)25
Tourists' overnight stays (thousands)	..	..	..	..	..	..	..	..
Total expenditure of visitors (millions of dollars)	..	..	..	..	..	..	..	..
Expenditure excluding transport (millions of dollars)	..	..	..	..	..	..	..	..
				Andorra - Andorre				
Arrivées des visiteurs (milliers)	..	(d)10 991	(d)11 351	(d)11 507	(d)11 601	(d)11 668	(d)11 049	(d)10 737
Nuitées des touristes (milliers)	..	8 628	9 809	9 336	7 745	7 322	6 762	6 284
Dépenses totales des visiteurs (millions de dollars)	..	..	..	..	..	..	..	..
Dépenses sans transport (millions de dollars)	..	..	..	..	..	..	..	..
				Angola				
Arrivals of visitors (thousands)	67	(a)51	(a)67	(a)91	(a)107	(a)194	(a)210	(a)121
Tourists' overnight stays (thousands)	..	77	112	207	217	149	182	231
Total expenditure of visitors (millions of dollars)	27	34	36	51	63	82	103	91
Expenditure excluding transport (millions of dollars)	13	18	22	37	49	66	88	75
				Anguilla				
Arrivées des visiteurs (milliers)	31	(d)112	(d)105	(d)111	(d)109	(d)121	(d)143	(d)167
Nuitées des touristes (milliers)	..	377	411	383	399	421	502	584
Dépenses totales des visiteurs (millions de dollars)	..	..	..	..	..	..	..	..
Dépenses sans transport (millions de dollars)	36	56	62	57	60	69	86	107
				Antigua and Barbuda - Antigua-et-Barbuda				
Arrivals of visitors (thousands)	206	(d)634	(d)624	(d)528	(d)623	(d)791	(d)734	(d)745
Tourists' overnight stays (thousands)	..	..	..	..	..	..	..	..
Total expenditure of visitors (millions of dollars)	273	..	..	..	..	..	..	..
Expenditure excluding transport (millions of dollars)	231	291	272	274	300	338	335	347
				Argentina - Argentine				
Arrivées des visiteurs (milliers)	1 930	(a)2 909	(a)2 620	(a)2 820	(a)2 995	(a)3 457	(a)3 823	(a)4 156
Nuitées des touristes (milliers)	..	..	26 986	27 636	31 148	36 576	40 097	45 547
Dépenses totales des visiteurs (millions de dollars)	1 292	3 195	2 756	1 716	2 306	2 660	3 209	3 863
Dépenses sans transport (millions de dollars)	903	2 904	2 642	1 535	2 006	2 235	2 729	3 308
				Armenia - Arménie				
Arrivals of visitors (thousands)	–	(a)45	(a)123	(a)162	(a)206	(a)263	(a)319	(a)381
Tourists' overnight stays (thousands)	–	151	200	202	343	385	420	840
Total expenditure of visitors (millions of dollars)	–	52	81	81	90	188	240	307
Expenditure excluding transport (millions of dollars)	–	38	65	63	73	171	220	271
				Aruba				
Arrivées des visiteurs (milliers)	433	(d)1 211	(d)1 178	(d)1 225	(d)1 184	(d)1 304	(d)1 286	(d)1 285
Nuitées des touristes (milliers)	3 380	5 248	5 145	4 863	5 098	5 640	5 695	5 471
Dépenses totales des visiteurs (millions de dollars)	..	851	826	835	859	..	..	1 076
Dépenses sans transport (millions de dollars)	349	815	822	834	859	1 056	1 094	1 076
				Australia - Australie				
Arrivals of visitors (thousands)	2 215	(d)4 931	(d)4 856	(d)4 841	(d)4 746	(d)5 215	(d)5 499	(d)5 532
Tourists' overnight stays (thousands)	22 950	67 037	69 849	74 610	70 688	76 247	..	..
Total expenditure of visitors (millions of dollars)	5 461	13 016	12 804	13 624	16 647	20 453	22 566	23 729
Expenditure excluding transport (millions of dollars)	4 247	9 289	9 224	9 971	12 438	15 214	16 868	17 854

For sources and notes, see end of table.

Pour les sources et les notes, se reporter à la fin du tableau.

	1990	2000	2001	2002	2003	2004	2005	2006
Austria - Autriche								
Arrivées des visiteurs (milliers)	19 011	(b)17 982	(b)18 180	(b)18 611	(b)19 078	(b)19 373	(b)19 952	(b)20 261
Nuitées des touristes (milliers)	94 788	64 468	65 523	67 346	68 217	68 270	69 733	70 017
Dépenses totales des visiteurs (millions de dollars)	..	11 483	12 033	13 046	16 342	18 385	19 310	18 890
Dépenses sans transport (millions de dollars)	13 417	9 998	10 291	11 136	13 842	15 290	15 589	16 510
Azerbaijan - Azerbaïdjan								
Arrivals of visitors (thousands)	–	(a)681	(a)767	(a)834	(a)1 014	(a)1 349	(a)1 177	(a)1 194
Tourists' overnight stays (thousands)	..	..	..	..	..	..	..	..
Total expenditure of visitors (millions of dollars)	–	68	57	63	70	79	100	201
Expenditure excluding transport (millions of dollars)	–	63	43	51	58	65	78	117
Bahamas								
Arrivées des visiteurs (milliers)	1 562	(d)4 204	(d)4 183	(d)4 406	(d)4 594	(d)5 004	(d)4 779	(d)4 731
Nuitées des touristes (milliers)	8 963	9 048	8 973	8 704	8 957	9 898	10 297	10 269
Dépenses totales des visiteurs (millions de dollars)	1 337	1 753	1 665	1 773	1 770	1 897	2 082	2 079
Dépenses sans transport (millions de dollars)	1 324	1 738	1 648	1 760	1 757	1 884	2 072	2 069
Bahrain - Bahreïn								
Arrivals of visitors (thousands)	1 376	(d)3 869	(d)4 388	(d)4 831	(d)4 844	(d)5 667	(d)6 313	(d)7 289
Tourists' overnight stays (thousands)	..	..	..	..	..	..	..	..
Total expenditure of visitors (millions of dollars)	332	854	886	985	1 206	1 504	1 603	1 786
Expenditure excluding transport (millions of dollars)	136	573	630	740	720	864	920	1 048
Bangladesh								
Arrivées des visiteurs (milliers)	115	(a)199	(a)207	(a)207	(a)245	(a)271	(a)208	(a)200
Nuitées des touristes (milliers)	..	..	..	..	..	..	..	..
Dépenses totales des visiteurs (millions de dollars)	..	..	..	59	59	76	79	80
Dépenses sans transport (millions de dollars)	19	50	48	57	57	67	70	80
Barbados - Barbade								
Arrivals of visitors (thousands)	432	(d)1 078	(d)1 035	(d)1 021	(d)1 090	(d)1 273	(d)1 111	(d)1 102
Tourists' overnight stays (thousands)	2 337	2 695	2 460	2 031	2 459	2 463	..	..
Total expenditure of visitors (millions of dollars)	..	734	706	666	767	785	905	..
Expenditure excluding transport (millions of dollars)	508	723	697	658	758	776	897	978
Belarus - Bélarus								
Arrivées des visiteurs (milliers)	–	(a)60	(a)61	(a)63	(a)64	(a)67	(a)91	(a)89
Nuitées des touristes (milliers)	–	..	..	..	..	..	..	..
Dépenses totales des visiteurs (millions de dollars)	–	188	273	295	339	362	346	386
Dépenses sans transport (millions de dollars)	–	93	212	234	267	270	253	272
Belgium - Belgique								
Arrivals of visitors (thousands)	–	–	–	(b)6 720	(b)6 690	(b)6 710	(b)6 747	(b)6 995
Tourists' overnight stays (thousands)	–	–	–	15 895	15 929	15 545	15 553	16 040
Total expenditure of visitors (millions of dollars)	–	–	–	7 598	8 848	10 089	10 881	11 556
Expenditure excluding transport (millions of dollars)	–	–	–	6 935	8 193	9 208	9 845	10 242
Belgium-Luxembourg - Belgique-Luxembourg								
Arrivées des visiteurs (milliers)	5 967	(b)7 309	(b)7 288	–	–	–	–	–
Nuitées des touristes (milliers)	15 316	17 934	17 795	–	–	–	–	–
Dépenses totales des visiteurs (millions de dollars)	..	..	..	–	–	–	–	–
Dépenses sans transport (millions de dollars)	..	8 278	8 667	–	–	–	–	–
Belize								
Arrivals of visitors (thousands)	88	(d)374	(d)385	(d)694	(d)999	(d)1 329	(d)1 037	(d)903
Tourists' overnight stays (thousands)	..	..	..	..	..	..	..	..
Total expenditure of visitors (millions of dollars)	38	..	..	..	..	..	..	..
Expenditure excluding transport (millions of dollars)	38	111	111	121	150	168	204	253
Benin - Bénin								
Arrivées des visiteurs (milliers)	110	(d)1 068	(d)1 155	(d)853	(d)850	(d)845	(d)960	(d)975
Nuitées des touristes (milliers)	406	200	190	144	219	215	348	321
Dépenses totales des visiteurs (millions de dollars)	..	77	86	95	108	121	108	..
Dépenses sans transport (millions de dollars)	55	77	85	93	106	118	103	..
Bermuda - Bermudes								
Arrivals of visitors (thousands)	435	(d)539	(d)458	(d)484	(d)483	(d)478	(d)517	(d)635
Tourists' overnight stays (thousands)	2 739	1 966	1 775	1 822	1 598	1 733	1 729	1 931
Total expenditure of visitors (millions of dollars)	..	431	351	378	348	426	429	508
Expenditure excluding transport (millions of dollars)	..	..	..	..	..	..	..	..

For sources and notes, see end of table.   Pour les sources et les notes, se reporter à la fin du tableau.

	1990	2000	2001	2002	2003	2004	2005	2006
				Bhutan - Bhoutan				
Arrivées des visiteurs (milliers)	2	(a)8	(a)6	(a)6	(a)6	(a)9	(a)14	(a)17
Nuitées des touristes (milliers)	..	..	..	..	..	..	..	..
Dépenses totales des visiteurs (millions de dollars)	..	10	9	8	8	13	19	24
Dépenses sans transport (millions de dollars)	..	..	..	..	..	..	..	..
				Bolivia - Bolivie				
Arrivals of visitors (thousands)	254	(a)319	(a)316	(a)334	(a)427	(a)480	(a)524	(a)515
Tourists' overnight stays (thousands)	..	..	..	..	..	..	..	..
Total expenditure of visitors (millions of dollars)	79	101	119	143	243	283	345	287
Expenditure excluding transport (millions of dollars)	58	68	76	100	166	192	239	201
				Bosnia and Herzegovina - Bosnie-Herzégovine				
Arrivées des visiteurs (milliers)	–	(b)171	(b)139	(b)160	(b)165	(b)190	(b)217	(b)256
Nuitées des touristes (milliers)	–	389	330	392	419	460	485	594
Dépenses totales des visiteurs (millions de dollars)	–	246	279	307	404	507	550	643
Dépenses sans transport (millions de dollars)	–	233	265	288	377	481	512	592
				Botswana				
Arrivals of visitors (thousands)	543	(d)1 306	(d)1 451	(d)1 485	(d)1 592	(d)1 727	(d)1 885	..
Tourists' overnight stays (thousands)	..	..	..	..	..	..	..	..
Total expenditure of visitors (millions of dollars)	129	227	235	324	459	582	561	539
Expenditure excluding transport (millions of dollars)	117	222	230	319	457	581	560	537
				Brazil - Brésil				
Arrivées des visiteurs (milliers)	1 091	(a)5 313	(a)4 773	(a)3 785	(a)4 133	(a)4 794	(a)5 358	(a)5 019
Nuitées des touristes (milliers)	..	..	..	..	..	..	..	..
Dépenses totales des visiteurs (millions de dollars)	1 415	1 969	1 844	2 142	2 673	3 389	4 168	4 577
Dépenses sans transport (millions de dollars)	1 383	1 810	1 731	1 998	2 479	3 222	3 861	4 316
				British Virgin Islands - Îles Vierges britanniques				
Arrivals of visitors (thousands)	160	(a)272	(a)296	(a)282	(a)318	(a)304	(a)337	(a)356
Tourists' overnight stays (thousands)	..	117	106	105	..	..	..	..
Total expenditure of visitors (millions of dollars)	..	345	401	345	342	393	437	..
Expenditure excluding transport (millions of dollars)	..	..	..	..	..	..	..	..
				Brunei Darussalam - Brunéi Darussalam				
Arrivées des visiteurs (milliers)	377	(d)984	(d)840	..	..	..	(d)815	(d)836
Nuitées des touristes (milliers)	..	..	..	..	..	..	..	..
Dépenses totales des visiteurs (millions de dollars)	..	..	..	..	..	..	..	..
Dépenses sans transport (millions de dollars)	..	..	155	114	124	181	191	224
				Bulgaria - Bulgarie				
Arrivals of visitors (thousands)	1 586	(d)4 922	(d)5 104	(d)5 563	(d)6 241	(d)6 982	(d)7 282	(d)7 499
Tourists' overnight stays (thousands)	12 759	5 170	6 190	7 055	9 142	10 304	11 624	11 960
Total expenditure of visitors (millions of dollars)	..	1 364	1 262	1 392	2 051	2 796	3 063	3 315
Expenditure excluding transport (millions of dollars)	320	1 074	994	1 096	1 621	2 202	2 412	2 610
				Burkina Faso				
Arrivées des visiteurs (milliers)	74	(c)126	(c)128	(c)150	(c)163	(c)222	(c)245	(c)264
Nuitées des touristes (milliers)	..	..	..	..	..	..	..	..
Dépenses totales des visiteurs (millions de dollars)	15	23	25	..	..	..	45	..
Dépenses sans transport (millions de dollars)	11	19	20	..	..	40	45	..
				Burundi				
Arrivals of visitors (thousands)	109	(a)29	(a)36	(a)74	(a)74	(a)133	(a)148	(a)201
Tourists' overnight stays (thousands)	..	..	..	..	..	..	..	..
Total expenditure of visitors (millions of dollars)	5	1	1	2	1	2	2	2
Expenditure excluding transport (millions of dollars)	3	1	1	1	1	1	2	1
				Cambodia - Cambodge				
Arrivées des visiteurs (milliers)	17	(a)466	(a)605	(a)787	(a)701	(a)1 055	(a)1 422	(a)1 700
Nuitées des touristes (milliers)	..	..	..	..	..	..	..	..
Dépenses totales des visiteurs (millions de dollars)	..	345	429	509	441	673	929	1 080
Dépenses sans transport (millions de dollars)	..	304	380	454	389	603	840	963
				Cameroon - Cameroun				
Arrivals of visitors (thousands)	89	(c)277	(c)221	(c)226	..	(c)190	(c)176	..
Tourists' overnight stays (thousands)	..	..	..	..	..	..	..	..
Total expenditure of visitors (millions of dollars)	97	132	182	124	266	212	..	..
Expenditure excluding transport (millions of dollars)	53	57	73	62	182	158	..	..

For sources and notes, see end of table.   Pour les sources et les notes, se reporter à la fin du tableau.

	1990	2000	2001	2002	2003	2004	2005	2006
Canada								
Arrivées des visiteurs (milliers)	15 209	(d)48 638	(d)47 147	(d)44 896	(d)38 903	(d)38 845	(d)36 160	(d)33 390
Nuitées des touristes (milliers)	82 177	119 381	125 022	122 150	107 698	123 426	125 656	120 703
Dépenses totales des visiteurs (millions de dollars)	7 391	13 035	12 680	12 744	12 236	14 953	16 006	16 976
Dépenses sans transport (millions de dollars)	6 360	10 778	10 623	10 687	10 602	12 847	13 768	14 678
Cape Verde - Cap-Vert								
Arrivals of visitors (thousands)	24	(a)115	(a)134	(a)126	(a)150	(a)157	(a)198	(a)242
Tourists' overnight stays (thousands)	..	..	..	..	..	..	..	..
Total expenditure of visitors (millions of dollars)	10	64	77	100	135	153	177	288
Expenditure excluding transport (millions of dollars)	6	41	54	65	87	99	122	215
Cayman Islands - Îles Caïmanes								
Arrivées des visiteurs (milliers)	253	(d)1 385	(d)1 549	(d)1 878	(d)2 113	(d)1 953	(d)1 967	(d)2 197
Nuitées des touristes (milliers)	..	..	..	..	..	..	..	..
Dépenses totales des visiteurs (millions de dollars)	..	559	585	607	518	523	356	509
Dépenses sans transport (millions de dollars)	..	..	..	..	..	..	..	..
Central African Republic - République centrafricaine								
Arrivals of visitors (thousands)	6	(a)11	(a)10	(a)3	(a)6	(a)8	(a)12	(a)14
Tourists' overnight stays (thousands)	..	..	..	..	..	..	..	..
Total expenditure of visitors (millions of dollars)	..	5	5	3	4	4	..	..
Expenditure excluding transport (millions of dollars)	3	..	..	..	..	..	..	..
Chad - Tchad								
Arrivées des visiteurs (milliers)	9	(d)94	(d)175	(d)149	(d)101	(d)106	(d)59	..
Nuitées des touristes (milliers)	..	..	..	..	..	..	..	..
Dépenses totales des visiteurs (millions de dollars)	12	14	23	25	..	..	..	..
Dépenses sans transport (millions de dollars)	8	..	..	..	..	..	..	..
Chile - Chili								
Arrivals of visitors (thousands)	943	(a)1 742	(a)1 723	(a)1 412	(a)1 614	(a)1 785	(a)2 027	(a)2 253
Tourists' overnight stays (thousands)	..	..	..	..	..	..	..	..
Total expenditure of visitors (millions of dollars)	666	1 179	1 184	1 221	1 309	1 571	1 652	1 816
Expenditure excluding transport (millions of dollars)	531	819	799	898	883	1 095	1 109	1 214
China - Chine								
Arrivées des visiteurs (milliers)	10 484	(d)83 444	(d)89 013	(d)97 908	(d)91 662	(d)109 038	(d)120 292	(d)124 942
Nuitées des touristes (milliers)	..	..	..	..	..	..	..	..
Dépenses totales des visiteurs (millions de dollars)	2 218	17 318	19 006	21 742	18 707	27 755	31 842	37 132
Dépenses sans transport (millions de dollars)	1 738	16 231	17 792	20 385	17 406	25 739	29 296	33 949
China, Hong Kong SAR - Chine (RAS de Hong Kong)								
Arrivals of visitors (thousands)	6 581	(d)13 059	(d)13 725	(d)16 566	(d)15 537	(d)21 811	(d)23 359	(d)25 251
Tourists' overnight stays (thousands)	..	..	..	..	..	..	..	..
Total expenditure of visitors (millions of dollars)	..	8 198	7 923	9 849	9 004	11 874	13 588	15 311
Expenditure excluding transport (millions of dollars)	..	5 868	5 904	7 410	7 072	8 918	10 179	11 461
China, Macao SAR - Chine (RAS de Macao)								
Arrivées des visiteurs (milliers)	2 513	(d)9 162	(d)10 279	(d)11 531	(d)11 888	(d)16 673	(d)18 711	(d)21 998
Nuitées des touristes (milliers)	..	..	..	..	..	..	..	..
Dépenses totales des visiteurs (millions de dollars)	..	3 205	3 745	4 440	5 303	7 344	7 757	9 337
Dépenses sans transport (millions de dollars)	..	..	..	..	..	..	..	..
China, Taiwan Province of - Province chinoise de Taiwan								
Arrivals of visitors (thousands)	1 934	(d)2 624	(d)2 831	(d)2 978	(d)2 248	(d)2 950	(d)3 378	(d)3 520
Tourists' overnight stays (thousands)	12 494	16 487	16 987	16 856	14 461	18 838	20 593	21 157
Total expenditure of visitors (millions of dollars)	..	4 253	4 849	5 077	3 578	4 670	5 740	5 956
Expenditure excluding transport (millions of dollars)	..	3 733	4 335	4 583	2 977	4 054	4 977	5 136
Colombia - Colombie								
Arrivées des visiteurs (milliers)	813	(d)557	(d)616	(d)567	(d)625	(d)791	(d)933	(d)1 053
Nuitées des touristes (milliers)	..	..	..	..	..	..	..	..
Dépenses totales des visiteurs (millions de dollars)	574	1 313	1 483	1 237	1 191	1 366	1 570	2 005
Dépenses sans transport (millions de dollars)	406	1 030	1 217	967	893	1 058	1 218	1 550
Comoros - Comores								
Arrivals of visitors (thousands)	8	(a)24	(a)19	(a)19	(a)21	(a)23	(a)26	(a)29
Tourists' overnight stays (thousands)	..	161	135	133	123	123	137	..
Total expenditure of visitors (millions of dollars)	3	15	9	11	16	21	24	27
Expenditure excluding transport (millions of dollars)	2	..	..	..	..	..	..	..

For sources and notes, see end of table.   Pour les sources et les notes, se reporter à la fin du tableau.

	1990	2000	2001	2002	2003	2004	2005	2006
				Congo				
Arrivées des visiteurs (milliers)	33	(c)19	(c)27	(c)22	..	..	..	..
Nuitées des touristes (milliers)	..	..	..	..	..	..	..	..
Dépenses totales des visiteurs (millions de dollars)	..	12	23	26	30	23	..	..
Dépenses sans transport (millions de dollars)	8	12	22	25	29	22	34	..
			Cook Islands - Îles Cook					
Arrivals of visitors (thousands)	34	(a)73	(a)75	(a)73	(a)78	(a)83	(a)88	(a)92
Tourists' overnight stays (thousands)	..	..	..	..	..	..	..	..
Total expenditure of visitors (millions of dollars)	..	36	38	46	69	72	91	90
Expenditure excluding transport (millions of dollars)	..	..	..	..	..	..	..	..
				Costa Rica				
Arrivées des visiteurs (milliers)	435	(d)1 278	(d)1 320	(d)1 335	(d)1 514	(d)1 771	(d)1 959	(d)2 071
Nuitées des touristes (milliers)	..	..	..	..	..	..	..	..
Dépenses totales des visiteurs (millions de dollars)	330	1 477	1 339	1 292	1 424	1 586	1 810	1 890
Dépenses sans transport (millions de dollars)	285	1 302	1 173	1 161	1 293	1 459	1 671	1 732
				Côte d'Ivoire				
Arrivals of visitors (thousands)	196	..	..	..	..	..	..	..
Tourists' overnight stays (thousands)	..	..	..	..	..	..	..	..
Total expenditure of visitors (millions of dollars)	55	53	58	56	76	91	93	..
Expenditure excluding transport (millions of dollars)	51	49	53	51	69	82	83	84
			Croatia - Croatie					
Arrivées des visiteurs (milliers)	–	(d)37 226	(d)40 129	(d)41 737	(d)42 857	(d)44 974	(d)45 762	(d)47 733
Nuitées des touristes (milliers)	–	34 045	38 384	39 711	41 323	42 516	45 987	47 022
Dépenses totales des visiteurs (millions de dollars)	–	2 871	3 463	3 952	6 513	6 945	7 625	8 296
Dépenses sans transport (millions de dollars)	–	2 758	3 335	3 811	6 310	6 727	7 370	7 990
				Cuba				
Arrivals of visitors (thousands)	327	(d)1 774	(d)1 775	(d)1 686	(d)1 906	(d)2 049	(d)2 319	(d)2 221
Tourists' overnight stays (thousands)	3 703	11 557	11 250	10 486	12 684	14 190	15 404	15 628
Total expenditure of visitors (millions of dollars)	..	1 948	1 840	1 769	1 999	2 114	2 399	2 404
Expenditure excluding transport (millions of dollars)	..	1 737	1 692	1 633	1 846	1 915	2 150	2 138
			Cyprus - Chypre					
Arrivées des visiteurs (milliers)	1 561	(d)2 912	(d)2 841	(d)2 495	(d)2 416	(d)2 478	(d)2 657	(d)2 629
Nuitées des touristes (milliers)	9 426	16 816	18 093	15 289	13 490	13 637	14 006	13 310
Dépenses totales des visiteurs (millions de dollars)	1 440	2 137	2 203	2 178	2 325	2 552	2 644	2 735
Dépenses sans transport (millions de dollars)	1 254	1 941	1 993	1 959	2 097	2 241	2 318	2 420
			Czech Republic - République tchèque					
Arrivals of visitors (thousands)	–	(b)4 666	(b)5 405	(b)4 743	(b)5 076	(b)6 061	(b)6 336	(b)6 435
Tourists' overnight stays (thousands)	–	15 831	17 255	15 569	16 511	18 980	19 595	20 090
Total expenditure of visitors (millions of dollars)	–	..	..	3 376	4 069	4 931	5 618	5 844
Expenditure excluding transport (millions of dollars)	–	2 973	3 106	2 964	3 566	4 187	4 659	5 026
		Dem. People's Rep. of Korea - Rép. populaire dém. de Corée						
Arrivées des visiteurs (milliers)	115	..	..	..	..	..	..	..
Nuitées des touristes (milliers)	..	..	..	..	..	..	..	..
Dépenses totales des visiteurs (millions de dollars)	..	..	..	..	..	..	..	..
Dépenses sans transport (millions de dollars)	..	..	..	..	..	..	..	..
			Dem. Rep. of the Congo - Rép. dém. du Congo					
Arrivals of visitors (thousands)	55	(a)103	(a)55	(a)28	(a)35	(a)36	(a)61	(a)55
Tourists' overnight stays (thousands)	..	46	175	163	150	99	165	189
Total expenditure of visitors (millions of dollars)	..	..	..	..	..	..	..	..
Expenditure excluding transport (millions of dollars)	..	..	..	..	..	..	..	..
			Denmark - Danemark (2)					
Arrivées des visiteurs (milliers)	1 838	(b)3 535	(b)3 684	(b)3 436	(b)3 474	(b)4 421	(b)4 699	(b)4 716
Nuitées des touristes (milliers)	9 338	26 280	25 456	25 663	26 152	24 925	23 012	23 371
Dépenses totales des visiteurs (millions de dollars)	3 471	..	..	..	..	..	..	..
Dépenses sans transport (millions de dollars)	3 338	3 671	4 003	4 791	5 271	5 652	5 293	5 587
				Djibouti				
Arrivals of visitors (thousands)	33	(c)20	(c)22	(c)23	(c)23	(c)26	(c)30	(c)40
Tourists' overnight stays (thousands)	..	..	..	..	..	..	..	..
Total expenditure of visitors (millions of dollars)	..	..	..	..	..	..	..	..
Expenditure excluding transport (millions of dollars)	..	8	9	9	7	7	7	9

For sources and notes, see end of table.   Pour les sources et les notes, se reporter à la fin du tableau.

	1990	2000	2001	2002	2003	2004	2005	2006
Dominica - Dominique								
Arrivées des visiteurs (milliers)	45	(d)312	(d)276	(d)208	(d)254	(d)466	(d)381	(d)465
Nuitées des touristes (milliers)	..	..	..	..	..	..	..	..
Dépenses totales des visiteurs (millions de dollars)	..	..	..	..	..	..	..	..
Dépenses sans transport (millions de dollars)	20	48	46	46	52	61	56	68
Dominican Republic - République dominicaine								
Arrivals of visitors (thousands)	1 305	(d)3 161	(d)3 090	(d)3 058	(d)3 680	(d)3 907	(d)3 981	(d)4 268
Tourists' overnight stays (thousands)	..	..	..	..	..	..	..	..
Total expenditure of visitors (millions of dollars)	..	..	..	..	..	..	..	..
Expenditure excluding transport (millions of dollars)	726	2 860	2 798	2 730	3 128	3 152	3 518	3 792
Ecuador - Équateur								
Arrivées des visiteurs (milliers)	362	(d)627	(d)641	(d)683	(d)761	(d)819	(d)860	(d)841
Nuitées des touristes (milliers)	..	..	..	..	..	..	..	..
Dépenses totales des visiteurs (millions de dollars)	266	451	438	449	408	464	488	492
Dépenses sans transport (millions de dollars)	188	402	430	447	406	462	486	490
Egypt - Égypte								
Arrivals of visitors (thousands)	2 411	(d)5 506	(d)4 648	(d)5 192	(d)6 044	(d)8 104	(d)8 608	(d)9 083
Tourists' overnight stays (thousands)	..	..	..	..	..	..	..	..
Total expenditure of visitors (millions of dollars)	1 530	4 657	4 119	4 133	4 704	6 328	7 206	8 133
Expenditure excluding transport (millions of dollars)	1 100	4 345	3 800	3 764	4 584	6 125	6 851	7 591
El Salvador								
Arrivées des visiteurs (milliers)	194	(a)795	(a)735	(a)798	(a)720	(a)812	(a)969	(a)1 133
Nuitées des touristes (milliers)	..	..	..	..	..	..	..	..
Dépenses totales des visiteurs (millions de dollars)	130	437	452	521	664	748	838	1 175
Dépenses sans transport (millions de dollars)	76	217	201	245	383	453	543	871
Equatorial Guinea - Guinée équatoriale								
Arrivals of visitors (thousands)	..	..	..	..	..	..	..	..
Tourists' overnight stays (thousands)	..	..	..	..	..	..	..	..
Total expenditure of visitors (millions of dollars)	..	5	14	..	..	..	..	..
Expenditure excluding transport (millions of dollars)	..	..	..	..	..	..	..	..
Eritrea - Érythrée								
Arrivées des visiteurs (milliers)	–	(d)70	(d)113	(d)101	(d)80	(d)87	(d)83	(d)78
Nuitées des touristes (milliers)	–	..	..	..	..	..	..	..
Dépenses totales des visiteurs (millions de dollars)	–	36	74	73	74	73	66	60
Dépenses sans transport (millions de dollars)	–	..	..	..	..	..	..	..
Estonia - Estonie								
Arrivals of visitors (thousands)	–	(a)1 220	(a)1 320	(a)1 362	(a)1 462	(a)1 750	(a)1 917	(a)1 940
Tourists' overnight stays (thousands)	–	1 598	1 911	1 998	2 268	2 747	2 982	3 020
Total expenditure of visitors (millions of dollars)	–	657	661	737	883	1 111	1 207	1 372
Expenditure excluding transport (millions of dollars)	–	508	507	555	671	887	948	1 035
Ethiopia - Éthiopie								
Arrivées des visiteurs (milliers)	–	(a)136	(a)148	(a)156	(a)180	(a)184	(a)227	(a)290
Nuitées des touristes (milliers)	–	..	..	..	..	..	..	..
Dépenses totales des visiteurs (millions de dollars)	–	205	218	261	336	458	533	639
Dépenses sans transport (millions de dollars)	–	57	51	72	114	174	168	162
Ethiopia (former) - Éthiopie (anc.)								
Arrivals of visitors (thousands)	79	–	–	–	–	–	–	–
Tourists' overnight stays (thousands)	..	–	–	–	–	–	–	–
Total expenditure of visitors (millions of dollars)	143	–	–	–	–	–	–	–
Expenditure excluding transport (millions of dollars)	5	–	–	–	–	–	–	–
Fiji - Fidji								
Arrivées des visiteurs (milliers)	279	(a)294	(a)348	(a)398	(a)431	(a)499	(a)550	(a)545
Nuitées des touristes (milliers)	..	..	..	..	..	..	..	..
Dépenses totales des visiteurs (millions de dollars)	271	285	309	379	490	585	676	636
Dépenses sans transport (millions de dollars)	200	184	198	255	340	420	439	433
Finland - Finlande								
Arrivals of visitors (thousands)	..	(a)2 714	(a)2 826	(a)2 875	(a)2 601	(a)2 840	(a)3 140	(a)3 375
Tourists' overnight stays (thousands)	..	4 066	4 183	4 290	4 331	4 383	4 499	5 036
Total expenditure of visitors (millions of dollars)	..	2 035	2 066	2 236	2 678	2 975	3 070	3 509
Expenditure excluding transport (millions of dollars)	..	1 406	1 438	1 578	1 870	2 067	2 180	2 380

For sources and notes, see end of table.   Pour les sources et les notes, se reporter à la fin du tableau.

	1990	2000	2001	2002	2003	2004	2005	2006
				France (3)				
Arrivées des visiteurs (milliers)	..	(a)79 049	(a)76 942	(a)78 213	(a)76 607	(a)76 728	(a)77 554	(a)80 553
Nuitées des touristes (milliers)	..	585 443	581 037	588 430	567 006	561 294	491 139	496 951
Dépenses totales des visiteurs (millions de dollars)	..	38 047	35 884	38 721	44 066	53 346	53 226	54 946
Dépenses sans transport (millions de dollars)	..	30 641	30 079	32 437	36 619	44 895	43 942	46 499
			French Polynesia - Polynésie française					
Arrivals of visitors (thousands)	132	(a)252	(a)228	(a)189	(a)213	(a)212	(a)208	(a)222
Tourists' overnight stays (thousands)	1 399	..	2 875	2 592	2 888	2 861	2 787	2 926
Total expenditure of visitors (millions of dollars)	..	..	..	471	651	737	751	785
Expenditure excluding transport (millions of dollars)	..	..	..	372	480	523	522	558
				Gabon				
Arrivées des visiteurs (milliers)	109	(d)230	(d)236	(d)269	(d)234	..	..	..
Nuitées des touristes (milliers)	..	..	..	..	..	..	..	..
Dépenses totales des visiteurs (millions de dollars)	33	99	46	77	84	74	..	..
Dépenses sans transport (millions de dollars)	3	20	15	18	15	10	..	..
				Gambia - Gambie				
Arrivals of visitors (thousands)	100	(a)79	(a)57	(a)81	(a)73	(a)90	(a)108	(a)125
Tourists' overnight stays (thousands)	..	..	..	..	..	..	..	..
Total expenditure of visitors (millions of dollars)	..	..	..	..	58	51	57	69
Expenditure excluding transport (millions of dollars)	46	..	..	..	56	47	56	66
				Georgia - Géorgie				
Arrivées des visiteurs (milliers)	–	(d)387	(d)302	(d)298	(d)313	(d)368	(d)560	(d)983
Nuitées des touristes (milliers)	–	..	..	..	..	..	..	..
Dépenses totales des visiteurs (millions de dollars)	–	107	136	144	172	209	287	361
Dépenses sans transport (millions de dollars)	–	97	117	126	147	177	241	313
				Germany - Allemagne				
Arrivals of visitors (thousands)	17 045	(b)18 983	(b)17 861	(b)17 969	(b)18 399	(b)20 137	(b)21 500	(b)23 569
Tourists' overnight stays (thousands)	39 146	42 629	40 798	40 655	41 746	45 374	48 246	52 947
Total expenditure of visitors (millions of dollars)	19 502	24 943	24 175	26 690	30 104	35 569	38 220	42 792
Expenditure excluding transport (millions of dollars)	14 330	18 611	18 031	19 278	23 125	27 613	29 121	32 846
				Ghana				
Arrivées des visiteurs (milliers)	146	(a)399	(a)439	(a)483	(a)531	(a)584	(a)429	..
Nuitées des touristes (milliers)	..	..	..	..	..	..	..	..
Dépenses totales des visiteurs (millions de dollars)	15	357	374	383	441	495	867	910
Dépenses sans transport (millions de dollars)	4	335	351	358	414	466	836	861
				Greece - Grèce				
Arrivals of visitors (thousands)	8 873	(d)13 567	(d)14 678	(d)14 918	(d)14 785	(d)14 268	(d)15 938	(d)17 284
Tourists' overnight stays (thousands)	..	47 024	42 494	40 953	40 407	38 796	40 734	43 055
Total expenditure of visitors (millions of dollars)	2 617	9 262	9 216	10 005	10 842	12 809	13 453	14 495
Expenditure excluding transport (millions of dollars)	2 587	9 219	9 155	9 909	10 766	12 715	13 334	14 402
				Grenada - Grenade				
Arrivées des visiteurs (milliers)	76	(d)316	(d)277	(d)271	(d)294	(d)370	(d)380	(d)342
Nuitées des touristes (milliers)	..	..	..	..	..	..	..	..
Dépenses totales des visiteurs (millions de dollars)	..	..	..	..	..	..	..	..
Dépenses sans transport (millions de dollars)	50	93	83	91	104	83	71	93
				Guam				
Arrivals of visitors (thousands)	780	(a)1 287	(a)1 159	(a)1 059	(a)910	(a)1 160	(a)1 228	(a)1 212
Tourists' overnight stays (thousands)	..	..	..	..	..	..	..	..
Total expenditure of visitors (millions of dollars)	..	..	..	..	..	..	..	..
Expenditure excluding transport (millions of dollars)	..	..	..	..	..	..	..	..
				Guatemala				
Arrivées des visiteurs (milliers)	509	(a)826	(a)835	(a)884	(a)880	(a)1 182	(a)1 316	(a)1 502
Nuitées des touristes (milliers)	3 201	..	..	..	..	..	..	..
Dépenses totales des visiteurs (millions de dollars)	..	498	588	647	646	806	883	1 008
Dépenses sans transport (millions de dollars)	118	482	562	620	621	776	846	969
				Guinea - Guinée				
Arrivals of visitors (thousands)	..	(a)33	(a)38	(a)43	(a)44	(a)45	(a)45	(a)46
Tourists' overnight stays (thousands)	..	698	526	600	928	1 233	1 318	959
Total expenditure of visitors (millions of dollars)	..	18	22	..	32	..	..	..
Expenditure excluding transport (millions of dollars)	..	12	14	43	31	30	..	70

For sources and notes, see end of table.   Pour les sources et les notes, se reporter à la fin du tableau.

	1990	2000	2001	2002	2003	2004	2005	2006
				Guinea-Bissau - Guinée-Bissau				
Arrivées des visiteurs (milliers)	..	..	(a)8	..	..	..	(a)5	(a)12
Nuitées des touristes (milliers)	..	..	..	..	..	..	..	..
Dépenses totales des visiteurs (millions de dollars)	..	..	..	..	2	2	..	..
Dépenses sans transport (millions de dollars)	..	..	3	2	2	1	2	..
				Guyana				
Arrivals of visitors (thousands)	64	(a)105	(a)99	(a)104	(a)101	(a)122	(a)117	(a)113
Tourists' overnight stays (thousands)	..	..	..	..	..	..	..	..
Total expenditure of visitors (millions of dollars)	..	80	65	53	28	29	37	40
Expenditure excluding transport (millions of dollars)	..	75	61	49	26	27	35	37
				Haiti - Haïti				
Arrivées des visiteurs (milliers)	144	(d)445	(d)499	(d)482	(d)518	(d)385	(d)480	..
Nuitées des touristes (milliers)	1 150	..	..	..	..	..	..	..
Dépenses totales des visiteurs (millions de dollars)	37	..	..	..	..	..	..	..
Dépenses sans transport (millions de dollars)	34	128	105	108	96	87	80	135
				Honduras				
Arrivals of visitors (thousands)	290	(a)471	(a)518	(a)550	(a)611	(a)641	(a)673	(a)739
Tourists' overnight stays (thousands)	..	..	..	..	..	..	..	..
Total expenditure of visitors (millions of dollars)	44	263	260	305	364	420	466	490
Expenditure excluding transport (millions of dollars)	29	260	256	301	356	414	464	488
				Hungary - Hongrie				
Arrivées des visiteurs (milliers)	3 693	(d)31 141	(d)30 679	(d)31 739	(d)31 412	(d)33 934	(d)36 173	(d)38 318
Nuitées des touristes (milliers)	13 618	10 514	10 894	10 361	10 040	10 508	10 779	10 046
Dépenses totales des visiteurs (millions de dollars)	..	3 809	4 191	3 774	4 119	4 129	4 717	4 943
Dépenses sans transport (millions de dollars)	985	3 733	4 154	3 728	4 061	4 034	4 120	4 254
				Iceland - Islande				
Arrivals of visitors (thousands)	142	(b)634	(b)672	(b)705	(b)771	(b)836	(b)871	(b)971
Tourists' overnight stays (thousands)	..	1 142	1 184	1 257	1 377	1 479	1 550	1 719
Total expenditure of visitors (millions of dollars)	234	386	383	415	486	558	630	663
Expenditure excluding transport (millions of dollars)	152	227	232	256	319	370	408	439
				India - Inde				
Arrivées des visiteurs (milliers)	1 707	(d)2 677	(d)2 591	(d)2 428	(d)2 774	(d)3 512	(d)4 038	(d)4 626
Nuitées des touristes (milliers)	..	..	..	..	..	..	..	..
Dépenses totales des visiteurs (millions de dollars)	..	3 718	3 342	3 300	4 560	6 307	7 652	9 227
Dépenses sans transport (millions de dollars)	1 558	3 460	3 198	3 102	4 463	6 170	7 493	8 934
				Indonesia - Indonésie				
Arrivals of visitors (thousands)	2 178	(a)5 064	(a)5 153	(a)5 033	(a)4 467	(a)5 321	(a)5 002	(a)4 871
Tourists' overnight stays (thousands)	..	..	..	..	..	..	..	..
Total expenditure of visitors (millions of dollars)	..	..	..	5 797	4 461	5 226	5 094	4 890
Expenditure excluding transport (millions of dollars)	2 153	4 975	5 277	5 285	4 037	4 798	4 522	4 448
				Iran (Islamic Rep. of) - Iran (Rép. islamique d')				
Arrivées des visiteurs (milliers)	154	(a)1 342	(a)1 402	(a)1 585	(a)1 546	(a)1 659	..	..
Nuitées des touristes (milliers)	..	..	..	..	..	..	..	..
Dépenses totales des visiteurs (millions de dollars)	64	677	1 122	1 607	1 266	1 305	1 364	1 513
Dépenses sans transport (millions de dollars)	28	467	891	1 357	1 033	1 044	1 069	1 194
				Iraq				
Arrivals of visitors (thousands)	748	(d)78	(d)127	..	..	..	..	..
Tourists' overnight stays (thousands)	..	..	..	..	..	..	..	..
Total expenditure of visitors (millions of dollars)	..	..	..	..	..	..	..	..
Expenditure excluding transport (millions of dollars)	..	2	15	45	..	..	..	..
				Ireland - Irlande				
Arrivées des visiteurs (milliers)	3 666	(a)6 646	(a)6 353	(a)6 476	(a)6 764	(a)6 953	(a)7 333	(a)8 001
Nuitées des touristes (milliers)	36 183	21 516	45 846	45 346	47 613	47 375	50 678	56 342
Dépenses totales des visiteurs (millions de dollars)	1 897	3 517	3 789	4 228	5 206	6 075	6 780	7 664
Dépenses sans transport (millions de dollars)	1 459	2 615	2 791	3 097	3 862	4 375	4 782	5 369
				Israel - Israël				
Arrivals of visitors (thousands)	1 063	(a)2 417	(a)1 196	(a)862	(a)1 063	(a)1 506	(a)1 903	(a)1 825
Tourists' overnight stays (thousands)	6 167	10 352	4 637	2 745	3 438	5 040	7 133	7 212
Total expenditure of visitors (millions of dollars)	1 757	4 611	2 855	2 426	2 473	2 863	3 358	3 319
Expenditure excluding transport (millions of dollars)	1 396	4 114	2 561	2 145	2 132	2 430	2 797	2 777

For sources and notes, see end of table.

Pour les sources et les notes, se reporter à la fin du tableau.

5

	1990	2000	2001	2002	2003	2004	2005	2006
Italy - Italie								
Arrivées des visiteurs (milliers)	26 679	(d)62 702	(d)60 960	(d)63 561	(d)63 026	(d)58 480	(d)59 230	(d)66 353
Nuitées des touristes (milliers)	84 720	140 357	146 672	145 560	139 653	141 169	148 501	156 861
Dépenses totales des visiteurs (millions de dollars)	18 300	28 706	26 916	28 192	32 591	37 870	38 374	41 644
Dépenses sans transport (millions de dollars)	16 460	27 493	25 822	26 873	31 247	35 378	35 319	38 257
Jamaica - Jamaïque								
Arrivals of visitors (thousands)	989	(d)2 230	(d)2 117	(d)2 131	(d)2 483	(d)2 515	(d)2 615	(d)3 016
Tourists' overnight stays (thousands)	9 194	12 327	12 109	12 038	12 844	13 134	13 608	15 465
Total expenditure of visitors (millions of dollars)	869	1 577	1 494	1 482	1 621	1 733	1 783	2 094
Expenditure excluding transport (millions of dollars)	751	1 333	1 232	1 209	1 355	1 438	1 545	1 870
Japan - Japon								
Arrivées des visiteurs (milliers)	3 236	(d)4 757	(d)4 772	(d)5 239	(d)5 212	(d)6 138	(d)6 728	(d)7 334
Nuitées des touristes (milliers)	..	..	..	..	..	..	..	..
Dépenses totales des visiteurs (millions de dollars)	..	5 970	5 750	6 069	11 475	14 343	15 555	11 490
Dépenses sans transport (millions de dollars)	..	3 373	3 306	3 497	8 848	11 265	12 430	8 470
Jordan - Jordanie								
Arrivals of visitors (thousands)	572	(d)2 700	(d)3 034	(d)4 677	(d)4 600	(d)5 587	(d)5 817	(d)6 573
Tourists' overnight stays (thousands)	..	..	..	..	..	..	..	..
Total expenditure of visitors (millions of dollars)	788	935	884	1 254	1 266	1 621	1 759	2 008
Expenditure excluding transport (millions of dollars)	511	723	700	1 048	1 062	1 330	1 441	1 642
Kazakhstan								
Arrivées des visiteurs (milliers)	–	(d)1 683	(d)2 693	(d)3 678	(d)3 237	(d)4 291	(d)4 365	(d)4 707
Nuitées des touristes (milliers)	–	..	..	..	..	..	..	..
Dépenses totales des visiteurs (millions de dollars)	–	403	502	680	638	803	801	973
Dépenses sans transport (millions de dollars)	–	356	452	622	564	718	701	838
Kenya								
Arrivals of visitors (thousands)	814	(d)1 037	(d)994	(d)1 001	(d)1 146	(d)1 359	(d)1 675	(d)1 840
Tourists' overnight stays (thousands)	..	..	..	..	..	..	..	..
Total expenditure of visitors (millions of dollars)	578	500	536	513	619	799	969	1 182
Expenditure excluding transport (millions of dollars)	465	283	309	276	347	486	579	688
Kiribati								
Arrivées des visiteurs (milliers)	3	(a)5	(a)5	(a)5	(a)5	(a)4	(a)3	(a)4
Nuitées des touristes (milliers)	..	..	..	..	..	..	..	..
Dépenses totales des visiteurs (millions de dollars)	2	3	3	..	..	..	..	..
Dépenses sans transport (millions de dollars)	1	..	..	..	..	..	..	..
Kuwait - Koweït								
Arrivals of visitors (thousands)	15	(d)1 944	(d)2 072	(d)2 316	(d)2 602	(d)3 056	(d)3 474	..
Tourists' overnight stays (thousands)	..	..	..	..	..	..	..	..
Total expenditure of visitors (millions of dollars)	471	394	286	320	328	412	410	470
Expenditure excluding transport (millions of dollars)	132	98	106	117	118	178	165	205
Kyrgyzstan - Kirghizistan								
Arrivées des visiteurs (milliers)	–	(a)59	(a)99	(a)140	(a)342	(a)398	(a)315	(a)766
Nuitées des touristes (milliers)	–	..	..	..	..	..	..	..
Dépenses totales des visiteurs (millions de dollars)	–	20	32	48	62	92	94	189
Dépenses sans transport (millions de dollars)	–	15	24	36	48	76	73	167
Lao People's dem. Rep. - Rép. dém. populaire lao								
Arrivals of visitors (thousands)	14	(d)737	(d)674	(d)736	(d)636	(d)895	(d)1 095	(d)1 215
Tourists' overnight stays (thousands)	..	..	..	..	..	..	..	..
Total expenditure of visitors (millions of dollars)	..	..	..	..	..	..	..	..
Expenditure excluding transport (millions of dollars)	3	114	104	113	87	119	147	173
Latvia - Lettonie								
Arrivées des visiteurs (milliers)	–	(d)1 882	(d)2 061	(d)2 297	(d)2 524	(d)3 127	(d)3 791	(d)4 649
Nuitées des touristes (milliers)	–	697	847	871	983	1 201	1 613	1 872
Dépenses totales des visiteurs (millions de dollars)	–	172	153	201	271	343	446	622
Dépenses sans transport (millions de dollars)	–	131	119	161	222	267	341	480
Lebanon - Liban								
Arrivals of visitors (thousands)	..	(a)742	(a)837	(a)956	(a)1 016	(a)1 278	(a)1 140	(a)1 063
Tourists' overnight stays (thousands)	..	..	..	..	..	..	..	..
Total expenditure of visitors (millions of dollars)	..	742	837	..	6 782	5 931	5 969	5 491
Expenditure excluding transport (millions of dollars)	..	..	..	4 284	6 374	5 411	5 532	5 015

For sources and notes, see end of table.   Pour les sources et les notes, se reporter à la fin du tableau.

	1990	2000	2001	2002	2003	2004	2005	2006
Lesotho (4)								
Arrivées des visiteurs (milliers)	171	(d)302	(d)295	(d)287	(d)329	(d)304	(d)304	(d)357
Nuitées des touristes (milliers)	359	..	..	..	..	..	..	..
Dépenses totales des visiteurs (millions de dollars)	22	..	..	..	..	..	..	..
Dépenses sans transport (millions de dollars)	17	24	23	20	28	34	30	23
Libyan Arab Jamahiriya - Jamahiriya arabe libyenne								
Arrivals of visitors (thousands)	96	(d)963	(d)953	(d)858	(d)958	(d)999	..	..
Tourists' overnight stays (thousands)	..	..	..	..	..	..	..	..
Total expenditure of visitors (millions of dollars)	15	84	90	202	243	261	301	244
Expenditure excluding transport (millions of dollars)	6	75	78	181	205	218	250	190
Lithuania - Lituanie								
Arrivées des visiteurs (milliers)	–	(a)1 083	(a)1 271	(a)1 428	(a)1 491	(a)1 800	(a)2 000	(a)2 180
Nuitées des touristes (milliers)	–	963	1 073	1 145	1 170	1 526	1 762	1 906
Dépenses totales des visiteurs (millions de dollars)	–	430	425	556	700	834	975	1 077
Dépenses sans transport (millions de dollars)	–	391	383	505	638	776	921	1 038
Luxembourg								
Arrivals of visitors (thousands)	–	–	–	(b)885	(b)867	(b)878	(b)913	(b)908
Tourists' overnight stays (thousands)	–	–	–	2 469	2 541	2 514	2 465	2 414
Total expenditure of visitors (millions of dollars)	–	–	–	2 547	3 149	3 880	..	..
Expenditure excluding transport (millions of dollars)	–	–	–	2 406	2 994	3 650	3 614	3 626
Madagascar								
Arrivées des visiteurs (milliers)	53	(a)160	(a)170	(a)62	(a)139	(a)229	(a)277	(a)312
Nuitées des touristes (milliers)	..	..	..	..	..	..	..	..
Dépenses totales des visiteurs (millions de dollars)	79	152	149	109	119	239	290	386
Dépenses sans transport (millions de dollars)	40	121	115	64	76	157	183	237
Malawi								
Arrivals of visitors (thousands)	130	(a)228	(a)266	(a)383	(a)424	(a)427	(a)438	..
Tourists' overnight stays (thousands)	1 178	1 325	2 029	2 893	3 259	3 617	..	..
Total expenditure of visitors (millions of dollars)	26	30	40	45	35	36	43	43
Expenditure excluding transport (millions of dollars)	16	26	25	33	23	24	24	24
Malaysia - Malaisie								
Arrivées des visiteurs (milliers)	7 446	(d)17 213	(d)22 995	(d)20 756	(d)16 293	(d)24 432	(d)24 209	(d)25 298
Nuitées des touristes (milliers)	..	..	..	..	..	..	..	..
Dépenses totales des visiteurs (millions de dollars)	2 131	5 873	7 627	8 084	6 799	9 183	10 389	12 355
Dépenses sans transport (millions de dollars)	1 684	5 011	6 863	7 118	5 901	8 203	8 846	10 427
Maldives								
Arrivals of visitors (thousands)	195	(a)467	(a)461	(a)485	(a)564	(a)617	(a)395	(a)602
Tourists' overnight stays (thousands)	..	..	..	..	..	..	..	..
Total expenditure of visitors (millions of dollars)	..	..	..	..	..	..	..	..
Expenditure excluding transport (millions of dollars)	89	321	327	337	402	471	287	434
Mali								
Arrivées des visiteurs (milliers)	44	(c)86	(c)89	(c)96	(c)110	(c)113	(c)143	(c)153
Nuitées des touristes (milliers)	..	..	..	..	..	..	..	..
Dépenses totales des visiteurs (millions de dollars)	40	47	91	105	136	142	149	..
Dépenses sans transport (millions de dollars)	38	40	88	104	128	140	148	167
Malta - Malte								
Arrivals of visitors (thousands)	872	(d)1 387	(d)1 439	(d)1 483	(d)1 516	(d)1 448	(d)1 491	(d)1 532
Tourists' overnight stays (thousands)	9 604	10 266	11 067	10 599	11 115	10 973	10 933	10 503
Total expenditure of visitors (millions of dollars)	613	731	704	757	869	953	923	970
Expenditure excluding transport (millions of dollars)	495	587	561	614	722	770	754	770
Marshall Islands - Îles Marshall								
Arrivées des visiteurs (milliers)	5	(a)5	(a)5	(a)6	(a)7	(a)9	(a)9	(a)6
Nuitées des touristes (milliers)	..	32	30	37	40	38	41	37
Dépenses totales des visiteurs (millions de dollars)	..	3	3	3	4	5	6	7
Dépenses sans transport (millions de dollars)	..	..	..	..	..	..	..	..
Mauritania - Mauritanie								
Arrivals of visitors (thousands)	..	(a)30	..	..	..	..	..	..
Tourists' overnight stays (thousands)	..	..	..	..	..	..	..	..
Total expenditure of visitors (millions of dollars)	..	..	..	..	..	..	..	..
Expenditure excluding transport (millions of dollars)	..	..	..	..	..	..	..	..

For sources and notes, see end of table. | Pour les sources et les notes, se reporter à la fin du tableau.

	1990	2000	2001	2002	2003	2004	2005	2006
				Mauritius - Maurice				
Arrivées des visiteurs (milliers)	292	(d)678	(d)675	(d)709	(d)722	(d)739	(d)782	(d)807
Nuitées des touristes (milliers)	..	..	..	..	..	..	..	..
Dépenses totales des visiteurs (millions de dollars)	385	732	820	829	960	1 156	1 189	1 302
Dépenses sans transport (millions de dollars)	244	542	623	612	697	856	871	1 005
				Mexico - Mexique				
Arrivals of visitors (thousands)	17 176	(d)105 673	(d)100 718	(d)100 153	(d)92 330	(d)99 250	(d)103 146	(d)97 701
Tourists' overnight stays (thousands)	..	..	..	..	..	..	..	..
Total expenditure of visitors (millions of dollars)	5 968	9 133	9 190	9 547	10 058	11 609	12 801	13 329
Expenditure excluding transport (millions of dollars)	5 527	8 294	8 401	8 858	9 362	10 796	11 803	12 177
				Micronesia (Federated States of) - Micronésie (États fédérés de)				
Arrivées des visiteurs (milliers)	..	(a)21	(a)15	(a)19	(a)18	(a)19	(a)19	(a)19
Nuitées des touristes (milliers)	..	..	..	..	..	..	..	..
Dépenses totales des visiteurs (millions de dollars)	..	15	15	17	17	17	17	..
Dépenses sans transport (millions de dollars)	..	..	..	..	..	..	..	..
				Moldova				
Arrivals of visitors (thousands)	–	(d)19	(d)16	(d)20	(d)24	(d)26	(d)25	(d)14
Tourists' overnight stays (thousands)	–	..	..	..	..	174	187	214
Total expenditure of visitors (millions of dollars)	–	57	58	72	79	112	138	145
Expenditure excluding transport (millions of dollars)	–	39	39	50	54	91	103	112
				Mongolia - Mongolie				
Arrivées des visiteurs (milliers)	147	(a)137	(a)166	(a)229	(a)201	(a)301	(a)338	(a)386
Nuitées des touristes (milliers)	..	..	..	..	..	..	..	..
Dépenses totales des visiteurs (millions de dollars)	..	43	49	143	154	205	203	261
Dépenses sans transport (millions de dollars)	5	36	39	130	143	185	177	225
				Montserrat				
Arrivals of visitors (thousands)	13	(d)14	(d)16	(d)15	(d)14	(d)15	(d)13	(d)10
Tourists' overnight stays (thousands)	..	..	..	..	..	..	..	..
Total expenditure of visitors (millions of dollars)	..	..	..	..	..	..	..	..
Expenditure excluding transport (millions of dollars)	11	9	8	9	7	9	9	8
				Morocco - Maroc				
Arrivées des visiteurs (milliers)	4 024	(d)4 458	(d)4 596	(d)4 709	(d)5 021	(d)5 732	(d)6 077	(d)6 777
Nuitées des touristes (milliers)	18 720	21 152	20 349	18 478	18 190	20 951	..	..
Dépenses totales des visiteurs (millions de dollars)	1 318	2 280	2 966	3 157	3 802	4 540	5 426	6 899
Dépenses sans transport (millions de dollars)	1 280	2 039	2 583	2 646	3 221	3 922	4 610	5 984
				Mozambique				
Arrivals of visitors (thousands)	..	..	(d)404	(d)943	(d)726	(d)711	(d)954	(d)1 095
Tourists' overnight stays (thousands)	..	..	..	..	..	..	..	..
Total expenditure of visitors (millions of dollars)	..	..	..	65	106	96	138	145
Expenditure excluding transport (millions of dollars)	..	74	64	63	98	95	130	140
				Myanmar				
Arrivées des visiteurs (milliers)	21	(d)416	(d)475	(d)487	(d)597	(d)657	(d)660	(d)630
Nuitées des touristes (milliers)	..	..	..	..	..	..	..	..
Dépenses totales des visiteurs (millions de dollars)	21	195	132	136	70	97	85	59
Dépenses sans transport (millions de dollars)	20	162	109	120	56	84	68	46
				Namibia - Namibie				
Arrivals of visitors (thousands)	..	(d)759	(d)861	(d)948	(d)917	(d)986	(d)973	(d)1 032
Tourists' overnight stays (thousands)	..	619	800	1 006	424	..	1 409	1 372
Total expenditure of visitors (millions of dollars)	..	..	264	251	383	426	363	473
Expenditure excluding transport (millions of dollars)	86	160	236	218	333	405	349	381
				Nepal - Népal				
Arrivées des visiteurs (milliers)	255	(a)464	(a)361	(a)275	(a)338	(a)385	(a)375	(a)384
Nuitées des touristes (milliers)	..	..	..	..	..	..	..	..
Dépenses totales des visiteurs (millions de dollars)	115	219	191	134	232	260	160	157
Dépenses sans transport (millions de dollars)	109	158	144	103	199	230	131	128
				Netherlands - Pays-Bas				
Arrivals of visitors (thousands)	5 795	(b)10 003	(b)9 500	(b)9 595	(b)9 181	(b)9 646	(b)10 012	(b)10 739
Tourists' overnight stays (thousands)	16 459	27 261	25 502	26 368	25 342	25 385	25 210	26 887
Total expenditure of visitors (millions of dollars)	5 944	11 285	11 147	11 745	..	..	..	..
Expenditure excluding transport (millions of dollars)	4 155	7 197	6 708	7 710	9 163	10 308	10 446	11 381

For sources and notes, see end of table.

Pour les sources et les notes, se reporter à la fin du tableau.

	1990	2000	2001	2002	2003	2004	2005	2006
Netherlands Antilles - Antilles néerlandaises (5)								
Arrivées des visiteurs (milliers)	..	(d)1 961	(d)1 938	(d)2 097	(d)2 236	(d)2 414	(d)2 594	(d)2 627
Nuitées des touristes (milliers)	..	2 038	2 194	2 301	2 493	2 498	2 545	2 777
Dépenses totales des visiteurs (millions de dollars)	..	..	..	..	..	..	..	..
Dépenses sans transport (millions de dollars)	..	..	..	..	..	..	..	..
New Caledonia - Nouvelle-Calédonie								
Arrivals of visitors (thousands)	87	(d)161	(d)152	(d)158	(d)166	(d)177	(d)182	(d)219
Tourists' overnight stays (thousands)	..	..	..	..	..	..	..	..
Total expenditure of visitors (millions of dollars)	..	..	..	..	..	..	..	..
Expenditure excluding transport (millions of dollars)	..	111	94	156	196	241	253	258
New Zealand - Nouvelle-Zélande								
Arrivées des visiteurs (milliers)	976	(d)1 787	(d)1 909	(d)2 045	(d)2 104	(d)2 334	(d)2 366	(d)2 409
Nuitées des touristes (milliers)	20 654	8 932	10 333	11 426	11 653	12 838	13 408	13 120
Dépenses totales des visiteurs (millions de dollars)	1 499	..	..	..	..	..	..	..
Dépenses sans transport (millions de dollars)	1 030	2 267	2 350	3 077	4 028	4 782	4 873	4 563
Nicaragua								
Arrivals of visitors (thousands)	106	(d)581	(d)584	(c)579	(d)646	(d)735	(d)804	(d)898
Tourists' overnight stays (thousands)	88	375	339	423	412	527	523	427
Total expenditure of visitors (millions of dollars)	..	133	138	138	164	196	210	237
Expenditure excluding transport (millions of dollars)	12	129	135	135	160	192	206	231
Niger								
Arrivées des visiteurs (milliers)	21	(a)50	(a)52	(a)39	(a)55	(a)57	(a)60	(a)60
Nuitées des touristes (milliers)	105	215	246	114	132	139	146	154
Dépenses totales des visiteurs (millions de dollars)	13	..	..	20	29	32	44	..
Dépenses sans transport (millions de dollars)	13	23	30	20	28	31	43	35
Nigeria - Nigéria								
Arrivals of visitors (thousands)	190	(d)1 492	(d)1 753	(d)2 046	(d)2 253	(d)2 646	(d)2 778	(d)3 056
Tourists' overnight stays (thousands)	..	..	..	..	..	..	..	..
Total expenditure of visitors (millions of dollars)	30	186	168	256	58	49	46	51
Expenditure excluding transport (millions of dollars)	25	101	91	139	30	21	18	21
Niue - Nioué								
Arrivées des visiteurs (milliers)	1	(a)2	(a)1	(a)2	(a)3	(a)3	(a)3	(a)3
Nuitées des touristes (milliers)	..	..	..	..	..	..	..	..
Dépenses totales des visiteurs (millions de dollars)	..	..	..	..	1	1	1	1
Dépenses sans transport (millions de dollars)	..	..	..	..	..	..	..	..
Northern Mariana Islands - Îles Mariannes du Nord								
Arrivals of visitors (thousands)	426	(d)529	(d)444	(d)476	(d)459	(d)536	(d)507	(d)436
Tourists' overnight stays (thousands)	..	..	..	..	..	..	..	..
Total expenditure of visitors (millions of dollars)	..	..	..	..	..	..	..	..
Expenditure excluding transport (millions of dollars)	..	..	..	..	..	..	..	..
Norway - Norvège								
Arrivées des visiteurs (milliers)	..	(a)3 104	(a)3 073	(a)3 111	(a)3 269	(a)3 628	(a)3 824	(a)3 945
Nuitées des touristes (milliers)	..	7 469	7 322	7 275	6 956	7 442	7 651	7 944
Dépenses totales des visiteurs (millions de dollars)	..	2 521	2 380	2 581	2 989	3 531	3 959	4 251
Dépenses sans transport (millions de dollars)	..	2 050	1 958	2 179	2 500	2 980	3 332	3 613
Occupied Palestinian territory - Territoire palestinien occupé								
Arrivals of visitors (thousands)	..	(c)310	(c)43	(c)33	(c)37	(c)56	(c)88	(c)123
Tourists' overnight stays (thousands)	..	1 106	217	..	..	..	..	..
Total expenditure of visitors (millions of dollars)	..	..	..	..	..	..	..	..
Expenditure excluding transport (millions of dollars)	..	283	35	33	107	56	121	..
Oman								
Arrivées des visiteurs (milliers)	149	(c)571	(a)829	(a)817	(a)1 039	(a)1 195	(a)1 114	..
Nuitées des touristes (milliers)	..	..	3 815	3 965	..	..	..	..
Dépenses totales des visiteurs (millions de dollars)	..	377	539	539	546	604	599	743
Dépenses sans transport (millions de dollars)	58	221	385	393	385	414	401	538
Pakistan								
Arrivals of visitors (thousands)	424	(a)557	(a)500	(a)498	(a)501	(a)648	(a)798	(a)898
Tourists' overnight stays (thousands)	..	1 901	1 583	1 096	1 577	2 773	..	..
Total expenditure of visitors (millions of dollars)	617	551	533	562	620	765	828	899
Expenditure excluding transport (millions of dollars)	147	81	88	97	122	179	182	255

For sources and notes, see end of table.   Pour les sources et les notes, se reporter à la fin du tableau.

	1990	2000	2001	2002	2003	2004	2005	2006
Palau - Palaos								
Arrivées des visiteurs (milliers)	33	(a)58	(a)54	(a)59	(a)68	(a)95	(a)86	(a)86
Nuitées des touristes (milliers)	..	..	..	..	..	..	..	..
Dépenses totales des visiteurs (millions de dollars)	..	53	59	57	76	97	97	90
Dépenses sans transport (millions de dollars)	..	..	..	..	..	..	..	..
Panama								
Arrivals of visitors (thousands)	214	(d)600	(d)737	(d)800	(d)897	(d)1 004	(d)1 070	(d)1 215
Tourists' overnight stays (thousands)	..	..	..	..	..	..	..	..
Total expenditure of visitors (millions of dollars)	179	628	665	710	804	903	1 108	1 450
Expenditure excluding transport (millions of dollars)	172	458	477	513	585	651	780	960
Papua New Guinea - Papouasie-Nouvelle-Guinée								
Arrivées des visiteurs (milliers)	41	(a)58	(a)54	(a)54	(a)56	(a)59	(a)69	(a)78
Nuitées des touristes (milliers)	..	..	..	..	..	..	..	..
Dépenses totales des visiteurs (millions de dollars)	38	..	..	..	..	6	4	..
Dépenses sans transport (millions de dollars)	24	7	5	3	4	6	4	..
Paraguay								
Arrivals of visitors (thousands)	280	(d)3 924	(d)3 550	(d)3 194	(d)2 859	(d)2 589	(d)2 648	(d)2 830
Tourists' overnight stays (thousands)	..	..	..	..	..	..	..	..
Total expenditure of visitors (millions of dollars)	140	88	91	76	81	87	96	111
Expenditure excluding transport (millions of dollars)	85	73	69	62	64	70	78	91
Peru - Pérou								
Arrivées des visiteurs (milliers)	317	(a)800	(a)901	(a)998	(a)1 070	(a)1 277	(a)1 487	(a)1 635
Nuitées des touristes (milliers)	..	..	..	..	..	..	..	..
Dépenses totales des visiteurs (millions de dollars)	262	861	763	836	1 023	1 232	1 438	1 586
Dépenses sans transport (millions de dollars)	217	837	733	787	963	1 142	1 308	1 381
Philippines								
Arrivals of visitors (thousands)	1 025	(a)1 992	(a)1 797	(a)1 933	(a)1 907	(a)2 291	(a)2 623	(a)2 843
Tourists' overnight stays (thousands)	..	..	..	..	..	..	..	..
Total expenditure of visitors (millions of dollars)	506	2 334	2 011	2 018	1 821	2 390	2 755	4 019
Expenditure excluding transport (millions of dollars)	466	2 156	1 742	1 761	1 544	2 017	2 265	3 501
Poland - Pologne								
Arrivées des visiteurs (milliers)	3 400	(d)84 515	(d)61 431	(d)50 735	(d)52 130	(d)61 918	(d)64 606	(d)65 115
Nuitées des touristes (milliers)	5 350	6 891	6 991	7 085	7 828	9 313	10 542	10 555
Dépenses totales des visiteurs (millions de dollars)	692	6 128	5 121	4 971	4 733	6 499	7 128	8 122
Dépenses sans transport (millions de dollars)	358	5 677	4 646	4 314	4 069	5 833	6 274	7 239
Portugal								
Arrivals of visitors (thousands)	8 020	(d)28 014	(d)28 150	(d)27 194	(d)27 532	(d)21 165	(d)21 172	(d)22 588
Tourists' overnight stays (thousands)	19 349	25 785	25 229	25 119	24 870	24 617	25 388	26 842
Total expenditure of visitors (millions of dollars)	3 652	6 027	6 236	6 595	7 634	8 863	9 009	10 036
Expenditure excluding transport (millions of dollars)	3 556	5 243	5 468	5 798	6 622	7 672	7 676	8 388
Qatar								
Arrivées des visiteurs (milliers)	136	(c)378	(c)376	(c)587	(c)557	(c)732	(c)913	(c)946
Nuitées des touristes (milliers)	795	..	..	..	..	..	..	..
Dépenses totales des visiteurs (millions de dollars)	..	..	..	..	..	..	..	..
Dépenses sans transport (millions de dollars)	..	128	272	285	369	498	760	374
Republic of Korea - République de Corée								
Arrivals of visitors (thousands)	2 959	(d)5 322	(d)5 147	(d)5 347	(d)4 753	(d)5 818	(d)6 023	(d)6 155
Tourists' overnight stays (thousands)	9 952	..	..	..	..	..	..	..
Total expenditure of visitors (millions of dollars)	4 010	8 527	7 919	7 621	7 005	8 226	8 290	8 069
Expenditure excluding transport (millions of dollars)	3 161	6 834	6 384	5 936	5 358	6 069	5 806	5 322
Romania - Roumanie (4)								
Arrivées des visiteurs (milliers)	3 009	(d)5 264	(d)4 938	(d)4 794	(d)5 595	(d)6 600	(d)5 839	(d)6 037
Nuitées des touristes (milliers)	4 238	2 149	2 391	2 534	2 766	3 333	3 464	3 242
Dépenses totales des visiteurs (millions de dollars)	..	394	419	400	523	607	1 325	1 676
Dépenses sans transport (millions de dollars)	106	359	362	335	449	503	1 052	1 308
Russian Federation - Fédération de Russie								
Arrivals of visitors (thousands)	–	(d)21 169	(d)21 595	(d)23 309	(d)22 521	(d)22 064	(d)22 201	(d)22 486
Tourists' overnight stays (thousands)	–	..	..	11 357	10 858	11 516	11 643	13 738
Total expenditure of visitors (millions of dollars)	–	..	4 726	5 428	5 879	7 262	7 806	9 720
Expenditure excluding transport (millions of dollars)	–	3 429	3 572	4 167	4 502	5 530	5 870	7 628

For sources and notes, see end of table.   Pour les sources et les notes, se reporter à la fin du tableau.

	1990	2000	2001	2002	2003	2004	2005	2006
Rwanda								
Arrivées des visiteurs (milliers)	..	(a)104	(a)113	..	..	..	..	..
Nuitées des touristes (milliers)	..	..	..	..	..	..	..	..
Dépenses totales des visiteurs (millions de dollars)	..	27	29	..	..	..	..	..
Dépenses sans transport (millions de dollars)	..	23	25	31	30	44	49	31
Saint Kitts and Nevis - Saint-Kitts-et-Nevis								
Arrivals of visitors (thousands)	73	(d)247	(d)334	(d)240	(d)241	(d)376	(d)347	(d)339
Tourists' overnight stays (thousands)	..	..	..	..	..	..	..	..
Total expenditure of visitors (millions of dollars)	..	..	..	..	..	..	..	..
Expenditure excluding transport (millions of dollars)	44	58	62	57	75	103	115	116
Saint Lucia - Sainte-Lucie								
Arrivées des visiteurs (milliers)	141	(d)727	(d)747	(d)648	(d)683	(d)791	(d)720	(d)670
Nuitées des touristes (milliers)	..	..	..	..	..	..	..	..
Dépenses totales des visiteurs (millions de dollars)	121	..	..	..	..	..	..	..
Dépenses sans transport (millions de dollars)	121	281	233	207	282	326	356	347
Saint Vincent and the Grenadines - Saint-Vincent-et-les Grenadines								
Arrivals of visitors (thousands)	54	(d)256	(d)254	(d)247	(d)242	(d)262	(d)256	(d)306
Tourists' overnight stays (thousands)	..	..	..	..	..	..	..	..
Total expenditure of visitors (millions of dollars)	31	..	..	..	..	..	..	..
Expenditure excluding transport (millions of dollars)	29	82	89	91	91	96	104	113
Samoa								
Arrivées des visiteurs (milliers)	48	(a)88	(a)88	(a)89	(a)92	(a)98	(a)102	(a)116
Nuitées des touristes (milliers)	..	..	..	..	..	..	..	..
Dépenses totales des visiteurs (millions de dollars)	22	..	..	..	..	70	78	91
Dépenses sans transport (millions de dollars)	21	41	39	45	54	69	77	90
San Marino - Saint-Marin								
Arrivals of visitors (thousands)	..	(d)3 071	(d)3 036	(d)3 102	(d)2 882	(d)2 812	(d)2 107	(d)2 136
Tourists' overnight stays (thousands)	..	..	..	..	..	..	..	..
Total expenditure of visitors (millions of dollars)	..	..	..	..	..	..	..	..
Expenditure excluding transport (millions of dollars)	..	..	..	..	..	..	..	..
Sao Tome and Principe - Sao Tomé-et-Principe								
Arrivées des visiteurs (milliers)	4	(a)7	(a)8	(a)9	(a)10	(a)11	(a)16	(a)12
Nuitées des touristes (milliers)	..	..	..	..	..	..	..	..
Dépenses totales des visiteurs (millions de dollars)	2	..	..	..	..	..	..	..
Dépenses sans transport (millions de dollars)	2	10	10	10	11	13	14	..
Saudi Arabia - Arabie saoucite								
Arrivals of visitors (thousands)	2 209	(a)6 585	(a)6 727	(a)7 511	(a)7 332	(a)8 599	(a)8 037	(a)8 620
Tourists' overnight stays (thousands)	..	..	..	..	..	111 810	91 359	112 383
Total expenditure of visitors (millions of dollars)	..	..	..	..	3 418	6 916	5 626	5 391
Expenditure excluding transport (millions of dollars)	..	..	..	..	..	6 486	5 149	4 955
Senegal - Sénégal								
Arrivées des visiteurs (milliers)	246	(c)389	(c)396	(c)427	(a)495	(a)667	(a)769	(a)866
Nuitées des touristes (milliers)	1 068	1 401	1 499	1 569	1 451	..	..	..
Dépenses totales des visiteurs (millions de dollars)	154	152	175	210	269	287	334	..
Dépenses sans transport (millions de dollars)	152	144	174	190	209	212	242	..
Serbia and Montenegro - Serbie-et-Monténégro								
Arrivals of visitors (thousands)	–	(b)239	(b)351	(b)448	(b)481	(b)580	(b)725	(b)847
Tourists' overnight stays (thousands)	–	865	1 281	1 650	1 708	2 075	2 576	3 211
Total expenditure of visitors (millions of dollars)	–	..	..	..	..	..	..	..
Expenditure excluding transport (millions of dollars)	–	30	54	97	201	..	..	..
Seychelles								
Arrivées des visiteurs (milliers)	104	(d)140	(d)138	(d)135	(d)127	(d)126	(d)135	(d)151
Nuitées des touristes (milliers)	1 048	1 352	1 350	1 336	1 233	1 208	1 248	1 378
Dépenses totales des visiteurs (millions de dollars)	141	225	221	247	258	256	269	323
Dépenses sans transport (millions de dollars)	122	139	146	164	171	172	192	228
Sierra Leone								
Arrivals of visitors (thousands)	98	(a)16	(a)24	(a)28	(a)38	(a)44	(a)40	(a)34
Tourists' overnight stays (thousands)	..	..	..	..	..	..	..	..
Total expenditure of visitors (millions of dollars)	..	..	..	..	..	..	..	..
Expenditure excluding transport (millions of dollars)	34	10	14	38	60	58	64	23

For sources and notes, see end of table.

Pour les sources et les notes, se reporter à la fin du tableau.

5

	1990	2000	2001	2002	2003	2004	2005	2006
				Singapore - Singapour				
Arrivées des visiteurs (milliers)	4 842	(d)7 691	(d)7 522	(d)7 567	(d)6 127	(d)8 329	(d)8 943	(d)9 751
Nuitées des touristes (milliers)	..							..
Dépenses totales des visiteurs (millions de dollars)	..	..	..	..	..	..	..	..
Dépenses sans transport (millions de dollars)	4 650	5 142	4 619	4 428	3 783	5 226	5 903	7 069
				Slovakia - Slovaquie				
Arrivals of visitors (thousands)	–	(d)28 769	(d)27 761	(d)26 450	(d)24 985	(d)26 415	(d)29 396	(d)30 592
Tourists' overnight stays (thousands)	–	3 743	4 378	5 043	4 964	4 675	4 872	5 134
Total expenditure of visitors (millions of dollars)	–	441	649	742	876	932	..	..
Expenditure excluding transport (millions of dollars)	–	433	641	736	865	901	1 210	1 513
				Slovenia - Slovénie				
Arrivées des visiteurs (milliers)	–	(d)63 580	(d)61 878	(d)60 031	(d)59 388	(d)63 013	(d)60 230	(d)58 274
Nuitées des touristes (milliers)	–	3 277	3 813	4 021	4 175	4 363	4 399	4 489
Dépenses totales des visiteurs (millions de dollars)	–	1 016	1 059	1 152	1 427	1 725	1 894	1 911
Dépenses sans transport (millions de dollars)	–	961	1 001	1 086	1 342	1 624	1 795	1 797
				Solomon Islands - Îles Salomon				
Arrivals of visitors (thousands)	9	(a)5	..	..	(a)7	..	(a)9	(a)12
Tourists' overnight stays (thousands)	..	..	..	..	..	..	..	..
Total expenditure of visitors (millions of dollars)	8	..	9	1	2	4	7	8
Expenditure excluding transport (millions of dollars)	7	4	5	1	2	4	2	2
				South Africa - Afrique du Sud				
Arrivées des visiteurs (milliers)	1 029	(d)6 001	(d)5 908	(d)6 550	(d)6 640	(d)6 815	(d)7 518	(d)8 509
Nuitées des touristes (milliers)	..							
Dépenses totales des visiteurs (millions de dollars)	2 167	3 338	3 256	3 695	6 533	7 380	8 448	8 967
Dépenses sans transport (millions de dollars)	1 835	2 677	2 569	2 923	5 571	6 322	7 335	7 876
				Spain - Espagne				
Arrivals of visitors (thousands)	34 085	(d)74 462	(d)75 678	(d)80 024	(d)82 326	(d)85 981	(d)92 563	(d)95 935
Tourists' overnight stays (thousands)	68 630	233 897	232 035	220 707	217 852	209 081	209 518	224 067
Total expenditure of visitors (millions of dollars)	..	32 656	33 829	35 468	43 863	49 996	53 066	57 537
Expenditure excluding transport (millions of dollars)	18 581	29 802	30 550	31 880	39 634	45 067	47 789	51 292
				Sri Lanka				
Arrivées des visiteurs (milliers)	298	(d)445	(d)397	(d)457	(d)583	(d)681	(d)669	(d)689
Nuitées des touristes (milliers)	3 225	4 056	3 342	3 989	5 093	5 742	4 754	5 794
Dépenses totales des visiteurs (millions de dollars)	224	388	347	594	709	808	729	733
Dépenses sans transport (millions de dollars)	128	248	213	363	441	513	429	410
				Sudan - Soudan				
Arrivals of visitors (thousands)	33	(a)38	(a)50	(a)52	(a)52	(a)61	(a)246	(a)328
Tourists' overnight stays (thousands)	..	..	..	..	..	..	..	..
Total expenditure of visitors (millions of dollars)	34	..	..	..	..	..	..	..
Expenditure excluding transport (millions of dollars)	21	5	3	108	17	21	89	126
				Suriname				
Arrivées des visiteurs (milliers)	46	(a)57	(a)54	(a)60	(a)82	(a)138	(a)160	..
Nuitées des touristes (milliers)	..	..	..	..	..	..	..	..
Dépenses totales des visiteurs (millions de dollars)	4	42	26	17	18	52	96	109
Dépenses sans transport (millions de dollars)	1	16	14	3	4	17	45	95
				Swaziland				
Arrivals of visitors (thousands)	263	(c)281	(c)283	(c)256	(c)461	(c)459	(c)839	(c)873
Tourists' overnight stays (thousands)	..	..	..	..	..	..	..	..
Total expenditure of visitors (millions of dollars)	35	24	23	45	70	75	78	74
Expenditure excluding transport (millions of dollars)	30	21	21	43	70	75	78	74
				Sweden - Suède				
Arrivées des visiteurs (milliers)	1 900	(b)2 746	(b)2 894	(b)2 989	(b)2 952	(b)3 003	(b)3 133	(b)3 270
Nuitées des touristes (milliers)	6 575	8 654	9 133	9 768	9 715	9 724	10 078	10 952
Dépenses totales des visiteurs (millions de dollars)	3 900	4 825	5 200	5 671	6 548	7 686	8 580	10 437
Dépenses sans transport (millions de dollars)	2 915	4 064	4 253	4 710	5 304	6 198	7 385	9 133
				Switzerland - Suisse (6)				
Arrivals of visitors (thousands)	..	(c)7 883	(c)7 512	(c)6 917	(c)6 579	..	(c)7 279	(c)7 918
Tourists' overnight stays (thousands)	..	32 844	32 111	29 641	28 569	..	..	..
Total expenditure of visitors (millions of dollars)	..	8 988	9 290	9 117	10 496	11 409	11 991	12 755
Expenditure excluding transport (millions of dollars)	..	6 652	6 782	7 260	8 617	9 600	10 095	10 640

For sources and notes, see end of table.   Pour les sources et les notes, se reporter à la fin du tableau.

	1990	2000	2001	2002	2003	2004	2005	2006
Syrian Arab Republic - République arabe syrienne								
Arrivées des visiteurs (milliers)	562	(d)3 015	(d)3 327	(d)4 273	(d)4 388	(d)6 154	(d)5 838	(d)6 009
Nuitées des touristes (milliers)	..	5 997	..	..	20 700	27 930	30 948	48 482
Dépenses totales des visiteurs (millions de dollars)	..	..	..	..	877	1 883	2 035	2 113
Dépenses sans transport (millions de dollars)	320	1 082	1 150	970	773	1 800	1 944	2 025
Tajikistan - Tadjikistan								
Arrivals of visitors (thousands)	–	(d)8	(d)5	..	..	..	..	..
Tourists' overnight stays (thousands)	–	..	..	..	..	..	..	..
Total expenditure of visitors (millions of dollars)	–	..	..	5	7	9	10	11
Expenditure excluding transport (millions of dollars)	–	..	..	2	2	1	2	2
Thailand - Thaïlande								
Arrivées des visiteurs (milliers)	5 299	(a)9 579	(a)10 133	(a)10 873	(a)10 082	(a)11 737	(a)11 567	(a)13 822
Nuitées des touristes (milliers)	..	..	..	..	..	..	..	..
Dépenses totales des visiteurs (millions de dollars)	4 987	9 936	9 380	10 388	10 456	13 054	12 102	15 653
Dépenses sans transport (millions de dollars)	4 325	7 483	7 076	7 901	7 856	10 043	9 577	12 432
TFY Rep. of Macedonia - ERY de Macédoine								
Arrivals of visitors (thousands)	–	(d)2 865	(d)1 730	(d)2 079	(d)2 183	(d)2 594	(d)3 246	(d)3 369
Tourists' overnight stays (thousands)	–	494	213	275	346	361	443	443
Total expenditure of visitors (millions of dollars)	–	88	49	55	65	77	92	156
Expenditure excluding transport (millions of dollars)	–	38	26	39	57	72	84	129
Togo								
Arrivées des visiteurs (milliers)	103	(c)60	(c)57	(c)58	(c)61	(c)83	(c)81	(c)94
Nuitées des touristes (milliers)	..	..	..	..	..	..	..	..
Dépenses totales des visiteurs (millions de dollars)	..	11	14	16	26	25	27	26
Dépenses sans transport (millions de dollars)	58	8	11	13	15	19	20	10
Tonga								
Arrivals of visitors (thousands)	21	(d)43	(d)38	(d)45	(d)51	(d)51	(d)60	(d)54
Tourists' overnight stays (thousands)	328	..	..	..	..	..	..	..
Total expenditure of visitors (millions of dollars)	7	..	..	..	..	..	..	..
Expenditure excluding transport (millions of dollars)	7	7	7	6	10	13	15	16
Trinidad and Tobago - Trinité-et-Tobago								
Arrivées des visiteurs (milliers)	195	(d)503	(d)465	(d)444	(d)465	(d)497	(d)530	(d)543
Nuitées des touristes (milliers)	..	..	..	..	..	..	..	..
Dépenses totales des visiteurs (millions de dollars)	221	371	361	402	437	568	593	357
Dépenses sans transport (millions de dollars)	95	213	201	242	249	341	453	177
Tunisia - Tunisie								
Arrivals of visitors (thousands)	3 204	(d)5 244	(d)5 663	(d)5 322	(d)5 492	(d)6 419	(d)6 975	(d)7 176
Tourists' overnight stays (thousands)	..	..	..	..	..	..	..	..
Total expenditure of visitors (millions of dollars)	1 197	1 978	2 061	1 831	1 935	2 432	2 800	2 999
Expenditure excluding transport (millions of dollars)	1 020	1 682	1 751	1 523	1 583	1 970	2 143	2 275
Turkey - Turquie								
Arrivées des visiteurs (milliers)	4 799	(d)10 428	(d)11 619	(d)13 256	(d)14 030	(d)17 517	(d)21 125	(d)19 820
Nuitées des touristes (milliers)	13 271	28 511	36 368	43 312	40 866	49 728	56 108	46 640
Dépenses totales des visiteurs (millions de dollars)	..	..	..	..	..	..	19 720	18 520
Dépenses sans transport (millions de dollars)	3 225	7 636	10 067	11 901	13 203	15 888	18 152	16 853
Turkmenistan - Turkménistan								
Arrivals of visitors (thousands)	–	(a)3	(a)5	(a)11	(a)8	(a)15	(a)12	..
Tourists' overnight stays (thousands)	–	..	..	..	..	..	..	..
Total expenditure of visitors (millions of dollars)	–	..	..	..	..	..	..	..
Expenditure excluding transport (millions of dollars)	–	..	..	..	..	..	..	..
Turks and Caicos Islands - Îles Turques et Caïques								
Arrivées des visiteurs (milliers)	49	(a)152	(a)166	(a)155	(a)164	(a)173	(a)176	(a)248
Nuitées des touristes (milliers)	..	1 142	1 239	1 172	..	..	..	..
Dépenses totales des visiteurs (millions de dollars)	..	285	311	292	..	..	..	..
Dépenses sans transport (millions de dollars)	..	..	..	..	..	..	..	..
Tuvalu								
Arrivals of visitors (thousands)	1	(a)1	(a)1	(a)1	(a)1	(a)1	(a)1	(a)1
Tourists' overnight stays (thousands)	..	..	..	..	..	..	..	..
Total expenditure of visitors (millions of dollars)	..	..	..	..	..	..	..	..
Expenditure excluding transport (millions of dollars)	..	..	..	..	..	..	..	..

For sources and notes, see end of table. Pour les sources et les notes, se reporter à la fin du tableau.

5

	1990	2000	2001	2002	2003	2004	2005	2006
				Uganda - Ouganda				
Arrivées des visiteurs (milliers)	69	(a)193	(a)205	(a)254	(a)305	(a)512	(a)468	(a)539
Nuitées des touristes (milliers)	..	772	820	1 016	..	..	..	..
Dépenses totales des visiteurs (millions de dollars)	..	..	187	194	185	257	383	356
Dépenses sans transport (millions de dollars)	..	165	165	171	184	256	381	355
				Ukraine				
Arrivals of visitors (thousands)	_	(d)11 691	(d)11 877	(d)12 793	(d)15 161	(d)18 583	(d)20 489	(d)21 714
Tourists' overnight stays (thousands)	_	5 053	5 177	4 757	4 479	4 188	3 895	..
Total expenditure of visitors (millions of dollars)	_	563	759	1 001	1 204	2 931	3 542	4 018
Expenditure excluding transport (millions of dollars)	_	394	573	788	935	2 560	3 125	3 485
				United Arab Emirates - Émirats arabes unis				
Arrivées des visiteurs (milliers)	633	(c)3 907	(c)4 134	(c)5 445	(c)5 871	(a)6 195	(a)7 126	..
Nuitées des touristes (milliers)	..	..	..	..	..	..	..	..
Dépenses totales des visiteurs (millions de dollars)	..	1 063	1 200	1 332	1 438	1 593	3 218	4 972
Dépenses sans transport (millions de dollars)	..	..	..	..	..	..	..	..
				United Kingdom - Royaume-Uni				
Arrivals of visitors (thousands)	18 013	(d)25 209	(d)22 835	(d)24 180	(d)24 715	(d)27 755	(d)29 970	(d)32 713
Tourists' overnight stays (thousands)	196 100	203 759	189 516	199 285	203 432	227 406	247 587	273 417
Total expenditure of visitors (millions of dollars)	21 268	29 978	26 137	27 819	30 736	37 166	39 569	43 041
Expenditure excluding transport (millions of dollars)	15 588	21 769	18 864	20 549	22 668	28 202	30 573	33 838
				United Republic of Tanzania - République-Unie de Tanzanie				
Arrivées des visiteurs (milliers)	153	(d)501	(d)525	(d)575	(d)576	(d)583	(d)613	(d)644
Nuitées des touristes (milliers)	1 265	1 677	2 632	4 459	5 500	5 525	6 130	7 729
Dépenses totales des visiteurs (millions de dollars)	..	381	626	639	654	762	835	950
Dépenses sans transport (millions de dollars)	48	377	615	635	647	746	824	914
				United States - États-Unis				
Arrivals of visitors (thousands)	..	(a)54 579	(a)50 478	(a)46 668	(a)44 456	(a)49 627	(a)52 892	(a)54 700
Tourists' overnight stays (thousands)	..	..	..	..	..	..	..	..
Total expenditure of visitors (millions of dollars)	..	121 018	109 433	104 284	101 884	116 411	126 332	132 291
Expenditure excluding transport (millions of dollars)	..	97 943	88 779	84 752	83 316	94 537	102 124	106 736
				United States Virgin Islands - Îles Vierges américaines				
Arrivées des visiteurs (milliers)	463	(d)2 396	(d)2 497	(d)2 337	(d)2 395	(d)2 620	(d)2 605	(d)2 575
Nuitées des touristes (milliers)	..	1 060	1 040	1 057	1 052	1 096	1 094	1 041
Dépenses totales des visiteurs (millions de dollars)	..	1 206	1 234	1 195	1 257	1 356	1 491	1 466
Dépenses sans transport (millions de dollars)	..	..	..	..	..	..	..	..
				Uruguay				
Arrivals of visitors (thousands)	1 267	(d)2 236	(d)2 136	(d)1 354	(d)1 508	(d)1 871	(d)1 917	(d)1 824
Tourists' overnight stays (thousands)	..	3 319	2 992	2 927	3 531	2 938	2 925	3 020
Total expenditure of visitors (millions of dollars)	303	827	700	409	419	591	699	706
Expenditure excluding transport (millions of dollars)	238	713	611	351	345	494	594	597
				Uzbekistan - Ouzbékistan				
Arrivées des visiteurs (milliers)	_	(a)302	(a)345	(a)332	(a)231	(a)262	(a)242	(a)281
Nuitées des touristes (milliers)	_	918	1 082	1 069	935	964	840	976
Dépenses totales des visiteurs (millions de dollars)	_	63	72	68	48	57	..	..
Dépenses sans transport (millions de dollars)	_	27	22	22	24	28	28	43
				Vanuatu				
Arrivals of visitors (thousands)	35	(d)106	(d)106	(d)99	(d)102	(d)99	(d)126	(d)154
Tourists' overnight stays (thousands)	..	..	..	..	..	..	..	..
Total expenditure of visitors (millions of dollars)	..	69	58	72	83	93	104	109
Expenditure excluding transport (millions of dollars)	39	56	46	54	64	75	85	92
				Venezuela (Bolivarian Rep. of) - Venezuela (Rép. bolivarienne du)				
Arrivées des visiteurs (milliers)	525	(d)604	(d)792	(d)590	(d)435	(d)618	(d)841	(d)911
Nuitées des touristes (milliers)	..	8 456	10 512	9 126	9 819	..	..	..
Dépenses totales des visiteurs (millions de dollars)	649	469	677	484	378	554	722	843
Dépenses sans transport (millions de dollars)	496	423	615	434	331	502	650	768
				Viet Nam				
Arrivals of visitors (thousands)	250	(d)2 140	(d)2 330	(d)2 628	(d)2 429	(d)2 928	(d)3 468	(d)3 583
Tourists' overnight stays (thousands)	..	..	..	..	..	..	..	..
Total expenditure of visitors (millions of dollars)	..	..	..	..	1 400	1 700	1 880	3 200
Expenditure excluding transport (millions of dollars)	..	..	..	..	..	..	..	..

For sources and notes, see end of table.   Pour les sources et les notes, se reporter à la fin du tableau.

	1990	2000	2001	2002	2003	2004	2005	2006
				Yemen - Yémen				
Arrivées des visiteurs (milliers)	52	(c)73	(c)76	(c)98	(c)155	(c)274	(c)336	(c)382
Nuitées des touristes (milliers)	..							
Dépenses totales des visiteurs (millions de dollars)	..	..	..	..	..	..	..	..
Dépenses sans transport (millions de dollars)	40	73	38	38	139	139	181	181
				Zambia - Zambie				
Arrivals of visitors (thousands)	141	(a)457	(a)492	(a)565	(a)413	(a)515	(a)669	(a)757
Tourists' overnight stays (thousands)	..							
Total expenditure of visitors (millions of dollars)	41	..	..	..	..	..	..	..
Expenditure excluding transport (millions of dollars)	13	133	80	64	88	92	98	110
				Zimbabwe				
Arrivées des visiteurs (milliers)	605	(d)1 967	(d)2 217	(c)2 041	(d)2 256	(d)1 854	(d)1 559	(d)2 287
Nuitées des touristes (milliers)	..			..			..	..
Dépenses totales des visiteurs (millions de dollars)	112	125	81	76	61	194	99	338
Dépenses sans transport (millions de dollars)	64	..	..	..	..	..	..	..

Sources:
- World Tourism Organisation (UNWTO), database
- International Monetary Fund (IMF), *Balance of Payments Statistics* on CD-ROM

Sources :
- Organisation mondiale du tourisme (UNWTO), base de données
- *Statistiques de la balance des paiements* sur CD-ROM du Fonds monétaire international (FMI)

Notes:

Arrivals of visitors represent the total number of non-resident visitors who arrived in a reporting economy during a given year. A visitor can remain in an economy for a short time and not spend a night there, in which case he is not considered a tourist. A tourist is a person who stays for at least one night. All tourists are also visitors. When the same person visits a country several times in a year, the total number of arrivals is counted. Similarly, when a person travels to several countries during one trip, her/his arrival in each country is recorded separately. Countries differ in the way in which they count arrivals. Most take into account all arrivals of non-resident visitors at national borders, while others count arrivals at hotels and other types of tourist accommodation. The different approaches are marked by footnotes.

Tourists' overnight stays refer to the number of nights spent by non-resident tourists in a reporting country and concern all types of tourism accommodation.

Total expenditure of visitors corresponds to the sum of items "Travel receipts" and "Passenger transport" in IMF balance-of-payments data. It refers to expenditures of non-resident visitors within the territory of a reporting economy, including the costs they pay for transportation.

Expenditure excluding transport corresponds to the item "Travel receipts" in IMF balance-of-payments data. It refers to expenditures of non-resident visitors within the territory of a reporting economy. Transport expenditures are not included.

(a)   Arrivals of non-resident tourists at national borders
(b)   Arrivals of non-resident tourists in all types of accommodation establishments
(c)   Arrivals of non-resident tourists in hotels and similar establishments
(d)   Arrivals of non-resident visitors at national borders

(1)   Arrivals - Data until 1994 (inclusive) concern only arrivals at hotels and similar establishments, while later figures cover arrivals at national borders.

(2)   Arrivals - Year 2000: break in series owing to new accommodation coverage.

(3)   Data for the overnight stays refer to the metropolitan France only.

(4)   Arrivals - Data until 1994 (inclusive) concern only arrivals of tourists at national borders, while later figures cover arrivals of visitors at national borders.

(5)   Data for the overnight stays of tourists include only Bonaire and Curaçao, while figures referring to visitors' arrivals cover all of the Netherlands Antilles.

(6)   Arrivals - Data until 1994 (inclusive) concern arrivals at national borders, while later figures cover only arrivals at hotels and similar establishments.
      Data for overnight stays cover Switzerland only; Liechtenstein is not included.

Notes :

Les **Arrivées des visiteurs** représentent le nombre total de visiteurs qui sont arrivés dans l'économie déclarante durant une année. Le visiteur peut rester dans une économie brièvement et ne pas y passer la nuit ; dans ce cas, il n'est pas considéré comme touriste. Le touriste passe au moins une nuit dans le pays. Tous les touristes sont aussi des visiteurs. Quand une personne se rend dans un pays plusieurs fois par année, chaque visite est comptée séparément. De même, si quelqu'un se rend dans plusieurs pays durant un voyage, son arrivée dans chaque pays est prise en compte. Les pays comptent les arrivées des visiteurs de manières différentes: la plupart des pays prennent en compte toutes les arrivées aux frontières nationales, tandis que les autres comptent les arrivées dans des hôtels et autres types de logements touristiques. Les approches différentes sont identifiées par des notes de bas de page.

Les **Nuitées des touristes** se réfèrent au nombre de nuits que les touristes non-résidents ont passées dans le pays déclarant et concernent tout type d'établissement touristique.

Les **Dépenses totales des visiteurs** correspondent à la somme des rubriques "Revenus des voyages" et "Transport des passagers" de la balance des paiements du FMI. Les dépenses totales des visiteurs se réfèrent aux dépenses des visiteurs non-résidents sur le territoire de l'économie déclarante, y compris les dépenses pour le transport.

Les **Dépenses sans transport** correspondent à la rubrique "Revenus des voyages" de la balance des paiements du FMI. Elles se réfèrent aux dépenses des visiteurs non-résidents sur le territoire de l'économie déclarante. Les dépenses pour le transport n'y sont pas incluses.

(a)   Arrivées de touristes non-résidents aux frontières nationales
(b)   Arrivées de touristes non-résidents à tout type de logement
(c)   Arrivées de touristes non-résidents aux hôtels et autres types de logement similaire
(d)   Arrivées de visiteurs non-résidents aux frontières nationales

(1)   Arrivées - Les données jusqu'à l'année 1994 (incluse) concernent seulement les arrivées aux hôtels, tandis que les chiffres des années d'après couvrent les arrivées aux frontières nationales.

(2)   Arrivées - Année 2000 : rupture de série, suite à une différente classification de logements.

(3)   Les données sur les nuitées des touristes se réfèrent seulement à la France métropolitaine.

(4)   Arrivées - Les données jusqu'à l'année 1994 (incluse) concernent seulement les arrivées des touristes, tandis que les chiffres des années d'après couvrent les arrivées des visiteurs.

(5)   Les données sur la durée moyenne de séjour et sur les nuitées des touristes comprennent Bonaire et Curaçao seulement, tandis que les chiffres concernant les arrivés des visiteurs couvrent la totalité des Antilles Néerlandaises.

(6)   Les données jusqu'à l'année 1994 (incluse) concernent les arrivées aux frontières nationales, tandis que les chiffres des années d'après couvrent seulement les arrivées aux hôtels et autres types d'accommodation similaires.
      Les données sur les nuitées des touristes se réfèrent à la Suisse et ne couvrent pas le Liechtenstein.

5

279

5.4 World merchant fleet by flag of registration and type of ship of countries and geographical regions

5.4 Flotte marchande mondiale par pavillons d'immatriculation et par types de navires des pays et des régions géographiques

Region, country or territory / Régions pays ou territoires	Year / Année	Total fleet (thousands of DWT) (1) / Flotte totale (milliers de TPL) (1)	As percentage of world total fleet / En pourcentage de la flotte mondiale					As percentage of the country or region total fleet / En pourcentage de la flotte totale du pays ou de la région				
			Oil tankers / Pétroliers	Bulk carriers / Vraquiers	General cargo / Navires de charge classique	Container ships / Porte-conteneurs	Other types / Autres navires	Oil tankers / Pétroliers	Bulk carriers / Vraquiers	General cargo / Navires de charge classique	Container ships / Porte-conteneurs	Other types / Autres navires
WORLD - MONDE	**1990**	**629 976.0**	**100.0**	**100.0**	**100.0**	**100.0**	**100.0**	**37.4**	**35.5**	**15.9**	**3.5**	**7.6**
	1995	**710 124.9**	**100.0**	**100.0**	**100.0**	**100.0**	**100.0**	**37.9**	**34.6**	**14.5**	**5.1**	**7.8**
	2000	**785 522.7**	**100.0**	**100.0**	**100.0**	**100.0**	**100.0**	**35.8**	**34.4**	**12.9**	**7.8**	**9.1**
	2007	**1 042 327.6**	**100.0**	**100.0**	**100.0**	**100.0**	**100.0**	**36.7**	**35.3**	**9.7**	**12.3**	**6.0**
DEVELOPING ECONOMIES - ÉCONOMIES EN DÉVELOPPEMENT (2)	1990	334 184.0	52.2	56.5	54.4	43.1	43.1	36.8	37.8	16.4	2.9	6.2
	1995	400 440.3	56.5	59.4	57.0	51.1	44.9	38.0	36.4	14.7	4.6	6.2
	2000	479 444.8	56.4	68.0	63.6	56.9	53.0	33.1	38.3	13.4	7.3	7.9
	2007	733 238.9	70.5	74.3	69.2	66.2	56.4	36.8	37.2	9.5	11.6	4.8
ECONOMIES IN TRANSITION - ÉCONOMIES EN TRANSITION	1990	35 090.0	2.9	4.4	12.4	3.2	11.0	19.2	28.4	35.4	2.0	15.0
	1995	24 852.7	1.6	2.1	10.2	1.8	7.4	17.8	20.8	42.2	2.7	16.5
	2000	13 598.3	0.9	0.9	5.4	0.8	3.8	18.5	18.0	40.2	3.4	19.9
	2007	13 118.1	0.8	0.8	5.1	0.1	3.0	24.2	21.5	38.9	1.3	14.2
DEVELOPED ECONOMIES - ÉCONOMIES DÉVELOPPÉES (2)	1990	260 702.0	45.0	39.1	33.2	53.7	45.8	40.7	33.5	12.8	4.6	8.4
	1995	284 831.9	41.8	38.5	32.8	47.1	47.8	39.6	33.2	11.9	6.0	9.3
	2000	292 479.6	42.7	31.1	31.0	42.4	43.2	41.1	28.7	10.7	8.9	10.5
	2007	291 284.9	28.4	24.7	23.9	33.6	39.3	37.4	31.1	8.3	14.8	8.4
Developing economies: Africa - Économies en développement : Afrique	**1990**	**97 139.0**	**23.1**	**12.7**	**6.1**	**5.4**	**14.6**	**56.0**	**29.3**	**6.4**	**1.2**	**7.2**
	1995	**102 952.3**	**20.8**	**11.9**	**5.9**	**10.1**	**14.5**	**54.3**	**28.3**	**5.9**	**3.6**	**7.9**
	2000	**91 552.9**	**14.7**	**9.9**	**6.5**	**9.8**	**15.1**	**45.3**	**29.2**	**7.2**	**6.6**	**11.8**
	2007	**111 188.8**	**14.3**	**6.1**	**4.8**	**18.1**	**9.4**	**49.2**	**20.2**	**4.4**	**20.9**	**5.3**
Eastern Africa - Afrique orientale	*1990*	*482.0*	*0.0*	*0.0*	*0.2*	*0.1*	*0.1*	*22.2*	*13.7*	*50.4*	*6.0*	*7.5*
	1995	*543.0*	*0.0*	*0.1*	*0.3*	*..*	*0.1*	*6.2*	*37.5*	*48.0*	*..*	*8.3*
	2000	*437.0*	*0.0*	*0.0*	*0.2*	*0.2*	*0.1*	*6.8*	*1.2*	*49.6*	*30.0*	*12.5*
	2007	*1 498.4*	*0.1*	*0.1*	*0.7*	*0.0*	*0.3*	*25.9*	*15.5*	*47.1*	*0.3*	*11.3*
Comoros - Comores	1990	3.0	..	..	0.0	..	..	..	..	100.0	..	..
	1995	3.0	..	..	0.0	..	0.0	..	..	77.6	..	22.4
	2000	1.0	..	..	0.0	..	..	..	..	100.0	..	..
	2007	1 010.1	0.1	0.1	0.5	0.0	0.1	24.1	22.2	47.6	0.5	5.7
Djibouti	1995	4.8	..	..	0.0	..	0.0	..	..	92.7	..	7.3
	2000	4.9	..	..	0.0	..	0.0	..	..	90.8	..	9.2
	2007	3.7	..	..	0.0	..	0.0	..	..	81.4	..	18.6
Eritrea - Érythrée	2007	24.9	0.0	..	0.0	..	0.0	12.8	..	75.9	..	11.4
Ethiopia - Éthiopie	1995	84.3	0.0	..	0.1	..	0.0	6.9	..	92.9	..	0.2
	2000	119.7	0.0	..	0.1	..	..	3.0	..	97.0	..	..
	2007	125.1	..	..	0.1	..	..	..	..	100.0	..	..
Ethiopia (former) - Éthiopie (anc.)	1990	94.0	0.0	..	0.1	..	..	2.1	..	96.8	..	..
Kenya	1990	5.0	..	..	..	..	0.0	..	..	..	..	100.0
	1995	15.6	0.0	..	0.0	..	0.0	41.2	..	9.8	..	49.1
	2000	19.1	0.0	..	0.0	..	0.0	40.0	..	10.4	..	49.7
	2007	15.6	0.0	..	0.0	..	0.0	48.9	..	12.7	..	38.4
Madagascar	1990	88.0	0.0	..	0.1	..	0.0	8.0	..	80.7	..	11.4
	1995	37.7	0.0	..	0.0	..	0.0	36.7	..	46.7	..	16.6
	2000	45.1	0.0	..	0.0	..	0.0	37.5	..	47.5	..	15.0
	2007	31.5	0.0	..	0.0	..	0.0	22.3	..	57.5	..	20.3
Mauritius - Maurice	1990	216.0	0.0	0.0	0.0	0.1	0.0	42.6	30.6	11.1	13.4	2.3
	1995	301.1	..	0.1	0.1	..	0.0	..	67.7	28.2	..	4.1
	2000	189.7	..	0.0	0.0	0.2	0.0	..	2.8	21.4	69.0	6.8
	2007	66.3	..	0.0	0.0	..	0.1	..	12.1	22.9	..	65.0
Mozambique	1990	27.0	0.0	..	0.0	..	0.0	7.4	..	66.7	..	25.9
	1995	26.1	0.0	..	0.0	..	0.0	1.6	..	66.1	..	32.2
	2000	25.2	..	..	0.0	..	0.0	..	..	49.9	..	50.1
	2007	27.5	..	..	0.0	..	0.0	..	..	38.5	..	61.5
Seychelles	1990	2.0	..	..	0.0	..	..	..	..	100.0	..	..
	1995	3.7	..	..	0.0	..	0.0	..	..	75.9	..	24.1
	2000	22.7	..	..	0.0	..	0.0	..	..	50.9	..	49.1
	2007	144.9	0.0	..	0.0	..	0.0	76.6	..	2.7	..	20.7

For sources and notes, see end of table.

Pour les sources et les notes, se reporter à la fin du tableau.

5.4 World merchant fleet by flag of registration and type of ship of countries and geographical regions

5.4 Flotte marchande mondiale par pavillons d'immatriculation et par types de navires des pays et des régions géographiques

Region, country or territory / Régions pays ou territoires	Year / Année	Total fleet (thousands of DWT) (1) / Flotte totale (milliers de TPL) (1)	As percentage of world total fleet / En pourcentage de la flotte mondiale					As percentage of the country or region total fleet / En pourcentage de la flotte totale du pays ou de la région				
			Oil tankers / Pétroliers	Bulk carriers / Vraquiers	General cargo / Navires de charge classique	Container ships / Porte-conteneurs	Other types / Autres navires	Oil tankers / Pétroliers	Bulk carriers / Vraquiers	General cargo / Navires de charge classique	Container ships / Porte-conteneurs	Other types / Autres navires
Somalia - Somalie	1990	14.0	..	..	0.0	..	0.0	..	..	71.4	..	28.6
	1995	17.3	..	..	0.0	..	0.0	..	..	68.8	..	31.2
	2000	6.8	0.0	..	0.0	..	0.0	22.6	..	59.5	..	17.9
	2007	10.1	0.0	..	0.0	..	0.0	15.1	..	49.3	..	35.7
Uganda - Ouganda	1990	1.0	..	..	..	..	0.0	..	..	..	..	100.0
	2000	2.7	..	..	0.0	..	..	..	..	100.0	..	..
United Republic of Tanzania - République-Unie de Tanzanie	1990	32.0	0.0	..	0.0	..	0.0	12.5	..	75.0	..	12.5
	1995	49.4	0.0	..	0.0	..	0.0	14.5	..	79.8	..	5.7
	2007	38.8	0.0	..	0.0	..	0.0	36.1	..	59.5	..	4.4
Middle Africa - Afrique centrale	*1990*	*285.0*	*0.0*	*..*	*0.2*	*..*	*0.1*	*0.7*	*..*	*82.8*	*..*	*16.5*
	1995	*226.0*	*0.0*	*0.0*	*0.1*	*..*	*0.1*	*1.5*	*8.4*	*68.2*	*..*	*21.8*
	2000	*143.3*	*0.0*	*..*	*0.1*	*0.0*	*0.1*	*4.9*	*..*	*65.6*	*1.0*	*28.5*
	2007	*212.4*	*0.0*	*0.0*	*0.1*	*..*	*0.1*	*36.2*	*3.3*	*27.3*	*..*	*31.2*
Angola	1990	122.0	0.0	..	0.1	..	0.0	1.6	..	86.9	..	11.5
	1995	116.3	0.0	..	0.1	..	0.0	2.3	..	86.3	..	11.4
	2000	69.7	0.0	..	0.0	..	0.0	6.5	..	69.1	..	24.4
	2007	47.2	0.0	..	0.0	..	0.0	17.9	..	26.1	..	56.0
Cameroon - Cameroun	1990	39.0	..	..	0.0	..	0.0	..	..	92.3	..	7.7
	1995	40.2	..	..	0.0	..	0.0	..	..	83.4	..	16.6
	2000	5.7	..	..	0.0	..	0.0	..	..	5.3	..	94.7
	2007	78.6	0.0	..	0.0	..	0.0	87.6	..	4.4	..	8.0
Congo	1990	11.0	..	..	..	..	0.0	..	..	..	..	100.0
	1995	11.0	..	..	..	..	0.0	..	..	..	..	100.0
	2000	0.7	..	..	..	..	0.0	..	..	..	..	100.0
	2007	0.7	..	..	..	..	0.0	..	..	..	..	100.0
Dem. Rep. of the Congo - Rép. dém. du Congo	1990	76.0	..	..	0.1	..	0.0	..	..	80.3	..	19.7
	1995	15.9	..	..	0.0	..	0.0	..	..	3.8	..	96.2
	2007	16.7	0.0	..	0.0	..	0.0	9.8	..	3.6	..	86.6
Equatorial Guinea - Guinée équatoriale	1990	7.0	..	..	0.0	..	..	..	..	100.0	..	..
	1995	3.3	..	..	0.0	..	..	..	..	100.0	..	..
	2000	19.4	..	..	0.0	..	0.0	..	..	53.1	..	46.9
	2007	19.1	0.0	..	0.0	..	0.0	3.0	..	29.6	..	67.4
Gabon	1990	29.0	..	..	0.0	..	0.0	..	..	89.7	..	10.3
	1995	37.0	0.0	0.0	0.0	..	0.0	2.0	51.6	40.9	..	5.5
	2000	11.6	0.0	..	0.0	..	0.0	6.4	..	61.0	..	32.6
	2007	7.9	0.0	..	0.0	..	0.0	9.4	..	49.1	..	41.6
Sao Tome and Principe - Sao Tomé-et-Principe	1990	1.0	..	..	..	..	0.0	..	..	..	..	100.0
	1995	2.3	..	..	0.0	..	0.0	..	..	56.4	..	43.6
	2000	36.3	0.0	..	0.0	0.0	0.0	4.8	..	77.6	4.1	13.5
	2007	42.3	0.0	0.0	0.0	..	0.0	2.4	16.3	75.9	..	5.4
Northern Africa - Afrique septentrionale	*1990*	*5 391.0*	*0.7*	*0.4*	*1.4*	*0.0*	*2.9*	*31.0*	*17.5*	*25.7*	*0.2*	*25.6*
	1995	*4 850.8*	*0.6*	*0.4*	*1.2*	*0.0*	*1.6*	*33.6*	*21.7*	*25.8*	*0.2*	*18.6*
	2000	*4 477.3*	*0.4*	*0.5*	*1.1*	*0.1*	*1.3*	*22.5*	*30.1*	*25.1*	*1.0*	*21.3*
	2007	*3 038.8*	*0.1*	*0.3*	*0.5*	*0.1*	*1.2*	*18.6*	*34.2*	*17.7*	*4.9*	*24.6*
Algeria - Algérie	1990	964.0	0.0	0.1	0.3	..	1.0	4.8	16.2	30.7	..	48.3
	1995	1 093.1	0.0	0.1	0.3	..	0.8	4.8	26.4	27.1	..	41.7
	2000	1 110.8	0.0	0.1	0.3	..	0.7	4.7	25.9	26.6	..	42.7
	2007	777.3	0.0	0.1	0.1	..	0.7	3.4	30.2	9.7	..	56.8
Egypt - Égypte	1990	1 796.0	0.2	0.3	0.7	..	0.2	25.9	31.5	37.4	..	5.3
	1995	1 899.1	0.2	0.3	0.6	..	0.2	23.7	37.2	32.9	..	6.2
	2000	2 092.6	0.1	0.4	0.5	0.0	0.2	17.4	49.5	26.0	0.8	6.3
	2007	1 646.4	0.1	0.2	0.3	0.0	0.2	20.9	47.2	20.1	3.5	8.1
Libyan Arab Jamahiriya - Jamahiriya arabe libyenne	1990	1 463.0	0.5	..	0.1	..	0.6	74.7	..	6.8	..	18.5
	1995	1 218.7	0.4	..	0.1	..	0.1	89.7	..	7.8	..	2.5
	2000	667.1	0.2	..	0.1	..	0.1	80.5	..	13.7	..	5.8
	2007	99.2	0.0	..	0.1	..	0.0	13.4	..	62.5	..	24.2

For sources and notes, see end of table.

Pour les sources et les notes, se reporter à la fin du tableau.

5

281

5.4 World merchant fleet by flag of registration and type of ship of countries and geographical regions

5.4 Flotte marchande mondiale par pavillons d'immatriculation et par types de navires des pays et des régions géographiques

Region, country or territory / Régions pays ou territoires	Year / Année	Total fleet (thousands of DWT) (1) / Flotte totale (milliers de TPL) (1)	As percentage of world total fleet / En pourcentage de la flotte mondiale					As percentage of the country or region total fleet / En pourcentage de la flotte totale du pays ou de la région				
			Oil tankers / Pétroliers	Bulk carriers / Vraquiers	General cargo / Navires de charge classique	Container ships / Porte-conteneurs	Other types / Autres navires	Oil tankers / Pétroliers	Bulk carriers / Vraquiers	General cargo / Navires de charge classique	Container ships / Porte-conteneurs	Other types / Autres navires
Morocco - Maroc	1990	594.0	0.0	0.1	0.1	0.0	0.6	3.2	27.4	21.7	1.7	46.0
	1995	391.3	0.0	..	0.1	0.0	0.4	6.4	..	27.5	2.6	63.5
	2000	383.8	0.0	..	0.1	0.0	0.3	5.3	..	29.2	6.6	58.9
	2007	365.5	0.0	..	0.0	0.1	0.2	30.8	..	11.2	24.6	33.4
Sudan - Soudan	1990	127.0	0.0	..	0.1	..	0.0	0.8	..	98.4	..	0.8
	1995	72.8	0.0	..	0.1	..	0.0	1.7	..	97.2	..	1.1
	2000	53.2	0.0	..	0.1	..	0.0	2.3	..	96.2	..	1.5
	2007	28.8	0.0	..	0.0	..	0.0	4.2	..	91.0	..	4.8
Tunisia - Tunisie	1990	447.0	0.0	0.0	0.1	..	0.6	10.5	13.2	14.8	..	61.5
	1995	175.9	0.0	0.0	0.1	..	0.1	5.7	33.3	33.3	..	27.7
	2000	169.9	0.0	0.0	0.0	..	0.1	19.1	15.5	17.9	..	47.5
	2007	121.7	0.0	0.0	0.0	..	0.0	55.0	21.7	2.7	..	20.6
Southern Africa - Afrique australe	*1990*	*352.0*	*0.0*	*..*	*..*	*1.1*	*0.2*	*9.1*	*..*	*..*	*68.2*	*22.7*
	1995	*285.0*	*0.0*	*..*	*0.0*	*0.5*	*0.2*	*0.8*	*..*	*0.0*	*69.7*	*29.5*
	2000	*369.0*	*0.0*	*..*	*0.0*	*0.4*	*0.1*	*1.4*	*..*	*0.0*	*71.1*	*27.4*
	2007	*165.7*	*0.0*	*..*	*0.0*	*0.0*	*0.2*	*6.1*	*..*	*2.3*	*17.9*	*73.7*
Namibia - Namibie	2007	55.6	..	..	0.0	..	0.1	..	..	6.5	..	93.5
South Africa - Afrique du Sud	1990	352.0	0.0	..	..	1.1	0.2	9.1	..	..	68.2	22.7
	1995	285.0	0.0	..	0.0	0.5	0.2	0.8	..	0.0	69.7	29.5
	2000	369.0	0.0	..	0.0	0.4	0.1	1.4	..	0.0	71.1	27.4
	2007	110.1	0.0	..	0.0	0.0	0.1	9.2	..	0.1	26.9	63.7
Western Africa - Afrique occidentale	*1990*	*90 629.0*	*22.3*	*12.3*	*4.3*	*4.2*	*11.3*	*58.0*	*30.2*	*4.7*	*1.0*	*6.0*
	1995	*97 047.5*	*20.2*	*11.4*	*4.3*	*9.5*	*12.6*	*55.9*	*28.7*	*4.6*	*3.6*	*7.2*
	2000	*86 126.4*	*14.4*	*9.4*	*5.1*	*9.1*	*13.5*	*47.0*	*29.4*	*6.0*	*6.5*	*11.2*
	2007	*106 273.5*	*14.0*	*5.8*	*3.6*	*18.0*	*7.6*	*50.5*	*19.9*	*3.4*	*21.7*	*4.5*
Benin - Bénin	1990	5.0	..	..	0.0	..	0.0	..	..	80.0	..	20.0
	1995	0.2	..	..	..	..	0.0	..	..	..	..	100.0
	2000	0.2	..	..	..	..	0.0	..	..	..	..	100.0
	2007	0.2	..	..	..	..	0.0	..	..	..	..	100.0
Cape Verde - Cap-Vert	1990	26.0	..	..	0.0	..	0.0	..	..	92.3	..	7.7
	1995	32.3	0.0	..	0.0	..	0.0	1.7	..	86.6	..	11.6
	2000	24.0	0.0	..	0.0	..	0.0	6.4	..	78.4	..	15.3
	2007	22.9	0.0	..	0.0	..	0.0	17.9	..	57.9	..	24.2
Côte d'Ivoire	1990	100.0	..	..	0.1	..	0.0	..	..	85.0	..	15.0
	1995	76.4	0.0	..	0.1	..	0.0	1.5	..	81.7	..	16.8
	2000	5.9	0.0	..	..	..	0.0	19.9	..	..	..	80.1
	2007	5.1	0.0	..	..	..	0.0	22.8	..	..	..	77.2
Gambia - Gambie	1990	2.0	..	..	..	..	0.0	..	..	..	..	100.0
	1995	2.7	..	..	..	..	0.0	..	..	..	..	100.0
	2000	1.9	..	..	..	..	0.0	..	..	..	..	100.0
	2007	11.7	0.0	..	0.0	..	0.0	42.7	..	38.4	..	18.9
Ghana	1990	114.0	0.0	..	0.1	..	0.1	0.9	..	69.3	..	29.8
	1995	92.5	0.0	0.0	0.0	..	0.1	1.3	0.3	43.1	..	55.4
	2000	92.1	0.0	0.0	0.0	..	0.1	9.3	0.3	19.2	..	71.1
	2007	87.0	0.0	0.0	0.0	..	0.1	5.2	0.3	17.8	..	76.7
Guinea - Guinée	1990	3.0	..	..	..	..	0.0	..	..	..	..	100.0
	1995	2.9	..	..	0.0	..	0.0	..	..	9.8	..	90.2
	2000	4.8	..	..	0.0	..	0.0	..	..	6.0	..	94.0
	2007	9.0	..	..	0.0	..	0.0	..	..	3.2	..	96.8
Guinea-Bissau - Guinée-Bissau	1990	2.0	..	..	..	..	0.0	..	..	..	..	100.0
	1995	1.8	..	..	0.0	..	0.0	..	..	29.3	..	70.7
	2000	2.2	..	..	0.0	..	0.0	..	..	24.7	..	75.3
	2007	2.2	..	..	0.0	..	0.0	..	..	10.2	..	89.8
Liberia - Libéria	1990	89 501.0	22.1	12.3	3.8	4.2	10.9	58.3	30.6	4.2	1.0	5.8
	1995	96 075.8	20.0	11.4	4.0	9.5	12.3	56.0	29.0	4.3	3.6	7.1
	2000	85 186.9	14.2	9.4	4.9	9.1	13.3	46.8	29.7	5.8	6.6	11.1
	2007	105 182.3	13.9	5.8	3.3	18.0	7.2	50.6	20.1	3.1	21.9	4.3

For sources and notes, see end of table.　　　　　Pour les sources et les notes, se reporter à la fin du tableau.

5.4 World merchant fleet by flag of registration and type of ship of countries and geographical regions

5.4 Flotte marchande mondiale par pavillons d'immatriculation et par types de navires des pays et des régions géographiques

Region, country or territory / Régions pays ou territoires	Year / Année	Total fleet (thousands of DWT) (1) / Flotte totale (milliers de TPL) (1)	As percentage of world total fleet / En pourcentage de la flotte mondiale					As percentage of the country or region total fleet / En pourcentage de la flotte totale du pays ou de la région				
			Oil tankers / Pétroliers	Bulk carriers / Vraquiers	General cargo / Navires de charge classique	Container ships / Porte-conteneurs	Other types / Autres navires	Oil tankers / Pétroliers	Bulk carriers / Vraquiers	General cargo / Navires de charge classique	Container ships / Porte-conteneurs	Other types / Autres navires
Mauritania - Mauritanie	1990	22.0	..	..	0.0	..	0.0	..	..	18.2	..	81.8
	1995	20.3	..	..	0.0	..	0.0	..	..	9.2	..	90.8
	2000	22.2	..	..	0.0	..	0.0	..	..	3.2	..	96.8
	2007	24.7	..	..	0.0	..	0.0	..	..	3.5	..	96.5
Nigeria - Nigéria	1990	737.0	0.2	..	0.3	..	0.1	59.0	..	35.7	..	5.3
	1995	699.6	0.2	0.0	0.2	..	0.1	67.8	0.2	25.8	..	6.2
	2000	677.9	0.2	..	0.1	..	0.1	76.6	..	17.0	..	6.4
	2007	524.2	0.1	0.0	0.0	..	0.2	73.3	2.5	5.3	..	18.9
Saint Helena - Sainte-Hélène	1990	2.0	..	..	..	..	0.0	..	..	..	..	100.0
	2000	0.5	..	..	..	..	0.0	..	..	..	..	100.0
	2007	1.2	..	..	..	..	0.0	..	..	..	..	100.0
Senegal - Sénégal	1990	36.0	..	..	0.0	..	0.0	..	..	47.2	..	52.8
	1995	27.6	..	..	0.0	..	0.0	..	..	22.4	..	77.6
	2000	22.4	..	..	0.0	..	0.0	..	..	9.1	..	90.9
	2007	18.4	0.0	..	0.0	..	0.0	1.5	..	8.4	..	90.0
Sierra Leone	1990	14.0	0.0	..	0.0	..	0.0	7.1	..	21.4	..	71.4
	1995	15.1	0.0	..	0.0	..	0.0	12.2	..	6.3	..	81.6
	2000	11.2	0.0	..	0.0	..	0.0	55.0	..	8.5	..	36.5
	2007	372.2	0.0	0.0	0.2	0.0	0.0	28.2	2.0	62.3	1.2	6.3
Togo	1990	65.0	0.0	..	0.0	..	0.1	1.5	..	32.3	..	67.7
	1995	0.1	..	..	..	..	0.0	..	..	..	..	100.0
	2000	74.4	..	0.0	..	..	0.0	..	99.1	..	..	0.9
	2007	12.4	..	..	0.0	..	0.0	..	..	35.5	..	64.5
Developing economies: America - Économies en développement : Amérique	**1990**	**119 936.0**	**16.4**	**20.2**	**24.0**	**19.3**	**16.2**	**32.2**	**37.6**	**20.1**	**3.6**	**6.4**
	1995	**162 514.9**	**23.0**	**22.3**	**27.0**	**22.9**	**17.4**	**38.1**	**33.6**	**17.1**	**5.1**	**6.0**
	2000	**237 755.2**	**26.9**	**35.0**	**31.7**	**29.8**	**23.7**	**31.9**	**39.8**	**13.5**	**7.7**	**7.1**
	2007	**327 939.0**	**25.2**	**39.5**	**33.1**	**27.8**	**27.3**	**29.5**	**44.3**	**10.2**	**10.9**	**5.2**
Caribbean - Caraïbes	*1990*	*24 104.0*	*5.1*	*2.7*	*4.3*	*1.1*	*3.0*	*49.8*	*25.2*	*18.0*	*1.0*	*5.9*
	1995	*47 569.9*	*8.0*	*4.6*	*10.4*	*4.4*	*4.3*	*45.3*	*23.7*	*22.6*	*3.3*	*5.1*
	2000	*62 854.5*	*9.5*	*5.4*	*13.5*	*6.4*	*5.4*	*42.6*	*23.4*	*21.7*	*6.2*	*6.1*
	2007	*83 755.8*	*7.8*	*6.2*	*15.2*	*6.7*	*11.1*	*35.9*	*27.3*	*18.3*	*10.3*	*8.3*
Anguilla	1990	4.0	..	..	0.0	..	..	..	..	75.0	..	..
	1995	3.6	..	..	0.0	..	0.0	..	..	97.4	..	2.6
	2000	2.0	..	..	0.0	..	..	..	..	100.0	..	..
	2007	0.9	..	..	0.0	..	..	..	..	100.0	..	..
Antigua and Barbuda - Antigua-et-Barbuda	1990	696.0	0.0	0.0	0.5	0.3	0.1	12.2	0.7	70.3	11.2	5.6
	1995	1 982.5	0.0	0.1	1.3	1.2	0.1	0.2	7.8	66.9	22.9	2.2
	2000	4 677.6	0.0	0.1	1.8	4.0	0.1	0.2	6.7	39.2	53.0	0.9
	2007	10 468.4	0.0	0.3	3.2	4.6	0.2	0.3	11.4	31.2	56.0	1.0
Aruba	2007	0.1	..	..	..	..	0.0	..	..	..	..	100.0
Bahamas	1990	19 228.0	4.8	2.2	1.8	0.4	2.2	59.2	25.3	9.6	0.5	5.4
	1995	35 740.8	7.3	3.1	5.7	2.5	3.2	54.9	21.1	16.6	2.5	5.0
	2000	44 941.4	8.8	3.2	7.3	1.9	3.9	55.4	19.3	16.5	2.7	6.1
	2007	55 394.9	6.9	3.8	6.6	1.8	9.4	47.7	25.5	12.0	4.1	10.6
Barbados - Barbade	1990	8.0	..	..	0.0	..	..	..	..	100.0	..	..
	1995	114.3	0.0	..	0.0	..	0.0	66.7	..	17.5	..	15.8
	2000	1 162.0	0.2	0.1	0.2	0.0	0.1	55.0	22.7	13.3	1.5	7.4
	2007	850.2	0.1	0.1	0.2	..	0.1	28.5	36.9	25.7	..	8.9
British Virgin Islands - Îles Vierges britanniques	1990	5.0	..	..	0.0	..	..	..	..	100.0	..	..
	1995	3.9	..	..	0.0	..	0.0	..	..	82.6	..	17.4
	2000	2.1	..	..	0.0	..	0.0	..	..	68.8	..	31.2
	2007	11.5	..	..	0.0	..	0.0	..	..	10.7	..	89.3
Cayman Islands - Îles Caïmanes	1990	566.0	0.0	0.1	0.2	..	0.2	11.0	33.2	38.9	..	17.0
	1995	538.0	0.0	0.1	0.2	0.0	0.1	1.7	44.6	38.2	0.4	15.2
	2000	1 756.2	0.1	0.3	0.4	0.1	0.3	11.9	52.7	22.1	2.2	11.1
	2007	4 666.2	0.6	0.5	0.5	..	0.2	47.9	38.6	10.5	..	3.0

For sources and notes, see end of table.

Pour les sources et les notes, se reporter à la fin du tableau.

5

5.4 World merchant fleet by flag of registration and type of ship of countries and geographical regions

5.4 Flotte marchande mondiale par pavillons d'immatriculation et par types de navires des pays et des régions géographiques

Region, country or territory / Régions pays ou territoires	Year / Année	Total fleet (thousands of DWT) (1) / Flotte totale (milliers de TPL) (1)	As percentage of world total fleet / En pourcentage de la flotte mondiale — Oil tankers / Pétroliers	Bulk carriers / Vraquiers	General cargo / Navires de charge classique	Container ships / Porte-conteneurs	Other types / Autres navires	As percentage of the country or region total fleet / En pourcentage de la flotte totale du pays ou de la région — Oil tankers / Pétroliers	Bulk carriers / Vraquiers	General cargo / Navires de charge classique	Container ships / Porte-conteneurs	Other types / Autres navires
Cuba	1990	1 198.0	0.0	0.0	0.8	..	0.3	9.8	8.3	68.1	..	13.8
	1995	543.0	0.0	0.0	0.3	..	0.3	18.8	0.1	55.0	..	26.1
	2000	156.3	0.0	0.0	0.1	..	0.1	3.0	2.0	53.3	..	41.6
	2007	82.2	0.0	0.0	0.0	..	0.0	39.4	10.9	12.4	..	37.3
Dominica - Dominique	1990	5.0	..	..	0.0	..	..	..	..	100.0	..	..
	1995	2.8	..	..	0.0	..	..	..	..	100.0	..	..
	2000	2.7	..	..	0.0	..	0.0	..	..	79.9	..	20.1
	2007	1 030.5	0.1	0.1	0.1	0.0	0.0	47.2	37.6	11.9	0.6	2.7
Dominican Republic - République dominicaine	1990	68.0	0.0	0.0	0.0	..	..	2.9	27.9	69.1	..	..
	1995	11.9	0.0	..	0.0	..	0.0	13.8	..	78.1	..	8.2
	2000	8.4	..	..	0.0	..	0.0	..	..	85.6	..	14.4
	2007	7.1	..	..	0.0	..	0.0	..	..	89.1	..	10.9
Grenada - Grenade	1990	1.0	..	..	..	..	0.0	..	..	..	..	100.0
	1995	0.6	..	..	0.0	..	..	..	..	100.0	..	..
	2000	1.0	..	..	0.0	..	..	..	..	100.0	..	..
	2007	1.0	..	..	0.0	..	0.0	..	..	95.5	..	4.5
Haiti - Haïti	1995	0.2	..	..	..	..	0.0	..	..	..	..	100.0
	2000	1.0	..	..	0.0	..	0.0	..	..	82.3	..	17.7
	2007	1.0	..	..	0.0	..	0.0	..	..	82.3	..	17.7
Jamaica - Jamaïque	1990	21.0	0.0	0.0	0.0	0.0	0.0	14.3	19.0	38.1	23.8	4.8
	1995	10.5	0.0	..	0.0	..	..	31.2	..	68.8	..	..
	2000	3.3	0.0	..	..	..	0.0	92.9	..	..	..	7.1
	2007	171.7	0.0	0.0	0.0	..	0.0	1.8	76.4	21.6	..	0.3
Montserrat	1990	1.0	..	..	0.0	..	..	..	..	100.0	..	..
Netherlands Antilles - Antilles néerlandaises	2007	1 849.6	0.0	0.1	0.8	0.3	0.5	3.1	16.2	45.3	19.9	15.6
Saint Kitts and Nevis - Saint-Kitts-et-Nevis	1990	1.0	..	..	0.0	..	..	..	..	100.0	..	..
	1995	0.6	..	..	0.0	..	..	..	..	100.0	..	..
	2000	0.6	..	..	0.0	..	..	..	..	100.0	..	..
	2007	677.8	0.1	0.0	0.3	..	0.0	30.5	15.8	51.7	..	2.0
Saint Lucia - Sainte-Lucie	1990	2.0	..	..	0.0	..	..	..	..	100.0	..	..
	1995	2.3	..	..	0.0	..	..	..	..	100.0	..	..
Saint Vincent and the Grenadines - Saint-Vincent-et-les Grenadines	1990	2 282.0	0.2	0.4	0.9	0.3	0.2	15.6	39.7	38.9	2.7	3.2
	1995	8 595.4	0.6	1.4	2.9	0.6	0.6	20.4	39.0	34.3	2.6	3.8
	2000	10 131.0	0.4	1.7	3.7	0.3	1.0	10.0	44.4	36.8	1.8	7.0
	2007	8 527.4	0.1	1.2	3.3	0.1	0.6	3.3	52.2	38.9	1.4	4.2
Trinidad and Tobago - Trinité-et-Tobago	1990	16.0	..	..	0.0	..	0.0	..	..	37.5	..	62.5
	1995	17.0	..	..	0.0	..	0.0	..	..	44.2	..	55.8
	2000	8.9	0.0	..	0.0	..	0.0	16.6	..	28.9	..	54.5
	2007	15.1	0.0	..	0.0	..	0.0	27.3	..	2.7	..	70.0
Turks and Caicos Islands - Îles Turques et Caïques	1990	2.0	..	..	0.0	..	0.0	..	..	50.0	..	50.0
	1995	2.6	0.0	..	0.0	..	0.0	52.8	..	38.0	..	9.3
	2000	0.2	..	..	0.0	..	..	..	..	100.0	..	..
	2007	0.2	..	..	0.0	..	..	..	..	100.0	..	..
Central America - Amérique centrale	*1990*	*78 245.0*	*8.9*	*14.3*	*16.4*	*17.2*	*10.3*	*27.0*	*40.7*	*21.1*	*4.9*	*6.3*
	1995	*101 670.0*	*13.1*	*15.7*	*15.1*	*17.6*	*10.7*	*34.7*	*37.8*	*15.3*	*6.3*	*5.9*
	2000	*164 753.9*	*15.9*	*28.4*	*17.2*	*23.1*	*16.5*	*27.2*	*46.6*	*10.6*	*8.6*	*7.1*
	2007	*236 035.0*	*16.3*	*32.8*	*17.1*	*20.8*	*14.0*	*26.5*	*51.1*	*7.3*	*11.3*	*3.7*
Belize	1995	430.0	0.0	0.0	0.2	0.0	0.1	25.3	1.7	57.5	4.1	11.4
	2000	3 052.4	0.2	0.1	1.7	0.1	0.6	18.8	10.6	55.5	1.8	13.2
	2007	1 693.8	0.0	0.1	1.0	0.0	0.4	3.2	20.1	61.4	0.9	14.5
Costa Rica	1990	7.0	..	..	0.0	..	0.0	..	..	42.9	..	57.1
	1995	2.9	..	..	0.0	..	0.0	..	..	23.8	..	76.2
	2000	1.2	..	..	..	..	0.0	..	..	..	..	100.0
	2007	0.4	..	..	..	..	0.0	..	..	..	..	100.0
El Salvador	1990	3.0	..	..	..	..	0.0	..	..	..	..	100.0
	2007	1.7	..	..	..	..	0.0	..	..	..	..	100.0

For sources and notes, see end of table.

Pour les sources et les notes, se reporter à la fin du tableau.

5.4 World merchant fleet by flag of registration and type of ship of countries and geographical regions

5.4 Flotte marchande mondiale par pavillons d'immatriculation et par types de navires des pays et des régions géographiques

Region, country or territory / Régions pays ou territoires	Year / Année	Total fleet (thousands of DWT) (1) / Flotte totale (milliers de TPL) (1)	As percentage of world total fleet / En pourcentage de la flotte mondiale					As percentage of the country or region total fleet / En pourcentage de la flotte totale du pays ou de la région				
			Oil tankers / Pétroliers	Bulk carriers / Vraquiers	General cargo / Navires de charge classique	Container ships / Porte-conteneurs	Other types / Autres navires	Oil tankers / Pétroliers	Bulk carriers / Vraquiers	General cargo / Navires de charge classique	Container ships / Porte-conteneurs	Other types / Autres navires
Guatemala	1990	7.0	..	..	0.0	..	0.0	..	..	85.7	..	14.3
	2000	3.8	..	..	..	..	0.0	..	..	..	..	100.0
	2007	4.5	0.0	..	..	..	0.0	21.1	..	..	..	78.9
Honduras	1990	982.0	0.1	0.1	0.6	0.0	0.1	14.1	17.6	62.8	0.9	4.6
	1995	1 753.5	0.1	0.1	1.2	0.0	0.2	9.1	11.8	71.6	0.5	7.0
	2000	1 520.7	0.1	0.1	0.9	0.0	0.3	15.8	14.6	57.0	0.5	12.1
	2007	837.7	0.1	0.0	0.3	0.0	0.2	33.5	12.9	41.5	0.3	11.9
Mexico - Mexique	1990	1 883.0	0.3	0.2	0.1	0 1	1.4	42.9	18.4	3.3	0.6	34.8
	1995	1 551.5	0.3	..	0.1	0 4	1.1	45.4	..	5.0	9.0	40.6
	2000	1 226.6	0.3	..	0.0	..	0.6	62.3	..	2.0	..	35.8
	2007	1 501.1	0.3	0.0	0.1	..	0.6	68.3	1.8	4.5	..	25.4
Nicaragua	1990	3.0	..	..	0.0	..	..	..	..	100.0	..	..
	1995	1.5	..	..	0.0	..	0.0	..	..	79.2	..	20.8
	2000	2.0	..	..	0.0	..	0.0	..	..	59.4	..	40.6
	2007	2.7	0.0	..	0.0	..	0.0	33.9	..	43.4	..	22.7
Panama	1990	75 360.0	8.5	14.0	15.7	17.1	8.8	26.7	41.6	21.0	5.1	5.6
	1995	97 930.7	12.7	15.6	13.5	17.2	9.3	35.0	39.1	14.3	6.4	5.3
	2000	158 947.3	15.3	28.2	14.6	23.0	15.0	27.2	47.9	9.3	8.9	6.7
	2007	231 993.2	16.0	32.7	15.7	20.8	12.8	26.4	51.8	6.8	11.5	3.5
South America - Amérique du Sud	*1990*	*17 587.0*	*2.4*	*3.2*	*3.3*	*1.0*	*2.9*	*31.6*	*40.5*	*18.9*	*1.3*	*7.8*
	1995	*13 274.9*	*1.9*	*2.0*	*1.5*	*0.9*	*2.4*	*38.8*	*37.0*	*11.6*	*2.6*	*10.0*
	2000	*10 146.7*	*1.5*	*1.2*	*1.0*	*0.4*	*1.9*	*42.5*	*32.0*	*10.2*	*2.3*	*13.0*
	2007	*8 148.2*	*1.1*	*0.4*	*0.8*	*0.2*	*2.3*	*50.2*	*19.6*	*9.5*	*3.3*	*17.4*
Argentina - Argentine	1990	2 764.0	0.4	0.4	0.8	0.3	0.5	32.6	29.1	27.6	2.6	8.2
	1995	949.2	0.1	0.0	0.3	0.2	0.4	22.6	11.1	36.2	7.9	22.2
	2000	599.3	0.1	0.0	0.1	..	0.3	30.1	8.7	21.9	..	39.3
	2007	1 162.9	0.2	0.0	0.1	0.0	0.4	53.9	14.6	9.9	1.6	19.9
Bolivia - Bolivie	1990	16.0	..	..	0.0	..	..	..	..	100.0	..	..
	2000	244.5	0.0	0.0	0.1	0.0	0.0	11.4	35.7	44.1	3.4	5.5
	2007	143.9	0.0	0.0	0.0	..	0.0	54.5	4.7	33.1	..	7.7
Brazil - Brésil	1990	10 063.0	1.4	2.3	1.1	0.5	1.1	32.2	50.6	10.9	1.1	5.2
	1995	8 887.6	1.4	1.6	0.5	0.7	0.8	42.8	44.0	5.5	2.7	5.0
	2000	6 383.6	1.1	0.9	0.4	0.3	0.3	48.0	39.8	6.1	2.6	3.5
	2007	3 314.6	0.4	0.2	0.3	0.2	0.5	50.2	24.7	8.6	6.9	9.6
Chile - Chili	1990	870.0	..	0.2	0.2	..	0.3	..	63.4	22.8	..	13.8
	1995	984.9	0.0	0.2	0.1	..	0.4	7.2	56.3	13.8	..	22.6
	2000	1 012.0	0.1	0.1	0.1	0.1	0.5	16.4	34.5	12.0	5.0	32.1
	2007	1 147.9	0.1	0.1	0.1	0.0	0.3	43.4	28.2	8.4	1.8	18.1
Colombia - Colombie	1990	546.0	0.0	0.1	0.4	.	0.0	2.7	28.8	65.0	..	3.5
	1995	183.1	0.0	..	0.2	.	0.0	5.3	..	84.9	..	9.8
	2000	119.4	0.0	..	0.1	.	0.0	8.3	..	67.7	..	24.1
	2007	121.3	0.0	..	0.1	.	0.1	10.6	..	52.8	..	36.6
Ecuador - Équateur	1990	531.0	0.1	0.0	0.2	..	0.1	39.4	7.2	47.1	..	6.4
	1995	358.5	0.0	0.0	0.2	..	0.1	36.8	10.5	44.0	..	8.7
	2000	446.6	0.1	..	0.0	..	0.1	86.3	..	0.8	..	12.9
	2007	355.0	0.1	..	0.0	..	0.1	82.0	..	0.9	..	17.1
Falkland Islands (Malvinas) - Îles Falkland (Malvinas)	1990	4.0	..	..	..	..	0.0	..	..	..	..	100.0
	1995	9.8	..	..	0.0	..	0.0	..	..	6.4	..	93.6
	2000	31.1	..	..	0.0	..	0.0	..	..	2.0	..	98.0
	2007	37.0	..	..	0.0	..	0.1	.	..	1.3	..	98.7
Guyana	1990	11.0	..	..	0.0	..	0.0	.	..	45.5	..	54.5
	1995	13.9	..	..	0.0	..	0.0	.	..	58.5	..	41.5
	2000	12.5	..	..	0.0	..	0.0	.	..	53.8	..	46.2
	2007	36.9	0.0	..	0.0	..	0.0	18.6	..	62.0	..	19.4
Paraguay	1990	44.0	0.0	..	0.0	..	0.0	2.3	..	59.1	..	38.6
	1995	36.2	0.0	..	0.0	..	0.0	7.9	..	82.3	..	9.9
	2000	48.8	0.0	..	0.0	0.0	0.0	18.2	..	73.3	4.5	4.0
	2007	50.6	0.0	..	0.0	0.0	0.0	7.7	..	85.7	4.3	2.3

For sources and notes, see end of table.

Pour les sources et les notes, se reporter à la fin du tableau.

5.4 **World merchant fleet by flag of registration and type of ship of countries and geographical regions**

5.4 **Flotte marchande mondiale par pavillons d'immatriculation et par types de navires des pays et des régions géographiques**

Region, country or territory / Régions pays ou territoires	Year / Année	Total fleet (thousands of DWT) (1) / Flotte totale (milliers de TPL) (1)	As percentage of world total fleet / En pourcentage de la flotte mondiale					As percentage of the country or region total fleet / En pourcentage de la flotte totale du pays ou de la région				
			Oil tankers / Pétroliers	Bulk carriers / Vraquiers	General cargo / Navires de charge classique	Container ships / Porte-conteneurs	Other types / Autres navires	Oil tankers / Pétroliers	Bulk carriers / Vraquiers	General cargo / Navires de charge classique	Container ships / Porte-conteneurs	Other types / Autres navires
Peru - Pérou	1990	841.0	0.1	0.1	0.2	..	0.1	40.1	25.7	28.2	..	6.1
	1995	317.3	0.0	0.0	0.1	..	0.1	41.2	15.9	24.2	..	18.7
	2000	267.0	0.0	0.0	0.1	..	0.1	29.7	9.6	30.4	..	30.4
	2007	151.1	0.0	..	0.0	..	0.1	17.9	..	24.5	..	57.6
Suriname	1990	15.0	0.0	..	0.0	0.0	0.0	13.3	..	66.7	13.3	6.7
	1995	9.7	0.0	..	0.0	0.0	0.0	31.3	..	42.5	18.3	7.9
	2000	7.2	0.0	..	0.0	..	0.0	42.1	..	43.8	..	14.2
	2007	6.8	0.0	..	0.0	..	0.0	49.9	..	46.4	..	3.7
Uruguay	1990	155.0	0.0	..	0.0	0.2	0.1	60.6	..	1.9	21.9	15.5
	1995	150.3	0.0	..	0.0	0.1	0.0	62.1	..	1.8	18.7	17.4
	2000	38.1	0.0	..	0.0	..	0.0	22.0	..	3.3	..	74.7
	2007	65.9	0.0	..	0.0	..	0.1	20.5	..	13.2	..	66.3
Venezuela (Bolivarian Rep. of) - Venezuela (Rép. bolivarienne du)	1990	1 727.0	0.3	0.1	0.4	0.0	0.7	43.9	15.3	21.1	0.2	19.5
	1995	1 374.3	0.3	0.1	0.1	0.0	0.5	50.1	18.4	10.5	0.1	20.9
	2000	936.7	0.1	0.1	0.1	0.0	0.4	40.1	20.7	8.1	0.1	31.0
	2007	1 554.3	0.2	0.1	0.0	0.0	0.6	55.5	17.6	3.0	0.2	23.6
Developing economies: Asia - Économies en développement : Asie	**1990**	**115 295.0**	**12.6**	**23.2**	**23.8**	**18.2**	**12.1**	**25.7**	**45.0**	**20.7**	**3.5**	**5.0**
	1995	**132 218.5**	**12.7**	**24.6**	**23.5**	**18.0**	**12.2**	**25.9**	**45.7**	**18.4**	**5.0**	**5.1**
	2000	**148 205.1**	**14.7**	**22.8**	**25.0**	**17.2**	**13.4**	**27.9**	**41.5**	**17.1**	**7.1**	**6.4**
	2007	**236 526.8**	**22.0**	**25.0**	**29.1**	**16.5**	**16.1**	**35.6**	**38.9**	**12.4**	**8.9**	**4.3**
Eastern Asia - Asie orientale	*1990*	*43 401.0*	*2.4*	*10.8*	*9.8*	*9.3*	*3.8*	*12.8*	*55.5*	*22.8*	*4.8*	*4.2*
	1995	*48 822.3*	*2.3*	*11.2*	*9.1*	*10.2*	*3.4*	*12.7*	*56.6*	*19.2*	*7.6*	*3.9*
	2000	*46 394.3*	*1.8*	*9.6*	*9.0*	*6.6*	*3.1*	*11.0*	*55.7*	*19.7*	*8.8*	*4.8*
	2007	*112 423.9*	*6.4*	*16.8*	*11.7*	*9.1*	*3.9*	*21.9*	*55.0*	*10.5*	*10.4*	*2.1*
China - Chine (c)	1990	20 200.0	1.1	3.6	7.7	4.0	1.8	13.2	39.9	38.2	4.5	4.2
	1995	23 357.0	1.4	4.1	6.9	4.5	1.7	15.7	42.8	30.4	7.1	4.0
	2000	23 701.2	1.2	4.1	6.4	2.7	1.6	14.3	46.8	27.2	7.0	4.7
	2007	39 159.5	2.4	4.9	6.4	3.5	1.8	23.3	45.9	16.6	11.4	2.9
China, Hong Kong SAR - Chine (RAS de Hong Kong)	1990	10 337.0	0.6	3.5	0.4	2.1	0.6	13.1	75.2	4.2	4.5	2.8
	1995	13 588.7	0.5	4.4	0.7	1.9	0.3	9.2	79.1	5.4	5.1	1.1
	2000	13 190.9	0.3	3.6	0.9	2.4	0.1	7.1	73.9	7.2	11.2	0.6
	2007	54 734.0	3.4	8.9	2.7	4.5	0.8	23.9	59.7	4.9	10.6	0.9
China, Macao SAR - Chine (RAS de Macao)	2007	2.2	..	..	..	..	0.0	..	..	..	..	100.0
Dem. People's Rep. of Korea - Rép. populaire dém. de Corée	1990	529.0	0.0	0.0	0.4	..	0.0	3.8	20.6	71.6	..	4.0
	1995	1 079.1	0.1	0.1	0.6	..	0.1	21.6	19.3	54.4	..	4.7
	2000	846.6	0.0	0.0	0.7	..	0.1	1.4	10.4	80.7	..	7.6
	2007	1 444.9	0.0	0.1	1.0	0.0	0.1	7.0	18.3	69.6	1.6	3.6
Mongolia - Mongolie	2007	627.0	0.0	0.1	0.3	..	0.0	7.1	36.7	53.7	..	2.4
Republic of Korea - République de Corée	1990	12 335.0	0.6	3.6	1.4	3.2	1.3	12.2	65.8	11.0	5.8	5.2
	1995	10 797.5	0.4	2.7	0.9	3.8	1.4	9.5	61.7	9.0	12.7	7.2
	2000	8 655.5	0.3	1.8	1.1	1.5	1.3	8.9	56.8	12.3	11.0	11.1
	2007	16 456.3	0.6	2.9	1.3	1.1	1.1	13.9	65.0	8.2	8.6	4.3
Southern Asia - Asie méridionale	*1990*	*20 524.0*	*3.9*	*3.2*	*3.5*	*..*	*1.4*	*45.3*	*34.6*	*16.9*	*..*	*3.3*
	1995	*19 013.2*	*3.3*	*2.8*	*2.4*	*0.3*	*1.6*	*46.3*	*35.6*	*13.0*	*0.5*	*4.6*
	2000	*18 704.6*	*3.0*	*2.4*	*2.4*	*0.3*	*1.7*	*45.2*	*34.5*	*13.1*	*1.0*	*6.3*
	2007	*24 504.6*	*4.0*	*1.5*	*1.8*	*0.5*	*2.0*	*62.7*	*22.2*	*7.3*	*2.6*	*5.2*
Bangladesh	1990	587.0	0.0	..	0.5	..	0.0	14.1	..	83.5	..	2.4
	1995	532.4	0.0	..	0.4	..	0.0	16.2	..	80.5	..	3.3
	2000	518.7	0.0	0.0	0.4	..	0.0	19.6	1.7	74.9	..	3.8
	2007	617.6	0.0	0.0	0.3	0.0	0.0	16.6	14.4	56.2	10.0	2.8
India - Inde	1990	10 207.0	1.2	2.3	1.6	..	1.0	28.5	50.9	15.9	..	4.7
	1995	10 508.4	1.6	1.9	0.9	0.3	1.2	39.7	44.2	8.7	1.0	6.4
	2000	11 209.3	1.7	1.7	0.6	0.2	1.4	43.1	41.3	5.9	1.2	8.6
	2007	13 904.4	2.3	1.0	0.3	0.1	1.8	63.1	25.7	2.1	1.2	7.9
Iran (Islamic Rep. of) - Iran (Rép. islamique d')	1990	8 685.0	2.6	0.8	0.6	..	0.3	71.3	20.4	6.5	..	1.8
	1995	6 840.0	1.6	0.7	0.6	0.0	0.3	63.0	25.7	9.0	0.0	2.3
	2000	6 097.3	1.2	0.6	0.9	0.0	0.2	55.9	26.4	14.8	0.2	2.6
	2007	8 952.8	1.6	0.5	0.7	0.3	0.2	67.9	19.1	7.7	3.9	1.4

For sources and notes, see end of table.

Pour les sources et les notes, se reporter à la fin du tableau.

5.4 World merchant fleet by flag of registration and type of ship of countries and geographical regions

5.4 Flotte marchande mondiale par pavillons d'immatriculation et par types de navires des pays et des régions géographiques

Region, country or territory / Régions pays ou territoires	Year / Année	Total fleet (thousands of DWT) (1) / Flotte totale (milliers de TPL) (1)	As percentage of world total fleet / En pourcentage de la flotte mondiale					As percentage of the country or region total fleet / En pourcentage de la flotte totale du pays ou de la région				
			Oil tankers / Pétroliers	Bulk carriers / Vraquiers	General cargo / Navires de charge classique	Container ships / Porte-conteneurs	Other types / Autres navires	Oil tankers / Pétroliers	Bulk carriers / Vraquiers	General cargo / Navires de charge classique	Container ships / Porte-conteneurs	Other types / Autres navires
Maldives	1990	148.0	0.0	0.0	0.1	..	0.0	6.8	48.6	43.2	..	1.4
	1995	106.8	0.0	0.0	0.1	..	0.0	11.9	18.3	62.7	..	7.2
	2000	132.8	0.0	..	0.1	..	0.0	6.5	..	88.5	..	4.9
	2007	132.6	0.0	..	0.1	..	0.0	13.3	..	82.7	..	4.0
Pakistan	1990	526.0	0.0	..	0.4	..	0.0	17.1	..	80.8	..	2.1
	1995	575.0	0.0	0.1	0.3	..	0.0	15.8	28.2	54.0	..	2.1
	2000	458.7	0.0	0.0	0.3	0.1	0.0	19.8	11.4	56.8	9.1	2.9
	2007	673.1	0.1	0.0	0.2	0.0	0.0	57.6	9.8	27.3	3.2	2.1
Sri Lanka	1990	371.0	0.0	0.0	0.3	..	0.0	4.0	14.8	80.1	..	1.1
	1995	450.6	0.0	0.1	0.1	..	0.0	29.2	40.0	29.9	..	0.9
	2000	287.6	0.0	0.1	0.1	..	0.0	3.5	52.0	42.2	..	2.4
	2007	224.1	0.0	0.0	0.2	0.0	0.0	6.5	5.5	68.3	14.3	5.3
South-Eastern Asia - Asie du Sud-Est	*1990*	*35 050.0*	*2.8*	*7.9*	*6.9*	*6.5*	*4.9*	*19.0*	*50.2*	*19.9*	*4.1*	*6.7*
	1995	*45 436.4*	*4.4*	*8.0*	*8.3*	*6.2*	*5.3*	*26.3*	*43.4*	*18.8*	*4.9*	*6.5*
	2000	*62 945.1*	*7.7*	*8.0*	*9.4*	*8.3*	*6.9*	*34.5*	*34.5*	*15.2*	*8.1*	*7.8*
	2007	*83 678.9*	*9.8*	*5.6*	*12.6*	*5.9*	*8.8*	*44.8*	*24.5*	*15.2*	*9.0*	*6.6*
Brunei Darussalam - Brunéi Darussalam	1990	346.0	..	..	0.0	..	0.7	..	..	0.3	..	99.7
	1995	352.8	0.0	..	0.0	..	0.6	0.1	..	1.4	..	98.6
	2000	349.6	0.0	..	0.0	..	0.5	0.1	..	0.7	..	99.2
	2007	420.7	0.0	..	0.0	..	0.7	0.4	..	0.5	..	99.2
Cambodia - Cambodge	1990	4.0	..	..	0.0	..	0.0	..	..	25.0	..	75.0
	2007	2 699.1	0.0	0.2	1.7	0.0	0.1	4.8	27.3	64.1	1.8	2.0
Indonesia - Indonésie	1990	2 742.0	0.4	0.1	1.2	0.3	0.5	35.2	7.7	45.4	2.7	9.0
	1995	3 403.6	0.4	0.1	1.6	0.3	0.6	31.4	7.5	49.1	2.7	9.4
	2000	4 153.7	0.5	0.2	1.8	0.1	0.5	32.1	14.8	43.5	1.4	8.2
	2007	6 268.3	0.5	0.2	2.5	0.4	0.7	32.7	12.6	40.4	7.4	6.9
Lao People's dem. Rep. - Rép. dém. populaire lao	2007	4.7	..	..	0.0	..	..	..	..	100.0	..	..
Malaysia - Malaisie	1990	2 364.0	0.1	0.3	0.7	1.0	1.1	12.0	26.9	29.6	9.8	21.8
	1995	4 134.2	0.2	0.6	0.7	1.0	1.8	15.8	35.0	16.7	8.5	24.0
	2000	7 577.5	0.6	1.0	0.9	1.3	2.3	21.6	35.3	11.4	10.5	21.3
	2007	8 570.8	1.2	0.2	0.6	0.7	3.3	52.0	6.9	6.9	9.8	24.3
Myanmar	1990	907.0	0.0	0.3	0.2	..	0.1	0.4	72.5	23.5	..	3.5
	1995	934.1	0.0	0.2	0.3	0.1	0.0	0.5	64.3	29.6	2.7	2.9
	2000	792.3	0.0	0.2	0.2	0.0	0.0	0.6	63.7	30.8	3.2	1.7
	2007	574.1	0.0	0.1	0.2	..	0.0	0.8	63.0	33.8	..	2.4
Philippines	1990	15 468.0	0.3	5.5	2.1	0.3	0.3	5.0	79.9	13.7	0.4	1.1
	1995	14 765.8	0.3	4.6	2.1	0.5	0.4	5.4	77.0	15.0	1.2	1.4
	2000	11 112.0	0.1	3.1	2.0	0.3	0.5	2.1	74.7	18.5	1.4	3.2
	2007	6 697.9	0.2	1.1	1.6	0.1	0.4	9.7	59.8	23.6	2.7	4.1
Singapore - Singapour	1990	11 888.0	1.9	1.7	1.7	4.6	2.1	37.6	31.2	14.2	8.6	8.4
	1995	18 520.0	3.3	2.3	1.8	4.1	1.1	48.0	30.4	10.2	8.1	3.3
	2000	34 635.5	6.3	3.2	2.6	6.3	2.6	50.9	25.0	7.5	11.2	5.4
	2007	50 981.1	7.6	3.3	2.6	4.3	3.0	56.8	23.6	5.1	10.9	3.6
Thailand - Thaïlande	1990	805.0	0.1	0.0	0.6	0.2	0.1	16.0	2.1	70.2	6.2	5.5
	1995	2 111.7	0.1	0.2	1.1	0.3	0.2	16.8	18.2	55.5	5.3	4.2
	2000	3 068.4	0.2	0.3	1.3	0.3	0.2	22.4	25.6	42.7	5.2	4.1
	2007	4 318.3	0.2	0.4	1.6	0.3	0.2	15.2	35.1	38.3	8.1	3.4
Viet Nam	1990	526.0	0.0	0.0	0.4	..	0.0	6.5	4.6	85.9	..	3.0
	1995	1 214.2	0.1	0.0	0.6	..	0.7	15.5	3.0	51.3	..	30.3
	2000	1 256.1	0.1	0.1	0.7	0.0	0.3	13.5	12.0	54.3	1.3	18.9
	2007	3 144.0	0.2	0.1	1.8	0.1	0.4	19.5	13.8	57.1	2.5	7.1
Western Asia - Asie occidentale	*1990*	*16 320.0*	*3.5*	*1.4*	*3.5*	*2.4*	*1.9*	*50.2*	*19.0*	*21.8*	*3.3*	*5.7*
	1995	*18 946.5*	*2.7*	*2.5*	*3.8*	*1.3*	*1.9*	*38.5*	*33.0*	*20.5*	*2.5*	*5.4*
	2000	*20 161.2*	*2.2*	*2.8*	*4.1*	*1.9*	*1.7*	*30.1*	*37.5*	*20.5*	*5.9*	*6.0*
	2007	*15 919.4*	*1.7*	*1.1*	*3.0*	*1.0*	*1.4*	*41.5*	*26.1*	*18.9*	*8.0*	*5.5*
Bahrain - Bahreïn	1990	65.0	0.0	0.0	0.0	..	0.0	3.1	30.8	41.5	..	24.6
	1995	243.3	0.0	0.0	0.1	..	0.1	40.4	5.4	40.6	..	13.6
	2000	369.8	0.0	0.0	0.1	0.2	0.0	26.2	11.9	26.5	27.0	8.3
	2007	410.1	0.0	0.0	0.1	0.0	0.1	37.5	20.8	1.0	24.3	16.3

For sources and notes, see end of table.

Pour les sources et les notes, se reporter à la fin du tableau.

5

5.4 World merchant fleet by flag of registration and type of ship of countries and geographical regions

5.4 Flotte marchande mondiale par pavillons d'immatriculation et par types de navires des pays et des régions géographiques

Region, country or territory / Régions pays ou territoires	Year / Année	Total fleet (thousands of DWT) (1) / Flotte totale (milliers de TPL) (1)	As percentage of world total fleet / En pourcentage de la flotte mondiale					As percentage of the country or region total fleet / En pourcentage de la flotte totale du pays ou de la région				
			Oil tankers / Pétroliers	Bulk carriers / Vraquiers	General cargo / Navires de charge classique	Container ships / Porte-conteneurs	Other types / Autres navires	Oil tankers / Pétroliers	Bulk carriers / Vraquiers	General cargo / Navires de charge classique	Container ships / Porte-conteneurs	Other types / Autres navires
Iraq	1990	1 813.0	0.7	..	0.1	..	0.3	85.6	..	7.5	..	6.9
	1995	1 548.0	0.5	..	0.1	..	0.2	87.3	..	7.0	..	5.7
	2000	834.7	0.2	..	0.1	..	0.1	79.0	..	12.6	..	8.4
	2007	175.8	0.0	..	0.1	..	0.1	29.0	..	31.3	..	39.7
Jordan - Jordanie	1990	48.0	..	0.0	..	..	0.0	..	91.7	..	..	8.3
	1995	113.3	0.0	0.0	..	..	0.0	85.8	13.9	..	..	0.2
	2000	59.3	..	0.0	0.0	0.0	0.0	..	56.3	32.1	11.2	0.4
	2007	543.3	0.1	0.0	0.1	0.0	0.0	53.9	9.7	26.4	6.2	3.8
Kuwait - Koweït	1990	2 887.0	0.8	..	0.5	0.7	0.6	65.9	..	18.8	5.1	10.2
	1995	3 236.4	0.9	..	0.3	0.3	0.7	74.8	..	11.1	2.8	11.2
	2000	3 884.4	1.1	0.0	0.3	0.4	0.5	76.2	0.7	7.9	5.8	9.4
	2007	3 442.8	0.7	0.0	0.1	0.2	0.4	80.6	2.7	2.5	6.6	7.6
Lebanon - Liban	1990	593.0	0.0	0.1	0.4	0.0	0.0	3.9	26.3	68.1	0.5	1.2
	1995	407.5	0.0	0.0	0.3	0.0	0.0	0.6	18.8	79.2	0.3	1.1
	2000	483.2	0.0	0.1	0.2	0.0	0.0	0.3	52.5	44.7	1.5	1.0
	2007	190.9	0.0	0.0	0.1	..	0.0	0.8	42.1	53.2	..	4.0
Oman	1990	13.0	..	..	0.0	..	0.0	..	..	53.8	..	46.2
	1995	10.6	0.0	..	0.0	..	0.0	4.3	..	28.3	..	67.4
	2000	10.9	0.0	..	0.0	..	0.0	4.2	..	27.5	..	68.2
	2007	13.2	0.0	..	0.0	..	0.0	9.3	..	12.5	..	78.2
Qatar	1990	459.0	0.1	..	0.2	0.4	0.0	43.8	..	32.9	20.0	3.3
	1995	915.7	0.1	0.1	0.2	0.3	0.0	36.2	29.5	22.6	10.0	1.6
	2000	1 154.0	0.2	0.1	0.2	0.3	0.0	40.4	23.4	17.5	17.1	1.5
	2007	932.6	0.2	0.0	0.1	0.2	0.1	62.3	2.3	5.6	21.6	8.1
Saudi Arabia - Arabie saoudite	1990	3 535.0	1.0	0.1	0.7	0.3	0.5	63.4	8.8	18.6	2.1	7.0
	1995	1 282.9	0.1	..	0.6	0.2	0.4	28.6	..	48.4	5.6	17.4
	2000	1 443.0	0.1	..	0.6	0.4	0.3	28.4	..	39.6	15.0	17.1
	2007	1 243.9	0.2	..	0.3	0.1	0.1	56.2	..	25.7	12.5	5.5
Syrian Arab Republic - République arabe syrienne	1990	102.0	..	..	0.1	..	0.0	..	..	97.1	..	2.9
	1995	445.4	..	0.0	0.4	..	..	..	17.1	82.9	..	..
	2000	679.4	..	0.0	0.6	..	0.0	..	6.5	92.1	..	1.4
	2007	569.1	0.0	0.0	0.5	0.0	0.0	0.4	12.5	85.4	1.5	0.3
Turkey - Turquie	1990	5 477.0	0.6	1.1	1.3	..	0.2	27.0	46.3	24.6	..	2.2
	1995	9 113.9	0.6	2.3	1.5	0.0	0.3	18.7	62.8	16.5	0.1	1.8
	2000	10 174.2	0.4	2.5	1.7	0.3	0.4	10.4	67.3	17.2	2.1	3.0
	2007	7 253.5	0.4	1.0	1.6	0.2	0.2	21.3	49.7	22.8	4.4	1.9
United Arab Emirates - Émirats arabes unis	1990	1 316.0	0.3	0.0	0.2	1.0	0.2	59.4	2.9	14.6	16.6	6.5
	1995	1 603.0	0.3	0.0	0.3	0.6	0.2	57.2	5.2	17.6	13.2	6.8
	2000	1 042.5	0.1	0.0	0.2	0.4	0.2	39.3	3.5	22.6	21.8	12.8
	2007	1 118.8	0.1	0.0	0.1	0.2	0.3	43.9	12.7	9.1	20.3	14.1
Yemen - Yémen	1990	12.0	0.0	..	0.0	..	0.0	25.0	..	33.3	..	41.7
	1995	26.4	0.0	..	0.0	..	0.0	12.1	..	10.9	..	77.0
	2000	25.8	0.0	..	0.0	..	0.0	12.3	..	11.9	..	75.8
	2007	25.5	0.0	..	0.0	..	0.0	66.7	..	9.1	..	24.2
Developing economies: Oceania - Économies en développement : Océanie (2)	**1990**	**1 814.0**	**0.1**	**0.4**	**0.4**	**0.2**	**0.3**	**15.5**	**48.5**	**24.9**	**2.8**	**8.4**
	1995	**2 754.7**	**0.0**	**0.7**	**0.6**	**0.1**	**0.8**	**1.1**	**60.6**	**21.6**	**1.1**	**15.6**
	2000	**1 931.6**	**0.0**	**0.3**	**0.5**	**0.1**	**0.7**	**1.2**	**44.4**	**25.4**	**1.8**	**27.2**
	2007	**57 584.2**	**9.0**	**3.7**	**2.2**	**3.9**	**3.6**	**60.0**	**23.4**	**3.9**	**8.7**	**4.0**
American Samoa - Samoa américaines	2007	0.9	..	..	..	..	0.0	..	..	..	..	100.0
Fiji - Fidji	1990	64.0	0.0	..	0.0	..	0.0	10.9	..	71.9	..	17.2
	1995	27.4	0.0	..	0.0	..	0.0	17.2	..	40.5	..	42.4
	2000	24.4	0.0	..	0.0	..	0.0	14.8	..	23.6	..	61.6
	2007	15.4	..	..	0.0	..	0.0	..	..	44.1	..	55.9
French Polynesia - Polynésie française	2007	31.2	..	..	0.0	..	0.0	..	..	78.2	..	21.8
Guam	2007	1.6	..	..	..	..	0.0	..	..	..	..	100.0
Kiribati	1990	3.0	..	..	0.0	..	..	..	..	100.0	..	..
	1995	4.7	..	..	0.0	..	0.0	..	..	85.2	..	14.8
	2000	4.1	..	..	0.0	..	0.0	..	..	84.0	..	16.0
	2007	40.8	0.0	0.0	0.0	..	0.0	2.4	66.1	29.9	..	1.6

For sources and notes, see end of table.

Pour les sources et les notes, se reporter à la fin du tableau.

5.4   World merchant fleet by flag of registration and type of ship of countries and geographical regions

5.4   Flotte marchande mondiale par pavillons d'immatriculation et par types de navires des pays et des régions géographiques

Region, country or territory / Régions pays ou territoires	Year / Année	Total fleet (thousands of DWT) (1) / Flotte totale (milliers de TPL) (1)	As percentage of world total fleet / En pourcentage de la flotte mondiale					As percentage of the country or region total fleet / En pourcentage de la flotte totale du pays ou de la région				
			Oil tankers / Pétroliers	Bulk carriers / Vraquiers	General cargo / Navires de charge classique	Container ships / Porte-conteneurs	Other types / Autres navires	Oil tankers / Pétroliers	Bulk carriers / Vraquiers	General cargo / Navires de charge classique	Container ships / Porte-conteneurs	Other types / Autres navires
Marshall Islands - Îles Marshall (2)	2007	54 278.1	8.9	3.2	1.6	3.9	2.6	63.0	21.9	2.9	9.1	3.0
Nauru	1990	45.0	..	0.0	0.0	..	0.0	..	60.0	42.2	..	2.2
New Caledonia - Nouvelle-Calédonie	2007	5.1	..	..	0.0	..	0.0	..	..	52.1	..	47.9
Papua New Guinea - Papouasie-Nouvelle-Guinée	1990	42.0	0.0	0.0	0.0	..	0.0	4.8	11.9	57.1	..	26.2
	1995	51.1	0.0	..	0.0	..	0.0	9.9	..	82.9	..	7.2
	2000	70.9	0.0	..	0.1	..	0.0	3.9	..	77.8	..	18.4
	2007	98.3	0.0	0.0	0.1	..	0.0	3.4	9.3	80.5	..	6.8
Samoa	1990	35.0	..	..	0.0	..	0.0	..	..	97.1	..	2.9
	1995	6.5	..	..	0.0	..	0.0	..	..	93.3	..	6.7
	2007	9.8	..	..	0.0	..	0.0	..	..	93.9	..	6.1
Solomon Islands - Îles Salomon	1990	7.0	..	..	0.0	..	0.0	..	..	71.4	..	28.6
	1995	5.7	..	..	0.0	..	0.0	..	..	54.9	..	45.1
	2000	6.9	..	..	0.0	..	0.0	..	..	35.9	..	64.1
	2007	5.4	..	..	0.0	..	0.0	..	..	34.6	..	65.4
Tonga	1990	43.0	..	..	0.0	0.1	0.0	..	..	27.9	69.8	2.3
	1995	12.3	..	..	0.0	..	0.0	..	..	89.7	..	10.3
	2000	29.3	..	..	0.0	..	0.0	..	..	63.1	..	36.9
	2007	88.1	0.0	0.0	0.1	..	0.0	1.3	7.6	81.2	..	9.8
Tuvalu	1990	1.0	..	..	0.0	..	..	..	..	100.0	..	..
	1995	77.2	..	..	0.0	..	0.1	..	..	24.0	..	76.0
	2000	68.4	..	..	0.0	..	0.1	..	..	37.6	..	62.4
	2007	519.2	0.0	0.0	0.2	0.0	0.0	33.3	16.8	42.8	2.4	4.8
Vanuatu	1990	1 574.0	0.1	0.4	0.3	0.1	0.3	17.3	53.9	19.5	1.3	8.0
	1995	2 569.8	0.0	0.7	0.5	0.1	0.6	0.8	65.0	19.4	1.2	13.6
	2000	1 727.7	0.0	0.3	0.4	0.1	0.6	1.0	49.7	21.9	2.0	25.4
	2007	2 490.1	0.0	0.4	0.2	0.0	0.9	7.7	58.4	9.4	1.2	23.3
Economies in transition: Asia - Économies en transition : Asie	**1995**	**1 131.2**	**0.2**	**0.1**	**0.1**	**..**	**0.3**	**50.8**	**23.4**	**10.1**	**..**	**15.6**
	2000	**732.5**	**0.1**	**0.0**	**0.2**	**..**	**0.3**	**48.6**	**0.9**	**22.4**	**..**	**28.0**
	2007	**2 335.5**	**0.1**	**0.2**	**0.8**	**0.0**	**0.4**	**24.2**	**27.6**	**35.3**	**1.1**	**11.8**
Azerbaijan - Azerbaïdjan	1995	476.6	0.1	..	0.1	..	0.3	48.4	..	21.7	..	29.9
	2000	507.5	0.1	..	0.1	..	0.2	45.8	..	20.2	..	33.9
	2007	602.0	0.1	..	0.1	..	0.3	52.3	..	18.6	..	29.1
Georgia - Géorgie	1995	634.6	0.1	0.1	0.0	..	0.0	54.0	41.8	0.4	..	3.9
	2000	183.8	0.0	0.0	0.0	..	0.0	65.3	0.1	24.8	..	9.8
	2007	1 605.4	0.0	0.2	0.7	0.0	0.1	11.2	39.9	43.4	1.6	3.9
Kazakhstan	1995	4.2	..	..	0.0	..	0.0	..	..	15.1	..	84.9
	2000	4.7	..	..	0.0	..	0.0	..	..	16.6	..	83.4
	2007	80.0	0.0	..	0.0	..	0.0	77.5	..	2.5	..	20.0
Turkmenistan - Turkménistan	1995	15.8	0.0	..	0.0	..	0.0	10.3	..	51.0	..	38.8
	2000	36.5	0.0	0.0	0.0	..	0.0	9.3	18.3	41.6	..	30.8
	2007	48.2	0.0	0.0	0.0	..	0.0	17.4	6.9	32.2	..	43.5
Economies in transition: Europe - Économies en transition : Europe	**1995**	**23 721.4**	**1.4**	**2.0**	**10.1**	**1.8**	**7.0**	**16.2**	**20.7**	**43.8**	**2.8**	**16.5**
	2000	**12 865.7**	**0.8**	**0.9**	**5.2**	**0.8**	**3.5**	**16.8**	**19.0**	**41.2**	**3.6**	**19.5**
	2007	**10 782.6**	**0.7**	**0.6**	**4.2**	**0.1**	**2.5**	**24.1**	**20.2**	**39.7**	**1.3**	**14.7**
Albania - Albanie	1990	63.0	..	..	0.1	..	..	..	..	100.0	..	..
	1995	81.0	..	..	0.1	..	..	..	..	100.0	..	..
	2000	20.1	..	..	0.0	..	0.0	..	..	93.8	..	6.2
	2007	107.4	..	..	0.1	..	0.0	..	..	98.7	..	1.3
Croatia - Croatie	1995	269.1	0.0	0.0	0.1	0.1	0.0	11.4	11.6	51.7	17.1	8.2
	2000	1 227.7	0.0	0.3	0.2	0.2	0.0	1.1	70.7	17.7	8.0	2.5
	2007	1 793.4	0.2	0.3	0.1	..	0.1	33.2	57.3	7.6	..	1.9
Moldova	2007	17.3	..	..	0.0	..	..	..	..	100.0	..	..
Russian Federation - Fédération de Russie	1995	17 182.1	1.4	1.2	6.6	1.3	5.9	21.5	16.6	39.9	2.8	19.1
	2000	9 950.4	0.7	0.5	4.1	0.5	2.9	20.6	13.2	42.0	3.2	21.0
	2007	7 723.0	0.5	0.3	3.3	0.1	2.2	25.3	12.8	43.0	1.5	17.4
Serbia and Montenegro - Serbie-et-Monténégro	2007	10.7	..	..	0.0	..	0.0	..	..	95.3	..	4.7

For sources and notes, see end of table.   Pour les sources et les notes, se reporter à la fin du tableau.

5.4 World merchant fleet by flag of registration and type of ship of countries and geographical regions

5.4 Flotte marchande mondiale par pavillons d'immatriculation et par types de navires des pays et des régions géographiques

Region, country or territory / Régions pays ou territoires	Year / Année	Total fleet (thousands of DWT) (1) / Flotte totale (milliers de TPL) (1)	As percentage of world total fleet / En pourcentage de la flotte mondiale					As percentage of the country or region total fleet / En pourcentage de la flotte totale du pays ou de la région				
			Oil tankers / Pétroliers	Bulk carriers / Vraquiers	General cargo / Navires de charge classique	Container ships / Porte-conteneurs	Other types / Autres navires	Oil tankers / Pétroliers	Bulk carriers / Vraquiers	General cargo / Navires de charge classique	Container ships / Porte-conteneurs	Other types / Autres navires
SFR of Yugoslavia (former) - RSF de Yougoslavie (anc.)	1990	5 815.0	0.2	1.5	1.8	0.5	0.1	9.1	57.2	30.9	2.0	0.8
Ukraine	1995	6 189.3	0.0	0.8	3.2	0.4	1.1	2.0	32.7	53.4	2.1	9.8
	2000	1 667.5	0.0	0.1	0.9	0.1	0.5	5.4	15.9	52.8	2.7	23.1
	2007	1 130.8	0.0	0.0	0.7	0.0	0.3	4.5	14.2	60.6	2.4	18.3
USSR (former) - URSS (anc.)	1990	29 212.0	2.6	3.0	10.5	2.7	10.9	21.2	22.7	36.2	2.1	17.9
Developed economies: America - Économies développées : Amérique (2)	**1990**	**31 335.0**	**9.0**	**0.9**	**2.0**	**13.0**	**6.7**	**67.6**	**6.3**	**6.5**	**9.3**	**10.2**
	1995	**27 067.0**	**6.0**	**0.9**	**2.1**	**8.3**	**6.2**	**59.9**	**8.4**	**7.9**	**11.1**	**12.7**
	2000	**37 163.0**	**7.3**	**2.5**	**2.0**	**7.1**	**5.1**	**55.4**	**17.8**	**5.4**	**11.7**	**9.7**
	2007	**25 007.9**	**2.0**	**2.1**	**1.2**	**3.1**	**7.5**	**30.4**	**30.5**	**4.7**	**15.7**	**18.7**
Bermuda - Bermudes	1990	7 625.0	2.8	0.1	0.2	0.1	1.0	86.7	3.6	2.8	0.4	6.4
	1995	4 566.8	1.2	0.1	0.1	0.4	1.5	70.3	6.0	1.8	3.3	18.7
	2000	10 468.5	1.9	1.4	0.3	0.9	0.8	51.0	35.3	3.0	5.3	5.4
	2007	9 361.5	0.5	1.0	0.2	0.6	4.4	21.9	38.2	2.0	8.6	29.2
Canada	1990	756.0	0.1	0.2	0.0	0.0	0.1	34.5	53.2	6.3	0.9	5.0
	1995	661.4	0.1	0.0	0.1	0.0	0.5	30.7	14.4	12.2	0.3	42.5
	2000	1 018.4	0.1	0.1	0.1	0.0	0.5	40.1	16.0	11.6	0.2	32.2
	2007	3 234.6	0.2	0.5	0.1	0.0	0.8	26.2	53.6	3.9	0.5	15.8
Saint Pierre and Miquelon - Saint-Pierre-et-Miquelon	2007	0.4	..	..	0.0	..	0.0	..	..	77.8	..	22.2
United States - États-Unis (2)	1990	22 954.0	6.1	0.6	1.8	12.8	5.6	62.4	5.7	7.8	12.5	11.7
	1995	21 838.8	4.8	0.8	1.9	7.8	4.1	58.6	8.7	9.1	13.1	10.5
	2000	25 676.0	5.3	1.0	1.6	6.2	3.8	57.8	10.8	6.2	14.7	10.5
	2007	(b)12 411.4	1.2	0.6	0.9	2.4	2.3	37.8	18.7	7.0	25.0	11.5
Developed economies: Asia - Économies développées : Asie	**1990**	**42 943.0**	**6.1**	**7.7**	**6.4**	**7.7**	**6.7**	**33.2**	**40.3**	**15.0**	**4.0**	**7.5**
	1995	**33 108.7**	**4.3**	**5.0**	**3.4**	**5.3**	**6.8**	**35.0**	**37.3**	**10.5**	**5.8**	**11.4**
	2000	**23 554.9**	**3.2**	**2.4**	**2.7**	**2.5**	**5.3**	**38.2**	**27.8**	**11.4**	**6.6**	**16.0**
	2007	**15 989.5**	**1.2**	**1.2**	**2.2**	**1.0**	**5.1**	**29.6**	**28.7**	**13.7**	**8.2**	**19.8**
Israel - Israël	1990	586.0	0.0	0.0	0.1	1.7	0.0	0.2	8.9	24.7	65.9	0.3
	1995	785.8	0.0	0.0	0.1	1.8	0.0	0.2	4.5	12.8	82.0	0.4
	2000	832.1	0.0	..	0.0	1.3	0.0	0.3	..	0.9	98.3	0.5
	2007	893.7	0.0	..	0.0	0.7	0.0	0.4	..	0.6	98.4	0.5
Japan - Japon	1990	42 357.0	6.1	7.7	6.3	6.0	6.7	33.7	40.7	14.8	3.2	7.6
	1995	32 322.9	4.3	5.0	3.3	3.5	6.8	35.8	38.1	10.4	4.0	11.7
	2000	22 722.9	3.2	2.4	2.6	1.2	5.3	39.6	28.8	11.8	3.3	16.5
	2007	15 095.8	1.2	1.2	2.2	0.3	5.0	31.3	30.4	14.5	2.9	20.9
Developed economies: Europe - Économies développées : Europe	**1990**	**182 418.0**	**29.4**	**29.6**	**24.5**	**32.4**	**31.5**	**38.0**	**36.3**	**13.5**	**4.0**	**8.2**
	1995	**220 178.6**	**31.0**	**31.8**	**27.2**	**33.2**	**33.1**	**37.9**	**35.5**	**12.8**	**5.5**	**8.4**
	2000	**228 742.9**	**32.1**	**25.7**	**26.3**	**32.7**	**31.4**	**39.4**	**30.4**	**11.6**	**8.8**	**9.8**
	2007	**247 877.7**	**25.1**	**21.1**	**20.3**	**29.5**	**25.2**	**38.7**	**31.4**	**8.3**	**15.3**	**6.4**
Austria - Autriche	1990	355.0	..	0.1	0.1	..	..	..	69.3	30.7	..	..
	1995	203.3	..	0.0	0.1	..	..	..	38.0	62.0	..	..
	2000	100.3	..	..	0.1	..	..	..	..	100.0	..	..
	2007	44.4	..	..	0.0	0.0	..	..	..	85.6	14.4	..
Belgium - Belgique	2007	6 981.9	0.7	0.8	0.0	0.2	1.5	39.3	42.3	0.7	4.5	13.2
Belgium-Luxembourg - Belgique-Luxembourg	1990	3 288.0	0.1	0.9	0.1	1.0	1.5	6.4	62.4	3.4	6.6	21.2
	1995	2 008.6	0.0	0.3	0.1	0.2	2.0	0.5	37.4	3.8	3.9	54.5
	2000	2 109.1	0.4	0.1	0.1	0.0	1.2	47.7	8.2	2.7	1.1	40.3
Bulgaria - Bulgarie	1990	1 956.0	0.2	0.4	0.4	0.1	0.2	23.6	49.5	22.3	0.9	3.7
	1995	1 841.9	0.2	0.4	0.4	0.2	0.1	22.7	49.4	21.6	3.4	2.8
	2000	1 501.6	0.1	0.3	0.3	0.1	0.1	18.0	54.1	20.8	4.5	2.7
	2007	1 248.5	0.0	0.3	0.1	0.1	0.0	2.5	78.8	10.9	6.2	1.6
Cyprus - Chypre	1990	32 699.0	4.7	7.1	4.9	1.9	0.9	33.9	48.5	14.9	1.3	1.3
	1995	39 325.2	3.3	8.9	6.4	3.5	1.5	22.6	55.4	16.7	3.2	2.1
	2000	36 669.4	2.4	7.3	5.7	4.7	1.7	18.8	54.1	15.9	7.9	3.4
	2007	30 067.8	1.6	4.7	2.3	3.1	0.3	20.8	57.4	7.8	13.4	0.7
Czechoslovakia (former) - Tchécoslovaquie (anc.)	1990	279.0	..	0.1	0.1	..	0.0	..	54.8	44.8	..	0.4
Czech Republic - République tchèque	1995	271.8	..	0.1	0.1	..	..	..	69.2	30.8	..	..

For sources and notes, see end of table.

Pour les sources et les notes, se reporter à la fin du tableau.

5.4 World merchant fleet by flag of registration and type of ship of countries and geographical regions

5.4 Flotte marchande mondiale par pavillons d'immatriculation et par types de navires des pays et des régions géographiques

Region, country or territory / Régions pays ou territoires	Year / Année	Total fleet (thousands of DWT) (1) / Flotte totale (milliers de TPL) (1)	As percentage of world total fleet / En pourcentage de la flotte mondiale					As percentage of the country or region total fleet / En pourcentage de la flotte totale du pays ou de la région				
			Oil tankers / Pétroliers	Bulk carriers / Vraquiers	General cargo / Navires de charge classique	Container ships / Porte-conteneurs	Other types / Autres navires	Oil tankers / Pétroliers	Bulk carriers / Vraquiers	General cargo / Navires de charge classique	Container ships / Porte-conteneurs	Other types / Autres navires
Denmark - Danemark	1990	6 926.0	1.2	0.3	0.8	5.5	2.8	42.0	8.7	12.0	17.7	19.6
	1995	7 246.8	0.6	0.4	0.9	5.9	2.9	20.6	14.4	12.8	29.8	22.4
	2000	7 420.8	0.4	0.3	0.8	5.1	2.0	16.1	11.8	10.8	42.5	18.8
	2007	10 436.2	0.8	0.2	0.4	4.4	0.9	30.2	6.2	3.8	54.4	5.3
Estonia - Estonie	1995	679.5	0.0	0.1	0.3	..	0.2	2.3	38.3	40.6	..	18.8
	2000	363.1	0.0	0.0	0.2	..	0.1	3.7	27.8	51.9	..	16.7
	2007	126.2	0.0	..	0.0	..	0.1	12.7	..	21.1	..	66.1
Finland - Finlande	1990	838.0	0.1	0.1	0.3	..	0.5	21.4	14.8	35.2	..	28.6
	1995	1 175.9	0.2	0.0	0.3	..	0.3	43.7	9.3	30.5	..	16.5
	2000	1 239.5	0.2	0.0	0.4	..	0.3	41.0	10.8	31.2	..	17.0
	2007	1 009.6	0.1	0.0	0.3	0.0	0.2	41.3	8.4	34.3	1.4	14.6
France	1990	6 653.0	1.6	0.5	0.6	2.6	1.1	57.3	16.3	9.4	8.8	8.2
	1995	6 454.8	1.5	0.3	0.4	1.7	1.0	62.5	13.0	6.2	9.7	8.7
	2000	7 292.5	1.6	0.4	0.4	0.8	1.4	60.8	14.0	4.9	7.1	13.2
	2007	7 635.4	1.2	0.1	0.1	1.4	1.5	58.7	4.5	0.9	23.3	12.6
Germany - Allemagne	1990	6 778.0	0.1	0.5	2.5	9.1	2.0	4.6	14.9	36.9	29.9	13.8
	1995	6 823.5	0.1	0.2	1.7	10.6	1.0	2.4	7.0	25.9	56.6	8.2
	2000	7 788.3	0.0	0.0	1.0	10.3	0.5	0.1	0.1	13.6	81.2	4.9
	2007	13 264.2	0.2	0.1	0.4	8.9	0.5	5.7	2.4	3.0	86.3	2.5
Gibraltar	1990	5 026.0	1.7	0.3	0.2	..	0.1	80.7	14.0	3.9	..	1.4
	1995	617.7	0.2	0.0	0.0	..	0.0	86.3	7.1	6.2	..	0.5
	2000	728.5	0.2	0.0	0.1	0.1	0.1	76.0	3.7	4.9	8.6	6.8
Greece - Grèce	1990	38 465.0	6.8	8.2	2.9	1.0	2.1	41.6	47.7	7.5	0.6	2.6
	1995	53 993.6	9.8	9.4	2.2	1.9	2.5	49.1	42.9	4.1	1.3	2.6
	2000	42 532.1	8.9	5.1	0.9	2.3	1.8	58.9	32.7	2.1	3.3	3.0
	2007	54 613.2	8.4	5.1	0.4	2.0	1.0	59.1	34.2	0.8	4.7	1.1
Hungary - Hongrie	1990	108.0	..	..	0.1	..	..	..	..	100.0	..	..
	1995	65.0	..	..	0.1	..	..	..	..	100.0	..	..
	2000	14.9	..	..	0.0	..	..	..	..	100.0	..	..
Iceland - Islande	1990	155.0	0.0	0.0	0.1	..	0.1	0.6	12.3	49.7	..	37.4
	1995	96.9	0.0	0.0	0.0	..	0.1	2.3	0.7	35.9	..	61.1
	2000	83.6	0.0	0.0	0.0	0.0	0.1	3.2	0.8	3.5	14.8	77.7
	2007	78.2	0.0	0.0	0.0	..	0.1	0.6	0.8	1.4	..	97.2
Ireland - Irlande	1990	178.0	0.0	..	0.1	0.1	0.1	6.2	..	55.1	14.0	24.7
	1995	187.1	0.0	0.0	0.1	0.0	0.1	7.6	2.2	62.8	5.4	22.0
	2000	154.4	0.0	0.0	0.1	0.0	0.0	0.2	7.9	65.5	4.4	22.0
	2007	183.9	0.0	..	0.1	0.0	0.1	10.0	..	66.9	4.1	18.9
Italy - Italie (a)	1990	11 524.0	1.8	1.9	1.2	1.5	2.9	37.7	36.5	10.7	2.9	12.2
	1995	9 334.6	1.4	1.2	0.8	1.2	2.8	39.8	30.4	8.5	4.6	16.7
	2000	9 768.8	1.0	1.3	0.9	1.1	2.7	28.7	35.8	9.5	6.7	19.4
	2007	13 278.9	1.4	1.1	1.5	0.8	2.0	41.7	29.7	11.1	8.0	9.5
Latvia - Lettonie	1995	1 177.2	0.3	..	0.3	..	0.2	62.0	..	28.1	..	10.0
	2000	101.5	0.0	..	0.0	..	0.1	15.1	..	47.0	..	37.9
	2007	379.4	0.1	..	0.0	..	0.1	64.5	..	12.4	..	23.0
Lithuania - Lituanie	1995	605.0	0.0	0.1	0.2	..	0.3	3.2	26.5	41.6	..	28.7
	2000	414.6	0.0	0.1	0.2	..	0.1	1.8	38.6	45.8	..	13.8
	2007	415.3	0.0	0.0	0.2	0.0	0.1	1.5	21.0	58.5	0.9	18.0
Luxembourg	2007	1 051.8	0.1	0.1	0.1	0.1	0.4	25.3	34.6	5.6	9.1	25.4
Malta - Malte	1990	5 691.0	1.1	0.9	1.1	0.0	0.3	43.5	35.2	19.0	0.1	2.2
	1995	26 267.7	4.0	4.4	3.6	1.2	1.0	40.5	41.6	14.0	1.7	2.2
	2000	46 749.4	7.9	6.3	5.3	1.5	1.7	47.4	36.5	11.5	2.0	2.6
	2007	40 440.2	3.6	5.7	3.6	1.2	0.8	33.7	52.2	9.1	3.8	1.3
Netherlands - Pays-Bas	1990	4 557.0	0.2	0.2	1.8	2.3	2.4	12.6	12.0	38.7	11.2	25.6
	1995	5 071.3	0.2	0.2	1.9	2.5	1.9	13.0	8.3	39.4	17.9	21.4
	2000	6 607.3	0.1	0.0	2.8	2.9	2.3	4.0	1.6	42.4	27.0	25.0
	2007	5 827.6	0.1	0.0	2.8	1.2	1.6	9.1	0.1	47.7	25.7	17.4

For sources and notes, see end of table.   Pour les sources et les notes, se reporter à la fin du tableau.

Region, country or territory / Régions pays ou territoires	Year / Année	Total fleet (thousands of DWT) (1) / Flotte totale (milliers de TPL) (1)	As percentage of world total fleet / En pourcentage de la flotte mondiale					As percentage of the country or region total fleet / En pourcentage de la flotte totale du pays ou de la région				
			Oil tankers / Pétroliers	Bulk carriers / Vraquiers	General cargo / Navires de charge classique	Container ships / Porte-conteneurs	Other types / Autres navires	Oil tankers / Pétroliers	Bulk carriers / Vraquiers	General cargo / Navires de charge classique	Container ships / Porte-conteneurs	Other types / Autres navires
Norway - Norvège	1990	26 568.0	5.5	3.5	1.7	0.3	8.3	48.9	29.6	6.3	0.2	14.9
	1995	34 569.7	6.4	3.5	3.4	0.3	9.3	49.7	24.9	10.1	0.3	15.0
	2000	35 388.0	6.2	2.6	3.8	0.2	9.8	49.2	19.9	10.8	0.3	19.7
	2007	23 950.3	3.0	1.3	3.2	0.2	6.7	48.5	19.5	13.7	0.8	17.5
Poland - Pologne	1990	4 490.0	0.1	1.2	1.4	0.2	0.5	4.9	57.6	31.6	1.0	4.9
	1995	3 556.3	0.1	1.0	0.7	..	0.3	4.3	69.7	21.1	..	4.9
	2000	1 855.4	0.0	0.6	0.1	..	0.2	0.4	88.8	3.8	..	6.9
	2007	126.3	0.0	..	0.0	..	0.1	10.5	..	32.6	..	56.8
Portugal	1990	1 102.0	0.3	0.1	0.1	0.0	0.2	54.8	26.3	9.5	0.9	8.4
	1995	1 449.2	0.4	0.1	0.1	0.1	0.2	70.0	11.5	10.3	1.5	6.7
	2000	1 630.0	0.3	0.1	0.4	0.1	0.3	44.9	17.6	23.7	2.5	11.3
	2007	1 413.2	0.2	0.0	0.2	0.0	0.2	58.5	12.0	15.3	3.1	11.0
Romania - Roumanie	1990	5 711.0	0.4	1.3	1.6	0.1	0.3	18.5	51.1	27.8	0.3	2.3
	1995	3 944.9	0.3	0.7	1.3	0.0	0.3	19.3	41.1	34.7	0.4	4.5
	2000	1 618.3	0.0	0.2	0.8	0.0	0.2	6.4	32.1	51.3	0.5	9.6
	2007	276.5	0.0	..	0.1	..	0.2	18.5	..	37.1	..	44.4
Slovakia - Slovaquie	2000	19.5	..	..	0.0	..	..	..	..	100.0	..	..
	2007	330.4	0.0	0.0	0.2	..	0.0	1.3	23.1	75.3	..	0.3
Slovenia - Slovénie	1995	9.1	..	..	0.0	..	0.0	..	..	90.2	..	9.8
	2000	0.8	..	..	0.0	..	0.0	..	..	29.9	..	70.1
	2007	0.4	..	..	..	..	0.0	..	..	..	..	100.0
Spain - Espagne	1990	6 461.0	1.3	0.8	0.8	0.5	1.6	47.4	27.3	12.0	1.7	11.6
	1995	1 817.2	0.3	0.0	0.3	0.3	1.0	41.9	5.7	15.3	6.0	31.1
	2000	2 053.0	0.4	0.0	0.3	0.2	0.7	51.1	3.4	14.3	6.6	24.6
	2007	2 689.2	0.3	0.0	0.2	0.3	1.6	40.5	1.6	8.1	12.4	37.4
Sweden - Suède	1990	1 995.0	0.1	0.1	0.9	0.3	0.9	14.6	13.7	46.8	3.6	21.3
	1995	2 293.8	0.2	0.0	1.0	..	1.0	28.6	2.7	44.6	..	24.2
	2000	1 846.0	0.1	0.0	1.0	..	0.9	8.7	2.4	55.9	..	33.0
	2007	2 484.0	0.3	0.0	1.2	..	0.4	39.4	1.9	48.0	..	10.7
Switzerland - Suisse	1990	363.0	..	0.1	0.0	..	0.1	..	83.7	9.4	..	6.9
	1995	654.5	..	0.3	0.0	..	0.1	..	93.8	1.9	..	4.3
	2000	779.0	..	0.3	0.0	..	0.1	..	91.7	3.6	..	4.7
	2007	809.9	0.0	0.1	0.1	0.2	0.0	3.5	55.7	11.1	29.1	0.6
United Kingdom - Royaume-Uni	1990	10 252.0	2.0	1.0	0.7	5.9	2.7	46.1	21.8	6.9	12.8	12.4
	1995	8 436.8	1.7	0.2	0.5	3.4	2.8	54.1	6.3	6.1	14.9	18.7
	2000	11 913.1	2.0	0.5	0.6	3.2	3.3	46.9	11.8	5.5	16.3	19.6
	2007	28 714.7	2.9	1.5	2.4	5.4	4.5	38.6	19.0	8.4	24.2	9.8
Developed economies: Oceania - Économies développées : Océanie	**1990**	**4 006.0**	**0.5**	**0.9**	**0.3**	**0.6**	**0.9**	**30.7**	**48.4**	**7.0**	**3.1**	**10.8**
	1995	**4 477.7**	**0.5**	**0.7**	**0.2**	**0.4**	**1.7**	**32.0**	**39.3**	**4.5**	**2.9**	**21.4**
	2000	**3 018.8**	**0.2**	**0.5**	**0.1**	**0.1**	**1.5**	**17.6**	**44.0**	**2.3**	**1.6**	**34.5**
	2007	**2 409.8**	**0.1**	**0.2**	**0.3**	**0.0**	**1.5**	**18.5**	**30.5**	**10.8**	**0.4**	**39.8**
Australia - Australie	1990	3 707.0	0.5	0.8	0.2	0.5	0.8	29.8	51.1	5.3	3.0	10.8
	1995	4 217.5	0.5	0.7	0.1	0.4	1.6	31.8	40.8	3.5	3.1	20.8
	2000	2 686.2	0.1	0.5	0.1	0.1	1.2	15.2	48.9	2.2	1.8	32.0
	2007	2 125.2	0.1	0.2	0.1	0.0	1.5	16.8	33.8	6.1	0.5	42.9
New Zealand - Nouvelle-Zélande	1990	299.0	0.1	0.0	0.1	0.1	0.1	42.1	14.0	27.8	4.7	11.4
	1995	260.2	0.0	0.0	0.0	..	0.1	36.2	14.3	19.7	..	29.8
	2000	332.7	0.0	0.0	0.0	..	0.3	37.1	5.1	3.2	..	54.6
	2007	284.6	0.0	0.0	0.1	..	0.1	31.3	6.0	46.0	..	16.7
Unallocated, unspecified or other economies - Non précisé, non ventilé ou autres économies	2007	4 685.8	0.2	0.3	1.9	0.0	1.3	18.3	23.1	40.2	1.1	17.3

For sources and notes, see end of table.

Pour les sources et les notes, se reporter à la fin du tableau.

5.4 World merchant fleet by flag of registration and type of ship of countries and geographical regions

5.4 Flotte marchande mondiale par pavillons d'immatriculation et par types de navires des pays et des régions géographiques

Region, country or territory / Régions pays ou territoires	Year / Année	Total fleet (thousands of DWT) (1) / Flotte totale (milliers de TPL) (1)	As percentage of world total fleet / En pourcentage de la flotte mondiale					As percentage of the country or region total fleet / En pourcentage de la flotte totale du pays ou de la région				
			Oil tankers / Pétroliers	Bulk carriers / Vraquiers	General cargo / Navires de charge classique	Container ships / Porte-conteneurs	Other types / Autres navires	Oil tankers / Pétroliers	Bulk carriers / Vraquiers	General cargo / Navires de charge classique	Container ships / Porte-conteneurs	Other types / Autres navires
Major 10 open and international registries - 10 principaux pays de libre immatriculation et de registre international (3)	*1990*	*233 082.0*	*44.2*	*37.0*	*28.9*	*24.4*	*24.4*	*44.7*	*35.5*	*12.4*	*2.3*	*5.0*
	1995	*310 485.0*	*49.1*	*44.9*	*37.4*	*36.2*	*29.5*	*42.6*	*35.5*	*12.4*	*4.2*	*5.3*
	2000	*397 771.6*	*50.9*	*57.6*	*43.7*	*45.5*	*37.4*	*36.0*	*39.1*	*11.1*	*7.0*	*6.7*
	2007	*559 935.6*	*53.8*	*59.4*	*40.4*	*54.3*	*40.3*	*36.8*	*39.0*	*7.3*	*12.4*	*4.5*
Developed economies excluding major open and international registries - Économies développées sans les principaux pays de libre immatriculation et de registre international	1990	207 020.0	35.8	29.2	25.0	51.4	43.2	40.7	31.6	12.2	5.6	10.0
	1995	208 885.5	33.0	24.0	21.1	41.8	43.3	42.5	28.2	10.4	7.3	11.5
	2000	195 472.5	30.4	15.6	18.5	35.1	38.7	43.8	21.5	9.6	11.0	14.1
	2007	195 668.6	20.3	12.1	16.9	28.4	31.5	39.8	22.8	8.7	18.6	10.1
Developing economies excluding major open and international registries - Économies en développement sans les principaux pays de libre immatriculation et de registre international	1990	147 117.0	16.5	27.6	31.7	20.8	20.9	26.4	42.0	21.6	3.2	6.8
	1995	160 115.1	15.9	28.0	29.6	20.0	19.5	26.7	42.9	19.1	4.6	6.8
	2000	175 560.6	17.6	25.5	31.2	18.5	19.8	26.3	39.2	18.0	6.5	8.0
	2007	267 394.6	24.7	27.2	35.6	17.1	23.7	35.4	37.4	13.4	8.2	5.5
Developing economies: Africa excluding major open and international registries - Économies en développement : Afrique sans les principaux pays de libre immatriculation et de registre international	1990	7 638.0	1.0	0.5	2.4	1.2	3.6	29.5	13.2	31.0	3.7	22.7
	1995	6 876.5	0.8	0.5	1.9	0.6	2.2	31.3	18.6	28.9	3.0	18.2
	2000	6 365.9	0.6	0.5	1.6	0.7	1.9	24.9	22.4	25.0	6.9	20.8
	2007	6 006.5	0.4	0.4	1.6	0.1	2.2	25.8	21.6	26.7	3.1	22.8
Developing economies: America excluding major open and international registries - Économies en développement : Amérique sans les principaux pays de libre immatriculation et de registre international	1990	22 370.0	2.8	3.6	5.1	1.1	4.9	29.9	35.5	22.9	1.1	10.5
	1995	18 265.5	2.3	2.2	3.6	1.4	4.3	34.6	29.4	20.2	2.8	13.0
	2000	19 057.9	2.4	1.8	4.2	0.6	3.8	35.4	26.2	22.4	1.8	14.2
	2007	21 555.1	2.3	1.4	4.3	0.5	4.4	40.4	23.8	20.0	3.1	12.7

Sources:
- *UNCTAD Review of Maritime Transport*, various editions
- *Lloyd's Register-Fairplay*, from 2004 onwards
- *Lloyd's Maritime Information Services* (London), from 1995 to 2003
- *Lloyd's Register of Shipping* (London) - Statistical tables and supplementary data regarding the Great Lakes Fleet of the United States and Canada and the United States Reserve Fleet, from 1980 to 1994

Notes:
(a) Including San Marino.
(b) Including United States Virgin Islands.
(c) Including Taiwan Province of China.
(1) Weight measure of a vessel's carrying capacity. It includes cargo, fuel and stores.

(2) From 2002 onwards, ships registered under the flag of the Marshall Islands (developing country) are shown separately; before they were included with the United States of America (developed country).

(3) Open-registry or international-registry country: A ship owner who registers his or her vessel in an open-registry or international-registry country does not need to have any connection with a country of registry. The number of open-registry countries has varied over the years. The following 10 economies appear in the group for this table: Antigua and Barbuda, Bahamas, Bermuda, Cyprus, Isle of Man, Liberia, Malta, Marshall Islands, Panama, and Saint Vincent and Grenadines.
The data for this group are not comparable with those presented in earlier editions, as the coverage of the group has changed and it now includes four more countries.
Data for the period 2002-2007 cover also the fleet of the Isle of Man, included otherwise with figures for the United Kingdom and not shown separately.

Sources :
- *Étude sur les transports maritimes* de la CNUCED, diverses éditions
- *Lloyd's Registry-Fairplay*, à partir de 2004
- *Services d'informations maritimes de Lloyd* (Londres), de 1995 à 2003
- *Le registre maritime de la Lloyd* (Londres) - Tableaux statistiques et les données supplémentaires concernant les flottes des Grands Lacs des États-Unis et du Canada et la flotte de réserve des États-Unis, de 1980 à 1994

Notes :
(a) Y compris Saint-Marin.
(b) Y compris les îles Vierges américaines.
(c) Y compris la Province chinoise de Taiwan.
(1) Mesure de poids de la capacité de charge d'un navire. Inclut la cargaison, le carburant et les magasins.

(2) Les navires immatriculés en Îles Marshall (pays en développement) sont présentés séparément à partir de 2002 ; avant, ils étaient compris dans les chiffres des États-Unis (pays développé).

(3) Pays de libre immatriculation ou de registre international : Un propriétaire qui enregistre son navire dans un pays "de libre immatriculation ou de registre international" ne doit avoir aucune relation avec ce pays. Le nombre de pays "libres d'immatriculation" a changé au cours des années. Les 10 pays suivants font partie du groupe dans ce tableau : Antigua-et-Barbuda, Bahamas, Bermudes, Chypre, Îles Marshall, Île de Man, Libéria, Malte, Panama et Saint-Vincent-et-les Grenadines.
Les données de ce groupe ne sont pas comparables à celles présentées dans les éditions précédentes parce que le groupe comprend maintenant quatre économies de plus.
Les données pour la période 2002-2007 comprennent aussi la flotte de l'Île de Man, qui est comptée avec la flotte du Royaume-Uni et qui n'est pas présentée séparément.

5

6 COMMODITIES

PRODUITS DE BASE

1
2
3
4
5
6
7
8

6.1 Annual and quaterly indices of free-market prices of selected primary commodities
2000 = 100

Commodity	Level (1) Niveau (1) 2000	1985	1990	1995	1999	2001	2002	2003	2004	2005	2006	2007
ALL COMMODITIES	_	**96.0**	**124.3**	**138.0**	**98.4**	**96.4**	**97.2**	**105.1**	**126.1**	**140.8**	**183.6**	**207.2**
All food	_	**103.4**	**121.8**	**138.9**	**102.8**	**99.6**	**102.5**	**106.8**	**120.8**	**128.4**	**149.4**	**169.2**
Food and tropical beverages	_	*98.8*	*123.5*	*135.5*	*100.1*	*100.4*	*100.8*	*103.1*	*116.7*	*127.0*	*149.6*	*162.5*
Food	_	*89.6*	*125.4*	*132.3*	*98.0*	*102.8*	*102.2*	*104.1*	*118.6*	*127.2*	*151.3*	*164.1*
1. Wheat*	119.6	91.4	88.9	139.4	96.0	99.5	108.2	126.8	114.9	109.2	128.5	209.1
2. Wheat	119.2	115.6	114.8	150.0	96.7	109.0	127.1	126.2	134.8	132.9	168.2	225.9
3. Maize	86.8	..	123.9	142.7	108.7	101.1	111.0	117.9	120.3	103.8	138.6	188.8
4. Maize*	90.0	..	121.9	139.0	102.9	101.2	111.7	118.9	124.9	109.9	136.8	189.0
5. Rice	203.8	106.7	140.9	157.8	122.3	84.7	94.1	97.9	120.6	141.2	149.0	163.1
6. Sugar (2)	8.2	49.6	153.4	162.4	76.7	105.6	84.2	86.7	87.6	120.9	180.6	123.3
7. Beef (2)	87.8	111.2	131.5	98.5	94.7	110.0	109.7	110.2	129.8	135.2	131.9	134.5
8. Bananas (2)	19.0	90.7	123.6	104.7	102.4	138.8	125.5	89.4	125.1	137.4	162.8	161.4
9. Pepper	4 341.6	93.0	41.3	87.3	157.2	57.0	53.1	64.7	59.1	57.1	74.5	109.3
10. Soybean meal	199.7	78.7	107.1	105.5	82.4	99.1	95.7	112.4	128.6	116.5	110.3	160.5
11. Fish meal	413.0	67.8	99.8	119.9	95.0	117.8	146.7	147.9	157.1	172.2	281.9	285.0
Tropical beverages	_	*179.1*	*107.6*	*163.3*	*118.2*	*79.4*	*88.7*	*94.1*	*100.2*	*125.7*	*134.1*	*148.0*
12. Coffee (2)	102.6	151.9	94.1	154.3	113.5	70.4	63.6	65.6	82.0	114.0	115.4	123.5
13. Coffee (2)	79.9	190.0	103.7	182.7	111.2	63.3	56.5	63.6	85.4	126.9	128.8	138.6
14. Coffee (2)	85.1	171.1	104.7	175.4	119.3	72.8	71.0	75.3	94.2	134.3	133.9	144.8
15. Coffee (2)	42.1	288.2	130.5	301.0	160.6	64.8	73.2	91.2	88.5	126.7	166.9	209.6
16. Coffee* (2)	63.6	209.8	113.3	217.0	133.0	70.2	71.8	80.6	92.3	131.8	144.8	166.3
17. Cocoa (2)	40.3	254.0	143.2	161.5	128.4	122.7	200.3	197.7	174.5	173.3	179.4	219.9
18. Tea (3)	248.1	..	..	71.1	93.7	79.9	72.2	78.3	79.9	87.2	97.4	85.4
Vegetable oilseeds and oils	_	*141.2*	*107.0*	*167.1*	*125.4*	*93.6*	*116.9*	*137.2*	*155.3*	*140.6*	*147.7*	*225.7*
19. Soybeans	211.8	106.3	116.5	122.4	95.2	92.5	100.4	124.6	144.7	129.7	126.8	181.3
20. Soybean oil	338.1	169.2	132.3	184.9	126.4	104.7	134.4	163.8	182.2	161.2	177.1	260.7
21. Sunflower oil	391.8	153.7	124.9	176.9	129.5	123.6	151.7	151.4	174.6	172.9	167.9	260.8
22. Groundnut oil	713.7	126.8	135.0	138.8	110.4	95.3	96.3	174.2	162.7	148.6	135.9	189.4
23. Copra	304.8	126.7	75.7	143.9	151.4	66.3	87.4	98.4	147.7	135.8	132.1	199.3
24. Coconut oil	450.3	131.1	74.8	148.7	163.7	70.6	93.5	103.8	146.7	137.0	134.8	204.1
25. Palm kernel oil	443.5	124.3	75.3	152.8	156.5	69.5	93.8	103.4	146.1	141.4	131.0	200.3
26. Palm oil	310.3	161.3	93.4	202.5	140.5	92.1	125.8	142.9	151.9	136.1	154.2	251.5
Agricultural raw materials	_	**92.5**	**130.2**	**153.1**	**97.0**	**96.1**	**93.8**	**112.4**	**127.4**	**132.3**	**152.2**	**169.3**
27. Linseed oil	398.4	157.5	177.9	165.0	128.5	96.2	130.4	170.2	218.5	276.5	168.6	251.3
28. Tobacco	2 988.1	87.4	113.7	88.5	103.8	100.0	91.8	88.6	91.7	93.4	99.4	110.9
29. Cotton (2)	83.8	117.6	112.1	133.8	84.9	94.8	79.4	88.8	97.1	88.0	102.5	..
30. Cotton (2)	65.5	108.9	127.9	159.4	85.1	81.0	72.5	105.9	95.8	89.9	92.8	98.8
31. Cotton (2)	57.3	111.8	138.4	176.0	96.6	79.1	76.5	105.5	107.3	97.6	101.6	111.2
32. Cotton* (2)	51.7	90.7	150.3	161.5	85.2	89.4	80.5	120.7	92.5	101.1	110.9	135.3
33. Cotton* (2)	59.2	101.0	139.5	164.4	89.7	81.0	78.1	107.1	103.6	91.5	97.0	106.8
34. Cotton (2)	108.5	147.9	236.0	..	106.6	108.6	94.4	103.5	109.5	93.2	126.3	114.8
35. Wool (4)	733.5	..	..	..	84.4	85.0	87.9	95.7	97.2	92.4	97.6	132.6
36. Wool (4)	281.0	..	..	..	98.4	118.3	201.3	234.5	196.9	188.8	192.4	272.2
37. Jute	278.8	204.2	146.5	131.2	98.9	118.2	97.2	86.8	100.5	104.0	104.0	104.0
38. Sisal	782.1	79.2	95.0	97.4	112.4	107.7	99.4	102.1	122.9	126.0	126.0	126.0
39. Sisal	628.7	83.6	113.7	113.0	110.7	111.2	105.0	111.1	137.0	140.8	140.8	140.8
40. Hides (2)	80.2	63.8	115.0	109.9	89.9	105.5	102.4	85.2	83.7	82.0	86.1	90.0
41. Non-coniferous woods*	100.0	..	..	107.8	104.0	98.0	105.4	118.0	136.0	143.9	165.3	197.6
42. Tropical logs (5)	244.6	71.1	140.4	139.4	96.4	106.4	95.2	114.3	136.3	136.7	130.2	155.7
43. Tropical sawnwood* (5)	531.8	51.9	98.6	144.2	97.8	95.7	94.3	102.2	103.4	103.4	103.4	103.4
44. Plywood* (6)	448.5	47.0	79.1	129.9	98.4	91.4	89.8	97.2	103.6	113.4	132.8	143.9
45. Rubber	669.2	112.8	129.4	239.2	92.7	85.9	114.3	162.0	194.9	224.4	315.2	342.3

For sources and notes, see end of table.

| 2005 | | | | 2006 | | | | 2007 | | | | Produits |
I	II	III	IV	I	II	III	IV	I	II	III	IV	
138.8	137.9	139.8	146.7	167.2	187.6	189.0	190.5	192.1	206.9	209.8	220.0	**TOTAL DES PRODUITS**
130.4	127.3	125.9	130.2	148.0	150.7	147.3	151.5	156.2	158.8	171.1	190.9	**Total des produits alimentaires**
129.3	*125.2*	*124.3*	*129.2*	*149.3*	*151.9*	*147.1*	*150.0*	*153.4*	*152.7*	*163.4*	*180.4*	***Produits alimentaires et boissons tropicales***
129.1	*124.5*	*124.8*	*130.3*	*150.8*	*154.5*	*148.7*	*151.3*	*154.7*	*153.9*	*164.9*	*183.1*	*Produits alimentaires*
97.3	110.2	117.4	111.7	112.8	117.0	127.1	157.2	151.3	186.7	239.3	259.1	1. Blé*
131.1	125.1	133.1	142.1	150.5	166.1	173.1	182.9	175.1	180.7	247.0	300.7	2. Blé
94.6	100.2	112.7	107.6	119.1	126.4	129.9	179.1	187.5	172.9	181.7	212.9	3. Maïs
108.2	107.4	112.6	111.5	117.8	122.9	130.8	175.5	192.2	178.5	177.1	208.2	4. Maïs*
143.1	144.1	138.9	138.6	143.7	148.2	153.4	150.5	156.2	158.5	162.6	175.0	5. Riz
108.8	106.9	121.8	145.9	207.6	202.6	169.5	142.6	130.3	115.9	121.3	125.6	6. Sucre (2)
133.6	136.3	137.8	132.8	129.5	128.3	133.3	136.7	134.8	134.4	134.4	134.4	7. Viande de boeuf (2)
182.4	135.6	110.2	121.4	189.0	185.1	133.2	143.9	154.6	168.3	166.6	156.0	8. Bananes (2)
58.7	57.6	56.6	55.6	57.6	60.3	81.5	98.7	91.3	109.9	118.7	117.3	9. Poivre
118.0	120.2	117.4	110.2	108.2	105.0	107.7	120.4	134.7	135.5	161.9	209.8	10. Farine de soja
155.1	160.6	172.5	200.6	217.8	285.3	323.1	301.2	303.0	305.1	271.8	260.3	11. Farine de poisson
131.4	*131.8*	*119.9*	*119.6*	*136.2*	*129.1*	*132.5*	*138.7*	*142.7*	*142.4*	*150.4*	*156.6*	*Boissons tropicales*
120.7	123.7	105.6	106.2	120.1	110.4	109.8	121.1	121.2	115.6	123.6	133.6	12. Café (2)
133.2	137.7	115.8	121.1	137.3	123.6	119.9	134.5	135.3	127.9	139.5	151.9	13. Café (2)
142.6	146.9	123.4	124.4	139.0	126.8	127.0	142.7	142.3	135.4	144.3	157.2	14. Café (2)
106.8	138.5	131.6	130.1	154.2	152.4	175.9	184.9	190.3	207.7	218.1	222.4	15. Café (2)
130.7	144.1	126.1	126.3	144.1	135.3	143.2	156.7	158.2	159.4	168.7	178.7	16. Café* (2)
185.5	174.1	168.0	165.4	175.3	179.3	182.3	180.7	204.3	225.3	225.0	225.1	17. Cacao (2)
99.0	82.5	85.6	81.8	102.7	96.5	99.6	90.9	89.5	78.5	87.7	86.0	18. Thé (3)
139.5	*144.2*	*139.7*	*139.0*	*137.1*	*140.7*	*149.3*	*163.5*	*179.1*	*209.5*	*235.9*	*278.3*	***Graines oléagineuses et huiles végétales***
127.9	137.2	131.4	122.2	121.3	124.5	124.6	136.9	150.0	159.7	186.8	228.8	19. Fèves de soja
154.2	162.1	163.2	165.2	158.3	170.5	183.5	196.1	209.9	234.9	271.4	326.7	20. Huile de soja
179.3	178.7	176.4	157.0	152.5	170.5	168.6	180.2	182.1	212.9	288.6	359.7	21. Huile de tournesol
161.5	154.3	143.6	134.9	128.6	125.6	132.5	157.0	163.9	166.7	195.7	231.4	22. Huile d'arachide
147.0	146.4	124.9	124.7	125.9	125.7	131.4	145.6	163.6	196.7	199.3	237.4	23. Coprah
148.2	145.5	126.9	127.4	128.4	128.5	133.1	149.1	167.5	199.9	205.0	243.8	24. Huile de coprah
149.3	147.9	131.3	137.0	136.8	125.6	126.1	135.7	152.8	197.5	206.7	244.3	25. Huile de palmiste
133.2	135.9	133.8	141.3	140.6	141.4	158.8	175.9	196.2	245.7	265.0	299.0	26. Huile de palme
126.1	**128.5**	**136.9**	**137.7**	**148.5**	**161.6**	**155.4**	**143.2**	**164.8**	**168.9**	**164.0**	**179.5**	**Matières premières d'origine agricole**
312.4	380.2	223.4	189.9	165.4	166.9	166.2	175.7	188.1	190.5	259.3	367.1	27. Huile de lin
91.5	93.7	92.6	95.7	96.4	94.9	101.7	104.5	106.8	113.4	111.3	112.2	28. Tabac
86.6	89.4	87.8	..	102.4	102.4	102.7	..	..	..	..	..	29. Coton (2)
85.9	90.9	88.8	93.4	94.4	90.2	94.9	91.7	94.5	89.5	103.9	107.4	30. Coton (2)
93.7	97.5	96.5	102.8	101.6	97.5	104.9	102.3	105.5	100.2	117.8	121.5	31. Coton (2)
97.4	103.5	97.6	104.7	110.9	..	..	..	..	..	131.7	136.4	32. Coton* (2)
88.3	91.9	90.4	95.5	98.8	93.3	98.0	97.9	98.7	97.5	114.0	117.2	33. Coton* (2)
89.7	95.1	98.0	..	126.9	129.7	129.8	119.8	119.3	117.5	114.9	104.0	34. Coton (2)
99.7	96.8	91.3	81.8	93.1	97.4	96.7	103.2	121.9	132.6	126.9	149.1	35. Laine (4)
195.9	194.6	191.4	173.4	183.4	184.3	187.3	214.6	254.7	275.0	268.1	291.0	36. Laine (4)
104.0	104.0	104.0	104.0	104.0	104.0	104.0	104.0	104.0	104.0	104.0	104.0	37. Jute
126.0	126.0	126.0	126.0	126.0	126.0	126.0	126.0	126.0	126.0	126.0	126.0	38. Sisal
140.8	140.8	140.8	140.8	140.8	140.8	140.8	140.8	140.8	140.8	140.8	140.8	39. Sisal
82.3	81.4	82.3	81.9	82.7	85.6	86.4	89.7	96.4	94.7	84.4	84.4	40. Cuirs (2)
143.7	145.4	142.5	144.1	148.6	159.2	170.1	183.3	192.0	196.5	200.2	201.8	41. Bois non conifères*
144.8	135.6	135.1	131.2	129.0	129.3	128.7	133.9	150.9	152.5	151.9	167.5	42. Grumes tropicales (5)
103.4	103.4	103.4	103.4	103.4	103.4	103.4	103.4	103.4	103.4	103.4	103.4	43. Grumes tropicales sciées* (5)
114.9	114.3	112.9	111.5	117.9	128.8	142.3	142.1	140.3	142.6	145.8	146.9	44. Contre-plaqué* (6)
189.1	207.0	250.3	251.3	302.4	367.2	328.1	262.9	333.8	349.3	319.7	366.4	45. Caoutchouc

Pour les sources et les notes, se reporter à la fin du tableau.

6

6.1 Annual and quaterly indices of free-market prices of selected primary commodities
2000 = 100

Commodity	Level (1) Niveau (1) 2000	1985	1990	1995	1999	2001	2002	2003	2004	2005	2006	2007
Minerals, ores and metals	_	**81.2**	**127.0**	**128.1**	**89.0**	**89.2**	**86.8**	**97.6**	**137.3**	**173.2**	**277.7**	**313.2**
46. Phosphate rock	43.8	76.6	92.6	80.0	100.4	95.5	92.3	86.9	93.7	96.0	101.1	162.1
47. Manganese ore	186.0	74.5	213.1	109.7	102.6	106.7	106.7	106.7	106.7	175.8	139.7	191.9
48. Iron ore (7)	27.7	96.0	111.3	97.4	97.4	104.5	103.4	112.2	131.7	225.9	268.8	294.4
49. Iron ore* (7)	27.5	96.5	109.8	97.4	99.8	104.3	103.5	109.8	126.2	201.0	256.4	286.1
50. Aluminium	1 549.2	69.8	105.8	116.6	87.9	93.2	87.1	92.4	110.8	122.5	165.9	170.3
51. Copper	1 813.1	78.2	146.8	161.8	86.7	87.0	86.0	98.1	158.0	202.9	370.7	392.6
52. Copper* (2)	86.8	75.6	140.4	158.4	85.9	87.0	85.8	96.6	152.8	198.4	361.2	376.5
53. Nickel*	8 637.7	56.8	102.6	95.3	69.6	68.8	78.4	111.5	160.0	170.6	280.7	430.9
54. Nickel (2)	397.9	56.8	102.3	98.1	69.1	69.0	77.8	111.7	159.4	171.2	276.0	424.8
55. Lead	454.0	86.1	178.5	138.9	110.7	104.9	99.7	113.5	195.2	215.0	283.8	568.2
56. Lead* (2)	43.6	43.8	103.4	96.3	100.4	100.2	100.0	100.4	126.6	140.1	178.0	284.2
57. Zinc	1 128.1	67.0	134.6	91.4	95.4	78.5	69.0	73.4	92.9	122.5	290.3	287.4
58. Zinc* (2)	55.6	72.6	134.1	95.9	96.2	79.0	69.5	73.1	94.4	120.7	285.7	277.6
59. Tin	5 432.8	221.8	114.8	114.3	99.4	82.5	74.7	90.0	156.5	135.8	161.5	267.4
60. Tin*	5 382.0	221.5	113.1	113.1	98.6	81.9	74.9	90.9	157.8	136.7	162.9	269.9
61. Tungsten (8)	44.9	150.9	103.4	141.2	89.2	145.6	84.8	100.0	122.9	271.3	369.7	367.4
62. Gold* (9)	279.0	113.7	137.4	137.7	99.9	97.1	111.1	130.3	146.6	159.4	216.6	249.7
63. Silver* (10)	499.9	122.9	96.4	103.8	105.0	87.8	92.6	98.2	133.3	146.8	231.4	268.3
MEMO ITEM:												
64. Crude petroleum (11)	28.2	95.6	78.1	59.9	64.3	86.7	88.4	102.4	133.8	189.1	227.8	252.1
65. Unit value index of manufactured goods exports	100.0	70.9	110.9	122.3	105.2	97.9	98.5	107.7	116.6	119.5	123.4	132.5

Sources:
- The prices used in the calculation of the indices shown in this table are extracted from the UNCTAD *Commodity Price Statistics* on-line.

Notes:

- The group indices have been re-based on 2000 using new weights. These indices include all commodities shown except for those with an asterisk (*).

- The average annual indices are calculated from monthly data and may not correspond to the average from quarterly data.

(1) Dollars per metric ton (if not indicated otherwise).
(2) Cents per pound .
(3) Cents per kilogram.
(4) Dollars per 100 kilograms.
(5) Dollars per cubic meter.
(6) Cents per sheet.
(7) Cents per Fe unit.
(8) Dollars per metric ton unit of WO3.
(9) Dollars per troy ounce.
(10) Cents per troy ounce.
(11) Dollars per barrel.

- For specifications, see next page.

2005				2006				2007				Produits
I	II	III	IV	I	II	III	IV	I	II	III	IV	
164.5	**166.9**	**172.8**	**188.6**	**220.5**	**285.1**	**301.2**	**304.0**	**288.1**	**336.1**	**321.4**	**307.1**	**Minéraux, minerais et métaux**
96.0	96.0	96.0	96.0	96.8	99.4	104.0	104.0	104.0	136.9	182.9	224.8	46. Phosphate brut
143.3	204.3	195.4	160.4	146.8	145.2	131.1	135.8	143.4	177.6	185.5	261.2	47. Minerai de manganèse
225.9	225.9	225.9	225.9	268.8	268.8	268.8	268.8	294.4	294.4	294.4	294.4	48. Minerai de fer (7)
130.9	224.4	224.4	224.4	224.4	267.1	267.1	267.1	267.1	292.4	292.4	292.4	49. Minerai de fer* (7)
122.6	115.5	118.0	134.0	156.3	171.3	160.2	175.8	180.8	178.3	164.3	157.7	50. Aluminium
180.2	186.9	207.1	237.2	272.4	397.6	423.0	389.8	327.2	421.4	425.3	396.4	51. Cuivre
173.6	181.0	200.5	238.3	264.7	394.1	413.0	372.9	316.4	403.9	406.2	379.3	52. Cuivre* (2)
177.6	189.9	168.6	146.4	171.4	230.6	337.3	383.4	479.6	556.1	349.6	338.2	53. Nickel*
178.6	192.4	170.0	144.0	170.0	228.4	328.3	377.1	466.8	547.6	345.6	339.3	54. Nickel (2)
215.6	217.3	196.3	231.0	273.4	242.5	262.2	357.0	393.5	479.2	692.5	707.6	55. Plomb
139.4	139.5	138.8	142.7	171.2	174.9	175.7	190.4	204.7	232.9	326.4	372.8	56. Plomb* (2)
116.7	112.8	115.0	145.4	198.7	291.8	298.2	372.6	306.4	324.7	286.0	232.5	57. Zinc
115.4	111.0	113.0	143.3	194.5	287.2	296.2	364.8	301.6	314.0	273.0	222.0	58. Zinc* (2)
148.7	146.4	129.6	118.3	139.9	156.8	159.1	190.1	234.2	259.4	275.6	300.6	59. Etain
149.7	147.3	130.3	119.5	140.9	159.4	160.2	191.2	234.6	262.9	277.0	305.1	60. Etain*
162.1	277.4	322.9	322.9	368.6	381.0	361.6	367.4	367.4	367.4	367.4	367.4	61. Tungstène (8)
153.1	153.1	157.5	174.0	198.6	224.8	222.8	220.2	233.0	239.1	244.1	282.4	62. Or* (9)
140.1	143.7	141.8	161.7	193.9	245.3	233.8	252.7	266.6	267.2	254.8	284.8	63. Argent* (10)
												POUR MÉMOIRE :
163.5	179.9	212.6	200.4	216.1	242.0	243.7	209.2	202.7	234.4	260.7	310.5	64. Pétrole brut (11)
123.0	120.0	118.0	117.0	119.0	123.0	124.0	127.0	128.0	131.0	133.0	138.0	65. Valeur unitaire des exportations d'articles manufacturés

Sources :
- Les prix utilisés pour le calcul des indices présentés dans ce tableau sont extraits des *Statistiques des prix des produits de base* en ligne de la CNUCED.

Notes :

- Les indices agrégés ont été calculés en utilisant 2000=100 comme année de base et une nouvelle pondération; ils recouvrent tous les produits présentés à l'exception de ceux munis d'un astérisque (*).
- Les indices moyens annuels sont calculés sur la base de données mensuelles et peuvent ne pas correspondre aux moyennes calculées sur la base des trimestres.

(1) Dollars par tonne métrique (sauf mention spéciale)
(2) Cents par livre.
(3) Cents par kilogramme.
(4) Dollars par 100 kilogrammes.
(5) Dollars par mètre cube.
(6) Cents par feuille.
(7) Cents par unité de Fe.
(8) Dollars par tonne métrique d'unité de WO3.
(9) Dollars par once "troy".
(10) Cents par once "troy".
(11) Dollars par baril.

- Pour les spécifications, se reporter à la page suivante.

Specifications

Food

1. Wheat: Argentina, Trigo Pan Upriver, f.o.b.
2. Wheat: United States, No. 2, Hard Red Winter (ordinary), f.o.b. Gulf ports.
3. Maize: Argentina, Rosario, f.o.b.
4. Maize: United States, No. 3 yellow, f.o.b. Gulf ports.
5. Rice: Thailand, white milled, 5 % broken, f.o.b. Bangkok.
6. Sugar: Caribbean ports, f.o.b. bulk basis (I.S.A.).
7. Beef: Australia and New-Zealand, frozen and boneless, 85 % visible lean, f.o.b. United States ports.
8. Bananas: Central America and Ecuador, fresh, f.o.b. United States ports.
9. Pepper: White Sarawak/Muntok, European market and spot London. Prior to June 2003, Singapore.
10. Soybean meal: Hamburg, 44/45 %, f.o.b. ex-mill.
11. Fish meal: Any origin, 64/65 %, Bremen free carrier price. Prior to March 2006, cost and freight Hamburg.

Tropical beverages

12. Coffee: Colombian mild Arabicas, ex-dock New York (I.C.A.).
13. Coffee: Brazilian and other natural Arabicas, ex-dock New York (I.C.A.).
14. Coffee: Other mild Arabicas, ex-dock New York (I.C.A.).
15. Coffee: Robustas, ex-dock New York (I.C.A.).
16. Coffee: Composite indicator price 1976 (I.C.A.).
17. Cocoa: Average of daily prices, New York/London, 3 months futures (I.C.C.A.).
18. Tea: Mombasa auction prices, Best Pekoe Fannings 1.

Vegetable oils and oilseeds

19. Soybeans: United States, No. 2 yellow, c.i.f. Rotterdam.
20. Soybean oil: Any origin, crude oil, the Netherlands, f.o.b. ex-mill.
21. Sunflower oil: European Union, f.o.b. N.W. European ports.
22. Groundnut oil: Any origin, c.i.f. Rotterdam.
23. Copra: Philippines/Indonesia, bulk, c.i.f. N.W. European ports.
24. Coconut oil: Philippines, c.i.f. Rotterdam.
25. Palm kernel oil: Malaysia, c.i.f. Rotterdam.
26. Palm oil: generally Indonesia, 5%, c.i.f. N.W. European ports.

Agricultural raw materials

27. Linseed oil: Any origin, ex-tank, c.i.f. Rotterdam.
28. Tobacco: Unmanufactured tobacco, US general import price.
29. Cotton: Sudan, Barakat, X4B, C/F Far Eastern quotations. Prior to August 2005, c.i.f. North Europe.
30. Cotton: United States, Memphis/Eastern Midd 1-3/32", c.i.f. North Europe.
31. Cotton: United States; Memphis/Orleans/Texas, Midd 1-3/32", C/F Far Eastern quotations. Prior to June 2005, Memphis/Orleans/Texas, Midd 1-3/32", c.i.f. North Europe.
32. Cotton: Pakistan, Sind/Punjab, Afzal 1-1/32", c.i.f. North Europe.
33. Cotton: Cotton Outlook Index A, Middling 1-3/32", C/F Far Eastern quotations. Prior to August 2004, c.i.f. North Europe.
34. Cotton: Egypt, Giza 88, good + 3/8, C/F Far Eastern quotations. Prior to August 2005, Giza 70, good + 3/8, f.o.b. Alexandria.
35. Wool: Australia, 19 microns.
36. Wool: Australia, 23 microns.
37. Jute: Bangladesh, B.W.D., f.o.b. Mongla.
38. Sisal: Tanzania/Kenya, No. 2 & 3 long, c.i.f. European ports. Prior to 1997, c.i.f. London.
39. Sisal: Tanzania/Kenya, No. 3 & UG, c.i.f. European ports. Prior to 1997, c.i.f. London.
40. Hides: US, Chicago packer's heavy native steers, wholesale dealer's price, f.o.b. shipping point.
41. Non-coniferous woods: United Kingdom, import price index 2000 = 100, dollar equivalent.
42. Tropical logs: Sapele, loyal and marchand, UK import price. Prior to June 2000, Cameroon f.o.b.
43. Tropical sawnwood: Malaysia, Dark Red Meranti, select and better, c.i.f. French ports.
44. Plywood: Southeast Asia, Lauan, 3-ply, Extra, 182 cm x 91 cm x 4 mm, wholesale price, spot Tokyo.
45. Rubber: Singapore, No. 1 RSS, f.o.b. in bales.

Spécifications

Produits alimentaires

1. Blé : Argentine, Trigo Pan Upriver, f.a.b.
2. Blé : États-Unis, Hard Red Winter, n° 2 (ordinaire), f.a.b. ports du Golfe.
3. Maïs : Argentine, Rosario, f.a.b.
4. Maïs : États-Unis, jaune n° 3, f.a.b. ports du Golfe.
5. Riz : Thaïlande, blanchi, 5 % brisures, f.a.b. Bangkok.
6. Sucre : Ports des Caraïbes, f.a.b. en vrac (A.I.S.).
7. Viande de boeuf : Australie et Nouvelle-Zélande, désossée et congelée, maigres à 85 % visibles, f.a.b. ports des États-Unis.
8. Bananes : Amérique centrale et Equateur, fraîches, f.a.b. ports des États-Unis.
9. Poivre : Sarawak blanc/Muntok, cours du disponible sur le marché européen et à Londres. Avant juin 2003, Singapour.
10. Farine de soja : Hambourg, 44/45 %, f.a.b. départ moulin.
11. Farine de poisson : Toutes origines, 64/65 %, Brême, prix franco transporteur. Avant mars 2006, coût et fret Hambourg.

Boissons tropicales

12. Café : Arabicas doux colombiens, ex-dock New York (A.I.C.).
13. Café : Brésilien et autres Arabicas naturels, ex-dock New York (A.I.C.).
14. Café : Autres Arabicas doux, ex-dock New York (A.I.C.).
15. Café : Robustas, ex-dock New York (A.I.C.).
16. Café : Prix indicatif composite de 1976 (A.I.C.).
17. Cacao : Moyenne des cours quotidiens New York/Londres, 3 mois à terme (A.I.C.C.).
18. Thé : Cours aux enchères à Mombasa, Best Pekoe Fannings 1.

Huiles végétales et graines oléagineuses

19. Fèves de soja : États-Unis, n° 2 jaune, c.a.f. Rotterdam.
20. Huile de soja : Toutes origines, huile brute, f.a.b. Pays-Bas, départ raffinerie.
21. Huile de tournesol : Union européenne, f.a.b. ports de l'Europe du Nord-Ouest.
22. Huile d'arachide : Toutes origines, c.a.f. Rotterdam.
23. Coprah : Philippines/Indonésie, en vrac, c.a.f. ports de l'Europe du Nord-Ouest.
24. Huile de coprah : Philippines, c.a.f. Rotterdam.
25. Huile de palmiste : Malaisie, c.a.f. Rotterdam.
26. Huile de palme : généralement Indonésie, 5 %, c.a.f. ports de l'Europe du Nord-Ouest.

Matières premières d'origine agricole

27. Huile de lin : Toutes origines, cours du disponible, c.a.f. Rotterdam.
28. Tabac : Tabac non fabriqué, prix général à l'importation aux États-Unis.
29. Coton : Soudan, Barakat, classe X4B, cotations coût et fret Extrême Orient. Avant août 2005, c.a.f. Europe septentrionale.
30. Coton : États-Unis, Memphis, oriental Midd 1-3/32", c.a.f. Europe septentrionale.
31. Coton : États-Unis, Memphis/Orléans/Texas, Midd 1-3/32", cotations coût et fret Extrême Orient. Avant juin 2005, Memphis/Orléans/Texas, Midd 1-3/32", c.a.f. Europe septentrionale.
32. Coton : Pakistan, Sind/Punjab, Afzal 1-1/32", c.a.f. Europe septentrionale.
33. Coton : Indice A de "Cotton Outlook", Middling 1-3/32", cotations coût et fret Extrême Orient. Avant août 2005, c.a.f. Europe septentrionale.
34. Coton : Égypte, Giza 88, good + 3/8, cotations coût et fret Extrême Orient. Avant août 2005, Giza 70, good + 3/8, f.a.b. Alexandrie.
35. Laine : Australie, 19 microns.
36. Laine : Australie, 23 microns.
37. Jute : Bangladesh, B.W.D., f.a.b. Mongla.
38. Sisal : Tanzanie/Kenya, n° 2 & 3 long, c.a.f. ports européens. Avant 1997, c.a.f. Londres.
39. Sisal : Tanzanie/Kenya, n° 3 & UG, c.a.f. ports européens. Avant 1997, c.a.f. Londres.
40. Peaux : États-Unis, bouvillons abattus à Chicago, prix de gros, f.a.b. point d'expédition.
41. Bois non conifères : Royaume-Uni, indice des prix à l'importation 2000 = 100, équivalent dollar.
42. Grumes tropicales : Sapelli, loyal et marchand, prix d'importation au Royaume-Uni. Avant juin 2000, Cameroun, f.a.b.
43. Grumes tropicales sciées : Malaisie, Meranti rouge foncé, select and better, c.a.f. ports français.
44. Contre-plaqué : Asie du Sud-Est, Lauan, 3-feuilles, extra, 182 cm x 91 cm x 4 mm, prix de gros, cours du disponible à Tokyo.
45. Caoutchouc : Singapour, n° 1 RSS, f.a.b. en balles.

Minerals, ores and metals

46. Phosphate rock: Khouribga, 70 % BPL, f.a.s. Casablanca.
47. Manganese ore: Metallurgical 48/50 % Mn content, f.o.b. United Kingdom.
48. Iron ore: Brazilian to Europe, fines, Vale, f.o.b.
49. Iron ore: Australian to Japan, fines, Hamersley, f.o.b.
50. Aluminium: London Metal Exchange, high grade, cash.
51. Copper: London Metal Exchange, grade A, cash.
52. Copper: United States producer, wire bars, f.o.b. refinery.
53. Nickel: London Metal Exchange, cash.
54. Nickel: New York dealer, 4x4 cathodes, free market.
55. Lead: London Metal Exchange, settlement and cash seller's price in warehouse, excluding duty, range main United Kingdom ports; purity 99.97 % Pb.
56. Lead: North America, producer price, refined.
57. Zinc: London Metal Exchange, cash settlement.
58. Zinc: North America, high grade, daily weighted average, delivered basis.
59. Tin: London Metal Exchange, high grade, cash.
60. Tin: Ex-smelter price Kuala Lumpur market.
61. Tungsten ore: wolframite and sheelite, c.i.f. European ports, basis minimum 65 % WO3. Prior to April 1992, Wolfram.
62. Gold: United Kingdom, 99.5 % fine, London afternoon fixing, average of daily rates.
63. Silver: Handy & Harman, 99.9 % grade refined, average of daily quotations, New York.

MEMO ITEM:

64. Crude petroleum: Average of Dubai, United Kingdom Brent and West Texas crude prices, reflecting relatively equal consumption of medium, light and heavy crudes worldwide.
65. Manufactured goods export unit value: Developed economies, sections 5-8 less 68 of the Standard International Trade Classification (SITC), Revision 2, 2000=100.

Minéraux, minerais et métaux

46. Phosphate brut : Khouribga, 70 % BPL, f.a.s. Casablanca.
47. Minerai de manganèse : 48/50 % teneur en Mn, f.a.b. Royaume-Uni.
48. Minerai de fer : Brésilien vers l'Europe, minerai fin, Vale, f.a.b.
49. Minerai de fer : Australien vers le Japon, minerai fin, Hamersley, f.a.b.
50. Aluminium : Bourse des métaux de Londres, haute qualité, cours au comptant.
51. Cuivre : Bourse des métaux de Londres, grade A, comptant.
52. Cuivre : Producteur États-Unis, barres à fil, f.a.b. sortie affinerie.
53. Nickel : Bourse des métaux de Londres, cours au comptant.
54. Nickel : Prix du négociant à New York, cathodes 4x4, marché libre.
55. Plomb : Bourse des métaux de Londres, prix vendeur, à terme et au comptant, à l'entrepôt, droits non acquittés, principaux ports du Royaume-Uni; pureté: 99,97 % Pb.
56. Plomb : Amérique du Nord, prix des producteurs, raffiné.
57. Zinc : Bourse des métaux de Londres, cours de vente au comptant.
58. Zinc : Amérique du Nord, haute qualité, moyenne pondérée des prix journaliers à la livraison.
59. Étain : Bourse des métaux de Londres, haute qualité, cours au comptant.
60. Étain : Prix départ fonderie, marché de Kuala Lumpur.
61. Minerai de tungstène : wolframite et scheelite, c.a.f. ports européens, minimum 65 % de WO3. Avant avril 1992, Wolfram.
62. Or : Royaume-Uni, 99,5 % fin, cotation de l'après-midi à Londres, moyenne des taux journaliers.
63. Argent : Handy & Harman, 99,9 % raffiné, moyenne des cotations journalières à New York.

POUR MÉMOIRE :

64. Pétrole brut : moyenne des prix du Dubaï, brent du Royaume-Uni et du Texas de l'Ouest, correspondant aux parts relatives de la consommation mondiale du brut moyen, léger et lourd.
65. Valeur unitaire des exportations de produits manufacturés : Économies développées, sections 5 à 8 moins 68 de la Classification type pour le commerce international (CTCI), révision 2, 2000=100.

6

6.2 **Instability indices and trends in free-market prices for selected primary commodities**
2000 = 100

6.2 **Indices d'instabilité et tendances des prix sur le marché libre d'une sélection de produits de base**
2000 = 100

Commodity	Price instability indices (1), (2) Indices d'instabilité des prix (1), (2)			Price trends (1), (3) Tendances des prix (1), (3) — In current dollars En dollars courants			In constant dollars (4) En dollars constants (4)			Produits
	78 - 87	88 - 97	98 - 07	78 - 87	88 - 97	98 - 07	78 - 87	88 - 97	98 - 07	
				Annual average rate of change in percentage / Taux de variation annuel en pourcentage						
ALL COMMODITIES	**10.4**	**6.8**	**13.3**	**-3.5**	**0.5**	**7.4**	**-5.8**	**-0.9**	**4.8**	**TOTAL DES PRODUITS**
All food	**11.6**	**6.8**	**10.9**	**-4.7**	**1.4**	**4.3**	**-6.9**	**0.0**	**1.6**	**Total des produits alimentaires**
Food and tropical beverages	*12.5*	*6.8*	*10.3*	*-4.5*	*1.1*	*4.3*	*-6.8*	*-0.3*	*1.6*	*Produits alimentaires et boissons tropicales*
Food	*14.8*	*6.7*	*9.7*	*-4.9*	*0.8*	*4.6*	*-7.2*	*-0.6*	*2.0*	*Produits alimentaires*
Wheat	11.5	13.0	10.8	-3.2	2.4	7.5	-5.5	1.0	4.9	Blé
Maize	15.8	11.2	12.5	-3.7	2.4	4.6	-6.2	1.0	1.9	Maïs
Rice	14.1	9.2	18.3	-7.7	0.7	3.0	-10.0	-0.8	0.4	Riz
Sugar	45.7	13.8	20.8	-10.6	1.2	4.6	-12.9	-0.2	2.0	Sucre
Beef	7.8	8.1	5.2	-1.6	-4.3	4.9	-3.9	-5.7	2.2	Viande de bœuf
Bananas	14.2	17.6	16.2	2.1	-1.0	4.2	-0.3	-2.4	1.5	Bananes
Pepper	30.0	39.3	35.9	11.3	6.9	-6.8	9.0	5.5	-9.4	Poivre
Soybean meal	11.0	11.9	10.9	-3.3	0.9	5.1	-5.5	-0.5	2.4	Farine de soja
Fishmeal	14.2	14.7	19.2	-3.3	2.1	9.9	-5.6	0.7	7.2	Farine de poisson
Tropical beverages	*12.1*	*22.0*	*18.8*	*-2.7*	*3.6*	*1.6*	*-5.0*	*2.2*	*-1.0*	*Boissons tropicales*
Coffee	14.7	30.6	26.9	-1.5	4.7	1.5	-3.8	3.3	-1.1	Café
Cocoa	13.5	12.1	18.1	-4.9	1.5	4.5	-7.1	0.1	1.9	Cacao
Tea	15.7	10.8	11.2	-1.3	1.6	-1.1	-3.2	-0.5	-3.7	Thé
Vegetable oilseeds and oils	**16.6**	**10.1**	**19.0**	**-5.7**	**3.8**	**4.3**	**-8.0**	**2.4**	**1.6**	**Graines oléagineuses et huiles végétales**
Soybeans	9.4	9.7	12.7	-3.5	0.6	5.4	-5.7	-0.8	2.7	Fèves de soja
Soybean oil	18.6	8.6	19.5	-5.5	3.8	5.9	-7.8	2.4	3.3	Huile de soja
Sunflower oil	17.5	9.6	16.8	-6.2	3.6	5.2	-8.5	2.2	2.5	Huile de tournesol
Groundnut oil	22.3	15.4	16.8	-5.7	4.1	5.5	-8.0	2.7	2.9	Huile d'arachide
Copra	30.7	18.0	26.3	-6.7	4.4	4.0	-9.0	3.0	1.4	Coprah
Coconut oil	32.6	17.9	25.8	-6.4	5.0	3.4	-8.7	3.6	0.8	Huile de coprah
Palm kernel oil	30.4	17.2	25.8	-8.3	5.6	3.2	-10.6	4.2	0.5	Huile de palmiste
Palm oil	20.5	15.7	25.3	-7.2	6.1	3.2	-9.5	4.7	0.6	Huile de palme
Cottonseed oil	15.0	8.9	22.6	-3.0	0.8	4.4	-5.4	-0.6	1.8	Huile de graines de coton
Agricultural raw materials	**9.1**	**6.7**	**8.8**	**-1.1**	**1.1**	**5.8**	**-3.4**	**-0.3**	**3.2**	**Matières premières d'origine agricole**
Linseed oil	19.2	20.3	26.4	-4.2	-0.2	7.5	-6.4	-1.6	4.9	Huile de lin
Tobacco	3.5	11.7	6.4	2.3	0.6	-0.6	0.0	-0.8	-3.2	Tabac
Cotton	14.6	13.3	11.9	-3.2	1.9	0.5	-5.5	0.5	-2.1	Coton
Wool	9.8	5.1	11.1	1.2	4.6	3.7	-1.2	3.2	1.1	Laine
Jute	27.0	18.0	7.7	-1.4	0.2	0.7	-3.7	-1.2	-2.0	Jute
Sisal	8.7	11.2	8.1	-0.6	3.5	1.6	-2.9	2.1	-1.1	Sisal
Hides and skins	20.5	7.9	7.8	3.5	-0.1	-1.6	1.2	-1.5	-4.2	Cuirs et peaux
Non-coniferous woods	9.8	5.1	8.8	1.2	4.6	7.3	-1.2	3.2	4.7	Bois non conifères
Tropical logs	14.3	9.9	8.0	0.3	-0.3	5.0	-1.9	-1.7	2.4	Grumes tropicales
Tropical sawnwood	11.2	12.6	4.0	-0.1	8.0	1.7	-2.4	6.6	-0.9	Grumes tropicales sciées
Plywood	15.0	14.6	8.5	3.3	6.0	4.9	1.1	4.6	2.3	Contre-plaqué
Rubber	15.6	20.3	16.0	-4.0	3.2	15.7	-6.3	1.8	13.0	Caoutchouc
Minerals, ores and metals	**10.8**	**10.5**	**20.8**	**-1.5**	**-2.3**	**14.1**	**-3.8**	**-3.7**	**11.4**	**Minéraux, minerais et métaux**
Phosphate rock	11.9	8.4	12.3	-2.1	-0.6	2.5	-4.4	-2.0	-0.2	Phosphate brut
Manganese ore	7.8	25.1	13.5	-1.5	-3.4	5.8	-3.8	-4.8	3.2	Minerai de manganèse
Iron ore	9.1	7.8	18.5	0.8	0.5	12.7	-1.5	-0.9	10.0	Minerai de fer
Aluminium	18.0	19.7	12.1	0.0	-3.2	7.2	-2.3	-4.6	4.6	Aluminium
Copper	13.9	12.6	25.0	-1.9	-1.5	17.4	-4.1	-2.9	14.8	Cuivre
Nickel	10.1	20.8	24.3	-4.5	-6.8	20.5	-6.8	-8.2	17.8	Nickel
Lead	23.9	16.0	26.0	-8.6	-0.6	16.0	-10.8	-2.0	13.4	Plomb
Zinc	10.4	15.1	34.8	1.5	-3.2	11.8	-0.7	-4.6	9.1	Zinc
Tin	17.9	10.9	22.2	-8.4	-0.9	9.8	-10.7	-4.2	7.1	Étain
Tungsten ore	11.8	15.0	28.7	-13.9	-1.2	16.0	-16.2	-2.6	13.3	Minerai de tungstène
Gold	24.0	6.2	11.9	3.2	-1.3	10.3	0.9	-2.7	7.6	Or
Silver	33.9	12.7	21.3	-4.9	-1.0	10.1	-7.2	-2.4	7.5	Argent
Crude petroleum	29.4	11.7	15.6	-2.5	1.4	17.7	-4.8	0.0	15.0	Pétrole brut

6.2 **Instability indices and trends in free-market prices for selected primary commodities**
2000 = 100

6.2 **Indices d'instabilité et tendances des prix sur le marché libre d'une sélection de produits de base**
2000 = 100

Sources:
- UNCTAD calculations based on UNCTAD *Commodity Price Statistics* on-line

Notes:

(1) Price instability indices and price trends reported here may not correspond to those published in the earlier issues of the *Handbook of Statistics*, since revised price indices, with a base year (2000=100), have been used for their calculations.

(2) The measure of price instability is

$$1/n\sum_{t=1}^{n}\left[\left(|Y(t)-y(t)|\right)/y(t)\right]*100$$

where

$Y(t)$ is the observed magnitude of the variable.

$y(t)$ is the magnitude estimated by fitting an exponential trend to the observed value and

n is the number of observations.

Accordingly, instability is measured as the percentage deviation of the variables concerned from their exponential trend levels for a given period.

(3) The growth rate of each period has been calculated using the formula:

$$\log(p)=a+b(t)$$

where

p is the price index and t is time.

(4) Constant 2000 dollars (current dollars divided by the United Nations unit value index of manufactured goods exported by developed economies)

Sources :
- Calculs du secrétariat de la CNUCED fondés sur les *Statistiques des prix des produits de base* en ligne de la CNUCED.

Notes :

(1) Les indices d'instabilité et les tendances des prix présentés ici ne correspondent pas à ceux publiés dans les versions antérieures du *Manuel de Statistiques*, car les indices des prix ont été révisés en utilisant 2000=100 comme année de base.

(2) L'indice d'instabilité des prix est calculé selon

$$1/n\sum_{t=1}^{n}\left[\left(|Y(t)-y(t)|\right)/y(t)\right]*100$$

où

$Y(t)$ est la valeur observée de la variable.

$y(t)$ est la valeur estimée par ajustement à la tendance exponentielle des valeurs observées et

n est le nombre d'observations.

L'instabilité est le pourcentage de déviation des variables en question par rapport à la ligne de tendance exponentielle pour une période donnée.

(3) Le taux de croissance de chaque période a été calculé selon la formule :

$$\log(p)=a+b(t)$$

où

p est l'indice de prix et t le temps.

(4) Dollars constants 2000 (dollar courant divisé par l'index des Nations Unies de la valeur unitaire des exportations des produits manufacturés par les économies développées)

6

Region, country or territory / Régions, pays ou territoires	Year / Année	Aluminium (Quantity) - Aluminium (Quantité)				Copper (Quantity) - Cuivre (Quantité)			
		Bauxite production / Production de bauxite (1)	Alumina production / Production d'alumine (2)	Primary aluminium production / Production d'aluminium de première fusion	Primary aluminium consumption / Consommation d'aluminium de première fusion (3)	Copper ore production / Production de minerai de cuivre (4)	Unrefined copper production / Production de cuivre non affiné (5)	Refined copper production / Production de cuivre affiné	Refined copper consumption / Consommation de cuivre affiné (3)
WORLD - MONDE	**94-96**	**119 681**	**22 088**	**20 022**	**20 123**	**10 310**	**10 435**	**11 959**	**12 074**
	99-01	**135 993**	**27 689**	**24 418**	**24 011**	**13 146**	**12 339**	**14 946**	**14 642**
	04-06	**176 263**	**34 045**	**31 958**	**31 793**	**15 077**	**12 122**	**16 565**	**16 865**
DEVELOPING ECONOMIES - ÉCONOMIES EN DÉVELOPPEMENT	94-96	66 130	6 989	6 112	5 477	5 655	4 134	4 428	3 757
	99-01	71 549	9 567	8 435	7 736	8 358	5 289	6 857	5 643
	04-06	100 666	13 429	15 101	13 680	10 343	5 925	8 923	8 025
ECONOMIES IN TRANSITION - ÉCONOMIES EN TRANSITION	94-96	6 992	2 315	3 149	552	912	981	999	283
	99-01	9 184	3 073	3 818	810	1 100	1 361	1 350	239
	04-06	12 613	3 711	4 429	1 211	1 278	1 480	1 523	798
DEVELOPED ECONOMIES - ÉCONOMIES DÉVELOPPÉES	94-96	46 558	12 784	10 761	14 094	3 743	5 320	6 532	8 034
	99-01	55 260	15 049	12 166	15 466	3 687	5 689	6 739	8 760
	04-06	62 983	16 905	12 428	16 902	3 456	4 717	6 119	8 042
Developing economies: Africa - Économies en développement : Afrique	**94-96**	**17 746**	**334**	**714**	**245**	**641**	**541**	**513**	**119**
	99-01	**18 100**	**319**	**1 205**	**324**	**496**	**492**	**407**	**128**
	04-06	**19 784**	**407**	**1 776**	**434**	**703**	**429**	**562**	**184**
Eastern Africa - Afrique orientale	*94-96*	*11*	*..*	*..*	*..*	*364*	*309*	*348*	*30*
	99-01	*8*	*..*	*160*	*..*	*279*	*321*	*279*	*25*
	04-06	*9*	*..*	*555*	*..*	*461*	*292*	*456*	*27*
Mozambique	94-96	11	..	..	..	..	..	..	..
	99-01	8	..	160	..	..	..	..	..
	04-06	9	..	555	..	..	..	..	..
United Republic of Tanzania - République-Unie de Tanzanie	94-96	..	..	..	..	..	..	..	..
	99-01	..	..	..	..	4	..	..	..
	04-06	..	..	..	..	4	..	..	..
Zambia - Zambie	94-96	..	..	..	..	355	297	327	15
	99-01	..	..	..	..	276	311	267	15
	04-06	..	..	..	..	454	290	450	17
Zimbabwe	94-96	..	..	..	..	9	12	21	15
	99-01	..	..	..	..	2	10	11	10
	04-06	..	..	..	..	3	3	6	10
Middle Africa - Afrique centrale	*94-96*	*..*	*..*	*81*	*19*	*39*	*36*	*35*	*1*
	99-01	*..*	*..*	*86*	*24*	*33*	*32*	*29*	*..*
	04-06	*..*	*..*	*88*	*19*	*100*	*..*	*2*	*..*
Cameroon - Cameroun	94-96	..	..	81	19	..	..	..	..
	99-01	..	..	86	24	..	..	..	..
	04-06	..	..	88	19	..	..	..	..
Dem. Rep. of the Congo - Rép. dém. du Congo	94-96	..	..	..	..	39	36	35	1
	99-01	..	..	..	..	33	32	29	..
	04-06	..	..	..	..	100	..	2	..
Northern Africa - Afrique septentrionale	*94-96*	*..*	*..*	*183*	*87*	*14*	*..*	*4*	*5*
	99-01	*..*	*..*	*189*	*97*	*6*	*..*	*..*	*25*
	04-06	*..*	*..*	*237*	*118*	*4*	*..*	*7*	*68*
Algeria - Algérie	94-96	..	..	..	7	..	..	..	..
	99-01	..	..	..	5	..	..	..	..
	04-06	..	..	..	6	..	..	..	..
Egypt - Égypte	94-96	..	..	183	79	..	..	4	4
	99-01	..	..	189	87	..	..	..	21
	04-06	..	..	237	102	..	..	7	63
Morocco - Maroc	94-96	..	..	..	2	14	..	..	..
	99-01	..	..	..	5	6	..	..	..
	04-06	..	..	..	10	4	..	..	..
Tunisia - Tunisie	94-96	..	..	..	..	..	..	..	3
	99-01	..	..	..	..	..	..	..	4
	04-06	..	..	..	..	..	..	..	5

For sources and notes, see end of table.

Pour les sources et les notes, se reporter à la fin du tableau.

Region, country or territory / Régions, pays ou territoires	Year / Année	Aluminium (Quantity) - Aluminium (Quantité)				Copper (Quantity) - Cuivre (Quantité)			
		Bauxite production / Production de bauxite	Alumina production / Production d'alumine	Primary aluminium production / Production d'aluminium de première fusion	Primary aluminium consumption / Consommation d'aluminium de première fusion	Copper ore production / Production de minerai de cuivre	Unrefined copper production / Production de cuivre non affiné	Refined copper production / Production de cuivre affiné	Refined copper consumption / Consommation de cuivre affiné
		(1)	(2)		(3)	(4)	(5)		(3)
Southern Africa - Afrique australe	*94-96*	..	..	*312*	*115*	*225*	*196*	*126*	*80*
	99-01	..	..	*675*	*170*	*177*	*161*	*109*	*75*
	04-06	..	..	*867*	*254*	*137*	*137*	*96*	*85*
Botswana	94-96	..	..	..	..	22	21	..	..
	99-01	..	..	..	..	20	20	..	..
	04-06	..	..	..	..	24	24	..	..
Namibia - Namibie	94-96		..	..	..	21	25	..	..
	99-01		..	..	..	10	11	..	..
	04-06		..	..	..	9	23	..	..
South Africa - Afrique du Sud	94-96		..	312	115	181	156	126	80
	99-01		..	675	170	151	130	109	75
	04-06		..	867	254	103	97	96	85
Western Africa - Afrique occidentale	*94-96*	*17 735*	*334*	*138*	*22*	..	..	..	..
	99-01	*18 092*	*319*	*149*	*26*	..	..	..	..
	04-06	*19 775*	*407*	*45*	*27*	*5*	..	..	..
Ghana	94-96	471	..	138	16	..	..	..	..
	99-01	517	..	144	16	..	..	..	..
	04-06	664	..	45	16	..	..	..	..
Guinea - Guinée	94-96	17 020	334	..	..	..	..	..	..
	99-01	17 574	319	..	..	..	..	..	..
	04-06	18 740	407	..	..	..	..	..	..
Mauritania - Mauritanie	94-96	..	..	..	..	..	..	..	..
	99-01	..	..	..	..	..	..	..	..
	04-06	..	..	..	..	5	..	..	..
Nigeria - Nigéria	94-96	..	..	..	6	..	..	..	..
	99-01	..	..	16	10	..	..	..	..
	04-06	..	..	..	11	..	..	..	..
Sierra Leone	94-96	735	..	..	..	..	..	..	..
	99-01	..	..	..	..	..	..	..	..
	04-06	557	..	..	..	..	..	..	..
Developing economies: America - Économies en développement : Amérique	*94-96*	*33 194*	*4 561*	*2 040*	*865*	*3 405*	*2 124*	*2 234*	*582*
	99-01	*35 700*	*5 757*	*2 089*	*891*	*5 707*	*2 397*	*3 752*	*951*
	04-06	*48 053*	*7 078*	*2 418*	*1 260*	*7 296*	*2 495*	*3 911*	*976*
Caribbean - Caraïbes	*94-96*	*11 417*	*1 667*	..	*1*	*2*	..	..	..
	99-01	*11 728*	*1 914*	..	*1*	*1*	..	..	*1*
	04-06	*14 093*	*2 188*	..	*3*	..	..	..	*1*
Cuba	94-96	..	..	..	1	2	..	..	..
	99-01	..	..	..	1	1	..	..	1
	04-06	..	..	..	3	..	..	..	1
Jamaica - Jamaïque	94-96	11 417	1 667	..	..	..	..	..	..
	99-01	11 728	1 914	..	..	..	..	..	..
	04-06	14 093	2 188	..	..	..	..	..	..
Central America - Amérique centrale	*94-96*	..	..	*36*	*71*	*327*	*295*	*242*	*191*
	99-01	..	..	*58*	*96*	*372*	*346*	*347*	*435*
	04-06	..	..	..	*151*	*390*	*321*	*354*	*427*
Mexico - Mexique	94-96	..	..	36	71	327	295	242	191
	99-01	..	..	58	96	372	346	347	435
	04-06	..	..	..	151	390	321	354	427
South America - Amérique du Sud	*94-96*	*21 778*	*2 894*	*2 016*	*793*	*3 076*	*1 829*	*1 992*	*390*
	99-01	*23 972*	*3 843*	*2 031*	*793*	*5 334*	*2 051*	*3 405*	*515*
	04-06	*33 960*	*4 890*	*2 418*	*1 107*	*6 906*	*2 173*	*3 557*	*548*
Argentina - Argentine	94-96	..	..	180	92	..	..	16	51
	99-01	..	..	237	73	178	..	16	44
	04-06	..	..	274	120	181	..	16	32
Bolivia - Bolivie	94-96	..	..	..	..	0	..	..	..
	99-01	..	..	..	..	..	..	..	..
	04-06	..	..	..	..	..	..	..	..

For sources and notes, see end of table.

Pour les sources et les notes, se reporter à la fin du tableau.

Region, country or territory / Régions, pays ou territoires	Year / Année	Aluminium (Quantity) - Aluminium (Quantité)				Copper (Quantity) - Cuivre (Quantité)			
		Bauxite production / Production de bauxite (1)	Alumina production / Production d'alumine (2)	Primary aluminium production / Production d'aluminium de première fusion	Primary aluminium consumption / Consommation d'aluminium de première fusion (3)	Copper ore production / Production de minerai de cuivre (4)	Unrefined copper production / Production de cuivre non affiné (5)	Refined copper production / Production de cuivre affiné	Refined copper consumption / Consommation de cuivre affiné (3)
Brazil - Brésil	94-96	11 336	1 194	1 190	471	45	169	169	204
	99-01	13 341	1 928	1 218	510	32	197	197	321
	04-06	21 940	2 786	1 520	728	271	206	209	337
Chile - Chili	94-96	..	..	..	13	2 608	1 295	1 506	88
	99-01	..	..	..	13	4 577	1 479	2 739	83
	04-06	..	..	..	20	5 365	1 547	2 824	105
Colombia - Colombie	94-96	..	..	..	32	3	..	4	1
	99-01	..	..	..	30	2	..	..	4
	04-06	..	..	..	56	1	..	..	14
Guyana	94-96	1 898	..	..	..	..	..	..	..
	99-01	2 353	..	..	..	..	..	..	..
	04-06	1 543	..	..	..	..	..	..	..
Peru - Pérou	94-96	..	..	..	5	420	366	300	29
	99-01	..	..	..	..	604	375	453	55
	04-06	..	..	..	..	1 089	420	508	55
Suriname	94-96	3 668	834	26	..	..	..	..	..
	99-01	3 906	1 010	7	..	..	..	..	..
	04-06	4 597	1 073	..	..	..	..	..	..
Venezuela (Bolivarian Rep. of) - Venezuela (Rép. bolivarienne du)	94-96	4 876	866	619	181	..	..	..	18
	99-01	4 371	904	574	168	..	..	..	9
	04-06	5 881	1 031	624	182	..	..	..	6
Developing economies: Asia - Économies en développement : Asie	**94-96**	**15 190**	**2 094**	**3 358**	**4 367**	**1 407**	**1 469**	**1 681**	**3 056**
	99-01	**17 750**	**3 492**	**5 140**	**6 521**	**1 957**	**2 399**	**2 698**	**4 564**
	04-06	**32 829**	**5 944**	**10 907**	**11 985**	**2 157**	**3 001**	**4 451**	**6 865**
Eastern Asia - Asie orientale	*94-96*	*7 919*	*1 157*	*1 765*	*2 765*	*556*	*1 027*	*1 236*	*2 158*
	99-01	*7 883*	*2 309*	*3 125*	*4 634*	*707*	*1 602*	*1 837*	*3 366*
	04-06	*17 839*	*4 184*	*7 948*	*8 921*	*892*	*1 872*	*3 136*	*5 089*
China - Chine	94-96	7 919	1 157	1 755	1 709	425	845	979	1 045
	99-01	7 883	2 309	3 125	3 306	567	1 180	1 356	1 907
	04-06	17 839	4 184	7 948	7 270	753	1 560	2 594	3 538
China, Hong Kong SAR - Chine (RAS de Hong Kong)	94-96	..	..	..	42	..	..	..	4
	99-01	..	..	..	49	..	..	..	5
	04-06	..	..	..	28	..	..	..	5
China, Taiwan Province of - Province chinoise de Taiwan	94-96	..	..	..	343	..	0	7	551
	99-01	..	..	..	429	..	..	..	608
	04-06	..	..	..	444	..	..	..	657
Dem. People's Rep. of Korea - Rép. populaire dém. de Corée	94-96	..	..	10	20	11	29	17	20
	99-01	..	..	..	22	11	15	15	16
	04-06	..	..	..	22	12	15	15	17
Mongolia - Mongolie	94-96	..	..	..	..	121	..	..	..
	99-01	..	..	..	..	129	..	1	..
	04-06	..	..	..	..	130	..	2	..
Republic of Korea - République de Corée	94-96	..	..	..	651	..	153	233	538
	99-01	..	..	..	829	..	408	465	832
	04-06	..	..	..	1 158	..	453	530	873
Southern Asia - Asie méridionale	*94-96*	*5 662*	*851*	*602*	*679*	*156*	*163*	*173*	*185*
	99-01	*8 237*	*1 101*	*767*	*706*	*178*	*407*	*446*	*370*
	04-06	*13 163*	*1 681*	*1 201*	*1 118*	*234*	*667*	*711*	*508*
Bangladesh	94-96	..	..	..	10	..	..	..	..
	99-01	..	..	..	..	..	..	..	..
	04-06	..	..	..	..	..	..	..	..
India - Inde	94-96	5 500	851	497	547	47	45	43	131
	99-01	7 798	1 101	624	587	37	258	274	265
	04-06	12 746	1 604	973	960	27	463	523	382

For sources and notes, see end of table.

Pour les sources et les notes, se reporter à la fin du tableau.

Region, country or territory / Régions, pays ou territoires	Year / Année	Aluminium (Quantity) - Aluminium (Quantité)				Copper (Quantity) - Cuivre (Quantité)			
		Bauxite production / Production de bauxite (1)	Alumina production / Production d'alumine (2)	Primary aluminium production / Production d'aluminium de première fusion	Primary aluminium consumption / Consommation d'aluminium de première fusion (3)	Copper ore production / Production de minerai de cuivre (4)	Unrefined copper production / Production de cuivre non affiné (5)	Refined copper production / Production de cuivre affiné	Refined copper consumption / Consommation de cuivre affiné (3)
Iran (Islamic Rep. of) - Iran (Rép. islamique d')	94-96	158	..	104	109	109	117	130	48
	99-01	410	..	143	119	141	150	172	97
	04-06	415	77	228	158	190	205	188	113
Pakistan	94-96	4	..	..	13	..	..	..	8
	99-01	29	..	..	..	..	..	..	7
	04-06	3	..	..	..	17	..	..	13
South-Eastern Asia - Asie du Sud-Est	*94-96*	*1 226*	*..*	*224*	*563*	*645*	*215*	*156*	*429*
	99-01	*1 327*	*..*	*171*	*569*	*1 002*	*335*	*331*	*439*
	04-06	*1 329*	*..*	*248*	*940*	*989*	*423*	*493*	*775*
Indonesia - Indonésie	94-96	1 028	..	224	172	526	..	..	83
	99-01	1 168	..	171	149	942	173	154	74
	04-06	1 305	..	248	268	907	229	230	211
Lao People's dem. Rep. - Rép. dém. populaire lao	94-96	..	..	..	..	..	..	..	..
	99-01	..	..	..	..	..	..	..	..
	04-06	..	..	..	..	31	..	46	..
Malaysia - Malaisie	94-96	188	..	..	99	22	..	..	121
	99-01	137	..	..	150	5	..	..	161
	04-06	4	..	..	120	..	..	..	211
Myanmar	94-96	..	..	..	..	5	..	..	..
	99-01	..	..	..	..	26	..	27	..
	04-06	..	..	..	..	29	..	29	..
Philippines	94-96	..	..	..	29	92	215	156	48
	99-01	..	..	..	31	30	162	150	35
	04-06	..	..	..	28	17	194	176	34
Singapore - Singapour	94-96	..	..	..	37	..	..	..	18
	99-01	..	..	..	23	..	..	..	10
	04-06	..	..	..	61	..	..	..	10
Thailand - Thaïlande	94-96	..	..	..	219	..	..	..	158
	99-01	..	..	..	193	..	..	..	145
	04-06	..	..	..	386	..	..	27	247
Viet Nam	94-96	30	..	..	7	..	..	..	1
	99-01	22	..	..	24	2	..	..	15
	04-06	20	..	..	76	6	..	..	61
Western Asia - Asie occidentale	*94-96*	*383*	*86*	*767*	*335*	*49*	*65*	*117*	*266*
	99-01	*303*	*82*	*1 077*	*526*	*70*	*55*	*83*	*383*
	04-06	*498*	*79*	*1 510*	*882*	*43*	*39*	*111*	*468*
Bahrain - Bahreïn	94-96	..	..	456	142	..	..	..	..
	99-01	..	..	511	242	..	..	..	..
	04-06	..	..	708	346	..	..	..	..
Iraq	94-96	..	..	..	1	..	..	..	..
	99-01	..	..	..	..	..	..	..	..
	04-06	..	..	..	..	..	..	..	..
Kuwait - Koweït	94-96	..	..	..	..	..	..	..	15
	99-01	..	..	..	..	..	..	..	9
	04-06	..	..	..	..	..	..	..	11
Lebanon - Liban	94-96	..	..	..	9	..	..	..	..
	99-01	..	..	..	..	..	..	..	..
	04-06	..	..	..	..	..	..	..	..
Oman	94-96	..	..	..	..	4	30	22	..
	99-01	..	..	..	..	..	22	22	..
	04-06	..	..	..	..	..	24	20	..
Saudi Arabia - Arabie saoudite	94-96	..	..	..	33	1	1	..	125
	99-01	..	..	..	60	1	..	..	160
	04-06	..	..	..	79	1	..	..	160

For sources and notes, see end of table.

Pour les sources et les notes, se reporter à la fin du tableau.

Region, country or territory / Régions, pays ou territoires	Year / Année	Aluminium (Quantity) - Aluminium (Quantité)				Copper (Quantity) - Cuivre (Quantité)			
		Bauxite production / Production de bauxite	Alumina production / Production d'alumine	Primary aluminium production / Production d'aluminium de première fusion	Primary aluminium consumption / Consommation d'aluminium de première fusion	Copper ore production / Production de minerai de cuivre	Unrefined copper production / Production de cuivre non affiné	Refined copper production / Production de cuivre affiné	Refined copper consumption / Consommation de cuivre affiné
		(1)	(2)		(3)	(4)	(5)		(3)
Turkey - Turquie	94-96	383	86	61	132	47	34	95	136
	99-01	303	82	62	185	69	33	61	214
	04-06	498	79	61	391	42	16	91	298
United Arab Emirates - Émirats arabes unis	94-96	..	..	251	19	..	..	..	..
	99-01	..	..	504	38	..	..	..	..
	04-06	..	..	741	66	..	..	..	..
Developing economies: Oceania - Économies en développement : Océanie	**94-96**	..	..	..	..	**202**	..	..	..
	99-01	..	..	..	..	**198**	..	..	..
	04-06	..	..	..	..	**187**	..	..	..
Papua New Guinea - Papouasie-Nouvelle-Guinée	94-96	..	..	..	..	202	..	..	..
	99-01	..	..	..	..	198	..	..	..
	04-06	..	..	..	..	187	..	..	..
Economies in transition: Asia - Économies en transition : Asie	**94-96**	**3 083**	**534**	**231**	..	**285**	**333**	**362**	**50**
	99-01	**3 674**	**685**	**285**	..	**513**	**495**	**468**	**30**
	04-06	**4 794**	**950**	**415**	..	**565**	**552**	**536**	**85**
Armenia - Arménie	94-96	..	..	..	..	1	..	..	..
	99-01	..	..	..	..	13	4	..	..
	04-06	..	..	..	..	17	9	..	..
Azerbaijan - Azerbaïdjan	94-96	..	18	11	..	..	..	..	..
	99-01	..	40	0	..	..	..	..	..
	04-06	..	148	31	..	..	..	..	..
Georgia - Géorgie	94-96	..	..	..	..	5	..	..	..
	99-01	..	..	..	..	7	..	..	..
	04-06	..	..	..	..	11	..	..	..
Kazakhstan	94-96	3 083	516	..	..	227	258	267	40
	99-01	3 674	644	..	..	424	410	394	20
	04-06	4 794	802	..	..	441	432	431	58
Tajikistan - Tadjikistan	94-96	..	..	224	..	..	..	..	..
	99-01	..	..	284	..	..	..	..	..
	04-06	..	..	384	..	..	..	..	..
Uzbekistan - Ouzbékistan	94-96	..	..	..	..	51	75	95	10
	99-01	..	..	..	..	69	82	74	10
	04-06	..	..	..	..	97	112	105	27
Economies in transition: Europe - Économies en transition : Europe	**94-96**	**3 910**	**1 781**	**2 918**	**552**	**628**	**648**	**637**	**233**
	99-01	**5 510**	**2 388**	**3 533**	**810**	**587**	**866**	**881**	**209**
	04-06	**7 820**	**2 761**	**4 014**	**1 211**	**712**	**928**	**986**	**713**
Albania - Albanie	94-96	0	..	..	1	3	2	2	0
	99-01	5	..	..	..	1	1	..	0
	04-06	..	..	..	..	1	..	..	0
Belarus - Bélarus	94-96	..	..	..	6	..	..	..	..
	99-01	..	..	..	10	..	..	..	..
	04-06	..	..	..	11	..	..	..	..
Bosnia and Herzegovina - Bosnie-Herzégovine	94-96	75	26	..	..	..	..	..	..
	99-01	172	50	87	..	..	..	..	..
	04-06	922	16	128	..	..	..	..	..
Croatia - Croatie	94-96	1	..	26	23	..	..	..	..
	99-01	..	..	..	32	..	..	..	..
	04-06	..	..	..	66	..	..	..	..
Russian Federation - Fédération de Russie	94-96	3 756	1 123	2 776	463	541	546	550	181
	99-01	4 802	1 537	3 233	699	535	818	839	192
	04-06	6 275	1 761	3 653	1 029	690	909	938	670
Serbia and Montenegro - Serbie-et-Monténégro	94-96	192	37	29	14	73	100	85	48
	99-01	588	97	95	16	43	48	43	13
	04-06	622	130	119	68	17	19	36	22

For sources and notes, see end of table.

Pour les sources et les notes, se reporter à la fin du tableau.

Region, country or territory Régions, pays ou territoires	Year Année	Aluminium (Quantity) - Aluminium (Quantité)				Copper (Quantity) - Cuivre (Quantité)			
		Bauxite production Production de bauxite (1)	Alumina production Production d'alumine (2)	Primary aluminium production Production d'aluminium de première fusion	Primary aluminium consumption Consommation d'aluminium de première fusion (3)	Copper ore production Production de minerai de cuivre (4)	Unrefined copper production Production de cuivre non affiné (5)	Refined copper production Production de cuivre affiné	Refined copper consumption Consommation de cuivre affiné (3)
TFYR of Macedonia - LERY de Macédoine	94-96	..	..	..	3	11	..	..	..
	99-01	..	..	..	3	9	..	..	..
	04-06	..	..	..	2	7	..	..	..
Ukraine	94-96	..	606	96	45	..	..	..	3
	99-01	..	704	119	50	..	..	..	3
	04-06	..	862	113	37	..	..	12	20
Developed economies: America - Économies développées : Amérique	**94-96**	**229**	**3 066**	**5 654**	**5 867**	**2 550**	**2 246**	**2 848**	**2 809**
	99-01	**223**	**3 108**	**5 810**	**6 623**	**2 099**	**1 691**	**2 463**	**3 144**
	04-06	**200**	**3 545**	**5 273**	**6 825**	**1 762**	**1 014**	**1 770**	**2 565**
Canada	94-96	..	581	2 237	597	677	595	561	202
	99-01	..	559	2 449	773	629	621	556	268
	04-06	..	693	2 846	803	588	492	514	296
United States - États-Unis	94-96	229	2 485	3 417	5 270	1 872	1 651	2 287	2 606
	99-01	223	2 549	3 361	5 850	1 470	1 070	1 907	2 876
	04-06	200	2 852	2 427	6 021	1 174	522	1 256	2 269
Developed economies: Asia - Économies développées : Asie	**94-96**	**..**	**246**	**17**	**2 392**	**3**	**1 175**	**1 186**	**1 423**
	99-01	**..**	**403**	**8**	**2 163**	**1**	**1 446**	**1 402**	**1 262**
	04-06	**..**	**406**	**7**	**2 353**	**1**	**1 537**	**1 436**	**1 263**
Israel - Israël	94-96	..	..	..	37	..	..	..	..
	99-01	..	..	..	46	..	..	..	..
	04-06	..	..	..	47	..	..	..	..
Japan - Japon	94-96	..	246	17	2 355	3	1 175	1 186	1 423
	99-01	..	403	8	2 117	1	1 446	1 402	1 262
	04-06	..	406	7	2 306	1	1 537	1 436	1 263
Developed economies: Europe - Économies développées : Europe	**94-96**	**3 583**	**2 537**	**3 486**	**5 456**	**742**	**1 626**	**2 170**	**3 638**
	99-01	**3 031**	**3 221**	**4 260**	**6 299**	**765**	**2 159**	**2 373**	**4 183**
	04-06	**3 068**	**3 719**	**4 891**	**7 304**	**808**	**1 881**	**2 447**	**4 059**
Austria - Autriche	94-96	..	..	..	150	..	56	58	27
	99-01	..	..	..	171	..	72	71	34
	04-06	..	..	..	240	..	75	73	34
Belgium - Belgique	94-96	–	–	–	–	–	–	–	–
	99-01	–	–	–	–	–	–	–	–
	04-06	..	..	..	437	..	103	383	328
Belgium-Luxembourg - Belgique-Luxembourg	94-96	..	..	..	338	..	172	379	367
	99-01	..	..	..	339	..	142	412	337
	04-06	–	–	–	–	–	–	–	–
Bulgaria - Bulgarie	94-96	..	..	..	6	79	100	25	18
	99-01	..	..	..	9	93	149	29	14
	04-06	..	..	..	25	86	239	60	31
Cyprus - Chypre	94-96	..	..	..	..	2	..	2	..
	99-01	..	..	..	..	5	..	5	..
	04-06	..	..	..	..	1	..	1	..
Czech Republic - République tchèque	94-96	..	..	..	56	..	22	..	11
	99-01	..	..	..	77	..	..	..	18
	04-06	..	..	..	126	..	..	..	5
Denmark - Danemark	94-96	..	..	..	27	..	..	..	0
	99-01	..	..	..	42	..	..	..	0
	04-06	..	..	..	66	..	..	..	0
Finland - Finlande	94-96	..	..	..	27	11	151	85	88
	99-01	..	..	..	37	11	160	115	111
	04-06	..	..	..	36	15	169	134	93
France	94-96	141	212	377	717	0	3	41	524
	99-01	169	266	452	766	..	1	2	554
	04-06	171	272	436	727	..	..	..	489

For sources and notes, see end of table.

Pour les sources et les notes, se reporter à la fin du tableau.

Region, country or territory / Régions, pays ou territoires	Year / Année	Aluminium (Quantity) - Aluminium (Quantité)				Copper (Quantity) - Cuivre (Quantité)			
		Bauxite production / Production de bauxite (1)	Alumina production / Production d'alumine (2)	Primary aluminium production / Production d'aluminium de première fusion	Primary aluminium consumption / Consommation d'aluminium de première fusion (3)	Copper ore production / Production de minerai de cuivre (4)	Unrefined copper production / Production de cuivre non affiné (5)	Refined copper production / Production de cuivre affiné	Refined copper consumption / Consommation de cuivre affiné (3)
Germany - Allemagne	94-96	..	411	552	1 407	..	328	626	1 007
	99-01	..	369	643	1 503	..	670	700	1 188
	04-06	..	449	610	1 797	..	520	651	1 205
Greece - Grèce	94-96	2 283	308	143	154	..	..	..	81
	99-01	1 868	274	164	220	..	..	..	126
	04-06	2 333	277	166	276	..	..	..	104
Hungary - Hongrie	94-96	970	90	33	136	..	0	..	14
	99-01	994	176	34	201	..	..	..	19
	04-06	563	163	22	225	..	..	..	3
Iceland - Islande	94-96	..	..	100	1	..	..	..	..
	99-01	..	..	231	..	..	..	..	..
	04-06	..	..	294	..	..	..	..	..
Ireland - Irlande	94-96	..	632	..	5	..	..	..	0
	99-01	..	760	..	9	..	..	..	..
	04-06	..	890	..	2	..	..	..	1
Italy - Italie	94-96	17	298	179	637	..	..	89	494
	99-01	..	534	188	757	..	..	31	662
	04-06	..	576	194	995	..	..	34	731
Malta - Malte	94-96	..	..	..	0	..	..	..	..
	99-01	..	..	..	..	..	..	..	..
	04-06	..	..	..	..	..	..	..	..
Netherlands - Pays-Bas	94-96	..	..	206	147	..	..	..	28
	99-01	..	..	294	155	..	..	..	51
	04-06	..	..	325	146	..	..	..	50
Norway - Norvège	94-96	..	..	856	179	7	33	36	1
	99-01	..	..	1 024	239	..	..	28	..
	04-06	..	..	1 374	251	..	..	38	..
Poland - Pologne	94-96	..	..	51	80	395	410	412	197
	99-01	..	..	53	144	464	497	485	256
	04-06	..	..	53	182	513	573	556	271
Portugal	94-96	..	..	..	63	123	0	0	3
	99-01	..	..	..	76	86	..	..	0
	04-06	..	..	..	91	88	..	..	1
Romania - Roumanie	94-96	178	156	134	30	25	27	24	25
	99-01	..	181	178	113	17	19	18	15
	04-06	..	337	241	208	16	0	22	29
Slovakia - Slovaquie	94-96	..	..	70	25	1	9	24	26
	99-01	..	..	108	33	..	10	6	6
	04-06	..	..	158	24	..	..	..	1
Slovenia - Slovénie	94-96	..	..	70	51	..	..	..	..
	99-01	..	..	76	91	..	..	..	..
	04-06	..	..	133	115	..	..	..	..
Spain - Espagne	94-96	..	373	354	354	23	202	206	181
	99-01	..	614	373	509	14	296	304	281
	04-06	..	755	387	616	4	234	266	301
Sweden - Suède	94-96	..	..	100	125	78	110	113	143
	99-01	..	..	100	133	74	151	154	192
	04-06	..	..	101	115	85	159	229	179
Switzerland - Suisse	94-96	..	..	24	148	..	..	..	6
	99-01	..	..	35	161	..	..	..	8
	04-06	..	..	35	175	..	..	..	5
United Kingdom - Royaume-Uni	94-96	..	56	236	587	..	50	52	390
	99-01	..	47	305	502	..	..	50	305
	04-06	..	..	363	385	..	..	..	194

For sources and notes, see end of table.

Pour les sources et les notes, se reporter à la fin du tableau.

6.3 Production and consumption of aluminium and copper of countries and geographical regions

6.3 Production et consommation d'aluminium et de cuivre des pays et des régions géographiques

Region, country or territory / Régions, pays ou territoires	Year / Année	Aluminium (Quantity) - Aluminium (Quantité)				Copper (Quantity) - Cuivre (Quantité)			
		Bauxite production / Production de bauxite	Alumina production / Production d'alumine	Primary aluminium production / Production d'aluminium de première fusion	Primary aluminium consumption / Consommation d'aluminium de première fusion	Copper ore production / Production de minerai de cuivre	Unrefined copper production / Production de cuivre non affiné	Refined copper production / Production de cuivre affiné	Refined copper consumption / Consommation de cuivre affiné
		(1)	(2)		(3)	(4)	(5)		(3)
Developed economies: Oceania - Économies développées : Océanie	**94-96**	**42 746**	**6 935**	**1 604**	**379**	**448**	**273**	**327**	**164**
	99-01	**52 006**	**8 317**	**2 087**	**381**	**823**	**394**	**501**	**170**
	04-06	**59 716**	**9 235**	**2 257**	**421**	**886**	**427**	**466**	**156**
Australia - Australie	94-96	42 746	6 935	1 329	340	448	273	327	155
	99-01	52 006	8 317	1 761	336	823	394	501	164
	04-06	59 716	9 235	1 910	351	886	427	466	156
New Zealand - Nouvelle-Zélande	94-96	..	..	275	39	..	..	..	9
	99-01	..	..	326	45	..	..	..	6
	04-06	..	..	347	69	..	..	..	0

Sources:
UNCTAD secretariat calculations based on:
- UNCTAD, *Commodity Yearbook*
- National sources
- British Geological Survey, *World Mineral Production*
- British Geological Survey, *World Mineral Statistics*
- Metallgesellschaft, *Metal Statistics*
- World Bureau of Metal Statistics, *World Metal Statistics Quarterly Summary*
- World Bureau of Metal Statistics, *World Metal Statistics Yearbook*
- United States Geological Survey (on-line) - *Minerals Yearbook Volume III. -- Area Reports: International*

Notes:
- Quantities are averages of three continuous years, and are expressed in thousand metric tons, unless otherwise indicated.
(1) Volume in gross weight
(2) UNCTAD estimates based on the data from *World Mineral Production* and *World Mineral Statistics*. Volume in metal content. Data for 2006 is not available.
(3) Only major consuming countries are reported. World and regional totals have been calculated by the UNCTAD secretariat, and include the data for countries which are not reported in this Handbook.
(4) Volume in metal content
(5) Includes production from both primary and secondary copper smelters

Sources :
Calculs du secrétariat de la CNUCED sur la base des données de :
- CNUCED, *Annuaire des produits de base*
- Sources nationales
- British Geological Survey, *World Mineral Production*
- British Geological Survey, *World Mineral Statistics*
- Metallgesellschaft, *Metal Statistics*
- World Bureau of Metal Statistics, *World Metal Statistics Quarterly Summary*
- World Bureau of Metal Statistics, *World Metal Statistics Yearbook*
- Service géologique des États-Unis (en ligne) - *Minerals Yearbook Volume III. -- Area Reports: International*

Notes :
- Les quantités représentent les moyennes de trois années continues et sont exprimées en milliers de tonnes métriques, sauf indication contraire.
(1) Volume en poids brut
(2) Les estimations de la CNUCED sont fondées sur les données des *World Mineral Production* et *World Mineral Statistics*. Les volumes sont exprimés en métal contenu. Les données pour 2006 ne sont pas disponibles.
(3) Seuls les principaux pays consommateurs sont rapportés. Les totaux pour le monde et les totaux régionaux ont été calculés par le secrétariat de la CNUCED et incluent les données des pays qui ne sont pas déclarés dans ce Manuel.
(4) Les volumes sont indiqués en métal contenu
(5) Inclut la production des fonderies de cuivre de première et seconde fusion

6

7

INTERNATIONAL **FINANCE**

FINANCE INTERNATIONALE

1
2
3
4
5
6
7
8

Country or territory Pays ou territoires	Year Année	Goods and services Biens et services			Income Revenu				Current transfers (net) Transfers courants (nets)	Current account balance Solde du compte des transactions courantes
					Debit / Débit		Credit / Crédit			
		Exports Exportations	Imports Importations	Balance on goods and services Balance des biens et services	Total	of which: / dont : Direct investment income Revenu d'investissement direct	Total	of which: / dont : Direct investment income Revenu d'investissement direct		
		(1)	(2)	(3)=(1)+(2)	(4)	(5)	(6)	(7)	(8)	
		Millions of dollars / Millions de dollars								
Albania - Albanie	1990	354	-485	-131	-2	..	..	..	15	-118
	2000	704	-1 499	-796	-9	0	116	..	533	-156
	2005	1 821	-3 860	-2 040	-53	-2	227	0	1 294	-571
	2006	2 297	-4 500	-2 204	-69	-5	332	13	1 270	-671
Algeria - Algérie	1990	13 462	-10 107	3 355	-2 341	-151	73	5	333	1 420
Angola	1990	3 992	-3 386	607	-776	-314	11	..	-77	-236
	2000	8 188	-5 739	2 449	-1 715	-929	34	..	28	796
	2005	24 286	-15 144	9 142	-4 057	-3 406	26	18	27	5 138
	2006	33 347	-16 289	17 058	-6 323	-5 278	145	..	-190	10 690
Anguilla	1990	41	-43	-2	-8	-7	2	..	0	-9
	2000	69	-124	-55	-13	-10	4	0	3	-61
	2005	114	-171	-57	-9	-6	12	..	1	-53
Antigua and Barbuda - Antigua-et-Barbuda	1990	345	-341	5	-48	-19	2	..	10	-31
	2000	467	-498	-32	-60	-22	16	..	9	-67
	2005	570	-598	-28	-60	-31	18	..	8	-62
Argentina - Argentine	1990	14 800	-6 846	7 954	-6 254	-637	1 854	2	998	4 552
	2000	31 277	-33 108	-1 832	-14 968	-3 086	7 420	978	399	-8 981
	2005	46 839	-34 940	11 899	-11 016	-4 856	4 279	987	529	5 691
	2006	54 123	-41 088	13 035	-10 851	-6 115	5 411	1 316	497	8 092
Armenia - Arménie	2000	447	-966	-519	-51	-22	104	..	188	-278
	2005	1 416	-2 124	-708	-325	-170	458	0	524	-52
	2006	1 510	-2 536	-1 026	-409	-244	624	1	694	-117
Aruba	1990	566	-716	-149	-23	..	15	..	-1	-158
	2000	3 534	-3 227	307	-73	-23	53	1	-76	211
	2005	4 787	-4 397	390	-503	-434	41	3	-130	-203
	2006	5 266	-4 823	443	-162	-90	58	14	-126	213
Australia - Australie	1990	49 846	-53 056	-3 210	-16 404	-4 488	3 228	760	439	-15 948
	2000	83 898	-87 799	-3 901	-19 791	-7 290	8 977	5 468	-47	-14 763
	2005	138 058	-150 888	-12 830	-44 166	-21 893	16 445	9 058	-403	-40 954
	2006	158 002	-166 759	-8 757	-54 018	-24 072	21 942	11 982	-213	-41 046
Austria - Autriche	1990	63 694	-61 580	2 114	-10 087	-933	9 145	313	-6	1 166
	2000	96 026	-97 074	-1 048	-14 456	-2 598	11 992	1 279	-1 352	-4 864
	2005	171 154	-162 913	8 241	-25 488	-6 939	24 151	7 014	-2 652	4 252
	2006	179 503	-166 059	13 445	-29 337	-7 104	27 506	7 269	-1 355	10 259
Azerbaijan - Azerbaïdjan	2000	2 118	-2 024	95	-391	-317	56	..	73	-168
	2005	8 332	-7 003	1 329	-1 847	-1 582	202	0	484	167
	2006	13 955	-8 133	5 822	-2 961	-2 624	280	1	566	3 708
Bahamas	1990	1 784	-1 653	131	-405	..	232	..	6	-37
	2000	2 438	-3 009	-571	-457	..	317	..	78	-633
	2005	3 034	-3 775	-741	-279	..	116	..	85	-819
	2006	3 141	-4 542	-1 401	-337	..	119	..	52	-1 567
Bahrain - Bahreïn	1990	4 119	-3 999	120	-5 275	-112	5 497	83	-272	70
	2000	7 176	-5 132	2 044	-6 552	-881	6 328	209	-990	830
	2005	11 794	-8 583	3 211	-5 428	-1 158	5 016	471	-1 223	1 575
	2006	13 552	-9 718	3 834	-8 019	-1 446	7 634	607	-1 531	1 918
Bangladesh	1990	2 064	-3 960	-1 896	-180	..	64	..	1 613	-398
	2000	7 214	-9 673	-2 459	-345	-149	78	2	2 420	-306
	2005	10 552	-14 708	-4 157	-910	-661	117	2	4 774	-176
	2006	12 888	-16 784	-3 896	-1 018	-765	177	11	5 933	1 196
Barbados - Barbade	1990	873	-878	-5	-76	-9	30	1	43	-8
	2000	1 377	-1 518	-141	-152	-17	70	6	78	-145
	2005	1 836	-2 144	-308	-257	-82	85	27	95	-385

For sources and notes, see end of table.

Pour les sources et les notes, se reporter à la fin du tableau.

Country or territory Pays ou territoires	Year Année	Goods and services Biens et services			Income Revenu				Current transfers (net) Transferts courants (nets)	Current account balance Solde du compte des transactions courantes
		Exports Exportations	Imports Importations	Balance on goods and services Balance des biens et services	Debit / Débit		Credit / Crédit			
					Total	of which: / dont : Direct investment income Revenu d'investissement direct	Total	of which: / dont : Direct investment income Revenu d'investissement direct		
		(1)	(2)	(3)=(1)+(2)	(4)	(5)	(6)	(7)	(8)	
		Millions of dollars / Millions de dollars								
Belarus - Bélarus	2000	7 641	-8 087	-446	-72	-5	26	0	155	-338
	2005	18 068	-17 859	209	-228	-135	283	1	169	434
	2006	22 137	-23 723	-1 586	-352	-219	245	1	182	-1 512
Belgium - Belgique	2005	319 200	-308 310	10 891	-53 604	-22 522	59 028	17 287	-6 369	9 945
	2006	340 727	-330 926	9 801	-62 736	-24 355	70 267	20 295	-6 661	10 671
Belgium-Luxembourg - Belgique-Luxembourg	1990	138 605	-135 098	3 507	-63 228	..	65 544	..	-2 197	3 627
	2000	214 466	-203 954	10 512	-70 625	-11 488	75 673	5 138	-4 179	11 381
Belize	1990	245	-248	-4	-21	-7	11	..	29	15
	2000	434	-601	-167	-60	-31	7	..	58	-162
	2005	618	-715	-97	-121	-35	7	1	51	-161
	2006	782	-763	19	-129	-45	10	1	74	-26
Benin - Bénin	1990	364	-454	-90	-38	0	12	..	97	-18
	2000	528	-708	-179	-36	1	23	0	111	-81
	2005	772	-1 145	-373	-43	-9	25	0	164	-226
	2006	..	..	..	..	..	..	..	..	-356
Bolivia - Bolivie	1990	977	-1 086	-110	-267	-17	19	..	159	-199
	2000	1 470	-2 078	-608	-365	-148	140	3	387	-446
	2005	3 280	-2 865	415	-498	-271	121	3	584	622
	2006	4 297	-3 437	861	-578	-321	215	3	822	1 319
Bosnia and Herzegovina - Bosnie-Herzégovine	2000	1 580	-4 157	-2 578	-76	..	667	..	1 591	-396
	2005	3 540	-8 002	-4 462	-212	-96	682	..	2 016	-1 976
	2006	4 496	-8 187	-3 691	-324	-188	733	0	2 049	-1 233
Botswana	1990	2 005	-1 987	18	-522	-407	416	30	69	-19
	2000	3 000	-2 321	679	-729	-658	378	25	217	545
	2005	5 298	-3 543	1 755	-1 292	-1 066	456	194	678	1 597
	2006	5 292	-3 451	1 841	-1 301	-1 043	529	150	871	1 940
Brazil - Brésil	1990	35 170	-28 184	6 986	-12 765	-1 892	1 157	27	799	-3 823
	2000	64 584	-72 444	-7 860	-21 507	-4 238	3 621	999	1 521	-24 225
	2005	134 356	-97 962	36 394	-29 162	-11 035	3 194	733	3 558	13 985
	2006	157 270	-120 466	36 804	-33 927	-13 884	6 438	1 073	4 306	13 622
Bulgaria - Bulgarie	1990	6 950	-8 027	-1 077	-878	..	120	..	125	-1 710
	2000	7 000	-7 670	-670	-644	-107	321	-2	290	-703
	2005	16 158	-20 608	-4 450	-1 323	-813	1 516	-2	1 013	-3 244
	2006	20 108	-25 985	-5 878	-1 555	-984	1 602	1	821	-5 010
Burkina Faso	1990	349	-758	-409	-18	-6	18	..	332	-77
	2000	237	-658	-421	-34	-3	14	0	122	-319
Burundi	1990	89	-318	-229	-23	-3	8	..	174	-69
	2000	53	-150	-97	-14	0	2	..	59	-50
	2005	92	-324	-232	-21	-2	3	..	239	-11
	2006	93	-448	-355	-13	-3	5	..	229	-135
Cambodia - Cambodge	2000	1 826	-2 263	-438	-190	-123	67	5	425	-136
	2005	4 028	-4 575	-547	-322	-227	68	8	440	-360
	2006	4 989	-5 539	-550	-380	-270	90	8	503	-337
Cameroon - Cameroun	1990	2 508	-2 475	32	-566	-138	8	2	-26	-551
	2000	2 576	-2 441	135	-519	-41	26	11	109	-249
Canada	1990	149 538	-149 118	419	-34 460	-5 730	15 072	3 890	-796	-19 764
	2000	329 252	-288 093	41 159	-47 036	-16 468	24 746	10 164	754	19 622
	2005	428 567	-385 908	42 659	-58 397	-28 260	39 860	21 516	-714	23 408
	2006	461 118	-429 289	31 829	-64 760	-27 428	54 344	28 761	-616	20 797
Cape Verde - Cap-Vert	1990	57	-149	-92	-4	0	6	0	86	-4
	2000	146	-326	-180	-18	-5	5	2	135	-58
	2005	366	-646	-280	-52	-10	19	0	279	-35
	2006	519	-809	-289	-64	-29	19	0	295	-40

For sources and notes, see end of table.

Pour les sources et les notes, se reporter à la fin du tableau.

Country or territory / Pays ou territoires	Year / Année	Goods and services / Biens et services Exports / Exportations (1)	Imports / Importations (2)	Balance on goods and services / Balance des biens et services (3)=(1)+(2)	Income / Revenu Debit / Débit Total (4)	of which: / dont : Direct investment income / Revenu d'investissement direct (5)	Credit / Crédit Total (6)	of which: / dont : Direct investment income / Revenu d'investissement direct (7)	Current transfers (net) / Transferts courants (nets) (8)	Current account balance / Solde du compte des transactions courantes
						Millions of dollars / Millions de dollars				
Central African Republic - République centrafricaine	1990	220	-410	-191	-22	-2	1	..	123	-89
Chad - Tchad	1990	271	-488	-216	-24	..	3	..	192	-46
	2000	..	..	..	..	..	..	..	..	-213
	2005	..	..	..	..	..	..	..	..	50
	2006	..	..	..	..	..	..	..	..	-105
Chile - Chili	1990	10 221	-9 166	1 055	-2 222	-387	484	2	198	-485
	2000	23 293	-21 893	1 400	-4 453	-2 539	1 598	568	558	-898
	2005	48 317	-38 148	10 169	-13 097	-11 377	2 452	1 063	1 791	1 315
	2006	65 620	-44 329	21 291	-22 734	-20 409	3 342	1 120	3 357	5 256
China - Chine	1990	57 374	-46 706	10 668	-1 962	-46	3 017	..	274	11 997
	2000	279 561	-250 688	28 874	-27 216	-20 198	12 550	62	6 311	20 518
	2005	836 888	-712 090	124 798	-28 324	-21 040	38 959	3 385	25 386	160 818
	2006	1 061 680	-852 769	208 912	-39 485	-29 237	51 240	4 429	29 199	249 866
China, Hong Kong SAR - Chine (RAS de Hong Kong)	2000	243 127	-235 589	7 538	-53 359	-34 183	54 483	19 748	-1 670	6 993
	2005	353 341	-331 185	22 156	-64 604	-50 800	64 806	35 046	-2 124	20 233
	2006	389 883	-368 167	21 716	-82 135	-61 617	82 792	43 366	-2 222	20 151
China, Macao SAR - Chine (RAS de Macao)	2005	11 091	-6 847	4 244	-1 582	-1 408	806	35	-101	3 367
	2006	13 097	-8 362	4 736	-2 981	-2 467	1 426	56	-235	2 946
China, Taiwan Province of - Province chinoise de Taiwan	1990	74 452	-67 295	7 157	-2 555	..	6 917	..	-596	10 923
	2000	171 909	-164 874	7 035	-4 698	-1 729	9 166	537	-2 604	8 899
	2005	224 283	-213 039	11 244	-8 355	-4 056	17 394	3 788	-4 264	16 019
	2006	253 061	-234 046	19 015	-9 757	-3 812	19 338	3 355	-3 935	24 661
Colombia - Colombie	1990	8 679	-6 858	1 821	-2 652	-964	347	20	1 026	542
	2000	15 771	-14 397	1 374	-3 331	-655	1 054	31	1 673	770
	2005	24 393	-24 900	-507	-6 531	-3 565	1 074	166	4 082	-1 881
	2006	28 554	-30 352	-1 798	-7 528	-4 664	1 525	359	4 743	-3 057
Comoros - Comores	1990	35	-89	-54	-4	-1	3	0	45	-10
Congo	1990	1 488	-1 282	206	-475	..	15	..	3	-251
	2000	2 628	-1 194	1 435	-819	-466	14	0	19	648
	2005	4 964	-2 917	2 048	-1 138	-1 093	15	4	-22	903
	2006	..	..	..	..	..	..	..	..	1 064
Costa Rica	1990	1 963	-2 346	-383	-363	-60	130	3	192	-424
	2000	7 750	-7 297	452	-1 495	-1 141	243	11	93	-707
	2005	9 721	-10 747	-1 026	-449	-170	234	19	270	-971
	2006	11 023	-12 422	-1 400	-408	-126	340	11	349	-1 118
Côte d'Ivoire	1990	3 503	-3 445	58	-1 149	-75	58	..	-181	-1 214
	2000	4 370	-3 629	742	-794	-284	142	3	-330	-241
	2005	8 530	-7 375	1 155	-847	-370	194	5	-462	40
	2006	9 010	-7 256	1 753	-926	..	198	..	-496	529
Croatia - Croatie	2000	8 645	-9 592	-947	-812	-161	346	10	880	-533
	2005	18 881	-21 702	-2 821	-1 982	-1 073	756	138	1 475	-2 571
	2006	21 454	-24 678	-3 225	-2 420	-1 321	1 036	115	1 389	-3 220
Cyprus - Chypre	1990	2 955	-3 178	-223	-217	-4	159	..	127	-154
	2000	5 019	-5 142	-123	-1 115	-846	572	39	177	-488
	2005	8 047	-8 498	-451	-2 247	-1 223	1 635	519	92	-971
	2006	8 690	-9 427	-736	-2 739	-1 461	2 175	618	210	-1 091
Czech Republic - République tchèque	2000	35 859	-37 551	-1 692	-3 323	-1 379	1 952	-11	373	-2 690
	2005	89 700	-85 647	4 053	-10 874	-6 641	4 390	489	492	-1 939
	2006	108 450	-103 940	4 510	-13 585	-8 056	5 381	410	-891	-4 586
Czechoslovakia (former) - Tchécoslovaquie (anc.)	1990	14 307	-15 529	-1 222	-709	..	498	..	206	-1 227

For sources and notes, see end of table.

Pour les sources et les notes, se reporter à la fin du tableau.

Country or territory Pays ou territoires	Year Année	Goods and services Biens et services			Income Revenu				Current transfers (net) Transferts courants (nets)	Current account balance Solde du compte des transactions courantes
		Exports Exportations	Imports Importations	Balance on goods and services Balance des biens et services	Debit / Débit		Credit / Crédit			
					Total	of which: / dont : Direct investment income Revenu d'investissement direct	Total	of which: / dont : Direct investment income Revenu d'investissement direct		
		(1)	(2)	(3)=(1)+(2)	(4)	(5)	(6)	(7)	(8)	
		Millions of dollars / Millions de dollars								
Denmark - Danemark	1990	48 902	-41 415	7 487	-11 719	..	6 011	..	-408	1 372
	2000	73 805	-64 506	9 300	-15 907	-6 539	11 883	5 108	-3 014	2 262
	2005	126 616	-112 817	13 799	-23 327	-8 956	24 928	12 271	-4 148	11 253
	2006	143 295	-134 061	9 234	-24 852	-9 467	27 463	13 563	-4 506	7 339
Djibouti	2000	193	-278	-84	-9	-4	25	..	50	-19
	2005	288	-361	-73	-11	-6	32	..	73	20
	2006	312	-431	-119	-12	-6	35	..	79	-17
Dominica - Dominique	1990	89	-134	-45	-9	-5	4	0	6	-44
	2000	145	-183	-39	-44	-33	5	0	18	-60
	2005	127	-198	-71	-48	-36	6	..	20	-93
Dominican Republic - République dominicaine	1990	1 832	-2 233	-402	-335	-90	86	..	371	-280
	2000	8 964	-10 852	-1 888	-1 341	-1 068	300	..	1 902	-1 027
	2005	10 058	-11 336	-1 278	-2 315	-1 763	418	..	2 697	-478
	2006	10 664	-12 748	-2 084	-2 292	-1 727	557	..	3 033	-786
Ecuador - Équateur	1990	3 262	-2 519	743	-1 235	-125	25	..	107	-360
	2000	5 906	-4 927	979	-1 476	-329	70	..	1 352	926
	2005	11 439	-11 837	-398	-2 029	-1 004	86	..	2 635	295
	2006	14 141	-13 737	404	-2 115	-977	165	..	3 049	1 503
Egypt - Égypte	1990	9 895	-14 091	-4 196	-1 879	-14	857	247	7 545	2 327
	2000	16 864	-22 895	-6 031	-983	-92	1 871	71	4 172	-971
	2005	30 716	-34 326	-3 611	-1 460	-647	1 425	92	5 748	2 103
	2006	36 680	-40 553	-3 873	-1 822	-915	2 560	110	5 770	2 635
El Salvador	1990	973	-1 624	-651	-161	-31	29	..	631	-152
	2000	3 662	-5 636	-1 975	-394	-60	141	..	1 797	-431
	2005	4 557	-7 744	-3 187	-754	-187	183	14	2 848	-911
	2006	5 070	-8 741	-3 671	-757	-90	238	19	3 335	-855
Equatorial Guinea - Guinée équatoriale	1990	42	-89	-47	-10	..	..	..	38	-19
Eritrea - Érythrée	2000	98	-500	-402	-11	-4	9	0	299	-105
	2005	..	..	..	..	..	..	..	..	-298
	2006	..	..	..	..	..	..	..	..	-325
Estonia - Estonie	2000	4 784	-4 965	-182	-322	-205	119	13	86	-299
	2005	10 939	-11 784	-845	-1 369	-1 066	669	256	100	-1 445
	2006	13 128	-14 833	-1 705	-1 730	-1 348	979	399	11	-2 446
Ethiopia - Éthiopie	2000	992	-1 621	-629	-52	-9	16	..	678	13
	2005	1 929	-4 895	-2 965	-48	-21	43	0	1 402	-1 568
	2006	2 199	-5 276	-3 078	-38	-24	56	0	1 274	-1 786
Ethiopia (former) - Éthiopie (anc.)	1990	597	-1 271	-674	-78	..	9	..	449	-294
Fiji - Fidji	1990	833	-899	-67	-75	-49	49	10	-1	-94
	2000	970	-1 107	-137	-36	-10	53	4	53	-67
	2005	1 507	-1 987	-479	-126	-114	80	6	129	-396
	2006	1 487	-2 183	-696	-184	-162	66	2	105	-709
Finland - Finlande	1990	31 180	-33 456	-2 276	-7 239	-277	3 505	-340	-952	-6 962
	2000	53 431	-40 459	12 973	-8 989	-2 837	7 265	3 825	-723	10 526
	2005	82 461	-71 089	11 371	-14 754	-4 829	14 406	7 030	-1 544	9 480
	2006	93 630	-81 955	11 675	-17 390	-6 210	18 275	9 199	-1 682	10 878
France	1990	285 389	-283 238	2 151	-59 632	-2 698	55 736	2 267	-8 199	-9 944
	2000	378 046	-361 421	16 625	-54 542	-5 395	73 995	14 745	-13 771	22 307
	2005	558 660	-573 973	-15 313	-121 764	-22 076	144 350	41 663	-27 295	-19 522
	2006	601 590	-628 801	-27 212	-159 712	-28 802	186 163	52 705	-27 555	-28 315
French Polynesia - Polynésie française	2005	1 284	-2 321	-1 037	-67	-2	588	1	524	9
	2006	1 299	-2 330	-1 031	-74	-5	647	..	496	38

For sources and notes, see end of table.

Pour les sources et les notes, se reporter à la fin du tableau.

Country or territory / Pays ou territoires	Year / Année	Goods and services / Biens et services — Exports / Exportations (1)	Imports / Importations (2)	Balance on goods and services / Balance des biens et services (3)=(1)+(2)	Income / Revenu — Debit / Débit — Total (4)	of which: / dont : Direct investment income / Revenu d'investissement direct (5)	Credit / Crédit — Total (6)	of which: / dont : Direct investment income / Revenu d'investissement direct (7)	Current transfers (net) / Transferts courants (nets) (8)	Current account balance / Solde du compte des transactions courantes
				Millions of dollars / Millions de dollars						
Gabon	1990	2 730	-1 812	919	-637	-116	20	13	-134	168
	2000	3 498	-1 656	1 843	-827	-473	48	12	-63	1 001
	2005	..	..	..	..	..	..	..	..	1 742
	2006	..	..	..	..	..	..	..	..	1 697
Gambia - Gambie	1990	168	-192	-24	-13	..	2	..	59	23
	2000	..	..	..	..	..	..	..	..	39
	2005	181	-261	-80	-35	-26	3	..	69	-44
	2006	201	-316	-115	-42	-33	4	..	87	-66
Georgia - Géorgie	2000	665	-1 187	-521	-61	0	179	..	135	-269
	2005	2 184	-3 318	-1 135	-188	-103	263	4	359	-701
	2006	2 567	-4 413	-1 845	-171	-89	339	..	522	-1 154
Germany - Allemagne	1990	473 672	-427 547	46 125	-49 209	-6 892	71 782	6 078	-21 954	46 745
	2000	626 435	-625 074	1 361	-114 297	-12 890	106 635	16 847	-25 654	-31 955
	2005	1 134 070	-992 457	141 617	-167 120	-37 400	192 808	52 567	-35 494	131 811
	2006	1 304 420	-1 149 110	155 311	-207 221	-47 028	236 026	58 731	-33 370	150 745
Ghana	1990	983	-1 506	-522	-77	-7	-34	..	411	-223
	2000	2 441	-3 350	-910	-123	..	16	..	530	-487
	2005	3 909	-6 620	-2 712	-230	..	43	..	1 794	-1 105
	2006	5 125	-8 286	-3 161	-201	..	73	..	2 248	-1 040
Greece - Grèce	1990	13 018	-19 564	-6 546	-2 024	-78	315	19	4 718	-3 537
	2000	29 440	-41 727	-12 286	-3 692	-319	2 807	48	3 352	-9 820
	2005	51 546	-66 642	-15 096	-11 102	-1 697	4 072	657	3 893	-18 233
	2006	56 063	-80 952	-24 889	-13 524	-1 569	4 566	681	4 282	-29 565
Grenada - Grenade	1990	93	-139	-46	-14	-8	3	0	11	-46
	2000	236	-310	-74	-39	-28	5	0	20	-88
	2005	149	-380	-231	-46	-23	11	0	78	-187
Guatemala	1990	1 568	-1 812	-244	-217	-37	21	1	227	-213
	2000	3 862	-5 567	-1 705	-424	-248	214	78	865	-1 050
	2005	6 611	-11 234	-4 623	-585	-374	253	128	3 523	-1 432
	2006	7 420	-12 750	-5 330	-734	-501	355	185	4 117	-1 592
Guinea - Guinée	1990	829	-953	-124	-162	-61	13	..	70	-203
	2000	734	-872	-138	-101	-8	23	..	75	-140
	2005	..	..	..	..	..	..	..	..	-123
	2006	..	..	..	..	..	..	..	..	-203
Guinea-Bissau - Guinée-Bissau	1990	26	-88	-62	-22	..	..	..	39	-45
Guyana	2000	672	-743	-71	-70	-6	12	..	47	-82
	2005	693	-918	-224	-42	-7	3	..	167	-96
	2006	743	-1 011	-268	-46	-9	3	..	200	-112
Haiti - Haïti	1990	318	-515	-197	-25	..	7	7	193	-22
	2000	504	-1 369	-865	-9	..	..	..	760	-114
	2005	597	-1 760	-1 163	-39	..	2	..	1 254	54
	2006	698	-2 086	-1 388	-12	..	19	..	1 332	1
Honduras	1990	1 033	-1 127	-94	-258	-72	21	..	280	-51
	2000	2 491	-3 278	-787	-252	-70	118	..	648	-273
	2005	3 493	-5 115	-1 621	-445	-321	105	..	1 830	-132
	2006	3 796	-6 055	-2 259	-465	-353	178	..	2 352	-195
Hungary - Hongrie	1990	12 035	-11 017	1 019	-1 707	-37	280	27	787	379
	2000	34 663	-36 449	-1 787	-3 740	-2 023	1 165	73	357	-4 004
	2005	75 022	-75 543	-520	-9 089	-5 900	1 931	649	215	-7 463
	2006	87 644	-87 169	475	-13 911	-10 208	5 567	3 786	449	-7 421
Iceland - Islande	1990	2 149	-2 065	83	-297	-8	83	6	-4	-134
	2000	2 946	-3 540	-595	-390	-16	147	13	-10	-847
	2005	5 149	-7 150	-2 001	-2 072	-1 044	1 456	966	-27	-2 645
	2006	5 311	-8 270	-2 959	-3 827	-1 365	2 587	1 323	-35	-4 234

For sources and notes, see end of table.

Pour les sources et les notes, se reporter à la fin du tableau.

Country or territory Pays ou territoires	Year Année	Goods and services Biens et services			Income Revenu				Current transfers (net) Transferts courants (nets)	Current account balance Solde du compte des transactions courantes
		Exports Exportations	Imports Importations	Balance on goods and services Balance des biens et services	Debit / Débit		Credit / Crédit			
					Total	of which: / dont : Direct investment income Revenu d'investissement direct	Total	of which: / dont : Direct investment income Revenu d'investissement direct		
		(1)	(2)	(3)=(1)+(2)	(4)	(5)	(6)	(7)	(8)	
		Millions of dollars / Millions de dollars								
India - Inde	1990	22 911	-29 527	-6 616	-3 693	..	436	..	2 837	-7 036
	2000	59 930	-73 073	-13 143	-7 414	..	2 521	..	13 435	-4 601
	2005	158 007	-182 691	-24 684	-11 475	-4 431	5 082	500	23 242	-7 835
	2006	198 971	-230 232	-31 261	-12 059	-5 278	7 795	1 039	26 109	-9 415
Indonesia - Indonésie	1990	29 295	-27 511	1 784	-5 599	-2 192	409	..	418	-2 938
	2000	70 622	-56 003	14 619	-10 901	-3 574	2 458	..	1 816	7 992
	2005	99 922	-91 511	8 411	-15 264	-9 525	2 338	209	4 793	278
	2006	115 032	-95 493	19 539	-17 042	-10 303	2 577	116	4 863	9 937
Iran (Islamic Rep. of) - Iran (Rép. islamique d')	1990	19 741	-22 292	-2 551	-78	..	456	..	2 500	327
	2000	29 727	-17 503	12 224	-604	..	404	..	457	12 481
Ireland - Irlande	1990	26 786	-24 576	2 211	-8 235	-4 350	3 280	395	2 384	-361
	2000	92 068	-79 792	12 276	-41 160	-21 707	27 613	3 061	915	-356
	2005	162 745	-139 166	23 579	-84 876	-40 889	53 862	8 017	284	-7 150
	2006	173 857	-151 307	22 550	-106 422	-39 461	75 321	10 560	-544	-9 095
Israel - Israël	1990	17 312	-20 228	-2 916	-3 571	-162	1 590	17	5 061	163
	2000	46 270	-46 633	-363	-10 719	-2 461	3 632	591	6 470	-980
	2005	57 548	-57 579	-31	-7 187	-781	5 579	2 356	5 972	4 334
	2006	62 992	-61 892	1 100	-8 497	-1 850	7 921	2 888	7 466	7 990
Italy - Italie	1990	219 971	-218 573	1 397	-33 709	-613	18 997	265	-3 164	-16 479
	2000	297 030	-286 526	10 504	-50 680	-3 535	38 671	1 936	-4 276	-5 781
	2005	461 582	-461 860	-277	-78 423	-5 819	61 288	4 976	-12 028	-29 441
	2006	515 634	-529 153	-13 519	-89 468	-6 801	72 350	7 652	-16 675	-47 312
Jamaica - Jamaïque	1990	2 217	-2 390	-173	-538	-189	108	1	291	-312
	2000	3 589	-4 427	-838	-543	-290	193	9	821	-367
	2005	3 994	-5 968	-1 974	-1 004	-454	328	24	1 578	-1 071
	2006	4 782	-7 098	-2 316	-981	-376	378	0	1 749	-1 170
Japan - Japon	1990	323 692	-297 306	26 386	-100 152	..	122 644	..	-4 800	44 078
	2000	528 751	-459 660	69 091	-36 799	-2 615	97 199	8 241	-9 831	119 660
	2005	677 782	-607 869	69 912	-37 618	-9 484	141 062	30 373	-7 573	165 783
	2006	733 111	-670 065	63 046	-47 647	-9 011	165 802	35 122	-10 684	170 517
Jordan - Jordanie	1990	2 511	-3 569	-1 058	-282	..	67	..	1 045	-227
	2000	3 539	-5 796	-2 257	-535	-1	668	..	2 184	60
	2005	6 635	-11 859	-5 224	-383	-1	791	..	2 588	-2 228
	2006	7 693	-12 973	-5 279	-451	-2	1 032	..	2 790	-1 909
Kazakhstan	2000	10 341	-8 970	1 371	-1 393	-1 046	139	..	249	366
	2005	30 529	-25 475	5 055	-6 377	-4 633	680	-162	-413	-1 056
	2006	41 570	-32 840	8 730	-10 758	-7 640	1 441	-183	-1 207	-1 795
Kenya	1990	2 228	-2 705	-477	-423	-132	5	..	368	-527
	2000	2 776	-3 763	-987	-178	-29	45	..	921	-199
	2005	5 335	-6 739	-1 405	-182	-35	73	..	1 253	-261
	2006	5 963	-8 200	-2 237	-170	-39	99	..	1 781	-526
Kiribati	1990	11	-46	-35	-2	-2	19	..	9	-9
Kuwait - Koweït	1990	8 268	-7 169	1 099	-846	..	8 584	..	-4 951	3 886
	2000	21 301	-11 372	9 929	-616	..	7 315	..	-1 956	14 672
	2005	51 694	-22 842	28 852	-556	..	9 413	..	-3 401	34 308
	2006	65 611	-24 542	41 068	-1 274	..	14 359	..	-3 457	50 996
Kyrgyzstan - Kirghizistan	2000	573	-654	-81	-99	-37	17	..	87	-76
	2005	942	-1 397	-454	-92	-34	17	..	500	-29
	2006	1 185	-2 253	-1 068	-70	-26	36	..	716	-386
Lao People's dem. Rep. - Rép. dém. populaire lao	1990	102	-212	-110	-3	..	2	..	56	-55
	2000	506	-578	-72	-60	..	7	..	116	-8
	2005	..	..	..	..	..	..	..	..	-214
	2006	..	..	..	..	..	..	..	..	-59

For sources and notes, see end of table.

Pour les sources et les notes, se reporter à la fin du tableau.

319

Country or territory Pays ou territoires	Year Année	Goods and services Biens et services			Income Revenu				Current transfers (net) Transferts courants (nets)	Current account balance Solde du compte des transactions courantes
		Exports Exportations	Imports Importations	Balance on goods and services Balance des biens et services	Debit / Débit		Credit / Crédit			
					Total	of which: / dont : Direct investment income Revenu d'investissement direct	Total	of which: / dont : Direct investment income Revenu d'investissement direct		
		(1)	(2)	(3)=(1)+(2)	(4)	(5)	(6)	(7)	(8)	
		Millions of dollars / Millions de dollars								
Latvia - Lettonie	2000	3 229	-3 813	-583	-198	-92	215	1	195	-371
	2005	7 523	-9 936	-2 413	-948	-617	772	35	596	-1 992
	2006	8 783	-13 251	-4 469	-1 610	-983	1 078	35	479	-4 522
Lebanon - Liban	1990	..	..	..	..	..	..	..	..	-6 106
	2000	..	..	..	..	..	..	..	..	-1 147
	2005	13 137	-16 291	-3 155	-1 919	-96	1 733	122	1 063	-2 279
	2006	14 417	-17 253	-2 837	-1 849	-96	2 059	79	1 280	-1 347
Lesotho	1990	100	-754	-654	-22	-13	455	..	286	65
	2000	254	-770	-516	-63	-15	289	..	139	-151
	2005	706	-1 409	-703	-65	-11	370	..	301	-98
	2006	754	-1 456	-702	-33	-12	412	..	390	67
Libyan Arab Jamahiriya - Jamahiriya arabe libyenne	1990	11 468	-8 960	2 508	-493	-436	666	18	-481	2 201
	2000	12 210	-5 024	7 186	-1 152	-1 143	723	..	-487	6 270
	2005	29 383	-13 523	15 860	-2 118	-2 058	1 837	224	-634	14 945
	2006	37 962	-15 783	22 179	-2 775	-2 710	2 180	320	586	22 170
Lithuania - Lituanie	2000	5 109	-5 833	-724	-379	-123	186	15	243	-675
	2005	14 879	-16 745	-1 866	-1 075	-711	448	10	662	-1 831
	2006	17 774	-20 900	-3 126	-1 407	-878	590	43	725	-3 218
Luxembourg	2005	55 377	-43 234	12 144	-82 141	-14 841	75 216	8 551	-1 129	4 088
	2006	67 378	-51 005	16 373	-110 322	-16 727	99 947	8 036	-1 627	4 370
Madagascar	1990	471	-809	-338	-176	-1	15	..	234	-265
	2000	1 188	-1 520	-332	-64	-4	22	..	113	-260
	2005	1 332	-2 042	-710	-104	-38	24	..	236	-554
	2006	..	..	..	..	..	..	..	..	-547
Malawi	1990	443	-549	-106	-89	-5	9	..	99	-86
	2000	437	-629	-192	-51	-15	33	..	135	-74
	2005	..	..	..	..	..	..	..	..	-294
	2006	..	..	..	..	..	..	..	..	-321
Malaysia - Malaisie	1990	32 665	-31 765	900	-3 721	-1 926	1 849	63	102	-870
	2000	112 370	-94 350	18 020	-9 594	-7 173	1 986	-222	-1 924	8 488
	2005	161 384	-130 609	30 776	-11 691	-8 330	5 373	1 087	-4 477	19 980
	2006	182 673	-147 865	34 809	-13 192	-8 924	8 463	3 247	-4 591	25 488
Maldives	1990	179	-159	20	-18	-14	5	..	4	10
	2000	452	-452	1	-40	-34	10	..	-27	-56
	2005	475	-860	-384	-42	-31	11	..	136	-279
	2006	689	-1 048	-359	-56	-41	15	..	22	-379
Mali	1990	420	-830	-410	-59	-4	23	..	225	-221
	2000	644	-927	-283	-119	-76	21	1	126	-255
	2005	1 375	-1 833	-458	-239	-155	32	0	228	-438
Malta - Malte	1990	1 950	-2 283	-333	-79	-74	269	248	37	-56
	2000	3 571	-3 993	-422	-1 009	-998	917	901	33	-480
	2005	4 586	-4 903	-317	-1 450	-553	1 206	28	44	-518
	2006	5 625	-5 852	-227	-2 049	-580	1 853	22	-11	-435
Mauritania - Mauritanie	1990	471	-520	-49	-50	-1	4	..	86	-10
Mauritius - Maurice	1990	1 722	-1 916	-194	-79	-22	56	2	97	-119
	2000	2 622	-2 707	-85	-65	-8	49	1	64	-37
	2005	3 756	-4 133	-377	-151	-34	143	4	61	-324
	2006	4 004	-4 736	-732	-324	-88	374	2	71	-611
Mexico - Mexique	1990	48 805	-51 915	-3 110	-11 589	-2 304	3 273	..	3 975	-7 451
	2000	179 876	-191 818	-11 942	-19 712	-6 017	5 977	..	6 994	-18 684
	2005	230 369	-243 259	-12 890	-18 378	-6 119	5 359	975	20 733	-5 176
	2006	266 390	-278 963	-12 574	-19 950	-6 097	6 406	653	24 124	-1 993

For sources and notes, see end of table.

Pour les sources et les notes, se reporter à la fin du tableau.

Country or territory / Pays ou territoires	Year / Année	Goods and services / Biens et services — Exports / Exportations (1)	Imports / Importations (2)	Balance on goods and services / Balance des biens et services (3)=(1)+(2)	Income / Revenu — Debit / Débit — Total (4)	of which: / dont : Direct investment income / Revenu d'investissement direct (5)	Credit / Crédit — Total (6)	of which: / dont : Direct investment income / Revenu d'investissement direct (7)	Current transfers (net) / Transferts courants (nets) (8)	Current account balance / Solde du compte des transactions courantes
Moldova	2000	641	-972	-331	-118	-3	139	..	211	-98
	2005	1 504	-2 716	-1 212	-129	-45	539	..	576	-226
	2006	1 542	-3 129	-1 587	-205	-109	606	..	800	-387
Mongolia - Mongolie	1990	493	-1 096	-603	-49	..	5	..	7	-640
	2000	614	-771	-158	-20	-9	13	..	94	-70
	2005	1 483	-1 574	-91	-61	-41	11	..	225	84
	2006	2 031	-1 880	151	-162	-145	17	..	215	222
Montserrat	1990	19	-55	-36	-3	-2	2	..	14	-23
	2000	17	-42	-24	-4	-3	1	..	19	-8
	2005	17	-52	-35	-5	-2	2	..	22	-16
Morocco - Maroc	1990	6 239	-7 783	-1 544	-1 071	-69	83	..	2 336	-196
	2000	10 453	-12 546	-2 093	-1 140	-268	276	13	2 483	-475
	2005	18 788	-22 739	-3 951	-1 003	-525	689	59	5 375	1 110
	2006	21 751	-25 811	-4 060	-1 169	-617	747	69	6 333	1 851
Mozambique	1990	229	-996	-766	-168	..	70	..	448	-415
	2000	689	-1 492	-802	-271	0	79	..	231	-764
	2005	2 087	-2 891	-804	-459	-284	99	..	403	-761
	2006	2 767	-3 407	-639	-655	-471	160	..	501	-634
Myanmar	1990	319	-603	-283	-194	-147	2	..	39	-436
	2000	2 139	-2 493	-354	-169	-137	35	..	276	-212
	2005	4 047	-2 261	1 786	-1 427	-1 402	56	..	174	588
	2006	4 834	-2 906	1 928	-1 346	-1 317	98	..	122	802
Namibia - Namibie	1990	1 220	-1 584	-364	-146	-67	183	3	354	28
	2000	1 531	-1 643	-111	-226	-194	128	0	436	227
	2005	2 483	-2 695	-212	-353	-285	225	8	673	334
	2006	3 177	-2 974	203	-319	-257	234	1	946	1 064
Nepal - Népal	1990	422	-834	-412	-11	..	25	..	109	-289
	2000	1 282	-1 790	-508	-35	..	72	..	340	-131
	2005	1 283	-2 711	-1 428	-92	-57	140	..	1 533	153
	2006	1 234	-2 934	-1 699	-96	-56	158	..	1 787	150
Netherlands - Pays-Bas	1990	159 304	-147 652	11 652	-26 869	-7 053	26 249	6 334	-2 943	8 089
	2000	254 590	-238 810	15 779	-47 803	-16 144	45 506	20 254	-6 219	7 264
	2005	423 818	-371 997	51 821	-93 529	-31 631	98 837	50 354	-11 406	45 723
	2006	469 195	-421 267	47 928	-110 715	-32 096	131 087	68 651	-12 504	55 795
Netherlands Antilles - Antilles néerlandaises	1990	1 464	-1 631	-166	-110	-73	126	15	106	-44
	2000	2 289	-2 388	-99	-103	-4	126	2	39	-37
	2005	2 818	-3 098	-280	-108	-6	103	1	136	-148
New Caledonia - Nouvelle-Calédonie	2005	1 573	-2 530	-958	-114	-42	596	3	417	-58
	2006	1 748	-3 107	-1 359	-163	-85	598	6	427	-496
New Zealand - Nouvelle-Zélande	1990	11 683	-11 699	-15	-2 295	-129	719	305	138	-1 453
	2000	17 862	-17 340	522	-4 137	-2 055	694	93	238	-2 683
	2005	30 262	-32 824	-2 562	-9 021	-5 132	1 451	126	376	-9 756
	2006	30 364	-32 376	-2 012	-9 308	-4 733	1 430	201	509	-9 381
Nicaragua	1990	392	-682	-290	-229	..	12	..	202	-305
	2000	1 102	-2 152	-1 050	-233	-69	31	..	410	-842
	2005	1 963	-3 404	-1 442	-150	-82	23	..	824	-745
	2006	2 319	-3 905	-1 586	-166	-85	41	..	856	-855
Niger	1990	533	-729	-196	-74	-23	20	0	14	-236
	2000	321	-456	-135	-30	-2	13	-1	47	-104
	2005	565	-1 049	-484	-47	-21	37	14	182	-312
Nigeria - Nigéria	1990	14 550	-6 909	7 642	-2 949	-135	211	..	85	4 988
	2000	20 965	-12 017	8 948	-3 365	-2 279	218	..	1 629	7 429
	2005	52 233	-24 609	27 624	-7 437	-7 437	705	705	3 310	24 202

For sources and notes, see end of table.

Pour les sources et les notes, se reporter à la fin du tableau.

Country or territory / Pays ou territoires	Year / Année	Goods and services / Biens et services			Income / Revenu				Current transfers (net) / Transferts courants (nets)	Current account balance / Solde du compte des transactions courantes
		Exports / Exportations	Imports / Importations	Balance on goods and services / Balance des biens et services	Debit / Débit		Credit / Crédit			
					Total	of which: / dont : Direct investment income / Revenu d'investissement direct	Total	of which: / dont : Direct investment income / Revenu d'investissement direct		
		(1)	(2)	(3)=(1)+(2)	(4)	(5)	(6)	(7)	(8)	
		Millions of dollars / Millions de dollars								
Norway - Norvège	1990	47 078	-38 911	8 168	-6 596	-798	3 896	86	-1 476	3 992
	2000	78 111	-49 476	28 635	-9 851	-3 499	7 546	1 920	-1 250	25 079
	2005	133 484	-84 039	49 446	-18 819	-8 231	18 764	8 344	-2 831	46 560
	2006	156 117	-94 890	61 227	-31 610	-13 431	30 988	12 172	-2 283	58 323
Occupied Palestinian territory - Territoire palestinien occupé	2000	988	-3 500	-2 512	-42	-34	867	28	640	-1 047
	2005	677	-3 537	-2 860	-36	-16	610	40	1 180	-1 107
Oman	1990	5 577	-3 342	2 235	-629	-390	375	..	-874	1 106
	2000	11 770	-6 352	5 418	-1 129	-830	291	..	-1 451	3 129
	2005	19 433	-11 080	8 353	-2 596	-2 401	676	..	-2 257	4 176
	2006	22 499	-13 636	8 864	-2 900	-2 622	1 202	..	-2 788	4 377
Pakistan	1990	6 835	-10 205	-3 371	-1 181	-53	96	..	2 794	-1 661
	2000	10 119	-12 148	-2 029	-2 336	-429	118	2	4 162	-85
	2005	19 110	-29 283	-10 173	-3 172	-1 871	658	18	9 079	-3 608
	2006	20 507	-35 113	-14 606	-3 996	-2 579	867	48	10 940	-6 795
Panama	1990	4 438	-4 193	245	-1 395	-196	1 139	..	219	209
	2000	7 833	-8 122	-289	-2 136	-562	1 575	..	177	-673
	2005	10 808	-10 688	120	-2 181	-1 048	1 056	..	245	-759
	2006	12 415	-11 928	488	-2 719	-1 273	1 422	..	258	-552
Papua New Guinea - Papouasie-Nouvelle-Guinée	1990	1 381	-1 509	-128	-210	-158	107	..	156	-76
	2000	2 337	-1 771	566	-242	-198	32	1	-5	351
	2005	3 580	-2 692	888	-565	-475	26	1	291	640
Paraguay	1990	2 514	-2 169	345	-115	-17	116	..	43	390
	2000	2 924	-3 286	-362	-238	-84	261	12	177	-163
	2005	4 045	-4 158	-113	-266	-161	193	25	224	37
	2006	5 645	-6 197	-552	-309	-191	258	24	386	-217
Peru - Pérou	1990	4 120	-4 087	33	-1 928	-15	195	..	281	-1 419
	2000	8 510	-9 648	-1 138	-2 146	-344	737	..	1 001	-1 546
	2005	19 657	-15 205	4 452	-5 701	-4 030	625	..	1 772	1 148
	2006	26 251	-18 266	7 985	-8 614	-6 741	1 033	..	2 185	2 589
Philippines	1990	11 430	-13 967	-2 537	-2 470	-311	1 598	17	714	-2 695
	2000	40 724	-48 565	-7 841	-3 363	-230	3 336	57	5 643	-2 225
	2005	44 788	-53 901	-9 113	-4 231	-1 391	3 937	19	11 391	1 984
	2006	52 979	-59 463	-6 484	-5 189	-1 723	4 390	53	13 180	5 897
Poland - Pologne	1990	19 037	-15 095	3 942	-3 989	-20	603	..	2 511	3 067
	2000	46 300	-57 202	-10 902	-3 709	-700	2 250	24	2 380	-9 981
	2005	112 653	-113 473	-820	-13 684	-9 267	2 795	126	6 934	-4 775
	2006	138 052	-142 839	-4 787	-18 647	-13 093	4 147	734	8 203	-11 084
Portugal	1990	21 554	-27 146	-5 592	-1 457	-102	1 360	1	5 507	-181
	2000	33 680	-46 248	-12 569	-7 177	-1 717	4 806	494	3 344	-11 595
	2005	53 430	-69 537	-16 106	-14 066	-4 342	9 297	2 770	2 827	-18 048
	2006	61 387	-76 063	-14 675	-19 062	-5 199	12 308	3 352	3 147	-18 281
Republic of Korea - République de Corée	1990	73 297	-76 373	-3 076	-2 982	-266	2 894	373	1 150	-2 014
	2000	206 754	-192 648	14 106	-8 797	-1 194	6 375	449	566	12 251
	2005	334 100	-315 075	19 025	-11 994	-4 351	10 432	1 748	-2 432	14 981
	2006	383 718	-373 268	10 451	-14 134	-4 572	13 596	1 753	-3 820	6 092
Romania - Roumanie	1990	6 380	-9 901	-3 521	-14	..	175	1	106	-3 254
	2000	12 113	-14 043	-1 930	-610	-72	325	8	860	-1 355
	2005	32 813	-42 866	-10 053	-4 432	-2 926	1 533	-76	4 449	-8 504
	2006	39 368	-54 199	-14 831	-6 255	-4 164	2 176	-21	6 125	-12 785
Russian Federation - Fédération de Russie	2000	114 598	-61 091	53 507	-11 489	-887	4 753	62	69	46 839
	2005	268 768	-164 299	104 470	-36 371	-19 483	17 382	8 092	-1 038	84 444
	2006	334 853	-209 431	125 422	-59 133	-34 601	29 505	12 357	-1 537	94 257

For sources and notes, see end of table.

Pour les sources et les notes, se reporter à la fin du tableau.

7.1 Balance of payments: current account summaries

7.1 Balance des paiements : sommaires des comptes des transactions courantes

Country or territory Pays ou territoires	Year Année	Goods and services Biens et services			Income Revenu				Current transfers (net) Transferts courants (nets)	Current account balance Solde du compte des transactions courantes
					Debit / Débit		Credit / Crédit			
		Exports Exportations	Imports Importations	Balance on goods and services Balance des biens et services	Total	of which: / dont : Direct investment income Revenu d'investissement direct	Total	of which: / dont : Direct investment income Revenu d'investissement direct		
		(1)	(2)	(3)=(1)+(2)	(4)	(5)	(6)	(7)	(8)	
					Millions of dollars / Millions de dollars					
Rwanda	1990	143	-354	-211	-21	-6	4	..	143	-85
	2000	128	-423	-295	-28	-3	14	..	216	-94
	2005	257	-659	-402	-44	-5	27	2	366	-52
	2006	276	-731	-455	-48	-4	27	1	296	-180
Saint Kitts and Nevis - Saint-Kitts-et-Nevis	1990	82	-132	-50	-8	-5	3	..	7	-47
	2000	150	-249	-99	-36	-21	6	..	63	-66
	2005	210	-277	-67	-45	-20	11	0	21	-80
Saint Lucia - Sainte-Lucie	1990	282	-320	-38	-32	-26	6	..	8	-57
	2000	377	-446	-69	-48	-33	4	..	19	-95
	2005	493	-589	-96	-79	-51	8	0	13	-154
Saint Vincent and the Grenadines - Saint-Vincent-et-les Grenadines	1990	130	-152	-22	-16	-13	5	0	10	-24
	2000	179	-200	-21	-22	-13	3	..	16	-24
	2005	202	-297	-95	-37	-24	12	0	18	-101
Samoa	1990	45	-95	-50	-2	..	7	..	54	9
	2005	124	-240	-116	-20	-8	6	..	106	-24
	2006	144	-276	-131	-18	-14	4	..	95	-50
Sao Tome and Principe - Sao Tomé-et-Principe	1990	8	-22	-14	0	..	0	..	2	-12
	2000	16	-36	-20	-4	..	..	..	4	-19
Saudi Arabia - Arabie saoudite	1990	47 381	-43 880	3 501	-1 219	-1 219	9 187	..	-15 616	-4 147
	2000	82 260	-52 932	29 328	-2 865	-2 865	3 345	..	-15 490	14 317
	2005	187 389	-83 234	104 155	-4 963	-4 963	4 964	..	-14 096	90 060
	2006	218 602	-104 466	114 136	-9 734	-9 734	10 376	..	-15 711	99 066
Senegal - Sénégal	1990	1 453	-1 840	-387	-213	-60	84	31	153	-363
	2000	1 307	-1 742	-435	-188	-75	76	2	214	-332
	2005	..	..	..	..	..	..	..	..	-693
	2006	..	..	..	..	..	..	..	..	-936
Serbia and Montenegro - Serbie-et-Monténégro	2000	..	..	..	..	..	..	..	..	35
	2005	..	..	..	..	..	..	..	..	-2 500
	2006	..	..	..	..	..	..	..	..	-3 894
Seychelles	1990	229	-247	-18	-18	-8	5	1	18	-13
	2000	482	-502	-20	-43	-8	10	4	11	-43
	2005	720	-906	-187	-50	-20	10	3	31	-195
	2006	853	-1 022	-168	-54	-25	10	3	48	-164
SFR of Yugoslavia (former) - RSF de Yougoslavie (anc.)	1990	20 682	-31 996	-11 314	-1 667	..	789	..	9 828	-2 364
Sierra Leone	1990	210	-215	-5	-72	-51	1	1	7	-69
	2000	55	-250	-195	-13	-2	7	1	88	-112
	2005	262	-452	-191	-56	-41	5	..	137	-104
	2006	313	-434	-122	-52	-27	11	0	62	-101
Singapore - Singapour	1990	67 489	-64 953	2 537	-5 502	..	6 508	..	-421	3 122
	2000	181 266	-168 644	12 622	-16 357	..	15 623	..	-1 160	10 728
	2005	284 865	-250 520	34 346	-30 244	..	25 680	..	-1 212	28 569
	2006	334 055	-292 161	41 894	-34 524	..	30 340	..	-1 383	36 326
Slovakia - Slovaquie	2000	14 137	-14 596	-459	-623	-43	268	27	120	-694
	2005	..	..	..	3 597	..	1 620	..	15	-4 090
	2006	..	..	..	4 043	..	1 955	..	-55	-4 562
Slovenia - Slovénie	2000	10 696	-11 385	-689	-408	-90	434	23	116	-548
	2005	22 122	-22 319	-198	-1 143	-458	781	82	-120	-681
	2006	25 741	-26 109	-368	-1 642	-710	1 135	257	-214	-1 088
Solomon Islands - Îles Salomon	1990	95	-156	-61	-8	-2	2	..	38	-28
	2000	122	-165	-43	-11	-8	7	3	7	-41
	2005	146	-243	-97	-7	-5	9	0	5	-90
	2006	181	-312	-131	-13	-11	19	5	28	-97

For sources and notes, see end of table.

Pour les sources et les notes, se reporter à la fin du tableau.

Country or territory Pays ou territoires	Year Année	Goods and services Biens et services			Income Revenu				Current transfers (net) Transferts courants (nets)	Current account balance Solde du compte des transactions courantes
		Exports Exportations	Imports Importations	Balance on goods and services Balance des biens et services	Debit / Débit		Credit / Crédit			
					Total	of which: / dont : Direct investment income Revenu d'investissement direct	Total	of which: / dont : Direct investment income Revenu d'investissement direct		
		(1)	(2)	(3)=(1)+(2)	(4)	(5)	(6)	(7)	(8)	
		Millions of dollars / Millions de dollars								
South Africa - Afrique du Sud	1990	27 160	-21 017	6 143	-4 928	-962	657	353	-321	1 552
	2000	36 995	-33 075	3 920	-5 696	-2 329	2 511	878	-927	-191
	2005	66 441	-68 434	-1 993	-9 569	-4 320	4 640	1 459	-2 801	-9 723
	2006	75 855	-84 232	-8 377	-11 238	-4 842	5 944	1 483	-2 817	-16 488
Spain - Espagne	1990	83 595	-100 870	-17 275	-11 350	-2 455	7 817	357	2 799	-18 009
	2000	168 221	-186 027	-17 805	-25 753	-6 121	18 904	5 477	1 469	-23 185
	2005	291 243	-348 912	-57 670	-60 701	-15 504	39 445	15 938	-4 463	-83 388
	2006	322 761	-395 527	-72 766	-75 597	-14 036	49 143	19 602	-7 125	-106 344
Sri Lanka	1990	2 293	-2 965	-672	-260	-25	93	0	541	-298
	2000	6 378	-8 105	-1 727	-449	-109	149	2	983	-1 044
	2005	7 887	-10 066	-2 179	-375	-115	76	3	1 828	-650
	2006	8 508	-11 621	-3 114	-700	-362	312	3	2 169	-1 334
Sudan - Soudan	1990	499	-877	-378	-148	..	12	..	141	-372
	2000	1 834	-2 014	-180	-580	..	5	..	237	-518
	2005	4 938	-7 790	-2 852	-1 406	-1 399	44	..	1 446	-2 768
	2006	5 862	-9 894	-4 032	-2 103	-2 093	89	..	1 324	-4 722
Suriname	1990	869	-840	29	-19	-3	4	..	53	67
	2000	490	-462	28	-7	..	13	..	-2	32
	2005	1 416	-1 541	-125	-64	-45	24	..	22	-144
	2006	1 408	-1 282	126	-80	-45	28	..	36	110
Swaziland	1990	658	-768	-110	-103	-85	162	9	102	51
	2000	1 240	-1 438	-198	-85	-66	136	1	101	-46
	2005	2 250	-2 356	-107	-96	-40	158	2	131	86
	2006	2 259	-2 329	-71	-167	-129	168	2	168	98
Sweden - Suède	1990	70 561	-70 490	70	-14 164	-473	9 691	3 690	-1 936	-6 339
	2000	107 683	-95 656	12 027	-22 137	-8 867	20 074	12 880	-3 348	6 617
	2005	174 266	-147 244	27 022	-35 708	-16 638	38 490	25 923	-4 574	25 230
	2006	199 130	-167 115	32 015	-44 215	-20 208	45 310	28 272	-4 696	28 413
Switzerland - Suisse	1990	97 033	-96 389	644	-20 808	-1 286	28 686	2 829	-2 398	6 124
	2000	123 537	-107 391	16 145	-40 676	-10 616	61 844	26 388	-4 483	32 830
	2005	198 534	-172 826	25 708	-65 565	-28 760	103 467	61 241	-11 918	51 692
	2006	219 219	-190 987	28 232	-73 339	-23 623	110 277	54 954	-10 321	54 849
Syrian Arab Republic - République arabe syrienne	1990	5 030	-2 955	2 075	-831	..	430	..	88	1 762
	2000	6 845	-5 390	1 455	-1 224	..	345	..	485	1 061
	2005	11 512	-11 101	411	-1 258	-1 220	395	330	751	299
	2006	13 169	-11 879	1 290	-1 363	-1 288	428	398	565	920
Tajikistan - Tadjikistan	2000	..	..	..	..	..	..	..	..	-62
	2005	1 254	-1 682	-428	-50	-2	10	..	450	-19
	2006	1 646	-2 349	-703	-76	-46	12	..	746	-21
Thailand - Thaïlande	1990	29 230	-35 871	-6 641	-2 913	-312	2 059	1	213	-7 281
	2000	81 762	-71 653	10 109	-5 616	..	4 235	..	586	9 313
	2005	129 362	-133 115	-3 753	-10 813	-4 501	3 640	249	3 004	-7 923
	2006	152 059	-146 408	5 651	-11 502	-4 165	4 659	163	3 368	2 175
TFYR of Macedonia - LERY de Macédoine	2000	1 637	-2 279	-642	-87	-7	42	0	615	-72
	2005	2 511	-3 602	-1 091	-153	-86	98	1	1 065	-81
	2006	2 998	-4 258	-1 260	-138	-39	135	1	1 239	-24
Togo	1990	663	-847	-184	-65	-15	33	..	132	-84
	2000	424	-602	-179	-62	-17	33	2	68	-140
	2005	837	-1 451	-614	-80	-46	46	7	188	-461
	2006	..	..	..	..	..	..	..	..	-492
Tonga	1990	38	-74	-36	-1	0	5	0	37	6
	2005	56	-150	-95	-2	-1	8	2	75	-14
	2006	41	-145	-104	-3	-1	11	3	80	-15

For sources and notes, see end of table.

Pour les sources et les notes, se reporter à la fin du tableau.

Country or territory Pays ou territoires	Year Année	Goods and services Biens et services			Income Revenu				Current transfers (net) Transferts courants (nets)	Current account balance Solde du compte des transactions courantes
		Exports Exportations	Imports Importations	Balance on goods and services Balance des biens et services	Debit / Débit		Credit / Crédit			
					Total	of which: / dont : Direct investment income Revenu d'investissement direct	Total	of which: / dont : Direct investment income Revenu d'investissement direct		
		(1)	(2)	(3)=(1)+(2)	(4)	(5)	(6)	(7)	(8)	
		Millions of dollars / Millions de dollars								
Trinidad and Tobago - Trinité-et-Tobago	1990	2 289	-1 427	862	-436	-197	40	..	-6	459
	2000	4 844	-3 709	1 135	-709	..	81	..	38	544
	2005	10 569	-6 265	4 304	-844	-292	84	..	50	3 594
	2006	..	..	..	..	..	..	..	..	4 655
Tunisia - Tunisie	1990	5 203	-6 039	-836	-552	-97	97	1	828	-463
	2000	8 607	-9 311	-705	-1 036	-468	94	3	825	-821
	2005	14 510	-14 647	-138	-1 786	-962	118	13	1 502	-304
	2006	15 802	-16 489	-687	-1 746	-930	160	7	1 639	-634
Turkey - Turquie	1990	21 042	-25 524	-4 482	-3 425	-161	917	..	4 365	-2 625
	2000	50 249	-60 834	-10 585	-6 839	-279	2 836	368	4 764	-9 824
	2005	103 597	-121 855	-18 258	-9 483	-1 011	3 684	277	1 454	-22 603
	2006	116 484	-144 361	-27 877	-11 057	-1 134	4 473	219	1 687	-32 774
Uganda - Ouganda	1990	178	-686	-509	-48	..	..	..	293	-263
	2000	663	-1 409	-745	-166	-19	53	..	499	-359
	2005	1 372	-2 567	-1 195	-299	-202	50	..	1 059	-386
	2006	1 494	-3 229	-1 735	-297	-235	72	..	1 720	-240
Ukraine	2000	19 522	-17 947	1 575	-1 085	-43	143	..	848	1 481
	2005	44 378	-43 707	671	-1 743	-268	758	5	2 845	2 531
	2006	50 239	-53 307	-3 068	-3 054	-996	1 332	8	3 173	-1 617
United Kingdom - Royaume-Uni	1990	239 226	-264 089	-24 863	-144 991	-13 960	139 837	29 032	-8 794	-38 811
	2000	404 775	-433 976	-29 201	-197 289	-41 526	204 239	68 175	-15 106	-37 357
	2005	593 753	-673 978	-80 225	-293 369	-64 893	340 528	144 413	-21 930	-54 996
	2006	679 164	-768 279	-89 114	-412 014	-87 614	445 524	166 970	-21 943	-77 548
United Republic of Tanzania - République-Unie de Tanzanie	1990	538	-1 474	-936	-191	..	6	..	562	-559
	2000	1 291	-2 050	-759	-180	-13	50	..	391	-499
	2005	2 945	-4 205	-1 260	-198	-66	81	..	496	-881
	2006	3 206	-5 113	-1 907	-165	-66	80	..	550	-1 442
United States - États-Unis (9)	1990	535 260	-616 120	-80 860	-143 190	-3 450	171 750	65 980	-26 660	-78 960
	2000	1 070 600	-1 450 330	-379 735	-329 863	-56 910	350 919	151 839	-58 645	-417 324
	2005	1 283 070	-1 997 440	-714 372	-457 428	-116 833	505 487	269 347	-88 536	-754 848
	2006	1 445 700	-2 204 230	-758 524	-613 820	-136 010	650 453	310 226	-89 595	-811 486
Uruguay	1990	2 158	-1 659	499	-580	..	258	..	8	186
	2000	3 660	-4 193	-533	-842	-89	782	1	28	-566
	2005	5 085	-4 693	393	-1 057	-228	563	5	144	42
	2006	5 660	-5 762	-101	-1 203	-292	734	10	134	-436
Uzbekistan - Ouzbékistan	2000	..	..	..	..	..	..	..	..	336
	2005	..	..	..	..	..	..	..	..	1 949
	2006	..	..	..	..	..	..	..	..	2 872
Vanuatu	1990	74	-103	-29	-33	-15	32	..	25	-6
	2000	157	-147	10	-32	-22	19	..	8	5
	2005	177	-205	-28	-54	-35	28	1	20	-34
	2006	184	-219	-35	-52	-34	32	1	25	-30
Venezuela (Bolivarian Rep. of) - Venezuela (Rép. bolivarienne du)	1990	18 806	-9 451	9 355	-3 432	-224	2 658	231	-302	8 279
	2000	34 711	-21 300	13 411	-4 437	-1 424	3 049	296	-170	11 853
	2005	56 988	-29 544	27 444	-6 411	-3 953	4 146	1 349	-69	25 110
	2006	66 782	-38 503	28 279	-9 026	-6 302	7 934	2 984	-38	27 149
Viet Nam	2000	17 150	-17 325	-175	-782	..	331	..	1 732	1 106
	2005	36 618	-38 562	-1 944	-1 583	..	364	..	3 380	217
	2006	..	..	..	..	..	..	..	..	191
Yemen - Yémen	1990	1 490	-2 170	-680	-409	-283	38	..	1 790	739
	2000	4 008	-3 294	714	-927	-855	150	..	1 399	1 337
	2005	6 785	-5 954	831	-1 791	-1 603	178	..	1 406	624
	2006	7 865	-7 781	84	-1 551	-1 403	316	..	1 356	206

For sources and notes, see end of table.

Pour les sources et les notes, se reporter à la fin du tableau.

Country or territory Pays ou territoires	Year Année	Goods and services Biens et services			Income Revenu				Current transfers (net) Transferts courants (nets)	Current account balance Solde du compte des transactions courantes
		Exports Exportations	Imports Importations	Balance on goods and services Balance des biens et services	Debit / Débit		Credit / Crédit			
					Total	of which: / dont : Direct investment income Revenu d'investissement direct	Total	of which: / dont : Direct investment income Revenu d'investissement direct		
		(1)	(2)	(3)=(1)+(2)	(4)	(5)	(6)	(7)	(8)	
		Millions of dollars / Millions de dollars								
Zambia - Zambie	1990	1 360	-1 897	-537	-439	-115	2	..	380	-594
	2000	872	-1 313	-441	-184	..	19	..	14	-591
	2005	2 483	-2 632	-150	-207	-60	37	..	107	-213
	2006	4 125	-3 222	902	-166	-87	43	..	171	950
Zimbabwe	1990	2 012	-2 001	11	-286	-92	23	1	112	-140

Sources:
- International Monetary Fund (IMF), *Balance of Payments Statistics* on CD-ROM.

Notes:

(1),(2),(3) Goods (f.o.b.) and services

The goods component - data on f.o.b. basis - includes general merchandise, goods for processing (gross value of goods before and after processing), repairs on goods (value of repairs only), goods procured in ports and non-monetary gold. The services component comprises 11 main BPM5 categories: transportation, travel, communications, construction, insurance, financial services, computer and information services, royalties and licence fees, other business services, personal-cultural-recreational services, and government services n.i.e. The statistics on services trade are presented separately in tables 5.1 and 5.2.

The credit (export) figures related to goods in table 7.1 differ from those reported in table 1.1 because of adjustments for coverage, valuation, timing, inland freight, etc. Such adjustments are necessary to make the trade statistics compatible with the concepts used in the balance of payments. Further adjustments are applied in cases in which the market price for goods differs from the price used for customs purposes. The valuation problem is probably more important for imports (debits) than for exports and is likely to be a factor whenever there is a long delay between the date of sale and the date on which the import duty becomes payable. In addition, an adjustment is made to convert imports from a c.i.f. to an f.o.b. basis for those countries reporting imports c.i.f. The balance of trade is also evaluated f.o.b./f.o.b.

(4),(6) Income

Income figures shown on the debit side comprise compensation of non-resident employees and investment income payments on external financial assets and liabilities. Included in the investment income are payments on direct investment (columns 5 and 7), and portfolio and other investments. Column 4 presents total payments for income. Column 6 is a counterpart to column 4 and shows total receipts for income.

(5),(7) Direct investment income

The heading includes two categories: income on equity and income on debt, as income accruing to a direct investor residing in one economy from the ownership of direct investment capital in another economy. Income on direct investment is presented on a net basis for both direct investment abroad and in the reporting economy (i.e. receipts of income on equity and income on debt less payments on income on equity and income on debt for each).

(8) Current transfers

Transfers are defined as economic values exchanged without quid pro quo (without reciprocity). BPM5 distinguishes current and capital transfers. Current transfers comprise two main categories: general government and other transfers. General government transfers include transfers – in cash or in kind – between governments of different economies or between governments and international organizations (international cooperation). Other transfers occur between other sectors of the economy and non-residents of that economy and can take place between individuals, non-governmental institutions, organizations and groups. Workers' remittances also fall into this category.

(9) Including United States Virgin Islands

Sources :
- Fonds monétaire international (FMI), *Statistiques de la balance des paiements* sur CD-ROM.

Notes :

(1),(2),(3) Biens (f.a.b.) et services

La partie relative aux biens comprend les marchandises générales, les biens importés ou exportés pour subir une transformation (valeur brute des biens avant et après transformation), la valeur des réparations de biens (seulement la valeur des réparations), les biens achetés dans les ports et l'or non-monétaire. La partie relative aux services couvre les 11 principales catégories selon le MBP5 : transports, voyages, communications, services de bâtiment et travaux publics, assurances, services financiers, services informatiques et d'information, redevances et droits de licence, autres services aux entreprises, services personnels, culturels et relatifs aux loisirs et services fournis ou reçus par les administrations publiques, n.c.a. Les données sur le commerce des services sont présentées séparément dans les tableaux 5.1 et 5.2.

Les chiffres relatifs aux exportations de biens dans le tableau 7.1 sont différents des données présentées dans le tableau 1.1. Ces différences sont dues principalement aux ajustements effectués sur la couverture, l'évaluation, la date d'enregistrement des transactions, le fret terrestre, etc. Les ajustements des données relatives aux importations et aux exportations sont nécessaires, car ils permettent de rendre les données du commerce extérieur compatibles avec les concepts employés dans les statistiques de balance des paiements. Les ajustements d'évaluation sont requis, en particulier dans les cas où les prix du marché auxquels les marchandises ont été vendues diffèrent des prix utilisés par les autorités douanières. Ce problème d'évaluation est probablement plus important pour les importations que pour les exportations et devient un facteur sérieux lorsque s'écoule une longue période entre la date de vente et la date à laquelle les importations sont soumises aux droits de douane. Par ailleurs, les importations déclarées sur la base c.a.f. sont converties sur la base f.a.b. pour les pays qui rapportent c.a.f. La balance du commerce est aussi évaluée f.a.b./f.a.b.

(4),(6) Revenu

Les chiffres relatifs au revenu et présentés comme débit, comprennent la rémunération des salariés non-résidents et les paiements du revenu des investissements afférents aux avoirs ou engagements financiers extérieurs. Le revenu des investissements se subdivise en paiements provenant d'investissement direct (colonnes 5 et 7), d'investissement de portefeuille et d'autres investissements. La colonne 4 présente les paiements totaux du revenu et la colonne 6 les recettes totales des revenus.

(5),(7) Revenu d'investissement direct

Deux catégories figurent sous cette rubrique : titres de participation et titres de créance. Ils recouvrent les revenus qui rapportent à un investisseur direct, résidant dans une économie, des capitaux d'investissement direct qu'il possède dans une entreprise située dans une autre économie. Aussi bien pour les investissements directs à l'étranger que pour ceux de l'étranger, c'est le montant net des revenus que l'on reporte (autrement dit : dans chaque cas, les revenus perçus moins les revenus versés).

(8) Transferts courants

Les transferts sont définis comme des valeurs économiques échangées sans quid pro quo (sans réciprocité). MBP5 distingue les transferts courants et les transferts de capitaux. Les transferts courants se répartissent en deux grandes catégories sectorielles : les administrations publiques et les autres secteurs. Parmi les transferts courants des administrations publiques, on trouve les transferts – en espèces ou en nature – entre les administrations publiques de différentes économies ou entre les administrations publiques et les organisations internationales (coopération internationale). Les transferts d'autres secteurs s'opèrent entre tous les autres secteurs d'une économie et les non-résidents de celle-ci. Ils peuvent avoir lieu entre les particuliers, les institutions non-gouvernementales, les organisations et les groupes. Les envois de fonds des travailleurs sont également inclus sous cette rubrique.

(9) Y compris les Îles Vierges américaines

Country or territory / Pays ou territoires	Year / Année	Capital account, net / Compte de capital, net (1)	Direct investment / Investissement direct — Abroad / À l'étranger (2)	Direct investment — In reporting economy / Dans l'économie déclarante (3)	Portfolio investment / Investissement de portefeuille — Assets / Avoirs (4)	Portfolio investment — Liabilities / Engagements (5)	Other investment / Autres investissements — Assets / Avoirs (6)	Other investment — Liabilities / Engagements (7)	Reserve assets / Avoirs de réserve (8)	Financial account, net / Compte financier, net (9)	Capital and financial account, net / Compte de capital et compte financier, net (10) = (1) + (9)
						Millions of dollars / Millions de dollars					
Albania - Albanie	1990	..	..	..	..	..	..	88	32	120	120
	2000	78	..	143	-25	..	-40	123	-132	69	147
	2005	123	-4	262	-6	..	7	136	-151	245	368
	2006	180	-11	325	34	..	-211	381	-265	254	434
Algeria - Algérie	1990	..	-5	0	..	..	-229	-712	-138	-1 084	-1 084
Angola	1990	..	-1	-335	..	..	-349	941	-2	255	255
	2000	18	..	879	..	..	-702	-309	-631	-763	-745
	2005	172	-219	-1 304	-1 267	..	-1 850	1 525	-1 817	-4 932	-4 760
	2006	23	-191	-38	-1 439	..	-1 633	-2 300	-5 402	-11 003	-10 980
Anguilla	1990	3	..	11	..	..	10	1	-3	19	23
	2000	10	..	40	..	..	-1	6	0	44	54
	2005	13	..	99	..	1	-9	-49	-5	36	49
Antigua and Barbuda - Antigua-et-Barbuda	1990	5	..	61	..	..	-2	2	1	61	66
	2000	39	..	43	0	2	0	-3	6	48	88
	2005	214	..	116	0	10	-56	-196	-7	-133	81
Argentina - Argentine	1990	..	..	1 836	-241	-1 068	661	-3 333	-3 121	-5 267	-5 267
	2000	106	-901	10 418	-1 252	-1 331	-1 368	3 060	403	9 029	9 135
	2005	89	-1 311	5 265	1 368	-1 755	1 935	-2 193	-9 088	-5 779	-5 690
	2006	97	-2 119	4 840	-1	7 835	-4 317	-11 870	-3 349	-9 108	-9 011
Armenia - Arménie	2000	28	..	104	-19	0	-9	177	-20	233	261
	2005	73	-7	239	-3	1	-171	78	-162	-24	49
	2006	86	-3	453	0	9	-176	129	-366	47	133
Aruba	1990	..	..	131	9	-15	-10	58	-12	161	161
	2000	11	-6	-120	-47	44	14	-87	15	-187	-175
	2005	18	-5	128	-14	21	48	-25	22	176	195
	2006	21	0	326	-79	41	-425	-42	-55	-237	-216
Australia - Australie	1990	1 516	-1 013	8 111	380	6 971	-2 735	4 521	-1 740	14 495	16 011
	2000	615	-3 275	13 618	-10 919	14 874	-4 887	4 416	1 365	14 318	14 933
	2005	963	33 940	-35 601	-21 271	58 979	-3 188	14 796	-7 256	40 361	41 324
	2006	1 603	-23 694	26 599	-44 210	97 375	-17 192	8 301	-9 722	39 908	41 511
Austria - Autriche	1990	8	-1 701	653	-1 608	3 239	-1 433	831	15	-4	4
	2000	-432	-5 599	8 523	-27 145	30 360	-16 334	13 790	746	4 153	3 721
	2005	-237	-10 078	9 057	-44 060	30 396	-29 966	42 870	750	-878	-1 115
	2006	-930	-4 017	157	-30 753	43 316	-66 032	49 647	862	-8 187	-9 117
Azerbaijan - Azerbaïdjan	2000	..	-1	130	..	..	-114	427	-274	168	168
	2005	41	-1 221	1 680	-48	78	-1 365	925	-132	-83	-42
	2006	-4	-705	-584	-34	22	-1 417	576	-1 306	-3 448	-3 452
Bahamas	1990	-8	0	-17	..	..	2 283	-2 199	-12	55	47
	2000	-16	..	250	..	..	-19 067	19 247	61	491	475
	2005	-60	..	564	..	..	-11 064	11 194	88	782	721
	2006	-64	..	706	-19	..	-9 017	9 533	80	1 283	1 219
Bahrain - Bahreïn	1990	457	-25	-183	698	..	10 769	-10 102	-796	361	818
	2000	50	-10	364	-88	283	-3 834	3 256	-200	-230	-180
	2005	50	-1 123	1 049	-7 036	2 422	-11 562	14 884	-294	-1 662	-1 612
	2006	75	-980	2 915	-10 255	1 696	-30 235	35 680	-822	-2 001	-1 926
Bangladesh	1990	..	..	3	..	0	-208	757	-79	474	474
	2000	249	..	280	..	1	-1 247	619	121	-225	23
	2005	262	-2	813	0	20	-865	274	319	558	820
	2006	153	..	697	-3	31	-1 353	894	-1 012	-745	-593
Barbados - Barbade	1990	..	-1	11	-3	-22	-22	76	48	86	86
	2000	2	-1	19	-29	100	53	147	-178	111	113
	2005	..	-9	62	-76	98	-239	548	-24	367	367
Belarus - Bélarus	2000	69	0	119	-6	50	42	-114	-76	15	84
	2005	41	-3	305	-3	-39	-492	185	-539	-586	-545
	2006	71	-3	354	6	-25	-137	1 508	1	1 691	1 762

For sources and notes, see end of table.

Pour les sources et les notes, se reporter à la fin du tableau.

Country or territory / Pays ou territoires	Year / Année	Capital account, net / Compte de capital, net (1)	Direct investment / Investissement direct		Portfolio investment / Investissement de portefeuille		Other investment / Autres investissements		Reserve assets / Avoirs de réserve (8)	Financial account, net / Compte financier, net (9)	Capital and financial account, net / Compte de capital et compte financier, net (10) = (1) + (9)
			Abroad / À l'étranger (2)	In reporting economy / Dans l'économie déclarante (3)	Assets / Avoirs (4)	Liabilities / Engagements (5)	Assets / Avoirs (6)	Liabilities / Engagements (7)			
					Millions of dollars / Millions de dollars						
Belgium - Belgique	2005	-894	-30 433	34 040	-43 491	-1 215	-87 399	125 017	2 176	-6 753	-7 648
	2006	-401	-55 300	61 990	-26 519	17 348	-91 915	81 520	-156	-12 099	-12 500
Belgium-Luxembourg - Belgique-Luxembourg	1990	..	-6 314	8 047	-9 443	7 946	-64 422	62 536	-404	-2 055	-2 055
	2000	-213	-207 472	214 941	-122 814	132 547	-39 033	14 999	959	-8 274	-8 487
Belize	1990	..	..	17	..	..	..	5	-12	10	10
	2000	-2	..	23	..	113	-51	119	-52	153	151
	2005	3	-1	127	0	18	-9	45	-19	156	159
	2006	9	-1	100	0	-21	-19	1	-49	11	20
Benin - Bénin	1990	125	..	62	-5	..	-6	-111	-58	-118	7
	2000	73	-4	60	6	-2	25	3	-87	1	74
	2005	122	0	53	15	2	7	131	-112	95	217
Bolivia - Bolivie	1990	7	-1	27	..	..	-32	214	-5	203	210
	2000	..	-3	736	55	..	-146	-180	39	501	501
	2005	9	-3	-239	-153	..	124	478	-463	-257	-248
	2006	1 813	-3	240	40	..	-270	-1 782	-1 286	-3 061	-1 248
Bosnia and Herzegovina - Bosnie-Herzégovine	2000	546	..	146	..	..	-675	628	-77	23	569
	2005	289	-1	590	-3	..	321	825	-461	1 271	1 561
	2006	231	-2	713	0	..	148	612	-790	681	912
Botswana	1990	65	-7	96	..	1	-137	130	-307	-225	-160
	2000	38	-2	57	-34	-6	-264	38	-367	-581	-543
	2005	31	56	279	-404	16	-152	260	-1 364	-1 310	-1 278
	2006	24	50	486	-593	36	-278	232	-1 756	-1 822	-1 798
Brazil - Brésil	1990	35	-665	989	-67	579	-2 864	6 587	-474	4 084	4 119
	2000	273	-2 282	32 779	-1 696	8 651	-2 989	-15 131	2 260	21 395	21 667
	2005	663	-2 517	15 066	-1 771	6 655	-5 035	-22 458	-4 324	-14 423	-13 760
	2006	869	-28 203	18 782	523	9 051	-8 914	23 491	-30 571	-15 458	-14 589
Bulgaria - Bulgarie	1990	..	..	4	..	..	384	374	878	1 640	1 640
	2000	25	-3	1 002	-62	-115	-332	566	-409	644	669
	2005	256	-308	4 252	29	-1 544	17	1 840	-415	3 760	4 016
	2006	228	-156	5 172	-273	578	-2 356	3 657	-1 924	4 528	4 756
Burkina Faso	1990	..	..	..	..	..	-7	89	-7	75	75
	2000	186	0	23	6	0	-10	77	31	127	314
Burundi	1990	-1	0	1	..	..	4	72	4	81	81
	2000	0	..	12	..	..	7	65	1	84	84
	2005	32	..	1	..	..	-8	99	-33	59	91
	2006	62	..	0	..	..	-30	116	-18	67	129
Cambodia - Cambodge	2000	36	-7	149	-7	..	-176	242	-109	92	127
	2005	95	-6	381	-7	..	-303	274	-78	260	355
	2006	268	-8	483	-12	..	-540	332	-139	116	383
Cameroon - Cameroun	1990	3	-15	-113	56	..	482	160	65	634	637
	2000	17	-10	159	-2	0	64	114	-206	120	137
Canada	1990	5 331	-5 229	7 581	-2 239	15 964	-8 442	9 648	-1 139	16 144	21 475
	2000	3 581	-44 487	66 144	-42 975	10 259	-4 195	754	-3 720	-18 220	-14 639
	2005	4 889	-33 584	29 142	-44 072	7 933	-16 567	26 997	-1 335	-31 485	-26 597
	2006	3 702	-45 391	69 068	-69 405	28 675	-30 375	28 212	-826	-20 041	-16 339
Cape Verde - Cap-Vert	1990	2	0	0	..	..	-29	4	12	-12	-11
	2000	11	-1	33	0	..	-22	39	10	59	70
	2005	20	..	17	..	..	-55	46	-56	-48	-28
	2006	27	..	123	..	0	15	-26	-58	53	81
Central African Republic - République centrafricaine	1990	..	-4	1	..	..	-16	98	9	88	88
Chad - Tchad	1990	..	..	..	..	..	..	75	4	79	79

For sources and notes, see end of table.

Pour les sources et les notes, se reporter à la fin du tableau.

Country or territory / Pays ou territoires	Year / Année	Capital account, net — Compte de capital, net (1)	Direct investment / Investissement direct — Abroad / À l'étranger (2)	Direct investment — In reporting economy / Dans l'économie déclarante (3)	Portfolio investment / Investissement de portefeuille — Assets / Avoirs (4)	Portfolio investment — Liabilities / Engagements (5)	Other investment / Autres investissements — Assets / Avoirs (6)	Other investment — Liabilities / Engagements (7)	Reserve assets / Avoirs de réserve (8)	Financial account, net / Compte financier, net (9)	Capital and financial account, net / Compte de capital et compte financier, net (10) = (1) + (9)
							Millions of dollars / Millions de dollars				
Chile - Chili	1990	..	-8	661	..	361	355	1 287	-2 121	535	535
	2000	..	-3 987	4 860	766	-127	-2 065	1 338	-317	471	471
	2005	41	-2 209	6 960	-4 218	1 594	-2 399	1 958	-1 711	-88	-47
	2006	13	-2 876	7 952	-10 851	843	-3 675	3 496	-1 998	-6 806	-6 793
China - Chine	1990	..	-830	3 487	-241	..	-231	578	-11 555	-8 792	-8 792
	2000	-35	-916	38 399	-11 308	7 317	-43 864	12 329	-10 693	-8 735	-8 770
	2005	4 102	-11 306	79 127	-26 157	21 224	-48 947	44 921	-207 342	-148 480	-144 378
	2006	4 020	-17 830	78 095	-110 419	42 861	-31 809	45 118	-246 855	-240 839	-236 819
China, Hong Kong SAR - Chine (RAS de Hong Kong)	2000	-1 546	-59 352	61 924	-22 022	46 508	18 279	-41 376	-10 044	-5 878	-7 424
	2005	-634	-27 201	33 618	-40 723	9 256	-18 750	18 432	-1 378	-22 825	-23 460
	2006	-286	-43 459	42 891	-50 563	17 376	-50 351	59 444	-6 016	-25 675	-25 961
China, Macao SAR - Chine (RAS de Macao)	2005	515	-60	1 767	-617	0	-4 428	3 599	-1 126	-1 388	-874
	2006	438	-512	2 654	-1 436	0	-5 520	4 220	-2 058	-2 865	-2 426
China, Taiwan Province of - Province chinoise de Taiwan	2000	-287	-6 701	4 928	-9 780	9 556	-8 368	2 650	-2 477	-10 496	-10 783
	2005	-117	-6 028	1 625	-33 902	31 045	-6 254	16 819	-20 056	-17 754	-17 871
	2006	-118	-7 399	7 424	-40 754	21 314	-1 266	1 551	-6 086	-25 681	-25 799
Colombia - Colombie	1990	..	-16	500	..	-4	-102	-380	-610	-612	-612
	2000	..	-325	2 436	-1 173	1 453	-551	-1 665	-862	-812	-812
	2005	..	-4 662	10 240	-1 689	-53	-181	-366	-1 726	1 502	1 502
	2006	..	-1 098	6 464	-3 334	902	-723	598	-32	2 769	2 769
Comoros - Comores	1990	..	-1	0	..	..	1	14	5	19	19
Congo	1990	..	..	..	..	..	-68	473	-113	292	292
	2000	17	-4	166	-4	0	-74	-488	-184	-588	-571
	2005	6	..	724	..	-13	..	-1 326	-619	-1 235	-1 229
Costa Rica	1990	..	-2	163	..	-28	-125	176	197	381	381
	2000	18	-5	409	-18	-50	-344	154	153	298	316
	2005	..	43	861	-681	336	141	508	-393	815	815
	2006	0	-98	1 469	-509	16	655	323	-1 031	825	825
Côte d'Ivoire	1990	..	..	48	4	..	-92	1 347	16	1 324	1 324
	2000	8	..	235	-13	5	-182	293	-89	246	254
	2005	185	..	312	-50	48	-374	-247	148	-167	18
	2006	28	..	315	-41	48	-568	-104	-259	-609	-581
Croatia - Croatie	2000	9	-5	1 110	-23	750	-888	981	-627	1 298	1 306
	2005	59	-237	1 788	-712	-798	1 308	3 462	-1 022	3 789	3 848
	2006	-175	-207	3 433	-587	-50	-942	4 855	-1 727	4 776	4 602
Cyprus - Chypre	1990	..	-5	127	..	-38	-115	467	-294	142	142
	2000	5	-172	855	-453	170	-1 285	1 413	8	538	543
	2005	87	-548	1 162	-1 620	1 567	-7 154	8 030	-703	719	806
	2006	34	-863	1 528	-4 839	4 081	-5 128	7 467	-1 027	1 239	1 272
Czech Republic - République tchèque	2000	-5	-43	4 987	-2 236	482	984	-300	-844	2 991	2 986
	2005	196	27	11 602	-3 467	79	-4 728	2 978	-3 879	2 500	2 696
	2006	380	-1 355	6 021	-3 004	1 877	-1 686	3 506	-92	4 980	5 361
Czechoslovakia (former) - Tchécoslovaquie (anc.)	1990	..	-20	207	..	..	-711	1 166	1 127	1 770	1 770
Denmark - Danemark	1990	..	-1 482	1 132	-1 168	4 068	-5 442	7 312	-3 385	1 035	1 035
	2000	-11	-28 381	36 013	-23 582	5 783	-2 025	8 554	5 521	2 210	2 199
	2005	307	-16 207	12 853	-32 807	21 038	-19 820	22 561	1 506	-8 716	-8 409
	2006	-44	-8 202	3 343	-26 033	7 890	-24 367	35 240	5 988	-3 238	-3 281
Djibouti	2000	9	..	3	..	..	0	34	2	40	50
	2005	27	..	22	..	..	-65	34	7	-1	25
	2006	17	..	108	..	..	-62	45	-33	58	75
Dominica - Dominique	1990	14	..	13	..	0	11	5	-4	24	38
	2000	11	..	18	0	14	-10	35	0	55	66
	2005	18	..	33	0	4	-13	56	-14	65	83

For sources and notes, see end of table.

Pour les sources et les notes, se reporter à la fin du tableau.

Country or territory / Pays ou territoires	Year / Année	Capital account, net / Compte de capital, net (1)	Direct investment / Investissement direct		Portfolio investment / Investissement de portefeuille		Other investment / Autres investissements		Reserve assets / Avoirs de réserve (8)	Financial account, net / Compte financier, net (9)	Capital and financial account, net / Compte de capital et compte financier, net (10) = (1) + (9)
			Abroad / À l'étranger (2)	In reporting economy / Dans l'économie déclarante (3)	Assets / Avoirs (4)	Liabilities / Engagements (5)	Assets / Avoirs (6)	Liabilities / Engagements (7)			
					Millions of dollars / Millions de dollars						
Dominican Republic - République dominicaine	1990	..	..	133	..	..	89	129	49	400	400
	2000	2	..	953	268	-4	-165	521	70	1 643	1 645
	2005	..	..	1 023	-82	331	236	460	-1 110	857	857
	2006	36	..	1 183	-328	910	-660	464	-319	1 250	1 286
Ecuador - Équateur	1990	..	..	126	..	..	..	369	-261	234	234
	2000	1 977	..	-23	..	-1 725	-473	-113	-307	-2 641	-664
	2005	70	..	493	-228	594	-845	-141	-714	-841	-771
	2006	21	..	271	-641	-743	-2 044	1 083	125	-1 948	-1 927
Egypt - Égypte	1990	10 610	-12	734	15	..	-1 921	-9 875	-2 508	-13 567	-2 957
	2000	..	-51	1 235	-3	269	-2 991	619	1 306	384	384
	2005	-40	-92	5 376	-60	3 528	-3 246	1 178	-6 319	364	324
	2006	-36	-148	10 043	-703	3	-9 743	923	-3 608	-3 234	-3 269
El Salvador	1990	..	..	2	..	..	-21	36	-165	-148	-148
	2000	109	5	173	-9	-17	-245	380	46	333	442
	2005	94	-217	605	94	86	-168	411	59	869	963
	2006	96	50	204	70	715	67	-88	-72	946	1 042
Equatorial Guinea - Guinée équatoriale	1990	..	..	11	..	..	..	10	-3	17	17
Eritrea - Érythrée	2000	..	..	28	..	..	-26	64	61	128	128
Estonia - Estonie	2000	26	-63	387	16	76	-167	139	-122	265	291
	2005	140	-609	2 997	-872	-1 360	-887	2 441	-386	1 316	1 456
	2006	412	-1 039	1 600	-1 230	43	124	3 227	-620	2 112	2 523
Ethiopia - Éthiopie	2000	..	..	..	..	..	116	210	-109	218	218
	2005	..	..	265	..	..	302	184	330	1 081	1 081
	2006	..	..	545	..	..	73	196	-190	625	625
Ethiopia (former) - Éthiopie (anc.)	1990	..	..	..	..	..	87	307	35	428	428
Fiji - Fidji	1990	48	-13	92	..	..	-18	-10	-34	17	65
	2000	-29	-2	-2	..	..	48	-46	-15	-17	-45
	2005	-18	-10	14	..	1	-50	23	131	109	91
	2006	-6	-1	157	0	146	13	63	-33	344	339
Finland - Finlande	1990	..	-2 782	812	-469	5 696	720	8 428	-3 931	8 474	8 474
	2000	103	-23 898	9 125	-18 920	17 116	-5 636	14 002	-351	-9 192	-9 089
	2005	336	-4 415	4 805	-17 624	10 485	-1 306	1 540	180	-4 167	-3 831
	2006	223	-1 706	5 311	-35 449	19 122	-16 367	13 277	4 321	-11 289	-11 065
France	1990	-4 133	-34 824	13 183	-8 409	43 219	-61 543	73 137	-10 947	13 817	9 684
	2000	1 350	-174 310	42 380	-97 433	132 322	1 272	59 020	2 437	-29 527	-28 177
	2005	662	-119 360	81 134	-242 174	224 863	-276 885	306 007	9 047	-11 012	-10 350
	2006	-259	-116 409	81 045	-338 591	265 847	-167 647	359 719	-11 783	76 316	76 057
French Polynesia - Polynésie française	2005	-1	-16	8	-66	..	-235	276	..	-32	-34
	2006	0	-10	31	4	..	90	-125	..	-11	-11
Gabon	1990	..	-29	73	..	..	-285	330	-219	-130	-130
	2000	0	-25	-43	-9	-2	-729	131	-172	-848	-849
Gambia - Gambie	1990	..	..	..	..	..	-1	-8	-3	-12	-12
	2005	1	..	52	..	..	14	41	-9	97	98
	2006	..	..	82	..	..	-14	24	-20	72	72
Georgia - Géorgie	2000	-5	1	131	3	..	-8	-60	20	86	82
	2005	59	89	453	13	2	-16	192	-111	623	682
	2006	171	16	1 060	-2	118	-46	218	-439	925	1 096
Germany - Allemagne	1990	-3 113	-24 484	3 004	-13 991	12 291	-74 668	42 552	-7 254	-62 582	-65 695
	2000	6 188	-59 745	210 085	-191 545	40 882	-80 178	120 924	5 222	34 209	40 398
	2005	-1 691	-56 946	35 297	-253 759	225 778	-161 315	69 201	2 601	-148 564	-150 255
	2006	-260	-78 949	43 410	-199 086	200 920	-252 689	114 286	3 652	-176 192	-176 452

For sources and notes, see end of table.

Pour les sources et les notes, se reporter à la fin du tableau.

Country or territory / Pays ou territoires	Year / Année	Capital account, net / Compte de capital, net (1)	Direct investment / Investissement direct — Abroad / À l'étranger (2)	Direct investment — In reporting economy / Dans l'économie déclarante (3)	Portfolio investment / Investissement de portefeuille — Assets / Avoirs (4)	Portfolio investment — Liabilities / Engagements (5)	Other investment / Autres investissements — Assets / Avoirs (6)	Other investment — Liabilities / Engagements (7)	Reserve assets / Avoirs de réserve (8)	Financial account, net / Compte financier, net (9)	Capital and financial account, net / Compte de capital et compte financier, net (10) = (1) + (9)
						Millions of dollars / Millions de dollars					
Ghana	1990	-1	..	15	..	..	-94	242	26	189	188
	2000	101	..	166	..	..	70	158	90	484	585
	2005	331	..	145	..	..	107	793	-297	748	1 079
	2006	230	..	435	..	..	135	338	-272	636	866
Greece - Grèce	1990	..	..	1 005	..	..	..	2 757	-40	3 722	3 722
	2000	2 112	-2 099	1 083	-1 184	9 262	6 970	-3 551	-2 573	8 257	10 370
	2005	2 563	-1 476	658	-23 194	32 308	-8 740	16 064	104	15 737	18 300
	2006	3 822	-4 226	5 401	-9 374	18 738	-7 336	21 539	-279	25 382	29 204
Grenada - Grenade	1990	22	..	13	..	0	-11	17	-2	16	38
	2000	32	..	37	0	20	-11	18	-7	57	89
	2005	54	..	72	1	17	-7	37	27	148	201
Guatemala	1990	..	..	48	-2	-15	-78	182	42	177	177
	2000	86	..	230	-36	79	213	1 035	-643	878	964
	2005	113	..	227	..	0	328	932	-255	1 232	1 345
	2006	259	..	354	..	1 715	309	-678	-278	1 421	1 680
Guinea - Guinée	1990	7	..	18	..	..	-53	182	-3	144	151
	2000	..	..	10	9	..	-17	4	50	56	56
Guinea-Bissau - Guinée-Bissau	1990	29	..	..	..	..	..	23	-5	18	47
Guyana	2000	16	..	67	3	-12	66	-30	-24	70	87
	2005	52	..	77	-34	17	..	77	-25	112	164
	2006	381	..	102	-6	1	..	-217	-32	-150	230
Haiti - Haïti	1990	..	8	..	..	..	-23	44	39	68	68
	2000	..	..	13	..	..	-43	14	57	41	41
	2005	..	..	26	..	..	-42	42	-22	4	4
	2006	..	..	160	..	..	-59	48	-108	41	41
Honduras	1990	..	..	44	0	..	-40	175	-20	159	159
	2000	129	..	282	-59	-1	-204	44	-32	29	158
	2005	849	..	372	-5	-12	-31	-638	-350	-664	184
	2006	1 651	..	385	-5	-10	3	-1 434	-302	-1 363	288
Hungary - Hongrie	1990	..	..	..	..	..	-524	-423	558	-388	-388
	2000	270	-589	2 770	-309	-141	939	2 232	-1 052	3 908	4 178
	2005	885	-2 256	7 626	-1 121	5 784	-2 122	6 769	-4 904	9 625	10 510
	2006	732	-16 385	20 655	-2 236	8 751	-5 360	6 491	-1 102	11 000	11 732
Iceland - Islande	1990	2	-12	22	..	25	-49	251	-74	163	165
	2000	-3	-375	155	-667	1 142	-79	671	74	921	917
	2005	-27	-7 114	3 124	-4 707	16 935	-10 922	5 038	-71	2 283	2 256
	2006	-26	-5 354	4 049	-3 092	14 396	-11 371	8 790	-1 252	6 165	6 139
India - Inde	1990	..	..	..	..	..	-611	5 281	2 798	7 468	7 468
	2000	716	-510	3 584	..	2 345	1 712	2 440	-6 017	3 555	4 270
	2005	..	-2 495	6 677	..	12 144	-5 580	10 876	-14 555	7 067	7 067
	2006	..	-9 670	17 453	..	9 549	-44	20 488	-23 737	14 039	14 039
Indonesia - Indonésie	1990	..	..	1 093	..	-93	..	3 332	-2 088	2 244	2 244
	2000	..	..	-4 550	..	-1 911	-150	-160	-5 051	-11 821	-11 821
	2005	334	-3 065	8 336	-1 080	5 270	-8 646	-1 948	657	-475	-141
	2006	350	-2 703	5 580	-1 933	6 058	-2 588	-10 258	-6 903	-12 747	-12 397
Iran (Islamic Rep. of) - Iran (Rép. islamique d')	1990	..	..	..	..	..	-1 510	1 805	325	620	620
	2000	..	..	39	..	..	-8 257	-1 971	-1 083	-11 273	-11 273
Ireland - Irlande	1990	387	-365	627	-465	266	-5 284	3 212	-626	-2 635	-2 248
	2000	1 074	-4 641	25 501	-83 075	77 906	-37 036	28 883	-121	7 791	8 865
	2005	323	-14 491	-30 334	-151 139	215 056	-133 298	119 746	1 776	-724	-402
	2006	283	-14 708	-882	-269 093	251 426	-126 184	168 124	112	10 844	11 127
Israel - Israël	1990	728	-199	151	-368	-171	-632	1 677	-511	-53	675
	2000	466	-3 338	5 130	-2 883	5 047	-4 131	2 019	-943	902	1 368
	2005	727	-2 930	4 792	-8 244	4 138	-5 144	541	-1 972	-8 791	-8 064
	2006	904	-14 399	14 302	-8 956	8 092	-10 112	2 729	-388	-8 754	-7 850

For sources and notes, see end of table.

Pour les sources et les notes, se reporter à la fin du tableau.

Country or territory Pays ou territoires	Year Année	Capital account, net Compte de capital, net (1)	Direct investment Investissement direct		Portfolio investment Investissement de portefeuille		Other investment Autres investissements		Reserve assets Avoirs de réserve (8)	Financial account, net Compte financier, net (9)	Capital and financial account, net Compte de capital et compte financier, net (10) = (1) + (9)
			Abroad À l'étranger (2)	In reporting economy Dans l'économie déclarante (3)	Assets Avoirs (4)	Liabilities Engagements (5)	Assets Avoirs (6)	Liabilities Engagements (7)			
					Millions of dollars / Millions de dollars						
Italy - Italie	1990	759	-7 394	6 411	-19 325	19 216	-13 894	57 542	-11 623	31 016	31 775
	2000	2 879	-12 078	13 176	-80 263	57 020	242	27 074	-3 247	4 257	7 136
	2005	1 239	-40 714	19 587	-108 077	164 399	-100 109	86 834	1 030	26 078	27 318
	2006	2 393	-42 407	38 884	-48 503	115 307	-142 315	123 223	567	44 165	46 558
Jamaica - Jamaïque	1990	-16	..	138	..	..	-3	229	-65	299	283
	2000	2	-74	468	-70	6	-96	600	-499	336	338
	2005	-3	-101	682	-1 406	1 280	-291	1 091	-228	1 028	1 025
	2006	0	-85	882	-506	378	-269	982	-230	1 150	1 150
Japan - Japon (11)	1990	-1 062	-50 497	1 777	-37 798	46 680	..	9 120	9 085	-30 710	-31 772
	2000	-9 259	-31 534	8 227	-83 362	47 387	-4 148	-10 211	-48 955	-127 268	-136 526
	2005	-4 878	-45 438	3 214	-196 397	183 129	-106 598	45 938	-22 325	-145 007	-149 885
	2006	-4 757	-50 171	-6 784	-71 036	198 556	-86 239	-89 124	-31 982	-134 324	-139 081
Jordan - Jordanie	1990	..	31	38	..	..	222	272	-412	152	152
	2000	65	-9	815	-38	-141	-942	589	-686	-412	-347
	2005	8	-163	1 774	144	169	-616	253	-184	1 377	1 386
	2006	63	138	3 219	-180	144	-1 148	733	-1 353	1 552	1 615
Kazakhstan	2000	-291	-4	1 283	-85	30	43	-400	-129	737	446
	2005	14	146	1 971	-5 157	1 204	-4 310	7 157	1 944	2 842	2 856
	2006	33	404	6 222	-9 177	4 669	-8 030	22 071	-11 075	5 017	5 049
Kenya	1990	7	..	57	..	..	73	265	59	453	460
	2000	50	..	111	-11	-4	-56	343	-107	277	327
	2005	103	-10	21	-46	15	-201	895	-281	394	498
	2006	168	-24	51	-24	3	-260	962	-616	92	261
Kiribati	1990	12	..	0	-8	..	..	3	7	2	14
Kuwait - Koweït	1990	..	-239	..	-919	537	829	205	897	1 310	1 310
	2000	2 217	303	16	-12 923	254	-1 109	-321	-2 268	-16 047	-13 830
	2005	797	-5 142	250	-10 006	-542	-19 965	4 260	-619	-31 764	-30 967
	2006	882	-7 892	110	-25 532	101	-23 683	8 896	-3 584	-51 584	-50 703
Kyrgyzstan - Kirghizistan	2000	-11	-5	-2	-2	0	-29	102	-21	69	58
	2005	-21	..	43	2	0	-52	80	-80	-8	-28
	2006	-44	..	182	-3	0	-20	151	-170	140	96
Lao People's dem. Rep. - Rép. dém. populaire lao	1990	11	..	6	..	..	-5	83	-1	84	95
	2000	..	..	34	..	..	19	66	-36	83	83
Latvia - Lettonie	2000	36	-12	413	-351	27	-389	714	7	410	446
	2005	212	-128	714	-270	131	-398	2 626	-524	2 076	2 288
	2006	239	-173	1 664	-246	294	-1 953	6 495	-1 979	4 162	4 401
Lebanon - Liban	2005	27	-122	2 751	-110	648	3 658	32	-458	6 399	6 426
	2006	1 940	-70	2 794	-238	1 308	-1 494	854	-250	2 904	4 844
Lesotho	1990	..	..	17	..	..	-110	51	-21	-62	-62
	2000	22	..	118	..	..	-19	-19	-13	67	89
	2005	21	..	93	..	..	0	-54	-44	-5	16
	2006	11	..	78	..	..	-88	-20	-190	-220	-209
Libyan Arab Jamahiriya - Jamahiriya arabe libyenne	1990	..	-105	159	-115	..	-715	-230	-1 158	-2 164	-2 164
	2000	..	-98	141	-706	..	-333	847	-5 357	-5 506	-5 506
	2005	..	-128	1 038	-393	..	-416	291	-13 840	-13 448	-13 448
	2006	..	-474	2 064	-5 198	..	-1 194	71	-19 447	-24 178	-24 178
Lithuania - Lituanie	2000	2	-4	379	-141	406	40	-5	-131	544	547
	2005	331	-343	1 032	-779	542	-786	2 557	-687	1 549	1 881
	2006	351	-290	1 840	-1 106	852	-476	3 852	-1 507	3 156	3 507
Luxembourg	2005	1 305	-121 511	114 307	-267 098	315 947	-215 605	173 023	48	-5 180	-3 875
	2006	-243	-109 614	126 459	-177 656	248 961	-265 130	163 232	28	-3 354	-3 597
Madagascar	1990	3	..	22	..	..	-7	78	167	260	263
	2000	115	..	83	..	..	-87	142	-30	107	222
	2005	192	..	85	..	..	11	184	-10	271	463

For sources and notes, see end of table.   Pour les sources et les notes, se reporter à la fin du tableau.

| Country or territory / Pays ou territoires | Year / Année | Capital account, net / Compte de capital, net (1) | Direct investment / Investissement direct | | Portfolio investment / Investissement de portefeuille | | Other investment / Autres investissements | | Reserve assets / Avoirs de réserve (8) | Financial account, net / Compte financier, net (9) | Capital and financial account, net / Compte de capital et compte financier, net (10) = (1) + (9) |
			Abroad / À l'étranger (2)	In reporting economy / Dans l'économie déclarante (3)	Assets / Avoirs (4)	Liabilities / Engagements (5)	Assets / Avoirs (6)	Liabilities / Engagements (7)			
						Millions of dollars / Millions de dollars					
Malawi	1990	..	..	..	..	1	34	100	-34	100	100
	2000	..	..	26	..	..	..	162	-91	97	97
Malaysia - Malaisie	1990	-48	..	2 332	..	-255	-205	-89	-1 951	-167	-215
	2000	..	-2 026	3 788	-387	-2 145	-5 565	..	1 009	-5 267	-5 267
	2005	..	-2 972	3 966	-715	-2 985	-4 877	-2 164	-3 620	-13 425	-13 425
	2006	..	-6 043	6 064	-2 123	5 593	-8 531	-6 883	-6 864	-18 758	-18 758
Maldives	1990	..	..	6	..	..	-2	5	0	8	8
	2000	..	..	13	..	..	23	4	4	44	44
	2005	..	..	9	..	..	162	98	17	287	287
	2006	..	..	14	..	..	113	164	-45	246	246
Mali	1990	117	..	6	..	..	-30	192	-55	112	229
	2000	105	-4	82	15	1	-87	204	-58	154	259
	2005	206	1	224	-18	3	-109	283	-123	261	467
Malta - Malte	1990	..	..	46	-2	..	-243	156	96	53	53
	2000	19	-21	601	-782	71	-222	585	222	454	472
	2005	193	24	660	-2 608	36	-2 806	5 309	-218	374	567
	2006	190	-7	1 789	-2 477	-19	-4 141	5 240	-112	305	495
Mauritania - Mauritanie	1990	..	..	7	..	..	206	-181	41	72	72
Mauritius - Maurice	1990	-1	-1	41	-2	..	-7	64	-188	-93	-94
	2000	-1	-13	266	-19	-120	-308	452	-231	27	27
	2005	-2	-47	42	-42	25	-231	394	165	307	305
	2006	-3	-10	107	-110	77	-371	367	140	200	198
Mexico - Mexique	1990	..	..	2 634	-7 354	3 369	-1 345	12 180	-3 261	6 223	6 223
	2000	..	..	17 923	1 290	-1 134	5 809	-4 182	-2 862	16 844	16 844
	2005	..	-6 474	20 960	..	8 366	-7 719	-1 124	-6 980	7 030	7 030
	2006	..	-5 759	19 212	..	1 296	-11 913	-4 999	1 288	-874	-874
Moldova	2000	-12	0	128	..	117	-36	-43	-47	119	107
	2005	-4	0	197	-1	-6	-78	70	-129	52	48
	2006	-23	1	242	0	-5	-73	280	-141	305	282
Mongolia - Mongolie	1990	..	..	..	..	..	-2	543	102	643	643
	2000	..	..	54	..	..	-44	82	-2	89	89
	2005	..	..	185	..	..	-125	-20	-48	-9	-9
	2006	..	..	344	..	..	-223	55	-389	-214	-214
Montserrat	1990	5	..	10	..	..	15	-1	-3	21	26
	2000	4	..	2	..	1	-5	4	4	6	10
	2005	10	..	1	..	0	-2	8	-1	5	15
Morocco - Maroc	1990	-5	..	165	..	..	-267	1 830	-1 537	191	186
	2000	-6	-59	427	..	18	..	-435	416	367	361
	2005	-5	-78	1 602	2	64	-891	958	-2 349	-691	-696
	2006	-3	-438	2 793	2	-309	-813	185	-2 772	-1 351	-1 354
Mozambique	1990	22	..	9	..	..	..	301	-18	293	315
	2000	306	..	139	..	..	-145	503	-77	420	726
	2005	194	..	108	-89	0	-78	215	130	286	480
	2006	2 278	0	154	-124	0	-14	-1 774	-29	-1 787	491
Myanmar	1990	235	..	163	..	..	..	22	-6	179	414
	2000	..	..	258	..	..	..	-45	23	236	236
	2005	..	..	237	..	..	..	-71	-144	23	23
	2006	..	..	279	..	..	..	-26	-423	-170	-170
Namibia - Namibie	1990	42	-1	30	-5	15	-328	87	-37	-240	-197
	2000	113	-2	186	-470	14	-156	109	-17	-336	-223
	2005	80	12	354	-1 053	7	43	59	-1	-577	-498
	2006	83	13	330	-1 066	7	-354	-48	-163	-1 282	-1 198
Nepal - Népal	1990	..	..	..	..	..	116	176	-8	284	284
	2000	..	..	0	..	..	129	148	-291	-15	-15
	2005	40	..	2	..	..	-242	78	-171	-332	-292
	2006	46	..	-7	..	..	-251	282	-329	-305	-259

For sources and notes, see end of table.   Pour les sources et les notes, se reporter à la fin du tableau.

Country or territory / Pays ou territoires	Year / Année	Capital account, net / Compte de capital, net (1)	Direct investment / Investissement direct — Abroad / À l'étranger (2)	Direct investment / Investissement direct — In reporting economy / Dans l'économie déclarante (3)	Portfolio investment / Investissement de portefeuille — Assets / Avoirs (4)	Portfolio investment / Investissement de portefeuille — Liabilities / Engagements (5)	Other investment / Autres investissements — Assets / Avoirs (6)	Other investment / Autres investissements — Liabilities / Engagements (7)	Reserve assets / Avoirs de réserve (8)	Financial account, net / Compte financier, net (9)	Capital and financial account, net / Compte de capital et compte financier, net (10) = (1) + (9)
						Millions of dollars / Millions de dollars					
Netherlands - Pays-Bas	1990	-301	-13 718	10 676	-3 547	-1 367	-25 277	28 376	-268	-5 190	-5 491
	2000	-97	-74 510	63 119	-65 635	55 242	-28 347	46 507	-219	-7 824	-7 921
	2005	-1 764	-133 929	47 235	-81 846	159 993	-52 628	29 609	1 790	-33 956	-35 720
	2006	-2 792	-46 474	7 197	-43 830	59 482	-185 690	162 461	-778	-54 570	-57 362
Netherlands Antilles - Antilles néerlandaises	1990	-2	-2	8	-50	1	-249	302	30	39	38
	2000	30	2	-13	-38	0	-41	36	48	-6	24
	2005	96	-72	73	-26	2	44	24	-74	-28	68
New Caledonia - Nouvelle-Calédonie	2005	9	-31	-7	241	..	-369	194	..	29	38
	2006	4	-31	749	-44	..	-208	9	..	476	480
New Zealand - Nouvelle-Zélande	1990	213	-1 594	1 735	-111	282	-81	1 479	-1 014	696	909
	2000	-180	-739	3 910	-2 188	76	-394	2 471	143	3 278	3 098
	2005	-197	1 130	1 690	-587	447	4 577	3 955	-2 410	8 803	8 606
	2006	-217	-737	7 941	-944	-377	-1 196	8 927	-4 258	9 356	9 139
Nicaragua	1990	..	..	..	..	..	..	447	7	454	454
	2000	322	..	267	..	35	-65	62	16	314	636
	2005	509	..	241	..	-8	-126	225	-60	273	781
	2006	1 510	..	282	..	-10	21	-944	-132	-783	727
Niger	1990	202	0	41	..	..	-2	23	-10	52	254
	2000	55	1	8	0	9	-15	104	-44	62	118
	2005	49	-9	44	-1	43	-19	120	-35	141	191
Nigeria - Nigéria	1990	..	..	588	..	-197	-2 886	-250	-2 478	-5 223	-5 223
	2000	33	..	1 140	502	..	-4 534	-1 958	-4 459	-9 309	-9 276
	2005	23	..	2 013	2 869	..	-15 786	-11 722	-11 357	-33 983	-33 960
Norway - Norvège	1990	31	-1 470	1 003	-987	1 548	-1 502	648	-414	-1 175	-1 144
	2000	-91	-9 433	6 962	-25 143	9 843	-15 746	19 173	-3 686	-18 490	-18 581
	2005	-290	-20 823	6 361	-39 534	32 376	-37 790	22 826	-4 511	-41 095	-41 385
	2006	-97	-20 505	6 916	-113 454	39 018	-31 794	79 731	-5 475	-45 564	-45 661
Occupied Palestinian territory - Territoire palestinien occupé	2000	198	-213	62	-113	12	1 084	58	-91	799	997
	2005	422	-9	47	-11	14	504	112	26	682	1 105
Oman	1990	..	..	142	..	..	-270	-369	-135	-633	-633
	2000	8	..	82	..	-36	-497	81	-2 263	-2 633	-2 626
	2005	-16	-114	900	-169	216	-2 528	947	-2 746	-3 495	-3 510
	2006	-96	-247	952	-549	1 020	-5 532	3 352	-2 200	-3 204	-3 300
Pakistan	1990	8	-2	245	..	87	-365	1 321	471	1 758	1 766
	2000	..	-11	308	..	9	-437	-348	7	-472	-472
	2005	202	-44	2 201	19	751	126	727	-176	3 604	3 806
	2006	347	-110	4 273	-4	1 975	-244	1 361	-1 544	5 706	6 053
Panama	1990	..	..	136	-200	-36	-1 422	1 806	-356	-72	-72
	2000	2	..	624	-93	184	489	-904	108	403	410
	2005	..	..	962	-1 103	402	-359	1 934	-523	1 313	1 313
	2006	..	..	2 574	-676	255	-3 645	2 154	-166	495	496
Papua New Guinea - Papouasie-Nouvelle-Guinée	1990	-37	0	155	..	..	..	113	-75	193	155
	2000	..	..	96	-124	..	-41	-167	-128	-364	-364
	2005	..	-7	34	27	-2	-640	-18	-82	-687	-687
Paraguay	1990	13	..	77	..	..	-50	-71	-220	-264	-252
	2000	3	-6	104	2	1	-212	305	210	403	406
	2005	20	-6	74	..	..	386	-153	-149	151	171
	2006	30	-4	189	..	..	125	53	-387	-24	6
Peru - Pérou	1990	-25	..	41	-48	..	468	1 384	-287	1 558	1 533
	2000	-258	..	810	-481	75	191	221	329	1 145	887
	2005	-22	..	2 579	-817	2 579	-1 084	-3 273	-1 472	-1 488	-1 510
	2006	-100	..	3 467	-1 829	155	8	-636	-3 209	-2 045	-2 145
Philippines	1990	..	..	530	..	-50	..	1 234	388	2 102	2 102
	2000	138	-125	2 240	-812	259	2 454	-418	69	3 711	3 849
	2005	40	-189	1 854	-145	3 621	-4 791	1 094	-1 622	-221	-181
	2006	138	-103	2 086	-1 567	3 927	-3 512	-3 135	-2 935	-5 378	-5 240

For sources and notes, see end of table.

Pour les sources et les notes, se reporter à la fin du tableau.

Country or territory / Pays ou territoires	Year / Année	Capital account, net / Compte de capital, net (1)	Direct investment / Investissement direct — Abroad / À l'étranger (2)	Direct investment — In reporting economy / Dans l'économie déclarante (3)	Portfolio investment / Investissement de portefeuille — Assets / Avoirs (4)	Portfolio investment — Liabilities / Engagements (5)	Other investment / Autres investissements — Assets / Avoirs (6)	Other investment — Liabilities / Engagements (7)	Reserve assets / Avoirs de réserve (8)	Financial account, net / Compte financier, net (9)	Capital and financial account, net / Compte de capital et compte financier, net (10) = (1) + (9)
						Millions of dollars / Millions de dollars					
Poland - Pologne	1990	..	..	89	..	..	-4 504	3 603	-2 418	-3 229	-3 229
	2000	34	-16	9 343	-84	3 423	-3 870	1 156	-624	9 597	9 631
	2005	995	-3 350	10 363	-2 509	15 109	-2 782	-1 729	-8 146	7 149	8 144
	2006	2 105	-9 161	19 198	-4 550	1 543	-3 734	9 572	-2 489	9 622	11 727
Portugal	1990	..	-163	2 610	..	961	-2 442	1 598	-3 542	-979	-979
	2000	1 512	-8 133	6 682	-4 582	2 792	-10 970	24 689	-371	10 378	11 890
	2005	2 139	-2 221	4 099	-19 659	18 141	-602	15 728	1 741	17 016	19 154
	2006	1 578	-3 507	7 366	-8 101	12 086	-18 195	23 335	2 357	15 028	16 606
Republic of Korea - République de Corée	1990	-331	-1 052	789	-500	662	-2 425	5 500	1 208	4 103	3 772
	2000	-615	-4 999	9 283	-520	12 697	-2 289	-1 268	-23 790	-11 065	-11 680
	2005	-2 340	-4 291	6 309	-14 136	14 114	-2 658	9 473	-19 864	-12 760	-15 100
	2006	-3 033	-7 126	3 645	-26 908	8 435	-8 759	56 438	-22 089	-435	-3 468
Romania - Roumanie	1990	..	-18	..	..	..	562	1 069	1 494	3 107	3 107
	2000	36	11	1 037	28	73	-407	1 380	-928	1 194	1 230
	2005	731	30	6 482	-140	1 089	-1 078	7 579	-6 777	7 160	7 891
	2006	-34	-422	11 393	-828	589	-1 323	9 431	-6 435	12 297	12 263
Russian Federation - Fédération de Russie	2000	10 955	-3 177	2 714	-411	-9 923	-17 086	-4 166	-16 009	-48 058	-37 103
	2005	-12 764	-12 768	12 886	-10 666	-828	-32 623	42 340	-61 461	-63 353	-76 117
	2006	191	-23 151	32 387	6 248	9 124	-49 280	30 340	-107 466	-101 898	-101 707
Rwanda	1990	-1	..	8	0	..	8	39	1	55	55
	2000	63	..	8	0	..	23	31	-53	10	73
	2005	93	..	8	..	..	-14	31	-92	-67	26
	2006	1 323	14	11	..	..	-30	-1 195	-31	-1 230	93
Saint Kitts and Nevis - Saint-Kitts-et-Nevis	1990	2	..	49	..	..	-1	3	0	51	53
	2000	6	..	96	0	5	-11	-14	4	81	87
	2005	15	..	85	0	-15	-13	-6	7	59	74
Saint Lucia - Sainte-Lucie	1990	4	..	45	..	0	2	5	-6	45	49
	2000	14	..	54	-1	29	-15	19	-13	73	87
	2005	5	..	82	0	11	-34	92	15	166	171
Saint Vincent and the Grenadines - Saint-Vincent-et-les Grenadines	1990	19	..	8	..	..	-11	5	-5	-3	15
	2000	6	..	38	-1	2	-9	-6	-14	11	16
	2005	14	..	56	-8	17	-5	19	3	82	96
Samoa	1990	..	..	..	..	..	0	9	-12	-3	-3
	2005	41	-2	-4	0	0	-1	-4	1	-9	31
	2006	42	..	21	0	0	3	-16	4	11	53
Sao Tome and Principe - Sao Tomé-et-Principe	1990	..	..	..	..	..	..	14	1	15	15
	2000	12	..	4	..	..	-5	11	-2	9	21
Saudi Arabia - Arabie saoudite	1990	..	..	1 861	-3 337	..	1 435	-1 181	5 373	4 150	4 150
	2000	..	..	-1 881	-9 378	..	-3 937	3 544	-2 665	-14 317	-14 317
	2005	..	..	464	-67 420	..	-28 717	5 149	465	-90 060	-90 060
	2006	..	..	660	-78 567	..	-17 664	-2 601	-894	-99 066	-99 066
Senegal - Sénégal	1990	172	10	57	-1	2	58	58	10	193	364
	2000	83	-1	63	11	12	-4	191	-14	258	341
Seychelles	1990	..	-1	20	2	0	-3	5	-4	19	19
	2000	1	-11	24	0	1	-15	58	-19	39	39
	2005	30	-7	86	0	1	-10	115	-22	163	193
	2006	13	-8	146	0	198	-8	-117	-62	149	162
SFR of Yugoslavia (former) - RSF de Yougoslavie (anc.)	1990	..	..	...	..	..	496	2 742	-1 102	2 136	2 136
Sierra Leone	1990	0	..	32	..	..	-20	13	-5	20	20
	2000	..	..	39	..	..	44	30	2	115	115
	2005	68	8	83	..	..	-2	63	-56	96	163
	2006	51	0	59	..	..	-7	-109	-11	-69	-18

For sources and notes, see end of table.

Pour les sources et les notes, se reporter à la fin du tableau.

Country or territory / Pays ou territoires	Year / Année	Capital account, net / Compte de capital, net (1)	Direct investment / Investissement direct Abroad / À l'étranger (2)	In reporting economy / Dans l'économie déclarante (3)	Portfolio investment / Investissement de portefeuille Assets / Avoirs (4)	Liabilities / Engagements (5)	Other investment / Autres investissements Assets / Avoirs (6)	Liabilities / Engagements (7)	Reserve assets / Avoirs de réserve (8)	Financial account, net / Compte financier, net (9)	Capital and financial account, net / Compte de capital et compte financier, net (10) = (1) + (9)
					Millions of dollars / Millions de dollars						
Singapore - Singapour	1990	-22	-2 034	5 575	-1 610	573	-220	1 664	-5 431	-1 484	-1 506
	2000	-163	-5 899	16 479	-13 371	-1 243	-15 824	14 097	-6 822	-12 582	-12 745
	2005	-202	-5 014	15 005	-13 819	5 532	-28 380	7 725	-12 315	-31 265	-31 466
	2006	-226	-8 631	24 191	-21 450	7 276	-49 368	27 228	-17 008	-37 762	-37 988
Slovakia - Slovaquie	2000	91	-22	2 052	-195	1 016	-973	-533	-794	553	644
	2005	-18	-157	2 107	-667	-315	-466	4 710	-2 572	2 607	2 589
	2006	-41	-368	4 165	-190	1 751	-1 114	-3 006	2 567	3 644	3 603
Slovenia - Slovénie	2000	3	-65	136	-59	246	-519	941	-178	502	506
	2005	-138	-629	540	-2 100	102	-1 899	4 842	-206	637	499
	2006	-169	-905	649	-2 677	849	-2 428	4 399	1 656	1 527	1 358
Solomon Islands - Îles Salomon	1990	0	..	10	..	..	-1	18	9	37	36
	2000	8	0	13	..	..	1	34	-20	28	36
	2005	28	-2	19	..	0	-12	-14	17	9	37
	2006	29	0	19	..	..	-18	-22	14	-6	23
South Africa - Afrique du Sud	1990	-56	-28	-76	-332	338	367	-1 650	-11	-1 391	-1 447
	2000	-52	-277	969	-3 672	1 807	34	1 354	-480	-406	-458
	2005	30	-909	6 522	-911	5 698	-3 503	5 686	-5 766	6 817	6 847
	2006	30	-6 536	-184	-2 231	21 814	-7 187	9 008	-3 711	10 974	11 004
Spain - Espagne	1990	1 451	-3 522	13 984	-1 357	10 382	-13 175	16 665	-7 188	15 782	17 232
	2000	4 797	-57 411	38 835	-59 318	58 146	-18 475	51 665	2 880	18 141	22 938
	2005	10 107	-41 922	24 573	-119 356	172 713	-42 199	79 803	1 920	75 804	85 912
	2006	7 831	-88 726	20 167	-9 978	240 716	-101 955	39 771	-578	102 003	109 834
Sri Lanka	1990	..	-1	43	..	..	-116	619	-132	413	413
	2000	49	..	173	19	-63	-244	477	447	808	857
	2005	250	-38	272	276	-216	-223	941	-540	473	723
	2006	291	-29	480	355	-304	297	578	-73	1 304	1 594
Sudan - Soudan	1990	..	..	..	..	..	-29	498	5	474	474
	2000	-119	..	392	..	..	-53	68	-108	299	179
	2005	..	..	2 305	51	..	1 135	-621	-828	2 041	2 041
	2006	..	..	3 534	0	-35	208	1 026	209	4 942	4 942
Suriname	1990	-5	..	-77	..	1	28	21	-18	-45	-50
	2000	2	..	-148	..	..	25	-16	-10	-149	-147
	2005	15	..	28	..	-2	-32	-15	-20	-40	-26
	2006	19	..	-163	..	0	8	-25	-94	-275	-255
Swaziland	1990	2	-8	30	-1	-2	-39	-20	-11	-50	-48
	2000	0	-17	91	-2	1	-184	41	-46	-116	-116
	2005	0	24	-50	4	1	-122	67	2	-74	-74
	2006	53	-2	36	0	0	-40	24	-141	-123	-70
Sweden - Suède	1990	-353	-14 629	1 982	-3 644	6 112	-9 618	39 074	-7 552	11 726	11 373
	2000	385	-39 962	22 125	-12 772	9 017	-16 000	34 609	-171	-3 467	-3 083
	2005	308	-26 968	10 252	-12 913	17 955	-13 363	1 717	-250	-24 500	-24 193
	2006	-2 585	-23 754	27 299	-36 489	14 175	-49 730	35 481	-1 289	-34 171	-36 756
Switzerland - Suisse	1990	..	-5 530	5 545	-746	-551	-28 697	19 920	-1 169	-11 227	-11 227
	2000	-3 541	-43 990	19 764	-23 169	10 247	-101 376	108 575	4 214	-25 734	-29 275
	2005	-665	-51 192	-1 118	-53 263	5 636	-70 620	83 278	18 215	-69 065	-69 729
	2006	-2 712	-70 584	27 185	-41 700	68	-42 151	59 924	-370	-70 536	-73 248
Syrian Arab Republic - République arabe syrienne	1990	..	..	..	..	..	-2 008	172	-36	-1 872	-1 872
	2000	63	..	270	..	..	1 206	-1 615	-814	-953	-890
	2005	18	..	500	..	..	-524	-138	-18	-180	-162
	2006	18	..	600	..	..	-733	-919	702	-350	-332
Tajikistan - Tadjikistan	2005	..	..	54	..	..	-71	138	-26	95	95
	2006	100	..	339	..	..	-302	157	-7	186	286
Thailand - Thaïlande	1990	-1	-140	2 444	..	-38	-164	6 722	-2 961	5 863	5 862
	2000	..	23	3 366	-153	-553	-2 109	-10 402	1 608	-8 219	-8 219
	2005	..	-501	8 055	-1 522	7 070	-1 726	232	-5 417	5 666	5 666
	2006	..	-1 033	9 004	-2 025	5 714	-10 005	3 641	-12 669	-7 020	-7 020

For sources and notes, see end of table.

Pour les sources et les notes, se reporter à la fin du tableau.

7.2 Balance of payments: capital and financial account summaries

7.2 Balance des paiements : sommaires des comptes de capital et d'opérations financières

Country or territory / Pays ou territoires	Year / Année	Capital account, net / Compte de capital, net (1)	Direct investment / Investissement direct — Abroad / À l'étranger (2)	In reporting economy / Dans l'économie déclarante (3)	Portfolio investment / Investissement de portefeuille — Assets / Avoirs (4)	Liabilities / Engagements (5)	Other investment / Autres investissements — Assets / Avoirs (6)	Liabilities / Engagements (7)	Reserve assets / Avoirs de réserve (8)	Financial account, net / Compte financier, net (9)	Capital and financial account, net / Compte de capital et compte financier, net (10) = (1) + (9)
						Millions of dollars / Millions de dollars					
TFYR of Macedonia - LERY de Macédoine	2000	0	1	175	-1	0	-78	178	-264	11	11
	2005	-2	-3	100	1	235	-89	268	-415	96	94
	2006	-1	0	351	0	83	-150	108	-376	15	14
Togo	1990	..	..	18	-2	4	25	87	-29	104	104
	2000	9	0	42	1	6	9	96	-28	126	135
	2005	51	13	78	-26	29	69	113	125	401	452
Tonga	1990	0	0	0	0	-8	5	1	-6	-8	-8
	2005	13	12	-5	..	..	2	-6	4	6	20
	2006	7	12	-2	..	..	8	-6	1	13	20
Trinidad and Tobago - Trinité-et-Tobago	1990	-19	..	109	..	..	63	-303	-198	-328	-347
	2000	..	-25	680	-30	..	398	-848	-441	-267	-267
	2005	..	341	940	-258	..	7	-1 483	-1 805	-2 259	-2 259
Tunisia - Tunisie	1990	-7	1	76	-1	3	-343	476	-220	-7	-14
	2000	3	-1	752	..	-20	-624	500	245	851	854
	2005	127	-10	723	..	12	17	394	-936	200	327
	2006	145	-30	3 270	..	65	19	-729	-2 082	513	658
Turkey - Turquie	1990	..	16	684	-134	681	-409	3 151	-895	3 094	3 094
	2000	..	-870	982	-593	1 615	-1 939	13 705	-383	12 518	12 518
	2005	..	-1 078	9 801	-1 233	14 670	259	15 946	-17 854	20 511	20 511
	2006	..	-934	20 070	-4 029	11 402	-12 420	27 186	-6 102	35 173	35 173
Uganda - Ouganda	1990	..	..	..	..	..	..	249	5	254	254
	2000	70	..	161	..	..	-1	134	-45	249	318
	2005	64	..	380	..	-13	-7	52	-92	319	384
	2006	3 232	..	392	..	22	-10	-3 053	-383	-3 033	199
Ukraine	2000	-8	-1	595	-4	-197	-449	-868	-401	-1 325	-1 333
	2005	-65	-275	7 808	..	2 757	-7 936	5 450	-10 425	-2 622	-2 687
	2006	3	133	5 604	-3	3 586	-15 424	9 779	-1 999	1 676	1 679
United Kingdom - Royaume-Uni	1990	888	-20 124	33 504	-29 952	23 846	-94 789	114 100	-131	26 454	27 341
	2000	2 569	-246 265	122 157	-97 188	255 647	-426 811	414 585	-5 300	19 088	21 657
	2005	2 801	-91 706	195 554	-291 523	240 339	-931 586	936 201	-1 732	72 072	74 873
	2006	1 259	-128 676	139 745	-368 488	294 361	-733 176	830 766	1 301	50 314	51 572
United Republic of Tanzania - République-Unie de Tanzanie	1990	338	..	..	..	..	..	324	-141	183	521
	2000	420	..	463	..	..	-134	364	-199	494	914
	2005	633	..	448	..	3	-61	284	247	919	1 552
	2006	5 293	..	474	..	3	-175	-4 900	-127	-4 725	568
United States - États-Unis (12)	1990	-6 578	-37 200	48 490	-28 771	22 010	-13 140	71 047	-2 233	60 203	53 625
	2000	-1 010	-159 212	321 274	-127 908	436 573	-273 113	289 049	-295	486 368	485 358
	2005	-4 057	7 662	108 995	-203 434	832 036	-245 198	263 199	14 100	777 360	773 304
	2006	-3 915	-235 359	180 580	-426 088	1 017 440	-396 104	661 573	2 392	833 200	829 285
Uruguay	1990	..	..	..	..	108	-632	343	-40	-222	-222
	2000	..	1	274	-98	290	-690	1 004	-166	613	613
	2005	4	-36	847	578	228	-1 113	244	-621	127	131
	2006	7	2	1 319	-77	1 808	1 387	-4 047	16	408	414
Vanuatu	1990	16	..	13	..	..	-1	2	-5	9	26
	2000	-24	..	20	1	..	-14	11	1	19	-4
	2005	13	-1	13	-1	0	27	0	-9	29	41
	2006	25	-1	43	0	-1	-27	18	-33	0	26
Venezuela (Bolivarian Rep. of) - Venezuela (Rép. bolivarienne du)	1990	..	-375	451	-1 952	17 928	-2 305	-15 908	-4 376	-6 537	-6 537
	2000	..	-521	4 701	-954	-2 180	-4 839	316	-5 449	-8 927	-8 927
	2005	..	-1 167	2 602	-2 297	3 225	-18 425	-418	-5 425	-21 905	-21 905
	2006	..	-2 076	-590	-5 382	-3 982	-7 020	-194	-5 077	-24 321	-24 321
Viet Nam	2000	..	..	1 298	..	..	-2 089	454	-89	-426	-426
	2005	..	-65	1 954	750	..	-634	913	-2 077	842	842

For sources and notes, see end of table.

Pour les sources et les notes, se reporter à la fin du tableau.

7

Country or territory Pays ou territoires	Year Année	Capital account, net Compte de capital, net (1)	Direct investment Investissement direct		Portfolio investment Investissement de portefeuille		Other investment Autres investissements		Reserve assets Avoirs de réserve (8)	Financial account, net Compte financier, net (9)	Capital and financial account, net Compte de capital et compte financier, net (10) = (1) + (9)
			Abroad À l'étranger (2)	In reporting economy Dans l'économie déclarante (3)	Assets Avoirs (4)	Liabilities Engagements (5)	Assets Avoirs (6)	Liabilities Engagements (7)			
		Millions of dollars / Millions de dollars									
Yemen - Yémen	1990	..	..	-131	2	..	-351	468	-51	-62	-62
	2000	339	..	6	0	..	-178	-370	-1 429	-1 971	-1 632
	2005	202	..	-302	-14	..	-82	72	-713	-1 040	-837
	2006	94	..	1 121	-34	..	-387	221	-1 401	-480	-385
Zambia - Zambie	1990	-3	..	203	..	..	-275	467	-119	275	272
	2000	153	..	122	..	6	-85	476	-245	273	426
	2005	2 560	..	262	..	122	-523	-2 010	-87	-2 235	325
	2006	2 658	..	575	..	50	-1 594	-2 291	-261	-3 521	-862
Zimbabwe	1990	-7	..	-12	10	-32	..	254	-63	157	150

For sources and notes, see end of table.

Pour les sources et les notes, se reporter à la fin du tableau.

338

7.2 Balance of payments: capital and financial account summaries

7.2 Balance des paiements : sommaires des comptes de capital et d'opérations financières

Sources:
- International Monetary Fund (IMF), *Balance of Payments Statistics* on CD-ROM.

Sources :
- Fonds monétaire international (FMI), *Statistiques de la balance des paiements* sur CD-ROM.

Notes:

(1) **Capital account**

The capital account consists of capital transfers and of acquisition or disposal of non-produced, non-financial assets. Transfers refer to transactions exchanged without quid-pro-quo (without reciprocity). Capital transfers include transfers of ownership of fixed assets or of funds linked to acquisition or disposal of fixed assets. They further incorporate cancellations of liabilities by creditors, where the later receive no counterpart value. Acquisitions/disposals of non-produced, non-financial assets mainly refer to intangibles, such as patents, leases, and goodwill. Items are entered in capital account as net credits or debits. Column 1, as presented here, shows the total net amounts (net credits less net debits).

(2),(3) **Direct investment**

Within the financial account, direct investment is firstly split according to its direction into direct investment abroad (column 2) and direct investment in reporting economy (column 3). Further subdivisions include: direct investment in equity capital, reinvested earnings and other direct investment capital (inter-company transactions.)
Direct investment is defined as investment that reflects a lasting interest of a resident entity of one economy (direct investor) in an entity resident in another economy (direct investment enterprise). It covers all the transactions between direct investors and direct investment enterprises. Direct investment implies a significant degree of influence by the investor on the management of the direct investment enterprise.

(4),(5) **Portfolio investment**

Within portfolio investment the distinction is being made between assets (column 4) and liabilities (column 5). Assets are claims on the rest of the world and liabilities represent indebtedness to the rest of the world. Portfolio investment covers transactions in equity securities and debt securities. The later are subdivided into bonds, notes, money market instruments and financial derivatives (when the derivatives generate financial claims or liabilities).

(6),(7) **Other investment**

Other investment is a residual category that covers all financial transactions not included under direct investment, portfolio investment or reserve assets. Assets (column 6) and liabilities (column 7) in this category are classified primarily on an instrument bases, such as trade credits, loans, currency and deposits.

(8) **Reserve assets**

Includes: monetary gold, special drawing rights, reserve position in the IMF, foreign exchange and other claims.

(9) **Financial account**

The financial account constituents are classified according to the type of investment or by a functional breakdown into four main components: direct investment, portfolio investment, other investment and reserve assets. Each component is further divided into relevant subcomponents. The sum of figures in columns 2 to 8 is equal to column 9 (financial account balance). Where the financial account subcomponents do not add up to the total net financial account, the difference can be attributed to financial derivatives that are not shown within this table.

(11) The financial account total for the year 1990 does not add up to the total of its subcomponents owing to data revision by the Japanese authorities; it is recommended to use the financial account sum as given rather than to sum up the sub-components for this year.

(12) Including United States Virgin Islands

Notes :

(1) **Compte de capital**

Le compte de capital est subdivisé en transferts de capital et en acquisitions ou cessions d'avoirs non-financiers non-produits. Les transferts sont les transactions échangées sans quid-pro-quo (sans réciprocité.) Les transferts de capitaux comprennent les transferts de propriété d'un actif fixe ou les transferts de fonds liés à l'acquisition ou à la cession d'un actif fixe. De plus, ils incorporent la remise d'une dette par un créancier, sans que celui-ci ne reçoive une valeur équivalente. Les acquisitions ou cession d'avoirs non-financiers non-produits se réfèrent aux avoirs incorporels tels que les brevets, les contrats de location et marques. Les éléments du compte de capital sont reportés comme les crédits ou les débits nets. La colonne (1) présente les totaux (crédits nets moins débits nets).

(2),(3) **Investissement direct**

Dans le Compte financier, l'investissement direct est d'abord divisé en fonction du sens des mouvements de capitaux entre investissement de l'économie déclarante à l'étranger (colonne 2) et celui en provenance de l'étranger investi dans l'économie déclarante (colonne 3). Les subdivisions suivantes incluent : capital social, bénéfices réinvestis et autres transactions. L'investissement direct étranger est accompagné d'un intérêt durable de la part d'une entité résidente d'une économie (l'investisseur direct) pour une entité résidente d'une autre économie (l'entreprise d'investissement direct.) Il recouvre toutes les transactions entre les investisseurs directs et les entreprises d'investissement direct. L'investissement direct donne à l'investisseur le privilège d'exercer une influence significative sur la gestion de l'entreprise dans laquelle il a investi.

(4),(5) **Investissement de portefeuille**

En investissement de portefeuille on distingue les avoirs (colonne 4) et les engagements (colonne 5). Les avoirs représentent les créances sur les non-résidents et les engagements les endettements envers les non-résidents. Les investissements de portefeuille couvrent les transactions portant sur les titres de participation et les titres de créances, ces dernières étant subdivisées en trois catégories : obligations et autres titres d'emprunt, instruments du marché monétaire et produits financiers dérivés (lorsque les dérivés résultent en créances ou en engagements financiers).

(6),(7) **Autres investissements**

Les autres investissements constituent une catégorie résiduelle qui comprend toutes les opérations sur actifs et passifs financiers qui ne figurent pas parmi les investissements directs, les investissements de portefeuille ou les avoirs de réserve. Les avoirs (colonne 6) et les engagements (colonne 7) sont répartis par instruments tels que les crédits commerciaux, les prêts, la monnaie fiduciaire et les dépôts.

(8) **Avoirs de réserve**

Comprend : l'or monétaire, droits de tirage spéciaux, position de réserve dans le FMI, devises et autres créances.

(9) **Compte financier**

Les éléments qui constituent le compte financier se divisent selon le type d'investissement ou selon une ventilation fonctionnelle en quatre principaux composants : investissements directs, investissements de portefeuille, autres investissements et avoirs de réserve. Chaque composant comprend plusieurs sous-groupes. La somme de tous les chiffres des colonnes 2 à 8 est égale à la colonne 9 (balance du compte financier). Dans le cas où la somme des éléments du compte financier ne correspond pas au total, la différence peut être attribuée aux instruments financiers dérivés, qui ne sont pas présentés dans ce tableau.

(11) Les données du compte financier net pour l'année 1990 ne correspondent pas à la somme des composants du compte financier à cause de révision des statistiques nationales du Japon ; il est préconisé d'utiliser les chiffres fournis pour ladite série, plutôt que de calculer la somme d'éléments composants pour cette année.

(12) Y compris les Îles Vierges américaines

Region, country or territory	Inward flows - Flux entrants Millions of dollars							
	1980	1990	2000	2002	2003	2004	2005	2006
WORLD	**55 262**	**201 594**	**1 411 366**	**621 995**	**564 078**	**742 143**	**945 795**	**1 305 852**
DEVELOPING ECONOMIES	7 664	35 877	256 096	166 275	178 705	283 006	314 279	379 052
ECONOMIES IN TRANSITION	24	75	6 930	11 279	19 877	30 289	30 824	52 717
DEVELOPED ECONOMIES	47 575	165 641	1 148 340	444 441	365 496	428 848	600 692	874 083
Developing economies: Africa	**400**	**2 806**	**9 685**	**13 570**	**18 677**	**18 018**	**29 648**	**35 544**
Eastern Africa	*197*	*389*	*1 390*	*1 484*	*1 834*	*1 965*	*1 833*	*2 667*
Burundi	5	1	12	0	0	0	1	290
Comoros	..	0	0	0	1	1	1	1
Djibouti	0	0	3	4	14	39	22	108
Eritrea	–	–	28	20	22	-8	-3	4
Ethiopia	–	–	135	255	465	545	221	364
Ethiopia (former)	1	12	–	–	–	–	–	–
Kenya	79	57	111	28	82	46	21	51
Madagascar	-1	22	83	61	95	95	86	230
Malawi	9	23	40	6	7	22	27	30
Mauritius	1	41	266	32	63	14	42	105
Mayotte	..	..	0	..	..	..	..	..
Mozambique	4	9	139	347	337	245	108	154
Rwanda	16	8	8	3	5	8	11	15
Seychelles	10	0	24	48	58	38	86	146
Somalia	0	6	0	0	-1	-5	24	96
Uganda	4	-6	181	185	202	222	257	307
United Republic of Tanzania	5	0	216	388	308	331	448	377
Zambia	62	203	122	82	172	364	380	350
Zimbabwe	2	12	23	26	4	9	103	40
Middle Africa	*353*	*-345*	*1 411*	*3 815*	*6 807*	*4 154*	*2 402*	*2 341*
Angola	37	-335	879	1 672	3 505	1 449	-1 303	-1 140
Cameroon	130	-113	159	602	383	319	225	309
Central African Republic	5	1	1	4	19	25	29	24
Chad	0	9	115	924	713	495	613	700
Congo	40	23	162	131	321	-13	724	344
Dem. Rep. of the Congo	110	-14	23	117	158	10	-79	180
Equatorial Guinea	..	11	111	323	1 444	1 651	1 873	1 656
Gabon	32	73	-43	39	263	219	321	268
Sao Tome and Principe	..	..	4	3	1	-2	-1	0
Northern Africa	*152*	*1 116*	*3 456*	*3 925*	*5 376*	*6 616*	*13 528*	*23 324*
Algeria	349	0	438	1 065	634	882	1 081	1 795
Egypt	548	734	1 235	647	237	2 157	5 376	10 043
Libyan Arab Jamahiriya	-1 089	159	141	145	143	357	1 038	1 734
Morocco	89	165	471	534	2 429	1 070	2 946	2 898
Sudan	9	-31	392	713	1 349	1 511	2 305	3 541
Tunisia	246	89	779	821	584	639	782	3 312
Southern Africa	*132*	*92*	*1 256*	*1 462*	*1 282*	*1 541*	*6 888*	*371*
Botswana	112	96	57	405	419	392	281	274
Lesotho	4	16	32	27	42	53	57	57
Namibia	..	30	188	182	149	226	348	327
South Africa	-10	-78	888	757	734	799	6 251	-323
Swaziland	26	28	91	92	-61	71	-50	36
Western Africa	*-434*	*1 553*	*2 172*	*2 884*	*3 377*	*3 743*	*4 997*	*6 841*
Benin	4	62	60	14	45	64	53	63
Burkina Faso	0	0	23	15	29	14	34	26
Cape Verde	..	0	33	10	16	20	76	122
Côte d'Ivoire	95	48	235	213	165	283	312	253
Gambia	0	14	44	43	15	49	45	70
Ghana	16	15	166	59	137	139	145	435
Guinea	1	18	10	30	83	98	102	108
Guinea-Bissau	..	2	1	4	4	2	9	42
Liberia	72	225	21	3	372	237	-479	-82
Mali	2	6	82	244	132	101	224	185
Mauritania	27	7	40	67	102	392	864	-3
Niger	49	41	8	2	11	20	30	20
Nigeria	-739	1 003	1 310	2 040	2 171	2 127	3 403	5 445
Saint Helena	..	..	-4	..	..	-1	0	0
Senegal	14	57	63	78	52	77	45	58
Sierra Leone	-19	32	39	10	9	61	59	43
Togo	43	23	41	53	34	59	77	57

For sources and notes, see end of table.

Outward flows - Flux sortants Millions de dollars								Régions, pays ou territoires
1980	1990	2000	2002	2003	2004	2005	2006	
53 829	229 598	1 239 190	540 714	560 087	877 301	837 194	1 215 789	**MONDE**
3 153	11 913	133 341	47 866	45 372	117 336	115 860	174 389	ÉCONOMIES EN DÉVELOPPEMENT
0	0	3 193	4 622	10 682	14 142	14 342	18 496	ÉCONOMIES EN TRANSITION
50 676	217 684	1 102 656	488 226	504 032	745 823	706 991	1 022 904	ÉCONOMIES DÉVELOPPÉES
1 090	655	1 526	305	1 286	2 059	2 272	8 186	**Économies en développement : Afrique**
5	*21*	*28*	*28*	*2*	*45*	*67*	*43*	*Afrique orientale*
..	0	0	0	0	..	..	0	Burundi
0	1	0	0	0	0	0	0	Comores
0	0	0	0	0	0	0	0	Djibouti
–	–	0	0	0	0	0	0	Érythrée
–	–	0	0	0	0	0	0	Éthiopie
0	0	–	–	–	–	–	–	Éthiopie (anc.)
1	0	0	7	2	4	10	24	Kenya
0	1	0	0	-5	0	0	0	Madagascar
0	0	-1	0	0	2	1	1	Malawi
..	1	13	9	-6	32	48	10	Maurice
0	0	0	0	0	0	0	0	Mayotte
0	0	0	0	0	0	0	0	Mozambique
0	0	0	0	0	0	0	0	Rwanda
4	1	8	9	8	8	7	8	Seychelles
0	0	0	0	0	0	0	0	Somalie
0	0	0	0	0	0	0	0	Ouganda
0	0	0	0	2	0	0	0	République-Unie de Tanzanie
0	0	0	0	0	0	0	0	Zambie
0	17	8	3	0	0	1	0	Zimbabwe
0	*52*	*12*	*-22*	*9*	*15*	*201*	*73*	*Afrique centrale*
0	1	-21	29	24	35	219	93	Angola
-8	15	10	-33	4	0	0	0	Cameroun
..	4	0	1	0	0	0	0	République centrafricaine
0	0	0	0	0	..	..	0	Tchad
..	3	4	6	2	5	4	3	Congo
0	0	-2	-2	0	0	0	0	Rép. dém. du Congo
..	0	-4	0	0	0	0	0	Guinée équatoriale
8	29	25	-23	-21	-25	-23	-23	Gabon
0	0	0	0	0	0	0	0	Sao Tomé-et-Principe
87	*135*	*227*	*52*	*123*	*167*	*464*	*834*	*Afrique septentrionale*
34	5	18	100	14	258	57	35	Algérie
7	12	51	28	21	159	92	148	Égypte
47	105	98	-136	63	-286	128	141	Jamahiriya arabe libyenne
..	13	60	54	20	32	174	468	Maroc
0	0	0	0	0	0	0	9	Soudan
..	0	0	7	5	4	13	33	Tunisie
766	*39*	*293*	*-362*	*778*	*1 300*	*949*	*6 685*	*Afrique australe*
2	7	2	43	206	-29	56	21	Botswana
0	0	0	0	0	0	0	0	Lesotho
..	1	3	-5	-10	-22	-13	-12	Namibie
755	27	271	-399	565	1 352	930	6 674	Afrique du Sud
9	3	17	-1	16	-1	-24	2	Swaziland
232	*407*	*966*	*610*	*375*	*532*	*591*	*551*	*Afrique occidentale*
..	0	4	1	0	-1	0	-1	Bénin
0	-1	0	2	2	-9	0	-2	Burkina Faso
..	0	0	1	0	..	0	0	Cap-Vert
0	0	8	-4	23	-26	-7	-6	Côte d'Ivoire
0	0	0	0	0	0	0	0	Gambie
0	0	0	-2	11	-1	0	0	Ghana
0	0	..	0	0	-1	-5	0	Guinée
..	..	0	1	1	-8	1	-4	Guinée-Bissau
231	-3	780	403	173	304	437	346	Libéria
0	0	4	2	1	1	-1	1	Mali
0	0	0	0	-1	4	2	0	Mauritanie
-4	0	-1	-2	0	7	-4	2	Niger
3	415	169	172	167	261	200	228	Nigéria
0	0	0	0	0	0	0	0	Sainte-Hélène
2	-10	1	34	3	13	-8	5	Sénégal
0	0	0	0	1	0	-8	3	Sierra Leone
0	5	0	2	-6	-13	-15	-20	Togo

Pour les sources et les notes, se reporter à la fin du tableau.

Region, country or territory	Inward flows - Flux entrants Millions of dollars							
	1980	1990	2000	2002	2003	2004	2005	2006
Developing economies: America	**6 483**	**9 733**	**97 810**	**54 274**	**44 698**	**94 266**	**75 505**	**83 735**
Caribbean	*390*	*828*	*20 125*	*4 478*	*3 643*	*30 875*	*7 118*	*14 352*
Anguilla	..	11	43	38	34	92	100	113
Antigua and Barbuda	20	59	67	80	179	95	133	207
Aruba	..	131	-120	337	160	152	128	326
Bahamas	4	-17	250	209	247	443	564	706
Barbados	3	11	19	17	58	-12	62	36
British Virgin Islands	-1	18	9 877	1 472	3 111	17 606	-8 013	6 463
Cayman Islands	20	49	7 627	-196	-2 689	9 659	10 931	2 878
Cuba	0	1	-10	3	-7	4	2	-1
Dominica	..	8	20	21	32	27	33	34
Dominican Republic	93	133	953	917	613	909	1 023	1 183
Grenada	..	13	39	57	91	66	86	119
Haiti	13	8	13	6	14	6	26	160
Jamaica	28	175	469	479	721	602	682	850
Montserrat	..	10	2	1	2	3	1	1
Netherlands Antilles	35	8	-1	75	11	41	83	47
Saint Kitts and Nevis	1	49	99	81	78	53	104	203
Saint Lucia	31	46	58	57	112	81	82	119
Saint Vincent and the Grenadines	1	8	38	34	55	66	42	85
Trinidad and Tobago	143	109	680	791	808	998	940	788
Turks and Caicos Islands	..	..	0	0	14	-15	108	36
Central America	*2 496*	*3 056*	*19 873*	*21 085*	*17 396*	*25 411*	*23 108*	*24 364*
Belize	..	19	23	24	-11	112	127	73
Costa Rica	53	162	409	659	575	794	861	1 469
El Salvador	6	2	173	470	142	376	518	204
Guatemala	111	59	230	111	131	155	227	354
Honduras	6	44	282	175	247	325	372	385
Mexico	2 090	2 633	17 789	19 363	15 340	22 396	19 736	19 037
Nicaragua	13	1	267	204	201	250	241	282
Panama, excl. Canal Zone (former)	219							
Panama	–	136	700	78	771	1 004	1 027	2 560
South America	*3 597*	*5 849*	*57 812*	*28 711*	*23 658*	*37 980*	*45 279*	*45 019*
Argentina	678	1 836	10 418	2 149	1 652	4 584	5 008	4 809
Bolivia	50	67	736	677	197	65	-239	240
Brazil	1 910	989	32 779	16 590	10 144	18 146	15 066	18 782
Chile	287	1 315	4 860	2 550	4 307	7 173	6 960	7 952
Colombia	157	500	2 395	2 139	1 758	3 084	10 255	6 295
Ecuador	70	126	720	1 275	1 555	1 160	1 646	2 087
Falkland Islands (Malvinas)	..	..	45	..	..	..	..	0
Guyana	1	8	67	44	26	30	77	102
Paraguay	30	71	104	10	27	38	98	130
Peru	27	41	810	2 156	1 335	1 599	2 579	3 467
Suriname	18	77	-97	146	201	286	399	323
Uruguay	290	42	273	194	416	332	847	1 374
Venezuela (Bolivarian Rep. of)	80	778	4 701	782	2 040	1 483	2 583	-543
Developing economies: Asia	**663**	**22 642**	**148 333**	**98 310**	**114 987**	**169 999**	**208 744**	**259 434**
Eastern Asia	*950*	*8 791*	*116 625*	*67 701*	*72 666*	*106 314*	*116 253*	*125 774*
China	57	3 487	40 715	52 743	53 505	60 630	72 406	69 468
China, Hong Kong SAR	710	3 275	61 924	9 682	13 624	34 032	33 618	42 892
China, Macao SAR	..	0	-1	375	411	484	1 322	739
China, Taiwan Province of	166	1 330	4 928	1 445	453	1 898	1 625	7 424
Dem. People's Rep. of Korea	..	-61	3	-16	158	197	50	135
Mongolia	..	..	54	78	132	93	182	167
Republic of Korea	17	759	9 002	3 395	4 384	8 980	7 050	4 950
Southern Asia	*284*	*213*	*4 688*	*7 087*	*5 858*	*7 883*	*10 226*	*23 176*
Afghanistan	9	..	0	1	2	1	4	2
Bangladesh	9	3	579	328	350	460	692	625
Bhutan	..	2	0	2	3	3	9	6
India	79	237	3 585	5 627	4 323	5 771	6 676	16 881
Iran (Islamic Rep. of)	81	-362	30	103	390	282	360	901
Maldives	0	6	13	12	14	15	9	14
Nepal	0	6	0	-6	15	0	2	-7
Pakistan	64	278	309	823	534	1 118	2 201	4 273
Sri Lanka	43	43	173	197	229	233	272	480

For sources and notes, see end of table.

Outward flows - Flux sortants Millions de dollars								Régions, pays ou territoires
1980	1990	2000	2002	2003	2004	2005	2006	
899	**300**	**49 577**	**12 114**	**21 641**	**27 762**	**35 743**	**49 132**	**Économies en développement : Amérique**
121	*-1 718*	*42 279*	*5 011*	*11 750*	*8 843*	*15 487*	*5 452*	*Caraïbes*
0	0	0	0	0	0	0	0	Anguilla
0	0	2	15	0	0	0	0	Antigua-et-Barbuda
0	487	6	2	6	0	-1	-2	Aruba
115	0	0	0	0	0	0	0	Bahamas
1	1	1	0	1	4	9	5	Barbade
..	-2 520	34 459	10 577	6 074	4 878	8 174	2 964	Îles Vierges britanniques
5	282	7 649	-5 778	5 366	3 862	6 771	1 950	Îles Caïmanes
0	0	0	0	3	0	-2	0	Cuba
0	0	0	0	0	0	0	0	Dominique
0	0	61	15	-41	-10	27	0	République dominicaine
0	0	0	0	0	0	0	0	Grenade
0	-8	0	0	0	0	0	0	Haïti
..	37	74	74	116	60	101	108	Jamaïque
0	0	0	0	0	0	0	0	Montserrat
1	2	-3	1	-1	22	65	56	Antilles néerlandaises
0	0	0	0	0	0	0	0	Saint-Kitts-et-Nevis
0	0	0	0	0	0	0	0	Sainte-Lucie
0	0	0	0	0	0	0	0	Saint-Vincent-et-les Grenadines
0	0	25	106	225	25	341	370	Trinité-et-Tobago
0	0	4	-2	0	2	1	1	Îles Turques et Caïques
358	*907*	*-591*	*2 988*	*4 922*	*6 258*	*8 313*	*6 960*	*Amérique centrale*
..	2	0	0	0	0	1	1	Belize
5	2	8	34	27	61	-43	98	Costa Rica
0	0	-5	-26	19	-53	217	-50	El Salvador
2	0	40	17	367	18	42	13	Guatemala
1	-1	-2	2	20	26	22	22	Honduras
3	223	363	891	1 253	4 432	6 474	5 758	Mexique
0	0	8	18	-6	8	7	3	Nicaragua
347		–	–	–	–	–	–	Panama, sans la zone du canal (anc.)
–	681	-1 004	2 053	3 243	1 767	1 594	1 115	Panama
420	*1 111*	*7 889*	*4 115*	*4 969*	*12 660*	*11 942*	*36 720*	*Amérique du Sud*
-110	35	901	-627	774	442	1 151	2 008	Argentine
1	1	3	3	3	3	3	3	Bolivie
367	625	2 282	2 482	249	9 807	2 517	28 202	Brésil
44	8	3 987	343	1 606	1 563	2 209	2 876	Chili
106	16	325	857	938	142	4 662	1 098	Colombie
1	2	10	-2	1	1	2	2	Équateur
0	0	0	0	0	0	0	0	Îles Falkland (Malvinas)
..	..	2	0	0	0	0	0	Guyana
0	0	6	2	6	6	6	16	Paraguay
0	50	-146	18	60	59	174	428	Pérou
0	0	0	0	0	0	0	0	Suriname
..	..	-1	14	15	18	36	-2	Uruguay
12	375	521	1 026	1 318	619	1 183	2 089	Venezuela (Rép. bolivarienne du)
1 146	**10 948**	**82 230**	**35 427**	**22 412**	**87 461**	**77 747**	**117 067**	**Économies en développement : Asie**
150	*9 574*	*71 973*	*27 555*	*17 447*	*62 924*	*49 836*	*74 099*	*Asie orientale*
..	830	916	2 518	2 855	5 498	12 261	16 130	Chine
82	2 448	59 352	17 463	5 492	45 716	27 201	43 459	Chine (RAS de Hong Kong)
0	0	0	71	-5	-95	47	-18	Chine (RAS de Macao)
42	5 243	6 701	4 886	5 682	7 145	6 028	7 399	Province chinoise de Taiwan
..	1	6	0	-1	2	0	0	Rép. populaire dém. de Corée
0	0	0	0	0	0	0	0	Mongolie
26	1 052	4 999	2 617	3 426	4 658	4 298	7 129	République de Corée
11	*10*	*546*	*1 778*	*1 590*	*2 314*	*3 031*	*10 206*	*Asie méridionale*
0	0	0	0	0	0	0	0	Afghanistan
..	1	2	4	6	6	2	8	Bangladesh
0	0	0	0	0	0	0	0	Bhoutan
4	6	509	1 679	1 879	2 179	2 495	9 676	Inde
7	0	22	55	-342	68	452	386	Iran (Rép. islamique d')
0	0	0	0	0	0	0	0	Maldives
0	0	0	0	0	0	0	0	Népal
0	2	11	28	19	56	44	107	Pakistan
..	1	2	11	27	6	38	29	Sri Lanka

Pour les sources et les notes, se reporter à la fin du tableau.

7

Region, country or territory	Inward flows - Flux entrants Millions of dollars							
	1980	1990	2000	2002	2003	2004	2005	2006
South-Eastern Asia	*2 756*	*12 821*	*23 540*	*18 024*	*24 491*	*35 245*	*41 071*	*51 483*
Brunei Darussalam	-20	7	549	1 035	3 375	334	289	434
Cambodia	1	..	149	145	84	131	381	483
Indonesia	300	1 092	-4 550	145	-597	1 896	8 337	5 556
Lao People's dem. Rep.	..	6	34	25	19	17	28	187
Malaysia	934	2 611	3 788	3 203	2 473	4 624	3 965	6 060
Myanmar	0	225	208	191	291	251	236	143
Philippines	114	550	2 240	1 542	491	688	1 854	2 345
Singapore	1 236	5 575	16 484	7 200	11 664	19 828	15 004	24 207
Thailand	189	2 575	3 349	3 335	5 235	5 862	8 957	9 751
Timor-Leste	..	..	..	1	5	3	0	3
Viet Nam	2	180	1 289	1 200	1 450	1 610	2 021	2 315
Western Asia	*-3 328*	*818*	*3 479*	*5 498*	*11 972*	*20 557*	*41 194*	*59 001*
Bahrain	-418	-183	364	217	517	865	1 049	2 915
Iraq	2	0	-3	-2	0	300	515	272
Jordan	34	38	815	74	436	651	1 532	3 121
Kuwait	1	6	16	4	-67	24	250	110
Lebanon	-12	6	964	1 336	2 977	1 993	2 751	2 794
Occupied Palestinian territory	..	..	62	9	18	49	47	38
Oman	98	125	83	122	494	229	900	952
Qatar	11	5	252	624	625	1 199	1 152	1 786
Saudi Arabia	-3 192	312	183	453	778	1 942	12 097	18 293
Syrian Arab Republic	0	71	270	115	180	275	500	600
Turkey	18	684	982	1 137	1 752	2 883	9 803	20 120
United Arab Emirates	98	-116	-515	1 307	4 256	10 004	10 900	8 386
Yemen (former Democratic)	34		–	–	–	–	–	–
Yemen	–	-131	6	102	6	144	-302	-385
Developing economies: Oceania	**118**	**696**	**268**	**121**	**343**	**723**	**383**	**339**
Cook Islands	..	4	-28	0	..	-1	1	0
Fiji	36	84	-18	21	26	94	-4	103
French Polynesia	..	22	2	11	58	6	8	0
Kiribati	..	0	18	15	16	19	1	12
Marshall Islands	..	1	125	-47	5	513	305	19
Micronesia (Federated States of)	..	..	..	..	..	..	0	..
Nauru	..	0	0	1	2	1	1	1
New Caledonia	2	31	22	59	116	27	-7	82
Niue	..	..	0	9	0	0	-1	0
Northern Mariana Islands	-1	124	12	..	..	..	..	..
Palau	..	1	15	1	2	7	1	1
Papua New Guinea	76	398	96	18	101	26	34	32
Samoa	0	7	-2	0	1	2	-4	-2
Solomon Islands	2	10	1	-4	-2	6	19	19
Tokelau	..	..	0	0	0	..	0	0
Tonga	..	0	5	0	3	5	17	11
Tuvalu	..	..	-1	25	0	0	0	0
Vanuatu	3	13	20	13	15	18	13	61
Economies in transition: Asia	**–**	**–**	**1 779**	**4 643**	**6 135**	**9 399**	**4 968**	**8 424**
Armenia	–	–	104	111	121	219	258	343
Azerbaijan	–	–	30	1 393	3 227	3 535	1 679	-601
Georgia	–	–	135	167	340	499	450	1 076
Kazakhstan	–	–	1 283	2 590	2 092	4 157	1 977	6 143
Kyrgyzstan	–	–	-2	5	46	175	43	182
Tajikistan	–	–	24	36	14	272	54	385
Turkmenistan	–	–	131	276	226	354	418	731
Uzbekistan	–	–	75	65	70	187	88	164
Economies in transition: Europe	**–**	**–**	**5 151**	**6 636**	**13 742**	**20 890**	**25 856**	**44 293**
Albania	..	..	143	135	178	338	277	325
Belarus	–	–	119	247	172	164	305	354
Bosnia and Herzegovina	–	–	146	265	381	668	521	423
Croatia	–	–	1 082	1 124	2 049	1 227	1 790	3 556
Moldova	–	–	128	84	74	149	199	222
Russian Federation	–	–	2 714	3 461	7 958	15 444	12 766	28 732
Serbia and Montenegro	–	–	50	549	1 410	1 029	2 090	5 128
SFR of Yugoslavia (former) (1)	24	71	–	–	–	–	–	–
TFYR of Macedonia	–	–	175	78	96	157	100	351
Ukraine	–	–	595	693	1 424	1 715	7 808	5 203
USSR (former)	..	4	–	–	–	–	–	–

For sources and notes, see end of table.

		Outward flows - Flux sortants Millions de dollars						Régions, pays ou territoires
1980	1990	2000	2002	2003	2004	2005	2006	
394	*2 328*	*8 225*	*4 681*	*5 286*	*14 212*	*11 918*	*19 095*	**Asie du Sud-Est**
..	..	20	24	76	4	35	38	Brunéi Darussalam
0	0	7	6	10	10	6	8	Cambodge
6	-11	150	182	213	3 408	3 065	3 418	Indonésie
0	0	4	0	0	0	0	0	Rép. dém. populaire lao
201	129	2 026	1 905	1 369	2 061	2 972	6 041	Malaisie
0	0	0	0	0	0	0	0	Myanmar
86	22	125	65	303	579	189	103	Philippines
98	2 034	5 915	2 329	2 695	8 074	5 034	8 626	Singapour
3	154	-22	171	621	76	552	790	Thaïlande
0	0	0	0	0	0	0	0	Timor-Leste
0	0	0	0	0	0	65	70	Viet Nam
591	*-964*	*1 485*	*1 412*	*-1 912*	*8 010*	*12 961*	*13 667*	**Asie occidentale**
..	25	10	190	741	1 036	1 123	980	Bahreïn
0	0	0	0	0	0	0	0	Iraq
3	-31	2	0	0	0	0	0	Jordanie
407	-239	-303	-77	-4 960	2 526	5 142	7 892	Koweït
2	-16	108	0	40	213	122	71	Liban
0	0	213	360	49	-51	9	2	Territoire palestinien occupé
1	0	-2	3	153	250	114	247	Oman
2	2	18	-21	88	192	352	379	Qatar
178	-634	112	211	368	709	1 183	753	Arabie saoudite
0	3	43	119	57	48	61	55	République arabe syrienne
0	-16	870	175	499	859	1 078	934	Turquie
-2	-58	424	413	991	2 208	3 750	2 316	Émirats arabes unis
0	–	–	–	–	–	–	–	Yémen (anc. démocratique)
–	0	-9	39	61	21	26	36	Yémen
18	*11*	*8*	*20*	*33*	*55*	*99*	*5*	**Économies en développement : Océanie**
0	0	0	1	0	2	0	0	Îles Cook
2	3	2	1	4	3	10	0	Fidji
0	0	0	14	6	9	16	1	Polynésie française
0	0	0	0	0	0	0	0	Kiribati
0	0	2	0	10	25	33	-18	Îles Marshall
0	0	0	0	0	0	0	0	Micronésie (États fédérés de)
0	0	0	0	0	0	0	0	Nauru
0	0	0	4	14	11	31	19	Nouvelle-Calédonie
0	0	5	0	1	4	1	0	Nioué
0	0	0	0	0	0	0	0	Îles Mariannes du Nord
0	0	-1	0	0	0	-2	0	Palaos
16	8	-1	-1	-3	0	6	1	Papouasie-Nouvelle-Guinée
0	0	0	0	0	0	2	1	Samoa
0	0	0	1	0	0	2	0	Îles Salomon
0	0	0	0	0	0	0	0	Tokélaou
0	0	0	0	0	0	0	0	Tonga
0	0	0	0	0	0	0	0	Tuvalu
..	..	..	1	1	1	1	1	Vanuatu
–	*–*	*8*	*758*	*816*	*-18*	*992*	*278*	**Économies en transition : Asie**
–	–	-1	1	0	2	7	3	Arménie
–	–	1	326	933	1 205	1 221	705	Azerbaïdjan
–	–	0	4	4	10	-89	-18	Géorgie
–	–	4	426	-121	-1 279	-146	-412	Kazakhstan
–	–	5	0	0	44	0	0	Kirghizistan
–	–	0	0	0	0	0	0	Tadjikistan
–	–	0	0	0	0	0	0	Turkménistan
–	–	0	0	0	0	0	0	Ouzbékistan
–	*–*	*3 185*	*3 864*	*9 867*	*14 160*	*13 350*	*18 218*	**Économies en transition : Europe**
0	0	6	0	0	14	4	11	Albanie
–	–	0	-206	2	1	3	3	Bélarus
–	–	0	0	0	2	1	0	Bosnie-Herzégovine
–	–	1	542	123	350	240	212	Croatie
–	–	0	0	0	3	0	-1	Moldova
–	–	3 177	3 533	9 727	13 782	12 763	17 979	Fédération de Russie
–	–	0	0	2	3	62	146	Serbie-et-Monténégro
0	0	–	–	–	–	–	–	RSF de Yougoslavie (anc.) (1)
–	–	-1	0	0	1	3	0	LERY de Macédoine
–	–	1	-5	13	4	275	-133	Ukraine
0	0	–	–	–	–	–	–	URSS (anc.)

Pour les sources et les notes, se reporter à la fin du tableau.

7.3.1 Foreign direct investment: inward and outward flows of countries and geographical regions

Region, country or territory	Inward flows - Flux entrants Millions of dollars							
	1980	1990	2000	2002	2003	2004	2005	2006
Developed economies: America	**23 665**	**56 823**	**392 964**	**98 070**	**63 445**	**160 986**	**121 294**	**251 256**
Bermuda	940	819	12 171	1 413	2 822	25 501	-8 689	6 803
Canada	5 807	7 582	66 795	22 156	7 482	-364	28 922	69 041
United States	16 918	48 422	313 997	74 501	53 141	135 850	101 061	175 412
Developed economies: Asia	**287**	**1 904**	**13 451**	**10 907**	**10 220**	**9 856**	**7 567**	**7 795**
Israel	9	151	5 128	1 668	3 896	2 040	4 792	14 301
Japan	278	1 753	8 323	9 239	6 324	7 816	2 775	-6 506
Developed economies: Europe	**21 578**	**97 058**	**724 044**	**316 696**	**281 385**	**219 172**	**505 325**	**582 955**
Austria	239	653	8 840	357	7 144	3 890	9 045	248
Belgium	–	–	–	16 251	33 476	43 558	33 918	71 997
Belgium-Luxembourg	1 545	8 047	88 739		–	–	–	–
Bulgaria	..	4	1 053	970	2 097	3 452	3 862	5 172
Cyprus	85	127	855	1 058	893	1 090	1 214	1 492
Czechoslovakia (former)	..	165		–	–	–	–	–
Czech Republic	–	–	4 986	8 483	2 101	4 974	11 658	5 957
Denmark	52	1 132	33 012	6 630	2 709	-10 442	13 103	7 032
Estonia	–	–	387	284	919	971	2 879	1 674
Finland	28	786	8 834	8 046	3 319	3 003	4 507	3 706
France	3 328	9 056	43 252	49 035	42 498	32 560	81 063	81 076
Germany (former Federal Rep.)	342	–	–	–	–	–	–	–
Germany	–	2 962	198 277	53 520	32 369	-9 195	35 867	42 870
Gibraltar	2	36	138	83	62	194	365	685
Greece	672	1 005	1 108	50	1 275	2 101	607	5 363
Hungary	1	623	2 764	2 994	2 137	4 506	7 619	6 098
Iceland	22	22	171	87	332	848	3 082	3 734
Ireland	286	622	25 779	29 324	22 781	-10 608	-31 132	12 811
Italy	577	6 345	13 375	14 545	16 415	16 815	19 971	39 159
Latvia	–	–	413	253	304	637	724	1 634
Lithuania	–	–	379	732	179	773	1 032	1 812
Luxembourg	–	–	–	4 093	2 917	5 823	7 246	29 309
Malta	27	46	618	-440	968	403	582	1 757
Netherlands	2 278	10 515	63 854	25 038	21 043	2 123	41 456	4 371
Norway	60	1 003	7 090	791	3 471	2 544	6 391	5 906
Poland	10	89	9 343	4 131	4 589	12 890	9 602	13 922
Portugal	157	2 610	6 635	1 799	8 593	2 327	3 965	7 371
Romania	..	0	1 057	1 144	2 213	6 517	6 483	11 394
Slovakia	–	–	1 925	4 123	2 160	3 031	2 107	4 165
Slovenia	–	–	136	1 636	333	827	496	363
Spain	1 493	13 294	39 575	39 214	25 820	24 761	25 020	20 016
Sweden	251	1 971	23 427	12 160	4 985	11 463	10 169	27 231
Switzerland	..	5 484	19 255	6 276	16 503	1 372	-1 266	25 089
United Kingdom	10 123	30 461	118 764	24 029	16 778	55 963	193 693	139 543
Developed economies: Oceania	**2 044**	**9 856**	**17 882**	**18 768**	**10 446**	**38 834**	**-33 494**	**32 077**
Australia	1 866	8 121	14 019	17 019	8 020	36 007	-35 160	24 022
New Zealand	178	1 735	3 863	1 749	2 426	2 827	1 666	8 055

Sources:
- UNCTAD, *World Investment Report 2007: Transnational Corporations, Extractive Industries and Development*

Notes:
(1) Data for 1990 refer to Slovenia only, except for the FDI inflows that also cover other Republics of the former SFR Yugoslavia.

FDI inward flows and outward flows comprise capital provided (either directly or through other related enterprises) by a foreign direct investor to a FDI enterprise, or capital received by a foreign direct investor from a FDI enterprise. FDI includes the three following components: equity capital, reinvested earnings and intra-company loans.

- Equity capital is the foreign direct investor's purchase of shares of an enterprise in a country other than that of its residence.
- Reinvested earnings comprise the direct investor's share (in proportion to direct equity participation) of earnings not distributed as dividends by affiliates or earnings not remitted to the direct investor. Such retained profits by affiliates are reinvested.

- Intra-company loans or intra-company debt transactions refer to short- or long-term borrowing and lending of funds between direct investors (parent enterprises) and affiliate enterprises.

Data on FDI flows are presented on net bases (capital transactions' credits less debits between direct investors and their foreign affiliates). Net decreases in assets or net increases in liabilities are recorded as credits (with a positive sign), while net increases in assets or net decreases in liabilities are recorded as debits (with a negative sign). Hence, FDI flows with a negative sign indicate that at least one of the three components of FDI is negative and not offset by positive amounts of the remaining components. These are called reverse investment or disinvestment.

7.3.1 Investissement étranger direct : flux entrants et sortants des pays et des régions géographiques

Outward flows - Flux sortants Millions de dollars								Régions, pays ou territoires
1980	1990	2000	2002	2003	2004	2005	2006	
23 601	**36 982**	**197 603**	**166 622**	**147 772**	**306 099**	**1 104**	**265 809**	**Économies développées : Amérique**
273	763	10 298	4 904	-4 504	4 442	-4 702	3 952	Bermudes
4 098	5 237	44 679	26 773	22 924	43 690	33 542	45 243	Canada
19 230	30 982	142 626	134 946	129 352	257 967	-27 736	216 614	États-Unis
2 382	**48 223**	**34 896**	**33 263**	**30 865**	**35 495**	**48 712**	**64 665**	**Économies développées : Asie**
-3	199	3 338	982	2 065	4 544	2 931	14 399	Israël
2 385	48 024	31 558	32 281	28 800	30 951	45 781	50 266	Japon
24 126	**129 892**	**866 232**	**280 085**	**308 607**	**394 320**	**691 495**	**668 891**	**Économies développées : Europe**
101	1 701	5 740	5 807	7 136	8 301	10 023	4 087	Autriche
			12 277	38 322	34 018	31 731	63 005	Belgique
196	6 314	86 362	–	–	–	–	–	Belgique-Luxembourg
0	-3	3	29	27	-217	308	156	Bulgarie
0	5	172	518	573	694	482	732	Chypre
..	20	–	–	–	–	–	–	Tchécoslovaquie (anc.)
–	–	43	206	206	1 014	-19	1 556	République tchèque
94	1 482	25 082	5 687	1 215	-10 364	15 030	8 181	Danemark
–	–	63	132	156	268	627	1 105	Estonie
137	2 702	24 030	7 371	-2 280	-1 079	4 477	9	Finlande
3 137	26 924	177 449	50 441	53 147	56 735	120 971	115 036	France
4 699	–	–	–	–	–	–	–	Allemagne (anc. Rép. fédérale d')
–	24 235	56 557	18 946	5 822	14 828	55 515	79 427	Allemagne
0	0	0	0	0	0	0	0	Gibraltar
..	11	2 137	655	412	1 029	1 451	4 167	Grèce
0	16	620	278	1 644	1 119	2 327	3 016	Hongrie
..	12	394	327	380	2 957	7 057	4 432	Islande
0	364	4 629	11 025	5 549	18 069	13 568	22 101	Irlande
740	7 614	12 316	17 123	9 071	19 262	41 822	42 035	Italie
–	–	12	3	49	103	127	146	Lettonie
–	–	4	18	37	263	343	276	Lituanie
–	–	–	9 416	-43	6 620	9 521	2 248	Luxembourg
..	..	21	-28	549	-2	-25	3	Malte
5 918	13 660	75 635	32 019	44 034	26 571	142 925	22 692	Pays-Bas
253	1 431	9 505	5 761	6 063	5 316	21 052	10 321	Norvège
21	5	16	230	305	793	3 024	4 266	Pologne
14	163	8 132	-149	8 028	7 845	2 078	3 508	Portugal
..	18	-13	17	39	70	-30	38	Roumanie
–	–	29	11	247	-21	157	368	Slovaquie
–	–	65	148	472	551	568	740	Slovénie
311	3 349	58 213	32 715	28 718	60 532	41 829	89 679	Espagne
625	14 746	40 971	10 599	21 099	21 754	26 540	24 600	Suède
..	7 176	44 673	8 203	15 442	26 274	54 309	81 505	Suisse
7 881	17 948	233 371	50 300	62 187	91 019	83 708	79 457	Royaume-Uni
567	**2 587**	**3 926**	**8 256**	**16 788**	**9 908**	**-34 320**	**23 538**	**Économies développées : Océanie**
460	993	3 174	7 863	16 264	10 813	-33 172	22 347	Australie
107	1 594	752	394	524	-905	-1 148	1 191	Nouvelle-Zélande

Sources :
- CNUCED, *World Investment Report 2007 : Transnational Corporations, Extractive Industries and Development*

Notes :
(1) Les données pour 1990 se réfèrent seulement à la Slovénie, à l'exception des flux entrants qui comprennent aussi d'autres Républiques de l'ex Yougoslavie (RSF).

Les flux entrants et sortants de l'IDE comprennent les capitaux fournis par l'investisseur direct (soit directement, soit par l'intermédiaire d'autres entreprises avec lesquelles il est lié) à l'entreprise d'investissement direct ou les capitaux reçus de cette entreprise par l'investisseur. L'IDE est composé des trois catégories suivantes : le capital social, les bénéfices réinvestis et les emprunts intra-compagnie.
- Le capital social inclut l'achat des actions d'une entreprise située à l'étranger par l'investisseur direct résident dans l'économie déclarante.
- Les bénéfices réinvestis correspondent à la part qui revient à l'investisseur direct (au prorata de sa participation directe au capital) sur les bénéfices qui ne sont pas distribués sous forme de dividendes par les entreprises apparentées, ainsi que les bénéfices des succursales qui ne sont pas versés à l'investisseur direct. Ces bénéfices retenus par les affiliés sont réinvestis.
- Les emprunts intra-compagnie ou les transactions intra-compagnie concernant les dettes ou les créances se réfèrent aux emprunts et prêts des fonds à court- ou long-terme entre l'investisseur direct (entreprise parente) et les entreprises apparentées (affiliées).

Les données sur l'IDE se présentent sur une base nette (les crédits moins les débits des transactions en capital entre l'investisseur direct et son entreprise apparentée). Les augmentations nettes en passifs et les décroissances nettes en actifs se déclarent comme crédits (avec le signe positif), tandis que les augmentations nettes en actifs et les décroissances nettes en passifs se déclarent comme débits (avec le signe négatif). Par conséquent, les flux de l'IDE avec un signe négatif indiquent qu'au moins une des trois catégories de l'IDE est négative et n'est pas contrebalancée par les valeurs positives des autres catégories. Il s'agit alors de désinvestissements ou de réductions d'investissement.

7

7.3.2 Foreign direct investment: inward and outward flows of economic groupings

Economic grouping	Inward flows - Flux entrants Millions of dollars							
	1980	1990	2000	2002	2003	2004	2005	2006
DEVELOPING ECONOMIES	**7 664**	**35 877**	**256 096**	**166 275**	**178 705**	**283 006**	**314 279**	**379 052**
Developing economies excluding China	7 607	32 390	215 381	113 532	125 200	222 376	241 873	309 584
Developing economies excluding LDCs	7 128	35 299	252 103	159 722	168 126	273 707	307 029	369 799
High-income developing countries	1 295	18 539	151 180	55 515	69 839	147 478	129 576	162 513
Middle-income developing countries	5 459	9 494	54 373	38 705	35 697	51 837	79 174	99 445
Low-income developing countries	910	7 844	50 542	72 055	73 169	83 691	105 530	117 094
Heavily indebted poor countries	794	837	4 014	5 780	6 497	6 613	7 418	9 938
Landlocked developing countries	387	603	3 803	7 693	8 520	11 762	7 118	11 366
Small island developing States	358	1 022	2 340	1 974	2 707	3 198	3 324	3 793
Least developed countries	*536*	*578*	*3 993*	*6 553*	*10 579*	*9 299*	*7 251*	*9 253*
Africa and Haiti	478	431	2 964	5 700	9 759	8 231	6 162	8 090
Asia	53	111	975	788	770	1 007	1 050	1 055
Islands	5	36	54	65	50	61	39	107
Major petroleum exporters	*-4 374*	*1 652*	*10 726*	*13 056*	*24 787*	*27 422*	*42 321*	*50 239*
Africa	-1 362	903	3 390	6 128	9 830	8 183	9 442	13 644
America	294	1 014	6 101	2 848	4 403	3 641	5 169	2 332
Asia	-3 306	-265	1 235	4 080	10 553	15 597	27 710	34 263
Major exporters of manufactured goods	*7 519*	*24 705*	*197 566*	*125 262*	*123 387*	*185 738*	*195 759*	*241 916*
America	4 000	3 622	50 569	35 953	25 484	40 542	34 803	37 820
Asia	3 520	21 083	146 997	89 309	97 903	145 197	160 957	204 097
Emerging economies	*7 533*	*19 664*	*104 208*	*61 386*	*56 987*	*95 090*	*85 949*	*106 438*
America	4 992	6 814	66 657	42 808	32 778	53 898	49 349	54 047
Asia	2 541	12 850	37 551	18 578	24 209	41 193	36 600	52 391
Newly industrialized economies	*3 665*	*17 767*	*97 165*	*29 947*	*37 726*	*77 809*	*80 409*	*103 184*
First tier	2 128	10 939	92 339	21 722	30 124	64 738	57 296	79 472
Second tier	1 537	6 828	4 827	8 226	7 602	13 070	23 113	23 711
Developing economies: Africa	**400**	**2 806**	**9 685**	**13 570**	**18 677**	**18 018**	**29 648**	**35 544**
Northern Africa excluding Sudan	144	1 147	3 064	3 212	4 027	5 105	11 224	19 782
Sub-Saharan Africa	257	1 659	6 621	10 358	14 650	12 913	18 424	15 762
Sub-Saharan Africa excluding South Africa	267	1 737	5 733	9 602	13 916	12 114	12 173	16 085
Developing economies: America	**6 483**	**9 733**	**97 810**	**54 274**	**44 698**	**94 266**	**75 505**	**83 735**
Central America and Greater Carribean Islands excluding Puerto Rico	2 629	3 372	21 298	22 489	18 736	26 931	24 841	26 557
Central America and Greater Carribean Islands excluding Mexico and Puerto Rico	539	739	3 508	3 126	3 396	4 535	5 105	7 519
South America and Central America	6 093	8 905	77 685	49 796	41 055	63 391	68 387	69 383
South America excluding Brazil	1 687	4 861	25 033	12 121	13 515	19 834	30 212	26 237
Developing economies: Asia	**663**	**22 642**	**148 333**	**98 310**	**114 987**	**169 999**	**208 744**	**259 434**
Eastern and South-Eastern Asia excluding China	3 649	18 125	99 450	32 982	43 651	80 929	84 918	107 789
Southern Asia excluding India	205	-24	1 103	1 460	1 535	2 112	3 550	6 295

Sources:
For sources and notes, see end of table 7.3.1.

Outward flows - Flux sortants Millions de dollars								Groupements économiques
1980	1990	2000	2002	2003	2004	2005	2006	
3 153	**11 913**	**133 341**	**47 866**	**45 372**	**117 336**	**115 860**	**174 389**	**ÉCONOMIES EN DÉVELOPPEMENT**
3 153	11 083	132 425	45 348	42 518	111 838	103 599	158 259	Économies en développement sans la Chine
2 924	11 921	132 576	47 343	45 099	116 963	115 203	173 902	Économies en développement sans les PMA
957	8 857	125 373	34 567	31 515	88 243	81 024	97 513	Pays en développement à revenu élevé
1 859	1 756	5 276	8 125	8 071	16 715	15 781	46 583	Pays en développement à revenu intermédiaire
338	1 300	2 692	5 175	5 787	12 378	19 055	30 293	Pays en développement à revenu faible
222	9	822	432	227	358	428	364	Pays pauvres très endettés
8	33	50	806	1 047	-45	1 123	338	Pays en développement sans littoral
137	53	127	215	356	157	558	486	Petits États insulaires en développement
229	*-8*	*765*	*523*	*273*	*373*	*658*	*487*	*Pays les moins avancés*
229	-10	761	472	195	335	619	432	Afrique et Haïti
0	1	4	49	77	37	34	53	Asie
0	1	0	2	1	1	4	3	Îles
698	*35*	*1 179*	*2 235*	*-973*	*7 953*	*14 351*	*16 030*	*Principaux exportateurs de pétrole*
91	558	289	148	249	248	586	485	Afrique
14	377	557	1 131	1 544	645	1 526	2 461	Amérique
593	-900	334	957	-2 765	7 060	12 239	13 083	Asie
912	*12 749*	*84 036*	*37 180*	*26 323*	*91 084*	*71 100*	*134 248*	*Principaux exportateurs d'articles manufacturés*
370	848	2 645	3 373	1 503	14 239	8 991	33 961	Amérique
542	11 901	81 391	33 807	24 820	76 845	62 109	100 287	Asie
673	*9 551*	*27 006*	*15 014*	*17 736*	*38 317*	*31 409*	*69 257*	*Économies émergentes*
303	940	7 386	3 107	3 943	16 303	12 524	39 272	Amérique
370	8 611	19 619	11 907	13 793	22 014	18 885	29 985	Asie
544	*11 070*	*79 246*	*29 617*	*19 800*	*71 717*	*49 340*	*76 965*	*Économies nouvellement industrialisées*
248	10 776	76 967	27 294	17 294	65 592	42 562	66 613	Première génération
296	294	2 279	2 323	2 506	6 124	6 778	10 352	Deuxième génération
1 090	**655**	**1 526**	**305**	**1 286**	**2 059**	**2 272**	**8 186**	**Économies en développement : Afrique**
87	135	227	52	123	167	464	825	Afrique septentrionale sans le Soudan
1 003	519	1 299	254	1 163	1 892	1 808	7 361	Afrique subsaharienne
248	492	1 028	653	598	540	878	687	Afrique subsaharienne sans l'Afrique du Sud
899	**300**	**49 577**	**12 114**	**21 641**	**27 762**	**35 743**	**49 132**	**Économies en développement : Amérique**
358	936	-456	3 077	5 001	6 308	8 440	7 068	Amérique centrale et Grandes Antilles sans Porto Rico
354	713	-819	2 187	3 747	1 876	1 966	1 310	Amérique centrale et Grandes Antilles sans le Mexique et Porto Rico
778	2 018	7 298	7 103	9 891	18 918	20 256	43 680	Amérique du Sud et Amérique centrale
54	486	5 608	1 633	4 720	2 853	9 426	8 517	Amérique du Sud sans le Brésil
1 146	**10 948**	**82 230**	**35 427**	**22 412**	**87 461**	**77 747**	**117 067**	**Économies en développement : Asie**
544	11 072	79 283	29 718	19 879	71 638	49 493	77 064	Asie orientale et Asie du Sud-Est sans la Chine
7	4	37	99	-289	135	536	530	Asie méridionale sans l'Inde

Sources :
Pour les sources et les notes, se reporter à la fin du tableau 7.3.1.

7

Trade group	Inward flows - Flux entrants Millions of dollars							
	1980	1990	2000	2002	2003	2004	2005	2006
AFRICA								
CEMAC (formerly UDEAC)	206	4	505	2 023	3 143	2 696	3 784	3 301
CEPGL	131	-6	43	120	163	18	-68	485
COMESA	-208	1 250	2 917	2 463	3 017	5 500	9 843	17 575
ECCAS	374	-336	1 431	3 818	6 812	4 161	2 413	2 646
ECOWAS	-461	1 547	2 136	2 817	3 275	3 352	4 133	6 845
MRU	54	276	70	43	464	396	-319	69
SADC	361	54	3 046	4 193	5 931	4 079	6 698	697
UEMOA	208	239	514	622	473	620	783	705
UMA	-378	420	1 868	2 633	3 892	3 339	6 712	9 736
AMERICA								
ANCOM	304	734	4 661	6 247	4 845	5 909	14 241	12 090
CACM	188	268	1 360	1 620	1 296	1 899	2 218	2 694
CARICOM	262	581	1 748	2 045	2 613	2 856	3 359	3 805
FTAA	29 155	65 510	461 138	149 201	104 685	202 211	202 148	318 325
LAIA	5 668	8 399	75 576	47 888	38 764	60 064	64 541	63 631
MERCOSUR	2 907	2 937	43 575	18 943	12 239	23 100	21 019	25 096
NAFTA	24 815	58 638	398 582	116 020	75 963	157 881	149 719	263 490
OECS	51	221	10 244	1 841	3 694	18 089	-7 430	7 343
ASIA								
APTA	204	4 536	54 088	62 315	62 810	76 092	87 123	92 591
ASEAN	2 756	12 821	23 540	18 022	24 486	35 242	41 071	51 480
ECO	172	600	2 861	6 428	8 352	12 964	16 627	32 300
GCC	-3 403	149	383	2 726	6 603	14 262	26 348	32 442
SAARC	194	575	4 658	6 983	5 467	7 600	9 862	22 272
EUROPE								
EFTA	82	6 509	26 517	7 155	20 306	4 763	8 207	34 728
EU	21 494	90 513	697 389	309 458	261 017	214 215	496 754	547 542
Euro zone	10 945	55 895	498 268	241 271	217 651	117 159	231 531	318 296
OCEANIA								
MSG	117	506	100	47	141	143	62	215
INTERREGIONAL								
ACP	729	2 883	9 545	13 374	18 040	17 371	23 188	21 009
APEC	31 231	93 441	572 985	237 138	202 491	369 156	296 463	504 644
BSEC	690	1 693	8 050	9 345	20 659	36 852	44 191	77 350
CIS	..	..	5 335	9 128	15 763	26 871	26 045	42 934

Sources:
For sources and notes, see end of table 7.3.1.

			Outward flows - Flux sortants Millions de dollars					Groupements commerciaux
1980	1990	2000	2002	2003	2004	2005	2006	
								AFRIQUE
0	51	35	-49	-15	-20	-19	-19	CEMAC (anc. UDEAC)
0	0	-2	-2	0	0	0	0	CEPGL
67	141	192	-83	100	-83	262	344	COMESA
0	52	12	-22	9	15	201	73	CEEAC
232	407	966	610	376	528	589	551	CEDEAO
231	-3	780	403	174	303	424	349	UFM
766	59	290	-324	793	1 368	1 219	6 789	SADC
-3	-5	16	36	24	-35	-35	-26	UEMOA
80	123	176	24	101	12	374	677	UMA
								AMÉRIQUE
108	69	192	875	1 001	205	4 840	1 531	ANCOM
8	1	50	44	426	59	245	86	MCAC
116	32	104	196	342	89	452	483	CARICOM
24 222	38 267	194 767	169 033	162 469	320 654	26 540	306 019	ZLEA
423	1 334	8 250	5 006	6 225	17 092	18 414	42 478	ALADI
257	660	3 188	1 871	1 044	10 272	3 710	30 224	MERCOSUR
23 332	36 442	187 668	162 610	153 530	306 089	12 280	267 616	ALENA
0	-2 520	34 461	10 592	6 074	4 878	8 174	2 964	OECO
								ASIE
30	1 889	6 432	6 829	8 193	12 347	19 094	32 972	ACAP
394	2 328	8 225	4 681	5 286	14 212	11 918	19 095	ANASE
7	-14	913	1 011	988	953	2 649	1 719	ECO
586	-903	258	719	-2 618	6 920	11 665	12 568	CCG
4	9	524	1 723	1 932	2 247	2 579	9 820	SAARC
								EUROPE
253	8 618	54 572	14 290	21 884	34 547	82 418	96 258	AELE
23 872	121 273	811 660	265 795	286 723	359 773	609 077	572 633	UE
15 253	87 036	511 199	197 646	197 917	252 729	475 912	447 993	Zone euro
								OCÉANIE
18	11	2	2	1	4	19	2	MSG
								INTERRÉGIONAUX
1 136	563	1 472	467	1 481	2 007	2 338	7 830	ACP
26 887	99 019	310 350	239 198	233 239	439 571	100 593	455 907	CEAP
0	10	6 180	4 736	11 654	16 760	16 987	23 840	CEMN
..	..	3 186	4 079	10 558	13 772	14 032	18 126	CEI

Sources :
Pour les sources et les notes, se reporter à la fin du tableau 7.3.1.

Top 50 developing countries ranked by 2005 values / 50 premiers pays en développement classés d'après les valeurs de 2005	Total amount (millions of dollars) / Montant total (millions de dollars)						As percentage of exports of goods and services (1) / En pourcentage des exportations de biens et services (1)					
	1990	1995	2000	2004	2005	2006	1990	1995	2000	2004	2005	2006
Mexico - Mexique	3 098	4 368	7 525	18 260	21 657	25 052	6.3	4.9	4.2	9.0	9.4	9.4
India - Inde	2 384	6 223	12 890	18 750	21 293	25 426	10.4	16.4	21.5	16.1	13.5	12.8
Philippines	1 465	5 360	6 924	11 468	13 561	15 239	12.8	20.0	17.0	26.8	30.3	28.8
China - Chine	124	350	758	6 641	8 832	11 150	0.2	0.2	0.3	1.0	1.1	1.1
Indonesia - Indonésie	166	651	1 190	1 866	5 420	5 722	0.6	1.2	1.7	2.3	5.4	5.0
Egypt - Égypte	4 284	3 226	2 852	3 341	5 017	5 330	43.3	24.3	16.9	12.6	16.3	14.5
Lebanon - Liban	..	..	..	5 591	4 924	5 202	..	..	..	47.6	37.5	36.1
Morocco - Maroc	2 006	1 970	2 161	4 221	4 589	5 454	32.2	21.8	20.7	25.4	24.4	25.1
Bangladesh	779	1 202	1 968	3 584	4 315	5 428	37.7	27.1	27.3	38.8	40.9	42.1
Pakistan	2 006	1 712	1 075	3 945	4 280	5 121	29.4	16.8	10.6	24.6	22.4	25.0
Colombia - Colombie	495	815	1 610	3 190	3 345	3 928	5.7	6.6	10.2	16.4	13.7	13.8
Nigeria - Nigéria	10	804	1 392	2 273	3 329	..	0.1	6.5	6.6	6.0	6.4	..
Guatemala	119	358	596	2 591	3 032	3 626	7.6	12.7	15.4	57.0	45.9	48.9
El Salvador	366	1 064	1 764	2 563	2 841	3 328	37.6	52.2	48.2	57.9	62.4	65.6
Brazil - Brésil	537	2 952	1 350	2 813	2 805	3 287	1.5	5.6	2.1	2.6	2.1	2.1
Dominican Republic - République dominicaine	315	839	1 839	2 501	2 719	3 044	17.2	14.6	20.5	26.5	27.0	28.5
Jordan - Jordanie	499	1 244	1 845	2 330	2 500	2 883	19.9	35.8	52.1	39.1	37.7	37.5
Ecuador - Équateur	51	386	1 322	1 838	2 460	2 922	1.6	7.4	22.4	20.5	21.5	20.7
Sri Lanka	401	801	1 154	1 574	1 976	2 331	17.5	17.3	18.1	21.6	25.0	27.4
Honduras	63	124	416	1 151	1 796	2 367	6.1	7.6	16.7	37.1	51.4	62.3
Jamaica - Jamaïque	229	639	878	1 601	1 762	1 924	10.3	18.8	24.5	41.1	44.1	40.2
Peru - Pérou	87	599	718	1 133	1 440	1 837	2.1	9.0	8.4	7.7	7.3	7.0
Tunisia - Tunisie	551	680	796	1 432	1 393	1 510	10.6	8.5	9.2	10.8	9.6	9.6
Yemen - Yémen	1 498	1 081	1 288	1 283	1 283	1 283	100.6	50.0	32.1	25.4	18.9	16.3
Nepal - Népal	..	57	112	823	1 212	1 453	..	5.5	8.7	66.7	94.4	117.7
Thailand - Thaïlande	973	1 695	1 697	1 622	1 187	1 333	3.3	2.4	2.1	1.4	0.9	0.9
Malaysia - Malaisie	185	116	342	802	1 117	1 364	0.6	0.1	0.3	0.6	0.7	0.7
Sudan - Soudan	62	346	641	1 403	1 016	1 156	12.4	50.8	34.9	36.7	20.6	19.7
Haiti - Haïti	..	..	578	932	985	1 070	..	..	114.8	182.6	165.0	153.2
Turkey - Turquie	3 246	3 327	4 560	804	851	1 111	15.4	9.1	9.1	0.9	0.8	1.0
Syrian Arab Republic - République arabe syrienne	385	339	180	855	823	795	7.7	5.9	2.6	8.7	7.1	6.0
Republic of Korea - République de Corée	1 030	1 065	645	743	809	823	1.4	0.7	0.3	0.2	0.2	0.2
Liberia - Libéria	..	..	..	484	620	685	..	..	..	..	..	..
South Africa - Afrique du Sud	108	83	325	468	614	692	0.4	0.2	0.9	0.8	0.9	0.9
Nicaragua	..	75	320	519	600	656	..	11.3	29.0	31.4	30.6	28.3
French Polynesia - Polynésie française	..	..	..	598	557	601	..	..	..	49.6	43.4	46.2
Occupied Palestinian territory - Territoire palestinien occupé	..	582	842	436	532	..	..	76.2	85.2	73.7	78.5	..
New Caledonia - Nouvelle-Calédonie	..	..	..	493	512	535	..	..	..	32.9	32.6	30.6
Argentina - Argentine	..	64	86	312	432	541	..	0.3	0.3	0.8	0.9	1.0
Kenya	0	..	..	376	425	570	0.0	..	..	8.8	8.0	9.6
Uganda - Ouganda	..	..	238	371	423	814	..	..	35.9	34.8	30.9	54.5
Costa Rica	12	123	136	320	420	513	0.6	2.8	1.8	3.7	4.3	4.7
Bolivia - Bolivie	4	5	127	211	337	603	0.4	0.4	8.6	8.2	10.3	14.0
Lesotho	428	411	252	355	327	361	427.6	206.3	99.4	46.0	46.2	48.0
China, Taiwan Province of - Province chinoise de Taiwan (2)	..	142	274	278	323	355	..	0.1	0.2	0.1	0.1	0.1
China, Hong Kong SAR - Chine (RAS de Hong Kong)	..	..	136	240	297	294	..	..	0.1	0.1	0.1	0.1
Paraguay	34	287	278	238	269	432	1.3	6.0	9.5	6.8	6.7	7.7
Guyana	..	..	27	153	201	218	..	..	4.1	20.5	29.0	29.4
Togo	27	15	34	179	193	..	4.1	3.2	8.1	23.8	23.0	..
Fiji - Fidji	21	33	43	171	182	164	2.6	3.0	4.4	12.8	12.1	11.0

Sources:
- International Monetary Fund (IMF), *Balance of Payments Statistics* on CD-ROM

Notes:
- Includes workers' remittances and compensation of employees.

(1) Trade data in this calculation correspond to IMF balance-of-payments series.

(2) National data.

Sources :
- Fonds monétaire international (FMI), *Statistiques de la balance des paiements* sur CD-ROM

Notes :
- Les valeurs dans ce tableau incluent les envois de fonds des travailleurs et la rémunération des salariés.

(1) Les données du commerce utilisées dans ce calcul proviennent de la série de la balance des paiements du FMI.

(2) Sources nationales.

Top 50 developing countries ranked by 2005 values / 50 premiers pays en développement classés d'après les valeurs de 2005	Total amount (millions of dollars) Montant total (millions de dollars)						As percentage of imports of goods and services (1) En pourcentage des importations de biens et services (1)					
	1990	1995	2000	2004	2005	2006	1990	1995	2000	2004	2005	2006
Saudi Arabia - Arabie saoudite	11 221	16 594	15 390	13 555	13 996	15 611	25.6	37.0	29.1	20.3	16.8	14.9
Malaysia - Malaisie (2)	182	1 329	599	5 064	5 679	5 560	0.6	1.5	0.6	4.3	4.3	3.8
Lebanon - Liban	..	..	..	4 233	4 012	4 134	..	..	..	25.3	24.6	24.0
Kuwait - Koweït	770	1 354	1 734	2 403	2 648	3 021	10.7	10.7	15.3	12.5	11.6	12.3
China - Chine	5	..	754	1 998	2 550	3 025	0.0	..	0.3	0.3	0.4	0.4
Oman	856	1 537	1 451	1 826	2 257	2 788	25.6	30.5	22.8	17.2	20.4	20.4
China, Taiwan Province of - Province chinoise de Taiwan (3)	..	945	1 544	1 251	1 342	1 370	.	0.8	0.9	0.6	0.6	0.6
India - Inde	106	419	486	1 653	1 341	1 580	0.4	0.9	0.7	1.3	0.7	0.7
Bahrain - Bahreïn	332	500	1 013	1 120	1 223	1 531	8.3	12.1	19.7	15.8	14.3	15.8
Indonesia - Indonésie	..	..	..	913	1 179	1 359	.	..	..	1.3	1.3	1.4
South Africa - Afrique du Sud	1 116	567	614	935	1 041	1 055	5.3	1.7	1.9	1.6	1.5	1.3
Republic of Korea - République de Corée	26	132	278	685	958	1 124	0.0	0.1	0.1	0.3	0.3	0.3
Libyan Arab Jamahiriya - Jamahiriya arabe libyenne	446	222	463	975	914	945	5.0	3.9	9.2	9.1	6.8	6.0
Liberia - Libéria	..	..	..	443	621	639	..	..	..	..	..	..
Côte d'Ivoire	471	457	390	591	597	17	13.7	12.0	10.7	9.4	8.1	0.2
Brunei Darussalam - Brunéi Darussalam	..	..	..	323	376	405	..	..	..	..	..	..
Brazil - Brésil	11	336	338	340	374	529	0.0	0.5	0.5	0.4	0.4	0.4
Jamaica - Jamaïque	11	50	152	391	369	358	0.5	1.3	3.4	7.4	6.2	5.0
Uganda - Ouganda	..	..	353	236	359	322	..	..	25.1	11.2	14.0	10.0
Jordan - Jordanie	71	107	197	272	349	402	2.0	2.2	3.4	2.9	2.9	3.1
China, Hong Kong SAR - Chine (RAS de Hong Kong)	..	..	225	321	348	377	..	..	0.1	0.1	0.1	0.1
Argentina - Argentine	..	195	268	234	314	366	..	0.7	0.8	0.8	0.9	0.9
Sri Lanka	..	13	14	230	249	274	..	0.2	0.2	2.5	2.5	2.4
Angola	150	210	266	296	215	413	4.4	6.0	4.6	2.8	1.4	2.5
Venezuela (Bolivarian Rep. of) - Venezuela (Rép. bolivarienne du)	701	203	331	214	211	253	7.4	1.2	1.6	1.0	0.7	0.7
China, Macao SAR - Chine (RAS de Macao)	..	..	..	132	210	476	..	..	..	2.2	3.1	5.7
Costa Rica	..	36	142	192	209	246	..	0.8	2.0	2.1	1.9	2.0
Papua New Guinea - Papouasie-Nouvelle-Guinée	..	..	11	117	128	..	..	..	0.6	4.8	4.8	..
Yemen - Yémen	106	61	61	108	110	120	4.9	2.5	1.8	2.2	1.8	1.5
Botswana	118	199	134	99	102	97	5.9	9.7	5.8	2.7	2.9	2.8
Turkey - Turquie	..	..	..	..	96	107	..	..	..	..	0.1	0.1
Zambia - Zambie	15	..	24	76	94	115	0.8	..	1.8	3.6	3.6	3.6
Cambodia - Cambodge	..	52	60	56	88	105	..	3.8	2.6	1.5	1.9	1.9
Panama	22	20	22	72	88	121	0.5	0.3	0.3	0.8	0.8	1.0
Bahamas	39	32	56	71	84	100	2.3	1.8	1.9	2.3	2.2	2.2
Maldives	8	27	46	62	70	84	5.2	8.6	10.3	8.5	8.1	8.0
Mali	45	42	26	64	69	..	5.5	4.3	2.8	3.9	3.8	..
Bolivia - Bolivie	8	9	37	51	67	73	0.7	0.6	1.8	2.2	2.3	2.1
Nepal - Népal	..	9	17	64	66	79	..	0.6	0.9	2.8	2.4	2.7
Aruba	..	5	44	49	64	73	..	0.2	1.4	1.3	1.5	1.5
Haiti - Haïti	..	..	11	39	59	68	..	..	0.8	2.5	3.4	3.3
Netherlands Antilles - Antilles néerlandaises	8	9	46	52	59	..	0.5	0.4	1.9	1.9	1.9	..
Egypt - Égypte	27	223	32	13	57	135	0.2	1.3	0.1	0.0	0.2	0.3
Kenya	6	4	..	34	56	25	0.2	0.1	..	0.6	0.8	0.3
Colombia - Colombie	44	150	219	50	56	66	0.6	0.9	1.5	0.3	0.2	0.2
Guyana	..	9	27	81	55	48	..	1.3	3.7	10.1	6.0	4.8
Ecuador - Équateur	2	4	6	7	54	62	0.1	0.1	0.1	0.1	0.5	0.5
French Polynesia - Polynésie française	..	..	..	46	47	51	..	..	..	2.2	2.0	2.2
Congo	55	27	37	49	45	..	4.3	2.0	3.1	2.5	1.5	..
Mongolia - Mongolie	..	..	3	49	40	77	..	..	0.4	3.5	2.6	4.1

Sources:
- International Monetary Fund (IMF), *Balance of Payments Statistics* on CD-ROM

Sources :
- Fonds monétaire international (FMI), *Statistiques de la balance des paiements* sur CD-ROM

Notes:
- Includes workers' remittances and compensation of employees.

(1) Trade data in this calculation correspond to IMF balance-of-payments series.

(2) For years 1990 and 2000, data include compensation of employees only; workers' remittances were not available.

(3) National data.

Notes :
- Les valeurs dans ce tableau incluent les envois de fonds des travailleurs et la rémunération des salariés.

(1) Les données du commerce utilisées dans ce calcul proviennent de la série de la balance des paiements du FMI.

(2) Pour les années 1990 et 2000, les données comprennent seulement la rémunération des salariés ; les envois de fonds des travailleurs n'étaient pas disponibles.

(3) Sources nationales.

Region, country or territory	Total reserves minus gold (1) - Réserves totales moins l'or (1) Millions of dollars - Millions de dollars							
	1980	1990	2000	2002	2003	2004	2005	2006
DEVELOPING ECONOMIES	153 353	290 509	923 573	1 219 795	1 558 835	1 997 424	2 356 461	2 919 163
Developing economies: Africa	**33 208**	**25 269**	**77 975**	**98 511**	**122 211**	**164 088**	**216 571**	**295 701**
Eastern Africa	*1 385*	*2 308*	*5 992*	*8 157*	*9 522*	*11 072*	*10 771*	*12 202*
Burundi	95	105	33	59	67	66	100	131
Comoros	6	30	43	80	94	104	86	94
Djibouti	..	94	68	74	100	94	89	120
Eritrea	–	–	26	30	25	35	28	25
Ethiopia	–	–	306	882	956	1 497	1 122	833
Ethiopia (former)	80	20	–	–	–	–	–	–
Kenya	492	205	898	1 068	1 482	1 519	1 799	2 416
Madagascar	9	92	285	363	414	504	481	583
Malawi	68	137	243	162	122	128	159	134
Mauritius	91	738	897	1 227	1 577	1 606	1 340	1 270
Mozambique	..	232	723	803	938	1 131	1 054	1 156
Rwanda	196	44	191	244	215	315	406	440
Seychelles	18	17	44	70	67	35	56	113
Somalia	15	..	..	..	..	..	..	..
Uganda	3	44	808	934	1 080	1 308	1 344	1 811
United Republic of Tanzania	20	193	974	1 529	2 038	2 296	2 049	2 259
Zambia	78	193	245	535	248	337	560	720
Zimbabwe	214	149	193	83	..	..	..	..
Middle Africa	*647*	*771*	*986*	*1 332*	*1 537*	*2 810*	*4 927*	*8 605*
Cameroon	189	26	212	630	640	829	949	1 716
Central African Republic	55	119	133	123	132	148	139	125
Chad	5	128	111	219	187	222	226	625
Congo	86	6	222	32	35	120	732	1 841
Dem. Rep. of the Congo	204	219	..	..	..	..	..	..
Equatorial Guinea	..	1	23	89	238	945	2 103	3 067
Gabon	108	274	190	140	197	443	669	1 113
Sao Tome and Principe	..	..	12	17	26	20	27	34
Northern Africa	*18 947*	*12 120*	*44 374*	*63 459*	*83 624*	*104 819*	*138 913*	*190 438*
Algeria	3 773	725	12 024	23 238	33 125	43 246	56 303	77 914
Egypt	1 046	2 684	13 118	13 242	13 589	14 273	20 609	24 462
Libyan Arab Jamahiriya	13 091	5 839	12 461	14 308	19 584	25 689	39 508	59 289
Morocco	399	2 067	4 823	10 133	13 851	16 337	16 188	20 341
Sudan	49	11	138	249	529	1 338	1 869	1 660
Tunisia	590	795	1 811	2 290	2 945	3 936	4 437	6 773
Southern Africa	*1 269*	*4 629*	*13 431*	*12 383*	*12 898*	*19 973*	*25 963*	*32 530*
Botswana	334	3 332	6 318	5 474	5 340	5 661	6 309	7 992
Lesotho	50	72	418	406	460	502	519	658
Namibia	..	..	260	323	325	345	312	450
South Africa	726	1 008	6 083	5 904	6 496	13 141	18 579	23 057
Swaziland	159	217	352	276	278	324	244	373
Western Africa	*10 961*	*5 441*	*13 192*	*13 179*	*14 630*	*25 416*	*35 997*	*51 926*
Benin	8	65	458	616	718	640	657	912
Burkina Faso	68	301	244	313	752	669	438	555
Cape Verde	42	77	28	80	94	140	174	255
Côte d'Ivoire	20	4	668	1 863	1 304	1 694	1 322	1 798
Gambia	6	55	109	107	59	84	98	121
Ghana	180	219	232	540	1 353	1 627	1 753	2 090
Guinea	..	..	148	171	..	111	95	..
Guinea-Bissau	..	18	67	103	33	73	80	82
Liberia	6	..	0	3	7	19	25	72
Mali	15	191	381	595	953	861	855	970
Mauritania	140	54	280	396	415	..	..	..
Niger	126	222	80	134	260	258	250	371
Nigeria	10 235	3 864	9 911	7 331	7 128	16 956	28 280	42 299
Senegal	8	11	384	637	1 111	1 386	1 191	1 334
Sierra Leone	31	5	49	85	67	125	171	184
Togo	78	353	152	205	205	360	195	375
Developing economies: America	**38 877**	**47 448**	**156 371**	**160 558**	**195 221**	**220 337**	**255 133**	**310 249**
Caribbean	*3 411*	*1 478*	*4 901*	*6 485*	*6 374*	*8 511*	*11 593*	*13 851*
Anguilla	..	7	20	26	33	34	40	42
Antigua and Barbuda	8	28	64	88	114	120	127	143
Aruba	..	98	208	340	295	295	274	338
Bahamas	92	158	350	381	491	674	586	461
Barbados	79	118	473	669	738	580	604	636
Dominica	5	15	29	46	48	42	49	63
Dominican Republic	202	62	627	468	253	798	1 843	2 116
Grenada	13	18	58	88	83	122	94	100
Haiti	16	3	182	82	62	114	133	253

For sources and notes, see end of table.

7.5.1 Réserves internationales des économies en développement par pays et régions géographiques

Annual change in reserves (millions of dollars) Variations annuelles des réserves (millions de dollars)				Number of months of imports (2) Nombre de mois d'importations (2)								Régions, pays ou territoires
2002-2003	2003-2004	2004-2005	2005-2006	1980	1990	2000	2002	2003	2004	2005	2006	
339 040	438 589	359 037	562 703	4.2	5 1	6.7	8.8	9.6	9.5	9.5	10.0	ÉCONOMIES EN DÉVELOPPEMENT
23 699	41 878	52 483	79 130	4.4	3.2	7.4	8.5	8.7	9.3	10.2	12.2	Économies en développement : Afrique
1 365	*1 550*	*-301*	*1 431*	*1.7*	*2.2*	*4.3*	*5.4*	*5.5*	*5.1*	*4.1*	*3.9*	*Afrique orientale*
8	-1	34	30	6.8	5.5	2.7	5.5	5.1	4.5	4.5	3.6	Burundi
14	9	-18	8	2.6	6.9	12.0	18.2	16.3	14.6	10.4	9.7	Comores
26	-6	-5	31	..	5.2	3.9	4.5	5.0	4.3	3.9	4.2	Djibouti
-6	10	-7	-3	–	–	0.6	0.7	0.7	0.9	0.7	(e)0.5	Érythrée
74	541	-375	-289	–	–	2.9	6.5	5.4	5.8	3.3	2.1	Éthiopie
–	–	–	–	1.3	0.2	–	–	–	–	–	–	Éthiopie (anc.)
414	37	280	617	2.8	1.1	3.5	3.9	4.8	4.0	3.5	4.0	Kenya
51	89	-22	102	0.1	2.0	3.4	7.2	3.8	3.6	3.4	3.9	Madagascar
-40	6	31	-25	1.9	2.9	5.5	2.8	1.9	1.6	1.6	1.3	Malawi
350	29	-266	-70	1.8	5.5	4.9	6.8	8.0	7.0	5.1	4.2	Maurice
135	194	-77	102	..	3.2	7.5	6.2	6.4	6.7	5.3	4.8	Mozambique
-29	100	91	34	9.0	1.9	10.7	11.8	9.9	13.3	12.1	10.6	Rwanda
-2	-33	22	57	2.2	1.1	1.5	2.0	2.0	0.8	1.0	1.8	Seychelles
..	..	..	..	0.4	..	..	..	..	..	..	..	Somalie
146	228	36	467	0.1	1.8	6.3	10.1	10.4	7.8	8.5	8.7	Ouganda
510	257	-247	211	0.2	1.7	7.7	11.0	11.3	10.8	7.5	6.1	République-Unie de Tanzanie
-287	89	223	160	0.9	1.9	3.3	5.8	1.9	1.9	2.6	2.8	Zambie
..	..	..	..	1.8	1.0	1.2	0.4	..	..	..	..	Zimbabwe
205	*1 273*	*2 117*	*3 678*	*1.7*	*1.8*	*2.6*	*2.3*	*2.4*	*3.7*	*5.3*	*7.5*	*Afrique centrale*
10	190	120	767	1.4	0.2	1.7	4.0	3.5	4.1	4.2	6.5	Cameroun
9	16	-9	-14	8.1	9.2	13.7	12.3	13.5	12.0	9.8	7.4	République centrafricaine
-32	35	4	400	0.8	5.4	4.2	1.6	2.9	2.8	2.8	5.7	Tchad
3	85	612	1 109	1.8	0.1	5.6	0.5	0.5	1.6	6.0	11.9	Congo
..	..	..	..	1.6	1.5	..	..	..	..	..	..	Rép. dém. du Congo
149	707	1 158	964	..	0.1	0.6	2.1	2.3	7.2	11.9	12.9	Guinée équatoriale
57	247	225	445	1.9	3.6	2.4	1.8	2.3	4.4	5.9	8.6	Gabon
8	-6	7	8	..	..	4.7	6.7	7.5	5.7	6.0	5.6	Sao Tomé-et-Principe
20 165	*21 195*	*34 094*	*51 526*	*7.2*	*3.2*	*10.9*	*14.3*	*17.2*	*16.8*	*18.2*	*22.8*	*Afrique septentrionale*
9 888	10 121	13 057	21 611	4.3	0.9	15.7	24.4	30.8	27.4	32.6	44.5	Algérie
346	685	6 336	3 852	2.6	1.9	11.2	12.7	14.6	13.3	12.5	14.2	Égypte
5 277	6 105	13 819	19 781	23.2	13.1	37.2	30.2	31.2	38.3	42.4	53.8	Jamahiriya arabe libyenne
3 718	2 486	-149	4 153	1.1	3.6	5.0	10.2	11.7	11.1	10.0	10.8	Maroc
281	809	531	-209	0.4	0.2	1.1	1.2	2.2	4.0	3.0	2.5	Soudan
655	990	501	2 337	2.0	1.7	2.5	2.9	3.2	3.7	4.0	5.5	Tunisie
515	*7 075*	*5 991*	*6 567*	*0.8*	*3.0*	*4.5*	*4.3*	*3.2*	*3.8*	*4.4*	*4.5*	*Afrique australe*
-134	322	648	1 683	..	..	30.7	35.6	26.2	21.0	24.1	31.3	Botswana
54	41	18	139	..	..	6.2	6.0	5.0	4.3	4.3	5.3	Lesotho
2	20	-33	138	..	..	2.0	3.0	2.0	1.7	1.5	2.0	Namibie
591	6 646	5 438	4 478	(a)0.8	(a)3.0	2.5	2.4	1.9	2.9	3.6	3.6	Afrique du Sud
2	46	-80	129	..	..	4.0	3.5	2.1	2.1	1.4	2.0	Swaziland
1 450	*10 786*	*10 582*	*15 929*	*5.1*	*4.8*	*7.4*	*6.0*	*5.4*	*7.9*	*8.9*	*11.6*	*Afrique occidentale*
102	-78	17	255	0.3	2.9	9.0	10.2	9.7	8.6	8.8	10.9	Bénin
439	-83	-231	117	2.3	6.7	4.8	5.1	9.8	6.3	3.8	4.7	Burkina Faso
14	46	35	81	7.5	6.8	1.5	3.5	3.2	4.3	4.8	5.6	Cap-Vert
-559	390	-372	476	0.1	0.0	2.9	9.1	4.8	4.7	3.1	3.7	Côte d'Ivoire
-48	25	15	22	0.4	3.5	7.0	8.0	4.6	4.4	5.0	5.9	Gambie
813	274	126	337	1.9	2.2	0.9	2.4	5.0	4.5	3.9	3.7	Ghana
..	..	-15	..	..	..	2.9	3.1	..	1.9	1.4	..	Guinée
-70	40	7	2	..	2.5	16.3	21.1	6.0	10.6	9.1	10.0	Guinée-Bissau
4	11	7	47	0.1	..	0.0	0.2	0.5	0.7	0.9	1.9	Libéria
358	-92	-6	115	0.4	3.8	5.7	7.7	9.1	8.0	6.4	6.6	Mali
19	..	..	..	5.9	2.9	7.4	11.0	9.2	..	..	..	Mauritanie
126	-2	-9	121	2.5	6.9	2.4	3.4	5.0	4.1	3.1	4.5	Niger
-203	9 827	11 324	14 019	7.4	8.2	13.6	6.5	5.0	10.5	13.4	18.5	Nigéria
474	276	-195	143	0.1	0.1	3.0	3.8	5.6	5.9	4.5	4.7	Sénégal
-18	59	45	13	0.9	0.4	4.0	3.8	2.6	5.2	5.9	5.7	Sierra Leone
0	155	-165	180	1.7	7.3	3.3	4.2	(e)3.2	(e)4.9	(e)2.1	(e)3.7	Togo
34 664	25 115	34 796	55 117	4.0	4.7	4.8	5.5	6.4	6.0	5.9	6.0	Économies en développement : Amérique
-111	*2 137*	*3 082*	*2 258*	*2.0*	*1.5*	*2.1*	*3.0*	*2.9*	*3.5*	*4.0*	*4.2*	*Caraïbes*
7	1	5	2	..	..	2.6	4.5	5.2	4.0	3.7	(e)2.9	Anguilla
26	6	7	15	1.1	1.3	1.9	2.6	3.2	3.2	3.1	3.1	Antigua-et-Barbuda
-45	0	-22	64	..	2.0	1.2	2.0	1.5	1.2	0.9	1.1	Aruba
111	183	-88	-125	0.1	1.7	2.0	2.6	3.3	4.2	2.9	2.0	Bahamas
69	-158	24	33	1.8	2.0	4.9	7.5	7.4	4.9	4.5	4.8	Barbade
2	-5	7	14	1.3	1.5	2.4	4.7	4.5	3.5	3.6	4.5	Dominique
-215	545	1 045	272	1.2	0.2	0.8	0.6	0.4	1.2	2.2	2.3	République dominicaine
-5	39	-27	6	3.1	2.0	2.8	5.3	3.9	5.8	3.9	4.2	Grenade
-20	52	19	120	0.5	0.1	2.1	0.9	0.6	1.1	1.1	1.6	Haïti

Pour les sources et les notes, se reporter à la fin du tableau.

Region, country or territory	Total reserves minus gold (1) - Réserves totales moins l'or (1) Millions of dollars - Millions de dollars							
	1980	1990	2000	2002	2003	2004	2005	2006
Jamaica	105	168	1 054	1 645	1 195	1 847	2 170	2 318
Montserrat	..	10	10	14	15	14	14	15
Netherlands Antilles	95	215	261	399	373	415	545	495
Saint Kitts and Nevis	..	16	45	66	65	79	72	89
Saint Lucia	8	45	79	94	107	133	116	135
Saint Vincent and the Grenadines	7	27	55	53	51	75	70	79
Trinidad and Tobago	2 781	492	1 386	2 028	2 451	3 168	4 856	6 570
Central America	*3 972*	*11 641*	*42 993*	*59 138*	*68 448*	*74 560*	*86 090*	*90 114*
Belize	13	70	123	115	85	48	71	114
Costa Rica	146	521	1 318	1 502	1 839	1 922	2 313	3 115
El Salvador	78	415	1 773	1 473	1 792	1 754	1 723	1 815
Guatemala	445	282	1 746	2 299	2 833	3 426	3 664	3 915
Honduras	150	40	1 313	1 524	1 430	1 970	2 327	2 629
Mexico	2 960	9 863	35 509	50 594	58 956	64 141	74 054	76 271
Nicaragua	65	107	489	448	502	668	728	922
Panama, excl. Canal Zone (former)	117	–	–	–	–	–	–	–
Panama	–	344	723	1 183	1 011	631	1 211	1 335
South America	*31 493*	*34 329*	*108 477*	*94 935*	*120 399*	*137 265*	*157 449*	*206 285*
Argentina	6 720	4 592	25 147	10 489	14 153	18 884	27 179	30 904
Bolivia	106	167	926	581	717	872	1 328	2 615
Brazil	5 769	7 441	32 434	37 462	48 847	52 462	53 245	85 156
Chile	3 123	6 069	15 035	15 341	15 840	15 994	16 929	19 392
Colombia	4 831	4 628	8 916	10 732	10 784	13 394	14 787	15 296
Ecuador	1 013	839	947	715	813	1 070	1 714	1 490
Guyana	13	29	305	285	276	232	252	280
Paraguay	762	661	763	629	969	1 168	1 297	1 702
Peru	1 980	1 040	8 374	9 339	9 777	12 176	13 599	16 733
Suriname	189	21	63	106	106	129	126	215
Uruguay	384	524	2 479	769	2 083	2 509	3 074	3 085
Venezuela (Bolivarian Rep. of)	6 604	8 321	13 089	8 487	16 035	18 375	23 919	29 417
Developing economies: Asia	**80 631**	**216 973**	**688 369**	**959 904**	**1 240 281**	**1 611 595**	**1 883 423**	**2 311 150**
Eastern Asia	*7 676*	*117 341*	*374 652*	*578 279*	*774 646*	*1 060 907*	*1 292 241*	*1 583 581*
China	2 546	29 586	168 277	291 128	408 151	614 500	821 514	1 068 493
China, Macao SAR	..	521	3 323	3 800	4 343	5 436	6 689	9 132
China, Taiwan Province of	2 205	72 441	106 742	161 656	206 632	241 738	253 290	266 148
Mongolia	..	..	179	350	236	236	430	926
Republic of Korea	2 925	14 793	96 131	121 345	155 284	198 997	210 317	238 882
Southern Asia	*8 540*	*3 543*	*43 561*	*80 799*	*116 705*	*143 996*	*149 763*	*191 434*
Afghanistan	371	266	..	..	..	..	..	..
Bangladesh	300	629	1 486	1 683	2 578	3 172	2 767	3 806
Bhutan	..	89	318	355	367	399	467	545
India	6 944	1 521	37 902	67 666	98 938	126 593	131 924	170 737
Maldives	1	24	123	133	160	204	186	231
Nepal	183	295	945	1 018	1 223	1 462	1 499	..
Pakistan	496	296	1 513	8 078	10 941	9 799	10 033	11 543
Sri Lanka	246	423	1 039	1 631	2 265	2 132	2 651	2 837
South-Eastern Asia	*21 013*	*59 547*	*183 380*	*199 804*	*231 817*	*277 536*	*288 239*	*348 055*
Brunei Darussalam	..	..	408	438	482	505	494	523
Cambodia	..	..	502	776	816	943	953	1 157
Indonesia	5 392	7 459	28 502	30 971	34 962	34 953	33 141	41 103
Lao People's dem. Rep.	..	2	139	192	209	223	234	327
Malaysia	4 387	9 754	28 330	33 361	43 822	65 881	69 858	82 132
Myanmar	261	313	223	470	550	672	771	1 236
Philippines	2 846	924	13 090	13 329	13 655	13 116	15 926	20 025
Singapore	6 567	27 790	80 170	82 221	96 245	112 579	116 172	136 259
Thailand	1 560	13 305	32 016	38 046	41 077	48 664	50 691	65 291
Western Asia	*43 403*	*36 542*	*86 776*	*101 022*	*117 112*	*129 156*	*153 180*	*188 081*
Bahrain	953	1 235	1 564	1 726	1 778	1 941	..	..
Iraq	..	..	..	..	..	7 824	12 104	19 535
Jordan	1 143	849	3 331	3 976	5 194	5 267	5 250	6 722
Kuwait	3 929	1 952	7 082	9 208	7 577	8 242	8 863	12 566
Lebanon	1 588	660	5 944	7 244	12 519	11 735	11 887	13 376
Oman	581	1 672	2 380	3 174	3 594	3 597	4 358	5 014
Qatar	343	631	1 158	1 567	2 944	3 396	4 542	5 383
Saudi Arabia (3)	23 437	11 668	19 586	20 611	22 620	27 291	26 530	27 523
Turkey	1 077	6 050	22 489	27 069	33 991	35 669	50 579	60 892
United Arab Emirates	2 015	4 584	13 523	15 219	15 088	18 530	21 010	27 618
Yemen (former Arab Republic)	1 283	–	–	–	–	–	–	–
Yemen (former Democratic)	234	–	–	–	–	–	–	–
Yemen	–	422	2 900	4 411	4 987	5 665	6 115	7 512

For sources and notes, see end of table.

Annual change in reserves (millions of dollars) Variations annuelles des réserves (millions de dollars)				Number of months of imports (2) Nombre de mois d'importations (2)								Régions, pays ou territoires
2002-2003	2003-2004	2004-2005	2005-2006	1980	1990	2000	2002	2003	2004	2005	2006	
-450	652	323	149	1.1	1.0	3.8	5.6	3.9	5.9	5.8	5.2	Jamaïque
1	-1	0	1	..	2.5	5.8	6.8	6.4	6.7	6.4	5.8	Montserrat
-26	43	130	-50	0.2	1.2	1.1	2.1	1.7	1.6	1.9	1.5	Antilles néerlandaises
-1	14	-7	17	..	1.8	3.1	4.4	4.4	5.4	4.6	(e)4.9	Saint-Kitts-et-Nevis
13	26	-16	18	0.8	2.0	2.7	3.6	3.2	3.5	2.5	2.7	Sainte-Lucie
-2	24	-6	9	1.5	2.3	4.1	3.6	3.1	4.0	3.5	3.8	Saint-Vincent-et-les Grenadines
423	717	1 688	1 713	10.5	5.3	5.0	6.7	7.6	7.8	10.2	12.1	Trinité-et-Tobago
9 311	*6 112*	*11 530*	*4 024*	*1.6*	*2.7*	*2.5*	*3.5*	*4.0*	*3.7*	*3.8*	*3.5*	**Amérique centrale**
-30	-36	23	42	1.0	4.0	2.8	2.6	1.8	1.1	1.4	2.0	Belize
338	83	391	802	1.1	3.1	2.5	2.5	2.9	2.8	2.8	3.2	Costa Rica
320	-38	-31	92	1.0	3.9	4.3	3.4	3.7	3.3	3.0	2.9	El Salvador
534	593	238	251	3.3	2.1	4.1	4.4	5.1	5.3	5.0	4.6	Guatemala
-94	540	357	301	1.8	0.5	5.5	6.1	5.2	6.0	6.1	5.8	Honduras
8 361	5 185	9 914	2 216	1.6	2.7	2.3	3.4	4.0	3.7	3.8	3.4	Mexique
54	166	60	194	0.9	2.0	3.2	3.1	3.2	3.6	3.3	3.7	Nicaragua
				1.0								Panama, sans la zone du canal (anc.)
-172	-380	580	125	_	2.7	2.6	4.8	3.9	2.1	3.5	3.3	Panama
25 464	*16 867*	*20 184*	*48 836*	*5.7*	*7.3*	*8.6*	*9.4*	*11.0*	*9.4*	*8.6*	*9.1*	**Amérique du Sud**
3 664	4 731	8 295	3 725	7.6	13.5	11.9	14.0	12.3	10.1	11.4	10.9	Argentine
136	156	455	1 287	1.9	2.9	6.1	3.9	5.3	5.7	6.8	11.1	Bolivie
11 385	3 615	783	31 911	2.8	4.0	6.6	9.0	11.5	9.5	8.2	10.7	Brésil
498	154	936	2 463	6.5	9.4	9.7	10.8	9.8	7.7	6.2	6.1	Chili
52	2 610	1 393	509	12.2	9.9	9.3	10.1	9.3	9.6	8.4	7.0	Colombie
98	257	645	-225	5.4	5.4	3.1	1.3	1.5	1.6	2.0	1.5	Équateur
-8	-45	20	28	0.4	1.1	5.6	5.9	5.8	4.3	3.8	3.9	Guyana
340	199	129	405	14.9	5.9	4.2	4.5	5.2	4.5	4.2	3.4	Paraguay
438	2 400	1 423	3 134	9.5	3.6	11.3	15.0	13.9	14.5	13.1	13.1	Pérou
0	24	-4	90	4.5	0.5	1.4	2.6	1.8	2.1	1.6	2.7	Suriname
1 314	425	566	11	2.7	4.7	8.6	4.7	11.4	9.7	9.5	7.8	Uruguay
7 548	2 341	5 543	5 499	6.7	13.6	9.7	8.6	18.4	13.2	11.9	10.5	Venezuela (Rép. bolivarienne du)
280 377	**371 314**	**271 828**	**427 727**	**4.2**	**5.7**	**7.3**	**9.9**	**10.6**	**10.4**	**10.2**	**10.7**	**Économies en développement : Asie**
196 367	*286 261*	*231 334*	*291 340*	*1.5*	*7.8*	*8.5*	*12.3*	*12.9*	*13.3*	*14.0*	*14.5*	**Asie orientale**
117 024	206 348	207 015	246 978	1.5	6.7	9.0	11.8	11.9	13.1	14.9	16.2	Chine
543	1 093	1 253	2 443	..	4.1	17.6	18.0	18.9	18.8	20.5	24.0	Chine (RAS de Macao)
44 975	35 107	11 551	12 858	1.3	15.9	9.2	17.2	19.5	17.3	16.6	15.8	Province chinoise de Taiwan
-114	0	194	496	..	..	3.5	6.1	3.5	2.8	4.4	7.5	Mongolie
33 939	43 713	11 321	28 565	1.6	2.5	7.2	9.6	10.4	10.6	9.7	9.3	République de Corée
35 907	*27 291*	*5 767*	*41 671*	*3.9*	*1.1*	*6.5*	*11.2*	*13.1*	*12.1*	*9.1*	*9.7*	**Asie méridionale**
..	..	..	..	5.3	3.4							Afghanistan
895	595	-405	1 038	1.4	2.1	2.0	2.4	3.0	3.2	2.4	2.8	Bangladesh
12	32	69	78	..	13.1	21.8	21.7	17.7	11.6	14.5	15.6	Bhoutan
31 273	27 655	5 331	38 813	5.6	0.8	8.8	14.4	16.4	15.2	11.1	11.7	Inde
26	44	-17	45	0.4	2.1	3.8	4.1	4.1	3.8	3.0	3.0	Maldives
205	240	37	..	6.4	5.3	7.2	8.6	8.4	9.4	9.7	..	Népal
2 863	-1 142	234	1 510	1.1	0.5	1.7	8.6	10.1	6.6	4.7	4.6	Pakistan
634	-133	519	186	1.4	1.9	2.0	3.2	4.1	3.2	3.6	3.3	Sri Lanka
32 013	*45 719*	*10 703*	*59 816*	*4.0*	*4.5*	*6.1*	*7.0*	*7.5*	*7.2*	*6.2*	*6.5*	**Asie du Sud-Est**
44	24	-11	29	..	..	4.4	3.4	4.4	4.3	4.0	3.6	Brunéi Darussalam
39	128	10	204	..	..	3.1	3.9	3.7	3.5	2.9	2.9	Cambodge
3 992	-10	-1 812	7 963	6.0	4.1	8.5	10.4	10.6	8.3	5.7	6.5	Indonésie
17	15	11	93	..	0.1	3.1	5.1	5.4	3.8	3.2	3.7	Rép. dém. populaire lao
10 461	22 059	3 977	12 274	4.9	4.0	4.1	5.0	6.4	7.5	7.3	7.5	Malaisie
80	122	99	465	8.8	13.8	1.1	2.4	3.2	3.7	4.8	7.0	Myanmar
326	-539	2 810	4 100	4.1	0.9	4.2	4.3	4.1	3.7	4.1	4.4	Philippines
14 024	16 334	3 593	20 087	3.3	5.5	7.2	8.5	9.0	8.2	7.0	6.8	Singapour
3 031	7 587	2 027	14 601	2.0	4.8	6.2	7.1	6.5	6.2	5.1	6.1	Thaïlande
16 090	*12 044*	*24 025*	*34 901*	*6.7*	*5.3*	*6.3*	*7.0*	*6.7*	*5.4*	*5.3*	*5.6*	**Asie occidentale**
53	162	..	..	3.3	4.0	4.1	4.1	3.8	3.5	..	..	Bahreïn
..	..	4 280	7 431	..	..	..	..	..	4.7	6.2	11.2	Iraq
1 218	72	-16	1 472	5.7	3.9	8.7	9.4	10.9	7.8	6.0	7.0	Jordanie
-1 631	665	621	3 703	7.2	5.9	11.9	12.3	8.3	7.8	6.1	9.4	Koweït
5 276	-785	153	1 489	5.2	3.1	11.4	13.3	20.5	14.7	14.8	16.6	Liban
420	4	761	656	4.0	7.5	5.7	6.3	6.6	4.9	5.9	5.5	Oman
1 377	452	1 147	840	2.8	4.5	4.3	4.6	7.2	6.8	5.4	3.9	Qatar
2 010	4 671	-761	993	9.3	5.8	7.8	7.7	7.4	7.3	5.4	4.7	Arabie saoudite (3)
6 922	1 678	14 910	10 313	1.6	3.3	5.0	6.5	6.2	4.4	6.1	5.5	Turquie
-132	3 442	2 480	6 607	2.8	4.9	4.6	4.3	3.5	3.1	2.8	3.4	Émirats arabes unis
_	_	_	_	10.1	_	_	_	_	_	_	_	Yémen (anc. République arabe du)
				2.9	_	_	_	_	_	_	_	Yémen (anc. démocratique)
576	678	451	1 396	_	3.2	15.0	18.1	16.3	17.6	15.6	14.7	Yémen

Pour les sources et les notes, se reporter à la fin du tableau.

7.5.1 International reserves of developing countries by country and geographical region

Region, country or territory	Total reserves minus gold (1) - Réserves totales moins l'or (1) Millions of dollars - Millions de dollars							
	1980	1990	2000	2002	2003	2004	2005	2006
Developing economies: Oceania	**637**	**819**	**858**	**823**	**1 123**	**1 404**	**1 335**	**2 064**
Fiji	168	261	412	359	424	478	315	..
Papua New Guinea	423	403	287	322	494	633	718	1 401
Samoa	3	69	64	63	84	96	92	91
Solomon Islands	30	18	32	18	37	81	95	104
Tonga	14	31	25	25	40	55	47	48
Vanuatu	..	38	39	37	44	62	67	105

Sources:
- International Monetary Fund (IMF), *International Financial Statistics* on CD-ROM

Notes:

(a)   Data refers to South Africa Customs Union (Botswana, Lesotho, Namibia, South Africa and Swaziland)

(1)   End of year data.
(2)   Reserve stock of the year, divided by the average monthly imports of the current year. Data on imports are based on figures shown in table 1.1.1.

(3)   Reserves data have been revised starting with 1996 because national financial authorities modified their methodolgy for classification of foreign assests.

Total reserves minus gold (1) - Réserves totales moins l'or (1)

Annual change in reserves (millions of dollars) Variations annuelles des réserves (millions de dollars)				Number of months of imports (2) Nombre de mois d'importations (2)								Régions, pays ou territoires
2002-2003	2003-2004	2004-2005	2005-2006	1980	1990	2000	2002	2003	2004	2005	2006	
300	**281**	**-69**	**729**	**4.0**	**4.5**	**4.4**	**3.9**	**4.5**	**4.6**	**4.0**	**5.2**	**Économies en développement : Océanie**
65	55	-163	..	3.6	4.2	5.8	4.8	4.2	4.0	2.3	..	Fidji
173	138	86	683	4.3	4.3	3.0	3.1	4.3	4.5	5.0	7.6	Papouasie-Nouvelle-Guinée
21	12	-3	-1	0.5	10.3	7.2	5.7	6.6	5.5	4.6	4.0	Samoa
19	43	15	9	4.0	2.3	4.2	3.2	4.8	7.9	6.2	5.8	Îles Salomon
15	16	-8	1	4.4	6.1	4.3	3.4	5.1	6.3	4.7	4.4	Tonga
7	18	5	38	..	4.7	5.4	4.9	5.0	5.8	5.4	7.9	Vanuatu

Sources :
- Fonds monétaire international (FMI), *International Financial Statistics* sur CD-ROM

Notes :
(a)   Donnée relative à l'Union Douanière d'Afrique du Sud (Afrique du Sud, Botswana, Lesotho, Namibie et Swaziland)

(1)   Données de fin d'année.
(2)   Montant des réserves de l'année, divisé par la moyenne mensuelle des importations de l'année en cours. Les données des importations se basent sur les chiffres présentés dans le tableau 1.1.1.
(3)   Les données des réserves ont été révisées à partir de 1996, en raison d'une modification par les autorités financières nationales, de leur méthodologie de classification des avoirs extérieurs.

7

Economic grouping	Total reserves minus gold (1) - Réserves totales moins l'or (1) Millions de dollars - Millions of dollars							
	1980	1990	2000	2002	2003	2004	2005	2006
DEVELOPING ECONOMIES	**153 353**	**290 509**	**923 573**	**1 219 795**	**1 558 835**	**1 997 424**	**2 356 461**	**2 919 163**
Developing economies excluding China	150 807	260 923	755 295	928 668	1 150 684	1 382 924	1 534 947	1 850 671
Developing economies excluding LDCs	149 254	285 316	909 155	1 200 064	1 534 767	1 968 011	2 325 918	2 882 005
High-income developing countries	80 518	174 374	444 726	532 458	660 589	785 247	858 141	971 857
Middle-income developing countries	31 386	58 993	192 625	233 830	284 007	348 587	403 560	520 968
Low-income developing countries	41 448	57 143	286 221	453 507	614 239	863 591	1 094 760	1 426 338
Heavily indebted poor countries	2 746	4 021	12 451	16 927	19 696	24 369	25 473	32 089
Landlocked developing countries	2 968	6 754	13 561	13 797	15 087	16 974	18 244	23 668
Small island developing States	3 894	2 788	5 597	7 586	8 483	10 350	11 948	14 653
Least developed countries	*4 099*	*5 194*	*14 418*	*19 731*	*24 068*	*29 413*	*30 543*	*37 158*
Africa and Haiti	1 428	2 999	7 358	10 244	12 661	16 077	16 947	20 183
Asia	2 631	2 016	6 748	9 139	10 963	12 772	13 042	16 316
Islands	40	178	312	348	444	565	554	659
Major petroleum exporters	*77 332*	*49 355*	*105 811*	*119 786*	*146 023*	*188 340*	*245 910*	*332 273*
Africa	27 340	10 720	34 969	45 385	60 836	88 737	129 462	187 183
America	10 398	9 651	15 422	11 229	19 298	22 613	30 489	37 476
Asia	39 595	28 984	55 421	63 172	65 889	76 990	85 958	107 614
Major exporters of manufactured goods	*39 786*	*193 468*	*653 090*	*923 877*	*1 205 597*	*1 574 340*	*1 847 570*	*2 270 287*
America	8 729	17 304	67 943	88 056	107 802	116 603	127 299	161 427
Asia	31 057	176 164	585 147	835 821	1 097 795	1 457 737	1 720 271	2 108 860
Emerging economies	*38 196*	*167 087*	*459 887*	*559 856*	*690 632*	*831 516*	*885 334*	*1 017 168*
America	20 552	29 004	116 499	123 226	147 572	163 657	185 007	228 455
Asia	17 644	138 083	343 389	436 630	543 060	667 859	700 327	788 713
Newly industrialized economies	*25 882*	*146 467*	*384 981*	*480 930*	*591 677*	*715 928*	*749 393*	*849 842*
First tier	11 697	115 024	283 043	365 223	458 161	553 314	579 778	641 289
Second tier	14 185	31 443	101 938	115 707	133 516	162 614	169 615	208 552
Developing economies: Africa	**33 208**	**25 269**	**77 975**	**98 511**	**122 211**	**164 088**	**216 571**	**295 701**
Northern Africa excluding Sudan	18 898	12 109	44 237	63 210	83 094	103 481	137 044	188 779
Sub-Saharan Africa	14 310	13 160	33 738	35 301	39 116	60 608	79 527	106 922
Sub-Saharan Africa excluding South Africa	13 585	12 152	27 656	29 397	32 621	47 467	60 948	83 866
Developing economies: America	**38 877**	**47 448**	**156 371**	**160 558**	**195 221**	**220 337**	**255 133**	**310 249**
Central America and Greater Carribean Islands excluding Puerto Rico	4 295	11 874	44 856	61 333	69 958	77 320	90 236	94 801
Central America and Greater Carribean Islands excluding Mexico and Puerto Rico	1 335	2 011	9 347	10 738	11 003	13 179	16 182	18 531
South America and Central America	35 466	45 970	151 470	154 073	188 847	211 826	243 540	296 399
South America excluding Brazil	25 724	26 889	76 043	57 473	71 552	84 803	104 204	121 129
Developing economies: Asia	**80 631**	**216 973**	**688 369**	**959 904**	**1 240 281**	**1 611 595**	**1 883 423**	**2 311 150**
Eastern and South-Eastern Asia excluding China	26 143	147 302	389 754	486 955	598 312	723 944	758 965	863 143
Southern Asia excluding India	1 596	2 022	5 659	13 133	17 767	17 403	17 839	20 696

Sources:
- International Monetary Fund (IMF), *International Financial Statistics* on CD-ROM

Notes:
(1) End of year data.
(2) Reserve stock of the year, divided by the average monthly imports of the current year. Data on imports are based on figures shown in table 1.1.1.

Annual change in reserves (millions of dollars) Variations annuelles des réserves (millions de dollars)				Number of months of imports (2) Nombre de mois d'importations (2)								Groupements économiques
2002-2003	2003-2004	2004-2005	2005-2006	1980	1990	2000	2002	2003	2004	2005	2006	
339 040	**438 589**	**359 037**	**562 703**	**4.2**	**5.1**	**6.7**	**8.8**	**9.6**	**9.5**	**9.5**	**10.0**	**ÉCONOMIES EN DÉVELOPPEMENT**
222 016	232 240	152 022	315 724	4.3	5.0	6.3	8.2	9.0	8.5	7.9	8.2	Économies en développement sans la Chine
334 703	433 244	357 907	556 087	4.3	5.2	6.8	9.0	9.7	9.7	9.6	10.1	Économies en développement sans les PMA
128 131	124 657	72 894	113 716	4.9	6.7	6.7	8.8	9.8	9.2	8.5	8.3	Pays en développement à revenu élevé
50 177	64 580	54 973	117 408	3.1	3.6	5.7	7.0	7.5	7.2	7.2	7.9	Pays en développement à revenu intermédiaire
160 732	249 352	231 169	331 578	4.1	4.1	7.6	10.2	10.7	11.4	11.8	13.0	Pays en développement à revenu faible
2 769	4 673	1 104	6 616	1.4	2.0	4.0	4.8	4.9	4.9	4.2	4.5	Pays pauvres très endettés
1 291	1 887	1 270	5 425	3.5	3.3	7.7	7.0	7.0	6.2	5.8	6.5	Pays en développement sans littoral
897	1 867	1 598	2 705	3.0	3.3	4.0	5.3	5.4	5.7	5.7	6.0	Petits États insulaires en développement
4 337	*5 345*	*1 130*	*6 616*	*2.4*	*2.8*	*4.3*	*5.1*	*5.3*	*5.4*	*4.6*	*4.8*	*Pays les moins avancés*
2 416	3 416	870	3 236	1.2	2.4	4.2	4.9	5.0	5.1	4.3	4.4	Afrique et Haïti
1 824	1 808	271	3 274	4.8	3.3	4.3	5.3	5.6	5.8	5.2	5.5	Asie
97	121	-11	106	2.3	4.7	5.0	5.4	5.7	5.5	4.5	4.5	Îles
26 237	*42 317*	*57 569*	*86 363*	*7.9*	*6.7*	*8.4*	*8.4*	*9.0*	*8.7*	*8.8*	*10.5*	*Principaux exportateurs de pétrole*
15 451	27 901	40 725	57 721	8.9	5.6	16.5	15.5	17.3	19.4	22.3	29.6	Afrique
8 069	3 315	7 876	6 987	7.2	11.2	8.0	6.1	11.0	9.1	9.1	8.6	Amérique
2 717	11 102	8 968	21 656	7.5	6.3	6.5	6.7	6.0	5.2	4.6	5.2	Asie
281 720	*368 742*	*273 230*	*422 717*	*2.6*	*5.4*	*6.6*	*9.3*	*10.2*	*10.3*	*10.4*	*10.8*	*Principaux exportateurs d'articles manufacturés*
19 746	8 800	10 697	34 127	2.2	3.1	3.4	4.7	5.6	5.1	4.9	5.3	Amérique
261 974	359 942	262 533	388 590	2.7	5.9	7.4	10.4	11.1	11.2	11.3	11.7	Asie
130 776	*140 884*	*53 818*	*131 834*	*3.0*	*6.1*	*6.3*	*8.6*	*9.6*	*9.2*	*8.4*	*8.3*	*Économies émergentes*
24 346	16 085	21 350	43 448	3.7	4.3	4.7	5.7	6.5	5.9	5.8	6.1	Amérique
106 430	124 799	32 468	88 386	2.5	6.7	7.1	10.0	11.0	10.6	9.6	9.4	Asie
110 747	*124 251*	*33 466*	*100 448*	*3.0*	*6.2*	*7.0*	*9.6*	*10.6*	*10.1*	*9.1*	*8.9*	*Économies nouvellement industrialisées*
92 938	95 153	26 465	61 511	2.1	7.4	7.8	11.5	12.7	11.9	10.8	10.2	Première génération
17 809	29 098	7 001	38 937	4.4	3.9	5.5	6.4	6.8	6.7	5.8	6.4	Deuxième génération
23 699	**41 878**	**52 483**	**79 130**	**4.4**	**3.2**	**7.4**	**8.5**	**8.7**	**9.3**	**10.2**	**12.2**	**Économies en développement : Afrique**
19 884	20 386	33 564	51 734	7.6	3.3	11.2	14.9	18.0	17.5	19.5	24.6	Afrique septentrionale sans le Soudan
3 815	21 492	18 919	27 396	2.8	3.1	5.1	4.8	4.2	5.2	5.6	6.4	Afrique subsaharienne
3 224	14 846	13 481	22 918	3.8	3.2	6.6	6.0	5.5	6.5	6.8	8.2	Afrique subsaharienne sans l'Afrique du Sud
34 664	**25 115**	**34 796**	**55 117**	**4.0**	**4.7**	**4.8**	**5.5**	**6.4**	**6.0**	**5.9**	**6.0**	**Économies en développement : Amérique**
8 626	7 361	12 917	4 565	1.5	2.5	2.4	3.4	3.8	3.7	3.8	3.5	Amérique centrale et Grandes Antilles sans Porto Rico
264	2 176	3 003	2 348	1.4	1.8	2.9	3.2	3.2	3.5	3.6	3.6	Amérique centrale et Grandes Antilles sans le Mexique et Porto Rico
34 774	22 979	31 714	52 859	4.4	5.1	5.1	5.7	6.7	6.1	6.0	6.1	Amérique du Sud et Amérique centrale
14 079	13 251	19 401	16 925	7.4	9.4	9.8	9.7	10.7	9.4	8.9	8.3	Amérique du Sud sans le Brésil
280 377	**371 314**	**271 828**	**427 727**	**4.2**	**5.7**	**7.3**	**9.9**	**10.6**	**10.4**	**10.2**	**10.7**	**Économies en développement : Asie**
111 357	125 632	35 022	104 177	3.0	6.2	7.0	9.6	10.5	10.1	9.1	9.0	Asie orientale et Asie du Sud-Est sans la Chine
4 634	-365	436	2 858	1.7	1.6	2.3	5.2	6.1	4.9	4.0	4.0	Asie méridionale sans l'Inde

Sources :
- Fonds monétaire international (FMI), *International Financial Statistics* sur CD-ROM

Notes :
(1) Données de fin d'année.
(2) Montant des réserves de l'année, divisé par la moyenne mensuelle des importations de l'année en cours. Les données des importations se basent sur les chiffres présentés dans le tableau 1.1.1.

7

7.6.1 Official financial flows from bilateral and multilateral sources to developing economies by country and geographical region

7.6.1 Flux financiers publics bilatéraux et multilatéraux à destination des économies en développement par pays et régions géographiques

Region, country or territory / Régions, pays ou territoires	Year / Année	Total official net (1) / Total secteur officiel net (1)	Total ODA Net / Total OA Net (2) — APD totale nette / AP totale nette (2)			Total OOF Net (3) / Flux AASP nets (3)		
			Total donors / Tous donneurs	DAC bilateral donors / Donneurs bilatéraux du CAD	Multilateral donors / Donneurs multilatéraux	Total donors / Tous donneurs	DAC bilateral donors / Donneurs bilatéraux du CAD	Multilateral donors / Donneurs multilatéraux
		Millions of dollars / Millions de dollars						
DEVELOPING ECONOMIES - ÉCONOMIES EN DÉVELOPPEMENT	1990	73 489.6	55 322.9	36 861.8	12 578.6	18 166.7	8 065.1	10 128.2
	1995	67 967.7	55 639.4	38 535.0	16 404.6	12 328.3	8 847.3	2 897.7
	2000	48 237.8	45 101.5	33 313.0	11 134.0	3 136.4	-4 522.3	8 332.8
	2006	88 467.3	98 917.2	72 966.0	21 892.1	-10 449.9	-9 259.7	-2 183.4
Developing economies: Africa - Économies en développement : Afrique	1990	28 024.2	25 077.3	15 817.3	6 126.3	2 946.9	847.9	1 950.3
	1995	25 150.9	21 781.1	13 223.1	8 410.6	3 369.8	3 574.0	-203.6
	2000	14 215.2	15 489.4	10 372.6	4 817.0	-1 274.2	-333.3	-930.8
	2006	31 058.1	43 402.0	31 514.8	11 367.9	-12 343.9	-10 864.6	-1 487.7
Eastern Africa - Afrique orientale	*1990*	*8 338.0*	*8 185.4*	*5 169.1*	*2 708.0*	*152.6*	*137.0*	*11.9*
	1995	*8 939.9*	*9 233.3*	*4 786.1*	*4 419.6*	*-293.4*	*-41.7*	*-251.7*
	2000	*6 465.9*	*6 569.7*	*4 295.8*	*2 219.6*	*-103.9*	*-37.7*	*-65.8*
	2006	*12 513.1*	*13 043.0*	*7 964.5*	*5 009.6*	*-529.9*	*-463.6*	*-66.3*
Burundi	1990	259.1	262.6	157.6	104.7	-3.4	1.0	-4.4
	1995	285.2	287.0	108.4	181.3	-1.8	0.2	-2.0
	2000	92.6	92.6	40.9	51.7	0.0	0.0	0.0
	2006	414.9	414.9	222.5	192.2	0.0	0.0	0.0
Comoros - Comores	1990	44.9	44.8	30.6	14.0	0.1	0.1	0.0
	1995	41.5	41.6	21.7	19.8	-0.1	-0.1	0.0
	2000	18.7	18.7	10.8	7.7	0.0	0.0	0.0
	2006	30.4	30.4	19.9	9.9	0.0	0.0	0.0
Djibouti	1990	193.6	193.7	88.3	17.3	-0.1	-0.1	0.0
	1995	104.9	104.7	79.6	21.9	0.2	0.2	0.0
	2000	71.4	71.4	42.1	19.7	0.0	0.0	0.0
	2006	131.4	117.2	89.5	26.0	14.2	6.2	8.0
Eritrea - Érythrée	1995	148.2	148.2	94.6	48.3	0.0	0.0	0.0
	2000	175.9	175.8	111.9	54.7	0.0	0.0	0.0
	2006	129.1	129.1	63.2	67.4	0.0	0.0	0.0
Ethiopia - Éthiopie	1995	899.0	876.5	525.5	350.4	22.5	5.5	17.1
	2000	667.3	686.1	379.5	291.6	-18.8	-1.0	-17.9
	2006	1 919.9	1 946.8	1 024.1	897.6	-26.9	-8.0	-18.9
Ethiopia (former) - Éthiopie (anc.)	1990	1 007.2	1 009.3	509.7	431.7	-2.0	-2.3	0.3
Kenya	1990	1 141.3	1 181.3	735.2	441.6	-40.0	15.4	-55.4
	1995	629.7	731.4	458.7	267.5	-101.7	-16.4	-85.3
	2000	476.1	509.9	293.0	212.1	-33.8	-4.6	-29.0
	2006	974.7	943.4	761.2	166.4	31.3	29.0	2.4
Madagascar	1990	411.9	397.0	268.2	129.9	14.9	11.2	3.2
	1995	299.7	299.4	194.9	104.4	0.3	4.8	-4.5
	2000	316.2	321.7	138.7	184.1	-5.5	1.4	-6.9
	2006	745.5	754.3	265.6	484.8	-8.8	-6.8	-2.0
Malawi	1990	486.3	500.4	216.2	283.6	-14.1	-5.8	-8.3
	1995	416.2	434.1	220.9	210.5	-18.0	-1.0	-17.0
	2000	443.8	446.2	269.2	170.7	-2.4	-0.1	-2.3
	2006	643.7	668.5	397.9	258.7	-24.8	-22.4	-2.4
Mauritius - Maurice	1990	107.2	88.3	75.7	11.9	18.9	16.2	2.7
	1995	3.7	23.1	11.0	13.5	-19.5	-1.2	-18.3
	2000	-17.9	20.4	12.4	7.4	-38.3	-20.7	-17.5
	2006	-9.8	18.6	8.5	12.0	-28.4	4.0	-32.4
Mayotte	1990	60.5	60.5	58.5	2.0	0.0	0.0	0.0
	1995	107.8	107.8	106.2	1.5	0.0	0.0	0.0
	2000	103.2	103.2	103.0	0.2	0.0	0.0	0.0
	2006	338.4	337.6	337.5	0.1	0.8	0.8	0.0

For sources and notes, see end of table.

Pour les sources et les notes, se reporter à la fin du tableau.

7.6.1 Official financial flows from bilateral and multilateral sources to developing economies by country and geographical region

7.6.1 Flux financiers publics bilatéraux et multilatéraux à destination des économies en développement par pays et régions géographiques

Region, country or territory / Régions, pays ou territoires	Year / Année	Total official net (1) / Total secteur officiel net (1)	Total CDA Net / Total OA Net (2) APD totale nette / AP totale nette (2)			Total OOF Net (3) Flux AASP nets (3)		
			Total donors / Tous donneurs	of which: / dont :		Total donors / Tous donneurs	of which: / dont :	
				DAC bilateral donors / Donneurs bilatéraux du CAD	Multilateral donors / Donneurs multilatéraux		DAC bilateral donors / Donneurs bilatéraux du CAD	Multilateral donors / Donneurs multilatéraux
		Millions of dollars / Millions de dollars						
Mozambique	1990	999.4	997.5	750.3	246.9	1.9	3.3	-1.5
	1995	1 035.6	1 062.4	698.3	361.9	-26.8	-23.4	-3.4
	2000	1 042.5	876.1	623.5	252.6	166.5	105.2	61.2
	2006	1 629.3	1 611.0	938.3	669.4	18.3	6.5	11.8
Rwanda	1990	286.9	287.9	183.2	94.5	-1.0	-0.1	-0.9
	1995	695.0	694.7	339.2	355.7	0.3	0.1	0.2
	2000	323.5	321.5	175.4	145.9	2.1	2.2	-0.2
	2006	610.5	584.9	321.1	263.3	25.6	25.6	0.0
Seychelles	1990	37.4	35.6	32.7	3.0	1.9	-0.8	-0.4
	1995	16.3	12.8	11.0	2.3	3.4	-0.4	3.9
	2000	14.5	18.3	3.3	8.4	-3.8	-0.7	-3.1
	2006	-11.2	14.0	7.1	7.5	-25.2	0.0	-25.2
Somalia - Somalie	1990	490.2	491.4	269.6	139.8	-1.2	-0.8	-0.4
	1995	188.0	187.8	119.2	68.6	0.2	0.2	0.0
	2000	101.0	101.0	56.4	44.4	0.0	0.0	0.0
	2006	391.9	391.9	263.1	125.3	0.0	0.0	0.0
Uganda - Ouganda	1990	665.2	663.1	244.4	376.1	2.1	9.4	-7.3
	1995	817.2	832.9	423.1	398.0	-15.7	-5.7	-9.9
	2000	773.5	817.1	578.2	233.2	-43.6	-46.3	2.8
	2006	1 546.4	1 550.6	938.2	609.5	-4.2	-4.7	0.5
United Republic of Tanzania - République-Unie de Tanzanie	1990	1 163.1	1 163.2	844.1	315.8	-0.1	28.2	-28.2
	1995	837.3	869.1	586.7	278.0	-31.9	-9.0	-22.9
	2000	1 046.5	1 019.4	778.7	243.3	27.1	32.1	-4.9
	2006	1 833.1	1 825.3	991.7	832.2	7.8	3.7	4.1
Zambia - Zambie	1990	540.8	474.8	408.9	65.9	66.0	47.2	18.8
	1995	1 963.6	2 030.7	439.5	1 591.0	-67.1	3.7	-70.8
	2000	674.5	794.7	486.2	308.1	-120.1	-104.4	-15.8
	2006	926.0	1 424.9	1 115.2	307.6	-498.9	-489.8	-9.1
Zimbabwe	1990	443.0	334.3	295.9	29.3	108.7	14.9	93.8
	1995	451.3	489.1	347.7	144.9	-37.8	1.0	-38.8
	2000	142.6	175.8	192.6	-16.1	-33.2	-0.9	-32.3
	2006	269.1	279.8	199.8	79.9	-10.8	-7.8	-3.0
Middle Africa - Afrique centrale	*1990*	*3 588.1*	*2 628.2*	*1 821.6*	*725.4*	*960.0*	*675.6*	*284.4*
	1995	*2 432.8*	*1 842.7*	*1 278.0*	*559.4*	*590.1*	*667.4*	*-77.3*
	2000	*972.5*	*1 165.1*	*658.8*	*502.2*	*-192.6*	*-52.5*	*-140.2*
	2006	*3 076.7*	*4 662.2*	*3 406.4*	*1 144.1*	*-1 585.5*	*-1 439.5*	*-146.0*
Angola	1990	343.5	265.8	163.2	100.8	77.7	76.2	1.5
	1995	489.6	416.4	241.7	174.5	73.1	73.1	0.0
	2000	256.3	302.2	189.1	107.1	-45.9	-23.3	-22.6
	2006	157.7	170.7	-55.2	123.8	-13.1	-11.4	-1.7
Cameroon - Cameroun	1990	607.2	444.4	339.1	107.9	162.8	75.1	87.7
	1995	578.2	442.8	345.5	95.8	135.4	235.2	-99.8
	2000	308.7	379.3	213.5	168.5	-70.6	9.4	-80.0
	2006	728.3	1 684.3	1 505.3	173.5	-956.0	-877.4	-78.6
Central African Republic - République centrafricaine	1990	248.6	248.9	99.9	146.7	-0.3	0.9	-1.1
	1995	167.0	167.8	122.4	42.0	-0.8	-0.8	0.0
	2000	74.0	75.3	53.1	22.4	-1.3	-1.3	0.0
	2006	134.6	133.9	65.3	68.6	0.8	0.8	0.0
Chad - Tchad	1990	310.5	310.6	183.3	125.0	-0.1	-0.1	0.0
	1995	237.2	235.0	127.0	107.4	2.2	2.2	0.0
	2000	129.2	130.2	53.3	76.1	-0.9	-0.9	0.0
	2006	272.9	283.7	152.5	127.8	-10.9	0.0	-10.8
Congo	1990	226.3	217.2	202.0	15.2	9.1	13.2	-4.1
	1995	394.0	124.9	105.0	19.8	269.2	287.2	-18.0
	2000	17.6	33.2	23.0	10.1	-15.6	-12.4	-3.2
	2006	209.0	254.4	169.1	84.4	-45.4	-27.8	-17.6

For sources and notes, see end of table.   Pour les sources et les notes, se reporter à la fin du tableau.

7.6.1 Official financial flows from bilateral and multilateral sources to developing economies by country and geographical region

7.6.1 Flux financiers publics bilatéraux et multilatéraux à destination des économies en développement par pays et régions géographiques

Region, country or territory / Régions, pays ou territoires	Year / Année	Total official net (1) / Total secteur officiel net (1)	Total ODA Net / Total OA Net (2) / APD totale nette / AP totale nette (2)			Total OOF Net (3) / Flux AASP nets (3)		
			Total donors / Tous donneurs	of which: / dont :		Total donors / Tous donneurs	of which: / dont :	
				DAC bilateral donors / Donneurs bilatéraux du CAD	Multilateral donors / Donneurs multilatéraux		DAC bilateral donors / Donneurs bilatéraux du CAD	Multilateral donors / Donneurs multilatéraux
			Millions of dollars / Millions de dollars					
Dem. Rep. of the Congo - Rép. dém. du Congo	1990	1 419.7	895.8	632.7	185.9	523.9	380.6	143.3
	1995	188.5	194.8	117.7	76.9	-6.3	-5.1	-1.2
	2000	173.7	177.1	102.7	74.3	-3.4	0.0	-3.4
	2006	1 390.4	2 055.7	1 500.4	556.0	-665.3	-640.6	-24.7
Equatorial Guinea - Guinée équatoriale	1990	60.8	60.2	43.6	16.5	0.6	0.0	0.6
	1995	35.2	33.4	21.7	11.7	1.8	1.8	0.0
	2000	20.2	21.3	18.2	3.3	-1.1	-0.7	-0.4
	2006	217.4	26.8	18.9	8.1	190.6	190.6	0.0
Gabon	1990	317.5	131.2	126.9	4.4	186.3	129.7	56.5
	1995	284.9	143.5	135.6	8.7	141.4	99.7	41.7
	2000	-42.1	11.7	-11.7	23.3	-53.7	-23.2	-30.5
	2006	-55.1	31.1	31.9	-1.3	-86.2	-73.5	-12.6
Sao Tome and Principe - Sao Tomé-et-Principe	1990	54.1	54.1	31.0	23.1	0.0	0.0	0.0
	1995	58.3	84.1	61.5	22.5	-25.8	-25.8	0.0
	2000	34.9	34.9	17.7	17.2	0.0	0.0	0.0
	2006	21.6	21.6	18.3	3.3	0.0	0.0	0.0
Northern Africa - Afrique septentrionale	*1990*	*7 994.0*	*7 817.8*	*4 501.3*	*653.2*	*176.2*	*-949.7*	*977.3*
	1995	*6 305.0*	*3 114.3*	*2 504.2*	*504.2*	*3 190.7*	*2 709.3*	*481.9*
	2000	*2 020.1*	*2 390.1*	*1 738.1*	*430.8*	*-370.0*	*101.0*	*-461.4*
	2006	*510.5*	*4 654.5*	*3 146.6*	*1 256.1*	*-4 144.0*	*-2 902.7*	*-1 248.2*
Algeria - Algérie	1990	675.6	131.7	102.2	21.5	543.9	114.2	283.3
	1995	1 986.1	293.9	275.3	30.7	1 692.2	1 325.6	366.6
	2000	-40.5	200.9	65.7	63.9	-241.4	-143.4	-98.0
	2006	-4 133.9	208.5	204.6	-3.5	-4 342.4	-2 885.9	-1 456.5
Egypt - Égypte	1990	4 153.9	5 425.8	3 163.1	76.2	-1 271.8	-1 234.0	-37.6
	1995	2 648.5	2 010.5	1 691.2	202.4	638.0	775.7	-137.7
	2000	1 367.6	1 327.7	1 138.9	134.9	39.9	220.5	-180.0
	2006	1 183.1	872.9	536.8	286.5	310.2	125.3	185.0
Libyan Arab Jamahiriya - Jamahiriya arabe libyenne	1990	8.3	8.3	7.6	0.7	0.0	0.0	0.0
	1995	5.8	5.8	3.2	2.6	0.0	0.0	0.0
	2006	37.3	37.3	33.4	2.7	0.0	0.0	0.0
Morocco - Maroc	1990	1 696.0	1 048.0	595.4	91.5	648.1	164.5	486.2
	1995	485.7	492.6	347.4	125.4	-6.9	-163.6	156.7
	2000	275.8	418.8	293.1	129.9	-143.0	-47.3	-95.7
	2006	1 253.9	1 045.6	566.7	362.5	208.4	-50.3	258.7
Sudan - Soudan	1990	810.6	813.1	420.0	385.2	-2.6	2.7	-5.2
	1995	250.7	237.0	130.6	102.8	13.7	-4.3	18.1
	2000	210.9	220.4	90.3	30.7	-9.5	0.0	-0.4
	2006	2 066.5	2 058.3	1 518.1	453.5	8.3	2.6	-1.3
Tunisia - Tunisie	1990	649.6	391.0	212.9	78.1	258.5	2.9	250.7
	1995	928.2	74.4	56.5	40.4	853.7	775.9	78.3
	2000	206.3	222.3	150.3	71.5	-16.0	71.2	-87.2
	2006	103.6	432.0	287.0	154.4	-328.5	-94.4	-234.1
Southern Africa - Afrique australe	*1990*	*460.8*	*457.6*	*281.9*	*177.8*	*3.2*	*-2.2*	*5.4*
	1995	*1 165.2*	*836.5*	*620.0*	*210.3*	*328.7*	*359.7*	*-30.9*
	2000	*843.2*	*720.1*	*498.5*	*220.5*	*123.2*	*-83.3*	*206.7*
	2006	*1 043.9*	*1 034.4*	*753.3*	*281.7*	*9.5*	*-70.6*	*78.5*
Botswana	1990	167.4	145.2	121.2	25.8	22.2	4.6	17.6
	1995	68.6	89.5	54.5	34.6	-20.9	18.5	-39.4
	2000	34.2	30.6	23.5	8.0	3.6	23.1	-19.5
	2006	64.6	65.1	36.3	30.5	-0.5	0.2	-0.8
Lesotho	1990	139.7	139.1	85.2	54.3	0.5	-1.5	2.0
	1995	134.1	112.7	61.6	51.0	21.5	12.6	8.9
	2000	47.1	36.7	21.8	16.1	10.4	-8.2	18.6
	2006	64.2	71.7	38.5	34.1	-7.5	0.2	-7.7

For sources and notes, see end of table.

Pour les sources et les notes, se reporter à la fin du tableau.

7.6.1 Official financial flows from bilateral and multilateral sources to developing economies by country and geographical region

7.6.1 Flux financiers publics bilatéraux et multilatéraux à destination des économies en développement par pays et régions géographiques

Region, country or territory / Régions, pays ou territoires	Year / Année	Total official net (1) / Total secteur officiel net (1)	Total ODA Net / Total OA Net (2) APD totale nette / AP totale nette (2)			Total OOF Net (3) Flux AASP nets (3)		
			Total donors / Tous donneurs	of which: / dont :		Total donors / Tous donneurs	of which: / dont :	
				DAC bilateral donors / Donneurs bilatéraux du CAD	Multilateral donors / Donneurs multilatéraux		DAC bilateral donors / Donneurs bilatéraux du CAD	Multilateral donors / Donneurs multilatéraux
			Millions of dollars / Millions de dollars					
Namibia - Namibie	1990	119.6	119.6	39.4	80.3	0.0	0.0	0.0
	1995	192.5	190.4	147.7	42.5	2.1	2.1	0.0
	2000	154.0	152.3	96.8	54.5	1.6	-0.5	2.1
	2006	165.6	145.3	105.7	37.8	20.4	-1.3	21.6
South Africa - Afrique du Sud	1995	712.7	386.2	318.5	64.7	326.6	326.6	0.0
	2000	592.1	487.3	353.6	131.7	104.8	-94.3	199.3
	2006	705.9	717.8	560.6	156.6	-11.9	-69.8	56.4
Swaziland	1990	34.1	53.6	36.1	17.4	-19.5	-5.3	-14.2
	1995	57.3	57.8	37.7	17.4	-0.5	0.0	-0.5
	2000	15.9	13.1	2.8	10.2	2.8	-3.5	6.2
	2006	43.5	34.5	12.3	22.8	9.0	0.0	9.0
Western Africa - Afrique occidentale	*1990*	*6 724.0*	*5 085.5*	*3 203.0*	*1 808.8*	*1 638.5*	*981.3*	*660.7*
	1995	*5 287.4*	*5 768.1*	*3 212.3*	*2 553.3*	*-480.7*	*-151.7*	*-329.0*
	2000	*2 879.5*	*3 612.1*	*2 333.6*	*1 272.2*	*-732.6*	*-267.6*	*-465.0*
	2006	*11 430.5*	*17 542.5*	*14 194.1*	*3 302.9*	*-6 111.9*	*-5 987.5*	*-124.5*
Benin - Bénin	1990	294.8	266.9	125.7	141.5	27.9	26.2	1.7
	1995	282.2	280.1	177.4	95.9	2.1	2.9	-0.8
	2000	227.5	238.4	190.5	49.0	-11.0	-11.0	0.0
	2006	373.9	374.7	228.4	146.7	-0.8	-0.7	-0.2
Burkina Faso	1990	328.0	326.5	238.7	76.5	1.4	1.3	0.1
	1995	487.6	490.0	252.3	229.9	-2.4	0.1	-2.5
	2000	329.4	334.9	227.8	103.4	-5.5	-3.5	-2.0
	2006	871.5	870.7	385.8	474.8	0.8	-0.3	1.0
Cape Verde - Cap-Vert	1990	103.9	105.3	75.9	29.0	-1.4	-0.2	-1.1
	1995	115.8	115.7	76.9	38.7	0.1	0.4	-0.3
	2000	92.4	93.9	69.7	24.6	-1.6	-0.1	-1.4
	2006	137.3	138.3	98.7	37.7	-1.0	0.0	-1.0
Côte d'Ivoire	1990	1 121.9	686.4	530.6	155.8	435.5	134.2	301.3
	1995	1 147.3	1 211.8	726.6	484.7	-64.5	31.6	-96.1
	2000	275.9	350.8	250.1	100.1	-74.9	17.8	-92.7
	2006	236.1	251.0	198.8	51.7	-14.9	-9.5	-5.4
Gambia - Gambie	1990	105.3	97.3	56.9	39.9	8.0	8.5	-0.5
	1995	43.1	45.4	25.1	21.8	-2.3	-0.4	-1.9
	2000	48.3	49.0	14.6	31.9	-0.7	0.0	-0.7
	2006	74.1	74.1	25.1	43.4	0.0	0.0	0.0
Ghana	1990	716.4	559.7	264.9	293.7	156.6	26.4	130.2
	1995	579.1	648.4	358.6	295.8	-69.3	10.7	-80.0
	2000	582.9	599.7	376.0	221.4	-16.8	8.6	-25.3
	2006	1 212.6	1 175.6	594.7	580.1	37.0	55.6	-18.6
Guinea - Guinée	1990	300.4	291.5	139.0	148.4	8.8	19.6	-10.8
	1995	432.7	415.9	220.4	189.7	16.8	-2.3	19.1
	2000	141.5	152.9	92.8	57.5	-11.4	-1.4	-10.0
	2006	156.4	163.5	102.9	57.7	-7.1	-0.7	-6.4
Guinea-Bissau - Guinée-Bissau	1990	125.0	126.4	75.4	51.0	-1.3	0.0	-1.3
	1995	114.3	117.6	76.9	37.7	-3.3	0.0	-3.3
	2000	80.3	80.3	41.6	38.7	0.0	0.1	-0.1
	2006	78.1	82.3	39.4	42.9	-4.3	-4.3	0.0
Liberia - Libéria	1990	66.5	113.7	42.3	69.2	-47.3	-12.5	-34.8
	1995	119.7	123.1	31.1	90.7	-3.4	-3.1	-0.4
	2000	69.1	67.4	23.8	43.6	1.6	-1.9	3.5
	2006	268.6	268.7	187.4	80.8	0.0	0.0	0.0
Mali	1990	480.1	479.0	312.5	151.1	1.1	1.9	-0.8
	1995	584.8	539.8	285.1	268.2	45.0	21.3	23.8
	2000	342.8	359.2	299.8	60.8	-16.4	-6.9	-9.5
	2006	819.4	825.4	398.4	418.2	-6.1	-5.1	-1.0

For sources and notes, see end of table.

Pour les sources et les notes, se reporter à la fin du tableau.

7.6.1   Official financial flows from bilateral and multilateral sources to developing economies by country and geographical region

7.6.1   Flux financiers publics bilatéraux et multilatéraux à destination des économies en développement par pays et régions géographiques

Region, country or territory / Régions, pays ou territoires	Year / Année	Total official net (1) / Total secteur officiel net (1)	Total ODA Net / Total OA Net (2) APD totale nette / AP totale nette (2)			Total OOF Net (3) Flux AASP nets (3)		
			Total donors / Tous donneurs	of which: / dont :		Total donors / Tous donneurs	of which: / cont :	
				DAC bilateral donors / Donneurs bilatéraux du CAD	Multilateral donors / Donneurs multilatéraux		DAC bilateral donors / Donneurs bilatéraux du CAD	Multilateral donors / Donneurs multilatéraux
				Millions of dollars / Millions de dollars				
Mauritania - Mauritanie	1990	224.8	236.1	106.4	105.1	-11.3	0.8	-12.1
	1995	218.4	229.8	126.0	119.7	-11.4	-9.0	-2.4
	2000	207.2	211.4	82.5	128.8	-4.2	6.8	-11.0
	2006	182.4	187.6	93.7	93.3	-5.1	3.7	-8.8
Niger	1990	392.9	387.6	254.6	129.4	5.3	6.7	-1.4
	1995	198.5	271.0	193.9	76.2	-72.6	-71.3	-1.2
	2000	184.2	208.5	105.8	102.6	-24.3	-24.3	0.0
	2006	392.0	401.3	235.2	165.9	-9.2	-6.7	-2.6
Nigeria - Nigéria	1990	1 307.7	255.1	172.7	73.4	1 052.6	739.4	313.2
	1995	-67.2	210.9	72.6	138.8	-278.1	-125.3	-152.8
	2000	-390.6	173.7	84.3	89.1	-564.3	-260.5	-303.8
	2006	5 339.9	11 433.9	10 819.6	612.7	-6 094.0	-6 018.8	-75.2
Saint Helena - Sainte-Hélène	1990	24.7	24.7	23.3	1.4	0.0	0.0	0.0
	1995	12.6	12.6	12.4	0.2	0.0	0.0	0.0
	2000	18.7	18.7	18.4	0.3	0.0	0.0	0.0
	2006	28.1	28.1	23.1	5.0	0.0	0.0	0.0
Senegal - Sénégal	1990	823.7	811.7	589.2	220.1	12.0	31.1	-15.6
	1995	632.8	659.3	399.4	247.3	-26.5	-0.4	-26.1
	2000	417.2	423.2	288.4	139.5	-6.0	9.2	-15.2
	2006	829.3	824.9	509.1	304.0	4.5	7.2	-2.8
Sierra Leone	1990	55.1	59.3	39.9	19.3	-4.3	-3.4	-0.9
	1995	200.4	205.3	59.6	145.1	-4.9	-1.4	-3.5
	2000	178.8	180.6	115.6	65.0	-1.8	-0.9	-0.9
	2006	363.8	363.9	199.1	164.3	-0.1	0.9	-1.0
Togo	1990	252.8	258.2	155.0	103.9	-5.4	1.3	-6.7
	1995	185.3	191.3	117.8	73.2	-6.0	-5.4	-0.6
	2000	74.1	69.6	51.9	16.2	4.5	0.4	4.1
	2006	67.1	78.7	54.8	23.9	-11.6	-9.1	-2.5
Developing economies: Africa unallocated - Économies en développement : Afrique, non ventilées	1990	919.3	902.8	840.4	53.1	16.5	5.8	10.6
	1995	1 020.7	986.4	822.6	163.8	34.3	30.9	3.5
	2000	1 034.0	1 032.3	847.7	171.8	1.7	6.9	-5.2
	2006	2 483.3	2 465.3	2 050.0	373.5	18.0	-0.7	18.7
Developing economies: America - Économies en développement : Amérique	**1990**	**13 524.8**	**5 190.4**	**4 146.3**	**1 032.0**	**8 334.4**	**3 730.0**	**4 634.3**
	1995	**8 022.0**	**6 386.5**	**4 809.4**	**1 543.2**	**1 635.6**	**81.2**	**1 557.5**
	2000	**10 363.1**	**4 831.9**	**3 846.2**	**935.1**	**5 531.2**	**-1 019.7**	**6 543.4**
	2006	**-423.7**	**6 909.7**	**5 235.7**	**1 634.0**	**-7 333.4**	**-1 300.3**	**-6 092.5**
Caribbean - Caraïbes	*1990*	*1 015.6*	*809.2*	*624.6*	*180.0*	*206.4*	*94.4*	*130.5*
	1995	*1 421.8*	*1 321.8*	*857.4*	*456.5*	*100.1*	*-75.9*	*176.0*
	2000	*575.5*	*420.7*	*279.0*	*123.1*	*154.8*	*-86.6*	*243.7*
	2006	*1 149.1*	*876.0*	*480.4*	*393.6*	*273.1*	*157.2*	*126.3*
Anguilla	1990	3.9	3.8	2.4	1.4	0.1	0.0	0.1
	1995	3.5	3.4	2.5	0.8	0.1	0.0	0.1
	2000	7.7	3.5	3.8	-0.3	4.2	0.0	4.2
	2006	4.1	4.4	0.3	4.1	-0.3	0.0	-0.3
Antigua and Barbuda - Antigua-et-Barbuda	1990	-2.7	4.6	2.9	1.7	-7.3	-7.3	0.0
	1995	-0.8	2.3	0.8	0.7	-3.1	-3.1	0.0
	2000	9.9	9.8	3.7	1.1	0.1	0.0	0.1
	2006	2.1	3.3	1.9	1.1	-1.2	-1.2	0.0
Aruba	1990	30.0	30.0	28.9	1.1	0.0	0.0	0.0
	1995	29.7	25.8	18.0	7.8	3.9	4.0	-0.1
Bahamas	1990	30.6	3.2	0.4	1.8	27.4	-0.6	28.0
	1995	6.7	4.3	1.3	2.2	2.4	-4.6	7.0
Barbados - Barbade	1990	21.4	2.6	1.4	1.2	18.8	10.7	8.1
	1995	8.2	-1.2	0.1	-1.3	9.4	-3.0	12.3
	2000	16.1	0.2	1.0	-0.8	15.9	3.1	12.8
	2006	53.3	-0.6	3.1	-3.7	53.8	63.6	-9.8

For sources and notes, see end of table.

Pour les sources et les notes, se reporter à la fin du tableau.

7.6.1 Official financial flows from bilateral and multilateral sources to developing economies by country and geographical region

7.6.1 Flux financiers publics bilatéraux et multilatéraux à destination des économies en développement par pays et régions géographiques

Region, country or territory / Régions, pays ou territoires	Year / Année	Total official net (1) / Total secteur officiel net (1)	Total ODA Net / Total OA Net (2) / APD totale nette / AP totale nette (2)			Total OOF Net (3) / Flux AASP nets (3)		
			Total donors / Tous donneurs	DAC bilateral donors / Donneurs bilatéraux du CAD	Multilateral donors / Donneurs multilatéraux	Total donors / Tous donneurs	DAC bilateral donors / Donneurs bilatéraux du CAD	Multilateral donors / Donneurs multilatéraux
			Millions of dollars / Millions de dollars					
British Virgin Islands - Îles Vierges britanniques	1990	9.4	5.6	3.0	2.5	3.9	1.6	2.3
	1995	2.6	1.4	0.3	1.1	1.2	0.0	1.2
Cayman Islands - Îles Caïmanes	1990	11.9	3.0	2.1	0.9	8.9	2.4	6.5
	1995	-0.1	-0.6	-0.6	0.0	0.5	0.7	-0.3
Cuba	1990	60.1	51.8	33.6	17.2	8.3	8.3	0.0
	1995	56.2	63.2	33.7	29.5	-7.1	-7.1	0.0
	2000	47.5	44.0	30.8	12.8	3.5	3.5	0.0
	2006	76.3	78.3	56.9	20.6	-1.9	-1.9	0.0
Dominica - Dominique	1990	19.4	19.6	10.8	8.4	-0.3	-0.4	0.1
	1995	24.3	25.0	9.5	14.4	-0.8	-1.2	0.4
	2000	18.5	15.2	5.9	6.4	3.3	-0.1	3.4
	2006	18.3	19.4	1.8	17.3	-1.1	0.0	-1.1
Dominican Republic - République dominicaine	1990	136.4	101.7	72.7	27.8	34.7	1.4	33.3
	1995	165.4	119.4	81.2	36.8	46.0	-12.1	58.1
	2000	73.0	56.1	44.6	11.5	16.9	-34.0	53.1
	2006	191.2	53.0	13.0	38.4	138.2	40.6	108.0
Grenada - Grenade	1990	12.9	13.8	5.0	8.7	-0.9	-1.1	0.2
	1995	8.3	10.8	5.6	4.5	-2.5	-0.6	-1.9
	2000	19.9	16.5	9.9	3.2	3.4	-0.2	3.6
	2006	43.7	26.8	3.4	23.6	16.9	6.9	9.9
Haiti - Haïti	1990	166.9	167.4	117.1	50.1	-0.5	0.0	-0.4
	1995	716.2	722.2	510.0	212.1	-6.0	-6.0	0.0
	2000	207.1	208.2	153.9	54.3	-1.1	-1.1	0.0
	2006	633.8	581.4	363.3	218.1	52.4	22.4	30.0
Jamaica - Jamaïque	1990	325.3	270.6	251.9	18.9	54.7	55.8	17.3
	1995	87.6	107.7	67.5	40.5	-20.1	-8.7	-11.5
	2000	130.2	10.0	-26.4	30.0	120.2	-19.9	140.1
	2006	8.7	36.7	-0.6	37.8	-28.0	-16.2	-11.8
Montserrat	1990	8.3	8.4	7.8	0.5	-0.1	0.0	-0.1
	1995	9.8	9.5	9.1	0.4	0.3	0.0	0.3
	2000	30.9	30.9	30.9	0.1	-0.1	0.0	-0.1
	2006	32.2	32.4	24.9	7.4	-0.2	0.0	-0.2
Netherlands Antilles - Antilles néerlandaises	1990	50.1	58.0	53.0	5.0	-7.9	-10.9	3.0
	1995	97.0	98.4	94.0	4.4	-1.4	0.0	-1.4
Saint Kitts and Nevis - Saint-Kitts-et-Nevis	1990	8.2	8.1	5.0	2.9	0.1	0.0	0.1
	1995	5.6	3.9	1.7	0.6	1.7	0.2	1.5
	2000	6.0	3.9	0.1	4.1	2.1	-1.3	3.3
	2006	4.2	5.2	3.6	3.2	-1.0	-1.8	0.8
Saint Lucia - Sainte-Lucie	1990	15.8	12.3	6.2	5.8	3.5	-0.4	3.9
	1995	52.8	48.2	12.7	34.6	4.6	0.1	4.5
	2000	13.5	11.0	7.1	4.4	2.5	0.0	2.5
	2006	19.0	18.5	2.4	14.2	0.6	0.1	0.5
Saint Vincent and the Grenadines - Saint-Vincent-et-les Grenadines	1990	15.4	15.4	5.2	9.7	0.0	0.0	0.0
	1995	48.2	47.6	6.3	40.7	0.6	0.4	0.2
	2000	9.7	6.2	3.8	1.1	3.5	0.0	3.5
	2006	9.4	4.7	2.3	3.0	4.7	0.0	4.7
Trinidad and Tobago - Trinité-et-Tobago	1990	80.8	17.8	6.1	11.7	63.0	34.8	28.2
	1995	95.1	24.9	-1.8	26.6	70.2	-35.1	105.4
	2000	-21.6	-1.5	4.4	-5.9	-20.1	-36.7	16.5
	2006	53.5	13.0	4.0	8.9	40.5	44.7	-4.1
Turks and Caicos Islands - Îles Turques et Caïques	1990	11.6	11.6	8.9	2.8	0.0	0.0	0.0
	1995	5.7	5.6	5.5	0.0	0.1	0.0	0.1
	2000	7.3	6.7	5.6	1.1	0.6	0.0	0.6
	2006	-0.6	-0.4	0.1	-0.5	-0.2	0.0	-0.2

For sources and notes, see end of table.

Pour les sources et les notes, se reporter à la fin du tableau.

7

7.6.1 Official financial flows from bilateral and multilateral sources to developing economies by country and geographical region

7.6.1 Flux financiers publics bilatéraux et multilatéraux à destination des économies en développement par pays et régions géographiques

Region, country or territory / Régions, pays ou territoires	Year / Année	Total official net (1) / Total secteur officiel net (1)	Total ODA Net / Total OA Net (2) APD totale nette / AP totale nette (2)			Total OOF Net (3) Flux AASP nets (3)		
			Total donors / Tous donneurs	of which: / dont :		Total donors / Tous donneurs	of which: / dont :	
				DAC bilateral donors / Donneurs bilatéraux du CAD	Multilateral donors / Donneurs multilatéraux		DAC bilateral donors / Donneurs bilatéraux du CAD	Multilateral donors / Donneurs multilatéraux
			Millions of dollars / Millions de dollars					
Central America - Amérique centrale	*1990*	*6 613.6*	*1 839.6*	*1 599.5*	*234.1*	*4 774.0*	*2 027.8*	*2 751.0*
	1995	*2 379.3*	*2 027.7*	*1 553.9*	*450.8*	*351.6*	*-834.9*	*1 187.7*
	2000	*1 730.0*	*1 440.1*	*1 002.4*	*421.5*	*289.9*	*-778.0*	*1 029.9*
	2006	*-6 065.1*	*2 273.0*	*1 617.9*	*644.7*	*-8 338.1*	*37.5*	*-8 416.6*
Belize	1990	38.5	30.3	18.8	11.3	8.1	4.1	4.1
	1995	23.4	18.2	8.8	6.3	5.2	-2.0	7.2
	2000	31.8	14.7	2.9	11.2	17.2	3.5	13.7
	2006	21.1	7.6	3.7	4.6	13.5	10.6	2.9
Costa Rica	1990	237.7	227.0	206.6	19.1	10.8	21.1	-10.3
	1995	79.6	29.7	16.6	0.1	49.9	-28.2	78.1
	2000	-37.9	11.3	17.2	-6.6	-49.2	-26.8	-22.3
	2006	-44.6	23.7	20.1	2.7	-68.3	4.3	-72.7
El Salvador	1990	308.3	347.3	312.0	34.3	-39.0	-0.9	-38.1
	1995	381.6	296.0	243.7	51.2	85.7	0.1	85.6
	2000	283.7	180.0	172.3	7.1	103.7	-13.1	117.2
	2006	144.1	157.3	150.6	6.1	-13.2	-0.7	-12.6
Guatemala	1990	221.5	201.4	149.5	50.5	20.1	6.2	13.9
	1995	206.0	208.4	161.4	45.1	-2.4	11.6	-14.0
	2000	321.5	263.5	230.3	32.7	58.0	7.5	51.4
	2006	692.7	487.2	445.1	39.6	205.5	-4.0	209.5
Honduras	1990	433.3	448.5	383.5	64.0	-15.2	-0.7	-14.6
	1995	394.0	402.4	232.9	168.1	-8.4	26.1	-33.9
	2000	396.8	449.0	310.6	133.8	-52.2	20.2	-71.7
	2006	536.9	587.4	384.7	204.0	-50.6	-39.6	-11.0
Mexico - Mexique	1990	5 024.2	156.3	144.7	11.5	4 868.0	2 034.9	2 837.9
	1995	407.8	384.1	365.1	19.0	23.7	-990.4	1 014.6
	2000	76.4	-55.5	-68.4	12.3	131.9	-751.7	842.6
	2006	-8 133.2	246.7	208.9	37.0	-8 379.9	94.9	-8 517.5
Nicaragua	1990	326.6	329.6	288.5	41.1	-2.9	-1.8	-1.1
	1995	823.0	649.1	492.1	155.9	173.9	165.1	8.8
	2000	553.0	561.2	325.9	234.9	-8.3	-6.2	-2.0
	2006	757.8	732.7	385.5	340.1	25.2	3.2	22.0
Panama	1990	23.5	99.3	96.0	2.4	-75.8	-35.0	-40.8
	1995	63.9	39.8	33.5	5.1	24.2	-17.2	41.3
	2000	104.7	16.0	11.7	-3.8	88.7	-11.5	101.1
	2006	-39.8	30.4	19.3	10.6	-70.2	-31.3	-37.3
South America - Amérique du Sud	*1990*	*5 246.1*	*2 030.9*	*1 569.5*	*460.0*	*3 215.2*	*1 608.0*	*1 613.8*
	1995	*3 590.5*	*2 457.0*	*1 910.0*	*544.9*	*1 133.5*	*864.1*	*271.4*
	2000	*6 902.9*	*1 853.6*	*1 562.0*	*275.8*	*5 049.3*	*-156.6*	*5 234.2*
	2006	*3 617.9*	*2 876.7*	*2 460.1*	*399.1*	*741.2*	*-1 494.9*	*2 207.3*
Argentina - Argentine	1990	903.8	168.7	166.2	2.6	735.1	411.9	323.2
	1995	2 529.4	142.6	110.3	32.2	2 386.9	719.6	1 667.1
	2000	677.4	52.8	43.5	1.8	624.6	-550.3	1 178.0
	2006	-842.9	114.1	81.0	33.8	-957.0	-119.7	-837.0
Bolivia - Bolivie	1990	576.2	545.4	364.7	180.7	30.8	10.4	20.4
	1995	712.4	711.5	518.0	193.2	0.9	-18.8	19.7
	2000	436.2	472.0	336.1	135.7	-35.8	-25.4	-10.4
	2006	498.6	580.7	569.7	6.3	-82.0	5.5	-87.5
Brazil - Brésil	1990	526.2	151.1	142.1	9.0	375.2	715.4	-334.5
	1995	-40.3	271.3	204.1	70.6	-311.6	-32.0	-278.6
	2000	4 098.6	232.3	222.5	8.2	3 866.3	440.5	3 435.4
	2006	2 043.9	82.4	74.8	6.4	1 961.5	-538.1	2 470.5
Chile - Chili	1990	787.2	103.5	83.3	20.2	683.7	207.9	475.8
	1995	-1 627.4	156.6	143.3	13.2	-1 783.9	-98.2	-1 685.8
	2000	-207.6	48.9	41.0	7.3	-256.5	-175.6	-80.8
	2006	122.8	83.0	64.3	17.8	39.8	33.5	6.3

For sources and notes, see end of table.   Pour les sources et les notes, se reporter à la fin du tableau.

7.6.1 Official financial flows from bilateral and multilateral sources to developing economies by country and geographical region

7.6.1 Flux financiers publics bilatéraux et multilatéraux à destination des économies en développement par pays et régions géographiques

Region, country or territory / Régions, pays ou territoires	Year / Année	Total official net (1) / Total secteur officiel net (1)	Total ODA Net / Total OA Net (2) APD totale nette / AP totale nette (2)			Total OOF Net (3) Flux AASP nets (3)		
			Total donors Tous donneurs	of which: / dont : DAC bilateral donors Donneurs bilatéraux du CAD	of which: / dont : Multilateral donors Donneurs multilatéraux	Total donors Tous donneurs	of which: / dont : DAC bilateral donors Donneurs bilatéraux du CAD	of which: / dont : Multilateral donors Donneurs multilatéraux
			Millions of dollars / Millions de dollars					
Colombia - Colombie	1990	-1.5	88.5	86.6	1.9	-90.0	-93.2	3.2
	1995	71.5	168.9	160.7	8.0	-97.4	131.3	-228.7
	2000	-24.3	186.5	178.5	7.4	-210.9	-276.7	66.0
	2006	2 236.4	988.0	917.1	69.7	1 248.4	-96.7	1 345.1
Ecuador - Équateur	1990	352.6	159.3	122.2	36.7	193.3	112.7	80.6
	1995	632.9	222.9	160.7	61.3	410.1	85.3	324.8
	2000	226.7	146.5	137.4	8.3	80.3	-16.0	108.7
	2006	177.3	188.8	170.5	17.6	-11.5	-6.9	-4.6
Falkland Islands (Malvinas) - Îles Falkland (Malvinas)	1990	1.8	1.8	1.3	..	0.0	0.0	..
	1995	1.7	1.7	0.1	1.6	0.0	0.0	0.0
Guyana	1990	221.5	168.3	35.3	132.5	53.2	72.0	-18.8
	1995	81.1	85.7	23.2	62.4	-4.6	11.3	-15.8
	2000	95.3	107.3	51.9	55.4	-11.9	-0.7	-11.2
	2006	177.8	172.9	46.6	126.3	4.9	0.0	4.9
Paraguay	1990	29.4	57.2	47.6	8.6	-27.8	1.6	-29.4
	1995	153.5	139.3	105.3	30.1	14.1	-20.1	34.2
	2000	202.0	81.6	72.9	8.2	120.5	8.3	112.2
	2006	87.3	56.1	62.1	-8.2	31.2	-4.9	36.1
Peru - Pérou	1990	398.3	397.1	350.4	46.7	1.2	-2.0	3.2
	1995	817.8	370.9	327.0	43.6	446.9	65.4	381.5
	2000	1 112.8	397.7	372.7	22.6	715.1	515.7	201.9
	2006	-6.9	467.9	374.9	87.0	-474.8	-638.7	163.9
Suriname	1990	64.3	61.1	51.2	10.0	3.1	-0.1	4.0
	1995	74.9	76.7	70.3	6.4	-1.8	0.0	-0.7
	2000	36.2	34.3	29.1	5.2	1.8	0.0	1.8
	2006	62.5	63.8	55.6	8.1	-1.3	-6.0	4.8
Uruguay	1990	86.6	52.4	41.7	10.7	34.2	1.1	33.1
	1995	52.6	65.7	57.5	8.1	-13.0	-2.6	-10.4
	2000	198.7	17.4	15.3	1.4	181.3	2.0	179.2
	2006	-548.2	20.8	10.8	9.6	-569.0	1.4	-570.4
Venezuela (Bolivarian Rep. of) - Venezuela (Rép. bolivarienne du)	1990	1 299.5	76.4	75.7	0.6	1 223.2	170.3	1 052.9
	1995	130.2	43.3	29.0	14.3	86.9	22.9	64.0
	2000	50.9	76.4	61.3	14.4	-25.5	-78.5	53.3
	2006	-390.7	58.3	32.9	24.7	-449.0	-124.3	-324.7
Developing economies: America unallocated - Économies en développement : Amérique, non ventilées	1990	649.5	510.7	352.8	157.9	138.8	-0.2	139.1
	1995	630.4	580.0	488.1	91.0	50.4	127.9	-77.6
	2000	1 154.7	1 117.5	1 002.7	114.8	37.2	1.5	35.7
	2006	874.4	884.0	677.2	196.6	-9.6	0.0	-9.6
Developing economies: Asia - Économies en développement : Asie	1990	24 239.3	17 828.2	10 544.6	4 600.1	6 411.1	3 075.4	3 481.1
	1995	24 178.8	17 377.6	11 754.6	5 193.1	6 801.2	5 104.2	1 555.2
	2000	13 538.1	14 996.1	10 322.4	4 254.0	-1 458.1	-3 507.3	2 717.7
	2006	40 371.9	31 542.3	21 533.9	7 275.2	8 829.6	2 774.1	5 408.9
Eastern Asia - Asie orientale	1990	2 879.4	2 177.9	1 553.3	605.2	701.6	662.3	39.3
	1995	6 909.4	3 764.0	2 688.1	1 044.0	3 145.4	1 766.2	1 275.8
	2000	1 467.9	2 018.3	1 433.9	562.9	-550.3	-2 140.4	1 639.1
	2006	2 580.3	1 502.6	1 329.3	81.5	1 077.7	-473.8	1 441.5
China - Chine	1990	3 294.5	2 030.4	1 465.5	570.1	1 264.1	835.9	428.2
	1995	7 041.6	3 470.6	2 476.6	952.5	3 571.0	1 839.6	1 627.9
	2000	1 176.4	1 727.5	1 256.2	456.0	-551.2	-2 141.3	1 639.1
	2006	2 332.0	1 245.5	1 173.7	12.0	1 086.5	-462.0	1 439.0
China, Hong Kong SAR - Chine (RAS de Hong Kong)	1990	31.4	38.2	19.4	18.7	-6.8	-6.8	0.0
	1995	2.3	17.7	11.5	6.2	-15.5	-15.5	0.0
China, Macao SAR - Chine (RAS de Macao)	1990	0.2	0.2	0.1	0.1	0.0	0.0	0.0
	1995	-4.0	-4.0	0.1	-4.1	0.0	0.0	0.0
China, Taiwan Province of - Province chinoise de Taiwan	1990	24.6	36.3	6.3	..	-11.7	-3.1	-8.6
	1995	10.1	0.2	11.0	..	9.9	9.9	..

For sources and notes, see end of table.

Pour les sources et les notes, se reporter à la fin du tableau.

7

7.6.1 Official financial flows from bilateral and multilateral sources to developing economies by country and geographical region

7.6.1 Flux financiers publics bilatéraux et multilatéraux à destination des économies en développement par pays et régions géographiques

Region, country or territory / Régions, pays ou territoires	Year / Année	Total official net (1) / Total secteur officiel net (1)	Total ODA Net / Total OA Net (2) APD totale nette / AP totale nette (2)			Total OOF Net (3) Flux AASP nets (3)		
			Total donors / Tous donneurs	of which: / dont :		Total donors / Tous donneurs	of which: / cont :	
				DAC bilateral donors / Donneurs bilatéraux du CAD	Multilateral donors / Donneurs multilatéraux		DAC bilateral donors / Donneurs bilatéraux du CAD	Multilateral donors / Donneurs multilatéraux
		Millions of dollars / Millions de dollars						
Dem. People's Rep. of Korea - Rép. populaire dém. de Corée	1990	6.9	7.7	0.9	6.9	-0.9	-0.9	0.0
	1995	17.0	13.5	1.5	11.9	3.5	3.5	0.0
	2000	74.2	73.3	26.9	46.4	0.9	0.9	0.0
	2006	50.3	54.5	28.9	23.3	-4.2	-4.2	0.0
Mongolia - Mongolie	1990	13.1	13.1	6.3	6.7	0.0	0.0	0.0
	1995	196.6	209.0	126.9	77.1	-12.4	-12.4	0.0
	2000	217.4	217.4	150.8	60.5	0.0	0.0	0.0
	2006	198.1	202.6	126.7	46.2	-4.6	-7.6	2.5
Republic of Korea - République de Corée	1990	-491.2	52.0	54.8	2.7	-543.2	-162.9	-380.3
	1995	-354.1	57.0	60.4	0.5	-411.1	-59.0	-352.1
Southern Asia - Asie méridionale	*1990*	*7 890.8*	*6 062.9*	*3 318.3*	*2 741.1*	*1 827.9*	*177.2*	*1 654.6*
	1995	*5 997.0*	*5 341.8*	*3 138.9*	*2 298.0*	*655.2*	*469.5*	*185.6*
	2000	*3 530.9*	*4 324.0*	*2 460.6*	*1 825.2*	*-793.1*	*-593.4*	*-130.9*
	2006	*12 099.2*	*9 312.5*	*5 599.6*	*3 462.5*	*2 786.7*	*384.8*	*2 073.1*
Afghanistan	1990	121.7	121.7	100.4	22.7	0.0	0.0	0.0
	1995	212.5	212.5	106.1	106.4	0.0	0.0	0.0
	2000	136.0	136.0	87.5	47.8	0.0	0.0	0.0
	2006	3 025.8	2 999.8	2 404.6	487.2	26.0	12.6	13.5
Bangladesh	1990	2 112.4	2 092.8	1 103.3	999.8	19.7	21.9	-2.2
	1995	1 272.8	1 281.5	727.4	563.2	-8.8	-3.3	-5.5
	2000	1 167.1	1 167.8	616.5	515.9	-0.7	-2.4	4.6
	2006	1 293.9	1 222.7	456.5	743.0	71.2	10.6	60.6
Bhutan - Bhoutan	1990	46.0	46.0	20.1	26.7	0.0	0.0	0.0
	1995	71.2	71.2	55.2	15.6	0.0	0.0	0.0
	2000	53.0	53.1	33.7	19.8	-0.1	-0.1	0.0
	2006	94.1	94.1	51.1	42.8	0.0	0.0	0.0
India - Inde	1990	2 900.2	1 398.9	751.8	644.6	1 501.2	255.5	1 248.3
	1995	1 769.6	1 729.0	1 060.8	695.1	40.6	41.4	-0.8
	2000	1 322.4	1 462.7	650.3	824.0	-140.3	20.7	-191.9
	2006	3 307.6	1 378.9	653.1	723.3	1 928.7	307.6	1 433.5
Iran (Islamic Rep. of) - Iran (Rép. islamique d')	1990	-96.1	104.8	34.8	35.7	-200.9	-133.9	-67.0
	1995	395.5	186.5	158.9	27.6	209.0	129.6	79.4
	2000	-582.5	129.9	112.8	17.0	-712.4	-668.8	44.4
	2006	465.5	121.0	70.8	44.2	344.5	61.5	115.2
Maldives	1990	24.9	20.9	11.6	9.9	4.1	4.1	0.0
	1995	59.1	57.8	30.4	21.3	1.3	1.3	0.0
	2000	16.2	19.2	13.3	7.1	-3.0	-1.8	-1.2
	2006	63.4	38.6	16.0	20.3	24.9	3.9	21.0
Nepal - Népal	1990	432.1	422.8	239.0	181.5	9.3	0.0	9.2
	1995	428.3	428.6	266.1	163.0	-0.3	0.7	-1.0
	2000	410.2	387.3	231.2	152.5	23.0	2.7	20.2
	2006	506.9	514.3	317.6	195.3	-7.4	0.9	-8.3
Pakistan	1990	1 631.1	1 126.6	653.5	492.3	504.5	31.2	474.7
	1995	1 241.8	820.9	360.1	525.5	421.0	299.9	121.1
	2000	755.7	692.4	475.1	216.4	63.3	81.1	-11.4
	2006	2 479.6	2 147.2	1 144.9	933.6	332.4	-25.2	383.4
Sri Lanka	1990	718.3	728.3	403.8	328.0	-10.0	-1.6	-8.5
	1995	546.2	553.8	374.0	180.2	-7.6	-0.1	-7.6
	2000	252.9	275.7	240.2	24.7	-22.8	-24.8	4.4
	2006	862.3	795.9	485.3	272.8	66.5	13.0	54.2
South-Eastern Asia - Asie du Sud-Est	*1990*	*7 777.3*	*4 783.1*	*4 085.8*	*677.7*	*2 994.1*	*1 561.3*	*1 456.8*
	1995	*7 567.2*	*5 012.2*	*4 099.6*	*909.7*	*2 555.0*	*2 021.7*	*488.8*
	2000	*4 317.8*	*5 669.0*	*4 741.6*	*904.6*	*-1 351.1*	*-1 137.7*	*334.6*
	2006	*3 648.7*	*5 087.4*	*3 252.8*	*1 652.6*	*-1 438.8*	*-1 057.5*	*-467.2*
Brunei Darussalam - Brunéi Darussalam	1990	-4.5	3.9	3.7	0.1	-8.4	-8.4	0.0
	1995	4.3	4.3	4.2	0.1	0.0	0.0	0.0

For sources and notes, see end of table.

Pour les sources et les notes, se reporter à la fin du tableau.

7.6.1 Official financial flows from bilateral and multilateral sources to developing economies by country and geographical region

7.6.1 Flux financiers publics bilatéraux et multilatéraux à destination des économies en développement par pays et régions géographiques

Region, country or territory / Régions, pays ou territoires	Year / Année	Total official net (1) / Total secteur officiel net (1)	Total CDA Net / Total OA Net (2) APD totale nette / AP totale nette (2)			Total OOF Net (3) Flux AASP nets (3)		
			Total conors / Tous donneurs	of which: / dont :		Total donors / Tous donneurs	of which: / dont :	
				DAC bilateral donors / Donneurs bilatéraux du CAD	Multilateral donors / Donneurs multilatéraux		DAC bilateral donors / Donneurs bilatéraux du CAD	Multilateral donors / Donneurs multilatéraux
			Millions of dollars / Millions de dollars					
Cambodia - Cambodge	1990	41.3	41.3	28.5	12.8	0.0	0.0	0.0
	1995	554.0	551.0	341.2	209.8	3.0	3.0	0.0
	2000	395.5	395.9	248.0	147.2	-0.4	-0.2	0.0
	2006	529.9	529.0	347.5	150.1	0.9	-0.1	1.0
Indonesia - Indonésie	1990	3 255.4	1 715.9	1 520.1	171.3	1 539.6	534.3	1 029.3
	1995	2 705.3	1 301.2	1 215.8	96.2	1 404.1	820.8	545.2
	2000	2 318.0	1 654.4	1 544.0	106.1	663.6	-6.7	721.0
	2006	1 505.2	1 404.5	688.4	657.0	100.7	248.0	-218.6
Lao People's dem. Rep. - Rép. dém. populaire lao	1990	149.1	149.1	51.2	96.9	0.0	0.0	0.0
	1995	307.0	306.9	170.0	136.8	0.1	0.1	0.0
	2000	281.3	281.6	194.9	85.9	-0.4	-0.3	0.2
	2006	412.5	364.2	187.6	124.1	48.3	9.8	38.6
Malaysia - Malaisie	1990	538.5	468.5	458.6	13.3	70.1	-6.3	76.4
	1995	399.9	108.1	106.9	7.3	291.8	412.8	-121.0
	2000	-117.6	45.4	43.3	3.3	-163.0	-80.2	-73.9
	2006	-233.7	240.3	230.2	8.9	-474.0	-323.0	-151.0
Myanmar	1990	184.0	160.8	83.1	77.7	23.2	23.6	-0.4
	1995	154.4	150.2	126.3	22.0	4.2	5.1	-0.9
	2000	125.8	105.6	68.1	36.6	20.2	1.3	0.0
	2006	91.0	146.6	92.0	41.4	-55.7	-55.7	0.0
Philippines	1990	2 176.9	1 270.6	1 102.1	167.3	906.3	411.7	494.6
	1995	675.3	902.1	764.5	128.8	-226.8	-169.5	-57.2
	2000	356.8	575.2	502.1	69.9	-218.4	-10.3	-198.1
	2006	-167.9	562.3	519.5	34.1	-730.2	-769.5	45.4
Singapore - Singapour	1990	152.1	-3.1	-3.2	0.1	155.2	193.2	-38.1
	1995	-49.0	16.7	13.9	2.8	-65.6	-65.6	0.0
Thailand - Thaïlande	1990	1 103.8	795.6	733.7	65.7	308.2	413.2	-104.9
	1995	1 765.7	837.0	807.2	35.1	928.7	821.9	106.9
	2000	-1 245.0	698.2	682.9	17.5	-1 943.2	-1 329.1	-159.7
	2006	-597.5	-215.6	-292.7	74.5	-381.9	-140.0	-225.2
Timor-Leste	1990	0.1	0.1	..	0.1	0.0	..	0.0
	1995	0.0	0.0	C.0	..	0.0	0.0	..
	2000	649.1	231.3	212.3	19.0	417.8	417.8	0.0
	2006	210.5	209.7	173.7	35.4	0.8	0.8	0.0
Viet Nam	1990	180.6	180.6	107.9	72.5	0.0	0.2	-0.1
	1995	1 050.4	834.8	549.7	270.9	215.6	193.2	15.8
	2000	1 553.9	1 681.4	1 246.2	419.1	-127.5	-129.9	45.1
	2006	1 898.6	1 846.4	1 306.5	527.2	52.2	-27.8	42.6
Western Asia - Asie occidentale	*1990*	*4 597.0*	*3 709.4*	*1 349.7*	*203.4*	*887.5*	*674.6*	*330.4*
	1995	*2 986.1*	*2 526.8*	*1 356.8*	*680.2*	*459.3*	*846.8*	*-381.4*
	2000	*3 587.8*	*2 352.1*	*1 255.0*	*834.5*	*1 235.7*	*355.2*	*883.0*
	2006	*18 553.8*	*12 337.6*	*10 259.9*	*1 752.0*	*6 216.2*	*3 930.6*	*2 163.5*
Bahrain - Bahreïn	1990	136.1	136.9	1.9	2.3	-0.8	-0.8	0.0
	1995	47.3	49.1	1.8	0.4	-1.8	-1.8	0.0
	2000	48.8	49.1	1.6	-0.1	-0.2	-0.2	0.0
Iraq	1990	700.0	63.1	-8.6	16.3	636.9	642.3	-5.4
	1995	322.3	332.8	238.9	81.7	-10.5	-10.5	0.0
	2000	99.6	99.6	84.1	15.4	0.0	0.0	0.0
	2006	7 993.0	8 661.3	8 487.8	17.9	-668.3	-668.3	0.0
Jordan - Jordanie	1990	1 080.0	886.0	435.0	25.0	194.1	126.1	75.5
	1995	1 031.8	539.1	392.1	144.1	492.7	410.0	82.7
	2000	552.2	552.5	385.3	168.0	-0.2	-21.4	21.2
	2006	566.5	579.6	361.8	156.5	-13.1	1.9	-15.0
Kuwait - Koweït	1990	5.7	5.7	2.2	3.5	0.0	0.0	0.0
	1995	19.6	3.1	2.1	1.0	16.5	16.5	0.0

For sources and notes, see end of table.

Pour les sources et les notes, se reporter à la fin du tableau.

7.6.1 Official financial flows from bilateral and multilateral sources to developing economies by country and geographical region

7.6.1 Flux financiers publics bilatéraux et multilatéraux à destination des économies en développement par pays et régions géographiques

Region, country or territory / Régions, pays ou territoires	Year / Année	Total official net (1) / Total secteur officiel net (1)	Total ODA Net / Total OA Net (2) APD totale nette / AP totale nette (2)			Total OOF Net (3) Flux AASP nets (3)		
			Total donors / Tous donneurs	of which: / dont :		Total donors / Tous donneurs	of which: / dont :	
				DAC bilateral donors / Donneurs bilatéraux du CAD	Multilateral donors / Donneurs multilatéraux		DAC bilateral donors / Donneurs bilatéraux du CAD	Multilateral donors / Donneurs multilatéraux
			Millions of dollars / Millions de dollars					
Lebanon - Liban	1990	229.6	252.1	64.9	39.0	-22.5	-13.6	-8.9
	1995	309.4	186.1	57.2	72.2	123.4	2.2	121.2
	2000	268.1	199.3	93.7	90.9	68.8	2.8	66.0
	2006	636.5	707.3	388.6	284.0	-70.8	-47.0	-23.8
Occupied Palestinian territory - Territoire palestinien occupé	1995	498.4	498.4	183.2	262.6	0.0	0.0	0.0
	2000	682.6	637.3	306.4	226.1	45.3	-0.1	45.4
	2006	1 449.1	1 448.8	754.4	671.6	0.3	0.3	0.0
Oman	1990	57.6	61.1	11.3	2.2	-3.5	6.0	-9.6
	1995	51.7	58.3	11.9	2.1	-6.6	-10.8	4.1
	2000	50.0	45.0	9.2	1.7	5.0	9.7	-4.7
	2006	373.0	34.8	-14.5	4.7	338.2	166.2	97.0
Qatar	1990	1.5	1.5	1.3	0.2	0.0	0.0	0.0
	1995	618.0	2.3	2.1	0.2	615.7	615.7	0.0
Saudi Arabia - Arabie saoudite	1990	14.0	14.6	12.8	1.7	-0.6	-0.6	0.0
	1995	6.4	16.9	14.5	1.9	-10.6	-10.6	0.0
	2000	48.0	21.9	18.0	2.1	26.1	26.5	0.0
	2006	4 740.3	24.9	11.2	2.8	4 715.4	4 645.6	17.0
Syrian Arab Republic - République arabe syrienne	1990	673.7	682.8	69.4	34.2	-9.1	0.5	-10.3
	1995	322.5	355.7	158.9	69.5	-33.2	-5.1	-21.9
	2000	485.8	157.9	97.3	38.1	327.9	342.1	-14.2
	2006	98.1	26.7	-11.4	64.2	71.4	-25.6	96.9
Turkey - Turquie	1990	1 292.3	1 202.3	587.9	-16.2	90.0	-88.5	289.1
	1995	-329.0	312.7	180.7	-12.7	-641.8	-74.2	-567.5
	2000	1 082.3	326.8	99.7	190.4	755.5	-4.1	761.6
	2006	2 414.2	569.9	147.2	401.4	1 844.2	-143.5	1 993.5
United Arab Emirates - Émirats arabes unis	1990	3.8	3.5	2.8	0.7	0.3	0.3	0.0
	1995	-77.6	5.4	4.8	0.4	-83.0	-83.0	0.0
Yemen - Yémen	1990	402.7	399.9	168.8	94.5	2.8	2.8	0.0
	1995	165.4	166.9	108.6	56.8	-1.6	-1.6	0.0
	2000	270.4	262.8	159.6	101.9	7.6	0.0	7.7
	2006	283.3	284.4	134.8	149.0	-1.1	0.9	-2.0
Developing economies: Asia unallocated - Économies en développement : Asie, non ventilées	1990	1 094.9	1 094.9	237.5	372.6	0.0	0.0	0.0
	1995	719.1	732.7	471.3	261.2	-13.7	0.0	-13.7
	2000	633.6	632.8	431.4	126.7	0.7	8.9	-8.2
	2006	3 489.9	3 302.1	1 092.3	326.5	187.8	-10.1	197.9
Developing economies: Oceania - Économies en développement : Océanie	*1990*	*1 495.0*	*1 372.5*	*1 214.7*	*154.6*	*122.5*	*60.0*	*62.5*
	1995	*1 974.0*	*1 865.7*	*1 710.9*	*150.3*	*108.3*	*119.6*	*-11.3*
	2000	*887.3*	*816.4*	*710.3*	*102.7*	*70.9*	*71.4*	*2.4*
	2006	*1 081.3*	*1 127.2*	*1 002.0*	*119.8*	*-45.9*	*-5.2*	*-37.0*
Cook Islands - Îles Cook	1990	11.4	12.1	10.1	2.0	-0.8	-0.8	0.0
	1995	13.0	13.0	10.4	2.6	0.0	0.0	0.0
	2000	4.2	4.3	3.4	0.9	-0.2	-0.2	0.0
	2006	24.1	32.3	31.0	1.3	-8.2	-8.2	0.0
Fiji - Fidji	1990	34.9	49.6	43.5	5.6	-14.7	-0.4	-14.3
	1995	41.9	44.4	39.1	4.0	-2.5	3.6	-6.0
	2000	22.8	29.1	28.7	0.2	-6.3	-0.1	-6.2
	2006	55.9	55.9	39.1	15.7	0.0	2.2	-2.2
French Polynesia - Polynésie française	1990	304.0	259.7	258.0	1.7	44.3	44.7	-0.4
	1995	434.3	450.9	444.4	6.5	-16.6	-16.1	-0.5
Kiribati	1990	20.2	20.2	17.7	2.5	0.0	0.0	0.0
	1995	15.3	15.3	11.4	3.9	0.0	0.0	0.0
	2000	17.9	17.9	14.8	3.1	0.0	0.0	0.0
	2006	-44.4	-44.9	-50.6	5.6	0.5	0.5	0.0
Marshall Islands - Îles Marshall	1995	38.9	38.9	32.1	6.7	0.0	0.0	0.0
	2000	57.2	57.2	47.1	10.1	0.0	0.0	0.0
	2006	55.0	55.0	55.0	0.0	0.0	0.0	0.0

For sources and notes, see end of table.

Pour les sources et les notes, se reporter à la fin du tableau.

7.6.1 Official financial flows from bilateral and multilateral sources to developing economies by country and geographical region

7.6.1 Flux financiers publics bilatéraux et multilatéraux à destination des économies en développement par pays et régions géographiques

Region, country or territory / Régions, pays ou territoires	Year / Année	Total official net (1) / Total secteur officiel net (1)	Total ODA Net / Total OA Net (2) APD totale nette / AP totale nette (2)			Total OOF Net (3) Flux AASP nets (3)		
			Total donors / Tous donneurs	of which: / dont :		Total donors / Tous donneurs	of which: / dont :	
				DAC bilateral donors / Donneurs bilatéraux du CAD	Multilateral donors / Donneurs multilatéraux		DAC bilateral donors / Donneurs bilatéraux du CAD	Multilateral donors / Donneurs multilatéraux
			Millions of dollars / Millions de dollars					
Micronesia (Federated States of) - Micronésie (États fédérés de)	1995	78.2	77.2	71.8	5.3	1.0	1.0	0.0
	2000	101.4	101.5	96.6	4.9	-0.1	0.0	0.0
	2006	108.7	108.5	105.9	2.5	0.2	0.5	0.0
Nauru	1990	0.2	0.2	0.2	..	0.0	0.0	..
	1995	2.7	2.7	2.2	..	0.0	0.0	..
	2000	4.0	4.0	3.9	0.1	0.0	0.0	0.0
	2006	18.1	17.4	17.3	0.1	0.7	0.7	0.0
New Caledonia - Nouvelle-Calédonie	1990	325.8	302.4	300.2	2.2	23.4	24.0	-0.6
	1995	548.8	451.2	442.3	8.9	97.6	98.7	-1.1
Niue - Nioué	1990	7.2	7.2	7.0	0.2	0.0	0.0	0.0
	1995	8.2	8.2	8.1	0.2	0.0	0.0	0.0
	2000	3.2	3.2	3.0	0.2	0.0	0.0	0.0
	2006	9.0	9.0	8.6	0.4	0.0	0.0	0.0
Northern Mariana Islands - Îles Mariannes du Nord	1990	63.1	63.1	61.9	1.2	0.0	0.0	0.0
	1995	18.8	-0.7	-0.2	-0.5	19.5	19.5	0.0
Palau - Palaos	1995	156.3	142.3	141.7	0.1	14.0	14.0	0.0
	2000	37.7	39.1	38.9	0.2	-1.5	-1.5	0.0
	2006	35.2	37.3	37.2	0.1	-2.1	-2.1	0.0
Papua New Guinea - Papouasie-Nouvelle-Guinée	1990	474.9	412.4	320.0	90.8	62.5	-15.3	77.8
	1995	365.3	370.3	300.5	68.9	-5.0	-1.3	-3.7
	2000	357.3	275.4	268.6	5.2	81.9	75.3	9.2
	2006	235.4	279.0	248.3	26.9	-43.6	-5.2	-34.9
Samoa	1990	47.4	47.6	27.7	19.5	-0.1	-0.1	0.0
	1995	43.2	43.2	31.3	12.1	0.0	0.0	0.0
	2000	27.8	27.4	18.1	9.2	0.4	0.3	0.1
	2006	47.6	47.1	38.3	8.7	0.5	0.5	0.0
Solomon Islands - Îles Salomon	1990	46.2	45.7	31.1	14.2	0.5	0.5	0.0
	1995	47.0	47.7	36.5	10.1	-0.7	-0.7	0.0
	2000	69.5	68.3	20.8	46.2	1.2	1.2	0.0
	2006	205.9	204.5	178.9	25.5	1.4	1.4	0.0
Tokelau - Tokélaou	1990	4.8	4.8	4.4	0.4	0.0	0.0	0.0
	1995	3.7	3.7	3.5	0.3	0.0	0.0	0.0
	2000	3.5	3.5	3.4	0.1	0.0	0.0	0.0
	2006	10.9	10.9	10.7	0.2	0.0	0.0	0.0
Tonga	1990	29.6	29.8	24.2	5.4	-0.2	-0.2	0.0
	1995	38.8	38.8	28.8	9.9	0.0	0.0	0.0
	2000	18.9	18.8	14.8	4.0	0.0	0.0	0.0
	2006	21.1	21.5	18.6	2.8	-0.4	-0.4	0.0
Tuvalu	1990	5.1	5.1	4.8	0.3	0.0	0.0	0.0
	1995	7.9	7.9	6.3	1.5	0.0	0.0	0.0
	2000	4.0	4.0	3.8	0.2	0.0	0.0	0.0
	2006	15.3	15.3	12.7	2.6	0.0	0.0	0.0
Vanuatu	1990	54.1	49.5	42.1	7.5	4.6	4.6	0.0
	1995	45.1	45.6	39.6	6.0	-0.5	-0.5	0.0
	2000	45.2	45.8	28.3	17.5	-0.7	0.0	-0.7
	2006	50.1	48.8	41.4	7.4	1.3	1.3	0.0
Wallis and Futuna Islands - Îles Wallis-et-Futuna	1990	3.9	0.9	0.0	0.9	3.0	3.0	0.0
	1995	0.5	1.0	0.1	0.8	-0.4	-0.4	0.0
	2000	53.3	52.1	52.1	0.0	1.2	1.2	0.0
	2006	100.6	102.4	102.0	0.4	-1.8	-1.8	0.0
Developing economies: Oceania unallocated - Économies en développement : Océanie, non ventilées	1990	62.4	62.4	61.9	0.1	0.0	0.0	0.0
	1995	65.9	64.0	61.1	3.0	1.9	1.9	0.0
	2000	59.5	64.7	64.0	0.7	-5.2	-5.0	0.0
	2006	132.8	127.3	107.8	19.5	5.5	5.5	0.0
Developing economies: Unspecified - Économies en développement : non spécifiées	1990	6 206.3	5 854.4	5 139.0	665.6	351.9	351.9	0.0
	1995	8 642.1	8 228.6	7 037.0	1 107.4	413.5	-31.7	0.0
	2000	9 234.2	8 967.6	8 061.6	1 025.3	266.6	266.6	0.0
	2006	16 379.7	15 936.1	13 679.7	1 495.2	443.6	136.3	25.0

For sources and notes, see next page.

Pour les sources et les notes, se reporter à la page suivante.

7.6.1 Official financial flows from bilateral and multilateral sources to developing economies by country and geographical region

7.6.1 Flux financiers publics bilatéraux et multilatéraux à destination des économies en développement par pays et régions géographiques

Sources:
- International Developement Statistics, Organisation for Economic Co-operation and Development (OECD)

Notes:

(1) Sum of "Total ODA/OA Net; total donors" and "Total OOF Net; total donors". It represents the total net disbursements by the official sector at large to the recipient country.

(2) Total ODA Net; total donors:
The Total Official Development Assistance (ODA) includes grants and loans to countries and territories on Part I of the "DAC List of Aid Recipients" which are:
undertaken by the official sector; with promotion of economic development and welfare as the main objective and at concessional financial terms (if a loan, have a grant element of at least 25 per cent).
Grants, loans and credits for military purposes are excluded.

"Total donors" is the sum of the three following donor types:
- DAC Bilateral donors: The Development Assistance Committee (DAC) is the Committee of the OECD which deals with development co-operation matters. It consists of 23 Member countries.
- Multilateral donors (i.e. African Development Bank, International Bank for Reconstruction and Development, International Monetary Fund, United Nations Development Programme).
- Other donors: the non-DAC Bilateral donors (i.e Hungary, Lithuania, Turkey).

(3) Total OOF Net; total donors:
The Other Official Flows (OOF) are transactions by the official sector whose main objective is other than development motivated, or, if development motivated, whose grant element is below the 25% threshold which would make them eligible to be recorded as ODA. The main classes of transactions included here are official export credits, official sector equity and portfolio investment, and debt reorganisation undertaken by the official sector at non-concessional terms (irrespective of the nature or the identity of the original creditor).

Total donors is the sum of the three following donor types:
- DAC Bilateral donors: The Development Assistance Committee (DAC) is the Committee of the OECD which deals with development co-operation matters. It consists of 23 Member countries.
- Multilateral donors (i.e. African Development Bank, International Bank for Reconstruction and Development, International Monetary Fund, United Nations Development Programme).
- Other donors: the non-DAC Bilateral donors (i.e Hungary, Lithuania, Turkey).

Sources :
- Statistiques sur le développement international, Organisation de coopération et de développement économique (OCDE)

Notes :

(1) Somme de "APD/AP totale nette ; tous donneurs" et de "Flux AASP nets ; tous donneurs". Cet agrégat correspond aux versements nets effectués par le secteur public dans son ensemble aux pays bénéficiaires considérés.

(2) AP totale nette ; tous donneurs :
Par aide publique (AP), on entend l'ensemble des apports de ressources qui sont fournis aux pays qui figurent à la Partie II de la "Liste des bénéficiaires de l'aide établie par le CAD" et qui répondent aux critères suivants :
a) être dispensés dans le but essentiel de favoriser le développement économique et l'amélioration du niveau de vie dans les pays en développement ; et
b) revêtir un caractère de faveur et comporter un élément de libéralité d'au moins 25 pour cent.

"Tous donneurs" est la somme des 3 types de donneurs suivants :
- Donneurs bilatéraux du CAD : Le Comité d'aide au développement (CAD) est la principale instance chargée, à l'OCDE, des questions relatives à la coopération avec les pays en développement. Le CAD regroupe 23 pays membres.
- Donneurs multilatéraux (i.e. Banque africaine de développement, Banque internationale pour la reconstruction et le développement, Fonds monétaire international, Programme des Nations Unies pour le développement).
- Autres donneurs : les donneurs bilatéraux non-membres du CAD (i.e. Hongrie, Lituanie, Turquie).

(3) Flux AASP nets ; tous donneurs :
Autres apports du secteur public (AASP) : il s'agit des opérations du secteur public dont le but essentiel est autre que le développement ou qui, tout en visant à favoriser le développement, sont assorties d'un élément de libéralité inférieur au seuil de 25 pour cent à partir duquel elles auraient pu être notifiées comme de l'APD. Les principales catégories d'opérations couvertes dans les AASP sont les crédits publics à l'exportation, les prises de participation et les investissements de portefeuille du secteur public et le réaménagement de la dette effectué par le secteur public aux conditions du marché (et ce, quelle que soit la nature ou l'identité du créancier initial).

Tous donneurs est la somme des 3 types de donneurs suivants :
- Donneurs bilatéraux du CAD : Le Comité d'aide au développement (CAD) est la principale instance chargée, à l'OCDE, des questions relatives à la coopération avec les pays en développement. Le CAD regroupe 23 pays membres.
- Donneurs multilatéraux (i.e. Banque africaine de développement, Banque internationale pour la reconstruction et le développement, Fonds monétaire international, Programme des Nations Unies pour le développement).
- Autres donneurs : les donneurs bilatéraux non-membres du CAD (i.e. Hongrie, Lituanie, Turquie).

7.6.2 Official financial flows from bilateral and multilateral sources to developing economies by economic grouping

7.6.2 Flux financiers publics bilatéraux et multilatéraux à destination des économies en développement par groupements économiques

Economic grouping / Groupements économiques	Year / Année	Total official net (1) / Total secteur officiel net (1)	Total ODA Net / Total OA Net (2) — APD totale nette / AP totale nette (2)			Total OOF Net (3) — Flux AASP nets (3)		
			Total donors / Tous donneurs	of which: / dont : DAC bilateral donors / Donneurs bilatéraux du CAD	of which: / dont : Multilateral donors / Donneurs multilatéraux	Total donors / Tous donneurs	of which: / dont : DAC bilateral donors / Donneurs bilatéraux du CAD	of which: / dont : Multilateral donors / Donneurs multilatéraux
					Millions of dollars / Millions de dollars			
DEVELOPING ECONOMIES - ÉCONOMIES EN DÉVELOPPEMENT	1990	73 489.6	55 322.9	36 861.8	12 578.6	18 166.7	8 065.1	10 128.2
	1995	67 967.7	55 639.4	38 535.0	16 404.6	12 328.3	8 847.3	2 897.7
	2000	48 237.8	45 101.5	33 313.0	11 134.0	3 136.4	-4 522.3	8 332.8
	2006	88 467.3	98 917.2	72 966.0	21 892.1	-10 449.9	-9 259.7	-2 183.4
Developing economies excluding China - Économies en développement sans la Chine	1990	61 262.7	44 867.2	28 765 0	10 759.1	16 395.4	6 871.7	9 550.3
	1995	49 848.1	41 577.1	27 178 3	13 825.8	8 270.9	6 878.7	1 357.6
	2000	34 945.4	31 559.0	21 649.4	9 238.8	3 386.5	-2 660.0	6 671.4
	2006	62 775.3	74 957.0	54 185 4	19 468.9	-12 181.7	-8 928.7	-3 854.4
Developing economies excluding LDCs - Économies en développement sans les PMA	1990	47 317.7	30 379.5	20 418.4	5 199.5	16 938.2	7 018.8	9 942.8
	1995	39 998.7	28 020.3	20 387 7	7 063.6	11 978.4	8 760.2	3 080.1
	2000	23 252.0	20 759.0	15 028.1	5 239.1	2 493.0	-5 140.1	8 313.3
	2006	37 934.1	48 159.4	38 227.5	9 089.6	-10 225.3	-8 438.1	-2 491.2
High-income developing countries - Pays en développement à revenu élevé	1990	9 294.9	2 013.8	1 485.5	173.5	7 281.1	2 926.6	4 356.2
	1995	3 583.0	2 506.0	2 092 3	274.5	1 077.0	123.7	953.7
	2000	1 352.5	593.6	323 7	147.3	758.9	-1 552.4	2 274.1
	2006	-3 769.8	1 480.9	904 6	483.1	-5 250.7	4 760.8	-10 181.7
Middle-income developing countries - Pays en développement à revenu intermédiaire	1990	16 257.8	14 916.3	9 432.6	1 156.5	1 341.6	319.2	1 016.2
	1995	15 556.6	10 060.1	7 686.5	1 918.0	5 496.5	5 008.1	497.3
	2000	10 966.9	8 105.0	6 117.9	1 676.1	2 861.9	-1 225.5	4 671.0
	2006	10 622.9	10 424.1	7 184.6	2 960.4	198.9	-4 709.1	4 744.4
Low-income developing countries - Pays en développement à revenu faible	1990	38 944.0	29 907.1	19 253.8	9 997.3	9 036.9	4 461.8	4 606.2
	1995	37 642.3	32 373.9	19 770.0	12 584.2	5 268.4	3 586.5	1 534.5
	2000	23 699.2	24 484.7	16 361.0	7 871.2	-785.4	-2 023.4	1 365.4
	2006	57 915.7	63 959.9	46 932.3	16 037.2	-6 044.2	-9 443.2	3 021.9
Heavily indebted poor countries - Pays pauvres très endettés	1990	17 597.7	16 180.0	10 250.7	5 569.4	1 417.8	885.7	535.2
	1995	18 432.3	18 176.2	10 077.0	8 058.0	256.1	615.4	-365.8
	2000	12 230.1	12 582.6	7 952.5	4 471.6	-352.4	-33.5	-309.0
	2006	27 969.9	30 246.7	19 337.8	10 481.8	-2 276.8	-2 002.5	-234.9
Landlocked developing countries - Pays en développement sans littoral	1990	7 157.4	6 978.2	4 176.7	2 635.9	179.3	84.9	94.4
	1995	11 176.4	10 628.4	5 283.6	5 299.6	548.0	159.3	400.1
	2000	7 970.4	7 624.2	4 831.6	2 654.1	346.2	27.3	334.6
	2006	15 520.0	16 112.7	10 116.3	5 473.7	-592.7	-444.4	-39.4
Small island developing States - Petits États insulaires en développement	1990	1 612.2	1 377.0	1 063.7	307.7	235.2	99.9	150.5
	1995	1 511.2	1 482.9	1 057.4	410.1	28.2	-65.3	93.5
	2000	1 773.4	1 196.3	933.3	235.6	577.1	414.8	165.0
	2006	1 458.2	1 443.4	1 106.1	329.6	14.8	104.0	-85.5
Least developed countries - Pays les moins avancés	*1990*	*17 239.5*	*16 518.1*	*9 812.1*	*6 129.8*	*721.4*	*688.9*	*35.6*
	1995	*16 890.9*	*17 027.4*	*9 267.2*	*7 714.6*	*-136.5*	*-41.9*	*-94.6*
	2000	*12 869.8*	*12 527.5*	*7 877.5*	*4 455.7*	*342.3*	*338.9*	*-2.9*
	2006	*27 173.1*	*28 043.0*	*17 131.5*	*10 391.2*	*-869.9*	*-952.7*	*75.8*
Africa and Haiti - Afrique et Haïti	1990	13 453.2	12 795.8	7 821.1	4 526.1	657.3	631.5	28.9
	1995	13 408.0	13 515.4	7 127.6	6 343.9	-107.4	-20.1	-87.3
	2000	9 147.5	9 270.1	5 898.1	3 220.9	-122.7	-79.6	-33.8
	2006	20 335.5	21 317.0	12 691.3	8 339.6	-981.5	-939.9	-48.5
Asia - Asie	1990	3 489.3	3 434.3	1 794.4	1 512.6	55.0	48.2	6.7
	1995	3 165.6	3 168.9	1 900.9	1 273.5	-3.3	4.0	-7.3
	2000	2 839.2	2 790.0	1 639.6	1 107.6	49.2	1.0	32.7
	2006	6 237.3	6 155.0	3 991.7	1 932.9	82.3	-21.1	103.3
Islands - Îles	1990	297.0	287.9	196.6	91.1	9.1	9.1	0.0
	1995	317.4	343.1	238.7	97.3	-25.8	-25.8	0.0
	2000	883.1	467.3	339.8	127.2	415.8	417.5	-1.8
	2006	600.3	571.0	448.5	118.7	29.3	8.3	21.0

For sources and notes, see end of table.

Pour les sources et les notes, se reporter à la fin du tableau.

7

7.6.2 Official financial flows from bilateral and multilateral sources to developing economies by economic grouping

7.6.2 Flux financiers publics bilatéraux et multilatéraux à destination des économies en développement par groupements économiques

Economic grouping / Groupements économiques	Year / Année	Total official net (1) / Total secteur officiel net (1)	Total ODA Net / Total OA Net (2) — APD totale nette / AP totale nette (2) — Total donors / Tous donneurs	of which: / dont : DAC bilateral donors / Donneurs bilatéraux du CAD	of which: / dont : Multilateral donors / Donneurs multilatéraux	Total OOF Net (3) / Flux AASP nets (3) — Total donors / Tous donneurs	of which: / cont : DAC bilateral donors / Donneurs bilatéraux du CAD	of which: / cont : Multilateral donors / Donneurs multilatéraux
			Millions of dollars / Millions de dollars					
Major petroleum exporters - *Principaux exportateurs de pétrole*	*1990*	*7 377.6*	*3 613.9*	*1 742.7*	*858.0*	*3 763.8*	*1 901.5*	*1 715.2*
	1995	*6 112.6*	*2 938.3*	*1 880.2*	*833.7*	*3 174.4*	*2 369.3*	*811.3*
	2000	*708.0*	*1 950.9*	*1 144.3*	*520.3*	*-1 242.8*	*-885.4*	*-247.3*
	2006	*17 632.1*	*23 634.2*	*21 626.6*	*1 614.2*	*-6 002.1*	*-4 730.4*	*-1 574.1*
Africa - Afrique	1990	3 750.2	1 882.6	1 238.2	617.6	1 867.6	1 075.5	645.7
	1995	3 379.1	1 465.9	985.7	489.6	1 913.2	1 657.7	255.6
	2000	31.9	963.3	458.8	327.4	-931.5	-463.4	-458.9
	2006	3 838.9	14 221.1	12 740.5	1 280.3	-10 382.2	-8 824.3	-1 564.8
America - Amérique	1990	1 733.0	253.5	204.1	48.9	1 479.5	317.8	1 161.7
	1995	858.3	291.0	187.8	102.3	567.2	73.1	494.1
	2000	256.0	221.4	203.0	16.7	34.7	-131.1	178.5
	2006	-159.9	260.1	207.4	51.2	-420.0	-86.5	-333.5
Asia - Asie	1990	1 894.5	1 477.8	300.4	191.5	416.7	508.2	-92.3
	1995	1 875.3	1 181.3	706.7	241.8	693.9	638.5	61.6
	2000	420.1	766.2	482.6	176.2	-346.1	-290.8	33.2
	2006	13 953.1	9 153.1	8 678.7	282.7	4 800.0	4 180.4	324.2
Major exporters of manufactured goods - *Principaux exportateurs d'articles manufacturés*	*1990*	*16 573.6*	*7 597.0*	*5 463.8*	*1 486.8*	*8 976.6*	*4 592.2*	*4 508.2*
	1995	*11 299.9*	*8 106.6*	*6 062.6*	*1 905.1*	*3 193.3*	*1 719.4*	*1 372.1*
	2000	*6 750.2*	*5 012.6*	*3 388.6*	*1 581.7*	*1 737.6*	*-3 855.4*	*6 055.2*
	2006	*965.4*	*4 110.4*	*2 714.6*	*1 297.5*	*-3 145.1*	*-1 973.6*	*-1 511.9*
America - Amérique	1990	5 550.5	307.3	286.8	20.5	5 243.2	2 750.3	2 503.4
	1995	367.6	655.5	569.2	89.6	-287.9	-1 022.4	736.0
	2000	4 175.0	176.8	154.1	20.5	3 998.2	-311.2	4 278.0
	2006	-6 089.4	329.1	283.7	43.4	-6 418.5	-443.2	-6 047.0
Asia - Asie	1990	11 023.1	7 289.7	5 177.0	1 466.3	3 733.4	1 841.9	2 004.7
	1995	10 932.3	7 451.2	5 493.5	1 815.5	3 481.2	2 741.8	636.1
	2000	2 575.3	4 835.8	3 234.5	1 561.2	-2 260.6	-3 544.3	1 777.2
	2006	7 054.7	3 781.4	2 430.9	1 254.2	3 273.4	-1 530.4	4 535.1
Emerging economies - *Économies émergentes*	*1990*	*8 967.7*	*2 326.0*	*2 137.1*	*171.6*	*6 641.7*	*3 802.1*	*2 850.1*
	1995	*3 860.1*	*2 344.5*	*2 149.2*	*224.3*	*1 515.5*	*784.4*	*732.7*
	2000	*4 395.0*	*1 419.7*	*1 337.4*	*73.0*	*2 975.3*	*-1 930.8*	*5 343.6*
	2006	*-7 647.5*	*1 018.8*	*741.3*	*265.4*	*-8 666.3*	*-1 631.1*	*-7 089.9*
America - Amérique	1990	7 639.8	976.7	886.8	89.9	6 663.1	3 368.0	3 305.7
	1995	2 087.4	1 325.5	1 149.8	178.6	761.9	-335.6	1 098.9
	2000	5 757.5	676.1	611.3	52.2	5 081.4	-521.4	5 577.1
	2006	-6 816.4	994.0	803.8	182.0	-7 810.4	-1 168.1	-6 713.8
Asia - Asie	1990	1 327.8	1 349.3	1 250.3	81.7	-21.5	434.1	-455.6
	1995	1 772.6	1 019.0	999.4	45.6	753.6	1 120.0	-366.3
	2000	-1 362.6	743.6	726.1	20.9	-2 106.2	-1 409.3	-233.6
	2006	-831.1	24.8	-62.5	83.4	-855.9	-463.0	-376.2
Newly industrialized economies - *Économies nouvellement industrialisées*	*1990*	*6 791.5*	*4 374.0*	*3 892.0*	*439.0*	*2 417.6*	*1 373.3*	*1 068.3*
	1995	*5 155.5*	*3 240.0*	*2 991.2*	*276.8*	*1 915.5*	*1 755.8*	*121.7*
	2000	*1 312.3*	*2 973.2*	*2 772.2*	*196.8*	*-1 660.9*	*-1 426.3*	*289.4*
	2006	*506.2*	*1 991.5*	*1 145.4*	*774.5*	*-1 485.3*	*-984.6*	*-549.4*
First tier - Première génération	1990	-283.1	123.4	77.4	21.5	-406.5	20.5	-427.0
	1995	-390.7	91.6	96.9	9.4	-482.3	-130.2	-352.1
Second tier - Deuxième génération	1990	7 074.7	4 250.6	3 814.6	417.6	2 824.1	1 352.8	1 495.3
	1995	5 546.2	3 148.4	2 894.3	267.4	2 397.8	1 886.0	473.8
	2000	1 312.3	2 973.2	2 772.2	196.8	-1 660.9	-1 426.3	289.4
	2006	506.2	1 991.5	1 145.4	774.5	-1 485.3	-984.6	-549.4
Developing economies: Africa - *Économies en développement : Afrique*	*1990*	*28 024.2*	*25 077.3*	*15 817.3*	*6 126.3*	*2 946.9*	*847.9*	*1 950.3*
	1995	*25 150.9*	*21 781.1*	*13 223.1*	*8 410.6*	*3 369.8*	*3 574.0*	*-203.6*
	2000	*14 215.2*	*15 489.4*	*10 372.6*	*4 817.0*	*-1 274.2*	*-333.3*	*-930.8*
	2006	*31 058.1*	*43 402.0*	*31 514.8*	*11 367.9*	*-12 343.9*	*-10 864.6*	*-1 487.7*

For sources and notes, see end of table.

Pour les sources et les notes, se reporter à la fin du tableau.

7.6.2 Official financial flows from bilateral and multilateral sources to developing economies by economic grouping

7.6.2 Flux financiers publics bilatéraux et multilatéraux à destination des économies en développement par groupements économiques

Economic grouping / Groupements économiques	Year / Année	Total official net (1) / Total secteur officiel net (1)	Total ODA Net / Total OA Net (2) APD totale nette / AP totale nette (2)			Total OOF Net (3) Flux AASP nets (3)		
			Total donors / Tous donneurs	of which: / dont :		Total donors / Tous donneurs	of which: / dont :	
				DAC bilateral donors / Donneurs bilatéraux du CAD	Multilateral donors / Donneurs multilatéraux		DAC bilateral donors / Donneurs bilatéraux du CAD	Multilateral donors / Donneurs multilatéraux
			Millions of dollars / Millions de dollars					
Northern Africa excluding Sudan - Afrique septentrionale sans le Soudan	1990	7 183.5	7 004.7	4 081.3	268.0	178.7	-952.3	982.5
	1995	6 054.2	2 877.2	2 373.6	401.4	3 177.0	2 713.7	463.9
	2000	1 809.2	2 169.7	1 647.9	400.2	-360.5	101.0	-461.0
	2006	-1 556.0	2 596.3	1 628.5	802.7	-4 152.3	-2 905.3	-1 246.9
Sub-Saharan Africa - Afrique subsaharienne	1990	19 921.4	17 169.7	10 895.6	5 805.2	2 751.7	1 794.4	957.1
	1995	18 076.0	17 917.5	10 027.0	7 845.4	158.5	829.4	-670.9
	2000	11 372 0	12 287.4	7 876.9	4 245.1	-915.4	-441.1	-464.6
	2006	30 130 8	38 340.4	27 836.4	10 191.8	-8 209.6	-7 958.5	-259.5
Sub-Saharan Africa excluding South Africa - Afrique subsaharienne sans l'Afrique du Sud	1990	19 921 4	17 169.7	10 895.6	5 805.2	2 751.7	1 794.4	957.1
	1995	17 363 3	17 531.4	9 708.5	7 780.8	-168.1	502.9	-670.9
	2000	10 779 9	11 800.1	7 523.4	4 113.4	-1 020.2	-346.8	-664.0
	2006	29 424.9	37 622.6	27 275.8	10 035.2	-8 197.7	-7 888.8	-315.9
Developing economies: America - Économies en développement : Amérique	**1990**	**13 524.8**	**5 190.4**	**4 146.3**	**1 032.0**	**8 334.4**	**3 730.0**	**4 634.3**
	1995	**8 022.0**	**6 386.5**	**4 809.4**	**1 543.2**	**1 635.6**	**81.2**	**1 557.5**
	2000	**10 363.1**	**4 831.9**	**3 846.2**	**935.1**	**5 531.2**	**-1 019.7**	**6 543.4**
	2006	**-423.7**	**6 909.7**	**5 235.7**	**1 634.0**	**-7 333.4**	**-1 300.3**	**-6 092.5**
Central America and Greater Carribean Islands excluding Puerto Rico - Amérique centrale et Grandes Antilles sans Porto Rico	1990	7 302.3	2 431.1	2 074.9	348.1	4 871.2	2 093.3	2 801.2
	1995	3 404.7	3 040.2	2 246.3	769.7	364.5	-868.7	1 234.4
	2000	2 187.8	1 758.4	1 205.3	530.0	429.3	-829.5	1 223.1
	2006	-5 155.0	3 022.4	2 050.4	959.5	-8 177.4	82.3	-8 290.4
Central America and Greater Carribean Islands excluding Mexico and Puerto Rico - Amérique centrale et Grandes Antilles sans le Mexique et Porto Rico	1990	2 278.0	2 274.8	1 930.2	336.6	3.2	58.4	-36.7
	1995	2 996.9	2 656.1	1 881.3	750.7	340.8	121.7	219.8
	2000	2 111.4	1 813.9	1 273.6	517.8	297.5	-77.9	380.5
	2006	2 978.2	2 775.7	1 841.5	922.5	202.5	-12.6	227.1
South America and Central America - Amérique du Sud et Amérique centrale	1990	11 859.7	3 870.5	3 168.9	694.1	7 989.2	3 635.8	4 364.7
	1995	5 969.8	4 484.7	3 463.9	995.7	1 485.1	29.2	1 459.0
	2000	8 632.9	3 293.7	2 564.4	697.2	5 339.2	-934.6	6 264.1
	2006	-2 447.2	5 149.7	4 078.0	1 043.8	-7 596.9	-1 457.4	-6 209.3
South America excluding Brazil - Amérique du Sud sans le Brésil	1990	4 719.9	1 879.9	1 427.4	451.0	2 840.0	892.6	1 948.2
	1995	3 630.8	2 185.7	1 705.9	474.3	1 445.1	896.1	550.0
	2000	2 804.3	1 621.3	1 339.6	267.5	1 183.0	-597.1	1 798.7
	2006	1 574.1	2 794.3	2 385.4	392.8	-1 220.3	-956.8	-263.2
Developing economies: Asia - Économies en développement : Asie	**1990**	**24 239.3**	**17 828.2**	**10 544.6**	**4 600.1**	**6 411.1**	**3 075.4**	**3 481.1**
	1995	**24 178.8**	**17 377.6**	**11 754.6**	**5 193.1**	**6 801.2**	**5 104.2**	**1 555.2**
	2000	**13 538.1**	**14 996.1**	**10 322.4**	**4 254.0**	**-1 458.1**	**-3 507.3**	**2 717.7**
	2006	**40 371.9**	**31 542.3**	**21 533.9**	**7 275.2**	**8 829.6**	**2 774.1**	**5 408.9**
Eastern and South-Eastern Asia excluding China - Asie orientale et Asie du Sud-Est sans la Chine	1990	7 362.2	4 930.6	4 173.7	712.8	2 431.6	1 387.7	1 067.9
	1995	7 435.1	5 305.7	4 311.0	1 001.3	2 129.4	1 948.2	136.6
	2000	4 609.4	5 959.7	4 919.3	1 011.5	-1 350.3	-1 136.8	334.6
	2006	3 897.0	5 344.6	3 408.4	1 722.2	-1 447.6	-1 069.4	-464.7
Southern Asia excluding India - Asie méridionale sans l'Inde	1990	4 990.6	4 664.0	2 566.5	2 096.5	326.6	-78.4	406.3
	1995	4 227.4	3 612.8	2 078.1	1 602.9	614.6	428.2	186.4
	2000	2 208.6	2 861.3	1 810.3	1 001.2	-652.8	-614.1	61.0
	2006	8 791.5	7 933.6	4 946.6	2 739.2	858.0	77.2	639.6

For sources and notes, see next page.

Pour les sources et les notes, se reporter à la page suivante.

7

Sources:
- International Developement Statistics, Organisation for Economic Co-operation and Development (OECD)

Notes:

- The groupings presented in this table do not include Unallocated/Unspecified recipient countries.

(1) Sum of "Total ODA/OA Net; total donors" and "Total OOF Net; total donors". It represents the total net disbursements by the official sector at large to the recipient country.

(2) Total ODA Net; total donors:
The Total Official Development Assistance (ODA) includes grants and loans to countries and territories on Part I of the "DAC List of Aid Recipients" which are:
undertaken by the official sector; with promotion of economic development and welfare as the main objective and at concessional financial terms (if a loan, have a grant element of at least 25 per cent).
Grants, loans and credits for military purposes are excluded.

"Total Donors" is the sum of the three following donor types:
- DAC Bilateral Donors: The Development Assistance Committee (DAC) is the Committee of the OECD which deals with development co-operation matters. It consists of 23 Member countries.
- Multilateral Donors (i.e. African Development Bank, International Bank for Reconstruction and Development, International Monetary Fund, United Nations Development Programme).
- Other Donors: the Non-DAC Bilateral Donors (i.e Hungary, Lithuania, Turkey).

(3) Total OOF Net; total donors:
The Other Official Flows (OOF) are transactions by the official sector whose main objective is other than development motivated, or, if development motivated, whose grant element is below the 25% threshold which would make them eligible to be recorded as ODA. The main classes of transactions included here are official export credits, official sector equity and ortfolio investment, and debt reorganisation undertaken by the official sector at non-concessional terms (irrespective of the nature or the identity of the original creditor).

Total Donors is the sum of the three following donor types:
- DAC Bilateral Donors: The Development Assistance Committee (DAC) is the Committee of the OECD which deals with development co-operation matters. It consists of 23 Member countries.
- Multilateral Donors (i.e. African Development Bank, International Bank for Reconstruction and Development, International Monetary Fund, United Nations Development Programme).
- Other Donors: the Non-DAC Bilateral Donors (i.e Hungary, Lithuania, Turkey).

Sources :
- Statistiques sur le développement international, Organisation de coopération et de développement économique (OCDE)

Notes :

- Les groupements présentés dans ce tableau n'incluent pas les pays bénéficiaires non-ventilé/non-spécifié.

(1) Somme de "APD/AP totale nette ; tous donneurs" et de "Flux AASP nets ; tous donneurs". Cet agrégat correspond aux versements nets effectués par le secteur public dans son ensemble aux pays bénéficiaires considérés.

(2) AP totale nette ; tous donneurs :
Par aide publique (AP), on entend l'ensemble des apports de ressources qui sont fournis aux pays qui figurent à la Partie II de la "Liste des bénéficiaires de l'aide établie par le CAD" et qui répondent aux critères suivants :
a) être dispensés dans le but essentiel de favoriser le développement économique et l'amélioration du niveau de vie dans les pays en développement ; et
b) revêtir un caractère de faveur et comporter un élément de libéralité d'au moins 25 pour cent.

"Tous Donneurs" est la somme des 3 types de donneurs suivants :
- Donneurs Bilatéraux du CAD : Le Comité d'aide au développement (CAD) est la principale instance chargée, à l'OCDE, des questions relatives à la coopération avec les pays en développement. Le CAD regroupe 23 pays membres.
- Donneurs Multilatéraux (i.e. Banque africaine de développppement, Banque internationale pour la reconstruction et le développement, Fonds monétaire international, Programme des Nations Unies pour le développement).
- Autres Donneurs : les Donneurs Bilatéraux non-membres du CAD (i.e. Hongrie, Lituanie, Turquie).

(3) Flux AASP nets ; tous donneurs :
Autres apports du secteur public (AASP) : il s'agit des opérations du secteur public dont le but essentiel est autre que le développement ou qui, tout en visant à favoriser le développement, sont assorties d'un élément de libéralité inférieur au seuil de 25 pour cent à partir duquel elles auraient pu être notifiées comme de l'APD. Les principales catégories d'opérations couvertes dans les AASP sont les crédits publics à l'exportation, les prises de participation et les investissements de portefeuille du secteur public et le réaménagement de la dette effectué par le secteur public aux conditions du marché (et ce, quelle que soit la nature ou l'identité du créancier initial).

Tous Donneurs est la somme des 3 types de donneurs suivants :
- Donneurs Bilatéraux du CAD : Le Comité d'aide au développement (CAD) est la principale instance chargée, à l'OCDE, des questions relatives à la coopération avec les pays en développement. Le CAD regroupe 23 pays membres.
- Donneurs Multilatéraux (i.e. Banque africaine de développppement, Banque internationale pour la reconstruction et le développement, Fonds monétaire international, Programme des Nations Unies pour le développement).
- Autres Donneurs : les Donneurs Bilatéraux non-membres du CAD (i.e. Hongrie, Lituanie, Turquie).

	Public and publicly guaranteed debt (1) / Dette publique et garantie par l'état (1)										Private non-guaranteed debt (4)
		Official creditors (2) / Créanciers publics (2)						Private creditors (3) / Créanciers (3)			Dette privée non garantie (4)
	Total creditors / Total créanciers	Total	Bilateral / Bilatéraux				Multilateral / Multilatéraux	Total	Bonds / Obligations	Commercial banks / Banques commerciales	
			Total	DAC / CAD	OPEC / OPEP	Other / Autres					
	Millions of dollars / Millions de dollars										
1990											
Debt outstanding (5)	905 658	505 210	308 920	209 326	18 380	81 214	196 290	400 448	97 364	196 392	56 129
Disbursments (6)	79 625	45 284	19 141	16 306	572	2 263	26 143	34 340	3 862	13 507	16 053
Debt service (7)	95 232	39 018	17 759	13 423	1 123	3 213	21 259	56 214	8 389	29 113	10 264
Principal repayments	54 704	21 827	10 562	7 544	871	2 147	11 265	32 876	4 367	15 145	6 069
Interest payments	40 529	17 191	7 197	5 879	253	1 066	9 994	23 337	4 022	13 969	4 195
Net transfers on debt (8)	-15 608	6 266	1 382	2 883	-551	-950	4 884	-21 874	-4 527	-15 607	5 789
1995											
Dette totale (5)	1 125 823	684 064	414 238	307 450	13 897	92 891	269 826	441 759	213 046	128 888	208 335
Décaissements (6)	120 668	60 484	32 124	26 182	535	5 407	28 360	60 184	22 001	21 916	53 384
Service de la dette (7)	134 428	66 484	34 696	26 209	944	7 543	31 788	67 944	24 241	22 619	37 275
Remboursement du principal	81 578	41 088	22 140	15 501	735	5 905	18 948	40 490	10 039	15 272	26 211
Paiement des intérêts	52 850	25 396	12 555	10 708	209	1 638	12 840	27 454	14 202	7 347	11 064
Transfers nets (8)	-13 760	-6 000	-2 572	-27	-409	-2 136	-3 428	-7 760	-2 240	-703	16 110
2000											
Debt outstanding (5)	1 141 257	660 317	353 538	253 639	14 580	85 318	306 779	480 941	294 233	121 872	446 380
Disbursments (6)	124 020	48 626	17 251	14 748	457	2 046	31 375	75 393	49 098	17 881	84 510
Debt service (7)	165 333	67 080	32 057	24 779	777	6 501	35 024	98 253	53 720	29 101	122 995
Principal repayments	107 633	43 175	22 273	16 819	593	4 861	20 903	64 457	31 577	20 953	94 358
Interest payments	57 700	23 905	9 784	7 960	184	1 640	14 121	33 795	22 143	8 149	28 637
Net transfers on debt (8)	-41 313	-18 454	-14 806	-10 031	-320	-4 454	-3 648	-22 859	-4 623	-11 221	-38 485
2002											
Dette totale (5)	1 183 991	667 185	338 664	246 121	14 365	78 178	328 521	516 808	319 272	141 662	415 688
Décaissements (6)	103 743	42 326	12 745	11 517	381	847	29 581	61 416	35 947	20 422	85 082
Service de la dette (7)	152 362	65 515	27 627	20 825	728	6 074	37 888	86 847	41 377	33 519	118 959
Remboursement du principal	105 096	45 642	20 226	14 996	575	4 656	25 416	59 454	23 549	26 007	97 972
Paiement des intérêts	47 266	19 872	7 401	5 829	153	1 418	12 472	27 393	17 828	7 512	20 988
Transfers nets (8)	-48 619	-23 188	-14 882	-9 308	-346	-5 227	-8 307	-25 431	-5 430	-13 097	-33 878
2003											
Debt outstanding (5)	1 240 807	699 176	357 198	286 390	13 664	57 144	341 977	541 633	345 052	145 617	416 920
Disbursments (6)	113 363	44 671	10 728	9 500	373	856	33 943	68 692	39 670	24 831	94 979
Debt service (7)	169 148	76 308	30 167	25 184	720	4 263	46 142	92 840	46 080	35 499	120 359
Principal repayments	120 683	56 728	21 880	18 329	571	2 981	34 848	63 955	26 201	28 660	99 211
Interest payments	48 465	19 580	8 286	6 855	149	1 282	11 294	28 885	19 879	6 838	21 149
Net transfers on debt (8)	-55 785	-31 637	-19 438	-15 684	-347	-3 407	-12 199	-24 148	-6 410	-10 668	-25 380
2004											
Dette totale (5)	1 268 393	704 921	355 875	287 713	13 334	54 827	349 046	563 474	361 760	153 703	425 176
Décaissements (6)	125 446	41 540	12 030	8 882	746	2 402	29 510	83 906	50 599	28 609	114 448
Service de la dette (7)	165 863	69 661	29 919	25 174	1 140	3 605	39 742	96 202	55 080	32 640	128 964
Remboursement du principal	115 938	51 693	21 923	18 694	1 000	2 229	29 769	64 245	32 572	24 945	109 553
Paiement des intérêts	49 925	17 969	7 996	6 480	140	1 376	9 973	31 956	22 507	7 695	19 411
Transfers nets (8)	-40 416	-28 121	-17 889	-16 292	-394	-1 203	-10 232	-12 295	-4 481	-4 031	-14 517
2005											
Debt outstanding (5)	1 166 240	636 887	294 449	241 154	13 435	39 860	342 438	529 353	331 092	156 222	444 415
Disbursments (6)	125 149	40 542	10 563	7 951	665	1 946	29 979	84 607	48 212	32 353	146 401
Debt service (7)	164 857	67 134	34 178	30 218	822	3 139	32 956	97 723	52 555	36 022	130 920
Principal repayments	113 002	47 046	23 593	20 717	694	2 183	23 452	65 956	29 240	28 970	112 812
Interest payments	51 855	20 088	10 585	9 501	128	956	9 503	31 767	23 315	7 053	18 108
Net transfers on debt (8)	-39 708	-26 592	-23 616	-22 267	-156	-1 192	-2 976	-13 116	-4 344	-3 669	15 481
2006											
Dette totale (5)	1 095 928	581 261	267 734	209 482	13 794	44 458	313 527	514 667	321 371	155 982	529 199
Décaissements (6)	119 997	53 300	11 944	6 778	1 045	4 121	41 356	66 697	40 680	21 468	193 431
Service de la dette (7)	209 513	80 045	36 439	32 982	765	2 692	43 607	129 468	87 342	32 101	142 709
Remboursement du principal	158 509	63 937	30 641	28 248	630	1 763	33 297	94 572	61 458	24 457	116 810
Paiement des intérêts	51 004	16 108	5 798	4 735	134	929	10 310	34 896	25 884	7 644	25 900
Transfers nets (8)	-89 516	-26 745	-24 494	-26 204	281	1 430	-2 251	-62 771	-46 662	-10 633	50 722

For sources and notes, see end of table 7.7.G.   Pour les sources et les notes, se reporter à la fin du tableau 7.7.G.

	Public and publicly guaranteed debt (1) / Dette publique et garantie par l'état (1)										Private non-guaranteed debt (4)
	Total creditors / Total créanciers	Official creditors (2) / Créanciers publics (2)						Private creditors (3) / Créanciers (3)			Dette privée non garantie (4)
		Total	Bilateral / Bilatéraux				Multilateral / Multilatéraux	Total	Bonds / Obligations	Commercial banks / Banques commerciales	
			Total	DAC / CAD	OPEC / OPEP	Other / Autres					
1990											
Debt outstanding (5)	228 691	157 999	107 383	77 559	11 464	18 360	50 616	70 692	1 721	24 622	6 694
Disbursments (6)	20 809	12 158	5 502	4 701	204	597	6 656	8 651	0	1 032	719
Debt service (7)	21 957	9 982	5 725	4 755	294	676	4 257	11 975	231	3 782	1 078
Principal repayments	14 038	5 402	3 013	2 521	210	283	2 389	8 636	108	2 517	643
Interest payments	7 919	4 580	2 712	2 234	84	393	1 868	3 339	123	1 265	435
Net transfers on debt (8)	-1 148	2 176	-223	-54	-90	-78	2 399	-3 324	-231	-2 750	-359
1995											
Dette totale (5)	268 778	206 964	133 600	106 612	8 502	18 487	73 364	61 814	5 319	22 067	12 550
Décaissements (6)	18 200	10 250	3 232	2 936	140	156	7 018	7 950	1 129	2 156	881
Service de la dette (7)	20 323	11 736	5 524	4 783	318	422	6 212	8 587	667	2 753	1 910
Remboursement du principal	12 033	6 480	2 707	2 162	246	299	3 773	5 553	318	1 728	1 372
Paiement des intérêts	8 290	5 256	2 817	2 621	72	123	2 440	3 034	348	1 025	538
Transfers nets (8)	-2 123	-1 487	-2 292	-1 847	-178	-266	805	-637	463	-597	-1 029
2000											
Debt outstanding (5)	237 709	197 243	124 127	78 852	9 710	35 565	73 115	40 467	10 630	15 341	14 610
Disbursments (6)	11 601	6 533	1 723	1 310	255	158	4 810	5 067	765	2 516	3 284
Debt service (7)	20 248	11 379	6 236	4 418	339	1 479	5 143	8 869	1 555	4 154	2 092
Principal repayments	13 801	6 996	3 718	2 453	255	1 011	3 278	6 805	881	3 423	1 589
Interest payments	6 446	4 383	2 518	1 965	84	468	1 865	2 064	674	731	503
Net transfers on debt (8)	-8 647	-4 846	-4 513	-3 109	-83	-1 321	-333	-3 802	-789	-1 638	1 192
2002											
Dette totale (5)	242 953	199 962	120 384	77 920	9 780	32 684	79 577	42 993	13 974	15 354	13 719
Décaissements (6)	13 333	7 155	1 164	764	249	151	5 991	6 179	3 122	1 796	2 568
Service de la dette (7)	18 441	11 480	5 819	5 033	353	433	5 661	6 961	1 731	2 808	4 361
Remboursement du principal	12 589	7 300	3 511	2 952	275	284	3 790	5 288	972	2 344	3 938
Paiement des intérêts	5 852	4 179	2 308	2 081	78	149	1 871	1 673	759	464	423
Transfers nets (8)	-5 108	-4 325	-4 655	-4 269	-104	-282	330	-782	1 391	-1 012	-1 793
2003											
Debt outstanding (5)	263 502	217 298	128 724	108 225	9 043	11 456	88 574	46 205	15 571	17 238	13 721
Disbursments (6)	14 222	7 804	1 253	887	187	179	6 551	6 418	2 498	2 404	2 933
Debt service (7)	20 532	12 861	7 133	6 363	335	434	5 728	7 672	1 632	3 261	2 209
Principal repayments	14 520	8 491	4 422	3 876	258	288	4 070	6 028	815	2 925	1 922
Interest payments	6 013	4 369	2 711	2 487	77	147	1 658	1 643	817	337	287
Net transfers on debt (8)	-6 311	-5 056	-5 879	-5 476	-148	-255	823	-1 254	867	-857	723
2004											
Dette totale (5)	268 421	221 487	125 855	106 762	8 906	10 187	95 632	46 936	13 715	21 093	15 804
Décaissements (6)	15 736	9 286	2 207	1 194	577	436	7 079	6 450	1 559	3 441	2 542
Service de la dette (7)	20 307	13 672	7 732	6 011	799	922	5 940	6 635	1 539	2 636	2 053
Remboursement du principal	15 067	10 024	5 738	4 279	722	737	4 286	5 044	688	2 359	1 672
Paiement des intérêts	5 240	3 648	1 994	1 731	78	185	1 654	1 592	851	277	381
Transfers nets (8)	-4 571	-4 386	-5 525	-4 817	-222	-486	1 139	-185	21	805	489
2005											
Debt outstanding (5)	237 593	191 311	99 340	81 009	8 882	9 449	91 972	46 281	11 968	23 877	16 051
Disbursments (6)	18 226	9 262	1 749	914	380	456	7 512	8 964	1 250	6 876	4 616
Debt service (7)	28 957	20 648	14 815	13 426	477	913	5 833	8 309	971	5 009	2 042
Principal repayments	19 356	12 844	8 534	7 365	408	761	4 309	6 512	178	4 445	1 425
Interest payments	9 602	7 805	6 281	6 060	69	152	1 524	1 797	793	564	617
Net transfers on debt (8)	-10 732	-11 386	-13 066	-12 512	-97	-457	1 680	655	279	1 868	2 574
2006											
Dette totale (5)	178 285	136 761	74 538	56 036	8 895	9 607	62 223	41 523	12 003	20 502	14 782
Décaissements (6)	17 140	13 578	2 137	855	417	865	11 441	3 562	1 876	1 156	4 175
Service de la dette (7)	36 902	25 808	18 463	17 364	495	604	7 345	11 094	2 914	5 725	4 299
Remboursement du principal	31 573	22 725	16 864	15 963	419	481	5 861	8 848	2 043	4 805	3 758
Paiement des intérêts	5 329	3 083	1 599	1 401	76	122	1 484	2 245	871	920	542
Transfers nets (8)	-19 762	-12 230	-16 326	-16 508	-79	261	4 096	-7 532	-1 038	-4 569	-124

For sources and notes, see end of table 7.7.G.

Pour les sources et les notes, se reporter à la fin du tableau 7.7.G.

	Total creditors Total créanciers	Public and publicly guaranteed debt (1) Dette publique et garantie par l'état (1)									Private non-guaranteed debt (4) Dette privée non garantie (4)
		Official creditors (2) / Créanciers publics (2)						Private creditors (3) / Créanciers (3)			
		Total	Bilateral / Bilatéraux				Multilateral Multilatéraux	Total	Bonds Obligations	Commercial banks Banques commerciales	
			Total	DAC CAD	OPEC OPEP	Other Autres					
	Millions of dollars / Millions de dollars										
1990											
Debt outstanding (5)	327 848	121 469	61 499	48 108	1 742	11 648	59 970	206 378	75 976	101 883	25 018
Disbursments (6)	23 033	13 183	4 198	3 245	211	742	8 986	9 850	1 938	4 803	4 698
Debt service (7)	32 124	11 950	3 075	2 368	182	524	8 875	20 174	4 406	11 917	4 476
Principal repayments	16 255	6 453	1 702	1 215	133	353	4 751	9 803	2 008	5 219	2 215
Interest payments	15 869	5 498	1 373	1 153	49	171	4 124	10 371	2 398	6 698	2 261
Net transfers on debt (8)	-9 091	1 233	1 123	876	29	218	110	-10 324	-2 468	-7 113	222
1995											
Dette totale (5)	374 206	160 181	87 407	76 752	1 327	9 328	72 775	214 025	165 484	35 374	87 394
Décaissements (6)	46 564	23 720	13 699	13 405	95	199	10 021	22 844	13 694	7 417	27 530
Service de la dette (7)	50 630	23 555	10 329	9 624	286	419	13 226	27 075	17 128	5 963	18 560
Remboursement du principal	27 859	14 628	6 290	5 777	230	283	8 338	13 231	5 839	4 333	12 724
Paiement des intérêts	22 771	8 927	4 039	3 847	56	136	4 888	13 844	11 289	1 630	5 836
Transfers nets (8)	-4 066	166	3 370	3 781	-191	-220	-3 205	-4 231	-3 434	1 454	8 970
2000											
Debt outstanding (5)	395 954	141 797	47 429	36 112	913	10 404	94 367	254 158	213 421	32 272	242 045
Disbursments (6)	58 953	16 539	2 907	2 257	39	611	13 632	42 414	34 644	6 987	58 065
Debt service (7)	81 764	25 510	9 259	8 221	122	916	16 251	56 254	43 609	10 227	76 138
Principal repayments	52 258	16 927	7 041	6 473	81	487	9 886	35 331	26 697	7 023	58 061
Interest payments	29 506	8 583	2 218	1 748	41	429	6 365	20 923	16 912	3 204	18 077
Net transfers on debt (8)	-22 810	-8 970	-6 352	-5 964	-82	-305	-2 619	-13 840	-8 965	-3 240	-18 073
2002											
Dette totale (5)	424 819	143 611	41 607	32 842	601	8 164	102 004	281 208	220 401	55 310	226 554
Décaissements (6)	45 220	15 723	4 168	3 958	28	182	11 555	29 497	16 273	12 667	38 156
Service de la dette (7)	67 590	22 390	7 013	5 429	98	1 487	15 377	45 201	25 386	17 297	59 883
Remboursement du principal	45 479	15 278	5 384	4 276	78	1 029	9 895	30 201	13 937	14 028	45 946
Paiement des intérêts	22 112	7 111	1 629	1 152	20	457	5 482	15 000	11 449	3 269	13 937
Transfers nets (8)	-22 370	-6 666	-2 845	-1 470	-70	-1 305	-3 822	-15 704	-9 113	-4 631	-21 727
2003											
Debt outstanding (5)	450 855	148 470	41 004	32 688	549	7 767	107 465	302 385	239 171	58 222	224 248
Disbursments (6)	60 353	19 206	1 850	1 679	49	123	17 356	41 147	26 660	13 443	41 547
Debt service (7)	73 350	26 611	6 154	4 890	125	1 139	20 457	46 738	30 966	13 987	56 457
Principal repayments	50 889	19 950	4 745	3 889	106	750	15 205	30 939	18 436	10 904	42 753
Interest payments	22 461	6 661	1 409	1 001	18	390	5 252	15 800	12 530	3 083	13 704
Net transfers on debt (8)	-12 997	-7 405	-4 304	-3 211	-75	-1 017	-3 102	-5 591	-4 307	-544	-14 910
2004											
Dette totale (5)	461 222	144 245	37 504	29 869	434	7 200	106 741	316 977	250 273	61 825	206 568
Décaissements (6)	54 399	12 572	1 988	1 729	35	224	10 583	41 827	24 790	16 141	48 746
Service de la dette (7)	68 998	22 211	5 672	4 775	67	831	16 538	46 788	30 242	15 452	72 055
Remboursement du principal	46 393	16 536	4 420	3 904	54	463	12 116	29 857	16 673	12 295	60 313
Paiement des intérêts	22 606	5 675	1 252	871	13	368	4 423	16 931	13 569	3 157	11 742
Transfers nets (8)	-14 600	-9 639	-3 684	-3 046	-31	-607	-5 955	-4 961	-5 452	690	-23 308
2005											
Debt outstanding (5)	419 480	134 415	30 340	23 886	478	5 976	104 075	285 065	217 288	63 339	208 183
Disbursments (6)	55 619	12 923	2 354	1 941	100	314	10 568	42 697	27 561	14 509	48 747
Debt service (7)	68 074	21 919	6 551	5 569	63	919	15 368	46 155	31 484	13 738	59 588
Principal repayments	43 662	16 330	5 441	4 840	51	550	10 888	27 333	16 220	10 366	49 772
Interest payments	24 412	5 589	1 110	728	12	370	4 480	18 823	15 263	3 372	9 816
Net transfers on debt (8)	-12 455	-8 996	-4 197	-3 627	37	-606	-4 800	-3 459	-3 922	772	-10 841
2006											
Dette totale (5)	399 101	123 037	26 903	20 055	762	6 087	96 134	276 064	204 475	68 536	230 494
Décaissements (6)	50 016	16 984	1 984	1 191	371	422	15 000	33 032	19 725	12 797	81 277
Service de la dette (7)	103 831	30 031	6 097	5 405	36	656	23 933	73 801	55 949	16 533	72 827
Remboursement du principal	79 081	24 068	5 118	4 757	27	334	18 949	55 013	40 971	12 880	57 216
Paiement des intérêts	24 751	5 963	979	648	9	322	4 984	18 788	14 978	3 652	15 611
Transfers nets (8)	-53 815	-13 047	-4 114	-4 214	335	-234	-8 933	-40 768	-36 224	-3 736	8 450

For sources and notes, see end of table 7.7.G.

Pour les sources et les notes, se reporter à la fin du tableau 7.7.G.

7

	Public and publicly guaranteed debt (1) Dette publique et garantie par l'état (1)										Private non-guaranteed debt (4)
	Total creditors Total créanciers	Official creditors (2) / Créanciers publics (2)						Private creditors (3) / Créanciers (3)			Dette privée non garantie (4)
		Total	Bilateral / Bilatéraux				Multilateral Multilatéraux	Total	Bonds Obligations	Commercial banks Banques commerciales	
			Total	DAC CAD	OPEC OPEP	Other Autres					
	Millions of dollars / Millions de dollars										
1990											
Debt outstanding (5)	347 034	224 149	139 592	83 247	5 164	51 181	84 557	122 885	19 628	69 557	23 384
Disbursments (6)	35 458	19 665	9 382	8 304	157	921	10 282	15 793	1 923	7 651	10 279
Debt service (7)	40 785	16 923	8 913	6 256	646	2 010	8 010	23 862	3 749	13 239	4 411
Principal repayments	24 160	9 874	5 822	3 783	527	1 511	4 053	14 285	2 251	7 271	2 989
Interest payments	16 626	7 049	3 091	2 473	119	499	3 958	9 577	1 498	5 968	1 422
Net transfers on debt (8)	-5 327	2 742	469	2 048	-490	-1 089	2 272	-8 069	-1 826	-5 588	5 868
1995											
Dette totale (5)	480 634	314 951	192 660	123 545	4 058	65 057	122 291	165 683	42 243	71 290	107 564
Décaissements (6)	55 722	26 350	15 124	9 775	300	5 049	11 226	29 372	7 178	12 329	24 916
Service de la dette (7)	63 135	30 996	18 782	11 743	338	6 701	12 214	32 139	6 412	13 830	16 458
Remboursement du principal	41 442	19 860	13 103	7 523	257	5 323	6 757	21 582	3 850	9 147	11 802
Paiement des intérêts	21 693	11 136	5 679	4 220	81	1 378	5 457	10 557	2 562	4 683	4 656
Transfers nets (8)	-7 413	-4 646	-3 658	-1 968	-38	-1 652	-988	-2 767	766	-1 501	8 459
2000											
Debt outstanding (5)	505 637	319 385	181 357	138 112	3 946	39 299	138 027	186 253	70 182	74 204	188 661
Disbursments (6)	53 210	25 311	12 475	11 048	160	1 267	12 836	27 898	13 688	8 364	23 126
Debt service (7)	63 116	30 011	16 493	12 079	315	4 098	13 519	33 105	8 557	14 708	44 642
Principal repayments	41 432	19 130	11 464	7 849	257	3 357	7 667	22 301	3 999	10 497	34 618
Interest payments	21 685	10 881	5 029	4 230	58	741	5 852	10 804	4 558	4 210	10 024
Net transfers on debt (8)	-9 907	-4 700	-4 018	-1 031	-156	-2 831	-682	-5 207	5 132	-6 343	-21 516
2002											
Dette totale (5)	514 231	321 716	176 080	134 842	3 974	37 264	145 636	192 515	84 897	70 911	174 565
Décaissements (6)	45 098	19 384	7 387	6 781	105	502	11 996	25 714	16 552	5 933	44 358
Service de la dette (7)	66 160	31 487	14 737	10 309	277	4 151	16 750	34 673	14 260	13 403	54 574
Remboursement du principal	46 913	22 956	11 292	7 731	221	3 340	11 664	23 957	8 640	9 628	47 966
Paiement des intérêts	19 247	8 531	3 444	2 578	55	811	5 086	10 716	5 620	3 775	6 608
Transfers nets (8)	-21 062	-12 103	-7 349	-3 529	-172	-3 649	-4 754	-8 959	2 292	-7 470	-10 216
2003											
Debt outstanding (5)	524 424	331 479	186 852	144 934	4 062	37 855	144 627	192 945	90 311	70 063	178 197
Disbursments (6)	38 716	17 603	7 611	6 924	137	551	9 992	21 113	10 512	8 970	50 499
Debt service (7)	75 064	36 661	16 803	13 859	259	2 685	19 858	38 403	13 482	18 224	61 573
Principal repayments	55 127	28 162	12 656	10 509	206	1 941	15 506	26 965	6 950	14 810	54 441
Interest payments	19 937	8 499	4 146	3 350	53	744	4 352	11 438	6 532	3 415	7 131
Net transfers on debt (8)	-36 348	-19 058	-9 191	-6 935	-123	-2 133	-9 867	-17 290	-2 969	-9 255	-11 074
2004											
Dette totale (5)	536 786	337 307	191 946	150 583	3 986	37 377	145 361	199 479	97 772	70 707	202 255
Décaissements (6)	55 257	19 633	7 831	5 955	133	1 743	11 801	35 624	24 249	9 021	63 160
Service de la dette (7)	76 356	33 603	16 429	14 310	273	1 847	17 174	42 752	23 299	14 526	54 608
Remboursement du principal	54 327	25 005	11 699	10 450	223	1 026	13 306	29 322	15 212	10 268	47 360
Paiement des intérêts	22 029	8 599	4 730	3 860	49	821	3 868	13 430	8 087	4 258	7 247
Transfers nets (8)	-21 099	-13 971	-8 598	-8 354	-140	-104	-5 373	-7 128	950	-5 505	8 552
2005											
Debt outstanding (5)	507 348	309 393	164 299	135 856	4 068	24 374	145 094	197 955	101 836	68 954	219 781
Disbursments (6)	51 220	18 274	6 451	5 093	186	1 172	11 823	32 946	19 400	10 967	93 038
Debt service (7)	67 645	24 412	12 746	11 165	281	1 300	11 666	43 233	20 101	17 253	69 115
Principal repayments	49 851	17 763	9 568	8 466	234	868	8 195	32 088	12 843	14 139	61 466
Interest payments	17 794	6 649	3 178	2 699	47	433	3 471	11 145	7 258	3 114	7 649
Net transfers on debt (8)	-16 425	-6 138	-6 295	-6 072	-95	-128	157	-10 287	-700	-6 286	23 923
2006											
Dette totale (5)	516 724	319 689	165 835	133 014	4 130	28 690	153 855	197 034	104 894	66 899	283 629
Décaissements (6)	52 729	22 631	7 808	4 731	258	2 819	14 823	30 099	19 079	7 512	107 979
Service de la dette (7)	68 597	24 034	11 834	10 174	233	1 427	12 200	44 563	28 479	9 833	65 456
Remboursement du principal	47 721	17 020	8 627	7 499	183	944	8 394	30 701	18 444	6 762	55 730
Paiement des intérêts	20 876	7 014	3 207	2 675	49	484	3 807	13 862	10 035	3 071	9 726
Transfers nets (8)	-15 868	-1 404	-4 026	-5 443	25	1 391	2 622	-14 464	-9 400	-2 321	42 524

For sources and notes, see end of table 7.7.G.

Pour les sources et les notes, se reporter à la fin du tableau 7.7.G.

	Total creditors / Total créanciers	Public and publicly guaranteed debt (1) / Dette publique et garantie par l'état (1)									Private non-guaranteed debt (4) / Dette privée non garantie (4)
		Official creditors (2) / Créanciers publics (2)						Private creditors (3) / Créanciers (3)			
		Total	Bilateral / Bilatéraux				Multilateral / Multilatéraux	Total	Bonds / Obligations	Commercial banks / Banques commerciales	
			Total	DAC CAD	OPEC OPEP	Other Autres					
	Millions of dollars / Millions de dollars										
1990											
Debt outstanding (5)	2 085	1 593	447	412	10	25	1 146	493	39	330	1 033
Disbursments (6)	325	279	59	57	0	2	219	46	0	21	358
Debt service (7)	366	163	47	44	0	3	116	203	3	175	299
Principal repayments	251	99	26	25	0	0	73	152	0	137	222
Interest payments	115	65	21	19	0	2	44	50	3	38	77
Net transfers on debt (8)	-42	115	12	13	0	0	103	-157	-3	-155	59
1995											
Dette totale (5)	2 205	1 967	571	541	11	19	1 396	237	0	157	828
Décaissements (6)	182	164	69	67	0	2	95	18	0	13	57
Service de la dette (7)	340	196	61	59	1	1	136	143	35	73	347
Remboursement du principal	243	120	40	39	1	1	80	124	32	63	313
Paiement des intérêts	96	77	21	20	0	0	56	19	2	9	34
Transfers nets (8)	-158	-33	8	8	-1	2	-41	-125	-35	-59	-290
2000											
Debt outstanding (5)	1 957	1 893	624	564	10	49	1 269	64	0	54	1 064
Disbursments (6)	256	243	146	134	2	10	97	13	0	13	35
Debt service (7)	205	181	69	60	1	8	112	25	0	13	123
Principal repayments	142	122	50	43	1	6	72	20	0	10	89
Interest payments	63	59	19	17	0	2	40	5	0	3	33
Net transfers on debt (8)	51	62	77	74	1	2	-15	-11	0	0	-88
2002											
Debt outstanding (5)	1988	1896	593	517	10	66	1304	92	0	87	851
Disbursments (6)	91	65	26	14	0	12	39	27	0	27	0
Debt service (7)	170	158	59	54	1	4	100	12	0	10	142
Principal repayments	116	107	40	37	1	2	68	8	0	7	122
Interest payments	55	51	19	18	0	1	32	4	0	4	20
Net transfers on debt (8)	-79	-94	-33	-40	-1	8	-61	15	0	16	-142
2003											
Dette totale (5)	2 026	1 928	618	542	9	66	1 310	98	0	94	754
Décaissements (6)	72	58	13	11	0	3	45	15	0	15	0
Service de la dette (7)	202	175	77	73	1	4	98	26	0	26	120
Remboursement du principal	147	124	57	54	1	2	67	23	0	23	95
Paiement des intérêts	55	51	20	18	0	2	31	4	0	4	25
Transfers nets (8)	-129	-117	-64	-62	-1	-2	-53	-12	0	-12	-120
2004											
Debt outstanding (5)	1 964	1 882	571	499	9	63	1 312	82	0	78	549
Disbursments (6)	55	50	3	3	0	0	47	5	0	5	0
Debt service (7)	201	175	85	79	1	6	90	26	0	26	249
Principal repayments	151	128	66	61	1	4	62	23	0	23	208
Interest payments	51	47	19	17	0	2	28	3	0	3	41
Net transfers on debt (8)	-146	-125	-82	-75	-1	-6	-43	-21	0	-21	-249
2005											
Dette totale (5)	1 820	1 768	471	403	7	60	1 297	52	0	51	399
Décaissements (6)	85	83	8	3	0	5	75	1	0	1	0
Service de la dette (7)	180	154	66	59	1	6	89	26	0	23	175
Remboursement du principal	133	109	50	45	1	4	59	23	0	21	150
Paiement des intérêts	47	45	16	14	0	2	29	2	0	2	25
Transfers nets (8)	-96	-71	-58	-56	-1	-1	-13	-25	0	-22	-175
2006											
Debt outstanding (5)	1 819	1 773	458	377	7	74	1 315	46	..	45	293
Disbursments (6)	111	107	15	0	0	15	92	4	..	4	0
Debt service (7)	183	172	44	39	1	5	128	11	..	10	127
Principal repayments	134	125	32	28	1	3	93	9	..	9	106
Interest payments	49	48	13	11	0	1	35	1	..	1	21
Net transfers on debt (8)	-71	-65	-29	-39	-1	11	-36	-6	..	-7	-127

For sources and notes, see end of table 7.7.G.

Pour les sources et les notes, se reporter à la fin du tableau 7.7.G.

7

7.7.F   External long-term debt by lending source
Developing economies:
Major petroleum exporters

7.7.F   Dette extérieure à long terme par catégories de prêt
Économies en développement :
Principaux exportateurs de pétrole

	Total creditors / Total créanciers	Public and publicly guaranted debt (1) / Dette publique et garantie par l'état (1)									Private non-guaranteed debt (4) / Dette privée non garantie (4)
		Official creditors (2) / Créanciers publics (2)						Private creditors (3) / Créanciers (3)			
		Total	Bilateral / Bilatéraux				Multilateral / Multilatéraux	Total	Bonds Obligations	Commercial banks Banques commerciales	
			Total	DAC CAD	OPEC OPEP	Other Autres					
					Millions of dollars / Millions de dollars						
1990											
Debt outstanding (5)	142 599	62 158	47 731	25 912	4 225	17 594	14 427	80 442	21 399	22 992	4 973
Disbursments (6)	13 140	4 957	2 081	1 638	47	396	2 875	8 183	599	463	30
Debt service (7)	20 283	5 865	4 214	2 560	90	1 564	1 650	14 418	586	6 666	698
Principal repayments	12 655	3 676	2 715	1 458	71	1 186	961	8 978	321	3 189	257
Interest payments	7 628	2 188	1 499	1 102	19	378	689	5 440	264	3 477	441
Net transfers on debt (8)	-7 143	-908	-2 133	-922	-42	-1 168	1 225	-6 235	14	-6 203	-668
1995											
Dette totale (5)	169 947	96 670	74 373	40 753	4 422	29 197	22 297	73 278	29 095	11 728	6 253
Décaissements (6)	9 219	4 715	1 700	1 435	181	85	3 015	4 505	349	1 396	605
Service de la dette (7)	17 942	8 848	6 097	1 571	79	4 447	2 752	9 094	2 958	1 341	1 259
Remboursement du principal	10 932	5 906	4 294	613	52	3 628	1 612	5 026	1 105	734	930
Paiement des intérêts	7 010	2 942	1 803	957	27	819	1 140	4 068	1 853	607	329
Transfers nets (8)	-8 722	-4 134	-4 396	-136	102	-4 362	263	-4 589	-2 609	55	-654
2000											
Debt outstanding (5)	148 499	97 775	76 111	26 631	4 688	44 792	21 664	50 725	23 319	14 057	11 240
Disbursments (6)	8 452	3 142	1 291	687	161	443	1 850	5 310	814	2 447	514
Debt service (7)	18 096	9 150	6 014	2 193	198	3 623	3 135	8 946	2 867	2 863	3 783
Principal repayments	12 367	6 200	4 357	1 207	137	3 013	1 843	6 167	1 241	2 240	2 843
Interest payments	5 729	2 950	1 658	987	61	610	1 292	2 779	1 627	622	940
Net transfers on debt (8)	-9 644	-6 008	-4 723	-1 507	-37	-3 180	-1 285	-3 636	-2 053	-415	-3 269
2002											
Dette totale (5)	139 318	92 494	70 634	25 356	5 074	40 204	21 859	46 824	21 224	13 378	11 113
Décaissements (6)	7 336	2 233	719	448	63	208	1 515	5 103	212	3 087	2 257
Service de la dette (7)	16 859	7 061	3 919	2 506	193	1 220	3 142	9 799	3 315	3 862	3 097
Remboursement du principal	11 998	4 816	2 756	1 621	136	1 000	2 059	7 182	1 855	3 105	2 458
Paiement des intérêts	4 862	2 245	1 162	885	57	221	1 083	2 617	1 460	757	638
Transfers nets (8)	-9 523	-4 827	-3 200	-2 058	-130	-1 013	-1 627	-4 696	-3 104	-775	-839
2003											
Debt outstanding (5)	146 784	97 513	74 778	51 485	5 061	18 233	22 734	49 272	22 341	14 907	11 897
Disbursments (6)	12 470	2 755	769	491	78	201	1 986	9 715	3 763	4 406	3 086
Debt service (7)	18 916	7 390	4 188	3 124	202	862	3 202	11 526	4 578	4 099	2 846
Principal repayments	14 019	5 176	3 004	2 149	146	709	2 173	8 843	3 074	3 272	2 162
Interest payments	4 897	2 214	1 184	975	56	153	1 030	2 683	1 504	827	683
Net transfers on debt (8)	-6 446	-4 635	-3 419	-2 634	-124	-661	-1 216	-1 811	-815	307	241
2004											
Dette totale (5)	152 083	98 318	75 956	52 072	5 182	18 702	22 362	53 765	24 537	16 582	12 664
Décaissements (6)	13 371	3 294	1 614	843	482	290	1 680	10 077	4 000	3 334	4 492
Service de la dette (7)	18 934	8 936	4 844	3 463	384	998	4 091	9 998	3 628	3 673	4 590
Remboursement du principal	13 991	6 769	3 612	2 475	331	805	3 158	7 222	1 901	3 036	3 823
Paiement des intérêts	4 943	2 167	1 233	987	52	193	934	2 776	1 727	637	768
Transfers nets (8)	-5 563	-5 642	-3 230	-2 620	98	-708	-2 412	78	372	-339	-98
2005											
Debt outstanding (5)	129 059	70 541	50 312	35 996	4 976	9 340	20 229	58 518	30 161	17 302	12 443
Disbursments (6)	16 356	2 911	1 107	411	114	582	1 804	13 445	6 793	5 013	3 658
Debt service (7)	25 917	16 112	12 171	10 889	305	977	3 941	9 805	3 139	4 030	4 627
Principal repayments	16 125	9 726	6 608	5 584	265	759	3 118	6 400	796	3 373	3 958
Interest payments	9 792	6 386	5 563	5 306	39	218	822	3 406	2 343	657	669
Net transfers on debt (8)	-9 561	-13 200	-11 064	-10 479	-190	-395	-2 137	3 640	3 654	983	-969
2006											
Dette totale (5)	97 212	46 516	27 219	12 122	4 875	10 222	19 296	50 697	23 911	16 136	14 753
Décaissements (6)	8 436	4 563	1 792	466	102	1 224	2 771	3 873	0	2 591	2 846
Service de la dette (7)	37 819	21 023	16 010	15 206	214	590	5 013	16 796	8 912	5 100	3 121
Remboursement du principal	32 312	19 265	15 027	14 470	169	388	4 239	13 047	6 474	4 234	2 078
Paiement des intérêts	5 507	1 758	984	736	45	202	774	3 749	2 438	866	1 043
Transfers nets (8)	-29 383	-16 460	-14 218	-14 740	-112	634	-2 242	-12 923	-8 912	-2 509	-275

For sources and notes, see end of table 7.7.G.   Pour les sources et les notes, se reporter à la fin du tableau 7.7.G.

7.7.G External long-term debt by lending source
Developing economies:
Major exporters of manufactured goods

7.7.G Dette extérieure à long terme par catégories de prêt
Économies en développement :
Principaux exportateurs d'articles manufacturés

	Total creditors / Total créanciers	Public and publicly guaranteed debt (1) / Dette publique et garantie par l'état (1)									Private non-guaranteed debt (4) / Dette privée non garantie (4)
		Official creditors (2) / Créanciers publics (2)						Private creditors (3) / Créanciers (3)			
		Total	Bilateral / Bilatéraux				Multilateral / Multilatéraux	Total	Bonds / Obligations	Commercial banks / Banques commerciales	
			Total	DAC CAD	OPEC OPEP	Other Autres					
1990											
Debt outstanding (5)	367 190	160 745	85 743	68 748	1 337	15 659	75 002	206 445	61 108	109 215	25 390
Disbursments (6)	38 238	18 060	7 572	6 729	48	795	10 488	20 178	3 098	10 415	8 160
Debt service (7)	41 702	15 988	6 242	5 212	326	704	9 746	25 714	5 239	14 045	4 775
Principal repayments	22 594	8 843	3 592	3 066	260	266	5 251	13 751	2 693	6 794	2 929
Interest payments	19 109	7 145	2 650	2 146	66	438	4 495	11 963	2 546	7 251	1 846
Net transfers on debt (8)	-3 464	2 072	1 331	1 518	-278	91	742	-5 536	-2 141	-3 631	3 386
1995											
Dette totale (5)	478 889	217 556	120 903	100 742	469	19 691	96 653	261 334	139 790	78 016	118 975
Décaissements (6)	72 494	31 808	21 527	16 665	6	4 856	10 280	40 686	14 992	16 389	35 207
Service de la dette (7)	71 469	27 896	14 737	12 432	157	2 148	13 159	43 573	18 111	14 140	22 781
Remboursement du principal	43 658	17 413	9 583	7 916	120	1 547	7 830	26 244	8 303	9 620	16 107
Paiement des intérêts	27 812	10 483	5 154	4 515	37	601	5 329	17 329	9 808	4 520	6 674
Transfers nets (8)	1 024	3 912	6 790	4 234	-151	2 707	-2 878	-2 887	-3 118	2 248	12 426
2000											
Debt outstanding (5)	496 907	217 224	104 374	90 394	655	13 325	112 850	279 683	168 151	75 641	304 139
Disbursments (6)	72 114	25 348	10 241	9 176	88	977	15 107	46 765	29 320	12 534	66 003
Debt service (7)	93 081	33 294	15 740	13 990	166	1 584	17 554	59 788	33 635	16 713	93 763
Principal repayments	63 154	23 129	11 876	10 558	130	1 188	11 253	40 025	21 107	11 628	73 551
Interest payments	29 927	10 165	3 863	3 432	36	396	6 301	19 763	12 529	5 085	20 213
Net transfers on debt (8)	-20 968	-7 945	-5 498	-4 814	-78	-607	-2 447	-13 022	-4 316	-4 179	-27 760
2002											
Dette totale (5)	512 092	210 967	93 325	84 870	375	8 080	117 642	301 125	170 929	99 962	282 252
Décaissements (6)	57 466	19 958	7 967	7 787	53	127	11 991	37 509	19 971	15 203	71 078
Service de la dette (7)	91 363	32 912	15 150	11 567	98	3 484	17 763	58 450	28 787	22 531	94 236
Remboursement du principal	63 985	24 823	12 347	9 123	82	3 142	12 476	39 162	16 192	16 993	77 674
Paiement des intérêts	27 377	8 089	2 803	2 444	16	343	5 286	19 288	12 595	5 539	16 562
Transfers nets (8)	-33 896	-12 955	-7 183	-3 780	-46	-3 358	-5 772	-20 942	-8 815	-7 328	-23 158
2003											
Debt outstanding (5)	519 265	207 430	94 632	86 406	365	7 861	112 798	311 836	182 751	103 482	281 631
Disbursments (6)	58 633	15 713	5 571	5 361	51	159	10 142	42 920	24 349	17 479	76 898
Debt service (7)	99 680	38 335	16 062	14 245	84	1 733	22 272	61 345	30 771	24 203	93 893
Principal repayments	72 077	30 900	13 101	11 649	69	1 383	17 798	41 177	17 129	18 957	77 059
Interest payments	27 603	7 435	2 961	2 596	15	350	4 474	20 168	13 642	5 246	16 834
Net transfers on debt (8)	-41 047	-22 622	-10 492	-8 884	-33	-1 574	-12 130	-18 425	-6 422	-6 724	-16 995
2004											
Dette totale (5)	524 747	207 593	97 860	83 789	318	13 752	109 734	317 153	185 516	109 279	290 091
Décaissements (6)	70 122	16 533	6 257	5 005	39	1 213	10 276	53 589	31 400	21 253	89 462
Service de la dette (7)	98 744	31 566	12 943	11 913	97	933	18 623	67 178	40 587	23 025	96 159
Remboursement du principal	69 241	24 937	10 174	9 536	85	553	14 764	44 303	24 885	16 656	82 029
Paiement des intérêts	29 503	6 628	2 769	2 377	12	380	3 859	22 875	15 702	6 368	14 129
Transfers nets (8)	-28 622	-15 033	-6 686	-6 908	-58	280	-8 347	-13 590	-9 186	-1 772	-6 697
2005											
Debt outstanding (5)	505 187	191 536	82 683	69 610	316	12 758	108 852	313 652	184 896	109 316	313 975
Disbursments (6)	64 422	15 269	5 268	4 464	31	773	10 001	49 153	25 792	21 794	116 338
Debt service (7)	88 660	22 698	11 332	10 504	44	785	11 366	65 961	36 641	24 878	102 027
Principal repayments	62 421	16 935	8 992	8 391	32	569	7 943	45 486	21 877	19 692	89 306
Interest payments	26 239	5 763	2 340	2 113	12	216	3 423	20 476	14 764	5 186	12 721
Net transfers on debt (8)	-24 237	-7 430	-6 065	-6 040	-13	-12	-1 365	-16 808	-10 849	-3 084	14 312
2006											
Dette totale (5)	485 681	187 815	80 187	64 433	251	15 503	107 628	297 866	165 738	115 078	394 075
Décaissements (6)	59 996	18 897	5 031	3 080	27	1 924	13 866	41 099	22 377	15 874	158 074
Service de la dette (7)	120 783	31 658	11 537	10 548	50	939	20 121	89 125	63 408	20 565	105 690
Remboursement du principal	91 554	25 675	9 546	8 831	40	675	16 130	65 879	46 335	14 884	86 864
Paiement des intérêts	29 229	5 983	1 991	1 717	10	265	3 991	23 247	17 073	5 681	18 826
Transfers nets (8)	-60 787	-12 761	-6 506	-7 467	-23	984	-6 255	-48 026	-41 031	-4 691	52 384

For sources and notes, see next page.

Pour les sources et les notes, se reporter à la page suivante.

7

7.7.G External long-term debt by lending source
Developing economies:
Major exporters of manufactured goods

7.7.G Dette extérieure à long terme par catégories de prêt
Économies en développement :
Principaux exportateurs d'articles manufacturés

Sources:
- World Bank, *Global Development Finance 2008*

Notes:

(1) Public and publicly guaranteed debt (PPG) are aggregated.
     - Public debt is an obligation of a public debtor, including the national government, a political subdivision (or an agency of either), and autonomous public bodies.
     - Publicly guaranteed debt is an external obligation of a private debtor that is guaranteed for repayment by a public entity.
     Data is shown by type of creditor: official creditors and private creditors.

(2) Public and publicly guaranteed debt from official creditors includes loans from Governments and loans from international organizations .
     Government loans include loans from governments and their agencies (including central banks), loans from autonomous bodies, and direct loans from official export credit agencies.
     Loans from international organizations include loans and credits from the World Bank, regional development banks, and other multilateral and intergovernmental agencies.
     Excluded are loans from funds administered by an international organization on behalf of a single donor Government; these are classified as loans from Governments.
     In this table, Governments are treated as bilateral creditors and international organizations are treated as multilateral creditors.

(3) Public and publicly guaranteed debt from private creditors includes:
     - Bonds that are either publicly issued or privately placed;
     - Commercial bank loans from private banks and other private financial institutions;
     - Other private credits from manufacturers, exporters, and other suppliers of goods, and bank credits covered by a guarantee of an export credit agency.

(4) Private nonguaranteed debt (PNG) is an obligation of a private debtor that is not guaranteed for repayment by a public entity.

(5) Long-term debt is defined as debt that has an original or extended maturity of more than one year and that is owed to nonresidents and repayable in foreign currency, goods, or services. Long-term debt has three components: Public debt, Publicly guaranteed debt, and Private nonguaranteed debt.
     Total outstanding long term debt at year end is long-term debt outstanding and disbursed.

(6) Disbursements on long-term debt are drawings on loan commitments during the year specified.

(7) Long-term debt service payments are the sum of principal repayments and interest payments in the year specified.

(8) Net transfers are disbursements minus debt service payments.

Sources :
- Banque mondiale, *Global Development Finance 2008*

Notes :

(1) La dette publique et garantie par l'État est une aggrégation de 2 composantes :
     - La dette publique qui est une dette contractée par le secteur public, y compris le gouvernement, une entité politique et d'autres organismes publics autonomes.
     - La dette garantie par l'État qui est une dette contractée par le secteur privé, dont l'amortissement est garanti par une entité publique.
     Les données sont indiquées par type de créanciers : créanciers publics et créanciers privés.

(2) La dette publique et garantie par l'État octroyée par les créanciers publics inclut les prêts des gouvernements et les prêts des organisations internationales.
     Les prêts des gouvernements incluent les prêts des gouvernements et des organismes publics (y compris les banques centrales), les prêts provenant d'entités autoromes et les prêts octroyés directement par des organismes publics de crédits à l'exportation.
     Les prêts des organisations internationales incluent les prêts et les crédits de la Banque mondiale, des banques régionales de développement, et d'autres organismes multilatéraux et intergouvernementaux. Ne sont pas compris les prêts provenant des fonds administrés par une organisation internationale, pour le compte d'un gouvernement ; ceux-ci sont classés sous la rubrique des prêts des gouvernements.
     Dans ce tableau, les gouvernements sont appelés créditeurs bilatéraux et les organisations internationales sont appelées créditeurs multilatéraux.

(3) La dette publique et garantie par l'État octroyée par les créanciers privés, comprend :
     - Les obligations qui sont soit des émissions publiques, soit des placements privés ;
     - Les prêts des banques commerciales octroyés par des banques privées et par d'autres entités financières ;
     - Les autres crédits privés provenant du secteur manufacturier, du secteur des exportations, et d'autres fournisseurs de biens, ainsi que des crédits bancaires couverts par un organisme de crédits à l'exportation.

(4) La dette du secteur privé non garantie est une dette contractée par le secteur privé, dont l'amortissement n'est pas garanti par une entité publique.

(5) La dette à long terme a une durée de remboursement (d'origine ou différée) supérieure à une année, et son amortissement est dû, en monnaies convertibles ou en nature, à des créanciers non-résidents. La dette à long terme a trois composantes : dette publique, dette garantie par l'État et dette du secteur privé non garantie.
     L'encours total de la dette à long terme à la fin de l'année est la somme de l'encours de la dette à long terme et de la dette décaissée à long terme.

(6) Les décaissements de la dette à long terme sont les tirages sur les engagements de la dette effectués au cours de l'année spécifiée.

(7) Les paiements du service de la dette à long terme sont la somme du remboursement du principal et du paiement des intérêts, effectués au cours de l'année spécifiée.

(8) Les transfers nets sont les décaissements moins les paiements du service de la dette.

8 DEVELOPMENT INDICATORS

INDICATEURS DU DÉVELOPPEMENT

8.1.1 Nominal gross domestic product: Total and per capita of countries and geographical regions

Region, country or territory	Total gross domestic product / Produit intérieur brut total (1) Millions of dollars / Millions de dollars							
	1980	1990	2000	2003	2004	2005	2006	2007
WORLD	**11 921 850**	**22 129 834**	**31 850 291**	**37 008 361**	**41 595 458**	**44 883 858**	**48 516 862**	**54 273 887**
DEVELOPING ECONOMIES	2 624 062	3 836 406	6 781 147	7 610 512	8 802 394	10 350 833	12 015 963	14 055 191
ECONOMIES IN TRANSITION	1 012 216	869 276	393 954	638 080	850 948	1 078 963	1 376 783	1 782 155
DEVELOPED ECONOMIES	8 285 572	17 424 153	24 675 189	28 759 769	31 942 115	33 454 062	35 124 116	38 436 541
Developing economies: Africa	**515 510**	**514 193**	**605 467**	**694 152**	**826 377**	**970 678**	**1 094 750**	**1 252 565**
Eastern Africa	*45 016*	*59 398*	*64 948*	*73 826*	*79 594*	*90 062*	*103 417*	*118 485*
Burundi	951	1 148	709	595	680	797	(e)923	(e)1 011
Comoros	124	244	204	318	369	382	398	(e)443
Djibouti	301	457	553	622	660	705	757	(e)827
Eritrea	–	–	637	754	944	(e)929	(e)1 088	(e)1 183
Ethiopia	–	–	7 837	8 012	9 467	11 354	13 288	(e)16 617
Ethiopia (former)	4 106	11 639	–	–	–	–	–	–
Kenya	9 165	11 035	12 604	14 986	16 199	18 730	23 753	(e)30 512
Madagascar	3 265	3 080	3 878	5 474	4 364	5 276	5 506	(e)7 380
Malawi	1 238	1 752	1 744	1 764	1 903	2 077	2 226	(e)2 480
Mauritius	1 146	2 588	4 583	5 641	6 386	6 288	6 413	(e)7 341
Mozambique	4 401	2 708	3 832	4 789	5 912	(e)6 730	(e)7 370	(e)8 427
Rwanda	1 383	2 541	1 749	1 684	1 826	2 085	2 290	(e)2 815
Seychelles	147	369	618	706	700	723	707	(e)648
Somalia	593	994	2 070	2 100	2 213	2 316	2 390	..
Uganda	2 747	3 652	5 734	6 498	7 793	9 190	10 340	(e)12 379
United Republic of Tanzania	6 226	4 683	9 331	10 573	11 668	12 937	13 228	(e)15 148
Zambia	3 885	3 742	3 239	4 305	5 440	7 315	10 974	(e)11 271
Zimbabwe	5 339	8 767	5 628	5 004	3 071	2 227	1 765	..
Middle Africa	*29 575*	*44 273*	*35 427*	*49 581*	*63 960*	*85 974*	*108 018*	*125 547*
Angola	5 415	10 295	9 130	13 956	19 775	32 811	47 268	(e)65 483
Cameroon	9 676	14 310	9 287	13 723	15 775	16 985	18 526	(e)21 296
Central African Republic	693	1 297	906	1 126	1 239	1 320	(e)1 431	(e)1 659
Chad	919	1 542	1 385	2 723	4 415	5 885	(e)6 485	(e)7 293
Congo	1 706	2 799	3 220	3 564	4 384	5 794	7 178	(e)7 140
Dem. Rep. of the Congo	6 139	8 352	5 256	5 636	6 591	7 102	(e)8 152	..
Equatorial Guinea	53	133	1 177	2 825	4 618	7 295	9 499	(e)11 471
Gabon	4 927	5 489	5 019	5 969	7 099	8 711	(e)9 406	(e)11 119
Sao Tome and Principe	47	58	46	59	64	71	74	(e)88
Northern Africa	*140 891*	*187 338*	*256 708*	*258 138*	*299 906*	*354 315*	*406 772*	*474 020*
Algeria	42 348	61 891	54 790	68 017	85 032	102 334	115 945	(e)131 866
Egypt	24 057	39 412	99 601	77 109	82 429	101 382	110 075	(e)132 507
Libyan Arab Jamahiriya	35 721	28 905	34 265	(e)22 093	(e)28 793	(e)37 969	(e)49 494	(e)55 953
Morocco	21 033	28 860	37 060	49 819	56 392	58 956	65 365	(e)73 744
Sudan	8 989	15 956	11 549	16 108	19 040	24 917	35 219	(e)45 272
Tunisia	8 743	12 314	19 444	24 993	28 221	28 758	30 673	(e)34 679
Southern Africa	*84 527*	*119 332*	*143 431*	*181 411*	*234 527*	*261 409*	*271 929*	*298 988*
Botswana	993	3 489	4 889	7 341	8 498	8 935	8 836	(e)9 894
Lesotho	380	618	863	1 039	1 319	1 457	1 446	(e)1 548
Namibia	2 021	2 340	3 414	4 473	(e)5 749	(e)6 240	(e)6 402	(e)6 826
South Africa	80 544	112 014	132 878	166 654	216 443	242 046	(e)252 502	(e)277 825
Swaziland	590	871	1 388	1 904	2 518	2 730	(e)2 742	(e)2 895
Western Africa	*215 501*	*103 852*	*104 955*	*131 195*	*148 390*	*178 918*	*204 614*	*235 525*
Benin	1 374	1 845	2 359	3 557	4 051	4 358	4 694	(e)5 505
Burkina Faso	1 287	3 120	2 415	4 028	4 945	5 397	5 976	(e)6 806
Cape Verde	142	308	539	814	925	983	1 116	(e)1 353
Côte d'Ivoire	10 176	11 893	10 682	14 255	16 064	16 960	18 014	(e)20 402
Gambia	239	333	421	367	401	461	511	(e)647
Ghana	3 252	6 226	4 978	7 624	8 869	10 695	12 245	(e)14 359
Guinea	1 360	2 818	3 134	3 446	3 839	2 927	(e)2 796	(e)4 292
Guinea-Bissau	163	233	215	239	270	301	322	(e)382
Liberia	917	384	561	435	497	548	687	(e)819
Mali	1 423	2 510	2 655	4 222	4 982	5 487	(e)6 005	(e)6 858
Mauritania	829	1 050	1 075	1 281	1 537	1 872	2 737	(e)2 832
Niger	2 538	2 506	1 666	2 523	2 792	3 245	3 388	(e)3 977
Nigeria	186 312	61 873	67 359	78 441	87 845	113 461	132 737	(e)151 312
Senegal	3 191	6 084	4 680	6 815	7 947	8 594	9 274	(e)11 267
Sierra Leone	1 168	941	921	1 421	1 416	1 523	1 828	(e)2 137
Togo	1 131	1 727	1 294	1 728	2 009	2 105	2 284	(e)2 577

For sources and notes, see end of table.

Per capita gross domestic product / Produit intérieur brut par habitant Dollars								Régions, pays ou territoires
1980	1990	2000	2003	2004	2005	2006	2007	
2 680	4 180	5 202	5 821	6 464	6 891	7 361	8 302	**MONDE**
795	943	1 400	1 503	1 713	1 987	2 274	2 688	ÉCONOMIES EN DÉVELOPPEMENT
3 496	2 756	1 288	2 099	2 804	3 562	4 552	5 948	ÉCONOMIES EN TRANSITION
9 659	19 147	25 398	29 092	32 123	33 459	34 949	38 067	ÉCONOMIES DÉVELOPPÉES
1 076	808	739	790	919	1 055	1 163	1 405	**Économies en développement : Afrique**
310	*303*	*254*	*267*	*281*	*310*	*347*	*399*	*Afrique orientale*
230	202	106	82	90	101	(e)113	(e)119	Burundi
319	463	292	419	475	479	486	(e)527	Comores
886	815	758	801	836	877	925	(e)993	Djibouti
–	–	173	181	217	(e)205	(e)232	(e)244	Érythrée
–	–	113	107	123	144	164	(e)200	Éthiopie
104	214	–	–	–	–	–	–	Éthiopie (anc.)
563	471	403	444	467	526	650	(e)813	Kenya
360	256	240	310	241	283	287	(e)375	Madagascar
199	186	150	140	148	157	164	(e)178	Malawi
1 186	2 449	3 864	4 625	5 189	5 067	5 124	(e)5 819	Maurice
363	200	211	244	294	(e)328	(e)351	(e)394	Mozambique
266	348	214	189	202	226	242	(e)289	Rwanda
2 229	5 118	7 619	8 399	8 249	8 449	8 209	(e)7 487	Seychelles
91	148	293	272	278	283	283	..	Somalie
217	205	232	239	278	317	346	(e)401	Ouganda
333	189	283	297	320	346	345	(e)386	République-Unie de Tanzanie
653	461	310	389	483	637	938	(e)945	Zambie
733	836	445	387	236	170	133	..	Zimbabwe
541	*601*	*362*	*467*	*585*	*764*	*933*	*2 224*	*Afrique centrale*
691	977	655	919	1 265	2 039	2 855	(e)3 846	Angola
1 066	1 169	586	806	906	954	1 019	(e)1 148	Cameroun
298	431	234	277	300	315	(e)335	(e)382	République centrafricaine
199	252	164	288	450	580	(e)619	(e)676	Tchad
946	1 156	1 005	1 033	1 242	1 605	1 946	(e)1 895	Congo
219	220	104	102	116	121	(e)134	..	Rép. dém. du Congo
251	392	2 734	6 116	9 765	15 069	19 166	(e)22 602	Guinée équatoriale
7 226	5 980	4 245	4 778	5 589	6 749	(e)7 176	(e)8 356	Gabon
495	496	331	400	423	465	480	(e)556	Sao Tomé-et-Principe
1 265	*1 301*	*1 472*	*1 408*	*1 609*	*1 869*	*2 110*	*2 417*	*Afrique septentrionale*
2 251	2 448	1 796	2 133	2 627	3 115	3 476	(e)3 895	Algérie
551	715	1 497	1 097	1 152	1 392	1 484	(e)1 755	Égypte
11 662	6 624	6 410	(e)3 888	(e)4 965	(e)6 416	(e)8 196	(e)9 083	Jamahiriya arabe libyenne
1 067	1 153	1 272	1 649	1 845	1 906	2 087	(e)2 326	Maroc
458	615	346	455	527	675	934	(e)1 174	Soudan
1 354	1 498	2 033	2 528	2 823	2 846	3 003	(e)3 358	Tunisie
2 563	*2 853*	*2 761*	*3 365*	*4 309*	*4 762*	*4 916*	*5 370*	*Afrique australe*
997	2 552	2 828	4 089	4 682	4 867	4 755	(e)5 259	Botswana
293	386	457	533	671	735	725	(e)771	Lesotho
2 035	1 651	1 816	2 272	(e)2 884	(e)3 090	(e)3 128	(e)3 291	Namibie
2 770	3 062	2 927	3 539	4 553	5 049	(e)5 230	(e)5 719	Afrique du Sud
959	1 007	1 311	1 727	2 260	2 428	(e)2 419	(e)2 536	Swaziland
1 599	*575*	*438*	*506*	*558*	*657*	*733*	*823*	*Afrique occidentale*
370	356	326	447	493	513	536	(e)609	Bénin
189	352	203	308	366	387	416	(e)460	Burkina Faso
492	867	1 197	1 683	1 867	1 940	2 153	(e)2 551	Cap-Vert
1 220	931	627	793	879	913	952	(e)1 059	Côte d'Ivoire
357	346	304	241	255	285	307	(e)379	Gambie
285	400	247	353	402	475	532	(e)612	Ghana
297	467	382	397	435	325	(e)305	(e)458	Guinée
206	230	157	159	174	189	196	(e)225	Guinée-Bissau
491	180	183	132	148	159	192	(e)218	Libéria
234	327	265	386	442	473	(e)502	(e)556	Mali
552	540	419	457	533	632	899	(e)907	Mauritanie
439	320	150	204	218	245	247	(e)280	Niger
2 622	655	540	583	637	803	917	(e)1 022	Nigéria
543	771	453	610	693	730	768	(e)910	Sénégal
361	230	204	275	263	273	318	(e)364	Sierra Leone
406	436	240	292	331	337	356	(e)391	Togo

Pour les sources et les notes, se reporter à la fin du tableau.

Region, country or territory	Total gross domestic product / Produit intérieur brut total (1) Millions of dollars / Millions de dollars							
	1980	1990	2000	2003	2004	2005	2006	2007
Developing economies: America	**765 041**	**1 122 097**	**2 007 926**	**1 810 446**	**2 082 925**	**2 528 463**	**3 029 628**	**3 534 209**
Caribbean	*42 862*	*59 953*	*89 919*	*96 462*	*104 896*	*124 582*	*137 967*	*149 510*
Anguilla	9	54	108	118	149	168	201	(e)207
Antigua and Barbuda	110	392	665	754	819	870	(e)1 002	(e)1 085
Aruba	493	828	1 859	2 011	2 134	2 258	2 380	(e)2 574
Bahamas	1 454	3 166	5 004	5 503	5 661	5 869	(e)6 175	(e)6 533
Barbados	865	1 720	2 559	2 695	2 816	3 062	3 446	(e)3 752
British Virgin Islands	28	105	784	782	873	972	1 034	..
Cayman Islands	132	708	1 734	1 924	2 027	2 309	2 447	..
Cuba	21 329	30 683	32 685	38 625	41 065	(e)44 911	(e)49 931	(e)55 293
Dominica	59	167	271	263	285	300	316	(e)325
Dominican Republic	6 761	7 074	19 772	16 325	18 452	29 101	31 593	(e)36 367
Grenada	71	177	335	357	345	404	(e)413	(e)436
Haiti	1 384	2 614	3 515	2 711	3 511	3 985	4 619	(e)5 688
Jamaica	2 689	4 271	7 889	8 190	8 837	9 715	10 316	(e)11 098
Montserrat	24	67	35	38	41	44	46	..
Netherlands Antilles	943	1 980	2 860	3 031	3 115	3 204	3 352	(e)3 482
Saint Kitts and Nevis	48	159	329	362	396	429	487	(e)529
Saint Lucia	135	416	707	746	798	882	933	(e)974
Saint Vincent and the Grenadines	59	198	335	382	415	(e)439	(e)480	(e)535
Trinidad and Tobago	6 236	5 068	8 154	11 236	12 673	15 089	18 147	(e)20 630
Turks and Caicos Islands	32	106	319	410	486	570	648	..
Central America	*233 784*	*294 714*	*649 483*	*718 243*	*768 718*	*862 120*	*941 561*	*1 006 783*
Belize	195	405	832	988	1 055	1 111	1 217	(e)1 284
Costa Rica	6 139	7 254	15 946	17 514	18 593	19 973	(e)22 333	(e)26 014
El Salvador	3 769	4 801	13 134	15 047	15 822	16 974	(e)18 485	(e)20 150
Guatemala	7 024	6 820	17 196	21 918	23 965	27 285	(e)30 608	(e)33 909
Honduras	2 566	3 049	6 025	6 945	7 538	8 372	9 301	(e)10 579
Mexico	207 663	262 710	580 792	638 797	683 070	767 970	(e)836 995	(e)889 180
Nicaragua	2 375	3 598	3 938	4 102	4 496	4 910	5 371	(e)5 793
Panama, excl. Canal Zone (former)	4 054	–	–	–	–	–	–	–
Panama	–	6 077	11 621	12 933	14 179	(e)15 525	(e)17 251	(e)19 875
South America	*488 394*	*767 430*	*1 268 524*	*995 741*	*1 209 311*	*1 541 761*	*1 950 100*	*2 377 916*
Argentina	75 492	141 353	284 346	129 596	153 129	183 196	(e)217 301	(e)266 041
Bolivia	2 696	4 868	8 398	8 089	(e)8 825	(e)9 442	(e)10 351	(e)12 075
Brazil	227 565	438 256	601 732	(e)512 410	(e)616 472	(e)819 429	(e)1 099 337	(e)1 346 927
Chile	29 479	33 507	75 197	73 986	95 844	118 908	(e)146 368	(e)164 522
Colombia	39 590	47 743	83 766	79 411	98 054	123 120	130 928	(e)165 807
Ecuador	12 351	11 248	15 934	28 636	32 636	(e)36 927	(e)41 225	(e)44 339
Guyana	591	396	713	743	788	826	901	(e)1 031
Paraguay	4 095	4 904	7 095	5 552	6 950	7 473	9 110	(e)11 561
Peru	16 740	29 281	53 336	61 504	69 662	79 382	(e)91 492	(e)107 192
Suriname	891	480	775	1 094	1 283	1 543	1 820	(e)1 997
Uruguay	9 636	8 366	20 086	11 191	13 216	16 615	19 308	(e)22 974
Venezuela (Bolivarian Rep. of)	69 268	47 028	117 148	83 529	112 451	(e)144 900	(e)181 959	(e)233 450
Developing economies: Asia	**1 336 372**	**2 188 999**	**4 154 224**	**5 089 097**	**5 873 681**	**6 830 822**	**7 869 727**	**9 244 809**
Eastern Asia	*452 895*	*927 892*	*2 212 093*	*2 735 395*	*3 129 324*	*3 620 654*	*4 130 243*	*4 811 351*
China	306 520	404 494	1 192 836	1 647 918	1 936 502	(e)2 282 554	(e)2 681 265	(e)3 286 881
China, Hong Kong SAR	28 934	75 934	168 754	158 364	165 743	(e)176 410	(e)188 381	(e)205 213
China, Macao SAR	944	2 990	6 102	7 925	10 359	11 603	14 293	..
China, Taiwan Province of	42 290	164 739	321 187	(e)300 705	(e)323 435	(e)348 135	(e)358 347	(e)375 827
Dem. People's Rep. of Korea	9 879	14 702	10 608	11 051	11 168	12 260	12 127	..
Mongolia	494	1 256	947	1 285	1 625	2 065	(e)3 041	(e)3 713
Republic of Korea	63 834	263 776	511 659	608 146	680 492	787 627	872 789	(e)939 717
Southern Asia	*340 663*	*523 129*	*725 095*	*914 815*	*1 060 715*	*1 235 059*	*1 405 703*	*1 748 714*
Afghanistan	3 639	3 622	2 963	4 786	5 700	6 840	(e)7 935	(e)9 785
Bangladesh	19 749	31 830	48 626	57 261	61 916	64 693	68 220	(e)77 763
Bhutan	131	279	446	628	710	837	922	(e)1 254
India	185 402	327 930	468 978	592 535	688 803	808 884	903 226	(e)1 136 921
Iran (Islamic Rep. of)	91 302	90 368	102 930	136 646	162 747	192 020	242 146	(e)314 334
Maldives	58	215	624	692	776	751	907	(e)1 049
Nepal	1 946	3 521	5 338	5 998	6 743	7 476	(e)8 085	(e)9 857
Pakistan	34 163	57 159	78 472	97 669	112 965	129 600	146 888	(e)167 310
Sri Lanka	4 273	8 204	16 717	18 600	20 355	23 958	27 373	(e)30 441

For sources and notes, see end of table.

Per capita gross domestic product / Produit intérieur brut par habitant Dollars								Régions, pays ou territoires
1980	1990	2000	2003	2004	2005	2006	2007	
2 123	2 552	3 875	3 358	3 815	4 573	5 411	6 234	Économies en développement : Amérique
1 654	2 000	2 655	2 761	2 972	3 496	3 836	4 130	Caraïbes
1 240	6 033	9 617	9 934	12 360	13 703	16 183	(e)16 418	Anguilla
1 523	6 324	8 665	9 334	9 988	10 481	(e)11 912	(e)12 753	Antigua-et-Barbuda
8 097	13 003	20 576	20 410	21 103	21 940	22 934	(e)24 775	Aruba
6 920	12 406	16 506	17 448	17 728	18 155	(e)18 869	(e)19 720	Bahamas
3 474	6 341	8 933	9 298	9 681	10 488	11 765	(e)12 768	Barbade
2 519	6 356	38 203	36 425	40 147	44 150	46 407	..	Îles Vierges britanniques
7 579	26 919	43 097	44 018	45 355	50 655	52 707	..	Îles Caïmanes
2 171	2 893	2 933	3 440	3 651	(e)3 989	(e)4 432	(e)4 907	Cuba
809	2 430	3 961	3 857	4 194	4 427	4 667	(e)4 829	Dominique
1 139	970	2 261	1 778	1 979	3 073	3 286	(e)3 726	République dominicaine
797	1 846	3 336	3 448	3 301	3 835	(e)3 910	(e)4 124	Grenade
243	368	410	301	384	429	489	(e)593	Haïti
1 261	1 803	3 047	3 094	3 316	3 622	3 823	(e)4 089	Jamaïque
2 033	6 253	7 014	7 590	7 656	7 813	7 967	..	Montserrat
5 433	10 388	15 830	16 619	16 909	17 188	17 750	(e)18 177	Antilles néerlandaises
1 109	3 910	7 149	7 560	8 153	8 724	9 776	(e)10 487	Saint-Kitts-et-Nevis
1 147	3 022	4 627	4 734	5 004	5 473	5 723	(e)5 905	Sainte-Lucie
589	1 812	2 891	3 243	3 501	(e)3 688	(e)4 010	(e)4 447	Saint-Vincent-et-les Grenadines
5 765	4 142	6 270	8 547	9 607	11 399	13 661	(e)15 473	Trinité-et-Tobago
4 284	9 177	16 931	18 283	20 621	23 316	25 811	..	Îles Turques et Caïques
2 534	2 614	4 790	5 110	5 410	5 996	6 467	6 823	Amérique centrale
1 354	2 183	3 400	3 752	3 917	4 032	4 320	(e)4 462	Belize
2 616	2 359	4 059	4 194	4 372	4 616	(e)5 077	(e)5 823	Costa Rica
822	939	2 120	2 320	2 406	2 545	(e)2 734	(e)2 938	El Salvador
1 002	766	1 531	1 813	1 933	2 147	(e)2 349	(e)2 539	Guatemala
706	623	972	1 057	1 125	1 225	1 335	(e)1 489	Honduras
2 995	3 127	5 823	6 231	6 610	7 365	(e)7 945	(e)8 346	Mexique
729	869	771	770	834	899	971	(e)1 034	Nicaragua
2 080	–	–	–	–	–	–		Panama, sans la zone du canal (anc.)
–	2 520	3 939	4 146	4 465	(e)4 804	(e)5 247	(e)5 944	Panama
2 016	2 583	3 638	2 738	3 281	4 128	5 154	6 205	Amérique du Sud
2 687	4 339	7 707	3 410	3 991	4 728	(e)5 553	(e)6 730	Argentine
503	730	1 010	916	(e)980	(e)1 028	(e)1 107	(e)1 268	Bolivie
1 871	2 931	3 455	(e)2 819	(e)3 345	(e)4 386	(e)5 807	(e)7 023	Brésil
2 638	2 543	4 879	4 638	5 944	7 297	(e)8 889	(e)9 890	Chili
1 396	1 369	2 010	1 818	2 213	2 739	2 874	(e)3 592	Colombie
1 551	1 095	1 295	2 242	2 526	(e)2 827	(e)3 123	(e)3 323	Équateur
777	542	970	1 007	1 067	1 117	1 219	(e)1 397	Guyana
1 281	1 155	1 326	977	1 200	1 266	1 514	(e)1 887	Paraguay
966	1 345	2 078	2 309	2 584	2 911	(e)3 316	(e)3 842	Pérou
2 500	1 192	1 775	2 449	2 853	3 410	3 998	(e)4 361	Suriname
3 307	2 694	6 053	3 366	3 976	4 996	5 796	(e)6 879	Uruguay
4 590	2 383	4 801	3 238	4 282	(e)5 422	(e)6 692	(e)8 441	Venezuela (Rép. bolivarienne du)
544	733	1 187	1 399	1 595	1 832	2 086	2 458	Économies en développement : Asie
428	760	1 639	1 985	2 257	2 596	2 944	3 470	Asie orientale
312	358	956	1 293	1 510	(e)1 769	(e)2 066	(e)2 517	Chine
5 743	13 311	25 330	22 935	23 740	(e)24 996	(e)26 413	(e)28 478	Chine (RAS de Hong Kong)
3 746	8 035	13 834	17 179	22 152	24 526	29 931	..	Chine (RAS de Macao)
2 375	8 075	14 418	(e)13 303	(e)14 255	(e)15 289	(e)15 683	(e)16 410	Province chinoise de Taiwan
642	735	462	471	473	517	509	..	Rép. populaire dém. de Corée
297	567	384	508	636	800	(e)1 168	(e)1 412	Mongolie
1 674	6 153	10 938	12 806	14 271	16 454	18 164	(e)19 487	République de Corée
362	439	496	595	679	778	872	1 067	Asie méridionale
261	286	143	207	237	273	(e)304	(e)360	Afghanistan
222	282	349	388	411	422	437	(e)490	Bangladesh
310	509	799	1 034	1 140	1 314	1 422	(e)1 904	Bhoutan
269	381	448	539	617	713	784	(e)973	Inde
2 321	1 595	1 557	2 009	2 370	2 766	3 446	(e)4 414	Iran (Rép. islamique d')
369	997	2 287	2 420	2 672	2 542	3 020	(e)3 433	Maldives
128	184	219	230	254	276	(e)293	(e)350	Népal
431	506	544	640	727	820	913	(e)1 021	Pakistan
286	479	893	981	1 069	1 253	1 425	(e)1 577	Sri Lanka

Pour les sources et les notes, se reporter à la fin du tableau.

8

Region, country or territory	Total gross domestic product / Produit intérieur brut total (1) Millions of dollars / Millions de dollars							
	1980	1990	2000	2003	2004	2005	2006	2007
South-Eastern Asia	*194 706*	*354 153*	*595 980*	*716 280*	*800 182*	*887 022*	*1 062 296*	*1 266 389*
Brunei Darussalam	4 724	3 441	6 001	6 557	7 872	9 531	11 481	(e)12 300
Cambodia	714	1 698	3 668	4 357	5 264	6 194	(e)6 648	(e)7 843
Indonesia	79 636	125 720	165 021	234 772	254 299	281 276	364 459	(e)432 607
Lao People's dem. Rep.	322	866	1 733	2 130	2 512	2 872	(e)3 484	(e)4 190
Malaysia	24 488	44 025	90 320	103 952	118 461	130 770	148 941	(e)177 891
Myanmar	5 905	5 179	7 275	10 000	10 254	11 900	13 612	(e)18 914
Philippines	32 450	44 312	75 031	79 634	86 703	98 371	116 931	(e)143 356
Singapore	11 718	36 901	92 717	92 350	107 405	116 704	132 155	(e)156 140
Thailand	32 354	85 361	122 725	142 640	161 349	176 222	206 247	(e)245 384
Timor-Leste	..	179	316	336	339	350	356	(e)415
Viet Nam	2 395	6 472	31 173	39 553	45 724	52 832	57 983	(e)67 348
Western Asia	*348 107*	*383 825*	*621 055*	*722 608*	*883 460*	*1 088 086*	*1 271 485*	*1 418 355*
Bahrain	3 292	4 293	7 971	9 699	11 013	13 381	(e)15 884	(e)19 674
Iraq	12 155	17 169	20 969	10 621	25 491	33 961	46 952	..
Jordan	4 013	4 020	8 461	10 196	11 398	12 711	14 336	(e)16 278
Kuwait	28 691	18 471	37 718	47 827	59 267	80 781	101 131	(e)113 912
Lebanon	4 074	2 812	16 679	19 802	21 464	21 802	22 064	(e)23 428
Occupied Palestinian territory	1 073	1 936	4 116	3 921	4 068	(e)4 222	(e)3 758	..
Oman	6 326	11 685	19 868	21 698	24 749	30 834	(e)36 443	(e)40 521
Qatar	7 838	7 360	17 760	23 534	31 734	42 463	52 722	(e)66 735
Saudi Arabia	164 540	116 622	188 442	214 573	250 339	(e)308 452	(e)357 170	(e)384 423
Syrian Arab Republic	13 062	11 152	19 651	20 724	(e)23 860	(e)27 393	(e)31 320	(e)36 168
Turkey	68 794	150 676	199 263	239 701	301 999	362 614	392 336	(e)484 976
United Arab Emirates	29 626	33 780	70 522	88 536	104 204	133 583	(e)178 826	(e)210 964
Yemen (former Arab Republic)	3 955	–	–	–	–	–	–	–
Yemen (former Democratic)	668	–	–	–	–	–	–	–
Yemen	–	3 847	9 636	11 778	13 874	15 890	18 543	(e)21 274
Developing economies: Oceania	*7 139*	*11 118*	*13 530*	*16 818*	*19 411*	*20 871*	*21 858*	*23 608*
Cook Islands	24	59	81	143	171	183	177	..
Fiji	1 203	1 337	1 686	2 309	2 728	2 998	3 103	(e)3 360
French Polynesia	1 260	2 930	3 242	4 471	5 144	5 388	5 643	(e)6 470
Kiribati	24	28	51	62	70	75	75	(e)88
Marshall Islands	23	69	99	109	115	123	128	..
Micronesia (Federated States of)	61	146	217	230	224	237	245	..
Nauru	36	51	33	44	51	54	55	..
New Caledonia	1 182	2 529	3 166	4 098	4 595	4 656	4 743	(e)5 272
Palau	26	77	117	117	134	145	156	..
Papua New Guinea	2 823	3 286	3 864	4 169	4 935	5 635	(e)6 068	(e)6 805
Samoa	155	112	231	319	377	417	(e)429	(e)479
Solomon Islands	144	208	338	289	334	374	416	(e)457
Tonga	60	124	148	163	189	215	232	(e)244
Tuvalu	5	10	12	19	23	25	26	..
Vanuatu	113	153	245	276	320	347	361	(e)432
Economies in transition: Asia	*–*	*–*	*48 681*	*63 319*	*81 676*	*105 290*	*138 182*	*175 247*
Armenia	–	–	1 912	2 807	(e)3 254	(e)4 191	(e)5 306	(e)7 636
Azerbaijan	–	–	5 273	7 276	8 680	13 245	19 851	(e)30 029
Georgia	–	–	3 058	3 991	5 126	6 411	(e)7 770	(e)10 307
Kazakhstan	–	–	18 292	30 834	43 152	57 124	77 237	(e)93 596
Kyrgyzstan	–	–	1 370	1 922	2 212	2 460	2 819	(e)3 724
Tajikistan	–	–	861	1 555	2 076	2 312	2 813	(e)3 195
Turkmenistan	–	–	4 157	4 779	5 160	5 795	6 500	(e)7 916
Uzbekistan	–	–	13 759	10 155	12 016	13 751	(e)15 885	(e)18 843
Economies in transition: Europe	*–*	*–*	*345 273*	*574 761*	*769 272*	*973 673*	*1 238 601*	*1 606 909*
Albania	2 219	2 184	3 709	5 859	7 549	8 488	(e)8 842	(e)10 411
Belarus	–	–	10 418	17 825	23 142	30 210	36 945	(e)44 753
Bosnia and Herzegovina (2)	–	–	5 047	7 757	9 318	10 040	11 326	(e)13 630
Croatia	–	–	18 425	29 593	35 269	38 498	(e)42 368	(e)50 614
Moldova	–	–	1 288	1 981	2 598	2 988	3 356	(e)4 159
Russian Federation	–	–	259 718	431 488	591 666	764 382	984 927	(e)1 284 698
Serbia and Montenegro	–	–	11 820	(e)25 495	(e)29 481	(e)27 110	(e)38 065	(e)50 295
SFR of Yugoslavia (former)	69 959	91 471	–	–	–	–	–	–
TFYR of Macedonia	–	–	3 587	4 630	5 369	5 816	6 304	(e)7 477
Ukraine	–	–	31 262	50 133	64 881	86 142	106 469	(e)140 872
USSR (former)	940 038	775 621	–	–	–	–	–	–

For sources and notes, see end of table.

Per capita gross domestic product / Produit intérieur brut par habitant Dollars								Régions, pays ou territoires
1980	1990	2000	2003	2004	2005	2006	2007	
542	*802*	*1 146*	*1 320*	*1 454*	*1 591*	*1 880*	*2 212*	**Asie du Sud-Est**
24 472	13 391	17 997	18 339	21 527	25 497	30 058	(e)31 534	Brunéi Darussalam
106	175	287	323	384	444	(e)468	(e)543	Cambodge
525	685	780	1 065	1 139	1 244	1 592	(e)1 868	Indonésie
104	212	332	388	451	507	(e)605	(e)715	Rép. dém. populaire lao
1 779	2 432	3 881	4 204	4 702	5 098	5 704	(e)6 695	Malaisie
177	129	159	212	216	248	281	(e)388	Myanmar
675	724	984	981	1 046	1 163	1 356	(e)1 630	Philippines
4 853	12 234	23 079	21 879	25 129	26 968	30 159	(e)35 196	Singapour
691	1 572	2 023	2 296	2 579	2 797	3 251	(e)3 841	Thaïlande
..	242	386	352	334	328	319	(e)360	Timor-Leste
45	98	394	479	545	621	673	(e)771	Viet Nam
3 552	*2 900*	*3 662*	*3 991*	*4 778*	*5 766*	*6 603*	*8 682*	**Asie occidentale**
9 487	8 709	12 261	13 952	15 507	18 462	(e)21 496	(e)26 140	Bahreïn
862	927	837	395	928	1 213	1 647	..	Iraq
1 803	1 235	1 763	1 958	2 122	2 293	2 502	(e)2 748	Jordanie
20 867	8 619	16 926	18 897	22 647	29 919	36 396	(e)39 953	Koweït
1 463	945	4 421	5 055	5 414	5 436	5 441	(e)5 715	Liban
727	899	1 307	1 117	1 119	(e)1 122	(e)966	..	Territoire palestinien occupé
5 327	6 340	8 271	8 823	9 985	12 299	(e)14 312	(e)15 614	Oman
34 161	15 747	28 797	32 378	41 521	53 333	64 193	(e)79 387	Qatar
17 132	7 174	9 057	9 545	10 862	(e)13 063	(e)14 774	(e)15 542	Arabie saoudite
1 456	877	1 190	1 158	(e)1 298	(e)1 450	(e)1 614	(e)1 815	République arabe syrienne
1 485	2 628	2 924	3 372	4 193	4 969	5 307	(e)6 477	Turquie
29 182	18 093	21 718	23 429	26 400	32 547	(e)42 092	(e)48 161	Émirats arabes unis
610		–	–	–	–	–		Yémen (anc. République arabe du)
352		–	–	–	–	–		Yémen (anc. démocratique)
–	312	530	593	677	753	853	(e)950	Yémen
1 449	*1 791*	*1 732*	*2 019*	*2 283*	*2 407*	*2 473*	*2 689*	**Économies en développement : Océanie**
1 329	3 293	5 055	9 705	11 940	13 098	13 005	..	Îles Cook
1 898	1 848	2 103	2 824	3 315	3 620	3 724	(e)4 006	Fidji
8 341	14 995	13 732	18 026	20 423	21 077	21 766	(e)24 624	Polynésie française
435	396	606	704	776	811	801	(e)928	Kiribati
765	1 453	1 896	2 000	2 074	2 166	2 204	..	Îles Marshall
842	1 512	2 027	2 121	2 051	2 154	2 212	..	Micronésie (États fédérés de)
4 796	5 588	3 283	4 326	5 023	5 351	5 474	..	Nauru
8 285	14 786	14 722	18 075	19 940	19 883	19 935	(e)21 810	Nouvelle-Calédonie
2 128	5 150	6 081	5 867	6 670	7 188	7 698	..	Palaos
882	795	718	719	832	928	(e)978	(e)1 075	Papouasie-Nouvelle-Guinée
997	694	1 301	1 759	2 064	2 267	(e)2 317	(e)2 564	Samoa
627	664	814	642	725	792	860	(e)922	Îles Salomon
622	1 309	1 513	1 648	1 906	2 159	2 328	(e)2 432	Tonga
564	1 012	1 204	1 815	2 191	2 385	2 441	..	Tuvalu
968	1 023	1 289	1 351	1 526	1 610	1 635	(e)1 908	Vanuatu
–	–	*683*	*869*	*1 110*	*1 418*	*1 844*	*2 316*	**Économies en transition : Asie**
–	–	620	924	(e)1 075	(e)1 389	(e)1 763	(e)2 543	Arménie
–	–	647	880	1 045	1 586	2 362	(e)3 547	Azerbaïdjan
–	–	648	875	1 135	1 433	(e)1 753	(e)2 345	Géorgie
–	–	1 223	2 055	2 856	3 756	5 043	(e)6 069	Kazakhstan
–	–	277	376	429	473	536	(e)701	Kirghizistan
–	–	139	243	321	353	424	(e)474	Tadjikistan
–	–	923	1 017	1 083	1 199	1 327	(e)1 594	Turkménistan
–	–	557	393	458	517	(e)589	(e)688	Ouzbékistan
–	–	*1 471*	*2 487*	*3 346*	*4 258*	*5 444*	*7 176*	**Économies en transition : Europe**
831	664	1 204	1 881	2 408	2 691	(e)2 787	(e)3 263	Albanie
–	–	1 036	1 801	2 350	3 084	3 792	(e)4 619	Bélarus
–	–	1 333	1 991	2 386	2 564	2 885	(e)3 464	Bosnie-Herzégovine (2)
–	–	4 089	6 544	7 769	8 458	(e)9 299	(e)11 111	Croatie
–	–	311	498	662	771	876	(e)1 096	Moldova
–	–	1 762	2 967	4 089	5 310	6 877	(e)9 016	Fédération de Russie
–	–	1 094	(e)2 409	(e)2 803	(e)2 589	(e)3 642	(e)6 259	Serbie-et-Monténégro
3 263	4 009			–	–	–		RSF de Yougoslavie (anc.)
–	–	1 785	2 285	2 644	2 860	3 096	(e)3 668	LERY de Macédoine
–	–	640	1 052	1 372	1 836	2 287	(e)3 049	Ukraine
3 542	2 681		–	–	–	–		URSS (anc.)

Pour les sources et les notes, se reporter à la fin du tableau.

Region, country or territory	Total gross domestic product / Produit intérieur brut total (1) Millions of dollars / Millions de dollars							
	1980	1990	2000	2003	2004	2005	2006	2007
Developed economies: America	**3 055 152**	**6 375 264**	**10 563 468**	**11 858 882**	**12 708 567**	**13 573 573**	**14 444 261**	**15 241 555**
Bermuda	931	2 023	3 476	4 176	4 450	4 857	5 194	(e)5 554
Canada	268 889	582 735	724 916	866 071	992 138	1 131 764	1 270 625	(e)1 419 952
Greenland	476	1 019	1 068	1 426	1 645	1 703	1 657	..
United States	2 784 856	5 789 487	9 834 008	10 987 209	(e)11 710 335	(e)12 435 249	(e)13 166 785	(e)13 816 049
Developed economies: Asia	**1 078 574**	**3 075 035**	**4 770 603**	**4 329 930**	**4 707 335**	**4 656 453**	**4 532 203**	**4 555 085**
Israel	23 369	56 923	120 989	115 101	122 476	129 753	140 294	(e)159 687
Japan	1 055 205	3 018 112	4 649 614	(e)4 214 828	(e)4 584 859	(e)4 526 700	(e)4 391 909	(e)4 395 398
Developed economies: Europe	**3 958 535**	**7 610 816**	**8 888 833**	**11 945 313**	**13 768 432**	**14 376 601**	**15 273 545**	**17 589 125**
Andorra	588	1 356	1 360	2 378	2 786	3 050	3 337	..
Austria	81 176	164 988	193 838	255 343	292 810	304 809	321 730	(e)371 105
Belgium	_	_	_	309 900	357 712	370 815	392 706	(e)447 307
Belgium-Luxembourg	131 170	215 359	252 203	_	_	_	_	_
Bulgaria	18 620	20 726	12 600	(e)19 968	(e)24 536	(e)27 076	(e)32 002	(e)40 174
Cyprus	2 230	5 777	9 294	13 269	15 770	16 941	18 221	(e)21 125
Czechoslovakia (former)	48 811	53 609	_	_	_	_	_	_
Czech Republic	_	_	56 717	91 358	108 214	123 981	141 249	(e)173 211
Denmark	69 709	135 839	160 081	(e)213 287	(e)245 234	(e)258 268	(e)278 782	(e)314 503
Estonia	_	_	5 627	9 592	11 646	13 753	(e)16 130	(e)20 659
Finland	53 115	139 561	121 865	164 709	188 654	195 713	209 678	(e)244 503
France	689 350	1 239 862	1 328 659	1 800 879	(e)2 064 079	(e)2 145 795	(e)2 254 582	(e)2 567 210
Germany (former Federal Rep.)	919 651	_	_	_	_	_	_	_
Germany	_	1 714 442	1 900 220	2 439 522	2 740 621	2 786 897	(e)2 900 829	(e)3 302 252
Greece	62 786	108 124	145 956	221 890	264 146	283 734	(e)309 146	(e)361 800
Hungary	25 183	36 754	47 958	84 419	102 159	110 364	111 990	(e)137 010
Iceland	3 331	6 371	8 641	10 828	13 040	16 071	(e)15 687	(e)18 817
Ireland	21 107	47 856	96 327	156 812	183 232	200 422	218 090	(e)256 987
Italy	459 811	1 133 465	1 097 346	1 507 109	1 724 522	1 762 473	1 848 001	(e)2 092 781
Latvia	_	_	7 833	11 186	13 762	16 042	20 101	(e)27 355
Lithuania	_	_	11 418	18 558	22 508	25 667	29 283	(e)37 741
Luxembourg	_	_	_	28 900	33 520	36 557	(e)40 741	(e)47 657
Malta	1 257	2 561	3 914	4 928	5 399	5 613	(e)6 021	(e)6 990
Netherlands	179 934	297 711	385 074	538 292	608 239	628 819	663 929	(e)760 605
Norway	63 646	116 107	166 906	222 698	254 706	295 513	333 924	(e)386 920
Poland	57 828	64 550	171 332	216 535	252 118	(e)303 687	(e)340 055	(e)418 054
Portugal	31 458	75 278	112 650	155 212	178 153	183 787	191 777	(e)219 499
Romania	34 599	38 510	37 025	59 507	75 489	98 566	(e)122 384	(e)165 620
San Marino	229	565	774	1 123	1 317	1 346	1 412	..
Slovakia	_	_	20 448	32 977	42 015	47 428	(e)56 048	(e)75 232
Slovenia	_	_	19 314	28 069	32 601	34 354	(e)37 207	(e)44 791
Spain	225 984	520 938	580 673	883 184	1 043 137	1 126 020	1 225 007	(e)1 430 435
Sweden	130 795	242 178	242 003	304 145	349 041	357 356	382 825	(e)447 427
Switzerland	109 788	237 236	248 528	325 919	363 160	369 387	378 166	(e)413 077
United Kingdom	536 376	991 091	1 442 249	1 812 816	2 154 107	2 226 298	2 372 504	(e)2 738 278
Developed economies: Oceania	**193 312**	**363 039**	**452 285**	**625 643**	**757 781**	**847 435**	**874 107**	**1 050 776**
Australia	170 327	319 140	399 612	544 962	659 361	737 677	(e)768 121	(e)921 725
New Zealand	22 985	43 898	52 673	80 681	98 420	109 757	105 986	(e)129 051

Sources:
- Data and UNCTAD secretariat estimates based on UN DESA Statistics Division data

Notes:
(1) GDP by expenditure, in current prices and current exchange rates.
(2) GDP data include the Federation of Bosnia and Herzegovina only. Data for the Republika Srpska are excluded.

Per capita gross domestic product / Produit intérieur brut par habitant Dollars								Régions, pays ou territoires
1980	1990	2000	2003	2004	2005	2006	2007	
11 808	**22 179**	**33 063**	**35 991**	**38 182**	**40 375**	**42 545**	**44 467**	**Économies développées : Amérique**
16 602	33 824	55 294	65 566	69 592	75 685	80 676	(e)86 027	Bermudes
10 968	21 037	23 621	27 379	31 048	35 071	39 004	(e)43 191	Canada
9 482	18 343	18 986	25 064	28 767	29 622	28 670	..	Groenland
11 895	22 299	34 064	36 902	(e)38 935	(e)40 933	(e)42 915	(e)44 594	États-Unis
8 946	**24 014**	**35 837**	**32 285**	**35 032**	**34 598**	**33 631**	**33 768**	**Économies développées : Asie**
6 209	12 611	19 886	17 831	18 630	19 389	20 601	(e)23 051	Israël
9 034	24 431	36 601	(e)33 016	(e)35 876	(e)35 393	(e)34 324	(e)34 348	Japon
8 591	**16 048**	**17 923**	**23 836**	**27 372**	**28 486**	**30 180**	**34 683**	**Économies développées : Europe**
15 761	25 699	20 470	33 623	38 535	41 503	44 962	..	Andorre
10 753	21 346	23 897	31 094	35 478	36 759	38 635	(e)44 387	Autriche
–	–	30 040	34 529	35 662	37 651	(e)42 774		Belgique
12 870	20 878	23 726				–		Belgique-Luxembourg
2 101	2 350	1 574	(e)2 546	(e)3 148	(e)3 496	(e)4 160	(e)5 259	Bulgarie
4 384	9 970	13 399	18 414	21 395	22 349	23 774	(e)27 271	Chypre
3 199	3 445	–	–	–	–	–	–	Tchécoslovaquie (anc.)
–	–	5 549	8 959	10 615	12 165	13 863	(e)17 004	République tchèque
13 607	26 428	30 004	(e)39 586	(e)45 389	(e)47 678	(e)51 341	(e)57 791	Danemark
–	–	4 108	7 093	8 638	10 230	(e)12 038	(e)15 471	Estonie
11 113	27 988	23 545	31 574	36 063	37 307	39 853	(e)46 335	Finlande
12 503	21 290	21 812	29 030	(e)33 054	(e)34 150	(e)35 677	(e)40 408	France
11 747		–	–	–	–	–	–	Allemagne (anc. Rép. fédérale d')
–	21 583	23 086	29 546	33 168	33 718	(e)35 102	(e)39 979	Allemagne
6 511	10 642	13 299	20 063	23 842	25 562	(e)27 795	(e)32 457	Grèce
2 352	3 546	4 695	8 326	10 101	10 942	11 134	(e)13 660	Hongrie
14 601	25 005	30 742	37 342	44 519	54 344	(e)52 564	(e)62 514	Islande
6 206	13 616	25 324	39 255	45 045	48 373	51 665	(e)59 752	Irlande
8 148	19 984	19 021	25 864	29 492	30 053	31 440	(e)35 545	Italie
–	–	3 293	4 802	5 944	6 969	8 781	(e)12 013	Lettonie
–	–	3 260	5 373	6 543	7 494	8 592	(e)11 133	Lituanie
–	–	–	64 413	74 091	80 062	(e)88 307	(e)102 145	Luxembourg
3 878	7 112	10 065	12 403	13 494	13 942	(e)14 875	(e)17 193	Malte
12 716	19 912	24 182	33 253	37 399	38 512	40 535	(e)46 325	Pays-Bas
15 578	27 374	37 183	48 646	55 268	63 704	71 525	(e)82 357	Norvège
1 626	1 694	4 458	5 655	6 592	(e)7 951	(e)8 916	(e)10 978	Pologne
3 221	7 540	11 015	14 910	17 013	17 457	18 129	(e)20 663	Portugal
1 558	1 659	1 673	2 726	3 475	4 557	(e)5 684	(e)7 726	Roumanie
10 696	23 371	28 720	38 796	44 443	44 562	46 083	..	Saint-Marin
–	–	3 795	6 122	7 800	8 804	(e)10 402	(e)13 958	Slovaquie
–	–	9 737	14 075	16 323	17 182	(e)18 596	(e)22 379	Slovénie
6 022	13 409	14 434	20 977	24 375	25 947	27 913	(e)32 305	Espagne
15 739	28 296	27 290	33 955	38 792	39 539	42 170	(e)49 066	Suède
17 304	34 567	34 063	44 091	48 902	49 522	50 491	(e)54 936	Suisse
9 525	17 315	24 500	30 378	35 923	36 954	39 207	(e)45 060	Royaume-Uni
10 890	**17 898**	**19 671**	**26 239**	**31 403**	**34 721**	**35 432**	**42 163**	**Économies développées : Océanie**
11 636	18 914	20 880	27 462	32 835	36 321	(e)37 414	(e)44 435	Australie
7 384	12 871	13 667	20 171	24 300	26 789	25 603	(e)30 884	Nouvelle-Zélande

Sources :
- Données et estimations du secrétariat de la CNUCED sur la base de données de ONU DAES Division de statistique

Notes :

(1) PIB par dépenses, aux prix et taux de change courants.
(2) Y compris le PIB de la Fédération de Bosnie-Herzégovine seulement. Non compris le PIB de la Republika Srpska.

8.1.2 Nominal gross domestic product: Total and per capita of economic groupings

Economic grouping	Total gross domestic product / Produit intérieur brut total (1) Millions of dollars / Millions de dollars							
	1980	1990	2000	2003	2004	2005	2006	2007
DEVELOPING ECONOMIES	**2 624 062**	**3 836 406**	**6 781 147**	**7 610 512**	**8 802 394**	**10 350 833**	**12 015 963**	**14 055 191**
Developing economies excluding China	2 317 542	3 431 912	5 588 311	5 962 594	6 865 893	8 068 279	9 334 698	10 768 311
Developing economies excluding LDCs	2 517 678	3 683 605	6 602 904	7 387 849	8 544 687	10 048 039	11 660 470	13 634 812
High-income developing countries	837 286	1 285 527	2 609 806	2 598 264	2 927 485	3 397 904	3 845 072	4 233 567
Middle-income developing countries	779 428	1 264 050	1 806 339	1 906 521	2 269 715	2 728 611	3 230 517	3 876 864
Low-income developing countries	1 007 348	1 286 829	2 365 002	3 105 727	3 605 195	4 224 318	4 940 375	5 944 760
Heavily indebted poor countries	101 331	143 833	141 927	177 041	203 521	232 247	267 228	303 294
Landlocked developing countries	41 794	68 508	120 224	147 174	178 468	214 190	261 117	316 515
Small island developing States	18 064	25 293	40 220	47 160	52 102	57 251	62 981	69 100
Least developed countries	*106 384*	*152 801*	*178 243*	*222 664*	*257 707*	*302 794*	*355 494*	*420 380*
Africa and Haiti	68 687	100 753	96 489	123 357	148 064	183 301	225 002	266 049
Asia	37 028	50 842	79 687	96 937	106 971	116 702	127 450	150 879
Islands	669	1 206	2 068	2 370	2 672	2 791	3 042	3 451
Major petroleum exporters	*739 504*	*568 875*	*829 213*	*926 567*	*1 129 497*	*1 418 496*	*1 740 696*	*1 998 342*
Africa	285 471	187 341	186 509	210 974	256 586	333 291	406 746	479 615
America	87 855	63 344	141 236	123 401	157 760	196 916	241 332	298 419
Asia	366 178	318 191	501 468	592 192	715 150	888 289	1 092 618	1 220 308
Major exporters of manufactured goods	*1 232 012*	*2 299 114*	*4 425 993*	*5 117 152*	*5 870 435*	*6 875 691*	*7 936 951*	*9 388 413*
America	435 227	700 966	1 182 524	1 151 207	1 299 541	1 587 399	1 936 332	2 236 107
Asia	796 785	1 598 148	3 243 470	3 965 945	4 570 893	5 288 292	6 000 619	7 152 306
Emerging economies	*731 623*	*1 499 909*	*2 734 010*	*2 664 085*	*3 009 320*	*3 528 343*	*4 109 971*	*4 668 821*
America	556 939	905 107	1 595 402	1 416 293	1 618 177	1 968 885	2 391 493	2 773 862
Asia	174 684	594 802	1 138 608	1 247 793	1 391 143	1 559 458	1 718 479	1 894 960
Newly industrialized economies	*315 704*	*840 768*	*1 547 414*	*1 720 563*	*1 897 888*	*2 115 515*	*2 388 250*	*2 676 136*
First tier	146 776	541 350	1 094 317	1 159 565	1 277 076	1 428 876	1 551 672	1 676 898
Second tier	168 929	299 417	453 097	560 998	620 812	686 639	836 579	999 239
Developing economies: Africa	**515 510**	**514 193**	**605 467**	**694 152**	**826 377**	**970 678**	**1 094 750**	**1 252 565**
Northern Africa excluding Sudan	131 902	171 382	245 159	242 031	280 866	329 398	371 553	423 748
Sub-Saharan Africa	383 608	342 811	360 308	452 121	545 511	641 280	723 197	823 818
Sub-Saharan Africa excluding South Africa	303 065	230 797	227 431	285 467	329 068	399 233	470 696	545 993
Developing economies: America	**765 041**	**1 122 097**	**2 007 926**	**1 810 446**	**2 082 925**	**2 528 463**	**3 029 628**	**3 534 209**
Central America and Greater Carribean Islands excluding Puerto Rico	265 948	339 355	713 344	784 094	840 583	949 831	1 038 020	1 115 230
Central America and Greater Carribean Islands excluding Mexico and Puerto Rico	58 285	76 645	132 552	145 298	157 514	181 862	201 025	226 050
South America and Central America	722 178	1 062 144	1 918 007	1 713 984	1 978 029	2 403 881	2 891 661	3 384 699
South America excluding Brazil	260 830	329 174	666 792	483 330	592 840	722 332	850 763	1 030 989
Developing economies: Asia	**1 336 372**	**2 188 999**	**4 154 224**	**5 089 097**	**5 873 681**	**6 830 822**	**7 869 727**	**9 244 809**
Eastern and South-Eastern Asia excluding China	341 081	877 551	1 615 238	1 803 756	1 993 004	2 225 122	2 511 274	2 790 859
Southern Asia excluding India	155 261	195 199	256 117	322 280	371 911	426 175	502 476	611 793

Sources:
- Data and UNCTAD secretariat estimates based on UN DESA Statistics Division data

Notes:
(1) GDP by expenditure, in current prices and current exchange rates.

Per capita gross domestic product / Produit intérieur brut par habitant Dollars								Groupements économiques
1980	1990	2000	2003	2004	2005	2006	2007	
795	**943**	**1 400**	**1 503**	**1 713**	**1 987**	**2 274**	**2 688**	**ÉCONOMIES EN DÉVELOPPEMENT**
999	1 167	1 553	1 573	1 781	2 058	2 342	2 745	Économies en développement sans la Chine
869	1 039	1 585	1 704	1 946	2 261	2 591	3 032	Économies en développement sans les PMA
3 939	4 973	8 627	8 296	9 249	10 621	11 886	12 965	Pays en développement à revenu élevé
1 556	2 005	2 413	2 441	2 866	3 399	3 971	4 726	Pays en développement à revenu intermédiaire
389	405	623	782	895	1 033	1 191	1 457	Pays en développement à revenu faible
341	369	274	316	354	393	441	550	Pays pauvres très endettés
274	342	361	413	490	575	685	811	Pays en développement sans littoral
1 681	1 868	2 508	2 788	3 025	3 267	3 536	3 866	Petits États insulaires en développement
263	*291*	*263*	*305*	*345*	*396*	*454*	*575*	*Pays les moins avancés*
294	324	236	279	326	392	469	631	Afrique et Haïti
218	240	298	342	370	396	424	493	Asie
556	524	736	770	839	849	899	997	Îles
3 188	*1 783*	*2 038*	*2 137*	*2 552*	*3 139*	*3 774*	*4 524*	*Principaux exportateurs de pétrole*
2 319	1 141	877	925	1 100	1 397	1 668	1 924	Afrique
3 640	2 029	3 716	3 094	3 896	4 790	5 784	7 050	Amérique
4 322	2 575	3 211	3 574	4 234	5 158	6 222	8 132	Asie
593	*925*	*1 539*	*1 718*	*1 950*	*2 259*	*2 580*	*3 020*	*Principaux exportateurs d'articles manufacturés*
2 279	3 002	4 317	4 049	4 518	5 453	6 571	7 496	Amérique
422	710	1 247	1 472	1 678	1 921	2 157	2 545	Asie
1 997	*3 411*	*5 373*	*5 064*	*5 662*	*6 570*	*7 573*	*8 513*	*Économies émergentes*
2 250	3 007	4 534	3 881	4 384	5 273	6 329	7 254	Amérique
1 469	4 289	7 252	7 742	8 566	9 531	10 425	11 414	Asie
975	*2 160*	*3 427*	*3 664*	*3 992*	*4 395*	*4 903*	*5 430*	*Économies nouvellement industrialisées*
2 316	7 520	13 724	14 277	15 645	17 420	18 828	20 260	Première génération
649	944	1 219	1 444	1 576	1 720	2 067	2 437	Deuxième génération
1 076	**808**	**739**	**790**	**919**	**1 055**	**1 163**	**1 405**	**Économies en développement : Afrique**
1 438	1 452	1 738	1 636	1 869	2 158	2 396	2 721	Afrique septentrionale sans le Soudan
990	662	531	619	728	836	920	1 122	Afrique subsaharienne
845	479	359	417	469	555	638	797	Afrique subsaharienne sans l'Afrique du Sud
2 123	**2 552**	**3 875**	**3 358**	**3 815**	**4 573**	**5 411**	**6 234**	**Économies en développement : Amérique**
2 296	2 422	4 281	4 542	4 817	5 382	5 811	6 165	Amérique centrale et Grandes Antilles sans Porto Rico
1 253	1 366	1 981	2 073	2 214	2 518	2 743	3 040	Amérique centrale et Grandes Antilles sans le Mexique et Porto Rico
2 159	2 592	3 961	3 399	3 873	4 647	5 519	6 377	Amérique du Sud et Amérique centrale
2 163	2 231	3 821	2 658	3 217	3 870	4 501	5 386	Amérique du Sud sans le Brésil
544	**733**	**1 187**	**1 399**	**1 595**	**1 832**	**2 086**	**2 458**	**Économies en développement : Asie**
780	1 647	2 599	2 792	3 047	3 361	3 748	4 271	Asie orientale et Asie du Sud-Est sans la Chine
616	587	618	737	836	941	1 090	1 303	Asie méridionale sans l'Inde

Sources :
- Données et estimations du secrétariat de la CNUCED sur la base de données de ONU DAES Division de statistique

Notes :
(1) PIB par dépenses, aux prix et taux de change courants.

8.2.1 Annual average growth rates of total and per capita real gross domestic product of countries and geographical regions

Region, country or territory	Total real gross domestic product / Produit intérieur brut réel total Percentage / En pourcentage										
	80-90	80-00	80-05	90-00	90-05	95-05	00-05	2004	2005	2006	2007
WORLD	**3.2**	**2.8**	**2.8**	**2.8**	**2.8**	**2.9**	**2.8**	**4.0**	**3.4**	**4.0**	**3.8**
DEVELOPING ECONOMIES	3.9	4.5	4.6	5.0	4.8	4.6	5.4	7.2	6.7	7.1	7.3
ECONOMIES IN TRANSITION	1.2	-5.5	-3.7	-4.8	-0.4	4.4	6.1	7.3	6.5	7.2	8.2
DEVELOPED ECONOMIES	3.2	2.8	2.7	2.5	2.4	2.4	1.9	2.9	2.3	2.8	2.5
Developing economies: Africa	**2.3**	**2.4**	**2.7**	**2.8**	**3.3**	**3.9**	**4.8**	**5.6**	**5.7**	**5.6**	**5.9**
Eastern Africa	***3.0***	***3.3***	***3.3***	***3.1***	***3.3***	***3.4***	***3.7***	***6.4***	***5.1***	***5.8***	***6.2***
Burundi	4.0	0.9	0.6	-2.6	-0.9	1.0	2.1	4.4	0.9	(e)5.1	(e)3.6
Comoros	2.7	1.7	1.7	1.2	1.6	2.1	2.2	1.9	2.8	1.2	(e)-1.0
Djibouti	0.5	1.0	1.3	1.3	1.6	1.8	2.9	3.0	3.2	4.2	(e)5.0
Eritrea	–	–	–	–	–	(e)1.2	(e)2.9	2.0	(e)0.5	(e)-1.0	(e)1.3
Ethiopia	–	–	–	–	–	4.2	4.8	13.1	10.3	10.6	(e)10.4
Ethiopia (former)	3.4	–	–	–	–	–	–	–	–	–	–
Kenya	4.4	3.2	3.0	2.1	2.4	2.6	3.5	4.9	5.8	5.4	(e)6.1
Madagascar	1.2	1.4	1.7	2.0	2.3	2.8	2.0	5.3	4.6	4.7	(e)6.4
Malawi	3.2	4.9	4.6	7.0	4.8	2.4	3.2	6.7	1.9	8.5	(e)6.6
Mauritius	6.3	5.8	5.5	5.1	4.8	4.6	3.3	5.4	1.4	4.2	(e)5.0
Mozambique	-0.1	3.1	(e)4.4	5.9	(e)7.1	(e)8.4	(e)8.6	7.5	(e)7.7	(e)7.9	(e)7.8
Rwanda	1.8	-0.5	0.9	0.1	3.2	7.2	5.0	3.8	6.0	3.0	(e)6.0
Seychelles	4.2	4.8	4.0	4.6	2.6	1.5	-2.5	-2.0	-2.3	-1.4	(e)5.3
Somalia	1.1	-1.7	-1.0	-3.2	-0.5	2.6	2.8	2.8	2.4	2.4	(e)-3.5
Uganda	3.5	5.7	5.9	7.4	6.8	6.1	5.8	5.6	6.5	6.2	(e)6.5
United Republic of Tanzania	2.8	3.8	4.2	3.7	4.6	5.5	6.9	6.7	6.9	5.9	(e)7.0
Zambia	1.0	0.6	1.2	0.5	1.9	3.4	4.7	6.2	5.1	6.0	(e)5.5
Zimbabwe	3.6	2.9	1.4	1.5	-1.0	-3.3	-4.9	0.7	-7.1	-4.8	(e)-5.0
Middle Africa	***2.6***	***0.8***	***1.5***	***1.4***	***2.9***	***4.3***	***6.4***	***8.6***	***8.7***	***6.6***	***8.2***
Angola	2.9	1.1	2.2	2.2	4.4	6.5	9.9	11.2	20.6	14.3	(e)17.8
Cameroon	3.4	1.0	1.7	2.6	3.5	4.5	4.2	5.1	2.6	4.2	(e)3.3
Central African Republic	1.4	0.7	0.7	1.3	0.8	0.6	-1.5	1.3	2.2	(e)4.1	(e)4.2
Chad	6.0	4.4	5.1	3.4	5.9	8.2	15.8	33.7	8.6	(e)0.5	(e)0.6
Congo	3.5	1.8	2.0	1.2	2.2	3.0	4.0	4.0	9.0	7.4	(e)-1.0
Dem. Rep. of the Congo	1.6	-2.9	-2.6	-4.9	-2.7	-0.7	4.4	6.6	6.5	(e)5.1	(e)6.3
Equatorial Guinea	2.0	9.6	14.4	23.7	26.4	30.1	24.8	30.0	9.3	-1.0	(e)11.1
Gabon	1.1	2.3	2.0	2.3	1.4	0.3	1.6	1.4	3.0	(e)1.2	(e)5.6
Sao Tome and Principe	-0.4	1.0	1.5	1.8	2.5	3.1	3.8	3.9	3.0	5.5	(e)6.2
Northern Africa	***2.4***	***2.5***	***2.9***	***3.2***	***3.7***	***4.2***	***4.9***	***5.2***	***5.5***	***6.0***	***6.1***
Algeria	2.7	1.7	2.1	1.9	2.8	3.9	5.1	5.2	5.3	2.7	(e)4.6
Egypt	7.0	5.6	5.3	4.9	4.6	4.5	4.5	4.5	6.8	6.7	(e)7.2
Libyan Arab Jamahiriya	-1.8	-0.5	(e)0.3	1.4	(e)2.2	(e)2.9	(e)4.7	(e)5.0	(e)6.3	(e)5.2	(e)5.5
Morocco	4.2	3.3	3.2	2.3	2.9	3.6	4.3	4.2	1.7	7.3	(e)2.7
Sudan	0.1	3.4	4.3	6.2	6.5	6.9	6.7	7.2	7.9	12.1	(e)11.6
Tunisia	3.3	4.1	4.3	4.7	4.7	4.9	4.5	6.0	4.2	5.1	(e)6.3
Southern Africa	***1.6***	***1.7***	***2.0***	***2.2***	***2.8***	***3.3***	***4.0***	***4.9***	***5.2***	***5.3***	***5.1***
Botswana	10.9	8.0	7.4	4.8	5.4	6.1	6.1	6.6	8.4	4.2	(e)5.6
Lesotho	4.5	5.0	4.4	3.9	3.2	2.3	3.0	4.0	2.9	1.6	(e)4.8
Namibia	2.3	3.5	(e)3.7	4.0	(e)4.0	(e)4.1	(e)4.9	(e)6.6	(e)4.7	(e)4.1	(e)4.2
South Africa	1.4	1.4	1.8	2.1	2.7	3.1	3.9	4.8	5.1	(e)5.4	(e)5.1
Swaziland	7.7	5.7	4.9	3.3	3.0	2.7	2.3	2.3	1.8	(e)2.1	(e)2.4
Western Africa	***2.5***	***3.0***	***3.3***	***2.9***	***3.5***	***4.2***	***5.4***	***5.4***	***5.5***	***5.0***	***5.3***
Benin	3.3	3.7	4.0	4.6	4.7	4.7	4.0	3.1	2.9	3.6	(e)4.4
Burkina Faso	2.5	4.4	4.6	5.4	5.0	4.7	6.3	6.6	5.9	5.9	(e)4.2
Cape Verde	5.4	5.4	5.8	7.1	6.9	7.0	5.1	4.4	5.8	5.5	(e)6.7
Côte d'Ivoire	3.3	2.8	2.5	3.3	2.3	1.4	0.7	1.8	1.9	1.9	(e)1.6
Gambia	3.8	3.3	3.5	3.2	3.6	4.2	3.6	5.1	5.0	5.6	(e)7.0
Ghana	3.0	4.0	4.1	4.3	4.4	4.6	5.0	5.2	5.8	6.0	(e)6.1
Guinea	3.2	3.9	3.9	4.4	3.9	3.6	2.9	2.7	3.3	(e)2.8	(e)1.5
Guinea-Bissau	4.3	3.0	2.1	1.1	0.3	-1.1	-0.5	2.2	3.5	4.6	(e)4.7
Liberia	-5.0	-10.3	-6.2	3.9	6.0	12.5	-6.9	2.6	5.3	7.0	(e)9.4
Mali	3.8	4.1	4.4	4.7	5.0	5.3	6.0	2.3	6.1	(e)5.3	(e)2.5
Mauritania	1.6	2.4	2.6	3.0	3.1	3.1	4.0	5.2	5.4	14.1	(e)0.9
Niger	-0.1	1.2	1.9	2.9	3.4	4.1	4.1	-0.6	7.1	3.5	(e)4.0
Nigeria	2.3	3.0	3.4	2.3	3.5	4.6	6.6	6.6	6.2	5.3	(e)6.3
Senegal	3.1	2.8	3.2	3.6	4.1	4.7	4.5	5.6	5.5	4.0	(e)5.2
Sierra Leone	2.6	-0.5	0.1	-7.2	-1.5	3.1	12.7	9.6	7.5	9.7	(e)6.8
Togo	1.8	1.6	1.7	1.4	1.7	1.8	2.2	3.0	0.8	4.2	(e)2.5

For sources and notes, see end of table.

Per capita real gross domestic product / Produit intérieur brut réel par habitant — Percentage / En pourcentage											Régions, pays ou territoires
80-90	80-00	80-05	90-00	90-05	95-05	00-05	2004	2005	2006	2007	
1.4	1.1	1.2	1.3	1.4	1.6	1.5	2.7	2.2	2.7	2.7	**MONDE**
1.7	2.5	2.7	3.2	3.1	3.0	3.9	5.7	5.2	5.6	5.9	ÉCONOMIES EN DÉVELOPPEMENT
0.3	-5.7	-3.8	-4.5	-0.2	4.6	6.3	7.5	6.6	7.3	9.2	ÉCONOMIES EN TRANSITION
2.6	2.1	2.0	1.9	1.8	1.9	1.3	2.3	1.8	2.3	2.0	ÉCONOMIES DÉVELOPPÉES
-0.5	-0.4	0.1	0.2	0.8	1.5	2.4	3.2	3.3	3.3	3.5	**Économies en développement : Afrique**
0.0	0.5	0.5	0.4	0.6	0.6	1.1	3.8	2.5	3.1	3.6	*Afrique orientale*
0.7	-1.5	-1.7	-4.0	-2.8	-1.3	-1.2	0.6	-2.9	(e)1.1	(e)-0.5	Burundi
-0.4	-1.3	-1.2	-1.6	-1.2	-0.6	-0.4	-0.7	0.2	-1.3	(e)-3.4	Comores
-4.5	-2.9	-2.3	-1.2	-0.9	-0.7	1.0	1.2	1.4	2.4	(e)3.2	Djibouti
–	–	–	–	–	(e)-2.3	(e)-1.3	-2.2	(e)-3.3	(e)-4.5	(e)-2.0	Érythrée
–	–	–	–	–	1.5	2.1	10.3	7.5	7.9	(e)7.7	Éthiopie
0.1	–	–	–	–	–	–	–	–	–	–	Éthiopie (anc.)
0.6	-0.1	-0.1	-0.8	-0.4	-0.1	0.8	2.1	3.1	2.7	(e)3.3	Kenya
-1.6	-1.5	-1.3	-1.0	-0.7	-0.2	-0.9	2.4	1.7	1.9	(e)3.6	Madagascar
-1.2	1.6	1.5	4.9	2.4	-0.4	0.6	4.1	-0.7	5.8	(e)3.8	Malawi
5.4	4.7	4.4	3.9	3.6	3.5	2.4	4.5	0.5	3.3	(e)4.2	Maurice
-1.0	1.1	(e)2.2	2.7	(e)4.1	(e)5.7	(e)6.0	5.0	(e)5.3	(e)5.6	(e)5.7	Mozambique
-1.9	-1.6	-0.9	-0.9	0.4	1.8	2.6	2.2	3.9	0.5	(e)3.2	Rwanda
3.3	3.7	2.8	3.4	1.4	0.2	-3.5	-3.0	-3.1	-2.1	(e)4.7	Seychelles
0.9	-1.8	-1.6	-3.5	-2.0	-0.3	-0.2	-0.2	-0.6	-0.6	(e)-6.3	Somalie
0.0	2.1	2.4	4.0	3.4	2.9	2.5	2.2	3.1	2.8	(e)3.1	Ouganda
-0.3	0.9	1.4	0.8	1.9	2.9	4.2	4.0	4.3	3.3	(e)4.6	République-Unie de Tanzanie
-2.1	-2.2	-1.5	-2.0	-0.4	1.2	2.8	4.3	3.2	4.1	(e)3.5	Zambie
-0.2	0.0	-1.0	-0.4	-2.4	-4.3	-5.6	0.0	-7.8	-5.6	(e)-5.9	Zimbabwe
-0.4	-2.2	-1.4	-1.4	0.1	1.6	3.4	5.5	5.7	3.6	5.1	*Afrique centrale*
-0.1	-1.7	-0.6	-0.6	1.6	3.7	6.8	7.9	17.2	11.1	(e)14.6	Angola
0.3	-1.8	-1.0	0.0	1.0	2.1	1.8	2.8	0.4	2.0	(e)1.2	Cameroun
-1.2	-1.8	-1.7	-1.3	-1.4	-1.3	-3.1	-0.2	0.5	(e)2.3	(e)2.3	République centrafricaine
3.1	1.3	1.8	0.1	2.4	4.4	11.7	29.0	5.0	(e)-2.6	(e)-2.3	Tchad
0.4	-1.1	-0.8	-1.6	-0.5	0.4	1.5	1.6	6.5	5.1	(e)-3.1	Congo
-1.4	-5.9	-5.5	-7.6	-5.3	-3.2	1.3	3.4	3.2	(e)1.8	(e)2.9	Rép. dém. du Congo
-2.7	6.3	11.2	20.8	23.4	27.0	21.9	27.0	6.8	-3.3	(e)8.5	Guinée équatoriale
-1.9	-0.5	-0.7	-0.3	-0.8	-1.7	-0.2	-0.3	1.4	(e)-0.4	(e)4.0	Gabon
-2.4	-1.0	-0.4	-0.1	0.6	1.3	2.1	2.2	1.3	3.8	(e)4.5	Sao Tomé-et-Principe
-0.2	0.3	0.8	1.2	1.8	2.5	3.2	3.4	3.8	4.2	4.3	*Afrique septentrionale*
-0.3	-0.8	-0.1	0.0	1.1	2.4	3.6	3.6	3.7	1.2	(e)3.0	Algérie
4.6	3.4	3.2	2.9	2.7	2.6	2.4	2.7	4.9	4.8	(e)5.3	Égypte
-5.2	-3.1	(e)-2.1	-0.6	(e)0.1	(e)0.8	(e)2.6	(e)2.9	(e)4.2	(e)3.1	(e)3.4	Jamahiriya arabe libyenne
1.8	1.3	1.4	0.8	1.5	2.3	3.0	3.0	0.5	6.0	(e)1.4	Maroc
-2.6	0.7	1.7	3.5	4.0	4.5	4.6	5.1	5.7	9.7	(e)9.1	Soudan
0.8	2.0	2.4	3.1	3.3	3.6	3.3	4.9	3.1	4.0	(e)5.2	Tunisie
-0.8	-0.7	-0.1	0.0	0.9	1.8	2.8	3.9	4.3	4.5	4.4	*Afrique australe*
7.5	5.0	4.7	2.4	3.3	4.5	4.9	5.5	7.1	2.9	(e)4.3	Botswana
2.3	3.2	2.7	2.2	1.6	0.8	2.0	3.2	2.2	0.9	(e)4.2	Lesotho
-1.4	0.0	(e)0.5	1.1	(e)1.6	(e)2.0	(e)3.5	(e)5.3	(e)3.4	(e)2.7	(e)2.8	Namibie
-0.9	-0.9	-0.3	-0.1	0.8	1.7	2.7	3.8	4.2	(e)4.6	(e)4.5	Afrique du Sud
4.1	2.8	2.3	1.3	1.2	1.0	1.0	1.2	0.9	(e)1.3	(e)1.7	Swaziland
-0.5	0.0	0.4	0.0	0.7	1.5	2.7	2.8	2.9	2.4	2.8	*Afrique occidentale*
-0.1	0.3	0.6	1.2	1.3	1.4	0.7	-0.2	-0.4	0.4	(e)1.2	Bénin
-0.1	1.5	1.6	2.4	1.9	1.6	3.0	3.2	2.6	2.7	(e)1.2	Burkina Faso
3.2	3.1	3.4	4.6	4.4	4.5	2.7	2.0	3.3	3.1	(e)4.3	Cap-Vert
-1.0	-0.8	-0.7	0.4	-0.2	-0.7	-1.0	0.1	0.2	0.2	(e)-0.3	Côte d'Ivoire
0.1	-0.4	-0.2	-0.5	0.0	0.8	0.5	1.9	2.0	2.7	(e)4.1	Gambie
-0.3	1.1	1.3	1.6	1.9	2.2	2.7	2.9	3.6	3.8	(e)4.0	Ghana
0.5	0.7	0.9	1.2	1.3	1.5	1.0	0.8	1.4	(e)0.8	(e)-0.5	Guinée
1.8	0.2	-0.8	-1.9	-2.7	-4.0	-3.5	-0.9	0.4	1.5	(e)1.6	Guinée-Bissau
-6.3	-11.7	-8.3	-0.2	1.7	7.3	-8.8	0.8	2.4	2.9	(e)4.4	Libéria
1.4	1.6	1.7	2.0	2.1	2.3	2.9	-0.8	3.0	(e)2.2	(e)-0.6	Mali
-1.0	-0.3	-0.1	0.2	0.3	0.2	1.1	2.2	2.5	11.1	(e)-1.6	Mauritanie
-3.1	-2.0	-1.4	-0.7	-0.2	0.5	0.5	-4.0	3.4	0.0	(e)0.4	Niger
-0.5	0.1	0.5	-0.5	0.8	1.9	3.9	4.0	3.7	2.9	(e)3.9	Nigéria
0.1	-0.1	0.3	0.9	1.3	2.0	1.9	2.9	2.8	1.4	(e)2.6	Sénégal
0.2	-2.1	-1.7	-8.0	-3.5	-0.1	8.0	5.0	3.7	6.8	(e)4.6	Sierra Leone
-1.8	-1.6	-1.5	-1.7	-1.5	-1.4	-0.6	0.2	-1.9	1.4	(e)-0.2	Togo

Pour les sources et les notes, se reporter à la fin du tableau.

Region, country or territory	Total real gross domestic product / Produit intérieur brut réel total Percentage / En pourcentage										
	80-90	80-00	80-05	90-00	90-05	95-05	00-05	2004	2005	2006	2007
Developing economies: America	1.7	2.4	2.4	3.2	2.8	2.4	2.7	6.1	4.7	5.4	5.7
Caribbean	2.3	0.9	1.6	1.9	2.9	4.1	3.8	4.2	7.2	8.6	6.2
Anguilla	9.4	7.8	6.9	5.1	4.9	5.2	6.6	21.6	8.8	0.1	(e)0.1
Antigua and Barbuda	6.9	4.8	4.4	3.4	3.5	3.9	4.5	7.2	4.6	(e)12.5	(e)6.0
Aruba	10.0	8.3	6.7	5.4	3.6	2.2	0.8	3.5	2.3	2.4	(e)2.0
Bahamas	3.1	1.9	2.1	2.8	2.8	2.9	1.8	1.8	2.7	(e)3.4	(e)3.3
Barbados	1.7	1.1	1.2	2.0	1.9	1.9	1.6	3.7	3.9	4.2	(e)4.1
British Virgin Islands	7.5	18.7	16.4	22.6	14.2	5.9	1.4	10.5	9.2	4.2	(e)4.2
Cayman Islands	9.2	8.3	7.1	7.0	4.9	3.0	2.1	0.9	6.5	4.2	(e)4.0
Cuba	3.4	-0.8	(e)0.0	-0.7	(e)1.6	(e)4.1	(e)4.3	5.4	(e)9.0	(e)10.0	(e)7.5
Dominica	5.2	3.4	2.6	2.0	1.2	0.7	0.8	6.3	3.3	4.1	(e)1.0
Dominican Republic	2.8	4.1	4.4	6.6	5.8	5.4	2.8	2.0	9.3	10.7	(e)8.5
Grenada	5.4	4.3	3.9	3.7	3.2	3.2	1.0	-6.9	12.1	(e)0.8	(e)3.0
Haiti	0.2	-0.8	-0.6	-0.8	-0.2	0.6	-0.7	-3.5	1.8	2.3	(e)3.2
Jamaica	2.0	2.5	2.1	1.2	1.1	0.8	1.5	1.0	1.4	2.9	(e)1.4
Montserrat	4.5	-1.7	-2.9	-9.5	-7.1	-5.7	1.4	6.8	2.0	1.1	..
Netherlands Antilles	-0.5	1.3	1.1	1.5	0.8	-0.3	1.0	1.1	0.9	0.9	(e)0.9
Saint Kitts and Nevis	7.2	5.9	4.9	3.0	2.5	1.7	2.1	7.3	4.1	4.4	(e)5.5
Saint Lucia	7.7	5.1	4.1	2.7	2.0	1.7	2.2	4.9	2.6	3.4	(e)4.0
Saint Vincent and the Grenadines	6.3	4.6	(e)4.2	3.2	(e)3.2	(e)3.3	(e)3.7	6.1	(e)3.6	(e)8.7	(e)6.6
Trinidad and Tobago	-3.4	0.2	2.1	4.6	6.1	8.0	9.2	8.8	8.0	12.0	(e)5.5
Turks and Caicos Islands	10.6	10.3	9.6	9.6	8.5	7.6	8.2	11.4	13.9	11.1	(e)10.0
Central America	1.1	2.4	2.6	3.2	3.1	3.4	2.1	4.2	3.2	5.1	3.6
Belize	4.7	5.3	5.3	3.9	4.6	5.1	5.5	4.7	3.1	5.3	(e)2.7
Costa Rica	3.0	4.4	4.4	5.3	4.7	4.5	4.3	4.3	5.9	(e)8.8	(e)6.8
El Salvador	0.6	3.1	3.2	4.8	3.7	2.6	2.2	1.8	2.8	(e)4.2	(e)4.5
Guatemala	0.8	2.9	3.1	4.1	3.8	3.5	3.1	3.2	3.5	(e)5.2	(e)5.7
Honduras	2.7	3.1	3.1	3.2	3.2	3.1	3.6	5.0	4.1	6.0	(e)6.3
Mexico	1.1	2.4	2.5	3.1	3.0	3.4	1.9	4.2	3.0	(e)4.9	(e)3.2
Nicaragua	-1.9	0.2	1.1	3.7	3.7	3.8	3.0	5.1	4.0	3.7	(e)3.5
Panama	–	–	–	4.7	(e)4.2	(e)4.1	(e)4.4	7.5	(e)7.2	(e)8.7	(e)11.2
South America	1.8	2.5	2.4	3.3	2.7	2.0	2.8	6.9	5.2	5.3	6.5
Argentina	-0.4	2.2	1.9	4.2	2.2	0.7	2.2	9.0	9.2	(e)8.5	(e)8.7
Bolivia	-0.2	2.5	(e)2.7	4.0	(e)3.4	(e)2.9	(e)3.0	(e)4.2	(e)4.0	(e)4.6	(e)4.2
Brazil	2.8	2.4	(e)2.4	2.9	(e)2.7	(e)2.3	(e)2.8	(e)5.7	(e)3.2	(e)3.7	(e)5.4
Chile	3.1	5.9	5.5	6.6	5.2	3.6	4.2	6.0	5.7	(e)4.3	(e)5.1
Colombia	3.6	3.6	3.2	2.9	2.5	1.8	3.5	4.9	5.3	4.8	(e)7.5
Ecuador	2.0	2.5	(e)2.6	2.2	(e)2.6	(e)2.8	(e)5.3	7.9	(e)6.0	(e)3.9	(e)2.7
Guyana	-3.1	1.4	1.7	5.4	3.3	1.2	0.3	1.6	-2.8	4.7	(e)5.4
Paraguay	2.6	2.9	2.5	2.2	1.6	0.8	2.6	4.1	2.9	4.0	(e)6.0
Peru	-0.3	1.3	1.9	4.7	4.0	2.9	4.3	5.2	6.4	(e)7.7	(e)9.0
Suriname	0.9	0.5	1.1	0.3	1.9	3.5	5.7	7.4	5.8	5.9	(e)5.0
Uruguay	1.0	2.7	2.1	3.4	1.5	0.1	0.9	11.9	6.4	7.0	(e)7.4
Venezuela (Bolivarian Rep. of)	0.7	1.9	(e)1.6	1.6	(e)1.0	(e)0.5	(e)1.5	18.3	(e)10.3	(e)10.3	(e)8.4
Developing economies: Asia	5.7	6.2	6.1	6.3	6.0	5.5	6.5	7.8	7.5	7.9	8.1
Eastern Asia	9.1	8.5	8.1	8.1	7.5	6.7	7.3	8.2	8.0	8.8	9.1
China	10.3	10.1	(e)9.9	10.6	(e)9.8	(e)8.9	(e)9.6	10.1	(e)10.4	(e)11.1	(e)11.4
China, Hong Kong SAR	6.9	5.6	(e)5.1	4.3	(e)4.0	(e)3.5	(e)4.2	8.2	(e)7.1	(e)7.0	(e)6.4
China, Macao SAR	7.4	5.5	5.4	2.2	4.1	5.5	13.5	28.6	6.7	16.6	(e)10.0
China, Taiwan Province of	8.5	7.6	(e)6.7	6.5	(e)5.2	(e)4.2	(e)3.6	(e)6.1	(e)4.2	(e)4.9	(e)5.7
Dem. People's Rep. of Korea	2.3	-1.0	-0.7	-2.8	-0.9	1.0	1.4	0.0	0.9	0.4	(e)0.0
Mongolia	5.7	1.6	2.0	1.0	2.5	3.9	6.1	10.8	7.0	(e)8.6	(e)9.9
Republic of Korea	9.0	7.7	7.0	5.8	5.3	4.5	4.6	4.7	4.0	5.0	(e)4.9
Southern Asia	4.6	4.9	5.0	5.1	5.3	5.5	6.5	7.5	7.7	8.2	8.6
Afghanistan	-1.6	-2.1	-1.4	-1.1	0.3	1.8	14.6	9.4	14.5	(e)6.1	(e)13.9
Bangladesh	3.9	4.4	4.6	4.9	5.1	5.4	5.6	5.4	6.7	6.5	(e)6.5
Bhutan	10.6	7.8	7.5	5.5	6.5	7.4	7.7	6.8	6.5	8.5	(e)17.6
India	5.8	5.7	5.8	6.0	6.0	6.0	6.9	8.5	8.8	9.2	(e)9.7
Iran (Islamic Rep. of)	1.0	2.9	3.3	3.2	3.9	4.6	5.6	4.4	4.5	5.4	(e)5.6
Maldives	11.9	9.7	8.9	7.8	7.2	6.9	6.1	11.3	-4.0	21.7	(e)6.6
Nepal	4.6	4.9	4.7	4.9	4.4	3.9	2.8	3.8	2.7	(e)2.8	(e)2.5
Pakistan	6.1	4.9	4.6	3.4	3.9	4.2	6.0	7.3	6.2	7.0	(e)6.5
Sri Lanka	4.0	4.6	4.5	5.3	4.7	4.2	4.3	5.4	6.2	7.5	(e)6.2

For sources and notes, see end of table.

80-90	80-00	80-05	90-00	90-05	95-05	00-05	2004	2005	2006	2007	Régions, pays ou territoires
-0.3	0.6	0.7	1.5	1.2	1.0	1.4	4.7	3.4	4.1	4.4	**Économies en développement : Amérique**
0.8	-0.4	0.3	0.7	1.7	2.9	2.7	3.2	6.2	7.6	5.2	*Caraïbes*
6.7	4.9	4.3	2.9	2.9	3.4	4.7	19.5	7.1	-1.5	(e)-1.4	Anguilla
8.7	4.6	3.6	1.0	1.3	1.8	2.9	5.7	3.2	(e)11.1	(e)4.7	Antigua-et-Barbuda
9.8	5.9	4.2	1.7	0.6	0.0	-1.9	0.9	0.5	1.5	(e)1.9	Aruba
1.2	0.1	0.3	1.1	1.2	1.5	0.5	0.6	1.5	(e)2.1	(e)2.1	Bahamas
0.8	0.3	0.6	1.5	1.4	1.5	1.2	3.3	3.5	3.8	(e)3.7	Barbade
3.1	14.9	13.2	20.0	12.0	4.1	0.0	9.1	7.8	2.9	(e)3.0	Îles Vierges britanniques
4.8	3.7	2.7	2.5	1.1	-0.3	-0.4	-1.3	4.4	2.3	(e)2.3	Îles Caïmanes
2.6	-1.5	(e)-0.6	-1.2	(e)1.2	(e)3.8	(e)4.1	5.2	(e)8.9	(e)9.9	(e)7.5	Cuba
5.9	3.8	3.0	2.0	1.3	0.8	1.0	6.5	3.6	4.4	(e)1.3	Dominique
0.7	2.1	2.5	4.7	4.0	3.6	1.1	0.4	7.6	9.1	(e)6.9	République dominicaine
4.6	4.0	3.5	3.2	2.5	2.5	0.0	-7.8	11.3	(e)0.4	(e)2.9	Grenade
-2.0	-2.8	-2.5	-2.7	-2.0	-1.1	-2.3	-5.0	0.2	0.7	(e)1.6	Haïti
0.9	1.5	1.2	0.3	0.2	0.0	0.8	0.3	0.8	2.3	(e)0.8	Jamaïque
5.7	1.5	1.1	-2.2	-0.6	1.1	-1.8	-0.4	-3.0	-1.7	..	Montserrat
-1.4	1.0	0.9	2.1	1.2	0.0	0.3	0.1	-0.3	-0.4	(e)-0.5	Antilles néerlandaises
7.9	5.6	4.3	1.6	1.2	0.4	0.7	6.0	2.7	3.1	(e)4.2	Saint-Kitts-et-Nevis
6.0	3.7	2.8	1.7	1.0	0.7	1.1	3.7	1.4	2.2	(e)2.8	Sainte-Lucie
5.4	3.9	(e)3.5	2.6	(e)2.6	(e)2.8	(e)3.2	5.6	(e)3.1	(e)8.1	(e)6.1	Saint-Vincent-et-les Grenadines
-4.6	-0.6	1.3	3.9	5.6	7.6	8.8	8.4	7.6	11.6	(e)5.1	Trinité-et-Tobago
6.1	5.3	4.6	4.4	3.3	2.6	2.6	6.0	9.7	8.2	(e)8.2	Îles Turques et Caïques
-0.9	0.5	0.8	1.3	1.4	1.9	0.9	3.1	2.0	3.8	2.3	*Amérique centrale*
2.1	2.5	2.5	1.1	1.8	2.5	3.1	2.3	0.8	3.0	(e)0.6	Belize
0.3	1.7	1.9	2.7	2.3	2.2	2.3	2.4	4.1	(e)7.0	(e)5.2	Costa Rica
-0.4	1.5	1.5	2.7	1.9	0.9	0.7	0.4	1.3	(e)2.8	(e)3.0	El Salvador
-1.6	0.5	0.7	1.8	1.4	1.1	0.6	0.6	0.9	(e)2.6	(e)3.1	Guatemala
-0.3	0.4	0.6	0.8	0.9	1.0	1.6	3.0	2.1	4.0	(e)4.2	Honduras
-0.8	0.5	0.8	1.3	1.4	2.1	1.0	3.3	2.0	(e)3.9	(e)2.0	Mexique
-4.2	-2.1	-1.0	1.5	1.8	2.2	1.6	3.8	2.7	2.4	(e)2.2	Nicaragua
–	–	–	2.6	(e)2.2	(e)2.1	(e)2.5	5.6	(e)5.3	(e)6.8	(e)9.3	Panama
-0.2	0.6	0.7	1.7	1.1	0.5	1.4	5.5	3.8	4.0	5.1	*Amérique du Sud*
-1.9	0.8	0.6	2.9	1.0	-0.4	1.2	8.0	8.1	(e)7.4	(e)7.6	Argentine
-2.4	0.2	(e)0.5	1.7	(e)1.3	(e)0.8	(e)1.0	(e)2.2	(e)2.0	(e)2.7	(e)2.3	Bolivie
0.6	0.6	(e)0.7	1.3	(e)1.2	(e)0.9	(e)1.4	(e)4.3	(e)1.8	(e)2.3	(e)4.0	Brésil
1.4	4.1	3.9	4.9	3.7	2.4	3.0	4.8	4.6	(e)3.3	(e)4.0	Chili
1.5	1.6	1.3	1.1	0.8	0.1	1.9	3.3	3.8	3.4	(e)6.1	Colombie
-0.6	0.2	(e)0.6	0.4	(e)1.0	(e)1.4	(e)4.1	6.7	(e)4.8	(e)2.8	(e)1.6	Équateur
-2.7	1.6	1.9	5.3	3.3	1.2	0.2	1.4	-2.9	4.8	(e)5.6	Guyana
-0.3	0.3	0.0	-0.1	-0.6	-1.3	0.6	2.1	0.9	2.1	(e)4.1	Paraguay
-2.6	-0.7	0.0	3.0	2.4	1.6	3.0	4.0	5.2	(e)6.5	(e)7.8	Pérou
-0.3	-0.5	0.2	-0.6	1.1	2.6	5.0	6.7	5.1	5.3	(e)4.4	Suriname
0.3	2.0	1.5	2.7	1.0	-0.2	0.9	11.9	6.3	6.8	(e)7.1	Uruguay
-1.9	-0.5	(e)-0.7	-0.5	(e)-1.0	(e)-1.4	(e)-0.3	16.2	(e)8.4	(e)8.4	(e)6.6	Venezuela (Rép. bolivarienne du)
3.7	4.3	4.3	4.6	4.4	4.1	5.2	6.5	6.2	6.6	6.8	**Économies en développement : Asie**
7.6	7.2	6.9	7.0	6.5	5.9	6.6	7.6	7.3	8.2	8.5	*Asie orientale*
8.8	8.8	(e)8.7	9.5	(e)8.9	(e)8.0	(e)8.9	9.4	(e)9.7	(e)10.4	(e)10.7	Chine
5.6	4.2	(e)3.7	2.7	(e)2.5	(e)2.1	(e)3.0	7.0	(e)6.0	(e)5.9	(e)5.3	Chine (RAS de Hong Kong)
3.1	2.5	2.8	0.5	2.6	4.0	11.9	26.9	5.5	15.5	(e)9.2	Chine (RAS de Macao)
7.1	6.5	(e)5.7	5.6	(e)4.4	(e)3.5	(e)3.1	(e)5.7	(e)3.8	(e)4.5	(e)5.5	Province chinoise de Taiwan
-0.3	-3.2	-2.6	-4.1	-2.0	0.2	0.7	-0.6	0.5	0.1	(e)0.1	Rép. populaire dém. de Corée
2.7	-0.4	0.2	0.0	1.5	3.1	5.2	9.7	6.0	(e)7.6	(e)8.9	Mongolie
7.7	6.6	6.0	4.8	4.6	3.9	4.1	4.3	3.6	4.6	(e)4.5	République de Corée
2.2	2.6	2.8	3.0	3.3	3.6	4.8	5.8	6.0	6.5	6.9	*Asie méridionale*
-0.2	-4.7	-4.3	-5.9	-3.8	-1.3	10.3	5.1	10.0	(e)2.0	(e)9.5	Afghanistan
1.4	2.0	2.3	2.8	3.0	3.4	3.6	3.4	4.8	4.7	(e)4.7	Bangladesh
7.6	6.6	6.2	5.5	5.2	4.8	4.9	4.1	4.2	6.5	(e)15.9	Bhoutan
3.4	3.5	3.6	3.9	4.1	4.2	5.2	6.8	7.2	7.6	(e)8.1	Inde
-2.7	0.3	1.1	1.7	2.5	3.5	4.6	3.4	3.4	4.1	(e)4.2	Iran (Rép. islamique d')
8.4	6.6	6.1	5.3	5.0	5.0	4.5	9.6	-5.6	19.7	(e)4.8	Maldives
2.2	2.4	2.2	2.4	2.0	1.6	0.6	1.7	0.7	(e)0.8	(e)0.5	Népal
2.4	1.8	1.8	0.9	1.5	2.0	4.1	5.5	4.4	5.1	(e)4.6	Pakistan
2.7	3.4	3.5	4.3	3.9	3.7	3.9	5.0	5.8	7.0	(e)5.7	Sri Lanka

Per capita real gross domestic product / Produit intérieur brut réel par habitant — Percentage / En pourcentage

Pour les sources et les notes, se reporter à la fin du tableau.

Region, country or territory	Total real gross domestic product / Produit intérieur brut réel total Percentage / En pourcentage										
	80 -90	80 -00	80 -05	90 -00	90 -05	95 -05	00 -05	2004	2005	2006	2007
South-Eastern Asia	*5.3*	*6.0*	*5.5*	*5.0*	*4.4*	*3.3*	*5.1*	*6.5*	*5.6*	*5.9*	*6.2*
Brunei Darussalam	-0.7	0.9	1.4	2.1	2.3	2.4	2.2	0.5	0.4	3.7	(e)0.4
Cambodia	6.6	6.5	6.7	6.4	7.1	7.9	9.0	14.9	13.4	(e)10.8	(e)9.6
Indonesia	5.9	6.0	5.2	4.2	3.5	2.2	4.7	5.1	5.6	5.6	(e)6.3
Lao People's dem. Rep.	5.1	5.8	5.9	6.5	6.3	6.1	6.3	6.9	7.3	(e)8.3	(e)8.0
Malaysia	5.2	6.9	6.5	7.0	5.7	4.1	4.8	7.3	5.2	5.9	(e)6.2
Myanmar	0.6	3.1	5.0	7.0	9.0	10.9	12.9	13.6	13.2	7.0	(e)4.2
Philippines	1.0	2.3	2.8	3.3	3.7	3.9	4.8	6.2	5.0	5.4	(e)7.3
Singapore	6.7	7.7	7.1	7.7	6.2	4.7	4.3	8.8	6.6	7.9	(e)7.7
Thailand	7.6	7.2	6.2	4.2	3.8	2.6	5.4	6.3	4.5	5.0	(e)4.8
Timor-Leste	..	(e)1.4	(e)0.1	1.4	0.1	-2.6	-0.6	0.4	2.2	-1.6	(e)7.8
Viet Nam	5.5	6.5	6.7	7.9	7.5	6.9	7.5	7.8	8.4	7.8	(e)8.5
Western Asia	*1.5*	*2.9*	*3.1*	*3.8*	*3.7*	*3.6*	*5.0*	*8.0*	*6.9*	*5.8*	*5.1*
Bahrain	0.1	3.5	4.0	4.8	4.9	4.8	6.1	5.4	7.9	(e)6.5	(e)6.3
Iraq	1.3	-2.0	-1.2	4.2	2.3	1.6	-6.3	23.0	3.3	4.0	(e)5.0
Jordan	1.4	2.6	3.2	4.7	4.8	4.6	6.1	8.4	7.2	6.3	(e)5.7
Kuwait	0.4	2.4	3.0	7.1	5.7	3.7	8.6	10.5	10.0	6.2	(e)5.7
Lebanon	-1.6	0.3	0.9	6.0	4.1	2.1	2.2	5.0	1.0	-3.2	(e)2.0
Occupied Palestinian territory	3.5	5.3	(e)4.6	6.0	(e)3.8	(e)2.6	(e)1.6	2.0	(e)6.0	(e)-8.8	(e)-2.2
Oman	7.7	5.8	5.3	4.5	4.3	3.9	4.2	5.8	5.8	(e)7.2	(e)5.5
Qatar	1.7	3.7	4.8	6.4	7.1	8.5	8.9	20.8	6.1	8.8	(e)12.5
Saudi Arabia	-1.4	1.6	(e)2.0	2.1	(e)2.4	(e)2.8	(e)4.1	5.3	(e)6.1	(e)4.3	(e)4.1
Syrian Arab Republic	0.6	3.5	(e)3.8	6.3	(e)5.0	(e)3.5	(e)4.5	(e)6.7	(e)4.5	(e)5.1	(e)4.5
Turkey	5.3	4.5	4.1	3.8	3.4	3.2	5.2	8.9	7.4	6.0	(e)4.5
United Arab Emirates	-1.5	3.2	4.1	5.5	5.9	6.3	6.8	7.4	8.4	(e)9.4	(e)7.4
Yemen	–	–	–	6.8	6.2	5.5	3.9	3.8	4.6	3.9	(e)2.9
Developing economies: Oceania	*3.7*	*3.7*	*3.3*	*3.0*	*2.6*	*2.3*	*2.4*	*2.9*	*2.5*	*2.5*	*3.0*
Cook Islands	7.0	4.2	4.0	1.5	2.8	4.1	4.4	4.3	0.1	1.8	(e)3.0
Fiji	1.7	2.5	2.5	2.7	2.5	2.3	2.6	5.3	0.7	3.4	(e)-3.9
French Polynesia	5.8	3.5	3.3	1.9	2.6	3.5	3.5	3.5	3.4	3.3	(e)3.0
Kiribati	0.8	2.8	3.3	5.3	4.9	4.8	2.5	-2.0	3.6	0.8	(e)2.3
Marshall Islands	8.2	3.3	2.1	-2.1	-1.2	-0.8	1.8	0.4	3.5	4.0	(e)2.0
Micronesia (Federated States of)	4.4	3.0	2.3	0.5	0.5	0.1	0.4	-4.4	1.5	-0.7	(e)-2.5
Nauru	4.4	-1.6	-1.9	-5.8	-3.6	-1.2	0.3	0.0	0.0	0.0	(e)0.0
New Caledonia	5.4	4.5	3.6	1.6	1.2	0.5	0.7	0.6	0.9	0.8	(e)0.8
Palau	1.1	1.4	1.3	1.6	1.1	0.4	0.9	4.9	5.5	5.0	(e)5.7
Papua New Guinea	1.9	4.0	3.8	5.0	3.8	2.7	2.5	2.9	3.1	(e)2.6	(e)6.2
Samoa	1.0	1.2	1.8	2.6	3.2	3.6	3.6	3.7	5.1	(e)2.6	(e)4.0
Solomon Islands	2.3	3.2	2.1	2.1	0.1	-1.9	2.2	8.0	5.0	5.0	(e)5.4
Tonga	3.9	2.5	2.5	2.2	2.4	2.4	2.3	1.3	2.3	1.9	(e)-3.5
Tuvalu	1.2	3.5	3.6	3.5	3.5	3.6	5.3	4.0	2.0	1.0	(e)2.0
Vanuatu	4.5	4.1	3.3	3.8	2.2	0.8	0.5	4.2	3.1	3.4	(e)6.6
Economies in transition: Asia	–	–	–	–	–	*6.2*	*8.5*	*8.7*	*10.3*	*11.8*	*11.1*
Armenia	–	–	–	–	–	(e)8.5	(e)12.4	(e)10.5	(e)13.9	(e)13.3	(e)13.8
Azerbaijan	–	–	–	–	–	9.9	12.7	10.2	26.4	34.5	(e)25.0
Georgia	–	–	–	–	–	5.8	7.6	6.3	9.6	(e)9.4	(e)12.7
Kazakhstan	–	–	–	–	–	6.9	10.1	9.6	9.7	10.6	(e)8.5
Kyrgyzstan	–	–	–	–	–	-0.5	4.1	7.0	-0.2	2.7	(e)8.2
Tajikistan	–	–	–	–	–	6.4	10.0	10.3	6.7	7.0	(e)7.8
Turkmenistan	–	–	–	–	–	4.6	3.9	5.0	9.0	9.0	(e)8.0
Uzbekistan	–	–	–	–	–	4.6	5.5	7.7	7.1	(e)7.3	(e)9.5
Economies in transition: Europe	–	–	–	–	–	*4.2*	*5.9*	*7.2*	*6.0*	*6.7*	*7.8*
Albania	1.5	-0.2	1.3	3.2	4.7	5.8	5.8	6.7	5.6	(e)5.2	(e)6.0
Belarus	–	–	–	–	–	6.6	7.5	11.4	9.4	9.9	(e)8.2
Bosnia and Herzegovina (1)	–	–	–	–	–	4.6	-6.3	-7.6	5.3	5.5	(e)5.7
Croatia	–	–	–	–	–	3.6	4.4	3.8	4.3	(e)4.8	(e)5.6
Moldova	–	–	–	–	–	2.4	7.1	7.4	7.5	4.0	(e)3.3
Russian Federation	–	–	–	–	–	4.4	6.2	7.1	6.4	6.7	(e)8.1
Serbia and Montenegro	–	–	–	–	–	(e)1.6	(e)4.9	(e)8.4	(e)6.1	(e)5.4	(e)7.0
SFR of Yugoslavia (former)	5.2	–	–	–	–	–	–	–	–	–	–
TFYR of Macedonia	–	–	–	–	–	2.0	1.8	4.1	4.1	4.0	(e)5.1
Ukraine	–	–	–	–	–	3.8	8.1	12.1	2.7	7.1	(e)7.6
USSR (former)	0.9	–	–	–	–	–	–	–	–	–	–

For sources and notes, see end of table.

8.2.1 Taux de croissance annuels moyens du produit intérieur brut réel total et par habitant des pays et des régions géographiques

Per capita real gross domestic product / Produit intérieur brut réel par habitant — Percentage / En pourcentage											Régions, pays ou territoires
80-90	80-00	80-05	90-00	90-05	95-05	00-05	2004	2005	2006	2007	
3.1	*4.0*	*3.6*	*3.3*	*2.8*	*1.8*	*3.6*	*5.1*	*4.2*	*4.5*	*4.9*	**Asie du Sud-Est**
-3.5	-1.8	-1.3	-0.5	-0.2	0.0	-0.1	-1.7	-1.8	1.5	(e)-1.7	Brunéi Darussalam
2.6	3.0	3.6	3.5	4.6	5.8	7.1	12.9	11.5	(e)8.9	(e)7.7	Cambodge
3.9	4.2	3.6	2.7	2.1	0.8	3.4	3.7	4.3	4.3	(e)5.0	Indonésie
2.2	2.9	3.3	3.9	4.0	4.1	4.6	5.3	5.6	(e)6.5	(e)6.2	Rép. dém. populaire lao
2.4	4.1	3.8	4.4	3.3	1.9	2.8	5.3	3.3	4.0	(e)4.4	Malaisie
-1.3	1.5	3.5	5.6	7.8	9.8	11.9	12.6	12.3	6.1	(e)3.3	Myanmar
-1.4	0.0	0.5	1.1	1.5	1.8	2.7	4.0	2.9	3.3	(e)5.3	Philippines
4.3	5.0	4.4	4.6	3.5	2.4	2.8	7.5	5.3	6.5	(e)6.4	Singapour
6.0	5.8	4.9	3.1	2.7	1.6	4.6	5.5	3.8	4.3	(e)4.1	Thaïlande
..	(e)0.6	(e)-1.6	0.6	-1.6	-4.8	-5.9	-5.5	-2.9	-5.7	(e)4.0	Timor-Leste
3.1	4.3	4.7	6.0	5.7	5.4	5.9	6.2	6.9	6.3	(e)7.0	Viet Nam
-1.3	*0.1*	*0.4*	*1.3*	*1.2*	*1.3*	*2.8*	*5.7*	*4.8*	*3.7*	*3.0*	**Asie occidentale**
-3.4	0.2	0.9	2.0	2.3	2.5	3.8	3.2	5.8	(e)4.5	(e)4.4	Bahreïn
-1.4	-4.7	-4.0	1.1	-0.6	-1.0	-8.3	20.4	1.3	2.1	(e)3.2	Iraq
-2.3	-1.6	-0.7	0.7	1.4	2.1	3.1	5.1	3.9	2.9	(e)2.2	Jordanie
-4.3	0.9	1.0	7.0	3.3	-1.2	4.6	6.9	6.6	3.2	(e)3.0	Koweït
-2.1	-1.4	-0.8	3.5	2.1	0.7	1.0	3.7	-0.2	-4.2	(e)0.9	Liban
-0.4	1.3	(e)0.7	2.0	(e)0.0	(e)-1.1	(e)-2.0	-1.5	(e)2.4	(e)-11.8	(e)-5.3	Territoire palestinien occupé
3.1	2.1	2.2	1.7	2.2	2.5	3.4	5.0	4.6	(e)5.5	(e)3.5	Oman
-5.4	-0.8	0.4	3.7	3.5	3.9	3.4	14.9	1.9	5.5	(e)9.9	Qatar
-6.5	-2.1	(e)-1.4	-0.3	(e)-0.1	(e)0.2	(e)1.5	2.7	(e)3.6	(e)1.9	(e)1.7	Arabie saoudite
-2.9	0.5	(e)0.8	3.6	(e)2.3	(e)0.9	(e)1.7	(e)3.8	(e)1.7	(e)2.3	(e)1.8	République arabe syrienne
3.1	2.5	2.2	2.0	1.7	1.6	3.8	7.5	6.0	4.7	(e)3.2	Turquie
-7.2	-2.4	-1.5	-0.2	0.3	0.8	1.9	2.8	4.3	(e)5.7	(e)4.2	Émirats arabes unis
–	–	–	2.7	2.6	2.4	0.9	0.8	1.5	0.9	(e)-0.1	Yémen
1.3	*1.3*	*1.0*	*0.6*	*0.3*	*0.1*	*0.2*	*0.8*	*0.5*	*0.6*	*1.2*	**Économies en développement : Océanie**
6.9	4.5	4.8	2.6	4.7	6.9	7.2	7.0	2.7	4.4	(e)5.4	Îles Cook
0.4	1.4	1.5	1.6	1.6	1.5	1.9	4.6	0.1	2.7	(e)-4.5	Fidji
3.2	1.2	1.2	0.0	0.8	1.8	1.9	2.0	1.9	1.9	(e)1.6	Polynésie française
-1.9	0.6	1.3	3.7	3.2	3.0	0.6	-3.8	1.8	-0.9	(e)0.6	Kiribati
3.4	0.5	-0.2	-2.9	-2.2	-1.8	0.1	-1.5	1.4	1.8	(e)-0.3	Îles Marshall
1.5	1.0	0.7	-0.5	-0.2	-0.1	-0.2	-5.0	0.9	-1.2	(e)-2.9	Micronésie (États fédérés de)
2.3	-3.2	-3.2	-6.7	-4.1	-1.3	0.1	-0.2	-0.2	-0.2	(e)-0.2	Nauru
3.6	2.4	1.4	-0.8	-1.0	-1.4	-1.0	-1.0	-0.7	-0.8	(e)-0.7	Nouvelle-Calédonie
-0.9	-0.9	-0.9	-1.1	-1.0	-1.2	0.1	4.3	5.0	4.5	(e)5.2	Palaos
-0.6	1.4	1.2	2.3	1.2	0.1	0.0	0.5	0.8	(e)0.4	(e)4.0	Papouasie-Nouvelle-Guinée
0.6	0.5	1.1	1.6	2.3	2.7	2.9	3.1	4.4	(e)1.8	(e)3.1	Samoa
-0.9	0.2	-0.8	-0.7	-2.6	-4.5	-0.4	5.3	2.4	2.5	(e)2.9	Îles Salomon
4.2	2.3	2.2	1.8	2.1	2.2	2.1	1.0	2.0	1.4	(e)-4.0	Tonga
-0.4	2.3	2.5	2.7	2.8	3.0	4.8	3.5	1.6	0.6	(e)1.6	Tuvalu
2.1	1.5	0.8	1.4	-0.1	-1.4	-2.1	1.5	0.5	0.9	(e)4.1	Vanuatu
–	–	–	–	–	*5.5*	*7.6*	*7.8*	*9.3*	*10.8*	*10.0*	**Économies en transition : Asie**
–	–	–	–	–	(e)9.2	(e)12.8	(e)10.9	(e)14.2	(e)13.6	(e)14.1	Arménie
–	–	–	–	–	9.2	12.1	9.6	25.8	33.6	(e)24.1	Azerbaïdjan
–	–	–	–	–	7.0	8.7	7.4	10.7	(e)10.4	(e)13.7	Géorgie
–	–	–	–	–	7.4	9.7	8.9	9.0	9.9	(e)7.7	Kazakhstan
–	–	–	–	–	-1.8	3.1	6.0	-1.2	1.6	(e)7.0	Kirghizistan
–	–	–	–	–	5.1	8.7	9.0	5.4	5.6	(e)6.3	Tadjikistan
–	–	–	–	–	3.1	2.4	3.5	7.5	7.5	(e)6.6	Turkménistan
–	–	–	–	–	3.1	4.0	6.2	5.6	(e)5.8	(e)7.9	Ouzbékistan
–	–	–	–	–	*4.7*	*6.4*	*7.8*	*6.6*	*7.2*	*9.5*	**Économies en transition : Europe**
-0.7	-0.8	0.8	4.0	5.1	5.8	5.3	6.0	5.0	(e)4.6	(e)5.4	Albanie
–	–	–	–	–	7.1	8.1	12.0	10.0	10.5	(e)8.8	Bélarus
–	–	–	–	–	2.9	-6.9	-7.8	5.0	5.2	(e)5.5	Bosnie-Herzégovine (1)
–	–	–	–	–	3.9	4.2	3.4	4.0	(e)4.7	(e)5.6	Croatie
–	–	–	–	–	3.7	8.6	8.8	8.8	5.2	(e)4.4	Moldova
–	–	–	–	–	4.8	6.8	7.7	6.9	7.2	(e)8.6	Fédération de Russie
–	–	–	–	–	(e)2.0	(e)5.6	(e)9.1	(e)6.6	(e)5.6	(e)39.2	Serbie-et-Monténégro
4.6	–	–	–	–	–	–	–	–	–	–	RSF de Yougoslavie (anc.)
–	–	–	–	–	1.6	1.5	3.9	3.9	3.9	(e)5.0	LERY de Macédoine
–	–	–	–	–	4.7	9.0	13.0	3.5	7.9	(e)8.4	Ukraine
0.0	–	–	–	–	–	–	–	–	–	–	URSS (anc.)

Pour les sources et les notes, se reporter à la fin du tableau.

Region, country or territory	Total real gross domestic product / Produit intérieur brut réel total Percentage / En pourcentage										
	80 -90	80 -00	80 -05	90 -00	90 -05	95 -05	00 -05	2004	2005	2006	2007
Developed economies: America	**3.6**	**3.2**	**3.1**	**3.5**	**3.2**	**3.1**	**2.4**	**3.6**	**3.1**	**2.9**	**2.2**
Bermuda	1.4	1.6	2.0	2.9	3.1	3.3	3.7	3.5	4.6	3.5	(e)3.0
Canada	3.2	2.7	2.8	3.1	3.2	3.5	2.6	3.3	2.9	3.1	(e)2.6
Greenland	2.0	1.0	1.3	1.9	2.1	2.5	0.7	2.7	2.0	4.1	..
United States	3.6	3.2	(e)3.2	3.5	(e)3.2	(e)3.1	(e)2.4	(e)3.6	(e)3.1	(e)2.9	(e)2.2
Developed economies: Asia	**3.9**	**2.9**	**2.4**	**1.2**	**1.1**	**1.0**	**1.4**	**2.8**	**2.0**	**2.5**	**2.2**
Israel	3.6	4.8	4.5	5.5	4.3	3.1	1.9	4.8	5.2	5.0	(e)5.2
Japan	3.9	2.8	(e)2.3	1.1	(e)1.0	(e)0.9	(e)1.3	(e)2.7	(e)1.9	(e)2.4	(e)2.1
Developed economies: Europe	**2.6**	**2.3**	**2.3**	**2.2**	**2.2**	**2.3**	**1.6**	**2.4**	**1.7**	**2.9**	**2.8**
Andorra	3.1	2.6	3.1	1.6	3.6	5.0	6.9	3.0	5.9	5.2	(e)5.0
Austria	2.2	2.5	2.4	2.4	2.2	2.2	1.4	2.4	2.0	3.1	(e)3.4
Belgium	–	–	–	–	–	–	–	2.6	1.2	2.7	(e)2.7
Belgium-Luxembourg	2.2	2.3	–	2.2	–	–	–	–	–	–	–
Bulgaria	3.4	-0.6	(e)0.1	-1.8	(e)0.7	(e)3.0	(e)5.3	(e)6.6	(e)6.2	(e)6.3	(e)6.2
Cyprus	6.3	5.6	5.1	4.6	4.2	3.6	3.0	4.2	3.9	3.8	(e)4.4
Czechoslovakia (former)	1.9	–	–	–	–	–	–	–	–	–	–
Czech Republic	–	–	–	–	–	2.3	3.5	4.2	6.1	6.0	(e)6.5
Denmark	2.4	2.2	(e)2.2	2.7	(e)2.3	(e)1.9	(e)1.2	(e)2.3	(e)2.5	(e)3 9	(e)1.8
Estonia	–	–	–	–	–	6.6	8.1	8.1	10.5	(e)11 2	(e)7.1
Finland	3.3	2.0	2.3	2.6	3.0	3.6	2.4	3.5	2.9	5 1	(e)4.3
France	2.6	2.2	(e)2.2	1.9	(e)2.1	(e)2.4	(e)1.6	(e)2.5	(e)1.9	(e)2 2	(e)2.1
Germany	–	–	–	1.8	1.6	1.4	0.5	1.2	0.9	(e)2 9	(e)2.5
Greece	0.9	1.5	2.1	2.2	3.1	4.0	4.4	4.7	3.7	(e)4 2	(e)4.0
Hungary	1.3	0.1	1.0	1.5	2.9	4.4	4.4	4.9	4.2	3 9	(e)1.3
Iceland	3.1	2.2	2.6	2.7	3.3	4.1	3.9	7.7	7.5	(e)4 4	(e)3.8
Ireland	3.2	5.1	5.8	7.5	7.4	7.5	5.1	4.3	5.5	5 3	(e)5.3
Italy	2.6	2.1	1.9	1.5	1.5	1.4	0.6	1.1	0.0	1 7	(e)1.5
Latvia	–	–	–	–	–	6.6	8.0	8.7	10.6	11 9	(e)10.3
Lithuania	–	–	–	–	–	5.9	7.9	7.3	7.6	7 8	(e)8.8
Luxembourg	–	–	–	–	–	–	–	3.6	4.0	(e)6 1	(e)4.5
Malta	3.6	4.9	4.4	5.1	3.7	2.5	0.1	0.1	2.2	(e)3 4	(e)3.8
Netherlands	2.4	2.8	2.7	3.1	2.7	2.6	1.0	2.0	1.5	3 0	(e)3.5
Norway	2.8	3.2	3.1	4.0	3.3	2.6	2.0	3.1	2.3	3 0	(e)3.5
Poland	1.6	1.7	(e)2.3	4.7	(e)4.2	(e)3.9	(e)3.2	5.3	(e)3.6	(e)6 2	(e)6.5
Portugal	3.2	3.2	3.0	2.8	2.5	2.4	0.5	1.2	0.4	1 2	(e)1.9
Romania	1.3	-1.2	-0.4	-0.6	1.1	2.1	5.8	8.4	4.1	(e)7 9	(e)6.0
San Marino	2.6	5.5	5.7	9.7	7.3	4.3	2.9	4.6	0.0	1 7	..
Slovakia	–	–	–	–	–	3.7	4.6	5.4	6.1	(e)8.5	(e)10.4
Slovenia	–	–	–	–	–	3.9	3.4	4.4	4.0	(e)5 7	(e)6.1
Spain	3.1	2.9	3.1	2.7	3.2	3.8	3.2	3.2	3.5	3.8	(e)3.8
Sweden	2.5	1.9	2.0	2.1	2.4	2.9	2.4	4.1	2.9	4.0	(e)3.6
Switzerland	2.2	1.6	1.6	1.0	1.3	1.6	1.0	2.3	1.9	2.7	(e)3.1
United Kingdom	3.1	2.5	2.6	2.7	2.8	2.9	2.5	3.3	1.9	2.8	(e)3.0
Developed economies: Oceania	**3.2**	**3.2**	**3.3**	**3.9**	**3.7**	**3.5**	**3.4**	**2.8**	**2.7**	**2.6**	**3.8**
Australia	3.4	3.3	3.4	4.0	3.8	3.6	3.3	2.7	2.8	(e)2.8	(e)3.9
New Zealand	1.9	2.1	2.4	3.2	3.3	3.2	3.7	3.7	1.9	1.3	(e)3.1

Sources:
- Data and UNCTAD secretariat estimates based on UN DESA Statistics Division data

Notes:
(1) GDP data include the Federation of Bosnia and Herzegovina only. Data for the Republika Srpska are excluded.

Per capita real gross domestic product / Produit intérieur brut réel par habitant Percentage / En pourcentage											Régions, pays ou territoires
80 -90	80 -00	80 -05	90 -00	90 -05	95 -05	00 -05	2004	2005	2006	2007	
2.5	**2.1**	**2.1**	**2.4**	**2.1**	**2.1**	**1.4**	**2.6**	**2.0**	**1.9**	**1.3**	**Économies développées : Amérique**
0.7	1.0	1.4	2.4	2.6	2.8	3.2	3.1	4.2	3.2	(e)2.7	Bermudes
2.0	1.5	1.7	2.1	2.2	2.5	1.5	2.3	1.9	2.1	(e)1.7	Canada
0.9	0.5	0.9	1.8	1.9	2.1	0.3	2.2	1.5	3.5	..	Groenland
2.6	2.2	(e)2.1	2.4	(e)2.1	(e)2.0	(e)1.4	(e)2.6	(e)2.0	(e)1.9	(e)1.2	États-Unis
3.3	**2.4**	**1.9**	**0.8**	**0.8**	**0.7**	**1.1**	**2.6**	**1.8**	**2.3**	**2.1**	**Économies développées : Asie**
1.8	2.2	1.9	2.4	1.6	0.9	0.0	2.9	3.4	3.1	(e)3.4	Israël
3.3	2.4	(e)2.0	0.8	(e)0.8	(e)0.7	(e)1.2	(e)2.6	(e)1.8	(e)2.4	(e)2.1	Japon
2.3	**1.9**	**1.9**	**1.8**	**1.9**	**2.1**	**1.3**	**2.0**	**1.4**	**2.7**	**2.6**	**Économies développées : Europe**
-0.3	-0.4	0.5	-0.7	1.6	3.8	4.7	0.8	4.2	4.1	(e)4.5	Andorre
2.0	2.0	2.0	1.9	1.8	1.9	1.0	1.9	1.6	2.7	(e)3.0	Autriche
–	–	–	–	–	–	–	2.2	0.9	2.4	(e)2.4	Belgique
2.1	2.1	–	1.9								Belgique-Luxembourg
3.4	0.0	(e)0.7	-0.8	(e)1.6	(e)3.8	(e)6.0	(e)7.3	(e)6.9	(e)7.0	(e)6.9	Bulgarie
5.0	3.8	3.4	2.8	2.5	2.2	1.2	1.8	1.0	2.6	(e)3.3	Chypre
1.8	–	–	–	–							Tchécoslovaquie (anc.)
–	–	–	–	–	2.4	3.6	4.2	6.1	6.0	(e)6.5	République tchèque
2.4	2.0	(e)1.9	2.3	(e)1.9	(e)1.6	(e)0.9	(e)2.0	(e)2.2	(e)3.6	(e)1.6	Danemark
–	–	–	–	–	7.3	8.5	8.4	10.8	(e)11.6	(e)7.5	Estonie
2.8	1.6	1.9	2.2	2.7	3.3	2.1	3.2	2.6	4.8	(e)4.0	Finlande
2.0	1.7	(e)1.7	1.4	(e)1.6	(e)1.9	(e)1.0	(e)1.8	(e)1.3	(e)1.6	(e)1.6	France
			1.4	1.3	1.3	0.5	1.2	0.9	(e)2.9	(e)2.6	Allemagne
0.4	0.8	1.5	1.4	2.5	3.6	4.2	4.5	3.5	(e)4.0	(e)3.8	Grèce
1.7	0.3	1.2	1.7	3.1	4.6	4.6	5.1	4.5	4.2	(e)1.6	Hongrie
1.9	1.2	1.5	1.7	2.2	3.0	2.9	6.6	6.5	(e)3.5	(e)2.9	Islande
2.9	4.7	5.1	6.6	6.2	6.0	3.3	2.4	3.6	3.3	(e)3.3	Irlande
2.6	1.9	1.7	1.3	1.3	1.2	0.2	0.7	-0.3	1.5	(e)1.3	Italie
–	–	–	–	–	7.4	8.7	9.4	11.2	12.5	(e)10.9	Lettonie
–	–	–	–	–	6.5	8.4	7.7	8.0	8.4	(e)9.4	Lituanie
–	–	–	–	–	–	–	2.8	3.0	(e)5.0	(e)3.3	Luxembourg
2.6	4.0	3.5	4.3	3.0	1.8	-0.6	-0.6	1.5	(e)2.9	(e)3.3	Malte
1.8	2.1	2.1	2.4	2.1	2.0	0.5	1.5	1.1	2.6	(e)3.2	Pays-Bas
2.4	2.7	2.5	3.4	2.7	2.0	1.3	2.4	1.6	2.3	(e)2.9	Norvège
0.9	1.3	(e)2.0	4.6	(e)4.3	(e)4.0	(e)3.3	5.4	(e)3.7	(e)6.4	(e)6.7	Pologne
3.0	3.1	2.8	2.5	2.1	1.9	-0.1	0.6	-0.1	0.8	(e)1.5	Portugal
0.8	-1.2	-0.3	-0.1	1.6	2.6	6.3	8.9	4.5	(e)8.4	(e)6.5	Roumanie
1.4	4.3	4.4	8.5	5.8	2.5	0.5	2.2	-1.9	0.3	..	Saint-Marin
–	–	–	–	–	3.7	4.6	5.4	6.1	(e)8.5	(e)10.4	Slovaquie
–	–	–	–	–	3.7	3.3	4.3	3.9	(e)5.6	(e)6.1	Slovénie
2.8	2.6	2.6	2.4	2.5	2.8	1.6	1.6	2.1	2.6	(e)2.9	Espagne
2.2	1.4	1.7	1.7	2.1	2.6	2.0	3.7	2.4	3.5	(e)3.1	Suède
1.4	0.8	0.9	0.4	0.7	1.2	0.5	1.8	1.5	2.3	(e)2.7	Suisse
3.0	2.3	2.3	2.4	2.4	2.5	2.0	2.8	1.4	2.4	(e)2.6	Royaume-Uni
1.8	**1.8**	**1.9**	**2.6**	**2.5**	**2.3**	**2.1**	**1.6**	**1.5**	**1.5**	**2.8**	**Économies développées : Océanie**
1.9	1.9	2.0	2.7	2.5	2.4	2.1	1.5	1.6	(e)1.7	(e)2.8	Australie
1.0	0.9	1.2	2.0	2.1	2.1	2.4	2.4	0.7	0.3	(e)2.1	Nouvelle-Zélande

Sources :
- Données et estimations du secrétariat de la CNUCED sur la base de données de ONU DAES Division de statistique

Notes :
(1) Y compris le PIB de la Fédération de Bosnie-Herzégovine seulement. Non compris le PIB de la Republika Srpska.

8.2.2 Annual average growth rates of total and per capita real gross domestic product of economic groupings

Region, country or territory	Total real gross domestic product / Produit intérieur brut réel total — Percentage / En pourcentage										
	80 - 90	80 - 00	80 - 05	90 - 00	90 - 05	95 - 05	00 - 05	2004	2005	2006	2007
DEVELOPING ECONOMIES	**3.9**	**4.5**	**4.6**	**5.0**	**4.8**	**4.6**	**5.4**	**7.2**	**6.7**	**7.1**	**7.3**
Developing economies excluding China	3.3	3.8	3.8	4.1	3.9	3.7	4.4	6.4	5.7	6.0	6.2
Developing economies excluding LDCs	3.9	4.6	4.6	5.0	4.8	4.6	5.4	7.2	6.6	7.1	7.3
High-income developing countries	2.9	4.2	4.1	4.6	4.0	3.5	3.7	6.4	5.3	5.9	5.5
Middle-income developing countries	3.1	3.1	3.2	3.3	3.3	3.1	4.1	5.9	4.8	5.0	5.5
Low-income developing countries	5.8	6.2	6.3	6.8	6.7	6.5	7.6	8.6	8.8	9.3	9.7
Heavily indebted poor countries	1.9	2.4	2.8	3.4	3.8	4.2	4.8	6.0	5.7	6.4	6.2
Landlocked developing countries	2.8	6.5	6.0	6.1	5.2	4.3	5.7	7.5	7.2	7.7	7.7
Small island developing States	1.4	2.6	2.9	3.5	3.6	3.8	4.0	4.6	3.8	6.0	4.3
Least developed countries	*2.2*	*2.8*	*3.4*	*4.0*	*4.7*	*5.4*	*6.3*	*7.3*	*7.9*	*7.4*	*7.6*
Africa and Haiti	1.9	2.4	3.1	3.4	4.2	5.1	6.0	7.6	7.9	8.1	8.6
Asia	2.7	3.5	4.1	5.1	5.5	6.0	6.8	6.9	7.9	6.4	6.2
Islands	4.4	4.9	4.3	3.5	2.9	2.1	3.0	5.8	1.1	8.2	5.0
Major petroleum exporters	*0.5*	*2.1*	*2.6*	*3.0*	*3.5*	*3.9*	*5.2*	*7.1*	*6.6*	*6.1*	*6.2*
Africa	1.4	1.8	2.4	2.4	3.4	4.4	6.0	6.3	6.9	5.8	7.1
America	0.5	1.8	1.8	2.0	1.8	1.6	3.1	14.9	9.2	9.3	7.0
Asia	-0.1	2.3	2.8	3.6	3.8	4.1	5.1	6.5	6.0	5.8	5.5
Major exporters of manufactured goods	*5.5*	*5.7*	*5.7*	*6.0*	*5.7*	*5.3*	*5.9*	*7.6*	*6.8*	*7.6*	*7.9*
America	2.1	2.4	2.4	3.0	2.8	2.7	2.5	5.1	3.1	4.2	4.5
Asia	7.5	7.3	7.1	7.1	6.6	6.0	6.8	8.2	7.8	8.4	8.7
Emerging economies	*3.7*	*4.3*	*4.1*	*4.5*	*3.9*	*3.2*	*3.4*	*5.8*	*4.3*	*5.1*	*5.4*
America	1.6	2.4	2.5	3.4	2.8	2.4	2.6	5.8	4.3	5.0	5.4
Asia	8.2	7.5	6.8	6.0	5.2	4.1	4.4	5.8	4.4	5.3	5.4
Newly industrialized economies	*7.2*	*6.8*	*6.2*	*5.5*	*4.8*	*3.8*	*4.4*	*5.9*	*4.8*	*5.4*	*5.7*
First tier	8.3	7.4	6.6	5.9	5.2	4.3	4.2	5.9	4.6	5.4	5.6
Second tier	5.3	5.9	5.3	4.5	4.0	2.8	5.0	6.0	5.1	5.4	6.0
Developing economies: Africa	**2.3**	**2.4**	**2.7**	**2.8**	**3.3**	**3.9**	**4.8**	**5.6**	**5.7**	**5.6**	**5.9**
Northern Africa excluding Sudan	2.7	2.5	2.8	2.8	3.3	3.9	4.7	4.9	5.2	5.1	5.3
Sub-Saharan Africa	2.1	2.3	2.7	2.7	3.3	3.9	4.8	5.9	5.9	5.9	6.2
Sub-Saharan Africa excluding South Africa	2.6	2.8	3.1	3.0	3.6	4.3	5.2	6.4	6.2	6.1	6.7
Developing economies: America	**1.7**	**2.4**	**2.4**	**3.2**	**2.8**	**2.4**	**2.7**	**6.1**	**4.7**	**5.4**	**5.7**
Central America and Greater Carribean Islands excluding Puerto Rico	1.3	2.2	2.4	3.0	3.0	3.5	2.2	4.1	3.7	5.6	4.0
Central America and Greater Carribean Islands excluding Mexico and Puerto Rico	2.2	1.7	2.1	2.7	3.2	3.8	3.5	4.0	6.4	7.9	6.9
South America and Central America	1.6	2.5	2.5	3.3	2.8	2.4	2.6	6.1	4.6	5.3	5.7
South America excluding Brazil	0.7	2.6	2.4	3.9	2.6	1.5	2.8	8.5	7.7	7.3	7.7
Developing economies: Asia	**5.7**	**6.2**	**6.1**	**6.3**	**6.0**	**5.5**	**6.5**	**7.8**	**7.5**	**7.9**	**8.1**
Eastern and South-Eastern Asia excluding China	7.0	6.6	6.0	5.4	4.8	3.9	4.6	6.0	4.9	5.5	5.7
Southern Asia excluding India	2.9	3.7	3.9	3.6	4.1	4.6	5.7	5.5	5.5	6.1	6.1

Sources:
- Data and UNCTAD secretariat estimates based on UN DESA Statistics Division data

8.2.2 Taux de croissance annuels moyens du produit intérieur brut réel total et par habitant des groupements économiques

Per capita real gross domestic product / Produit intérieur brut réel par habitant — Percentage / En pourcentage											Régions, pays ou territoires
80 - 90	80 - 00	80 - 05	90 - 00	90 - 05	95 - 05	00 - 05	2004	2005	2006	2007	
1.7	**2.5**	**2.7**	**3.2**	**3.1**	**3.0**	**3.9**	**5.7**	**5.2**	**5.6**	**5.9**	**ÉCONOMIES EN DÉVELOPPEMENT**
0.9	1.6	1.7	2.0	2.0	1.8	2.6	4.6	3.9	4.3	4.5	Économies en développement sans la Chine
1.8	2.7	2.8	3.4	3.3	3.1	4.0	5.8	5.3	5.8	6.0	Économies en développement sans les PMA
0.9	2.4	2.4	2.9	2.5	2.2	2.6	5.2	4.2	4.7	4.4	Pays en développement à revenu élevé
0.8	1.1	1.2	1.6	1.6	1.6	2.7	4.4	3.4	3.6	4.1	Pays en développement à revenu intermédiaire
3.6	4.2	4.4	4.9	5.0	4.9	6.0	7.0	7.2	7.7	8.1	Pays en développement à revenu faible
-0.8	-0.5	0.0	0.5	1.0	1.5	2.1	3.3	3.0	3.6	3.5	Pays pauvres très endettés
0.0	1.7	1.8	1.4	1.6	2.0	3.4	5.1	4.9	5.2	5.2	Pays en développement sans littoral
-0.6	0.4	0.8	1.8	1.9	2.0	2.1	2.8	2.1	4.3	2.6	Petits États insulaires en développement
-0.4	*0.2*	*0.8*	*1.3*	*2.1*	*2.9*	*3.7*	*4.7*	*5.3*	*4.9*	*5.1*	*Pays les moins avancés*
-1.0	-0.4	0.2	0.6	1.4	2.3	3.2	4.7	5.0	5.2	5.7	Afrique et Haïti
0.7	1.1	1.7	2.6	3.2	3.9	4.7	4.8	5.8	4.4	4.2	Asie
-0.1	-0.4	-0.3	1.5	0.7	-0.1	-0.2	2.3	-2.0	5.2	2.3	Îles
-2.6	*-0.7*	*-0.1*	*0.6*	*1.1*	*1.7*	*3.0*	*4.9*	*4.4*	*4.0*	*4.0*	*Principaux exportateurs de pétrole*
-1.5	-0.9	-0.3	-0.2	0.9	2.0	3.6	3.9	4.6	3.5	4.8	Afrique
-2.0	-0.5	-0.3	0.0	0.0	-0.1	1.5	13.1	7.5	7.7	5.5	Amérique
-3.5	-0.8	0.0	1.2	1.6	2.0	3.1	4.4	4.0	3.7	3.5	Asie
3.6	*4.0*	*4.0*	*4.4*	*4.2*	*4.0*	*4.7*	*6.4*	*5.7*	*6.4*	*6.7*	*Principaux exportateurs d'articles manufacturés*
0.1	0.6	0.7	1.3	1.3	1.3	1.2	3.9	1.9	2.9	3.3	Amérique
5.6	5.6	5.4	5.5	5.2	4.7	5.6	7.0	6.7	7.3	7.5	Asie
1.8	*2.6*	*2.5*	*3.0*	*2.5*	*2.0*	*2.3*	*4.7*	*3.3*	*4.0*	*4.3*	*Économies émergentes*
-0.4	0.6	0.8	1.8	1.4	1.1	1.4	4.6	3.1	3.8	4.2	Amérique
6.5	6.1	5.4	4.7	4.0	3.1	3.6	5.0	3.6	4.5	4.7	Asie
5.2	*5.1*	*4.5*	*3.9*	*3.3*	*2.4*	*3.1*	*4.6*	*3.5*	*4.2*	*4.5*	*Économies nouvellement industrialisées*
7.0	6.2	5.6	4.9	4.3	3.5	3.6	5.3	4.1	4.9	5.1	Première génération
3.2	4.0	3.5	2.9	2.4	1.3	3.5	4.5	3.7	4.0	4.6	Deuxième génération
-0.5	**-0.4**	**0.1**	**0.2**	**0.8**	**1.5**	**2.4**	**3.2**	**3.3**	**3.3**	**3.5**	**Économies en développement : Afrique**
0.1	0.3	0.7	1.0	1.6	2.3	3.0	3.3	3.6	3.5	3.7	Afrique septentrionale sans le Soudan
-0.8	-0.5	-0.1	0.0	0.7	1.3	2.3	3.4	3.3	3.4	3.7	Afrique subsaharienne
-0.4	-0.1	0.3	0.2	0.9	1.6	2.6	3.7	3.6	3.5	4.0	Afrique subsaharienne sans l'Afrique du Sud
-0.3	**0.6**	**0.7**	**1.5**	**1.2**	**1.0**	**1.4**	**4.7**	**3.4**	**4.1**	**4.4**	**Économies en développement : Amérique**
-0.6	0.4	0.7	1.2	1.4	2.1	1.1	3.0	2.5	4.3	2.7	Amérique centrale et Grandes Antilles sans Porto Rico
0.3	-0.2	0.3	0.9	1.4	2.2	1.9	2.5	4.8	6.3	5.4	Amérique centrale et Grandes Antilles sans le Mexique et Porto Rico
-0.4	0.6	0.7	1.6	1.2	0.9	1.3	4.8	3.3	3.9	4.3	Amérique du Sud et Amérique centrale
-1.3	0.7	0.7	2.1	1.0	0.0	1.4	7.1	6.3	5.9	6.4	Amérique du Sud sans le Brésil
3.7	**4.3**	**4.3**	**4.6**	**4.4**	**4.1**	**5.2**	**6.5**	**6.2**	**6.6**	**6.8**	**Économies en développement : Asie**
4.9	4.7	4.3	3.8	3.3	2.5	3.2	4.7	3.6	4.3	4.5	Asie orientale et Asie du Sud-Est sans la Chine
0.1	1.1	1.4	1.4	2.0	2.6	3.9	3.7	3.7	4.3	4.3	Asie méridionale sans l'Inde

Sources :
- Données et estimations du secrétariat de la CNUCED sur la base de données de ONU DAES Division de statistique

8.3.1 Nominal gross domestic product by type of expenditure and by kind of economic activity of countries and geographical regions

8.3.1 Produit intérieur brut nominal par catégories de dépenses et par branches d'activité économique des pays et des régions géographiques

Region, country or territory / Régions, pays ou territoires	Year / Année	Total GDP / PIB total	GDP by type of expenditure (1) / PIB par catégories de dépense (1)					GDP by kind of economic activity (2) / PIB par branches d'activité économique (2)			
			Final consumption / Consommation finale		Gross capital formation / Formation brute de capital	Exports / Exportations	Less imports / Moins les importations	Agriculture (3)	Industry (4) / Industrie (4)		Services (5)
			Government / Administration publique	Household / Ménages		Of goods and services / Des biens et services			Total	Manufacturing / Activités de fabrication	
			Percentage / En pourcentage								
WORLD - MONDE	**1990**	**100.0**	**17.3**	**59.3**	**23.7**	**20.0**	**20.2**	**5.5**	**33.1**	**22.2**	**61.4**
	1995	**100.0**	**16.8**	**59.9**	**22.9**	**21.7**	**21.4**	**4.3**	**30.7**	**20.6**	**65.0**
	2000	**100.0**	**16.4**	**61.1**	**22.4**	**25.2**	**25.1**	**3.7**	**29.1**	**19.3**	**67.2**
	2006	**100.0**	**17.2**	**59.7**	**22.6**	**30.8**	**30.3**	**3.9**	**29.1**	**18.0**	**67.0**
DEVELOPING ECONOMIES - ÉCONOMIES EN DÉVELOPPEMENT	1990	100.0	14.0	59.3	25.8	27.4	26.1	14.8	35.6	22.0	49.6
	1995	100.0	13.7	58.9	28.5	30.2	30.9	12.6	35.6	22.8	51.8
	2000	100.0	14.3	58.0	25.0	36.1	33.3	10.7	36.7	22.8	52.6
	2006	100.0	13.9	53.0	27.4	44.1	38.5	10.3	38.9	23.6	50.8
ECONOMIES IN TRANSITION - ÉCONOMIES EN TRANSITION	1990	100.0	20.0	52.7	28.9	24.1	26.1	18.8	45.4	35.9	35.8
	1995	100.0	19.5	55.5	24.6	32.3	31.8	10.5	36.3	27.4	53.2
	2000	100.0	16.1	52.2	19.4	45.2	32.9	10.2	36.4	27.4	53.4
	2006	100.0	17.3	51.5	22.4	37.5	29.4	6.5	37.4	18.6	56.1
DEVELOPED ECONOMIES - ÉCONOMIES DÉVELOPPÉES	1990	100.0	17.9	59.7	22.9	18.1	18.7	2.7	32.0	21.5	65.3
	1995	100.0	17.5	60.3	21.5	19.4	18.8	2.2	29.4	20.0	68.4
	2000	100.0	17.0	62.1	21.7	21.9	22.7	1.7	27.0	18.2	71.3
	2006	100.0	18.4	62.3	21.0	26.0	27.5	1.6	25.5	16.1	72.9
Developing economies: Africa - Économies en développement : Afrique	**1990**	**100.0**	**15.9**	**64.0**	**19.1**	**32.0**	**30.0**	**18.8**	**37.5**	**16.5**	**43.7**
	1995	**100.0**	**15.5**	**69.2**	**18.6**	**27.2**	**30.8**	**17.4**	**34.0**	**15.1**	**48.6**
	2000	**100.0**	**14.8**	**62.5**	**17.4**	**32.6**	**27.2**	**16.2**	**36.9**	**13.0**	**46.9**
	2006	**100.0**	**14.9**	**58.7**	**20.7**	**38.2**	**32.1**	**16.8**	**38.5**	**11.6**	**44.7**
Eastern Africa - Afrique orientale	*1990*	*100.0*	*15.7*	*75.6*	*17.9*	*18.3*	*26.8*	*37.0*	*21.0*	*13.8*	*42.0*
	1995	*100.0*	*13.9*	*77.8*	*18.3*	*25.2*	*34.7*	*34.3*	*18.9*	*11.4*	*46.8*
	2000	*100.0*	*13.7*	*77.5*	*19.0*	*21.9*	*31.4*	*32.9*	*18.1*	*10.6*	*49.0*
	2006	*100.0*	*13.6*	*77.2*	*21.2*	*24.8*	*37.4*	*31.2*	*19.5*	*10.1*	*49.3*
Burundi	1990	100.0	19.5	83.0	15.8	8.0	26.2	52.4	21.1	16.8	26.5
	1995	100.0	13.4	91.6	9.3	12.9	27.3	48.2	19.2	12.1	32.6
	2000	100.0	14.8	91.1	7.5	7.8	21.3	40.5	18.8	13.2	40.7
	2006	100.0	26.3	83.8	23.2	9.3	39.3	38.4	19.3	13.2	42.3
Comoros - Comores	1990	100.0	25.7	79.7	20.2	11.7	37.3	40.4	8.1	4.1	51.5
	1995	100.0	22.3	83.1	19.5	19.8	44.6	39.9	11.7	4.1	48.5
	2000	100.0	13.3	88.3	13.1	15.1	27.0	47.7	11.3	4.5	41.0
	2006	100.0	13.2	93.6	13.8	12.1	30.8	49.1	11.6	4.2	39.4
Djibouti	1990	100.0	33.6	67.2	27.1	81.4	109.3	3.1	22.0	3.6	74.9
	1995	100.0	35.4	62.6	18.7	39.2	55.8	3.2	15.4	2.9	81.3
	2000	100.0	30.1	67.5	19.1	39.4	60.3	3.5	15.2	3.0	81.3
	2006	100.0	28.9	62.4	19.7	42.2	54.9	3.7	16.8	2.8	79.5
Eritrea - Érythrée	1995	100.0	56.6	80.5	23.3	22.3	82.7	20.9	16.8	9.0	62.3
	2000	100.0	75.5	58.2	20.0	10.7	64.4	15.1	23.0	11.2	61.9
	2006	100.0	36.9	82.1	18.1	5.2	42.3	17.1	24.6	10.4	58.3
Ethiopia - Éthiopie	1995	100.0	8.2	89.9	11.7	10.7	19.7	56.7	10.0	4.4	33.2
	2000	100.0	18.5	77.0	19.2	12.5	24.8	46.9	12.6	5.7	40.5
	2006	100.0	12.4	80.0	19.8	15.1	32.6	47.5	12.4	4.6	40.1
Ethiopia (former) - Éthiopie (anc.)	1990	100.0	16.8	82.1	9.6	6.9	14.0	57.0	9.5	4.3	33.5
Kenya	1990	100.0	18.4	69.1	18.0	20.2	24.7	29.9	20.9	13.9	49.2
	1995	100.0	14.5	76.5	16.2	25.4	30.4	32.6	17.8	11.9	49.6
	2000	100.0	15.3	78.1	17.6	22.3	30.5	32.8	17.3	11.5	49.9
	2006	100.0	15.9	79.9	18.2	23.3	37.7	27.7	17.8	11.1	54.5
Madagascar	1990	100.0	8.0	86.0	17.0	15.9	26.9	28.6	12.8	11.6	58.6
	1995	100.0	6.2	89.9	11.3	24.1	31.4	32.3	14.8	13.5	52.8
	2000	100.0	6.8	85.5	15.0	30.7	38.0	30.0	16.7	14.9	53.4
	2006	100.0	8.4	82.6	21.7	27.4	40.4	27.6	18.7	15.4	53.8

For sources and notes, see end of table.   Pour les sources et les notes, se reporter à la fin du tableau.

8.3.1 Nominal gross domestic product by type of expenditure and by kind of economic activity of countries and geographical regions

8.3.1 Produit intérieur brut nominal par catégories de dépenses et par branches d'activité économique des pays et des régions géographiques

Region, country or territory / Régions, pays ou territoires	Year / Année	Total GDP / PIB total	GDP by type of expenditure (1) / PIB par catégories de dépense (1)					GDP by kind of economic activity (2) / PIB par branches d'activité économique (2)			
			Final consumption / Consommation finale		Gross capital formation / Formation brute de capital	Exports / Exportations / Of goods and services / Des biens et services	Less imports / Moins les importations	Agriculture (3)	Industry (4) / Industrie (4)		Services (5)
			Government / Administration publique	Household / Ménages					Total	Manufacturing / Activités de fabrication	
			Percentage / En pourcentage								
Malawi	1990	100.0	16.2	91.6	17.1	25.3	36.2	45.0	28.9	19.5	26.1
	1995	100.0	20.6	76.1	17.1	33.0	46.7	30.4	19.6	15.8	50.0
	2000	100.0	14.6	81.1	14.5	25.1	35.3	39.5	17.9	12.9	42.5
	2006	100.0	16.2	104.3	10.5	24.3	55.3	38.3	17.1	11.6	44.6
Mauritius - Maurice	1990	100.0	12.7	64.6	30.3	66.8	74.3	12.1	33.7	25.9	54.3
	1995	100.0	13.1	63.7	25.6	58.6	61.1	10.0	30.9	22.2	59.1
	2000	100.0	14.1	60.3	26.1	61.4	61.9	6.6	29.3	22.2	64.1
	2006	100.0	14.3	72.4	23.4	61.8	71.9	5.1	25.8	18.5	69.1
Mozambique	1990	100.0	12.0	102.3	19.7	6.1	38.3	37.1	18.4	11.7	44.5
	1995	100.0	9.7	99.4	30.6	12.6	52.4	33.9	14.2	7.4	51.9
	2000	100.0	11.5	80.1	33.5	12.7	37.8	23.6	24.1	12.0	52.3
	2006	100.0	11.6	60.7	24.8	42.3	37.5	21.5	26.5	13.0	52.0
Rwanda	1990	100.0	10.2	84.4	13.9	5.7	14.1	43.6	23.6	15.8	32.8
	1995	100.0	9.2	100.6	13.5	5.8	29.1	44.0	16.0	10.2	40.0
	2000	100.0	8.9	90.2	18.0	6.3	23.4	40.7	19.7	10.0	39.7
	2006	100.0	13.8	90.4	20.8	9.6	34.5	41.8	20.3	9.2	37.9
Seychelles	1990	100.0	27.7	52.0	24.6	62.5	66.7	5.7	19.1	11.9	75.2
	1995	100.0	27.7	51.0	30.1	53.4	60.1	4.5	24.4	13.6	71.1
	2000	100.0	26.2	38.2	35.1	77.7	79.6	3.0	31.0	20.5	66.0
	2006	100.0	22.1	50.0	15.6	106.1	95.7	2.6	27.7	15.1	69.6
Somalia - Somalie	1990	100.0	10.3	71.0	23.6	0.9	5.7	69.3	6.0	2.0	24.7
	1995	100.0	8.5	72.2	20.7	0.3	1.7	60.1	7.3	2.5	32.6
	2000	100.0	8.6	72.4	20.4	0.3	1.7	60.1	7.3	2.5	32.6
	2006	100.0	8.7	72.4	20.3	0.3	1.7	60.1	7.3	2.5	32.6
Uganda - Ouganda	1990	100.0	9.7	82.0	14.7	6.9	17.7	52.8	12.5	6.4	34.7
	1995	100.0	11.6	77.4	16.8	10.9	19.4	46.5	16.0	7.9	37.5
	2000	100.0	13.7	80.6	18.9	10.7	23.6	36.9	20.1	9.3	43.0
	2006	100.0	13.7	78.1	24.8	14.4	32.2	32.2	21.4	9.0	46.4
United Republic of Tanzania - République-Unie de Tanzanie	1990	100.0	10.3	76.0	35.0	11.8	33.5	44.2	15.3	8.3	40.6
	1995	100.0	15.3	83.9	19.8	24.1	41.5	44.9	14.1	6.9	41.0
	2000	100.0	6.6	83.4	17.6	14.6	23.0	43.7	15.3	7.3	41.0
	2006	100.0	7.7	81.3	22.5	23.5	32.9	44.5	16.3	6.9	39.2
Zambia - Zambie	1990	100.0	19.0	64.4	17.3	35.9	36.6	20.6	51.3	36.1	28.1
	1995	100.0	15.5	72.3	15.9	36.1	39.8	17.3	33.6	10.6	49.1
	2000	100.0	9.5	82.2	18.7	21.1	31.4	21.0	23.8	10.8	55.2
	2006	100.0	13.5	68.2	25.9	18.8	26.7	21.8	26.8	11.2	51.3
Zimbabwe	1990	100.0	19.4	63.1	17.4	22.9	22.8	16.1	32.4	22.3	51.5
	1995	100.0	17.9	59.3	25.4	38.0	40.7	14.9	28.5	21.4	56.6
	2000	100.0	16.4	70.7	13.1	32.7	32.9	20.2	16.5	11.7	63.3
	2006	100.0	31.2	73.3	9.6	49.8	60.7	15.2	25.7	17.3	59.1
Middle Africa - Afrique centrale	*1990*	*100.0*	*20.8*	*60.1*	*16.8*	*39.1*	*37.6*	*20.1*	*34.5*	*11.2*	*45.4*
	1995	*100.0*	*18.8*	*56.0*	*20.1*	*41.9*	*36.9*	*25.2*	*38.1*	*11.0*	*36.8*
	2000	*100.0*	*19.1*	*47.1*	*17.8*	*52.1*	*36.1*	*19.2*	*49.6*	*8.8*	*31.3*
	2006	*100.0*	*14.3*	*42.3*	*18.7*	*63.8*	*39.2*	*14.5*	*56.8*	*7.5*	*28.6*
Angola	1990	100.0	28.6	44.8	11.7	39.0	23.7	18.0	40.8	4.9	41.2
	1995	100.0	52.3	21.9	27.9	76.2	78.2	7.4	67.4	4.0	25.2
	2000	100.0	42.5	15.6	15.1	89.6	62.8	5.7	73.1	2.9	21.2
	2006	100.0	20.4	39.1	13.1	74.2	46.8	8.0	66.1	3.8	26.0
Cameroon - Cameroun	1990	100.0	11.4	76.7	15.0	17.9	21.1	18.2	32.9	19.2	48.9
	1995	100.0	8.7	72.2	13.3	23.6	17.8	23.5	31.1	21.5	45.4
	2000	100.0	9.5	70.2	16.7	23.3	19.7	22.0	35.5	20.7	42.5
	2006	100.0	10.7	66.8	21.5	27.2	26.1	22.2	31.9	20.5	45.9

For sources and notes, see end of table.

Pour les sources et les notes, se reporter à la fin du tableau.

8.3.1 Nominal gross domestic product by type of expenditure and by kind of economic activity of countries and geographical regions

8.3.1 Produit intérieur brut nominal par catégories de dépenses et par branches d'activité économique des pays et des régions géographiques

Region, country or territory / Régions, pays ou territoires	Year / Année	Total GDP / PIB total	GDP by type of expenditure (1) / PIB par catégories de dépense (1)					GDP by kind of economic activity (2) / PIB par branches d'activité économique (2)			
			Final consumption / Consommation finale		Gross capital formation / Formation brute de capital	Exports / Exportations	Less imports / Moins les importations	Agriculture (3)	Industry (4) / Industrie (4)		Services (5)
			Government / Administration publique	Household / Ménages		Of goods and services / Des biens et services			Total	Manufacturing / Activités de fabrication	
			Percentage / En pourcentage								
Central African Republic - République centrafricaine	1990	100.0	14.9	85.7	12.3	14.8	27.6	43.0	16.8	9.8	40.2
	1995	100.0	14.7	80.4	13.8	15.2	25.8	41.8	18.1	10.6	40.1
	2000	100.0	15.3	83.4	9.1	13.3	22.2	51.2	17.6	10.3	31.2
	2006	100.0	7.1	97.8	5.7	11.5	22.6	51.8	19.2	11.2	29.0
Chad - Tchad	1990	100.0	47.3	51.7	7.2	19.0	24.8	39.2	17.0	14.6	43.8
	1995	100.0	50.1	54.8	9.7	22.8	37.2	36.8	13.8	11.9	49.4
	2000	100.0	39.4	65.8	17.5	20.0	42.7	42.3	11.3	9.1	46.4
	2006	100.0	24.0	24.0	23.6	55.7	27.4	21.3	53.8	6.7	24.9
Congo	1990	100.0	20.1	52.9	15.9	50.2	39.1	12.9	40.6	9.7	46.5
	1995	100.0	12.6	35.2	50.6	64.7	63.1	10.9	46.9	8.5	42.2
	2000	100.0	11.1	27.7	19.7	81.8	40.3	5.4	73.9	3.6	20.7
	2006	100.0	7.5	23.5	25.2	90.6	46.7	6.1	62.0	5.5	31.9
Dem. Rep. of the Congo - Rép. dém. du Congo	1990	100.0	28.3	56.7	25.0	75.0	90.0	28.6	28.6	9.5	42.9
	1995	100.0	4.9	79.3	11.0	28.5	23.7	57.0	17.0	4.9	26.0
	2000	100.0	7.5	81.7	11.0	6.5	6.7	50.0	20.3	4.8	29.7
	2006	100.0	7.5	87.1	16.7	31.4	42.6	51.2	22.4	5.4	26.4
Equatorial Guinea - Guinée équatoriale	1990	100.0	11.4	69.2	54.4	31.8	66.8	61.9	10.6	1.6	27.6
	1995	100.0	13.0	41.2	79.2	55.9	89.3	55.3	28.2	1.0	16.5
	2000	100.0	4.9	19.0	61.9	105.2	90.9	8.3	88.1	0.2	3.7
	2006	100.0	2.8	6.5	33.2	95.1	37.7	4.4	91.8	5.0	3.8
Gabon	1990	100.0	13.4	49.7	21.7	46.0	30.9	7.3	43.0	6.2	49.7
	1995	100.0	14.1	38.6	23.7	57.5	33.9	8.0	52.4	7.9	39.6
	2000	100.0	9.7	32.0	21.6	69.7	33.0	6.4	53.2	8.1	40.4
	2006	100.0	8.0	25.8	21.5	74.3	29.5	7.8	55.5	8.4	36.7
Sao Tome and Principe - Sao Tomé-et-Principe	1990	100.0	27.6	100.8	29.5	14.5	72.5	27.6	17.9	4.3	54.5
	1995	100.0	27.6	83.8	68.1	20.6	100.1	26.4	19.6	5.0	53.9
	2000	100.0	31.6	80.2	35.8	33.4	81.0	20.0	17.3	4.4	62.6
	2006	100.0	45.4	79.3	67.6	30.7	123.1	17.7	15.3	3.9	67.0
Northern Africa - Afrique septentrionale	*1990*	*100.0*	*14.8*	*62.0*	*25.3*	*26.9*	*28.8*	*15.7*	*38.1*	*13.5*	*46.2*
	1995	*100.0*	*14.6*	*67.0*	*21.5*	*25.3*	*29.2*	*15.5*	*35.2*	*14.1*	*49.4*
	2000	*100.0*	*14.1*	*61.8*	*20.2*	*29.2*	*25.3*	*13.7*	*38.7*	*12.9*	*47.7*
	2006	*100.0*	*13.9*	*50.3*	*25.1*	*43.3*	*31.3*	*14.3*	*43.0*	*11.5*	*42.7*
Algeria - Algérie	1990	100.0	16.2	56.6	28.9	23.4	25.1	11.9	48.3	11.6	39.8
	1995	100.0	17.0	55.6	31.6	26.6	30.7	10.3	47.9	8.9	41.8
	2000	100.0	13.6	41.6	23.5	42.1	20.7	8.8	56.7	6.0	34.5
	2006	100.0	12.1	28.7	32.3	49.8	23.0	9.4	56.3	6.0	34.3
Egypt - Égypte	1990	100.0	8.6	71.5	28.3	27.4	33.8	16.2	34.0	18.6	49.8
	1995	100.0	10.4	76.9	16.6	20.8	26.6	17.3	31.6	17.7	51.1
	2000	100.0	11.1	76.8	17.7	19.1	24.7	14.1	31.4	16.9	54.5
	2006	100.0	12.6	75.2	20.5	27.8	31.9	13.9	35.9	17.4	50.1
Libyan Arab Jamahiriya - Jamahiriya arabe libyenne	1990	100.0	24.4	48.4	18.6	39.7	31.1	8.7	46.0	6.3	45.4
	1995	100.0	22.3	58.8	12.2	29.2	22.4	8.7	46.4	7.0	44.9
	2000	100.0	20.6	46.4	13.0	35.2	15.3	8.1	53.7	5.0	38.2
	2006	100.0	14.4	18.6	14.4	83.1	30.5	4.6	68.1	2.6	27.4
Morocco - Maroc	1990	100.0	14.4	61.1	29.6	26.5	30.9	20.0	28.4	18.0	51.6
	1995	100.0	16.5	64.8	24.3	24.7	30.6	16.4	27.6	17.9	55.9
	2000	100.0	18.4	61.5	25.5	27.9	33.3	14.2	27.7	16.6	58.1
	2006	100.0	16.7	61.2	29.9	32.5	39.9	15.0	27.0	16.2	58.1
Sudan - Soudan	1990	100.0	7.3	84.5	7.3	4.5	5.5	33.8	16.3	8.7	49.9
	1995	100.0	6.0	82.0	20.4	9.4	18.5	39.8	11.6	5.7	48.5
	2000	100.0	7.6	76.5	18.3	15.3	17.7	46.4	21.4	7.5	32.2
	2006	100.0	17.1	56.8	23.8	27.1	23.5	45.8	25.0	8.3	29.2

For sources and notes, see end of table.

Pour les sources et les notes, se reporter à la fin du tableau.

8.3.1 Nominal gross domestic product by type of expenditure and by kind of economic activity of countries and geographical regions

8.3.1 Produit intérieur brut nominal par catégories de dépenses et par branches d'activité économique des pays et des régions géographiques

Region, country or territory / Régions, pays ou territoires	Year / Année	Total GDP / PIB total	GDP by type of expenditure (1) / PIB par catégories de dépense (1)					GDP by kind of economic activity (2) / PIB par branches d'activité économique (2)			
			Final consumption / Consommation finale		Gross capital formation / Formation brute de capital	Exports / Exportations / Of goods and services / Des biens et services	Less imports / Moins les importations	Agriculture (3)	Industry (4) / Industrie (4)		Services (5)
			Government / Administration publique	Household / Ménages					Total	Manufacturing / Activités de fabrication	
			Percentage / En pourcentage								
Tunisia - Tunisie	1990	100.0	16.4	63.6	27.1	43.6	50.6	17.2	32.1	20.2	50.7
	1995	100.0	16.3	62.9	24.7	44.9	48.8	12.6	32.5	22.0	54.9
	2000	100.0	15.6	60.7	27.3	44.5	48.2	13.8	31.9	21.9	54.3
	2006	100.0	15.1	63.8	23.1	50.3	52.3	12.0	31.8	18.4	56.3
Southern Africa - Afrique australe	*1990*	*100.0*	*20.0*	*60.5*	*18.8*	*26.0*	*21.7*	*4.9*	*40.7*	*22.9*	*54.4*
	1995	*100.0*	*18.9*	*62.2*	*18.7*	*24.5*	*24.5*	*4.2*	*35.2*	*20.7*	*60.6*
	2000	*100.0*	*18.8*	*62.2*	*16.3*	*30.0*	*27.2*	*3.6*	*32.4*	*18.4*	*63.9*
	2006	*100.0*	*20.9*	*62.5*	*19.1*	*30.1*	*32.5*	*3.4*	*31.8*	*18.4*	*64.8*
Botswana	1990	100.0	24.0	31.8	38.0	56.4	50.1	4.9	61.1	5.2	34.0
	1995	100.0	28.9	34.7	25.7	49.5	38.9	4.1	49.6	5.3	46.2
	2000	100.0	30.2	31.4	20.4	61.4	41.3	2.8	48.8	5.2	48.4
	2006	100.0	37.0	28.8	20.3	49.2	33.5	2.5	49.6	4.3	47.9
Lesotho	1990	100.0	13.9	137.4	53.2	16.6	121.1	20.8	29.9	12.2	49.3
	1995	100.0	17.9	120.4	60.5	21.3	120.2	17.2	38.0	15.4	44.7
	2000	100.0	19.1	101.1	42.1	29.7	92.1	17.2	39.8	16.3	43.0
	2006	100.0	19.3	82.6	41.1	41.8	86.7	16.2	39.5	17.4	44.2
Namibia - Namibie	1990	100.0	30.8	50.7	33.8	52.1	67.7	11.9	38.6	14.0	49.5
	1995	100.0	30.2	56.6	21.7	49.5	55.7	12.0	27.6	12.9	60.4
	2000	100.0	28.8	59.9	19.5	45.6	51.2	10.8	28.0	11.0	61.2
	2006	100.0	24.3	54.7	26.0	41.9	44.2	10.6	30.2	11.7	59.2
South Africa - Afrique du Sud	1990	100.0	19.7	61.0	17.7	24.2	18.8	4.6	40.1	23.6	55.3
	1995	100.0	18.3	62.6	18.2	22.8	22.1	3.9	34.8	21.2	61.3
	2000	100.0	18.1	63.0	15.9	27.9	24.9	3.3	31.8	19.0	64.9
	2006	100.0	20.2	63.7	18.8	28.4	31.1	3.2	31.0	19.0	65.8
Swaziland	1990	100.0	18.4	79.2	19.4	73.4	88.9	12.9	42.8	34.9	44.4
	1995	100.0	19.2	79.5	19.9	74.7	93.4	15.4	44.4	36.4	40.3
	2000	100.0	20.0	75.4	19.9	80.6	96.0	15.6	44.9	36.0	39.5
	2006	100.0	27.0	62.0	17.4	90.5	96.8	11.6	47.8	38.9	40.6
Western Africa - Afrique occidentale	*1990*	*100.0*	*11.3*	*66.6*	*9.7*	*52.9*	*40.6*	*28.8*	*43.4*	*18.7*	*27.8*
	1995	*100.0*	*10.8*	*86.7*	*11.4*	*32.9*	*41.7*	*32.0*	*37.7*	*10.9*	*30.3*
	2000	*100.0*	*10.4*	*60.6*	*10.8*	*44.5*	*26.4*	*27.9*	*45.3*	*8.9*	*26.7*
	2006	*100.0*	*10.0*	*69.7*	*15.2*	*31.8*	*26.8*	*32.5*	*37.1*	*6.2*	*30.3*
Benin - Bénin	1990	100.0	13.2	80.4	14.2	20.4	28.2	35.4	12.7	7.5	51.9
	1995	100.0	14.4	73.2	21.4	27.4	36.4	35.4	14.3	8.6	50.3
	2000	100.0	12.6	73.1	18.7	25.4	29.7	38.5	14.2	9.0	47.3
	2006	100.0	12.1	76.2	21.0	18.5	27.8	37.3	14.4	8.3	48.3
Burkina Faso	1990	100.0	21.5	72.7	18.8	10.9	23.9	28.6	20.8	14.2	50.6
	1995	100.0	23.1	66.7	21.4	12.6	23.8	31.4	18.9	12.0	49.7
	2000	100.0	24.3	66.6	26.5	9.8	27.2	34.6	17.9	11.1	47.4
	2006	100.0	22.3	68.1	24.5	9.1	24.0	26.1	20.3	13.3	53.6
Cape Verde - Cap-Vert	1990	100.0	18.9	88.9	43.6	17.1	68.6	15.2	22.6	7.9	62.3
	1995	100.0	22.8	86.3	40.8	16.6	66.5	14.6	20.4	7.3	65.1
	2000	100.0	18.9	86.7	30.7	20.9	57.3	13.9	16.5	5.6	69.7
	2006	100.0	20.5	76.3	38.7	16.3	51.8	11.5	15.6	4.6	72.9
Côte d'Ivoire	1990	100.0	20.7	69.1	6.1	28.8	24.6	29.7	24.0	19.8	46.3
	1995	100.0	16.9	64.1	14.1	37.0	32.1	26.7	22.4	18.2	50.9
	2000	100.0	15.5	67.2	11.3	39.8	33.8	24.8	27.4	22.5	47.8
	2006	100.0	15.7	66.8	12.0	47.0	41.7	28.6	24.4	18.4	47.0
Gambia - Gambie	1990	100.0	14.5	82.1	17.9	43.2	57.7	22.2	11.0	5.6	66.8
	1995	100.0	11.6	73.9	26.6	42.0	54.0	30.0	13.4	6.1	56.7
	2000	100.0	11.2	79.4	17.6	44.9	53.1	35.8	13.1	5.4	51.1
	2006	100.0	10.3	84.0	24.1	51.5	69.9	32.4	13.5	5.3	54.2

For sources and notes, see end of table.

Pour les sources et les notes, se reporter à la fin du tableau.

8.3.1 Nominal gross domestic product by type of expenditure and by kind of economic activity of countries and geographical regions

8.3.1 Produit intérieur brut nominal par catégories de dépenses et par branches d'activité économique des pays et des régions géographiques

Region, country or territory / Régions, pays ou territoires	Year / Année	Total GDP / PIB total	GDP by type of expenditure (1) / PIB par catégories de dépense (1)					GDP by kind of economic activity (2) / PIB par branches d'activité économique (2)			
			Final consumption / Consommation finale		Gross capital formation / Formation brute de capital	Exports / Exportations	Less imports / Moins les importations	Agriculture (3)	Industry (4) / Industrie (4)		Services (5)
			Government / Administration publique	Household / Ménages		Of goods and services / Des biens et services			Total	Manufacturing / Activités de fabrication	
			Percentage / En pourcentage								
Ghana	1990	100.0	10.9	85.5	12.3	15.4	24.0	44.8	16.8	9.8	38.4
	1995	100.0	12.1	76.2	20.0	24.5	32.8	42.7	26.7	10.3	30.6
	2000	100.0	7.8	86.7	24.0	49.0	67.5	36.0	25.4	9.0	38.6
	2006	100.0	14.3	75.8	26.8	35.1	52.0	37.5	24.7	8.6	37.8
Guinea - Guinée	1990	100.0	8.8	75.9	17.0	28.3	30.0	23.8	33.3	4.6	42.9
	1995	100.0	7.4	85.1	12.6	17.5	22.6	21.5	33.1	4.9	45.4
	2000	100.0	6.5	73.7	21.5	18.6	22.1	21.6	33.8	3.8	44.5
	2006	100.0	4.4	84.9	21.5	26.1	36.1	25.2	37.1	4.1	37.7
Guinea-Bissau - Guinée-Bissau	1990	100.0	11.4	100.9	14.7	12.0	39.0	44.6	18.2	..	37.2
	1995	100.0	6.4	94.8	22.3	11.7	35.1	55.1	12.2	..	32.7
	2000	100.0	17.6	71.5	15.1	31.8	36.0	58.8	12.3	..	28.9
	2006	100.0	16.1	82.4	15.7	35.4	49.5	60.8	12.2	..	27.0
Liberia - Libéria	1990	100.0	13.0	69.8	10.8	34.3	27.8	53.4	16.5	11.2	30.0
	1995	100.0	13.0	69.6	10.8	35.7	29.0	80.5	5.2	2.7	14.3
	2000	100.0	13.9	82.6	6.9	26.5	29.9	72.0	11.6	9.5	16.4
	2006	100.0	9.5	91.0	12.3	33.9	46.6	65.2	13.3	10.2	21.5
Mali	1990	100.0	15.2	79.0	22.2	17.3	33.7	47.8	13.5	8.1	38.8
	1995	100.0	19.3	71.8	27.6	19.2	38.6	43.1	16.1	8.2	40.7
	2000	100.0	16.4	73.4	19.8	24.3	34.9	36.3	20.9	7.2	42.9
	2006	100.0	16.3	66.3	22.5	28.6	34.6	38.3	23.5	9.0	38.2
Mauritania - Mauritanie	1990	100.0	16.6	78.3	19.5	43.4	57.8	37.5	24.2	9.0	38.3
	1995	100.0	23.3	72.5	9.8	37.1	42.6	37.4	25.1	8.3	37.4
	2000	100.0	27.6	74.2	18.6	35.6	56.0	27.7	29.7	9.0	42.6
	2006	100.0	17.5	59.4	29.0	54.9	60.8	25.6	27.0	5.7	47.4
Niger	1990	100.0	17.2	74.1	12.8	16.8	20.9	35.3	16.2	7.3	48.6
	1995	100.0	15.8	77.7	14.3	20.0	27.9	35.1	15.4	6.9	49.6
	2000	100.0	19.0	75.2	13.9	19.2	27.3	38.8	13.2	6.7	47.9
	2006	100.0	17.6	73.3	22.8	18.9	31.6	43.2	12.8	6.5	44.0
Nigeria - Nigéria	1990	100.0	8.1	60.2	7.6	73.0	49.0	26.4	58.7	22.8	14.9
	1995	100.0	6.9	98.8	6.4	38.2	50.3	32.3	51.3	10.2	16.4
	2000	100.0	8.3	52.5	7.0	51.7	19.7	26.8	57.1	7.0	16.1
	2006	100.0	7.0	68.1	11.9	31.5	18.8	33.1	44.4	3.5	22.5
Senegal - Sénégal	1990	100.0	16.3	77.4	11.4	23.8	28.4	19.4	22.0	15.0	58.7
	1995	100.0	13.8	80.2	13.9	30.1	37.6	19.6	23.1	15.8	57.2
	2000	100.0	12.6	76.2	20.5	27.9	37.2	18.8	22.8	14.4	58.4
	2006	100.0	16.6	74.8	25.6	26.6	43.5	16.3	24.4	16.2	59.3
Sierra Leone	1990	100.0	7.8	84.0	10.0	22.4	23.8	39.6	11.6	3.7	48.8
	1995	100.0	8.8	86.2	5.5	19.8	20.4	41.4	10.7	3.4	47.9
	2000	100.0	14.3	105.8	1.1	18.1	39.4	43.1	10.1	2.9	46.8
	2006	100.0	14.7	90.8	16.5	16.5	40.0	47.2	12.0	2.5	40.9
Togo	1990	100.0	13.4	72.7	25.1	31.6	42.7	36.6	23.9	6.6	39.5
	1995	100.0	10.6	79.9	13.1	29.4	32.9	40.7	23.3	6.4	36.0
	2000	100.0	10.0	87.9	16.9	32.8	47.6	37.4	19.0	5.2	43.6
	2006	100.0	8.8	87.5	20.8	39.1	56.2	43.1	22.2	6.1	34.7
Developing economies: America - Économies en développement : Amérique	**1990**	**100.0**	**14.1**	**62.8**	**21.1**	**16.5**	**14.7**	**7.9**	**33.2**	**22.3**	**58.8**
	1995	**100.0**	**15.5**	**63.8**	**21.4**	**16.7**	**17.7**	**8.0**	**31.8**	**20.1**	**60.2**
	2000	**100.0**	**14.9**	**64.7**	**21.1**	**21.8**	**22.6**	**6.4**	**31.9**	**19.3**	**61.6**
	2006	**100.0**	**15.2**	**62.7**	**19.3**	**26.1**	**23.5**	**7.1**	**34.0**	**19.1**	**58.9**
Caribbean - Caraïbes	*1990*	*100.0*	*26.0*	*53.4*	*24.7*	*38.9*	*43.5*	*9.6*	*23.7*	*11.4*	*66.7*
	1995	*100.0*	*20.4*	*62.7*	*16.8*	*34.0*	*36.7*	*6.9*	*25.6*	*14.8*	*67.4*
	2000	*100.0*	*20.6*	*64.6*	*19.8*	*36.7*	*41.5*	*7.1*	*27.3*	*14.5*	*65.7*
	2006	*100.0*	*23.1*	*59.1*	*17.4*	*35.5*	*36.6*	*5.8*	*25.6*	*12.4*	*68.6*

For sources and notes, see end of table.

Pour les sources et les notes, se reporter à la fin du tableau.

8.3.1 Nominal gross domestic product by type of expenditure and by kind of economic activity of countries and geographical regions

8.3.1 Produit intérieur brut nominal par catégories de dépenses et par branches d'activité économique des pays et des régions géographiques

Region, country or territory / Régions, pays ou territoires	Year / Année	Total GDP / PIB total	GDP by type of expenditure (1) / PIB par catégories de dépense (1)					GDP by kind of economic activity (2) / PIB par branches d'activité économique (2)			
			Final consumption / Consommation finale		Gross capital formation / Formation brute de capital	Exports / Exportations	Less imports / Moins les importations	Agriculture (3)	Industry (4) / Industrie (4)		Services (5)
			Government / Administration publique	Household / Ménages		Of goods and services / Des biens et services			Total	Manufacturing / Activités de fabrication	
			Percentage / En pourcentage								
Anguilla	1990	100.0	13.4	51.6	40.8	75.6	79.7	4.9	21.0	0.7	74.1
	1995	100.0	17.6	77.5	29.0	76.0	100.1	3.5	16.5	0.7	80.0
	2000	100.0	17.1	90.2	43.4	64.2	114.9	2.4	19.0	1.2	78.5
	2006	100.0	15.7	96.9	33.7	54.0	100.3	1.8	21.0	2.0	77.1
Antigua and Barbuda - Antigua-et-Barbuda	1990	100.0	18.0	47.6	32.4	89.0	87.0	4.0	19.0	3.2	77.0
	1995	100.0	21.4	50.5	36.9	81.4	90.1	3.6	17.2	2.2	79.2
	2000	100.0	22.3	34.5	48.0	70.2	74.9	3.6	18.3	2.1	78.1
	2006	100.0	19.8	35.9	53.6	61.4	70.6	3.4	20.0	2.0	76.6
Aruba	1990	100.0	18.6	50.2	30.0	83.2	81.9	0.5	15.9	2.1	83.6
	1995	100.0	20.0	50.5	31.1	84.9	86.5	0.5	15.6	2.7	83.9
	2000	100.0	22.0	50.0	24.6	74.4	71.0	0.4	16.0	3.8	83.6
	2006	100.0	26.5	52.5	33.1	63.2	75.3	0.4	15.4	3.4	84.2
Bahamas	1990	100.0	12.9	62.8	29.4	54.2	56.0	2.3	14.6	3.9	83.1
	1995	100.0	13.9	68.1	27.7	49.5	54.9	2.8	13.8	3.5	83.4
	2000	100.0	13.6	67.1	38.6	47.2	63.4	2.4	16.6	3.9	81.0
	2006	100.0	14.5	68.3	32.9	45.5	57.9	2.2	16.2	4.5	81.5
Barbados - Barbade	1990	100.0	20.2	63.6	18.8	49.1	51.7	5.4	18.3	8.0	76.3
	1995	100.0	20.1	61.6	15.2	58.2	55.0	6.3	15.6	6.7	78.2
	2000	100.0	21.2	66.9	18.5	50.5	57.0	4.3	16.3	6.4	79.4
	2006	100.0	20.2	67.2	19.3	50.2	60.4	4.0	16.2	6.8	79.8
British Virgin Islands - Îles Vierges britanniques	1990	100.0	14.0	45.4	25.7	101.0	86.2	3.2	10.6	2.5	86.1
	1995	100.0	13.9	49.9	25.4	92.2	81.4	1.8	13.3	3.6	84.9
	2000	100.0	10.5	40.5	23.2	104.3	78.6	1.1	11.4	3.4	87.5
	2006	100.0	9.4	37.7	22.6	108.2	77.9	1.0	10.7	3.0	88.3
Cayman Islands - Îles Caïmanes	1990	100.0	14.2	62.5	21.4	64.1	58.5	0.3	14.6	1.5	85.0
	1995	100.0	14.6	63.2	22.2	62.0	60.2	0.4	14.8	1.7	84.8
	2000	100.0	14.6	63.3	22.4	61.9	61.1	0.4	14.9	1.7	84.7
	2006	100.0	14.6	63.4	22.4	61.9	61.3	0.4	15.0	1.7	84.6
Cuba	1990	100.0	37.9	42.5	26.6	27.7	36.1	10.1	18.9	9.6	71.0
	1995	100.0	29.8	55.5	9.6	12.3	14.1	6.0	24.2	17.3	69.8
	2000	100.0	34.2	56.8	11.7	13.2	15.8	6.2	24.2	15.5	69.6
	2006	100.0	39.4	51.5	8.7	15.0	14.6	3.4	19.5	10.7	77.1
Dominica - Dominique	1990	100.0	20.3	64.1	40.8	50.1	75.3	24.1	17.1	6.6	58.8
	1995	100.0	20.8	63.8	31.5	50.9	67.0	17.3	20.1	6.8	62.7
	2000	100.0	22.0	63.1	27.5	53.3	67.5	16.7	21.4	8.1	62.0
	2006	100.0	18.4	71.4	26.9	44.2	60.9	17.1	21.7	7.5	61.2
Dominican Republic - République dominicaine	1990	100.0	2.7	79.4	21.6	43.7	47.2	13.3	31.5	21.6	55.3
	1995	100.0	5.1	78.8	19.5	47.5	50.9	10.1	30.3	19.6	59.6
	2000	100.0	8.4	77.8	23.8	44.9	54.9	11.1	34.0	22.3	54.8
	2006	100.0	9.7	74.9	17.9	33.4	40.1	11.8	28.7	18.8	59.5
Grenada - Grenade	1990	100.0	20.5	64.9	42.0	44.4	71.8	12.6	17.0	6.2	70.4
	1995	100.0	16.6	67.5	32.1	44.8	60.9	9.6	19.0	6.2	71.4
	2000	100.0	14.7	59.7	43.8	57.6	75.7	7.2	22.5	7.1	70.3
	2006	100.0	17.5	67.8	50.0	39.4	74.7	4.9	31.0	5.4	64.1
Haiti - Haïti	1990	100.0	7.7	81.6	14.3	18.1	21.7	35.8	22.6	15.5	41.6
	1995	100.0	8.3	100.0	13.8	10.9	33.0	33.2	18.0	7.5	48.8
	2000	100.0	7.9	98.0	12.9	13.8	31.7	31.4	23.2	7.6	45.3
	2006	100.0	8.4	91.9	28.6	14.2	43.1	30.8	23.8	7.8	45.4
Jamaica - Jamaïque	1990	100.0	14.0	62.3	27.7	51.7	55.8	6.0	40.4	18.4	53.5
	1995	100.0	11.1	70.4	28.8	50.7	61.0	8.4	34.5	15.1	57.0
	2000	100.0	15.8	68.8	26.8	43.1	54.5	6.3	29.6	13.0	64.1
	2006	100.0	15.3	72.3	30.7	39.9	58.1	5.6	30.6	13.0	63.8

For sources and notes, see end of table.

Pour les sources et les notes, se reporter à la fin du tableau.

8.3.1 Nominal gross domestic product by type of expenditure and by kind of economic activity of countries and geographical regions

8.3.1 Produit intérieur brut nominal par catégories de dépenses et par branches d'activité économique des pays et des régions géographiques

Region, country or territory / Régions, pays ou territoires	Year / Année	Total GDP / PIB total	GDP by type of expenditure (1) / PIB par catégories de dépense (1)					GDP by kind of economic activity (2) / PIB par branches d'activité économique (2)			
			Final consumption / Consommation finale		Gross capital formation / Formation brute de capital	Exports / Exportations	Less imports / Moins les importations	Agriculture (3)	Industry (4) / Industrie (4)		Services (5)
			Government / Administration publique	Household / Ménages	Formation brute de capital	Of goods and services / Des biens et services			Total	Manufacturing / Activités de fabrication	
			Percentage / En pourcentage								
Montserrat	1990	100.0	17.7	61.6	73.4	28.6	81.4	2.5	37.6	2.3	60.0
	1995	100.0	22.7	61.8	35.4	61.2	81.1	5.4	13.0	3.0	81.6
	2000	100.0	49.6	73.8	46.6	49.8	119.8	1.3	20.6	0.7	78.0
	2006	100.0	49.8	73.3	44.9	42.0	110.1	1.2	20.6	0.7	78.2
Netherlands Antilles - Antilles néerlandaises	1990	100.0	40.7	40.1	29.8	82.8	92.8	0.6	15.2	7.4	84.1
	1995	100.0	25.6	62.6	24.2	76.7	90.1	0.7	16.5	7.7	82.8
	2000	100.0	23.2	52.6	27.6	80.2	83.5	0.7	16.2	6.9	83.1
	2006	100.0	21.5	55.0	24.8	92.0	93.3	0.7	16.2	5.9	83.2
Saint Kitts and Nevis - Saint-Kitts-et-Nevis	1990	100.0	18.0	57.9	55.4	51.7	83.1	6.1	27.4	12.1	66.5
	1995	100.0	20.4	56.5	46.5	51.5	74.9	5.0	23.5	10.0	71.6
	2000	100.0	21.1	59.3	49.6	45.6	75.6	2.6	27.1	9.8	70.3
	2006	100.0	17.7	57.1	46.4	45.4	66.6	2.2	26.1	8.7	71.8
Saint Lucia - Sainte-Lucie	1990	100.0	15.2	69.8	24.6	68.5	78.1	13.7	16.8	7.7	69.5
	1995	100.0	17.4	58.7	24.6	69.6	70.3	8.9	17.9	6.5	73.3
	2000	100.0	18.5	65.8	25.7	53.1	63.1	6.6	17.5	4.5	75.9
	2006	100.0	18.4	52.2	40.8	61.7	73.1	4.3	16.6	4.7	79.1
Saint Vincent and the Grenadines - Saint-Vincent-et-les Grenadines	1990	100.0	20.9	68.4	31.0	65.8	76.8	20.0	21.7	8.1	58.3
	1995	100.0	20.2	64.0	30.2	51.6	66.1	13.3	23.6	8.0	63.1
	2000	100.0	19.4	59.3	27.3	53.6	59.7	10.1	22.6	5.7	67.3
	2006	100.0	20.3	68.0	31.9	48.2	67.9	7.8	23.1	5.4	69.0
Trinidad and Tobago - Trinité-et-Tobago	1990	100.0	16.2	54.7	13.8	49.1	33.5	2.6	46.4	13.8	51.0
	1995	100.0	15.9	48.8	20.8	53.8	39.2	1.9	41.7	16.5	56.3
	2000	100.0	12.0	57.4	16.8	59.2	45.3	1.2	44.8	16.9	53.9
	2006	100.0	13.9	36.6	15.2	68.8	39.0	1.0	46.0	16.6	53.1
Turks and Caicos Islands - Îles Turques et Caïques	1990	100.0	15.2	26.8	24.1	58.7	35.6	1.3	16.4	4.4	82.3
	1995	100.0	14.0	29.3	25.5	60.4	38.5	1.3	16.4	4.3	82.3
	2000	100.0	15.2	30.8	26.3	78.5	50.8	1.5	15.6	3.5	82.9
	2006	100.0	17.0	33.0	39.2	67.2	56.5	1.2	19.6	2.3	79.2
Central America - Amérique centrale	*1990*	*100.0*	*9.1*	*70.1*	*22.5*	*20.7*	*22.3*	*8.7*	*27.8*	*20.4*	*63.5*
	1995	*100.0*	*10.5*	*68.3*	*20.0*	*32.1*	*30.8*	*6.5*	*26.6*	*19.7*	*66.9*
	2000	*100.0*	*11.2*	*67.9*	*23.5*	*32.1*	*34.7*	*4.8*	*27.7*	*20.0*	*67.4*
	2006	*100.0*	*11.2*	*69.6*	*21.6*	*33.2*	*35.6*	*4.6*	*26.4*	*17.8*	*68.9*
Belize	1990	100.0	14.4	60.4	26.1	60.3	61.3	20.7	25.4	14.9	53.8
	1995	100.0	14.3	72.0	21.7	48.0	49.2	16.9	19.1	10.3	64.0
	2000	100.0	12.9	75.2	32.0	52.0	73.6	16.5	20.6	10.6	62.9
	2006	100.0	12.7	75.4	18.9	60.1	67.5	15.3	17.8	9.3	66.9
Costa Rica	1990	100.0	15.0	74.9	19.6	29.9	39.0	12.1	29.3	22.0	58.6
	1995	100.0	13.5	71.1	18.2	37.6	40.4	13.3	28.7	21.2	58.0
	2000	100.0	13.3	67.0	16.9	48.6	45.8	9.1	31.0	24.5	59.9
	2006	100.0	13.6	65.8	27.6	49.7	56.7	8.3	28.7	21.1	63.1
El Salvador	1990	100.0	9.9	88.9	13.9	18.6	31.2	17.1	26.8	21.8	56.1
	1995	100.0	8.6	87.4	20.0	21.6	37.8	14.0	28.7	22.3	57.3
	2000	100.0	10.2	87.9	16.9	27.4	42.4	10.0	30.3	23.6	59.7
	2006	100.0	10.1	94.0	15.7	26.5	46.2	9.7	28.4	21.6	61.9
Guatemala	1990	100.0	9.1	82.4	15.0	29.6	33.9	17.1	29.0	20.6	54.0
	1995	100.0	7.4	84.8	16.6	28.9	36.3	15.8	28.6	20.4	55.5
	2000	100.0	9.4	82.6	19.7	30.3	41.3	14.9	28.7	20.1	56.4
	2006	100.0	9.0	85.8	20.3	25.9	41.1	13.6	28.8	19.8	57.6
Honduras	1990	100.0	12.9	66.8	23.0	37.2	39.9	22.4	26.4	16.3	51.2
	1995	100.0	9.3	63.5	31.6	43.7	48.1	21.5	30.7	17.8	47.8
	2000	100.0	12.5	70.6	30.7	41.3	55.2	16.2	31.6	19.6	52.2
	2006	100.0	14.0	78.8	32.9	40.8	66.5	13.8	31.1	19.7	55.1

For sources and notes, see end of table.

Pour les sources et les notes, se reporter à la fin du tableau.

8.3.1 Nominal gross domestic product by type of expenditure and by kind of economic activity of countries and geographical regions

8.3.1 Produit intérieur brut nominal par catégories de dépenses et par branches d'activité économique des pays et des régions géographiques

Region, country or territory / Régions, pays ou territoires	Year / Année	Total GDP / PIB total	GDP by type of expenditure (1) / PIB par catégories de dépense (1)					GDP by kind of economic activity (2) / PIB par branches d'activité économique (2)			
			Final consumption / Consommation finale		Gross capital formation / Formation brute de capital	Exports / Exportations / Of goods and services / Des biens et services	Less imports / Moins les importations	Agriculture (3)	Industry (4) / Industrie (4)		Services (5)
			Government / Administration publique	Household / Ménages					Total	Manufacturing / Activités de fabrication	
			Percentage / En pourcentage								
Mexico - Mexique	1990	100.0	8.4	69.6	23.1	18.6	19.7	7.8	28.1	20.6	64.1
	1995	100.0	10.5	67.1	19.8	30.4	27.8	5.2	26.5	19.8	68.3
	2000	100.0	11.2	67.1	23.8	31.0	33.0	4.0	27.7	20.1	68.3
	2006	100.0	11.2	68.4	21.5	33.0	34.1	3.8	26.4	17.8	69.8
Nicaragua	1990	100.0	33.5	66.3	20.5	25.7	46.1	30.0	21.5	16.9	48.5
	1995	100.0	14.9	78.6	22.0	19.1	34.7	22.8	26.6	18.2	50.5
	2000	100.0	17.2	79.0	31.0	23.9	51.1	20.1	27.2	16.4	52.7
	2006	100.0	19.6	80.2	29.1	30.1	59.1	18.9	27.9	17.6	53.2
Panama	1990	100.0	15.7	63.5	14.7	77.9	70.5	9.0	17.7	13.3	73.2
	1995	100.0	13.1	57.4	26.5	90.5	87.8	7.4	19.9	12.5	72.7
	2000	100.0	13.2	59.9	24.1	72.6	69.8	7.0	18.5	9.7	74.5
	2006	100.0	9.9	66.5	21.1	35.9	33.4	6.7	16.3	6.9	77.0
South America - Amérique du Sud	*1990*	*100.0*	*15.1*	*60.7*	*20.3*	*13.2*	*9.5*	*7.5*	*35.8*	*23.8*	*56.7*
	1995	*100.0*	*16.5*	*62.7*	*22.0*	*11.9*	*13.3*	*8.4*	*33.5*	*20.5*	*58.1*
	2000	*100.0*	*16.4*	*63.1*	*19.9*	*15.4*	*15.1*	*7.2*	*34.4*	*19.2*	*58.4*
	2006	*100.0*	*16.6*	*59.6*	*18.3*	*22.0*	*16.6*	*8.4*	*38.3*	*20.2*	*53.4*
Argentina - Argentine	1990	100.0	12.8	66.9	14.0	10.3	4.6	8.0	35.6	26.5	56.4
	1995	100.0	13.3	68.6	17.9	9.7	10.1	5.7	28.0	18.4	66.3
	2000	100.0	13.8	69.3	16.2	11.0	11.8	5.0	27.6	17.5	67.4
	2006	100.0	12.2	63.6	16.4	23.0	15.0	9.3	32.9	21.9	57.9
Bolivia - Bolivie	1990	100.0	11.8	76.9	12.5	22.8	23.9	16.4	34.2	18.2	49.4
	1995	100.0	13.6	75.8	15.2	22.6	27.2	16.4	32.1	18.4	51.5
	2000	100.0	14.5	76.4	18.1	18.3	27.3	14.3	28.3	14.6	57.4
	2006	100.0	15.9	68.6	13.2	30.7	28.4	14.6	29.7	14.0	55.7
Brazil - Brésil	1990	100.0	16.9	58.5	22.9	7.9	6.1	6.0	34.3	24.1	59.7
	1995	100.0	19.6	59.9	22.3	7.7	9.5	8.5	34.5	22.5	57.1
	2000	100.0	19.1	60.9	21.5	10.7	12.2	7.7	36.1	21.6	56.3
	2006	100.0	19.9	60.4	16.8	14.7	11.7	9.0	37.3	23.0	53.7
Chile - Chili	1990	100.0	10.4	60.1	25.6	33.1	29.4	7.1	41.2	18.0	51.7
	1995	100.0	10.5	60.8	26.3	29.2	26.9	6.1	40.8	19.0	53.1
	2000	100.0	12.5	63.8	21.9	31.6	29.7	5.9	37.0	18.7	57.1
	2006	100.0	10.1	55.0	20.4	45.4	30.9	4.1	47.7	13.5	48.2
Colombia - Colombie	1990	100.0	11.4	63.8	22.2	18.6	16.0	18.2	32.6	18.0	49.1
	1995	100.0	14.9	65.7	25.8	14.5	21.0	14.4	30.1	15.2	55.5
	2000	100.0	21.2	63.0	13.7	21.5	19.4	13.5	29.2	15.2	57.3
	2006	100.0	19.0	61.6	21.1	22.5	24.3	11.9	32.0	15.4	56.2
Ecuador - Équateur	1990	100.0	13.0	67.0	17.0	31.4	28.6	13.9	39.5	20.1	46.6
	1995	100.0	12.5	68.5	21.6	25.7	28.3	17.6	26.2	11.9	56.2
	2000	100.0	9.8	64.0	20.1	37.1	31.0	11.5	37.6	5.5	50.9
	2006	100.0	10.8	64.1	23.9	34.0	32.8	6.5	37.5	1.9	56.0
Guyana	1990	100.0	13.6	60.9	42.3	55.1	78.5	43.2	19.7	5.2	37.0
	1995	100.0	16.0	46.3	45.4	79.7	84.9	48.8	25.1	3.8	26.1
	2000	100.0	27.5	49.9	38.5	63.1	81.5	36.1	24.1	3.2	39.9
	2006	100.0	24.6	64.7	45.9	90.1	116.5	34.9	19.4	3.6	45.7
Paraguay	1990	100.0	6.2	77.2	22.9	33.2	39.5	27.8	25.6	17.3	46.6
	1995	100.0	7.2	85.3	23.9	35.0	51.2	24.8	26.2	15.6	49.0
	2000	100.0	12.7	79.2	18.8	38.1	48.8	18.5	24.8	17.2	56.7
	2006	100.0	10.1	65.6	20.3	33.5	35.6	20.5	24.5	16.6	55.0
Peru - Pérou	1990	100.0	11.5	71.2	18.1	15.1	14.5	7.7	30.4	19.4	61.9
	1995	100.0	9.8	71.1	24.8	12.5	18.2	8.8	31.0	16.8	60.2
	2000	100.0	10.6	71.2	20.2	16.0	18.0	8.5	29.9	15.8	61.6
	2006	100.0	9.9	63.1	17.6	27.6	20.7	7.4	32.9	16.1	59.7

For sources and notes, see end of table.

Pour les sources et les notes, se reporter à la fin du tableau.

8.3.1 Nominal gross domestic product by type of expenditure and by kind of economic activity of countries and geographical regions

8.3.1 Produit intérieur brut nominal par catégories de dépenses et par branches d'activité économique des pays et des régions géographiques

Region, country or territory / Régions, pays ou territoires	Year / Année	Total GDP / PIB total	Final consumption / Consommation finale Government / Administration publique	Household / Ménages	Gross capital formation / Formation brute de capital	Exports / Exportations Of goods and services / Des biens et services	Less imports / Moins les importations	Agriculture / Agriculture (3)	Industry (4) / Industrie (4) Total	Manufacturing / Activités de fabrication	Services (5)
						Percentage / En pourcentage					
Suriname	1990	100.0	24.4	53.8	20.8	27.4	26.6	9.9	27.6	11.7	62.4
	1995	100.0	18.1	14.8	47.3	91.6	80.2	18.3	38.3	16.0	43.4
	2000	100.0	5.6	19.5	68.7	62.6	56.4	12.5	28.7	16.3	58.8
	2006	100.0	5.3	18.4	84.6	53.6	61.8	6.1	42.2	16.8	51.7
Uruguay	1990	100.0	13.9	69.1	11.0	26.2	20.1	10.7	30.2	24.8	59.1
	1995	100.0	11.8	72.9	15.4	19.0	19.1	8.4	28.1	19.1	63.6
	2000	100.0	13.2	74.5	14.0	19.3	21.0	5.9	26.0	16.1	68.1
	2006	100.0	11.0	73.1	16.4	29.9	30.3	9.1	32.0	22.9	58.9
Venezuela (Bolivarian Rep. of) - Venezuela (Rép. bolivarienne du)	1990	100.0	16.8	46.6	13.4	40.6	20.4	5.9	57.3	27.1	36.8
	1995	100.0	14.8	54.1	23.8	27.9	22.1	5.9	47.1	23.4	47.0
	2000	100.0	12.4	51.7	24.2	29.7	18.1	4.1	48.4	19.3	47.5
	2006	100.0	11.3	48.3	24.7	36.6	21.0	4.2	51.8	17.5	44.0
Developing economies: Asia - Économies en développement : Asie	**1990**	**100.0**	**13.4**	**56.4**	**29.8**	**31.8**	**30.9**	**17.6**	**36.5**	**23.2**	**45.9**
	1995	**100.0**	**12.4**	**54.8**	**33.6**	**37.3**	**37.5**	**14.1**	**37.8**	**25.3**	**48.0**
	2000	**100.0**	**13.8**	**54.1**	**28.0**	**43.6**	**39.4**	**11.9**	**38.8**	**25.9**	**49.3**
	2006	**100.0**	**13.2**	**48.4**	**31.4**	**51.8**	**45.1**	**10.6**	**40.8**	**26.8**	**48.6**
Eastern Asia - Asie orientale	*1990*	*100.0*	*13.3*	*51.1*	*32.8*	*35.7*	*33.0*	*15.6*	*39.9*	*31.6*	*44.5*
	1995	*100.0*	*12.5*	*50.7*	*36.5*	*37.5*	*37.1*	*11.5*	*40.7*	*31.8*	*47.7*
	2000	*100.0*	*14.2*	*51.2*	*31.9*	*41.3*	*38.5*	*9.8*	*40.0*	*33.0*	*50.2*
	2006	*100.0*	*14.3*	*43.3*	*37.1*	*51.8*	*45.6*	*9.4*	*41.6*	*35.0*	*49.0*
China - Chine	1990	100.0	13.6	48.8	34.9	18.4	15.0	26.9	41.3	36.7	31.8
	1995	100.0	13.3	44.9	40.3	19.4	17.9	19.8	47.2	41.0	33.1
	2000	100.0	15.9	46.4	35.3	23.4	21.0	14.8	45.9	40.4	39.3
	2006	100.0	14.7	36.3	42.9	40.7	32.9	12.8	46.6	41.1	40.7
China, Hong Kong SAR - Chine (RAS de Hong Kong)	1990	100.0	7.7	56.7	27.4	130.9	123.2	0.2	24.1	16.6	75.7
	1995	100.0	8.4	62.0	34.1	143.2	147.6	0.1	15.2	7.7	84.7
	2000	100.0	9.1	58.9	27.5	143.6	139.1	0.1	13.3	5.4	86.6
	2006	100.0	8.4	58.5	21.6	205.8	194.3	0.1	8.5	3.2	91.5
China, Macao SAR - Chine (RAS de Macao)	1990	100.0	9.9	39.2	25.0	110.0	84.0	..	23.8	16.5	76.2
	1995	100.0	8.4	33.6	29.5	74.2	45.7	..	15.6	7.6	84.4
	2000	100.0	12.3	40.2	11.6	100.4	64.6	..	14.8	9.5	85.2
	2006	100.0	7.7	24.4	34.2	91.6	57.9	..	12.7	5.0	87.3
China, Taiwan Province of - Province chinoise de Taiwan	1990	100.0	17.6	54.6	23.0	45.7	40.8	4.2	40.2	32.7	55.6
	1995	100.0	15.0	58.2	25.2	47.2	45.6	3.5	34.3	26.5	62.2
	2000	100.0	13.9	60.7	23.3	53.8	51.6	2.1	30.1	24.6	67.9
	2006	100.0	13.0	61.1	20.3	71.7	66.1	1.6	25.8	22.1	72.6
Dem. People's Rep. of Korea - Rép. populaire dém. de Corée	1990	100.0	..	..	..	7.5	11.8	27.4	54.6	31.8	18.0
	1995	100.0	..	..	..	3.8	5.7	27.6	42.0	22.5	30.3
	2000	100.0	..	..	..	4.2	10.0	30.4	37.1	17.7	32.4
	2006	100.0	..	..	..	5.7	11.2	27.3	40.2	18.5	32.4
Mongolia - Mongolie	1990	100.0	22.6	67.1	33.4	19.5	42.6	15.2	30.6	10.3	54.3
	1995	100.0	12.3	59.2	29.6	44.8	46.0	37.6	27.4	12.2	35.0
	2000	100.0	16.5	65.7	33.2	59.5	74.7	32.7	23.2	5.2	44.1
	2006	100.0	28.8	28.8	40.7	80.8	77.9	21.0	26.8	5.9	52.2
Republic of Korea - République de Corée	1990	100.0	11.8	50.9	37.5	28.0	29.0	8.9	41.6	27.3	49.5
	1995	100.0	11.2	52.3	37.7	28.8	29.9	6.3	41.9	27.6	51.8
	2000	100.0	12.1	54.0	31.0	40.8	37.7	4.9	40.7	29.4	54.4
	2006	100.0	14.7	54.5	29.6	43.7	43.1	3.2	39.6	27.8	57.2
Southern Asia - Asie méridionale	*1990*	*100.0*	*11.3*	*66.5*	*27.3*	*9.6*	*13.3*	*27.7*	*26.9*	*15.5*	*45.4*
	1995	*100.0*	*11.2*	*63.1*	*27.6*	*13.9*	*14.4*	*25.4*	*28.2*	*16.0*	*46.5*
	2000	*100.0*	*11.7*	*64.1*	*24.9*	*15.6*	*16.5*	*22.3*	*27.6*	*15.3*	*50.1*
	2006	*100.0*	*10.8*	*59.0*	*29.8*	*23.7*	*26.3*	*18.4*	*29.8*	*15.2*	*51.8*

For sources and notes, see end of table.

Pour les sources et les notes, se reporter à la fin du tableau.

8.3.1 Nominal gross domestic product by type of expenditure and by kind of economic activity of countries and geographical regions

8.3.1 Produit intérieur brut nominal par catégories de dépenses et par branches d'activité économique des pays et des régions géographiques

Region, country or territory / Régions, pays ou territoires	Year / Année	Total GDP / PIB total	GDP by type of expenditure (1) / PIB par catégories de dépense (1)					GDP by kind of economic activity (2) / PIB par branches d'activité économique (2)			
			Final consumption / Consommation finale		Gross capital formation / Formation brute de capital	Exports / Exportations / Of goods and services / Des biens et services	Less imports / Moins les importations / Of goods and services / Des biens et services	Agriculture (3)	Industry (4) / Industrie (4)		Services (5)
			Government / Administration publique	Household / Ménages					Total	Manufacturing / Activités de fabrication	
			Percentage / En pourcentage								
Afghanistan	1990	100.0	5.6	83.9	13.4	11.5	14.4	35.7	23.7	20.6	40.6
	1995	100.0	7.2	101.6	13.1	23.6	45.5	65.7	10.5	5.4	23.8
	2000	100.0	8.8	119.3	12.9	35.7	76.7	57.0	23.2	16.9	19.8
	2006	100.0	9.6	121.1	17.3	32.9	80.9	42.4	22.4	14.7	35.2
Bangladesh	1990	100.0	4.4	83.3	16.4	6.7	12.3	30.8	21.4	13.4	47.7
	1995	100.0	4.4	80.7	20.0	11.1	18.7	25.7	24.9	15.4	49.5
	2000	100.0	4.5	77.5	23.1	15.4	21.5	24.1	25.9	15.6	50.0
	2006	100.0	5.6	73.5	25.6	18.0	25.5	20.2	27.3	16.6	52.5
Bhutan - Bhoutan	1990	100.0	17.5	54.2	36.3	28.9	33.0	39.0	28.0	8.4	33.0
	1995	100.0	18.6	41.6	48.6	38.9	43.9	34.0	34.8	10.9	31.2
	2000	100.0	21.6	46.9	47.4	28.5	52.6	28.6	35.7	8.4	35.7
	2006	100.0	22.0	48.8	53.5	40.4	64.7	22.2	39.2	7.6	38.5
India - Inde	1990	100.0	11.8	66.2	27.9	7.1	8.5	30.6	27.3	16.9	42.1
	1995	100.0	10.8	63.0	29.3	10.9	12.1	27.4	27.7	17.6	45.0
	2000	100.0	12.5	63.8	24.3	13.2	14.1	23.7	26.3	15.6	50.0
	2006	100.0	11.6	56.7	32.2	22.3	26.3	19.6	27.1	15.8	53.3
Iran (Islamic Rep. of) - Iran (Rép. islamique d')	1990	100.0	12.1	57.9	34.8	14.8	27.4	17.9	28.2	10.6	53.9
	1995	100.0	16.0	46.3	30.5	21.4	12.9	18.3	34.1	11.8	47.6
	2000	100.0	14.0	46.9	34.5	22.3	17.2	13.3	36.6	13.4	50.1
	2006	100.0	11.7	45.9	27.9	33.5	22.7	10.9	41.6	11.0	47.5
Maldives	1990	100.0	17.2	35.9	31.5	92.0	76.5	14.9	12.8	7.5	72.3
	1995	100.0	16.8	36.5	31.3	92.7	77.2	11.0	13.0	7.6	76.0
	2000	100.0	22.9	32.9	26.3	89.5	71.6	8.4	14.5	7.7	77.1
	2006	100.0	37.9	29.8	55.6	82.6	105.9	8.4	16.8	6.6	74.8
Nepal - Népal	1990	100.0	8.7	83.5	18.4	10.5	21.1	50.6	15.9	6.0	33.5
	1995	100.0	9.2	75.9	25.2	24.2	34.6	40.8	22.2	9.3	37.0
	2000	100.0	8.9	75.9	24.3	23.3	32.4	39.6	21.5	9.2	38.9
	2006	100.0	10.2	78.7	30.3	18.6	37.7	38.1	20.3	7.5	41.5
Pakistan	1990	100.0	11.0	69.2	20.4	13.9	15.1	24.9	25.9	16.7	49.2
	1995	100.0	9.8	73.8	20.4	13.9	17.5	24.7	24.2	15.4	51.1
	2000	100.0	7.8	76.3	17.0	14.7	15.7	24.1	24.0	15.5	51.9
	2006	100.0	6.4	82.0	20.5	15.8	24.7	21.6	26.7	17.8	51.7
Sri Lanka	1990	100.0	12.7	75.2	20.5	29.5	37.3	25.3	29.8	20.8	44.9
	1995	100.0	14.2	71.2	25.3	34.7	44.0	20.5	30.1	19.3	49.4
	2000	100.0	13.7	70.9	25.4	38.2	48.4	17.6	29.9	19.5	52.5
	2006	100.0	12.9	70.4	26.7	32.6	44.4	14.6	31.3	20.2	54.1
South-Eastern Asia - Asie du Sud-Est	*1990*	*100.0*	*9.6*	*56.4*	*36.9*	*50.5*	*51.0*	*16.0*	*35.8*	*22.8*	*48.2*
	1995	*100.0*	*9.3*	*55.2*	*39.0*	*60.7*	*62.1*	*13.6*	*37.5*	*25.1*	*48.9*
	2000	*100.0*	*9.9*	*55.7*	*24.8*	*86.5*	*76.2*	*11.7*	*40.3*	*27.2*	*48.0*
	2006	*100.0*	*10.3*	*56.6*	*23.2*	*85.1*	*75.4*	*11.8*	*41.3*	*27.7*	*46.9*
Brunei Darussalam - Brunéi Darussalam	1990	100.0	19.7	18.4	14.3	70.5	29.6	2.3	53.6	8.8	44.1
	1995	100.0	23.5	31.6	27.4	60.7	48.2	2.5	42.8	11.7	54.7
	2000	100.0	25.8	24.8	13.1	67.3	35.8	1.0	63.7	15.4	35.3
	2006	100.0	21.5	25.4	13.3	69.4	31.7	1.1	67.9	13.6	31.0
Cambodia - Cambodge	1990	100.0	7.2	90.4	8.3	2.4	8.4	50.1	11.7	7.3	38.2
	1995	100.0	5.1	90.9	13.4	32.7	43.9	51.4	12.9	7.4	35.7
	2000	100.0	5.2	88.8	16.9	49.8	61.7	37.9	23.0	16.9	39.1
	2006	100.0	0.0	92.5	19.3	69.0	78.6	29.6	29.2	20.9	41.2
Indonesia - Indonésie	1990	100.0	7.8	54.2	42.4	24.2	21.6	16.6	36.8	21.7	46.6
	1995	100.0	7.1	56.5	44.1	25.1	25.2	14.6	39.6	25.3	45.7
	2000	100.0	6.5	61.7	22.2	41.0	30.5	14.9	43.7	26.4	41.4
	2006	100.0	8.6	62.7	24.6	30.9	26.1	13.7	42.4	26.8	44.0

For sources and notes, see end of table.

Pour les sources et les notes, se reporter à la fin du tableau.

8.3.1 Nominal gross domestic product by type of expenditure and by kind of economic activity of countries and geographical regions

8.3.1 Produit intérieur brut nominal par catégories de dépenses et par branches d'activité économique des pays et des régions géographiques

Region, country or territory / Régions, pays ou territoires	Year / Année	Total GDP / PIB total	GDP by type of expenditure (1) / PIB par catégories de dépense (1)					GDP by kind of economic activity (2) / PIB par branches d'activité économique (2)			
			Final consumption / Consommation finale		Gross capital formation / Formation brute de capital	Exports / Exportations	Less imports / Moins les importations	Agriculture (3)	Industry (4) / Industrie (4)		Services (5)
			Government / Administration publique	Household / Ménages		Of goods and services / Des biens et services			Total	Manufacturing / Activités de fabrication	
			Percentage / En pourcentage								
Lao People's dem. Rep. - Rép. dém. populaire lao	1990	100.0	9.5	92.1	11.3	11.8	24.7	61.2	14.5	10.0	24.3
	1995	100.0	9.7	93.0	11.3	23.2	37.3	55.0	19.0	14.1	26.0
	2000	100.0	8.9	85.0	10.4	30.1	34.4	52.6	22.9	17.0	24.6
	2006	100.0	7.8	59.0	30.7	32.0	29.0	46.8	27.6	20.1	25.7
Malaysia - Malaisie	1990	100.0	13.8	51.8	32.4	74.5	72.4	15.0	41.5	23.8	43.5
	1995	100.0	12.4	47.9	43.6	94.1	98.0	12.7	40.5	25.8	46.8
	2000	100.0	10.4	42.4	27.3	124.4	104.5	8.4	48.4	31.1	43.1
	2006	100.0	12.9	43.7	20.0	122.2	98.8	8.8	50.0	29.4	41.2
Myanmar	1990	100.0	88.3	..	13.4	1.9	3.6	57.3	10.5	7.8	32.2
	1995	100.0	86.6	..	14.2	0.8	1.7	60.0	9.9	6.9	30.1
	2000	100.0	87.7	..	12.4	0.5	0.6	57.2	9.7	7.2	33.1
	2006	100.0	84.7	..	15.2	0.1	0.1	52.6	13.4	9.3	34.0
Philippines	1990	100.0	10.1	71.2	24.2	27.5	33.3	21.9	34.5	24.8	43.6
	1995	100.0	11.4	74.1	22.5	36.4	44.2	21.6	32.1	23.0	46.3
	2000	100.0	13.2	70.4	19.5	56.1	54.1	16.0	31.5	22.5	52.6
	2006	100.0	9.7	70.4	14.8	46.6	48.3	14.2	32.1	23.3	53.7
Singapore - Singapour	1990	100.0	10.1	46.1	36.4	182.9	176.1	0.3	32.7	25.5	67.0
	1995	100.0	8.5	41.3	34.2	187.7	171.7	0.1	33.7	25.0	66.1
	2000	100.0	10.8	42.2	33.3	195.6	182.0	0.1	33.5	26.2	66.4
	2006	100.0	11.3	40.2	18.8	252.6	220.9	0.1	33.0	27.7	66.9
Thailand - Thaïlande	1990	100.0	9.4	56.5	41.3	34.1	41.6	14.4	35.9	24.9	49.7
	1995	100.0	9.9	53.2	42.1	41.8	48.6	10.8	40.2	28.6	49.0
	2000	100.0	11.3	56.1	22.8	66.8	58.1	9.0	42.0	33.6	49.0
	2006	100.0	11.6	56.1	27.9	73.7	69.8	10.7	44.6	35.1	44.7
Timor-Leste	1990	100.0	15.0	81.1	35.0	-31.1	..	29.5	25.4	2.9	45.1
	1995	100.0	15.0	81.1	35.0	-31.1	..	29.4	25.5	3.2	45.1
	2000	100.0	35.2	111.6	25.6	0.4	72.8	25.8	18.5	2.8	55.8
	2006	100.0	50.1	68.5	19.0	2.2	39.7	32.2	12.8	2.6	55.0
Viet Nam	1990	100.0	7.5	89.6	14.4	26.4	35.7	38.7	22.7	12.3	38.6
	1995	100.0	8.2	73.6	27.1	32.8	41.9	27.2	28.8	15.0	44.1
	2000	100.0	6.4	66.5	29.6	55.0	57.5	24.5	36.7	18.6	38.7
	2006	100.0	6.3	63.9	34.7	75.0	79.1	21.7	40.2	20.5	38.0
Western Asia - Asie occidentale	*1990*	*100.0*	*20.2*	*55.5*	*19.8*	*36.0*	*31.6*	*11.0*	*41.5*	*13.9*	*47.5*
	1995	*100.0*	*18.2*	*58.5*	*23.5*	*34.6*	*34.1*	*9.8*	*40.4*	*14.7*	*49.8*
	2000	*100.0*	*19.0*	*51.3*	*21.0*	*43.7*	*34.3*	*7.9*	*45.6*	*12.1*	*46.5*
	2006	*100.0*	*15.1*	*46.7*	*21.9*	*55.0*	*39.5*	*5.5*	*48.9*	*12.8*	*45.6*
Bahrain - Bahreïn	1990	100.0	23.8	56.0	16.9	91.9	90.3	0.8	36.5	11.0	62.7
	1995	100.0	20.9	53.0	14.6	82.0	70.5	0.8	35.8	16.0	63.4
	2000	100.0	17.6	47.1	10.3	89.4	64.4	0.7	40.0	10.3	59.4
	2006	100.0	14.3	34.1	21.3	97.2	66.9	0.4	37.4	10.5	62.1
Iraq	1990	100.0	20.6	16.9	19.0	113.9	70.3	18.9	30.0	8.4	51.1
	1995	100.0	36.9	52.7	5.0	21.1	15.6	18.9	30.0	8.4	51.1
	2000	100.0	14.7	16.8	36.2	93.9	61.6	4.6	84.6	0.9	10.8
	2006	100.0	27.9	52.7	22.2	90.2	93.0	7.5	68.4	1.5	24.2
Jordan - Jordanie	1990	100.0	24.9	74.1	31.9	61.9	92.7	7.5	30.9	17.0	61.7
	1995	100.0	23.6	64.6	33.0	51.7	72.9	4.3	27.5	13.9	68.3
	2000	100.0	23.7	80.2	22.4	41.8	68.1	2.3	24.4	14.8	73.3
	2006	100.0	20.5	96.6	26.4	51.5	95.0	2.6	26.3	16.4	71.1
Kuwait - Koweït	1990	100.0	38.6	58.6	15.9	44.8	57.8	0.9	51.7	11.5	47.4
	1995	100.0	33.0	41.3	15.1	53.6	43.0	0.4	52.8	11.1	46.7
	2000	100.0	21.5	41.5	10.7	56.5	30.1	0.3	57.2	6.7	42.5
	2006	100.0	13.4	28.0	16.7	67.9	26.4	0.4	56.8	7.7	42.8

For sources and notes, see end of table.   Pour les sources et les notes, se reporter à la fin du tableau.

8.3.1 Nominal gross domestic product by type of expenditure and by kind of economic activity of countries and geographical regions

8.3.1 Produit intérieur brut nominal par catégories de dépenses et par branches d'activité économique des pays et des régions géographiques

Region, country or territory / Régions, pays ou territoires	Year / Année	Total GDP / PIB total	GDP by type of expenditure (1) / PIB par catégories de dépense (1)					GDP by kind of economic activity (2) / PIB par branches d'activité économique (2)			
			Final consumption / Consommation finale		Gross capital formation / Formation brute de capital	Exports / Exportations / Of goods and services / Des biens et services	Less imports / Moins les importations	Agriculture (3)	Industry (4) / Industrie (4)		Services (5)
			Government / Administration publique	Household / Ménages					Total	Manufacturing / Activités de fabrication	
			Percentage / En pourcentage								
Lebanon - Liban	1990	100.0	25.1	123.3	28.7	22.2	99.2	8.8	21.2	12.6	70.0
	1995	100.0	9.9	107.7	36.3	11.0	64.9	12.4	26.6	17.3	61.0
	2000	100.0	17.6	85.6	20.3	13.6	37.1	6.4	20.9	12.0	72.7
	2006	100.0	14.8	87.0	21.8	15.6	34.7	5.3	19.2	11.4	75.5
Occupied Palestinian territory - Territoire palestinien occupé	1990	100.0	11.8	112.1	30.3	27.5	81.7	14.2	28.8	17.5	57.0
	1995	100.0	18.5	98.2	35.4	15.5	67.6	12.9	31.3	19.5	55.8
	2000	100.0	27.0	95.5	32.6	16.0	71.1	11.4	24.0	15.2	64.6
	2006	100.0	30.8	97.5	24.4	11.6	64.4	9.4	17.6	11.8	73.0
Oman	1990	100.0	26.6	41.4	12.3	47.2	27.6	2.6	53.4	2.9	44.0
	1995	100.0	27.5	49.0	15.0	44.0	35.6	2.7	45.8	4.6	51.5
	2000	100.0	20.7	40.2	11.9	59.2	32.0	1.9	56.1	5.3	42.0
	2006	100.0	20.8	46.2	14.8	63.7	45.5	1.7	55.1	8.3	43.2
Qatar	1990	100.0	32.9	27.8	18.0	53.5	32.1	0.8	55.7	12.7	43.6
	1995	100.0	31.9	32.1	35.1	44.3	43.3	1.0	52.1	8.2	46.9
	2000	100.0	19.7	15.2	20.2	67.3	22.3	0.4	69.5	5.3	30.1
	2006	100.0	13.3	17.4	34.6	64.7	30.0	0.2	74.1	6.0	25.8
Saudi Arabia - Arabie saoudite	1990	100.0	29.2	46.7	15.1	40.6	31.6	5.7	48.6	8.6	45.7
	1995	100.0	23.6	46.9	19.8	37.6	27.9	5.9	48.6	9.6	45.5
	2000	100.0	26.0	36.5	18.7	43.7	24.9	4.9	53.6	9.6	41.5
	2006	100.0	19.9	27.1	18.9	65.2	31.1	3.6	60.1	9.8	36.3
Syrian Arab Republic - République arabe syrienne	1990	100.0	14.3	68.7	16.5	28.3	28.0	28.3	24.2	5.5	47.6
	1995	100.0	13.4	66.2	27.2	31.0	37.9	28.2	18.1	6.2	53.7
	2000	100.0	12.4	63.4	17.3	36.1	29.2	24.8	33.3	1.5	41.9
	2006	100.0	12.5	65.1	18.7	40.3	37.2	23.5	29.7	3.8	46.8
Turkey - Turquie	1990	100.0	11.0	68.6	24.3	13.3	17.6	17.6	32.1	22.2	50.3
	1995	100.0	10.8	70.3	25.5	19.9	24.4	15.7	31.9	22.6	52.4
	2000	100.0	14.1	71.5	24.5	24.0	31.5	14.2	28.7	19.3	57.1
	2006	100.0	12.3	69.8	24.2	26.0	34.3	9.4	31.6	21.6	59.0
United Arab Emirates - Émirats arabes unis	1990	100.0	16.3	38.6	20.4	65.4	40.8	1.6	62.2	7.2	36.2
	1995	100.0	16.4	47.9	29.7	69.0	63.0	2.8	51.0	10.2	46.1
	2000	100.0	15.4	43.5	23.2	73.7	55.8	3.5	54.8	13.3	41.8
	2006	100.0	8.5	40.0	23.9	81.9	55.2	2.6	53.9	12.7	43.6
Yemen - Yémen	1990	100.0	17.0	72.1	15.2	13.9	19.5	25.7	25.7	8.3	48.6
	1995	100.0	14.3	83.0	21.8	21.7	41.9	20.1	31.0	12.7	48.9
	2000	100.0	13.6	60.3	18.9	41.4	34.2	13.6	45.8	5.7	40.7
	2006	100.0	15.6	60.6	21.5	47.2	44.9	12.6	44.0	6.4	43.4
Developing economies: Oceania - Économies en développement : Océanie	**1990**	**100.0**	**31.4**	**60.1**	**23.3**	**30.3**	**45.3**	**14.9**	**22.5**	**7.8**	**62.6**
	1995	**100.0**	**28.4**	**56.1**	**20.4**	**35.7**	**39.2**	**16.6**	**22.4**	**7.6**	**61.0**
	2000	**100.0**	**28.7**	**59.5**	**20.1**	**33.4**	**41.7**	**15.0**	**24.9**	**9.2**	**60.1**
	2006	**100.0**	**27.5**	**61.1**	**18.9**	**32.0**	**42.7**	**16.5**	**23.9**	**8.1**	**59.6**
Cook Islands - Îles Cook	1990	100.0	42.9	107.3	21.0	4.7	76.0	11.6	8.2	4.1	80.2
	1995	100.0	27.8	69.5	13.6	47.7	58.7	9.7	7.6	2.8	82.6
	2000	100.0	22.3	55.9	10.9	95.0	84.2	13.0	8.1	3.4	78.9
	2006	100.0	22.4	56.1	11.0	73.6	63.1	13.6	8.7	3.5	77.7
Fiji - Fidji	1990	100.0	17.5	69.0	18.3	62.3	67.2	18.7	20.4	10.5	60.9
	1995	100.0	15.9	74.0	13.6	54.7	58.3	18.8	22.8	13.1	58.3
	2000	100.0	17.2	70.6	17.2	65.1	70.2	16.5	21.5	13.5	62.0
	2006	100.0	15.8	78.3	20.1	56.3	70.5	14.1	21.6	13.5	64.3
French Polynesia - Polynésie française	1990	100.0	40.4	61.3	20.0	9.4	31.7	4.5	15.3	7.3	80.2
	1995	100.0	41.5	57.8	15.3	12.5	27.0	4.1	13.3	6.3	82.6
	2000	100.0	42.1	49.7	13.2	20.9	26.0	4.0	14.5	6.5	81.5
	2006	100.0	44.4	48.9	13.0	20.6	26.9	3.5	14.4	6.6	82.1

For sources and notes, see end of table.

Pour les sources et les notes, se reporter à la fin du tableau.

8.3.1 Nominal gross domestic product by type of expenditure and by kind of economic activity of countries and geographical regions

8.3.1 Produit intérieur brut nominal par catégories de dépenses et par branches d'activité économique des pays et des régions géographiques

Region, country or territory / Régions, pays ou territoires	Year / Année	Total GDP / PIB total	GDP by type of expenditure (1) / PIB par catégories de dépense (1)					GDP by kind of economic activity (2) / PIB par branches d'activité écconomique (2)			
			Final consumption / Consommation finale		Gross capital formation / Formation brute de capital	Exports / Exportations	Less imports / Moins les importations	Agri-culture (3)	Industry (4) / Industrie (4)		Services (5)
			Government / Administration publique	Household / Ménages		Of goods and services / Des biens et services			Total	Manu-facturing / Activités de fabrication	
			Percentage / En pourcentage								
Kiribati	1990	100.0	52.8	89.6	93.1	11.6	147.2	18.6	7.6	1.2	73.8
	1995	100.0	45.4	76.9	53.3	14.5	90.1	20.3	4.9	1.2	74.8
	2000	100.0	36.1	61.2	43.2	26.6	67.0	14.7	8.7	0.7	76.6
	2006	100.0	36.4	61.7	43.6	30.2	71.9	9.7	12.0	0.8	78.3
Marshall Islands - Îles Marshall	1990	100.0	50.2	97.6	88.4	11.0	147.2	13.9	12.9	1.0	73.2
	1995	100.0	54.2	91.0	56.3	12.5	114.0	14.9	15.0	2.6	70.0
	2000	100.0	54.1	91.1	56.8	12.4	114.5	10.0	19.2	4.6	70.8
	2006	100.0	54.1	91.1	56.8	12.4	114.5	10.1	19.2	4.4	70.7
Micronesia (Federated States of) - Micronésie (États fédérés de)	1990	100.0	58.3	83.9	37.7	3.4	84.3	19.2	4.0	1.4	76.8
	1995	100.0	58.3	83.9	37.7	3.4	84.3	19.2	4.0	1.4	76.8
	2000	100.0	58.3	83.9	37.7	3.4	84.3	19.2	4.0	1.4	76.8
	2006	100.0	58.3	83.9	37.7	3.4	84.3	19.2	4.0	1.4	76.8
Nauru	1990	100.0	52.8	89.6	93.1	11.6	147.2	18.6	7.6	1.2	73.8
	1995	100.0	45.4	76.9	53.3	14.5	90.1	20.3	4.9	1.2	74.8
	2000	100.0	36.1	61.2	43.2	26.6	67.0	14.7	8.7	0.7	76.6
	2006	100.0	36.4	61.7	43.6	30.2	71.9	9.7	12.0	0.8	78.3
New Caledonia - Nouvelle-Calédonie	1990	100.0	32.6	57.3	23.3	22.0	35.4	2.0	24.9	6.4	73.1
	1995	100.0	33.3	56.0	24.1	19.1	26.2	1.8	22.0	6.0	76.2
	2000	100.0	33.2	55.8	24.2	16.4	28.7	2.4	26.0	10.9	71.6
	2006	100.0	33.2	55.8	24.2	15.4	28.9	2.5	23.7	9.6	73.8
Palau - Palaos	1990	100.0	47.9	51.4	22.0	25.4	46.8	25.9	15.5	0.7	58.6
	1995	100.0	59.6	69.9	19.5	14.6	63.5	5.9	9.4	0.9	84.7
	2000	100.0	61.5	107.8	29.3	9.8	108.4	4.1	12.3	1.5	83.6
	2006	100.0	46.1	40.8	21.1	76.3	84.2	3.6	16.5	0.7	79.8
Papua New Guinea - Papouasie-Nouvelle-Guinée	1990	100.0	26.2	51.6	24.0	43.0	45.4	29.7	31.2	9.2	39.0
	1995	100.0	17.1	42.7	21.9	59.3	41.1	35.1	33.3	8.3	31.6
	2000	100.0	16.2	60.1	21.3	43.9	41.5	31.7	39.2	9.9	29.1
	2006	100.0	11.9	63.0	18.3	40.2	44.6	39.5	37.1	6.6	23.4
Samoa	1990	100.0	28.6	82.8	22.9	29.0	63.3	20.5	28.8	19.2	50.6
	1995	100.0	24.6	80.5	19.6	32.9	57.6	18.4	29.4	19.2	52.2
	2000	100.0	24.0	85.2	14.2	30.6	53.9	16.5	25.6	14.6	57.8
	2006	100.0	22.1	91.8	9.8	30.2	53.9	13.0	27.1	15.2	59.9
Solomon Islands - Îles Salomon	1990	100.0	31.1	57.4	20.1	46.5	56.8	45.5	7.9	3.7	46.6
	1995	100.0	32.9	48.9	19.2	57.7	58.8	44.7	9.9	5.8	45.3
	2000	100.0	31.8	48.5	19.6	59.1	59.1	44.5	10.1	5.9	45.4
	2006	100.0	31.9	48.5	19.6	59.1	59.1	44.5	10.1	5.9	45.4
Tonga	1990	100.0	19.1	93.6	18.5	33.9	65.1	35.1	14.4	6.1	50.4
	1995	100.0	19.7	107.1	22.2	20.2	69.2	23.7	11.1	3.4	65.2
	2000	100.0	14.9	103.4	19.2	15.7	54.0	28.6	16.7	5.3	54.6
	2006	100.0	13.0	117.3	13.5	21.2	62.1	28.1	14.9	4.5	57.0
Tuvalu	1990	100.0	52.8	102.9	93.1	11.6	147.2	25.6	14.5	3.1	59.8
	1995	100.0	54.2	91.1	56.3	12.6	114.0	24.0	14.0	3.9	62.0
	2000	100.0	54.2	91.1	54.7	12.6	114.0	17.3	13.1	3.2	69.7
	2006	100.0	54.2	91.1	55.7	12.6	114.0	16.7	13.6	3.4	69.7
Vanuatu	1990	100.0	28.2	62.9	43.2	46.4	76.6	20.0	13.5	5.9	66.5
	1995	100.0	25.4	46.9	31.9	44.2	53.6	15.6	11.6	4.4	72.8
	2000	100.0	23.1	57.6	22.1	43.0	56.7	14.9	8.9	4.2	76.3
	2006	100.0	22.8	61.2	20.2	42.9	58.7	14.4	8.5	3.5	77.1
Economies in transition: Asia - Économies en transition : Asie	**1995**	**100.0**	**15.5**	**67.0**	**24.0**	**41.0**	**46.4**	**23.5**	**30.7**	**23.2**	**45.8**
	2000	**100.0**	**14.5**	**63.7**	**20.7**	**46.6**	**44.8**	**20.4**	**34.6**	**17.7**	**45.0**
	2006	**100.0**	**11.2**	**51.8**	**28.9**	**52.0**	**43.2**	**12.2**	**40.4**	**14.5**	**47.4**
Armenia - Arménie	1995	100.0	11.2	106.3	18.4	23.9	62.2	40.8	31.0	24.4	28.2
	2000	100.0	11.8	97.1	18.6	23.4	50.5	25.2	35.0	23.9	39.8
	2006	100.0	11.4	72.2	32.8	21.6	34.4	19.2	47.3	11.3	33.5

For sources and notes, see end of table.

Pour les sources et les notes, se reporter à la fin du tableau.

8.3.1 Nominal gross domestic product by type of expenditure and by kind of economic activity of countries and geographical regions

8.3.1 Produit intérieur brut nominal par catégories de dépenses et par branches d'activité économique des pays et des régions géographiques

Region, country or territory / Régions, pays ou territoires	Year / Année	Total GDP / PIB total	GDP by type of expenditure (1) / PIB par catégories de dépense (1)					GDP by kind of economic activity (2) / PIB par branches d'activité économique (2)			
			Final consumption / Consommation finale		Gross capital formation / Formation brute de capital	Exports / Exportations	Less imports / Moins les importations	Agri-culture (3)	Industry (4) / Industrie (4)		Services (5)
			Government / Administration publique	Household / Ménages		Of goods and services / Des biens et services			Total	Manu-facturing / Activités de fabrication	
			Percentage / En pourcentage								
Azerbaijan - Azerbaïdjan	1995	100.0	12.8	84.3	23.8	32.5	53.4	26.9	32.9	12.2	40.3
	2000	100.0	15.2	64.4	20.7	40.2	38.4	17.0	45.1	5.6	37.9
	2006	100.0	8.0	35.6	31.6	70.3	41.0	7.5	69.3	5.7	23.2
Georgia - Géorgie	1995	100.0	8.0	83.2	24.0	14.0	28.5	44.4	12.7	10.3	43.0
	2000	100.0	8.5	90.5	26.6	23.0	39.7	21.7	22.1	12.9	56.1
	2006	100.0	16.4	74.3	28.0	32.9	56.9	12.8	24.6	12.6	62.5
Kazakhstan	1995	100.0	13.6	71.1	23.3	39.0	43.5	12.8	31.2	24.4	56.0
	2000	100.0	12.1	61.9	18.1	56.6	49.1	8.6	40.1	17.5	51.3
	2006	100.0	9.9	49.0	30.7	53.7	42.3	7.5	37.7	13.8	54.9
Kyrgyzstan - Kirghizistan	1995	100.0	19.5	75.0	18.3	29.5	42.4	43.1	20.1	13.6	36.8
	2000	100.0	20.0	65.7	20.0	41.8	47.6	36.6	31.3	19.4	32.1
	2006	100.0	18.9	97.1	21.1	39.3	76.5	33.0	20.1	12.9	46.9
Tajikistan - Tadjikistan	1995	100.0	10.9	60.5	28.7	112.0	121.2	35.9	36.4	33.3	27.7
	2000	100.0	11.6	87.7	9.4	92.4	100.2	27.3	38.4	36.1	34.3
	2006	100.0	12.9	77.9	11.3	59.0	72.0	24.1	34.1	29.7	41.8
Turkmenistan - Turkménistan	1995	100.0	8.4	60.6	33.6	142.5	145.0	16.9	64.8	58.8	18.3
	2000	100.0	14.5	35.3	35.4	97.2	82.4	22.9	41.8	35.0	35.2
	2006	100.0	12.7	54.9	23.9	63.4	55.0	20.3	41.2	36.6	38.5
Uzbekistan - Ouzbékistan	1995	100.0	22.3	50.6	24.2	31.6	28.7	31.4	28.1	20.2	40.5
	2000	100.0	18.7	61.9	19.6	26.5	26.7	34.9	22.8	15.8	42.3
	2006	100.0	17.0	52.7	22.6	39.1	31.3	30.7	25.8	20.5	43.4
Economies in transition: Europe - Économies en transition : Europe	**1995**	**100.0**	**19.8**	**54.5**	**24.6**	**31.5**	**30.5**	**9.3**	**36.8**	**27.8**	**53.9**
	2000	**100.0**	**16.4**	**50.6**	**19.2**	**45.0**	**31.2**	**8.7**	**36.7**	**28.8**	**54.6**
	2006	**100.0**	**18.0**	**51.4**	**21.6**	**35.9**	**27.3**	**5.8**	**37.0**	**19.1**	**57.1**
Albania - Albanie	1990	100.0	10.2	72.7	24.4	14.9	22.2	40.2	43.8	..	16.0
	1995	100.0	13.3	88.4	20.8	12.2	33.3	54.6	22.0	..	23.4
	2000	100.0	10.6	67.5	41.7	17.5	37.3	25.5	15.7	4.7	58.8
	2006	100.0	10.2	62.8	51.1	23.3	46.5	22.7	22.2	5.2	55.1
Belarus - Bélarus	1995	100.0	20.6	59.1	24.8	49.7	54.1	16.8	35.7	30.0	47.4
	2000	100.0	19.5	56.9	25.4	64.7	68.2	13.9	38.5	31.1	47.6
	2006	100.0	19.9	52.4	30.4	59.9	64.2	9.2	41.5	32.4	49.3
Bosnia and Herzegovina - Bosnie-Herzégovine	1995	100.0	27.4	103.7	20.0	20.4	71.5	13.6	26.9	11.9	59.6
	2000	100.0	23.0	88.0	21.2	28.0	60.3	11.8	25.4	11.3	62.7
	2006	100.0	23.3	85.6	20.8	26.8	56.6	10.0	24.3	11.2	65.7
Croatia - Croatie	1995	100.0	28.2	65.1	17.6	38.6	49.5	10.4	33.4	23.6	56.3
	2000	100.0	24.8	60.1	20.2	47.1	52.3	8.8	29.3	21.0	61.9
	2006	100.0	19.6	55.2	27.5	46.5	54.1	7.3	28.1	18.6	64.6
Moldova	1995	100.0	25.9	57.0	24.9	60.1	67.9	32.2	31.4	25.1	36.4
	2000	100.0	14.7	88.4	23.9	49.6	76.6	28.3	21.2	15.8	50.6
	2006	100.0	18.3	95.1	34.3	46.7	94.4	17.6	21.4	14.1	61.0
Russian Federation - Fédération de Russie	1995	100.0	19.1	52.1	25.4	29.3	25.9	7.6	37.0	27.9	55.5
	2000	100.0	15.1	46.2	18.7	44.1	24.0	6.7	37.9	31.4	55.4
	2006	100.0	17.5	48.7	20.2	33.9	21.2	4.8	38.4	18.9	56.8
Serbia and Montenegro - Serbie-et-Monténégro	1995	100.0	22.9	74.5	12.8	18.7	29.0	16.2	28.7	20.0	55.1
	2000	100.0	20.9	79.3	11.9	11.9	24.9	18.0	30.0	20.0	52.0
	2006	100.0	22.5	71.1	27.6	26.1	47.3	13.1	27.6	15.4	59.3
SFR of Yugoslavia (former) - RSF de Yougoslavie (anc.)	1990	100.0	22.6	68.4	15.3	43.0	49.8	12.2	33.5	24.8	54.3
TFYR of Macedonia - LERY de Macédoine	1995	100.0	18.6	70.4	20.8	33.0	42.8	12.8	33.6	24.7	53.7
	2000	100.0	18.2	74.4	22.3	48.6	63.5	11.7	32.9	20.2	55.4
	2006	100.0	18.7	78.5	21.1	48.2	66.3	12.8	29.2	17.7	57.9

For sources and notes, see end of table.

Pour les sources et les notes, se reporter à la fin du tableau.

8.3.1 Nominal gross domestic product by type of expenditure and by kind of economic activity of countries and geographical regions

8.3.1 Produit intérieur brut nominal par catégories de dépenses et par branches d'activité économique des pays et des régions géographiques

Region, country or territory / Régions, pays ou territoires	Year / Année	Total GDP / PIB total	GDP by type of expenditure (1) / PIB par catégories de dépense (1)					GDP by kind of economic activity (2) / PIB par branches d'activité économique (2)			
			Final consumption / Consommation finale		Gross capital formation / Formation brute de capital	Exports / Exportations — Of goods and services / Des biens et services	Less imports / Moins les importations	Agriculture (3)	Industry (4) / Industrie (4)		Services (5)
			Government / Administration publique	Household / Ménages					Total	Manufacturing / Activités de fabrication	
			Percentage / En pourcentage								
Ukraine (6)	1995	100.0	21.3	55.1	26.7	47.1	50.2	15.0	41.7	34.2	43.2
	2000	100.0	18.6	56.6	19.7	62.4	57.4	16.8	37.6	21.3	45.5
	2006	100.0	18.9	59.7	24.3	47.2	50.1	8.4	33.4	20.0	58.1
USSR (former) - URSS (anc.)	1990	100.0	19.7	50.8	30.6	21.9	23.3	19.5	46.8	37.2	33.7
Developed economies: America - Économies développées : Amérique	**1990**	**100.0**	**17.5**	**65.8**	**17.9**	**11.4**	**12.6**	**2.0**	**27.8**	**18.2**	**70.2**
	1995	**100.0**	**15.8**	**66.9**	**18.2**	**13.3**	**14.2**	**1.6**	**26.2**	**17.8**	**72.2**
	2000	**100.0**	**14.6**	**68.0**	**20.5**	**14.0**	**17.1**	**1.1**	**24.2**	**16.2**	**74.7**
	2006	**100.0**	**16.2**	**68.9**	**19.7**	**13.8**	**18.6**	**1.0**	**22.9**	**13.6**	**76.1**
Bermuda - Bermudes	1990	100.0	12.5	69.1	16.4	47.5	43.7	0.8	10.4	2.4	88.8
	1995	100.0	11.8	64.3	14.0	45.5	36.0	0.8	10.5	2.4	88.7
	2000	100.0	10.9	51.5	20.1	47.3	34.4	0.7	11.1	2.5	88.2
	2006	100.0	11.0	58.5	19.1	47.3	36.3	0.8	9.8	1.9	89.4
Canada	1990	100.0	22.3	56.7	20.9	25.8	25.7	2.9	31.3	16.9	65.8
	1995	100.0	21.3	56.9	18.8	37.3	34.1	2.9	30.7	18.4	66.4
	2000	100.0	18.6	55.4	20.2	45.6	39.8	2.3	33.2	19.2	64.5
	2006	100.0	19.1	55.7	21.9	37.0	33.7	2.2	31.7	18.0	66.1
Greenland - Groenland	1990	100.0	53.4	27.0	19.0	44.3	43.7	7.3	20.9	11.9	71.8
	1995	100.0	54.0	34.8	16.3	30.7	35.9	7.4	20.9	11.9	71.7
	2000	100.0	52.4	33.3	22.9	25.5	34.1	6.8	20.4	10.9	72.8
	2006	100.0	53.6	32.4	30.2	23.8	33.5	5.8	19.5	10.1	74.7
United States - États-Unis	1990	100.0	17.0	66.7	17.6	10.0	11.3	1.9	27.5	18.3	70.6
	1995	100.0	15.3	67.7	18.1	11.4	12.6	1.5	25.9	17.8	72.6
	2000	100.0	14.4	68.9	20.5	11.7	15.4	1.0	23.6	16.6	75.4
	2006	100.0	15.9	70.2	19.5	11.6	17.2	0.9	22.1	13.3	77.0
Developed economies: Asia - Économies développées : Asie	**1990**	**100.0**	**13.7**	**52.6**	**32.9**	**10.9**	**10.0**	**2.5**	**38.2**	**25.9**	**59.3**
	1995	**100.0**	**15.4**	**55.0**	**28.4**	**9.5**	**8.3**	**1.9**	**33.1**	**22.4**	**65.1**
	2000	**100.0**	**17.2**	**56.3**	**25.1**	**11.7**	**10.3**	**1.7**	**30.9**	**21.2**	**67.4**
	2006	**100.0**	**18.0**	**57.1**	**23.6**	**16.7**	**15.5**	**1.6**	**28.8**	**20.0**	**69.7**
Israel - Israël	1990	100.0	28.5	55.0	19.8	31.0	34.9	3.1	28.2	20.9	68.7
	1995	100.0	28.0	55.2	25.1	29.1	37.3	2.1	26.1	16.9	71.8
	2000	100.0	26.8	52.6	20.9	38.2	38.5	1.7	24.6	17.5	73.7
	2006	100.0	27.0	54.8	17.2	44.8	43.7	1.6	22.2	15.2	76.2
Japan - Japon	1990	100.0	13.4	52.5	33.1	10.5	9.5	2.5	38.4	26.0	59.2
	1995	100.0	15.1	55.0	28.4	9.2	7.8	1.9	33.2	22.4	64.9
	2000	100.0	16.9	56.4	25.2	11.0	9.6	1.7	31.1	21.3	67.2
	2006	100.0	17.7	57.2	23.8	15.8	14.6	1.6	28.9	20.2	69.5
Developed economies: Europe - Économies développées : Europe	**1990**	**100.0**	**19.9**	**57.5**	**23.1**	**26.7**	**27.2**	**3.4**	**33.0**	**22.9**	**63.5**
	1995	**100.0**	**20.2**	**57.8**	**20.4**	**29.9**	**28.3**	**2.9**	**30.0**	**20.7**	**67.1**
	2000	**100.0**	**19.6**	**58.4**	**21.3**	**36.5**	**35.9**	**2.4**	**28.2**	**19.3**	**69.5**
	2006	**100.0**	**20.5**	**57.7**	**21.0**	**40.6**	**39.8**	**2.1**	**27.0**	**17.7**	**71.0**
Andorra - Andorre	1990	100.0	16.7	60.4	26.1	16.1	19.4	1.1	17.1	5.3	81.9
	1995	100.0	18.1	60.0	21.9	22.4	22.4	1.0	17.4	5.2	81.6
	2000	100.0	17.2	59.7	26.3	29.0	32.2	0.9	17.3	4.5	81.8
	2006	100.0	18.1	57.6	30.7	26.2	32.5	0.6	17.2	5.0	82.2
Austria - Autriche	1990	100.0	18.7	56.9	23.9	37.7	36.8	4.0	31.8	21.4	64.2
	1995	100.0	20.1	57.1	23.4	35.1	35.4	2.7	30.4	19.3	66.9
	2000	100.0	18.4	56.8	23.4	45.4	44.1	2.1	30.9	20.3	67.0
	2006	100.0	18.0	55.7	21.2	55.2	50.2	1.8	29.8	19.4	68.3
Belgium - Belgique	2006	100.0	22.9	53.1	21.0	90.4	87.4	1.1	24.4	17.3	74.4
Belgium-Luxembourg - Belgique-Luxembourg	1990	100.0	19.7	54.8	22.4	71.4	68.7	1.9	31.4	21.7	66.7
	1995	100.0	21.2	53.4	20.0	70.4	64.9	1.5	27.9	19.8	70.7
	2000	100.0	20.8	52.9	21.9	89.9	85.5	1.3	26.3	18.6	72.4

For sources and notes, see end of table.

Pour les sources et les notes, se reporter à la fin du tableau.

8.3.1 Nominal gross domestic product by type of expenditure and by kind of economic activity of countries and geographical regions

8.3.1 Produit intérieur brut nominal par catégories de dépenses et par branches d'activité économique des pays et des régions géographiques

Region, country or territory / Régions, pays ou territoires	Year / Année	Total GDP / PIB total	GDP by type of expenditure (1) / PIB par catégories de dépense (1)					GDP by kind of economic activity (2) / PIB par branches d'activité économique (2)			
			Final consumption / Consommation finale		Gross capital formation / Formation brute de capital	Exports / Exportations	Less imports / Moins les importations	Agriculture (3)	Industry (4) / Industrie (4)		Services (5)
			Government / Administration publique	Household / Ménages		Of goods and services / Des biens et services			Total	Manufacturing / Activités de fabrication	
			Percentage / En pourcentage								
Bulgaria - Bulgarie	1990	100.0	7.2	66.8	30.4	33.1	37.5	18.3	50.9	35.1	30.8
	1995	100.0	15.3	70.7	15.7	44.7	46.3	13.4	32.4	21.9	54.3
	2000	100.0	17.9	69.2	18.3	55.7	61.1	13.9	30.1	17.8	56.0
	2006	100.0	17.6	70.8	30.2	63.9	82.3	10.6	30.0	18.3	59.4
Cyprus - Chypre	1990	100.0	17.3	59.9	27.0	51.5	57.0	7.1	27.0	14.7	65.9
	1995	100.0	13.7	64.8	21.8	50.2	50.5	5.1	22.8	12.1	72.0
	2000	100.0	16.0	64.8	18.3	55.4	54.5	3.6	19.1	9.9	77.3
	2006	100.0	17.9	65.7	21.1	50.3	53.9	2.8	19.6	8.6	77.6
Czechoslovakia (former) - Tchécoslovaquie (anc.)	1990	100.0	23.9	50.8	26.0	37.4	38.2	7.6	44.0	24.7	48.4
Czech Republic - République tchèque	1995	100.0	20.9	50.9	32.6	50.7	55.1	5.0	38.3	24.3	56.7
	2000	100.0	21.1	52.5	29.5	63.4	66.4	3.9	38.1	26.8	58.0
	2006	100.0	22.0	49.1	26.4	74.1	71.7	3.1	37.2	25.4	59.7
Denmark - Danemark	1990	100.0	25.1	50.3	19.9	37.2	32.6	4.0	25.6	17.4	70.4
	1995	100.0	25.2	51.2	19.5	37.6	33.5	3.5	25.1	17.1	71.5
	2000	100.0	25.1	47.7	21.2	46.6	40.6	2.6	26.8	16.2	70.6
	2006	100.0	25.3	48.4	22.4	53.1	49.3	1.8	24.5	14.0	73.7
Estonia - Estonie	1995	100.0	26.8	53.5	27.5	66.1	73.5	7.2	30.8	19.2	62.0
	2000	100.0	19.9	55.0	28.7	85.4	89.0	4.9	27.8	17.8	67.3
	2006	100.0	16.2	53.4	38.5	83.8	92.1	4.0	28.4	17.6	67.6
Finland - Finlande	1990	100.0	21.7	50.7	28.6	22.5	23.9	6.3	33.3	22.6	60.3
	1995	100.0	22.8	51.9	17.7	36.4	28.8	4.3	32.8	25.3	62.8
	2000	100.0	20.3	49.4	20.1	43.5	33.4	3.5	33.7	26.2	62.8
	2006	100.0	21.6	51.0	20.9	44.5	38.0	3.0	31.6	23.6	65.4
France	1990	100.0	21.7	57.3	22.3	21.3	22.7	3.7	28.4	20.1	68.0
	1995	100.0	23.6	56.6	18.6	22.8	21.6	3.2	26.3	18.5	70.5
	2000	100.0	22.9	55.7	20.5	28.6	27.7	2.8	22.9	16.0	74.3
	2006	100.0	23.4	57.2	20.9	27.5	28.9	2.4	21.1	13.7	76.5
Germany - Allemagne	1990	100.0	19.3	57.8	23.2	24.8	24.9	1.5	37.3	28.0	61.2
	1995	100.0	19.6	57.7	22.2	24.0	23.5	1.3	32.1	22.6	66.6
	2000	100.0	19.0	58.9	21.8	33.4	33.0	1.3	30.3	22.9	68.5
	2006	100.0	18.5	58.5	18.0	44.9	40.0	1.0	30.0	23.7	69.1
Greece - Grèce	1990	100.0	13.3	72.8	24.3	15.3	25.3	8.1	25.9	13.7	65.9
	1995	100.0	13.6	74.3	19.8	14.9	22.7	7.8	21.5	11.4	70.7
	2000	100.0	15.7	70.4	25.0	21.6	32.7	5.7	21.2	10.3	73.1
	2006	100.0	14.0	68.4	25.3	19.0	26.6	3.3	20.8	9.5	75.9
Hungary - Hongrie	1990	100.0	22.2	48.6	24.6	27.3	23.8	10.6	34.9	20.8	54.6
	1995	100.0	23.7	53.9	22.3	43.1	43.1	6.7	30.9	22.5	62.3
	2000	100.0	20.9	52.2	30.5	72.0	75.7	5.4	32.4	23.5	62.2
	2006	100.0	22.8	54.3	22.1	78.0	77.1	4.3	30.5	22.5	65.3
Iceland - Islande	1990	100.0	19.9	59.8	19.0	33.7	32.3	11.3	30.0	16.4	58.7
	1995	100.0	22.0	58.0	16.3	35.5	31.9	11.0	27.9	16.0	61.1
	2000	100.0	23.4	61.0	22.9	33.8	41.1	8.5	25.5	13.7	65.9
	2006	100.0	24.0	60.2	30.2	34.3	47.5	7.3	24.6	12.8	68.2
Ireland - Irlande	1990	100.0	16.2	59.3	20.8	56.7	51.8	8.9	35.1	27.5	56.0
	1995	100.0	16.3	54.3	18.2	76.2	64.4	7.0	38.0	30.2	55.0
	2000	100.0	13.8	47.1	25.1	98.4	84.8	3.4	42.5	33.5	54.1
	2006	100.0	16.1	44.9	28.0	80.9	69.5	2.4	37.2	26.5	60.5
Italy - Italie	1990	100.0	20.1	57.3	22.3	19.2	19.0	3.5	32.1	23.3	64.4
	1995	100.0	18.0	58.4	19.8	25.7	21.9	3.3	30.3	22.2	66.4
	2000	100.0	18.4	59.9	20.7	27.1	26.1	2.8	28.4	21.0	68.8
	2006	100.0	20.3	59.0	21.2	28.0	28.5	2.4	27.1	18.8	70.5

For sources and notes, see end of table.

Pour les sources et les notes, se reporter à la fin du tableau.

8.3.1 Nominal gross domestic product by type of expenditure and by kind of economic activity of countries and geographical regions

8.3.1 Produit intérieur brut nominal par catégories de dépenses et par branches d'activité économique des pays et des régions géographiques

Region, country or territory / Régions, pays ou territoires	Year / Année	Total GDP / PIB total	GDP by type of expenditure (1) / PIB par catégories de dépense (1)					GDP by kind of economic activity (2) / PIB par branches d'activité économique (2)			
			Final consumption / Consommation finale		Gross capital formation / Formation brute de capital	Exports / Exportations	Less imports / Moins les importations	Agriculture (3)	Industry (4) / Industrie (4)		Services (5)
			Government / Administration publique	Household / Ménages		Of goods and services / Des biens et services			Total	Manufacturing / Activités de fabrication	
			Percentage / En pourcentage								
Latvia - Lettonie	1995	100.0	24.5	62.9	15.0	41.9	44.3	9.1	30.4	20.7	60.6
	2000	100.0	20.8	62.5	23.7	41.6	48.7	4.6	23.6	13.7	71.8
	2006	100.0	16.9	65.2	38.0	44.2	64.4	3.7	21.5	11.8	74.8
Lithuania - Lituanie	1995	100.0	21.7	65.9	23.5	49.2	60.3	11.4	32.8	19.9	55.8
	2000	100.0	21.3	65.1	19.8	44.8	51.1	7.9	29.8	19.4	62.3
	2006	100.0	16.3	66.8	26.0	63.2	72.2	6.0	33.0	20.8	61.0
Luxembourg	2006	100.0	16.6	39.1	19.3	180.5	155.5	0.4	14.6	8.1	85.0
Malta - Malte	1990	100.0	17.2	65.3	29.5	75.2	87.6	3.2	31.3	23.6	65.5
	1995	100.0	20.1	63.8	28.3	82.7	95.1	2.6	28.3	21.2	69.2
	2000	100.0	19.0	65.1	26.6	91.4	102.1	2.2	28.8	22.9	69.0
	2006	100.0	21.7	66.6	20.6	72.1	82.3	2.5	24.1	18.0	73.4
Netherlands - Pays-Bas	1990	100.0	23.2	50.0	23.3	56.3	52.9	4.4	29.4	18.6	66.2
	1995	100.0	23.8	49.5	21.0	59.4	53.7	3.5	27.4	17.4	69.2
	2000	100.0	22.0	50.4	22.0	70.1	64.5	2.6	24.9	15.6	72.4
	2006	100.0	25.0	47.3	19.4	75.5	67.2	2.3	24.6	14.5	73.2
Norway - Norvège	1990	100.0	21.2	49.1	23.1	40.4	33.9	3.4	33.9	12.5	62.7
	1995	100.0	21.6	49.3	22.9	38.0	31.7	3.0	34.1	13.3	62.9
	2000	100.0	19.1	42.6	21.0	46.7	29.4	2.1	41.8	10.7	56.1
	2006	100.0	19.8	41.0	21.0	45.5	27.4	1.6	44.9	13.0	53.6
Poland - Pologne	1990	100.0	20.7	47.6	24.3	26.2	19.7	8.1	52.4	33.6	39.5
	1995	100.0	18.7	60.4	18.7	23.2	21.0	8.0	35.2	21.1	56.8
	2000	100.0	17.5	64.0	24.8	27.1	33.5	5.0	31.7	18.5	63.3
	2006	100.0	17.9	62.8	20.1	40.9	41.6	4.7	31.4	18.6	63.9
Portugal	1990	100.0	15.6	64.2	26.7	31.2	37.9	9.0	28.3	19.3	62.8
	1995	100.0	17.9	65.2	23.3	28.6	35.0	5.7	28.4	18.6	65.9
	2000	100.0	19.3	63.9	27.7	29.8	40.6	3.8	27.6	17.1	68.6
	2006	100.0	20.7	65.9	21.5	30.9	39.0	2.8	24.9	15.7	72.4
Romania - Roumanie	1990	100.0	13.6	65.7	29.9	16.1	25.4	23.6	47.6	36.9	28.8
	1995	100.0	14.0	67.5	24.0	26.6	32.3	21.0	40.4	26.1	38.6
	2000	100.0	16.1	70.1	19.5	32.9	38.5	12.4	35.9	24.5	51.7
	2006	100.0	19.7	67.4	24.5	34.0	45.6	12.5	34.9	23.1	52.6
San Marino - Saint-Marin	1990	100.0	14.0	64.2	23.4	268.5	269.1	3.5	32.1	23.3	64.4
	1995	100.0	9.5	68.5	18.0	236.7	232.7	3.3	30.3	22.2	66.4
	2000	100.0	15.4	40.0	50.4	193.7	199.4	2.8	28.4	21.0	68.8
	2006	100.0	13.8	35.5	57.4	181.2	187.9	2.4	27.1	18.8	70.5
Slovakia - Slovaquie	1995	100.0	21.3	52.2	24.3	57.4	55.2	5.9	37.8	26.8	56.3
	2000	100.0	19.9	56.6	25.9	70.3	72.8	4.5	36.2	24.7	59.3
	2006	100.0	18.1	57.0	29.2	80.2	84.4	4.5	35.3	23.5	60.2
Slovenia - Slovénie	1995	100.0	19.1	59.8	22.9	51.2	53.0	4.2	35.3	26.4	60.5
	2000	100.0	19.3	57.4	26.8	55.6	59.1	3.2	36.2	26.5	60.6
	2006	100.0	19.5	54.7	26.1	68.5	68.8	2.6	34.9	25.6	62.5
Spain - Espagne	1990	100.0	16.7	60.4	26.1	16.1	19.4	5.5	33.0	21.3	61.5
	1995	100.0	18.1	60.0	21.9	22.4	22.4	4.5	29.4	19.5	66.1
	2000	100.0	17.2	59.7	26.3	29.0	32.2	4.4	29.2	18.6	66.4
	2006	100.0	18.1	57.6	30.7	26.2	32.5	3.5	29.2	16.2	67.3
Sweden - Suède	1990	100.0	27.2	49.2	23.3	29.8	29.7	3.3	30.5	20.0	66.2
	1995	100.0	27.0	49.5	17.0	39.2	32.7	2.7	30.3	22.3	67.0
	2000	100.0	26.4	49.4	18.3	45.9	40.0	1.9	28.6	22.0	69.5
	2006	100.0	26.8	47.7	17.6	51.2	43.2	1.6	27.6	20.1	70.8
Switzerland - Suisse	1990	100.0	11.1	57.0	30.5	35.7	34.4	2.8	31.3	20.8	65.9
	1995	100.0	11.7	59.8	23.4	35.4	30.3	2.0	29.8	20.0	68.2
	2000	100.0	11.1	60.0	23.2	45.7	40.0	1.5	26.8	18.8	71.7
	2006	100.0	11.2	59.9	21.8	53.9	46.7	1.3	26.4	18.5	72.4

For sources and notes, see end of table.

Pour les sources et les notes, se reporter à la fin du tableau.

8.3.1 Nominal gross domestic product by type of expenditure and by kind of economic activity of countries and geographical regions

8.3.1 Produit intérieur brut nominal par catégories de dépenses et par branches d'activité économique des pays et des régions géographiques

Region, country or territory / Régions, pays ou territoires	Year / Année	Total GDP / PIB total	GDP by type of expenditure (1) / PIB par catégories de dépense (1)					GDP by kind of economic activity (2) / PIB par branches d'activité économique (2)			
			Final consumption / Consommation finale		Gross capital formation / Formation brute de capita	Exports / Exportations	Less imports / Moins les importations	Agri-culture (3)	Industry (4) / Industrie (4)		Services (5)
			Government / Administration publique	Household / Ménages	Formation brute de capita	Of goods and services / Des biens et services			Total	Manu-facturing / Activités de fabrication	
			Percentage / En pourcentage								
United Kingdom - Royaume-Uni	1990	100.0	20.1	62.3	20.1	24.0	26.6	1.8	34.0	22.4	64.2
	1995	100.0	19.9	63.6	17.0	28.4	28.8	1.8	30.9	21.1	67.3
	2000	100.0	19.1	65.5	17.5	28.1	30.1	1.0	27.2	17.4	71.8
	2006	100.0	22.0	64.3	17.6	30.3	34.3	0.9	24.0	14.0	75.1
Developed economies: Oceania - Économies développées : Océanie	**1990**	**100.0**	**18.6**	**58.8**	**22.9**	**17.5**	**17.6**	**4.0**	**29.7**	**15.0**	**66.3**
	1995	**100.0**	**18.2**	**59.1**	**22.9**	**20.6**	**20.8**	**4.3**	**28.0**	**15.1**	**67.7**
	2000	**100.0**	**18.1**	**59.4**	**22.0**	**24.2**	**23.7**	**4.5**	**25.9**	**13.1**	**69.5**
	2006	**100.0**	**18.1**	**56.7**	**26.5**	**22.0**	**23.0**	**3.8**	**26.6**	**12.2**	**69.7**
Australia - Australie	1990	100.0	18.5	58.6	23.3	16.2	16.4	3.6	30.1	14.5	66.2
	1995	100.0	18.3	59.2	22.8	19.2	19.6	3.8	28.4	14.6	67.8
	2000	100.0	18.2	59.5	22.1	22.7	22.4	4.0	26.1	12.7	69.9
	2006	100.0	18.0	56.3	26.8	21.1	21.9	3.3	27.0	11.7	69.8
New Zealand - Nouvelle-Zélande	1990	100.0	19.1	60.7	20.1	26.8	26.6	6.7	26.8	18.0	66.6
	1995	100.0	17.5	58.4	23.3	29.0	28.2	7.2	25.9	17.9	66.9
	2000	100.0	17.5	59.2	21.6	35.5	33.8	8.6	24.4	16.3	66.9
	2006	100.0	18.9	59.7	24.3	28.4	31.2	7.0	24.0	15.4	69.0

Sources:
- UN DESA Statistics Division

Sources :
- ONU DAES Division de statistique

Notes:

(1) The breakdown in shares might not add-up to 100 percent due to statistical discrepancies.

(2) Refers to Total Value Added.

(3) Includes agriculture, hunting, forestry and fishing (ISIC Revision 3 divisions 01-05).

(4) Includes mining and quarrying, manufacturing, electricity, gas and water supply, and construction (ISIC Revision 3 divisions 10-45).

(5) Include all other economic activities (ISIC Revision 3 divisions 50-99).

(6) GDP data include the Federation of Bosnia and Herzegovina only. Data for the Republika Srpska are excluded.

Notes :

(1) La somme des pourcentages du PIB peut ne pas être égale à 100 à cause des écarts statistiques.

(2) Renvoie à la valeur ajoutée totale.

(3) Inclut l'agriculture, la chasse, la sylviculture et la pêche (CITI Révision 3 divisions 01-05).

(4) Inclut les activités extractives, les activités de fabrication, la production et distribution d'électricité, de gaz et d'eau et la construction (CITI Révision 3 divisions 10-45).

(5) Incluent toutes les autres activités économiques (CITI Révision 3 divisions 50-99).

(6) Y compris le PIB de la Fédération de Bosnie-Herzégovine seulement. Non compris le PIB de la Republika Srpska.

8.3.2 Nominal gross domestic product by type of expenditure and by kind of economic activity of economic groupings

8.3.2 Produit intérieur brut nominal par catégories de dépenses et par branches d'activité économique des groupements économiques

Economic grouping / Groupements économiques	Year / Année	Total GDP / PIB total	Final consumption / Consommation finale — Government / Administration publique	Final consumption — Household / Ménages	Gross capital formation / Formation brute de capital	Exports / Exportations — Of goods and services / Des biens et services	Less imports / Moins les importations — Of goods and services / Des biens et services	Agriculture / Agriculture (3)	Industry (4) / Industrie (4) — Total	Industry — Manufacturing / Activités de fabrication	Services (5)
						Percentage / En pourcentage					
DEVELOPING ECONOMIES - **ÉCONOMIES EN DÉVELOPPEMENT**	**1990**	**100.0**	**14.0**	**59.3**	**25.8**	**27.4**	**26.1**	**14.8**	**35.6**	**22.0**	**49.6**
	1995	**100.0**	**13.7**	**58.9**	**28.5**	**30.2**	**30.9**	**12.6**	**35.6**	**22.8**	**51.8**
	2000	**100.0**	**14.3**	**58.0**	**25.0**	**36.1**	**33.3**	**10.7**	**36.7**	**22.8**	**52.6**
	2006	**100.0**	**13.9**	**53.0**	**27.4**	**44.1**	**38.5**	**10.3**	**38.9**	**23.6**	**50.8**
Developing economies excluding China - Économies en développement sans la Chine	1990	100.0	14.1	60.6	24.7	28.4	27.4	13.4	34.9	20.3	51.7
	1995	100.0	13.7	61.0	26.7	31.8	32.9	11.5	33.9	19.9	54.6
	2000	100.0	13.9	60.5	22.8	38.8	36.0	9.8	34.6	18.9	55.6
	2006	100.0	13.7	57.8	22.9	45.0	40.1	9.6	36.6	18.3	53.8
Developing economies excluding LDCs - Économies en développement sans les PMA	1990	100.0	14.1	58.6	26.2	27.8	26.1	13.9	36.2	22.5	49.9
	1995	100.0	13.7	58.3	28.8	30.5	30.9	11.9	36.1	23.1	52.0
	2000	100.0	14.3	57.6	25.1	36.4	33.4	10.1	37.0	23.2	52.9
	2006	100.0	14.0	52.6	27.5	44.3	38.6	9.8	39.1	24.0	51.1
High-income developing countries - Pays en développement à revenu élevé	1990	100.0	14.7	56.6	24.2	41.3	37.2	6.1	38.6	21.7	55.3
	1995	100.0	13.5	57.6	27.0	46.1	44.2	4.7	35.3	20.3	59.9
	2000	100.0	13.7	57.6	23.8	50.1	45.3	3.7	35.1	19.3	61.2
	2006	100.0	13.1	53.0	22.7	63.6	52.6	3.2	38.3	18.0	58.5
Middle-income developing countries - Pays en développement à revenu intermédiaire	1990	100.0	15.1	60.9	25.5	20.1	21.8	11.1	34.2	20.8	54.7
	1995	100.0	16.0	61.1	25.6	22.6	25.4	11.1	34.1	20.7	54.8
	2000	100.0	16.1	61.7	22.0	29.5	29.0	9.9	35.0	19.9	55.1
	2006	100.0	16.3	59.7	21.2	32.9	30.6	9.4	36.9	20.0	53.7
Low-income developing countries - Pays en développement à revenu faible	1990	100.0	12.3	60.5	27.8	20.5	19.0	27.3	34.1	23.6	38.6
	1995	100.0	11.4	58.0	33.2	20.1	21.5	22.9	37.6	27.7	39.5
	2000	100.0	13.5	55.8	28.6	25.7	23.3	18.8	39.5	28.6	41.7
	2006	100.0	13.0	48.6	35.1	36.0	32.6	16.3	40.6	29.9	43.1
Heavily indebted poor countries - Pays pauvres très endettés	1990	100.0	14.8	76.7	14.8	20.9	27.5	34.0	22.1	12.7	43.9
	1995	100.0	12.3	77.6	17.6	23.4	30.9	35.8	20.7	10.9	43.4
	2000	100.0	12.4	77.0	18.9	23.9	32.1	33.2	23.8	11.4	42.9
	2006	100.0	13.8	71.9	22.4	30.0	38.0	32.9	25.1	11.0	42.0
Landlocked developing countries - Pays en développement sans littoral	1990	100.0	15.7	74.7	17.1	19.6	26.7	35.2	24.7	13.8	40.1
	1995	100.0	15.4	71.8	21.4	33.1	41.3	28.3	27.2	17.0	44.5
	2000	100.0	15.6	70.5	19.6	35.6	41.2	26.0	28.1	14.1	46.0
	2006	100.0	13.9	60.6	25.8	42.0	42.1	20.1	34.0	12.9	45.9
Small island developing States - Petits États insulaires en développement	1990	100.0	18.0	60.8	24.7	51.9	54.9	11.0	30.7	12.4	58.3
	1995	100.0	16.4	60.3	24.7	53.7	54.6	12.6	28.4	11.9	58.9
	2000	100.0	16.5	63.4	25.5	51.3	56.4	8.6	29.2	12.0	62.2
	2006	100.0	16.2	59.1	24.0	53.6	55.2	8.5	31.1	11.9	60.4
Least developed countries - *Pays les moins avancés*	*1990*	*100.0*	*13.2*	*77.3*	*15.6*	*17.8*	*24.5*	*35.7*	*21.1*	*10.5*	*43.2*
	1995	*100.0*	*11.3*	*79.8*	*18.6*	*19.9*	*30.4*	*35.8*	*21.0*	*10.0*	*43.3*
	2000	*100.0*	*11.6*	*74.7*	*20.0*	*24.1*	*30.8*	*32.1*	*25.7*	*10.2*	*42.2*
	2006	*100.0*	*12.7*	*66.3*	*22.5*	*34.7*	*36.8*	*28.1*	*32.3*	*9.8*	*39.6*
Africa and Haiti - Afrique et Haïti	1990	100.0	16.2	75.0	15.3	21.9	28.8	35.5	21.7	9.7	42.8
	1995	100.0	14.7	78.3	17.7	22.4	33.2	37.2	20.2	7.6	42.6
	2000	100.0	15.2	73.0	18.6	24.8	31.6	34.6	25.4	7.7	40.0
	2006	100.0	15.0	61.7	21.2	38.2	36.2	29.1	35.2	7.5	35.7
Asia - Asie	1990	100.0	6.2	82.6	16.0	8.1	14.0	36.2	20.0	12.1	43.8
	1995	100.0	6.1	82.5	19.7	15.4	25.6	34.2	22.1	12.9	43.7
	2000	100.0 ·	6.5	77.4	21.7	22.4	28.8	29.4	26.4	13.2	44.2
	2006	100.0	7.7	75.6	24.7	27.4	37.0	26.4	27.7	13.8	45.9
Islands - Îles	1990	100.0	26.8	65.5	29.5	42.8	64.2	29.4	14.8	6.1	55.8
	1995	100.0	25.3	56.8	27.2	53.0	63.0	26.3	16.1	6.7	57.6
	2000	100.0	26.2	63.8	22.8	48.2	62.0	22.7	14.7	6.4	62.6
	2006	100.0	31.5	60.3	30.2	45.5	68.6	23.2	15.1	6.4	61.7

For sources and notes, see end of table.

Pour les sources et les notes, se reporter à la fin du tableau.

8.3.2 Nominal gross domestic product by type of expenditure and by kind of economic activity of economic groupings

8.3.2 Produit intérieur brut nominal par catégories de dépenses et par branches d'activité économique des groupements économiques

Economic grouping / Groupements économiques	Year / Année	Total GDP / PIB total	Final consumption / Consommation finale — Government / Administration publique	Household / Ménages	Gross capital formation / Formation brute de capital	Exports / Exportations — Of goods and services / Des biens et services	Less imports / Moins les importations	Agriculture (3)	Industry (4) — Total	Manufacturing / Activités de fabrication	Services (5)
Major petroleum exporters -	*1990*	*100.0*	*19.1*	*51.8*	*19.2*	*41.3*	*33.1*	*12.2*	*45.6*	*12.2*	*42.3*
Principaux exportateurs de pétrole	*1995*	*100.0*	*18.7*	*54.0*	*22.7*	*35.6*	*31.0*	*11.4*	*43.8*	*11.5*	*44.8*
	2000	*100.0*	*17.2*	*43.9*	*20.8*	*45.5*	*27.3*	*8.6*	*51.8*	*10.1*	*39.6*
	2006	*100.0*	*14.0*	*39.9*	*22.0*	*56.1*	*32.6*	*8.4*	*53.4*	*9.1*	*38.2*
Africa - Afrique	1990	100.0	14.7	58.0	17.1	42.6	32.6	18.2	47.9	13.6	33.9
	1995	100.0	14.9	70.2	18.7	33.0	37.0	19.6	46.5	8.4	34.0
	2000	100.0	13.8	46.7	15.0	46.8	22.3	17.2	55.2	6.1	27.5
	2006	100.0	11.7	43.2	20.1	51.2	26.3	19.3	53.2	4.7	27.4
America - Amérique	1990	100.0	16.1	50.9	14.1	39.7	22.9	7.0	53.4	24.9	39.6
	1995	100.0	14.4	56.7	23.2	28.9	24.2	8.0	42.7	20.8	49.3
	2000	100.0	12.1	53.5	23.3	32.3	21.1	4.7	47.0	17.7	48.2
	2006	100.0	11.5	50.1	23.9	38.6	24.4	4.3	49.0	14.8	46.7
Asia - Asie	1990	100.0	22.2	48.4	21.5	40.9	35.4	9.8	42.7	9.0	47.5
	1995	100.0	21.1	47.4	24.0	38.3	30.6	9.5	43.2	10.2	47.4
	2000	100.0	19.9	40.1	22.2	48.7	30.9	6.6	51.9	9.6	41.6
	2006	100.0	15.3	36.4	22.3	61.8	36.8	5.3	54.4	9.5	40.3
Major exporters of manufactured goods -	*1990*	*100.0*	*12.8*	*58.4*	*28.8*	*25.7*	*25.1*	*14.5*	*34.8*	*25.6*	*50.7*
Principaux exportateurs d'articles manufacturés	*1995*	*100.0*	*13.2*	*56.3*	*31.3*	*32.6*	*33.1*	*12.1*	*36.3*	*26.6*	*51.6*
	2000	*100.0*	*14.0*	*57.0*	*27.8*	*37.8*	*36.4*	*10.2*	*36.0*	*27.1*	*53.8*
	2006	*100.0*	*14.1*	*51.8*	*30.3*	*45.3*	*41.6*	*9.8*	*37.4*	*28.5*	*52.8*
America - Amérique	1990	100.0	13.7	62.6	23.0	11.9	11.2	6.6	32.2	22.9	61.2
	1995	100.0	17.0	62.0	21.6	14.3	14.8	7.5	32.1	21.7	60.4
	2000	100.0	15.2	63.9	22.6	20.6	22.4	5.9	32.0	20.8	62.1
	2006	100.0	16.1	63.9	18.8	22.7	21.5	6.8	32.6	20.7	60.6
Asia - Asie	1990	100.0	12.4	56.6	31.3	31.8	31.3	18.4	36.0	26.9	45.6
	1995	100.0	11.8	54.1	34.9	39.5	40.0	13.8	37.9	28.4	48.3
	2000	100.0	13.6	54.4	29.6	44.1	41.6	11.7	37.4	29.3	50.9
	2006	100.0	13.5	48.0	33.9	52.4	48.0	10.7	38.8	30.9	50.4
Emerging economies -	*1990*	*100.0*	*13.3*	*59.1*	*26.3*	*26.1*	*25.0*	*7.4*	*35.5*	*25.0*	*57.1*
Économies émergentes	*1995*	*100.0*	*13.9*	*58.6*	*27.7*	*31.3*	*31.7*	*6.8*	*35.0*	*23.6*	*58.2*
	2000	*100.0*	*13.7*	*60.6*	*24.1*	*38.9*	*37.4*	*5.2*	*34.1*	*23.5*	*60.7*
	2006	*100.0*	*14.5*	*59.4*	*21.7*	*46.1*	*41.8*	*5.7*	*35.4*	*23.4*	*59.0*
America - Amérique	1990	100.0	13.4	63.5	21.5	12.5	10.9	6.9	33.0	23.2	60.2
	1995	100.0	15.7	63.5	21.3	14.1	14.7	7.1	31.8	20.7	61.1
	2000	100.0	14.6	65.1	21.4	19.3	20.7	5.8	31.4	20.0	62.8
	2006	100.0	15.1	63.3	18.6	24.3	21.5	6.9	33.6	20.2	59.6
Asia - Asie	1990	100.0	13.1	52.5	33.6	46.8	46.4	8.2	39.8	28.1	52.0
	1995	100.0	11.8	52.7	35.5	52.1	52.3	6.3	39.0	27.1	54.7
	2000	100.0	12.3	54.2	27.8	66.5	60.8	4.4	37.9	28.4	57.7
	2006	100.0	13.6	54.0	25.8	76.0	69.6	4.1	37.7	27.7	58.1
Newly industrialized economies -	*1990*	*100.0*	*11.7*	*54.1*	*33.8*	*50.0*	*49.0*	*9.6*	*37.5*	*25.8*	*52.9*
Économies nouvellement industrialisées	*1995*	*100.0*	*10.8*	*55.1*	*36.0*	*55.9*	*56.9*	*7.8*	*36.6*	*24.9*	*55.6*
	2000	*100.0*	*11.4*	*56.3*	*26.8*	*71.7*	*65.8*	*5.8*	*35.6*	*25.3*	*58.7*
	2006	*100.0*	*12.2*	*56.5*	*24.7*	*78.0*	*71.8*	*5.9*	*35.9*	*25.3*	*58.2*
First tier - Première génération	1990	100.0	12.9	52.5	31.6	58.4	55.9	5.5	37.8	27.2	56.6
	1995	100.0	11.6	54.3	33.5	63.0	62.5	4.1	35.2	24.2	60.7
	2000	100.0	12.1	55.7	28.4	73.6	69.6	2.8	32.5	23.8	64.7
	2006	100.0	13.3	55.3	25.5	87.7	82.0	2.2	31.7	23.3	66.2
Second tier - Deuxième génération	1990	100.0	9.5	57.0	37.9	34.9	36.5	16.6	36.9	23.3	46.5
	1995	100.0	9.4	56.5	40.5	42.8	46.5	14.2	38.9	26.0	46.9
	2000	100.0	9.7	57.8	23.0	67.1	56.6	12.2	42.3	28.6	45.6
	2006	100.0	10.3	58.8	23.2	59.9	52.9	12.2	42.9	28.8	45.0

For sources and notes, see end of table.

Pour les sources et les notes, se reporter à la fin du tableau.

8.3.2 Nominal gross domestic product by type of expenditure and by kind of economic activity of economic groupings

8.3.2 Produit intérieur brut nominal par catégories de dépenses et par branches d'activité économique des groupements économiques

Economic grouping / Groupements économiques	Year / Année	Total GDP / PIB total	Final consumption / Consommation finale — Government / Administration publique	Household / Ménages	Gross capital formation / Formation brute de capital	Exports / Exportations — Of goods and services / Des biens et services	Less imports / Moins les importations	Agriculture / Agriculture (3)	Industry / Industrie (4) — Total	Manufacturing / Activités de fabrication	Services (5)
							Percentage / En pourcentage				
Developing economies: Africa -	**1990**	**100.0**	**15.9**	**64.0**	**19.1**	**32.0**	**30.0**	**18.8**	**37.5**	**16.5**	**43.7**
Économies en développement : Afrique	**1995**	**100.0**	**15.5**	**69.2**	**18.6**	**27.2**	**30.8**	**17.4**	**34.0**	**15.1**	**48.6**
	2000	**100.0**	**14.8**	**62.5**	**17.4**	**32.6**	**27.2**	**16.2**	**36.9**	**13.0**	**46.9**
	2006	**100.0**	**14.9**	**58.7**	**20.7**	**38.2**	**32.1**	**16.8**	**38.5**	**11.6**	**44.7**
Northern Africa excluding Sudan -	1990	100.0	15.5	59.9	27.0	29.0	30.9	14.1	40.1	14.0	45.8
Afrique septentrionale sans le Soudan	1995	100.0	15.2	66.2	21.5	26.2	29.8	13.9	36.6	14.7	49.4
	2000	100.0	14.4	61.1	20.3	29.8	25.7	12.1	39.5	13.2	48.4
	2006	100.0	13.6	49.7	25.2	44.8	32.0	11.3	44.7	11.8	44.0
Sub-Saharan Africa - Afrique subsaharienne	1990	100.0	16.1	66.0	15.1	33.5	29.6	21.3	36.1	17.8	42.6
	1995	100.0	15.6	70.9	17.0	27.7	31.3	19.3	32.5	15.3	48.2
	2000	100.0	15.1	63.5	15.4	34.4	28.3	19.2	35.1	12.8	45.7
	2006	100.0	15.6	63.3	18.4	34.8	32.2	19.8	35.2	11.5	45.0
Sub-Saharan Africa excluding South Africa -	1990	100.0	14.4	68.4	13.8	38.0	34.8	28.9	34.3	15.1	36.8
Afrique subsaharienne sans l'Afrique du Sud	1995	100.0	13.5	77.5	16.1	31.5	38.5	30.9	30.8	10.8	38.3
	2000	100.0	13.3	63.8	15.1	38.3	30.3	28.1	36.9	9.4	35.0
	2006	100.0	13.1	63.1	18.3	38.1	32.7	28.1	37.2	7.7	34.7
Developing economies: America -	**1990**	**100.0**	**14.1**	**62.8**	**21.1**	**16.5**	**14.7**	**7.9**	**33.2**	**22.3**	**58.8**
Économies en développement : Amérique	**1995**	**100.0**	**15.5**	**63.8**	**21.4**	**16.7**	**17.7**	**8.0**	**31.8**	**20.1**	**60.2**
	2000	**100.0**	**14.9**	**64.7**	**21.1**	**21.8**	**22.6**	**6.4**	**31.9**	**19.3**	**61.6**
	2006	**100.0**	**15.2**	**62.7**	**19.3**	**26.1**	**23.5**	**7.1**	**34.0**	**19.1**	**58.9**
Central America and Greater Carribean Islands	1990	100.0	11.6	67.8	22.9	22.2	24.5	9.1	27.1	19.2	63.8
excluding Puerto Rico - Amérique centrale et	1995	100.0	11.9	67.8	19.2	31.0	30.4	6.8	26.6	19.3	66.7
Grandes Antilles sans Porto Rico	2000	100.0	12.2	67.8	22.9	31.7	34.6	5.2	27.7	19.7	67.0
	2006	100.0	12.7	69.0	21.0	32.3	35.0	4.9	26.2	17.4	68.9
Central America and Greater Carribean Islands	1990	100.0	22.7	61.7	21.9	34.4	41.0	13.5	23.8	14.9	62.7
excluding Mexico and Puerto Rico -	1995	100.0	16.1	69.7	17.5	32.7	37.8	11.2	26.7	18.1	62.1
Amérique centrale et Grandes Antilles sans	2000	100.0	17.0	71.1	19.3	34.7	41.9	10.4	27.8	18.3	61.8
le Mexique et Porto Rico	2006	100.0	18.5	71.1	18.9	29.2	38.3	9.2	25.2	15.8	65.5
South America and Central America -	1990	100.0	13.4	63.3	20.9	15.3	13.1	7.8	33.8	23.0	58.4
Amérique du Sud et Amérique centrale	1995	100.0	15.3	63.8	21.6	16.0	16.9	8.0	32.1	20.3	59.9
	2000	100.0	14.6	64.7	21.1	21.1	21.7	6.4	32.2	19.5	61.5
	2006	100.0	14.8	62.9	19.4	25.7	22.9	7.2	34.4	19.5	58.4
South America excluding Brazil -	1990	100.0	12.8	63.6	16.8	20.3	14.1	9.8	38.2	23.4	52.0
Amérique du Sud sans le Brésil	1995	100.0	13.0	66.0	21.6	16.7	17.7	8.3	32.5	18.2	59.2
	2000	100.0	14.0	65.1	18.4	19.7	17.7	6.7	32.9	17.2	60.4
	2006	100.0	12.4	58.7	20.3	31.2	22.8	7.5	39.5	16.8	53.0
Developing economies: Asia -	**1990**	**100.0**	**13.4**	**56.4**	**29.8**	**31.8**	**30.9**	**17.6**	**36.5**	**23.2**	**45.9**
Économies en développement : Asie	**1995**	**100.0**	**12.4**	**54.8**	**33.6**	**37.3**	**37.5**	**14.1**	**37.8**	**25.3**	**48.0**
	2000	**100.0**	**13.8**	**54.1**	**28.0**	**43.6**	**39.4**	**11.9**	**38.8**	**25.9**	**49.3**
	2006	**100.0**	**13.2**	**48.4**	**31.4**	**51.8**	**45.1**	**10.6**	**40.8**	**26.8**	**48.6**
Eastern and South-Eastern Asia excluding China -	1990	100.0	11.7	54.3	33.5	49.9	48.8	10.6	37.5	25.5	51.9
Asie orientale et Asie du Sud-Est sans la Chine	1995	100.0	10.8	55.3	35.7	55.6	56.5	8.6	36.3	24.5	55.2
	2000	100.0	11.3	56.4	26.7	71.3	65.5	6.7	35.5	25.0	57.8
	2006	100.0	12.1	56.4	25.0	77.9	71.7	6.8	36.0	25.0	57.2
Southern Asia excluding India -	1990	100.0	10.4	67.0	26.3	13.8	21.5	23.2	26.2	13.2	50.6
Asie méridionale sans l'Inde	1995	100.0	11.8	63.2	25.0	18.2	17.9	22.6	28.8	13.7	48.6
	2000	100.0	10.1	64.7	25.9	20.1	20.8	20.0	29.9	14.7	50.2
	2006	100.0	9.4	63.2	25.3	26.0	26.3	16.3	34.2	14.1	49.4

For sources and notes, see end of table.

Pour les sources et les notes, se reporter à la fin du tableau.

8.3.2 Nominal gross domestic product by type of expenditure and by kind of economic activity of economic groupings

8.3.2 Produit intérieur brut nominal par catégories de dépenses et par branches d'activité économique des groupements économiques

Sources:
- UN DESA Statistics Division

Notes:

(1) The breakdown in shares might not add-up to 100 percent due to statistical discrepancies.

(2) Refers to Total Value Added

(3) Includes agriculture, hunting, forestry and fishing (ISIC Revision 3 divisions 01-05)

(4) Includes mining and quarrying, manufacturing, electricity, gas and water supply, and construction (ISIC Revision 3 divisions 10-45)

(5) Include all other economic activities (ISIC Revision 3 divisions 50-99)

Sources :
- ONU DAES Division de statistique

Notes :

(1) La somme des pourcentages du PIB peut ne pas être égale à 100 à cause des écarts statistiques.

(2) Renvoie à la valeur ajoutée totale

(3) Inclut l'agriculture, la chasse, la sylviculture et la pêche (CITI Révision 3, divisions 01-05)

(4) Inclut les activités extractives, les activités de fabrication, la production et distribution d'électricité, de gaz et d'eau et la construction (CITI Révision 3, divisions 10-45)

(5) Incluent toutes les autres activités économiques (CITI Révision 3, divisions 50-99)

Region, country or territory Régions, pays ou territoires	Year Année	Population		Total labour force Main d'œuvre totale		Agriculture labour force Main d'œuvre dans l'agriculture	
		Total (thousands) Total (milliers) (1)	Urban population (7) (% of total population) Population urbaine (7) (en % de la population totale) (2)	Total (thousands) Total (milliers) (3)	Female labour (% of total labour force) Main d'œuvre féminine (en % de la main d'œuvre totale) (4)	Total (thousands) Total (milliers) (5)	Female labour (% of total agriculture labour force) Main d'œuvre féminine (en % de la main d'œuvre totale dans l'agriculture) (6)
WORLD - MONDE	**1990**	**5 294 879**	**43.0**	**2 405 619**	**39.8**	**1 224 371**	**42.7**
	2000	**6 124 123**	**46.8**	**2 818 456**	**39.8**	**1 323 353**	**43.7**
	2005	**6 514 751**	**48.8**	**3 050 420**	**40.1**	**1 359 802**	**44.0**
	2007	**6 671 226**	**49.6**	**3 143 748**	**40.1**	**..**	**..**
DEVELOPING ECONOMIES - ÉCONOMIES EN DÉVELOPPEMENT	1990	4 068 994	35.0	1 788 670	38.4	1 163 858	42.9
	2000	4 846 278	40.2	2 173 688	38.4	1 277 573	43.9
	2005	5 211 595	42.8	2 383 899	38.6	1 319 816	44.3
	2007	5 358 921	43.8	2 469 498	38.7	..	..
ECONOMIES IN TRANSITION - ÉCONOMIES EN TRANSITION	1990	315 460	62.5	156 160	47.8	29 691	38.9
	2000	305 902	63.8	141 977	47.6	22 887	36.1
	2005	302 902	63.5	146 514	48.0	20 672	34.7
	2007	302 038	63.4	147 938	48.1	..	..
DEVELOPED ECONOMIES - ÉCONOMIES DÉVELOPPÉES	1990	910 425	72.1	444 815	42.4	30 822	38.6
	2000	971 943	74.5	481 941	44.0	22 893	37.4
	2005	1 000 255	75.5	496 128	44.8	19 314	36.6
	2007	1 010 267	76.0	501 021	45.1	..	..
Developing economies: Africa - Économies en développement : Afrique	**1990**	**636 817**	**31.9**	**230 981**	**40.3**	**169 453**	**46.5**
	2000	**820 235**	**36.2**	**301 556**	**39.7**	**202 027**	**47.6**
	2005	**921 225**	**38.3**	**340 646**	**39.6**	**218 384**	**47.8**
	2007	**964 166**	**39.2**	**357 756**	**39.6**	**..**	**..**
Eastern Africa - Afrique orientale	*1990*	*196 640*	*17.7*	*87 714*	*47.5*	*77 861*	*49.6*
	2000	*256 570*	*20.5*	*114 652*	*47.1*	*96 351*	*49.5*
	2005	*291 754*	*21.9*	*130 092*	*46.8*	*106 051*	*49.1*
	2007	*307 054*	*22.5*	*137 068*	*46.7*	*..*	*..*
Burundi	1990	5 692	6.3	2 799	52.6	2 795	52.4
	2000	6 668	8.6	3 111	53.0	3 061	53.5
	2005	7 859	10.0	3 833	51.9	3 591	53.2
	2007	8 508	10.6	4 202	51.5	..	..
Comoros - Comores	1990	527	28.2	208	42.7	184	50.5
	2000	699	33.8	287	40.5	241	51.0
	2005	798	37.0	335	40.1	271	50.9
	2007	839	38.3	356	39.9	..	..
Djibouti	1990	561	76.0	217	40.8	230	48.7
	2000	730	83.3	280	39.9	282	48.6
	2005	804	86.1	315	39.3	309	48.5
	2007	833	87.0	329	39.2	..	..
Eritrea - Érythrée	2000	3 684	17.8	1 451	41.5	1 345	51.6
	2005	4 527	19.4	1 788	41.1	1 634	51.3
	2007	4 851	20.2	1 920	40.9	..	..
Ethiopia - Éthiopie	2000	69 388	14.9	30 160	44.9	24 755	40.9
	2005	78 986	16.0	34 331	44.9	27 528	40.2
	2007	83 099	16.5	36 256	44.9	..	..
Ethiopia (former) - Éthiopie (anc.)	1990	54 306	12.8	23 777	44.8	20 660	42.4
Kenya	1990	23 447	18.2	9 830	46.0	8 937	49.6
	2000	31 252	19.7	13 631	44.3	11 809	49.5
	2005	35 599	20.7	15 500	43.8	12 714	48.8
	2007	37 538	21.3	16 327	43.5	..	..
Madagascar	1990	12 033	23.6	5 364	49.2	4 564	50.5
	2000	16 187	26.0	7 329	48.7	5 745	50.0
	2005	18 643	26.8	8 589	48.4	6 461	49.6
	2007	19 683	27.3	9 129	48.3	..	..
Malawi	1990	9 446	11.6	4 454	50.3	4 080	54.4
	2000	11 623	15.1	5 383	49.9	4 581	55.7
	2005	13 226	17.2	5 932	49.8	4 903	56.4
	2007	13 925	18.1	6 207	49.8	..	..

For sources and notes, see end of table.   Pour les sources et les notes, se reporter à la fin du tableau.

Region, country or territory / Régions, pays ou territoires	Year / Année	Population		Total labour force / Main d'œuvre totale		Agriculture labour force / Main d'œuvre dans l'agriculture	
		Total (thousands) / Total (milliers)	Urban population (7) (% of total population) / Population urbaine (7) (en % de la population totale)	Total (thousands) / Total (milliers)	Female labour (% of total labour force) / Main d'œuvre féminine (en % de la main d'œuvre totale)	Total (thousands) / Total (milliers)	Female labour (% of total agriculture labour force) / Main d'œuvre féminine (en % de la main d'œuvre totale dans l'agriculture)
		(1)	(2)	(3)	(4)	(5)	(6)
Mauritius - Maurice	1990	1 057	43.9	460	33.9	72	26.4
	2000	1 186	42.7	529	34.2	61	24.6
	2005	1 241	42.4	569	35.6	54	24.1
	2007	1 262	42.5	583	36.1	..	..
Mozambique	1990	13 544	21.1	6 330	54.0	5 723	58.7
	2000	18 194	30.7	8 569	53.7	7 580	59.6
	2005	20 533	34.5	9 288	53.5	8 250	59.5
	2007	21 397	36.1	9 623	53.3	..	..
Rwanda	1990	7 294	5.4	3 071	51.0	3 238	52.5
	2000	8 176	13.8	3 600	51.9	3 820	54.1
	2005	9 234	19.3	4 181	51.2	4 376	53.8
	2007	9 725	21.1	4 418	50.9	..	..
Seychelles	1990	72	49.3	..	..	35	48.6
	2000	81	51.0	..	..	37	48.6
	2005	86	52.9	..	..	39	48.7
	2007	87	53.8	..	..	..	..
Somalia - Somalie	1990	6 717	29.7	2 839	39.9	2 300	50.3
	2000	7 055	33.3	3 014	39.4	2 285	50.4
	2005	8 196	35.2	3 523	39.2	2 572	50.3
	2007	8 699	36.1	3 744	39.2	..	..
Uganda - Ouganda	1990	17 841	11.1	7 813	47.4	7 548	49.9
	2000	24 690	12.1	10 157	48.0	9 341	49.5
	2005	28 947	12.6	11 858	48.3	10 566	49.1
	2007	30 884	12.8	12 662	48.5	..	..
United Republic of Tanzania - République-Unie de Tanzanie	1990	25 494	18.9	12 817	50.2	11 571	53.3
	2000	33 849	22.3	17 315	49.8	14 609	53.6
	2005	38 478	24.2	19 338	49.4	15 802	53.6
	2007	40 454	25.0	20 228	49.3	..	..
Zambia - Zambie	1990	8 122	39.4	3 475	43.2	2 672	48.8
	2000	10 451	34.8	4 498	42.7	3 129	47.8
	2005	11 478	35.0	4 951	42.2	3 293	46.9
	2007	11 922	35.2	5 157	42.1	..	..
Zimbabwe	1990	10 487	29.0	4 260	47.2	3 252	52.5
	2000	12 656	33.8	5 337	45.1	3 670	53.9
	2005	13 120	35.9	5 761	44.0	3 688	53.6
	2007	13 349	36.8	5 927	43.5	..	..
Middle Africa - Afrique centrale	*1990*	*73 632*	*32.5*	*14 186*	*44.3*	*22 261*	*51.0*
	2000	*97 765*	*37.3*	*18 857*	*43.7*	*26 536*	*51.8*
	2005	*112 505*	*39.9*	*21 175*	*43.7*	*28 632*	*52.1*
	2007	*119 096*	*41.0*	*22 250*	*43.7*	*..*	*..*
Angola	1990	10 534	37.1	4 545	46.4	3 663	53.4
	2000	13 930	50.0	6 079	46.0	4 610	53.8
	2005	16 095	53.3	7 034	45.8	5 218	53.8
	2007	17 024	54.6	7 471	45.7	..	..
Cameroon - Cameroun	1990	12 239	40.7	4 411	41.5	3 252	44.0
	2000	15 861	50.0	5 747	40.1	3 637	45.3
	2005	17 795	54.6	6 297	39.9	3 695	45.1
	2007	18 549	56.4	6 563	39.9	..	..
Central African Republic - République centrafricaine	1990	3 008	36.8	1 350	47.1	1 166	51.2
	2000	3 864	37.6	1 704	46.6	1 288	51.4
	2005	4 191	38.0	1 826	46.1	1 281	51.1
	2007	4 343	38.3	1 888	45.8	..	..
Chad - Tchad	1990	6 113	20.8	2 348	46.0	2 357	48.3
	2000	8 465	23.4	3 169	46.2	2 809	50.8
	2005	10 146	25.3	3 669	46.9	3 085	52.1
	2007	10 781	26.1	3 857	47.1	..	..

For sources and notes, see end of table.

Pour les sources et les notes, se reporter à la fin du tableau.

Region, country or territory / Régions, pays ou territoires	Year / Année	Population		Total labour force / Main d'œuvre totale		Agriculture labour force / Main d'œuvre dans l'agriculture	
		Total (thousands) / Total (milliers) (1)	Urban population (7) (% of total population) / Population urbaine (7) (en % de la population totale) (2)	Total (thousands) / Total (milliers) (3)	Female labour (% of total labour force) / Main d'œuvre féminine (en % de la main d'œuvre totale) (4)	Total (thousands) / Total (milliers) (5)	Female labour (% of total agriculture labour force) / Main d'œuvre féminine (en % de la main d'œuvre totale dans l'agriculture) (6)
Congo	1990	2 422	54.3	960	41.5	500	60.6
	2000	3 203	58.3	1 406	40.7	566	60.2
	2005	3 610	60.2	1 506	40.3	584	59.6
	2007	3 768	60.9	1 587	40.2	..	..
Dem. Rep. of the Congo - Rép. dém. du Congo	1990	37 942	27.8	..	..	10 957	52.5
	2000	50 689	29.8	..	..	13 243	52.9
	2005	58 741	32.1	..	..	14 433	53.1
	2007	62 636	33.3	..	..	..	..
Equatorial Guinea - Guinée équatoriale	1990	340	34.8	140	35.9	112	42.9
	2000	431	38.8	177	36.6	130	45.4
	2005	484	38.9	197	36.8	139	46.0
	2007	507	39.2	205	36.9	..	..
Gabon	1990	918	69.1	398	43.9	219	50.2
	2000	1 182	80.1	534	43.5	212	49.1
	2005	1 291	83.6	596	43.4	197	48.2
	2007	1 331	84.7	626	43.2	..	..
Sao Tome and Principe - Sao Tomé-et-Principe	1990	116	43.6	34	33.4	35	51.4
	2000	140	53.4	42	29.6	41	51.2
	2005	153	58.0	49	29.3	..	..
	2007	158	59.8	52	29.3	..	..
Northern Africa - Afrique septentrionale	*1990*	*143 963*	*44.8*	*43 212*	*24.7*	*21 181*	*40.6*
	2000	*174 435*	*48.9*	*56 141*	*24.5*	*24 053*	*45.1*
	2005	*189 562*	*51.1*	*64 785*	*25.3*	*25 103*	*47.1*
	2007	*196 108*	*52.1*	*68 358*	*25.7*	*..*	*..*
Algeria - Algérie	1990	25 283	52.1	7 227	22.6	1 818	46.6
	2000	30 506	59.8	11 069	28.0	2 563	51.1
	2005	32 854	63.3	13 417	30.6	2 916	52.4
	2007	33 858	64.6	14 339	31.5	..	..
Egypt - Égypte	1990	55 137	43.5	16 577	26.3	7 596	41.1
	2000	66 529	42.5	20 009	21.7	8 346	46.5
	2005	72 850	42.8	22 881	21.8	8 599	48.6
	2007	75 498	43.1	24 085	21.8	..	..
Libyan Arab Jamahiriya - Jamahiriya arabe libyenne	1990	4 364	78.6	1 257	17.3	140	46.4
	2000	5 346	83.1	1 918	23.8	109	62.4
	2005	5 918	84.8	2 338	27.1	92	67.4
	2007	6 160	85.4	2 520	28.9	..	..
Morocco - Maroc	1990	24 808	48.4	7 779	23.7	4 081	49.0
	2000	28 827	55.1	10 459	25.5	4 215	54.6
	2005	30 495	58.7	11 605	25.4	4 241	58.1
	2007	31 224	60.0	12 125	25.6	..	..
Sudan - Soudan	1990	25 933	26.6	7 810	26.0	6 711	32.8
	2000	33 349	36.1	9 225	25.1	7 835	36.7
	2005	36 900	40.8	10 515	24.8	8 220	38.5
	2007	38 560	42.6	11 022	24.9	..	..
Tunisia - Tunisie	1990	8 219	59.6	2 462	21.5	801	43.4
	2000	9 564	63.4	3 327	25.4	944	42.4
	2005	10 105	65.3	3 875	27.6	990	41.4
	2007	10 327	66.0	4 095	28.4	..	..
Western Sahara - Sahara occidental	1990	221	88.5	99	32.7	34	35.3
	2000	315	91.2	135	32.2	41	41.5
	2005	440	91.6	154	31.4	45	44.4
	2007	480	91.7	172	31.3	..	..
Southern Africa - Afrique australe	*1990*	*41 828*	*48.9*	*16 875*	*41.9*	*2 857*	*35.7*
	2000	*51 950*	*53.8*	*21 490*	*39.4*	*2 900*	*35.9*
	2005	*54 900*	*56.1*	*21 991*	*38.6*	*2 654*	*35.6*
	2007	*55 682*	*57.1*	*22 020*	*38.2*	*..*	*..*

For sources and notes, see end of table.

Pour les sources et les notes, se reporter à la fin du tableau.

Region, country or territory / Régions, pays ou territoires	Year / Année	Population Total (thousands) / Total (milliers) (1)	Population Urban population (7) (% of total population) / Population urbaine (7) (en % de la population totale) (2)	Total labour force — Main d'œuvre totale Total (thousands) / Total (milliers) (3)	Total labour force — Main d'œuvre totale Female labour (% of total labour force) / Main d'œuvre féminine (en % de la main d'œuvre totale) (4)	Agriculture labour force — Main d'œuvre dans l'agriculture Total (thousands) / Total (milliers) (5)	Agriculture labour force — Main d'œuvre dans l'agriculture Female labour (% of total agriculture labour force) / Main d'œuvre féminine (en % de la main d'œuvre totale dans l'agriculture) (6)
Botswana	1990	1 367	41.9	514	45.2	286	54.9
	2000	1 729	53.2	625	43.9	361	56.5
	2005	1 836	57.4	616	41.7	354	56.8
	2007	1 882	58.9	611	41.1	..	..
Lesotho	1990	1 601	17.2	605	46.5	246	58.9
	2000	1 886	17.8	647	45.3	277	58.8
	2005	1 981	18.7	634	44.5	276	58.3
	2007	2 008	19.2	631	44.0	..	..
Namibia - Namibie	1990	1 417	27.7	446	44.2	279	44.8
	2000	1 879	32.4	607	44.3	314	42.7
	2005	2 020	35.1	647	43.6	311	40.8
	2007	2 074	36.2	665	43.4	..	..
South Africa - Afrique du Sud	1990	36 577	52.0	15 054	41.6	1 934	27.7
	2000	45 398	56.9	19 310	39.0	1 829	26.4
	2005	47 939	59.3	19 786	38.3	1 598	25.2
	2007	48 577	60.2	19 801	37.9	..	..
Swaziland	1990	865	22.9	254	38.1	112	51.8
	2000	1 058	23.3	301	34.4	119	47.9
	2005	1 125	24.1	308	32.8	115	46.1
	2007	1 141	24.6	311	32.3	..	..
Western Africa - Afrique occidentale	*1990*	*180 754*	*33.0*	*68 994*	*39.6*	*45 293*	*42.5*
	2000	*239 515*	*39.6*	*90 417*	*39.1*	*52 187*	*43.7*
	2005	*272 505*	*42.7*	*102 604*	*38.7*	*55 944*	*44.1*
	2007	*286 227*	*44.0*	*108 061*	*38.7*	*..*	*..*
Benin - Bénin	1990	5 179	34.5	2 009	40.8	1 503	49.4
	2000	7 227	38.4	2 793	39.3	1 779	47.3
	2005	8 490	40.1	3 296	38.4	1 919	46.0
	2007	9 033	40.9	3 522	38.1	..	..
Burkina Faso	1990	8 871	13.8	3 798	46.3	4 085	47.1
	2000	11 882	16.5	4 904	47.0	5 019	47.2
	2005	13 933	18.3	5 835	46.6	5 793	46.8
	2007	14 784	19.1	6 218	46.7	..	..
Cape Verde - Cap-Vert	1990	355	44.1	113	38.4	38	39.5
	2000	451	53.4	144	34.6	40	37.5
	2005	507	57.3	165	33.8	41	39.0
	2007	530	58.8	175	33.8	..	..
Côte d'Ivoire	1990	12 780	39.7	4 606	30.2	2 946	37.6
	2000	17 049	43.0	6 147	29.3	3 287	39.5
	2005	18 585	45.0	6 796	29.3	3 224	40.0
	2007	19 262	45.8	7 093	29.3	..	..
Gambia - Gambie	1990	962	38.3	394	43.4	383	50.1
	2000	1 384	49.1	562	42.1	524	51.0
	2005	1 617	53.9	657	41.6	597	51.4
	2007	1 709	55.7	695	41.5	..	..
Ghana	1990	15 579	36.5	6 709	48.8	4 349	46.1
	2000	20 148	44.0	8 658	48.5	5 563	45.3
	2005	22 535	47.8	9 802	48.0	6 245	44.7
	2007	23 478	49.3	10 313	47.9	..	..
Guinea - Guinée	1990	6 033	28.0	2 993	46.2	2 802	48.8
	2000	8 203	31.0	3 992	46.4	3 508	48.7
	2005	9 003	33.0	4 417	46.5	3 788	48.5
	2007	9 370	33.9	4 612	46.7	..	..
Guinea-Bissau - Guinée-Bissau	1990	1 017	28.1	412	40.3	391	45.5
	2000	1 370	29.7	552	41.0	491	47.0
	2005	1 597	29.6	636	40.9	551	47.7
	2007	1 695	29.7	672	40.9	..	..

For sources and notes, see end of table.

Pour les sources et les notes, se reporter à la fin du tableau.

Region, country or territory / Régions, pays ou territoires	Year / Année	Population		Total labour force Main d'œuvre totale		Agriculture labour force Main d'œuvre dans l'agriculture	
		Total (thousands) / Total (milliers)	Urban population (7) (% of total population) / Population urbaine (7) (en % de la population totale)	Total (thousands) / Total (milliers)	Female labour (% of total labour force) / Main d'œuvre féminine (en % de la main d'œuvre totale)	Total (thousands) / Total (milliers)	Female labour (% of total agriculture labour force) / Main d'œuvre féminine (en % de la main d'œuvre totale dans l'agriculture)
		(1)	(2)	(3)	(4)	(5)	(6)
Liberia - Libéria	1990	2 137	45.3	787	39.5	610	46.4
	2000	3 071	54.3	1 128	39.7	793	46.0
	2005	3 442	58.1	1 196	39.9	796	45.5
	2007	3 750	59.5	1 248	40.0	..	..
Mali	1990	7 669	23.3	3 760	46.0	3 800	47.9
	2000	10 004	27.9	4 821	46.5	4 483	47.0
	2005	11 611	30.5	5 460	47.5	4 978	46.1
	2007	12 337	31.6	5 745	48.1	..	..
Mauritania - Mauritanie	1990	1 945	39.7	805	40.6	511	50.5
	2000	2 566	40.0	1 033	40.7	627	52.2
	2005	2 963	40.4	1 202	40.4	705	53.0
	2007	3 124	40.7	1 274	40.3	..	..
Niger	1990	7 822	15.4	3 565	42.6	3 640	46.3
	2000	11 124	16.2	5 017	42.0	4 854	47.2
	2005	13 264	16.8	5 936	41.9	5 635	47.9
	2007	14 226	17.2	6 347	41.9	..	..
Nigeria - Nigéria	1990	94 454	35.0	32 712	36.2	15 438	35.7
	2000	124 773	43.9	42 561	35.5	15 468	37.5
	2005	141 356	48.2	47 835	34.8	15 191	38.3
	2007	148 093	49.8	50 259	34.5	..	..
Saint Helena - Sainte-Hélène	1990	5	41.6	..	..	2	50.0
	2000	6	39.2	..	..	1	100.0
	2005	6	38.9	..	..	1	100.0
	2007	7	39.1	..	..	..	..
Senegal - Sénégal	1990	7 896	39.0	3 117	43.4	2 655	49.1
	2000	10 334	40.6	4 071	42.6	3 338	49.1
	2005	11 770	41.6	4 594	42.4	3 746	48.8
	2007	12 379	42.0	4 844	42.5	..	..
Sierra Leone	1990	4 087	30.1	1 694	38.5	1 068	42.0
	2000	4 521	37.0	1 930	38.5	1 067	45.0
	2005	5 586	40.7	2 358	38.4	1 249	46.8
	2007	5 866	42.2	2 478	38.4	..	..
Togo	1990	3 961	30.1	1 520	38.5	1 072	39.4
	2000	5 403	36.6	2 104	37.4	1 345	41.3
	2005	6 239	40.1	2 419	36.9	1 485	42.3
	2007	6 585	41.5	2 566	36.8	..	..
Developing economies: America - Économies en développement : Amérique	**1990**	**439 876**	**70.8**	**171 546**	**34.1**	**44 624**	**16.9**
	2000	**518 242**	**75.2**	**228 519**	**38.8**	**43 832**	**17.3**
	2005	**553 005**	**77.2**	**255 179**	**40.6**	**42 626**	**17.5**
	2007	**567 170**	**77.9**	**265 675**	**41.3**		
Caribbean - Caraïbes	*1990*	*30 074*	*53.2*	*11 882*	*37.1*	*3 934*	*26.6*
	2000	*33 976*	*57.0*	*14 143*	*38.3*	*3 906*	*28.1*
	2005	*35 743*	*58.9*	*15 264*	*39.0*	*3 878*	*28.5*
	2007	*36 412*	*59.5*	*15 749*	*39.4*	*..*	*..*
Anguilla	1990	9	100.0	..	..	1	..
	2000	11	100.0	..	..	1	..
	2005	12	100.0	..	..	1	..
	2007	13	100.0	..	..	..	..
Antigua and Barbuda - Antigua-et-Barbuda	1990	62	35.4	..	..	8	25.0
	2000	77	32.1	..	..	8	25.0
	2005	83	30.7	..	..	9	22.2
	2007	85	30.5	..	..	..	..
Aruba	1990	64	50.3	..	..	8	25.0
	2000	90	46.7	..	..	10	30.0
	2005	103	46.6	..	..	10	30.0
	2007	104	46.7	..	..	..	..

For sources and notes, see end of table.

Pour les sources et les notes, se reporter à la fin du tableau.

Region, country or territory / Régions, pays ou territoires	Year / Année	Population		Total labour force / Main d'œuvre totale		Agriculture labour force / Main d'œuvre dans l'agriculture	
		Total (thousands) / Total (milliers)	Urban population (7) (% of total population) / Population urbaine (7) (en % de la population totale)	Total (thousands) / Total (milliers)	Female labour (% of total labour force) / Main d'œuvre féminine (en % de la main d'œuvre totale)	Total (thousands) / Total (milliers)	Female labour (% of total agriculture labour force) / Main d'œuvre féminine (en % de la main d'œuvre totale dans l'agriculture)
		(1)	(2)	(3)	(4)	(5)	(6)
Bahamas	1990	255	83.6	119	45.4	7	14.3
	2000	303	88.8	145	49.2	5	20.0
	2005	323	90.4	156	49.8	5	..
	2007	331	90.9	161	49.9	..	..
Barbados - Barbade	1990	271	44.8	130	46.6	9	44.4
	2000	286	49.9	149	48.1	6	50.0
	2005	292	52.7	156	47.4	5	40.0
	2007	294	53.9	157	47.2	..	..
British Virgin Islands - Îles Vierges britanniques	1990	17	37.8	..	..	2	50.0
	2000	21	39.4	..	..	2	50.0
	2005	22	39.9	..	..	2	50.0
	2007	23	40.3	..	..	..	..
Cayman Islands - Îles Caïmanes	1990	26	..	..	..	3	33.3
	2000	40	..	..	..	4	25.0
	2005	46	..	..	..	5	20.0
	2007	47	..	..	..	..	..
Cuba	1990	10 605	73.4	4 545	34.8	864	16.6
	2000	11 142	75.6	5 249	36.8	782	18.5
	2005	11 260	75.5	5 376	37.4	710	18.9
	2007	11 268	75.2	5 430	37.8	..	..
Dominica - Dominique	1990	69	67.7	..	..	9	22.2
	2000	68	71.1	..	..	9	22.2
	2005	68	72.9	..	..	8	25.0
	2007	67	73.6	..	..	..	..
Dominican Republic - République dominicaine	1990	7 295	55.2	2 630	29.7	685	10.4
	2000	8 744	62.4	3 386	33.7	583	15.6
	2005	9 470	66.8	3 849	35.9	532	19.2
	2007	9 760	68.3	4 050	37.0	..	..
Grenada - Grenade	1990	96	32.2	..	..	12	25.0
	2000	100	31.0	..	..	11	27.3
	2005	105	30.6	..	..	11	27.3
	2007	106	30.7	..	..	..	..
Haiti - Haïti	1990	7 110	29.5	2 642	43.3	1 950	36.8
	2000	8 573	35.6	3 207	41.8	2 129	35.2
	2005	9 296	38.8	3 667	41.7	2 239	34.0
	2007	9 598	40.1	3 860	41.9	..	..
Jamaica - Jamaïque	1990	2 369	49.4	1 113	46.8	276	27.9
	2000	2 589	51.8	1 165	44.8	260	28.8
	2005	2 682	53.1	1 166	43.5	248	29.8
	2007	2 714	53.7	1 177	43.3	..	..
Montserrat	1990	11	12.5	..	..	1	..
	2000	5	11.0	..	..	..	..
	2005	6	13.5	..	..	..	..
	2007	6	13.8	..	..	..	..
Netherlands Antilles - Antilles néerlandaises	1990	191	68.3	88	44.1	1	..
	2000	181	69.3	81	46.5	..	..
	2005	186	70.4	83	46.1	..	..
	2007	192	70.9	84	46.0	..	..
Saint Kitts and Nevis - Saint-Kitts-et-Nevis	1990	41	34.6	..	..	5	20.0
	2000	46	32.8	..	..	4	25.0
	2005	49	32.2	..	..	4	25.0
	2007	50	32.2	..	..	..	..
Saint Lucia - Sainte-Lucie	1990	138	29.3	55	39.0	15	26.7
	2000	153	28.0	69	41.1	16	25.0
	2005	161	27.6	76	41.5	16	31.3
	2007	165	27.7	79	41.7	..	..

For sources and notes, see end of table.

Pour les sources et les notes, se reporter à la fin du tableau.

Region, country or territory Régions, pays ou territoires	Year Année	Population		Total labour force Main d'œuvre totale		Agriculture labour force Main d'œuvre dans l'agriculture	
		Total (thousands) Total (milliers)	Urban population (7) (% of total population) Population urbaine (7) (en % de la population totale)	Total (thousands) Total (milliers)	Female labour (% of total labour force) Main d'œuvre féminine (en % de la main d'œuvre totale)	Total (thousands) Total (milliers)	Female labour (% of total agriculture labour force) Main d'œuvre féminine (en % de la main d'œuvre totale dans l'agriculture)
		(1)	(2)	(3)	(4)	(5)	(6)
Saint Vincent and the Grenadines - Saint-Vincent-et-les Grenadines	1990	109	40.6	42	36.3	12	25.0
	2000	116	44.4	51	39.1	12	25.0
	2005	119	45.9	57	40.9	12	25.0
	2007	120	46.6	59	41.7	..	..
Trinidad and Tobago - Trinité-et-Tobago	1990	1 224	8.5	469	36.1	52	17.3
	2000	1 301	10.8	589	39.0	50	16.0
	2005	1 324	12.2	628	38.9	47	17.0
	2007	1 333	12.9	640	38.9	..	..
Turks and Caicos Islands - Îles Turques et Caïques	1990	12	74.3	..	..	1	0.0
	2000	19	84.6	..	..	2	50.0
	2005	24	89.7	..	..	3	33.3
	2007	26	91.3	..	..	..	..
United States Virgin Islands - Îles Vierges américaines	1990	103	87.7	48	45.2	13	30.8
	2000	110	92.6	52	46.0	12	25.0
	2005	111	94.2	52	46.6	11	27.3
	2007	111	94.7	52	46.9	..	..
Central America - Amérique centrale	*1990*	*112 724*	*65.8*	*39 768*	*30.5*	*12 457*	*11.4*
	2000	*135 587*	*68.8*	*53 548*	*33.4*	*13 011*	*11.9*
	2005	*143 775*	*70.0*	*59 430*	*35.2*	*13 015*	*12.0*
	2007	*147 554*	*70.6*	*61 890*	*36.1*	*..*	*..*
Belize	1990	186	47.5	60	27.2	20	5.0
	2000	245	47.7	89	31.6	26	3.8
	2005	276	48.3	107	34.1	29	3.4
	2007	288	48.7	115	34.8	..	..
Costa Rica	1990	3 076	50.7	1 155	27.6	307	6.8
	2000	3 929	59.0	1 593	30.9	324	9.0
	2005	4 327	61.7	1 956	35.1	327	10.4
	2007	4 468	62.8	2 088	36.5	..	..
El Salvador	1990	5 110	49.2	1 961	41.2	709	6.1
	2000	6 195	58.4	2 503	38.1	785	7.5
	2005	6 668	59.8	2 772	40.2	805	8.3
	2007	6 857	60.4	2 893	41.3	..	..
Guatemala	1990	8 908	41.1	2 869	24.7	1 604	7.2
	2000	11 229	45.1	3 566	30.3	1 783	8.6
	2005	12 710	47.2	4 074	31.3	1 929	9.1
	2007	13 354	48.1	4 325	31.6	..	..
Honduras	1990	4 891	40.3	1 611	27.7	693	16.5
	2000	6 196	44.4	2 494	33.7	764	19.9
	2005	6 834	46.5	3 131	37.7	785	21.8
	2007	7 106	47.4	3 398	38.9	..	..
Mexico - Mexique	1990	84 002	72.5	29 915	30.6	8 473	12.7
	2000	99 735	74.7	40 300	33.6	8 684	12.7
	2005	104 266	76.0	43 888	35.2	8 509	12.6
	2007	106 535	76.5	45 353	36.1	..	..
Nicaragua	1990	4 141	53.1	1 272	30.1	406	9.9
	2000	5 108	57.2	1 730	29.8	394	9.9
	2005	5 463	59.0	2 034	29.8	384	10.2
	2007	5 603	59.8	2 174	30.0	..	..
Panama	1990	2 411	53.9	925	32.5	245	4.1
	2000	2 950	65.8	1 273	35.4	251	3.6
	2005	3 232	70.8	1 466	38.8	247	3.6
	2007	3 343	72.5	1 542	39.9	..	..
South America - Amérique du Sud	*1990*	*297 077*	*74.5*	*119 896*	*34.9*	*28 233*	*18.0*
	2000	*348 679*	*79.4*	*160 827*	*40.6*	*26 915*	*18.4*
	2005	*373 487*	*81.7*	*180 484*	*42.5*	*25 733*	*18.6*
	2007	*383 204*	*82.5*	*188 036*	*43.2*	*..*	*..*

For sources and notes, see end of table.   Pour les sources et les notes, se reporter à la fin du tableau.

Region, country or territory / Régions, pays ou territoires	Year / Année	Population		Total labour force / Main d'œuvre totale		Agriculture labour force / Main d'œuvre dans l'agriculture	
		Total (thousands) / Total (milliers)	Urban population (7) (% of total population) / Population urbaine (7) (en % de la population totale)	Total (thousands) / Total (milliers)	Female labour (% of total labour force) / Main d'œuvre féminine (en % de la main d'œuvre totale)	Total (thousands) / Total (milliers)	Female labour (% of total agriculture labour force) / Main d'œuvre féminine (en % de la main d'œuvre totale dans l'agriculture)
		(1)	(2)	(3)	(4)	(5)	(6)
Argentina - Argentine	1990	32 581	87.0	13 006	34.4	1 482	6.7
	2000	36 896	89.2	16 233	40.0	1 445	8.0
	2005	38 747	90.1	18 351	42.9	1 427	8.8
	2007	39 531	90.4	19 174	43.7	..	..
Bolivia - Bolivie	1990	6 669	55.6	2 511	39.2	1 249	35.5
	2000	8 317	61.8	3 553	43.2	1 497	35.5
	2005	9 182	64.2	4 158	43.5	1 650	35.3
	2007	9 525	65.2	4 414	43.7	..	..
Brazil - Brésil	1990	149 522	74.8	62 430	35.1	15 241	20.4
	2000	174 161	81.2	83 387	41.2	13 265	19.6
	2005	186 831	84.2	91 377	42.8	11 933	19.0
	2007	191 791	85.2	94 207	43.4	..	..
Chile - Chili	1990	13 179	83.3	5 002	30.5	947	9.5
	2000	15 412	85.9	6 081	33.4	1 001	11.7
	2005	16 295	87.6	6 516	35.1	1 019	13.2
	2007	16 635	88.2	6 682	36.0	..	..
Colombia - Colombie	1990	34 875	68.7	14 083	36.9	3 696	17.5
	2000	41 683	71.2	19 435	42.4	3 719	19.3
	2005	44 946	72.7	22 325	44.4	3 650	20.1
	2007	46 156	73.3	23 498	45.0	..	..
Ecuador - Équateur	1990	10 272	55.1	3 682	27.8	1 202	11.9
	2000	12 306	60.3	5 584	40.5	1 228	14.6
	2005	13 061	62.8	6 355	42.5	1 207	16.2
	2007	13 341	63.8	6 723	43.4	..	..
Falkland Islands (Malvinas) - Îles Falkland (Malvinas)	1990	2	74.5	..	..	..	..
	2000	3	85.8	..	..	..	..
	2005	3	90.2	..	..	..	..
	2007	3	91.5	..	..	..	..
Guyana	1990	731	29.5	268	32.8	58	12.1
	2000	734	28.6	312	36.3	55	10.9
	2005	739	28.2	329	36.9	..	..
	2007	738	28.2	335	37.1	..	..
Paraguay	1990	4 248	48.7	1 649	38.4	595	5.4
	2000	5 349	55.3	2 390	41.3	706	5.0
	2005	5 904	58.5	2 875	43.5	768	4.7
	2007	6 127	59.7	3 080	44.1	..	..
Peru - Pérou	1990	21 762	68.9	8 507	36.9	2 654	16.9
	2000	25 663	71.6	11 558	40.0	2 965	19.5
	2005	27 274	72.6	13 352	42.0	3 095	20.7
	2007	27 903	73.0	14 125	42.7	..	..
Suriname	1990	402	68.3	134	36.1	29	24.1
	2000	436	72.1	143	36.9	31	22.6
	2005	452	73.9	153	34.9	32	25.0
	2007	458	74.6	157	35.0	..	..
Uruguay	1990	3 106	89.0	1 379	39.9	193	10.9
	2000	3 318	91.3	1 623	42.7	190	12.1
	2005	3 326	92.0	1 753	44.2	189	13.2
	2007	3 340	92.2	1 804	44.7	..	..
Venezuela (Bolivarian Rep. of) - Venezuela (Rép. bolivarienne du)	1990	19 731	84.0	7 247	31.8	887	4.8
	2000	24 402	91.1	10 528	36.8	813	5.3
	2005	26 726	93.4	12 940	40.9	763	5.5
	2007	27 657	94.1	13 836	42.0	..	..
Developing economies: Asia - Économies en développement : Asie	**1990**	**2 985 852**	**30.4**	**1 383 595**	**38.6**	**947 770**	**43.5**
	2000	**3 499 689**	**36.0**	**1 640 396**	**38.1**	**1 029 359**	**44.3**
	2005	**3 728 361**	**38.8**	**1 784 419**	**38.1**	**1 056 243**	**44.6**
	2007	**3 818 239**	**40.0**	**1 842 217**	**38.1**	**..**	**..**

For sources and notes, see end of table.

Pour les sources et les notes, se reporter à la fin du tableau.

Region, country or territory Régions, pays ou territoires	Year Année	Population		Total labour force Main d'œuvre totale		Agriculture labour force Main d'œuvre dans l'agriculture	
		Total (thousands) Total (milliers)	Urban population (7) (% of total population) Population urbaine (7) (en % de la population totale)	Total (thousands) Total (milliers)	Female labour (% of total labour force) Main d'œuvre féminine (en % de la main d'œuvre totale)	Total (thousands) Total (milliers)	Female labour (% of total agriculture labour force) Main d'œuvre féminine (en % de la main d'œuvre totale dans l'agriculture)
		(1)	(2)	(3)	(4)	(5)	(6)
Eastern Asia - *Asie orientale*	*1990*	*1 220 374*	*30.5*	*694 191*	*44.6*	*500 864*	*47.3*
	2000	*1 349 261*	*38.7*	*783 240*	*44.5*	*516 988*	*47.7*
	2005	*1 394 576*	*43.2*	*822 816*	*44.3*	*514 444*	*47.6*
	2007	*1 410 960*	*45.0*	*837 273*	*44.2*	*..*	*..*
China - Chine	1990	1 128 790	27.9	661 448	44.8	493 124	47.4
	2000	1 247 777	36.4	745 715	44.7	510 910	47.7
	2005	1 290 249	41.1	782 782	44.5	509 215	47.7
	2007	1 305 728	43.0	796 468	44.4	..	..
China, Hong Kong SAR - Chine (RAS de Hong Kong)	1990	5 704	99.5	2 852	36.3	..	..
	2000	6 662	100.0	3 375	42.4	..	..
	2005	7 057	100.0	3 714	46.6	..	..
	2007	7 206	100.0	3 828	47.7	..	..
China, Macao SAR - Chine (RAS de Macao)	1990	372	99.8	160	40.6	..	..
	2000	441	100.0	224	44.7	..	..
	2005	473	100.0	259	47.2	..	..
	2007	481	100.0	272	48.2	..	..
China, Taiwan Province of - Province chinoise de Taiwan (8)	1990	20 279	..	..	..	..	..
	2000	22 185	..	..	..	..	..
	2005	22 730	..	..	..	..	..
	2007	22 902	..	..	..	..	..
Dem. People's Rep. of Korea - Rép. populaire dém. de Corée	1990	20 143	58.4	9 720	39.3	3 859	48.1
	2000	22 946	60.2	10 323	38.8	3 389	46.5
	2005	23 616	61.6	10 697	38.7	3 097	45.8
	2007	23 790	62.3	10 857	38.8	..	..
Mongolia - Mongolie	1990	2 216	57.0	884	41.0	326	43.9
	2000	2 470	56.6	1 101	40.3	310	44.5
	2005	2 581	56.7	1 245	40.2	299	45.2
	2007	2 629	56.9	1 305	40.1	..	..
Republic of Korea - République de Corée	1990	42 869	73.8	19 128	39.3	3 555	43.9
	2000	46 780	79.6	22 501	40.3	2 379	45.2
	2005	47 870	80.8	24 121	40.9	1 833	45.7
	2007	48 224	81.3	24 543	41.0	..	..
Southern Asia - *Asie méridionale*	*1990*	*1 192 558*	*26.5*	*449 785*	*29.4*	*306 267*	*37.3*
	2000	*1 460 857*	*28.9*	*552 958*	*29.0*	*354 190*	*39.1*
	2005	*1 587 400*	*30.2*	*618 572*	*29.6*	*377 859*	*39.8*
	2007	*1 638 396*	*30.8*	*646 455*	*29.8*	*..*	*..*
Afghanistan	1990	12 659	18.3	5 007	28.4	4 076	40.9
	2000	20 737	21.3	8 001	28.4	6 122	44.1
	2005	25 067	22.9	10 221	29.3	7 529	45.7
	2007	27 145	23.6	11 177	29.8	..	..
Bangladesh	1990	113 049	19.8	46 940	40.1	33 667	46.8
	2000	139 434	23.2	57 239	37.6	36 879	50.1
	2005	153 281	25.1	63 845	36.9	37 874	51.8
	2007	158 665	25.9	66 911	36.9	..	..
Bhutan - Bhoutan	1990	547	7.2	576	28.9	774	40.8
	2000	559	9.6	688	30.6	898	41.3
	2005	637	11.1	845	36.5	1 015	41.4
	2007	658	11.8	923	39.1	..	..
India - Inde	1990	860 195	25.5	329 760	28.7	229 986	36.3
	2000	1 046 235	27.7	398 363	28.0	264 347	37.2
	2005	1 134 403	28.7	438 766	28.3	280 716	37.6
	2007	1 169 016	29.2	455 348	28.4	..	..
Iran (Islamic Rep. of) - Iran (Rép. islamique d')	1990	56 674	56.3	16 264	20.2	5 403	27.3
	2000	66 125	64.2	22 787	29.5	6 163	38.4
	2005	69 421	66.9	28 040	33.8	6 689	44.3
	2007	71 208	68.0	30 230	35.2	..	..

For sources and notes, see end of table.

Pour les sources et les notes, se reporter à la fin du tableau.

Region, country or territory / Régions, pays ou territoires	Year / Année	Population		Total labour force / Main d'œuvre totale		Agriculture labour force / Main d'œuvre dans l'agriculture	
		Total (thousands) / Total (milliers)	Urban population (7) (% of total population) / Population urbaine (7) (en % de la population totale)	Total (thousands) / Total (milliers)	Female labour (% of total labour force) / Main d'œuvre féminine (en % de la main d'œuvre totale)	Total (thousands) / Total (milliers)	Female labour (% of total agriculture labour force) / Main d'œuvre féminine (en % de la main d'œuvre totale dans l'agriculture)
		(1)	(2)	(3)	(4)	(5)	(6)
Maldives	1990	216	25.8	58	19.4	29	34.5
	2000	273	27.5	90	32.9	27	37.0
	2005	295	29.6	117	38.9	27	37.0
	2007	306	30.5	129	40.5	..	..
Nepal - Népal	1990	19 114	8.9	7 122	37.9	8 506	41.9
	2000	24 419	13.4	9 178	40.1	10 673	43.8
	2005	27 094	15.8	10 526	40.5	12 078	44.2
	2007	28 196	16.7	11 160	40.6	..	..
Pakistan	1990	112 991	30.6	36 469	23.3	20 292	34.1
	2000	144 360	33.1	48 238	24.8	25 020	40.0
	2005	158 081	34.9	57 340	27.0	27 701	42.5
	2007	163 902	35.7	61 519	28.0	..	..
Sri Lanka	1990	17 114	17.2	7 591	34.8	3 534	33.8
	2000	18 714	15.7	8 374	31.5	4 061	34.8
	2005	19 121	15.1	8 873	30.4	4 230	35.1
	2007	19 299	15.1	9 058	30.4	..	..
South-Eastern Asia - Asie du Sud-Est	*1990*	*440 574*	*31.6*	*196 761*	*41.9*	*121 822*	*42.6*
	2000	*519 996*	*39.7*	*247 707*	*41.5*	*136 967*	*43.6*
	2005	*557 669*	*44.0*	*276 141*	*41.9*	*142 242*	*44.0*
	2007	*572 500*	*45.7*	*287 898*	*42.2*	*..*	*..*
Brunei Darussalam - Brunéi Darussalam	1990	257	65.8	110	32.1	2	50.0
	2000	333	71.1	147	34.4	1	..
	2005	374	73.5	164	34.1	1	..
	2007	390	74.4	171	34.1	..	..
Cambodia - Cambodge	1990	9 698	12.6	4 381	52.5	3 463	57.2
	2000	12 780	16.9	5 848	51.8	4 582	55.9
	2005	13 956	19.7	6 814	51.4	5 107	55.3
	2007	14 444	20.9	7 218	51.1	..	..
Indonesia - Indonésie	1990	182 847	30.6	76 615	38.5	44 068	39.0
	2000	211 693	42.0	98 742	37.8	49 225	42.2
	2005	226 063	48.1	108 361	37.9	50 539	43.8
	2007	231 627	50.4	112 518	38.1	..	..
Lao People's dem. Rep. - Rép. dém. populaire lao	1990	4 076	15.4	1 544	41.3	1 585	48.3
	2000	5 224	18.9	2 023	40.8	2 007	48.5
	2005	5 664	20.6	2 355	40.7	2 278	48.6
	2007	5 859	21.4	2 500	40.6	..	..
Malaysia - Malaisie	1990	18 103	49.8	7 122	34.8	1 985	32.7
	2000	23 274	61.8	9 684	35.3	1 843	28.5
	2005	25 653	67.3	11 013	35.9	1 712	26.2
	2007	26 572	69.3	11 561	36.3	..	..
Myanmar	1990	40 147	24.9	20 000	44.6	15 381	45.8
	2000	45 884	28.0	24 832	44.8	18 174	45.7
	2005	47 967	30.6	27 427	45.0	19 479	45.8
	2007	48 798	31.9	28 495	45.1	..	..
Philippines	1990	61 226	48.8	23 439	36.6	11 001	24.6
	2000	76 213	58.5	30 761	37.4	12 421	24.5
	2005	84 566	62.7	37 093	39.8	13 086	24.5
	2007	87 960	64.2	39 521	40.7	..	..
Singapore - Singapour	1990	3 016	100.0	1 541	38.7	6	16.7
	2000	4 017	100.0	2 059	40.0	3	..
	2005	4 327	100.0	2 207	39.9	2	..
	2007	4 436	100.0	2 270	40.2	..	..
Thailand - Thaïlande	1990	54 291	29.4	30 442	46.6	20 055	47.7
	2000	60 666	31.1	33 586	45.5	20 761	46.8
	2005	63 003	32.3	35 715	46.2	20 197	46.2
	2007	63 884	32.9	36 552	46.5	..	..

For sources and notes, see end of table.

Pour les sources et les notes, se reporter à la fin du tableau.

Region, country or territory Régions, pays ou territoires	Year Année	Population		Total labour force Main d'œuvre totale		Agriculture labour force Main d'œuvre dans l'agriculture	
		Total (thousands) Total (milliers)	Urban population (7) (% of total population) Population urbaine (7) (en % de la population totale)	Total (thousands) Total (milliers)	Female labour (% of total labour force) Main d'œuvre féminine (en % de la main d'œuvre totale)	Total (thousands) Total (milliers)	Female labour (% of total agriculture labour force) Main d'œuvre féminine (en % de la main d'œuvre totale dans l'agriculture)
		(1)	(2)	(3)	(4)	(5)	(6)
Timor-Leste	1990	740	20.8	284	37.0	322	49.7
	2000	819	24.5	256	34.9	293	47.1
	2005	1 067	26.5	383	37.6	375	48.3
	2007	1 155	27.3	440	38.3	..	..
Viet Nam	1990	66 173	20.3	31 284	48.4	23 954	49.6
	2000	79 094	24.3	39 770	48.5	27 657	49.2
	2005	85 029	26.4	44 608	48.5	29 466	49.0
	2007	87 375	27.3	46 651	48.5	..	..
Western Asia - *Asie occidentale*	*1990*	*132 346*	*60.5*	*42 857*	*24.1*	*18 817*	*47.4*
	2000	*169 574*	*63.4*	*56 491*	*23.2*	*21 214*	*55.4*
	2005	*188 717*	*64.7*	*66 890*	*24.0*	*21 698*	*59.0*
	2007	*196 383*	*65.2*	*70 590*	*24.3*	*..*	*..*
Bahrain - Bahreïn	1990	493	88.1	220	16.8	4	..
	2000	650	94.6	311	18.3	4	..
	2005	725	96.5	337	18.7	3	..
	2007	753	97.0	350	18.9	..	..
Iraq	1990	18 515	69.7	4 726	16.8	751	40.1
	2000	25 052	67.8	6 963	19.2	691	50.5
	2005	27 996	66.9	8 353	20.2	651	55.1
	2007	28 993	66.7	8 946	20.6	..	..
Jordan - Jordanie	1990	3 254	72.2	773	18.8	123	46.3
	2000	4 799	80.4	1 569	22.7	184	64.1
	2005	5 544	82.3	1 919	24.5	194	70.1
	2007	5 924	83.0	2 056	25.2	..	..
Kuwait - Koweït	1990	2 143	98.0	859	21.8	11	..
	2000	2 228	98.2	1 165	22.3	13	..
	2005	2 700	98.3	1 457	25.4	15	..
	2007	2 851	98.3	1 549	26.6	..	..
Lebanon - Liban	1990	2 974	83.1	942	31.7	62	35.5
	2000	3 772	86.0	1 265	29.4	45	37.8
	2005	4 011	86.6	1 408	30.4	35	40.0
	2007	4 099	86.9	1 480	31.2	..	..
Occupied Palestinian territory - Territoire palestinien occupé	1990	2 154	67.9	430	12.0	..	..
	2000	3 149	71.5	656	13.0	..	..
	2005	3 762	71.6	783	13.1	..	..
	2007	4 017	71.7	839	13.3	..	..
Oman	1990	1 843	65.3	567	11.1	257	4.3
	2000	2 402	71.6	912	12.7	337	5.0
	2005	2 507	71.5	957	16.4	317	6.6
	2007	2 595	71.5	1 017	18.0	..	..
Qatar	1990	467	92.2	256	10.5	7	..
	2000	617	94.9	320	14.5	4	..
	2005	796	95.4	472	13.7	5	..
	2007	841	95.6	498	14.3	..	..
Saudi Arabia - Arabie saoudite	1990	16 256	76.6	5 098	11.4	1 031	7.2
	2000	20 807	79.8	6 716	13.5	717	8.6
	2005	23 612	81.0	7 925	15.2	600	9.0
	2007	24 735	81.4	8 447	15.8	..	..
Syrian Arab Republic - République arabe syrienne	1990	12 721	48.9	3 670	26.2	1 185	51.6
	2000	16 511	50.1	6 036	29.3	1 505	61.3
	2005	18 894	50.6	7 580	30.6	1 690	66.1
	2007	19 929	51.0	8 180	31.1	..	..
Turkey - Turquie	1990	57 345	59.2	21 402	29.4	13 163	53.1
	2000	68 158	64.7	23 877	26.2	14 767	61.3
	2005	72 970	67.3	27 060	26.5	14 994	64.9
	2007	74 877	68.2	27 876	26.5	..	..

For sources and notes, see end of table.　　　　　　　　　　　　　Pour les sources et les notes, se reporter à la fin du tableau.

Region, country or territory / Régions, pays ou territoires	Year / Année	Population		Total labour force / Main d'œuvre totale		Agriculture labour force / Main d'œuvre dans l'agriculture	
		Total (thousands) / Total (milliers)	Urban population (7) (% of total population) / Population urbaine (7) (en % de la population totale)	Total (thousands) / Total (milliers)	Female labour (% of total labour force) / Main d'œuvre féminine (en % de la main d'œuvre totale)	Total (thousands) / Total (milliers)	Female labour (% of total agriculture labour force) / Main d'œuvre féminine (en % de la main d'œuvre totale dans l'agriculture)
		(1)	(2)	(3)	(4)	(5)	(6)
United Arab Emirates - Émirats arabes unis	1990	1 867	79.1	953	9.8	74	..
	2000	3 247	77.4	1 875	12.4	92	..
	2005	4 104	76.7	2 700	13.4	103	..
	2007	4 380	76.7	2 898	14.2	..	..
Yemen - Yémen	1990	12 314	20.9	2 963	27.4	2 149	39.9
	2000	18 182	25.4	4 824	27.0	2 855	42.9
	2005	21 096	27.3	5 937	27.9	3 091	44.2
	2007	22 389	28.1	6 454	28.3	..	..
Developing economies: Oceania - Économies en développement : Océanie	**1990**	**6 449**	**22.5**	**2 549**	**43.7**	**2 011**	**43.6**
	2000	**8 113**	**22.8**	**3 217**	**45.0**	**2 355**	**46.2**
	2005	**9 003**	**23.0**	**3 655**	**44.9**	**2 563**	**47.2**
	2007	**9 345**	**23.2**	**3 851**	**45.0**	**..**	**..**
American Samoa - Samoa américaines	1990	47	80.9	..	..	8	37.5
	2000	57	88.8	..	..	8	37.5
	2005	64	91.3	..	..	8	37.5
	2007	67	92.0	..	..	..	..
Cook Islands - Îles Cook	1990	18	56.9	..	..	3	33.3
	2000	16	63.9	..	..	2	50.0
	2005	14	70.6	..	..	2	50.0
	2007	13	73.0	..	..	..	..
Fiji - Fidji	1990	724	41.6	289	37.6	115	14.8
	2000	802	48.3	354	38.0	129	19.4
	2005	828	50.8	387	38.5	135	22.2
	2007	839	51.8	400	38.8	..	..
French Polynesia - Polynésie française	1990	195	55.9	78	37.2	34	29.4
	2000	236	52.4	99	37.8	35	31.4
	2005	256	51.7	111	38.3	35	31.4
	2007	263	51.6	116	38.5	..	..
Guam	1990	134	90.8	63	35.3	21	23.8
	2000	155	93.2	72	38.6	20	25.0
	2005	169	94.0	78	38.8	21	23.8
	2007	173	94.3	81	39.2	..	..
Kiribati	1990	72	35.0	..	..	9	33.3
	2000	84	43.0	..	..	11	27.3
	2005	92	43.6	..	..	12	25.0
	2007	95	43.7	..	..	..	..
Marshall Islands - Îles Marshall	1990	47	..	..	..	6	33.3
	2000	52	..	..	..	6	33.3
	2005	57	..	..	..	7	28.6
	2007	59	..	..	..	..	..
Micronesia (Federated States of) - Micronésie (États fédérés de)	1990	96	25.8	..	..	11	27.3
	2000	107	22.3	..	..	11	27.3
	2005	110	22.3	..	..	11	27.3
	2007	111	22.4	..	..	..	..
Nauru	1990	9	100.0	..	..	1	..
	2000	10	100.0	..	..	1	..
	2005	10	100.0	..	..	2	..
	2007	10	100.0	..	..	..	..
New Caledonia - Nouvelle-Calédonie	1990	171	59.6	69	37.5	37	45.9
	2000	215	61.9	89	37.2	41	46.3
	2005	234	63.7	98	37.0	42	45.2
	2007	242	64.4	102	36.9	..	..
Niue - Nioué	1990	2	30.9	..	..	..	..
	2000	2	33.7	..	..	..	..
	2005	2	36.7	..	..	..	..
	2007	2	38.0	..	..	..	..

For sources and notes, see end of table.

Pour les sources et les notes, se reporter à la fin du tableau.

Region, country or territory / Régions, pays ou territoires	Year / Année	Population		Total labour force / Main d'œuvre totale		Agriculture labour force / Main d'œuvre dans l'agriculture	
		Total (thousands) Total (milliers) (1)	Urban population (7) (% of total population) Population urbaine (7) (en % de la population totale) (2)	Total (thousands) Total (milliers) (3)	Female labour (% of total labour force) Main d'œuvre féminine (en % de la main d'œuvre totale) (4)	Total (thousands) Total (milliers) (5)	Female labour (% of total agriculture labour force) Main d'œuvre féminine (en % de la main d'œuvre totale dans l'agriculture) (6)
Northern Mariana Islands - Îles Mariannes du Nord	1990	44	..	..	..	6	33.3
	2000	69	..	..	..	8	25.0
	2005	80	..	..	..	9	22.2
	2007	84	..	..	..	..	..
Palau - Palaos	1990	15	69.6	..	..	2	50.0
	2000	19	69.9	..	..	2	50.0
	2005	20	77.1	..	..	2	50.0
	2007	20	79.6	..	..	..	..
Papua New Guinea - Papouasie-Nouvelle-Guinée	1990	4 131	13.1	1 771	46.4	1 564	46.0
	2000	5 381	13.2	2 244	47.8	1 855	48.6
	2005	6 070	13.4	2 575	47.5	2 032	49.5
	2007	6 331	13.6	2 726	47.5	..	..
Pitcairn	1990	0	..	..	..	..	..
	2000	0	..	..	..	..	..
	2005	0	..	..	..	..	..
	2007	0	..	..	..	..	..
Samoa	1990	161	21.2	56	31.5	24	33.3
	2000	177	21.9	63	32.1	22	31.8
	2005	184	22.4	65	31.9	20	35.0
	2007	187	22.7	66	32.0	..	..
Solomon Islands - Îles Salomon	1990	314	13.7	118	39.3	125	52.8
	2000	415	15.7	166	38.8	159	53.5
	2005	472	17.0	195	38.6	178	53.9
	2007	496	17.6	207	38.5	..	..
Tokelau - Tokélaou	1990	2	..	..	..	..	..
	2000	2	..	..	..	..	..
	2005	1	..	..	..	..	..
	2007	1	..	..	..	..	..
Tonga	1990	95	22.7	33	32.6	14	35.7
	2000	98	23.2	37	37.8	12	33.3
	2005	99	24.0	40	37.8	12	33.3
	2007	100	24.4	41	37.8	..	..
Tuvalu	1990	9	40.7	..	..	2	50.0
	2000	10	46.0	..	..	1	0.0
	2005	10	48.1	..	..	1	0.0
	2007	11	49.0	..	..	..	..
Vanuatu	1990	149	18.7	71	46.3	27	48.1
	2000	190	21.7	92	46.6	30	46.7
	2005	215	23.5	107	46.7	32	46.9
	2007	226	24.3	113	46.8	..	..
Wallis and Futuna Islands - Îles Wallis-et-Futuna	1990	14	..	..	..	2	50.0
	2000	15	..	..	..	2	50.0
	2005	15	..	..	..	2	50.0
	2007	15	..	..	..	..	..
Economies in transition: Asia - Économies en transition : Asie	**2000**	**71 244**	**44.4**	**30 810**	**46.0**	**7 828**	**43.4**
	2005	**74 234**	**44.1**	**33 750**	**46.3**	**7 758**	**43.1**
	2007	**75 677**	**44.2**	**35 208**	**46.5**	**..**	**..**
Armenia - Arménie	2000	3 082	65.1	1 300	47.8	182	24.2
	2005	3 018	64.1	1 280	49.1	162	21.0
	2007	3 002	63.8	1 290	49.2	..	..
Azerbaijan - Azerbaïdjan	2000	8 143	50.9	3 711	46.7	963	52.0
	2005	8 352	51.5	4 140	47.7	982	52.4
	2007	8 467	51.6	4 356	48.1	..	..

For sources and notes, see end of table.

Pour les sources et les notes, se reporter à la fin du tableau.

Region, country or territory / Régions, pays ou territoires	Year / Année	Population		Total labour force / Main d'œuvre totale		Agriculture labour force / Main d'œuvre dans l'agriculture	
		Total (thousands) / Total (milliers)	Urban population (7) (% of total population) / Population urbaine (7) (en % de la population totale)	Total (thousands) / Total (milliers)	Female labour (% of total labour force) / Main d'œuvre féminine (en % de la main d'œuvre totale)	Total (thousands) / Total (milliers)	Female labour (% of total agriculture labour force) / Main d'œuvre féminine (en % de la main d'œuvre totale dans l'agriculture)
		(1)	(2)	(3)	(4)	(5)	(6)
Georgia - Géorgie	2000	4 720	52.7	2 356	46.2	465	40.9
	2005	4 473	52.2	2 256	43.4	395	39.5
	2007	4 395	52.3	2 224	42.6	..	..
Kazakhstan	2000	14 954	56.3	7 608	48.6	1 289	28.1
	2005	15 211	57.3	7 953	49.6	1 187	25.7
	2007	15 422	57.8	8 135	49.8	..	..
Kyrgyzstan - Kirghizistan	2000	4 946	35.4	2 091	44.7	554	37.7
	2005	5 204	35.8	2 318	44.2	552	35.7
	2007	5 317	36.1	2 421	44.1	..	..
Tajikistan - Tadjikistan	2000	6 173	25.9	1 971	42.5	789	50.7
	2005	6 550	24.7	2 149	43.7	806	52.6
	2007	6 736	24.4	2 252	43.9	..	..
Turkmenistan - Turkménistan	2000	4 502	45.1	1 915	46.1	664	51.5
	2005	4 833	46.2	2 197	46.7	716	52.0
	2007	4 965	46.9	2 320	46.6	..	..
Uzbekistan - Ouzbékistan	2000	24 724	37.3	9 858	44.3	2 922	46.1
	2005	26 593	36.7	11 457	44.6	2 958	45.2
	2007	27 372	36.7	12 211	44.9	..	..
Economies in transition: Europe - Économies en transition : Europe	**2000**	**234 658**	**70.0**	**111 167**	**48.0**	**15 059**	**32.4**
	2005	**228 668**	**70.1**	**112 763**	**48.5**	**12 914**	**29.7**
	2007	**226 361**	**70.1**	**112 730**	**48.6**	**..**	**..**
Albania - Albanie	1990	3 289	36.4	1 564	40.2	857	44.3
	2000	3 080	41.8	1 347	41.7	708	45.2
	2005	3 154	45.4	1 359	42.2	693	44.7
	2007	3 190	46.9	1 377	42.3	..	..
Belarus - Bélarus	2000	10 052	70.0	4 770	48.8	699	25.5
	2005	9 795	72.2	4 769	49.2	581	21.9
	2007	9 689	73.2	4 757	49.3	..	..
Bosnia and Herzegovina - Bosnie-Herzégovine	2000	3 787	43.2	1 966	45.7	90	52.2
	2005	3 915	45.7	2 054	48.2	61	52.5
	2007	3 935	46.9	2 075	48.7	..	..
Croatia - Croatie	2000	4 506	55.6	1 994	44.2	180	35.6
	2005	4 551	56.5	2 002	45.0	131	32.8
	2007	4 555	56.9	1 993	45.4	..	..
Moldova	2000	4 145	46.1	2 056	48.2	495	33.7
	2005	3 877	46.7	2 159	47.7	421	29.7
	2007	3 794	47.1	2 192	47.4	..	..
Russian Federation - Fédération de Russie	2000	147 423	73.3	71 319	48.5	8 175	29.7
	2005	143 953	73.0	73 270	49.0	7 163	27.1
	2007	142 499	72.8	73 368	49.1	..	..
Serbia and Montenegro - Serbie-et-Monténégro	2000	10 801	..	4 868	40.6	1 008	42.0
	2005	10 471	..	5 120	42.2	823	39.6
	2007	10 456	..	5 241	43.3	..	..
SFR of Yugoslavia (former) - RSF de Yougoslavie (anc.)	1990	22 817	27.2	10 017	42.9	2 196	45.1
TFYR of Macedonia - LERY de Macédoine	2000	2 009	64.9	..	..	120	39.2
	2005	2 034	68.9	..	..	94	38.3
	2007	2 038	70.3	..	..	..	..
Ukraine	2000	48 854	67.1	22 847	48.9	3 584	33.4
	2005	46 918	67.8	22 031	49.1	2 947	30.4
	2007	46 205	68.2	21 727	48.9	..	..
USSR (former) - URSS (anc.)	1990	289 353	65.5	144 579	48.2	26 638	38.2

For sources and notes, see end of table.

Pour les sources et les notes, se reporter à la fin du tableau.

Region, country or territory / Régions, pays ou territoires	Year Année	Population Total (thousands) Total (milliers) (1)	Urban population (7) (% of total population) Population urbaine (7) (en % de la population totale) (2)	Total labour force Main d'œuvre totale Total (thousands) Total (milliers) (3)	Female labour (% of total labour force) Main d'œuvre féminine (en % de la main d'œuvre totale) (4)	Agriculture labour force Main d'œuvre dans l'agriculture Total (thousands) Total (milliers) (5)	Female labour (% of total agriculture labour force) Main d'œuvre féminine (en % de la main d'œuvre totale dans l'agriculture) (6)
Developed economies: America - Économies développées : Amérique	**1990**	**287 448**	**75.4**	**148 132**	**44.3**	**4 195**	**22.6**
	2000	**319 506**	**79.3**	**166 469**	**45.8**	**3 453**	**26.2**
	2005	**336 192**	**80.9**	**175 420**	**46.2**	**3 113**	**27.8**
	2007	**342 822**	**81.5**	**179 111**	**46.4**	..	..
Bermuda - Bermudes	1990	60	100.0	..	..	1	..
	2000	63	100.0	..	..	1	..
	2005	64	100.0	..	..	1	..
	2007	65	100.0	..	..	..	..
Canada	1990	27 701	76.6	14 665	44.1	494	32.2
	2000	30 689	79.4	16 224	45.7	389	42.2
	2005	32 271	80.1	17 639	46.3	347	47.0
	2007	32 876	80.3	18 150	46.6	..	..
Greenland - Groenland	1990	56	79.7	..	..	1	..
	2000	56	81.6	..	..	1	..
	2005	57	82.8	..	..	1	..
	2007	58	83.3	..	..	..	..
Saint Pierre and Miquelon - Saint-Pierre-et-Miquelon	1990	6	88.9	..	..	..	..
	2000	6	88.9	..	..	..	..
	2005	6	89.0	..	..	..	..
	2007	6	89.1	..	..	..	..
United States - États-Unis	1990	259 625	75.3	133 467	44.3	3 699	21.3
	2000	288 691	79.3	150 244	45.8	3 062	24.1
	2005	303 793	81.0	157 780	46.2	2 764	25.4
	2007	309 817	81.6	160 961	46.4	..	..
Developed economies: Asia - Économies développées : Asie	**1990**	**128 051**	**64.0**	**65 502**	**40.6**	**4 742**	**45.2**
	2000	**133 118**	**66.4**	**70 077**	**40.7**	**2 840**	**43.0**
	2005	**134 589**	**67.1**	**69 352**	**41.3**	**2 106**	**41.8**
	2007	**134 894**	**67.5**	**68 689**	**41.6**	..	..
Israel - Israël	1990	4 514	90.4	1 597	40.6	73	20.5
	2000	6 084	91.4	2 373	45.6	70	20.0
	2005	6 692	91.6	2 650	47.1	64	20.3
	2007	6 928	91.6	2 762	47.6	..	..
Japan - Japon	1990	123 537	63.1	63 905	40.6	4 669	45.6
	2000	127 034	65.2	67 705	40.6	2 770	43.6
	2005	127 897	65.8	66 702	41.1	2 042	42.5
	2007	127 967	66.2	65 927	41.4	..	..
Developed economies: Europe - Économies développées : Europe	**1990**	**474 642**	**71.7**	**221 171**	**41.8**	**21 252**	**40.5**
	2000	**496 326**	**72.9**	**233 988**	**43.7**	**15 990**	**38.9**
	2005	**505 067**	**73.6**	**238 978**	**44.6**	**13 494**	**37.7**
	2007	**507 630**	**73.9**	**240 487**	**45.0**	..	..
Andorra - Andorre	1990	53	94.7	..	..	4	25.0
	2000	66	92.4	..	..	3	33.3
	2005	73	90.3	..	..	2	50.0
	2007	75	89.3	..	..	..	..
Austria - Autriche	1990	7 729	65.8	3 558	40.8	276	46.7
	2000	8 111	65.8	3 917	43.1	192	44.3
	2005	8 292	66.0	3 958	44.6	156	42.9
	2007	8 361	66.2	3 993	45.1	..	..
Belgium - Belgique	2005	10 398	97.2	4 472	43.5	65	27.7
	2007	10 457	97.3	4 501	43.9	..	..
Belgium-Luxembourg - Belgique-Luxembourg	1990	10 315	95.8	4 108	38.8	112	26.8
	2000	10 630	96.6	4 636	42.7	82	28.0

For sources and notes, see end of table.   Pour les sources et les notes, se reporter à la fin du tableau.

Region, country or territory / Régions, pays ou territoires	Year / Année	Population		Total labour force / Main d'œuvre totale		Agriculture labour force / Main d'œuvre dans l'agriculture	
		Total (thousands) / Total (milliers)	Urban population (7) (% of total population) / Population urbaine (7) (en % de la population totale)	Total (thousands) / Total (milliers)	Female labour (% of total labour force) / Main d'œuvre féminine (en % de la main d'œuvre totale)	Total (thousands) / Total (milliers)	Female labour (% of total agriculture labour force) / Main d'œuvre féminine (en % de la main d'œuvre totale dans l'agriculture)
		(1)	(2)	(3)	(4)	(5)	(6)
Bulgaria - Bulgarie	1990	8 819	66.4	4 436	48.0	597	46.6
	2000	8 003	68.9	3 208	46.6	291	39.2
	2005	7 745	70.0	3 106	46.0	204	34.8
	2007	7 639	70.5	3 027	45.6	..	..
Cyprus - Chypre	1990	681	66.8	324	37.7	44	43.2
	2000	786	68.6	370	41.2	34	38.2
	2005	836	69.3	413	45.1	29	37.9
	2007	855	69.7	428	46.1	..	..
Czechoslovakia (former) - Tchécoslovaquie (anc.)	1990	15 559	68.9	8 049	47.0	933	38.0
Czech Republic - République tchèque	2000	10 220	74.0	5 181	44.4	472	31.6
	2005	10 192	73.5	5 194	45.1	400	28.0
	2007	10 186	73.5	5 192	45.6	..	..
Denmark - Danemark	1990	5 140	84.8	2 912	46.1	162	24.1
	2000	5 335	85.1	2 864	46.6	111	24.3
	2005	5 417	85.6	2 849	46.7	90	24.4
	2007	5 442	85.8	2 843	46.9	..	..
Estonia - Estonie	2000	1 370	69.4	669	48.8	83	32.5
	2005	1 344	69.1	655	49.4	73	28.8
	2007	1 335	69.1	658	49.4	..	..
Faeroe Islands - Îles Féroé	1990	47	30.6	..	..	1	..
	2000	46	36.3	..	..	1	..
	2005	48	39.8	..	..	1	..
	2007	49	40.9	..	..	..	..
Finland - Finlande	1990	4 986	61.4	2 574	47.3	216	35.2
	2000	5 176	61.1	2 599	47.7	143	35.7
	2005	5 246	61.1	2 658	47.8	113	35.4
	2007	5 277	61.2	2 663	47.8	..	..
France	1990	58 237	74.4	25 420	43.3	1 409	34.9
	2000	60 915	76.2	27 071	45.4	933	33.9
	2005	62 835	77.1	27 682	46.0	736	33.2
	2007	63 532	77.6	27 742	46.2	..	..
Germany - Allemagne	1990	79 433	73.4	38 304	40.5	1 588	42.6
	2000	82 309	75.1	40 464	43.7	1 013	38.7
	2005	82 652	75.2	41 067	45.2	805	37.0
	2007	82 599	75.3	41 379	45.8	..	..
Gibraltar	1990	27	100.0	..	..	2	50.0
	2000	27	100.0	..	..	1	100.0
	2005	29	100.0	..	..	1	..
	2007	29	100.0	..	..	..	..
Greece - Grèce	1990	10 161	58.8	4 185	36.1	963	44.7
	2000	10 975	58.8	4 894	39.2	809	48.2
	2005	11 100	59.0	5 154	40.9	707	49.4
	2007	11 147	59.2	5 262	41.7	..	..
Holy See - Saint-Siège	1990	1	100.0	..	..	..	..
	2000	1	100.0	..	..	..	..
	2005	1	100.0	..	..	..	..
	2007	1	100.0	..	..	..	..
Hungary - Hongrie	1990	10 365	65.8	4 531	44.5	721	30.5
	2000	10 214	64.6	4 235	44.5	523	26.2
	2005	10 086	66.3	4 212	45.1	431	24.1
	2007	10 030	67.1	4 199	45.3	..	..
Iceland - Islande	1990	255	90.8	142	45.6	16	18.8
	2000	281	92.3	165	47.0	13	15.4
	2005	296	92.8	175	46.7	12	16.7
	2007	301	93.0	180	46.7	..	..

For sources and notes, see end of table.

Pour les sources et les notes, se reporter à la fin du tableau.

Region, country or territory / Régions, pays ou territoires	Year / Année	Population		Total labour force / Main d'œuvre totale		Agriculture labour force / Main d'œuvre dans l'agriculture	
		Total (thousands) / Total (milliers)	Urban population (7) (% of total population) / Population urbaine (7) (en % de la population totale)	Total (thousands) / Total (milliers)	Female labour (% of total labour force) / Main d'œuvre féminine (en % de la main d'œuvre totale)	Total (thousands) / Total (milliers)	Female labour (% of total agriculture labour force) / Main d'œuvre féminine (en % de la main d'œuvre totale dans l'agriculture)
		(1)	(2)	(3)	(4)	(5)	(6)
Ireland - Irlande	1990	3 515	56.9	1 335	34.3	188	6.9
	2000	3 804	59.1	1 757	40.7	164	6.7
	2005	4 143	60.5	2 075	43.0	156	6.4
	2007	4 301	61.0	2 180	43.9	..	..
Italy - Italie	1990	56 719	66.7	23 915	37.1	2 101	38.6
	2000	57 692	67.2	23 837	38.3	1 353	41.2
	2005	58 646	67.6	24 245	40.0	1 048	42.0
	2007	58 877	67.9	24 304	40.7	..	..
Latvia - Lettonie	2000	2 379	68.1	1 092	49.0	153	32.7
	2005	2 302	67.8	1 097	48.6	133	29.3
	2007	2 277	67.9	1 100	48.6	..	..
Lithuania - Lituanie	2000	3 503	67.0	1 681	48.7	219	28.3
	2005	3 425	66.6	1 628	49.2	180	25.0
	2007	3 390	66.4	1 632	49.3	..	..
Luxembourg	2005	457	82.8	205	42.0	3	33.3
	2007	467	82.5	212	42.7	..	..
Malta - Malte	1990	360	90.4	127	23.6	3	..
	2000	389	93.4	153	28.9	2	..
	2005	403	95.3	169	33.6	2	..
	2007	407	95.8	175	35.7	..	..
Netherlands - Pays-Bas	1990	14 952	68.7	6 932	39.1	315	28.6
	2000	15 924	76.8	8 128	42.9	248	30.6
	2005	16 328	80.2	8 603	44.2	214	32.2
	2007	16 419	81.3	8 712	44.5	..	..
Norway - Norvège	1990	4 241	72.0	2 217	44.7	134	27.6
	2000	4 489	76.1	2 411	46.6	106	34.0
	2005	4 639	77.4	2 523	47.3	93	36.6
	2007	4 698	77.5	2 559	47.5	..	..
Poland - Pologne	1990	38 111	61.3	18 584	45.9	5 144	45.5
	2000	38 433	61.7	17 567	45.7	4 333	41.9
	2005	38 196	62.1	17 506	45.7	3 909	39.5
	2007	38 082	62.3	17 478	45.9	..	..
Portugal	1990	9 983	47.9	4 836	42.8	864	50.6
	2000	10 227	54.4	5 228	45.4	662	56.5
	2005	10 528	57.6	5 534	46.5	571	59.2
	2007	10 623	58.9	5 627	46.8	..	..
Romania - Roumanie	1990	23 207	54.3	10 965	44.3	2 551	51.3
	2000	22 138	54.6	11 454	46.0	1 589	47.5
	2005	21 628	53.7	10 308	46.1	1 239	45.0
	2007	21 438	54.0	10 118	46.4	..	..
San Marino - Saint-Marin	1990	24	90.4	..	..	2	50.0
	2000	27	93.4	..	..	1	100.0
	2005	30	94.1	..	..	1	..
	2007	31	94.2	..	..	..	..
Slovakia - Slovaquie	2000	5 388	56.3	2 611	45.6	268	30.2
	2005	5 387	56.2	2 683	45.2	238	26.9
	2007	5 390	56.4	2 701	45.1	..	..
Slovenia - Slovénie	2000	1 984	50.8	963	46.2	20	45.0
	2005	1 999	51.0	1 015	46.1	12	41.7
	2007	2 002	51.3	1 023	46.2	..	..
Spain - Espagne	1990	38 851	75.4	16 179	34.4	1 892	30.4
	2000	40 229	76.3	18 661	39.5	1 335	32.8
	2005	43 397	76.7	20 675	41.1	1 115	33.3
	2007	44 279	77.0	21 151	41.7	..	..

For sources and notes, see end of table.

Pour les sources et les notes, se reporter à la fin du tableau.

Region, country or territory Régions, pays ou territoires	Year Année	Population		Total labour force Main d'œuvre totale		Agriculture labour force Main d'œuvre dans l'agriculture	
		Total (thousands) Total (milliers)	Urban population (7) (% of total population) Population urbaine (7) (en % de la population totale)	Total (thousands) Total (milliers)	Female labour (% of total labour force) Main d'œuvre féminine (en % de la main d'œuvre totale)	Total (thousands) Total (milliers)	Female labour (% of total agriculture labour force) Main d'œuvre féminine (en % de la main d'œuvre totale dans l'agriculture)
		(1)	(2)	(3)	(4)	(5)	(6)
Sweden - Suède	1990	8 559	83.1	4 745	47.7	204	28.4
	2000	8 868	84.0	4 609	47.3	151	32.5
	2005	9 038	84.2	4 690	47.4	129	34.9
	2007	9 119	84.3	4 718	47.4	..	..
Switzerland - Suisse	1990	6 863	68.1	3 744	40.4	201	30.3
	2000	7 296	72.8	4 003	45.0	159	35.3
	2005	7 459	74.8	4 085	46.7	141	38.3
	2007	7 519	75.6	4 105	47.3	..	..
United Kingdom - Royaume-Uni	1990	57 449	88.4	29 050	44.0	609	20.4
	2000	59 091	89.1	29 558	45.5	523	22.6
	2005	60 472	89.5	30 339	46.0	485	23.7
	2007	60 997	89.6	30 624	46.2	..	..
Developed economies: Oceania - Économies développées : Océanie	**1990**	**20 284**	**85.3**	**10 011**	**41.6**	**633**	**29.4**
	2000	**22 993**	**86.9**	**11 407**	**44.6**	**610**	**36.4**
	2005	**24 407**	**87.9**	**12 379**	**45.7**	**601**	**39.4**
	2007	**24 922**	**88.2**	**12 734**	**46.1**	**..**	**..**
Australia - Australie	1990	16 873	85.4	8 353	41.3	463	28.9
	2000	19 139	87.2	9 498	44.4	440	37.5
	2005	20 310	88.2	10 261	45.5	431	41.3
	2007	20 743	88.6	10 551	45.9	..	..
New Zealand - Nouvelle-Zélande	1990	3 411	84.7	1 658	43.1	170	30.6
	2000	3 854	85.7	1 909	45.4	170	33.5
	2005	4 097	86.2	2 117	46.5	170	34.7
	2007	4 179	86.4	2 183	46.9	..	..

Sources:
- UN DESA Population Division, *World Population Prospects: The 2006 Revision*
- UN DESA Population Division, *World Urbanization Prospects: The 2007 Revision*
- ILO, online database
- FAO, online database

Notes:
(1) Total population: de facto population in a country, area or region as of 1 July of the year indicated.

(2) Urban population as percentage of total population: population living in areas classified as urban according to the criteria used by each area or country. Data refer to 1st July of the year indicated.

(3) Total labour force: comprises all persons (both sexes) of age 15 and over.

(4) Female labour force as percentage of total labour force: comprises all persons of sex feminine of age 15 and over.

(5) Total labour force in agriculture: is that part (male and female) of the total labour force engaged in or seeking work agriculture, hunting, fishing and forestry. These estimates are related neither to the agriculture nor to the rural population.

(6) Female labour force as percentage of total agriculture labour force: is that part (female) of the total labour force engaged or seeking work in agriculture, hunting, fishing and forestry.

(7) For the following countries the source is: World Urbanization Prospects: The 2007 Revision
American Samoa, Andorra, Anguilla, Antigua and Barbuda, Aruba, Bermuda,Cayman Islands, Cook Islands, Dominica, Faeroe Islands, Falkland Islands (Malvinas), Gibraltar, Greenland, Grenada, Kiribati, Liechtenstein, Marshall Islands, Monaco, Montserrat, Nauru, Niue, Northern Mariana Islands, Palau, Saint Helena, Saint Kitts and Nevis, Saint-Pierre-et-Miquelon, San Marino, Seychelles, Turks and Caicos Islands, Tuvalu.

(8) National source.

Sources :
- ONU DAES Division de la population, *World Population Prospects: The 2006 Revision*
- ONU DAES Division de la population, *World Urbanization Prospects: The 2007 Revision*
- BIT, base de données en ligne
- FAO, base de données en ligne

Notes :
(1) Population totale : de facto la population dans un pays ou région au 1er juillet de l'année indiquée.

(2) Population urbaine en pourcentage de la population totale : la population au 1er juillet vivant dans une région classée comme urbaine selon les critères définis par une région ou un pays.

(3) Main-d'œuvre totale : toutes les personnes (hommes et femmes) de 15 ans et plus.

(4) Main-d'œuvre féminine en pourcentage de la main d'œuvre totale : toutes les personnes de sexe féminin de 15 ans et plus.

(5) Main-d'œuvre totale en agriculture : la part (hommes et femmes) du total de la main d'œuvre qui travaille ou cherche du travail dans l'agriculture, la chasse, la pêche et la sylviculture. Ces estimations ne sont reliées ni à l'agriculture ni à la population rurale.

(6) Main-d'œuvre totale féminine en pourcentage du total de la main-d'œuvre en agriculture : la part (femmes) du total de la main d'œuvre qui travaille ou cherche du travail dans l'agriculture, la chasse, la pêche et la sylviculture.

(7) Pour les pays suivants la source est : World Urbanization Prospects : The 2007 Revision
Samoa américaines, Andorre, Anguilla, Antigua-et-Barbuda, Aruba, Bermudes, Îles Caïmanes, Îles Cook, Dominique, Îles Féroé, Îles Falkland (Malouines), Gibraltar, Groenland, Grenade, Kiribati, Liechtenstein, Îles Marshall, Monaco, France, Montserrat, Nioué, Îles Mariannes septentrionales, Palaos, Sainte-Hélène, Saint-Kitts et-Nevis, Saint-Pierre-et-Miquelon, Saint-Marin, Seychelles, Îles Turques et Caïques, Tuvalu.

(8) Sources nationales.

Economic grouping Groupements économiques	Year Année	Population		Total labour force Main d'œuvre totale		Agriculture labour force Main d'œuvre dans l'agriculture	
		Total (thousands) Total (milliers)	Urban population (% of total population) Population urbaine (en % de la population totale)	Total (thousands) Total (milliers)	Female labour (% of total labour force) Main d'œuvre féminine (en % de la main d'œuvre totale)	Total (thousands) Total (milliers)	Female labour (% of total agriculture labour force) Main d'œuvre féminine (en % de la main d'œuvre totale dans l'agriculture)
		(1)	(2)	(3)	(4)	(5)	(6)
DEVELOPING ECONOMIES - **ÉCONOMIES EN DÉVELOPPEMENT**	**1990**	**4 068 994**	**35.0**	**1 788 670**	**38.4**	**1 163 858**	**42.9**
	2000	**4 846 278**	**40.2**	**2 173 688**	**38.4**	**1 277 573**	**43.9**
	2005	**5 211 595**	**42.8**	**2 383 899**	**38.6**	**1 319 816**	**44.3**
	2007	**5 358 921**	**43.8**	**2 469 498**	**38.7**	**..**	**..**
Developing economies excluding China - Économies en développement sans la Chine	1990	2 940 204	37.7	1 127 222	34.6	670 734	39.7
	2000	3 598 501	41.5	1 427 973	35.1	766 663	41.4
	2005	3 921 346	43.4	1 601 117	35.7	810 601	42.1
	2007	4 053 193	44.1	1 673 030	35.9	..	..
Developing economies excluding LDCs - Économies en développement sans les PMA	1990	3 543 877	37.1	1 582 057	37.8	978 437	42.1
	2000	4 167 282	42.7	1 908 076	37.8	1 053 876	43.0
	2005	4 445 286	45.6	2 081 203	38.0	1 075 031	43.3
	2007	4 555 001	46.7	2 150 265	38.1	..	..
High-income developing countries - Pays en développement à revenu élevé	1990	258 702	77.9	91 610	31.9	17 412	18.1
	2000	302 830	81.2	118 899	34.6	16 119	16.9
	2005	320 325	82.5	132 944	36.3	15 198	16.3
	2007	327 574	83.0	138 166	37.0	..	..
Middle-income developing countries - Pays en développement à revenu intermédiaire	1990	630 318	57.4	240 329	33.8	88 895	36.1
	2000	748 302	62.3	310 849	36.2	92 827	39.8
	2005	802 301	64.7	348 906	37.3	92 465	41.6
	2007	824 049	65.6	363 547	37.8	..	..
Low-income developing countries - Pays en développement à revenu faible	1990	3 179 754	27.3	1 456 632	39.6	1 057 517	43.9
	2000	3 794 831	32.8	1 743 805	39.1	1 168 586	44.6
	2005	4 088 528	35.6	1 901 894	39.0	1 212 108	44.8
	2007	4 206 818	36.8	1 967 613	38.9	..	..
Heavily indebted poor countries - Pays pauvres très endettés	1990	390 042	23.9	146 461	43.3	137 066	46.7
	2000	519 552	27.9	194 445	43.3	168 777	47.2
	2005	591 954	29.8	222 797	43.2	186 473	47.3
	2007	623 604	30.7	235 438	43.2	..	..
Landlocked developing countries - Pays en développement sans littoral	1990	200 035	18.2	85 135	43.9	77 048	45.9
	2000	333 418	26.0	140 878	44.4	101 758	45.8
	2005	372 736	26.7	161 009	44.5	112 957	45.7
	2007	390 166	27.1	170 172	44.6	..	..
Small island developing States - Petits États insulaires en développement	1990	13 538	29.0	5 424	42.3	3 020	42.3
	2000	16 034	30.3	6 473	42.8	3 360	44.3
	2005	17 522	30.9	7 224	42.7	3 616	45.5
	2007	18 087	31.2	7 560	42.8	..	..
Least developed countries - *Pays les moins avancés*	*1990*	*525 473*	*21.0*	*206 613*	*43.1*	*185 421*	*47.4*
	2000	*679 447*	*24.7*	*265 612*	*42.5*	*223 697*	*48.3*
	2005	*766 816*	*26.7*	*302 696*	*42.3*	*244 785*	*48.5*
	2007	*804 450*	*27.6*	*319 232*	*42.3*	*..*	*..*
Africa and Haiti - Afrique et Haïti	1990	311 210	22.1	117 250	45.2	115 063	48.2
	2000	408 970	25.9	151 982	45.1	140 682	48.6
	2005	468 260	27.9	173 474	44.9	155 418	48.5
	2007	494 293	28.8	183 031	44.9	..	..
Asia - Asie	1990	211 604	19.3	88 534	40.4	69 601	45.9
	2000	267 219	22.7	112 633	39.0	82 190	47.8
	2005	294 762	24.7	127 971	38.7	88 451	48.7
	2007	306 155	25.6	134 839	38.8	..	..
Islands - Îles	1990	2 304	23.6	829	37.8	757	49.1
	2000	2 807	27.5	997	37.7	825	48.6
	2005	3 287	29.5	1 251	38.7	916	49.1
	2007	3 472	30.4	1 363	39.0	..	..

For sources and notes, see end of table.

Pour les sources et les notes, se reporter à la fin du tableau.

Economic grouping / Groupements économiques	Year / Année	Population		Total labour force / Main d'œuvre totale		Agriculture labour force / Main d'œuvre dans l'agriculture	
		Total (thousands) / Total (milliers)	Urban population (% of total population) / Population urbaine (en % de la population totale)	Total (thousands) / Total (milliers)	Female labour (% of total labour force) / Main d'œuvre féminine (en % de la main d'œuvre totale)	Total (thousands) / Total (milliers)	Female labour (% of total agriculture labour force) / Main d'œuvre féminine (en % de la main d'œuvre totale dans l'agriculture)
		(1)	(2)	(3)	(4)	(5)	(6)
Major petroleum exporters - **Principaux exportateurs de pétrole**	**1990**	**319 023**	**49.1**	**102 133**	**28.2**	**41 616**	**35.0**
	2000	**406 881**	**55.6**	**141 728**	**30.9**	**45 966**	**39.6**
	2005	**451 843**	**58.3**	**167 284**	**32.2**	**47 739**	**41.9**
	2007	**470 697**	**59.3**	**177 967**	**32.6**	**..**	**..**
Africa - Afrique	1990	164 247	38.1	55 050	33.5	28 601	38.6
	2000	212 719	46.8	72 969	33.8	31 493	41.4
	2005	238 508	50.7	83 439	33.7	32 557	42.6
	2007	249 302	52.2	88 029	33.8	..	..
America - Amérique	1990	31 226	71.5	11 398	30.7	2 141	9.1
	2000	38 009	78.4	16 701	38.1	2 091	11.0
	2005	41 110	81.1	19 923	41.4	2 017	12.1
	2007	42 331	82.0	21 198	42.3	..	..
Asia - Asie	1990	123 549	58.2	35 685	19.3	10 874	30.6
	2000	156 154	62.0	52 058	24.6	12 382	39.9
	2005	172 225	63.3	63 922	27.2	13 165	44.7
	2007	179 064	63.8	68 740	28.2	..	..
Major exporters of manufactured goods - **Principaux exportateurs d'articles manufacturés**	**1990**	**2 485 343**	**33.9**	**1 189 477**	**38.9**	**796 589**	**43.0**
	2000	**2 875 863**	**39.6**	**1 393 607**	**38.8**	**849 380**	**43.5**
	2005	**3 043 926**	**42.5**	**1 497 736**	**38.9**	**862 197**	**43.5**
	2007	**3 109 130**	**43.6**	**1 537 527**	**38.9**	**..**	**..**
America - Amérique	1990	233 524	74.0	92 345	33.6	23 714	17.7
	2000	273 895	78.8	123 687	38.7	21 949	16.9
	2005	291 097	81.3	135 266	40.3	20 442	16.3
	2007	298 326	82.1	139 560	41.0	..	..
Asia - Asie	1990	2 251 820	29.7	1 097 132	39.4	772 875	43.8
	2000	2 601 968	35.4	1 269 921	38.8	827 431	44.2
	2005	2 752 829	38.3	1 362 470	38.7	841 755	44.2
	2007	2 810 804	39.5	1 397 968	38.6	..	..
Emerging economies - Économies émergentes	**1990**	**439 605**	**68.4**	**177 092**	**36.7**	**54 398**	**30.5**
	2000	**508 787**	**72.9**	**225 390**	**39.8**	**52 346**	**30.2**
	2005	**536 997**	**75.1**	**246 540**	**41.2**	**49 727**	**29.9**
	2007	**548 412**	**75.9**	**254 468**	**41.8**	**..**	**..**
America - Amérique	1990	301 046	75.4	118 859	33.8	28 797	16.8
	2000	351 865	79.7	157 559	38.8	27 360	16.5
	2005	373 414	81.8	173 484	40.5	25 983	16.3
	2007	382 394	82.6	179 542	41.3	..	..
Asia - Asie	1990	138 559	50.4	58 233	42.6	25 601	46.0
	2000	156 921	55.3	67 831	42.1	24 986	45.3
	2005	163 583	57.2	73 056	42.7	23 744	44.7
	2007	166 018	58.0	74 926	42.9	..	..
Newly industrialized economies - **Économies nouvellement industrialisées**	**1990**	**388 336**	**41.1**	**161 138**	**39.6**	**80 670**	**39.3**
	2000	**451 490**	**50.0**	**200 708**	**39.3**	**86 632**	**40.6**
	2005	**481 270**	**54.4**	**222 223**	**39.9**	**87 369**	**41.1**
	2007	**492 811**	**56.1**	**230 793**	**40.3**	**..**	**..**
First tier - Première génération	1990	71 869	78.2	23 521	38.9	3 561	43.9
	2000	79 644	83.4	27 936	40.5	2 382	45.1
	2005	81 985	84.5	30 041	41.5	1 835	45.6
	2007	82 768	84.9	30 641	41.8	..	..
Second tier - Deuxième génération	1990	316 467	35.0	137 617	39.7	77 109	39.0
	2000	371 845	44.9	172 773	39.1	84 250	40.4
	2005	399 285	50.0	192 182	39.7	85 534	41.0
	2007	410 043	51.9	200 152	40.0	..	..

For sources and notes, see end of table.   Pour les sources et les notes, se reporter à la fin du tableau.

Economic grouping Groupements économiques	Year Année	Population		Total labour force Main d'œuvre totale		Agriculture labour force Main d'œuvre dans l'agriculture	
		Total (thousands) Total (milliers)	Urban population (% of total population) Population urbaine (en % de la population totale)	Total (thousands) Total (milliers)	Female labour (% of total labour force) Main d'œuvre féminine (en % de la main d'œuvre totale)	Total (thousands) Total (milliers)	Female labour (% of total agriculture labour force) Main d'œuvre féminine (en % de la main d'œuvre totale dans l'agriculture)
		(1)	(2)	(3)	(4)	(5)	(6)
Developing economies: Africa -	**1990**	**636 817**	**31.9**	**230 981**	**40.3**	**169 453**	**46.5**
Économies en développement : Afrique	**2000**	**820 235**	**36.2**	**301 556**	**39.7**	**202 027**	**47.6**
	2005	**921 225**	**38.3**	**340 646**	**39.6**	**218 384**	**47.8**
	2007	**964 166**	**39.2**	**357 756**	**39.6**	..	..
Northern Africa excluding Sudan -	1990	117 809	48.8	35 302	24.3	14 436	44.2
Afrique septentrionale sans le Soudan	2000	140 771	51.8	46 781	24.4	16 177	49.2
	2005	152 222	53.5	54 116	25.4	16 838	51.3
	2007	157 068	54.3	57 164	25.8	..	..
Sub-Saharan Africa - Afrique subsaharienne	1990	519 007	28.1	195 678	43.1	155 017	46.7
	2000	679 464	33.0	254 775	42.6	185 850	47.4
	2005	769 004	35.3	286 530	42.2	201 546	47.5
	2007	807 098	36.2	300 592	42.2	..	..
Sub-Saharan Africa excluding South Africa -	1990	482 430	26.3	180 624	43.2	153 083	47.0
Afrique subsaharienne sans l'Afrique du Sud	2000	634 066	31.3	235 466	42.8	184 021	47.7
	2005	721 065	33.7	266 744	42.5	199 948	47.7
	2007	758 522	34.7	280 791	42.5	..	..
Developing economies: America -	**1990**	**439 876**	**70.8**	**171 546**	**34.1**	**44 624**	**16.9**
Économies en développement : Amérique	**2000**	**518 242**	**75.2**	**228 519**	**38.8**	**43 832**	**17.3**
	2005	**553 005**	**77.2**	**255 179**	**40.6**	**42 626**	**17.5**
	2007	**567 170**	**77.9**	**265 675**	**41.3**	..	..
Central America and Greater Carribean Islands	1990	140 103	63.7	50 699	31.9	16 232	15.0
excluding Puerto Rico - Amérique centrale et	2000	166 634	66.9	66 556	34.3	16 765	15.5
Grandes Antilles sans Porto Rico	2005	176 484	68.3	73 487	35.9	16 744	15.7
	2007	180 893	68.9	76 407	36.6	..	..
Central America and Greater Carribean Islands	1990	56 100	50.6	20 784	33.7	7 759	17.4
excluding Mexico and Puerto Rico -	2000	66 900	55.3	26 256	35.4	8 081	18.6
Amérique centrale et Grandes Antilles sans	2005	72 217	57.2	29 599	36.8	8 235	19.1
le Mexique et Porto Rico	2007	74 358	57.9	31 053	37.5	..	..
South America and Central America -	1990	409 802	72.1	159 664	33.8	40 690	16.0
Amérique du Sud et Amérique centrale	2000	484 266	76.4	214 375	38.8	39 926	16.3
	2005	517 262	78.5	239 914	40.7	38 748	16.4
	2007	530 758	79.2	249 926	41.5	..	..
South America excluding Brazil -	1990	147 556	74.2	57 466	34.8	12 992	15.2
Amérique du Sud sans le Brésil	2000	174 519	77.6	77 441	39.9	13 650	17.2
	2005	186 656	79.2	89 107	42.3	13 800	18.3
	2007	191 413	79.8	93 829	43.1	..	..
Developing economies: Asia -	**1990**	**2 985 852**	**30.4**	**1 383 595**	**38.6**	**947 770**	**43.5**
Économies en développement : Asie	**2000**	**3 499 689**	**36.0**	**1 640 396**	**38.1**	**1 029 359**	**44.3**
	2005	**3 728 361**	**38.8**	**1 784 419**	**38.1**	**1 056 243**	**44.6**
	2007	**3 818 239**	**40.0**	**1 842 217**	**38.1**	..	..
Eastern and South-Eastern Asia excluding China -	1990	532 158	37.1	229 504	41.5	129 562	42.8
Asie orientale et Asie du Sud-Est sans la Chine	2000	621 480	44.4	285 232	41.3	143 045	43.7
	2005	661 996	48.1	316 175	41.8	147 471	44.0
	2007	677 732	49.6	328 703	42.0	..	..
Southern Asia excluding India -	1990	332 363	28.8	120 026	31.3	76 281	40.5
Asie méridionale sans l'Inde	2000	414 622	32.2	154 595	31.7	89 843	44.5
	2005	452 996	33.8	179 807	32.7	97 143	46.4
	2007	469 380	34.6	191 107	33.2	..	..

For sources and notes, see end of table.

Pour les sources et les notes, se reporter à la fin du tableau.

8.4.2 Population and labour force of economic groupings

8.4.2 Population et main-d'œuvre des groupements économiques

Sources:
- UN DESA Population Division, World Population Prospects: The 2006 Revision
- UN DESA Population Division, World Urbanization Prospects: The 2007 Revision
- ILO, online database
- FAO, online database

Notes:

(1) Total population: de facto population in a country, area or region as of 1 July of the year indicated. Figures are presented in thousands.

(2) Urban population as percentage of total population: population living in areas classified as urban according to the criteria used by each area or country. Data refer to 1st July of the year indicated.

(3) Total labour force: comprises all persons (both sexes) of age 15 and over.

(4) Female labour force as percentage of total labour force: comprises all persons of sex feminine of age 15 and over.

(5) Total labour force in agriculture: is that part (male and female) of the total labour force engaged in or seeking work agriculture, hunting, fishing and forestry. These estimates are related neither to the agriculture nor to the rural population.

(6) Female labour force as percentage of total agriculture labour force: is that part (female) of the total labour force engaged or seeking work in agriculture, hunting, fishing and forestry.

Sources :
- ONU DAES Division de la population, World Population Prospects: The 2006 Revision
- ONU DAES Division de la population, World Urbanization Prospects: The 2007 Revision
- BIT, base de données en ligne
- FAO, base de données en ligne

Notes :

(1) Population totale : de facto la population dans un pays ou région au 1er juillet de l'année indiquée.

(2) Population urbaine en pourcentage de la population totale : la population au 1er juillet vivant dans une région classée comme urbaine selon les critères définis par une région ou un pays.

(3) Main-d'œuvre totale : toutes les personnes (hommes et femmes) de 15 ans et plus.

(4) Main-d'œuvre féminine en pourcentage de la main d'œuvre totale : toutes les personnes de sexe féminin de 15 ans et plus.

(5) Main-d'œuvre totale en agriculture : la part (hommes et femmes) du total de la main d'œuvre qui travaille ou cherche du travail dans l'agriculture, la chasse, la pêche et la sylviculture. Ces estimations ne sont reliées ni à l'agriculture ni à la population rurale.

(6) Main-d'œuvre totale féminine en pourcentage du total de la main-d'œuvre en agriculture : la part (femmes) du total de la main d'œuvre qui travaille ou cherche du travail dans l'agriculture, la chasse, la pêche et la sylviculture.

8.5.1 Demographic indicators of countries and geographical regions

8.5.1 Indicateurs démographiques des pays et des régions géographiques

Region, country or territory / Régions, pays ou territoires	Year / Année	Population growth rate / Taux d'accroissement de la population (1)	Natural increase rate per 1000 inhabitants / Taux d'évolution naturel pour 1000 habitants (2)	Net migration rate per 1000 inhabitants / Taux net de migration pour 1000 habitants (3)	Crude birth rate per 1000 inhabitants / Taux de natalité brut pour 1000 habitants (4)	Crude death rate per 1000 inhabitants / Taux de mortalité brut pour 1000 habitants (5)	Infant mortality rate per 1000 live births / Taux de mortalité infantile pour 1000 naissances vivantes (6)	Life expectancy at birth / Espérance de vie à la naissance (7)
WORLD - MONDE	**1995 - 2000**	**1.37**	**13.68**	**0.00**	**22.57**	**8.89**	**58.40**	**65**
	2000 - 2005	**1.24**	**12.36**	**0.00**	**21.12**	**8.76**	**54.32**	**65**
	2005 - 2010	**1.17**	**11.68**	**0.00**	**20.32**	**8.64**	**49.71**	**66**
DEVELOPING ECONOMIES - ÉCONOMIES EN DÉVELOPPEMENT	1995 - 2000	1.65	17.03	-0.42	25.68	8.65	63.99	62
	2000 - 2005	1.45	15.24	-0.61	23.72	8.48	59.63	63
	2005 - 2010	1.37	..	-0.48	25.03	..	54.55	65
ECONOMIES IN TRANSITION - ÉCONOMIES EN TRANSITION	1995 - 2000	-0.15	-0.48	-1.03	11.72	12.20	38.06	66
	2000 - 2005	-0.20	-1.24	-0.52	11.82	13.06	32.67	66
	2005 - 2010	-0.12	..	-0.64	12.54	..	29.95	66
DEVELOPED ECONOMIES - ÉCONOMIES DÉVELOPPÉES	1995 - 2000	0.50	2.61	2.39	11.79	9.18	6.83	77
	2000 - 2005	0.57	2.42	3.34	11.47	9.05	5.90	79
	2005 - 2010	0.46	..	2.51	11.29	..	5.47	79
Developing economies: Africa - Économies en développement : Afrique	**1995 - 2000**	**2.45**	**25.16**	**-0.37**	**39.38**	**14.22**	**98.82**	**50**
	2000 - 2005	**2.32**	**24.00**	**-0.51**	**38.14**	**14.14**	**93.03**	**49**
	2005 - 2010	**2.26**	**..**	**-0.40**	**36.61**	**..**	**86.90**	**50**
Eastern Africa - Afrique orientale	*1995 - 2000*	*2.75*	*26.98*	*0.89*	*43.12*	*16.14*	*97.23*	*46*
	2000 - 2005	*2.57*	*26.11*	*-0.09*	*41.75*	*15.64*	*89.07*	*46*
	2005 - 2010	*2.54*	*..*	*-0.23*	*39.98*	*..*	*81.54*	*47*
Burundi	1995 - 2000	1.32	25.58	-12.39	43.83	18.25	117.47	42
	2000 - 2005	3.29	27.51	5.28	44.17	16.66	105.95	43
	2005 - 2010	3.90	31.50	7.43	47.09	15.59	97.29	46
Comoros - Comores	1995 - 2000	2.82	29.99	-1.84	38.51	8.52	68.05	61
	2000 - 2005	2.65	29.09	-2.67	36.53	7.44	58.11	63
	2005 - 2010	2.46	26.88	-2.35	33.33	6.45	49.17	65
Djibouti	1995 - 2000	3.13	22.33	8.86	34.59	12.26	104.52	52
	2000 - 2005	1.94	19.42	0.00	31.40	11.98	94.86	53
	2005 - 2010	1.74	17.35	0.00	28.68	11.32	86.40	54
Eritrea - Érythrée	1995 - 2000	2.74	27.83	-0.52	39.64	11.82	75.51	52
	2000 - 2005	4.12	29.87	11.17	40.47	10.60	62.15	54
	2005 - 2010	3.24	30.10	2.23	39.28	9.18	54.95	56
Ethiopia - Éthiopie	1995 - 2000	2.81	28.29	-0.24	44.05	15.76	104.85	47
	2000 - 2005	2.59	26.25	-0.38	40.69	14.44	95.95	48
	2005 - 2010	2.51	25.28	-0.17	38.23	12.95	87.09	49
Kenya	1995 - 2000	2.65	26.56	-0.15	37.96	11.40	66.73	50
	2000 - 2005	2.61	25.86	0.15	39.11	13.25	68.48	47
	2005 - 2010	2.65	27.47	-0.99	39.24	11.77	64.30	50
Madagascar	1995 - 2000	2.98	29.81	-0.08	42.30	12.49	84.46	54
	2000 - 2005	2.83	28.26	-0.06	39.26	10.99	75.27	55
	2005 - 2010	2.66	26.66	-0.05	36.36	9.70	66.02	56
Malawi	1995 - 2000	2.83	29.79	-1.57	47.00	17.21	117.30	42
	2000 - 2005	2.58	26.28	-0.48	43.79	17.51	101.79	40
	2005 - 2010	2.57	25.91	-0.28	40.72	14.82	89.99	41
Mauritius - Maurice	1995 - 2000	1.06	10.94	-0.35	17.63	6.70	18.23	71
	2000 - 2005	0.91	9.12	0.00	15.89	6.77	15.65	72
	2005 - 2010	0.78	7.83	0.00	14.87	7.04	14.07	73
Mozambique	1995 - 2000	2.64	25.50	0.88	43.50	18.00	118.68	44
	2000 - 2005	2.42	24.36	-0.21	43.53	19.17	106.41	42
	2005 - 2010	1.95	19.66	-0.19	39.48	19.81	97.37	42
Rwanda	1995 - 2000	7.41	16.07	57.22	40.18	24.11	123.75	37
	2000 - 2005	2.43	23.31	0.99	41.74	18.43	113.10	44
	2005 - 2010	2.76	27.27	0.31	44.47	17.20	111.31	45
Seychelles	1995 - 2000	1.39	..	..	..	..	..	..
	2000 - 2005	1.06	..	..	..	..	..	..
	2005 - 2010	0.49	..	..	..	..	..	..
Somalia - Somalie	1995 - 2000	2.45	27.45	-3.01	47.73	20.28	142.59	44
	2000 - 2005	3.00	27.31	2.62	45.83	18.52	126.35	46
	2005 - 2010	2.92	26.36	2.83	42.92	16.56	116.36	49

For sources and notes, see end of table.

Pour les sources et les notes, se reporter à la fin du tableau.

8.5.1 Demographic indicators of countries and geographical regions

8.5.1 Indicateurs démographiques des pays et des régions géographiques

Region, country or territory / Régions, pays ou territoires	Year / Année	Population growth rate / Taux d'accroissement de la population	Natural increase rate per 1000 inhabitants / Taux d'évolution naturel pour 1000 habitants	Net migration rate per 1000 inhabitants / Taux net de migration pour 1000 habitants	Crude birth rate per 1000 inhabitants / Taux de natalité brut pour 1000 habitants	Crude death rate per 1000 inhabitants / Taux de mortalité brut pour 1000 habitants	Infant mortality rate per 1000 live births / Taux de mortalité infantile pour 1000 naissances vivantes	Life expectancy at birth / Espérance de vie à la naissance
		(1)	(2)	(3)	(4)	(5)	(6)	(7)
Uganda - Ouganda	1995 - 2000	3.02	30.49	-0.40	48.23	17.74	88.69	43
	2000 - 2005	3.18	31.79	-0.04	47.27	15.49	83.53	47
	2005 - 2010	3.24	33.20	-0.86	46.57	13.38	76.44	52
United Republic of Tanzania - République-Unie de Tanzanie	1995 - 2000	2.48	26.05	-1.29	41.50	15.45	90.91	48
	2000 - 2005	2.56	27.51	-1.91	42.12	14.61	78.40	46
	2005 - 2010	2.47	26.16	-1.46	39.04	12.88	72.51	47
Zambia - Zambie	1995 - 2000	2.42	22.49	1.69	43.75	21.26	105.00	39
	2000 - 2005	1.88	20.23	-1.49	41.92	21.69	101.28	37
	2005 - 2010	1.91	20.45	-1.41	39.28	18.84	93.57	39
Zimbabwe	1995 - 2000	1.42	16.61	-2.45	31.91	15.30	61.91	44
	2000 - 2005	0.72	8.35	-1.16	28.90	20.55	65.06	37
	2005 - 2010	0.95	9.98	-0.45	27.85	17.87	58.78	37
Middle Africa - Afrique centrale	*1995 - 2000*	*2.41*	*27.36*	*-3.01*	*46.73*	*19.37*	*123.10*	*43*
	2000 - 2005	*2.81*	*28.30*	*0.21*	*46.98*	*18.68*	*117.50*	*43*
	2005 - 2010	*2.83*	*..*	*0.27*	*45.98*	*..*	*110.64*	*45*
Angola	1995 - 2000	2.46	26.41	-1.83	48.99	22.58	148.50	40
	2000 - 2005	2.89	26.51	2.33	48.60	22.09	139.30	41
	2005 - 2010	2.78	26.81	0.93	47.31	20.50	131.36	42
Cameroon - Cameroun	1995 - 2000	2.41	24.10	0.00	37.89	13.79	90.46	49
	2000 - 2005	2.30	22.92	0.07	37.87	14.95	88.70	46
	2005 - 2010	2.00	20.14	-0.20	34.53	14.39	87.81	46
Central African Republic - République centrafricaine	1995 - 2000	2.27	22.01	0.62	40.02	18.01	104.31	42
	2000 - 2005	1.63	18.51	-2.24	37.92	19.41	101.90	39
	2005 - 2010	1.83	18.02	0.23	36.15	18.13	97.02	40
Chad - Tchad	1995 - 2000	3.37	31.88	1.78	47.60	15.72	122.87	45
	2000 - 2005	3.62	31.41	4.71	47.43	16.03	121.93	44
	2005 - 2010	2.88	30.09	-1.37	45.47	15.38	118.53	44
Congo	1995 - 2000	2.74	24.56	2.77	37.19	12.63	75.52	51
	2000 - 2005	2.39	24.48	-0.59	37.16	12.68	74.07	52
	2005 - 2010	2.11	23.69	-2.62	35.09	11.39	70.60	54
Dem. Rep. of the Congo - Rép. dém. du Congo	1995 - 2000	2.23	28.03	-5.74	49.17	21.14	128.55	42
	2000 - 2005	2.95	30.30	-0.87	49.57	19.27	121.49	43
	2005 - 2010	3.22	31.47	0.69	49.57	18.10	111.87	45
Equatorial Guinea - Guinée équatoriale	1995 - 2000	2.39	23.89	0.00	41.35	17.46	109.55	46
	2000 - 2005	2.34	23.40	0.00	39.77	16.37	101.14	43
	2005 - 2010	2.38	23.76	0.00	38.54	14.79	92.33	42
Gabon	1995 - 2000	2.26	20.00	2.57	30.18	10.18	59.90	58
	2000 - 2005	1.76	15.99	1.55	27.67	11.68	60.83	55
	2005 - 2010	1.48	14.04	0.75	25.75	11.71	54.90	53
Sao Tome and Principe - Sao Tomé-et-Principe	1995 - 2000	1.82	27.15	-8.95	36.02	8.87	80.79	62
	2000 - 2005	1.71	26.63	-9.56	34.87	8.24	76.76	63
	2005 - 2010	1.61	24.87	-8.81	32.40	7.53	72.79	64
Northern Africa - Afrique septentrionale	*1995 - 2000*	*1.80*	*19.84*	*-1.69*	*27.12*	*7.28*	*56.10*	*65*
	2000 - 2005	*1.66*	*18.63*	*-1.86*	*25.37*	*6.74*	*45.91*	*67*
	2005 - 2010	*1.69*	*..*	*-0.81*	*24.29*	*..*	*38.64*	*68*
Algeria - Algérie	1995 - 2000	1.53	16.20	-0.95	21.61	5.41	48.97	69
	2000 - 2005	1.48	15.71	-0.88	20.74	5.03	38.01	71
	2005 - 2010	1.51	15.87	-0.82	20.81	4.94	31.22	72
Egypt - Égypte	1995 - 2000	1.85	20.23	-1.73	26.82	6.60	49.64	68
	2000 - 2005	1.82	19.65	-1.51	25.51	5.87	36.80	70
	2005 - 2010	1.76	18.60	-1.05	24.22	5.61	29.61	71
Libyan Arab Jamahiriya - Jamahiriya arabe libyenne	1995 - 2000	2.02	19.77	0.39	23.77	4.00	24.32	72
	2000 - 2005	2.04	19.98	0.36	24.03	4.05	20.66	73
	2005 - 2010	1.97	19.33	0.32	23.40	4.08	18.20	75
Morocco - Maroc	1995 - 2000	1.35	17.04	-3.59	23.42	6.38	48.27	68
	2000 - 2005	1.13	14.96	-3.71	20.91	5.95	38.76	70
	2005 - 2010	1.20	14.70	-2.70	20.54	5.83	30.91	71

For sources and notes, see end of table.

Pour les sources et les notes, se reporter à la fin du tableau.

8

Region, country or territory Régions, pays ou territoires	Year Année	Population growth rate Taux d'accroissement de la population (1)	Natural increase rate per 1000 inhabitants Taux d'évolution naturel pour 1000 habitants (2)	Net migration rate per 1000 inhabitants Taux net de migration pour 1000 habitants (3)	Crude birth rate per 1000 inhabitants Taux de natalité brut pour 1000 habitants (4)	Crude death rate per 1000 inhabitants Taux de mortalité brut pour 1000 habitants (5)	Infant mortality rate per 1000 live births Taux de mortalité infantile pour 1000 naissances vivantes (6)	Life expectancy at birth Espérance de vie à la naissance (7)
Sudan - Soudan	1995 - 2000	2.46	25.99	-1.44	37.92	11.92	80.71	55
	2000 - 2005	2.02	23.25	-3.03	34.42	11.17	73.26	56
	2005 - 2010	2.22	21.48	0.69	31.55	10.07	65.50	57
Tunisia - Tunisie	1995 - 2000	1.27	13.07	-0.38	18.56	5.50	27.84	72
	2000 - 2005	1.10	11.60	-0.59	17.07	5.47	22.65	73
	2005 - 2010	1.08	11.16	-0.39	16.73	5.57	19.81	74
Western Sahara - Sahara occidental	1995 - 2000	3.93	20.64	18.56	28.27	7.63	65.33	61
	2000 - 2005	6.68	18.59	47.64	25.08	6.50	53.31	64
	2005 - 2010	3.72	17.51	19.57	23.34	5.83	44.01	66
Southern Africa - Afrique australe	*1995 - 2000*	*1.83*	*16.87*	*1.53*	*26.38*	*9.51*	*52.34*	*57*
	2000 - 2005	*1.10*	*10.88*	*0.20*	*24.73*	*13.85*	*53.31*	*48*
	2005 - 2010	*0.61*	*..*	*0.08*	*22.96*	*..*	*47.90*	*43*
Botswana	1995 - 2000	1.98	16.97	2.78	29.07	12.10	58.72	52
	2000 - 2005	1.20	9.77	2.24	26.04	16.28	59.33	37
	2005 - 2010	1.23	10.74	1.58	24.86	14.11	48.22	34
Lesotho	1995 - 2000	1.81	22.10	-3.99	34.03	11.93	71.74	49
	2000 - 2005	0.99	13.59	-3.72	31.27	17.68	74.06	37
	2005 - 2010	0.63	9.87	-3.58	29.04	19.17	66.42	34
Namibia - Namibie	1995 - 2000	2.52	23.35	1.82	32.71	9.36	57.63	58
	2000 - 2005	1.44	14.49	-0.10	27.41	12.93	55.35	49
	2005 - 2010	1.32	13.25	-0.10	25.68	12.43	43.95	46
South Africa - Afrique du Sud	1995 - 2000	1.79	16.14	1.78	25.34	9.21	49.84	58
	2000 - 2005	1.09	10.57	0.32	24.07	13.51	50.91	49
	2005 - 2010	0.55	5.31	0.21	22.34	17.04	46.30	44
Swaziland	1995 - 2000	1.98	22.13	-2.38	33.32	11.20	80.46	45
	2000 - 2005	1.22	13.26	-1.10	30.42	17.16	85.12	33
	2005 - 2010	0.63	7.34	-1.05	28.54	21.20	74.02	30
Western Africa - Afrique occidentale	*1995 - 2000*	*2.77*	*28.15*	*-0.09*	*44.44*	*16.29*	*115.66*	*47*
	2000 - 2005	*2.58*	*26.58*	*-0.46*	*42.60*	*16.01*	*111.06*	*46*
	2005 - 2010	*2.41*	*..*	*-0.69*	*40.18*	*..*	*105.65*	*47*
Benin - Bénin	1995 - 2000	3.04	31.20	-0.87	44.04	12.84	109.75	54
	2000 - 2005	3.22	29.63	2.52	42.20	12.57	104.97	54
	2005 - 2010	3.02	29.02	1.09	40.18	11.16	97.90	56
Burkina Faso	1995 - 2000	2.91	31.26	-2.18	47.70	16.44	114.95	46
	2000 - 2005	3.19	30.24	1.55	45.93	15.69	109.30	47
	2005 - 2010	2.89	29.68	-0.87	44.03	14.35	103.79	49
Cape Verde - Cap-Vert	1995 - 2000	2.33	25.59	-2.35	31.67	6.08	36.78	69
	2000 - 2005	2.35	25.57	-2.09	30.89	5.32	29.70	70
	2005 - 2010	2.23	24.17	-1.86	28.91	4.73	25.00	72
Côte d'Ivoire	1995 - 2000	2.58	23.58	2.19	39.28	15.70	117.79	47
	2000 - 2005	1.73	21.04	-3.80	37.53	16.49	120.16	46
	2005 - 2010	1.84	19.87	-1.49	35.29	15.43	117.55	46
Gambia - Gambie	1995 - 2000	3.55	28.29	7.08	40.62	12.33	83.92	54
	2000 - 2005	3.11	26.89	4.15	38.09	11.20	79.48	55
	2005 - 2010	2.63	24.58	1.73	34.94	10.36	74.43	58
Ghana	1995 - 2000	2.38	24.31	-0.54	34.27	9.95	67.99	57
	2000 - 2005	2.24	22.27	0.11	32.25	9.98	62.99	57
	2005 - 2010	1.99	20.30	-0.43	29.63	9.34	57.35	58
Guinea - Guinée	1995 - 2000	2.27	28.50	-5.85	43.65	15.15	124.37	52
	2000 - 2005	1.86	28.48	-9.88	41.99	13.51	113.63	54
	2005 - 2010	2.16	27.85	-6.31	39.78	11.93	103.20	54
Guinea-Bissau - Guinée-Bissau	1995 - 2000	2.80	29.67	-1.67	50.10	20.43	129.30	44
	2000 - 2005	3.06	30.37	0.16	49.88	19.52	120.57	45
	2005 - 2010	2.98	31.15	-1.43	49.59	18.45	111.61	45
Liberia - Libéria	1995 - 2000	7.19	28.58	42.58	49.74	21.16	155.23	42
	2000 - 2005	2.28	30.06	-7.29	49.87	19.81	139.34	42
	2005 - 2010	4.50	31.28	13.55	49.56	18.27	131.60	43

For sources and notes, see end of table.

Pour les sources et les notes, se reporter à la fin du tableau.

Region, country or territory / Régions, pays ou territoires	Year / Année	Population growth rate / Taux d'accroissement de la population (1)	Natural increase rate per 1000 inhabitants / Taux d'évolution naturel pour 1000 habitants (2)	Net migration rate per 1000 inhabitants / Taux net de migration pour 1000 habitants (3)	Crude birth rate per 1000 inhabitants / Taux de natalité brut pour 1000 habitants (4)	Crude death rate per 1000 inhabitants / Taux de mortalité brut pour 1000 habitants (5)	Infant mortality rate per 1000 live births / Taux de mortalité infantile pour 1000 naissances vivantes (6)	Life expectancy at birth / Espérance de vie à la naissance (7)
Mali	1995 - 2000	2.71	33.13	-6.06	51.19	18.06	145.73	47
	2000 - 2005	2.98	32.22	-2.43	48.59	16.37	138.40	48
	2005 - 2010	3.02	33.39	-3.21	48.10	14.71	127.24	49
Mauritania - Mauritanie	1995 - 2000	2.85	27.61	0.83	37.23	9.62	74.59	50
	2000 - 2005	2.88	26.55	2.17	35.28	8.74	68.00	52
	2005 - 2010	2.53	24.65	0.63	32.50	7.85	63.12	54
Niger	1995 - 2000	3.61	35.54	0.47	53.82	18.28	149.29	43
	2000 - 2005	3.52	35.57	-0.47	51.16	15.59	121.72	44
	2005 - 2010	3.49	35.18	-0.39	48.96	13.78	109.02	45
Nigeria - Nigéria	1995 - 2000	2.70	27.13	-0.16	44.49	17.36	116.18	45
	2000 - 2005	2.50	25.18	-0.26	42.67	17.48	114.47	43
	2005 - 2010	2.27	23.03	-0.40	39.88	16.84	109.82	44
Saint Helena - Sainte-Hélène	1995 - 2000	2.73	..	..	..	..	..	..
	2000 - 2005	1.46	..	..	..	..	..	..
	2005 - 2010	1.23	..	..	..	..	..	..
Senegal - Sénégal	1995 - 2000	2.64	28.46	-2.06	39.01	10.55	77.71	55
	2000 - 2005	2.60	27.81	-1.81	37.60	9.79	69.31	56
	2005 - 2010	2.46	26.17	-1.60	35.18	9.01	65.40	57
Sierra Leone	1995 - 2000	1.75	22.57	-5.08	47.09	24.52	174.74	40
	2000 - 2005	4.23	23.45	18.69	46.93	23.47	162.82	41
	2005 - 2010	2.04	24.10	-3.76	46.16	22.05	158.38	42
Togo	1995 - 2000	3.59	30.63	5.15	41.33	10.70	96.19	56
	2000 - 2005	2.88	28.83	-0.12	39.64	10.81	92.90	54
	2005 - 2010	2.65	26.62	-0.16	36.75	10.14	88.75	56
Developing economies: America - Économies en développement : Amérique	**1995 - 2000**	**1.56**	**17.31**	**-1.56**	**23.44**	**6.13**	**32.22**	**70**
	2000 - 2005	**1.30**	**15.62**	**-2.56**	**21.65**	**6.03**	**26.23**	**71**
	2005 - 2010	**1.25**	**..**	**-1.49**	**20.03**	**..**	**21.99**	**73**
Caribbean - Caraïbes	*1995 - 2000*	*1.14*	*14.62*	*-3.32*	*22.43*	*7.81*	*42.91*	*66*
	2000 - 2005	*1.01*	*13.16*	*-3.10*	*21.01*	*7.85*	*35.66*	*66*
	2005 - 2010	*0.90*	*..*	*-3.12*	*19.58*	*..*	*31.12*	*68*
Anguilla	1995 - 2000	1.71	..	..	..	..	..	..
	2000 - 2005	1.74	..	..	..	..	..	..
	2005 - 2010	1.41	..	..	..	..	..	..
Antigua and Barbuda - Antigua-et-Barbuda	1995 - 2000	2.44	..	..	..	..	..	..
	2000 - 2005	1.57	..	..	..	..	..	..
	2005 - 2010	1.16	..	..	..	..	..	..
Aruba	1995 - 2000	1.67	10.68	6.03	17.71	7.03	19.02	..
	2000 - 2005	2.61	9.29	16.72	16.19	6.91	18.92	..
	2005 - 2010	0.01	7.01	-6.93	14.08	7.08	17.39	..
Bahamas	1995 - 2000	1.56	14.24	1.37	21.30	7.07	17.99	68
	2000 - 2005	1.29	11.59	1.28	18.12	6.53	15.79	69
	2005 - 2010	1.20	10.80	1.20	16.90	6.10	13.78	72
Barbados - Barbade	1995 - 2000	0.46	5.48	-0.88	13.00	7.52	13.69	75
	2000 - 2005	0.38	4.67	-0.86	11.93	7.27	12.46	75
	2005 - 2010	0.32	4.02	-0.85	11.04	7.03	10.40	76
British Virgin Islands - Îles Vierges britanniques	1995 - 2000	2.12	..	..	..	..	..	..
	2000 - 2005	1.41	..	..	..	..	..	..
	2005 - 2010	1.13	..	..	..	..	..	..
Cayman Islands - Îles Caïmanes	1995 - 2000	4.04	..	..	..	..	..	..
	2000 - 2005	2.50	..	..	..	..	..	..
	2005 - 2010	1.51	..	..	..	..	..	..
Cuba	1995 - 2000	0.38	6.04	-2.19	13.06	7.02	10.68	76
	2000 - 2005	0.21	4.40	-2.30	11.98	7.58	6.47	77
	2005 - 2010	-0.01	2.77	-2.81	10.33	7.56	5.24	79
Dominica - Dominique	1995 - 2000	-0.08	..	..	..	..	..	..
	2000 - 2005	-0.18	..	..	..	..	..	..
	2005 - 2010	-0.29	..	..	..	..	..	..

For sources and notes, see end of table.

Pour les sources et les notes, se reporter à la fin du tableau.

455

Region, country or territory / Régions, pays ou territoires	Year / Année	Population growth rate / Taux d'accroissement de la population (1)	Natural increase rate per 1000 inhabitants / Taux d'évolution naturel pour 1000 habitants (2)	Net migration rate per 1000 inhabitants / Taux net de migration pour 1000 habitants (3)	Crude birth rate per 1000 inhabitants / Taux de natalité brut pour 1000 habitants (4)	Crude death rate per 1000 inhabitants / Taux de mortalité brut pour 1000 habitants (5)	Infant mortality rate per 1000 live births / Taux de mortalité infantile pour 1000 naissances vivantes (6)	Life expectancy at birth / Espérance de vie à la naissance (7)
Dominican Republic - République dominicaine	1995 - 2000	1.75	20.77	-3.33	26.74	5.97	41.35	67
	2000 - 2005	1.59	19.18	-3.24	25.22	6.05	35.49	67
	2005 - 2010	1.47	17.53	-2.85	23.47	5.94	30.09	69
Grenada - Grenade	1995 - 2000	0.42	11.97	-7.78	21.12	9.15	40.79	..
	2000 - 2005	0.94	9.64	-0.25	18.41	8.77	38.66	..
	2005 - 2010	0.02	9.66	-9.50	17.97	8.31	34.15	..
Haiti - Haïti	1995 - 2000	1.80	21.28	-3.31	32.66	11.37	71.52	50
	2000 - 2005	1.62	19.34	-3.14	29.80	10.47	58.00	51
	2005 - 2010	1.58	18.68	-2.89	27.92	9.24	49.15	53
Jamaica - Jamaïque	1995 - 2000	0.82	16.07	-7.88	22.88	6.81	15.33	72
	2000 - 2005	0.71	14.68	-7.59	21.79	7.12	14.60	71
	2005 - 2010	0.54	12.75	-7.36	19.88	7.13	13.83	71
Montserrat	1995 - 2000	-14.49	..	..	..	..	..	..
	2000 - 2005	2.54	..	..	..	..	..	..
	2005 - 2010	1.15	..	..	..	..	..	..
Netherlands Antilles - Antilles néerlandaises	1995 - 2000	-1.08	9.39	-20.16	16.34	6.95	15.82	75
	2000 - 2005	0.62	6.99	-0.75	14.51	7.52	15.24	76
	2005 - 2010	1.33	4.57	8.76	12.46	7.89	14.91	77
Saint Kitts and Nevis - Saint-Kitts-et-Nevis	1995 - 2000	1.33	..	..	..	..	..	..
	2000 - 2005	1.30	..	..	..	..	..	..
	2005 - 2010	1.27	..	..	..	..	..	..
Saint Lucia - Sainte-Lucie	1995 - 2000	0.88	12.39	-3.57	19.45	7.06	16.93	72
	2000 - 2005	1.09	12.16	-1.27	19.12	6.96	14.80	72
	2005 - 2010	1.12	12.41	-1.21	19.05	6.64	12.66	73
Saint Vincent and the Grenadines - Saint-Vincent-et-les Grenadines	1995 - 2000	0.52	13.93	-8.74	20.76	6.83	28.79	70
	2000 - 2005	0.54	13.93	-8.51	20.83	6.90	26.54	71
	2005 - 2010	0.50	13.30	-8.29	20.08	6.78	23.78	72
Trinidad and Tobago - Trinité-et-Tobago	1995 - 2000	0.48	7.86	-3.11	14.99	7.12	16.02	71
	2000 - 2005	0.35	6.58	-3.05	14.46	7.88	15.19	70
	2005 - 2010	0.37	6.68	-2.99	14.82	8.14	12.68	70
Turks and Caicos Islands - Îles Turques et Caïques	1995 - 2000	4.16	..	..	..	..	..	..
	2000 - 2005	5.19	..	..	..	..	..	..
	2005 - 2010	1.37	..	..	..	..	..	..
United States Virgin Islands - Îles Vierges américaines	1995 - 2000	0.65	11.92	-5.45	17.15	5.24	12.12	77
	2000 - 2005	0.16	8.86	-7.21	14.61	5.75	9.63	78
	2005 - 2010	-0.03	6.86	-7.19	13.43	6.57	8.69	79
Central America - Amérique centrale	*1995 - 2000*	*1.78*	*20.80*	*-2.89*	*25.86*	*5.06*	*30.92*	*72*
	2000 - 2005	*1.17*	*18.55*	*-6.76*	*23.50*	*4.95*	*24.62*	*74*
	2005 - 2010	*1.33*	*..*	*-3.21*	*21.55*	*..*	*20.00*	*75*
Belize	1995 - 2000	2.67	27.51	-0.87	31.65	4.14	23.67	73
	2000 - 2005	2.38	24.52	-0.77	28.29	3.78	18.97	72
	2005 - 2010	2.08	21.43	-0.69	25.19	3.76	16.61	72
Costa Rica	1995 - 2000	2.46	17.63	6.89	21.45	3.81	12.14	77
	2000 - 2005	1.93	15.23	4.07	19.11	3.88	10.60	78
	2005 - 2010	1.50	13.70	1.33	17.77	4.07	9.87	79
El Salvador	1995 - 2000	1.91	21.63	-2.57	27.62	5.99	32.51	70
	2000 - 2005	1.47	19.16	-4.45	25.08	5.92	26.92	71
	2005 - 2010	1.37	16.95	-3.24	22.83	5.88	22.06	72
Guatemala	1995 - 2000	2.31	30.44	-7.35	37.34	6.90	46.18	65
	2000 - 2005	2.48	29.75	-5.01	35.78	6.03	38.73	67
	2005 - 2010	2.47	27.58	-2.95	33.25	5.67	30.85	68
Honduras	1995 - 2000	2.13	27.37	-6.12	33.52	6.15	36.27	67
	2000 - 2005	1.96	24.21	-4.61	30.16	5.95	31.90	68
	2005 - 2010	1.95	22.26	-2.78	27.88	5.63	28.44	69
Mexico - Mexique	1995 - 2000	1.65	19.02	-2.50	23.72	4.71	28.27	74
	2000 - 2005	0.89	16.70	-7.81	21.41	4.71	21.52	75
	2005 - 2010	1.12	14.59	-3.36	19.35	4.75	17.01	76

For sources and notes, see end of table.

Pour les sources et les notes, se reporter à la fin du tableau.

Region, country or territory Régions, pays ou territoires	Year Année	Population growth rate Taux d'accroissement de la population	Natural increase rate per 1000 inhabitants Taux d'évolution naturel pour 1000 habitants	Net migration rate per 1000 inhabitants Taux net de migration pour 1000 habitants	Crude birth rate per 1000 inhabitants Taux de natalité brut pour 1000 habitants	Crude death rate per 1000 inhabitants Taux de mortalité brut pour 1000 habitants	Infant mortality rate per 1000 live births Taux de mortalité infantile pour 1000 naissances vivantes	Life expectancy at birth Espérance de vie à la naissance
		(1)	(2)	(3)	(4)	(5)	(6)	(7)
Nicaragua	1995 - 2000	1.82	24.73	-6.55	30.24	5.50	35.51	68
	2000 - 2005	1.34	21.35	-7.95	26.32	4.96	27.11	70
	2005 - 2010	1.31	20.17	-7.08	24.86	4.69	21.82	71
Panama	1995 - 2000	1.99	19.11	0.78	24.12	5.01	23.85	74
	2000 - 2005	1.82	17.70	0.52	22.68	4.98	20.89	75
	2005 - 2010	1.65	15.80	0.65	20.82	5.02	18.39	76
South America - Amérique du Sud	*1995 - 2000*	*1.52*	*16.22*	*-0.87*	*22.60*	*6.38*	*31.75*	*70*
	2000 - 2005	*1.37*	*14.72*	*-0.89*	*21.00*	*6.28*	*26.01*	*71*
	2005 - 2010	*1.25*	*..*	*-0.68*	*19.49*	*..*	*21.96*	*73*
Argentina - Argentine	1995 - 2000	1.15	12.05	-0.56	19.73	7.68	21.72	73
	2000 - 2005	0.98	10.32	-0.53	18.02	7.70	16.31	74
	2005 - 2010	1.00	9.87	0.15	17.52	7.66	13.27	75
Bolivia - Bolivie	1995 - 2000	2.12	23.67	-2.53	32.59	8.92	67.22	62
	2000 - 2005	1.98	22.07	-2.29	30.25	8.18	56.52	64
	2005 - 2010	1.77	19.76	-2.08	27.35	7.59	46.73	66
Brazil - Brésil	1995 - 2000	1.50	15.20	-0.25	21.59	6.39	34.60	69
	2000 - 2005	1.41	14.29	-0.25	20.62	6.33	27.96	70
	2005 - 2010	1.26	12.84	-0.24	19.17	6.33	23.86	72
Chile - Chili	1995 - 2000	1.37	12.84	0.81	18.02	5.18	11.78	76
	2000 - 2005	1.12	10.77	0.38	15.73	4.97	8.60	78
	2005 - 2010	1.00	9.68	0.36	15.04	5.36	7.11	79
Colombia - Colombie	1995 - 2000	1.71	17.88	-0.75	23.63	5.74	24.17	71
	2000 - 2005	1.51	15.62	-0.55	21.19	5.57	20.98	72
	2005 - 2010	1.27	13.20	-0.52	18.73	5.53	19.19	73
Ecuador - Équateur	1995 - 2000	1.54	20.41	-5.06	25.60	5.20	34.14	72
	2000 - 2005	1.19	18.22	-6.31	23.19	4.97	25.94	74
	2005 - 2010	1.07	15.86	-5.22	20.99	5.13	21.37	75
Falkland Islands (Malvinas) - Îles Falkland (Malvinas)	1995 - 2000	3.34	..	..	..	..	..	..
	2000 - 2005	0.52	..	..	..	..	..	..
	2005 - 2010	0.59	..	..	..	..	..	..
Guyana	1995 - 2000	-0.12	15.05	-16.29	24.20	9.15	57.71	60
	2000 - 2005	0.14	12.23	-10.86	21.34	9.10	51.16	63
	2005 - 2010	-0.22	8.66	-10.88	17.05	8.39	44.98	65
Paraguay	1995 - 2000	2.17	23.39	-1.69	29.26	5.88	39.47	70
	2000 - 2005	1.97	21.31	-1.58	26.92	5.61	35.82	71
	2005 - 2010	1.80	19.28	-1.29	24.82	5.54	32.34	72
Peru - Pérou	1995 - 2000	1.46	18.99	-4.41	25.37	6.38	39.50	68
	2000 - 2005	1.22	16.03	-3.85	22.19	6.15	31.24	70
	2005 - 2010	1.15	14.74	-3.21	20.87	6.13	22.36	71
Suriname	1995 - 2000	0.96	17.15	-7.51	23.68	6.53	33.00	68
	2000 - 2005	0.72	14.41	-7.20	21.20	6.79	32.32	69
	2005 - 2010	0.56	12.56	-6.97	19.49	6.94	28.48	70
Uruguay	1995 - 2000	0.61	7.71	-1.59	16.95	9.24	16.41	74
	2000 - 2005	0.05	6.71	-6.26	16.02	9.30	14.38	75
	2005 - 2010	0.29	5.84	-2.99	15.09	9.25	13.27	76
Venezuela (Bolivarian Rep. of) - Venezuela (Rép. bolivarienne du)	1995 - 2000	2.00	19.66	0.34	24.49	4.83	20.89	72
	2000 - 2005	1.82	17.86	0.31	22.87	5.01	18.95	73
	2005 - 2010	1.67	16.35	0.29	21.44	5.09	17.15	74
Developing economies: Asia - Économies en développement : Asie	**1995 - 2000**	**1.48**	**15.12**	**-0.26**	**22.88**	**7.76**	**55.16**	**65**
	2000 - 2005	**1.27**	**13.07**	**-0.34**	**20.57**	**7.49**	**50.03**	**67**
	2005 - 2010	**1.17**	**..**	**-0.33**	**22.50**	**..**	**44.12**	**68**
Eastern Asia - Asie orientale	*1995 - 2000*	*0.91*	*9.28*	*-0.18*	*15.99*	*6.71*	*28.08*	*71*
	2000 - 2005	*0.66*	*6.87*	*-0.25*	*13.54*	*6.66*	*26.33*	*72*
	2005 - 2010	*0.57*	*..*	*-0.34*	*20.73*	*..*	*23.14*	*74*
China - Chine	1995 - 2000	(b)0.91	(b)9.27	(b)-0.22	(b)15.98	(b)6.71	(b)28.26	(b)70
	2000 - 2005	(b)0.67	(b)6.96	(b)-0.29	(b)13.60	(b)6.65	(b)26.45	(b)71
	2005 - 2010	(b)0.58	(b)6.05	(b)-0.26	(b)13.11	(b)7.06	(b)23.18	(b)73

For sources and notes, see end of table.

Pour les sources et les notes, se reporter à la fin du tableau.

Region, country or territory / Régions, pays ou territoires	Year / Année	Population growth rate / Taux d'accroissement de la population (1)	Natural increase rate per 1000 inhabitants / Taux d'évolution naturel pour 1000 habitants (2)	Net migration rate per 1000 inhabitants / Taux net de migration pour 1000 habitants (3)	Crude birth rate per 1000 inhabitants / Taux de natalité brut pour 1000 habitants (4)	Crude death rate per 1000 inhabitants / Taux de mortalité brut pour 1000 habitants (5)	Infant mortality rate per 1000 live births / Taux de mortalité infantile pour 1000 naissances vivantes (6)	Life expectancy at birth / Espérance de vie à la naissance (7)
China, Hong Kong SAR - Chine (RAS de Hong Kong)	1995 - 2000	1.42	4.86	9.33	9.98	5.13	4.22	80
	2000 - 2005	1.15	2.78	8.75	8.08	5.30	3.89	82
	2005 - 2010	1.00	1.71	8.29	7.59	5.87	3.66	82
China, Macao SAR - Chine (RAS de Macao)	1995 - 2000	1.38	6.68	7.13	10.90	4.22	9.21	79
	2000 - 2005	1.40	3.08	10.94	7.38	4.31	8.12	80
	2005 - 2010	0.70	2.85	4.15	7.54	4.69	6.88	81
China, Taiwan Province of - Province chinoise de Taiwan (8)	1995 - 2000	0.84	..	..	..	..	..	..
	2000 - 2005	0.49	..	..	..	..	..	..
Dem. People's Rep. of Korea - Rép. populaire dém. de Corée	1995 - 2000	1.10	11.03	0.00	18.95	7.92	47.80	63
	2000 - 2005	0.58	5.75	0.00	15.07	9.32	51.22	63
	2005 - 2010	0.34	3.36	0.00	13.24	9.89	49.14	64
Mongolia - Mongolie	1995 - 2000	0.66	14.01	-7.41	21.21	7.20	54.97	62
	2000 - 2005	0.88	12.77	-3.96	19.65	6.89	43.80	64
	2005 - 2010	0.96	11.83	-2.27	18.38	6.55	40.53	66
Republic of Korea - République de Corée	1995 - 2000	0.77	8.07	-0.35	13.53	5.46	9.31	75
	2000 - 2005	0.46	4.94	-0.34	10.39	5.45	5.31	77
	2005 - 2010	0.33	3.45	-0.12	9.30	5.85	4.07	78
Southern Asia - Asie méridionale	*1995 - 2000*	*1.89*	*19.49*	*-0.46*	*28.64*	*9.15*	*73.75*	*65*
	2000 - 2005	*1.66*	*17.24*	*-0.49*	*25.91*	*8.67*	*66.40*	*66*
	2005 - 2010	*1.55*	*..*	*-0.32*	*24.09*	*..*	*59.03*	*68*
Afghanistan	1995 - 2000	2.55	29.53	-4.07	51.96	22.43	165.62	46
	2000 - 2005	3.79	28.10	9.71	49.75	21.64	167.08	46
	2005 - 2010	3.85	28.30	10.08	48.22	19.92	155.88	48
Bangladesh	1995 - 2000	1.98	20.23	-0.45	29.44	9.21	75.54	60
	2000 - 2005	1.89	19.61	-0.68	27.80	8.20	61.69	63
	2005 - 2010	1.67	17.33	-0.63	24.83	7.50	53.62	65
Bhutan - Bhoutan	1995 - 2000	1.94	19.29	0.05	29.28	9.99	73.34	60
	2000 - 2005	2.63	14.54	11.70	22.37	7.83	55.49	63
	2005 - 2010	1.43	11.28	3.03	18.48	7.20	46.08	65
India - Inde	1995 - 2000	1.84	18.67	-0.28	27.72	9.06	70.49	61
	2000 - 2005	1.62	16.42	-0.25	25.14	8.72	63.20	63
	2005 - 2010	1.46	14.79	-0.21	23.00	8.21	55.84	65
Iran (Islamic Rep. of) - Iran (Rép. islamique d')	1995 - 2000	1.22	13.89	-1.66	19.52	5.63	48.40	68
	2000 - 2005	0.97	13.41	-3.69	18.96	5.54	36.82	70
	2005 - 2010	1.35	14.91	-1.39	20.35	5.44	30.74	72
Maldives	1995 - 2000	1.93	19.30	0.00	26.58	7.28	57.71	64
	2000 - 2005	1.57	15.71	0.00	22.17	6.46	47.05	66
	2005 - 2010	1.76	17.63	0.00	23.38	5.75	34.65	69
Nepal - Népal	1995 - 2000	2.39	24.71	-0.86	34.49	9.79	75.23	59
	2000 - 2005	2.08	21.54	-0.78	30.25	8.70	65.18	61
	2005 - 2010	1.97	20.39	-0.70	28.08	7.70	54.84	64
Pakistan	1995 - 2000	2.44	24.45	-0.06	33.30	8.85	82.69	61
	2000 - 2005	1.82	19.79	-1.64	27.46	7.68	77.91	63
	2005 - 2010	1.84	20.14	-1.71	27.24	7.11	67.25	65
Sri Lanka	1995 - 2000	0.69	11.23	-4.35	18.19	6.95	15.21	73
	2000 - 2005	0.43	8.97	-4.67	16.31	7.34	12.83	74
	2005 - 2010	0.47	7.81	-3.10	15.02	7.21	11.17	75
South-Eastern Asia - Asie du Sud-Est	*1995 - 2000*	*1.55*	*15.90*	*-0.32*	*22.97*	*7.08*	*42.21*	*66*
	2000 - 2005	*1.40*	*14.68*	*-0.61*	*21.43*	*6.75*	*33.69*	*67*
	2005 - 2010	*1.27*	*..*	*-0.56*	*19.77*	*..*	*27.97*	*69*
Brunei Darussalam - Brunéi Darussalam	1995 - 2000	2.45	22.26	2.24	25.12	2.86	6.69	75
	2000 - 2005	2.29	20.84	1.99	23.60	2.77	6.06	76
	2005 - 2010	2.05	18.72	1.78	21.53	2.81	5.61	77
Cambodia - Cambodge	1995 - 2000	2.29	21.59	1.32	31.97	10.38	85.36	55
	2000 - 2005	1.76	17.45	0.15	27.49	10.04	74.43	56
	2005 - 2010	1.74	17.45	-0.07	26.43	8.97	63.17	58

For sources and notes, see end of table.

Pour les sources et les notes, se reporter à la fin du tableau.

Region, country or territory / Régions, pays ou territoires	Year / Année	Population growth rate / Taux d'accroissement de la population (1)	Natural increase rate per 1000 inhabitants / Taux d'évolution naturel pour 1000 habitants (2)	Net migration rate per 1000 inhabitants / Taux net de migration pour 1000 habitants (3)	Crude birth rate per 1000 inhabitants / Taux de natalité brut pour 1000 habitants (4)	Crude death rate per 1000 inhabitants / Taux de mortalité brut pour 1000 habitants (5)	Infant mortality rate per 1000 live births / Taux de mortalité infantile pour 1000 naissances vivantes (6)	Life expectancy at birth / Espérance de vie à la naissance (7)
Indonesia - Indonésie	1995 - 2000	1.40	14.85	-0.88	22.00	7.15	46.44	65
	2000 - 2005	1.31	14.05	-0.91	20.67	6.62	35.00	67
	2005 - 2010	1.16	12.40	-0.77	18.73	6.32	27.42	69
Lao People's dem. Rep. - Rép. dém. populaire lao	1995 - 2000	2.15	24.98	-3.53	34.47	9.50	75.64	52
	2000 - 2005	1.62	20.39	-4.23	28.42	8.04	64.18	54
	2005 - 2010	1.72	19.73	-2.54	26.79	7.07	52.03	56
Malaysia - Malaisie	1995 - 2000	2.45	19.89	4.54	24.55	4.66	12.13	72
	2000 - 2005	1.95	18.23	1.23	22.74	4.51	10.08	73
	2005 - 2010	1.69	16.18	0.75	20.65	4.47	9.05	74
Myanmar	1995 - 2000	1.24	12.34	0.02	22.13	9.79	77.40	59
	2000 - 2005	0.89	9.30	-0.42	19.54	10.24	75.16	60
	2005 - 2010	0.85	8.54	-0.04	18.19	9.65	67.21	62
Philippines	1995 - 2000	2.11	23.55	-2.49	29.05	5.50	35.23	69
	2000 - 2005	2.08	23.02	-2.24	28.08	5.06	28.13	70
	2005 - 2010	1.90	21.03	-2.03	25.82	4.79	23.45	72
Singapore - Singapour	1995 - 2000	2.88	9.15	19.64	13.96	4.81	3.93	77
	2000 - 2005	1.49	5.28	9.59	10.13	4.85	3.07	79
	2005 - 2010	1.19	2.90	8.97	8.16	5.26	3.02	79
Thailand - Thaïlande	1995 - 2000	1.06	8.89	1.75	16.98	8.09	16.09	69
	2000 - 2005	0.76	6.81	0.75	15.37	8.56	12.48	70
	2005 - 2010	0.66	6.08	0.55	14.55	8.47	10.60	72
Timor-Leste	1995 - 2000	-0.76	33.16	-40.75	45.75	12.59	97.56	53
	2000 - 2005	5.31	31.55	21.21	41.71	10.16	81.20	55
	2005 - 2010	3.50	33.16	1.71	42.10	8.94	65.18	58
Viet Nam	1995 - 2000	1.51	15.65	-0.53	21.39	5.74	30.65	69
	2000 - 2005	1.45	14.95	-0.49	20.15	5.20	22.73	70
	2005 - 2010	1.32	13.68	-0.46	18.76	5.08	19.67	72
Western Asia - Asie occidentale	*1995 - 2000*	*2.37*	*22.99*	*1.01*	*29.50*	*6.51*	*51.15*	*66*
	2000 - 2005	*2.14*	*20.52*	*1.08*	*26.66*	*6.13*	*46.90*	*67*
	2005 - 2010	*1.95*	*..*	*0.30*	*25.13*	*..*	*39.80*	*69*
Bahrain - Bahreïn	1995 - 2000	2.36	18.21	5.38	21.26	3.05	14.83	73
	2000 - 2005	2.18	16.21	5.53	19.30	3.09	12.69	74
	2005 - 2010	1.79	13.89	3.95	17.13	3.24	11.37	75
Iraq	1995 - 2000	2.94	28.28	1.02	38.31	10.03	90.67	59
	2000 - 2005	2.22	25.03	-2.83	35.59	10.56	94.66	59
	2005 - 2010	1.84	22.68	-4.33	31.73	9.05	82.99	61
Jordan - Jordanie	1995 - 2000	2.18	27.89	-6.15	32.44	4.55	27.58	70
	2000 - 2005	2.89	23.80	5.03	27.93	4.13	24.06	71
	2005 - 2010	3.04	21.96	8.34	25.89	3.93	19.48	72
Kuwait - Koweït	1995 - 2000	5.12	18.80	32.13	20.56	1.76	9.92	76
	2000 - 2005	3.84	16.83	21.45	18.56	1.73	8.46	77
	2005 - 2010	2.44	16.05	8.35	17.91	1.86	7.97	78
Lebanon - Liban	1995 - 2000	1.55	15.51	0.00	22.58	7.08	27.92	71
	2000 - 2005	1.23	12.26	0.00	19.30	7.05	25.90	72
	2005 - 2010	1.05	11.12	-0.61	18.16	7.04	22.27	73
Occupied Palestinian territory - Territoire palestinien occupé	1995 - 2000	3.70	36.92	0.00	41.97	5.05	24.73	71
	2000 - 2005	3.56	34.83	0.62	39.06	4.23	21.11	72
	2005 - 2010	3.18	32.18	-0.49	35.86	3.68	17.69	73
Oman	1995 - 2000	2.02	26.27	-6.12	29.40	3.13	19.40	73
	2000 - 2005	0.86	20.77	-12.22	23.54	2.78	16.12	74
	2005 - 2010	1.97	19.35	0.38	22.07	2.72	12.46	75
Qatar	1995 - 2000	3.19	16.76	15.10	19.95	3.19	13.45	72
	2000 - 2005	5.11	15.22	35.59	17.81	2.60	10.06	73
	2005 - 2010	2.11	13.89	7.14	16.24	2.35	8.23	74
Saudi Arabia - Arabie saoudite	1995 - 2000	2.62	25.46	0.72	29.46	4.00	26.61	71
	2000 - 2005	2.53	22.70	2.57	26.51	3.81	22.57	72
	2005 - 2010	2.24	21.22	1.20	24.88	3.66	19.06	73

For sources and notes, see end of table.

Pour les sources et les notes, se reporter à la fin du tableau.

Region, country or territory / Régions, pays ou territoires	Year / Année	Population growth rate / Taux d'accroissement de la population (1)	Natural increase rate per 1000 inhabitants / Taux d'évolution naturel pour 1000 habitants (2)	Net migration rate per 1000 inhabitants / Taux net de migration pour 1000 habitants (3)	Crude birth rate per 1000 inhabitants / Taux de natalité brut pour 1000 habitants (4)	Crude death rate per 1000 inhabitants / Taux de mortalité brut pour 1000 habitants (5)	Infant mortality rate per 1000 live births / Taux de mortalité infantile pour 1000 naissances vivantes (6)	Life expectancy at birth / Espérance de vie à la naissance (7)
Syrian Arab Republic - République arabe syrienne	1995 - 2000	2.45	26.10	-1.67	29.98	3.88	24.06	72
	2000 - 2005	2.70	24.66	2.26	28.23	3.56	18.88	73
	2005 - 2010	2.52	23.30	1.84	26.73	3.42	16.02	74
Turkey - Turquie	1995 - 2000	1.66	16.27	0.30	22.48	6.21	41.45	68
	2000 - 2005	1.36	13.72	-0.09	19.48	5.76	32.81	69
	2005 - 2010	1.26	12.49	0.08	18.42	5.93	27.51	70
United Arab Emirates - Émirats arabes unis	1995 - 2000	5.79	17.17	40.29	18.80	1.64	11.18	76
	2000 - 2005	4.69	15.24	31.40	16.66	1.42	8.95	78
	2005 - 2010	2.85	14.83	13.58	16.21	1.38	8.03	79
Yemen - Yémen	1995 - 2000	3.16	32.74	-1.19	42.88	10.14	80.40	58
	2000 - 2005	2.97	30.69	-1.02	39.30	8.61	69.90	60
	2005 - 2010	2.97	30.85	-1.19	38.26	7.41	58.80	63
Developing economies: Oceania - Économies en développement : Océanie	**1995 - 2000**	**2.25**	**24.32**	**-2.21**	**33.04**	**8.72**	**57.95**	**58**
	2000 - 2005	**2.08**	**21.90**	**-1.59**	**30.41**	**8.52**	**56.71**	**59**
	2005 - 2010	**1.78**	**..**	**-1.19**	**26.83**	**..**	**53.35**	**61**
American Samoa - Samoa américaines	1995 - 2000	1.61	..	..	..	..	..	..
	2000 - 2005	2.31	..	..	..	..	..	..
	2005 - 2010	2.01	..	..	..	..	..	..
Cook Islands - Îles Cook	1995 - 2000	-2.46	..	..	..	..	..	..
	2000 - 2005	-2.67	..	..	..	..	..	..
	2005 - 2010	-2.23	..	..	..	..	..	..
Fiji - Fidji	1995 - 2000	0.86	19.30	-10.70	25.52	6.22	26.32	67
	2000 - 2005	0.65	16.78	-10.31	23.15	6.37	21.68	68
	2005 - 2010	0.62	14.52	-8.32	21.11	6.59	19.89	69
French Polynesia - Polynésie française	1995 - 2000	1.80	16.58	1.42	21.36	4.79	9.65	72
	2000 - 2005	1.59	14.37	1.50	19.31	4.94	8.80	73
	2005 - 2010	1.31	13.13	0.00	18.34	5.21	8.09	74
Guam	1995 - 2000	1.28	19.20	-6.45	23.90	4.70	11.02	74
	2000 - 2005	1.66	15.59	0.98	20.66	5.07	10.29	75
	2005 - 2010	1.30	13.00	0.00	18.46	5.46	9.20	76
Kiribati	1995 - 2000	1.68	..	..	..	..	..	..
	2000 - 2005	1.82	..	..	..	..	..	..
	2005 - 2010	1.58	..	..	..	..	..	..
Marshall Islands - Îles Marshall	1995 - 2000	0.44	..	..	..	..	..	..
	2000 - 2005	1.68	..	..	..	..	..	..
	2005 - 2010	2.23	..	..	..	..	..	..
Micronesia (Federated States of) - Micronésie (États fédérés de)	1995 - 2000	-0.02	25.19	-25.42	31.48	6.29	40.14	67
	2000 - 2005	0.55	23.35	-17.89	29.70	6.35	38.14	68
	2005 - 2010	0.46	19.85	-15.27	25.94	6.09	35.18	68
Nauru	1995 - 2000	0.15	..	..	..	..	..	..
	2000 - 2005	0.15	..	..	..	..	..	..
	2005 - 2010	0.29	..	..	..	..	..	..
New Caledonia - Nouvelle-Calédonie	1995 - 2000	2.15	16.04	5.46	21.56	5.53	8.46	74
	2000 - 2005	1.71	12.77	4.30	17.99	5.22	6.98	75
	2005 - 2010	1.54	10.84	4.52	16.38	5.54	6.22	76
Niue - Nioué	1995 - 2000	-3.59	..	..	..	..	..	..
	2000 - 2005	-2.80	..	..	..	..	..	..
	2005 - 2010	-1.85	..	..	..	..	..	..
Northern Mariana Islands - Îles Mariannes du Nord	1995 - 2000	3.57	..	..	..	..	..	..
	2000 - 2005	3.02	..	..	..	..	..	..
	2005 - 2010	1.95	..	..	..	..	..	..
Palau - Palaos	1995 - 2000	2.45	..	..	..	..	..	..
	2000 - 2005	0.86	..	..	..	..	..	..
	2005 - 2010	0.41	..	..	..	..	..	..
Papua New Guinea - Papouasie-Nouvelle-Guinée	1995 - 2000	2.67	26.67	0.00	36.87	10.20	66.22	54
	2000 - 2005	2.41	24.05	0.00	33.97	9.92	65.08	55
	2005 - 2010	2.00	19.98	0.00	29.57	9.59	61.64	57

For sources and notes, see end of table.

Pour les sources et les notes, se reporter è la fin du tableau.

Region, country or territory Régions, pays ou territoires	Year Année	Population growth rate Taux d'accroissement de la population	Natural increase rate per 1000 inhabitants Taux d'évolution naturel pour 1000 habitants	Net migration rate per 1000 inhabitants Taux net de migration pour 1000 habitants	Crude birth rate per 1000 inhabitants Taux de natalité brut pour 1000 habitants	Crude death rate per 1000 inhabitants Taux de mortalité brut pour 1000 habitants	Infant mortality rate per 1000 live births Taux de mortalité infantile pour 1000 naissances vivantes	Life expectancy at birth Espérance de vie à la naissance
		(1)	(2)	(3)	(4)	(5)	(6)	(7)
Pitcairn	1995 - 2000	-1.01	..	..	..	..	..	..
	2000 - 2005	-2.97	..	..	..	..	..	..
Samoa	1995 - 2000	1.07	26.90	-16.23	33.10	6.20	29.61	68
	2000 - 2005	0.71	23.66	-16.61	29.36	5.70	26.47	70
	2005 - 2010	0.87	19.31	-10.64	24.67	5.35	23.09	71
Solomon Islands - Îles Salomon	1995 - 2000	2.76	27.59	0.00	36.33	8.74	67.61	61
	2000 - 2005	2.57	25.68	0.00	33.56	7.88	60.26	62
	2005 - 2010	2.33	23.23	0.00	30.48	7.25	54.89	63
Tokelau - Tokélaou	1995 - 2000	0.52	..	..	..	..	..	..
	2000 - 2005	-1.59	..	..	..	..	..	..
	2005 - 2010	-0.03	..	..	..	..	..	..
Tonga	1995 - 2000	0.14	20.89	-19.50	26.64	5.75	23.73	71
	2000 - 2005	0.26	18.67	-16.10	24.34	5.67	21.47	72
	2005 - 2010	0.50	19.93	-14.91	25.62	5.69	18.47	73
Tuvalu	1995 - 2000	0.75	..	..	..	..	..	..
	2000 - 2005	0.50	..	..	..	..	..	..
	2005 - 2010	0.42	..	..	..	..	..	..
Vanuatu	1995 - 2000	1.94	27.24	-7.89	33.94	6.70	39.95	66
	2000 - 2005	2.54	25.32	0.00	31.04	5.72	35.76	68
	2005 - 2010	2.38	23.74	0.00	28.76	5.03	28.64	70
Wallis and Futuna Islands - Îles Wallis-et-Futuna	1995 - 2000	0.78	..	..	..	..	..	..
	2000 - 2005	0.24	..	..	..	..	..	..
	2005 - 2010	0.66	..	..	..	..	..	..
Economies in transition: Asia - Économies en transition : Asie	**1995 - 2000**	**0.51**	**13.24**	**-8.11**	**21.65**	**8.41**	**62.62**	**65**
	2000 - 2005	**0.82**	**12.07**	**-3.81**	**20.21**	**8.14**	**56.32**	**66**
	2005 - 2010	**0.99**	**..**	**-2.54**	**20.66**	**..**	**51.04**	**66**
Armenia - Arménie	1995 - 2000	-0.92	5.07	-14.27	13.50	8.42	37.51	70
	2000 - 2005	-0.42	2.34	-6.56	11.19	8.85	31.43	71
	2005 - 2010	-0.21	2.92	-5.00	12.54	9.61	28.10	72
Azerbaijan - Azerbaïdjan	1995 - 2000	0.88	12.03	-3.20	18.89	6.85	81.82	66
	2000 - 2005	0.51	7.49	-2.43	14.35	6.86	79.39	67
	2005 - 2010	0.75	8.67	-1.18	16.24	7.57	70.10	67
Georgia - Géorgie	1995 - 2000	-1.28	1.54	-14.36	11.76	10.22	42.35	70
	2000 - 2005	-1.07	0.06	-10.79	11.13	11.07	40.39	70
	2005 - 2010	-0.79	-1.04	-6.84	10.79	11.83	39.22	71
Kazakhstan	1995 - 2000	-1.25	4.60	-17.11	16.22	11.62	46.45	63
	2000 - 2005	0.34	6.05	-2.65	16.67	10.61	33.27	63
	2005 - 2010	0.71	9.66	-2.58	19.72	10.06	24.02	64
Kyrgyzstan - Kirghizistan	1995 - 2000	1.49	16.02	-1.13	24.18	8.16	59.71	66
	2000 - 2005	1.01	13.09	-2.96	20.98	7.90	56.92	67
	2005 - 2010	1.10	13.76	-2.80	21.82	8.06	52.13	68
Tajikistan - Tadjikistan	1995 - 2000	1.34	24.96	-11.55	32.68	7.72	80.38	63
	2000 - 2005	1.19	22.71	-10.85	29.36	6.65	66.07	64
	2005 - 2010	1.51	20.93	-5.88	27.34	6.41	59.82	64
Turkmenistan - Turkménistan	1995 - 2000	1.42	16.52	-2.30	24.49	7.96	78.59	63
	2000 - 2005	1.42	14.62	-0.43	22.89	8.27	77.12	62
	2005 - 2010	1.32	13.61	-0.40	21.84	8.23	75.14	63
Uzbekistan - Ouzbékistan	1995 - 2000	1.52	18.51	-3.36	25.24	6.72	60.23	67
	2000 - 2005	1.46	16.91	-2.34	23.67	6.76	57.33	66
	2005 - 2010	1.44	15.85	-1.45	22.60	6.75	55.28	67
Economies in transition: Europe - Économies en transition : Europe	**1995 - 2000**	**-0.35**	**-4.54**	**1.06**	**8.78**	**13.32**	**20.17**	**67**
	2000 - 2005	**-0.52**	**-5.38**	**0.51**	**9.21**	**14.59**	**16.50**	**67**
	2005 - 2010	**-0.50**	**..**	**0.00**	**9.83**	**..**	**15.14**	**67**
Albania - Albanie	1995 - 2000	-0.45	13.39	-17.88	19.42	6.02	28.49	73
	2000 - 2005	0.47	11.76	-7.03	17.24	5.48	22.87	74
	2005 - 2010	0.57	10.39	-4.69	16.25	5.86	19.27	74

For sources and notes, see end of table.

Pour les sources et les notes, se reporter à la fin du tableau.

461

8

Region, country or territory / Régions, pays ou territoires	Year / Année	Population growth rate / Taux d'accroissement de la population (1)	Natural increase rate per 1000 inhabitants / Taux d'évolution naturel pour 1000 habitants (2)	Net migration rate per 1000 inhabitants / Taux net de migration pour 1000 habitants (3)	Crude birth rate per 1000 inhabitants / Taux de natalité brut pour 1000 habitants (4)	Crude death rate per 1000 inhabitants / Taux de mortalité brut pour 1000 habitants (5)	Infant mortality rate per 1000 live births / Taux de mortalité infantile pour 1000 naissances vivantes (6)	Life expectancy at birth / Espérance de vie à la naissance (7)
Belarus - Bélarus	1995 - 2000	-0.42	-4.22	0.00	9.45	13.67	14.78	68
	2000 - 2005	-0.52	-5.18	0.00	9.27	14.45	10.50	68
	2005 - 2010	-0.55	-5.32	-0.21	9.39	14.71	9.22	69
Bosnia and Herzegovina - Bosnie-Herzégovine	1995 - 2000	2.03	3.99	16.33	11.96	7.97	15.08	73
	2000 - 2005	0.67	0.67	5.98	9.40	8.73	13.93	74
	2005 - 2010	0.13	-0.70	2.04	8.79	9.49	12.16	75
Croatia - Croatie	1995 - 2000	-0.71	-0.59	-6.54	10.48	11.07	9.19	74
	2000 - 2005	0.20	-2.39	4.42	9.10	11.49	7.59	75
	2005 - 2010	-0.09	-3.05	2.20	9.02	12.07	6.34	76
Moldova	1995 - 2000	-1.10	0.76	-11.73	12.64	11.88	23.04	66
	2000 - 2005	-1.34	-0.94	-12.47	11.42	12.35	18.02	67
	2005 - 2010	-0.90	-1.04	-7.91	11.43	12.47	15.71	70
Russian Federation - Fédération de Russie	1995 - 2000	-0.23	-5.25	2.96	8.95	14.20	21.49	66
	2000 - 2005	-0.48	-6.02	1.26	9.89	15.91	17.59	65
	2005 - 2010	-0.51	-5.47	0.35	10.68	16.15	16.37	65
Serbia and Montenegro - Serbie-et-Monténégro	1995 - 2000	-0.03	..	..	..	..	..	72
	2000 - 2005	-0.62	..	..	..	..	..	73
TFYR of Macedonia - LERY de Macédoine	1995 - 2000	0.46	5.11	-0.50	13.36	8.25	19.99	73
	2000 - 2005	0.24	3.40	-0.99	11.99	8.59	16.49	74
	2005 - 2010	0.08	1.74	-0.98	10.89	9.16	15.13	74
Ukraine	1995 - 2000	-0.87	-6.47	-2.19	8.63	15.09	17.52	67
	2000 - 2005	-0.81	-7.37	-0.72	8.45	15.81	14.13	66
	2005 - 2010	-0.76	-7.16	-0.43	9.20	16.35	12.53	66
Developed economies: America - Économies développées : Amérique	**1995 - 2000**	**1.04**	**5.94**	**4.47**	**14.19**	**8.25**	**7.41**	**77**
	2000 - 2005	**1.02**	**5.62**	**4.61**	**13.84**	**8.22**	**6.74**	**78**
	2005 - 2010	**0.95**	**..**	**4.08**	**13.69**	**..**	**6.23**	**78**
Bermuda - Bermudes	1995 - 2000	0.47	..	..	..	..	..	..
	2000 - 2005	0.41	..	..	..	..	..	..
	2005 - 2010	0.25	..	..	..	..	..	..
Canada	1995 - 2000	0.93	4.36	4.89	11.59	7.23	5.70	79
	2000 - 2005	1.01	3.43	6.62	10.65	7.22	5.11	80
	2005 - 2010	0.90	2.92	6.06	10.34	7.42	4.81	81
Greenland - Groenland	1995 - 2000	0.23	..	..	..	..	..	..
	2000 - 2005	0.43	..	..	..	..	..	..
	2005 - 2010	0.60	..	..	..	..	..	..
Saint Pierre and Miquelon - Saint-Pierre-et-Miquelon	1995 - 2000	0.05	..	..	..	..	..	..
	2000 - 2005	0.07	..	..	..	..	..	..
	2005 - 2010	0.07	..	..	..	..	..	..
United States - États-Unis	1995 - 2000	1.05	6.11	4.43	14.47	8.36	7.56	77
	2000 - 2005	1.02	5.85	4.40	14.17	8.32	6.87	77
	2005 - 2010	0.96	..	3.87	14.05	..	6.35	78
Developed economies: Asia - Économies développées : Asie	**1995 - 2000**	**0.34**	**2.60**	**0.84**	**10.13**	**7.53**	**4.01**	**80**
	2000 - 2005	**0.22**	**1.62**	**0.58**	**9.53**	**7.91**	**3.49**	**82**
	2005 - 2010	**0.07**	**..**	**0.53**	**8.90**	**..**	**3.34**	**83**
Israel - Israël	1995 - 2000	2.48	15.15	9.65	21.46	6.31	6.19	78
	2000 - 2005	1.91	15.43	3.60	21.07	5.64	5.04	80
	2005 - 2010	1.66	14.17	2.44	19.65	5.48	4.75	81
Japan - Japon	1995 - 2000	0.25	2.03	0.44	9.61	7.58	3.79	81
	2000 - 2005	0.14	0.93	0.42	8.95	8.02	3.31	82
	2005 - 2010	-0.02	-0.64	0.42	8.31	8.95	3.16	83
Developed economies: Europe - Économies développées : Europe	**1995 - 2000**	**0.17**	**0.35**	**1.39**	**10.64**	**10.29**	**7.09**	**77**
	2000 - 2005	**0.35**	**0.37**	**3.12**	**10.38**	**10.01**	**5.81**	**78**
	2005 - 2010	**0.20**	**..**	**1.89**	**10.24**	**..**	**5.32**	**79**
Andorra - Andorre	1995 - 2000	0.54	..	..	..	..	..	..
	2000 - 2005	2.01	..	..	..	..	..	..
	2005 - 2010	0.36	..	..	..	..	..	..
Austria - Autriche	1995 - 2000	0.16	0.37	1.24	10.35	9.98	5.90	78

For sources and notes, see end of table.

Pour les sources et les notes, se reporter à la fin du tableau.

Region, country or territory Régions, pays ou territoires	Year Année	Population growth rate Taux d'accroissement de la population	Natural increase rate per 1000 inhabitants Taux d'évolution naturel pour 1000 habitants	Net migration rate per 1000 inhabitants Taux net de migration pour 1000 habitants	Crude birth rate per 1000 inhabitants Taux de natalité brut pour 1000 habitants	Crude death rate per 1000 inhabitants Taux de mortalité brut pour 1000 habitants	Infant mortality rate per 1000 live births Taux de mortalité infantile pour 1000 naissances vivantes	Life expectancy at birth Espérance de vie à la naissance
		(1)	(2)	(3)	(4)	(5)	(6)	(7)
	2000 - 2005	0.44	0.01	4.39	9.47	9.45	4.81	79
	2005 - 2010	0.36	-0.24	3.83	9.18	9.41	4.37	80
Belgium - Belgique	2005 - 2010	0.24	0.45	1.91	10.44	9.99	4.18	80
Belgium-Luxembourg - Belgique-Luxembourg	1995 - 2000	0.26	1.06	1.55	11.31	10.25	5.58	..
Bulgaria - Bulgarie	1995 - 2000	-0.87	-6.13	-2.53	8.19	14.31	15.87	71
	2000 - 2005	-0.66	-5.48	-1.09	8.74	14.19	12.80	72
	2005 - 2010	-0.72	-5.87	-1.31	8.92	14.79	11.77	73
Cyprus - Chypre	1995 - 2000	1.46	6.96	7.63	14.02	7.06	6.55	78
	2000 - 2005	1.23	5.19	7.13	12.14	6.96	6.07	79
	2005 - 2010	1.06	4.74	5.82	12.19	7.45	5.77	79
Czech Republic - République tchèque	1995 - 2000	-0.17	-1.97	0.23	8.68	10.65	6.00	74
	2000 - 2005	-0.06	-1.88	1.31	8.95	10.83	3.91	75
	2005 - 2010	-0.03	-1.70	1.38	9.16	10.87	3.69	76
Denmark - Danemark	1995 - 2000	0.41	1.29	2.78	12.65	11.36	5.27	76
	2000 - 2005	0.30	1.34	1.70	12.01	10.67	4.63	77
	2005 - 2010	0.21	0.95	1.10	11.25	10.30	4.40	78
Estonia - Estonie	1995 - 2000	-0.98	-4.55	-5.21	9.15	13.69	11.15	70
	2000 - 2005	-0.38	-3.91	0.13	9.79	13.70	7.60	71
	2005 - 2010	-0.35	-3.47	0.00	10.79	14.26	7.00	73
Faeroe Islands - Îles Féroé	1995 - 2000	1.05	..	..	..	..	..	..
	2000 - 2005	0.76	..	..	..	..	..	..
	2005 - 2010	0.68	..	..	..	..	..	..
Finland - Finlande	1995 - 2000	0.27	1.89	0.76	11.49	9.61	4.49	77
	2000 - 2005	0.27	1.41	1.28	10.95	9.54	3.97	78
	2005 - 2010	0.29	1.38	1.51	11.11	9.72	3.70	79
France	1995 - 2000	0.36	3.31	0.33	12.76	9.44	5.36	78
	2000 - 2005	0.62	3.87	2.35	12.97	9.10	4.65	79
	2005 - 2010	0.51	..	1.56	12.39	..	4.49	80
Germany - Allemagne	1995 - 2000	0.16	-1.19	2.77	9.50	10.68	5.07	77
	2000 - 2005	0.08	-1.59	2.43	8.67	10.26	4.55	79
	2005 - 2010	-0.07	-2.51	1.82	8.19	10.70	4.33	79
Gibraltar	1995 - 2000	0.05	..	..	..	..	..	..
	2000 - 2005	1.22	..	..	..	..	..	..
	2005 - 2010	0.08	..	..	..	..	..	..
Greece - Grèce	1995 - 2000	0.59	0.35	5.55	9.67	9.32	8.07	78
	2000 - 2005	0.23	-0.53	2.80	9.38	9.91	7.72	78
	2005 - 2010	0.21	-0.62	2.69	9.26	9.88	6.88	79
Holy See - Saint-Siège	1995 - 2000	0.15	..	..	..	..	..	..
	2000 - 2005	-0.10	..	..	..	..	..	..
	2005 - 2010	0.05	..	..	..	..	..	..
Hungary - Hongrie	1995 - 2000	-0.22	-3.89	1.66	9.87	13.75	10.31	71
	2000 - 2005	-0.25	-3.80	1.28	9.46	13.26	7.45	73
	2005 - 2010	-0.29	-3.93	1.00	9.25	13.18	6.75	74
Iceland - Islande	1995 - 2000	0.99	8.77	1.15	15.50	6.73	3.76	79
	2000 - 2005	1.02	8.33	1.83	14.43	6.09	3.08	81
	2005 - 2010	0.84	8.05	0.33	14.29	6.24	3.01	81
Ireland - Irlande	1995 - 2000	1.05	5.58	4.94	14.14	8.56	6.17	76
	2000 - 2005	1.71	7.61	9.47	15.17	7.56	5.43	78
	2005 - 2010	1.77	8.45	9.23	15.50	7.05	4.88	78
Italy - Italie	1995 - 2000	0.14	-0.73	2.09	9.22	9.95	5.91	79
	2000 - 2005	0.33	-0.59	3.87	9.35	9.94	5.17	80
	2005 - 2010	0.13	-1.32	2.63	9.15	10.48	4.97	81
Latvia - Lettonie	1995 - 2000	-0.91	-5.83	-3.28	8.03	13.86	14.49	70
	2000 - 2005	-0.66	-4.91	-1.67	8.73	13.64	11.37	71
	2005 - 2010	-0.52	-4.28	-0.88	9.35	13.62	10.48	73
Lithuania - Lituanie	1995 - 2000	-0.72	-0.99	-6.16	10.60	11.58	13.29	71
	2000 - 2005	-0.45	-2.76	-1.72	9.05	11.81	9.93	72

For sources and notes, see end of table.

Pour les sources et les notes, se reporter à la fin du tableau.

463

8

Region, country or territory / Régions, pays ou territoires	Year / Année	Population growth rate / Taux d'accroissement de la population	Natural increase rate per 1000 inhabitants / Taux d'évolution naturel pour 1000 habitants	Net migration rate per 1000 inhabitants / Taux net de migration pour 1000 habitants	Crude birth rate per 1000 inhabitants / Taux de natalité brut pour 1000 habitants	Crude death rate per 1000 inhabitants / Taux de mortalité brut pour 1000 habitants	Infant mortality rate per 1000 live births / Taux de mortalité infantile pour 1000 naissances vivantes	Life expectancy at birth / Espérance de vie à la naissance
		(1)	(2)	(3)	(4)	(5)	(6)	(7)
	2005 - 2010	-0.53	-3.22	-2.07	9.07	12.29	8.52	73
Luxembourg	2005 - 2010	1.13	2.78	8.51	11.46	8.68	4.53	79
Malta - Malte	1995 - 2000	0.58	4.50	1.30	12.28	7.78	8.08	77
	2000 - 2005	0.69	2.38	4.55	10.04	7.66	7.20	78
	2005 - 2010	0.43	1.84	2.46	9.81	7.98	6.36	79
Netherlands - Pays-Bas	1995 - 2000	0.59	3.61	2.32	12.43	8.82	5.46	78
	2000 - 2005	0.50	3.64	1.37	12.35	8.71	4.97	78
	2005 - 2010	0.21	2.49	-0.37	11.08	8.59	4.82	79
Norway - Norvège	1995 - 2000	0.59	3.47	2.38	13.37	9.90	5.43	78
	2000 - 2005	0.66	2.88	3.70	12.35	9.47	4.17	79
	2005 - 2010	0.62	2.83	3.40	11.92	9.10	3.29	80
Poland - Pologne	1995 - 2000	-0.08	0.72	-1.56	10.55	9.84	11.12	73
	2000 - 2005	-0.12	-0.20	-1.04	9.36	9.55	7.71	74
	2005 - 2010	-0.15	-0.49	-1.05	9.53	10.02	6.60	75
Portugal	1995 - 2000	0.39	0.43	3.46	11.17	10.74	6.58	76
	2000 - 2005	0.58	0.48	5.32	10.89	10.41	5.51	77
	2005 - 2010	0.37	-0.06	3.76	10.55	10.61	5.07	78
Romania - Roumanie	1995 - 2000	-0.49	-1.73	-3.12	10.48	12.21	20.77	70
	2000 - 2005	-0.47	-2.19	-2.47	10.01	12.21	17.42	71
	2005 - 2010	-0.45	-2.62	-1.87	9.82	12.44	14.99	72
San Marino - Saint-Marin	1995 - 2000	0.95	..	..	..	..	..	..
	2000 - 2005	2.29	..	..	..	..	..	..
	2005 - 2010	0.81	..	..	..	..	..	..
Slovakia - Slovaquie	1995 - 2000	0.09	0.89	0.00	10.82	9.94	9.84	73
	2000 - 2005	0.00	-0.13	0.11	9.68	9.81	7.72	74
	2005 - 2010	0.03	-0.04	0.37	9.96	10.00	6.82	75
Slovenia - Slovénie	1995 - 2000	0.20	-0.49	2.45	9.15	9.64	6.07	75
	2000 - 2005	0.16	-0.57	2.16	8.87	9.44	5.40	76
	2005 - 2010	0.01	-0.89	1.00	8.98	9.87	4.81	77
Spain - Espagne	1995 - 2000	0.42	0.26	3.97	9.34	9.08	5.13	78
	2000 - 2005	1.52	1.54	13.61	10.24	8.70	4.33	79
	2005 - 2010	0.77	2.08	5.65	10.84	8.76	4.17	80
Sweden - Suède	1995 - 2000	0.09	-0.19	1.11	10.38	10.57	4.69	79
	2000 - 2005	0.38	0.40	3.40	10.87	10.46	3.40	80
	2005 - 2010	0.45	1.17	3.28	11.27	10.09	3.13	81
Switzerland - Suisse	1995 - 2000	0.36	2.76	0.83	11.16	8.40	4.92	79
	2000 - 2005	0.44	1.66	2.72	9.78	8.12	4.43	80
	2005 - 2010	0.38	..	2.66	9.19	..	4.16	81
United Kingdom - Royaume-Uni	1995 - 2000	0.31	1.41	1.70	12.18	10.77	6.22	77
	2000 - 2005	0.46	1.44	3.18	11.64	10.19	5.27	78
	2005 - 2010	0.42	..	2.14	11.96	..	4.80	79
Developed economies: Oceania - Économies développées : Océanie	**1995 - 2000**	**1.12**	**6.64**	**4.57**	**13.78**	**7.14**	**6.24**	**79**
	2000 - 2005	**1.19**	**6.11**	**5.90**	**13.02**	**6.91**	**5.18**	**80**
	2005 - 2010	**0.99**	**..**	**4.42**	**12.64**	**..**	**4.53**	**81**
Australia - Australie	1995 - 2000	1.15	6.43	5.04	13.46	7.03	6.17	79
	2000 - 2005	1.19	5.87	6.01	12.69	6.83	5.07	80
	2005 - 2010	1.01	5.30	4.80	12.36	7.06	4.41	81
New Zealand - Nouvelle-Zélande	1995 - 2000	0.96	7.49	2.11	14.92	7.44	6.57	78
	2000 - 2005	1.22	7.11	5.12	14.20	7.09	5.65	79
	2005 - 2010	0.90	6.58	2.39	13.68	7.10	5.06	80

For sources and notes, see end of table.

Pour les sources et les notes, se reporter à la fin du tableau.

Sources:
- UN DESA Population Division, *World Population Prospects: The 2004 Revision*
- UN DESA Population Division, *World Population Prospects: The 2006 Revision*
- UNCTAD secretariat calculations

Notes:

(a) Including Taïwan

(1) Population growth rate: Average exponential rate of growth of the population over a given period. It is calculated as ln(Pt/P0)/t where t is the length of the period. It is expressed as a percentage.
(2) Natural increase rate per 1 000 inhabitants: Crude birth rate minus the crude death rate.
(3) Net migration rate per 1 000 inhabitants: Net number of migrants over a given period divided by the person-years lived by the population over that period. It is expressed as net number of migrants per 1 000 population.
(4) Crude birth rate per 1 000 inhabitants: Number of births over a given period divided by the person-years lived by the population over that period. It is expressed as number of births per 1 000 population.
(5) Crude death rate per 1 000 inhabitants: Number of deaths over a given period divided by the person-years lived by the population over that period. It is expressed as number of deaths per 1 000 population.
(6) Infant mortality rate per 1 000 live births: The number of deaths under one year of age in a given period of time divided by the number of live-births in the same period. It is expressed as number of deaths under one year per 1 000 births.

(7) Life expectancy at birth: The average number of years a newborn infant would to be expected to live if current mortality trends were to continue for the rest of that person's life.
(8) National sources.

Sources :
- ONU DAES Division de la population, *World Population Prospects: The 2004 Revision*
- ONU DAES Division de la population, *World Population Prospects: The 2006 Revision*
- Calculs du secrétariat de la CNUCED

Notes :

(a) Y compris Taïwan

(1) Taux d'accroissement de la population : le taux exponentiel d'accroissement de la population pour une période donnée, calculé comme ln(Pt/P0)/t, où le t est la longueur de la période, et exprimé en pourcentage.
(2) Taux d'évolution naturelle pour 1 000 habitants : le taux de natalité brut moins le taux de mortalité brut.
(3) Taux net de migration pour 1 000 habitants : le rapport entre le nombre net des migrants pour une période donnée et l'effectif de la population vivant durant la période considérée. Il est exprimé en nombre net des migrants pour 1 000 habitants.
(4) Taux de natalité brut pour 1 000 habitants : le rapport entre le nombre de naissances vivantes pour une période donnée et l'effectif de la population durant la période considérée. Il est exprimé en nombre de naissances pour 1 000 habitants.
(5) Taux de mortalité brut pour 1 000 habitants : c'est le rapport entre le nombre de décès pour une période donnée et l'effectif de la population durant la période considérée. Il est exprimé en nombre de décès pour 1 000 habitants.
(6) Taux de mortalité infantile pour 1 000 naissances vivantes : il est défini par le nombre des décès d'enfants âgés de moins d'un an pour une période donnée, rapporté au nombre de naissances vivantes durant la période considérée. Il est exprimé en nombre de décès d'enfants âgés de moins d'un an pour 1 000 naissances.
(7) Espérance de vie à la naissance : nombre moyen d'années à vivre pour un nouveau-né soumis aux conditions de mortalité de l'année de sa naissance.

(8) Sources nationales.

Economic grouping / Groupements économiques	Year / Année	Population growth rate / Taux d'accroissement de la population (1)	Natural increase rate per 1,000 inhabitants / Taux d'évolution naturel pour 1 000 habitants (2)	Net migration rate per 1,000 inhabitants / Taux net de migration pour 1 000 habitants (3)	Crude birth rate per 1,000 inhabitants / Taux de natalité brut pour 1 000 habitants (4)	Crude death rate per 1,000 inhabitants / Taux de mortalité brut pour 1 000 habitants (5)	Infant mortality rate per 1,000 live births / Taux de mortalité infantile pour 1 000 naissances vivantes (6)	Life expectancy at birth / Espérance de vie à la naissance (7)
DEVELOPING ECONOMIES - ÉCONOMIES EN DÉVELOPPEMENT	**1995 - 2000**	**1.65**	**17.03**	**-0.42**	**25.68**	**8.65**	**63.99**	**62**
	2000 - 2005	**1.45**	**15.24**	**-0.61**	**23.72**	**8.48**	**59.63**	**63**
	2005 - 2010	**1.37**	**..**	**-0.48**	**25.03**	**..**	**54.55**	**65**
Developing economies excluding China - Économies en développement sans la Chine	1995 - 2000	1.91	19.73	-0.49	29.02	9.29	71.17	60
	2000 - 2005	1.72	18.00	-0.71	27.07	9.06	65.41	61
	2005 - 2010	1.52	..	-0.49	25.56	..	59.84	62
Developing economies excluding LDCs - Économies en développement sans les PMA	1995 - 2000	1.52	15.71	-0.40	23.45	7.74	53.41	..
	2000 - 2005	1.29	13.68	-0.69	21.33	7.65	49.11	..
	2005 - 2010	1.20	..	-0.59	22.77	..	43.91	..
High-income developing countries - Pays en développement à revenu élevé	1995 - 2000	1.54	14.60	0.21	19.48	4.88	22.33	74
	2000 - 2005	1.12	12.55	-1.64	17.40	4.85	17.80	75
	2005 - 2010	-0.30	..	-0.41	16.46	..	14.69	76
Middle-income developing countries - Pays en développement à revenu intermédiaire	1995 - 2000	1.59	16.73	-0.73	23.23	6.50	37.94	68
	2000 - 2005	1.39	15.05	-1.02	21.65	6.60	31.12	68
	2005 - 2010	1.31	..	-0.66	20.54	..	26.27	69
Low-income developing countries - Pays en développement à revenu faible	1995 - 2000	1.67	17.28	-0.41	26.66	9.38	70.91	61
	2000 - 2005	1.49	15.49	-0.45	24.63	9.14	66.91	62
	2005 - 2010	1.51	..	-0.45	26.79	..	61.55	63
Heavily indebted poor countries - Pays pauvres très endettés	1995 - 2000	2.65	27.49	-0.60	43.31	15.83	106.92	48
	2000 - 2005	2.61	26.72	-0.29	41.67	14.95	99.72	48
	2005 - 2010	2.58	..	0.01	39.85	..	92.86	49
Landlocked developing countries - Pays en développement sans littoral	1995 - 2000	2.23	24.19	-1.66	38.66	14.47	102.77	50
	2000 - 2005	2.23	22.93	-0.38	36.87	13.94	96.88	50
	2005 - 2010	2.29	..	-0.15	36.09	..	89.79	51
Small island developing States - Petits États insulaires en développement	1995 - 2000	1.55	20.60	-5.31	28.84	8.24	52.25	62
	2000 - 2005	1.77	19.05	-1.47	27.11	8.06	49.18	63
	2005 - 2010	1.52	..	-2.25	25.06	..	45.10	65
Least developed countries - Pays les moins avancés	*1995 - 2000*	*2.45*	*25.04*	*-0.57*	*39.26*	*14.22*	*103.28*	*50*
	2000 - 2005	*2.42*	*24.28*	*-0.12*	*37.61*	*13.33*	*94.94*	*51*
	2005 - 2010	*2.37*	*23.66*	*0.04*	*35.91*	*12.25*	*87.85*	*52*
Africa and Haiti - Afrique et Haïti	1995 - 2000	2.74	28.16	-0.37	45.15	16.98	110.67	46
	2000 - 2005	2.71	27.78	-0.34	43.66	15.87	101.87	47
	2005 - 2010	2.69	..	-0.17	41.87	..	94.40	48
Asia - Asie	1995 - 2000	2.03	21.15	-0.71	31.75	10.60	88.05	57
	2000 - 2005	1.96	19.64	0.17	29.53	9.89	79.53	59
	2005 - 2010	1.86	..	0.38	27.53	..	72.32	61
Islands - Îles	1995 - 2000	1.36	28.34	-15.11	37.58	9.24	75.15	64
	2000 - 2005	3.15	27.02	4.55	35.02	7.99	64.40	65
	2005 - 2010	2.56	..	-0.98	33.56	..	54.64	67
Major petroleum exporters - Principaux exportateurs de pétrole	*1995 - 2000*	*2.29*	*23.41*	*-0.26*	*34.04*	*10.63*	*84.46*	*59*
	2000 - 2005	*2.10*	*21.85*	*-0.68*	*32.43*	*10.58*	*81.01*	*60*
	2005 - 2010	*2.03*	*..*	*-0.45*	*31.03*	*..*	*74.93*	*61*
Africa - Afrique	1995 - 2000	2.45	25.35	-0.52	40.18	14.83	105.89	48
	2000 - 2005	2.29	23.73	-0.59	38.52	14.79	102.61	47
	2005 - 2010	2.18	..	-0.21	36.37	..	97.28	48
America - Amérique	1995 - 2000	1.80	19.65	-1.55	24.73	5.08	25.29	72
	2000 - 2005	1.57	17.74	-1.94	22.87	5.13	21.16	73
	2005 - 2010	1.44	..	-1.56	21.24	..	18.37	74
Asia - Asie	1995 - 2000	2.19	21.72	0.42	28.03	6.31	55.80	65
	2000 - 2005	1.96	20.27	-0.49	26.38	6.11	50.27	67
	2005 - 2010	1.96	..	-0.52	25.91	..	42.22	69
Major exporters of manufactured goods - Principaux exportateurs d'articles manufacturés	*1995 - 2000*	*1.37*	*14.01*	*-0.24*	*21.47*	*7.46*	*48.36*	*66*
	2000 - 2005	*1.14*	*11.93*	*-0.52*	*19.23*	*7.30*	*43.75*	*68*
	2005 - 2010	*1.03*	*..*	*-0.40*	*21.69*	*..*	*38.37*	*69*
America - Amérique	1995 - 2000	1.55	16.70	-1.07	22.53	5.82	32.16	70
	2000 - 2005	1.22	15.25	-3.00	21.03	5.78	25.58	72
	2005 - 2010	1.21	..	-1.36	19.35	..	21.40	73

For sources and notes, see end of table.

Pour les sources et les notes, se reporter à la fin du tableau.

8.5.2 Demographic indicators of economic groupings

8.5.2 Indicateurs démographiques des groupements économiques

Economic grouping Groupements économiques	Year Année	Population growth rate Taux d'accroissement de la population (1)	Natural increase rate per 1,000 inhabitants Taux d'évolution naturel pour 1 000 habitants (2)	Net migration rate per 1,000 inhabitants Taux net de migration pour 1 000 habitants (3)	Crude birth rate per 1,000 inhabitants Taux de natalité brut pour 1 000 habitants (4)	Crude death rate per 1,000 inhabitants Taux de mortalité brut pour 1 000 habitants (5)	Infant mortality rate per 1,000 live births Taux de mortalité infantile pour 1 000 naissances vivantes (6)	Life expectancy at birth Espérance de vie à la naissance (7)
Asia - Asie	1995 - 2000	1.35	13.73	-0.15	21.36	7.63	50.15	63
	2000 - 2005	1.13	11.58	-0.25	19.04	7.46	45.87	65
	2005 - 2010	1.01	..	-0.27	22.00	..	40.32	66
Emerging economies - *Économies émergentes*	*1995 - 2000*	*1.40*	*13.99*	*-0.28*	*19.89*	*5.90*	*26.93*	*71*
	2000 - 2005	*1.08*	*12.28*	*-1.65*	*18.19*	*5.91*	*21.44*	*72*
	2005 - 2010	*0.20*	*..*	*-0.73*	*17.04*	*..*	*17.73*	*74*
America - Amérique	1995 - 2000	1.49	16.23	-1.18	22.27	6.04	31.06	71
	2000 - 2005	1.19	14.61	-2.66	20.59	5.98	24.61	72
	2005 - 2010	1.18	..	-1.27	19.11	..	20.21	74
Asia - Asie	1995 - 2000	1.19	9.01	1.72	14.61	5.60	12.94	72
	2000 - 2005	0.83	7.03	0.63	12.77	5.74	9.90	73
	2005 - 2010	-2.23	..	0.55	12.17	..	8.54	75
Newly industrialized economies - *Économies nouvellement industrialisées*	*1995 - 2000*	*1.44*	*14.19*	*-0.09*	*20.53*	*6.34*	*35.12*	*..*
	2000 - 2005	*1.28*	*13.09*	*-0.47*	*19.15*	*6.06*	*27.29*	*..*
	2005 - 2010	*0.21*	*..*	*-0.43*	*17.76*	*..*	*21.93*	*..*
First tier - Première génération	1995 - 2000	0.95	5.63	1.52	9.52	3.89	8.48	..
	2000 - 2005	0.58	3.41	1.04	7.31	3.90	5.02	..
	2005 - 2010	-6.02	..	1.20	6.87	..	3.95	..
Second tier - Deuxième génération	1995 - 2000	1.55	16.06	-0.44	22.93	6.87	37.54	..
	2000 - 2005	1.42	15.13	-0.79	21.64	6.52	28.87	..
	2005 - 2010	1.28	..	-0.74	19.85	..	23.12	..
Developing economies: Africa - **Économies en développement : Afrique**	**1995 - 2000**	**2.45**	**25.16**	**-0.37**	**39.38**	**14.22**	**98.82**	**50**
	2000 - 2005	**2.32**	**24.00**	**-0.51**	**38.14**	**14.14**	**93.03**	**49**
	2005 - 2010	**2.26**	**..**	**-0.40**	**36.61**	**..**	**86.90**	**50**
Northern Africa excluding Sudan - Afrique septentrionale sans le Soudan	1995 - 2000	1.64	18.34	-1.79	24.51	6.17	47.16	68
	2000 - 2005	1.56	17.46	-1.70	23.11	5.65	36.04	70
	2005 - 2010	1.56	..	-1.24	22.41	..	29.22	72
Sub-Saharan Africa - Afrique subsaharienne	1995 - 2000	2.62	26.61	-0.07	42.55	15.94	105.17	47
	2000 - 2005	2.48	25.33	-0.27	41.19	15.86	99.54	46
	2005 - 2010	2.39	.	-0.24	39.37	..	93.29	47
Sub-Saharan Africa excluding South Africa - Afrique subsaharienne sans l'Afrique du Sud	1995 - 2000	2.68	27.38	-0.21	43.81	16.43	107.54	46
	2000 - 2005	2.57	26.36	-0.32	42.38	16.03	101.47	46
	2005 - 2010	2.51	..	-0.27	40.46	..	94.95	47
Developing economies: America - **Économies en développement : Amérique**	**1995 - 2000**	**1.56**	**17.31**	**-1.56**	**23.44**	**6.13**	**32.22**	**70**
	2000 - 2005	**1.30**	**15.62**	**-2.56**	**21.65**	**6.03**	**26.23**	**71**
	2005 - 2010	**1.25**	**..**	**-1.49**	**20.03**	**..**	**21.99**	**73**
Central America and Greater Carribean Islands excluding Puerto Rico - Amérique centrale et Grandes Antilles sans Porto Rico	1995 - 2000	1.67	19.74	-2.97	25.34	5.60	33.25	71
	2000 - 2005	1.15	17.65	-6.11	23.16	5.51	26.74	72
	2005 - 2010	1.26	..	-3.22	21.29	..	22.11	73
Central America and Greater Carribean Islands excluding Mexico and Puerto Rico - Amérique centrale et Grandes Antilles sans le Mexique et Porto Rico	1995 - 2000	1.69	20.64	-3.66	27.54	6.90	39.71	67
	2000 - 2005	1.53	18.97	-3.56	25.63	6.66	33.19	68
	2005 - 2010	1.45	..	-2.99	23.90	..	28.08	70
South America and Central America - Amérique du Sud et Amérique centrale	1995 - 2000	1.60	17.50	-1.43	23.51	6.01	31.50	70
	2000 - 2005	1.32	15.79	-2.53	21.70	5.91	25.59	72
	2005 - 2010	1.27	..	-1.38	20.06	..	21.38	73
South America excluding Brazil - Amérique du Sud sans le Brésil	1995 - 2000	1.55	17.13	-1.49	23.45	6.32	29.12	71
	2000 - 2005	1.34	15.05	-1.52	21.23	6.18	24.11	72
	2005 - 2010	1.23	..	-1.11	19.70	..	20.10	74
Developing economies: Asia - **Économies en développement : Asie**	**1995 - 2000**	**1.48**	**15.12**	**-0.26**	**22.88**	**7.76**	**55.16**	**65**
	2000 - 2005	**1.27**	**13.07**	**-0.34**	**20.57**	**7.49**	**50.03**	**67**
	2005 - 2010	**1.17**	**..**	**-0.33**	**22.50**	**..**	**44.12**	**68**
Eastern and South-Eastern Asia excluding China - Asie orientale et Asie du Sud-Est sans la Chine	1995 - 2000	1.44	14.41	-0.22	21.12	6.71	40.62	..
	2000 - 2005	1.26	12.98	-0.45	19.47	6.49	32.96	..
	2005 - 2010	0.46	.	-0.40	18.10	..	27.57	..
Southern Asia excluding India - Asie méridionale sans l'Inde	1995 - 2000	2.01	21.15	-0.90	30.33	9.17	81.36	..
	2000 - 2005	1.77	18.96	-1.11	27.34	8.38	73.85	..
	2005 - 2010	1.78	..	-0.60	26.40	..	65.98	..

For sources and notes, see end of table.

Pour les sources et les notes, se reporter à la fin du tableau.

Sources:
- UN DESA Population Division, *World Population Prospects: The 2004 Revision*
- UN DESA Population Division, *World Population Prospects: The 2006 Revision*
- UNCTAD secretariat calculations

Notes:

(1) Population growth rate: Average exponential rate of growth of the population over a given period. It is calculated as ln(Pt/P0)/t where t is the length of the period. It is expressed as a percentage.

(2) Natural increase rate per 1 000 inhabitants: Crude birth rate minus the crude death rate.

(3) Net migration rate per 1 000 inhabitants: Net number of migrants over a given period divided by the person- years lived by the population over that period. It is expressed as net number of migrants per 1 000 population.

(4) Crude birth rate per 1 000 inhabitants: Number of births over a given period divided by the person-years lived by the population over that period. It is expressed as number of births per 1 000 population.

(5) Crude death rate per 1 000 inhabitants: Number of deaths over a given period divided by the person-years lived by the population over that period. It is expressed as number of deaths per 1 000 population.

(6) Infant mortality rate per 1 000 live births: The number of deaths under one year of age in a given period of time divided by the number of live-births in the same period. It is expressed as number of deaths under one year per 1 000 births.

(7) Life expectancy at birth: The average number of years a newborn infant would to be expected to live if current mortality trends were to continue for the rest of that person's life.

Sources :
- ONU DAES Division de la population, *World Population Prospects: The 2004 Revision*
- ONU DAES Division de la population, *World Population Prospects: The 2006 Revision*
- Calculs du secrétariat de la CNUCED

Notes :

(1) Taux d'accroissement de la population : le taux exponentiel d'accroissement de la population pour une période donnée, calculé comme ln(Pt/P0)/t, où le t est la longueur de la période, et exprimé en pourcentage.

(2) Taux d'évolution naturelle pour 1 000 habitants : le taux de natalité brut moins le taux de mortalité brut.

(3) Taux net de migration pour 1 000 habitants : le rapport entre le nombre net des migrants pour une période donnée et l'effectif de la population vivant durant la période considérée. Il est exprimé en nombre net des migrants pour 1 000 habitants.

(4) Taux de natalité brut pour 1 000 habitants : le rapport entre le nombre de naissances vivantes pour une période donnée et l'effectif de la population durant la période considérée. Il est exprimé en nombre de naissances pour 1 000 habitants.

(5) Taux de mortalité brut pour 1 000 habitants : c'est le rapport entre le nombre de décès pour une période donnée et l'effectif de la population durant la période considérée. Il est exprimé en nombre de décès pour 1 000 habitants.

(6) Taux de mortalité infantile pour 1 000 naissances vivantes : il est défini par le nombre des décès d'enfants âgés de moins d'un an pour une période donnée, rapporté au nombre de naissances vivantes durant la période considérée. Il est exprimé en nombre de décès d'enfants âgés de moins d'un an pour 1 000 naissances.

(7) Espérance de vie à la naissance : nombre moyen d'années à vivre pour un nouveau-né soumis aux conditions de mortalité de l'année de sa naissance.